Combating Violent Extremism and Radicalization in the Digital Era

Majeed Khader
Home Team Behavioural Sciences Centre, Ministry of Home Affairs, Singapore

Loo Seng Neo
Home Team Behavioural Sciences Centre, Ministry of Home Affairs, Singapore

Gabriel Ong
Home Team Behavioural Sciences Centre, Ministry of Home Affairs, Singapore

Eunice Tan Mingyi
Home Team Behavioural Sciences Centre, Ministry of Home Affairs, Singapore

Jeffery Chin
Home Team Behavioural Sciences Centre, Ministry of Home Affairs, Singapore

A volume in the Advances in Religious and
Cultural Studies (ARCS) Book Series

Information Science
REFERENCE
An Imprint of IGI Global

Published in the United States of America by
      Information Science Reference (an imprint of IGI Global)
      701 E. Chocolate Avenue
      Hershey PA, USA 17033
      Tel: 717-533-8845
      Fax: 717-533-8661
      E-mail: cust@igi-global.com
      Web site: http://www.igi-global.com

Library of Congress Cataloging-in-Publication Data

Names: Khader, Majeed, 1966- editor.
Title: Combating violent extremism and radicalization in the digital era /
  Majeed Khader, Loo Seng Neo, Gabriel Ong, Eunice Tan Mingyi, and Jeffery
  Chin, editors.
Description: Hershey, PA : Information Science Reference, [2016] | Includes
  bibliographical references and index.
Identifiers: LCCN 2015051297| ISBN 9781522501565 (hardcover) | ISBN
  9781522501572 (ebook)
Subjects: LCSH: Cyberterrorism. | Internet and terrorism. | Extremist Web
  sites. | Terrorists--Recruiting. | Radicalism. | Terrorism--Prevention.
Classification: LCC HV6773.15.C97 C65 2016 | DDC 363.325--dc 3 LC record available at http://lccn.loc.gov/2015051297

This book is published in the IGI Global book series Advances in Religious and Cultural Studies (ARCS) (ISSN: Pending; eISSN: Pending)

British Cataloguing in Publication Data
A Cataloguing in Publication record for this book is available from the British Library.

For electronic access to this publication, please contact: eresources@igi-global.com.

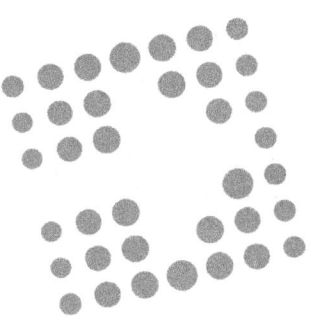

Advances in Religious and Cultural Studies (ARCS) Book Series

ISSN: Pending
EISSN: Pending

MISSION

In the era of globalization, the diversity of the world and various cultures becomes apparent as cross-cultural interactions turn into a daily occurrence for individuals in all professions. Understanding these differences is necessary in order to promote effective partnerships and interactions between those from different religious and cultural backgrounds.

The **Advances in Religious and Cultural Studies (ARCS)** book series brings together a collection of scholarly publications on topics pertaining to religious beliefs, culture, population studies, and sociology. Books published within this series are ideal for professionals, theorists, researchers, and students seeking the latest research on collective human behavior in terms of religion, social structure, and cultural identity and practice.

COVERAGE

- Politics and Religion
- Cults and Religious Movements
- Group Behavior
- Globalization and Culture
- Sociology
- Gender
- Cross-Cultural Interaction
- Human Rights and Ethics
- Cultural Identity
- Stereotypes and Racism

IGI Global is currently accepting manuscripts for publication within this series. To submit a proposal for a volume in this series, please contact our Acquisition Editors at Acquisitions@igi-global.com or visit: http://www.igi-global.com/publish/.

Titles in this Series

For a list of additional titles in this series, please visit: www.igi-global.com

www.igi-global.com

701 E. Chocolate Ave., Hershey, PA 17033
Order online at www.igi-global.com or call 717-533-8845 x100
To place a standing order for titles released in this series, contact: cust@igi-global.com
Mon-Fri 8:00 am - 5:00 pm (est) or fax 24 hours a day 717-533-8661

Table of Contents

Section 1
Exploitation of the Internet by Violent Extremists

Section 2
Understanding the "Person" within Online Violent Extremism

Section 3
Countering Violent Extremism and Radicalisation

Section 4
Emerging Trends

Section 5
Summary and Future Directions

Detailed Table of Contents

Section 1
Exploitation of the Internet by Violent Extremists

    Loo Seng Neo, Home Team Behavioural Sciences Centre, Ministry of Home Affairs,
        Singapore
    Leevia Dillon, Home Team Behavioural Sciences Centre, Ministry of Home Affairs,
        Singapore
    Priscilla Shi, Home Team Behavioural Sciences Centre, Ministry of Home Affairs, Singapore
    Jethro Tan, Home Team Behavioural Sciences Centre, Ministry of Home Affairs, Singapore
    Yingmin Wang, Home Team Behavioural Sciences Centre, Ministry of Home Affairs,
        Singapore
    Danielle Gomes, Home Team Behavioural Sciences Centre, Ministry of Home Affairs,
        Singapore

Exploiting the benefits afforded by the Internet, violent extremists have created and utilised a myriad of online platforms (e.g., websites, forums, blogs, social media) that have abetted and enhanced their recruitment campaigns across the world. While the idea of countering violent extremists' online presence is a matter of considerable security interest, the paucity of research analysing the persuasiveness of their online platforms to certain target audiences impedes law enforcement agencies' capability to deal with them. There is a need to understand why their online platforms are so persuasive to certain target audiences. Focusing on these online platforms, this chapter will examine the features of these platforms that enhance the appeal of violent extremist messages.

Chapter 2

Thomas Steinfatt, University of Miami, USA
Dana Janbek, Lasell College, USA

This chapter focuses on the use of propaganda during times of war, prejudice, and political unrest. Part one distinguishes between persuasion and one of its forms, propaganda. The meaning-in-use of the term 'propaganda' is essential to understanding its use over time. Part two presents relevant examples of propaganda from the past several centuries in the United States and Europe. These examples include episodes from World War I and II, among others. Propaganda is not a new tool of persuasion, and learning about its use in the past provides a comparison that helps in understanding its use in the present and future. Part three looks at recent examples of how propaganda occurs in actual use in online terrorist mediums by Al-Qaeda and by the Islamic State in Iraq and Syria (ISIS).

Chapter 3

Robyn Torok, Edith Cowan University, Australia

This chapter examines the shift toward the use of social media to fuel violent extremism, what the key discursive markers are, and how these key discursive markers are used to fuel violent extremism. The chapter then addresses and critiques a number of radicalisation models including but not limited to phase based models. Discursive markers are covered under three broad narrative areas. Narratives of grievance are designed to stimulate strong emotive responses to perceived injustices. Based on these grievances, active agency is advocated in the form of jihad as a path that one should follow. Finally, a commitment to martyrdom is sought as the goal of these discursive markers.

Chapter 4

Fajar Erikha, Universitas Indonesia, Indonesia
Idhamsyah Eka Putra, Persada Indonesia University, Indonesia
Sarlito Wirawan Sarwono, Universitas Indonesia, Indonesia & Persada Indonesia
    University, Indonesia

This article aims to understand how discourses about Islamic State in Iraq and Syria (ISIS) are supported and/or rejected by radical Islamic groups. Data were collected from two Islamic news website: Voa-Islam and Arrahmah. Both websites are categorised as radical Islamic sites. By using the discursive psychology approach, it was found that when ISIS is viewed as a group that actualised the establishment of an Islamic State, it is praised and supported. However, when ISIS is deemed to have killed other fellow Muslims, it is opposed and its movement is considered to be 'out of Islamic corridors'. Practical implications of these findings are identified and discussed.

In this chapter, we discuss how terrorists can use the Internet as a source of information to plan for terrorist attacks. Online anonymity services such as virtual private network (VPN) are discussed, along with advantages and disadvantages of using these services. We also discuss online bomb-making instructions and highlight ways in which these can be used to the advantage of law enforcement. Finally, the use of the Internet as a reconnaissance tool for target selection is discussed, with descriptions of current and past research in this field to identify key information that is available to terrorists, and how this information can be manipulated to reduce the likelihood or severity of a terrorist attack.

Section 2
Understanding the "Person" within Online Violent Extremism

The chapter aims to provide an opinion on major challenges for ongoing personality research on cyber security, especially in the area of insider threat. While research on the prevention and perpetuation of insider threat activity within cyberspace has grown substantially in the recent decade, there remain many unanswered challenges and unchartered territories of knowledge in the field. Specifically, compared to the amount of work done on algorithmic modelling approaches, much of the psychological data is scant and focuses on correlations between the so-called Big Five personality traits (i.e., extraversion, openness to experience, agreeableness, emotional stability, conscientiousness) or demographic variables (e.g., gender, age) with insider threat activity. Thus, the focus of this article is to articulate the major challenges for understanding insider threat in the context of cyber security, particularly from a personality and person-specific perspective that emphasises internal characteristics of the individual actor as explanations of actions and events.

This chapter will explore possible factors (both online and real world) that can 'tip' an 'armchair jihadi' towards real world extremism. This entails examining social psychological research on tipping points that can be translated to the process of radicalisation. Prominent cases of jihadists will then be examined to illustrate the physiognomies behind their tipping points and the applicability of such theories. Finally, strategies to incorporate tipping point mechanisms towards countering violent extremism will be discussed. This chapter emphasises how the key to understanding tipping points in extremism lies in understanding the cognitive, social and emotive barriers to extremist thinking and action. There is thus an imperative need for more research and experimentation on persuasion tactics and in particular tipping points. Extremist counter-narratives can only be successful if they incorporate the energies of youth and other key individuals at the grassroots towards crafting, spreading and adding credibility to counter-narratives.

Since the Islamic State in Iraq and Syria (ISIS) became prominent after the release of beheading videos of its prisoners, many have been confused over how to describe this development in relation to the way the Internet is exploited by violent extremists. While the element of surprise and horror lingered on the minds of many observers, a more pressing question facing the law enforcement is: how does ISIS attract foreign fighters using such videos and online propaganda? As countries around the globe grapple with the security threat posed by their nationals travelling to join ISIS, the need to be au fait with the appeal of ISIS and its ability to use the Internet to recruit new members and sympathisers becomes even more apparent. This chapter uses a behavioural sciences lens to explicate how individual and organisational motivational factors may contribute to the overall appeal of joining ISIS.

The threat of violent extremism has been considerably influenced by the self-proclaimed Islamic State in Iraq and Syria (ISIS), its inhumane brutal killings in Iraq and Syria, and exploitation of social media to recruit large numbers of foreign fighters in a scale never seen before. This development has serious implications for Singapore's security landscape. This aggressive promotion of fighting in Syria has resonated with a handful of Singaporeans, who were radicalised by radical online propaganda. In this psychological study of the Singapore cases, there are five psychological drivers that have contributed to the radicalisation process of these cases. They are: (1) justifying violence, (2) romanticising the notion of a utopian state, (3) desire to be a 'good' Muslim, (4) escaping the 'unbearable present' world, and (5) existential anxiety in relation to End Times prophecies. The preliminary findings further indicate that most of these radicalised individuals have engaged in negative activism.

Women have long been a blind spot for security, academic and think tank sectors in relation to the growing threat of global extremism. The recent spike in female recruitment to the terrorist organisation, Islamic State in Iraq and Syria (ISIS), is a strong indicator of this dangerous trend. While often assumed to be passive agents, women continue to play strong roles in online and offline recruitment to violent extremist organisations. However, women can also act as strong counter-extremism agents in the fight against radicalisation and terrorism. Looking at the issue of gender, there is a new ability through online research to retrieve valuable insight into terrorist strategies around recruitment of women from online propaganda. This chapter aims to address questions of gender within current radicalisation trends through an analysis of online data, and through tracking Western females who are migrating to territories under the control of ISIS.

Chapter 11

This chapter proposes an Internet-mediated radicalisation model, RECRO. It consists of five phases: (1) the Reflection phase details the triggers, needs, and vulnerabilities that an individual may have which increase one's receptiveness towards alternative belief systems; (2) the Exploration phase details the period where the individual begins making sense of the information put forth by violent extremists; (3) the Connection phase details the influence of like-minded individuals and the online community on the individual's new worldview; (4) the Resolution phase details the period during which the individual gains the momentum to translate one's radical beliefs into action; and finally (5) the Operational phase details the period during which the individual is ready to commit violence to further one's radical objectives. This model provides a basis for understanding and informing judgements about an individual's level of involvement, and paves the way for future empirical work.

Section 3
Countering Violent Extremism and Radicalisation

Chapter 12

This chapter argues that 'framing' the challenges posed by radicalised individuals 'online' where the path to violent extremism is just a click away, is as much about getting the framing right as it is about getting the operational plans right. A general framework based on 4 P's (Policing-Public-Policies-Politics) is proposed as the conceptual 'frame' for combating violent extremism. The metaphor of a compass is used to examine this 4P's framework from the perspective of knowledge management. The key notions of 'violent extremism', 'radicalisation' and 'digital era' are deconstructed before presenting a neurocognitive-based model of 'self-indoctrination' by those who 'inspire' a violently extreme narrative through social media technologies using the 'dark net' of cyberspace. Law enforcement's use of communication interception technologies and data retention laws is critically examined. The chapter concludes with operational implications for Policing the Public with Policy tools in the context of Political realities.

Chapter 13

Based on the assumption that ideology is the centre of gravity of a violent Islamist terrorist network, this chapter proposes a Counter-Ideological Response (CIR) Model for countering violent extremism (CVE) in Southeast Asia. The Model seeks to gradually diminish the appeal of violent extremist ideology. It comprises of five conceptual Spaces of Sender, Message, Mechanism, Recipient and Context, within which ideology-relevant policy interventions may be attempted, so as to impact the overall reach and appeal of the violent extremist narrative vis-a-vis any countervailing narrative put out against it. The model is applied to the Indonesian CVE milieu in this chapter.

State action is an important form of strategic communication and therefore, significant to Countering Violent Extremism (CVE) initiatives on and offline. While non-state actors often use state action (and sometimes inaction) to incite and legitimise violence against the state as well as its citizens, generating this sort of negative sentiment does not require instigation. This is especially the case when the action(s) of a state are deemed so unacceptable and repulsive that a public backlash automatically ensues. As many violent extremists (including lone wolves) have been radicalised as a result of such controversies, it is necessary for positive state action to be carried out as well as widely publicised at the macro and micro levels. This is envisaged to counter negative narratives as well as address real world issues that push individuals towards violent extremism.

The threat of violent extremism in the Internet age has undoubtedly become one important focus of research, policy, and government bodies all over the world. Understandably, many resources have been invested into counter violent extremism efforts, such as the identification of possible radicalised individuals, and understanding the psychology behind violent extremism. These methods adopt a resistance stance and attempt to prevent violent extremism. However, this chapter argues that resilience is equally, if not more important given the unpredictable nature of violent extremism. The first part examines 'systems' within a nation such as critical infrastructure and how concepts such as 'resilient-by-design' can be incorporated to ensure continuity in times of attacks. The second part will explore 'person' factors of crisis communication, cohesion, and social capital, and how these factors can afford a cohesive society that can overcome the cracks in social order and harmony often caused by violent extremism.

Social media analytics are increasingly incorporated into security practices due to the rise in online criminal and extremist activities. Social media research, however, has not become established in either intelligence practice or academic-based approach. This chapter aims to fill the gap by discussing collection methods and analytical tools for the study of social media data for intelligence and countering violent extremism: social network analysis, sentiment analysis, multilingual analysis, geo-coding, automated entity extraction, semantic search, and multimedia analysis. While technological capabilities of social media analytics are improving rapidly, it needs to be complemented with nuanced perspectives from the social sciences. Understanding of the epistemology of social media and dynamics between the online-offline interaction as well as data access will put practitioners in a better position to reap the benefits of the social media. Attention should be given to train practitioners in relevant technological skills while also incorporating social science knowledge.

Online behaviour can provide a unique window from which we can glean intent. From an intelligence standpoint it provides an important source of open-source information. However, making inference of intent from online activity is inherently difficult. Yet elsewhere progress is being made in incorporating information online into decisions regarding risk and offender prioritisation. This chapter synthesises lessons learnt from studies of risk assessment of violent extremists, risk assessment online, and the form and function of extremist materials online in order to begin to approach the issue of online risk assessment of violent extremism. In doing so it highlights issues associated with the diversity of online extremist behaviour, the diversity of offline extremist behaviour and the general lack of understanding related to the interaction of online and offline experiences, and how this contributes to the wider psychological process of 'radicalisation'. Implications for practitioners are discussed.

The ability to disseminate information instantaneously over vast geographical regions makes the Internet a key facilitator in the radicalisation process and preparations for terrorist attacks. This can be both an asset and a challenge for security agencies. One of the main challenges for security agencies is the sheer amount of information available on the Internet. It is impossible for human analysts to read through everything that is written online. In this chapter we will discuss the possibility of detecting violent extremism by identifying signs of warning behaviours in written text – what we call linguistic markers – using computers, or more specifically, natural language processing.

This chapter introduces a new approach to the risk assessment for violent extremism that is focused on cyber-related behaviour and content. The Violent Extremist Risk Assessment (VERA-2) protocol, used internationally, is augmented by an optional cyber-focused risk indicator protocol referred to as CYBERA. The risk indicators of CYBERA are elaborated and the application of CYBERA, conjointly with the VERA-2 risk assessment protocol, is described. The combined use of the two tools provides

(1) a robust and cyber-focused risk assessment intended to provide early warning indicators of violent extremist action, (2) provides consistency and reliability in risk and threat assessments, (3) determines risk trajectories of individuals, and (4) assists intelligence and law enforcement analysts in their national security investigations. The tools are also relevant for use by psychologists, psychiatrists, communication analysts and provide relevant information that supports Terrorism Prevention Programs (TPP) and countering violent extremism (CVE) initiatives.

With today's technological advancements, common online platforms, such as Gmail, forum, websites, Facebook, Twitter, Instagram and YouTube, are used by millions to communicate and share information in the form of text, image or both with varying synchronicity. In a similar way, violent extremists are also bringing their radical agenda online. As more individuals become radicalised by online violent extremist propaganda, the need to counter such propaganda and manage existing threats, such as incarcerated detainees who are more technology-savvy, becomes increasingly urgent. This chapter propounds the idea of online deradicalisation. First, the online milieu and its concomitant social phenomena will be discussed. Second, an overview of existing elements of deradicalisation and its target audience will be covered. Third, the chapter will delve into online psychotherapy and its potential applicability to deradicalisation. Last, the chapter will conclude with relevant implications and future research directions.

Section 4
Emerging Trends

The cyber threat landscape has continued to evolve with time and enhanced technology. With the advent of new breeds of terrorists and cybercriminals, the cyberterrorism debate has again wielded global attention. In this chapter, the author will attempt to delve deeper into the concept of cyberterrorism. Firstly, it will discuss the related issues which include the definition consensus, perception, and media abuse problems. The next section draws on parallels from research on cyber threats and terrorism based on six themes (i.e., modus operandi, domain, targets, impact, antagonists and motivations) to formulate a cyberterrorism conceptual framework. The third section will provide a hypothetical four-step cyberterrorism attack sequence and suggestions for countering cyberterrorism. This chapter will then conclude by highlighting several implications of interest.

Innovation and technological advancements have seen many devices and systems being linked up on to the Internet. Such devices and systems include personal medical devices like insulin pumps and pacemakers, cars, as well as critical infrastructure like power grids and traffic light systems. However, recent research by cyber security experts has revealed that these critical devices and systems are highly vulnerable to being hacked into and manipulated. Should such an attack be carried out successfully by bad actors, like violent extremists, this could result in physical injury or even death. Hence, this chapter aims to bring awareness on the kinetic cyber threat by highlighting various forms of kinetic cyber, and the vulnerabilities that make these devices and systems susceptible. In addition, this chapter introduces the motivations and characteristics of violent extremists who might engage in kinetic cyber, and ends off by proposing some recommended directions to counter this threat.

The ubiquitous use of the Internet has made it possible for terrorist groups to remotely foment attacks with little risk of capture. Among the newest forms of attacks is cyber hacking, which has seen increased use by terrorist groups for acts ranging from pinpointing targets for assassination to holding organisations hostage and embarrassing governments. In almost all these attacks, spear phishing is the vector used to gain access to a computer network – making it imperative that policymakers find ways to stop it. This chapter provides an overview of the different types of spear phishing attacks and the reasons they succeed. The chapter then provides an overview of the different strategies being used to combat it and their relative effectiveness. Drawing from the latest social science research and from initiatives that have worked around the world, the chapter culminates with six policy suggestions, which could significantly reduce the effectiveness of spear phishing and protect nations from a major cyber attack.

Section 5
Summary and Future Directions

This concluding chapter is an attempt made to summarise and analyse the chapters provided by the various authors in this book. The analysis used in this chapter is based on a public health prevention model. The value of this approach is the systemic prevention angle that it undertakes to examine problems and solutions.

Foreword

I congratulate the team from the Home Team Behavioural Sciences Centre for the publication of this book *Combating Violent Extremism and Radicalization in the Digital Era*.

Violent extremists are increasingly using the cyber medium to maximise their outreach. This book provides a reminder that online radicalisation poses a serious threat to safety and security all over the world. Violent extremism has continued to evolve with new forms of social media. There is therefore a critical need for governments and communities across the world to step up their counter terrorism efforts.

In addressing this threat, evidence-based research findings are critical to inform both policy making and operational tactics. This book contains many articles by both international as well as Singapore experts in the field. I am delighted that the Singapore Home Team psychologists and behavioural science researchers have made an important contribution to this book.

I am confident that this book will provide readers with a better understanding of this important subject, and contribute to efforts to deal with the threat of online violent extremism.

Leo Yip
Permanent Secretary, Ministry of Home Affairs, Singapore & Permanent Secretary, Prime Minister's Office, Singapore & Permanent Secretary, National Security and Intelligence Coordination, Singapore

Preface

Wicked problems are large and intractable issues – highly complex problems, often framed in political, social, economic and scientific dimensions that have multiple stakeholders who see the problem in different ways. Wicked problems require a high degree of process knowledge about creativity and collaboration in order to make even a dent in them. (Former Head of Civil Service Singapore, Peter Ho, 2008)

Rittel and Webber (1973) coined the term 'wicked problem' to refer to issues that are difficult to solve, not because the problem is inherently difficult, but because such problems do not offer themselves up to solutions. A wicked problem may be hard to define, and its causes may be complex and nebulous. Conventional solutions are unlikely to bring about a wicked problem's resolution, and there are unlikely any definitive answers. Rittel and Webber (1973) described ten properties of wicked problems that make them distinct from ordinary problems:

1. We can define an ordinary problem, but a definitive formulation of a wicked problem will remain elusive. The formulation of a wicked problem is the problem!
2. We will know when a solution to an ordinary problem has been found; with wicked problems, we never really know when to stop searching for the solution.
3. With ordinary problems, we may objectively determine whether a solution was correct or incorrect; with wicked problems, it is a judgment call whether the solution was satisfactory or not.
4. We can tell if a solution has been effective in resolving an ordinary problem. On the other hand, solutions to wicked problems will generate consequences over an extended period of time, making it very difficult to measure the solution's effectiveness.
5. With ordinary problems, we can apply solutions and learn by trial and error; with wicked problems, every trial must count because of the consequences that follow.
6. Ordinary problems come with a limited set of potential solutions, whereas wicked problems may not.
7. Every wicked problem is unique – we may learn to solve ordinary problems through experience over time, but with wicked problems, experience may not be as helpful.
8. A wicked problem is intertwined with other problems, whereas an ordinary problem may not.
9. There are many ways to explain wicked problems, and the choice adopted to explain the problem will determine the choice of solution in resolving it.
10. Solvers of wicked problems have to get it right, as they will be held responsible for the consequences of their actions, which have a large impact that are hard to justify.

Violent extremism is one such wicked problem.

It has persisted over time, and continues to evolve in its manifestation over time. This is made more daunting by the problematic nature of defining violent extremism and its closely-related phenomenon, especially terrorism[1]. There is no consensus in the literature regarding a universally accepted definition of violent extremism and terrorism in spite of decades of research. For the purposes of this book titled 'Combating Violent Extremism and Radicalisation in the Digital Era', a working definition of violent extremism would be "a willingness to use or support the use of violence to further particular beliefs, including those of a political, social or ideological nature. This may include acts of terrorism." (Nasser-Eddine, Garnham, Agostino, & Caluya, 2011, p. 9). Online radicalisation can be defined as "the process by which an individual is introduced to an ideological message and belief system that encourages movement from mainstream beliefs toward extreme views, primarily through the use of online media such as Facebook, Twitter, and YouTube" (Community Oriented Policing Services, 2014, p. 1).

Having said that, ideologically motivated violence defies conventional categorisation and definition. It may be perpetrated by individuals or by groups; it may be motivated by various belief systems; it may be discriminate or indiscriminate. Violent ideologies attract a diverse audience – the religious, the thrill seekers, the humanitarians, the martyrs, the anti-establishment, the naïve. With the advent of the Internet and social media, this wicked problem is swaddled with an added layer of complexity.

In recent years, the violent extremism threat landscape has evolved rapidly. The threat of the past decade, Al-Qaeda, appears to have rescinded somewhat, although it has not been eradicated. In its place, various Salafi Jihadi groups, supposed affiliates of Al-Qaeda, have sprouted to continue applying the pressure of violent extremism. Exploits of the Boko Haram and Al-Shabab, for instance, continue to grab headlines and occupy news space. While most of the expression of violent extremist ideology has its epicentre in the Middle East region, the trend of lone wolf terror attacks in traditionally Western countries such as Australia, Canada, the United Kingdom, the United States and France, has also emerged. Such attacks, although limited in the scale of damage, are hard to detect and thwart, and bring the war on terror uncomfortably close to home. More importantly, these drive home the point how social media has expanded the reach of violent extremist ideology.

Alongside these developments is the emergence of the Islamic State in Iraq and Syria (ISIS), which signalled its arrival and determination with decisive military victories in Iraq and Syria. In fact, the expansion of ISIS influence into other countries in the Middle East and beyond suggests that it is still on an ascendant trajectory, and this is unlikely to abate any time soon. An incipient ISIS presence in the Southeast Asia region provides some proof of this growth.

ISIS is a particularly interesting case study because of its sophisticated use of social media to communicate its violent extremist ideologies. Using the Internet to its advantage, ISIS appears successful in putting forward an effective media campaign to raise its profile, attract and recruit fighters to its ranks, share practical information on performing jihad, and push out propaganda materials coupled with up-to-date videos, posts and images of its soldiers fighting at the warfront for a noble cause. In this digital era, ISIS appears highly successful in attracting foreign fighters to join them, and numerous violent extremist groups have affiliated themselves to it. A large part of ISIS success may be attributed to its online presence. While it may be argued that individual dispositions and vulnerabilities may cause one to decide to become a violent extremist, the ISIS example paints an equally compelling picture that online system factors may enlarge these vulnerabilities, increasing an individual's susceptibility to persuasion by violent extremist ideologies. What, then, are the individual motivations and psychological attributes that increase one's likelihood of becoming involved in violent extremism? How have online platforms been exploited by violent extremists to their advantage? How do both these circles of influence interact, and how does the interplay between the person factor and the system factor result in involvement in violent extremism and online radicalisation?

Owing to the complexity of the wicked problem of violent extremism, a creative and collaborative effort is required to conceive answers. This means that problem solvers need to look further beyond traditional boundaries of thinking and work further beyond conventional partners to exact that dent in violent extremism. Knowledge drawn from diverse fields, such as psychology, sociology, economics, history, political science, technology, communications, statistics, and more, are vital and needed to contribute pieces to the puzzle of violent extremism. For an effective resolution of this wicked problem, interdisciplinary collaboration must take place.

This book was put together with the aim to help understand and address this wicked problem. There are three ways in which this book adds unique value.

1.   We adopted a multidisciplinary approach, and asked experts and researchers in various fields to share their perspectives on the issue of violent extremism. Contributors to this book include psychologists, historians, experts in cyber systems, linguistics experts, and researchers in behavioural sciences. Each discipline provides a unique perspective of the wicked problem, and the confluence of perspectives through a multidisciplinary approach will give us greater confidence on the steps that need to be taken to resolve this problem.

2.   With wicked problems, we only have one shot at them, because any actions we take to address them may result in further consequences. Bearing this in mind, we asked the contributors to this book to search wide and look deep into their respective fields to look for solutions. The end objective was to arrive at a collection of thoughts that is solution driven and deeply considered.

3.   With ISIS theatre of operations taking a foothold in the Southeast Asia region, it is critical to revisit this wicked problem from an Asian perspective. Most of the literature on violent extremism has largely come from Western perspectives. To this end, this book aims to present some of the thinking from an Asian lens, in the hope that the concurrence of ideas, or a counterpoint as the case may be, may lend to more holistic points of view.

ORGANISATION OF THE BOOK: SUMMARY OF CHAPTERS

To facilitate your understanding of issues pertaining to countering violent extremism and radicalisation in the digital era, the chapters in this book have been organised broadly in the following themes, demarcated by sections. These sections are:

Section 1: Exploitation of the Internet by Violent Extremists (Chapters 1-5)
Section 2: Understanding the 'Person' within Online Violent Extremism (Chapters 6-11)
Section 3: Countering Violent Extremism and Radicalisation (Chapters 12-20)
Section 4: Emerging Trends (Chapters 21-23)
Section 5: Summary and Future Directions (Chapter 24)

Section 1 on the theme of 'Exploitation of the Internet by violent extremists' comprises a group of chapters that discuss the role of online platforms and how violent extremists can leverage – and in many cases, have leveraged – on these online media for their needs and to propel their cause. Loo Seng Neo and his team in their chapter 'Understanding the Psychology of Persuasive Violent Extremists Online Platforms' highlight how violent extremist groups have not just exploited, but also created, online platforms that enhanced their recruitment campaigns across the world. The chapter examines the features of these platforms which enhance the appeal of violent extremist messages. Thomas Steinfatt and Dana Janbek focus on the history and use of propaganda in their chapter 'Persuasion and Propaganda in War and Terrorism', and discuss recent examples of how propaganda is used in online violent extremist mediums by terrorist groups such as Al-Qaeda and ISIS. Robyn Torok in her chapter 'Social Media and the Use of Discursive Markers of Online Extremism and Recruitment' examines the shift in recent years towards the use of social media to fuel violent extremism. The chapter discusses key discursive markers based on existing radicalisation models and how these markers are used to fuel violent extremism. Fajar Erikha, Idhamsyah Eka Putra, and Sarlito Sarwono in 'ISIS Discourse in Radical Islamic Online News Media in Indonesia: Supporter or Opponent' examine how discourses about ISIS based on two Islamic news websites are supported or rejected by radical Islamic groups. Finally, David Romyn and Mark Kebbell in their chapter 'Using the Internet to Plan for Terrorist Attack' discuss how terrorists can use the Internet as a source of information to plan for terrorist attacks, and how this information can be manipulated to reduce the likelihood or severity of a terrorist attack.

Countries and nations have treated and managed terrorism as a military issue, but it is a primarily human-cultural-psychosocial issue. Hence, there is a need to focus on the human actor. Section 2 is thus the theme of 'Understanding the 'person' within Online Violent Extremism', providing a person-specific focus on the issue of online violent extremism. This section contains chapters which examine the motivations and psychological attributes of the individual who may increase his/her likelihood of becoming involved in online violent extremism. Joyce Pang in her chapter 'Understanding Personality and Person-specific Predictors of Cyber-based Insider Threat' discusses the major challenges for understanding insider threat in the context of cyber security. It examines cyber-based insider threat from a personality and person-specific perspective that emphasises internal characteristics of the individual actor as explanations of actions and events. Omer Saifudeen in his chapter 'Getting out of the Armchair - Potential Tipping Points for Online Radicalisation' highlights another interesting angle affecting the human actor, that is, how the key to understanding tipping points in online violent extremism lies in understanding the cognitive, social and emotive barriers to violent extremist thinking and action. He discusses the need for research and experimentation on persuasion tactics for countering online extremism. Loo Seng Neo and colleagues in their chapter on 'Why is ISIS so Psychologically Attractive?' use a behavioural sciences perspective to explicate how individual motivational factors and organisational factors may contribute to the overall appeal of ISIS. Adding to this person-centric theme, Weiying Hu in her chapter on 'Psychological Effects of the Threat of ISIS: A Preliminary Inquiry of Singapore Case Studies' identifies five psychological drivers that have contributed to the radicalisation process of the cases of Singaporean individuals who had been attracted by ISIS radical online propaganda. Erin Saltman in her chapter 'Western Female Migrants to ISIS: Propaganda, Radicalisation and Recruitment' highlights how women continue to play strong roles in online and offline recruitment to violent extremist organisations. The chapter addresses questions of gender within current radicalisation trends through an analysis of online data that tracks Western females migrating to territories under the control of ISIS. Finally, Loo Seng Neo in his chapter on 'An Internet-mediated Pathway for Online Radicalisation: RE-CRO' introduces a framework to explain the interaction between cyber systems and person factors, and highlight how this framework can be used to guide the identification of key behavioural markers for an individual's involvement in online violent extremism.

In Section 3, the theme of 'Countering Violent Extremism and Radicalisation' comprises of chapters that bring us into the thick of key areas valuable for implementing measures to counter online violent extremism. Geoff Dean in his chapter on 'Framing the Challenges of Online Violent Extremism: 'Policing-Public-Policies-Politics' Framework' uses a framework to expound real and relevant implications surrounding efforts to combat online violent extremism. Kumar Ramakrishna in his chapter on 'Towards a Comprehensive Approach to Combating Violent Extremist Ideology in the Digital Space: The Counter-Ideological Response (CIR) Model' introduces a model aimed to gradually diminish the appeal of violent extremist ideology. This model can potentially guide ideology-relevant policy interventions to impact the overall reach and appeal of the violent extremist narrative vis-a-vis any countervailing narrative put out against it. Damien Cheong in his chapter on 'Countering Online Violent Extremism: State Action as Strategic Communication' focuses on the utility of strategic communication strategies, particularly state action, in countering violent extremism both online and offline, while Jethro Tan and his team in their chapter 'Building National Resilience in the Digital Era of Violent Extremism: Systems and People' focus on building national resilience as a macro-level strategy for countering violent extremism. The latter chapter examines the 'systems' within a nation such as critical infrastructures and how they can be built 'resilient-by-design' to ensure continuity in times of crisis, and also explores 'person' factors of crisis communication, cohesion, and social capital, and discuss how instilling these factors can engender a cohesive society that can overcome the cracks in social order and harmony often caused by violent extremism. Jennifer Yang in her chapter on 'Social Media Analytics for Intelligence and Countering Violent Extremism' discusses collection methods and analytical tools for the study of social media data to facilitate intelligence-gathering and efforts to counter violent extremism. The coverage in this chapter includes social network analysis, sentiment analysis, multilingual analysis, geo-coding, automated entity extraction, semantic search and multimedia analysis.

There are also chapters in this section which introduce tools for assessing risk of online violent extremism and which discuss the challenges of making assessments in the online domain. Neil Shortland in his chapter on '"On the Internet, nobody knows you're a dog": The Online Risk Assessment of Violent Extremists' draws links on how psychology can contribute to conducting online risk assessment of violent extremism. Fredick Johannson and colleagues in their chapter on 'Detecting Linguistic Markers of Violent Extremism in Online Environments' discuss the use of linguistic markers in natural language processing as warning behaviours to detect online violent extremism. Elaine Pressman and Cristina Ivan in their chapter 'Internet Use and Violent Extremism: A Cyber-VERA Risk Assessment Protocol' introduce a new tool named CYBERA (adapted from the pre-existing tool VERA-2), which is designed to be a systematic, empirically-grounded, cyber-focused assessment guide to assess the risk of online violent extremism. CYBERA focuses on cyber-related behaviours and content to guide assessment of early signs of online violent extremism. Finally, Priscilla Shi in her chapter 'A Supplementary Intervention to Deradicalisation: CBT-based Online Forum' propounds the idea of online deradicalisation and delves into online therapeutic engagement and its potential applicability to deradicalisation.

Section 4 on the theme of 'Emerging Trends' comprises of chapters that highlight the potential threat posed by violent extremists as they adopt modus operandi commonly associated with cyber criminals. Leevia Dillon in her chapter on 'Cyberterrorism: Using the Internet as a weapon of destruction' focuses on cyberterrorism and draws on parallels from research on cyber threats and terrorism based on six themes (i.e., modus operandi, domain, targets, impact, antagonists and motivations) to formulate a cyberterrorism conceptual framework. The chapter provides a hypothetical four-step cyberterrorism attack sequence and suggestions for best practice. Penelope Wang in her chapter on 'Death by Hacking: The Emerging Threat of Kinetic Cyber' focuses on kinetic cyber threat and highlights various forms of kinetic cyber as well as the vulnerabilities that make devices and systems (e.g., personal medical devices, cars, critical infrastructures) susceptible. The chapter introduces motivations and characteristics of violent extremists who might engage in kinetic cyber attacks. Arun Vishwanath in his chapter on 'Spear Phishing: The Tip of the Spear Used by Cyber Terrorists' focuses on spear phishing, which is an email spoofing fraud attempt that seeks unauthorised access to confidential data, highlighting it as the vector used to gain access to a computer network in almost all forms of cyber attacks. The chapter, which emphasises the need for policy interventions, provides an overview of the different strategies being used to combat it and their relative effectiveness.

The final section, Section 5, brings the discourse on combating online violent extremism and radicalisation to a close by summarising the key learning lessons from the preceding chapters, as well as identifying future research directions. This concluding chapter on 'What we know and what else we need to do to address the problem of violent extremism online' by Majeed Khader, highlights potential future trends for online violent extremism and in tackling these trends, the need to understand the critical catalysts for change of which violent extremists can exploit. The chapter also discusses the need to evaluate counter violent extremism measures and identifies areas for future research.

In closing, we cite Brian Michael Jenkins, senior advisor to the president of the RAND Corporation, who wrote that:

[C]ounterterrorist efforts focus on only the operational portion of this cycle, the visible tip of the iceberg: from late in the recruitment process to death or capture. Insufficient attention is paid to defeating radicalisation, indoctrination, and recruitment at the front end or to developing a coherent strategy for dealing with detainees at the back end. We have concentrated on degrading the jihadists' operational capabilities by eliminating jihadists, but not by impeding recruiting, inducing defections, or getting detainees to renounce jihad … this narrow vision is understandable. It reflects the traditional law enforcement approach in which the task of the police is to apprehend criminals and gather evidence for their prosecution. It comes from a narrow military approach in which the armed forces close with and kill or capture enemy soldiers and interrogate them for operational intelligence but do not consider prisoners a possible resource. (Jenkins, 2006, p. 124)

These comments greatly echo the sentiment of the editors of this book, who are psychologists and behavioural scientists by training. As co-labourers in this wicked problem of violent extremism, then, our counter-terrorism strategy must adjust to also address the sociological and psychological dynamics of violent extremism and radicalisation, and focus more at the front end.

Majeed Khader
Home Team Behavioural Sciences Centre, Ministry of Home Affairs, Singapore

Loo Seng Neo
Home Team Behavioural Sciences Centre, Ministry of Home Affairs, Singapore

Gabriel Ong
Home Team Behavioural Sciences Centre, Ministry of Home Affairs, Singapore

Eunice Tan Mingyi
Home Team Behavioural Sciences Centre, Ministry of Home Affairs, Singapore

Jeffery Chin
Home Team Behavioural Sciences Centre, Ministry of Home Affairs, Singapore

REFERENCES

Community Oriented Policing Services. (2014). *Online radicalisation to violent extremism: Awareness brief.* Washington, DC: Office of Community Oriented Policing Services.

Jenkins, B. M. (2006). *Unconquerable nation: Knowing our enemy, strengthening ourselves.* Santa Monica, CA: RAND Corporation.

Nasser-Eddine, M., Garnham, B., Agostino, K., & Caluya, G. (2011). Countering violent extremism (CVE) literature review. Edinburgh, Australia: Australian Government, Department of Defence, Command and Control Division, Defence Science and Technology Organisation (DSTO).

Rittel, H. W. J., & Webber, M. M. (1973). Dilemmas in a general theory of planning. *Policy Sciences, 4,* 155–169.

Schmid, A. P. (Ed.). (2011). *The Routledge handbook of terrorism research.* New York: Routledge.

ENDNOTE

[1]   According to Schmid (2011), the revised academic consensus definition of terrorism is: "Terrorism refers on the one hand to a doctrine about the presumed effectiveness of a special form or tactic of fear-generating, coercive political violence and, on the other hand, to a conspiratorial practice of calculated, demonstrative, direct violent action without legal or moral restraints, targeting mainly civilians and non-combatants, performed for its propagandistic and psychological effects on various audiences and conflict parties" (p. 86).

Acknowledgment

During the course of this project, the editors have received generous help and support from dozens of remarkable people. We would like to acknowledge the time and effort of all the people involved in this project. Without their support, this book would not have become a reality.

To begin with, we would like to take this opportunity to thank IGI Global, the publisher of this book, and in particular, Ms Caitlyn Martin and Ms Eleana Wehr who have supported us tirelessly throughout this book project.

We would like to thank each one of the authors for their contributions. Thank you all for giving generously your time and talents to this project.

Next, we wish to take this opportunity to express our sincere thanks for the valuable contributions of the EAB members (Dr Geoff Dean, Dr Vincent Egan, Dr Lisa Kaati, Dr Mark Kebbell, Dr Kumar Ramakrishna, and Ms Susan Sim) and authors that took part in the review process. Their expertise and valuable insights have enhanced the quality, coherence, and content presentation of the chapters.

Most importantly, we would like to express our most sincere gratitude to the Permanent Secretary of the Ministry of Home Affairs, Mr Leo Yip, former Permanent Secretary of the Ministry of Home Affairs, Mr Tan Tee How, and Deputy Secretary (Policy) of the Ministry of Home Affairs, Ms Goh Soon Poh for their support and guidance which have greatly contributed to the rigour of this project. In addition, we would like to thank the Permanent Secretary of the National Security and Intelligence Coordination, Mr Benny Lim, and Senior Director of the National Security Research Centre, Mr Gabriel Wong for their valuable support. We would also like to express our appreciation to the support provided by our valued-partners from the Internal Security Department.

Furthermore, we wish to convey our heartfelt appreciation to our colleagues at the Home Team Behavioural Sciences Centre for their personal and professional support. Their moral support and dedicated involvement were our motivational force.

Finally, we would like to take this opportunity to thank the members of our families for their unwavering love and support that made this book project an enjoyable experience for us.

Majeed Khader
Home Team Behavioural Sciences Centre, Ministry of Home Affairs, Singapore

Loo Seng Neo
Home Team Behavioural Sciences Centre, Ministry of Home Affairs, Singapore

Gabriel Ong
Home Team Behavioural Sciences Centre, Ministry of Home Affairs, Singapore

Eunice Tan Mingyi
Home Team Behavioural Sciences Centre, Ministry of Home Affairs, Singapore

Jeffery Chin
Home Team Behavioural Sciences Centre, Ministry of Home Affairs, Singapore

Section 1
Exploitation of the Internet by Violent Extremists

Chapter 1
Understanding the Psychology of Persuasive Violent Extremist Online Platforms

Loo Seng Neo
*Home Team Behavioural Sciences Centre,
Ministry of Home Affairs, Singapore*

Jethro Tan
*Home Team Behavioural Sciences Centre,
Ministry of Home Affairs, Singapore*

Leevia Dillon
*Home Team Behavioural Sciences Centre,
Ministry of Home Affairs, Singapore*

Yingmin Wang
*Home Team Behavioural Sciences Centre,
Ministry of Home Affairs, Singapore*

Priscilla Shi
*Home Team Behavioural Sciences Centre,
Ministry of Home Affairs, Singapore*

Danielle Gomes
*Home Team Behavioural Sciences Centre,
Ministry of Home Affairs, Singapore*

ABSTRACT

Exploiting the benefits afforded by the Internet, violent extremists have created and utilised a myriad of online platforms (e.g., websites, forums, blogs, social media) that have abetted and enhanced their recruitment campaigns across the world. While the idea of countering violent extremists' online presence is a matter of considerable security interest, the paucity of research analysing the persuasiveness of their online platforms to certain target audiences impedes law enforcement agencies' capability to deal with them. There is a need to understand why their online platforms are so persuasive to certain target audiences. Focusing on these online platforms, this chapter will examine the features of these platforms that enhance the appeal of violent extremist messages.

INTRODUCTION

The ease with which violent extremist groups have utilised the Internet highlights the growing volatility of threats facing law enforcement today. The Internet has allowed violent extremist groups to disseminate their propaganda messages more easily, and has become the ideal platform to communicate with one another and with their followers (Aly, Weimann-Saks, & Weimann, 2014; Hussain & Saltman, 2014;

DOI: 10.4018/978-1-5225-0156-5.ch001

Weimann, 2004; Weimann & von Knop, 2008). Based on this line of thought, a significant amount of research and analysis has gone into the question of how the Internet has enhanced and contributed to the persuasiveness of violent extremist online propaganda.

In general, research trying to decipher the factors underlying the persuasiveness of violent extremist online propaganda can be attributed to a range of factors, two of which is of interest to this chapter: understanding the messages, and the online platforms that house these messages.

In terms of the message, insights derived from the research on 'sticky ideas' suggest that the persuasiveness of online propaganda messages can, to some extent, be attributed to the presentation and structuring of the message. For example, Heath and Heath (2008) in their book titled 'Made to Stick' identified six principles that would enhance the appeal of a message. A persuasive message would be characterised by its simplicity (i.e., contain content that is simple and easy to remember); its unexpectedness (i.e., contain counter-intuitive content that catch the target audience's attention); its concreteness (i.e., contain content that the target audience can relate to); its credibility (i.e., contain content that needs to be perceived as legitimate to the target audience); its emotional content (i.e., contain content that must appeal emotionally to the target audience); and the presence of stories (i.e., contain stories that aid the target audience in recalling the message). Similarly, Gladwell (2004) highlighted that message that provides practical advice and has personal alignment would appeal more as compared to one that does not. This suggests that the way a message is packaged may influence the appeal of the message to its targeted audience.

In the context of violent extremism, analysis (e.g., Al Raffie, 2012; Lia, 2008; Saifudeen, 2014) of the propagandistic messages released by groups suggests that they have leveraged on some of the principles put forth by Gladwell (2004), and Heath and Heath (2008). A related literature also focuses on the wider role of the creator and sender of the messages on the persuasiveness of the violent extremist online propaganda (see Ramakrishna, 2015).

However, it is instructive to consider the target audience as individuals who are active both in the selection of the information they pay attention to and in the interpretation of the messages. If so, this seems to suggest that the medium through which the messages are presented would also influence the persuasiveness of the online propaganda. That is to say, there is a need to look not only at the factors underlying the appeal of the messages, but also at the nature of the online platforms (which is the focus of this chapter) that enhances the appeal of these messages.

Online Violent Extremists' Platforms

Much has been written about the wide repository of online platforms utilised by violent extremist groups. However, less has been written about how violent extremists have been able to exploit the features of these platforms to enhance the appeal of their propaganda messages. Research into hypermedia seduction for violent extremist recruiting (e.g., Conway, 2005; Dauber & Winkler, 2014; Hussain & Saltman, 2014; Rogan, 2006) has hinted that features of these online platforms may influence how an individual reacts to violent extremist online propaganda.

Some have focused on the initial response of the user when one comes into contact with violent extremist online platforms. After the brief initial confrontation with online radical content, it is envisaged that the individual would experience a range of emotions from apathy to repulsion to exhilaration that might influence one's decision to either ignore the materials, or to continue the search for more relevant materials (Neo, Singh, Khader, Ang, & Ong, 2013). Fighel (2007) in his research on radical Islamic Internet propaganda also suggested that the presence of additional materials (e.g., images, videos) that can substantiate the narratives presented is an important feature of attractive online platforms that may encourage users to further explore violent extremist content.

Others have looked at the usability of the online platforms and have found that users would not spend much time in trying to navigate a platform which is not user-friendly as there are plenty of alternatives available online (Duarte, 2007). Other studies have also examined the users' initial impression of the online platforms' perceived credibility. Salamon (2007) using the example of television commercials, argued that the commercials will not work unless the audience perceives some level of authenticity in them. In the context of violent extremism, individuals who are interested in radical rhetoric are more likely to explore the online platforms that included a video of Osama bin Laden as compared to one that contains sports-related videos.

Overview of Chapter

Based on this line of thinking, it can be seen that the features of various online platforms and the messages used by violent extremist groups online are intended to attract, incite negative sentiment toward enemies (or perceived enemies) and mobilise potential recruits. While the idea of countering violent extremists' online presence is a matter of considerable security interest, the paucity of research analysing the persuasiveness of their online propaganda material to certain target audiences impedes law enforcement agencies' capability to deal with them. There is a need to identify the role played by the online platforms, and understand how they have afforded violent extremist messages so much traction.

Focusing on the online platforms, this chapter will examine the features of these platforms that enhance the appeal of violent extremist messages online. For the purpose of this chapter, online platforms refer to websites, forums, blogs and social media that violent extremists create and/or exploit to propagate their radical messages (i.e., videos, images, and articles etc. that contain radical ideology, belief systems, and skewed interpretation of facts). The second section will explore several features of the online platforms that may contribute to the appeal of violent extremist online propaganda: (1) regular updates; (2) online tools to control and manipulate message; (3) easy access to wide repository of messages; (4) interactive features; and (5) online anonymity. The final section will highlight implications for countering online violent extremism.

PERSUASIVE FEATURES OF VIOLENT EXTREMIST ONLINE PLATFORMS

Regular Updates on Violent Extremist Activities

One of the features that shapes the appeal of a violent extremist online platform is the frequency of which new information and activities are being uploaded. These uploaded content may range from news emerging from conflict zones (e.g., Iraq, Syria, Myanmar) to incidences of discriminations (e.g., indiscriminate killings, Islamophobia), and episodes of the groups' accomplishments (e.g., successful attacks on enemies).

This line of inquiry is based on the observations (e.g., Community Oriented Policing Services [COPS], 2014; Dauber & Winkler, 2014; Neo, Khader, Shi, Dillon, & Ong, 2015) that prominent violent extremist groups would regularly update their activities on their online platforms. Conway (2005, p. 196) in her analysis of ten violent extremist websites found that "sites that are regularly updated will create more interest than those that are not". She used a six-point scale to determine the extent to which each of the website was updated: '6' for daily; '5' for every one to two days; '4' for every three to seven days; '3' for every two weeks; '2' for monthly; '1' for every one to six months; and '0' for no updates for more than six months. In other words, the findings suggest that the regularity of the updates may attract the attention of users who are interested in the violent extremist groups' activities.

Thus, the act of updating their activities online epitomises an active form of agency that allows violent extremist groups the means to connect with potential recruits and garner more publicity for their causes. It is essential to note that traditional means of updating new information via physical interactions would not be able to achieve the same level of currency (i.e., up-to-date), accessibility (i.e., widely available), and speed (i.e., instantaneous) afforded by the online platforms.

From a psychological perspective, this has three implications. Firstly, these updates provide a biased perspective which is tailored to magnify the impact of the violent extremist groups' activities. The recent furore of reports on Somalia-based Al-Shabab, for example, exemplified how violent extremist groups have exploited Twitter to update their followers (Egan, 2013). Through its Twitter account, Al-Shabab was able to capitalise on the heightened media attention during the Westgate shopping mall attack in 2013 by providing news updates from the group's perspective (Osman, 2013). The group used Twitter to claim responsibility for the attack, spread misinformation about the enemies, praised the perpetrators, and provided links to videos taken by the group about the attacks. Thus, Twitter with its feature to provide instantaneous updates, has allowed Al-Shabab to exaggerate its offline activities. This, in turn, may increase its appeal and legitimacy among its followers.

Secondly, the ability to share information in real-time via these online platforms has become an essential source of information and inspiration for potential violent extremist wannabes. For example, Carter, Maher, and Neumann (2014) opined that Islamic State in Iraq and Syria (ISIS) fighters' constant real-time documentation of their involvement in the Syrian conflict have provided their followers with a unique glimpse of what is happening on the ground (e.g., battle victories, life in the Islamic State). In many instances, these updates will provide the followers with the perception that the group is capable and active in fighting for their cause (COPS, 2014). For some individuals, these updates may act as a form of inspiration, and a valuable data source to acquire information. In other words, violent extremist wannabes who are looking for a potential group to join would be more attracted towards online platforms that belong to groups which constantly update their status and activities, as compared to one which does not. Furthermore, regular updates by violent extremist groups on social media platforms such as Twitter would allow sympathiser (e.g., who has difficulty gaining access to messages via the secured forums) to obtain the information quickly and easily (McFarlane, 2010).

Lastly, there is a need for violent extremist groups to disseminate updates on their activities regularly enough to retain recognition and stay connected with its followers. This suggests that online platforms that do not update their content frequently may not be able to gain traction with their target audience. Take for example, the Indonesian-based jihadi blog, At-Taujih; despite functioning as a news site on jihadi-related news in Indonesia, the blog receives very little traffic (i.e., it is not traceable on general analytic trackers such as Alexa due to its low usage). This may be attributed to the lack of update on its online content; the most recent article posted on the blog was dated 29 October 2014. Put another way, visitors to the blog may not be able to find the latest jihadi-related developments in Indonesia and derive any gratification from the content shared on the outdated blog. These users may have moved on to other violent extremist online platforms.

Thus, it is not just the need for violent extremist groups to establish a plethora of violent extremist online platforms that matter, but the need for them to ensure that these online platforms are updated regularly to enhance the appeal of their messages.

Online Tools to Control and Manipulate Messages

The next feature focuses on the tools afforded by the online platforms that allow violent extremist groups to control and manipulate the messages that they disseminate online. Based on their analysis of jihadi video content on YouTube, Conway and McInerney (2008, p. 108) opined, "technological advances, particularly the increased availability of sophisticated, but cheap and easy to use video capturing hardware … and editing software meant that moving images began to play a much greater role in the jihadists information strategy from 2003".

With access to such online tools, violent extremist groups can select any content, manipulate it, and reproduce it to frame their ideals more effectively for their followers as part of their online visual persuasion strategy (Balkesim, 2014; Bowman-Grieve, 2013; Torok, 2013). This presents an apt illustration of how violent extremist online platform has evolved from traditional form of website (i.e., contains mostly texts) to one that contains professionally made videos and images (i.e., to augment the texts).

For example, in a study of 450 non-radicalised adults responses' to jihadi and right-wing violent extremist videos, Rieger, Frischich, and Bente (2013) found that the production style of the videos was cited as a dominant reason for the attitudes developed towards these videos. The authors noted that those violent extremist videos that were professionally made and directly addressed the recipients received less pronounced unpleasant ratings (i.e., neutral attitudes) as compared to other videos that did not. It would therefore be reasonable to acknowledge that the production style of these messages does play a role in facilitating a climate of receptivity in the recipient. These professionally made videos were also found to stimulate some degree of interest in the violent extremist messages.

Furthermore, findings by Lee and Leets (2002, p. 950) on the persuasiveness of online hate groups on young adolescent teens opined that "of additional concern, neutral adolescents appear vulnerable to hate groups' persuasive strategies. Both high-narrative [rich in text] and implicit message [rich in graphics] approaches swayed them, with the two strategies interacting for greater persuasion". Indeed, this ability to exercise ownership over the message underscores the violent extremist groups' ability to frame a radical worldview that may appeal viscerally and emotionally to the target audience (Rogan, 2007).

From a psychological perspective, such framing of violent extremist messages online amounts to generating interest within their target audience about their ideology and worldviews. Underlying the transformation of online platforms from crude statements to sophisticated impression management tool is intended to gather sympathy, incite negative sentiment toward enemies (or perceived enemies), and enhance the appeal of the messages online. Thus, it suggests that the use of such manipulated messages may increase the psychological appeal for some sympathisers and followers to join violent extremist groups (Kruglanski, 2014).

Another line of evidence comes from studies that have shown how such manipulated content may be used to better justify the use of violence as compared to other communication tools (e.g., mainstream media). In his analysis on right-wing violent extremists in the United States, Waltman (2014) noted that messages found on these online platforms have been reframed to highlight that violence is the only solution to challenges faced by white people in an attempt to influence the users' perceptions and opinions.

Similarly, in the context of violent jihadi extremists in Germany, Rieger and colleagues (2013) observed that messages were:

[A]imed at making the subtle and non-verbalised messages in propaganda footage visible. The catalogue reaches from symbols of nature, geography and politics to people, weapons, warfare and afterlife, to gestures and colours. Many motives are immanent in the Islamic culture and combined with selective picture elements, are used by the jihadists to suggest a certain extremist interpretation ... for instance, the depiction of a waterfall symbolises spiritual progress, the spirit which is ultimately raised to paradise and is therefore often used in conjunction with martyrdom. (p. 23)

On a broader level, the ability of violent extremist groups to adopt the use of these online tools to incorporate relevant cultural markers into their messages can make a big difference in ensuring that their messages do not lose their currency over time. Given that the act of interpreting messages online do not occur in an emotional vacuum and is heavily influenced by how the user developed meaning based on what one has seen, the presence of cultural visual markers may provide the contextual information user would require to make sense of the messages (Mielczarek & Perlmutter, 2014). Therefore, the tools afforded by the online platforms may suffice as the ideal conduit for violent extremist groups to enhance the appeal of violent extremist messages online.

In essence, the feature of the online platforms that allows violent extremist groups to control and manipulate their messages (i.e., via the online tools) may have enhanced the appeal of their propaganda messages online. The leverage afforded by these tools allows groups to create the visceral and emotional connections with their target audience.

Easy Access to Wide Repository of Messages

A third feature of the online platforms is the ease with which online messages created by violent extremist groups can be accessed by users. These propagandistic messages can take on many forms (e.g., videos, audiotapes, images, books, magazines, training manuals) and be embedded within the online platforms and/or accessed via the web-links provided. Unlike traditional hard copy versions of violent extremist propaganda, these online messages are relatively easy to locate and access via numerous online platforms (Bergin, Osman, Ungerer, & Yasin, 2009; Neo et al., 2015).

Given that radical messages are primarily accessed by individuals who actively search for them (Hussain & Saltman, 2014; Lennings, Amon, Brummert, & Lennings, 2010), the ease with which these individuals can navigate and obtain information from the online platforms will bear a significant influence on the likelihood of them further exploring the violent extremist messages. Similarly, in his analysis of the Internet as a tool for violent extremist persuasion, Duarte (2007) underscored the importance of the usability of the online platforms as there are plenty of alternative online platforms available if the user experienced difficulties trying to navigate an online platform which is not user-friendly. This suggests that the accessibility and usability of the online platforms may influence the user's online behaviour.

Given the potential role this feature of the online platforms may play in attracting individuals to view the entirety of their messages, it is therefore not surprising that violent extremist groups have endeavoured to organise their online platforms in ways that would increase the ease of navigating these online platforms. For instance, the Liberation Tigers of Tamil Eelam (LTTE) has provided numerous web-links to online materials for Tamils living abroad to stay connected to the Tamil community in Sri Lanka

(Tekwani, 2007). In doing so, it assured continuity, not only in terms of extending the outreach of their radical rhetoric, but also allowing violent extremist groups to maintain links with its sympathisers and members across the world.

It is also important to recognise that the wide assortment of messages and web-links found on these online platforms can be an indication of the violent extremist group's level of online sophistication as well as an indication of the group's legitimacy and credibility (Conway, 2006). As Lennings and colleagues (2010, p. 429) averred, "[T]he use of hyperlinks may increase credibility but also provide for ease of access to ideologically motivated websites that increase their utility as a 'first go' place". This may include access to insightful articles (e.g., topics chosen to elicit sympathy which are accompanied by elaborate religious, historical and/or political legitimisation), or other useful facts which members of the target audience are likely to find useful (e.g., information censored by the mainstream media). Thus, the presence of these web-links lends academic or authoritative support to the online platform and its associated violent extremist group.

One such example is the e-book titled 'Hijrah to the Islamic State'. This e-book, which was produced and disseminated by ISIS supporters, aims to provide operational guidance to potential recruits who are interested to perform hijrah (emigration) to the Islamic State. The easy access to such information online has therefore facilitated violent extremist groups' capability to connect with supporters and followers, and provided more opportunities for them to be radicalised.

Furthermore, insights gathered from the authors' research on online violent extremism suggest that attractive violent extremist online platforms are similar in nature to popular mainstream online mediums (Neo et al., 2015). In terms of the layout, violent extremist online platforms that attract users typically possess the following features:

- Laid out in a visually appealing manner with a modern professional presentation format;
- Demarcated with clear sections which is easy for users to navigate;
- Contain bite-sized barrage of factual and verifiable messages that are easily absorbed;
- Provide good levels of interactivity;
- A wide range of resources (i.e., offered in various digital resolution qualities as well as in a variety of formats to cater to the preference of the user) would be embedded within the online platforms, some of which are available for download and/or sharing via social media; and
- Contain web-links, which are functional and well-maintained, to similar online platforms, archives, libraries, and/or bookstores.

The Indonesia-based jihadi website, Voice of al-Islam, for example contains most of these features. In fact, data from analytic monitoring sites such as Alexa suggest that Voice of al-Islam has been widely viewed and received a consistent and high volume of visitor traffic since its inception[1]. The website, which aims to highlight the struggles of Islam from an alternative perspective (Sim & Ismail, 2012), is professionally designed with multiple web-links to other violent extremist online platforms, and has a wide variety of materials embedded within. The articles found on the site are presented in bite-size formats coupled with attractive imagery. This in turn makes it easier for users to digest the information.

In sum, the accessibility and usability of the violent extremist online platforms make it easier for individuals to navigate and find relevant information that they are searching for. Furthermore, it may increase the likelihood of users spending more time exploring the messages housed on these online platforms.

Interactive Features of Violent Extremist Online Platforms

The next feature of interest pertains to the presence of interactive communication features of violent extremist online platforms. Violent extremist groups have been known to utilise online platforms that are interactive (e.g., bulletin boards, forums, social media) to extent their outreach and influence.

In a recent study looking at the contents of 29 violent extremist online forums, the Dark Web team from the University of Arizona suggested that these interactive platforms serve as an effective channel to garner support and to intimidate enemies (Hsinchun et al., 2011). Similarly, in their annual terrorism trend report, Europol (2014, p. 14) reported that "Internet forums continue to be crucial in the dissemination of propaganda by religiously inspired terrorist groups. These forums connect terrorist groups to thousands of Internet users, who in turn can relay the content to a potentially unlimited audience".

Similar to how a mainstream online forum functions, an online violent extremist forum would also contain a spectrum of sections where different topics of interest are discussed. Forum users have to create a new thread to start a discussion or reply to other users' discussion threads. However, in many cases, users are required to register and log in in order to achieve the right to post a comment or start a new thread (Holtz, Kronberger, & Wagner, 2012). As compared to offline discussions, online forums provide a number of additional benefits. Firstly, posts remain on forum boards indefinitely, allowing for re-reading and re-posting. Secondly, individuals can observe the community interactions without explicitly joining in the discussion – i.e., unobtrusive lurking (Shi, Neo, Ong, & Khader, 2014). Thus, anyone with a computer and Internet access is capable of uploading and retrieving radical messages and is at risk of being influenced by violent extremist groups. Thirdly, no turn-taking defines cyberspace communication; anyone can post a message whenever one has questions to ask or comments to make (Ridings, Gefen, & Arinze, 2002).

In many respects, these interactive online platforms form an 'echo chamber' which allow for the development of interactive communication and opportunities for one to reinforce one's beliefs and worldviews with like-minded individuals (Hussain & Saltman, 2014; Lennings et al., 2010; Neo et al., 2015). For instance, in the aftermath of the 2015 Charlie Hebdo shootings, some Twitter users with or without links to violent extremist groups were seen celebrating the attack and praising the Kouachi brothers as martyrs. From a psychological perspective, such behaviours seemed to suggest that the interactivity afforded by these online platforms (i.e., the tweets being retweeted by others) allowed users (especially those without any connections to known violent extremist groups) the chance to voice their support and network with others who shared similar concerns or aspirations.

In other words, the interactive feature of the online platform allows for the exchange of ideas and validation of beliefs between like-minded individuals; which in the past would have been possible only through elaborate and often clandestine physical interactions (Sageman, 2008). More importantly, the act of deliberating the messages via these online platforms is considered to be potentially more compelling and persuasive than passively receiving information (Duarte, 2007).

Further to this, research has also found that interactions via these interactive platforms play an integral role in the creation of an online community (e.g., Conway & McInerney, 2008; Hussain & Saltman, 2014). These interactive features have the potential to reinforce a sense of community and belonging among the members in the shared online milieu. For example, Sageman (2008) noted that individuals become radicalised not simply by reading radical messages online, but instead through discussions with others. The report by U.S. Department of Justice on online violent extremism cited the interactive capability of the forums as a dominant reason in some cases to "move individuals from passively discussing violence and attacks to actively plotting with others" (COPS, 2014, p. 2).

Thus, these interactive features of the online platforms create the required social environment, which aim to cultivate partisanships and facilitate the assimilation of new social conduct, routines and behaviours. Furthermore, these interactions may create a sphere of influence where violent extremist groups socialise their online members to radical worldview thereby creating a ready-made antecedent for more radical ideology. And in doing so, member of the online community may regress from a myriad of mainstream influences to a narrow radical frame of reference (Geeraerts, 2012).

This has two operational implications. On the one hand, it has the potential to facilitate and lower the barrier for violent extremist groups to connect and influence their target audience. On the other hand, it also increases the possibility for violent extremist wannabes to contact the groups directly. Thus, the key perceivable danger is not that the online community serves as repositories for radical messages, but that it allows the individual to gain access to a community of like-minded individuals. Even in cases of lone-wolf attacks, the report by the General Intelligence and Security Service [AIVD] (2012) noted that these perpetrators rarely radicalise in complete isolation; there will be some form of interactions with like-minded individuals in these online communities.

In sum, the capacity to engage in interactive communication via the online platforms may have enhanced the appeal of the messages online. As Powers and Armstrong (2014, p. 184) pointed out in their analysis of visual propaganda and violent extremism, "this 'soft' side of power [use of interactive communication tools], typically seen as a subsidiary to the use of force, is increasingly capable of engendering hard-power responses". Thus, it underscores the utility of using these interactive channels as a tool to build an online proselytising community to maximise violent extremist groups' reach and influence.

Online Anonymity Afforded by Online Platforms

The last feature of violent extremist online platforms revolves around the sense (or perceived sense) of anonymity associated with the use of these online platforms. In utilising the Internet, individuals are under the perception that they are operating in a safe and secure environment and that makes the online search for mainstream-ostracised content or engagement in criminal activities a psychologically safer endeavour (Benson, 2014). Users would believe that no one knows what they are doing online and there will be little or no consequences in their illegal online engagements.

For example, individuals can utilise services such a virtual private network (VPN) to encrypt their online activities and hide their identity online (Larsson, Svensson, de Kaminski, Rönkkö, & Olsson, 2012). The VPN would make it difficult for the Internet service provider or any other agency to identify which users have accessed particular information online, as the identifying information will be referred to the VPN itself, rather than the user who was using that VPN.

In the context of violent extremism, this feature of online anonymity has a number of implications. First, it provides violent extremist groups with the sense of security as the chance of being detected by law enforcement agencies is made more unlikely by the use of services such as VPN. Thus, it may encourage more antisocial behaviours among violent extremist groups, especially when such behaviours are the group norm (Demetriou & Silke, 2003).

Secondly, the anonymity offered by the online platforms provides the opportunity for individuals (with no connections to violent extremist groups) to exist and become active within the online violent extremist community in a way that is not possible offline. This may encourage individuals who would not normally engage in accessing violent extremist online platforms to do so, comforted by the fact that their behaviours will go unnoticed and undetected. For instance, Bermingham, Conway, McInerney, O'Hare, and Smeaton (2009) in their analysis of YouTube for the potential for online radicalisation, found more extreme and less tolerant views among female users as compared to male users – e.g., female users expressed more positive opinions towards Al-Qaeda. In addition, they observed "a potentially increased leadership role for women online than they would generally be held to have within jihadi circles" (p. 7). It is reasonable therefore to suggest that the anonymity of the Internet may have offered greater opportunity for individuals (i.e., who would not normally engage in violent extremism) such as female users to become active online.

In sum, the feature of online anonymity may increase the likelihood of individuals who espouse deviant or alternate views not accepted by the mainstream society, to visit violent extremist online platforms and become involved in violent extremism.

CONCLUSION

Technological innovations have inadvertently allowed new ways for violent extremist groups to present themselves to the global audience that might not otherwise be possible a decade ago. Besides offering violent extremist groups a variety of online platforms to disseminate propagandistic messages online, the Internet has afforded these groups the opportunity to connect and alter the relationships between them and their potential followers. Indeed, law enforcement agencies across the world are confronting and grappling with the threat of online propaganda campaign by violent extremist groups, and its potential impact of the internet on the radicalisation process. Thus, there is the need for law enforcement agencies to understand how violent extremist groups gain traction with their followers – especially in terms of the messages, and the online platforms that house these messages.

Recognising the paucity of research analysing the persuasiveness of violent extremist online platforms, this chapter has identified five features of the violent extremist online platforms that may contribute to a climate of receptivity for radical messages. The five features of online platforms are: (1) regular updates; (2) tools to control and manipulate message; (3) easy access to wide repository of messages; (4) interactive features; and (5) online anonymity.

While the identified features of the online platforms may play a role in enhancing the appeal of violent extremist messages online, it is also important to acknowledge the attributes (i.e., needs and vulnerabilities) of the users visiting these online platforms. Aly and colleagues (2014) argued that individuals played an important role in the process of receiving and digesting the message online. They reasoned that for any effective communication to occur, the audience should have the freedom to choose what they want to read which is shaped by "social roles that are gratified by the attributes, content and the context of different media platforms" (p. 34). Therefore, it is important to recognise that the identified features alone should not be used to determine persuasiveness, or for that matter, the likelihood of any individual becoming radicalised. This underscores the need to consider other factors (e.g., person-centric, political context) in order to gain a better comprehension of the persuasiveness of violent extremist online propaganda.

Having said that, law enforcement agencies could use insights about how violent extremist groups are designing their online platforms to develop interventions so as to enhance their counter violent extremism strategies. Based on the features of the online platforms examined in this chapter, two implications have been identified.

The Need to Disrupt Key Violent Extremist Online Platforms

The nature of the Internet makes it easy for violent extremist groups to evade detection. For example, little can be done about violent extremist online platforms that fall outside the jurisdiction of one's country (Seib & Janbek, 2011). Another challenge resides in the nature of these online platforms which are known to evolve and change their Uniform Resource Locator (URL) frequently. Thus, approaches aimed at restricting and removing violent extremist messages from the Internet is not only the least effective, but it is also the most labour-intensive endeavour.

However, none of this is meant to imply that disruptions of violent extremist online platforms are not effective or necessary. On the contrary, successful disruptions of prominent violent extremist online platforms can be quite useful in signalling the types of content that the country regards as offensive or harmful (Neo et al., 2015). Moreover, it may also undermine inadvertent viewing. In other words, restricting the access to some of these attractive violent extremist online platforms (i.e., contains the features identified earlier) presents the opportunity to prevent Internet users from chancing upon these online platforms. Alternatively, it serves to send out a strong message that the country does not condone such violent extremist messages. Thus, law enforcement agencies should not shy away from making the effort to disrupt online platforms that contravene existing violent extremism legislations when necessary, and to adopt this measure in conjunction with other countering violent extremism initiatives.

Work Together with the Internet Industry

There is a need to engage the Internet industry companies such as YouTube, Twitter, and Facebook for assistance to remove unlawful violent extremist messages. Due to the nature of the Internet, countering online violent extremism must be a joint effort between the law enforcement agencies and private sector (Benson, 2014). Hussain and Saltman (2014) in their report on countering online violent extremism opined that:

Governments [law enforcement agencies] need to have established channels of communication with private sector technology companies, such as Google, YouTube and Facebook. These channels will allow them to raise concerns and establish procedures through which dialogue over contentious content or polices can be held. (p. 112)

This serves to obstruct violent extremist groups' exploitation of the Internet and subvert the redistribution of undesirable radical messages.

The appreciation of the role played by the Internet industry in countering online violent extremism may encourage law enforcement agencies to work together with these companies to introduce new ideas to regulate and manage the Internet infrastructure (Conway, 2007). Internet industry companies may consider manipulating their search engine algorithms so that the search for violent extremist related messages are interrupted, and only results that do not include violent extremist online platforms are returned. Similarly, in a recent BBC report, it was mentioned that Facebook has begun placing warnings over violent videos uploaded to its site in an attempt to make it harder for people to find violent-laden materials (Kelion, 2015).

More importantly, law enforcement should leverage on the technical expertise of these private companies to develop appealing online platforms to disseminate counter-narratives in an attempt to reduce the appeal and reach of the violent extremist messages online (The Online Radicalisation Research Community of Practice [ORRCOP], 2014). Furthermore, the knowledge gained from such collaborations may provide law enforcement agencies with valuable insights of how new technological developments (e.g., communication technology) can be exploited by violent extremist groups.

ACKNOWLEDGMENT

The views expressed in this chapter are the authors' only and do not represent the official position or view of the Ministry of Home Affairs, Singapore.

REFERENCES

Al Raffie, D. (2012). Whose hearts and minds? Narratives and counter-narratives of Salafi Jihadism. *Journal of Terrorism Research*, *3*(2), 13–31. doi:10.15664/jtr.304

Aly, A., Weimann-Saks, D., & Weimann, G. (2014). Making 'noise' online: An analysis of the say no to terror online campaign. *Perspective on Terrorism*, *8*(5), 33–47.

Balkesim, S. (2014). Semantic processing of visual propaganda in the online environment. In C. K. Winkler & C. E. Dauber (Eds.), *Visual propaganda and extremism in the online environment* (pp. 193–214). Carlisle, PA: Strategic Studies Institute and U.S. Army War College Press.

Benson, D. C. (2014). Why the Internet is not increasing terrorism. *Security Journal*, *23*, 293–328.

Bergin, A., Osman, S. B., Ungerer, C., & Yasin, N. A. M. (2009). *Countering Internet radicalisation in Southeast Asia. Special Report*. Australia: Australian Strategic Policy Institute.

Bermingham, A., Conway, M., McInerney, L., O'Hare, N., & Smeaton, A. F. (2009). *Combining social network analysis and sentiment analysis to explore the potential for online radicalisation*. Paper presented at Advances in Social Networks Analysis and Mining, Athens, Greece. doi:10.1109/ASONAM.2009.31

Bowman-Grieve, L. (2013). A psychological perspective on virtual communities supporting terrorist & extremist ideologies as a tool for recruitment. *Security Informatics*, *2*(9), 1–5.

Carter, J. A., Maher, S., & Neumann, P. R. (2014). *Greenbirds: measuring importance and influence in Syrian foreign fighter networks*. London: The International Centre for the Study of Radicalisation and Political Violence.

Community Oriented Policing Services (COPS). (2014). *YouTube and violent extremism: Awareness brief*. Washington, DC: U.S. Department of Justice.

Conway, M. (2005). Terrorist web sites: Their contents, functioning, and effectiveness. In P. Seib (Ed.), *Media and conflict in the twenty-first century* (pp. 185–215). New York, NY: Palgrave.

Conway, M. (2006). Terrorism and the Internet: New media – new threat. *Parliamentary Affairs*, *59*(2), 283–298. doi:10.1093/pa/gsl009

Conway, M. (2007). Terrorist use of the Internet and the challenges of governing cyberspace. In D. Myriam, V. Mauer, & F. Krishna-Hensel (Eds.), *Power and security in the information age: Investigating the role of the state in cyberspace* (pp. 95–127). London: Ashgate.

Conway, M., & McInerney, L. (2008). Jihadi video & auto-radicalisation: Evidence from an exploratory YouTube study. *Intelligence and Security Informatics, 5376*, 108–118.

Dauber, C. E., & Winkler, C. K. (2014). Radical visual propaganda in the online environment: An introduction. In C. K. Winkler & C. E. Dauber (Eds.), *Visual propaganda and extremism in the online environment* (pp. 1–30). Carlisle, PA: Strategic Studies Institute and U.S. Army War College Press.

Demetriou, C., & Silke, A. (2003). A criminological Internet 'sting'. Experimental evidence of illegal and deviant visits to a website trap. *The British Journal of Criminology, 43*(1), 213–222. doi:10.1093/bjc/43.1.213

Duarte, C. (2007). The seductive web: Technology as a tool for persuasion. In B. Ganor, K. von Knop, & C. Duarte (Eds.), Hypermedia seduction for terrorist recruiting (pp. 169-187). Washington, DC: IOS Press.

Egan, M. (2013, October 9). Does Twitter have a terrorism problem? *Fox Business*. Retrieved from http://www.foxbusiness.com/technology/2013/10/09/does-twitter-have-terrorism-problem/

Europol. (2014). *TE-SAT 2014. European Union terrorism situation and trend report 2014*. European Law Enforcement Agency.

Fighel, J. (2007). Radical Islamic Internet propaganda: Concepts, idioms and visual motifs. In B. Ganor, K. von Knop, & C. Duarte (Eds.), *Hypermedia seduction for terrorist recruiting* (pp. 34–38). Washington, DC: IOS Press.

Geeraerts, S. (2012). Digital radicalisation of youth. *Social Cosmos, 3*(1), 25–32.

General Intelligence and Security Service (AIVD). (2012). *Jihadism on the web: A breeding ground for jihad in the modern age*. The Hague: Algemene Inlichtingen en Veiligheidsdienst.

Gladwell, M. (2004). *The tipping point: How little things can make a big difference*. London: Abacus.

Heath, C., & Heath, D. (2008). *Made to stick: Why some ideas take hold and others come unstuck*. London: Arrow.

Holtz, P., Kronberger, N., & Wagner, W. (2012). Analysing Internet forums: A practical guide. *Journal of Media Psychology, 24*(2), 55–66. doi:10.1027/1864-1105/a000062

Hsinchun, C., Denning, D., Roberts, N. N., Larson, C. A., Yu, X., & Huang, C. (2011). The Dark Web Forum Portal: From multi-lingual to video. In *Proceedings on the 2011 IEEE International Conference on Intelligence and Security Informatics*. Beijing: IEEE.

Hussain, G., & Saltman, E. M. (2014). *Jihad trending: a comprehensive analysis of online extremism and how to counter it*. Quilliam Foundation.

Kelion, L. (2015, January 13). Facebook restricts violent video clips and photos. *BBC News*. Retrieved from http://www.bbc.com/news/technology-30793702

Kruglanski, A. W. (2014, October 28). Psychology not theology: Overcoming ISIS' secret appeal. *E-International Relations*. Retrieved from http://www.e-ir.info/2014/10/28/psychology-not-theology-overcoming-isis-secret-appeal/

Larsson, S., Svensson, M., de Kaminski, M., Rönkkö, K., & Olsson, J. A. (2012). Laws, norms, piracy and online anonymity: Practices of de-identification in the global file sharing community. *Journal of Research in Interactive Marketing, 6*(4), 260–280. doi:10.1108/17505931211282391

Lee, E., & Leets, L. (2002). Persuasive story telling by hate groups on line. *The American Behavioral Scientist, 45*, 927–957. doi:10.1177/0002764202045006003

Lennings, C. J., Amon, K. L., Brummert, H., & Lennings, N. J. (2010). Grooming for Terror: The Internet and Young People. *Psychiatry, Psychology and Law, 17*(3), 424–437. doi:10.1080/13218710903566979

Lia, B. (May 2008). Al-Qaida's appeal: Understanding its unique selling points. *Perspectives on Terrorism, 2*(8).

McFarlane, B. (2010). *Online violent radicalisation (OVeR): Challenges facing law enforcement agencies and policy stakeholders*. Peer reviewed conference paper. Global Terrorism Research Centre, Monash University.

Mielczarek, N., & Perlmutter, D. D. (2014). Big pictures and visual propaganda: The lessons of research on the "effects" of photojournalistic icons. In C. K. Winkler & C. E. Dauber (Eds.), *Visual propaganda and extremism in the online environment* (pp. 215–232). Carlisle, PA: Strategic Studies Institute and U.S. Army War College Press.

Neo, L. S., Khader, M., Shi, P., Dillon, L., & Ong, G. (2015). *Extremist cyber footprints: A guide to understanding and countering online extremism*. Singapore: Home Team Behavioural Sciences Centre.

Neo, L. S., Singh, K., Khader, M., Ang, J., & Ong, G. (2013). *Understanding Internet-mediated radicalisation: A theoretical C3PO pathway framework. Research report No. 05/2013*. Singapore: Home Team Behavioural Sciences Centre.

Online Radicalisation Research Community of Practice (ORRCOP). (2014, November). *ISIS and its formula for recruitment effectiveness in the online realm*. ORRCOP Commentary 1/15. Singapore: National Security Coordination Secretariat.

Osman, J. (2013). Al-Shabaab: Using social media to fight the jihad. *Channel 4*. Retrieved from: http://www.channel4.com/news/al-shabaab-jihadist-kenya-westgate-kenya-nairobi-twitter

Powers, S., & Armstrong, M. (2014). Conceptualising radicalisation in a market for loyalties. In C. K. Winkler & C. E. Dauber (Eds.), *Visual propaganda and extremism in the online environment* (pp. 165–192). Carlisle, PA: Strategic Studies Institute and U.S. Army War College Press.

Ramakrishna, K. (2015). *Islamist Terrorism and Militancy in Indonesia: The Power of the Manichean Mindset*. Singapore: Springer. doi:10.1007/978-981-287-194-7

Ridings, C. M., Gefen, D., & Arinze, B. (2002). Some antecedents and effects of trust in virtual communities. *The Journal of Strategic Information Systems, 11*(3-4), 271–295. doi:10.1016/S0963-8687(02)00021-5

Rieger, D., Frischich, L., & Bente, G. (2013). *Propaganda 2.0 Psychological effects of right-wing and Islamic extremist Internet videos*. German Federal Criminal Police Office.

Rogan, H. (2006). Jihadism online – A study of how al-Qaeda and radical Islamist groups use the Internet for terrorist purposes. Norwegian Defence Research Establishment (FFI).

Rogan, H. (2007). Al-Qaeda's online media strategies: From Abu Reuter to Irhabi 007. Norwegian Defence Research Establishment (FFI).

Sageman, M. (2008). *Leaderless jihad*. Philadelphia, PA: Pennsylvania University Press. doi:10.9783/9780812206784

Saifudeen, O. A. (2014). *The cyber extremism orbital pathways model*. Singapore: S. Rajaratnam School of International Studies.

Salamon, K. L. G. (2007). Design and identity – Visual culture and identity politics. In B. Ganor, K. von Knop, & C. Duarte (Eds.), *Hypermedia seduction for terrorist recruiting* (pp. 267–280). Washington, DC: IOS Press.

Seib, P., & Janbek, D. M. (2011). *Global terrorism and new media: The post-Al Qaeda generation*. New York, NY: Routledge.

Shi, P., Neo, L. S., Ong, G., & Khader, M. (2014). *Understanding online protest: A system-person perspective. Research report No. 15/2014*. Singapore: Home Team Behavioural Sciences Centre.

Sim, S., & Ismail, N. H. (2012). *Online jihad in Indonesia*. Singapore: Strategic Nexus Consultancy.

Tekwani, S. (2007). Online networks of terrorist groups and their implications for security: a case study of Sri Lanka's Liberation Tigers of Tamil Eelam. In I. Banerjee (Ed.), *The Internet and governance in Asia: A critical reader* (pp. 173–188). Singapore: National Technological University of Singapore.

Torok, R. (2013). Developing an explanatory model for the process of online radicalisation and terrorism. *Security Informatics*, *2*(1), 1–10. doi:10.1186/2190-8532-2-6

Waltman, M. S. (2014). Teaching hate: The role of Internet visual imagery in the radicalisation of white ethno-terrorists in the United States. In C. K. Winkler & C. E. Dauber (Eds.), *Visual propaganda and extremism in the online environment* (pp. 83–104). Carlisle, PA: Strategic Studies Institute and U.S. Army War College Press.

Weimann, G. (2004). *How modern terrorism uses the Internet. Special Report No.116*. Washington, DC: United States Institute of Peace; www.terror.net

Weimann, G., & von Knop, K. (2008). Applying the notion of noise to countering online terrorism. *Studies in Conflict and Terrorism*, *31*(10), 883–902. doi:10.1080/10576100802342601

ENDNOTE

[1.] The global rank of the jihadi website, Voice of al-Islam, stood at 46,731 accurate as of August 3, 2015.

Chapter 2
Persuasion and Propaganda in War and Terrorism

Thomas Steinfatt
University of Miami, USA

Dana Janbek
Lasell College, USA

ABSTRACT

This chapter focuses on the use of propaganda during times of war, prejudice, and political unrest. Part one distinguishes between persuasion and one of its forms, propaganda. The meaning-in-use of the term 'propaganda' is essential to understanding its use over time. Part two presents relevant examples of propaganda from the past several centuries in the United States and Europe. These examples include episodes from World War I and II, among others. Propaganda is not a new tool of persuasion, and learning about its use in the past provides a comparison that helps in understanding its use in the present and future. Part three looks at recent examples of how propaganda occurs in actual use in online terrorist mediums by Al-Qaeda and by the Islamic State in Iraq and Syria (ISIS).

PROPAGANDA AS HUMAN COMMUNICATION

Propaganda is useful in a dictatorship, but essential in a democracy. It is an ancient tool used by state and non-state actors during times of peace and of war. The messages used by power groups and by those aspiring to power are seldom random statements made in haste and anger.

This chapter considers the use of propaganda during times of war and power struggles. The introduction to propaganda may serve as background to introduce considerations as to how terrorist groups have operated prior to their introduction by newer terrorist groups such as Al-Qaeda and the Islamic State in Iraq and Syria (ISIS) in current online forums. Terrorist groups thrive on disseminating propagandistic content to their followers. Thus, a review of how propaganda has been used historically by governments and individuals should assist in understanding how it is used today by modern terrorist organisations. Most writings on terrorism focus on the present and seldom borrow from historical examples in explaining the how and why of terrorism. It is important to remember that terrorist groups did not invent

DOI: 10.4018/978-1-5225-0156-5.ch002

propaganda. This chapter offers a unique perspective in thinking about terrorism which is one of the great challenges that faces societies today.

The first part of this chapter traces propaganda into its earliest forms. It delves into the various definitions of propaganda and adopts one for our discussion here. It then proceeds to discuss propaganda in specific terms through a number of historical examples starting with the late 1800s. While there are thousands of examples one could use, the authors focus on 11 cases, ten of which we regard as propaganda cases and one case we do not. In considering modern day terrorist communication habits, the authors invite readers to link what is happening today in the terrorism world to some of the examples shared here.

Propaganda is a form of persuasion and persuasion is a form of communication. Communication among humans began about 500,000 years ago in its spoken form, and at least several hundred thousand years later in its written form. Humans use words to bring objects and ideas into our minds, not just into our hands. Words do not 'mean', in the sense of having a fixed meaning such that a call to arms or a call to peace will have the same or even necessarily similar meanings to others who hear or read the same messages. Only people have the power to create meaning, and that meaning is in their minds. Meaning is phenomenological, not physical. Meanings are in people, not in words.

Written symbols developed about 30,000 years ago, likely as methods of keeping track of numbers of sheep, harvests, debts, and similar important items. Most languages and societies we know about necessarily had a written form, which provided humanity with much of our knowledge of those cultures and societies. Oral culture and language survived only in stories, and these changed somewhat with almost every telling.

The surviving pictograph records of many early societies provide evidence of systems of belief illustrating the prowess and skills of the hunters among meat eating groups, and depictions concerning beliefs and conceptions of the weather and seasons in agricultural societies. Without outside corroboration, it is difficult to tell if the hieroglyphs are accurate representations of the abilities of the hunters, and of the size and methods of the harvest to bring food to their respective groups, or if they are exaggerations of what commonly occurred. Exaggerations and misrepresentations, to the extent they occurred, might represent simply the artistic license of the artists. But they could also be the earliest form of propaganda as the term is commonly used today.

What evidence is there that might suggest that the early messages that survived were intended as relatively accurate depictions, or if they tended towards the exaggerative end of the scale? What would suggest that they were relatively accurate, or that alternately they were tending towards the propagandistic? The modern notion of 'propaganda', including its principles and how to recognise, defend against, and create it, developed much later.

Propaganda has not always been a negative term. Some conceptions and definitions have equated propaganda with any forms of mass messages. And in some languages spoken today, the term closest in meaning to propaganda is advertising. The term is not necessarily seen as negative in several Spanish and Portuguese speaking countries. Though there were many instances in history where propaganda was considered to be a positive term by those producing it, only two of these are commonly cited as examples today. These are the Roman Catholic Church in the 17th century, and quite independently, the beginnings of Russian Communism in the 1920s. ISIS likely considers its propaganda as positive.

The first known use of the term propaganda as a positive formal concept in the Western world occurred through its use in the Latin title of the newly formed Council of Bishops, created in the 17th century by Pope Gregory XV. This *Congregation de propaganda fide*, or *Congregation for Propagation of the Faith* of the Roman Catholic Church, was a formal recognition by the Church that conversion to Roman Catholicism by force and the sword was not as effective as desired, since many proposed converts preferred to die rather than to convert. The new method involved conversion without coercion, representing the benefits of voluntarily accepting the 'one true faith'. The Congregation de propaganda fide's task was to seek ways of convincing people to convert without the use of violence, replacing it with *propaganda* (i.e., messages about the joy of eternal salvation through belief in Christ as the saviour).

The other major positive connotations historically are found in Communist agitprop strategies, where agitation, the repetition of slogans without accompanying reasoning or rationale, was proposed for use with the masses. Propaganda, defined as a one-sided discussion involving a minor rationale and reasoning, was to be used for the more educated classes.

Definition of Propaganda

Propaganda is one form of persuasion. In many academic discussions of the term, propaganda is poorly defined in ways that do not distinguish it from other forms involving communication with large groups of people. These non-distinguishing definitions include, but are not limited to: the systematic propagation of a doctrine or cause; communication's role in social struggle; mass suggestion of influence through the manipulation of symbols and psychology.

These definitions relegate the term propaganda to nothing more than a synonym for 'sets of repeated messages over time'. Sets such as these occur in advertising, public relations, religion, and education. Such definitions fail to recognise what the term propaganda denotes and connotes to most speakers of English. Lacking such clarity, the distinction as employed between propaganda and education may simply be: 'what your schools teach is propaganda, what our schools teach is education'. In some cases, propaganda, as defined here, may be found in education and other applications. But not all education is propaganda and not all propaganda is education. Using any of the above definitions of propaganda implies that propaganda is just another persuasion campaign. But the term propaganda, as used, designates a very specific subset of persuasion. A number of propaganda campaigns are considered below that illustrate the distinctions between persuasion together with 'any mass communication campaign' on the one side, and propaganda on the other.

A More Useful Definition

Persuasion refers to a subset of communication involving the intent to support or change people's beliefs and behaviours. In its most common current usage, propaganda refers to:

- A form of persuasion,
- Usually distinguished by a mass persuasion campaign,
- Often one-sided and fear-based,
- Which attempts to subvert rational processes,
- Often by hiding relevant information, and
- That may occur by lying or deception (Steinfatt, 2016).

In addition, two distinct but related persuasion campaigns often exist in developed propaganda systems. The first (i.e., which always exists) is a propaganda system laudatory of the cause, position, religion, political party, etc., which is supported by that propaganda. Almost all of the messages in this pro-campaign are simply a one-sided message set supporting the view or cause in question, with no mention or consideration that there might be another side or sides. Any few messages that do allude to another side or sides will be very brief, and/or mention only absurdly flawed reasons for supporting that other side, or discuss silly reasons for rejecting the desired/supported side.

Second, one or more negative campaigns may be developed that attack the views of the other side or sides. These are intended for messages directed to outsiders, persons who are not true believers of the belief system in question. In some cases, a propaganda campaign may begin by using this second message system as an attempt to entice those from opposing sides or with opposing views into switching sides. Such an approach will at least provide considerations of the benefits of the propagandist's side, hoping to convert disbelievers later. Message campaigns involving only 'positive' messages that do not disparage opposing views may also be considered propaganda when opposing opinions are discouraged or outlawed.

Public relations, religion, advertising, and education can each involve propaganda as defined above. They can also be distinguished from it to the extent that they are not one-sided and/or fear-based, and do not attempt to subvert rational processes. In theory, education should promote the search for and evaluation of all available evidence and to promote rational thought, attempting to separate it from emotion in order to create a balanced understanding of the subject matter. Advertising and public relations may become propaganda to the extent that they employ fear, and/or attempt to subvert logical processes in the way in which they treat negative consequences of the product or idea advertised. Religion may avoid being propaganda to the extent that it attempts to rationally consider evidence for and against its propositions.

Given a definition of propaganda, specific historical cases that involved propaganda used in attempts at governmental control are considered below, in preparation for examining the current use of the Internet by terrorist groups as a propaganda tool.

PROPAGANDA: HISTORICAL EXAMPLES

Major Governmental Propaganda Episodes: 1890 to World War II

Propaganda could not exist, as defined, until the earth had a sufficient population to support mass persuasion campaigns. As indicted in historical records, it did exist throughout most of recorded history. Anti-Semitic propaganda alone appears to have occurred from well before the time of Jesus. Its effect, and the relationship between propaganda and terrorism, may be noted when during the first Crusades Christians leaving their homes to fight for the Holy Land, paused to sack and burn nearby Jewish settlements before heading towards Jerusalem. Propaganda's history over the past 200 odd years can hardly be covered adequately in any single book, let alone chapter. The use of propaganda in terrorism is likely as old as terrorism itself. This is illustrated in the cases below, presented in order to place our research on the use of the Internet by terrorist groups in context.

By the late 1800s, lists and codifications of propaganda techniques were published, by Tarde (1890), and Le Bon (1896). These lists influenced psychoanalysis through Freud's writings and lectures, and influenced Hitler in portions of *Mein Kampf*. The selected propaganda episodes considered below begin in the 1800s and concentrate on war, political, and anti-Semitic propaganda, and terrorism. These are followed by the results of an empirical study of terrorist use of propaganda to recruit on the Internet.

The Protocols of the Learned Elders of Zion

The case of *The Protocols* serves to illustrate some of the staying properties of propaganda after its initial introduction and acceptance, and despite its refutation. In 1864, Maurice Joly, a French writer, published the novel *Dialogue in Hell between Machiavelli and Montesquieu*, protesting the rule of Napoleon III (Joly, 1864). Four years later, Hermann Goedsche, also known as Sir John Retcliffe, wrote the novel *Biarritz*, clearly presented as fiction, in which Goedsche plagiarised liberally and without citation from Joly's 1864 work, as well as from Dumas' *Joseph Balsamo* (Goedsche, 1868). Goedsche also changed a major section of the work when he added the chapter 'At the Jewish Cemetery in Prague'. The chapter was presented in large part as though it were a word for word record of a supposed secret meeting of a cabal representing the 'Twelve Tribes of Israel' which occurred at midnight in a Prague cemetery. In it, the representatives discuss their progress in achieving the long-term conspiratorial goal of world domination by many methods, including owning land, controlling the press, reducing master craftsmen to common industrial workers, and making their way into high office. The meeting notes conclude by reaffirming the 'Jewish Goal' of world domination within a century. Neither *Dialogue in Hell* nor *Biarritz* were major successes; most copies were eventually relegated to dusty back shelves in a few libraries.

In Russia one quarter century later, the stirrings of Bolshevism, Lenin's doctrine proposing and ultimately forming a party composed of disciplined professional revolutionaries in his branch of the Russian Social-Democratic Workers' Party, created a growing apprehension of a threat to the rule of Czar Nicholas II. Rasputin had the ear of the Czar's wife concerning their haemophiliac son. And the Czar's secret police, the Okhrana, became increasingly concerned with the Czar's failure to see the Bolshevists as a growing terrorist threat not just to the Czar, but to the monarchy itself.

The Czar was resisting attempts by his militarists to convince him that the Bolsheviks could become a major threat both to his rule and to mother Russia itself. The goal of *The Protocols*' author appears to be to move the Czar towards acting forcefully against the Bolsheviks, and further attempting to discredit Bolshevism by tying it to Judaism.

While there is no absolute evidence of its authorship, a bound manuscript appeared in Russia in the mid-1890s and was presented to the Czar: *The Protocols of the Learned Elders of Zion* (Anonymous, 1895). The manuscript was written as though it were the minutes of a secret meeting of Jewish leaders, plotting in some detail the takeover of the world through domination of its financial systems, and using direct quotes from the participants. In *The Protocols* there were 'written proof' of the Jews' evil intentions. The Jews were seen as behind it all. Except that *The Protocols* was for the most part a word for word copy of one scene from *Biarritz*.

The first Zionist Congress had been recently held in Basil, Switzerland, and the names of its leaders were substituted in *The Protocols* for Goedsche's original characters in *Biarritz*. Many historians suspect Pyotr Rachkovsky, Chief of the Okhrana, as the author of *The Protocols* since he was an expert forger, creating ID cards and other false documents for his secret police, and a principal advocate of crushing the Bolsheviks, several of whose leaders were Jewish. The propaganda connection between *The Protocols* and the Bolsheviks was Judaism. Others believe that Matvei Golovinski, an Okhrana agent, created the first edition as instructed by Rachkovsky.

That it was a single copy, loosely bound and printed not as an attack on Jews but as a document written by them representing their innermost thoughts that they wished to conceal: that created the special propaganda appeal of *The Protocols*. Here was clear support for people's hatred and prejudice against the Jews – the Jews were clearly admitting to the evil seen in them through the prejudices of others.

The Czar initially waivered on the authenticity of *The Protocols* but this did not prevent the Russian Orthodox Church from reading excerpts of it during Sunday Services through the early 1900s. A Czarist commission appointed to study the work eventually exposed it as propaganda in 1903, and the Czar accepted that judgment. As with most propaganda, its exposure as fraud did little to influence the beliefs and behaviour of the true believers who flocked to *The Protocols* as truth after its exposure. Nor did the Czar heed the views of the Okhrana, falsely supported though they were, that Bolshevism was a major threat.

While in circulation in Russia throughout the early 1900s, *The Protocols* was generally unknown in other countries. When Germany funded the Bolshevists late in World War I as an attempt to remove Russia as an Eastern Front, the fall of the Czar and the terror that followed led Czarist loyalists to pack what they could and flee the mother country. Most carried little but their valuables and the Bible with them. But as the rumour spread that the Czar had taken only the Bible and his copy of *The Protocols* with him to the Katchaturin Forest, many White Russians added their copy of *The Protocols* in their hurried packing. This process served to spread the Protocols across Europe and to America as well. German, English, and Spanish translations rapidly became available and reached most Western countries by 1920.

In Britain, Winston Churchill, Under Secretary of the Admiralty, initially expressed belief in *The Protocols* authenticity, withdrawing that opinion several months later. Government figures in Europe and America also initially saw *The Protocols* as authentic. In 1920, *The Protocols* was exposed as a forgery by a Jewish committee, which did little to change public belief. In 1921, London based reporter Philip Graves located copies of *Biarritz* and of *Dialogue in Hell between Machiavelli and Montesquieu* and published a clear refutation of *The Protocols* in a *Times of London* article, which was later reprinted by the *New York Times* (Graves, 1921). But exposure of propaganda as propaganda has seldom been persuasive to true believers. Perhaps because a document reflects and offers support for an individual's views, prejudiced though those views may be, what is clear evidence against the Protocols to the rational, becomes accepted truth to believers. This occurs in the process of religious belief as well as in racial and political beliefs.

In America, Henry Ford, founder and developer of the first American car intended for the masses and not just for the rich, was a believer in the myths of Jewish Domination theories. He had excerpts of *The Protocols* placed in each of his Ford Model-T showrooms, next to the blurb extoling his cars. And he purchased the *Dearborn Independent*, becoming its editor and publisher. The *Dearborn Independent* served as Ford's vehicle for disseminating the anti-Semitic propaganda of *The Protocols*. He wrote and published many anti-Jewish editorials which he had leather-bound in a set of volumes containing portions of *The Protocols*, and Ford's editorials for the *Dearborn Independent*. The copyright page of the volumes stated clearly that they were not copyrighted, and readers were encouraged to copy and disseminate everything within. He used his own money both to publish and to have the documents leather bound, and shipped copies to every major library in the world. In 1927, Ford finally was forced to agree that *The Protocols* was likely a forgery, but he still believed in its essential truth, a specific instance where, though there was clear rational evidence against *The Protocols* authenticity, it became accepted truth to believers. Similarly, rational evidence establishing evil thought, motives, or deeds behind terrorist organisations may not be convincing evidence for the organisations' believers.

One copy of Henry Ford's leather bound volumes was available in a library in Berlin in the 1920s. It may have been the copy initially seen by Adolph Hitler and referred to in Mein Kampf. Hitler clearly regarded Ford as a hero, and is rumoured to have kept a picture of *My Dear Heinrich* above his bed in the 1920s. While Hitler and his propaganda minister Josef Goebbels recognised *The Protocols* as a forgery and seldom if ever based their propaganda on it, Julius Streicher, editor of the viscously anti-Semitic newspaper *Der Stürmer,* occasionally relied on *The Protocols* while producing issues of *Der Stürmer* in the 1930s. Many terrorist attacks on individual Jews and their possessions were processed through the German courts in the 1920s, with *The Protocols* commonly mentioned as one justification in defence of the attack.

Though denounced as a forgery by each of many investigations beginning with the Czarist committee in 1903, continued through Phillip Graves's intensive work, and that of many others including a U.S. Senate investigation in 1964, *The Protocols* still appears on many Internet hate sites represented as the truth. Few hate sites on the web fail to contain a reference or link to *The Protocols* or a copy of the document, and they are well-known by and circulated within the Ku Klux Klan and similar hate based organisations. An extensive 2013 study of the many New York City corner newsstands in Manhattan between Little Italy and 59th Street was unable to locate a single stand that did not have a copy of *The Protocols* available for sale (Daugherty, 2013).

The case of *The Protocols* illustrates the use of a single document that is held to be the basis for a set of beliefs and corresponding actions (i.e., based on those beliefs) over time.

American Propaganda: 1914 to 1919

The Birth of a Nation

In 1914, Woodrow Wilson, the former President of Princeton University, was elected President of the United States. While outwardly liberal in his thinking, Wilson accepted D.W. Griffith's offer to exhibit his 1915 masterpiece, *The Birth of a Nation* which extoled the virtues of the Ku Klux Klan, particularly in protecting white women from rape by non-whites. Following the viewing, Wilson remarked of the blatant racism and glorification of the Ku Klux Klan in the film, that he was afraid it was all too true. The propaganda of inequality of the races was so ingrained in American culture that even the clearest instances of propaganda in racist literature were accepted as true and 'common knowledge', even by a highly educated former university president.

The case of *The Birth of a Nation* illustrates the use of an entertainment film to provide continued support of discriminatory laws against and treatment of a disenfranchised minority.

World War I and the Zimmerman Telegram

Wilson had run on a 'peace' platform, advocating an isolationist policy for the country. But the massive loss of life and stalemate in Europe during the early stages of World War I eventually moved him to consider intervening in the conflict with American forces. His decision to intervene created a distinct communication problem: how to move the citizenry from an isolationist to an interventionist position regarding the War in Europe. The Zimmerman Telegram, sent by German Foreign Minister Arthur Zimmermann to the German Minister in Mexico in early 1917, proposed that Mexico declare war and attack the United States across the Rio Grande. The anti-German outcry this generated gave Wilson the opening he needed to propose United States intervention.

While the telegram itself does not qualify as propaganda, the American cover-up of the method of access to its information does. The United States created a faked burglary of the German Embassy in Mexico City to provide a cover story for how the Zimmerman Telegram was obtained by the Americans. This protected their story of how the knowledge was obtained. When the telegram's contents were revealed to the American people, it took little more than this to move many of them from pacifism towards a demand for war against Germany. But such initial fervour is often followed by a change of heart, and the American people's continued support for entrance to the war was required.

The case of World War I and The Zimmerman Telegram illustrates one method of moving the citizenry from an isolationist to an interventionist position regarding War in Europe.

The Creel Committee

To continue and to broaden this support, Wilson appointed George Creel, a newspaperman and former Police Commissioner of Denver, tasking him with heading 'The Committee of Public Information,' which was intended to discuss America's mission in joining World War I. Rather than suppressing information given to the American people, the commission was intended to create both a communication strategy, and the tactics needed to move American sentiment from pacifist to interventionist and support it at that level. The sinking of the RMS Lusitania (i.e., a British ocean liner sunk by German U-boat), considered as terrorism by the Americans but as a legitimate target by the Germans, added to Wilson's arguments.

Creel sought journalists, writers, and advertising people to brainstorm and then implement strategies and tactics that would bring the American people to see that avoidance of participation in World War I was no longer possible. The Committee employed various communication techniques, some of which could be classified as propaganda. These included posters, one form of which depicted a German soldier as a giant gorilla holding a blond female, clothes in disarray while reaching for her child as the gorilla salivated its lust for her, the child impaled on the Gorilla's bayonet. Clearly, this together with similar messages constituted a form of persuasion which was part of a mass persuasion campaign, one-sided and fear-based, that attempted to subvert rational processes.

The Committee also conducted brief *4-minute men* lectures at church socials and parent teacher association meetings, and ran articles in American newspapers advocating anti-German intervention. These tactics were so successful that strong anti-German feelings arose in America by 1917. American parents applauded their children who threw mud, rocks, and feces at the homes of Americans of German ancestry, whose own children were no longer welcome to come out and play with their long-time friends.

Americans moved towards strong support of Wilson's war effort and America's entry to World War I. Wilson defended his flip from pacifism to war supporter by arguing that American intervention was an acceptable peacetime strategy since we would make this 'The War to End All Wars'. The best known Creel Commission appointees were journalist Walter Lippmann, on his way to becoming America's political philosopher (Lippmann, 1922), and Sigmund Freud's nephew Edward Bernays, who by his account and that of others, became the father of public relations (Bernays, 1928). The reaction against the work of the Commission when it became known in America following World War I was so strong that Congress provided no funding to catalogue its records. Most of these have been lost to time.

The case of 'The Creel Committee' and American Propaganda during World War I illustrates the use of an appointed committee to create and disseminate many messages and message types through multiple channels designed to continue, and to increase the level of support for an existing war.

Hitler and the Nazis: *Mein Kampf* (My Fight), *Der Stuermer* (The Stormtrooper), and Hitler's Public Statements

Perhaps the most significant example of Adolf Hitler's action-based propaganda concerned his political promises, those which framed land grabs as justified and necessary for Germany, and simple lies such as a mutual non-aggression pact with Joseph Stalin. Used to buy time, these promises expired whenever Hitler had no further use for them.

In Hitler's Germany, propaganda was perceived as a positive term by those employing it. Goebbels was openly referred to as Hitler's Propaganda Minister, in charge of all messages to the public. These messages touted the benefits of National Socialism over other governmental forms. Nazi propaganda used simple words associating them with emotions and fears, and repeating them in various messages and forms. Propaganda related to Hitler's military attacks on most early targets always offered a motive for conducting the action, and the motive, judged independently, was always 'good', in the sense of being humanitarian and protective. He needed to invade the *Sudetenland* (northern part of Czech Republic) to stop the ethnic cleansing of Germans, often so identified by their speech and accent. And the conquered would reap benefits too, of German protection and artistic cultural achievements.

Rather than judge whether a specific message such as *Mein Kampf* (Hitler, 1925, 1926) or Goebbels' Nazi version of the movie *Titanic*, or a related set of messages (such as the set of *Der Stuermer* [Nazi newspaper] issues) is propaganda, it is clear that the Nazi's language-based public messages in general, both internally within the party and those intended for the masses, are largely propaganda. That is, together with, and as combined with Hitler's and Goebbels' speeches, they constituted a form of persuasion distinguished by a mass persuasion campaign, which was one-sided, fear-based, certainly involved lies, and which attempted to subvert rational processes and hid information.

The fear involved in the messages, especially in the early years of the Reich, was of two forms. For Germans it was: What would continue to happen if Germany did not act? For the conquered to be, it was: The supposed evil of their current leaders, and/or evil from other conquerors who were about to strike. Germany is presented as their saviour and protector from these 'evils'. The use and existence of concentration camps was downplayed or hidden, and justified only when required by circumstances. Justification was tied to the need for racial purity, and alleged crimes of disloyalty.

As with Stalin, Hitler's action based propaganda was implemented through murder and terror. In addition to fear of the Gestapo, the Secret Police, the propaganda involved creating paramilitary groups of fanatic loyalists, first the brown shirted paramilitary *Sturmabteilung* (SA), and later the black shirted *Schutzstaffel* (SS). As Hitler's paranoia increased over time, the SA's allegiance to Hitler alone came into question and the members of the SA were eliminated. This introduced a combination of pride and fear in SS members that further increased their open expression of fanaticism towards Hitler. This process created a gap of safety between Hitler and any person or group likely to get close to him; warned others that true fanaticism and not just loyalty was required, and at the same time made Hitler more exalted as a leader.

In addition to the reassuring work of Goebbels' propaganda ministry, the case of Hitler and the Nazis illustrates knowledge of the use of the military and police power of the state, the willingness to use it, and rationally driven fear, as bases for propaganda.

Stalin and Soviet Propaganda

After Hitler abandoned his 1939 alliance with Stalin by attacking Russia in June 1941, Marshall Georgy Zhukov was clearly the hero in organising supply chains, mustering and distributing troops and supplies, and all other aspects of the Russian fight against the Nazi invasion. Stalin cowered in the Kremlin during the initial Nazi thrust, but continued to create and spread the myth that it was he who had saved Moscow and Mother Russia from the Nazis. It was unusual for Stalin not to have the real hero or power figure murdered, as he simply had with most of his rivals and with other large masses, who might have supported a rival. As with Hitler, communist word-based propaganda under Stalin was always more inner directed at the Soviet people than towards countries and persons outside the Soviet Bloc, and propaganda was perceived as a positive term by those employing it. This propaganda urged continued maximum effort by all in the struggle against Germany, with the Russian people seen as waging a war of liberation of other smaller countries that had been overrun by the Nazis.

Stalin's fear-based propaganda worked more through acts of terror and assassination than through speeches and writings, as did a portion of Hitler's propaganda related to the Gestapo and the SS. And Stalin's goal in his propaganda was both to exalt his standing and to create massive levels of fear among anyone who might even think of any form of action against him. Knowledge of his purges by those who were close to him, perhaps especially of the murders of those who had been close to him, spread quickly among insiders, but was somewhat slower to spread to the population in general, particularly outside the cities. Insiders were commanded to entertain him, often until late in the evening, such as with Nikita Khrushchev who was ordered to play the fool at after-hours parties or some other often demeaning role. This served to illustrate Stalin's absolute power over those within his inner circle.

The case of Stalin and Soviet Propaganda illustrates a use of propaganda similar to that of Hitler: the military and police power of the state, the willingness to use it, and rationally driven fear, as bases for propaganda.

As propaganda came to be perceived as a more negative term, particularly following World Wars I and II, its users became less likely to accept the term to label their actions. American revulsion towards both Hitler and Stalin led to a particular antipathy in the West towards propaganda, as a term reflecting 'what dictators do'. In the United States, hate messages produced by the various Ku Klux Klan and White Supremacist groups against Blacks and immigrants are generally classed as propaganda, and not perceived as positive outside of those groups and their fellow travellers.

Propaganda Examples Following World War II

The Undeclared Korean War

After World War II, US Government-involved propaganda became continuously more sophisticated in its placement and delivery methods. Less change occurred in its construction and content. While U.S. General Douglas McArthur's end-run attack on Incheon was heavily covered in the U.S. press, the terrible suffering of United States and of Chinese troops in the cold that led to many of the deaths of these troops was seldom discussed. As with agencies that employ it, propaganda normally ignores negative news. News and rumours of the slaughter of American prisoners of war (POWs) was covered, but United States retaliation in kind was not. In the 1990s, silent black-and-white films surfaced apparently showing unarmed captured Chinese troops shot by allied troops by order of high ranking U.S. officers, who are seen standing and watching. Were these old black-and-white films manufactured by the Chinese or North Koreans? If so, it was a masterful job as the films appear very authentic.

The Vietnam War and Southeast Asia

Propaganda involved in the United States War with Vietnam is as long and complicated as would seem possible. Briefly, it began in 1873 with the start of the French incursion into Indochine following Britain's long term relationship with China as the 'first prize in the pacific'. The Japanese threw out French rule in Indochine in 1941; and in 1945 were kept in place by the United States for six months as an armed police force in Vietnam following the Japanese surrender.

Vietnamese leader Ho Chi Minh had worked against the Japanese with the forerunner of the CIA, the U.S. Office of Strategic Services (OSS) and its Commander, William Donovan. Ho promulgated a Constitution for all of Vietnam modelled on and largely copied from the U.S. Constitution. Donovan and other former OSS men lobbied U.S. President Truman for siding with Ho, and refusing to aid the French in Southeast Asia who 'wanted their country back'. The French government had few funds after the German occupation of World War II and needed United States money to retake at least Vietnam, ignoring for the most part what became Cambodia and Laos. Given a choice between supporting the Vietnamese versus supporting white skin, plus a familiar view of government and of Euro-American life, Truman opted for France.

Beginning in 1947, the first fledging agents of the newly created CIA entered Vietnam to assist the French. Despite American funding and CIA help, the French continued to lose their battle for pacification, as would the Americans 25 years later. Several of the Kennedy children, including John F. Kennedy (JFK) and his brother Robert Kennedy, visited Southeast Asia after World War II, lending JFK's administration greater knowledge and understanding of the situation and culture than other presidents.

After the fall of their presumed impregnable fort at *Dien Bien Phu* in 1954, the French withdrew and the CIA entered Vietnam in earnest. The CIA built up slowly from 1954 to the1960s, supporting Ngo Dinh Diem and his brother Ngô Đình Nhu as puppets. The Ngo's were Catholic, a belief system understood by Americans. They were both assassinated on November 2, 1963, with the covert understanding and perhaps instigation, of the U.S. ambassador to Saigon Henry Cabot Lodge II, but without President Kennedy's approval. This further cleared the road for the expansion of the war. In Vietnam, the will of the Vietnamese people, prodded by Ho, General Giap, and North Vietnamese propaganda, ultimately was stronger than were the 'pacification' tactics of U.S. Ambassador Henry Cabot Lodge II, General William Westmoreland, and the U.S. Military.

This expansion of the Vietnam War illustrates the importance of similar cultural belief systems and cultural familiarity in susceptibility to influence, as well as the influence of massive amounts of money in American politics. Dealing with Christians was dealing with trustworthy people, or so it seemed to many Americans. Messages from clearly native Vietnamese leaders such as Ho and Giap were less believable than messages mouthed by American puppets. The money to be made by Brown & Root and related construction companies in building Cam Ranh Bay, and many other U.S. military installations in the Philippines and Thailand as well as in Vietnam was not discussed, only the 'need to stop communist expansion.'

United States home front war propaganda was extensive from 1965 to 1968, continuing in a different direction between 1968 and 1973 under President Nixon, who ordered the bombing of Cambodia in 1970. The Khmer Rouge had been in a standoff with Lon Nol's Cambodian forces prior to Nixon's bombing, but the Khmer people turned towards the Khmer Rouge when Nixon's bombings fell into the pattern Pol Pot's propaganda had ascribed to the United States. Estimates are that the reign of terror of the Khmer Rouge killed some three million of Cambodia's six million people between 1975 and 1979. Yet the actions of the Ohio National Guard in 1970, shooting down four peaceful Americans of student age walking across the Kent State University campus added to the horror. News coverage of Kent State, even more than that of the Cambodian bombing, signalled the beginning of the end of the American people's faith in Nixon's 'end the war by bombing and then stopping it' strategy. Kent State illustrates the importance of cultural similarity in what is sometimes called the 'closeness to home' effect. The death of over three million was treated as a statistic. The death of four young white Americans in this way was treated as a major tragedy.

The Cover-up of the JFK Assassination

U.S. President John F. Kennedy was assassinated in Dallas, Texas at 12:30 p.m., November 22, 1963. The cover-up of the assassination illustrates how perfectly propaganda can be employed in the process of political change. The report of the Warren Commission on the JFK assassination became one of the most important documents in the history of the United States. The report was believed by some, but seen as propaganda of the worst form by others. The claim is made here that the Warren Commission was a cover-up, and that the Commission never in fact actually conducted an investigation of the evidence that might have shown that there were multiple shooters. There is strong evidence for the multiple shooters claim. The 1964 Warren Commission Report said there was only one shooter. More than one shooter would indicate a conspiracy. The report's objectivity was questioned during the 1977 U.S. Congressional Investigation of the Warren Report.

Norman Redlich, soon to be Dean of the Law School at New York University (NYU), testified during the 1977 Investigation of the Warren Report. Redlich was in charge of the Warren Commission investigators' day-to-day operations in 1963-1964. In formal questioning of Redlich during the 1977 investigation, Harold S. Sawyer, a member of the 1977 Congressional Commission, asked: "Can you tell me why the decision was made that the people primarily concerned on the staff were not allowed to see the X-rays or the photos of the autopsy and who made the decision?" Redlich replied that "the Chief Justice himself held that the publication of the autopsy film and the X-rays would be a great disservice to Mrs. Kennedy, the Kennedy family".

Thus, by request rather than order of Chief Justice Earl Warren of the United States, the Warren Commission failed to look at perhaps the most important evidence in any murder, the autopsy report, among many other evidentiary threads. Warren's request not to look, together with his stated reasoning that presenting the autopsy to the public, as the committee would have to do if they looked at the autopsy report (i.e., it would upset the dead President's wife), is a master stroke in the creation of the propaganda. Whom in hindsight would believe that 'not upsetting the dead President's wife' would possibly trump 'let us find out who did this, how, and why', as the basis for operations in investigating the assassination of the President of the United States? This rationale originated not with Earl Warren, but with Lyndon B. Johnson (LBJ), the primary beneficiary of JFK's death.

Summary/Chronology of the Propaganda Creation Method in the Warren Report

The method of construction of the Warren Commission propaganda is instructive. First, news media around the world were provided with prepared information on Lee Harvey Oswald as the assassin within hours of the act. The murder was 'solved'.

Second, the proposed assassin was murdered. This removed the possibility of continued statements from him claiming lack of responsibility.

Third, control was obtained over all official messages concerning the assassination. The principal beneficiary of the assassination, LBJ, became the new President of United States.

Fourth, when an uncontrollable source, the U.S. Congress as the second branch of government, began to create an investigation of the assassination independent of the principal beneficiary, LBJ announced that an official Presidential investigation of the death was already under way. This stopped the Congressional investigation.

Fifth, the new President appointed an 'unimpeachable source' to head the Presidential investigation, the highly respected and honest Earl Warren, Chief Justice of the United States Supreme Court. While an honest man, Warren had great sympathy for the dead President's widow Jackie Kennedy, as did the entire country.

Sixth, playing on this sympathy, LBJ strongly suggested to Warren personally that they must not increase the suffering of JFK's family, suggesting "that must be our principal concern now that we have the assassin." The goal is manipulated and altered, from studying the evidence and finding the assassin, to assuring that the President's widow will not have to experience more suffering.

Seventh, the Warren Commission was formed. Former U.S. Solicitor General and highly respected attorney James Lee Rankin was unanimously selected by the Commission as its General Counsel. Rankin appointed Norman Redlich, later to become Dean of the Law School of NYU, as special assistant on the Warren Commission, in charge of investigating the factual aspects of the assassination itself.

Eighth, General Counsel Rankin addressed the first meeting of Redlich's factual aspects group in late January 1964, stating: "Gentlemen, your only client is the truth", as the opening words of his talk.

Ninth, Chief Justice Warren addressed Redlich's factual aspects group concerning its mission several days later. During the 1977 House Select Committee on Assassinations hearings, House Committee member Harold Sawyer questioned Redlich about Warren's early 1964 instructions concerning the mission of the factual aspects group. Sawyer asked why the Warren Commission investigators were not allowed to see the X-rays or photos of the autopsy, and who made the decision. Contrary to Rankin's 'your only client is the truth' instructions, Redlich replies that Chief Justice Warren argued that the publication of the autopsy film and X-rays would be a great disservice to the dead President's widow Jackie Kennedy and her family.

In conclusion, the Warren Commission never looked at evidence concerning major physical aspects of the assassination itself, yet advertised the Warren Report as the complete, extensive, comprehensive, and accurate report of how the JFK assassination occurred. U.S. news media in general still accept the Warren Report's claim that it is a full and accurate accounting of the JFK assassination. In fact, none of the crucial evidence concerning Oswald as the possible assassin was even examined or considered, a stunning propaganda success.

Wilbur Schramm and the Development of Doctoral Programs in Communication

Early in World War II, 1941, Wilbur Schramm served for two years as Director of Education in the U.S. Office of Facts and Figures. Promoted to Director of the U.S. Office of War Information, he led the American war information campaign until 1943. United States war information during World War II had a similar ring to any war propaganda campaign, and consisted largely of radio announcements and posters, with some communication research sponsored as well. Even though speakers similar to Creel's '4-minute men' were available, their use was limited. Calling Schramm's information work propaganda would be a stretch since it did not, by all indications, attempt to subvert rational processes.

Following the war, Schramm oversaw initial research on the effects of propaganda. He became Director of the School of Journalism at the University of Iowa in 1943, and in 1947, Director of the Institute of Communications Research at the University of Illinois at Urbana-Champaign. Eventually offering the Doctorate of Philosophy (PhD), graduates from these programs established other departments of communication at universities in the United States, including Hawaii and Michigan State University. Most studies of propaganda and many of persuasion since World War II have been influenced by or conducted by graduates from these programs.

Schramm's grant proposed engaging in studies of persuasion rather than focusing on propaganda messages alone, since it was proposed that propaganda effects occur through the persuasion of individuals; as groups do not think but are collections of individuals. 'Group think' is a convenient fiction, as is 'the sun will rise tomorrow'. The sun does not in fact rise, nor do groups think. Individual people think. In the same way, as long as we recognise that propaganda works through the persuasion of individuals, not of groups or populations of people, which serve as convenient fictions, we can discuss propaganda effects, knowing that they are in fact affecting the internal phenomenological processes of individual human beings.

Glander (2000) presents a reasoned argument that this chain of events constitutes the creation of American schools that teach about propaganda, its history and uses, and how to form and counteract it, under the heading of persuasion. Based on direct personal experience with these programs, the authors believe Glander's proposition that these schools teach or taught the creation of propaganda for U.S. government purposes is not supported. Rather, we believe that the formation of the communication discipline paved the way for scholars to study terrorism and its messages through this communication lens.

CONCLUSION

This section considered the use of propaganda during times of war and war preparation, both abroad and in the United States, from the late 1800s through 1975. It provided examples of how propaganda is constructed, some of its goals and targets, its effects and in some cases its lack of desired effect, and cautionary examples of how propaganda can produce unexpected and undesired effects.

PERSUASIVENESS OF ONLINE VIOLENT TERRORIST MESSAGES AND THEIR IMPACT

Many cases of propaganda from 1980 onward exist; among the most important is the current case concerning the use of the Internet by terrorist groups.

Use of the Internet by Terrorist Groups: Overview

The use of the Internet by terrorist groups has evolved over the past 25 years. Much has changed since media reported in the late 1980s that Osama bin Laden, founder of Al-Qaeda and mastermind of the 9/11 attacks against the United States, had used a computer to maintain a database of those who volunteered for the Afghan War (Encyclopaedia Britannica, 2014). Today, the threats of terrorism online are far more varied and widespread than a simple database. Here, we will look at how terrorist groups take advantage of the Internet to spread their propaganda and how their use has evolved over time. As mentioned above, propaganda refers to a form of persuasion that is often one-sided and fear-based, which attempts to subvert rational processes.

The extent of Internet use, as indexed by the Internet adoption rate, continues to grow globally. It is estimated that 42 percent of the world is connected to the Internet today (Internet World Stats, 2014). As with print, radio, and television, governments attempt to regulate this new medium. However, unlike more established media outlets, the Internet has unique features, such as its relative anonymity and global reach that make it hard to govern. This makes it easier for groups that operate illegally, like terrorist groups, to use the Internet to achieve political and religious goals. This also means that in democratic states, prosecuting individuals based on their intentions to commit an act of terror is no easy task. Thus, the Internet continues to be a practical and sometimes effective tool for terrorist groups to further their missions.

What determines whether an organisation is a terrorist one or not is a matter of great debate. The U.S. Department of States currently has 59 organisations designated as Foreign Terrorist Organisations (U.S. Department of State, 2014). U.S. Code defines terrorism as activities that:

Involve violent acts or acts dangerous to human life that violate federal or state law ... Appear to be intended (i) to intimidate or coerce a civilian population; (ii) to influence the policy of a government by intimidation or coercion; or (iii) to affect the conduct of a government by mass destruction, assassination, or kidnapping. (Federal Bureau of Investigation, n.d., para. 2)

Terrorist organisations that maintain an online presence use the Internet today to communicate or to inform, to radicalise and to recruit, to educate and to plan, and to fundraise (Seib & Janbek, 2010). In their online activities, they target a wide range of audience members including their supporters, the media, and their enemies. Each group is targeted using carefully crafted messages that are often one-sided and fear-based. Over the years, researchers have documented how the Internet is used to achieve these multiple functions by terrorist groups as they closely monitored their websites. This form of data mining is beneficial to the counterterrorism community: "[A] significant amount of knowledge about the functioning, activities and sometimes the targets of terrorist organisation is derived from website, chat room and other Internet communications" (United Nations Office on Drugs and Crime, 2012, p. 12).

Internet as a Platform for Communication

In principle, the Internet is seen by terrorist groups as a platform for communication. These groups communicate online for a variety of reasons:

Sometimes this is done as sheer propaganda, other times as a means of claiming credit (real or false) for an attack, and still others for the purpose of communicating a threat -- as with the rash of communiqués from al Qaeda in Iraq fighters, concerning the fate of the kidnap victims, some of whom were later beheaded on camera and online. (Tuman, 2010, p. 200)

Terrorist groups communicate their ideologies and their missions to a number of audiences, such as those sympathetic to the organisations' message, people who are curious about the group and people who oppose the group.

The biggest advantage of such communication is that the message reaches its intended audience unfiltered. Groups labelled by states as terrorist groups no longer need to rely on media outlets to communicate their message. Instead, they can control the content, how it is presented, and when it is communicated. While groups like Al-Qaeda now have the option to send an unfiltered message online to their audiences, they still cannot ignore the power of traditional media outlets which have a wider reach. After all, their main purpose is to maximise their visibility, and media groups can help them with this task.

Something happens to an online message published by terrorist groups when it gets noticed by the media. Instead of being consumed by only hundreds or even thousands of audience members, the message becomes available to hundreds of thousands or even millions of people. An online post picked up by media organisations could make headlines for days, weeks, or even months. In general, the lifespan of some stories related to terrorism, such as the 2013 Boston Marathon bombings or the 9/11 attacks in New York, could last for years, especially when court proceedings are involved.

Over the years, websites of organisations that engage in terrorism have become informative and user-friendly. These websites have evolved away from only using text for their content. Various tools are now used to present the message. As an example:

Hezbollah continues to maintain an extensive media and public relations operation and has periodically posted a Web site. When active, the Web site contains a great deal of pro-Hezbollah information, including political statements, reports from the 'front', audio links, video links, photographs, and e-mail links. (Martin, 2006, p. 390)

To attract their audiences, these websites must be relevant and engaging. Martin (2006) writes that "[m]usic, photographs, videos, and written propaganda are easily posted on Web pages" (p. 399). With some technical skills, an individual sympathetic to a terrorist organisation's mission can help the organisation to maintain an active and appealing website. Posting multimedia content was one of the main changes that took place when terrorist organisations started their migration from Web 1.0 to Web 2.0: "While much of the original content on the terrorist-linked sites was text-based, videos began to play a much larger role after 2003" (Mantel, 2009, p. 299).

Internet as a Platform to Recruit and to Radicalise

Terrorist organisations recognise that they cannot use a single message to reach their diverse target audiences. Instead, they strategically craft specific messages to appeal to varied groups. They often translate these messages to multiple languages including English, French, and German to influence a wider group of people. Such translations will allow a group to reach possible sympathisers in foreign countries. All of these pro-campaign messages are one-sided and support the cause in question, with no mention or consideration that there might be another side or sides.

In the first part of 2015, it was estimated that ISIS had successfully recruited between 16,000 and 17,000 fighters from 90 countries ("Legion of fighters", 2015). ISIS claims to have recruited supporters from the United Kingdom, France, Germany, and other European countries, as well as the United States, the Arab world, and the Caucasus. Others estimated the number of foreigners joining ISIS as well as other groups at 20,000 ("20,000 foreign fighters", 2015).

While the number of recruits from the United States represents a very small percentage of the overall number of foreign recruits, it remains significant and alarming: "Intelligence agencies now believe that as many as 150 Americans have tried and some have succeeded in reaching in the Syrian war zone" ("20,000 foreign fighters", 2015, para. 2). Those interested in joining ISIS and many other terrorist groups can gain more information about them online: "Today, many Islamic State recruits find their way to the group in web forums and on Twitter, where they can easily connect to fighters and networks in Iraq and Syria" (Dickinson, 2015, para. 12).

Though information is readily available, those sincerely interested in joining a group like ISIS may face many obstacles. Not every supporter can easily leave his/her country and move to Syria or Iraq. Younger recruits may feel the need to run their radical idea by their family members. In a jihadi magazine titled *Sawt al-Jihad* which is Arabic for 'The Voice of Martyrdom', "Sheikh Youssef al-Ayeri told mujahid youths not to ask their parents for permission to join jihad. At the same time, he calls upon parents not to prevent their sons from fulfilling their religious duty" (Moghadam, 2008, p. 145). In this instance, the Sheikh appealed to young recruits with a clear message about their obligation to join jihad and directly addresses the issue of gaining their parents' permission. He also urged parents not to serve as an obstacle to their children joining the movement. Such propagandistic messages of course hide relevant information about the legal implications of someone leaving their country, and about what life is really like under ISIS rule. Nevertheless, referring to jihad as a religious obligation is widespread in online rhetoric, as are conspiracy theories against Islam. Such theories can motivate terrorists to join jihadi groups (Moghadam, 2008).

International terrorist organisations do not have a monopoly on the use of the Internet to spread hateful messages and recruit sympathisers. Local hate groups also rely on the same tools to find sympathisers. Referring to White Aryan Resistance (WAR) and their online recruitment efforts, Martin (2006) writes: "WAR publishes neo-Nazi propaganda, manages an active Web site, and has tried to recruit and organise racist skinheads" (p. 455). Those interested in the movement and sympathetic to its message can seek out information online to learn more about the organisation.

Internet as a Platform to Educate and to Plan Attacks

Bates and Mooney (2014) liken some of terrorist organisations' online efforts to online education: "Al-Qaeda and other jihadist organisations are offering their own form of distance learning" (para. 22). By providing materials that reinforce the organisations' message and offer how-to manuals online, they are basically delivering an education at no charge: "[t]hese online training facilities are mostly offered for free and are accessible through semi-centralised, password-protected forums" (para. 24). Groups that have access to Internet can benefit from the wealth of information available to them for planning an attack: "[a] great deal of useful information is available for terrorists on the Internet, including instructions for bomb assembly, poisoning, weapons construction, and mixing lethal chemicals" (Martin, 2006, p. 542). In April 2013, two brothers detonated two pressure cooker bombs near the finish line of the annual Boston marathon which resulted in the death of three spectators and injuries to hundreds of others. Investigators discovered that the brothers learned how to prepare the pressure cookers through reading Al-Qaeda's online magazine titled *Inspire* (Khan, 2013).

Al-Qaeda's other periodical entitled *The Al-Batter Training Camp* also includes similar information that can help a supporter plan and execute an attack. The publication includes advice on: "… how to pre-examine targets for attacks, remain vigilant during the planning phase, organise small, compartmentalised cells, mislead the enemy, and conduct surprise attacks" (Moghadam, 2008, p. 148). Training lessons and videos teach recruits the technical side of terrorism including producing hard to notice suicide belts. The promise of heaven in afterlife is essential to those who commit suicide attacks.

Internet as a Platform to Fundraise

It is hard for terrorist organisations to survive without capital. While expenses vary from one organisation to the next, they usually include salaries, payments to families of members who were killed, training costs, and operational costs, among others. Online, terrorist organisations have relied on asking for donations directly to support the cause, on using a front social or religious organisation to raise funds, on stealing identities, or on a combination of these methods. Terrorist organisations "… increasingly conduct identity theft of ordinary Web users, including the stealing of credit card information, to help them finance terrorist attacks" (Moghadam, 2008, p. 149).

Conclusion

There are many cases that demonstrate how the Internet plays a role in communicating messages, radicalising and recruiting individuals, planning attacks, and fund raising. This section focused on how these functions play out in the online world. And all of them also take place in the offline world.

It is important to note that while the Internet played a role, the cases above do not prove that the Internet caused terrorist activity. As Benson (2014) reminds us, "merely establishing that the Internet played a role does not preclude the possibility the terrorists were first motivated offline to attack and only later used the Internet as one tool among many to attempt to carry out that attack" (p. 311). The Internet is one factor among many that may contribute to persuade potential recruits to join the groups:

Although one cannot isolate the Internet as the main or only factor that causes individuals to commit an act of terrorism, one can confirm from documented cases that the Internet has been used in various ways to facilitate different aspects of terrorism. (Janbek & Williams, 2014, p. 302)

But we also know that the Internet is the future in many areas of life and terrorism is no exception. As Martin (2006, p. 542) asserted, "[T]he increasing availability of new technologies, when combined with the motivations and morality of the New Terrorism, suggests very strongly that technology will be an increasingly potent weapon in the arsenals of terrorists".

A Case Study of ISIS Online Propaganda

In Islam, the Quran is the most trusted source of religious text followed by *Hadith*, a collection of teachings and sayings of Prophet Muhammad. Like all religious text, the way the two are interpreted plays a great role in determining what the adherents of that religion will believe. If a question arises that cannot be answered by reading the Quran or Hadith, then Muslims rely on a religious legal opinion on that matter to be issued by a mufti, a respected Islamic scholar. This is how Muslims learn about what is permissible, and what is not according to Islam. Since religious interpretations and legal opinions are issued by people and people are subjective, it is not uncommon to have two muftis issue different religious legal opinions on the same matter.

Terrorist organisations benefit from this subjective process of interpreting religious text to advance their political agendas. Similar to the Protocols, a narrow reading of the holy text by terrorist groups is held to be the basis for a set of beliefs and corresponding actions (i.e., based on those beliefs). We regard this as a very significant point that can assist in understanding terrorist groups, and how they justify violence in the name of their religion.

ISIS is a jihadist group consisting primarily of Sunni fighters and operating mainly in Iraq and Syria. Terrorist organisations, like ISIS, usually have two characteristics in common: a desire to achieve political objectives, and spread fear in the process.

ISIS has high aspirations of building an Islamic State across two countries, Syria and Iraq, based on the Sharia law. It proudly uses the word 'Islam' in its title. While it often presents itself as a religious group to appeal to disenfranchised Muslims around the world, it is in fact a political group with political aspirations camouflaged as a religious one. It insists that all Muslims have a duty to support the group. The Internet serves as a tool to spread its version of religion, and to bond with those who find the message appealing: "The Internet helps generate a forum where individuals who feel humiliated and jilted can regain a sense of community, solidarity, brotherhood, and a new identity" (Moghadam, 2008, p. 150).

Similar to other terrorist religious groups, ISIS relies on a specific interpretation of religious text to justify the use of violence. A close look at ISIS messages reveals that they are one-sided and fear-based. ISIS also attempts to subvert rational processes since its organisation is founded on a religious directive. ISIS religious interpretation is rejected by Muslim leaders around the world (Mandhai, 2014). Nevertheless, the organisation can only advance through the use of this narrow reading. ISIS version of what the Quran demands of Muslims secures its existence.

ISIS has relied on barbaric methods to torture and kill its victims. This includes Muslims and non-Muslims who do not agree with ISIS. ISIS used media outlets to spread fear to the rest of the world. In late 2014, ISIS beheaded a number of foreigners, including journalists and aid workers, and produced high-quality videos of the beheadings. The videos usually end with a stern warning to the United States and its allies, where ISIS would advise them to end their presence in the region. Sometimes the videos mentioned Guantanamo prison, and at other times they mentioned American troops in the region. The overall anti-American message, however, was loud and clear: leave ISIS alone. Similar to 'Birth of a Nation' as mentioned earlier, these videos are produced to provide continued support for the discriminatory treatment of non-ISIS followers.

A major purpose of such barbaric videos is to garner media attention. This is exactly what ISIS was able to achieve successfully in 2014 when the beheading videos were circulated widely online and discussed for months by news media organisations. ISIS has since continued to rely on this strategy. This is similar to the strategy used by Hitler and Stalin to spread fear which was discussed earlier. ISIS is willing to use power and rationally driven fear, as bases for propaganda. Some of the victims, who were beheaded by ISIS, were targeted because they represented American and foreign interests. They were a symbol of the enemy. Terrorism works by targeting such symbols.

The Use of Magazines in Terrorism

One online communication tool used by terrorist organisations to promote their mission is through the use of online magazines. The strategic use of a magazine can help an organisation reach its diverse audiences on a regular basis with tailored messages. ISIS launched *Dabiq* magazine in 2014. The publication covers military achievements, political news, and religious interpretations which is not unusual for a terrorist magazine. A good amount of effort has gone into producing the content for this magazine which is tens of pages long. Much of the information in Dabiq is current and reflects events that happened recently in the region. Most legitimate, large organisations today recognise the need to rely on multiple channels to communicate their messages to various members of public. ISIS, although not a legitimate organisation, is no exception.

ISIS uses the magazine to explain the Caliphate concept, and to distinguish itself from other jihadi groups by publicising its strategy and vision. The group is positioning itself as the one and only jihadi group "that will lead the Muslim community into worldwide domination" (Gambhir, 2014, p. 3). This is important as there are many terrorist groups that compete for recruits besides ISIS.

ISIS is known for having taken its global outreach efforts seriously. Its magazine is available in English. Through such efforts, ISIS hopes to appeal to a wide range of recruits. For the group to grow in significance and power, it must increase its population by converting locals and replacing those they killed with like-minded immigrant supporters from foreign countries. Muslims from all over the world are encouraged to migrate with their families. Those who cannot migrate are encouraged to ask others to do so. These calls, when successful, coupled with military gains, help ISIS grow and expand its influence.

ISIS wants to be perceived as a religious organisation with political aspirations. This is similar to rhetoric published by other well-known jihadi groups. As mentioned earlier, it is essential for ISIS, which is best viewed as a political organisation with a religious justification, to rely heavily on its interpretation of religion to govern regions it controls: "As ISIS recruits followers from around the globe, including English speakers, it needs to not only publicise its victories, but also to frame those successes as inevitable results of God's approval" (Gambhir, 2014, p. 2). Such propaganda may resonate with its followers.

As with many organisations labelled as terrorists, terrorism represents one part of their overall daily activities. In addition to its terrorist activities, ISIS also serves as a provider of goods for its 'citizens', much like a government would: "… creating law enforcement forces and providing aid to civilians are key ways that ISIS establishes territorial control and citizen dependency and trust" (Gambhir, 2014, p. 5). To provide such public services, ISIS needs to collect taxes from its residents.

Gambhir (2014) sheds light on the difference between Inspire Magazine by Al-Qaeda, and Dabiq by ISIS. Inspire aimed to motivate Western recruits to act against the perceived enemies of Al-Qaeda, and provided guides on how to conduct attacks. However, "Dabiq series is farther-reaching, laying out the religious underpinning of the Caliphate and encouraging all believing Muslims to support ISIS and emigrate from their homes to the Islamic State" (Gambhir, 2014, p. 1-2).

An online magazine is only one of the many communication tools available to terrorist groups to tell their story. Twitter, Facebook, and YouTube are other tools that have been used by ISIS and its supporters. While ISIS is not the first group to rely on the Internet and on social media to spread its message, it has been consistent and relentless in its online efforts. ISIS battle on the ground is paralleled by a battle online, and the group has made gains in the former and mastered the latter. ISIS online storytelling efforts deserve special attention: "as well as being one of the most savage terrorist groups in the world today, ISIS also has the slickest propaganda" (Cottee, 2015, para. 2).

Unlike some of the other terrorist organisations, ISIS has consistently produced powerful images and videos that seem to resonate with its followers and sympathisers. It is estimated that ISIS and its supporters produce "as many as 90,000 tweets and other social media responses every day" (Schmitt, 2015, para. 4). These materials are uploaded and distributed by a dedicated network of followers. Identifying and countering these messages is no easy task for the United States government and its allies. The U.S. Center for Strategic Counterterrorism Communications (CSCC) works to combat the dominant narrative produced by ISIS and other similar groups. They "coordinate, orient, and inform government-wide foreign communications activities targeted against terrorism and violent extremism, particularly al-Qaida and its affiliates and adherents" (U. S. Department of State, n.d., para. 1).

The head of CSCC has reached out informally to marketers and advertising agencies as he believes communication experts can help analyse and possibly generate messages that can counter ISIS propaganda (Bruell & Sebastian, 2015). CSCC "has produced well over 50,000 online 'engagements' in four languages – Arabic, Urdu, Somali, and English" – to counter terrorist groups' narrative and highlight their hypocrisies (Cottee, 2015, para. 5). These include sharing images and videos as well as engaging in Twitter wars with ISIS and responding to pro-ISIS messages. The group also crashes pro-ISIS forums.

Terrorism is a symptom of certain ills in a society. Communication tools, whether online or offline, provide a medium for communicating terrorist propaganda. More important than these tools are the messages that are communicated through them. ISIS has a compelling message to its followers concerning Muslim power and empowerment. The group is unlikely to cease its propaganda or its attacks unless its political demands are met or its military power is weakened to a degree such that it can no longer operate effectively. Those against ISIS are tasked with not only defeating the group militarily, but also defeating it ideologically. The latter challenge may be more difficult than the former. Funding of further empirical studies concerning the effects of terrorist propaganda, of possible counter propaganda effectiveness, and ways of constructing and carrying out such studies is in order.

SUMMARY

This chapter considered how propaganda has been used during times of war and war preparation by states and by terrorist organisations. Propaganda is often a label applied from an 'outside' perspective. These states and other entities rely on propaganda to further their missions. Whether they would apply such a description to their own communication behaviour or not is irrelevant, as the appellation depends upon whether the behaviour empirically fits the definition, and not on self-ascription. The chapter examined how propaganda was involved in spreading anti-Semitism across Europe, and in fuelling the Nazi movement. It also considered its use in moving the United States citizenry into accepting involvement in World War I, and through the JFK assassination, and in the Vietnam War. Propaganda, available to both state and non-state actors, has also been used by modern terrorist groups to communicate their messages. Our concluding section discussed the results of a search of websites used by ISIS, well-known as a 21st century terrorist group, to distribute propaganda online. This use was largely for two purposes: to spread fear, and to achieve political goals.

REFERENCES

20,000 foreign fighters flock to Syria, Iraq to join terrorists. (2015, February 10). *CBS News*. Retrieved from http://www.cbsnews.com/news/ap-20000-foreign-fighters-flock-to-syria-iraq-to-join-terrorists/

Anonymous. (1895). *The protocols of the learned elders of Zion*. Author.

Bates, R., & Mooney, M. (2014). Distance learning and jihad: The dark side of the force. *Online Journal of Distance Learning Administration*, *17*(3). Retrieved from http://www.westga.edu/~distance/ojdla/fall173/Bates_Mooney173.html

Benson, D. (2014). Why the Internet is not increasing terrorism. *Security Studies*, *23*(2), 293–328. doi :10.1080/09636412.2014.905353

Bernays, E. (1928). *Propaganda*. New York, NY: Horace Liveright.

Bruell, A., & Sebastian, M. (2015, March 2). Should Adland join the communications war on ISIS? *Ad Age*. Retrieved from http://adage.com/article/news/adland-join-communications-war-isis/297365/

Cottee, S. (2015, March 2). Why it is so hard to stop ISIS propaganda. *The Atlantic*. Retrieved from http://www.theatlantic.com/international/archive/2015/03/why-its-so-hard-to-stop-isis-propaganda/386216/

Daugherty, J. (2013). *A study of the availability of the Protocols at Manhattan newsstands*. Coral Gables, FL: University of Miami, School of Communication.

Dickinson, E. (2015, May 22). The Islamic State brings the war to Saudi Arabia. *Foreign Policy*. Retrieved from http://foreignpolicy.com/2015/05/22/isis-brings-the-war-to-saudi-arabia-qatif-mosque-bombing/

Encyclopedia Britannica. (2014). *Osama bin Laden: Saudi Arabian militant*. Retrieved from http://www.britannica.com/EBchecked/topic/65507/Osama-bin-Laden

Federal Bureau of Investigation. (n.d.). *Definitions of terrorism in the U. S. Code*. Retrieved from http://www.fbi.gov/about-us/investigate/terrorism/terrorism-definition

Gambhir, H. (2014). Backgrounder-Dabiq: The strategic messaging of the Islamic State. *Institute for the Study of War*. Retrieved from http://www.understandingwar.org/sites/default/files/Dabiq%20Backgrounder_Harleen%20Final.pdf

Glander, T. (2000). *Origins of mass communications research during the American Cold War: Educational effects and contemporary implications*. Mahwah, NJ: Lawrence Erlbaum Associates, Inc.

Goedsche, H. (1868). *Biarritz*. Author.

Graves, P. (1921). *The truth about the Protocols: A literary forgery*. London: The Times.

Hitler, A. (1925). *Mein Kampf* (Vol. 1). Munich.

Hitler, A. (1926). *Mein Kampf* (Vol. 2). Munich.

Internet World Stats. (2014). *Internet usage statistics: The internet big picture*. Retrieved from http://www.internetworldstats.com/stats.htm

Janbek, D., & Williams, V. (2014). The role of the internet post-9/11 in terrorism and counterterrorism. *The Brown Journal of World Affairs*, *20*(2), 297–308.

Joly, M. (1864). *Dialogue in hell between Machiavelli and Montesquieu*. Brussels: A. Mertens and Son.

Khan, A. (2013, April 30). The magazine that 'inspired' the Boston bombers. *PBS: Frontline*. Retrieved from http://www.pbs.org/wgbh/pages/frontline/iraq-war-on-terror/topsecretamerica/the-magazine-that-inspired-the-boston-bombers/

Le Bon, G. (1896). *The crowd: A study of the popular mind*. New York, NY: Macmillan & Co.

Legion of fighters battles for ISIS. (2015, May 20). *Al-Arabiya*. Retrieved from http://english.alarabiya. net/en/perspective/features/2015/05/20/Legion-of-foreign-fighters-battles-for-ISIS.html

Lippmann, W. (1922). *Public Opinion*. New York, NY: Harcourt, Brace and Co.

Mandhai, S. (2014). Muslim leaders reject Baghdadi's caliphate. *Al-Jazeera*. Retrieved from http://www. aljazeera.com/news/middleeast/2014/07/muslim-leaders-reject-baghdadi-caliphate-20147744058773906. html

Mantel, B. (2009). Terrorism and the internet: Should web sites that promote terrorism be shut down? *CQ Researcher*, *3*(1), 285–310.

Martin, G. (2006). *Understanding terrorism: Challenges, perspectives, and issues* (2nd ed.). Thousand Oaks, CA: Sage Publications.

Moghadam, A. (2008). *The globalization of martyrdom*. Baltimore, MD: The Johns Hopkins University Press.

Schmitt, E. (2015, February 16). U. S. intensifies effort to blunt ISIS' message. *The New York Times*. Retrieved from http://www.nytimes.com/2015/02/17/world/middleeast/us-intensifies-effort-to-blunt-isis-message.html?_r=0

Seib, P., & Janbek, D. (2010). *Global terrorism and new media: The post-Al Qaeda generation*. Abingdon, UK: Routledge.

Steinfatt, T. (2016). Measuring propaganda. In M. R. Allen (Ed.), *The Sage encyclopedia of communication research methods*. Thousand Oaks, CA: Sage Publications.

Tarde, G. (1890). *Les lois de l'imitation*. Paris: Félix Alcan.

Tuman, J. (2010). *Communicating terror: The Rhetorical dimensions of terrorism* (2nd ed.). Thousand Oaks, CA: Sage Publications.

U. S. Department of State. (2014). Foreign terrorist organizations. *Bureau of Counterterrorism*. Retrieved from http://www.state.gov/j/ct/rls/other/des/123085.htm

U. S. Department of State. (n.d.). *Center for Strategic Counterterrorism Communications*. Retrieved from http://www.state.gov/r/cscc/

United Nations Office on Drugs and Crime (UNODC). (2012). *The use of the Internet for terrorist purposes*. Retrieved from http://www.unodc.org/documents/frontpage/Use_of_Internet_for_Terrorist_Purposes.pdf

Chapter 3
Social Media and the Use of Discursive Markers of Online Extremism and Recruitment

Robyn Torok
Edith Cowan University, Australia

ABSTRACT

This chapter examines the shift toward the use of social media to fuel violent extremism, what the key discursive markers are, and how these key discursive markers are used to fuel violent extremism. The chapter then addresses and critiques a number of radicalisation models including but not limited to phase based models. Discursive markers are covered under three broad narrative areas. Narratives of grievance are designed to stimulate strong emotive responses to perceived injustices. Based on these grievances, active agency is advocated in the form of jihad as a path that one should follow. Finally, a commitment to martyrdom is sought as the goal of these discursive markers.

INTRODUCTION

Social media has now become the mainstream recruitment platform for online radicals and extremists. In order to better understand this phenomenon, it is necessary to map the discursive markers that are present online. In addition, it is important to understand the models that help to contextualise these discursive markers. Consequently, this chapter covers these three broad areas: the shift towards social media; the main discursive narratives both from the literature as well as a longitudinal study of Facebook; and finally a review of several models as they relate to the discursive markers and how these apply to radicalisation.

SHIFT TOWARDS SOCIAL MEDIA

In order to propagate their discourses toward as wide an audience as possible, online terrorist strategies have undergone significant evolution in recent years. In their initial stages, the main source of jihad

DOI: 10.4018/978-1-5225-0156-5.ch003

propaganda was from terrorist websites with most in Arabic and very few in English (Awan, 2007). However, not only has there been an exponential growth in the number of websites but also a shift in how terrorists use online media (McNeal, 2007). Increasingly, there has been a shift towards incorporating more interactive and Western forms of social media such as Myspace, YouTube, Facebook, Yahoo services and Twitter (Michael, 2009; O'Rourke, 2007; Weimann, 2010). These social media services provide new opportunities for terrorists including greater anonymity and protection from law enforcement (Dean, Bell, & Newman, 2012). Consequently, terrorist organisations including jihadist groups have been very quick to take advantage of them.

As an example, Weimann (2011) notes Al-Qaeda's use of Yahoo services including chat, email and Yahoo Groups. Another case in point is Facebook. As the largest social media site in the world, Facebook is a useful terrorist tool to attract like-minded radicals especially through its group pages (Dean et al., 2012). Networks and group pages can quickly grow with more moderate or sympathiser pages being linked to more hard line propaganda pages (Dean et al., 2012; Holtmann, 2011). Given these benefits of social media, it is no surprise that the latest research indicates that 90 percent of terrorist activity on the Internet takes place using some type of social networking tool (Weimann, 2012).

Not only do these forms of media allow for more savvy forms of presentation, but also more interactivity and participation from potential recruits (O'Rourke, 2007). Radicals can actively participate by creating and uploading videos from smartphones or computers, other propaganda or useful terrorist links (Brachman, 2012). Additionally, they allow an easy medium to display propaganda in a variety of formats aimed at attracting young recruits (Brachman, 2012).

Spiritual mentoring is regarded as an important process in online radicalisation and is well accommodated in social media forums (Michael, 2009). In essence, this means that online jihadists can make contact directly with terrorist representatives to receive instruction, mentoring or learn how they can make a contribution to the cause of jihad (Weimann, 2012).

Social media forums provide an easy means for those who are like-minded to easily connect (O'Rourke, 2007) as well as provide a strategy for terrorists to specifically target certain population subgroups using sophisticated narrowcasting strategies (Weimann, 2010). Social media is specifically designed for like-minded people to collaborate and share ideas and files (Dean et al., 2012). This is especially problematic for individuals who may think twice normally before sharing extremist views; who on social media can easily gain confidence with like-minded extremists with the possibility of leading to violent acts (Weimann, 2012). However, it is important to note that the shift towards social media forums does not mean that traditional jihad websites are obsolete; in fact, there is often an overlap and cross links between different media forums where links are made to these traditional sites for important propaganda or practical information (Michael, 2009).

According to Sageman (2008), the most significant threat is from terrorist wannabes that are recruited online especially via social media forums. Such individuals, as previously mentioned, have no direct organisational affiliations but have been recruited, socialised and trained online. Similarly, Weimann (2012) terms this threat the lone wolf terrorist. In fact lone wolf terrorists rely heavily on social media networks for support and backing, and are part of a virtual community of extremists with similar ideologies (Weimann, 2012). Social media communities are becoming more important to terrorists for recruiting and indoctrination (Weimann, 2012). Terrorist attacks and cases of those recruited online who have been convicted on terrorism charges reveal that this is a real and ongoing threat. Significantly, almost all lone wolf attacks in recent years have involved the use of electronic social media (Weimann, 2012).

Sociological Research on Internet Use

Although little research has been conducted on the mechanisms of online radicalisation, there are studies that do give some general insights into some of the mechanisms of online socialisation.

Group polarisation is a phenomenon both in real world and online contexts when group exposure to debates simply results in the reinforcing of current beliefs in addition to a shift towards a more extreme position (Yardi & Boyd, 2010). Group polarisation stems from homophily, where like-minded individuals seek each other out, resulting in a mutual reinforcement of beliefs and opinions (Yardi & Boyd, 2010). This phenomenon is well suited to recruiting and radicalising individuals on the path to jihad and terrorism.

Given the increasing emphasis on the use of Western social media, there has been a corresponding need for terrorists groups to open up these pages in order to attract new recruits (Weimann, 2010). Many terrorist organisations now have open Facebook groups, which makes it much easier for radicals to enter these pages without the previous restrictions that often applied to specialised Internet sites (Weimann, 2010). In addition, many of these sites are becoming much more media savvy, targeting and appealing to marginalised and disaffected youth. Despite these benefits, there is also the increased risk that terrorist organisations face of being infiltrated by intelligence agencies, and even prominent jihadi figures have warned their members and recruits about these potential dangers (Weimann, 2010). Nevertheless, given the membership of social media sites such as Facebook (more than 500 million active users) and Twitter (more than 40 million active users) these are important tools for finding and recruiting subjects. These facts, in conjunction with the shift toward lone jihad wannabes targeting heroic fantasies (Sageman, 2008), make this risk a necessary one for terrorist organisations to take.

Marginalised and disaffected individuals join interest groups that allow terrorists to specifically target individuals in a manner similar to the way a marketing group would target consumers (Weimann, 2010). Many of these are young males and females who are socially isolated and hence are seeking an identity. The danger here is that these individuals are visiting these radical pages or sites with a high degree of disciplined regularity. This disciplined or obsessive regularity is better known as problematic Internet usage (PIU).

There have been a number of studies conducted on PIU especially in relation to loneliness and isolation. In terms of predictors of PIU on a group of university students, loneliness, depression and computer self-efficacy were the main predictors with loneliness and then depression being the most significant (Ceyhan & Ceyhan, 2008). For a younger cohort of secondary students, a strong relationship was found between hours of Internet engagement and levels of loneliness (Deniz, 2010). This relationship in itself is problematic; nonetheless, other research studies also suggest that a negative spiral can occur. Those who were lonely or had poor social skills could develop PIU and this in turn had negative impacts on lifestyle factors such as home, school, work and relationships leading in further social isolation and loneliness (Kim, LaRose, & Peng, 2009). Another study also supported the link between high Internet use and poor social ties (Sanders, Field, Diego, & Kaplan, 2000). Consequently, those most likely to enter the obsessive regularity of online social media are also those most vulnerable with problematic psychological antecedents. Others have also found that PIU is associated with low psychological well-being (Kang, 2007).

To further elaborate on the vulnerability of the disaffected, online interaction becomes a form of compensation for an individual's poor social skills (Kim et al., 2009). Furthermore, the freedom of online interaction without the need for non-verbal cues often compounds the problems of real world interactions reinforcing the attraction of Internet usage (Kang, 2007). Unfortunately such individuals, in addition to those who have shown sympathy to terrorist causes, are particularly vulnerable for recruitment and training, given that they actually prefer online interaction.

DISCURSIVE MARKERS

A discursive marker will be defined as discourse that links radical Islam to its context and role in the world. In other words, what is the role of a radical (or true) Muslim in this world? Discursive markers will look at both literature insights as well as a longitudinal study of Facebook over three years. Both sources indicate a high level of congruence with each other in terms of overall discursive themes. However, closer inspection of Facebook discourses indicate that these are tailored toward specific global political situations, most notably the conflict in Syria.

Literature on Online Propaganda and Discourses

Terrorist leaders create discourses through their interpretations or those of others of both religious and political spheres (Gunaratna, 2005). Both aspects are important given that Islam fuses religious and political ideologies. Understanding the cultural context in which narratives and discourses are housed is just as important as understanding the narratives themselves (Al Raffie, 2012).

Historically, medieval Islamic discourses were developed through a consensus of interpretation of scholars that were well grounded in the fundamental principles of Islam and involved a thorough and well balanced process (Al Raffie, 2012). However, over time this religious authority was degraded due to the belief that governments were apostates and puppets of the West, and consequently government-supported Islamic institutions were regarded as corrupt (Al Raffie, 2012). Individualisation of interpretation resulted with individual scholars, including radical sheiks, making major contributions to Islamic thought without the usual consensus of a wider group of scholars (Al Raffie, 2012).

Discourse and propaganda has been used by Al-Qaeda and other radical Islamic groups both defensively and offensively. Defensively, it has been used to prevent what is perceived as an increasing corrupt influence of the West impacting on Islamic ideology, institutions and ideals (Lachow & Richardson, 2007). Offensively, propaganda is used to recruit, fundraise and achieve set goals related to strengthening the Islamic Caliphate (Lewis, 2005). In addition, propaganda seeks to undermine public opinions in the West such as the war in Iraq (Maher, 2007). In fact, terrorists leaders such as Osama bin Laden have made it clear that the "media jihad" is just as important as the "battlefield jihad" (McNeal, 2007, p. 794). Media jihad and terrorism itself can be viewed as being constructed from discourses (Tripathy, 2010). So the question arises, what are these discourses?

Sunni Salafist Based Discourse

One of the most important points that must be made at the outset is that discourses of radical Islam and Jihad spread online do not represent the views of the majority of Muslims. In fact, radical Islamists seek to propagate a fundamentalist, homogenised view of Islam that has little to do with traditional Islam (Ariza, 2006). Nonetheless, radical narratives cannot stray too far from traditional Islam without becoming overtly nullified (Al Raffie, 2012). Radical ideas must be gradually embedded within and upon traditional discourse, and have the support or at least the perceived support of important Islamic texts (Al Raffie, 2012). The more subtly and skilfully this is done, the more the seduction of radicalised narratives and discourses.

Although there are many branches of Islam and also forms of radical Islam, this chapter will focus on Al-Qaeda and associated groups that make up the "global jihadi movement" (Wiktorowicz, 2005, p. 75). These are known as Sunni Salafist (or salafi) who believe that Islam has been compromised over time and must be returned to its historical purity by following the Qur'an (Holy Book), the Hadith (Book of Law), the example and teachings of the prophet Mohammed's original companions (salaf) (Al Raffie, 2012; Wiktorowicz, 2005). Particular emphasis is given on following the earliest followers of Mohammed as well as making Islam a total way of life in contrast to Western ideas (Al Raffie, 2012).

A final point needs to be made on the relationship between Salafi jihadists and Wahhabism. While these forms of discourse share many similarities and are often regarded as the same for practical analysis (Al Raffie, 2012), they are historically derived from different key thinkers. Wahhabsim is based on the Saudi reformer Muhammad Bin Abdul Wahhab, while Salafist ideology is based on a number of key reformers including Ibn Taymiyya and Syed Qutb.

Discourse of Grievance (Humiliation, Oppression and Shame)

As previously stated, discourses can be categorised as defensive, a response to foreign hostilities; and offensive, seeking to achieve the Islamic caliphate. Naturally, there is also an element of overlap between such discourses. Defensive discourses begin with the idea of grievance or what some term "grievance narratives" (Jandora, 2006, p. 41). Grievances, based on the teachings of bin Laden cover a wide range of issues that include U.S. troop presence near holy sites in Saudi Arabia, dispossessing native Muslims, undervaluing oil and Israeli aggression against Palestine (Jandora, 2006). Overall, grievances are based on the colonial occupation of many Muslim lands that is perceived to have led to humiliation, poverty, corrupt governments, and the decline of Islam (Al Raffie, 2012). Furthermore, these grievances are framed in such a way so as to gain a wide support base using concepts similar to the anti-globalisation movement, and then embedding these within a social justice and religious narrative (Gunaratna, 2005). Discontent and grievance are essentially motivating factors towards collective action and terrorism (Oberschall, 2004).

Fatwa Discourses

A fatwa is a written legal opinion on a matter of Islamic law (Sharia) (Bar, 2006; Weimann, 2011). More specifically, it is a legal opinion or jurisprudence aimed at applying the principles of Islamic (Sharia) law to today's complex world and therefore provides guidance (Bar, 2006). Obligations of fatwas vary between sects with fatwas being non-binding in Sunni Islam, and may be binding in Shia Islam depending on the scholars relation to the individual (Weimann, 2011). Given the obvious complexities of making such rulings, fatwas should only be given by Islamic scholars with a detailed understanding of Islamic law (Bar, 2006). Nevertheless, in practice because there is no institutionalised priesthood, there is no universal agreement about who should issue a fatwa and who should not (Weimann, 2011).

Many Internet sites and social media pages are dedicated solely to fatwas to promoting jihad (Weimann, 2011). In the same manner as the aforementioned section on the myth of homogeneous discourse, fatwas issued by different individuals may not only be inconsistent or contradictory, but may also be explicitly directed against each other (Weimann, 2011).

Discourse of Active Agency (Jihad)

Jihad can be understood in a variety of ways in Islam ranging from a personal, spiritual struggle to a strictly physical struggle (Bar, 2006). Importantly, jihad is undertaking a course of action; it epitomises an active form of agency. The radical definition of jihad views it as a strictly military or armed struggle between Muslims and the Kuffur (Infidel, non-believer or non-Muslim) (Bar, 2006). This view of jihad is justified by the example of Muhammad and the early followers, as well as key verses in the Qur'an and Hadith (Bar, 2006).

Fundamentalist Islam through fatwas and other means elevates jihad to a central status, essentially as a pillar of Islam (Wiktorowicz, 2005). Nonetheless, this jihad cannot be separated from the discourse of grievance as bin Laden indicates: "No, we fight because we are free men who don't sleep under oppression. We want to restore freedom to our nation, just as you lay waste to our nation"; and similarly: "What we want and what we are demanding are the rights of every living being. We demand that our land be freed from our enemies and that our land be freed from Americans" (as cited in Aboul-Enein, 2004, p. 110). Hence, the fight for freedom from oppression is strongly encased in the notion of jihad (Gunaratna, 2005). Also strongly encapsulated in the notion of jihad is the notion of justice for the ummah (Islamic peoples) (Gunaratna, 2005).

Discourses of Martyrdom

Martyrdom brings together the discourses of humiliation and the discourse of active agency. It should be noted that martyrdom is not necessarily seen as a response to localised oppression, although this may be the case; on the global jihad front, it can be more generalised in response to an overall perceived humiliation of Muslims (Moghadam, 2006).

Al-Jihad fi Sabilillah

The Arabic phrase Al-Jihad fi Sabilillah means striving or fighting in the path of Allah (Gawrych, 2002) and is referred to in the Qur'an (Holbrook, 2010). Fundamental to this fight is an underlying just cause. It is a test of devotion and self-sacrifice for the individual (Minzili, 2007). There are two outcomes from this just fight: that is either victory, or martyrdom and paradise (Bar, 2006). This willingness to fight and die for a just cause is viewed as a major tactical advantage by terrorist leaders (Schweitzer, 2006), and is closely related to the next concept – Istishhad.

Istishhad

Istishhad is a discourse that seeks to evoke a very sharp contrast between the faithful and the infidel. Simply put, it contrasts the faithful Muslim as one that loves death and eagerly awaits death with the West – who value and love life (Schweitzer & Ferber, 2005). It is a rejection of the temporal world and a focus on the eternal. Jihad in Shia discourse shares many similarities with that of Sunni salafists (despite extreme Sunni salafists viewing Shias as heretics), with one of the most important being that success of operations depends on being able to focus a warrior towards the goal of paradise (Litvak, 2010). Perhaps the most important aspect of this concept is that it is independent of any forms of structured leadership which has been imperative for Al-Qaeda since the global war on terror (Schweitzer, 2006). The goal of one that holds a strong view of Istishhad is to become a martyr (shaheed).

Shaheed

Shaheed or martyr is the name given to anyone who has died fighting for the cause of Allah (Gawrych, 2002). Shaheed is much more than a term; it encapsulates a whole range of imagery. It is a brave soul who has fought an oppressive enemy at close range (Raja, 2005). Moreover, Shaheed encompasses a passage (Shahaadat) between life and paradise bypassing the place of judgement, indicating a cleansing and forgiveness of sin (Raja, 2005). They also receive a place of elevation amongst other Muslims (Minzili, 2007). This concept of rewards and guidance for those who sacrifice themselves for the sake of Allah is firmly embedded in the minds of Al-Qaeda and other jihadist groups (Gunaratna, 2005).

History and Justification of Jihad and Martyrdom

Historically, the term jihad has undergone many transformations. Whilst jihad has connotations to both internal and external struggles, nonetheless, the ultimate model of a martyr's death is based on the earliest martyrs who first battled for the Islamic cause (Heck, 2004). Even so, the most important aspect of jihad is the fact that it must be considered a just or righteous cause (Heck, 2004). One aspect that has been consistent throughout history is the rewards of martyrdom which have always held a prominent emphasis (Hoffman, 2006). Justification for jihad and martyrdom is often argued from both the Qu'ran and the Hadith (Bar, 2006). For example Qur'an 9:38:

O you who believe! What is the matter with you, that when you are asked to march forth in the Cause of Allah (i.e., Jihad) you cling heavily to the earth? Are you pleased with the life of this world rather than the Hereafter? But little is the enjoyment of the life of this world as compared with the Hereafter.

Nevertheless, it is the Hadith that carries much of the discourse related to martyrdom (Bar, 2006). In addition, both early writings and more recent fatwas by clerics both declare jihad as a legal and religious obligation as well as an act that attracts many heroic rewards (Bar, 2006). Holbrook (2010) argues that martyrdom is based less on the teachings of the Qur'an and more on the Hadith and supporting writings which may be simply narratives about the acts of heroic martyrs.

DISCURSIVE MARKERS FROM A LONGITUDINAL STUDY ON FACEBOOK

Having outlined the main discursive markers found in the literature, it is time to compare these to those found on Facebook over a period of three years using a longitudinal study. Collection of data was limited to posts in English only and focused on a broad range of extremist profiles and group pages related to Sunni Salafist style discourses.

Narratives of Grievance

Social media was filled with narratives of grievance and these ranged from broad narratives of oppression down to specific examples in a particular context. What was interesting is even in cases where grievances were described in a specific context such as the internal conflict in Syria, these grievances were still broadened to encompass a general, more global, and specifically Western assault on Islam.

Another important aspect of these narratives of grievance was that in many cases it was Western news sources that were used to describe oppression of Muslims. These included reports of brutality and maltreatment by U.S. soldiers presented on major news networks such as CNN. Amnesty International was another important source used to highlight the suffering of Muslims. The use of multiple sources including Western media and independent organisations, helped to provide a high degree of credibility to these narratives of grievance.

Persecution of Muslims and Interference in Muslim Lands

A meta-narrative was found to be built up telling a story of continual persecution and oppression of Muslims across the globe.

While the Palestinian conflict was featured on social media as a source of oppression, it did not feature as heavily as expected. Instead, other perhaps less known areas of persecution were highlighted. These included less known cases such as Nigeria, China, and Myanmar (see Table 1).

Anti-Islamic Attitudes of Western Society

Another important narrative is that of the anti-Islamic attitudes of Western society. Posts on social media ranged from dealing with more public events such as a U.S. preacher threatening to burn the Qur'an to more personalised adversarial interactions.

Perhaps the most significant activity took place following the September 2012 protests in Sydney, Australia over an anti-Islamic film. Similar protests took place around the globe. This event was an opportunity taken to promote the narrative of anti-Islamic values in the West but also to promote jihad (see Table 2).

Table 1. Posts highlighting oppression of Muslims

Muslims captured and tortured as Nigerian troops committing atrocities in fight against Islamic uprising. (linked with photos & story) ZM
Israeli Police and army guilty of torturing, detaining, threatening and sexual assault on Palestinian children in Israeli Prisons according to UN report.
He did say the Syrian government made mistakes, even the Syrian government acknowledged mistakes. He did also say this is not the reason that the West with their head chopping heart eating extremists are fighting the Syrian people, he said the West is funding foreign fighters because Bashar won't stop supporting the Lebanese & Palestinian resistance and won't recognise Israel like the rest of the Arab puppets.
Sources: Moderate and extremist Facebook pages on Syria

Table 2. Posts highlighting anti-Islamic values

We must stand against the infidels who defame our prophet ...jihad is more than a duty it is our 6th pillar
yet another attack on islam from kuffur scum. government swine won't stop the film so we must fight until our prophet is no longer under attack by the kuffur scum
Sources: Moderate and extremist Facebook pages

Military Action in Iraq and Afghanistan

As indicated in Table 3, military action in Iraq and Afghanistan was presented as a form of oppression in Muslim lands. Grievance narratives were subsequently developed from this military action. Further to this, inappropriate behaviour by soldiers is also highlighted as is the contrast between the strong and the weak.

Inaction of Western Governments in Syria

On examining Facebook profiles relating to Syria, the first key theme emerging from the coding was the failure of governments to act and intervene in Syria. Coupled with this is the criticism of governments for condemning those who do act. This narrative is combined with the anti-Islamic attitudes of the West to paint a picture that Western governments do not care about the suffering of Muslims (see Table 4).

Table 3. Posts relating to military intervention in Iraq and Afghanistan

THE KUFAR ARE MAKING THE MUSLIMS EXTREME HOW? I WILL TELL YOU HOW BY KILLING AND RAPING AND BOMBING AND DESTROYING OUR HOMES OUR SISTERS OUR BROTHERS OUR KIDS OUR BABIES THIS IS HOW THE KUFAR ARE MAKING THE MUSLIMS EXTREME ITS THEM THAT ARE MAKING US EXTREME NOT THE PREACHERS !!!!!!!!!!!!!!!!!!!!!!!!!!!!!!!
This house [US White House] is the house of international bullying of anyone who dares to dissent, expose, or leak information against the US policy, lawmakers and its Intelligence agency. The case of former NSA employee Snowden who leaked information
Western foreign policy and the double standards towards the Muslim world is to be blamed for the brutal hacking of British soldier and now, the French soldier who, according to reports, was knifed in the neck by a Muslim.
Sources: Extremist group pages

Table 4. Posts highlighting inaction of Western governments

How could we have leaders who urge the government to ban Muslims who return from syria. This is disgusting. Shows there hypocrisy. Watch out from these paid sheiks. (Youth for Syria)
What more can we add?!?! Of course, the stats don't include the number of injured, how many have been raped, the number of buildings destroyed and more..... Where is the rush to put an end to the rising numbers? Enough with the fake & useless political solutions!!!
when 1 dog from the other side dies its ok but when the whole sunna nation from syria dies know 1 cares
Women in Syria are being forced to stand in front of tanks and act as human shields before they're stripped and raped by soldiers. This is the depravity humanity has sunk to in Syria as the war there drags on. (Youth for Syria)
WHAT ABOUT THE SYRIAN PEOPLE??? BEING SLAUGHTERED LIKE SHEEP BY THE DISGUSTING DICTATOR BASHAR AL ASSAD. ITS ABSOLUTELY INHUMANE AND REVOLTING TO SEE AT LEAST 100 DEAD IN SYRIA EVERY SINGLE DAY DUE TO BLATANT MURDERS OF THE ASSAD REGIME
Amnesty International Australia
Sources: Youth for Syria Pages (Australia) and moderate pages on Syria

The atrocities in Syria are well documented both outside and within the social media jihad community. Given this fact, outside sources were often included to give greater legitimacy as well as the presentation of shocking statistics outlining the number of deaths.

While the tragedies in Syria are unquestionable, the narrative surrounding these can be constructed in many ways, laying the blame on different actors. Another dimension to this narrative was the criticism of the Australian government for both preventing Muslims from going to Syria as well as condemning those who return.

Perceived Targeting of the Muslim Community

Coupled with inaction of Western governments was the perceived targeting of the Muslim community. This targeting was found to take two directions. First, was the lack of inclusion of the Muslim community (see first post in Table 5) especially by security agencies in Western nations. Following Australian government talks with Islamic leaders to try and stop the flow of fighters to Islamic State in Syria and Iraq, as expected many negative comments were found on Facebook indicating it was not done in the interests of the Muslim community.

Second, there was the strong criticism of the Australian government's crackdown on those trying to leave the country to fight overseas (see last post in Table 5). Laws such as these are promoted in social media as anti-Islamic rather than anti-terrorism laws. Furthermore, government actions to stop Muslims leaving the country to fight in Iraq and Syria were combined with discourses of oppression, as well as the inaction of Western governments in order to create a strong picture of anti-Western sentiment.

Narratives of Jihad

Jihad was a fundamental concept for the promotion of Islamic extremism. Although jihad can be interpreted differently in moderate Islam, extremists subscribe to the fundamentalist meaning of a physical or military struggle against the infidel (unbeliever). Following the Sydney riots in September 2012, there was wide circulation on both social media and the news media about the sixth pillar of Islam which is Jihad. In the context of the anti-Islamic film, the narrative was one of not just protesting but taking action through jihad.

The phrase Al-Jihad fi Sabilillah was widely circulated on Facebook and means undertaking jihad as a path to Allah. It is this concept of jihad as a violent struggle that separates the moderate from the extremist.

Table 5. Post highlighting perceived targeting of the Muslim community

This guy has sent out a message to CIA, ASIO, FBI, MI5, SECURITY SERVICES - except Islam. Direct invite to Islam. A call for these ppl in these agencies to leave and not obey the worldly law system. One cannot obey a man, we must come under Shariah.
Turn to Islam now. Become a stranger of this world. Glad tidings to the strangers. Become a Muslim or die by the sword....Allah is best of planners - victory for Islam and Muslims....don't sugar coat Da'wah of Allah. Who are you to legislate, man does not have the right to do that, only Allah on orders - law and orders. Secret services can't handle the truth, that is why you put them in jail for speaking the truth (haqq).
Some brothers in Aust have had their passports cancelled from speaking the truth....security, take my message seriously. laws of democracy are based on killing the innocent. Islam is not terrorism or based on killing innocent but based on shariah - laws that are just.
Sources: Extremist profile pages

Call to Action: Obligation of Jihad

Congruent with the philosophy of the sixth pillar of jihad, a significant and recurrent theme was the obligation of Muslims to undertake jihad. It is presented not as an option but as a compulsory obligation. This obligation has been subdivided into key categories that emerged from the data.

Obligation from Personal Posts and Those from Martyrs

The first category was discourses posted by those committed to jihad. This also included the examples and words from those who had been martyred in the cause of jihad (see Table 6).

This concept of martyr discourse will be discussed more fully in the next section on martyrdom. Of particular interest here is the attempt to unify Muslims by stating that if you do not wish to participate, at least do not stand in the way or be critical of those who do.

Obligation from Qur'an

In Islam, the Qur'an is regarded as the highest authority being the sacred text of the religion. Hence, it is not surprising that no argument outlining the obligation to participate in jihad would be complete without support from the Qur'an. The following verses in Table 7 are a summary of the primary texts on social media used to support jihad.

Table 6. Personal posts highlighting the obligation of jihad

How can you dare to prevent people from carrying out an act of obedience which Allah loves, Has commanded His Slaves and Has obligated in the likes of these circumstances? [0107]   O Muslims, we are fighting in defense of our religion and your religion, our honor and your honor. If you do not fight with us, at least do not stand in our way as we fight those criminal traitors [quote from martyr Ibn Hazm] [0108]   And wanted to point out that we (muslims) are not in any position to criticise or blacklist these people as bad people. Mujahideens never fight for their own desires [02113]   Death is only once so let it be in the path of Allah [0704]   Jihad FI Sabilillah Let us sell our lives to our Lord to gain His mercy and devote our life for One who deserve [0706]   *Sources*: Moderate Muslim discussion pages and extremist pages on Facebook

Table 7. Qur'an verses justifying jihad found on social media

Qur'an 9:38 – o you believe! What is the matter with you, that when you are asked to march forth in the Cause of Allah (Jihad) you cling heavily to the earth? Are you pleased with the life of this world rather than the hereafter? But little is the enjoyment of the life of this world compared to the hereafter.   Qur'an 9:24 – say: if your fathers and your sons, your brothers, your wives, your kindred, the wealth that you have gained, the commerce in which you fear a decline, and the dwellings in which you delight are dearer to you than ALLAH and His messenger, and striving hard and fighting in his cause, then wait until ALLAH brings about His decision (torment). And ALLAH guides not the people who are Al-Fasiqun (the rebellious, disobedient to ALLAH)   Qur'an 4:74 – So let those fight in the cause of ALLAH who sell the life of this world for the Hereafter. And he who fights in the cause of ALLAH and is killed or achieves victory we will bestow upon him a great reward.   Qur'an 9:111 – Indeed, ALLAH has purchased from the believers their lives and properties (in exchange) for that they will have Paradise. They fight in the cause of ALLAH, so they kill and are killed. (It is) a true promise (binding) upon Him in the Torah and the Gospel and the Qur'an. And who is truer to his covenant than ALLAH? So rejoice in your transaction which you have contracted. And it is that which is the great attainment   Qur'an 2:216 – Fighting is enjoined on you, and it is an object of dislike to you; and it may be that you dislike a thing while it is good for you, and it may be that you love a thing while it is evil for you, and Allah knows, while you do not know.   *Sources*: Qur'an online and Extremist personal and group Facebook pages

Obligation from the Hadith

The Hadith or book of law is another important text in Islam and also contains justifications for jihad as illustrated below in Table 8. What is particularly interesting was the social media contexts that used the Hadith varied significantly. General posts relating to carrying out jihad as well as those relating to the conflicts in Iraq and Afghanistan contained a significant number of posts using the Hadith. In fact, the Hadith was used more than the Qur'an itself to authorise the use of jihad. On the other hand, the obligation of jihad in Syria used almost exclusively the Qur'an, with very few references to the Hadith.

Obligation from General Legal References and Sharia Law

During the Syrian conflict, there was a lot of material circulating on the obligation to participate in jihad. One of the most important references was to Sharia (Islamic) law. In fact, references to Sharia law were common on both profile and group pages of extremists.

As Table 9 indicates, justification for action against rulers in Syria and Iraq was to label them as *taghut* rulers. The last post in Table 9 gives the definition of a taghut ruler which has been verified correct from other sources. Not only are these rulers labelled, but associated with that label come certain obligations.

Table 8. Hadith verses justifying jihad found on social media

I asked the Prophet, "What is the best deed?" He replied, "To believe in Allah and to fight for His Cause." (*Sahih Bukhari,* 3:46:694, *Sahih Muslim,* 1:149)   A man came to the Prophet and asked, "A man fights for war booty; another fights for fame and a third fights for showing off; which of them fights in Allah's Cause?" The Prophet said, "He who fights that Allah's Word (i.e. Islam) should be superior, fights in Allah's Cause." (*Sahih Bukhari,* 4:52:65)   *Sources*: Hadith online and extremist Facebook profile pages

Table 9. Posts outlining the obligation of Muslims to fight against certain rulers

WHY JIHAD?   -By Shaykh Abu Qatadah Al Filistini(May Allah hasten his release)   Statements of the Scholars Regarding the Replacers of the Sharee'ah   Our scholars have spoken about the Kufur of these religions and void legislations — and they judged those who legislate it and act upon it, to be disbelievers and apostates.   Someone might ask: What's the importance of this knowledge? Is it obligatory upon a Muslim to do Takfeer of these Taghut rulers?   The answer: Yes. For it is necessary for each Muslim to know that Takfeer of the Kufur and infidels is a pillar of a Muslim's creed. This is because there are obligations resulting from this Takfeer.   So the obligation upon every Muslim is to wage Jihad against these rulers until they are removed and eliminated from authority over the Muslims. It is also obligatory upon all the Muslims to dedicate their efforts to preparing the tools of Jihaad as much as possible so as to return the authority of the Muslims to the earth which they conquered with their blood, then these accursed rulers came along and changed the faith and religion, replaced the Sharee'ah, and returned the authority of the Mushriks over the lands.   The definition of TAGHUT in the Shariah is 'anyone who exceeds the proper limits by ascribing to himself any of the rights of Allah (Subhana wa ta'ala) and makes himself a partner with Allah (Subhana wa ta'ala)'.   The second: 2. The oppressive ruler who changes the laws of Allah (Subhana wa ta'ala).   The third: 3. The one who does not govern by what Allah(Subhana wa ta'ala) has revealed.   *Sources*: radical group and profile pages

This includes the takfir (excommunication of the apostate) and the removal of such rulers by jihad. In essence, a legal case is made by charging rulers with apostasy, labelling them as taghut rulers and then proceeding with takfir and jihad against them.

Narratives of Martyrdom

Narratives of martyrdom were more prolific on extremist pages than narratives of jihad. Since martyrdom was so heavily featured on profile and group pages, it has been subdivided into further categories that emerged during the coding process. These narratives became especially significant during the conflict in Syria.

Announcement of Martyrdom

A very important aspect of social media posts on the war on Syria was the announcement of martyrs. This was also found to be the case for martyrs in the Iraq and Syrian conflicts, but was much more pronounced during the Syrian conflict due to the high number of foreign fighters. In addition to details about a martyr's death, almost always a photo and YouTube video link are given as shown in Table 10. The last post of Table 10 also demonstrates comments posted by some about this desire for martyrdom. However, the extent of this desire and willingness of individuals to follow through cannot be determined.

Martyrdom as an Obligation and the Outcome of Jihad

On analysis of profile and group pages pertaining to the Syrian conflict, the most significant theme to emerge from the coding is that of the call to martyrdom. In other words, there was not so much the call for soldiers to fight, rather the call to give one's life as a martyr. Also worthy of note is the fact that Facebook pages dedicated to martyrdom in Syria in most cases contained a YouTube link that was designed to convey powerful imagery to enforce the rewards of being a martyr.

Table 10. Posts on the announcement of martyrdom

Some names of Shuhada (Martyrs in shaaAllah) of Islamic State of Iraq and ash-Shaam…[LIST]
Among the believers are men true to what they promised Allah . Among them is he who has fulfilled his vow [to the death], and among them is he who awaits [his chance]. And they did not alter [the terms of their commitment] by any alteration. [Qur'an 33:23]
The blood of the martyrs are on our neck, we promise you this – we will rise.
Oh, allah, my son is a martyr, all praise to allah, my son is a martyr. My son is going to paradise.
Saif Al-Maliky, an honorable mujahid martyred yesterday. He's from the Land of the Haramain, the Land of the Prophet Muhammad (SAW). May Allah reward him and all the mujahideen who have sacrificed everything in the name of Allah. May Allah cast His mercy on them, and elevate their ranks on the day of Judgement [with photo of him and his baby]
#Syria – The martyrdom of Abu Hamza – One of the champions of Jabhat Al-Nusrah after clashes today with PKK Terrorists
MashaAllah the lion has a beautiful smile on his face
Video of martyrdom: http://www.youtube.com/watch?v=-403mF0MHFk
HOW ALLAH REWARDS THE SHUHADA (THE MARTYRS). IMAAN BOOSTER!
http://www.youtube.com/watch?v=ae8_j5...
I really want to go ...doing jihad is one of my first and foremost wish in my life, and want to be martyred....
Sources: Extremist Facebook pages on Syria with embedded YouTube links

The concept of embracing death (Istishhad) was present on many extremist pages (see Table 11), which also incorporated the notion of death for the sake of Allah. Extremists viewed death as a passionate desire, a process to not only acknowledge, but undertake with fervent love. Further to this, an emphasis was placed on the concept of Shaheed or martyrdom.

Another important aspect of martyrdom as an outcome of jihad was the important emphasis on the words of those who had been martyred (see Table 12). Their action appeared to give their words a high degree of symbolic authority. This included Anwar al-Awlaki whose words still have an important role even years after his death.

Rewards of Martyrs

The benefits or rewards of shaheed are clearly spelt out on extremist individual and group pages. Sorting of data into categories saw three main areas: the joy of shaheed, the specific rewards of Shaheed, and finally the transition to shaheed. This last category had been discussed in a subsequent section due to the significant imagery involved.

Martyrdom is viewed as a joyful event, a transition into happiness. In addition, specific rewards are listed for the martyr (see Table 13). Overall, shaheed is presented as a positive and rewarding experience that one should not only work towards, but encourage others to seek as well.

Table 11. Posts in embracing death

"...the caravan (of martyrs) is moving, the more you delay joining it, the further it will get away, and the harder it will be for you to catch up"...in other words, don't miss the opportunity now to join the caravan of martyrs.
All good signs of death – to die on the battlefield, this is a very, very good sign. And this is a testimony for those people who have belittled, and mocked and condemned us, they are the fake salifs or the so called moderate muslims. When a persons dies on the battlefield, that is a tremendous sign
What a great thing it is to be a shaheed – yet few people want to be it martyr. I was asked a question – why do all believers EXCEPT the shaheed tremble in their grave? All believers face fitnah in the grave EXCEPT the shaheed. What makes shaheed exempt and will not be tested in the grave? Because of the flashing of the swords over his head in battle, the flying F16 and bombs falling to his right and left was enough fitna for him.
Every muslims should want martyrdom – only a foolish person would not want it.
"There is only one death, so let it be in the path of Allah"
- Shaykh Abdallah Azzam
"Oh you Muslims! You have slept for a long time, long enough for the tyrants to take control over you. You accepted to live as slaves and submitted to tyrants. Now the time has come to revolt and destroy the shackle of slavery."
- Shaykh Abdallah Azzam
What are the things you would sacrifice for the #Religion of #Allah to be Supreme??
Some sit and just #talk!
Others #Pay with their #Lives
Which #category do u belong to?
"O you who believe! What is the matter with you, that when you are asked to march forth in the Cause of Allah (i.e. Jihad) you cling heavily to the earth? Are you pleased with the life of this world rather than the Hereafter?" [Al-Tawbah: 38]a [0625]
The cowards are afraid to fight and they do not yearn for martyrdom [0834]
Muslims love death more than life [0315]
We love death (in the path of Allah) just as much as you (kuffar) love life [0317]
Sources: Extremist pages on Facebook
a. From Qur'an
b. Meaning apostates

Table 12. Martyrdom in the words of martyrs

There is no one closer to the status of the prophets than the scholars and the mujahideen the mujahideen are the ONES WHO FIGHT FOR WHAT THE PROPHETS HAVE BROUGHT And they strive to make the word of Allah the highest while the word of the non believers the lowest [Imam anwar al awlaki]

"We stress the Importance of Martyrdom Operations against the enemy, These Attacks that have scared Americans and Israelis like never before."

[Shaykh ul Jihad (rh) (May Allah accept him as Shaheed)]

#Running away from #Jihad won't save you from #Death

You can die as a #Coward or you can die as a #Martyr

[Imam Anwar Al-Awlaki (rh)]

And an even smaller group from this elite group is the ones who sacrifice their SOULS and their BLOOD in order to bring Victory to these convictions and ambitions. So they are the Cream of the Cream of the Cream

[Abu Hamzah Al-Muhajir (May Allah accept him as Martyr)]

I was merely discharging a religious obligation by waging Jihad against those who attacked Muslims. It does not matter if I die in the course of fulfilling this responsibility; my death and the death of others like me will one day awaken millions of Muslims from apathy

[Ibn Khattab (may Allah accept him as Martyr)]

Sources: Extremist Facebook group pages

Table 13. Rewards of martyrdom

Lovely women of paradise, the most beautiful, the shaheed gets them

The most beautiful of virgins waits them in jannah

Allah grant them [the martyr] the highest parts of Jannah

A martyr has six bounties[1]:

● He will be forgiven with the first drop of his blood that is spilt;

● He will see his place in Paradise (at the time of death);

● He will be saved from the 'Great Horror' (on the Day of Judgment):

● A Crown of Dignity will be placed on his head, which contains many corundums, each one being more precious than this life and all that it contains;

● He will have seventy two Women of Paradise;

● And, he will be allowed to intercede for seventy of his family members (who would have otherwise gone to hell). (Tirmidhi & Ibn Maajah).

From: Virtues of martyrdom

Source: http://www.alminbar.com/khutbaheng/1478.htm (link found on Extremist Facebook page)

Notes: 1. Elsewhere there is noted 7 favours (bounties), the additional favour noted is being saved from the fitnah of the grave, the interrogation or great questioning, see below.

Sources: Extremist Facebook group and profile pages

Mystic Dimensions of Martyrs

Another interesting pattern found on analysis was a mystic dimension of shaheed. These narratives seemed designed to give evidence that martyrs were both special and had attained paradise without pain and suffering. The two key mystic dimensions are now outlined below.

Smell of the Martyrs Blood

Musk scented blood was another narrative found to illustrate this mystic dimension of shaheed which seems designed to give evidence to support the concept (see Table 14).

Table 14. Mythic dimension of the smell of the martyrs blood

Dr. Abdullah Azzam conveyed, "Subhanallah! Indeed, we have witnessed it on most of the people who have died shaheed. The smell of their blood are like the aroma of musk. And indeed, in my pocket is a piece of letter – on it are drops of blood belongings to Abdul Wahid (Al Shaheed, insha Allah) – it has been 2 months, but the scent is very fragrant like that of musk."   *Sources*: Extremist profile page

The Martyrs Smile

In Table 15, there is a post noting that martyrs die with a smile on their face. This was found to be a very important theme with many posts showing photos of dead martyrs smiling. Additionally, this is captured in narratives such as the one given in Table 15.

Transition of a Martyr: Under the Shadow of the Sword

One of the most critical aspects of martyrdom presented is the reconceptualisation of death as a transition from this world to the next. This concept is coupled with an attitude of willingness to undertake martyrdom operations. Perhaps most importantly is the transition to the next world. Imagery of a bridge is used to symbolise this transition in one post (see Table 16). Furthermore, attempts are made to allay fears associated with death such as whether or not the experience will be painful, as well as being exempt from the fear of judgement. Imagery of the shadow or shades of swords is found in the Hadith as follows:

Table 15. Mythic dimension of the martyrs smile

Humaydullah was honoured with Shahaadat whilst amongst us. When burying him, I found him smiling. I thought I was imagining. I therefore came out and wiped my eyes. I then found him to be the same. Fathullah, one of Haqqani's senior leaders, narrated to me: I saw the Shaheed, Suhait Khan 4 days after his burial. We opened his grave and he was smiling. Khairullah says: "I saw him looking at me." See. Why do they die with a smile on their face. Why they so happy that they are dead. Why they look at peace. They have their reward from the most merciful allah.   *Sources*: Extremist profile pages

Table 16. Posts relating to symbolism of the shadow of the sword

Think not of those who are killed in the Way of Allah as dead. Nay, they are alive, with their Lord, and they have provision   'paradise under the shade of swords' - is the second code for wanting martyrdom. The first is: 'in the heart of green birds..'   Think not of those who are killed in the Way of Allah as dead…   Those men and women! in the Judgement day! no fear will touch them!   Forget the term "terrorism" how we understand it. Everyone is going to be terrified on the day of judgment except the shaeed - no fear on the Day of Judgment for the shaheed   Allah's statement, 'They rejoice in what Allah has bestowed upon them' indicates that the martyrs who were killed in Allah's cause are alive with Allah, delighted because of the bounty and happiness they are enjoying. They are also awaiting their brethren, who will die in Allah's cause after them, for they will be meeting them soon.   What will cleanse our sins? What will purify our mistakes? And what will clean out dirt? It will not be washed except with the blood of martyrdom, and know that there is no path except this Path. If not, then the Accountability will be difficult, the Scale awaits, the Bridge is ready and your time is running out, so consider it…   Indeed, death in the way of Allah is not as frightening as people have imagined. They are a lot of hadiths which relate that the Shuhada's do not feel the pain when finding martyrdom, except like that of a pinch.   "A martyr only feels from the effect of being killed that which one would when being stung by a mosquito."   *Sources*: Extremist Facebook group and profile pages

Allah's Apostle said, "Know that Paradise is under the shades of swords". (Sahih Bukhari, 4:52:73)

This verse was found to be interpreted by extremists as attainment of paradise is achieved through the action of jihad symbolised by the imagery of swords. As stated, not only will the outcome of death be pleasant (paradise and associated rewards), but also the mechanism of death will not be in any way unpleasant. As stated in the last post in Table 16, 'under the shadow of swords' is the first of two key martyrdom metaphors. The second metaphor is 'in the heart of green birds' which will be outlined in the next section.

Destination of the Martyr: In the Heart of Green Birds

Being carried in the heart of a green bird was a very important part of shaheed found on Facebook sites with both literary descriptions as well as actual images of green birds. This concept is originally founded in the following verse of the Hadith Qudsi 27:

Their souls are in the insides of green birds having lanterns suspended from the Throne, roaming freely in Paradise where they please, then taking shelter in those lanterns. So their Lord cast a glance at them (1) and said: 'Do you wish for anything?' They said: 'What shall we wish for when we roam freely in Paradise where we please?'

This verse or slight variations of it were found in many pages and profiles associated with martyrdom (see Table 17). Even the name – green bird, as well as variations of it, were utilised as a user name on Facebook.

Table 17. Posts relating to green bird imagery and martyrdom

Real Soldiers don't reside within the depths of the ghettos;
Real Soldiers are Slave of Allah...
Real Soldiers Reside within the Hearts of Green Birds!
I learned so many things here…Green Birds changed me inside out… At times I thought that my studies, my work, my earnings will be of no use if I don't have treasure of Iman…
The souls of the martyrs live in the bodies of green birds who have their nests in chandeliers hung from the throne of the Almighty. They eat the fruits of Paradise wherever they like and then nestle in these chandeliers. Once, their Lord cast a glance at them and said: "Do you want anything?" They said: "What more can we desire? We eat the fruit of Paradise wherever we like."
The arwah of the Shuhada's are with Allah on Judgement Day inside the belly of green birds. They have lanterns suspended from the 'Asrh. They fly in Paradise to where ever they want
Surely in the hearts of green bird we will meet For Allah is pleased for we have done the righteous deed
Insh'Allah a martyr and now in the hearts of green birds flying in paradise. May Allah grant this brother Jannatul Firdaus.
"Their (i.e., the martyrs souls) will live inside green birds that dwell in designated lamps which hang on the throne of Allaah, they will roam freely in Paradise as they please, then return to these lamps"
like a bird returning to their nest, so is the brother who just died as a shaheed – he will return back to allah. They go back to allah's throne flying free like a bird.
ALSO When your brothers were killed in Uhud, Allah placed their souls inside green birds that tend to the rivers of Paradise and eat from its fruits.
'The soul of the believer becomes a bird that feeds on the trees of Paradise, until Allah sends him back to his body when He resurrects him.'
They are the Martyrs! Shuhadah! -->> the Green Birds of Paradise flying over the seas of Paradise..
Some of the sahaba Asked the Prophet(sa), after the battle of Uhud! where are our death brothers! and then the deaths brothers answered themselves, from Jannah, in the hearts of the green birds! they said who will tell our brothers that we live in Paradise! "how beautiful"! and that the food we eat are great!
Sources: extremist group pages

Although Anwar Awlaki has been killed (to extremists he is a worthy martyr), his work continues to be one of the most important and commonly endorsed by extremists, as well as the most quoted, including his imagery of birds in which he contrasts the freedom of birds with the limitations of man. Others also created posts capturing a magical or fairy tale aspect to the whole green bird experience of the martyr (see Table 18).

Repeating the Cycle of Martyrdom

Imagery was an essential aspect of martyrdom and one aspect that came up was the concept of martyrs wanting to repeat this cycle again because it was such an honour. From such discourses, it became clear that martyrdom was not just a goal or a desire but an obsession. Superiority of martyrdom and the desire to repeat this act is found in the following verse of the Hadith:

The Prophet said, "Nobody who dies and finds good from Allah (in the Hereafter) would wish to come back to this world even if he were given the whole world and whatever is in it, except the martyr who, on seeing the superiority of martyrdom, would like to come back to the world and get killed again (in Allah's Cause)". (Sahih Bukhari, 4:52:53)

This verse or variations were found to be commonly re-quoted on Facebook and indicated a high level of extremism (see Table 19).

Love of Martyrdom

This final theme can perhaps better be described as a summary theme rather than one that is separate. It captures the whole philosophy of the path of jihad with martyrdom as the destination. The following poem (see Table 20) found on post captures this whole desire for martyrdom as well as many of the other aforementioned narratives including grievances, jihad, and the heart of green birds. Essentially, it provides a story of why an individual wants to be a martyr.

Table 18. Posts highlighting capturing the fairytale aspect of green birds

Do you wonder what its like to be amongst the "Green Birds of Paradise"
As we speak, some of our brothers have experienced, one of the most beautiful journeys of Islam, and the best, Magical and wonderful journey of the entire world..
Sometimes when we hear about this beautiful and magical journey, we think it's a fairytale!! because its so beautiful...
Imagine angels flying over you, calling O you the friend of Allah! and after that flying straight to Paradise, without ever entering the grave! and Allah(swt) will speak to you in paradise 3 Times! asking you O' my servant what more do you like, and you will answer O Allah you have given me everything..
After that you will become the green Bird of Paradise, you will live in a Nest on the Throne of Allah(swt) itself Subhanalllah.. By night you will sleep on that Nest on the Throne and by day you will travel, to see the seas of Paradise.. Thats so beautiful, its even better than Fairy tales!
The bird has an honor that man does not have,
Man lives in the traps of his abdicated laws and traditions;
but the birds live according to the natural law of ALLAH,
The Almighty--Who causes the earth to turn around the sun
Sources: Extremist Facebook group and profile pages

Table 19. Posts indicating the desire to repeat the cycle of martyrdom

"I swear by the One in Whose Hands my soul is, I wish that I would fight for the sake of Allah (i.e., Jihad) and get martyred, then return and fight again and get martyred, then return and fight again and get martyred" (Bukhaari & Muslim)

Imam Ahmad recorded that Anas said that the Messenger of Allah (sallallaahu 'alayhi wa sallam) said, 'No soul that has a good standing with Allah and dies would wish to go back to the life of this world, except for the martyr. He would like to be returned to this life so that he could be martyred gain, for he tastes the honor achieved from martyrdom.'

"Nobody who enters Paradise would ever wish to return to this life again, even if he was to be given the whole world and everything in it – except for a martyr; for he would wish to return and get killed ten times due to the honour that he received (in Paradise)."

Martyrs ask: what more could we wish for, what more could they (martyrs wish for) wish for when their souls are in green birds? Could you imagine? How many of you when you were a child you wished you were a "green bird"? How many of you? Did any of you wish you were a worm or an ant? No! But when you are young and you see that bird you wish you were that bird so you could fly. That's why they create all those movies, "Superman". It's amazing to be able to fly. It would be incredible. So the shaeed will be in these green birds – their souls. And Allah will ask them: "is there anything you wish?". They reply, 'what else can we have when we can fly over all paradise?'

The shaeed realise Allah will continue to ask them three times is there anything they want or wish. And when the shaeed realise Allah will not stop asking them they will reply – 'we wish for our souls to go back to our bodies so we can be killed again for your sake'. No other person not even a righteous person will want to come back to this dunya except the shaheed.

We wish our souls could be returned back to our bodies so that we could be killed again in your name, for your names sake. Not even a pious, righteous person will want to come back to life again, only the shaheed will want to come back. The martyr understands why he wants to come back again, because he has experienced what it is to die for the honor and sake of allah. They have seen the reward to die for the sake of allah. The martyr is protected from the fitnah and fear of the grave, the questioning and interrogations from allah. The martyr will be saved from the day of terror (Day of Judgment).

Sources: Extremist Facebook group and profile pages

MODELS OF ONLINE RADICALISATION

In recent years, during the course of this research project a number of radicalisation models have been developed. It is important to examine these models in light of research data as well as critiques by fellow researchers. The common element of these models is that they are phase models demonstrating the phases that an individual goes through on the path to radicalisation (Veldhuis & Staun, 2009). Most researchers agree that radicalisation is a gradual path with individuals going through certain stages with varying timeframes (Borum, 2003; Moghaddam, 2005). However, it is not just the phases themselves that are important, rather the key assumptions or foundations of a model are just as, if not more important than the description of the phases. Consequently when each model is outlined, its fundamental assumptions will also be analysed.

Discursive Markers and Models of Online Radicalisation

Prior to outlining some of the models of online radicalisation, it is important to first look at the relationship between the aforementioned discursive markers and their role in forming these models. Firstly, it should be noted that these models are not fundamentally based on discursive markers, yet these markers are incorporated as an important part of these models. Showing the progression of radicalisation is the key focus in many of the following models which have often been constructed without a detailed knowledge of the discursive markers.

Perhaps the most fundamental and foundational discursive marker present in these models is that of grievance. Essentially, the first phase in many of these following models utilises this discourse. Following on from this foundation, later phases in many of these models tend to reflect the outcomes of engaging with the discursive markers rather than the markers themselves, and this is one of the limitations of these

Table 20. Poem capturing a love of martyrdom

The land of Jihad
The love for Jihad runs through my veins
And not going there brings so much pains
I feel so sorry when I see Muslims die
You all feel helpless, so do I
It's hard to see all the blood that is shed
"Respect human rights", is what they said
The dirty and devilish Kuffar
May Allah grant us victory in this war
For Allah I will sacrifice my wealth (In sha'ALLAH)
My life, my luxury and my health
The trade has a very good price
Give up the Dunya for Paradise
My heart yearns to go out in His Way
In the land of Kufr how can we stay?
On Qiyamah Allah will ask
Why we didn't fulfil our task!
Do not forget what Allah has said
"Those who die fisabilillah are not dead"
It cannot be described with words
What they feel inside the Green Birds
From Jannah I want my share
Dunya is nothing in compare
Eternal bliss and to see Allah's Face
That happiness this world can never replace
In the battle of Badr they were 313
Even the young ones were very keen
To fight and give their lives for Islam
But today there is no Taqwa or Iman
In front of Allah, what will we say
When we're asked about this on Judgement Day
Muslim Blood is running on the Earth
It has more value that the Kaba's worth
To die as Shaheed and then rise
And directly go into Paradise
And to drink from it's indescribable streams
That is the greatest of all my dreams
The Mujahideen are the best of men
May Allah let me soon join them
Half my Deen I need to complete
With a Mujahid with whom I can compete…
Sources: Extremist Facebook profile page

models. Notwithstanding these limitations, these models do provide important insight into the processes of radicalisation that are ultimately built on these discursive markers.

Borum's Four-Stage Model into a Terrorist's Mindset (2003)

Borum's four-stage model was designed to give law enforcement officials insights into the radicalisation process, and was developed as a conceptual rather than as an empirical model (Borum, 2003). The main theoretical underpinning of the model was to demonstrate how grievances can be turned into hatred against a particular group (Borum, 2011). Borum's four-stage model is shown in Figure 1.

One of the strongest aspects of Borum's model is that it begins with the focus on grievance and injustice. Research data from this study strongly supports this starting point. Nonetheless, the transformation

Figure 1. Borum's four-stage model (Borum, 2003, 2011)

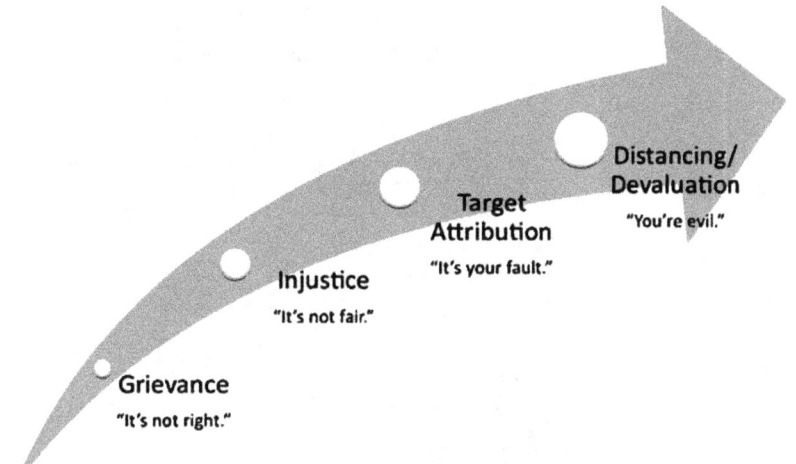

to action has more to do with embracing radical discourses of jihad and martyrdom rather than ascribing hate. Even so, as part of these blame was ascribed to the West and in particular the United States and Israel, with action against them framed in terms of an execution of judgement. Overall, the model gives an accurate starting point for radicalisation and serves as a simplistic albeit incomplete tool.

Moghaddam's Terrorism Staircase (2005)

Mohaddam's model outlines the path to terrorism as a staircase of stages with fewer and fewer individuals progressing onto each of the following stages in the staircase (Moghaddam, 2005). Figure 2 illustrates these six stages.

Rather than discuss in detail each stage, it is more useful to examine problems with this model as well as any salient aspects. The assumptions underlying the model especially at the first stage are very limited and assume a personalised adversity. As indicated both in this study and by other researchers, people's reasons for engaging with radical Islam are many and varied, and cannot be narrowed down to a particular set of circumstances. Another problem with this model is the first floor which outlines violent action as an option rather than as this study found – i.e., a discursive narrative that imparted the violence of jihad as an obligation based more on religious rather than circumstantial grounds.

Despite the flaws of this model, it does provide some salient insights into the radicalisation process. The metaphor of the staircase is particularly useful as it highlights the fact that there are a number of obstacles to overcome in the pathway to terrorism which fortunately prevents a greater number of individuals becoming terrorists. A second useful aspect of the model is its recognition of the moral aspect of the transformation into terrorism. Despite some salient points, overall, this model is inadequate primarily due to its assumptions and its hyperfocus on psychological rather than social dimensions. However, it should be noted that some researchers actually prefer this model due to its detailed psychological focus (Young, Zwenk, & Rooze, 2013).

Figure 2. Moghaddam's staircase model (Moghaddam, 2005)

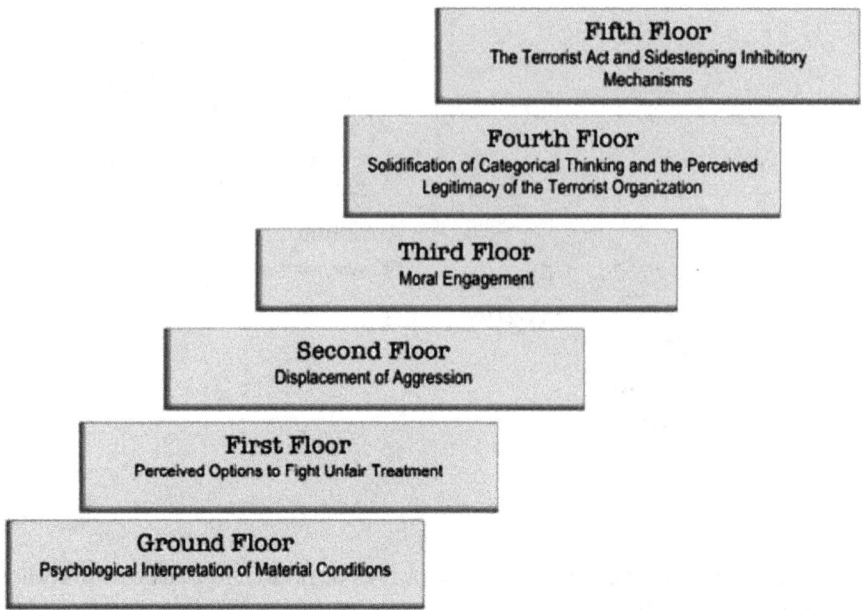

Wiktorowicz's Analytical Model Based on British Extremists (2005)

Wiktorowic's model was based on a study of radical extremists in Britain (Young et al., 2013). Similar to the previous two models, it is also a phase based model. This model has been influential amongst researchers given its detailed stages and use of a solid research base (Schmid, 2013).

Wiktorowic's model has a number of interesting facets that are worth further exploring (see Figure 3). One of the major differences with this model is the need to emphasise the religious seeking aspect (Schmid, 2013). This follows what is termed a cognitive opening where a realisation of the need to change one's worldview arises in order to make sense of one's existence (Schmid, 2013). Data from this study supports the idea of participants identifying meaning from a radical form of Islam. In addition, one of the important symbolic messages was to create dissatisfaction with this world (dunya) and instead focus on the next (jannah).

Perhaps one of the most congruent facets of the model was the religious seeking aspect where all narratives are framed clearly and explicitly in a religious context. Interestingly, studies have found that individuals with a less rigorous understanding of Islam were more susceptible to radicalisation compared to those with a more detailed understanding (Schmid, 2013). Data from this study only partially supported this notion with a case study of a new revert showing high susceptibility to the radicalisation process. However, another case study demonstrated radicalisation of individual with significant and strong understanding of Islam albeit from a more radical perspective. Framing or perhaps better expressed as reframing and socialisation are also important aspects of radicalisation supported by this study.

One significant point of difference is the socialisation process which Wiktorowic lists as the final step; it was shown to be an important aspect of radicalisation throughout a participant's journey in this study. Nevertheless, this difference can be easily explained given that Wiktorowic's model is in general a more street-based model as compared to this study which focused solely on online radicalisation.

Figure 3. Wiktorowic's model (Schmid, 2013)

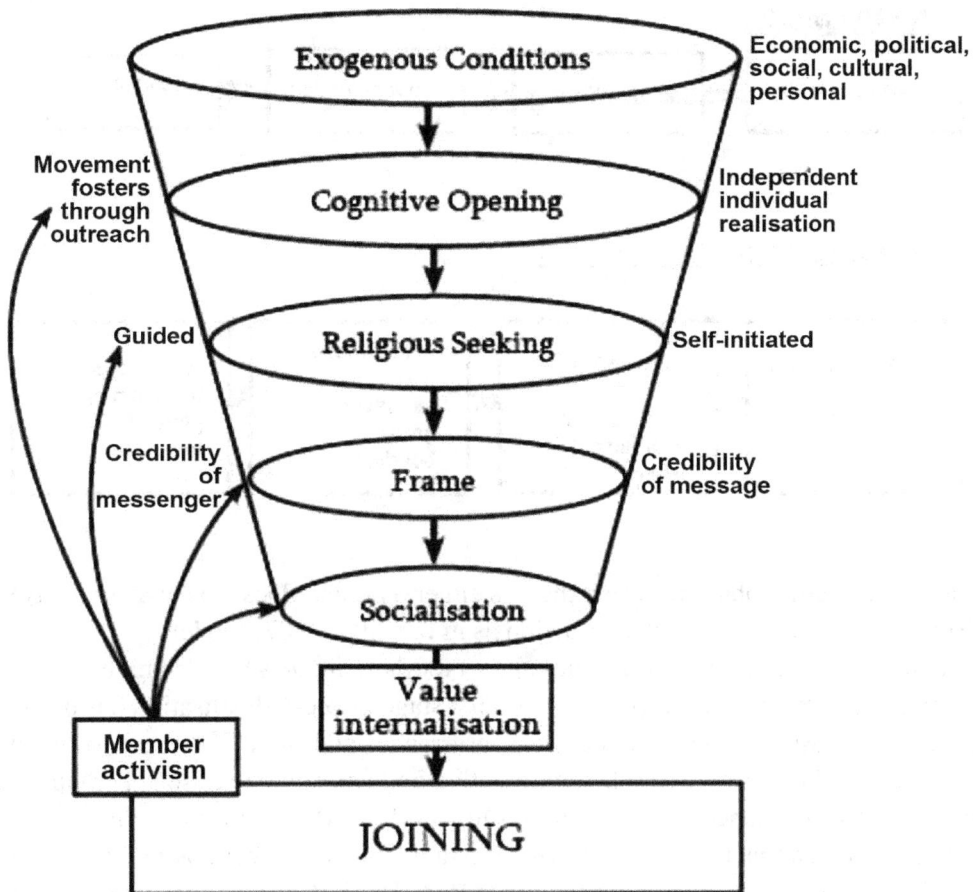

Although this model has many strengths especially its consideration of wider factors as well as the religious dimension, it does neglect the moral dimension found in Moghaddam (2005)'s model. Perhaps the most significant issue is that as stated, this is a general street model of radicalisation as opposed to a solely Internet or social media model which is developed in this chapter.

New York Police Department (NYPD) and Precht's Four Stage Models (2007)

These two models have been grouped together due to the similarity of their four stages. The NYPD model was developed based on case studies (Silber & Bhatt, 2007) and Precht's model developed in Europe through a qualitative review commissioned by the Danish government (Borum, 2011; Precht, 2007). These models are illustrated in Figure 4 based on steps listed in Precht (2007) and Silber and Bhatt (2007).

In the first stage of pre-radicalisation, an individual is exposed to extremist ideology which often occurs via the Internet or social media. The second stage involves an adoption of the tenets of radical Islam which Precht (2007) puts forward as a conversion. Third is the indoctrination stage which is an intensification of belief and which Precht (2007) also views as a process of increased group bonding.

Figure 4. Four stage models of radicalisation by NYPD and Precht

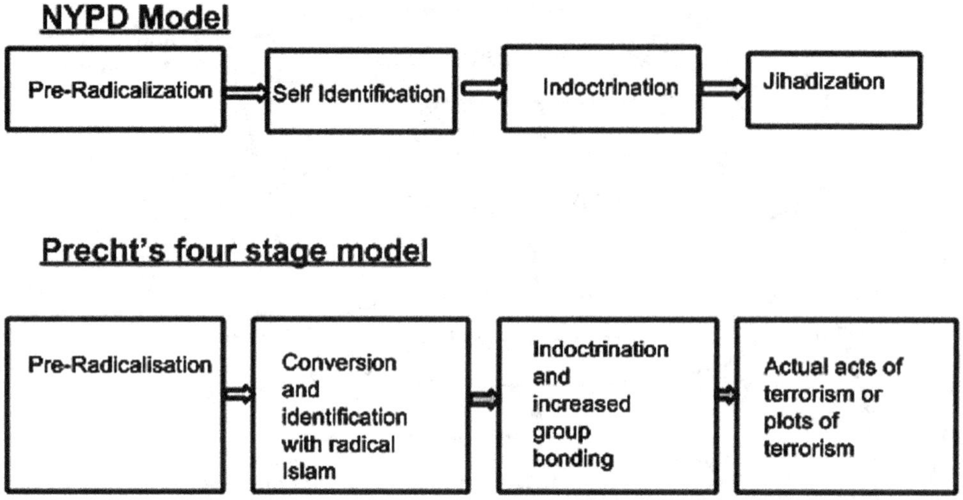

NYPD Model

Pre-Radicalization	⇒	Self Identification	⇔	Indoctrination	⇒	Jihadization

Precht's four stage model

Pre-Radicalisation	⇒	Conversion and identification with radical Islam	⇒	Indoctrination and increased group bonding	⇒	Actual acts of terrorism or plots of terrorism

The final stage is the action phase in which there is either a preparedness to act as in the NYPD model (Silber & Bhatt, 2007), or an actual plan or action as in Precht's (2007) model.

The research data in this study shows some support for these models but also highlights some issues. Exposure to extremist ideology as proposed in the first stage of pre-radicalisation has been found to be very limited in some cases. In fact in some cases, grievances and the ills of the government were the only initial aspects of this phase. The self-identification and conversion phase is perhaps the strongest aspect of these models. Evidence from this study supported the idea that individuals gave clear indications from their discourse that they had subscribed to radical Islam. Facebook names were also important self-identifiers of those who had become radicalised. The last phase is appropriate and is a test of radicalisation. The NYPD view of this stage is preferred given that a preparedness to undertake jihad is an indicator of radicalisation. In addition, there is a discrepancy between the last stages of the NYPD and Precht's model. An individual may accept his/her duty to jihad but may not progress to plot acts of terrorism as indicated in the last stage of Precht's model. This may be due to any number of reasons such as lack of opportunity, insufficient expertise, contacts or resources, or even surveillance concerns from law enforcement. In other words, a radicalised individual will not necessarily become a terrorist.

Perhaps the biggest issue with these two models is the placement of self-identification before indoctrination and group bonding. Social media evidence from this study found this progression flawed. Indoctrination and in particular group bonding was an important aspect in recruiting. In fact, embedding an individual within a group of radicalised individuals and beginning the intensification process was critical in gaining a full commitment or self-identification. In other words, self-identification or conversion could take place anywhere from pre-indoctrination all the way through to the later stages of the indoctrination process. Consequently, while these middle two stages do occur, they were found not to be discrete or progressive stages but rather intertwined with each other. While these models have been widely circulated, new and improved models are continually being developed.

A Root Cause Model (2009)

The root cause model is a deviation away from the more common phase based models of radicalisation. In its justification for moving away from a phase based model, certain shortcomings are argued with one of the most significant being the assumption of a linear process (Veldhuis & Staun, 2009). While researchers of these models do acknowledge the various speeds at which individuals go through the phases and even the fact that some individuals may skip certain phases, there is no acknowledgement of regression of phases. Another limitation pointed out of several phase models is that they are based on post fact data or successful cases of radicalisation without considering non-successful radicalisation (Veldhuis & Staun, 2009).

Figure 5 illustrates the root cause model as a series of concentric circles with the individual at the centre with his/her own personal characteristics surrounded by a number of social causes including interactions and issues of identity; the individual is further surrounded by more macro factors including global relations (Veldhuis & Staun, 2009).

Given that events in Iraq and Syria, particularly the formation and growth of the Islamic State and the significant impact that this has had on social media, research data strongly supports the broader global and geo-political context as a key root cause. Research evidence also supported the fact that this information is mediated through social media networks which have significant influences on individuals. Individual characteristics and in particular vulnerabilities were important in determining how quickly and effectively an individual was socialised.

Figure 5. Root Cause Model (Veldhuis & Staun, 2009)

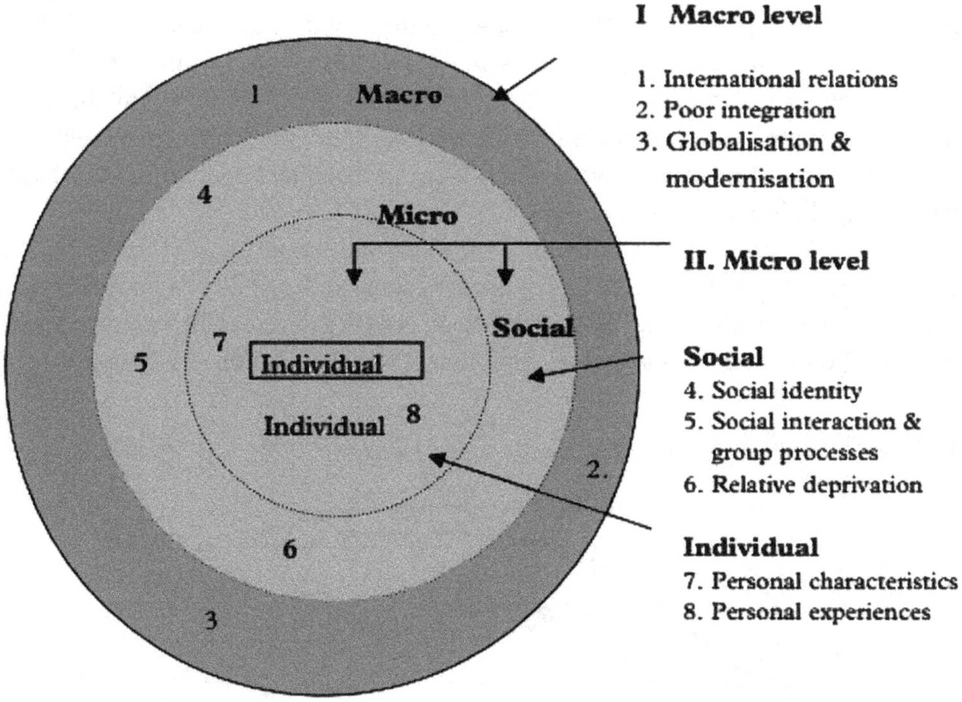

As its name suggests, the root cause model is an excellent tool for describing the particular root causes of radicalisation and the layers involved. All these complex micro and macro variables become push and pull factors of radicalisation (Veldhuis & Staun, 2009). While this model is able to capture these variables and the relational levels of variables, it does not give the same insight as phase based models into the actual process of radicalisation.

Helfstein's Four Stage Model (2012)

Helfstein's four stage model is a newer phase model with some important differences (Helfstein, 2012). Unlike previous phase models that have been criticised for being too linear, Helfstein's model views the phases as cyclic and dynamic rather than linear, and includes regression as well as revisiting previous stages (see Figure 6). The most significant differences or more accurately, developments, are the assumptions underlying the model. Helfstein (2012, p. 2) argues that radicalisation cannot be seen as purely a social or ideological process; rather it is a "coevolutionary" process that needs to account for both streams of influence.

Before discussing the model itself, it is important to look at other key findings or underlying assumptions of this model. Helfstein (2012) noted that while Internet sites, YouTube and online magazines such as Inspire carry and convey the ideology of radicals, it is Facebook that makes it interactive and facilitates the social process. Another important finding was that those who are radicalised or prone to radicalisation often had a counterculture background (Helfstein, 2012). Moreover, radicalisation can have an important self-serving element which is distinct from the religious or ideological motivations (Helfstein, 2012).

Comparison of these key findings and assumptions with the research data found a strong congruence. Facebook as the focus of the study was not only critical in the institutional process of socialisation but also very much linked to Helfstein's (2012) ideology sources with key links to YouTube videos and Internet discourses. Additionally, radical recruiters were found on anti-government and new world order websites which not only confirms Helfstein's findings that many radicals have this history, but it also indicates that recruiters are well aware of this target audience and are using strategies to engage with these individuals. Finally, evidence was found of a self-serving element confirming this as an important dimension for some individuals.

The model itself is based on case studies of radicalised individuals and plots in the United States (Helfstein, 2012). Awareness is seen as the first important stage and covers the exposure to radical ideology. From here, individuals move to the interest phase where they have a willingness to alter their belief systems. It is at this point where an individual enters the virtual institution. Individuals may go back to

Figure 6. Helfstein's four stage model of radicalisation (Helfstein, 2012)

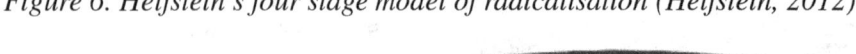
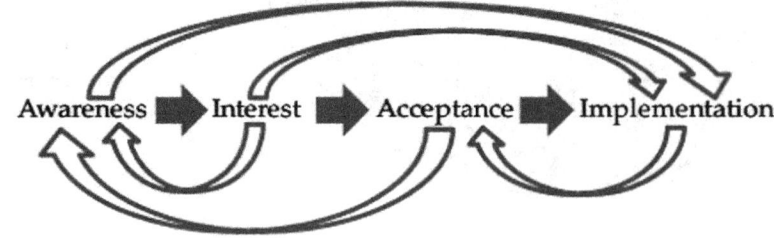

the awareness phase until sufficient interest is regained. Following interest and the socialisation of the individual is the acceptance stage where social norms are internalised and violent actions are sanctioned. Helfstein (2012) also makes an important distinction between radical norms and violent radical norms. For example, some groups believe in the Islamic Caliphate but shun the use of violence (Helfstein, 2012). Finally, there is the implementation phase based on these internalised values.

Torok's Explanatory Model Utilising Psychiatric Power (2011, 2013)

The author's explanatory model (Torok, 2011, 2013) is an alternative model that is not a phased based model like many of the aforementioned models. Rather it looks at power relationships online and how discourses are formed and propagated online. Like the previous models, it is important to understand the assumptions underlying this model.

Most significant is that it takes a view of power based on Foucault's (2006) research that utilises a circular and networked nature of power, and more significantly discourse formation. This model is based on three key foundations.

- The social media environment is viewed as an online institution that isolates an individual in terms of regular exposure to a narrow range of discourses.
- Discourses are normalised. In other words, extremist discourses are conveyed as those with authority and truth.
- Power is networked with individuals being radicalised by homogeneous extreme discourses from a large number of different sources rather than just a singular individual.

Essentially, an individual enters the online institution of social media with disciplined regularity, and with isolation from competing discourses his/her belief system becomes more normalised toward extremist thinking – i.e., the individual is influenced by a whole network of constructed discourses. This model gives an alternative lens where the discursive markers are central to the process of radicalisation. Furthermore, these discursive markers are central to the model in terms of the normalised discourses used to transform individuals.

CONCLUSION

In conclusion, the shift towards social media for propagating radical discourses has necessitated the need to understand the key discursive markers. While categorisations of key discursive markers have been stable, they have also adapted to global political contexts, most notably the situation in Syria and Iraq.

Discursive markers are designed along a progression of narratives beginning with grievances. Narratives of grievance form the foundation for discourses of active agency that promote a commitment to jihad. However, it is narratives of martyrdom that are the ultimate goal of discourses where the aim is to gain a commitment to give one's life for the cause of Islamic extremism. With the recent formation of the Islamic State in Iraq and Syria, the goal becomes to maintain a pure Islamic State under the Sharia Law.

Understanding discursive markers is the first step in understanding the complex phenomenon known as radicalisation. Utilising these discursive markers, a number of radicalisation models have been discussed. Most are phase based models viewing radicalisation as a progression of steps. Some of the models take a different approach including the author's explanatory model of online radicalisation. Despite progress made in understanding discourses as well as a number of important models relating to the process of radicalisation, there is still much work to be done in terms of not only further understanding but also in applying this to policy formation to prevent and reduce radicalisation.

REFERENCES

Aboul-Enein, Y. H. (2004). Osama bin-Laden interview, June 1999: Entering the mind of an adversary. *Military Review, 84*(Sep-Oct), 109–112.

Al Raffie, D. (2012). Whose hearts and minds? Narratives and counter-narratives of salafi jihadism. *Journal of Terrorism Research, 3*(2), 13–31. doi:10.15664/jtr.304

Ariza, L. M. (2006). Virtual Jihad. *Scientific American, 294*(1), 18–21. doi:10.1038/scientificamerican0106-18 PMID:16468423

Awan, A. N. (2007). Virtual jihadist media: Function, legitimacy, and radicalising efficacy. *European Journal of Cultural Studies, 10*(3), 389–408. doi:10.1177/1367549407079713

Bar, S. (2006). *Jihad ideology in light of contemporary fatwas*. Washington, DC: Hudson Institute.

Borum, R. (2003). Understanding the terrorist mindset. *FBI Law Enforcement Bulletin, 72*(7), 7–10.

Borum, R. (2011). Radicalization into violent extremism II: A review of conceptual models and empirical research. *Journal of Strategic Security, 4*(4), 37–62. doi:10.5038/1944-0472.4.4.2

Brachman, J. (2012, February 3). The jihad hobbyists who've moved on from watching al-Qaida videos. *The Guardian*. Retrieved from http://www.guardian.co.uk/commentisfree/2012/feb/03/jihad-hobbyists-al-qaida?utm_source=twitterfeed&utm_medium=twitter

Ceyhan, A. A., & Ceyhan, E. (2008). Loneliness, depression, and computer self-efficacy as predictors of problematic Internet use. *Cyberpsychology & Behavior, 11*(6), 699–701. doi:10.1089/cpb.2007.0255 PMID:19072150

Dean, G., Bell, P., & Newman, J. (2012). The dark side of social media: Review of online terrorism. *Pakistan Journal of Criminology, 3*(3), 107–126.

Deniz, L. (2010). Excessive Internet use and loneliness among secondary school students. *Journal of Instructional Psychology, 37*(1), 20–23.

Foucault, M. (2006). Lectures at the College de France 1973-1974. In J. LaGrange (Ed.), *Michel Foucault: Psychiatric power* (G. Burchell, Trans.). New York, NY: Palgrave MacMillan.

Gawrych, G. W. (2002). Jihad, war, and terrorism. *Small Wars Journal*. Retrieved from www.smallwarsjournal.com/documents/gawrych.pdf

Gunaratna, R. (2005). *Ideology in terrorism and counter terrorism: Lessons from combating Al Qaeda and Al Jemaah Al Islamiyah in Southeast Asia*. Retrieved from http://kms1.isn.ethz.ch/serviceengine/Files/ISN/44015/ichaptersection_singledocument/0d07f910-03a4-4cc7-86ea-5b754a6e04fa/en/07.pdf

Heck, P. L. (2004). Jihad revisited. *The Journal of Religious Ethics, 32*(1), 95–128. doi:10.1111/j.0384-9694.2004.00156.x

Helfstein, S. (2012). *Edges of radicalization: Ideas, individuals and networks in violent extremism.* Retrieved from https://www.hsdl.org/?view&did=700228

Hoffman, B. (2006). Inside terrorism (Revised and Expanded Ed.). New York, NY: Columbia University Press.

Holbrook, D. (2010). Using the Qur'an to justify terrorist violence: Analysing selective application of the Qur'an in English-language militant Islamist discourse. *Perspectives on Terrorism, 4*(3), 15–28.

Holtmann, P. (2011). *No threat at first sight: Invisible terrorist environments on Facebook and YouTube.* Retrieved from http://www.univie.ac.at/jihadism/blog/wp-content/uploads/2011/03/Philipp-Holtmann-No-threat-at-first-sight-Invisible-terrorist-environments-on-Facebook-and-Youtube.pdf

Jandora, J. W. (2006). Osama bin Laden's global jihad: Myth and movement. *Military Review, 86*(6), 41–50.

Kang, S. (2007). Disembodiment in online social interaction: Impact of online chat on social support and psychosocial well-being. *Cyberpsychology & Behavior, 10*(3), 475–477. doi:10.1089/cpb.2006.9929 PMID:17594274

Kim, J., LaRose, R., & Peng, W. (2009). Loneliness as the cause and the effect of problematic Internet use: The relationship between Internet use and psychological well-being. *Cyberpsychology & Behavior, 12*(4), 451–455. doi:10.1089/cpb.2008.0327 PMID:19514821

Lachow, I., & Richardson, C. (2007). Terrorist use of the Internet: The real story. *Joint Force Quarterly, 45*, 100–103.

Lewis, J. A. (2005). The Internet and terrorism. *Proceedings of the Annual Meeting (American Association of University Teachers of Insurance), 99*, 112–115.

Litvak, M. (2010). "Martyrdom is life": Jihad and martyrdom in the ideology of Hamas. *Studies in Conflict and Terrorism, 33*(8), 716–734. doi:10.1080/1057610X.2010.494170

Maher, S. (2007). Road to jihad. *Index on Censorship, 36*(4), 144–147. doi:10.1080/03064220701740590

McNeal, G. S. (2007). Cyber embargo: Countering the Internet jihad. *Case Western Reserve University School of Law, 39*(3), 789–826.

Michael, G. (2009). Adam Gadahn and Al-Qaeda's Internet strategy. *Middle East Policy, 16*(3), 135–152. doi:10.1111/j.1475-4967.2009.00409.x

Minzili, Y. (2007). *Strategic thinking of the salafi-jihadi movement.* Retrieved from http://www.herzliya-conference.org/_Uploads/2817ShmuelBarIslamistStrategic.pdf

Moghadam, A. (2006). Suicide terrorism, occupation and the globalisation of martyrdom: A critique of dying to win. *Studies in Conflict and Terrorism, 29*(8), 707–729. doi:10.1080/10576100600561907

Moghaddam, F. M. (2005). The staircase to terrorism: A psychological exploration. *The American Psychologist, 60*(2), 161–169. doi:10.1037/0003-066X.60.2.161 PMID:15740448

O'Rourke, S. (2007). *Virtual radicalisation: Challenges for police.* Paper presented at the 8th Australian Information Warfare and Security Conference, Perth, Australia.

Oberschall, A. (2004). Explaining terrorism: The contribution of collective action theory. *Sociological Theory, 22*(1), 26–37. doi:10.1111/j.1467-9558.2004.00202.x

Precht, T. (2007). *Home grown terrorism and Islamist radicalization in Europe: From conversion to terrorism.* Denmark: Danish Ministry of Justice.

Raja, M. A. (2005). Death as a form of becoming: The Muslim imagery of death and necropolitics. *Domes, 14*(2), 1–11. doi:10.1111/j.1949-3606.2005.tb00894.x

Sageman, M. (2008). *Leaderless jihad: Terror networks in the twenty-first century.* Philadelphia, PA: University of Pennsylvania Press. doi:10.9783/9780812206784

Sanders, C. E., Field, T. M., Diego, M., & Kaplan, M. (2000). The relationship of Internet use to depression and social isolation among adolescents. *Adolescence, 35*(138), 237–242. PMID:11019768

Schmid, A. P. (2013). *Radicalisation, de-radicalisation and counter-radicalisation: A conceptual discussion and literature review.* The Hague: ICCT.

Schweitzer, Y. (2006). Istishad as an ideological and practical tool in the hands of Al-Qaeda. *Journal of National Defense Studies, 6*, 113–138.

Schweitzer, Y., & Ferber, S. G. (2005). *Al-Qaeda and the internationalization of suicide terrorism.* Retrieved from http://ics-www.leeds.ac.uk/papers/pmt/exhibits/2809/memo78.pdf

Silber, M., & Bhatt, A. (2007). *Radicalization in the West: The homegrown threat.* New York, NY: New York Police Department.

Torok, R. (2011). *The online institution: Psychiatric power as an explanatory model for the normalisation of radicalisation and terrorism.* Paper presented at the European Intelligence and Security Informatics Conference (EISIC), Athens, Greece. doi:10.1109/EISIC.2011.43

Torok, R. (2013). Developing an explanatory model for the process of online radicalisation and terrorism. *Security Informatics, 2*(6).

Tripathy, J. (2010). What is a terrorist? *International Journal of Cultural Studies, 13*(3), 219–234. doi:10.1177/1367877909359731

Veldhuis, T., & Staun, J. (2009). *Islamist radicalisation: A root cause model.* Retrieved from http://subweb.diis.dk/graphics/_IO_indsatsomraader/Religion_og_social_konflikt_og_Mellemosten/Islamist%20Radicalisation.Veldhuis%20and%20Staun.pdf

Weimann, G. (2010). Terror on Facebook, Twitter, and YouTube. *The Brown Journal of World Affairs, 16*(2), 45–54.

Weimann, G. (2011). Cyber-Fatwas and terrorism. *Studies in Conflict and Terrorism, 34*(10), 765–781. doi:10.1080/1057610X.2011.604831

Weimann, G. (2012). Lone wolves in cyberspace. *Journal of Terrorism Research, 3*(2), 75–90. doi:10.15664/jtr.405

Wiktorowicz, Q. (2005). A genealogy of radical Islam. *Studies in Conflict and Terrorism, 28*(2), 75–97. doi:10.1080/10576100590905057

Yardi, S., & Boyd, D. (2010). Dynamic debates: An analysis of group polarization over time on Twitter. *Bulletin of Science, Technology & Society, 30*(5), 316–327. doi:10.1177/0270467610380011

Young, H. F., Zwenk, F., & Rooze, M. (2013). *A review of the literature on radicalisation; and what it means for TERRA*. Retrieved from http://www.terra-net.eu/files/publications/20140227160036Literature%20review%20incl%20cover%20in%20color.pdf

Chapter 4
ISIS Discourse in Radical Islamic Online News Media in Indonesia:
Supporter or Opponent

Fajar Erikha
Universitas Indonesia, Indonesia

Idhamsyah Eka Putra
Persada Indonesia University, Indonesia

Sarlito Wirawan Sarwono
Universitas Indonesia, Indonesia & Persada Indonesia University, Indonesia

ABSTRACT

This article aims to understand how discourses about Islamic State in Iraq and Syria (ISIS) are supported and/or rejected by radical Islamic groups. Data were collected from two Islamic news website: Voa-Islam and Arrahmah. Both websites are categorised as radical Islamic sites. By using the discursive psychology approach, it was found that when ISIS is viewed as a group that actualised the establishment of an Islamic State, it is praised and supported. However, when ISIS is deemed to have killed other fellow Muslims, it is opposed and its movement is considered to be 'out of Islamic corridors'. Practical implications of these findings are identified and discussed.

INTRODUCTION

The Islamic State in Iraq and Syria (ISIS), an Islamic terrorist group, is currently under great scrutiny as a result of numerous violent acts that have been perpetrated around Iraq and Syria. ISIS has asked other Muslims around the world to join and support its movement. As a result, a lot of Muslims from different countries have joined ISIS.

DOI: 10.4018/978-1-5225-0156-5.ch004

Indonesia is one of the most populated Muslim countries in the world (88.2 percent of the 250 million Indonesians; Pew Forum on Religion & Public Life, 2009) with the majority identifying themselves as being Sunni Islam. Presently, there are two major schools of thought (*madhhab*) in Islam, namely Sunni and Shia Islam. Both schools have each further spawned various other schools of thought. Each has a different interpretation of Islam. Normally, differences in thoughts and Islamic law are understandable; as long as the Al-Quran and Hadith are used as the foundation (Okon, 2012), they will still be regarded as being Muslim thinking.

ISIS has branded itself as one of the many schools of thought in Sunni Islam. This is appealing to some and hence, Indonesia is considered as a fertile ground for ISIS to recruit new followers. It is interesting to note that the majority of Muslims in Indonesia are moderate, and most of them rejected ISIS ideology and movement. However, radical groups, which make up the minority, are more aggressive in spreading their ideology. This is why, many Islamic news sites in Indonesia are categorised as radical in nature. To the best of our knowledge, radical groups in Indonesia are actively discussing about the ISIS phenomenon. So far, radical Islamic groups have been found to have different perspectives with regards to ISIS. The present article discusses the discourses about ISIS in radical Islamic online news media in Indonesia.

LITERATURE REVIEW

The Islamic State in Iraq and Syria (ISIS)

ISIS is a state as well as a political-military organisation with an orientation towards militant *Salafi-jihadism* that is not recognised by the Iraqi and Syrian authority (The Clarion Project, 2015). The name ISIS was used from 2013 to 2014, and changed into 'The Islamic State' after it was declared on June 29, 2014. Abu Bakar Al-Bagdadi was officially appointed as the leader of this group (*Caliph*). The Islamic State originally annexed Iraq and Syria because the two countries are considered to be important for the world jihad movement (Gerges, 2014).

In its journey, ISIS uses the legal interpretation of Islam (*Sharia*) and imposes its application in areas under its territorial control. ISIS performs extreme and oppressive acts such as suicide bombings, bank looting, and executions against those considered as its enemies – such as the West (e.g., America, Europe), as well as other Islamic groups (in Sunni or Shia sub-schools). Furthermore, ISIS propaganda materials (e.g., execution of all prisoners) have been shared and propagated through print media, Internet, and video.

Terrorism and ISIS in Indonesia

Ever since Abu Bakar Bashir (a former leader of Jemaah Islamiyah and Indonesian Mujahidin Council; currently, a leader of Jemaah Ansharut Tauhid [JAT]) pledged an allegiance to ISIS in Nusakambangan prison on July 18, 2014, ISIS has attracted the attention of the Indonesian government (Feillard, 2014). The Indonesian government immediately took a stand on this matter, and recognise the need to reject, prevent, and combat ISIS ideology.

On the one hand, opposition to ISIS has been seen across Indonesia. Major religious institutions such as Nadlatul Ulama (NU) and Muhammadiyah are supporting the stance adopted by the Indonesian government ("PBNU: Ulama Besar", 2014; Putra & Sukabdi, 2014). Furthermore, anti-terror Special

Detachment from Indonesian National Police (Densus 88) has arrested 14 people suspected to be ISIS members and sympathisers (T. Sembiring, personal communication, May 17, 2015). On the other hand, support from Indonesian Muslims towards ISIS has been seen in the form of recognising ISIS as the Islamic Caliphate. These Muslims pledge allegiance (via an oath of support) to ISIS, and send fighters to join ISIS in Iraq and Syria.

Discourse Analysis and Discursive Psychology as an Approach

In this chapter, discourse analysis will be employed. A discourse is defined as written or spoken form of communication about a topic. Discourse is a way or a product of thinking that is expressed through languages; it can be an ideology, notions, or opinion. In order to achieve a wide influence, an ideology or notion requires an institution to convey the messages to the public. On this matter, as a tool that can reach a large audience, mass media have been utilised by institutions, groups, and individuals to spread their ideas. It is no doubt that currently mass media is playing an increasingly important role because it is easily accessible. Hence, a discourse can be disseminated to large segments of the population through mass media (Cotter, 2001).

Some topics that have been discussed using discourse analysis pertain to the construction of facts from news agencies covering the events of:

- September 11, 2001 attacks,
- The New Labour political discourse and political arguments against the expansion of the European Union,
- Conversation between Oprah Winfrey and the Queen of Jordan (Saj, 2012),
- President Barack Obama's speech (Ferencik & Horváth, 2009), and
- The death of Princess Diana (MacMillan & Edwards, 1999).

Discourse analysis was introduced and primarily used for linguistic studies. However, discourse analysis is currently used in other area of studies such as sociology, psychology, communication research (van Dijk, 1998), history, and political science (Fairclogh, 1992). Usually, studies analysing a discourse cover a number of themes, namely cohesion and conformity, anaphora, information structure, and segmentation (i.e., paragraph) as well as conclusions, implications, prejudices, conversations, relevance, courtesy and narrative, and many others (Brinton, 2001). Other than that, discourse analysis has also been used as a methodological tool in analysing social power and oppressions (Edwards, 2005; Fairclough, 1992).

Discursive Psychology

In its development, discourse analysis is developed in several forms; one of those is discursive psychology, which is an attempt to analyse discourse using psychological approaches. Discursive psychology tends to emphasise on analysing implicit and explicit messages of texts and talks (Edwards & Potter, 2005); it examines how people carry out psychological activities such as justification and rationalisation. It starts to see psychological variables as things that are constructed, observable, and discussed. Usually, sentences, phrases, and idioms within texts and talks are used to track expressions, attitudes, or perceptions. More often, some discrete set of words correspond to a discrete act (Potter & Edwards, 2001).

Discursive psychology is used to examine action-orientation and reality-construction of written or spoken communication. To begin with, a research using discursive psychology approach can start by asking what is the 'talk doing', what strategies the speakers are using, what is the 'hidden' meaning beyond the texts, and how do people manage their interest.

FOCUS OF THE PRESENT PAPER

This article aims to understand how discourses about ISIS are supported by *Voa-Islam* and rejected by *Arrahmah* (although it supported ISIS in the beginning) in their online news media – *da'wah* (missionary endeavour).

Online da'wah

The emergence of the Internet has been well received and used by Muslims around the world. It has been used for preaching (Adam, Anuar, & Ali, 2014) and organising social movements (Mousa, 2011). Radical groups, on the other hand, use the Internet as a propaganda tool for their ideology (National Coordinator for Counterterrorism, 2010). This is why the Internet is considered to play an important role as a vehicle for radicalisation (Aly, 2010; Brahman, 2009; Friedland & Rogerson, 2009; Homeland Security Institute, 2009; Jenkins, 2011; Neumann, 2013; O'Rourke, 2007; Solahudin, 2013; Tucker, 2010; Yasin, 2014).

According to Solahudin (2013), there are four types of *jihad media* in Indonesia which purport to be the voice of Islam. The first type refers to jihadist news sites, such as Arrahmah[1], *Muslim Daily*[2], and *Al-mustaqbal*[3]. The second type of jihad media refers to propaganda sites that provide explanations about preaching jihad. One of these is *Millah Ibrahim*[4]. The third type refers to jihadist forums containing information related to practical military knowledge in preparation for acts of terrorism. Members of these forums are exclusive and selected. Examples of such forums are *Albusyro*[5] and *At-tawbah*[6]. The last type refers to jihad media which is a mixture of various other jihad media. One such site is *Anshorut Tauhid Was Sunnah Wal Jihad*[7].

In January 2015, the Institute for Policy Analysis of Conflict (IPAC) visited a number of sites that explicitly supported ISIS ("Inilah Situs Online", 2014). Among them are Al-mustaqbal, Arrahmah, *Compass Islam*, Millah Ibrahim, *Prisonerjoy*, *Shautussalam*, and Voa-Islam[8]. Of the seven media, Voa-Islam and Arrahmah are most often referred to Islamic extremist websites (Solahudin, 2013). Both are popular radical militant media which overtly provide support to ISIS. Currently, these online media are being monitored by the Indonesian government and are considered as dangerous sites.

Blocking the Radical Islamic Sites

The issue of ISIS is gaining prominence as more people have been arrested on suspicion of involvement with ISIS. At the end of March 2015, the National Counter Terrorism Agency (Badan Nasional Penanggulangan Terorisme/BNPT) requested the Ministry of Communication and Information to block 22 more websites pertaining to radical Islam (Ningrum, 2015). Among those were Voa-Islam and Arrahmah websites. As a result, a counter movement was started which opposed the blocking of these radical Islamic sites; the reason was that this initiative to block radical Islamic sites also led to Islamic sites that do not support ISIS being blocked as well. In short, both Voa-Islam and Arrahmah, and some other sites were reopened after a dialogue between the sites' managers and the Indonesian government (Ngazis & Haryanto, 2015).

Voa-Islam

Voa-Islam was founded by Sabrun Jamil Abu Ammar, Abu Faris, and Abu Vakha (one of the current leadership council) in Bekasi on April 2009. It was officially opened on June 1, 2009. Based on information on its official Facebook page, Voa-Islam was created as a reference for Islamic information and to act as the defender of Muslims so that Islam can stand tall and firm. They have two official fan pages on Facebook (Voice of Al-Islam and Voa-Islam). The main official Facebook account, Voice of Al-Islam has 87,681 followers, while the second official account, Voa-Islam has only 4,385. Furthermore, Voa-Islam has a Twitter account, which was created on April 5, 2010 (@voaislam), with 67,421 followers. Five years since this account was created, the administrator has issued 23,915 tweets.

Arrahmah

Arrahmah was founded by Muhammad Jibril (son of Abu Jibril who was one of the founders of Jemaah Islamiyah) in 2012. Similar to Voa-Islam, Arrahmah has a fan page on Facebook under the account, Arrahmah.com, with 8,082 followers. This is only ten percent of Voa-Islam followers. They also have a Twitter account as another propaganda tool. The account name is @Arrahmah with 55,985 followers. Since it was created on June 1, 2009, the Twitter account has issued 26,173 tweets. It produces approximately 11 tweets a day. Beside Twitter and Facebook, Arrahmah also uses an application that can be downloaded for free from Android and Windows operating system.

METHOD

Procedure

This study used a discourse analysis approach to analyse the ISIS discourse in Voa-Islam and Arramah website. Although both sites have other social media sources such as Facebook and Twitter, the articles from both websites were used as the primary source.

News articles were collected from each website through search engine using the keyword 'ISIS'. Afterwards, the articles were sorted. Although ISIS has changed their name since June 29, 2014 to The Islamic State (IS), the use of ISIS as a keyword is still considered effective and relevant as both websites still continue to use the word ISIS. Each selected article was broken down into pieces or excerpts based on similar themes, typically in the form of single or multiple paragraphs that will be called extract.

Of the 139 articles in Voa-Islam that were associated with ISIS, three articles showed Voa-Islam's support for ISIS. Whereas from the 204 Arrahmah collected data, six articles strongly exhibited support for ISIS, and three articles demonstrated rejection of ISIS. For the purpose of this chapter, the authors decided not to use the remaining articles as extracts for analysis. The articles from both websites were collected from August 2013 until April 2015 – i.e., when ISIS started to gain attention in news media coverage. Extracts that were featured were exactly the same as how they were presented in the article in its original state. The publication date and time of the article are highlighted in the extracts to facilitate the analysis process. Extracts found in articles by Arrahmah that supported ISIS were marked as SA (Support of Arrahmah). SV (Support of Voa-Islam) was marked for all supporting points given by Voa-Islam towards ISIS. As for extracts which opposed ISIS (i.e., found in articles by Arrahmah), they were marked as OA (Opponent of Arrahmah).

Ethics in Data Collection

Voa-Islam and Arrahmah websites published news with the purpose of preaching through the media. At the end of each news article, they inserted a statement: 'Spread! Earn deeds, spread this information' for Arrahmah; and 'Spread this information, may we become pious charity!' for Voa-Islam. We decided not to ask for permission in advance to the sites' managers because after considering the statements, we concluded that no personal information will be mentioned or discussed.

ANALYSIS

The data identified in the analysis was categorised into themes. Two attitudes were found which represented these Internet media on the issue of ISIS: supporting ISIS or opposing ISIS. Voa-Islam exhibited an attitude of supporting all ISIS propaganda. Any act performed by ISIS, regardless of whether it was an act of violence or provision of aid, was supported by Voa-Islam.

In this regards, what we found on Arrahmah website was interesting. Initially, Arrahmah shared a similar attitude with Voa-Islam in terms of its support towards ISIS. In fact, from the data we obtained, Arrahmah had intensely and positively preached about ISIS initially. Between August 2013 to February 2014 (i.e., seven months), Arrahmah was very supportive of ISIS. However, ever since one of the Sunni Muslim groups affiliated with Al-Qaeda (Jabhat al-Nusra) was attacked by ISIS, Arrahmah started to criticise ISIS, especially towards its leader, Abu Bakr Al-Bagdadi. Since then, Arrahmah began to oppose ISIS.

The next section will provide an in-depth analysis of the two main themes of discourse about ISIS: to support ISIS and to reject ISIS.

RESULTS

Supporting ISIS Means Supporting the Caliphate of Islam

Many Islamic radical groups gave support to ISIS mainly because they viewed ISIS as a group that had fought for Islam, and could actualise the dream of establishing an Islamic state. They adored ISIS heroic acts in attacking those who are considered as the enemies. Extracts of Arrahmah and Voa-Islam news articles, which are engaged in discussing ISIS ideology, are highlighted as follows:

Extract 1[9]: SA1 – Support of Arrahmah, September 16, 2013, 6:28 a.m.

Original - Bahasa Indonesia:

Alhamdulillah, mujahidin ISIS merebut markas Pasukan Pertahanan Udara dan gudang-gudang senjata Brigade 66 di Hamah Timur.

Sekali lagi rezim Nushairiyah Suriah merasakan pukulan paling menyakitkan dari mujahidin Islam. Dalam sebuah operasi jihad dengan skala besar di pinggiran Hamah Timur, mujahidin Daulah Islam Irak dan Syam (ISIS) berhasil merebut markas Pasukan Pertahanan Udara dan gudang-gudang senjata milik Brigade 66 pasukan Nushairiyah Suriah. Kemenangan spektakuler mujahidin Islam ini semakin menggoyahkan kedudukan rezim teroris Bashar Asad.

Translated:

Alhamdulillah, ISIS Mujahideen seized the headquarters of the Air Defence Forces and weapons warehouses of Brigade 66 in East Hamah.

Once again Nushairiyah Syrian regime felt the most painful blow from the Mujahideen of Islam. In a large-scale jihad operation on the outskirts of East Hamah, Mujahideen of the Islamic State of Iraq and Sham (ISIS) took control of the Air Defense Force headquarters and weapon warehouses belonging to Brigade 66 force of Nushairiyah Syrian. Spectacular victory is increasingly destabilising the Islamic Mujahideen terrorist regime of Bashar Asad position.

Based on the SA1 extract above, it illustrated Arrahmah's support for ISIS. Arrahmah used words such as 'succeed', 'spectacular winning', and 'terrorist regime'. The words 'succeed' and 'spectacular winning' reflected a positive emotion and faith towards ISIS in its endeavour to establish the caliphate or Islamic state. The use of the word 'terrorist' to label the Nushairiyah *Suriah* regime suggested that the actions of ISIS were seen as an attempt to defend Islam. Nushairiyah regime was perceived as a regime that is justified to be attacked. The text also highlighted conflict between two major ideologies or school in Islam, namely Sunni, represented by ISIS, and Suriah, represented by Nushairiyah regime.

Extract 2[10]: SA2 – Support of Arrahmah, October 8, 2013, 8:18 a.m.

Original - Bahasa Indonesia:

100 tentara Kurdistan Irak tewas dan cedera oleh serangan mujahidin ISIS di Erbil.

Dalam sebuah operasi serangan yang berkualitas dan berani, yang Allah memudahkan sarana-sarana taufik-Nya dan setelah melakukan usaha intelijen selama lebih dari satu bulan; para singa Daulah Islam Irak dan Syam dalam rangkaian serial operasi 'memetik tentara-tentara' berhasil mengguncangkan dan menghantam salah satu markas kejahatan yang selama ini menjadi alat kriminal guna menindas, menzalimi dan memerangi Islam dan kaum muslimin di kawasan Kurdistan Irak, yaitu Markas Komando Keamanan Kurdistan di kota Erbil.

Translated:

100 soldiers of Iraqi Kurdistan army were killed and wounded by ISIS Mujahideen attack in Erbil.

In a high quality operation and daring attacks, which Allah facilitate with His blessings and after intelligence operation for more than one month; the lions of the Islamic State of Iraq and Sham in series of operation successfully 'pluck' the soldiers, shaken and hit one of the headquarters of evil that have become a criminal tool to repress, oppress, and fight against Islam and the Muslims in the Kurdistan region of Iraq, that is the Kurdistan Security Command Headquarters in the city of Erbil.

The above extract clearly showed that ISIS is adored because of its bravery in opposing 'the tyrants'. The use of the words 'quality' and 'brave' reflected the support Arrahmah has for ISIS. Moreover, the Iraqi government is labelled as non-Muslim and evil since the Iraqi government often oppressed Sunni Muslims.

Besides accepting ISIS as a jihadist group that represents Muslims struggling to establish an Islamic state, ISIS was supported by Arrahmah since the group also wanted to free the Syrians from a tyrant.

Extract 3[11]: SA3 – Support of Arrahmah, November 5, 2013, 2:13 p.m.

Original - Bahasa Indonesia:

Sambut tahun baru 1435 H, Mujahidin ISIS rilis video 'Potret-potret Dari Bumi Jihad # 2'

Video eksklusif tersebut merekam suasana kebersamaan mujahidin ISIS di bumi jihad Suriah. Mujahidin dari beragam negara, bahasa, dan suku bangsa bahu-membahu dalam barisan ISIS untuk menolong saudara-saudara muslim Suriah yang tertindas. Hal yang menarik dari video ini adalah kemunculan sejumlah kakek-kakek berusia tua renta yang tak kalah semangatnya dari para pemuda. Para kakek itu tetap memanggul senjata, bermandikan peluh dan debu di medan hijrah, ribath dan jihad Suriah. Mereka rela mempersembahkan nyawa dan harta mereka demi menegakkan syariat Allah di bumi Suriah. Allahu akbar!

Translated:

Greet the new year 1435 H, ISIS Mujahideen release video 'portraits of Earth Jihad # 2'

The exclusive video showed togetherness of ISIS mujahideen in the land of jihad, Syria. Mujahideen from various countries, with various languages, and ethnicity shoulder to shoulder within the rank of ISIS to help the Syrian Muslim brothers who are oppressed.

The interesting thing about this video was the increasing number of elderly people who are as spirited as the youth. The elders bear arms, bathed in sweat and dust on the field of migration, ribath and jihad in Syria. They were willing to dedicate their lives and property for the sake of enforcing the law of God on the land of Syria. Allah is the Greatest!

For this extract, Arrahmah's form of support towards ISIS is seen through the use of positive words, such as 'togetherness', 'cooperate' (i.e., show cooperation to achieve future goals which is deemed to be good), 'helping brothers' (i.e., help by killing enemies who are also Muslims, but are not considered brothers since they belong to a different sect, namely the Suriah Muslims sect).

Extract 4[12]: SA4 – Support of Arrahmah, November 13, 2013, 4:00 p.m.

Original - Bahasa Indonesia:

Video terbaru ISIS, 'Potret-potret Dari Bumi Jihad # 2'

Hal menarik lainnya dari video ini adalah kemuliaan akhlak mujahidin ISIS. Mereka dikenal luas sebagai orang-orang yang menyayangi orang yang lebih muda dan menghormati orang yang lebih tua

Translated:

Latest Video ISIS, 'portraits of Earth Jihad # 2'

Another interesting thing about this video was the moral glory of ISIS mujahideen. They are widely known as the people who care for those who are younger and respect for the elderly.

Mass media as a funnel of information and ideology has a big impact on which discourse they want to present (van Dijk, 1998). The discourse is also portrayed equally with a negative nuance such as news coverage on an attack, war, and murder. Furthermore, the media also has the power to portray a discourse in a positive way, such as mutual help, affection, and mutual respect; as it is outlined in this SA4 extract. This is important as it may abet in making reader (who still have doubt about ISIS movement) to view ISIS in a more positive light; usually, positive nuances expressed in a text or story made it easier for the message to resonate with the readers.

Extract 5[13]: SA5 – Support of Arrahmah, December 27, 2013, 8:30 a.m.

Original - Bahasa Indonesia:

MasyaAllah, Mujahid ISIS mengajari anak-anak di jalanan tata cara wudhu dan shalat

Keseriusan Mujahidin ISIS dalam menggarap bidang dakwah di medan jihad Suriah tidak diragukan lagi. Mujahidin ISIS tidak hanya mendatangi masjid-masjid dan menggelar tabligh akbar. Di tempat-tempat umum seperti pasar dan jalan raya pun, Mujahidin ISIS turut memberikan pengajaran dan dakwah kepada masyarakat muslim Suriah. ... MasyaAllah, di tengah kesibukan berperang demi membela agama dan rakyat muslim Suriah, Mujahidin ISIS tak lupa menyempatkan diri dalam aktivitas dakwah lapangan.

Translated:

MasyaAllah, ISIS Mujaheed teach the children in the street ordinances ablution and prayer

The seriousness of ISIS Mujahideen in the field of da'wah for jihad in Syria cannot be doubted. ISIS Mujahideen not only came to mosques and held Tabligh Akbar (great movement). In public places such as markets and highways, ISIS Mujahideen also provides teaching and sermons for the Syrian Muslim community. ... MasyaAllah, in the midst of their fighting for the defence of the religion and the Muslim people of Syria, ISIS Mujahideen did not forget to perform missionary activity.

In the extract above, Arrahmah supported ISIS by creating a good image of ISIS by portraying ISIS attention to education, especially religious education for children. It seemed that by associating ISIS with religious education, Arrahmah believed that it can touch the readers' affection or emotion. Thus, Arrahmah can portray that ISIS activity is not just about war and violence, but also about care toward children's education. This type of information has the potential to influence the perception of Muslims by highlighting that ISIS may be good even though its ideology and worldview are opposed by the majority of the world.

Extract 6[14]: SA6 – Support of Arrahmah, February 6, 2014, 8:30 a.m.

Original - Bahasa Indonesia:

Mujahidin ISIS merilis video 'Pertempuran Terbesar Anbar'

Dalam pesan audionya Syaikh Abu Bakar Al-Baghdadi hafizhahullah mengucapkan terima kasih dan memuji penduduk dan suku-suku Anbar, yang telah menerima mujahidin dan mendukung mereka. Realita persatuan antara penduduk dan suku-suku Anbar dengan mujahidin ISIS merupakan bukti tak terbantahkan bahwa mujahidin adalah bagian dari masyarakat muslim Irak, bukan teroris seperti yang digambarkan oleh media massa Barat dan rezim Syiah.

Translated:

ISIS Mujahideen released a video 'The Greatest Anbar Battle'

In his audio message, Shaykh Abu Bakr al-Baghdadi hafizhahullah, thanked and praised the people and tribes of Anbar, who has received the mujahedeen and supported them. The unity between people and the tribes of Anbar with the ISIS mujaheedin was irrefutable evidence that they were part of Iraqi Muslim, not terrorist as portrayed by the Western media and the Shiite regime.

From the SA6 extract, Arrahmah was very firm in arguing that the terrorist label of ISIS was one that was given by the West and Shia regime in Iraq. The article directly quoted an audio message from ISIS leader, Abu Bakar Al-Bagdhdadi. The quote implied Arrahmah's support for ISIS. Arrahmah added the word 'hafizhahullah' which means 'may God guard him' after mentioning the name of the ISIS leader. This illustrated Arrahmah's respect for the caliphate which has been coveted by Muslims since the fall of the Ottoman Caliphate in 1924.

A positive impression was also portrayed in the second sentence which stated that ISIS is part of Islam in Iraq. This statement indicates that Arrahmah does not label ISIS as a terrorist group (Clarion Project, 2015; The Meir Amit Intelligence and Terrorism Information Center, 2014). The issue raised by Arrahmah is considered important as it may help ISIS gain more support in Indonesia, and tackle the negative labelling of ISIS as 'terrorist'.

In line with Arrahmah, Voa-Islam supported every ISIS activity. The support was shown through its intention of rejecting the terrorist label given by the Western mass media, and by supporting ISIS in its fight against the Western power, Iraq and Syria tyranny.

Extract 7[15]: SV1 – Support of Voa-Islam, September 16, 2014, 7:00 a.m.

Original - Bahasa Indonesia:

Dapatkah 40 Negara Barat dan Arab Mengalahkan ISIS?

Sekarang lahir kelompok baru ISIS yang lebih menakutkan terhadap Barat. ISIS lebih kuat dan canggih. ISIS mendapatkan dukungan senjata yang sangat luar biasa, dana, pasukan, dan menguasai wilayah yang sangat luas, Irak dan Suriah. Barat dan Arab menggigil melihat ISIS, dan sekarang sudah menjadi Daulah Islam Irak dan Suriah. Barat dan Arab akan menghadapi ancaman yang bersifat laten, yaitu ancaman ideologi, dan tak pernah bisa dihapus. Sekarang berbagai kelompok jihad di berbagai negara telah bergabung dengan Daulah Islam Irak dan Suriah. Sebuah perkembangan yang sangat dramatik.

Translated:

Can the 40 countries of Western and Arab Beat ISIS?

Now a new ISIS group that is more frightening to the West is born. ISIS is more powerful and sophisticated. ISIS have extraordinary support of weapons, funds, troops, and controlled a vast territory: Iraq and Syria. The West and Arab shiver (when they) see ISIS, and (they) now have become the Islamic State of Iraq and Syria. The West and Arab will face a latent threat, the threat of ideology, and can never be erased. Now various jihadist groups in various countries have joined the Islamic State of Iraq and Syria. A very dramatic development.

This SV1 extract depicted a sense of intimidation that ISIS would direct towards the West and Arab coalition who stand against it. This intimidation indicated the belief that ISIS can defeat the coalition. Some phrases, which reflected the sense of intimidation, are 'ISIS is stronger and sophisticated' and 'incredible weaponry and the West and Arab quivers seeing ISIS'. Such information has the potential to influence readers' perception towards ISIS in a positive light. Voa-Islam utilised its online media to report every bit of information about ISIS activities.

Extract 8[16]: SV2 – Support of Voa-Islam, March 24, 2015, 1:01 p.m.

Original - Bahasa Indonesia:

Berita Soal ISIS di Indonesia Lebay dan Mencurigakan!

Sebagai negara dengan umat Islam terbesar di dunia, mewabahnya berita soal Negara Islam Irak dan Syuriah (ISIS) belakangan ini justru menimbulkan kecurigaan dari dari berbagai kalangan. Apalagi, negara-negara tetangga juga tidak ada yang menghebohkan soal ini, kecuali mungkin Australia, meng-ingat keterlibatannya sebagai negara sekutu Amerika Serikat.

Translated:

News Problem ISIS in Indonesia is Exaggerating and Suspicious!

As the country with the largest Muslim community in the world, the spreading of news about Islamic State of Iraq and Syria (ISIS) recently raises suspicion from various circles. Especially when neighbouring countries also did not exaggerate about it, except perhaps Australia, given its involvement as allies of the United States.

In this extract, Voa-Islam emphasised that the issues raised by the Indonesian government about ISIS are exaggerated. This shows how Voa-Islam had defended ISIS; it blamed the Indonesian government. The use of the words 'lebay' (i.e., a slang word used widely in Jakarta to mean 'exaggerating') and 'suspicious' served as a form of justification that the Indonesian government should not follow other countries that are opposing ISIS, just for the sake of it. Voa-Islam accused Indonesia of following the West (especially the United States). Voa-Islam argued that the image of Islam in Indonesia is becoming negative since the government demonised ISIS. This suggests that Voa-Islam is worried that supports towards ISIS may be prohibited in Indonesia in the future.

Extract 9[17]: SV3 – Support of Voa-Islam, November 18, 2014, 4:24 p.m.

Original - Bahasa Indonesia:

Dibalik Kampanye Militer Amerika Melawan ISIS

Wahai kaum muslim, bukalah mata untuk melihat dan membongkar makar sebuah permusuhan. Bukalah telinga untuk mendengar kebenaran di dunia. Dan bukalah mulut kita untuk menyuarakan kebenaran itu dengan lantang tanpa gentar. Sungguh apa yang sedang Amerika dan sekutunya lakukan sekarang adalah untuk memicu perang persaudaraan. Kita lihat bagaimana pemimpin negeri-negeri islam diadu domba dan didesain untuk saling melawan satu sama lain. Butuh berapa nyawa kaum muslim lagi yang perlu dikorbankan agar kita sadar? Butuh berapa liter lagi darah kaum muslim yang mengucur agar kita peduli? Sungguh, Rasulullah tercinta berkata nyawa seorang kaum muslim lebih berharga bahkan dibandingkan dengan runtuhnya ka'bah. Oleh karena itu, kekuatan negara adidaya butuh dilawan dengan negara adidaya pula. Kekuatan sebuah persatuan musuh, butuh dilawan oleh sebuah persatuan pula. Negara adidaya dan persatuan itu tidak lain adalah negara Khilafah sesuai manhaj kenabian yang didirikan sesuai dengan metode Rasulullah. Hanya Khilafah lah yang akan mampu melawan kekuatan besar dunia dan kembali melindungi seluruh kaum muslim di manapun dia berada. Sungguh khilafah adalah janji Allah, dan Allah adalah sebaik-baik penepat janji.

Translated:

Behind the Campaign of US Military Against ISIS

O Muslims, open your eyes to see and dismantle the treason of a feud. Open your ears to hear the truth in the world. And open our mouth to speak the truth out loud without trepidation. What America and its allies are doing now is to trigger a civil war. We see how leaders of Islamic countries are being pitted against each another and engineered to fight one another. How many more Muslims lives need to be sacrificed so that we are aware? How many more litre of Muslim bloods that need to be shed so that we care? Indeed, the beloved Messenger (Prophet Muhammad, pbuh) said the life of a Muslim is more valuable than even the collapse of the Ka'bah. Therefore, the strength of a superpower country requires another superpower country to confront them. The strength of a united enemy, need to be challenged with a union as well. Superpower country and unity is none other than the Khilafah according prophetic manhaj which was established in accordance with the method of the Prophet. Only the Khilafah will be able to battle the great powers of the world and re-protect all Muslims wherever they are. Indeed Caliphate is the promise of Allah, and Allah is the Best at keeping a promise.

The above extract underscored the importance of ISIS ideology in depicting the enemies of ISIS as the enemies of Islam. This extract is filled with provocative phrases such as 'out loud without trepidation', 'against each other and one another', and 'how many more Muslims lives need to be sacrificed'. In the opinions of the authors, these phrases may increase the likelihood of the readers to develop sympathy towards ISIS.

Rejecting ISIS as Its Ideology Contradicts with Islamic Teaching

Our analysis also indicated that after supporting ISIS for several months via its online news media, Arrahmah changed its attitude and started criticising and rejecting ISIS movement. This rejection started from a critic to ISIS after it attacked the Jabhat al-Nusra group (affiliated with Al-Qaeda and supported by Arrahmah; Al-Majdi, 2014). This suggests that news media may also reject an ideology if it felt that the ideology is no longer important or due to other things that had happened (van Dijk, 1998).

After this attack, Arrahmah showed remorse and apologised for its support for ISIS. Arrahmah then started to oppose and reject every single action of ISIS. Arrahmah covered news highlighting that ISIS had gone against Islamic teaching. Some of these examples include the killing of infidels who had helped in humanitarian actions (which in Islamic teaching is considered haram to kill them), the burning of a Jordanian Muslim Pilot, and the killing of Syrian jihadists who are affiliated with Al-Qaeda.

Extract 10[18]: OA1 – Opponent of Arrahmah, October 4, 2014, 1:21 p.m.

Original - Bahasa Indonesia:

Alan Hening, petugas kemanusian itu telah tewas disembelih ISIS.

Yakinlah bahwa dengan insiden pelanggaran syari'at perlindungan dan keselamatan terhadap non-Muslim ini (amaan), maka akan ada perlawanan dari setiap jiwa Ummat Islam. Allah pasti tidak akan membiarkan Ummat Islam dicoreng citranya oleh segelintir manusia yang melakukan penistaan agama dengan menumpahkan darah yang tidak halal, bahkan di Hari 'Arafah, dimana manusia semestinya menyucikan dirinya, bersebab manusia berimanan berharap dosanya akan diampuni Allah subhanahu wata'ala. Subhanallah.

Translated:

Alan Hening, the humanitarian officer had been killed, slaughtered by ISIS.

Rest assured that the incident on the violation of protection and safety syari'at against non-Muslim (amaan), will then cause resistance from the soul of every Muslim. God will not let Muslims' image be tarnished by a handful of humans who commit blasphemy by spilling the blood that is not halal, even at 'Arafah Day, where man should actually purify themselves, devoted believers hope they will be forgiven by Allah Subhanahu wata'ala. Subhanallah.

The OA1 extract showed Arrahmah's attitude in opposing ISIS. It informed that ISIS actions are outside of Islamic teaching. The use of negative words and phrases such as 'the incident of syari'at protection', 'resistance from the soul of every Muslim', and 'blasphemy' reflected the sense of disappointment that Arrahmah wanted to share with its readers. These phrases are thick with psychological nuance (Edward, 2005), which is expected to make an impression to the readers. The phrase 'spilling the blood that is not halal' underscored Arrahmah's disappointment towards the actions of ISIS. According to Arrahmah, ISIS slaughtered a non-Muslim humanitarian worker whom Arrahmah considered as a peaceful non-Muslim. Thus, even though Arrahmah is considered supports Al-Qaeda's ideology, it is still of the view that killing a good non-Muslim is forbidden. Such attitudes represent a clear stance by Arrahmah in stating that it is different from ISIS.

Extract 11[19]: OA2 – Opponent of Arrahmah, February 7, 2015, 6:03 p.m.

Original - Bahasa Indonesia:

Analisa: ISIS 'Sedang Mengencingi Mata Air Zam Zam

Kontroversi atas eksekusi membakar hidup-hidup pilot Jordania bukanlah sekedar persoalan boleh atau tidaknya eksekusi ini dalam tinjauan syari'at. Tidak diragukan lagi bahwa keturutsertaan dalam memerangi kaum muslimin adalah kejahatan keji dan munkar, yang hukumnya dalam syari'at adalah murtad. Akan tetapi yang menjadi perhatian kita pada jama'ah ini adalah kebijakan-kebijakan mereka yang penuh kontroversi. Para Ulama dan peneliti Islam telah membahas panjang lebar tentang sepak terjang Jama'ah ini dalam upaya mereka merusak jihad, merusak citra Mujahidin di mata umum dan kaum muslimin, dan khususnya dimata selain kaum muslimin yang tidak melihat Islam kecuali melalui gambaran keji dan adegan beringas yang jama'ah ini suguhkan.

Translated:

Analysis: ISIS 'peed on Zam Zam Spring

The controversy over the execution by burning alive a Jordanian pilot is not just a question of whether or not the execution is allowed in the view of shari'ah. No doubt that the participation in fighting against other Muslims is an evil and heinous crime, which in the Shari'ah is considered as apostates. But what concerns us in this congregation is their controversial policy. Islamic scholars and researchers have discussed regarding the actions of this Jama'ah in their efforts to undermine jihad, damaging the Mujahideen image in the eyes of the public and other Muslims, and especially in the eyes of others aside from Muslim who do not see Islam except through the cruel imagery and violent scenes presented by this jama'ah.

ISIS was negatively depicted in this extract. Starting from the extract's title 'ISIS Urinating on the Zamzam Spring', which is a stern reprimand to ISIS for damaging the purity of Islamic teaching. For Muslims, Zamzam Spring is perceived to be holy water which can only be found in Saudi Arabia, the holy land of Muslims. Moreover, Arrahmah used words such as 'controversy' and 'execution' in discussing the burning of the Jordanian pilot. Those statements contained a critique and censure regarding the execution. Arrahmah questioned the justification of the action since the person that had been burned by ISIS was also a Muslim.

Furthermore in Islam, there is a value to prioritise brotherhood among Muslims (*Ukhuwah Islamiyah*). This extract used the word vile and evil (*munkar*) to illustrate ISIS actions. These two words reflected an understanding that ISIS ideology was deemed as inhumane, as Arrahmah even used the word *murtad* (apostate), which is considered to be a rude and negative word in Muslims culture. This meant that Arrahmah has equated ISIS with other enemies of Islam (e.g., the West). Other negative phrases such as 'cruel imagery' and 'violent scenes' were also expressed by Arrahmah. Both phrases are a repetition of Arrahmah's resentment towards the killing of the Jordanian pilot, and reaffirming that ISIS is not worth following.

It is interesting to note the differences in the words used by Arrahmah as it changed its discourse about ISIS. While it was supporting ISIS (see extract SA1), Arrahmah dubbed ISIS as Mujahiddin, which sounds very positive. However, as seen in this extract, Arrahmah expressed its opposition towards ISIS and dubbed it as a *Jamaah* (congregation).

Extract 12[20]: OA3 – Opponent of Arrahmah, October 17, 2014, 2:52 p.m.

Original - Bahasa Indonesia:

Mengapa ISIS menyerang Kobane?

Hampir setengah tahun sebelum ISIS dikenali dunia, Mujahidin dan tentara pembebasan Suriah telah mengetahui bahwa rezim Assad melindungi, menyokong dan membantu ISIS. Sungguh keberadaan ISIS adalah musuh Islam sebenar-benarnya bagi Suriah dan Ummat Islam sedunia. Maka dari tulisan di atas, hanya dunia luar yang luput dari pengetahuan bahwa ISIS sengaja disempalkan ke dalam cabang Al-Qaeda oleh musuh Islam. Pun dengan ini, kita ketahui bagaimana perasaan Muslimin dan Mujahidin Suriah, serta Al-Qaeda yang dikhianati ISIS dengan sedemikian liciknya. Sedikit demi sedikit kedok para agen dajjal terbuka satu persatu. Wallahua'lam bishowab

Translated:

Why ISIS attack Kobane?

Almost half a year before ISIS was recognised by the world, the Mujahideen and the Syrian liberation army has learned that the Assad regime protected, supported and assisted ISIS. Indeed the existence of ISIS is truly an enemy of Islam, Syria, and Muslims worldwide. Based on the above writing, only the outside world missed the knowledge that ISIS is deliberately thrust into a branch of Al-Qaeda by the enemies of Islam. Even with this, we know the feeling Muslims and Mujahideen of Syria, as well as Al-Qaeda which were betrayed by ISIS with such cunning. Little by little the guise of dajjal's (lucifer) agents was open one by one. Wallahua'lam bishowab.

This extract explained that there are two enemies of Islam: ISIS and Assad's regime. Therefore, Arrahmah is clearly demarcating ISIS as an enemy. Furthermore, the *dajjal* (Lucifer) analogy stated by Arrahmah reflected something with two faces; in which ISIS previously seemed very kind and helpful to the Syrian jihadists, but now it is attacking other jihadists.

DISCUSSION AND CONCLUSION

The findings of this chapter have provided evidence showing how and why Islamic radical groups support and oppose ISIS. Since the beginning, Voa-Islam has consistently broadcasted news in favour of ISIS. Voa-Islam considers ISIS as Islamic fighters because it believes that ISIS goes to war in order to establish an Islamic State. On the other hand, Arrahmah's portrayal of ISIS was very positive in the beginning but later turned to criticise and reject the ISIS movement. Arrahmah considers ISIS as a group that is doing more harm than good. For Arrahmah, it deemed that ISIS does not have clear guidelines to build an Islamic State.

These radical groups also tend to be paradoxical (Keller & Pfattheicher, 2013) in the way they view ISIS; negative actions are paired with positive perceptions. For example, if ISIS is perceived to be helping Muslims or as Muslim warriors, ISIS would be loved by its supporters even when it brutally killed people labelled as enemies of Islam. For supporters of ISIS, it is viewed as a group that embodies the Islamic State. Massacres done to enemies of Islam are considered reasonable and morally justified.

Voa-Islam and Arrahmah (when they were supporting ISIS) regarded ISIS as Islamic fighters because of its struggle to establish an Islamic State. Arrahmah (when they started rejecting ISIS) viewed ISIS as a blind Islamic movement that is doing more harm than good. van Dijk (1988) explained that a group's ideology or attitude can change due to changes in social situations, and social relations between groups. With regard to Arrahmah's rejection of ISIS, Arrahmah believed that ISIS is going down the wrong path. Furthermore, Arrahmah believed in a conspiracy theory that ISIS was built by the Assad regime (see extract 12) to ruin Islam. Usually groups that are considered as conspirators are also regarded as enemies. For example, a research conducted by Putra, Mashuri, and Zaduqisti (2015) found that when Ahmadiyya, a minority of Islamic groups, is believed to be conspirator trying to undermine Islam, Ahmadiyya members are still blamed even though they are on the receiving end of violent attacks. The violent attacks are considered to be the result of the conspiracy that was devised by Ahmadiyya.

When ISIS is seen as Islamic militants, ISIS activities are viewed positively, even though a lot of news has highlighted how ISIS had killed or beheaded innocent people. In fact, such information is not considered negative and deemed as something which is common in war. The enemies must be confronted and friends or relatives should be defended. Enemies are those who are considered to be non-Muslim or non-Muslims' henchmen (i.e., those who are understood to have oppressed Muslims). When Arrahmah was still supporting ISIS, Arrahmah saw ISIS as a hope which could realise Arrahmah's dream of establishing an Islamic State. However, this sense of hope disappeared when Arrahmah saw that innocent Muslims and peaceful non-Muslim groups were killed by ISIS; for Arrahmah, a group that is at peace with Islam should be protected and should never be killed. Thus, Arrahmah considered ISIS to be 'out of Islamic corridors'.

Practical Implications

On the basis of the above findings, some practical implications have been identified. First, we must realise that it is almost impossible to eradicate and combat radical ideology. The most likely thing that can be done is to stem the radical ideology before it becomes radical action. Learning from the attitude changes towards ISIS by Arrahmah, we see that a radical ideology can be prevented by providing information that Islam has boundaries in humanity. For example, when Arrahmah sees Muslims or non-Muslims who are at peace with Islam, being killed by ISIS, it assesses that ISIS has strayed out of Islamic values.

Second, by utilising conflict of interpretations within the radical groups and exposing those who oppose ISIS more than those that support ISIS, other radical groups may be force to rethink their stance on the issue of ISIS.

Third, deploy moderate clerics who are more aggressive in preaching Islamic ideas of peace and tolerance on Islamic online sites (i.e., counter-narratives). Because Islamic online news is dominated by fundamentalists and radicals, the presence of counter-narratives becomes an important measure to offset the influence of ISIS and other radical groups.

Fourth, limiting freedom of speech and deleting radical Internet content is not only disliked by majority of people, but also far from effective (Neumann, 2013; Yasin, 2011). Hence, the most prudent way is by encouraging the government to challenge the younger generation to be vigilant of the danger of extremism (Neumann, 2013). In addition, radical sites can become a 'goldmine' that contains information about all radical activities and developments. So sites that are considered dangerous can directly become tracking targets by the authority (whether it is the Anti-terror Special Detachment or the National Counterterrorism Agency).

Finally, we see that several implications of the research findings can become considerations for the policymaker. This is especially so now given that the use of Internet is more intensive and has become an important medium in radicalisation. In addition, these findings can become a starting point for subsequent research, especially in investigating whether the suggested implications of this chapter have led to a reduction of radical concepts or actions.

Mass media plays a role in the (re)production of power and ideology. Through information and news forums as well as the Internet, mass media can easily represent an ideology and a group's idea. As a result, the media have the power to raise the discourse they wanted. It certainly will benefit a group if it has its own media capability. That means, the more the media is in power, the less freedom is attached to the audience and vice versa (van Dijk, 1995). In doing so, the more the moderate Islamic media is in power, the better they can educate Muslims to be tolerant.

REFERENCES

Adam, F., Anuar, M., & Ali, A. H. (2014). The use of blog as a medium of Islamic da'wah in Malaysia, The use of blog as a medium of Islamic da'wah in Malaysia. *International Journal of Sustainable Human Development*, 2(2), 74–80.

Al-Majdi, M. (2014, February 8). Inna lillah, saat Jabhah Nushrah membebaskan ribuan tawanan dari penjara pusat Aleppo, ISIS menyerbu dan mengepung Jabhah Nushrah di Hasakah. *Arrahmah*. Retrieved from http://www.arrahmah.com/news/2014/02/08/inna-lillah-saat-jabhah-nushrah-membebaskan-ribuan-tawanan-dari-penjara-pusat-aleppo-isis-menyerbu-dan-mengepung-jabhah-nushrah-di-hasakah.html#sthash.RxIqckP5.dpuf

Aly, A. (2010). The Internet as ideological battleground. In *Proceedings of the 1st Australian Counter Terrorism Conference*. Perth, Australia: Edith Cowan University.

Brachman, J. (2009). A survey of Southeast Asian global jihadist websites. In S. Helfstein (Ed.), *Radical Islamic ideology in Southeast Asia* (pp. 95–114). West Point: Combating Terrorism Center.

Brinton, L. J. (2001). Historical discourse analysis. In D. Schiffrin, D. Tannen, & H. Hamilton (Eds.), *The handbook of discourse analysis* (pp. 138–160). Massachusetts, MA: Blackwell Publishers.

Cotter, C. (2001). Discourse and media. In D. Schiffrin, D. Tannen, & H. Hamilton (Eds.), *The handbook of discourse analysis* (pp. 416–436). Massachusetts, MA: Blackwell Publishers.

Edwards, D. (2005). Discursive psychology. In K. L. Fitch & R. E. Sanders (Eds.), *Handbook of language and social interaction* (pp. 257–273). Hillsdale, NJ: Erlbaum.

Edwards, D., & Potter, J. (2005). Discursive psychology, mental states and descriptions. In L. Molder & J. Potter (Eds.), *Conversation and cognition* (pp. 241–259). Cambridge: Cambridge University Press. doi:10.1017/CBO9780511489990.012

Fairclough, N. (1992). *Discourse and social change*. Cambridge: Polity Press.

Feillard, G. N. (2014). Responses to the challenge of ISIS in Indonesia. In T. C. Tion (Ed.), *ISEAS Perspective* (pp. 11–18). Singapore: Institute of Southeast Asian Studies.

Ferencik, M., & Horvath, J. (2009). Critical discourse analysis of Obama's. In *Political Discourse, Language, Literature and Culture in a Changing Transatlantic World, International Conference Proceedings*. Presov: University of Presov.

Friedland, J., & Rogerson, K. (2009). *How political and social movements form on the Internet and how they change over time*. Washington, DC: Institute for Homeland Security Solutions.

Gerges, F. A. (2014). ISIS and the third wave of jihadism. *Current History (New York, N.Y.)*, *113*(767), 339–343.

Homeland Security Institute. (2009). *The Internet as a terrorist tool for recruitment and radicalization of youth (HSI Publication Number: RP08-03.02.17-01)*. Arlington, VA: Homeland Security Institute.

Inilah Situs Online Radikal dan Pendukung ISIS. (2014, August 5). *Satu Islam*. Retrieved from http://www.satuislam.org/nasional/inilah-situs-online-radikal-dan-pendukung-isis/

Jenkins, B. M. (2011). *Stray dogs and virtual armies: Radicalization and recruitment to jihadist terrorism in the United States since 9/11*. Santa Monica, CA: RAND Corporation.

Keller, J., & Pfattheicher, S. (2013). The compassion-hostility paradox: The interplay of vigilant, prevention-focussed self-regulation, compassion, and hostility. *Personality and Social Psychology Bulletin*, *39*(11), 1518–1529. doi:10.1177/0146167213499024

MacMillan, K., & Edwards, D. (1999). Who killed the princess? Description and blame in the British press. *Discourse Studies*, *1*(2), 151–174. doi:10.1177/1461445699001002002

Moussa, M. B. (2011). The use of the internet by Islamic social movements in collective action: The case of justice and charity. *Westminster Papers in Communication and Culture*, *8*(2), 154–177.

National Coordinator for Counterterrorism. (2010, May). *Jihadists and the Internet 2009 update*. Retrieved from http://fas.org/irp/world/netherlands/jihadists.pdf

Neumann, P. R. (2013). Options and strategies for countering online radicalization in the United States. *Studies in Conflict and Terrorism*, *36*(6), 431–459. doi:10.1080/1057610X.2013.784568

Ngazis, A. N., & Haryanto, A. T. (2015, April 9). Pemerintah buka 12 Situs Islam yang. *Berita VIVA*. Retrieved from http://news.viva.co.id/news/read/611803-pemerintah-buka-12-situs-islam-yang-diblokir

Ningrum, B. W. (2013, March 30). Kominfo blokir 22 situs yang dianggap radikal. *Liputan6.com*. Retrieved from http://tekno.liputan6.com/read/2199730/kominfo-blokir-22-situs-yang-dianggap-radikal

O'Rourke, S. (2007). Virtual radicalisation: Challenges for police. In *Proceedings of the 8th Australian Information Warfare and Security Conference*. Perth: Edith Cowan University.

Okon, E. (2012). The sources and schools of Islamic jurisprudence. *American Journal of Social and Management Sciences*, *3*(3), 106–111. doi:10.5251/ajsms.2012.3.3.106.111

PBNU. Ulama besar dunia tolak ISIS. (2014, August 8). *Tribunnews.com*. Retrieved from http://www.tribunnews.com/nasional/2014/08/08/pbnu-ulama-besar-dunia-tolak-isis

Pew Forum on Religion & Public Life. (2009). *Mapping the global Muslim population*. Washington, DC: Pew Research Center.

Potter, J., & Edwards, D. (2001). Discursive social psychology. In W. P. Robinson & H. Giles (Eds.), *The new handbook of language and social psychology* (pp. 103–118). London: John Wiley & Sons Ltd.

Putra, I. E., Mashuri, A., & Zaduqisti, E. (2015). Demonising the victm: Seekig the answer for how a group as the violent victim is blamed. *Psychology and Developing Societies*, *27*(1), 31–57. doi:10.1177/0971333614564741

Putra, I. E., & Sukabdi, Z. A. (2013). Basic concepts and reasons behind the emergence of religious terror activities in Indonesia: An inside view. *Asian Journal of Social Psychology*, *16*(2), 83–91. doi:10.1111/ajsp.12001

Saj, H. E. (2012). Discourse analysis: Personal pronouns in Oprah Winfrey hosting Queen Rania of Jordan. *International Journal of Social Science and Humanity*, 2(6), 529–532.

Solahudin. (2013). www.teror.co.id. Depok: Center for Terrorism and Social Conflict Studies Fakultas Psikologi Universitas Indonesia.

The Clarion Project. (2015). Special report: The Islamic State. Clarion Project, Inc.

The Meir Amit Intelligence and Terrorism Information Center. (2014). *ISIS: Portrait of a jihadi terrorist organization*. Retrieved from http://www.terrorism-info.org.il/Data/articles/Art_20733/101_14_Ef_1329270214.pdf

Tucker, D. (2010). *Jihad dramatically transformed? Sageman on Jihad and the Internet*. Washington, DC: Homeland Security Affairs.

van Dijk. T. A. (1998). Ideology: A multidisciplinary approach. London: Sage Publications.

van Dijk, T. A. (1988). *News as discourse*. Lawrence Erlbaum Associates, Inc.

van Dijk, T. A. (1995). The mass media today: Discourse of domination or diversity. *Communication Beyond the Nation-State*, 2(2), 27–45.

Yasin, N. A. M. (2011). *Online Indonesian Islamist extremism: A gold mine of information. RSIS Commentaries (114/2011)*. Singapore: S. Rajaratnam School of International Studies.

Yasin, N. A. M. (2014). Understanding the contents in bahasa Indonesia extremist websites. *Counter Terrorist Trends and Analysis*, 6(3), 18–24.

ENDNOTES

[1]. Refer to link: www.arrahmah.com
[2]. Refer to link: www.muslimdaily.net
[3]. Refer to link: www.al-mustaqbal.net
[4]. Refer to link: www.millahibrahim.wordpress.com
[5]. Refer to link: www.albusyro.org
[6]. Refer to link: www.at-tawbah.net
[7]. Refer to link: www.anshoruttauhidwassunnahwaljihad.blogspot.com
[8]. Refer to link: www.voa-islam.com
[9]. Refer to link: http://www.arrahmah.com/jihad/mujahidin-isis-merebut-markas-pasukan-pertahanan-udara-gudang-gudang-senjata-brigade-66-hamah-timur.html
[10]. Refer to link: http://www.arrahmah.com/news/2013/10/08/100-tentara-kurdistan-irak-tewas-cedera-serangan-mujahidin-isis-erbil.html
[11]. Refer to link: http://www.arrahmah.com/news/2013/11/05/sambut-1435-mujahidin-isis-rilis-video-potret-potret-bumi-jihad-2.html
[12]. Refer to link: http://www.arrahmah.com/video/video-terbaru-isis-potret-potret-bumi-jihad-2.html
[13]. Refer to link: http://www.arrahmah.com/news/2013/12/27/masyaallah-mujahid-isis-mengajari-anak-anak-di-jalanan-tata-cara-wudhu-dan-shalat.html

14. Refer to link: http://www.arrahmah.com/jihad/mujahidin-isis-merilis-video-pertempuran-terbesar-anbar.html

15. Refer to link: http://www.voa-islam.com/read/opini/2014/09/16/32876/dapatkah-40-negara-barat-dan-arab-mengalahkan-isis/#sthash.7OLqN0bN.dpbs

16. Refer to link: http://www.voa-islam.com/read/indonesiana/2015/03/24/36057/berita-soal-isis-di-indonesia-lebay-dan-mencurigakan/#sthash.mOGrsWz0.dpbs

17. Refer to link: http://www.voa-islam.com/read/world-analysis/2014/11/18/33954/dibalik-kampanye-militer-amerika-melawan-isis/#sthash.zyjobEsU.dpbs

18. Refer to link: http://www.arrahmah.com/news/2014/10/04/alan-hening-petugas-kemanusian-itu-telah-tewas-disembelih-isis.html

19. Refer to link: http://www.arrahmah.com/news/2015/02/07/analisa-isis-sedang-mengencingi-mata-air-zam-zam-b1.html

20. Refer to link: http://www.arrahmah.com/news/2014/10/17/mengapa-isis-menyerang-kobane.html

Chapter 5
Using the Internet to Plan for Terrorist Attack

David Romyn
Griffith University, Australia

Mark Kebbell
Griffith University, Australia

ABSTRACT

In this chapter, we discuss how terrorists can use the Internet as a source of information to plan for terrorist attacks. Online anonymity services such as virtual private network (VPN) are discussed, along with advantages and disadvantages of using these services. We also discuss online bomb-making instructions and highlight ways in which these can be used to the advantage of law enforcement. Finally, the use of the Internet as a reconnaissance tool for target selection is discussed, with descriptions of current and past research in this field to identify key information that is available to terrorists, and how this information can be manipulated to reduce the likelihood or severity of a terrorist attack.

INTRODUCTION

The Internet has been used in a variety of ways by terrorists, including the provision of information to others, financing terrorist organisations, communication between terrorists, the recruitment of new potential terrorists, and as an information gathering tool (Conway, 2006; Keene, 2011; United Nations Office on Drugs and Crime [UNODC], 2012). It has also been argued by some that the Internet provides a mechanism by which individuals, who would otherwise not have conducted a terrorist attack, can self-radicalise and access the information they require to carry out an attack (Benson, 2014).

In this chapter, we will discuss aspects of how the Internet can be used by terrorists to prepare for terrorist attacks. We will also discuss how the Internet can be used by law enforcement to increase the chance of detecting terrorism before it happens, or to reduce the effectiveness of attacks when they occur. Specifically, we will discuss the use of online anonymity services such as virtual private network (VPN) and the onion router (TOR). We will also discuss the use of the Internet for instructions on how to make explosive devices. Prior research based on a 'red-team' design to investigate terrorist target

DOI: 10.4018/978-1-5225-0156-5.ch005

selection and the use of the Internet as a reconnaissance tool will also be described. Finally, ways that these factors can be manipulated to reduce the likelihood and effectiveness of terrorist attacks will be explored. We conclude that while the Internet is a valuable source of information for those planning a terrorist attack, the accuracy and availability of this information can be manipulated to reduce the likelihood and effectiveness of an attack.

TRACING TERRORIST ACTIVITY ONLINE

While some authors (e.g., Conway, 2006; Keene, 2011; Thomas, 2003) discuss ways in which the Internet can facilitate aspects of planning and conducting a terrorist attack, other authors (e.g., Benson, 2014; Kenney, 2010; Torres-Soriano, 2012) argue that the Internet poses a risk to terrorists that use it, and a method by which law enforcement can identify and track terrorists. Both of these conclusions are partly correct.

Benson (2014) notes that while the Internet can give the perception of anonymity to those who use it, it is still possible for law enforcement to trace where information has come from and where it has gone. While this is true of the ability to monitor and trace general Internet traffic, this assertion may not be true in all cases if someone takes steps to remain anonymous online and hide their identity. An investigation of the use of online anonymity practices amongst those involved with online piracy, found a portion (17.8%) of those involved with the practice, used services such a VPN to hide their identity online (Larsson, Svensson, de Kaminski, Rönkkö, & Olsson, 2012). Antoniades, Markatos, and Dovrolis (2010) note that there are over 100,000 Internet users who are using TOR on a daily basis to hide their identity. Those involved with terrorism, who are also motivated to hide their identity online, could use these same methods to make tracking them more difficult.

The use of a VPN is a reasonably robust method to ensure online anonymity. All traffic sent between a user and a VPN is encrypted, so that the content of this traffic is hidden from the Internet service provider (ISP) or any other agency that may be collecting metadata (Larsson et al., 2012). The use of a VPN also makes it difficult to identify which individuals have accessed particular information online, as the identifying information will be referred to the VPN itself, rather than the person who was using that VPN. It has also been found that as the efforts of authorities to track particular individuals increase, so does the use of VPN to hide people's identity.

Larsson and Svensson (2010) investigated the use of online anonymity services, such as VPN, to hide the identity of those involved in file sharing in Sweden. Specifically, the authors surveyed a very large sample ($N=1047$) of computer users two months prior to the implementation of a policy aimed at stopping online piracy. They then surveyed a sample ($N=1042$) of computer users seven months following the implementation of the policy. The survey also gauged how frequently participants were engaged in online file sharing. Overall, the study found that among those who were not heavily involved in file sharing, there was no significant increase in use of VPN following the implementation of the new policy. However, there was a significant increase in the use of VPN among those in the sample that had been identified as being frequently involved in file sharing following the implementation of the policy (Larsson & Svensson, 2010). This study demonstrates that the use of anonymity services such as VPNs increases among those motivated to hide their identity, as measures to track those people online are increased. However, the use of a VPN is still not a perfect solution for anonymity.

The provider of the VPN service still has full access to all of the information regarding their users' actions on the service; so users are placing a great deal of trust in the service that they use (Larsson et al., 2012). It is also possible for law enforcement agencies to subpoena the information held by VPN services that fall within their jurisdiction (Benson, 2014). It is also possible for an ISP to block its customers from accessing a particular service such as a VPN (Edman & Yener, 2009; Rescorla, 2008). Because of this, it may be possible in some jurisdictions for governments to require a locally-based ISP to block customers' access to a VPN, if it is found that the service is being used to facilitate terrorism-related activities (Edman & Yener, 2009). Another possible solution, where user access to the VPN itself cannot be controlled, is for governments to block the actual VPN service from being able to access key services. In that instance, while users would still be able to access the VPN, any traffic identified as being from that VPN would be blocked from accessing those services. A further way of reducing the use of VPN to hide a terrorist's identity online, is to give the impression to the wider community that it is a less-secure method than it actually is.

There has been much discussion in recent years regarding the ability of the U.S. National Security Agency (NSA) to use a 'back door' to break through encryption services (Schneier, 2007; Soghoian, 2010). Without discussing which encrypted traffic the NSA is or is not able to access, the belief that governments are able to view encrypted information may lead some away from using services such as VPN when using the Internet (Torres-Soriano, 2012). For this reason, it would be useful to give the impression to those engaged in terrorist activities that VPN are not a reliable method of ensuring anonymity. Doing this may encourage some terrorists to avoid the use of the Internet altogether. While this would mean that they are also unable to be monitored using the Internet, as we shall see later, it also means that they would be removing themselves from a useful medium to facilitate terrorist attacks.

Another commonly used method of maintaining online anonymity is TOR. TOR is a method of online browsing that randomly routes a user's traffic through multiple points, or 'nodes', before it reaches its online destination (Antoniades et al., 2010; Dingledine, Mathewson, & Syverson, 2004). This routing makes it impossible for an outside observer to identify the origin of the traffic. Unlike VPN services, TOR does not function well for moving large volumes of data, and is more suited to Internet web-browsing than for piracy (Antoniades et al., 2010; "The Tor Project", n.d.). However, an advantage with TOR is that it is freely available to anyone and does not require a high level of skill to use. Most people are able to access TOR simply by installing a particular type of browser on their computers ("The Tor Project", n.d.). TOR also has some advantages over VPNs to a would-be terrorist, in that it does not require all of a user's traffic to pass through a single service provider that could pass that information on to the authorities. However, there are also some weaknesses with TOR that have been exploited by government agencies.

Murdoch and Danezis (2005) note that while it is impossible to observe traffic and identify a particular source, it is possible to identify which traffic has come from the same source and attempt to use the content of that traffic to identify the source itself. This form of traffic monitoring allows for an observer to build a profile of a particular user, and to sift through the content of their traffic for identifying information. While using TOR itself does not require much technical skill, maintaining an online presence without providing identifying information can be difficult (Murdoch & Danezis, 2005; "The Tor Project", n.d.). Another weakness that has been identified is the use of malicious exit nodes (Chakravarty, Portokalidis, Polychronakis, & Keromytis, 2011). When traffic passes through TOR, it must exit TOR through what is known as an exit node, which is a random router that can be set up by anyone who wishes to be a part of TOR. Antoniades et al. (2010) estimate that in 2009, there were over 600 of these exit nodes located in 48 different countries. It is possible for whoever is controlling the exit node to insert malicious code into the traffic and identify the origin (Chakravarty et al., 2011). This fact has been exploited by government agencies to identify individuals using TOR.

Although the identity of the original user is hidden in TOR, an observer knows the identity of the exit node that the traffic is coming from. While the selection of exit nodes is essentially random within TOR, Jansen, Tschorsch, Johnson, and Scheuermann (2014) describe a method, known as a sniper attack, which can be used to exploit exit nodes and identify an individual using TOR. A sniper attack involves a government agency identifying, overloading and shutting down specific exit nodes being used by an individual. This action then forces the individual's traffic to route through a different exit node. By overloading the exit node that that an individual is using, the user's traffic can eventually be routed through an exit node that is being monitored by the government agency (Jansen et al., 2014). At this point, the original user can be identified.

In summary, it should not be assumed that the Internet provides a completely safe environment for terrorists to organise terrorist attacks, or that the Internet provides a sound method by which law enforcement can trace the online presence of those involved in terrorist activities. While it is possible to trace an individual's activity online, it is also possible for an individual to use services like VPN or TOR to hide their identity from those who are monitoring their activity online.

However, depending on jurisdiction, there are still measures that can be used to trace the identity of people using a VPN. It is also possible to either block access to the VPN service itself, or to block the VPN service from being able to access particular information. Likewise, TOR does provide a level of anonymity to a user, but it is possible to still profile a user or exploit weaknesses in TOR to identify an individual. Finally, if those who are utilising VPN or TOR to hide their identity, are given the impression that this is not a reliable method of ensuring anonymity, they may avoid using these sorts of services, or from using the Internet altogether.

USING THE INTERNET TO PREPARE FOR TERRORIST ATTACKS

Regarding the planning of attacks, the Internet has been described as being an invaluable tool for the gathering of information such as how to create weapons for an attack, and to identify and conduct reconnaissance on likely targets for an attack (Barnes, 2012; Brunst, 2010). Romyn and Kebbell (2013) conducted a 'red-team' experiment to investigate the order and importance of particular tasks when planning a terrorist attack. A red-team is where participants play the role of an enemy – in this case a terrorist. In the experiment, soldiers and civilians were given the roles of trained and untrained terrorists respectively, and participants were asked to list the order and importance of specific tasks related to planning a terrorist attack. These tasks included: identifying a target, searching for information online, conducting reconnaissance on the target, acquiring weapons, and testing weapons.

The results of this experiment showed that regardless of whether participants were military trained or civilians, they tended to identify targets before working towards acquiring weapons (Romyn & Kebbell, 2013). The results also indicated that the acquisition of weapons and the identification of a target were considered significantly more important than other tasks, such as acquiring other equipment or finding a location to prepare for an attack. Because of the importance of acquiring weapons and identifying targets, we will discuss each in turn.

Using the Internet to Construct Weapons

The most common method of terrorist attack in Europe and Australia is using an explosive device (Mullins, 2011; Nesser, 2008). In the United States, the most common method of terrorist attack is using a firearm, with explosives the second most frequent method (Spaaij, 2010). Spaaij (2010) suggests the difference for the method of attacks within the U.S. compared to other countries is due to the lack of firearm restrictions in the United States. Barnes (2012) notes the ease with which one can use the Internet to access technical information, such as how to build an explosive device. Some of this technical information provides instruction not only on how to build the device, but also how to acquire the necessary parts.

Explosives can generally be categorised into one of two broad categories: high explosives, such as dynamite and Trinitrotoluene (TNT), which undergo an explosive reaction when initiated; and low explosives, such as black powder or compressed gas, which burn rapidly instead of exploding. High explosives have a detonation force and burn rate that is many times greater than that of low explosives[1], and comparably sized devices based on high explosives create a far larger impact than those based on low explosives. Fertiliser based explosives, such as ammonium nitrate fuel oil (ANFO), are generally considered to be high explosives, and have been used in a number of attacks and attempts in the past.

While ANFO is categorised as a high explosive, it has a burn rate about half of that of other high explosives – though it is still far greater than low explosives. However, high explosives are far more difficult to create and initiate than low explosives (Benson, 2014). While ANFO is one of the simplest high explosives to make, as it requires access to specific forms of fertiliser and fuel to create, it is also one of the most difficult to actually detonate. Given ANFO has a slower burn rate than other high explosives, far more of it is required to construct an effective explosive device. For this reason, ANFO-based explosive devices are usually too large to be easily carried, and require a vehicle to be moved around, limiting their use.

Devices based on low explosives are far easier to construct and initiate, but are far less effective than comparably sized devices based on high explosives. These devices can be constructed by placing any readily available incendiary material, such as black powder, into a compressed space. When initiated, the material undergoes a very rapid burn and expansion, which causes the explosive effect. While an advantage of low explosive devices is that they are easier to initiate than high explosive devices, in turn this means that they are also easier to initiate prematurely, and if not constructed carefully, can be more dangerous to the person using it than to any would-be targets. Therefore, construction of explosive devices (i.e., based on either high or low explosives) require access to sound technical information and a degree of skill on the part of the person constructing the device.

Kenney (2010) suggests that much of the information available online would pose more of a risk to a would-be terrorist than to the general public. Many of the instructions for explosive devices that are available online would result in devices with a high likelihood of premature detonation, or a high likelihood of failing to detonate at all (Kenney, 2010). It is often difficult for someone who is searching online to build an explosive device, to gauge the quality of that information (Benson, 2014). Also, while some guides include information on how to acquire the parts needed to construct an explosive device, there are some common parts such as blasting caps (i.e., required to detonate high explosives) that are extremely difficult to acquire or construct (Barnes, 2012; Benson, 2014). This has meant that terrorists have to rely on less effective explosive devices, such as those based on chemical mixes, compressed flammable gas, or compressed gunpowder.

There have been a number of cases, such as the attempted public transport bombings in London on July 21, 2005, the attempted car bombings in London and Glasgow in 2007, and the car bombing of Times Square in New York in 2010; where the attacks failed because the explosive devices failed to detonate (Segell, 2006; West & Stewart, 2010).

The attempted terrorist attack carried out in London on July 21, 2005 was an attempt to mimic the attack carried out two weeks prior on July 7, 2005, where 52 civilians had been killed in a number of coordinated attacks on public transport around London (Segell, 2006). Similar to the July 7 attacks, the July 21 attacks consisted of four different bomb attacks carried out on public transport targets around London. Segell (2006) reports that the July 21 attacks relied on devices that were similar, but not identical to those used in the July 7 attacks. The fact that all of the devices used in the July 21 attack failed to detonate demonstrates that either the skill of those constructing the devices and/or the instructions they were relying on were inadequate.

Another similar example is the attempted attack on Times Square in New York City. On May 1, 2010, Faisal Shahzad, a U.S. citizen of Pakistani descent, parked a car loaded with two separate explosive devices and some fuel cans in the middle of Times Square in New York City (West & Stewart, 2010). West and Stewart (2010) describe the two devices as 113 kilograms of fertiliser and three 75-litre propane tanks. If Shahzad had managed to initiate the fertiliser or propane within the car, the resulting explosion would have caused considerable casualties and damage to the surrounding area. However, despite having received training overseas and being able to access instructions on the Internet on how to construct these devices, these devices failed to detonate and there were no casualties from this attack. It is unclear whether the device failed because the fertiliser had not been mixed properly, or because the initiating device was not large enough, or whether the initiating device simply failed to function; but it was this failure that led to the failure of the attack and the perpetrator was arrested soon after (West & Stewart, 2010).

There has been one recent incident (i.e., Boston Marathon bombing in 2013) where terrorists have successfully used an explosive device that was believed to have been based on an Internet-based design (Benson, 2014). However, it has since been suggested that the perpetrators of that attack had also received training overseas rather than relying solely on plans that they had viewed online, and that this may explain why their device worked correctly (Benson, 2014). It is also noted that the devices used in the Boston bombing were based on low explosives such as gunpowder rather than high explosives, indicating the difficulty with building explosive devices based on high explosives. If a comparably sized device based on high explosives was detonated in the Boston attack instead, there would have been many times more casualties as a result.

An example of the type of information (i.e., instructions for various devices) available online to terrorists can be found in 'Inspire', Al-Qaeda's English-language online magazine. A specific example is a device referred to as an 'ember bomb', which is designed to ignite and spread embers in a forest environment and start a forest fire. This device was tested by the California Department of Forestry and Fire Protection (CAL FIRE) (California Department of Forestry and Fire Protection, 2012). The ember bomb relies on a timer and electric initiator, made from a broken light bulb and match-heads, to ignite a liquid fuel mix. Staff at CAL FIRE constructed the device according to the instructions provided in the magazine. However, the initiator for the device failed to ignite the fuel. The fuel was then lit using a match, to observe the effect the fuel would have once ignited. Rather than spreading embers, the fuel created a small fire, which burned for less than 12 minutes over an area of approximately 8 inches. The

CAL FIRE staff concluded that the ember bomb was impractical, compared with starting a fire using a cigarette lighter, and would probably leave valuable physical evidence behind that would be useful for identifying the perpetrator.

Another bomb-making example available from Inspire magazine, involves rigging gas bottles with a mix of flammable gases to serve as a car bomb. This device relied on using the same broken light bulb and match-heads initiator that was suggested for the ember bomb. The likelihood that the bulb and match-heads would actually function and ignite the gas cylinder is low, given that the design relies on an unprotected and fragile filament to remain intact and produce enough heat to ignite the match heads. There is also a risk that even if the initiator for that device was made effectively, the device could still detonate prematurely due to extraneous current in the circuit. For these reasons, the would-be terrorists may well blow themselves up simply from static electricity while detonating the bomb.

A separate issue with accessing specific terrorism-related information online, is that it provides a method for law enforcement to identify those planning an attack (Torres-Soriano, 2012). Given the content on these sites is designed specifically to facilitate a terrorist attack, the monitoring of IP addresses of people who access these sites could assist in identifying those who are planning an attack. This method has been used to identify individuals involved in terrorist activities in the past (UNODC, 2012). However, as previously discussed, this method would not identify possible terrorists if they are using a VPN, unless the VPN's user data can be compromised (Larsson et al., 2012). With TOR users, it may be possible to identify those accessing terrorism literatures using a sniper attack (Jansen et al., 2014). Torres-Soriano (2012) also notes that many terrorists are aware of the ability of law enforcement to monitor activity on particular websites, and are avoiding these sources of information for this reason. One particular incident, where MI6 was able to replace part of a bomb instruction in Inspire magazine with instructions for making cupcakes, led to many in jihadi terrorist groups to advocate avoiding that magazine as a source of information (Torres-Soriano, 2012).

The difficulty in constructing high explosive devices and the fear that the websites providing this sort of information may be monitored, may be the reason why some terrorists have recently been leaning towards the use of attacks based on less conventional weapons. An example of this, is the attacks in France in December 2014, where cars were driven into crowded markets in different locations, injuring dozens of people ("France attack: Van", 2014). Another example is the use of knives rather than firearms or explosives, such as the attack in Kunming, China, where 29 people were killed with knives (Gracie, 2014); or a recent attack in Melbourne, Australia where two police officers were stabbed with a knife, and where others have been accused of plotting attacks based on the use of knives or swords ("Melbourne shooting: Man", 2014). Similarly the killing of a soldier, Lee Rigby, in London, United Kingdom was committed with a machete. This may indicate that some terrorists are leaning towards simpler but less-effective methods to carry out attacks. While this does create a difficulty, in that it is easier to monitor firearms and explosives than it is to monitor cars and knives, these simpler methods also have a much smaller impact than those based on explosives.

In summary, while there is a lot of technical information available to would-be terrorists, the quality of this information is often poor (Benson, 2014; Kenney, 2010). There can also be a risk to terrorists who are accessing this sort of information, particularly if they are not using an online anonymity service, as it may be used to identify those who are planning a terrorist attack (Benson, 2014; Torres-Soriano, 2012). By monitoring who is accessing particular types of information, law enforcement may be able to identify those who are planning a terrorist attack. Because of the difficulty in creating high explosive devices, some terrorists have moved towards devices based on low explosives, or to unconventional methods such as cars and knives. While these methods are more difficult to trace and prevent, they also pose far greater risk to the perpetrators, and are far less effective.

Target Selection Preferences

Romyn and Kebbell (2013) investigated how terrorists select targets by providing several groups of participants with a list of generic locations, and asking them to rank those locations in order of preference for a bomb attack and explain why they selected those targets. The locations used in this research, in descending order of preference, were: an underground train station, a football grand final, a military parade, an airport, a religious gathering, an electrical substation, and a military base. It was found that an underground train station was the most preferred target. The reasons provided by participants for selecting this location were that it was considered to be very crowded and likely to cause high number of casualties, and that it was more likely that the attack would be successful because security personnel would not be able to identify them. A military base was the least preferred target. Participants who avoided this target did so because they believed it would not cause enough casualties or that the target was not an easy one to attack.

A later experiment (Romyn & Kebbell, 2015) also placed participants in the role of would-be terrorists, and asked them to select from a list of prospective targets, which they would prefer to attack. As with the previous experiment, participants were required to rank all the locations in the list from most to least preferred, then to explain why they selected their most and least preferred targets. This later experiment differed from Romyn and Kebbell (2013), in that the participants were provided with specific locations in a specific city that most participants were not familiar with. To inform their decisions, participants were provided a photo and brief description of each location, and with links to publicly available online information.

The links provided for participants included the specific website for that location, Google Maps, street-view images, government information pages, and security information. Participants were also able to use Google to search independently for any further information on the target locations. The Internet browser history was recorded for each participant, which provided insight into which of the links they had viewed, as well as which other information they had sought to inform their decision. It was found that almost all participants relied heavily on Google maps and street-view images to learn more about the target locations. Many participants were also found to have independently searched for information regarding the security of locations, and the number of people who visit each of the locations. It was also found that there was a significant moderate correlation between the number of websites for each location that a participant looked at, and the participant's preference for that location as a target. It was also found that participants tended to revisit information for locations that they preferred to attack. As well as providing insight into which information terrorists may view online to learn about potential targets, this experiment identified which targets were significantly more or less preferred, and what attributes of those targets informed participants' choices.

The most preferred target was a public pedestrian shopping mall in the middle of the city. Participants selected this location because it was easily accessible, had relatively low security, and a high volume of traffic. Participants selected this location over a nearby railway station, generally because there was a perception of less security in the mall than at the railway station. The target considered to be the least preferred by participants was the international airport. Participants who selected this location as their least preferred location were nearly unanimous in their reason why. The airport was the location that was perceived to have the greatest level of security.

One thing that needs to be noted regarding aspects of target vulnerability is that these assessments are very subjective, and are based heavily on how the individual perceives the location. This was demonstrated by participant responses in the research by Romyn and Kebbell (2015), where many of the participants who selected the university as their most preferred target stated that they believed the location was quite crowded; while those who selected that same target as their least preferred stated that they did so because they believed the target was not crowded. While a significant majority of people selected the pedestrian mall as their most preferred target (i.e., over 70 percent of those stated that they would attack that location because they perceived it to be an easy target), of the few who selected the pedestrian mall as their least preferred target, nearly half said that their decision was because it would not be an easy target to attack (Romyn & Kebbell, 2015). This means that one does not necessarily need to alter the features of a location to make it less vulnerable to an attack. By altering the perception of key features, such as altering online information describing how crowded the location is or the level of security present, a location can be made to appear less attractive as a target location.

While the research by Romyn and Kebbell (2013), and Romyn and Kebbell (2015) does indicate which features of a location are likely to make a terrorist more or less inclined to want to target it for an attack, it is still nearly impossible to predict which location will actually be attacked (Mueller, 2010). This is because there are arguably a near-infinite number of possible locations that a terrorist could attack, and the likelihood of any particular location coming under an attack is incredibly small. Altering the features of one location so as to make it less vulnerable to a terrorist attack would only serve to shift the attention of a would-be terrorist to a different location (Mueller, 2010).

However, there are still key public locations, such as centrally located public-transport hubs and vital infrastructure, where the impact of an attack would be amplified, when compared to other locations. Addressing vulnerability issues at these key locations may increase the likelihood of an attack occurring somewhere else, the analogy used in crime prevention is that reducing vulnerability in one area merely increases it in another – i.e., like air moving in a squeezed balloon. However, research indicates that this is not necessarily the case (for a review see Crawford, 2007). In some instances, crime prevention initiatives reduce crime not only where they are applied but this also extends to include areas where the crime prevention initiatives are not in effect. In addition, some offenders seem to give up when they find offending too difficult and not worthwhile.

Target Reconnaissance Using the Internet

Another widely cited way that terrorists could use the Internet to help facilitate an attack is through the use of Internet-based reconnaissance (Keene, 2011). Conway (2006) refers to an Al-Qaeda manual that was captured prior to 2003, which states "Using public sources openly and without resorting to illegal means, it is possible to gather at least eighty percent of information about the enemy" (p. 290). There have since been numerous incidents overseas where people involved in planning terrorist attacks were found to possess information they had sourced online regarding specific targets and locations (Brunst, 2010; Conway, 2006; Thomas, 2003).

Some examples include an online Al-Qaeda manual that contains structural plans for a dam in the United States (Thomas, 2003); Muhammad Naeem Noor Khan, who was arrested in Pakistan in 2004 with floor plans for public buildings in the United States (Conway, 2006); and insurgents in Iraq found with Google Maps images of British military bases, which were in enough detail to identify where the accommodation, amenities and vehicle storages were located within each base (Brunst, 2010). In Australia, convicted terrorist Faheed Khalid Lodhi was found to have utilised the Internet to access electricity grid maps (Conway, 2006; Urbas & Choo, 2008). The Internet has since been utilised in some form in most cases of terrorism in Australia (Mullins, 2011). Finally, those interested in planning an assassination of a public figure can often easily find information on the upcoming locations of their target through online sources.

To investigate how the Internet can be used to plan a terrorist attack, the authors conducted an experiment to observe differences between tourists and terrorists in Internet usage in terms of gathering information on a particular location. The aim of the experiment was to observe how people use the Internet to find information about specific locations, and how this usage may differ depending on the reason for looking for that information. To investigate this, participants were randomly allocated to either a 'tourist' or 'terrorist' group, and asked to look for information on an international airport in a distant city. Participants were required to explain how they would travel to and from the airport, and where they would leave their bag or bomb (i.e., depending on the group they were assigned to). The actual Internet browsing for each participant was captured by video and analysed to identify patterns within the groups, and differences between the groups.

Both groups indicated that they were generally satisfied with the level of information they were able to access via the Internet to inform their decisions. There were no significant differences between the groups regarding how many websites they looked at, or in the number or length of Internet searches conducted. However, some valuable insights were made regarding the amount and type of information that a would-be terrorist have access to. Websites such as Google Maps, as well as websites specific to the airport, provided detailed maps of buildings and surrounding areas. These maps include details regarding the location of security within the airport, and allowed terrorist participants to identify the best place to leave an explosive device.

Further Internet searches conducted by participants, provided terrorist participants with information on: whether or not CCTV was used in a particular location; the number and type of security personnel present; and which modes of transport were more or less likely to include security that would positively identify passengers. For example, one of the terrorist participants explained his choice of transport by stating "… my name is not on any records, and I have a higher chance of getting away with it", while another stated "… you can purchase a ticket on the day from the driver of the bus, this means that you would not have to provide any information therefore there will be no record of your name". Overall, while tourists identified modes of transport that were fast or cheap, terrorists identified modes where they were not required to provide identification in order to ride, which did not include cameras on-board (so that they could blend in with the crowd).

Participants in both the tourist and terrorist groups were compared on their Internet browsing habits. Specifically, the research investigated the number of unique websites participants looked at, and the time spent searching for information. The number of Google searches conducted did not significantly differ between participants in the tourist or terrorist groups. The results from this experiment suggest that it may be difficult to identify someone conducting terrorism-related reconnaissance among all of the other Internet traffic, simply by the pattern in which individuals look for information.

However, the research has also highlighted the types of information that can be freely accessed, and how this information can be used to inform terrorist's decisions when planning an attack. Using the Internet alone, it is possible to find out the layout of a location, what sort of security exists at a particular location, the number of people who visit a location, transport to and from a location, and many other very relevant pieces of information. Because of this, care must be taken to ensure information that may be useful to those planning a terrorist attack is limited wherever possible. Finally, while the findings of this research suggest that it is not possible to identify terrorist suspects involved in online reconnaissance by monitoring all Internet traffic, monitoring the browsing habits of those already suspected of being involved in terrorism has been used many times in the past to identify which locations are likely to be targets for an attack (Mullins, 2011; Urbas & Choo, 2008).

SOLUTIONS AND RECOMMENDATIONS

The Internet does provide a large amount of information that is useful to someone planning a terrorist attack, including information on key locations, and instructions on how to make and use weapons for an attack. By monitoring individuals who are accessing terrorist-specific information, such as bomb-building instructions, it may be possible to identify those involved in terrorism activities. While it may be possible to track the activities of individuals online, it is also a relatively simple process to ensure anonymity online using services such as VPN or TOR (Dingledine et al., 2004; Larsson et al., 2012). For those who are using a VPN to hide their activities online, authorities may be able to legally require the VPN services to allow them access to their records (Benson, 2014). It may also be possible to block an individual's access to the VPN service, or in the case of VPN and individuals that exist in a different jurisdiction, it may be possible to block that VPN's access to key online information. TOR users can possibly be identified by building a profile of their activities online, or by using a sniper attack (Jansen et al., 2014; Murdoch & Danezis, 2005). Finally, by giving the impression that VPN and TOR are not entirely anonymous sources and this being a reality, authorities may be able to reduce the use of such services by terrorists.

Some terrorists, when planning an attack, have certainly used online information both to learn more about specific locations, and how to construct explosive devices and other weapons. However, acquiring the materials to construct an explosive device and assembling one that will actually function as intended, is not a simple process (Benson, 2014). Much of the information available online is considered to be of poor quality, and is more likely to fail or cause injury to the terrorist than to harm others (Kenney, 2010). Given how difficult it is for non-experts to tell the difference between good and bad information on how to build explosives, law enforcement could further reduce the usefulness of this information by including misinformation regarding how to construct explosive devices. This reduces the likelihood that a device would function, and that terrorists would base a device on one of these instructions. Providing misinformation regarding how to make bombs would also reduce the credibility of this source of information generally among terrorists, which in turn means that terrorists would need to rely on more reliable but less effective methods (Torres-Soriano, 2012).

Given the numerous recent examples of failed terrorist attacks, such as the Times Square attack, it may be useful to focus more public attention on these failures. By highlighting the likelihood of failure, those considering involvement in terrorism may be dissuaded. Also, playing down the possible severity of the attacks, while highlighting their failures, would serve to reduce public fear regarding such attacks. In the end, given that the aim of these attacks is to induce fear in a wider audience, this would reduce the effectiveness of these actions.

Regarding the selection of targets, the Internet does provide a wealth of extremely useful information for those planning a terrorist attack. This information can be used to inform decisions regarding which target should or should not be attacked. In particular, Romyn and Kebbell (2015) found that locations that were considered to be very crowded and with relatively low security were more attractive as terrorist targets. Conversely, locations that were seen to have very high security were perceived as being significantly less attractive as possible terrorist targets. Security aspects such as the presence of security personnel on the ground, the location of nearby police stations, or the presence or absence of CCTV can influence the decisions of those planning an attack.

With this in mind, it may be useful to either increase security, or at least give the impression of increased security on key locations so as to deter a would-be attacker. Likewise, the information regarding the number of people who visit a location strongly influences the decision to select it as a target. To reduce how attractive a target appears to those planning an attack, it would be best to omit this data from websites wherever possible.

These suggestions all work towards influencing aspects of rational choice theory to make terrorist attacks less likely (Clarke & Newman, 2006). In the context of crime, rational choice theory asserts that would-be criminals weigh up the possible costs and benefits of committing a crime prior to actually committing it. This theory is based on an individual's perception of the costs and benefits of an act, and individual's perceptions can be changed. The actions suggested in this chapter all seek to change the perceptions of those involved in terrorism:

- Giving the impression that Internet anonymity services are not effective,
- Providing false information regarding how to make explosive devices (and other potential weapons),
- Making locations appear less attractive to a would-be terrorist, and
- Playing down the impact of terrorist attacks while highlighting their failures.

Specifically, by increasing the perceived cost of an action, while reducing the perceived benefit, some may be turned away from following that course of action.

FUTURE RESEARCH DIRECTIONS

Whilst in its infancy, the use of a red-team design for research investigating how terrorists plan attacks has provided valuable insight into aspects of terrorism, particularly in highlighting how attacks can be planned and conducted, and has the potential to inform how security may be enhanced to reduce the likelihood of a terrorist attack. However, other sources of information regarding how attacks are planned and conducted are also crucial in identifying key aspects of the planning process of terrorist attacks. For example, interviews with those arrested for terrorism offences would certainly provide very valid insight into common aspects of the planning process. This information could also be used to further inform future red-team research designs.

Another example is to investigate the Internet usage habits of past terrorists in various settings around the world, to identify key points that could be used to identify those currently involved. Using information from primary sources such as terrorist interviews and terrorist Internet usage, future red-team designs could be focused on specific aspects of the terrorism attack planning. The results from this research can further highlight aspects of the planning process that can be influenced to reduce the likelihood of an attack occurring, or to reduce the impact of an attack if one is to occur.

CONCLUSION

To conclude, the Internet can be used to facilitate terrorist attacks through obtaining and developing weapons, selecting targets, and supplying reconnaissance. While some argue that terrorists are at a disadvantage using the Internet because of their likelihood to be identified and monitored, it is possible for those involved to either hide their identity entirely, or to make it much more difficult to be identified. The availability of technical and reconnaissance information, and the ability to increase anonymity while using the Internet, will continue to pose a persistent challenge for disrupting terrorism.

Nevertheless, there are many ways (some that we have identified in this chapter) to disrupt and weaken terrorists. Focusing on (1) terrorist's ability to use anonymity services, (2) the reliability of online bomb-making instructions, and (3) altering specific online information about key locations will increase the likelihood of detection while decreasing the likelihood and severity of an attack occurring. While terrorism has been a persistent problem, and is one that is not likely to disappear in the near future, steps can be made to increase the difficulty in conducting attacks, while reducing the effectiveness of those attacks when they occur.

REFERENCES

Antoniades, D., Markatos, E. P., & Dovrolis, C. (2010). MOR: Monitoring and measurements through the onion router. In A. Krishnamurthy & B. Plattner (Eds.), *Passive and active measurement* (pp. 131–140). Berlin: Springer-Verlag. doi:10.1007/978-3-642-12334-4_14

Barnes, B. (2012). Confronting the one-man wolf pack: Adapting law enforcement and prosecution responses to the threat of lone wolf terrorism. *Boston University Law Review. Boston University. School of Law, 92*, 1613–1662.

Benson, D. C. (2014). Why the Internet is not increasing terrorism. *Security Studies, 23*(2), 293–328. doi:10.1080/09636412.2014.905353

Brunst, P. W. (2010). Terrorism and the Internet: New threats posed by cyberterrorism and terrorist use of the Internet. In M. Wade & A. Maljević (Eds.), *A war on terror?: The European stance on a new threat, changing laws and human rights implications* (pp. 51–78). New York, NY: Springer. doi:10.1007/978-0-387-89291-7_3

California Department of Forestry and Fire Protection (CAL FIRE). (2012). *A practical test of the 'Ember Bomb' as described in Inspire, Issue 9*. California State Threat Assessment Center.

Chakravarty, S., Portokalidis, G., Polychronakis, M., & Keromytis, A. D. (2011). Detecting traffic snooping in Tor using decoys. In *Proceedings of the 14th International Conference on Recent Advances in Intrusion Detection*. Berlin: Springer. doi:10.1007/978-3-642-23644-0_12

Clarke, R. V., & Newman, G. R. (2006). *Outsmarting the terrorists*. Westport, CA: Greenwood Publishing Group.

Conway, M. (2006). Terrorism and the Internet: New media - new threat? *Parliamentary Affairs, 59*(2), 283–298. doi:10.1093/pa/gsl009

Crawford, A. (2007). Crime prevention and community safety. In M. Maguire, R. Morgan, & R. Reiner (Eds.), *The oxford handbook of criminology* (4th ed.; pp. 866–909). Oxford, UK: Oxford University Press.

Dingledine, R., Mathewson, N., & Syverson, P. (2004). *Tor: The second-generation onion router*. Washington, DC: Naval Research Lab.

Edman, M., & Yener, B. (2009). On anonymity in an electronic society: A survey of anonymous communication systems. *ACM Computing Surveys, 42*(1), 1–35. doi:10.1145/1592451.1592456

France attack: Van driven into shoppers in Nantes. (2014, December 23). *BBC News*. Retrieved from http://www.bbc.com/news/world-europe-30583390

Gracie, C. (2014, July 16). The knife attack that changed Kunming. *BBC News*. Retrieved from http://www.bbc.com/news/world-asia-28305109

Jansen, R., Tschorsch, F., Johnson, A., & Scheuermann, B. (2014). *The sniper attack: Anonymously deanonymizing and disabling the Tor Network*. Arlington, VA: Office of Naval Research.

Keene, S. D. (2011). Terrorism and the Internet: A double-edged sword. *Journal of Money Laundering Control, 14*(4), 359–370. doi:10.1108/13685201111173839

Kenney, M. (2010). Beyond the Internet: Mētis, techne, and the limitations of online artifacts for Islamist terrorists. *Terrorism and Political Violence, 22*(2), 177–197. doi:10.1080/09546550903554760

Larsson, S., & Svensson, M. (2010). Compliance or obscurity? Online anonymity as a consequence of fighting unauthorised file-sharing. *Policy and Internet, 2*(4), 77–105. doi:10.2202/1944-2866.1044

Larsson, S., Svensson, M., de Kaminski, M., Rönkkö, K., & Olsson, J. A. (2012). Laws, norms, piracy and online anonymity: Practices of de-identification in the global file sharing community. *Journal of Research in Interactive Marketing, 6*(4), 260–280. doi:10.1108/17505931211282391

Melbourne shooting: Man being investigated over terrorism shot dead after stabbing police officers outside Endeavour Hills police station. (2014, September 24). *ABC News*. Retrieved from http://www.abc.net.au/news/2014-09-23/one-person-shot-dead-two-stabbed-endeavour-hills/5764408

Mueller, J. (2010). Assessing measures designed to protect the homeland. *Policy Studies Journal: the Journal of the Policy Studies Organization, 38*(1), 1–21. doi:10.1111/j.1541-0072.2009.00341.x

Mullins, S. (2011). Islamist terrorism in Australia: An empirical examination of the 'Home grown' threat. *Terrorism and Political Violence, 23*(2), 254–285. doi:10.1080/09546553.2010.535717

Murdoch, S. J., & Danezis, G. (2005). *Low-cost traffic analysis of TOR*. Paper presented at the 2005 IEEE Symposium on Security and Privacy, Oakland, CA. doi:10.1109/SP.2005.12

Nesser, P. (2008). Chronology of jihadism in Western Europe 1994–2007: Planned, prepared, and executed terrorist attacks. *Studies in Conflict and Terrorism, 31*(10), 924–946. doi:10.1080/10576100802339185

Rescorla, E. (2008). *Notes on P2P blocking and evasion.* IETF P@P Infrastructure Workshop (P2Pi). Retrieved from http://64.170.98.42/area/rai/trac/raw-attachment/wiki/PeerToPeerInfrastructure/27 rescorla-p2pi.pdf

Romyn, D., & Kebbell, M. R. (2013). Terrorists' planning of attacks: A simulated 'red-team' investigation into decision-making. *Psychology, Crime & Law, 20*(5), 480–496. doi:10.1080/1068316X.2013.793767

Romyn, D., & Kebbell, M. R. (2015). *Use of Internet to inform terrorist target selection.* Australia: Griffith University.

Schneier, B. (2007). Did NSA put a secret backdoor in new encryption standard? *Wired.* Retrieved from http://www.wired.com/politics/security/commentary/securitymatters/2007/11/securitymatters_1115

Segell, G. M. (2006). Terrorism on London public transport. *Defense and Security Analysis, 22*(1), 45–49. doi:10.1080/14751790600577132

Soghoian, C. (2010). Caught in the cloud: Privacy, encryption and government back doors in the Web 2.0 era. *Journal on Telecommunications & High Technology Law, 8,* 359–423.

Spaaij, R. (2010). The enigma of lone wolf terrorism: An assessment. *Studies in Conflict and Terrorism, 33*(9), 854–870. doi:10.1080/1057610X.2010.501426

Thomas, T. L. (2003). Al Qaeda and the Internet: The dangers of 'cyberplanning'. *Parameters, 33*(1), 112–123.

Tor Project. (n.d.). Retrieved from https://www.torproject.org/index.html.en

Torres-Soriano, M. R. (2012). The vulnerabilities of online terrorism. *Studies in Conflict and Terrorism, 35*(4), 263–277. doi:10.1080/1057610X.2012.656345

United Nations Office on Drugs and Crime (UNODC). (2012). *The use of the internet for terrorist purposes.* Retrieved from http://www.unodc.org/documents/frontpage/Use_of_Internet_for_Terrorist_Purposes.pdf

Urbas, G., & Choo, K. R. (2008). *Resource materials on technology-enabled crime (Technical and Background Paper no.28).* Canberra: Australian Institute of Criminology.

West, B., & Stewart, S. (2010). Uncomfortable truths and the Times Square attack. *Stratfor.* Retrieved from https://www.stratfor.com/weekly/20100505_uncomfortable_truths_times_square_attack

ENDNOTE

[1.] High explosives burn rate is between 4,000 and 8,000 meters per second, while low explosives burn rate is around 500 meters per second.

Section 2

Understanding the "Person" within Online Violent Extremism

Chapter 6

Understanding Personality and Person–Specific Predictors of Cyber–Based Insider Threat

Joyce S. Pang
Nanyang Technological University, Singapore

ABSTRACT

The chapter aims to provide an opinion on major challenges for ongoing personality research on cyber security, especially in the area of insider threat. While research on the prevention and perpetuation of insider threat activity within cyberspace has grown substantially in the recent decade, there remain many unanswered challenges and unchartered territories of knowledge in the field. Specifically, compared to the amount of work done on algorithmic modelling approaches, much of the psychological data is scant and focuses on correlations between the so-called Big Five personality traits (i.e., extraversion, openness to experience, agreeableness, emotional stability, conscientiousness) or demographic variables (e.g., gender, age) with insider threat activity. Thus, the focus of this article is to articulate the major challenges for understanding insider threat in the context of cyber security, particularly from a personality and person-specific perspective that emphasises internal characteristics of the individual actor as explanations of actions and events.

INTRODUCTION AND GENERAL APPROACH

The aim of this chapter is to provide an opinion on the major challenges for ongoing personality research on cyber security, especially in the area of insider threat. Cyber security refers to the field involved in the monitoring of criminal activities in cyberspace, in order to maintain a safe environment for the transfer of resources and for the dissemination and protection of information. Insider threat refers to the presence of trusted individuals who are either members of an organisation or who have privileged access to organisation resources, and who engage in activities from within the organisation to threaten the interests of that organisation (cf. Probst, Hunker, Gollmann, & Bishop, 2010). In relation to cyber security, the major categories of insider threat are IT sabotage, fraud, theft of intellectual property (IP

DOI: 10.4018/978-1-5225-0156-5.ch006

theft), and espionage. While research on the prevention and perpetuation of insider threat activity within cyberspace has grown substantially in the recent decade, there remain many unanswered challenges and unchartered territories of knowledge in the field. Specifically, compared to the amount of work done on logging software and algorithmic modelling approaches, relatively less work has been carried out to clarify the important psychological and sociological factors for cyber security and for insider threat. Importantly, much of the psychological data is scant and focuses on correlations between the so-called Big Five personality traits (i.e., extraversion, openness to experience, agreeableness, emotional stability, conscientiousness; John & Srivastava, 1999; see Axelrad, Sticha, Brdiczka, & Shen, 2013, for an example of a Bayesian network model of insider threat using the Big Five traits) or demographic variables (e.g., gender and age; see Chang & Lim, 2014) with insider threat activity. Thus, the focus of this chapter is to articulate the major challenges for understanding insider threat in the context of cyber security, particularly from a personality and person-specific perspective.

By a 'personality and person-specific perspective', I am referring to a perspective that emphasises internal characteristics of the individual actor as explanations of actions and events. These internal characteristics can come from personality dimensions – which are a system of thoughts, feelings, and behaviours that an individual exhibits consistently across time and over situations – or they can come from person-specific dimensions that are externally ascribed to an individual usually because of his or her social category. Examples of personality dimensions are traits (e.g., extraversion), explanatory styles (e.g., pessimism), motives (e.g., power motivation), skills and competencies (e.g., intelligence, creativity), and values (e.g., benevolence). Individuals differ on these personality dimensions because of biology, influence from social contexts, upbringing, and exposure to significant others, as well as through a combination of learning experiences and interaction with social and physical environments. Examples of person-specific dimensions include gender, age, and socioeconomic class.

There are two major decisions for a behavioural scientist who is trying to understand person-specific characteristics of cyber-based insider threat; these involve the questions of what and how to study cybercrime and insider threat. In considering the question of what should be studied, I will make use of the excellent groundwork carried out recently by researchers in the fields of cyber security and insider threat. I will conduct a targeted review of recently published frameworks for understanding insider threat, specifically the models of Nurse et al. (2014) and Moore et al. (2011).

Whilst Nurse and colleagues did an admirable job of summarising main themes in the field, their framework is relatively general and thus allows for much more categories of study to be uncovered. Hence, Nurse at al.'s (2014) model can be a jumping off point, from which I will discuss more context-specific areas for future research inquiry, such as regarding the motivation of offenders.

I will also discuss offender profiles and types of cyber-insiders, using recent work by Moore and colleagues. Moore, Cappelli, and Trzeciak (2008) and Moore et al. (2011) have provided some insight into offender profiles in insider crime, specifically in the areas of fraud and IP theft. Using research in the related fields of organisational psychology and personality psychology (e.g., Murphy & Dacin, 2011), I suggest some extensions of Moore and colleagues' work by identifying some other promising variables and/or productive dimensions for categorising cyber offenders of insider attacks.

For the question of how to study cyber-based insider attacks, in the latter part of the chapter, I will discuss some methodological considerations, such as how to derive an approach for the field that is both theory and data driven, and how psychological and behavioural data should be collected and/or treated for validation purposes and for application purposes.

NURSE ET AL.'S (2014) MODEL FOR CHARACTERISING INSIDER ATTACKS

Nurse and his colleagues (2014) set out to formulate a framework of the insider threat problem. In order to do so, they collected a dataset of 80 insider threat cases from various sources, including CERT (Computer Emergency Response Team; for more information, see Cappelli, Moore, & Trzeciak, 2012) and CPNI (Centre for the Protection of National Infrastructure), as well as various news sources in the United States and the United Kingdom. They then analysed each case, as well as consulted literature in order to come up with consistent themes and relationships.

There are four major sections in Nurse et al.'s (2014) framework: the *catalyst* or precipitating event that triggers the insider attack; *actor* characteristics of the offender; *attack* characteristics; and *organisational* characteristics. For this review, since we are concerned with the personality of the offender, we will limit our discussion to the portion of the model that discusses actor characteristics.

Nurse et al. (2014) take a dimensional approach to understand the person characteristics of the offender in insider attacks. There are 12 elements in the insider/actor characteristics in Nurse et al.'s model. These are: personality characteristics, historical behaviour, psychological state, attitude towards work, motivation to attack, skill set, opportunity, enterprise role, type of actor, state of relationship, observed physical behaviour, and observed cyber behaviour. In general, all these elements also apply to cyber-based offenders conducting insider attacks. However, I propose that further research is needed, particularly in three key elements of personality – personality characteristics of the actor, the actor's current psychological state, and the actor's motivation to attack – before personality researchers can adapt the model more specifically to cyber security.

Personality Characteristics

Personality characteristics discussed by Nurse et al. (2014) mostly belong to the category of dispositions best described as static. Specifically, static notions of personality see dispositional characteristics as being relatively stable and enduring. In other words, it is assumed that, after a certain period of development, there is a stability of beliefs, attitudes, cognitions, and emotions in the style and content of interactions between an individual and his/her environment. Moreover, there is also the assumption that static personality is resistant to change (such as via the process of maturation, or because of exposure to traumatic and/or significant life events). This view of personality is encapsulated in James' (1890) famous comment that most of the character is 'set in plaster' by the age of thirty. In this type of conceptualisation, assessments of personality display relatively high test-retest and inter-rater reliability[1].

There are some dimensions of personality (e.g., traits, temperaments), which display relatively high temporal stability, and thus can be easily classified as static. Specifically, there is ample evidence that the traits of neuroticism, extroversion, and openness exhibit only small declines, and that agreeableness and conscientiousness exhibit only small increases from ages 20 to 40, and moreover, there is little change thereafter (Duggan, 2004).

However, most personality characteristics tend to be dynamic. In dynamic notions of personality (e.g., Costa & McCrae, 1994), basic tendencies and innate characteristics such as biological tendencies, temperaments, intelligence, gender, etc. interact with the environment to produce so-called characteristic adaptations. These adaptations manifest in the form of dimensions of personality, such as attitudes, values, and other traits. For instance, the person might possess a certain degree of general intelligence (basic tendency) which, when exposed to a stimulating home environment and a challenging school environment, produces conscientiousness (a trait) and high need for achievement (a motive), both of which are characteristic adaptations. Following this line of reasoning, even though there are some personality dimensions that are relatively stable (e.g., a controlled temperament), these stable dimensions could still lead to a variety of different behavioural outcomes (e.g., depression versus overachievement), depending on the specific environment to which the person is exposed (troubled home environment versus competitive school environment). Another particularly important point which Moore, Detert, Treviño, Baker, and Mayer (2012) also mention is that all the person-specific and personality dimensions, whether they are basic tendencies or characteristic adaptations, are interlinked and interact with each other. In this way, personality characteristics are dynamic and mutually interacting, which makes them more difficult to assess or to model. Nonetheless, there is evidence of some predictive validity for a combination of personality traits that seem to go together in predicting unethical work or counterproductive work behaviours. Specifically, counterproductive workplace behaviours are typically perpetrated by those with high negative emotionality or high neuroticism, low agreeableness, and low conscientiousness (see Salgado, 2002; Marcus, Lee, & Ashton, 2007).

Another reason that many actor characteristics should be treated as dynamic is because of the need to consider the local context when considering the interaction of all the actor characteristics. For instance, a practitioner who is seeking to use personality research to predict behavioural outcomes would not only need to know the type of behaviour a personality trait predicts, but also the specific environmental condition that is most likely to cause the behaviour to manifest. It is precisely because of the influence of context and the dynamic nature of many personality traits, that many researchers of criminal behaviour have found that risk assessments that are based on personality inventories exhibit only moderate levels of inter-rater and field reliability ranging around 0.6-0.75 (e.g., Miller, Kimonis, Otto, Kline, & Wasserman, 2012). It is likely that some items on these personality based risk assessments are less susceptible to contextual influences than others, and these items would hence display relatively higher inter-rater and field reliabilities. Future research is needed to assess which particular items of standard risk assessment instruments display better rater agreement than others. Another precaution that practitioners interested in personality based risk assessments of insider threat can take is to bear in mind that such instruments should only play a secondary role in informing decisions about personnel selection and monitoring, especially in high-pressure, high-stakes environments, like legal judgments and national security.

Regrettably, most of the work done on insider threat and in the related field of counterproductive work behaviour (see Sackett, Berry, Wiemann, & Laczo, 2006) has focused on static personality characteristics like the Big Five personality traits of extraversion, conscientiousness, openness to experience, emotional stability, and agreeableness. In this line of research, typical findings are that personality traits such as Machiavellianism and neuroticism are positively associated with counterproductive work behaviour (e.g., Marcus & Schuler, 2004) or with insider threat activity (e.g., Axelrad et al., 2013). While they are helpful in describing the structure of personality and in developing typologies for typical offender profiles, conceptions of personality that are solely trait-based have limited field validity because a purely descriptive taxonomy of between-person individual differences does not address why the same person will behave differently across different situations (Cervone, Shoda, & Downey, 2007; cf. Graber, Laurenceau, & Carver, 2011).

Instead of seeing personality as a constellation of traits, popular contemporary notions of personality (e.g., the Cognitive-Affective Processing System [CAPS]; Mischel & Shoda, 1995) emphasise a more process-oriented view that represents the individual as a combination of different dimensions (which includes traits but also other dimensions of personality) that continually interact and transact with the environment. In these process-oriented models, individuals exhibit behavioural signatures, which work in a contingent, if-then fashion. In other words, traits can predict behavioural outcomes only in certain situations, and only if the traits are activated within and/or applicable to that specific situation. For instance, following Mischel and Shoda's (1995) CAPS model, Graber et al. (2011) developed a multilevel-modelling framework for studying personality and close dyadic relationships. In their model, personality is conceptualised as the person-specific factor of relationship satisfaction. Specifically, individuals may differ in the general degree to which they experience relationship satisfaction. Graber et al.'s (2011) final multilevel model showed that degree of relationship satisfaction is related to person-specific differences in propensity to experience relationship satisfaction as well as the outcome of negative behaviours towards one's partner, in a complex fashion. Specifically, there is within-person variability in relationship satisfaction on a day-to-day level over the 21 days of their study, and there is also between-person variability in relationship threat (i.e., the amount of conflict the couple experiences during each day). The day-to-day variation in relationship satisfaction is related to the day-to-day variation in between-person variability in relationship threat, which in turn is related to the overall between-person variation in amount of negative behaviours each individual expresses to their partner.

This type of analysis of personality in research like Graber et al.'s (2011; see also Cooper, Barber, Zhaoyang, & Talley, 2010, for an example with multilevel modelling of sexually deviant behaviour) illustrates that personality and person-specific variables are linked to behavioural outcomes through a complex series of interactions with the environment (e.g., the level of conflict with one's partner on a day-to-day basis). Accordingly, in order to increase the predictive value of trait-based conceptualisations of personality, researchers should focus on developing process-based models of insider threat behaviour that takes into account interactions with elements of the environment (e.g., day-to-day social interactions with co-workers, superiors, and subordinates). Researchers could also search for other trait-based variables that have specifically been developed to explain the behaviours that are more relevant to insider threats. For instance, subclinical psychopathy has been examined as a better predictor than Big Five traits in the specific context of counterproductive work behaviours (Scherer, Baysinger, Zolynsky, & LeBreton, 2013). By examining more specific traits that incorporate psychological elements related to the environment of interest (rather than broad super-traits), savvy researchers would improve the external validity of their predictive models.

Certain personality elements, however, are relatively easier to quantify since they are likely to exhibit minimal change over time and/or are unlikely to fluctuate highly alongside micro-contextual variations. Some examples of these person-specific elements in Nurse et al.'s (2014) model which are relatively resistant to change – and thus more easy to assess and to include in an algorithmic predictive model – include historical behaviour and skill set.

Historical behaviour, particularly, could be an area where large knowledge increments can be accrued, and where improvements to modelling approaches can be made easily. For instance, in general, historical behaviour refers to a set of behaviours that the insider has engaged in during the immediate past, and which taken together suggest a consistent pattern of responses that are indicative of the insider's personality characteristics. Specifically, historical behaviours could include previous criminal acts, risky or addictive practices, and other serious rule violations that may or may not be classified as insider threat behaviours. These kinds of behaviours are all indicative of an underlying personality characteristic, which could arguably be described as anti-social tendency.

The idea of historical behaviours is conceptually equivalent to the habit construct in personality psychology. Habits are behaviours that are performed frequently in stable contexts (Hull, 1943; see

Wood & Neal, 2007). As a part of personality, habits are defined as "learned dispositions to repeat past responses. They are triggered by features of the context that have covaried frequently with past performance" (Wood & Neal, 2007, p. 843). Because a habit tends to be formed through the frequent, unintentional, and repeated occurrences of a response in a specific context, habits are often stable and resistant to long-term change. In situations that do not engender much deliberated action, habits guide behaviour rapidly and efficiently. Researchers interested in assessing historical behaviours and habits can easily do so by assessing frequencies of behaviours that are assumed to be related to insider threat[2].

Psychological State

In Nurse et al.'s (2014) model, the psychological state refers to the insider's short-term emotional and psychological state. This is the aspect that is perhaps the most difficult to assess and to quantify, because of the nature of emotional states being automatic, transient and rapidly cycling, as well as relatively inaccessible to conscious awareness. More research is needed in order to either develop relevant implicit measures of affect or to validate the use of standardised implicit measures of affect in psychological studies of cyber security and of insider attacks. The problem is that questionnaire measures of affect are reactive measures, in the sense that respondents often react to the act of taking the test, and this awareness of their responses is likely to cause them to subtly alter their responses. Most respondents of questionnaire measures would be reluctant to report extreme negative emotion, for example. Additionally, the possibility of response sets, for instance, the tendency to 'fake-good' or 'fake-bad' on Likert-type personality tests has been consistently demonstrated (cf. Bagby, Buis, & Nicholson, 1995). Hence, there is a need to select measures of emotion that are non-reactive. However, the good news is that non-reactive measures of affect and emotion are already readily available in psychological research, and can easily be transplanted for use in cyber security research. Examples of non-reactive measures of affect and emotion include the Implicit Positive and Negative Affect Test [IPANAT] (Quirin & Bode, 2014) and the Emotion Regulation Implicit Association Test [ER-IAT] (Mauss, Evers, Wilhelm, & Gross, 2006)[3].

Another interesting point about the study of emotional states of cyber-based insiders is the distinction between the actor's emotional content and his or her emotional style. This is a distinction (i.e., about emotions) that could be useful, but which is not commonly embraced by current researchers of cyber security. Specifically, while emotional content typically refers to the emotional state of an individual, which is susceptible to rapid moment-to-moment changes, emotional style refers to a stable characteristic way of reacting emotionally to events. Different emotional styles can be described, such as the tendency to react with positive emotions frequently and in response to ambiguous events (positive emotional style), or the tendency to react with negative emotions frequently and in response to ambiguous events (negative emotional style), or the tendency towards experiencing strong negative as well as strong positive emotions frequently and in response to ambiguous events (dialectical emotional style). While emotional content – currently commonly assessed in insider threat research – might differ dramatically from moment-to-moment, emotional style is relatively stable and influenced by other personality attributes as well as by culturally appropriate norms for emotional expressiveness (e.g., Miyamoto & Ryff, 2011).

Motivation to Attack

Motivation to attack refers to the specific reason for an insider attack. At present, most researchers of insider threat define motivation as the explicit reasons for the attack, which the attackers attribute to themselves or which investigators might attribute to the insiders, through extrapolation from personal circumstances and known external triggers of the attack. Common reasons include financial gain, revenge, political advantage, curiosity, boredom, etc. However, this way of looking at motivation (as self-attributed or other-declared reasons for the attack) primarily deals with the short-term motivational state of the offender, at the moment of the attack. These reasons for offending are state-like, most likely triggered by the circumstances, actors, and events in the immediate context, and hence difficult to assess before the fact. I would like to propose that, instead of studying state-based reasons for offending, researchers should turn their attention to trait-based notions of the motives of the offenders. In other words, individuals could be chronically motivated to fulfil certain needs. Moreover, there would be individual differences for these motives such that some people are perpetually more motivated than others by certain psychological needs. For instance, personality research suggests that people are differentially motivated by their need for power, affiliation, or achievement (McClelland, 1987).

Classic personality research shows that individual differences in these needs affect people's long-term goal-directed behaviour in important personal and social domains. Of particular relevance is power motivation: people motivated by their need for power are more likely to engage in antisocial and dominance-seeking aggressive behaviours. For instance, U.S. presidents with high power motivation tend to be more war mongering but are also more likely to be seen as effective leaders from a historical perspective (Winter, 1987). The level of power motivation between parties in a dyadic negotiation has also been shown to determine whether or not the conflict will escalate – an increase in power motivation of one party in the negotiation is typically followed by concomitant conflict-escalating behaviour of the other party (Winter, 2004). On the other hand, when communications between parties in a negotiation contain relatively more affiliation motive imagery than power motive imagery, the conflict tends to de-escalate. This and other research on motivation, illustrate the importance of accounting for the context when predicting behaviour from personality. Specifically, the motives of important others in the social interaction affect whether one's motives manifest in behaviour. Thus, motives are often seen as dynamic personality variables that wax and wane according to the degree to which environmental conditions encourage their expression.

A major problem for using self-attributed, short-term reasons to understand the motivation behind insider attacks, is that measures of these reasons are typically self-report, questionnaire measures. Once again, the issue of respondent reactivity applies. Moreover, people are notoriously unreliable in reporting their motives since motives tend to operate at an implicit level, largely away from conscious cognition (cf. McClelland, Koestner, & Weinberger, 1989). As discussed later, in personality research, non-reactive measures of chronic dispositions like motives for power, affiliation, and achievement are readily available (e.g., Schultheiss & Pang, 2007), and could be used for future investigations of motivations behind insider threat.

MOORE ET AL.'S (2011) MODEL OF INSIDER IP THEFT

IP theft, a major category of insider cyber attacks, refers to "crimes in which current or former employees, contractors, or business partners intentionally exceeded or misused an authorised level of access to networks, systems, or data to steal confidential or proprietary information from the organisation" (Moore et al., 2011, p. 1). Moore et al.'s work comes from the well-known CERT program at Carnegie Mellon University, whose aim is to gather data on and analyse malicious insider incidents. The CERT Insider

Threat Center collaborates with the U.S. Department of Homeland Security, and is primarily involved in using system dynamics modelling to characterise and study insider threats (see Cappelli, Moore, & Trzeciak, 2012, for a more detailed description of CERT). Although the group at Carnegie Mellon has published work on other examples of insider threat (e.g., IT sabotage and fraud; Moore et al., 2008; Rich et al., 2005), the 2011 paper is the first one that uses a primarily personological approach, emphasising within-person specific characteristics more than the attack characteristics.

CERT's research is partially funded by the U.S. Army Research Office. Thus, the group at CERT had access to, and analysed hundreds of cases of insider threat, which were gathered from various sources across different United States infrastructure sectors. Moore et al. (2011) conducted follow-up work on 48 cases of IP theft using detailed group modelling procedures. Through this work, Moore et al. (2011) developed dynamics systems models for two major profiles of attackers for IP theft, specifically, the 'entitled independent' and the 'ambitious leader'.

The entitled independent refers to an insider who acts alone in order to obtain proprietary information that is beneficial to his or her personal interests in a new job or for a side business. The entitled independent is mainly characterised by his/her feeling of entitlement to access the information, and it is this sense of entitlement that justifies his/her actions. Typically, these offenders steal information that they were at least partially responsible for developing or safeguarding, and this partial investment of energy, time, and resources contributes to a sense of ownership of the information, which in turn feeds the feeling of entitlement. An example of an entitled independent individual might be a software programmer who leaves a virtual 'back door' to programs that he/she created. These programs could be portions of a larger system of infrastructure that is proprietary to the organisation, and the 'back door' serves as a threat to cyber security because it enables the programmer to obtain privileged but unsanctioned and/or unregulated access.

On the other hand, the ambitious leader recruits other insiders in order to obtain proprietary information to serve some larger purpose, such as the interests of a competing organisation or a foreign government. There are at least two ways to interpret the underlying motives of the ambitious leader type of cyber-criminals – they could see their role as a facilitator for the machinations of a larger power such as the competitor company that they are aiding and aligning with, or the ambitious leaders could see the outside company as a tool for obtaining greater power for themselves. However, these distinctions are not discussed in Moore et al.'s (2011) typology. What matters in Moore et al.'s (2011) model is that the act of betrayal is in service of an external organisation that will give the ambitious leader access to greater power.

Personality Differences between Ambitious Leader-type versus Entitled Independent-type Insiders

There are two major differences between the ambitious leader model and the entitled independent model for IP theft. First, insider attacks by entitled independents are typically preceded by the attackers experiencing dissatisfaction with their organisations, whereas such dissatisfaction is absent in ambitious leaders. Second, the attacks by ambitious leaders are executed with a great amount of prior planning that typically involve the recruitment of other insiders as well as the use of deception in order to obscure the theft. In contrast, attacks by entitled independents typically involve little planning or deception.

Although Moore and colleagues (2011) take a typological approach by essentially constructing profiles of different types of offenders, what is most interesting about their categorisation of IP theft attacks is that it reveals some common dimensions with which different types of insider attackers can be distinguished.

The first dimension is the presence and degree of negative emotionality. In the entitled independent model, the insider experiences some sort of triggering event (e.g., loss of a promotion opportunity), which leads him or her to experience dissatisfaction with the organisation. It is this dissatisfaction that provides the motivation for the act of disloyalty in stealing proprietary information. However, in the ambitious leader model, the attacker's decision to commit IP theft is motivated by the insider's commitment to an entity (another organisation) or a cause (a political agenda) other than the insider's organisation. This sense of commitment is not typically accompanied by negative emotion. In fact, there is a very deliberate, carefully thought-out plan to execute the theft, which suggests a low level of emotionality. Thus, one might describe the distinction between entitled independents' and ambitious leaders' motives as the difference between 'hot' and 'cold' – on one hand, entitled independents' actions are accompanied by arousing negative emotions of dissatisfaction and disgruntlement, while ambitious leaders actions are calculated and dispassionate.

The second dimension is the level of organisation of the attack. The ambitious leader undertakes a complex, well-planned, and drawn-out process of recruiting and coordinating other insiders into his or her cause, whereas the entitled independent executes the IP theft typically within a short period of time after the precipitating event, and without much prior planning or coordination.

Since Moore et al. (2011) take a system dynamics perspective, their model assumes that each offender is predisposed to engage in IP theft, but only acts on this propensity once there is some kind of triggering event. In the case of the entitled independent, the catalyst is an event that leads him or her to feel undervalued by the organisation (e.g., being passed over for promotion) and to start to shift his or her loyalties to a new organisation. In the case of the ambitious leader, a proposal by a competing cause or organisation leads him or her to form a plan for the attack in service of the competing organisation. Regardless, both scenarios work on a principle commonly referred to in clinical psychology as the diathesis-stress model. In the diathesis-stress model, individuals have internal attributes (diathesis – e.g., hormone dysregulation) that act as risk factors for certain conditions. The predisposing internal attributes, which could be due to biological, societal, or cultural causes, put the individual at risk for developing the conditions (of illness or clinical symptoms – e.g., anxiety disorders) but only under certain resource-demanding environmental context (stress). In Moore et al.'s (2011) model, both types of insiders are assumed to have predisposing characteristics (diathesis) that lead them to be susceptible to triggering events (stress) such as the loss of a promotion or the proposal from a competing company, which in turn leads to the insider attack.

Furthermore, the principle of differential susceptibility (Belsky, 1997) states that individuals differ in the degree to which they are susceptible to the effects of stressful events. That is, there are varying degrees of risk (diathesis) in a population, such that for certain individuals with greater risk factors (e.g., low socioeconomic status combined with cultural norms for depression, combined with biological vulnerability), the likelihood of developing symptoms are higher than for those individuals with fewer risk factors.

Specifically, according to Moore et al. (2011), the entitled independent has a predisposition that leads him or her to become more easily entitled. However, Moore and colleagues do not go on to discuss what these predispositions might be.

Following the principles of diathesis-stress and differential susceptibility, one might argue that entitled independents possess key personality and person-specific factors that are different from those of ambitious leaders, and that these person-specific factors make entitled independents particularly susceptible to feeling entitled but dissatisfied at work, and to act on their dissatisfaction in ways that are harmful to their organisations. Accordingly, ambitious leaders should also be more likely to possess personality attributes that are different from those of entitled independents, and these attributes should make ambitious leader types more susceptible to counter-proposals from competing organisations, and more willing to engage in deceptive behaviour in service of those competing organisations.

For instance, as argued above, the entitled independent model of IP theft is distinguished from the ambitious leader model by the presence of negative emotionality. This suggests that individuals who are more likely to fall into the role of entitled independent are more reactive to negative emotions, or perhaps are more emotionally unstable. It could be argued that these individuals are less adept at the emotion-regulation aspect of coping with emotionally aversive events. Conversely, individuals who have relatively fewer negative emotions on average, or who have fewer fluctuations in their emotions on a daily basis, or have greater resources for coping with negative emotions would be more likely to be resilient to triggering incidents at work (e.g., being passed over for a promotion, a perception of a lack of respect or injustice in the organisation) that could threaten their loyalty to the organisation. Of course, there is an alternative explanation of events, in which the entitled independent is not necessarily more prone to negative emotionality, but where they have been repeatedly thwarted in their work efforts and general agency by systematic factors, such as an unequitable remuneration or promotion system, exploitative or unappreciative bosses, or corporate indifference. In these cases, however, there would still be mean level differences in negative emotionality between loyal employees and disgruntled ones, albeit differences caused by the immediate work context. Regardless of whether there is a dispositional style towards negative emotionality or there are higher-than normal context-dependent levels of negative emotionality, it seems likely that entitled independents would exhibit higher mean levels than their colleagues.

On the other hand, the ambitious leader model is distinguished by the presence of a high level of organisation. Accordingly, insiders who are emotionally stable, possess sufficient organisational and coordination skills, have a certain degree of influence in the organisation in order to recruit other insiders, and who enjoy the process of planning covert and complicated operations, would be more likely to fall under the ambitious leader model than their more neurotic, less skilled, less organised, and less socially-influential counterparts.

Literature in a wide range of related fields such as that of organisational citizenship behaviours, counterproductive work behaviours, personality psychology, forensic psychology, and business ethics is replete with evidence for profiles of criminal behaviour. These lines of research, while not being directly related to cyber security and/or insider threat might help researchers interested in insider attacks that take place in cyber arenas, particularly when the work includes related insider activities such as fraud and industrial sabotage. For instance, Murphy and Dacin (2011) illustrate the value of constructing overarching dimensions to organise the decision-making processes of perpetrators of fraud. In their framework, individuals first have to become aware that certain behaviours constitute as fraud. Next, the insider needs to make a judgment about whether the fraudulent act is an acceptable behaviour, according to the norms of the organisation. Next, the insider needs to evaluate the relative costs and risks versus the benefits of the fraudulent action. Finally, the insider needs to decide how to deal with the negative emotions (e.g., guilt, shame) that accompany the fraud. If the fraudsters are able to rationalise their actions in a way that minimises personal responsibility for any negative consequences or in a way that diminishes their moral culpability, then they are likely to continue engaging in the fraudulent behaviour.

Murphy and Dacin's (2011) paper reveals some common personality and person-specific dimensions that help to differentiate between different perpetrators of insider attacks. These dimensions are:

- **Awareness**: First, individuals who engage in insider attacks typically possess some minimum degree of social acumen, such that they have awareness of the social norms regarding ethical behaviour within their organisation, as well as the boundaries of acceptable work behaviour. This necessitates a certain level of social, emotional, and analytical intelligence. Furthermore, every organisation's normative culture is idiosyncratic and developed from a combination of the micro-level group dynamics and daily work culture, the larger institutional demands and goals, and macro-level moral, ethical, and social codes within the proximal geographical context. These ethical norms for acceptable work behaviour would be generally endorsed by insiders at all levels of the organisation, implicitly known to all the members of the organisation, and finally, transmitted quickly to any new uninitiated members of the organisation – even though they would not be communicated or immediately obvious to outsiders. As a result, researchers seeking to understand norms for ethical behaviour in an organisation would need to survey a large number of insiders of the organisation from different levels of the organisation structure in order to determine the level of awareness a true insider would need to possess.

- **Value System**: Second, individuals who engage in insider attacks tend to possess a value system that allows them to overlook the goals of their organisation in order to serve their own needs and/or the needs of a competing organisation. Two scenarios could occur. Either the insiders possess a set of values that causes them to place their personal interests above the interests of others (e.g., the value of ambition), or the insiders possess a set of values which conflicts with the normative value system of the organisation (i.e., culturally sanctioned values). Specifically, in the first scenario, employees of an organisation who value personal ambition over communal growth would be more willing to engage in insider activities that damage the interests of their organisation. In the second scenario, employees who possess work goals which conflict with the goals of their work-group would feel alienated from their colleagues, and this alienation could lessen the insiders' allegiance to their group and to their organisation.

- **Negative Emotionality**: Third, as mentioned earlier, insiders who engage in insider attacks are likely to be more susceptible to negative emotions. In personality psychology, generally the disposition to be more reactive to negative emotions such as anxiety, shame, and depression, can either be described by the personality trait of neuroticism (e.g., as assessed by the NEO-FFI; McCrae & Costa, 2004), or by the temperament of negative emotionality. Negative emotionality is assumed to be a stable emotional style that is present at a very young age, even before early socialisation and before the development of language. Hence, personality assessments for negative emotionality and related constructs (e.g., irritability – Stringaris et al., 2012; rumination – Nolen-Hoeksema, 1998; NEO-PI assessed neuroticism – Reise, Smith, & Furr, 2001) could easily be adapted for use in cyber security research.

- **Rationalisation/Moral Disengagement**: Finally, individuals who initiate an insider attack are likely to possess a personality characteristic that allows them to rationalise their actions in a way that absolves them of personal responsibility for any wrongdoing. A candidate personality variable that describes such a process is the dispositional propensity for moral disengagement. Specifically, people differ in the degree to which they disengage from morally dubious outcomes. Insiders who engage in insider attacks could be high in moral disengagement, which lessens their moral culpability for their actions, and this in turn makes it easier for them to continue their attacks. Moore et al. (2012) have developed an 8-item measure of the propensity for moral disengagement that has been used to predict unethical organisational behaviour. Accordingly, this and other conceptually equivalent measures of moral disengagement could be included in screening and personnel assessments. Of relevance are personality profiles of individuals who are more likely to engage in moral disengagement. For instance, individuals who score highly on measures for the 'dark triad' characteristics of psychopathy, Machiavellianism, and narcissism have been found to be more likely to morally disengage and to endorse unethical consumer attitudes (Egan, Hughes, & Palmer, 2015). Certainly, more research is needed on how individual differences in the propensity to morally disengage affect social interactions. Of particular interest would be whether ethical decision-making processes are predicted by the greater tendency to morally disengage, and whether the mode of interaction – face-to-face versus computer-mediated – would moderate these relationships.

RELATING CYBER-BASED INSIDER THREAT AND THREATS FROM RADICALISATION

Broadly speaking, radicalisation refers to the process of individuals becoming increasingly committed to attitudes and behaviours that are judged by larger society as non-normative (Bhui, Warfa, & Jones, 2014; cf. Kruglanski et al., 2014). As Silke (2008) has argued, while the recent burgeoning interest in radicalisation can be attributed to its link to terrorism, not all individuals who become radicalised will eventually engage in terrorist acts. As such, radicalised attitudes and behaviours can include – besides terrorism – extreme criminal activity, participation in religious cults, self-harming behaviour, suicidal ideation, and substance and behavioural addiction, amongst others. When conceptualised in this manner, it is clear that some perpetrators of cyber-based insider criminal activity could be radicalised individuals who see cyberspace as a suitable avenue for accomplishing their focal goals.

As such, as long as there is an accompanying process of personal and/or political transformation into an identity that deviates from the norm and which leads to commitment to intergroup conflict in order to protect the beliefs of the group to which these non-normative ideals are ascribed (cf. Christmann, 2012), the insider threat issue can be viewed using the same lens as the issue of the threat of radicalisation. Using Moore et al.'s (2011) terminology, radicalised insiders would qualify as ambitious leader-types who perpetrate the insider attack in support of some larger organisation. In this case, the 'organisation' refers to the group to which these non-normative ideologies or identities are attributed.

A key finding in radicalisation research is that certain person-specific demographic factors seem to emerge robustly as correlates of radical behaviour – although there is considerable inter-individual variation, broadly speaking, these individuals tend to be male, young (under 25 years old), and highly educated (or at least have some degree of intellectual aptitude in order to contemplate doctrine and ideology) (cf. Young, Rooze, & Holsappel, 2015). The significance of the under-25 age factor is likely due to the possibility that individuals in this age group are actively developing their personal identities, thus this is a sensitive period of life where youth might be more susceptible to the extreme political, social, or theological ideologies that underpin radicalised criminal or terrorist activity. Additionally, the emotional skill set of young males in this age group are also likely to still be developing, which contributes to their vulnerability to the persuasive potential of extremist messages that are often couched in emotionally evocative language.

Besides documenting some of these important person-specific, socioeconomic variables, recent research has also produced some psychologically grounded models of the process of developing radicalised identities (e.g., Doosje & de Wolf, 2010; Moghadam, 2005) that might also present some points of relevance for the present discussion. For instance, in Doosje and de Wolf's (2010) model, the radicalisation process is structured around six levels of increasing radicalisation, in which the earlier levels (0, 1, 2) contain socio-psychological processes tied to how an individual process his/her environment, and the middle and higher levels (3, 4, 5, 6) involve increasing degrees of influence of the group and social context, and the associated ideologies, actors, and mores of the group. In this model, some factors that exist at the lowest levels are directly relevant to personality. For instance, on the ground floor of Doosje and de Wolf's (2010) model, the prominent psychological factors governing entry into a radicalisation process are the individuals' frustration at being deprived or discriminated by society, their feelings of personal uncertainty, either about their identities or their social status, and finally their degree of openness towards the influence of close others.

There are established personality measures for assessing individual differences in the levels of frustration (e.g., Harrington, 2005), in subscription to prevailing social norms and values and degree of identification with the prevailing cultural identity (e.g., Hu, Wang, & Li, 2014; Wan & Chew, 2013), and non-hypnotic or imaginative suggestibility (e.g., Braffman & Kirsch, 2001) which could be useful to researchers interested in assessing individual differences in susceptibility to radicalisation. Furthermore, it is likely that these feelings of deprivation and discrimination, feelings of uncertainty, and an unstable identity accompanied by the intellectual openness would lead insiders to become vulnerable to feelings of entitlement and/or a loss of identification with the organisation to which they belong, and hence be vulnerable to the orchestrations of malicious outsiders who might exploit these insiders' access.

There is a fragmented but highly relevant set of literature on personality, anti-sociality, extremism, and radicalisation that researchers interested in building psychological and personality based models of cyber-based insider threat can refer to. Case studies are particularly useful in this regard (e.g., Mastors & Siers, 2014), as are a wide variety of papers that examine different individual motives for extremism and/or terrorism. For instance, promising examples of constructs examined in these literatures include moral disengagement (cf. Bandura, 2004), frustration and anger (cf. Davie, 1973), honour-based notions of aggression (Nisbett & Cohen, 1996), personal injustice (Moghaddam, 2007), personal uncertainty (Doosje, Loseman, & van de Bos, 2013), need for closure (Kruglanski, Pierro, Mannetti, & de Grada, 2006), self-deception (von Hippel & Trivers, 2011), terror management theory (Pyszczynski, Rothschild, & Abdollahi, 2008), psychopathy and associated traits such as callous-unemotional traits (Kimonis et al., 2008), and anti-social tendencies such as the so-called dark triad (Paulhus, 2014).

To illustrate the relevance of these literatures, let us turn to Kruglanski et al. (2014) who argued that the underlying personal motivation for radicalised individuals is an underlying need for personal significance. This search for personal significance is reminiscent of classic constructs in personality psychology that speak to an intrinsic and universal need for building a sense of self-worth; for example, Maslow's (1943) needs for self-esteem and self-actualisation, Frankl's (2000) *Being* need, and Deci and Ryan's (2000) basic need for competence. In relation to cyber-based insider crime, this quest for personal significance could also drive some individuals belonging to Moore et al.'s (2011) ambitious leader type. Specifically, when the work environment does not contain the necessary means for individuals to feel effective in their environment or to achieve personal meaning, these individuals might become more susceptible to external influences and ideologies that provide a larger significance to their lives, and hence embark on a process of radicalisation.

Finally, as mentioned earlier, case studies of radicalised individuals are particularly useful for theory generation, especially in establishing early detection models, provided that there is enough information about the personal histories of these individuals. These cases studies provide the benefit of determining – albeit retrospectively – trajectories, and examining the dynamic interaction of various personality and person-specific factors in an integrative manner.

Some examples of high profile cases that involved cyber-based insider activity include Edward Snowden, Bradley/Chelsea Manning, and Robert Hanssen. Although none of these individuals mentioned involved violent acts of terrorism and hence are not extreme radicals, I would argue that they could be described as radicalised, given that they all committed their acts of data theft and espionage in the service of an external organisation (the Soviet Union for Hanssen) or identity (transgender identity for Manning; larger American society for Snowden), and possessed varying degrees of feelings of perceived injustice or discrimination (in the case of Snowden, the perceptions of the United States intelligence community's failure to preserve global privacy, and in Manning's case, perceptions of discrimination based on sexual orientation), or deprivation (monetary in Hanssen's case) in their interaction with the institutions (the CIA and NSA for Snowden, the FBI for Hanssen, and the U.S. Army for Manning) to which they belonged, and subsequently betrayed.

For instance, Bradley/Chelsea Manning was a U.S. Army intelligence officer who provided classified military information to the whistle-blower website, WikiLeaks. Written accounts of Manning's case revealed that she was unhappy with having to hide her homosexuality and her transgendered identity given the 'Don't Ask Don't Tell' policy of the U.S. Army, and its hyper-masculine social landscape. Additionally, she perceived some discrimination and injustices in her work life that drove her to become increasingly isolated from other soldiers in her unit. As such, it might be helpful for researchers to study these cases for commonalities in personality and other person-specific characteristics.

GUIDELINES FOR INVESTIGATING CYBER-BASED INSIDER THREAT FROM A PERSONALITY PERSPECTIVE

As personality psychologists interested in cyber-based insider threat, we are in the midst of a field of research that must keep up with a moving target composed of an expanding and rapidly changing group of qualified insiders who are increasingly familiar with information technology, with cyberspace, and the ways to exploit it. Additionally, low bases rates for cyber-based insider activity pose a major challenge to developing models for personality precursors of insider threat behaviour before rather than after an attack. Finally, environments in which cyber-based insider activity occurs are often restricted-access, high-stakes, and low-transparency environments, such as the higher levels in the hierarchy of a multi-national corporation or in national security contexts. As a result, it is often difficult to obtain access to insiders, and even after access is granted, there is a strong likelihood that self-presentational concerns would jeopardise the veridicality of self-report measures of personality. In some cases, peer ratings, direct observations, and other non-self-report measures may require more invasive access into the subject's life than he or she is willing or able to accommodate. Clearly, there are a myriad of difficulties when undertaking research with a personality or person-based perspective on cyber-based insider threat.

In the following section, I discuss three major guidelines for personality based research that might help researchers interested in insider threat and cyber security to improve the psychological realism, and the reliability and validity of their models.

Incorporating the Person-Situation Interaction into Analyses

In order to understand processes related to cyber-based insider attacks from a personality and person-specific perspective, researchers need to develop a more contextualised research approach to understanding the influence of personality variables on behavioural and social outcomes. Specifically, because insider attacks happen usually as a result of a triggering event, the immediate context has a large influence on the initiation as well as maintenance of behaviour that would lead to insider attacks and threats to cyber security. Research that assesses personality variables or demographic factors related to questions of cyber security tends to underemphasise the interaction between the person and the situation as a source of the threat. Specifically, research on offender profiling (e.g., Kapardis & Krambia-Kapardis, 2004; Knapp, Smith, & Sprinkle, 2014) tends to generate types of offenders based on a combination of personality (e.g., traits, motives, cognitive indicators) and person-specific characteristics (e.g., gender, work role, duration with organisation), and uses these combinations of personality dimensions directly as single predictors of insider attacks.

However, as argued above, the integration of the context into understanding the effect of personality on insider attacks is particularly important in cyber-based attacks, since cyber-environments evolve more rapidly than physical environments. The key is to be mindful of the context when applying personality and dispositional measures in predictive models. Given the dynamic interplay between person-factors and the environment, it is unlikely that researchers would be able to comprehensively measure all the relevant dispositional and demographic variables; nonetheless, researchers should still apply prudence and sensitivity when adapting personality based explanations and personality precursors from the research to the immediate context.

Developing Culturally Informed Explanations

Related to the above point, there is a need for more specialised explanations of cyber-based insider threats, particularly explanations that take the local cultural norms, conventions, and values into account. Due to the low base rates for insider attacks and the difficulty of gaining access to insider information within many corporate organisations, extant research has relied heavily on national defence-related sectors for funding and for sources of data on insider attacks (e.g., CERT, CPNI). However, this creates explanations and models that are heavily rooted in the cultural and social mores for acceptable work-related behaviour and for personal ethics. Frequently, as can be seen from Moore et al.'s (2011) work, the insiders create a sense of self-entitlement in order to justify their actions, suggesting that they are at least appreciative of the possible ethical transgressions of their actions. Thus, before using personality to predict behaviour, researchers should take care to establish the meaning of the behaviour, as ascribed to it by significant others within the immediate social context. Researchers should lay the groundwork for every research program by first assessing the norms for acceptable work behaviour, the consensus view of clear transgressions within the organisation, as well as the core ethical principles within the organisation and for the larger cultural milieu.

Moving Away from Correlation-based Research that uses only Reactive Measures of Personality

As discussed above, most research on insider threat and cyber security uses questionnaire measures of personality variables, which are highly susceptible to response biases, self-monitoring and self-presentational concerns, amongst other problems. There are already many well-established measures of personality that are non-self-report – e.g., for motives and for emotions. Researchers would do well to utilise these and other similar instruments. This is not to say that researchers should do away with self-report or questionnaire measures altogether, but to caution against solely relying on self-report data, especially in a sensitive area of study that generates wariness in participants. In general, an approach that uses multiple sources of data (e.g., self, observers, subordinates, superiors, peers), multiple methods of inquiry (e.g., experimental, modelling, content analysis of freely generated text documents, correlational analyses of survey data, behavioural coding) and that relies on interdisciplinary (e.g., mathematical, computer science, information science, psychology, sociology) collaborations should be encouraged.

For instance, the popular corporate practice of having 360-degree assessments of performance appraisal has addressed some of the concerns of self-report, questionnaire, and retrospective assessment. Briefly, the 360-degree assessment method relies on using competence-based survey instruments to solicit confidential evaluations from the full range of working relationships a worker encounters. At minimum, these relationships include those with subordinates, peers, and supervisors. Each targeted individual in turn receives a numerical as well as a descriptive assessment of his/her capability to effectively demonstrate specific competences based on the perceptions of those people with whom he/she closely works with. By relying on the testimonies of the network of close associates, and by triangulating measurement across different sources and perspectives of the work-group (each source involved in different physical or knowledge-based aspects of the production process), the 360-degree approach is able to decrease data distortions due to reporting biases and thus improve the validity and reliability of performance measurement (see Toegel & Conger, 2003, for a more comprehensive discussion of the pros and cons of adopting this assessment method). In the same spirit, there are many merits to incorporate a multi-source approach to personality and psychometric assessment, while still preserving the convenience and ease of administration of questionnaire-based measures.

Specific to the cyber-arena, researchers could also adopt methodologies that have been used by personality and social psychologists interested in social media platforms such as Facebook, Twitter, Instagram, etc. The area of work that is particularly relevant to non-reactive assessments of personality is based on the principle of assessing behavioural residues in naturally occurring verbal content on online social networking sites (see Gosling, Augustine, Vazire, Holtzman, & Gaddis, 2011, for a representative study on assessing personality traits from Facebook activity). Briefly, researchers assume that personality characteristics manifest themselves in behaviours that individuals engage in when participating on these social networking sites. In other words, there is a residue of the traits that is left behind in the observable remnants of online behaviours. Facebook posts, for instance, are a log of online activity and can be collected and analysed for varying degrees of trait-relevant content. This work on coding freely generated content for personality characteristics is not new – there is a long tradition of at-a-distance personality measurement (cf. Winter, 2005) of individuals who are not easily accessible (e.g., because they are historical figures or because they are socially prominent individuals for which access is difficult to obtain). For instance, researchers have conducted personality assessments of U.S. presidents – e.g., Winter's (2011) assessment of Barack Obama's personality.

Finally, validation of any theories and models should take place ideally by the collection of new data from realistic environments within a different organisation which belongs nonetheless to the same cultural context, rather than by way of simulations or re-analyses of data from the same organisation. This practice will improve the validity of models, as well as provide greater generalisability for the theories.

REFERENCES

Axelrad, E. T., Sticha, T. J., Brdiczka, O., & Shen, J. (2013). A Bayesian network model for predicting insider threats. In *IEEE Symposium on Security and Privacy Workshops*. San Francisco, CA: IEEE. doi:10.1109/SPW.2013.35

Bagby, R. M., Buis, T., & Nicholson, R. A. (1995). Relative effectiveness of the standard validity scales in detecting fake-bad and fake-good responding: Replication and extension. *Psychological Assessment*, 7(1), 84–92. doi:10.1037/1040-3590.7.1.84

Bandura, A. (2004). The role of selective moral disengagement in terrorism and counterterrorism. In F. M. Moghaddam & A. J. Marsella (Eds.), *Understanding terrorism: Psychosocial roots, causes and consequences* (pp. 121–150). Washington, DC: American Psychological Association. doi:10.1037/10621-006

Belsky, J. (1997). Theory testing, effect-size evaluation, and differential susceptibility to rearing influence: The case of mothering and attachment. *Child Development*, 68(4), 598–600. doi:10.2307/1132110

Bhui, K., Warfa, N., & Jones, E. (2014). Is violent radicalisation associated with poverty, migration, poor self-reported health and common mental disorders? *PLoS ONE*, 9(3), 1–10. doi:10.1371/journal.pone.0090718

Braffman, W., & Kirsch, I. (2001). Reaction time as a predictor of imaginative suggestibility and hypnotizability. *Contemporary Hypnosis*, 18(3), 107–119. doi:10.1002/ch.224

Cappelli, D., Moore, A., & Trzeciak, R. (2012). *The CERT guide to insider threats: How to Prevent, Detect, and Respond to Information Technology Crimes*. Boston, MA: Pearson Education, Inc.

Cervone, D., Shoda, Y., & Downey, G. (2007). Construing persons in context: On building a science of the individual. In Y. Shoda, D. Cervone, G. Downey, Y. Shoda, D. Cervone, & G. Downey (Eds.), *Persons in context: Building a science of the individual* (pp. 3–15). New York, NY: Guilford Press.

Chang, M., & Lim, Y. (2014). Late disclosure of insider trades: Who does it and why? *Journal of Business Ethics*, 1–13.

Christmann, K. (2012). *Preventing religious radicalisation and violent extremism: A systematic review of the research evidence*. London: Youth Justice Board.

Cooper, M. L., Barber, L. L., Zhaoyang, R., & Talley, A. E. (2011). Motivational pursuits in the context of human sexual relationships. *Journal of Personality*, 79(6), 1031–1066. doi:10.1111/j.1467-6494.2010.00713.x

Costa, P. T. Jr, & McCrae, R. R. (1994). Stability and change in personality from adolescene through adulthood. In C. F. Halverson, G. A. Kohnstamm, & R. P. Martin (Eds.), *The developing structure of temperament and personality from infancy to adulthood* (pp. 139–150). Hillsdale, NJ: Erlbaum.

Davie, J. C. (1973). Aggression, violence, revolution and war. In J. N. Knutsen (Ed.), *Handbook of political psychology* (pp. 234–260). San Francisco, CA: Jossey-Bass.

Deci, E. L., & Ryan, R. M. (2000). The 'what' and 'why' of goal pursuits: Human needs and the self-determination of behaviour. *Psychological Inquiry, 11*(4), 227–268. doi:10.1207/S15327965PLI1104_01

Doosje, B., & de Wolf, A. (2010). *Dealing with radicalism: A psychological analysis.* Amsterdam: SWP.

Doosje, B., Loseman, A., & van de Bos, K. (2013). Determinants of radicalization of Islamic youth in the Netherlands: Personal uncertainty, perceived injustice, and perceived group threat. *The Journal of Social Issues, 69*(3), 586–604. doi:10.1111/josi.12030

Duggan, C. (2004). Does personality change and, if so, what changes? *Criminal Behaviour and Mental Health, 14*(1), 5–16. doi:10.1002/cbm.556

Egan, V., Hughes, N., & Palmer, E. J. (2015). Moral disengagement, the dark triad, and unethical consumer attitudes. *Personality and Individual Differences, 76*, 123–128. doi:10.1016/j.paid.2014.11.054

Fiedler, K., Messner, C., & Bluemke, M. (2006). Unresolved problems with the "I," the "A" and the "T": Logical and psychometric critique of the Implicit Association Test (IAT). *European Review of Social Psychology, 17*(1), 74–147. doi:10.1080/10463280600681248

Frankl, V. (2000). *Recollections: An autobiography.* New York, NY: Perseus Books.

Gosling, S., Augustine, A. A., Vazire, S., Holtzman, N., & Gaddis, S. (2011). Manifestations of personality in online social networks: Self-reported Facebook-related behaviors and observable profile information. *Cyberpsychology, Behavior, and Social Networking, 14*(9), 483–488. doi:10.1089/cyber.2010.0087

Graber, E. C., Laurenceau, J., & Carver, C. S. (2011). Integrating the dynamics of personality and close relationship processes: Methodological and data analytic implications. *Journal of Personality, 79*(6), 1101–1137. doi:10.1111/j.1467-6494.2011.00725.x

Harrington, N. (2005). The frustration discomfort scale: Development and psychometric properties. *Clinical Psychology & Psychotherapy, 12*(5), 374–387. doi:10.1002/cpp.465

Hu, F., Wang, P., & Li, L. (2014). Psychometric structure of the Chinese Multiethnic Adolescent Cultural Identity Questionnaire. *Psychological Assessment, 26*(4), 1356–1368. doi:10.1037/a0037690

Hull, C. L. (1943). *Principles of behavior.* Oxford, England: Appleton-Century.

James, W. (1890). *The principles of psychology* (Vol. I). New York, NY, US: Henry Holt and Co. doi:10.1037/11059-000

John, O. P., & Srivastava, S. (1999). The Big Five trait taxonomy: History, measurement and theoretical perspectives. In L. A. Pervin & O. P. John (Eds.), *Handbook of personality: Theory and Research* (pp. 102–138). New York, NY: The Guildford Press.

Kapardis, A., & Krambia-Kapardis, M. (2004). Enhancing fraud prevention and detection by profiling fraud offenders. *Criminal Behaviour and Mental Health, 14*(3), 189–201. doi:10.1002/cbm.586

Kimonis, E. R., Frick, P. J., Skeem, J. L., Marsee, M. A., Cruise, K., Munoz, L. C., & Morris, A. S. et al. (2008). Assessing callous-unemotional traits in adolescent offenders: Validation of the inventory of callous-unemotional traits. *International Journal of Law and Psychiatry, 31*(3), 241–252. doi:10.1016/j.ijlp.2008.04.002

Knapp, J. R., Smith, B. R., & Sprinkle, T. A. (2014). Clarifying the relational ties of organizational belonging: Understanding the roles of perceived insider status, psychological ownership, and organizational identification. *Journal of Leadership & Organizational Studies, 21*(3), 273–285. doi:10.1177/1548051814529826

Kruglanski, A. W., Gelfand, M. J., Bélanger, J. J., Sheveland, A., Hetiarachchi, M., & Gunaratna, R. (2014). The psychology of radicalization and deradicalisation: How significance quest impacts violent extremism. *Political Psychology, 35*(S1), 69–93. doi:10.1111/pops.12163

Kruglanski, A. W., Pierro, A., Mannetti, L., & de Grada, E. (2006). Groups as epistemic providers: Need for closure and the unfolding of group-centrism. *Psychological Review, 113*(1), 84–100. doi:10.1037/0033-295X.113.1.84

Lilienfeld, S. O., Wood, J. M., & Garb, H. N. (2000). The scientific status of projective techniques. *Psychological Science in the Public Interest, 1*, 27–66.

Lucas, R. E., & Donnellan, M. B. (2011). Personality development across the life span: Longitudinal analyses with a national sample from Germany. *Journal of Personality and Social Psychology, 101*(4), 847–861. doi:10.1037/a0024298

Marcus, B., Lee, K., & Ashton, M. C. (2007). Personality dimensions explaining relationships between integrity tests and counterproductive behavior: Big five, or one in addition? *Personnel Psychology, 60*(1), 1–34. doi:10.1111/j.1744-6570.2007.00063.x

Marcus, B., & Schuler, H. (2004). Antecedents of counterproductive behavior at work: A general perspective. *The Journal of Applied Psychology, 89*(4), 647–660. doi:10.1037/0021-9010.89.4.647

Maslow, A. (1943). A theory of motivation. *Psychological Review, 50*(4), 370–396. doi:10.1037/h0054346

Mastors, E., & Siers, R. (2014). Omar al-Hammami: A case study in radicalization. *Behavioral Sciences & the Law, 32*(3), 377–388. doi:10.1002/bsl.2108

Mauss, I. B., Evers, C., Wilhelm, F. H., & Gross, J. J. (2006). How to bite your tongue without blowing your top: Implicit evaluation of emotion regulation predicts affective responding to anger provocation. *Personality and Social Psychology Bulletin, 32*(5), 589–602. doi:10.1177/0146167205283841

McClelland, D. C. (1987). *Human motivation*. New York, NY: Cambridge University Press.

McClelland, D. C., Koestner, R., & Weinberger, J. (1989). How do self-attributed and implicit motives differ? *Psychological Review, 96*(4), 690–702. doi:10.1037/0033-295X.96.4.690

McCrae, R. R., & Costa, P. J. Jr. (2004). A contemplated revision of the NEO Five-Factor Inventory. *Personality and Individual Differences, 36*(3), 587–596. doi:10.1016/S0191-8869(03)00118-1

Miller, C. S., Kimonis, E. R., Otto, R. K., Kline, S. M., & Wasserman, A. L. (2012). Reliability of risk assessment measures used in sexually violent predator proceedings. *Psychological Assessment*, *24*(4), 944–953. doi:10.1037/a0028411

Mischel, W., & Shoda, Y. (1995). A cognitive-affective system theory of personality: Reconceptualizing situations, dispositions, dynamics, and invariance in personality structure. *Psychological Review*, *102*(2), 246–268. doi:10.1037/0033-295X.102.2.246

Miyamoto, Y., & Ryff, C. D. (2011). Cultural differences in the dialectical and non-dialectical emotional styles and their implications for health. *Cognition and Emotion*, *25*(1), 22–39. doi:10.1080/02699931003612114

Moghaddam, F. M. (2005). The staircase to terrorism: A psychological exploration. *The American Psychologist*, *60*(2), 161–169. doi:10.1037/0003-066X.60.2.161

Moghaddam, F. M. (2007). The staircase to terrorism: A psychological exploration. In B. Bongar, L. M. Brown, L. E., Beutler, J. N. Breckenridge, & P. G. Zimbardo (Eds.), Psychology of terrorism (pp. 69-80). New York, NY: Oxford University Press.

Moore, A. P., Cappelli, D. M., Caron, T. C., Shaw, E. D., Spooner, D., & Trzeciak, R. F. (2011). *A preliminary model of insider theft of intellectual property (Technical report: CMU/SEI-2011-TN-013)*. Pittsburgh, PA: Software Engineering Institute.

Moore, A. P., Cappelli, D. M., & Trzeciak, R. F. (2008). *The "Big Picture" of insider IT sabotage across U.S. critical infrastructures (Technical report: CMU/SEI-2008-TR-009)*. Pittsburgh, PA: Software Engineering Institute.

Moore, C., Detert, J. R., Treviño, L. K., Baker, V. L., & Mayer, D. M. (2012). Why employees do bad things: Moral disengagement and unethical organizational behavior. *Personnel Psychology*, *65*(1), 1–48. doi:10.1111/j.1744-6570.2011.01237.x

Murphy, P. R., & Dacin, M. T. (2011). Psychological pathways to fraud: Understanding and preventing fraud in organization. *Journal of Business Ethics*, *101*(4), 601–618. doi:10.1007/s10551-011-0741-0

Nisbett, R. E., & Cohen, D. (1996). *Culture of honor: The psychology of violence in the South*. Boulder, CO: Westview Press.

Nolen-Hoeksema, S. (1998). The other end of the continuum: The costs of rumination. *Psychological Inquiry*, *9*(3), 216–219. doi:10.1207/s15327965pli0903_5

Nurse, J. R. C., Buckley, O., Legg, P. H., Goldsmith, M., Creese, S., Wright, G. R. T., & Whitty, M. (2014). Understanding insider threat: A framework for characterizing attacks. In *IEEE Computer Society Security and Privacy Workshops*. San Francisco, CA: IEEE. doi:10.1109/SPW.2014.38

Paulhus, D. L. (2014). Toward a taxonomy of dark personalities. *Current Directions in Psychological Science*, *23*(6), 421–426. doi:10.1177/0963721414547737

Probst, C. W., Hunker, J., Bishop, M., & Gollmann, D. (Eds.). (2010). *Insider threats in cyber security*. New York, NY: Springer. doi:10.1007/978-1-4419-7133-3

Pyszczynski, T., Rothschild, Z., & Abdollahi, A. (2008). Terrorism, violence, and hope for peace: A terror management perspective. *Current Directions in Psychological Science, 17*(5), 318–322. doi:10.1111/j.1467-8721.2008.00598.x

Quirin, M., & Bode, R. C. (2014). An alternative to self-reports of trait and state affect: The Implicit Positive and Negative Affect Test (IPANAT). *European Journal of Psychological Assessment, 30*(3), 231–237. doi:10.1027/1015-5759/a000190

Reise, S. P., Smith, L., & Furr, R. M. (2001). Invariance on the NEO PI-R neuroticism scale. *Multivariate Behavioral Research, 36*(1), 83–110. doi:10.1207/S15327906MBR3601_04

Rich, E., Martinez-Moyano, I. J., Conrad, S., Cappelli, D. M., Moore, A. P., Shimeall, T. J., & Wilk, J. et al. (2005). Simulating insider cyber-threat risks: A model-based case and a case-based model. In *Proceedings of the 16th International Conference of the System Dynamics Society*. Quebec City, Canada: System Dynamics Society.

Sackett, P. R., Berry, C. M., Wiemann, S. A., & Laczo, R. M. (2006). Citizenship and counterproductive behavior: Clarifying relations between the two domains. *Human Performance, 19*(4), 441–464. doi:10.1207/s15327043hup1904_7

Salgado, J. (2002). The Big Five personality dimensions and counterproductive behaviors. *International Journal of Selection and Assessment, 10*(1-2), 117–125. doi:10.1111/1468-2389.00198

Scherer, K. T., Baysinger, M., Zolynsky, D., & LeBreton, J. M. (2013). Predicting counterproductive work behaviors with sub-clinical psychopathy: Beyond the Five Factor Model of personality. *Personality and Individual Differences, 55*(3), 300–305. doi:10.1016/j.paid.2013.03.007

Schultheiss, O. C., & Pang, J. S. (2007). Measuring implicit motives. In R. W. Robins, R. C. Fraley, & R. Krueger (Eds.), *Handbook of research methods in personality psychology* (pp. 322–344). New York, NY: Guilford.

Silke, A. (2008). Holy warriors: Exploring the psychological processes of jihadi radicalisation. *European Journal of Criminology, 5*(1), 99–123. doi:10.1177/1477370807084226

Stringaris, A., Goodman, R., Ferdinando, S., Razdan, V., Muhrer, E., Leibenluft, E., & Brotman, M. A. (2012). The Affective Reactivity Index: A concise irritability scale for clinical and research settings. *Journal of Child Psychology and Psychiatry, and Allied Disciplines, 53*(11), 1109–1117. doi:10.1111/j.1469-7610.2012.02561.x

Toegel, G., & Conger, J. (2003). 360-degree feedback: Time for reinvention. *Academy of Management Learning & Education, 2*(3), 297–311. doi:10.5465/AMLE.2003.10932156

von Hippel, W., & Trivers, R. (2011). The evolution and psychology of self-deception. *Behavioral and Brain Sciences, 34*(1), 1–16. doi:10.1017/S0140525X10001354

Wan, C., & Chew, P. Y. (2013). Cultural knowledge, category label, and social connections: Components of cultural identity in the global, multicultural context. *Asian Journal of Social Psychology, 16*(4), 247–259. doi:10.1111/ajsp.12029

Winter, D. G. (1987). Leader appeal, leader performance, and the motive profiles of leaders and followers: A study of American presidents and elections. *Journal of Personality and Social Psychology, 52*(1), 196–202. doi:10.1037/0022-3514.52.1.196

Winter, D. G. (2004). Motivation and the escalation of conflict: Case studies of individual leaders. *Peace and Conflict, 10*(4), 381–398. doi:10.1207/s15327949pac1004_8

Wood, W., & Neal, D. T. (2007). A new look at habits and the habit-goal interface. *Psychological Review, 114*(4), 843–863. doi:10.1037/0033-295X.114.4.843

Young, H. F., Rooze, M., & Holsappel, J. (2015). Translating conceptualizations into practical suggestions: What the literature on radicalization can offer to practitioners. *Peace and Conflict, 21*(2), 212–225. doi:10.1037/pac0000065

ENDNOTES

[1.] The issue of personality stability, personality change, and personality coherence is a perennial topic for discussion, and one that has yet to be irrefutably resolved within the field. Whilst there is relatively high test-retest reliability and relatively high life-span stability for the Big Five personality traits (e.g., Lucas & Donnellan, 2011), contemporary personality psychologists understand that even these traits continue to develop and change over the lifespan and are also susceptible to short term changes due to demand characteristics and 'strong situation' context effects. The predominant view is that of dynamic interactionism, where individuals select, react to, and directly change the environments that they are in depending on their stable dispositional characteristics, and the resulting environments in turn affect the quantity and quality of the dispositional trait that the individuals are expressing.

[2.] However, the sheer number of possible antecedents and habits makes this task tedious, laborious, and challenging. Research that takes the time to catalogue the habits relevant to cyber-based insider crime is surely something worthwhile exploring, but which is likely to be neglected by busy researchers, academics, and policy makers with competing demands and limited time and resources.

[3.] Users of implicit measures of personality should be aware of some of the controversies of implicit measures. Since these are indirect measures of personality, they utilise less obvious measures of psychological constructs – such as reaction time or through content coding of imaginative material. Hence, there is healthy discussion amongst researchers about the psychometric properties of these measures (e.g., Fiedler, Messner, & Bluemke, 2006; Lilienfeld, Wood, & Garb, 2000).

Chapter 7
Getting out of the Armchair:
Potential Tipping Points for Online Radicalisation

Omer Ali Saifudeen
National Security Coordination Secretariat, Prime Minister's Office, Singapore

ABSTRACT

This chapter will explore possible factors (both online and real world) that can 'tip' an 'armchair jihadi' towards real world extremism. This entails examining social psychological research on tipping points that can be translated to the process of radicalisation. Prominent cases of jihadists will then be examined to illustrate the physiognomies behind their tipping points and the applicability of such theories. Finally, strategies to incorporate tipping point mechanisms towards countering violent extremism will be discussed. This chapter emphasises how the key to understanding tipping points in extremism lies in understanding the cognitive, social and emotive barriers to extremist thinking and action. There is thus an imperative need for more research and experimentation on persuasion tactics and in particular tipping points. Extremist counter-narratives can only be successful if they incorporate the energies of youth and other key individuals at the grassroots towards crafting, spreading and adding credibility to counter-narratives.

INTRODUCTION

Online militant jihadi sympathisers are at times reproached by those more active in the real world for being an 'armchair jihadi[1]'. This chapter will begin by exploring the concept of 'tipping points[2]' from a multidisciplinary perspective that analyses the epistemology behind this term and its subsequent development. It will also examine and illustrate via case studies the challenges involved in identifying tipping points in radicalisation cases, and the kind of surface inferences such analyses produce. This will be juxtaposed against the current understanding of attitude shifts based on social psychology, and how the Internet presents an ideal environment for transforming and creating new beliefs. If tipping points do matter in the process of radicalisation, then this inevitably brings in the question of how one goes about identifying them. A framework for identifying tipping points can primarily be of use in extremism risk

DOI: 10.4018/978-1-5225-0156-5.ch007

assessment models that can help identify individuals who are about to move from 'talking about it' to 'doing something'.

This will be followed by further illustrations describing why the Islamic State in Iraq and Syria's (ISIS) messaging strategies have been so persuasive and how jihadi messaging has incorporated strategies for creating tipping points towards an extremist trajectory. Finally, the chapter will explore practical applications for countering violent extremism that can be built around the concept of the tipping points and resultant factors for creating persuasive messaging. This will culminate towards suggestions for reworking current counter-narrative strategies. These suggested changes aim to promote initiatives for the development of effective and credible counter-narratives, platforms that can reach and resonate with targeted individuals at risk, and the creation of an exponential counter-extremism momentum with the potential to overwhelm extremist voices and arguments.

EPISTEMOLOGY OF TIPPING POINTS

One of the earliest uses of the term 'tipping points' in sociology can be seen in the pioneering work of Morton Grodzins who observed how in a particular neighbourhood in the late 1950s, white individuals who lived in areas dominated by non-whites started moving out in droves when the number of non-whites exceeded a certain threshold (Grodzins, 1958, 2007; "The original tipping point", 2009). Mark Granovetter (1978) later expanded on this concept in his threshold model. In this model, Granovetter stated that individual behaviour is contingent on those who are already partaking in that behaviour. It is not simply about following others or about being influenced by them. Rather, the tipping point depends on the number of individuals who eventually ascribe to the act and is based on a cost-benefit calculation for partaking in the act or leaving it.

Applying this to the radicalisation process, an individual may choose to join an extremist group at a threshold point where the cost of partaking is low compared to the benefits of being in the group, and vice-versa for leaving. Different individuals naturally have varying thresholds (Granovetter, 1978). The key contribution from the threshold model is in revealing the importance of barriers to action as compared to simply focusing on forces of attraction. These barriers (i.e., threshold points) are in fact synonymous with the idea of what tipping points actually constitute. Over time, social interaction models have also recognised that one's choices are at times dependant on the choices of others following their interactions, and this leads to a complex dynamic with 'multiple equilibrium and tipping points' (Card, Mas, & Rothstein, 2007).

Various disciplines in social psychology have attempted to elucidate the myriad factors leading to this elusive tipping point. What is less emphasised are the factors that keep this individual at 'equilibrium'. Again in reference to the radicalisation process, this would refer to the competing forces that balance and maintain the individual at a particular stage of radicalisation. The Cyber Extremism Orbital Pathways (CEOP) model is essentially an inferential pathway model for online radicalisation based on the characteristics of the Internet (Saifudeen, 2014). The rationale for using circular orbits in this model is to emphasise how for every stage of radicalisation, there are competing forces that maintain that stage and keep it in equilibrium. However, there can be influences which culminate towards tipping points that upset the equilibrium at each stage of radicalisation. These influences ultimately steer an individual who may have initially only harboured radical thoughts at the cognitive level towards actual violent behaviour.

Identity tensions as a result of socially imposed identities coming into conflict with personal identities is one of many equilibrium breaking tipping point influences. Thomas Schelling's work on segregation taps on the notion of 'meaningful differences' such as gender, age, race, ethnicity, language, sexual orientation or religion (Martinez, 2005; Schelling, 1971). Schelling observed how seemingly small, innocuous personal or group preferences based on such differences may lead to a chain of events and a cycle of segregation with a self-sustaining momentum (Schelling, 2006). Schelling's work demonstrates how minor and seemingly insignificant choices and actions by individuals or groups may often evolve into considerable unintended consequences for the larger collective (Schelling, 2006).

Applying Schelling's idea to the radicalisation process would involve asking what other attributes can constitute 'meaningful differences'? Such differences could extend to political preferences or even one's position on controversial issues. The supposition is that resultant effects based on any meaningful difference can be overwhelming and exponential. For instance, an individual who is not radical or extremist to begin with, may get caught in resultant waves of overpowering events sparked by identity issues emphasising such differences, despite having neutral thoughts to begin with. The emphasis here is on the self-sustaining momentum seemingly insignificant events or individual actions can have, when they touch on meaningful differences stemming from in-group or individual preferences. The limits of tolerance over tensions created by such meaningful differences is the tipping point in this case, and tipping points can take a life of their own once they begin. This is why knowing what can constitute tipping points is crucial as one event or narrative that overwhelms cognitive barriers sustaining prior notions and limits of acceptance is all that is needed to produce an exponential wave of changes.

This viral effect of tipping points can be of value to counter-radicalisation projects. For the counter-radicalisation process, this can come in the form of 'narratives of disillusionment[3]' that makes the individual rethink his or her extremist path (see Venugopala, 2014). If a powerful enough narrative of disillusionment can be constructed based on perhaps one or a few significant meaningful differences, then the resultant viral effect will allow just a few narratives to have far-reaching consequences against a whole range of extremist arguments. The current drawback with a lot of counter-narrative strategies is that they can end up in a narrative 'arms race' or war of attritions countering each point posed by extremists with another.

If the idea of tipping points were to be employed, then a far more efficient strategy for counter-narratives would be to incorporate only a few viral tipping points against extremist narratives, which are then strategically placed in appropriate platforms to have far-reaching effects against a whole range of extremist narratives. The viral effect of such counter-narrative tipping points will do the rest of the job. As a working reference for the chapter, tipping points for radicalisation are to be seen either as strategic influences/occurrences that can shift attitude or behaviour or as a threshold that needs to be crossed before an attitudinal or behavioural shift occurs.

AN ILLUSTRATION OF TIPPING POINTS IN FOREIGN FIGHTER RADICALISATION

Months went by; I got involved in work and in a daily routine life, however, I kept watching mujahidin videos. In one of these days, and after I returned from work at night, I watched a YouTube video[4] that was released by Jabhat al-Nusra … this video has changed me forever. This video was like a lightning that hit my heart in a way that brought it to life again[5]. (Saudi Foreign Fighter, Abu Thabit al-Jazrawi)

Taken at face value, the above quote apparently demonstrates how just one idea disseminated over cyberspace can create the cognitive opening leading to real world actions. However, Abu Thabit in this case did not immediately jump into joining the Syrian jihad after watching the video. Apparently only after some time had passed and after further discourse with one of his friends who returned from Syria, did he firmly decide that he would attempt to go for jihad in Syria.

The case example of Abu Thabit is being used here to raise a number of questions on the process of how tipping points contribute to radicalisation. The quote below by Abu Thabit describes his initial forays into the jihadi world prior to the events in Syria:

… I was visited by one of my friends who started to show me mujahidin releases. I pretended that I was touched with what I saw, but deep inside me I didn't want to be involved in jihad, moreover, I wasn't even a committed Muslim as I used to shave my beard. This friend kept his attempts with me, until I was guided to the right path in 2009, and gradually I became more committed until the events of the Levant took place. ("Hijrah to the Islamic State", 2015, p. 28)

If an idea presented in the Jabhat al-Nusra video featured on YouTube was the defining trigger for Abu Thabit, would it have been as effective if the preceding activities contributing to the infusion of extremist ideas had not taken place, and what exactly was this idea that caused an epiphany? Abu Thabit was already exploring extremist ideas by exposing himself to mujahidin videos prior to being awestruck by the video in question. However, what the video managed to achieve was to introduce a new idea to Abu Thabit that being sympathetic or having beliefs alone was not enough – beliefs needed to be demonstrated (Carré, 2003; Qutb & Salahi, 1979); "I finally realised that Qur'an and the sword [should work] together" ("Hijrah to the Islamic State", 2015, p. 28).

The second question that arises from the case example of Abu Thabit is whether his online triggers were propped up by real world influences. Abu Thabit was already exposed to the worldviews of political Islam and supportive of the idea of militant jihad, even though his early worldview was almost anti Al-Qaeda. Abu Thabit mentioned,

When I was 15, I used to think of Usama bin Ladin as the person who transferred the reality of this umma to a nightmare. He is the reason behind all the problems of the Islamic world. Although I used to like Khattab[6] and the old day of jihad, but I never supported the Manhattan raid [the 9/11 attacks]. During the events that took place in Saudi Arabia when al-Miqrin[7] waged his campaign, I believed that we had to expel terrorists [out of Saudi Arabia]. ("Hijrah to the Islamic State", 2015, p. 28)

One of his initial tipping points was when one of his real world contacts first introduced him to the world of mujahidin releases and alternative perspectives. There was no pause to this kind of jihadi exposure by his real world friends until he reached a point that was akin to a 'stable' sympathiser.

Finally taking a step back even further, what was the personal and social historical context under which Abu Thabit's cognitive triggers were able to work so effectively? The socio-political landscape of Saudi Arabia has historically been receptive to the idea of militant jihad in foreign theatres of conflict. This was an accepted idea in Abu Thabit's society[8], provided that the 'jihad' did not threaten the monarchy and worked against its enemies instead (Boghardt, 2014; Hegghammer, 2010). Thus, Abu Thabit's predisposition to the idea of militant jihad for a legitimate cause is a manifestation of this inherent socio-political environment, as evidenced by him citing how he "used to like Khattab and the old day of jihad" ("Hijrah to the Islamic State", 2015, p. 28).

This case example demonstrates how problematic the concept of tipping points is when applied to the process of radicalisation. The first conundrum we run into from this example is whether the apparent tipping point that led Abu Thabit towards real world action was the only one. Were there many other tipping points or cognitive triggers prior to and after the video that resulted in his move to the Syrian jihad, and how can one possibly identify these tipping points apart from making narrative inferences? Secondly, would this tipping point been as effective if there was no continual reinforcement or ideological grooming by real world or online influencers? Finally, would the tipping point be as effective if the socio-political environment he was in was not conducive to the idea of militant jihad?

A prelude to answering these questions would require an examination of how attitudinal shifts occur, and what creates the impetus for corresponding behaviour. For now, based on the case example of Abu Thabit, we have the following preliminary inferences:

- There is no one tipping point, but many with perhaps varying effects. The confluence of all of them results in the expected behaviour.
- These tipping points cannot work in isolation. They require reinforcement from influential actors, narratives or situations. We can assume for now that without such reinforcement, counter-acting forces could upset any behavioural trajectories initiated by these tipping points.
- Tipping points work better when there is a conducive environment for the behaviour trajectory.

WHAT CAUSES ATTITUDINAL SHIFTS?

Carl Jung defines attitude as a "readiness of the psyche to act or react in a certain way" (as cited in Lenhart, 1996). Attitudes can also be viewed as how one approves or disapproves any entity, occurrence or issue (McLeod, 2009). Icek Ajzen's Theory of Planned Behaviour (TPB) takes this further to illustrate how beliefs shape attitude and subsequent behaviour. He describes three kinds of beliefs (Ajzen, n.d.). One is 'behavioural belief', which is the subjective probability of a behaviour actually manifesting in an expected outcome. People naturally have many beliefs and they do not turn to all of them at once in a given situation; there is thus a limited set of accessible beliefs. However, there are salient beliefs that dominate one's thinking and are the ones most accessed (Chaiken, 1999). Behavioural belief, in combination with accessible salient beliefs, shapes the prevailing attitude towards behaviour. This attitude towards a particular behaviour can be either positive or negative, and also takes outcome into consideration (Chaiken, 1999).

'Normative beliefs' are the perceived behavioural expectations of significant individuals in one's life. Normative beliefs, combined with an individual's motivation to conform according to these significant individuals, determine the subjective norm. The subjective norm is thus based on the social pressure to partake or not partake in certain behaviour (Chaiken, 1999).

'Control beliefs' help or hinder the execution of a particular behaviour. The perceived power of each of these 'controls' plays a part in whether the behaviour is actually manifested. Perceived behavioural controls refer to one's perception of his/her ability to carry out a given behaviour. Intention precedes actual behaviour and is a reflection of one's readiness to carry out that behaviour. Actual behavioural control refers to how much one has the skills, resources, and other attributes needed to carry out a given behaviour. Finally, the end result behaviour is simply the cumulative manifestation of all these factors and beliefs, and is the observable response of the individual in question (Chaiken, 1999).

If the idea of a tipping point were to be applied to the TPB model, then one might want to look at junctures where these three belief categories (i.e., behavioural, normative, control) could possibly shift. One theoretical inference based on the characteristics underpinning these belief categories would point to issues of accessibility, social expectations and controls as possible determinants of a tipping point. Put simply, one would need to create a situation where such behaviours can actually be realised with any barriers (individually or socially imposed) minimised or removed. It would also require an environment with influential individuals that promote such behaviour. The Internet is one such ready environment that provides all these determinants. However to partake in the planned behaviour, the influence of the online environment becomes contingent on real world issues of accessibility.

HOW THE INTERNET CONTRIBUTES TO ATTITUDINAL SHIFTS

There are characteristics of the Internet that enhance one's beliefs, attitude and corresponding behaviour. The CEOP model suggests three triggers that cause one to shift attitudes.

The first entails a case of loss of credibility or doubt in the ideas or solutions proposed by the current worldview one ascribes to. It is referred to as a 'cognitive rethink' which leads one to question accepted norms and beliefs (Saifudeen, 2014). The online realm presents many opportunities for a cognitive re-think, given the multitude of ideas one can encounter that can offer a credible challenge to one's present worldview. Furthermore, the slackening or total relinquishment of social restrictions and inhibitions due to the online disinhibition effect creates an environment where the individual is able to experiment with a whole array of alternate ideas with little regard for repercussions on oneself or consequences affecting others (Suler, 2004). A lot of emotive triggers affecting cognition can also thrive on the Internet given the multitude of sources for emotion laden visual stimuli. There is also some realisation now that both emotion and cognition working evenly and in unison can contribute to resultant thinking and behaviour (Gray, Braver, & Raichle, 2002). What needs to be stressed here is that in many ways, the Internet is the realm for counterculture (Breton, 2000), and there are many opportunities for both cognitive as well as emotional triggers stemming from alternate ideas to thrive on the Internet.

Attitudinal shifts can also occur when social ties with the population in one's current real world or online environment start to ebb or when bad relations arise with 'significant others' in that environment. This in the CEOP model is referred to as 'resonance loss' (Saifudeen, 2014). Over the Internet whenever resonance loss occurs, there are many options for alternate forms of socialisation online. Furthermore, there is recourse to various countercultures that espouse alternate norms and values that may be preferred by the individual.

Finally, attitudinal shifts online are more likely to occur when 'social anchors' like one's lifestyle, family or career, which entrench one to the present population and their worldviews, become consider-ably weaker or less important (Saifudeen, 2014). Conversely, online counterculture social anchors might at the same time become stronger and create new social anchors within the new sub-culture.

The concept of cognitive rethink, resonance loss, and social anchors are adaptations that leverage on major socio-psychological theories that have attempted to explain attitudinal change ("Theories of Attitude Change", 2001). These include:

- Consistency theories such as Balance Theory (Himmelfarb & Eagly, 1974; Kiesler, Collins, & Miller, 1969; O'Keefe, 1990) which emphasise the individual's need to maintain consistency with various attitudes and behaviours. This can include the positive or negative attitudes of others who perceive them (Heider, 1958).
- Learning theories (Hovland, Janis, & Kelley, 1953) which look at how attitudes persist unless they are provided with new learning experiences or conditioning. For learning theories, persuasive communications play a major part.
- Social judgement theories (Eagly & Chaiken, 1993) which emphasise the importance of entrenched prior attitudes and how it can serve as a judgemental anchor that determines the extent to which new attitudes are accepted – depending how close they are to one's initial position.
- Functional theories (Katz, 1960) which place emphasis on the function that the attitude plays. New attitudes are likely to be accepted when there is a need or utility value to be gained by moving towards this new attitude position.

Cognitive rethink borrows on learning theories, which entail the importance of new ideas in forming new attitudes. It also entails the incorporation of functional theories especially when new ideas offer to achieve the utility or need in question. On the Internet, this utility can be in the form of instant gratification that one is seeking (voyeurism, being able to express repressed angst, etc.), or quick answers to difficult questions that were not credibly answered by others. Such needs and utilities may not be achievable in the real world. Resonance loss emphasises the acceptance of an attitude within the social milieu in question, and borrows on consistency theories. Social anchors emphasise the importance of prior attitudes towards an object or relationship. This can be one's lifestyle or relationship with key individuals, and borrows on social judgement theories.

All three 'attitude change' triggers in the CEOP model (cognitive rethink, resonance loss, and social anchors) can be drilled down towards looking at attitude change by virtue of appealing to one's reasoning (logic), emotions, or relationships. The Internet offers a dynamic platform where avenues for attitude change as a result of all three factors are easily accessible, and with a wide range of options. The availability of such easily accessible options entrenches the Internet as an instrument and platform with a high capacity for attitude change.

IDENTIFYING THE ELUSIVE 'TIPPING POINT' IN RADICALISATION

Going back to the example of Abu Thabit, we see how his belief is incrementally reinforced (both online and real world) to the point when the last barrier to action is removed. In his case, this would be the moment when it is put to him that his faith needs to be demonstrated by action. Thus one possible way to identify tipping points leading to extremist behaviours would require examining barriers to escalating extremist attitudes and action, rather than focusing primarily on motivations. For instance, they can be belief barriers arising out of parental objection to militant jihadism, doubt over one's ability to undertake such violent actions, uncertainty of one's ability to carry out the journey to jihadi theatres or simply fear of 'loss' (i.e., this can be anything from fear over losing aspects of one's life to fear of harming those who matter in one's life due to one's actions).

The case of Roshonara Choudhry[9] offers another illustration of how these barriers were overcome. In her case, it was an online video by Abdullah Azzam that apparently tipped that last cognitive barrier, namely her initial belief that women need not partake in actual militant jihad. The message by Azzam helped to remove this cognitive barrier when he declared in his video that jihad was the individual duty of every able man, woman and child to defend Muslim lands (Carter, 2013; Dodd, 2010).

However, we do not know enough about other intrinsic barriers Roshonara might have overcome before proceeding to attack MP Stephen Timms. It could have perhaps been the actions she did to reassure herself that her family would be all right, no matter what happened to her, that helped to remove one such barrier – she paid off her school fees and any debts her family and siblings might have had. What would be more interesting to find out is not why martyrdom was more appealing to her, but rather why she felt her existing life was no longer one to look forward to or strive towards. The latter might represent the key tipping point if there were far more 'push' factors in her life and environment as compared to 'pull' factors that made the extremist option more attractive.

If we assume there are multiple tipping points in one's radical journey, then the move towards more extremist actions could either be the cumulative effect of push factors towards such actions that overwhelm pull factors (i.e., attractiveness of alternate actions) or barriers/opportunity costs keeping one away from it. Such competing forces exist in online communities as well (Chang, Liu, & Chen, 2014). A move towards extremism could also happen during a temporal state of such imbalance, and actual behaviour during this period might serve to reinforce such beliefs if the extremist action is successful or encouraged (McLeod, 2015). Thus, tipping points as a result of push/pull factors are most effective during a weakening of barriers to such behaviour, or when cost calculations predict a high degree of success. The latter is in line with research concerning positive reinforcement and operant conditioning (McLeod, 2015).

INCORPORATING TIPPING POINTS INTO EXTREMISM RISK ASSESSMENT TOOLS

The Violent Extremist Risk Assessment or VERA (see Pressman, 2009) based on a structured professional judgement (SPJ) protocol was designed to be applied to individuals with a history of extremist violence, or having been convicted for terrorist offences for the purpose of determining their propensity for future extremist violence or potential for rehabilitation. VERA-2 (see Pressman & Flockton, 2012) delineates the risk assessment factors according to five categories specific to violent extremism, namely attitude items (e.g., attachment to ideology justifying violence), context and intent items (e.g., user of extremist websites), history and capability (e.g., prior criminal violence/experience), commitment and motivation (e.g., being driven by the thrill and adventure that militancy might offer), protective items (e.g., having access to significant other/community support to deter them), and demographic items (e.g., sex, marital status, age). VERA-2 also provides a scoring guide for rating each of the items in this category as 'low', 'moderate' or 'high' (Pressman & Flockton, 2012).

If we incorporate intrinsic barriers to violence as a possible tipping point that needs to be breached for radicalisation to take place, then the focus would skew towards looking at the intrinsic factors in the 'protective items' category that hinder one from pursuing the extremist track – i.e., mitigation of extremist risk (Pressman & Flockton, 2012). Adapting the concept of tipping points and VERA 2 to specifically assess at-risk 'fence-sitters' in online communities would then require us to utilise factors in the 'protective items' group as they could represent thresholds/tipping points to radicalisation that are easier to track than the myriad number of factors that promote radicalisation.

To demonstrate how this could be applied for assessing specific online communities, take for example the 'rejection of violence to obtain goals' criteria that comes under the category of 'protective items'. If the violence rejection criteria were to be applied to assess an online community or platform, and it was revealed that:

1. The majority of members,
2. Prominent members with a lot of followers,
3. The administrator[10] setting the tone for the discussions,

did not advocate violence despite sympathising with radical grievances, then the online community or platform being assessed could be rated low in its capacity to produce members who would tip towards violence. This is because factors 1-3 act as a bulwark against any radicalising influences, and changes to any of these factors might 'tip the balance'. What is needed is further research aimed at looking for other protective factors specific to online communities premised on the concept of intrinsic barriers. This could then be extended towards developing an actuarial assessment tool specifically for assessing suspected online communities where fence-sitters congregate, and may potentially get radicalised.

ISIS AND ITS POSITIONING AND MARKET SEGMENTATION STRATEGIES FOR PERSUASIVE ONLINE MESSAGING

In a recent study (see Penrose, 2014) analysing ISIS YouTube video clips targeting those from the West, established ideas about social media, theories of persuasion, and the 'psychology of scarcity' came into question. The videos analysed in this study featured 'target audience native speakers' speaking in a calm and rational manner that challenged socially constructed conventional perceptions of a fanatical extremist (Penrose, 2014). Furthermore, these videos were professionally done in a manner that might make it identifiable with Western mainstream media (Penrose, 2014).

It was also evident from this study that ISIS media or that of ISIS 'fanboys' took into mind their intended objective or target audience to determine the message, 'tone of voice', and type of production value. They were clearly demarcating desired audience segments akin to how public relations firms might go about it. In these aspects, their media tactics were unprecedented as compared to other Middle Eastern extremist organisations. They were also deliberately targeting the young, and Western social media accounts were ripe targets to recruit for their propaganda efforts (Penrose, 2014).

The study also revealed a number of counter-intuitive findings. One had to do with the viewer numbers of these video clips featuring Western foreign fighters. These numbers were low compared to ISIS videos done by associated accounts, and ISIS videos meant for large mass distribution via Twitter. The study found that such low 'hits' combined with professional production and audience segmentation was meant to leverage on the social psychology concept of scarcity (i.e., the idea being that if the item was hard to come and scarce, it will be valued highly), and make the audience feel as they were part of a highly select group that got to see these messages (Worchel, Lee, & Adewole, 1975). It seemed that only select 'dummy' social media profiles set up in the study that seemed to match ISIS recruitment patterns were given 'private invitations' to view such exclusive content. This demonstrates how online ISIS propagandists have a demographic and behaviour selection bias for online recruits.

These dummy accounts, when active online, were then invited to add temporary ISIS accounts to their profiles that allowed them to have exclusive access to the content. The ISIS accounts issuing the invites themselves were temporal in nature (Penrose, 2014). The study suggested that ISIS had found a niche via YouTube for recruitment and testing the usefulness of audience targeting (Penrose, 2014). Twitter on the other hand was used for large-scale information dissemination (Penrose, 2014). They also knew how to attach their Twitter accounts with popular social media campaign to get more notice (Nordland, 2014).

JIHADI MESSAGING USING TIPPING POINTS

Malcolm Gladwell in his aptly named book titled 'the tipping point: how little things can make a big difference' emphasises three concepts for creating messages and ideas that go 'viral' and win many advocates (Crossman, n.d.; Gladwell, 2000). These concepts can also be used to explain the wide reach and appeal of online extremist jihadi materials.

Law of the Few

This is meant to illustrate how certain people are key points for information dissemination and/or because of their extensive networks, are able to make an idea go viral. ISIS social media fanboys are perfect examples of how a few strategically placed 'connectors' have been instrumental in having their propaganda have the reach it has today.

Jihadists who offer experiential accounts to bring jihad experience closer to their audience and offer practical knowledge based on this experience represent the 'Mavens' or 'Information Brokers' (according to Gladwell, 2000). The Maven's deep understanding is a big selling point. Connectors who feature the advice of Mavens are able to create a wide reach for their ideas.

Finally, there are the 'Salesmen' who have the persuasive skills to make a message 'sticky' by framing it to be more simple and attractive than it actually is. Often the idea that sells is one that is easily understandable and appeals to basic logic and ideals. Good Salesmen know how to target the 'essentials' the customer is actually looking for. This is no different for persuasive online jihadi advocators. Radical preacher Anwar al-Awlaki is an example of a Salesman who in his lectures was able to put complex Islamic concepts and doctrines in an easy-to-understand manner that one could find personal alignment with as well (Meleagrou-Hitchens, 2011). He was certainly a Maven as well, given his portrayal of himself as a well-educated Islamic scholar (Meleagrou-Hitchens, 2011). Jihadi social media Connectors were more than happy to feature his videos on their page to extend their reach. Online jihadi Connectors, Mavens, and Salesmen working in unison offer the perfect combination for extremist jihadi ideas to go viral online, and 'tip' whomever comes across it towards their worldview.

The Stickiness Factor

Often, the idea that is persuasive, memorable and sells is the one that gives practical advice and has personal alignment. But in addition to this, it is packaged into bite-sized portions that are easily absorbed, is repetitive at key points and packaged in a manner that incorporates other factors to make the message sticky (e.g., punctuated pauses, a running story line). Some of the more popular Jihadi video clips often incorporate these features. Jihadi narratives sometimes use analogies to package their worldviews into a form that is easy to relate with (Al Raffie, 2012; Lia, 2008). Suicide bomber videos also show the attack repeatedly from multiple angles if necessary to glorify the impact of the attack ("Double Truck Bombing", 2007). Jihadi ideologues such as Anwar al-Awlaki understood the concerns of Western Muslims and their lifestyles (Meleagrou-Hitchens, 2011). He was then able to package his messaging into a storyline that they could relate to.

The Power of Context

This factor emphasises how individuals are highly sensitive to their environment and situational pressures. Certain situations can be so powerful that they can overtake our inherent nature or nurtured predispositions to produce a behaviour that is totally contrary to it. To illustrate this, imagine a well-integrated Muslim youth living in the West who was brought up according to Western cultural norms and values. He or she may already be acclimatised to random incidents of mild or subtle racism, but is able to tolerate it. But one day, this individual encounters an overwhelming situation that puts his/her Muslim identity at the forefront. For example, it can be a case of extreme racist bullying where he/she was taunted or vilified for his/her Muslim identity. Subsequently, it comes as a big surprise to everyone when he or she joins a radical Muslim group when there were apparently no prior warning indicators. The common perception then becomes that this individual 'snapped'.

There are many examples of seemingly innocuous individuals who never demonstrated any penchant for violence who snapped and went on a rampage. It is to be noted that in any case of someone snapping, it is usually the cumulative effect of prior incidents and influences (Swink, 2010). However a single event or situation can contain all the ingredients necessary to overwhelm any built up resistance to contrary behaviours. Thus it is important to keep in mind that any resistance to contrary behaviours get weakened if the attacks are prolonged and constant.

In such a case, it will not take a major incident to tip the balance, and move an individual to behave in a manner that he or she has been resistant to for so long. The power of context reminds us that the key to their snapping or tipping towards violence is not simply the result of a psychological build-up towards a violent outburst, but has a great deal to do with the fact that the individuals remained in the same environment/situation promoting such tensions. The chances of the outburst actually materialising increases with every action the individual does to reinforce the thought – e.g., fantasising about it, or actually taking concrete steps towards fulfilling it such as buying a weapon or finding out information about the victims (Landau, 2009; Swink, 2010).

EXTREMISTS LEVERAGING ON THE INHERENT ADVANTAGE OF THE ONLINE REALM

Extremist counter-narratives, despite innovative attempts to produce 'catchy' messages are still not able to have the same traction as extremist narratives on the Internet that are seemingly more persuasive. This uphill battle that extremist counter-narratives face is partly the result of counter-culture narratives having a distinct advantage by virtue of identifying themselves as alternate voices to an audience that is already distrustful of mainstream sources of information[11] (Venitism, n.d.).

Rushkoff (2002) in his description of the ideals of 'Technological Utopianism' described how netizens who advocate for a free Internet and against censorship have the notion that technology democratises society. People with online technology have greater access to knowledge and skills that previously might have been the purview of the elite. Netizens feel they are now able to hear voices that may have been suppressed in the real world, and are also able to voice their own opinions freely in the online world (Rushkoff, 2002). This creates the impression of an environment where everyone is seemingly equal. This is something which netizens advocating the Internet might feel is severely lacking in the real world.

Riding on this inherent advantage of the online realm, extremist narratives enhance their messaging by incorporating persuasion and messaging techniques which reflect the factors mentioned in earlier sections (i.e., factors which influence attitude, behaviour shifts, and tipping points). This can be seen in many of the propaganda products produced by ISIS social media fanboys who act as a force multiplier for ISIS propaganda. Take for example, the rise in videos produced by ISIS supporters that cites fake news about ISIS (some taken from mainstream sources) to discredit every criticism about ISIS; it is also increasing in popularity[12]. The following encompass the various features of such video narratives that facilitate attitudinal shifts:

- It strategically weaves in the prominent United Kingdom-based Islamist Faizur Rahman[13] only at selected spots. The 'law of the few' applies here.
- It produces a constant bite-sized barrage of factual and verifiable information to support its points. This reinforces earlier points and produces new ideas that appear to credibly challenge earlier perceptions (i.e., learning theories).
- It aligns itself with the broader counter-cultural view of distrusting mainstream information (i.e., social judgement theories).
- Finally, slick video and sound choreography at the start of the video initially ridicules mainstream criticism of ISIS followed by direct contrasts that 'prove' how each mainstream news content presented is 'fake'. This enhances the 'stickiness factor' that catches on the memory of viewers, even if they cannot remember each point. Subsequent ideas then become more believable.

PRACTICAL APPLICATION OF TIPPING POINTS IN COUNTERING VIOLENT EXTREMISM (CVE) ONLINE

Taking a leaf from Gladwell (2000)'s idea of the tipping points entails treating extremist online narratives as an 'epidemic' in which seemingly insignificant and inconsequential details have an overwhelming effect on the message. Similarly, small changes to current messaging strategies can have a huge impact. This should essentially be aimed at finding factors that can help to shift extremist attitudes, inoculate one to never think positively about extremist narratives, or at the very least create obstacles in one's thinking that will prevent one ascribing to violent behaviours[14] as a solution. In this chapter, the label Counter Violent Extremist Messaging (CVEM) is used to describe this whole spectrum of outcomes. But first, we need to identify what these small changes or possible tipping points are.

Retrospective Approach

The first approach to finding CVEM tipping points entails looking at the online narratives of extremists who have actually manifested their intentions into real world actions. This is unfortunately highly contingent on actually having the full set of their online discourses and being able to juxtapose it with significant events and interactions in their real world. It would also help if the subjects themselves voice the key events that led them down the extremist path. But such accounts need to be treated with caution as many of them represent an impression the individual seeks to portray, as part of the extremist propaganda, or to paint a noble picture of oneself.

Complete case study data sets are few and the other main limitation of such an approach would naturally be one of representativeness. This has not stopped many studies from formulating anticipatory inferences based on many of these extremist biographies and accounts. Such inferences derived from data collated from this retrospective approach set the stage for the next approach, which is forward-looking.

Anticipatory Approach

Linguistic Markers

Meloy, Hoffmann, Guldimann, and James (2012) described eight warning behaviours for violence that can be inferred from narratives. Cohen, Fredrik, Lisa and Jonas (2014) proposed how such warning behaviours can be adapted to identify linguistic markers for violence in social media. The warning behaviours are:

1. **Pathway Warning Behaviour:** Any behaviour that demonstrates the collation of information that could be used for an attack or militant actions (e.g., probing questions about roads near key installations, questions on where to meet key personalities).
2. **Fixation Warning Behaviour:** Pathological preoccupation with a person, issue, object etc. usually followed by increasing negative descriptions, an obsession with getting information and detailed facts about the subject.
3. **Identification Warning Behaviour:** This entails identifying oneself with a radical role model, group or radical action that espouses the 'warrior mentality'. The individual portrays oneself as a saviour or hero in a narcissistic and grandiose manner, usually accompanied with a fetish for anything military.
4. **Novel Aggression Warning Behaviour:** An act of violence committed for the first time that usually is indicative of a self-assessment of one's ability to actually carry out the violent act (e.g., a sudden interest in hunting/slaughtering animals, or actually getting into places or situations to test one's ability to fight, or picking up martial arts skills with a particular interest in offensive/attack tactics).
5. **Energy Burst Warning Behaviour:** Noticeable increase in activity monitoring the individual of interest.
6. **Leakage Warning Behaviour:** Actual disclosure of one's intent to commit violence to a third party, usually done implicitly out of bravado or as a threat.
7. **Last Resort Warning Behaviour:** Words that indicate desperation, feeling trapped or that there is no viable recourse other than violence.
8. **Directly Communicated Threat Warning Behaviour:** Implicit or explicit threat directly communicated to the target or law enforcement.

Cohen and colleagues (2014) felt that out of these eight indicators, *leakage*, *fixation*, and *identification* warning behaviours are more likely to be discovered via social media narrative analysis. Incorporating observations from retrospective case studies with such warning behaviours can potentially help determine tipping points which signify an imminent escalation towards real world violence. This is done by analysing the archived online narratives of individuals radicalised online to determine the frequency at which such linguistic markers appear before actual real world violence occurs. However, these linguistic markers are more useful as indicators for violent behaviour rather than indicative of the factors that caused the attitude shift towards extremist ideas in the first place. The latter might entail an experimental approach using social media.

Experimentation

If attitudes are a direct product of experience and conditioning (Cherry, n.d.), then a more forward-looking approach towards CVEM would entail discovering factors that lead to the formation of extremist attitudes, and how these factors can be manifested online.

The precursor to this would be to find a suitable platform where extremist counter-narratives can be tested in an online community where there are predominantly fence-sitters who are at the activist stage, rather than actually making plans for militant actions. These ideas also cannot be explicitly counter-extremist but subtle in their approach. The CEOP model stresses the need to 'seed doubts' in the extremist conversations that are known to be taking place (Saifudeen, 2014). The online identity for such an experiment would also need to be a 'dummy' account meant purely for testing CVEM approaches. A very likely end-result at the onset would be getting kicked out of the online forum or being blacklisted. But the idea is to observe the initial effect of the subtle CVEM narrative being planted. Subsequent dummy accounts can then be used to further test subtle 'doubt-seeding' narratives.

CONCLUSION: RE-WORKING COUNTER-NARRATIVE STRATEGIES BASED ON TIPPING-POINTS

It is now almost axiomatic to say that more effective counter-narratives are needed to stem the growing tide of extremist ideologies. But for the longest time, a lot of counter-narrative approaches have relied on trial-and-error approaches ranging from the conventional to the creative based on well-intended but assumed notions of what would work. In all fairness, dismal results can to some extent be attributed to the difficulties involved in challenging entrenched extremist beliefs, which leverage on popular grievances that are exploited by extremists. Justifications to conventional approaches can also come from the need to have, at the very least, mainstream counter-extremist presence in the online space that would otherwise be totally uncontested.

As noble as these intentions are, they might inevitably end up preaching to the converted. This end-result should not be taken too harshly either as the 'crowding out' of extremist voices by mainstream voices and the inoculation of potential recruits by more louder mainstream voices are vital strategies as well. However, this in itself is not enough to stem the overwhelming influence of online extremist voices despite recognising the fact that extremist voices are the minority (Briggs, Carlile, Shiraz, & Frank, 2015). While it may be true that mainstream voices have to some extent numerical superiority on the Internet (Briggs et al., 2015), Gladwell (2000)'s 'law of the few' reminds us that all it takes is a few influential individuals to turn the tide. The question now is how to apply this same strategy to counter-narratives.

Counter-narratives represent a range of measures to be employed both online and in the real world. Given the blurring of lines today between both realms, it is inconsequential trying to figure out where counter-narratives are best placed. Counter-narrative strategies are needed for both realms, and have to be structured such that they mutually reinforce each other, instead of being isolated strategies. A key arsenal in this would be the identification of factors that would serve as tipping points towards moving away from extremist worldviews. These tipping points are not simply messages and messaging strategies, but would also require identifying platforms and messengers who would be best placed to deliver it (Briggs et al., 2015).

Some of the key recommendations arising from the United Nations Counterterrorism Implementation Task Force (CTITF), Working Group on Use of the Internet for Terrorist Purposes entailed some key recommendations that to this day need to be further reinforced. One would be to "build a hub for deconstructing extremist narratives on the Internet, providing counter narratives and training workshops for practitioners, students, journalists" (United Nations Counterterrorism Implementation Task Force [UN CTITF], 2011). This hub should ideally come from the grassroots and civil society with the government at the most playing a silent facilitation role by providing required resources and tools for such capacity building.

Next, there has to be research to identify online and real world platforms where sympathisers can be best reached, and counter-narratives crafted in such a manner that aligns and credibly addresses their specific grievances and influences. Online industry partners should be roped in to see how their engineering capabilities can be used to create an online environment where search engines are able to display counter-narratives near search results producing extremist content. This can be extended to social media platforms to ensure a counter-narrative appears in the very same space and every time new extremist messages appear on YouTube, Facebook or similar platforms (UN CTITF], 2011). Mobilising and tapping on the creative potential of youth to come up with these counter-narratives is another useful recommendation arising out of the CTITF working group.

But ultimately, the success of a lot of these initiatives mentioned require identifying and 'testing' the kind of message or messaging (incorporating tipping points) that works before launching it. This should be followed up by testing the actual effects of the message or messaging strategy to refine and alter it entirely if necessary. Such an initiative is predicated on designing effective online experiments to test actual counter-narrative messaging and the effects of online disruption techniques (Briggs et al., 2015), instead of relying on untested assumptions about what works. An example of such a CVEM experiment is 'Abdullah X' – a fictional animated character who counters the reasons posted by ISIS to go and fight in Syria. Abdullah X's narratives were inserted into the same online spaces used by extremists, and this resulted in responses that actually advocated countering the reasons cited by him ("Anti-ISIS tests show", 2015).

This is only the beginning. We should keep pushing the boundaries of crafting credible counter-narratives, given the highly dynamic and fluid nature of issues and events that feed extremist thought. The litmus test for the effectiveness for any of such CVEM is whether they are actually noticed and taken seriously enough to warrant a response from extremist sympathisers or the extremists themselves, as was the case for Abdullah X. What such an approach needs is further momentum from multiple online platforms from different regions of the world to allow experiments to test CVEM in extremist online spaces specific to that region. The online space in Southeast Asia has much potential for the incorporation of such experimentation to identify credible CVEM, and the kind of tipping points that will create a counter-extremist momentum. Such an ideological momentum against them is exactly the kind of 'epidemic' extremists fear the worst. This energy created by a dynamic movement[15] behind CVEM initiatives is precisely what we need so desperately, and what tipping points help create when messaging takes a life of its own (Atran, 2015). It is something that will make youths spending much of their lives in the virtual world to 'get out of the armchair' as a force of resistance against extremism instead of tipping towards terrorism.

REFERENCES

Ajzen, I. (n.d.). *Theory of planned behavior diagram.* Retrieved from http://people.umass.edu/aizen/tpb.diag.html

Al Raffie, D. (2012). Whose hearts and minds? Narratives and counter-narratives of salafi jihadism. *Journal of Terrorism Research, 3*(2), 13–31. doi:10.15664/jtr.304

Anti-ISIS tests show winning the Internet war is key to beating militants: Experts. (2015, February 20). *The Straits Times.* Retrieved from http://www.straitstimes.com/news/world/united-states/story/anti-isis-tests-show-winning-the-internet-war-key-beating-militants-experts/

Atran, S. (2015, April 25). Here's what the social science says about countering violent extremism. *Huffington Post.* Retrieved from http://www.huffingtonpost.com/scott-atran/violent-extremism-social-science_b_7142604.html

Boghardt, L. (2014, June 23). Saudi funding of ISIS. *The Washington Institute for Near East Policy.* Retrieved from http://www.washingtoninstitute.org/policy-analysis/view/saudi-funding-of-isis

Breton, P. (2000, October 1). Wired to the counterculture. *Le Monde diplomatique.* Retrieved from http://mondediplo.com/2000/10/06internet

Briggs, R., Carlile, L., Maher, S., & Gardner, F. (2015, March 2). *Digital jihad: How online networks are changing extremists.* London: Chatham House, the Royal Institute of International Affairs.

Card, D., Mas, A., & Rothstein, J. (2007). *Tipping and the dynamics of segregation* (Working paper 13052). Cambridge, MA: National Bureau of Economic Research.

Carré, O. (2003). *Mysticism and politics: A critical reading of Fi Zilal al-Qur'an by Sayyid Qutb (1906-1966).* Leiden: Brill.

Carter, J. (2013, January 23). Case study: Roshonara Choudhry. *The Risky Shift.* Retrieved from http://theriskyshift.com/2013/01/case-study-roshonara-choudhry/

Chaiken, S. (1999). *Dual-process theories in social psychology.* New York, NY: Guilford Press.

Chang, I., Liu, C., & Chen, K. (2014). The push, pull and mooring effects in virtual migration for social networking sites. *Information Systems Journal, 24*(4), 323–346. doi:10.1111/isj.12030

Cherry, K. (n.d.). How attitudes form, change and shape behavior. *about education*. Retrieved from http://psychology.about.com/od/socialpsychology/a/attitudes.htm

Cohen, K., Fredrik, J., Lisa, K., & Jonas, C. M. (2014). Detecting linguistic markers for radical violence in social media. *Terrorism and Political Violence*, *26*(1), 246–256. doi:10.1080/09546553.2014.849948

Crossman, A. (n.d.). The tipping point: An overview of the book by Malcolm Gladwell. *about education*. Retrieved from http://sociology.about.com/od/Works/a/The-Tipping-Point.htm

Dodd, V. (2010, November 3). Roshonara Choudhry: Police interview extracts. *The Guardian*. Retrieved from http://www.theguardian.com/uk/2010/nov/03/roshonara-choudhry-police-interview

Double truck bombing on CIA HQ - Multiple angles. (n.d.). *Live Leak*. Retrieved from http://www.liveleak.com/view?i=0d8_1184205759

Eagly, A., & Chaiken, S. (1993). *The psychology of attitudes*. Fort Worth, TX: Harcourt, Brace.

Gladwell, M. (2000). *The tipping point: How little things can make a big difference*. Boston: Little, Brown.

Granovetter, M. (1978). Threshold models of collective behavior. *American Journal of Sociology*, *83*(6), 1420–1420. doi:10.1086/226707

Gray, J. R., Braver, T. S., & Raichle, M. E. (2002). Integration of emotion and cognition in the lateral prefrontal cortex. *Proceedings of the National Academy of Sciences of the United States of America*, *99*(6), 4115–4120. doi:10.1073/pnas.062381899

Grodzins, M. (1958). *The metropolitan area as a racial problem*. Pittsburgh: University of Pittsburgh Press.

Grodzins, M. (2007, September 18). 50 years ago in Scientific American: Metropolitan Segregation. *Scientific American*. Retrieved from http://www.scientificamerican.com/article/50-years-ago-in-scientific-american-white-flight-1/

Hegghammer, T. (2010). *Jihad in Saudi Arabia: Violence and pan-Islamism since 1979*. Cambridge, UK: Cambridge University Press. doi:10.1017/CBO9780511809439

Heider, F. (1958). *The psychology of interpersonal relations*. New York, NY: Wiley. doi:10.1037/10628-000

Himmelfarb, S., & Eagly, A. H. (1974). *Readings in attitude change*. New York, NY: Wiley.

Hovland, C., Janis, I., & Kelley, H. (1953). *Communication and persuasion*. New Haven, CT: Yale University Press.

Katz, D. (1960). The functional approach to the study of attitudes. *Public Opinion Quarterly*, *24*(2, Special Issue: Attitude Change), 163–204. doi:10.1086/266945

Kiesler, C. A., Collins, B. E., & Miller, N. (1969). *Attitude change*. New York, NY: Wiley.

Landau, E. (2009, May 26). Insights on why people 'snap' and kill. *CNN*. Retrieved from http://edition.cnn.com/2009/HEALTH/05/26/snap.moments/index.html?iref=newssearch

Lenhart, G. (1996, March 1). *Chapter 1: Introduction - Jung and the four psychological functions*. Retrieved from http://sulcus.berkeley.edu/flm/SH/MDL/GAL/GalDisChapts/galdis.chapter1.html

Lia, B. (2008). Al-Qaida's appeal: Understanding its unique selling points. *Perspectives on Terrorism, 2*(8). Retrieved from http://www.terrorismanalysts.com/pt/index.php/pot/issue/view/14

Martinez, J. (2005). *Spatial dynamics of human populations: Some basic models.* Retrieved from http://faculty.ucr.edu/~hanneman/spatial/schelling/schelling.html

McLeod, S. (2009). Attitudes and behavior. *Simply Psychology.* Retrieved from http://www.simplypsychology.org/attitudes.html

McLeod, S. (2015). B. F. Skinner, operant conditioning. *Simply Psychology.* Retrieved from http://www.simplypsychology.org/operant-conditioning.html

Meleagrou-Hitchens, A. (2011, September 11). *As American as apple pie: How Anwar al-Awlaki became the face of Western jihad* (ICSR Policy Report). London: The International Centre for the Study of Radicalisation.

Meloy, J. R., Hoffmann, J., Guldimann, A., & James, D. (2012). The role of warning behaviors in threat assessment: An exploration and suggested typology. *Behavioral Sciences & the Law, 30*(3), 256–279. doi:10.1002/bsl.999

Muhammad, A. (2014, August 27). Stories of foreign fighter migration to Syria. *CTC Sentinel, 7*(8), 11–13.

Nordland, R. (2014, June 28). Iraq's Sunni militants take to social media to advance their cause and intimidate. *The New York Times.* Retrieved from http://www.nytimes.com/2014/06/29/middleeast/iraqs-sunni-militants-take-to-social-media-to-advance-their-cause-and-intimidate.html?_r=0

O'Keefe, D. (1990). *Persuasion.* Newbury Park, CA: Sage.

Penrose, G. (2014, July 23). Precision guided message - Radical Islam, social media and building a sleeper 'army'. *Quora.* Retrieved from http://tmgcorporateservices.quora.com/Precision-Guided-Message-Radical-Islam-Social-Media-and-Building-a-Sleeper-Army

Pressman, D., & Flockton, J. (2012). Calibrating risk for violent political extremists and terrorists: The VERA 2 structured assessment. *British Journal of Forensic Practice, 14*(4), 237–251. doi:10.1108/14636641211283057

Pressman, E. (2009, October 1). *Risk assessment decisions for violent political extremism 2009-02.* Retrieved from http://www.publicsafety.gc.ca/cnt/rsrcs/pblctns/2009-02-rdv/index-eng.aspx

Qutb, S., & Salahi, M. (1979). *In the shade of the Qur'ān.* London: MWH.

Rouse, M. (2006). Definition: Tipping points. *WhatIs.com.* Retrieved from http://whatis.techtarget.com/definition/tipping-point

Rushkoff, D. (2002). Renaissance Now! Media ecology and the new global narrative. *Explorations in Media Ecology, 1*(1), 21–32. doi:10.1386/eme.1.1.41_1

Saifudeen, O. A. (2014). *The cyber extremism orbital pathways model* (Working paper 283). Singapore: S.Rajaratnam School of International Studies.

Schelling, T. (1971). Dynamic models of segregation. *The Journal of Mathematical Sociology, 1*(2), 143–186. doi:10.1080/0022250X.1971.9989794

Schelling, T. (2006). Micromotives and macrobehaviour: With a new preface and the Nobel lecture (New ed.). New York, NY: W.W Norton & Co.

Suler, J. (2004). The online disinhibition effect. *Cyberpsychology & Behavior, 7*(3), 321–326. doi:10.1089/1094931041291295

Swink, D. (2010, March 6). The Pentagon shooting: They don't "just snap". *Psychology today.* Retrieved from http://www.psychologytoday.com/blog/threat-management/201003/the-pentagon-shooting-they-don-t-just-snap

The Islamic State of Iraq and Syria. (2015). *Hijrah to the Islamic State.* Author.

The original tipping point wasn't one. (2009, July 13). *The Economist.* Retrieved from http://www.economist.com/blogs/freeexchange/2009/07/the_original_tipping_point_was

Theories of attitude change. (2001, August 3). *The Association for Educational Communications and Technology.* Retrieved from http://www.aect.org/edtech/ed1/34/34-03.html

TODAY just published the worst article of the year. Singapore netizens tear it to shreds. (2014, November 15). *Must Share News.* Retrieved May 13, 2015, from http://mustsharenews.com/worse-story-of-year/

United Nations Counterterrorism Implementation Task Force (UN CTITF). (2011). *Use of the Internet to Counter the Appeal of Extremist Violence: Conference Summary and Follow-up/ Recommendations.* Retrieved from http://www.un.org/terrorism/pdfs/CTITF%20Riyadh%20Conference%20-%20Summary%20&%20Recommendations.pdf

Venitism. (n.d.). *Distrust of mainstream media.* Retrieved from http://venitism.blogspot.sg/2011/09/distrust-of-mainstream-media.html

Venugopala, B. N. (2014). Post war disillusionment and English poetry. *International Journal of Language & Linguistics, 1*(1), 11–14.

Worchel, S., Lee, J., & Adewole, A. (1975). Effects of supply and demand on ratings of object value. *Journal of Personality and Social Psychology, 32*(5), 906–914. doi:10.1037/0022-3514.32.5.906

ENDNOTES

[1.] This is meant to describe a person who talks a lot about jihad over the Internet, but does very little in the real world to achieve jihadi ideals.

[2.] The term is believed to have started in epidemiology and has been borrowed over to many other fields such as the social sciences and physics. It often refers to a turning point in an evolving situation that leads to a new development or a threshold/ tolerance point if crossed would lead to changes to the original state (Rouse, 2006).

3. Akin to narratives of disillusionment characteristic of Post-war Modernist literature in the aftermath of the First World War.

4. The video was delivered by Abd al-Majid al-Utaybi (also known as Qarin al-Klash), and produced by al-Manara al-Bayda, the media wing of Jabatul Nusra, in February 2013 (see Muhammad, 2014).

5. The story of Abu Thabit al-Jazrawi was cited in the Islamic State e-book 'Hijrah to the Islamic State' released in February 2015 that offered travel advisories on how to get to Syria, and stories from those who successfully made the journey (see "Hijrah to the Islamic State", 2015).

6. Ibn al-Khattab – deceased leader of the Arab Mujahideen in Chechnya who was a veteran of the Afghan jihad as well (Muhammad, 2014).

7. Abd al-Aziz al-Miqrin – Amir of the AQAP during its inception (Muhammad, 2014).

8. Back during the Afghan – Russian conflict, Saudi Arabia was open to calling the struggle a legitimate jihad. Today, private Saudi donors still continue to constitute part of the funding of Sunni groups in Syria. Even though it is in the Saudi government's interests to see its enemies like Shia Iraq and Assad being defeated by Sunni militant groups like ISIS, it nonetheless realises that ISIS poses a direct threat to the Kingdom hence takes a hard stance against it.

9. The young British Muslim Woman who apparently became radicalised purely online by watching the videos of Anwar Awlaki, and proceeded to carry out a knife attack on British member of parliament, Stephen Timms in 2010.

10. These represent possible 'mavens' and 'connectors'. See subsequent section 'Jihadi messaging using tipping points'.

11. To not trust mainstream news is a tagline often voiced by online counter-culture groups. This sentiment is also shared by Singaporean counterculture netizens ("TODAY Just Published", 2014).

12. The Facebook site for the jihadi supporter media production house that produced videos (e.g., "Satan's Whisper's: Lies against the Islamic State") and others similar to it, is called the 'The Light Revelations'. This Facebook site has 6,171 likes and is growing. The "Repelling the swords of Irjaa" video made by the same media production house that focuses on counter-arguments from a religious frame of reference has a sizable 15,575 views. This is considerably more than non-religious counter-arguments from other videos by the light series judging purely based on YouTube views. These videos by 'The Light Revelations' have been reproduced with Malay subtitles, and have been circulating on many jihadi supporter social media platforms. This diversified dissemination strategy has helped promote these videos even when the websites are taken down.

13. United Kingdom-based Islamist Mizanur Rahman, has an impressive 28,600 plus (and growing) followers on Twitter, and has high 'Twitterstats' figures for popularity.

14. This last part is a disengagement strategy in which the individual in question is still an extremist at heart and mind, but will not engage or condone violent actions as an approach to make his worldview a reality.

15. Scott Atran in his speech to the United Nation security council on April 25, 2015, spoke of how a dynamic movement that is "intimately personal and global – involving not just entrepreneurial ideas, but also physical activity, music and entertainment – to counter the growing global counterculture of violent extremism".

Chapter 8
Why Is ISIS so Psychologically Attractive?

Loo Seng Neo
Home Team Behavioural Sciences Centre,
Ministry of Home Affairs, Singapore

Jethro Tan
Home Team Behavioural Sciences Centre,
Ministry of Home Affairs, Singapore

Priscilla Shi
Home Team Behavioural Sciences Centre,
Ministry of Home Affairs, Singapore

Yingmin Wang
Home Team Behavioural Sciences Centre,
Ministry of Home Affairs, Singapore

Leevia Dillon
Home Team Behavioural Sciences Centre,
Ministry of Home Affairs, Singapore

Danielle Gomes
Home Team Behavioural Sciences Centre,
Ministry of Home Affairs, Singapore

ABSTRACT

Since the Islamic State in Iraq and Syria (ISIS) became prominent after the release of beheading videos of its prisoners, many have been confused over how to describe this development in relation to the way the Internet is exploited by violent extremists. While the element of surprise and horror lingered on the minds of many observers, a more pressing question facing the law enforcement is: how does ISIS attract foreign fighters using such videos and online propaganda? As countries around the globe grapple with the security threat posed by their nationals travelling to join ISIS, the need to be au fait with the appeal of ISIS and its ability to use the Internet to recruit new members and sympathisers becomes even more apparent. This chapter uses a behavioural sciences lens to explicate how individual and organisational motivational factors may contribute to the overall appeal of joining ISIS.

INTRODUCTION

Much has been said and written about the influx of foreign fighters to Iraq and Syria, particularly about the scale of jihadist volunteerism to join violent extremist groups such as the Islamic State in Iraq and Syria (ISIS) and Jabhat al-Nusra. As of 2015, approximately 20,000 individuals from 90 countries have travelled to join the fight in Iraq and Syria (van Ginkel, 2015).

DOI: 10.4018/978-1-5225-0156-5.ch008

Notably, these groups have attracted much attention not only due to the huge influx of foreign fighters, but more importantly, through their sophisticated use of social media to convey messages about the jihad that they are fighting for. As Shiraz Maher from the International Centre for the Study of Radicalisation had put it, this can be considered the "most socially-mediated conflict in history" (Casciani, 2014, para. 14).

While violent extremist groups in general have exploited the Internet, it is noteworthy that ISIS, in particular, has been using the Internet very effectively both to lure foreign fighters as well as sow terror through its polished online propaganda (e.g., Altman, 2014; Carter, Maher, & Neumann, 2014; Hegghammer, 2013; Rose, 2014). For instance, in terms of attracting foreign supporters and fighters, a German fighter was featured in a series of short videos titled 'Muhatweets' describing his wonderful experience of living in the Islamic Caliphate established by ISIS (Reuter, Salloum, & Shafy, 2014).

Such videos, which are uploaded by ISIS fighters, are targeted at Muslims living beyond the conflict zone. By presenting themselves as "defenders of Syria's Sunni majority against the tyrannical Shiite regime", these foreign fighters serve as an essential source of information and inspiration to jihadist wannabes (Carter et al., 2014, p. 7). It appears that ISIS had effectively leveraged on the benefits of the Internet to create online platforms and propaganda content to encourage potential supporters to adopt its views and participate in the conflict (Shi et al., 2014).

Furthermore, ISIS has propagated extreme forms of content (e.g., beheading of prisoners and rebels videos) and yet is able to attract and recruit new followers (Kruglanski, 2014). While the modus operandi shown in these propaganda materials may be brutal, the messages inherent in these materials do capture the attention of the world – as evidenced by the re-circulation of these materials on various social media platforms including mainstream news channels.

Thus, the dissemination of propaganda online has become one of its most important recruiting tools to enlist new members to its rank. ISIS has succeeded in not merely intimidating people, but also attracting foreign fighters to their strongholds in Iraq and Syria, and even inspiring established violent extremist groups across the world to pledge their alliance to the group (Neo, Shi et al., 2014). From a counter violent extremism perspective, the appeal of ISIS and its online propaganda campaign reflects a set of interests and priorities, which needs to be explained and understood. This concern will be the overriding focus of this chapter.

By utilising a psychological and behavioural sciences approach, this chapter seeks to examine how (1) individual motivational factors and (2) organisational motivational factors may contribute to the overall appeal and attractiveness of joining ISIS as a foreign fighter. Specifically, this chapter makes the case that it is important for the law enforcement to be aware of these factors in order to better inform and develop effective countermeasures. However, it must be emphasised that this chapter is not an attempt to discover or construct a profile of an individual susceptible to joining ISIS, and that the list of factors identified in this chapter is not an exhaustive one.

Defining Foreign Fighter

It is important to define the term 'foreign fighter' because the definition will allow researchers to scope the population of individuals considered for analysis – e.g., in terms of their motives and potential impacts of their actions.

From the literature, various definitions of foreign fighter have been identified. For example, Cillufo, Cozzens, and Ranstorp (2010, p. 3) in their report 'Foreign Fighters: Trends, Trajectories & Conflict

Zones' defined these individuals as "violent extremists who leave their Western states of residence with the aspirations to train or take up arms against non-Muslim factions in jihadi conflicts". In his doctoral dissertation on the analysis of modern civil wars with transnational insurgents, Malet (2009, pp. 57-58) defined a foreign fighter as "an agent who has joined, and operates within the confines of, an insurgency, lacks citizenship of the conflict state or kinship links to its warring factions, lacks affiliation to an official military organization, and is unpaid". Further refining Malet's definition of foreign fighter, Hegghammer (2013), director of terrorism research at the Norwegian Defence Research Establishment, suggested that a foreign fighter has the following attributes: (i) individuals who try to leave the West to fight elsewhere; (ii) the act of foreign fighting, be it training or fighting, is a military activity that uses any tactic against the Western or non-Western target; and (iii) it happens outside of the West.

However, the consideration of citizenship and kinship, as well as the rigid dichotomy between Western and non-Western targets complicate the examination of foreign fighters. The double nature of the Syria conflict, both sectarian and socio-revolutionary, makes such considerations 'disadvantageous' as some populations of foreign fighters might be left out (Skidmore, 2014). Furthermore, not all foreign fighters enter Iraq and Syria with a full-fledged jihadist worldview (Zelin, 2013a).

Considering the aforementioned concerns, Skidmore (2014, p. 13) further refined the definition of a foreign fighter as "any unpaid individual who voluntarily joins, operates within, a third party conflict using any tactic, regardless of kinship ties". In like manner, Malet (2013, p. 4) redefined his original definition of foreign fighter by describing one as "an individual from outside the conflict zone who fights in a conflict while he does not have a direct stake in the conflict outcome nor is he being paid for it".

From these definitions and insights, three common themes have been identified by the authors:

- The context of the conflict, such as the fighting being location-specific and not related to international terrorism;
- Voluntary participation and unpaid; and
- Attacks perpetrated within the conflict zone.

Based on these identified themes, the present chapter defined a foreign fighter as an unpaid individual from outside the conflict zone who voluntarily joins and operates in a third party conflict in which he/she does not have a direct stake.

INDIVIDUAL MOTIVATIONAL FACTORS

There has been an influx of foreign fighters to Iraq and Syria since the civil movement began, with foreigners reported to have joined both pro-government and rebel groups in the region (e.g., Hegghammer, 2013; Meir Amit Intelligence and Terrorism Information Center [MAITIC], 2013; Nuraniyah, 2014; Zelin, 2013b). For this reason, the phenomenon of foreign fighters has been repeatedly flagged by law enforcement agencies worldwide as one of the most serious concerns in the current fight against violent extremism.

In response, law enforcement agencies have tried to discern the dynamic processes and factors that drive individuals to leave their countries of origin and fight as foreign fighters for violent extremist groups such as ISIS. While it is appealing to identify an overarching factor that motivates individuals to join ISIS, it is essential to recognise that there is no single radicalisation pathway and individuals become involved in violent extremism for a variety of reasons.

Based on this line of thought, a significant amount of research and analysis has gone into the questions of how an individual's propensity for involvement with violent extremist groups and actions may increase as a result of one's vulnerabilities and worldviews. For example, Horgan (2008) averred that vulnerabilities factors may be used to explain why certain individuals have a greater propensity to become involved in violent extremism than others. In his analysis on the psychology of violent extremism, Borum (2014) argued for the need to focus on:

[A]n individual psychology of terrorism that explores how otherwise normal mental states and processes, built on characteristic attitudes, dispositions, inclinations, and intentions, might affect a person's propensity for involvement with violent extremist groups and actions. It uses the concepts of "mindset" – a relatively enduring set of attitudes, dispositions, and inclinations – and worldview as the basis of a psychological "climate," within which various vulnerabilities and propensities shape ideas and behaviours in ways that can increase the person's risk or likelihood of involvement in violent extremism. (p.286)

There is therefore a need to be cognisant of these factors that may shape one's ideas and behaviours in ways that increase receptivity to violent extremist ideology and likelihood of involvement in violent extremism. With that in mind, five key motivations have been identified.

Motivated by Ideology

Research suggests that the role of ideology is to provide meaning and value to its believers (e.g., Borum, 2004; Neo, Khader, Ang, Ong, & Tan, 2014). For example, Alex Schmid (2011, pp. 643-644), director of the Terrorism Research Initiative, defined ideology as "patterns of beliefs and expressions that people use to interpret and evaluate the world in a way designed to shape, mobilise, direct, organize and justify certain modes and courses of action". In this regard, ideology influences the attitudes and behaviours of its adherents by providing them with a template of how they should behave and think.

In the case of ISIS foreign fighters, some of the ideologies that motivate them to travel to Iraq and Syria include: the establishment of an Islamic Caliphate in Greater Syria and Middle East that is driven by the Salafi jihadi worldview (MAITIC, 2014); and participation in the final victory to defeat Assad regime that is driven by end-time prophetic narrative (Ali, 2014).

From a psychological perspective, adherents of these ideologies may derive gratifications by becoming involved in beliefs that is 'beyond their own lives'. In the context of the establishment of an Islamic Caliphate, individuals who exhibit the desire to live under true Sharia may be motivated to travel to the Islamic Caliphate established by ISIS (Wood, 2015). For instance, British national Abdul Raqib Amin left Aberdeen to join ISIS in Iraq. The psychological longing to participate in the 'holy war' and live in a country governed by Islamic laws may have motivated Amin to join ISIS. In the ISIS's recruitment video titled 'There is No Life without Jihad', Amin explained:

Are you willing to sacrifice the fat job you've got, the big car, the family you have? Are you willing to sacrifice this for the sake of Allah? If you do, Allah will give you back 700 times more … In the Aberdeen mosque there is not one person with the same mentality as me. They don't agree with jihad and disagree with all these extremists ... I left with the intention not to go back, I'm going to stay and fight until the Khilafah [rule of Islam] is established or I die ... I left UK to give everything I have for the sake of Allah. One of the happiest moments in my life was when the plane took off from Gatwick Airport ... As a Muslim you cannot live in the country of Kuffars [disbelievers]. (Byrne, 2014; para. 7-14)

In the context of the end-time prophecies, some foreign fighters are attracted by the opportunity to participate in the final battle against the enemies of Islam. For example, Zelin (2013c) explained that

There are end-time prophecies related to Syria, and more specifically Bilad al-Sham (or greater Syria, which encompasses modern-day Syria, Lebanon, Jordan, Israel/Palestine, and western Iraq), that state Jesus will descend from the white minaret at the Great Mosque in Damascus and fight the dajjal (false messiah), and this will hasten the Day of Judgement from God. This, coupled with the Hadith (sayings of the Prophet Muhammad) about the black banners being raised in Khurasan (historically in parts of Iran, Central Asia, and most importantly for jihadis, Afghanistan), is also related to the end times, and jihadis view it as a reference to the jihad that started in Afghanistan in the 1980s. These signs are leading some militant Salafists to believe that they are hastening the Day of Judgement. (para. 2)

Thus, for adherents for such end-time prophecies, these ideologies help to explain their current situation and provide them with a sense of direction. Musa Cerantonio, an Australian online preacher who supports ISIS, presents an apt example of how end-time prophetic narratives have been used to motivate others to join ISIS. Via YouTube videos, Cerantonio expressed the deepest interest in end-time prophecies and described ISIS as warriors of Islam who carry the black banners as described in the Hadith (Ali, 2014).

In sum, ideology epitomises an active form of agency that can bind its followers from diverse backgrounds and geographical locations together. This, in turn, may be exploited by violent extremist groups such as ISIS to attract new fighters who want to live in an Islamic Caliphate, and/or fulfil the end-time prophecies.

Motivated by Perceived Injustice

Press releases and personal narratives of the atrocities committed by the Assad regime towards the Syrians are widespread (e.g., Engel, 2013; Sorko-Ram, 2012). The perceived sense of injustice towards the Syrians drives not only the Muslims, but also the desires of secular-minded individuals and humanitarian organisations to defend the weak and vulnerable (Siegel, 2014). Of particular interest here is the possibility that individuals who experienced feelings of perceived injustice may take action against those whom they deemed responsible for the wrongdoings.

In the case of ISIS foreign fighters, they may be motivated to fight for the rights of the Muslims who are being suppressed by the Syrian government. This, as Post, Ruby, and Shaw (2002) suggested, creates an enabling environment that reduces one's inhibition for violence and provides meaning to one's actions. For instance, Canadian national Andre Poulin outlined the perceived injustice he felt in an ISIS recruitment video titled 'The Chosen Few of Different Lands':

I was like any other regular Canadian; I watched hockey, I went to cottage in the summertime, I loved to fish, I wanted to go hunting, I like outdoors, I liked sports ... life in Canada was good. I had money,

I had good family, but at the end of the day ... how can you answer to Allah the Almighty when you live on the same street, when using their [government] light and paying taxes to them, and they use these taxes for war on Islam. (Kohlmann & Alkhouri, 2014, p. 4)

Given the wide variety of interactive digital platforms that has been ceded to radical ideology, it opens up the probability that individuals and groups may be exposed to ISIS online propaganda that reinforce and validate their perceived sense of injustice. Besides promoting new information, acts of discussing negative sentiments also create an opportunity for one to personalise larger societal problems that may resonate with them (Gupta, 2011). These perceptions in turn may create the emotional push for one to embrace a violent extremism-justifying ideology that advocates the use of violence (Brown & Abernethy, 2010). Thus, the Internet increases the likelihood for ISIS to reach out to potential recruits using these perceptions of injustice.

However, it is essential to note that our conceptualisation of the influence of perceived injustice largely hinges on how these sentiments relate to one's life experiences and sense of self. This as Borum (2014, p. 293), in his analysis on the psychological vulnerabilities and propensities for involvement in violent extremism, argued: "The power of injustice over an individual, then, comes from how sensitive a person is to detecting injustices, and how much that person rehearses, ruminates and fuels them".

When this happens, it provides a contact point that increases the potential for one to make connections in a manner that has well-defined consequences. It allows one to extract new meaning with the potential to exert control over one's subsequent decisions, actions, and behaviours and prompt powerful, moral emotions that potentiate a drive to punish the wrongdoer (Neo, Khader et al., 2014). Thus, it may increase the likelihood of the individual to re-negotiate their identity within the violent extremist movement and become more supportive of ISIS.

In sum, the perception of injustice may stimulate strong emotive responses that mobilise the individual and provide the justification for him/her to join ISIS.

Motivated by Need for Significance and Identity

Prior research on violent extremist motivations suggests that individuals who are motivated by the need for significance and identity have an increased likelihood to seek a greater purpose and significance in their life (Kruglanski, 2014; Samuel, 2015).

From a psychological perspective, such individuals are driven by a need to define their identities or sense of self (Neo, Khader, Shi, Dillon, & Ong, 2015). For example, Venhaus (2010) in his analysis of 2,032 affiliated Al-Qaeda foreign fighters found that:

[T]he recurring theme was that they all were looking for something ... they want to understand who they are, why they matter, and what their role in the world should be. They have an unfulfilled need to define themselves, which al-Qaida offers to fill. (p. 8)

In many instances, these individuals are substantially influenced by who they perceive to be their 'in-group'; where they would not feel marginalised and alienated. In this regards, the narratives disseminated by violent extremist groups such as ISIS provide an attractive alternative for their adherents to instil a sense of identity that they desire (Kruglanski, 2014). This is especially so when individuals look towards highly regarded in-group members, such as martyrs and glorified jihadists, and model their actions.

For certain ISIS foreign fighters, the act of joining the fight against the infidels may fulfil a deep psychological need for significance and identity. For example, the foreign fighters may be drawn to the conflict by the glorification of martyrs and other jihadi fighters. In the case of British national Reyaad Khan, he left Cardiff to join ISIS because he was keen to become a martyr. Khan tweeted "Spent the day with 2 German brothers waiting 2 do martyrdom ops. The waiting list is so long, we got fireworks for us when they return" (Williams & Marsden, 2014, para. 5). Thus, ISIS provided Khan with the opportunity to engage in activities that would allow him to earn the status of heroes and martyrs.

In sum, the desire to seek a greater purpose and significance in their life may motivate jihadist wannabes to adopt the worldview of ISIS and join the group in Iraq and Syria.

Motivated by Need for Belonging

Humans have an innate and universal need for coherent and meaningful relationships with another person or group (Lavigne, Vallerand, & Crevier-Braud, 2011; Maslow, 1943). Fowler and Christakis (2008), for example, noted an innate tendency for individuals to engage in behaviours that increase the potential for them to foster a sense of belonging to a larger social entity.

This need for belonging has been identified as a key motivator for one's behaviours, emotions and cognitions (Baumeister & Leary, 1995; Stillman & Baumeister, 2009). For example, Crenshaw (2007) concluded that individuals sometimes are drawn to violent extremist groups because they feel a need for belonging which the group can provide. Furthermore, Walton, Cohen, Cwir, and Spencer (2012) found that a mere sense of belonging is sufficient for people to adopt the goals and motivation of others for themselves. This underscores the power of social connections and that motivation to join a group is highly sensitive to social relationships. Thus, the individual's initial engagement with violent extremist groups may be driven by one's need to form and maintain significant interpersonal relationships.

While some ISIS foreign fighters seek membership in the groups to gain peer approval, reduce their loneliness and boost their self-esteem, others do so to network with like-minded others and experience interpersonal closeness and connectedness to the cause. Thus, it can be envisaged that the need to establish meaningful relationships with like-minded individuals may have motivated some prospective fighters to join the group.

Being part of ISIS, these foreign fighters would spend a lot of time living, training and fighting with like-minded peers. Over time, they would reinforce each other's or the group's beliefs and develop positive interpersonal relationships through shared experiences. In fact, this enhanced sense of belonging would give the fighters an identity to associate themselves with and enable them to function optimally. Thus, a prospective fighter who is in contact with ISIS may then choose to define one's identity simply through the worldview of the group (Shi et al., 2014).

Of interest, current leader of ISIS, Abu Bakr al-Baghdadi also recognised the importance of the need for belonging as exemplified in his statement ("Abu-Bakr al-Baghdadi", 2014):

O Muslims everywhere, glad tidings to you and expect good ... you have a state and khilafah [an Islamic Caliphate] which will return your dignity, might, rights and leadership. It is a state where the Arab and non-Arab, the white man and black man, the easterner and westerner are all brothers. It is a khilafah that gathered the Caucasian, Indian, Chinese, Shāmi, Iraqi, Yemeni, Egyptian, Maghribī [North African], American, French, German and Australian ... loving each other for the sake of Allah, standing in a single trench, defending and guarding each other, and sacrificing themselves for one another ...

In sum, the need for belonging may motivate an individual to join ISIS if the group can meet the needs of these individuals by providing a ready network of like-minded others.

Motivated by Excitement and Adventure

Research suggests that some individuals became involved in violent extremism because of the prospects for excitement, adventure, and glory (e.g., Borum, 2014; Jenkins, 2015; Neo, Shi et al., 2014), and that such sensation-seeking opportunities suffice as a motivating factor for these violent extremists to stay engaged regardless of the radical ideology or cause itself.

In the context of ISIS foreign fighters, the social media campaigns have romanticised the conflict and played up the thrills and pleasure of participating in it (Friedman & Siemaszko, 2014; Singal, 2014). This in turn may attract individuals who are interested in sensation-seeking and adventure for which the sensationalised portrayal of the conflict by ISIS has great appeal.

French national Mehdi Nemmouche presents an apt example of someone who is motivated by excitement and adventure. Nemmouche, who became an ISIS foreign fighter in Syria, was described as someone who "went to Syria to achieve recognition to fulfil every violent fantasy" (Calais, 2014, para. 8). Another line of evidence comes from the freed French journalist Nicolas Henin who was under the watch of Nemmouche during his time in prison:

Nemmouche earned a reputation as a violent and provocative thug who took pleasure in torturing hostages ... It seemed to us that he did not leave for Syria because of some grand ideals but, above all, to make this mark, to carry out a murderous path that he had traced. (Kohlmann & Alkhouri, 2014, p. 4)

From a psychological perspective, research has shown how individuals, who exhibit such sensation-seeking behaviours, are defined by their need for novel and intense experiences and their willingness to take on these risks for the sake of such experiences (Zuckerman, 1994).

Furthermore, the appeal of the excitement and adventure outweighs the potential consequences of becoming a foreign fighter. The possibility of relieving boredom, apathy and/or frustration may motivate the jihadi wannabes by providing them with a sense of direction and drama to their life which they enjoy (National Offender Management Service, 2011). In some instances, such needs for excitement and adventure are conscious reasons for individuals to commit to the use of violence, as there are limited opportunities for them to meet these needs through legitimate means.

This is why violent extremist groups such as ISIS try to create opportunities to meet the needs of these individuals. As Bartlett (2008) in his report on the appeal of violent extremism outlined:

For some young people, violent jihadi is exciting. It offers glamorous trips around the world to meet some of the world's most infamous men, running around with an AK-47 in mysterious locations. It offers the chance to becoming a hero who wins respect and admiration amongst peers. Anyone remotely familiar with Western popular culture will find that pretty exhilarating. (p. 4)

In sum, it is reasonable to suggest that the motivating factor of excitement and adventure may contribute to the overall appeal and attractiveness of joining ISIS as a foreign fighter. In addition, it is essential to note that an individual may be motivated by more than one factor and that these factors may work in tandem to shape one's ideas and behaviours in ways that increase receptivity to ISIS's ideology and likelihood of involvement in violent extremism.

ORGANISATIONAL MOTIVATIONAL FACTORS

While it is tempting to attribute the influx of foreign fighters to the presence of individual motivational factors, should the mere presence of these factors be the determining element in understanding the appeal of ISIS?

In addressing this question, it is important to first recognise that the involvement in violent extremism tends to be characterised as something to be understood out of an individual's personal (e.g., personal grievances) and social (e.g., need for belonging) context. This leads to a focused attempt to identify unique personal and social qualities which may not necessarily contribute to the overall appeal and attractiveness of joining ISIS as a foreign fighter.

Alternatively, there is a need to appreciate the equally important role played by the violent extremist group in providing the context to choices (e.g., in terms of involvement with, knowledge and expectations of, access to ideology and materials of violent extremist group) made by the individual. This implies a focus not only on the personal and social qualities of an individual, but also on the organisational qualities of the violent extremist group that resonates with the individual.

This highlights the role of organisational factors that makes ISIS appealing to the foreign fighters. Such factors may shape its followers' attitudes toward the group's ideas, perceptions of the group, or appraisals of threats and grievances. This section examines how three organisational motivational factors might affect the likelihood of an individual's propensity to become a foreign fighter.

The Ability to Establish and Govern an Islamic Caliphate

As a violent extremist group, ISIS has managed to rivet the world's attention with its ability to establish and govern an Islamic Caliphate. It has consistently portrayed itself as a group that delivers results within the jihadi enclaves, thereby increasing its appeal for prospective foreign fighters.

Firstly, ISIS has achieved what other violent extremist groups were not capable of: the establishment of an Islamic Caliphate. The Islamic Caliphate, which is a state governed in accordance to the Islamic law, is created for Muslims to practice the traditions and texts of early Islam, and defend the Muslim community against infidels and apostates ("What is Islamic State", 2015). For example, it was noted by ISIS supporters that "the world is starting to search about Islam a lot more now that it is a real practical entity (State) instead of just an idea" ("The Islamic State", 2015, p. 81). Signifying a new beacon of hope, ISIS serves as an ideal alternative for Muslims who want to live in an Islamic Caliphate – i.e., live the life of a good Muslim. In fact, ISIS successes on the battlefield have validated its followers' conviction that ISIS is indeed the prophesised caliphate. Thus, the establishment of an Islamic Caliphate by ISIS may present the group as an attractive destination for individuals who are interested to live under the Islamic law.

Secondly, ISIS has demonstrated its commitment to develop and govern the land it has conquered. ISIS adopts a departmentalised hierarchical organisational structure with tight command and control governed by a leadership core (Gorman, Malas, & Bradley, 2014; Wood, 2015). Although the leader of ISIS, Abu Bakr al-Baghdadi, seems to allow its members some degree of freedom in self-expression on social media platforms and ground operations, he maintains control and delivers direct command to his members in a top-down manner (Hall, 2014). As ISIS spreads its control over more territories, it also exploits local alliances either by coercion or mutual collaboration to govern these newly acquired territories (Gorman et al., 2014). In these ways, ISIS is able to portray itself to be in control of its territory.

Furthermore, ISIS has described life in the Islamic Caliphate as a supposed 'utopian lifestyle' where the basic necessities are provided for. Examples include the free provision of necessities (e.g., electricity, food, water, transportation and medicines), introduction of its own currency, and even education for females ("The Islamic State", 2015). In like manner, after ISIS has gained control of the city of Ramadi, the group has initiated several public work projects to repair key infrastructures and rebuild the city (Cunningham, 2015). Thus, ISIS has portrayed itself as a genuine state capable of providing effectively for its Muslim citizens. Its claim to legitimacy has rested in large part on its ability to govern the Islamic Caliphate.

Thirdly, ISIS has showcased its ability to thrive on adversity. Despite the countermeasures (e.g., decapitate ISIS leadership, drone strikes) implemented by the United States led coalition against ISIS, the group has remarkably continued to seize more territory within Iraq and Syria, and maintain continued functioning of its Islamic Caliphate. In fact, due to its strategic occupation of large territories across Iraq and Syria, the group has since seen considerable military and financial success ("Despite Tikrit Loss, ISIS Still", 2014). This inability to cause critical disturbance to the functioning of the Islamic Caliphate and compromise its integrity has inevitably enhanced the legitimacy and credibility of the group. In fact, evidence from the e-book titled 'The Islamic State (2015)' released by ISIS supporters, emphasised that ISIS is a resilient group which is capable of defending and expanding the territory it controls.

Lastly, many established violent extremist groups such as Al-Qaeda in the Islamic Maghreb (Zelin, 2014), Al-Qaeda in the Arabian Peninsula (Goodenough, 2014), Tehrik-e-Taliban Pakistan (Young, 2014), Islamic Movement of Uzbekistan ("The Islamic movement", 2014), and Philippines-based Bangsamoro Islamic Freedom Movement (Masi, 2014) have pledged alliance to show support for ISIS. Such developments indicate the increasing appeal of ISIS within the jihadist enclave and prospective foreign fighters. More importantly, the pledge of allegiance by other violent extremist groups has further abetted ISIS legitimacy and credibility as a group (Ali, 2014).

As countries around the globe grapple with the security threat posed by their nationals travelling to join ISIS, there is a need to be au fait with the appeal of ISIS, and its ability to glorify and validate its achievements and its visions for the future. As Emile Nakhleh, a former CIA analyst (as cited in Shane & Hubbard, 2014, para. 9) opined, "the overriding point is that success breeds success ... The perception of quick victories and territory and weapons and bases means they don't need to try hard to recruit". Thus, ISIS ability to establish and govern an Islamic Caliphate may increase its appeal for prospective foreign fighters.

The Ability to Implement Effective Recruitment Strategies

ISIS provides accessible avenues for prospective foreign fighters to fulfil their individual agenda (e.g., need for significance, need for belonging). Employing complex recruitment strategies, vulnerable individuals are targeted and manipulated. For example, by exploiting people's poor understanding of the Islam religion and their need for empowerment, ISIS offers these individuals the opportunities and shortcuts to learn about their religion and fulfil their needs (Singal, 2014). Such almost-immediate gratification of needs adds to the appeal of ISIS because it creates the impression that ISIS is able to meet their needs and solve their problems.

Most importantly, ISIS is skilled in the manipulation of religious texts to legitimise and offer justifications for its violent actions (Siddiqui, 2014). In many instance, by tailoring its ideological rationale via effective framing to create powerful positive feelings (e.g., portraying acts of oppression and killing of non-Muslims as acts of honour and victory), ISIS seeks to rationalise the appeal of becoming a foreign fighter. Thus, the ability to introduce carefully thought-out worldviews for its potential recruits has allowed ISIS the adeptness to tailor its messages to offer something for everyone.

For example, Stern and Berger (2015) in their analysis of ISIS and the foreign fighter phenomenon, observed that the goal of ISIS has shifted from overthrowing Assad regime to establishing an Islamic Caliphate govern by Islamic law. Similarly, Skinner (2015, para. 3) noted that ISIS has tailored its propaganda messages to meet the needs of its target audience:

- Feeling like an outcast? ISIS will accept you.
- Feeling persecuted? ISIS will empower you.
- Want to be loved? ISIS will love you.
- Want to be famous? ISIS will guarantee you a spotlight and your own Wikipedia page.
- Want your life to mean something? Kill for ISIS.
- Want to live forever? Die for ISIS.

This, in turn, increases the likelihood that an individual will be able to find some form of gratification and fulfil one's needs when one encounters ISIS propaganda. Hence, these developments may explain the growing appeal of ISIS worldwide. By focusing the call for jihad on a grander scale (i.e., establishing an Islamic Caliphate) and branding itself as a legitimate state, ISIS effective recruitment strategies have allowed it to entice a wider audience with its online propaganda and draw in prospective foreign fighters with a myriad of motivations.

The Adept Use of Social Media

ISIS is highly efficacious in harnessing the power of social media to inspire and attract foreign fighters to join its ranks. Exploiting the outreach afforded by social media platforms, ISIS has managed to gain access and prominence among certain demographics of the Muslim community – i.e., targeting women and the young (Maher, 2014).

Furthermore, ISIS has effectively packaged its radical narrative, as well as adapted its propaganda to 'fit' the profile of its target audience. For example, ISIS has crafted a formula to normalise the experience of a foreign fighter, while also motivating and inspiring the audience about the stability and dignity of living in the Islamic Caliphate. ISIS portrays its fighters as 'enlightened' and offers interested individuals a limited-time offer to join ISIS and experience the 'enlightenment' in the Islamic Caliphate (Singal, 2014). Another line of evidence comes from images of ISIS fighters posing with their pet cats, Snicker bars, and other commonly used items, which are constantly uploaded onto various social media platforms (Wagner, 2014). These posts, which are tagged with short messages, are meant to illustrate the 'good' times that the fighters are having.

Similarly, ISIS also engages its target audience in dialogues via social media platforms such as ask. fm and Kik Messenger, where it attempts to answer queries posed by curious individuals (Miller, 2014).

These online voices "have been essential to spreading propaganda and ensuring that newcomers know what to believe" (Wood, 2015, para. 33). Furthermore, the e-book titled 'Hijrah to the Islamic State' has been disseminated by ISIS supporters to inform readers of the how-to and must-have for the hijrah (emigration) to Iraq and Syria for jihad, and share numerous success stories of those who had made the trip. This, in turn, may move the bar for prospective recruits to identify with the foreign fighters and the Islamic Caliphate.

Interestingly, ISIS has also created online tools to manage and circumvent the limitations of social media (Behn, 2014). For example, Berger (2014) observed that ISIS has created an Android application titled 'The Dawn of the Glad Tidings' and rode on popular hashtags to maximise the outreach of its radical narratives. As a result, ISIS is able to manipulate the technological advancement of social media to inflate and amplify the reach of its radical narratives.

Besides normalising the experience of becoming a foreign fighter, ISIS has crafted images and videos that glorify the brutal use of force (e.g., beheading) towards its prisoners. This form of propaganda is aimed at a different set of audience: to intimidate the enemies of ISIS (Reuter et al., 2014). Similarly, through its online magazine, Dabiq, ISIS has called upon its followers worldwide to conduct attacks in their home countries. ISIS has also disseminated many e-books which attempt to glorify and validate the group's actions, its achievements and its visions for the future.

IMPLICATIONS

The threat of ISIS has steadily increased over the past few years. Through its well-honed online propaganda campaign, ISIS has attracted and recruited many foreign fighters to travel to Syria and Iraq for jihad. In fact, there are a larger number of foreign fighters joining ISIS in comparison to other violent extremist groups involved in the Syria conflict (al-Tamimi, 2013; Watts, 2014). Thus, there is a need to examine the factors that may contribute to the overall appeal and attractiveness of joining ISIS as a foreign fighter. The knowledge gleaned from the understanding of the appeal of ISIS could aid in the endeavour to anticipate and manage the threat that ISIS may pose.

Based on the findings of this chapter, the authors posit that for an individual to be attracted to the appeal of any violent extremist groups, factors at both the individual level and organisational level must be present.

At the individual level, the motivational factors may shape attitudes, beliefs and behaviours in ways that can increase an individual's risk or likelihood of involvement in violent extremism. While the identified individual motivational factors can be used to explain why a prospective foreign fighter may be inclined to join ISIS, it is also important to note that these factors are not necessarily unique to the context of ISIS (i.e., individuals joining other violent extremist groups have also manifested these motivations).

Besides understanding the motivational factors at the individual level, there is also a need to appreciate the organisational factors that may contribute to the appeal of a violent extremist group. These factors provide the context which influence and determine the 'connection' that an individual may develop towards the group. This implies a focus to see involvement in violent extremism, at least in psychological terms, as an interaction between the individual and the group rather than as a static process.

In the case of ISIS, the overall appeal and attractiveness of joining the group can be attributed to the presence of the following factors:

- At the *individual* level: The individual must manifest at least one of the five individual motivational factors – i.e., ideology; perceived injustice; need for significance and identity; need for belonging; desire for excitement and adventure.
- At the *organisational* level: ISIS appeal is facilitated by three organisational motivational factors – i.e., ability to establish and govern an Islamic Caliphate; the ability to implement effective recruitment strategies; adept use of social media.

Taken together, the presence and interaction of these factors (i.e., five individual motivational factors and three organisational factors) may enhance the appeal of ISIS to prospective foreign fighters. They may then complete the 'connection' by making the physical journey to Iraq and Syria.

FUTURE DIRECTION

It is hoped that this chapter may help law enforcement agencies better understand the psychological appeal of ISIS. Given that the threat of individuals becoming foreign fighters is real, the ability to reduce the appeal of ISIS and de-incentivise individuals to heed the call for jihad by ISIS is fast becoming a key area of concern for many countries.

Firstly, there is a need to appreciate the essential differences between ISIS and other violent extremist groups. ISIS has evolved beyond the 'traditional mound' of a violent extremist group to boost an effective online propaganda campaign and more importantly, a physical state in the form of an Islamic Caliphate. This implies that the knowledge which was previously utilised to address the threat of Al-Qaeda and its affiliated groups may not be useful in countering the threat of ISIS. To increase our understanding of ISIS, future studies should investigate and compare ISIS with other violent extremist groups such as Jabhat al-Nusra and al-Shabaab in order to identify any unique factors that underlined its psychological appeal.

Secondly, the fluency in which ISIS has utilised the social media highlights the growing volatility and threats facing law enforcement agencies today. In response, efforts should be taken to formulate counter narratives to mitigate ISIS online propaganda campaign by using the online platforms that ISIS has exploited. This may allow law enforcement agencies to match the volume of ISIS propaganda online. Future studies should also examine the way ISIS has exploited the Internet to better identify (1) who is its target audience, (2) what narrative is being exploited by ISIS, and (3) what online medium is used to deliver the narrative.

Lastly, law enforcement agencies have to act before an individual becomes attracted to ISIS. However, the huge amount of available intelligence makes the identification of such individuals among the general population a daunting task. To increase the chances of managing the threat, authorities need to involve the local community (e.g., family, friends, colleagues) to look out for behavioural indicators that is associated with the individual motivational factors as identified in this chapter. This, in turn, may aid in the early identification of individuals who may be attracted to violent extremist groups such as ISIS.

ACKNOWLEDGMENT

Views expressed in this chapter belong to the authors only and do not represent the official position or views of the Ministry of Home Affairs, Singapore.

REFERENCES

Abu Bakr al-Baghdadi urges Muslims to make hijrah to the Islamic State. (2014). *5 Pillarz*. Retrieved from http://www.5pillarz.com/2014/07/02/abu-bakr-al-baghdadi-urges-muslims-to-make-hijrah-to-the-islamic-state/

al-Tamimi, A. J. (2013, December 24). The Syrian rebel groups pulling in foreign fighters. *BBC News*. Retrieved from http://www.bbc.com/news/world-middle-east-25460397

Ali, M. (2014). *'Jihad' in Syria: Fallacies of ISIS' end time prophecies. RSIS Commentaries (149/2014)*. Singapore: S. Rajaratnam School of International Studies.

Altman, A. (2014, September 22). Government veterans to take fight to extremists on online battleground. *Time*. Retrieved from http://time.com/3418918/counter-extremism-group-isis-twitter-Internet/

Bartlett, J. (2008). *'Wicked' jihad and the appeal of violent extremism*. London: DEMOS.

Baumeister, R., & Leary, M. R. (1995). The need to belong: Desire for interpersonal attachments as fundamental human motivation. *Psychological Bulletin, 117*(3), 497–529. doi:10.1037/0033-2909.117.3.497 PMID:7777651

Behn, S. (2014, September 5). ISIS militants use 'Jihadi cool' to recruit globally. *Voices of America (VOA)*. Retrieved from http://www.thecuttingedgenews.com/index.php?article=85237

Berger, J. M. (2014). How ISIS games Twitter. *The Atlantic*. Retrieved from http://www.theatlantic.com/international/archive/2014/06/isis-iraq-twitter-social-media-strategy/372856/

Borum, R. (2004). *Psychology of terrorism*. Tampa: University of South Florida.

Borum, R. (2014). Psychological vulnerabilities and propensities for involvement in violent extremism. *Behavioral Sciences & the Law, 32*(3), 286–305. doi:10.1002/bsl.2110 PMID:24652686

Brown, A., Abernethy, A., Gorsuch, R., & Dueck, A. C. (2010). Sacred violations, perceptions of injustice, and anger in Muslims. *Journal of Applied Social Psychology, 40*(5), 1003–1027. doi:10.1111/j.1559-1816.2010.00608.x

Byrne, P. (2014, July 15). British ISIS militant Abdul Raqib Amin believed killed by Iraqi soldiers. *Mirror*. Retrieved from http://www.mirror.co.uk/news/uk-news/british-isis-militant-abdul-raqib-3866692

Calais, D. C. (2014, September 7). Brussels museum shooting suspect 'beheaded baby'. *The Telegraph*. Retrieved from http://www.telegraph.co.uk/news/worldnews/middleeast/syria/11080079/Brussels-museum-shooting-suspect-beheaded-baby.html

Carter, J. A., Maher, S., & Neumann, P. R. (2014, April 15). *ICSR Insight: Who inspires the Syrian foreign fighters?* The International Centre for the Study of Radicalisation. Retrieved from http://icsr.info/category/icsr-news/insights/

Casciani, D. (2014, October 9). How the battle against IS is being fought online. *BBC News*. Retrieved from http://www.bbc.com/news/magazine-29535343

Cilluffo, F. J., Cozzens, J. B., & Ranstorp, M. (2010). *Foreign fighters: Trends, trajectories & conflict zones*. Homeland Security & Policy Institutes. Retrieved from http://www.gwumc.edu/hspi/policy/report_foreignfighters501.pdf

Crenshaw, M. (2007). *The debate over 'new' vs 'old' terrorism*. Paper presented at the annual meeting of the American Political Science Association, Chicago, IL.

Cunningham, E. (2015, July 2). In Ramadi, the Islamic State settles in, fixing roads and restoring electricity. *The Washington Post*. Retrieved from https://www.washingtonpost.com/world/middle_east/in-ramadi-the-islamic-state-settles-in-fixing-roads-and-restoring-electricity/2015/07/01/db32ccec-19e2-11e5-bed8-1093ee58dad0_story.html

Despite Tikrit loss, ISIS still holds large swaths of Iraq. (2015). *The New York Times*. Retrieved from http://www.nytimes.com/interactive/2014/06/12/world/middleeast/the-iraq-isis-conflict-in-maps-photos-and-video.html?_r=0

Engel, R. (2013, November 3). Analysis: Did Syria's Assad get away with chemical weapons attack? *NBC News*. Retrieved from http://www.nbcnews.com/news/other/analysis-did-syrias-assad-get-away-chemical-weapons-attack-f8C11519031

Friedman, D., & Siemaszko, C. (2014, June 19). Home-grown terror: American jihadist wannabes flock to ISIS-like groups in Iraq and Syria. *Daily News*. Retrieved from http://www.nydailynews.com/news/national/jihadist-wannabes-u-s-flock-isis-like-groups-overseas-article-1.1837013

Goodenough, P. (2014, August 20). Al-Qaeda in Yemen announces 'solidarity' with 'our Muslims Brothers in Iraq'. *CNS News*. Retrieved from http://www.cnsnews.com/news/article/patrick-goodenough/al-qaeda-yemen-announces-solidarity-our-muslim-brothers-iraq

Gorman, S., Malas, N., & Bradley, M. (2014). Brutal Efficiency: The secret to Islamic State's Success. *The Wall Street Journal*. Retrieved from http://online.wsj.com/articles/the-secret-to-the-success-of-islamic-state-1409709762

Gupta, D. K. (2011). Waves of international terrorism: An exploration of the process by which ideas flood the world. In J. E. Rosenfeld (Ed.), *Terrorism, identity and legitimacy: The four waves theory and political violence* (pp. 30–43). New York, NY: Routledge.

Hall, J. (2014, September 19). The ISIS family tree: Sinister and organised network that begins with 'the caliph' and continues with a rigid chain of command down to foot soldiers. *Mail Online*. Retrieved from http://www.dailymail.co.uk/news/article-2761071/The-ISIS-family-tree-Sinister-organised-network-begins-caliph-continues-rigid-chain-command-level-foot-soldiers.html

Hegghammer, T. (2013). Should I stay or should I go. Explaining variation in western jihadists' choice between domestic and foreign fighting. *The American Political Science Review, 107*(01), 1–15. doi:10.1017/S0003055412000615

Horgan, J. (2008). From profiles to pathways and roots to routes: Perspectives from psychology on radicalization into terrorism. *The Annals of the American Academy of Political and Social Science, 618*(1), 80–94. doi:10.1177/0002716208317539

Jenkins, B. M. (2015, March 20). *The allure of ISIS for young recruits.* RAND Commentary. Retrieved from http://www.rand.org/blog/2015/03/the-allure-of-isis-for-young-recruits.html

Kohlmann, E., & Alkhouri, L. (2014, September 29). Profiles of Foreign Fighters in Syria and Iraq. *CTC Sentinel, 7*(9), 1–4.

Kruglanski, A. W. (2014, October 28). Psychology not theology: Overcoming ISIS' secret appeal. *E-International Relations.* Retrieved from http://www.e-ir.info/2014/10/28/psychology-not-theology-overcoming-isis-secret-appeal/

Lavigne, G. L., Vallerand, R. J., & Crevier-Braud, L. (2011). The fundamental need to belong: On the distinction between growth and deficit-reduction orientations. *Personality and Social Psychology Bulletin, 37*(9), 1185–1201. doi:10.1177/0146167211405995 PMID:21540365

Maher, S. (2014, November 6). From Portsmouth to Kobane: the British Jihadis fighting for ISIS. *NewStatesman.* Retrieved from http://www.newstatesman.com/2014/10/portsmouth-kobane

Malet, D. (2009). *Foreign fighters: Transnational identity in civil conflicts* (Doctoral dissertation). Retrieved from http://davidmalet.com/uploads/Why_Foreign_Fighters_Malet.pdf

Malet, D. (2013). *Foreign fighters: Transnational identity in civil conflicts.* New York, NY: Oxford University Press. doi:10.1093/acprof:oso/9780199939459.001.0001

Masi, A. (2014, October 9). Where to find ISIS supporters: A map of militant groups aligned with the Islamic State group. *International Business Times.* Retrieved from http://www.ibtimes.com/where-find-isis-supporters-map-militant-groups-aligned-islamic-state-group-1701878

Maslow, A. H. (1943). A theory of human motivation. *Psychological Review, 50*(4), 370–396. doi:10.1037/h0054346

Meir Amit Intelligence and Terrorism Information Center (MAITIC). (2013, December). *Foreign fighters in Syria.* Retrieved from http://www.terrorism-info.org.il/en/article/20607

Miller, J. (2014, June 25). Can Iraqi militants be kept off social media sites? *BBC News.* Retrieved from http://www.bbc.com/news/technology-28016834

National Offender Management Service. (2011). *Extremism risk guidance 22.* London: Ministry of Justice Publications.

Neo, L. S., Khader, M., Ang, J., Ong, G., & Tan, E. (2014). Developing an early screening guide for jihadi terrorism: A behavioural analysis of 30 terror attacks. *Security Journal.* doi:10.1057/sj.2014.44

Neo, L. S., Khader, M., Shi, P., Dillon, L., & Ong, G. (2015). *Extremist cyber footprints: A guide to understanding and countering online extremism.* Singapore: Home Team Behavioural Sciences Centre.

Neo, L. S., Shi, P., Dillon, L., Ong, G., Tan, E., & Khader, M. (2014). *Why is ISIS so psychologically attractive? A behavioural sciences perspective (Research report no. 18/2014).* Singapore: Home Team Behavioural Sciences Centre.

Nuraniyah, N. (2014, February 24). *Syrian conflict fallout: Time to contain hate speech in Indonesia.* RSIS Commentaries (038/2014). Singapore: S. Rajaratnam School of International Studies.

Post, J. M., Ruby, K. G., & Shaw, E. C. (2002). The radical group in context: 1. An integrated framework for the analysis of group risk for terrorism. *Studies in Conflict and Terrorism, 25*(2), 73–100. doi:10.1080/105761002753502466

Reuter, C., Salloum, R., & Shafy, S. (2014, October 8). Inside Islamic State's Savvy PR War. *Spiegel.* Retrieved from http://www.spiegel.de/international/world/the-professional-pr-strategies-of-isis-in-syria-and-iraq-a-995611.html

Rose, S. (2014, October 7). The Isis propaganda war: a hi-tech media jihad. *The Guardian.* Retrieved from http://www.theguardian.com/world/2014/oct/07/isis-media-machine-propaganda-war

Samuel, T. K. (2015). *M.A.D. (making a difference) Amidst Mad People: Addressing Foreign Fighter Involvement in Terrorist Campaigns.* Paper presented at CENS Workshop on Countering Extremism: Islamic State and Beyond, Singapore.

Schmid, A. (Ed.). (2011). *The Routledge Handbook of Terrorism Research.* New York, NY: Routledge.

Shane, S., & Hubbard, B. (2014, August 30). ISIS displaying a deft command of varied media. *The New York Times.* Retrieved from http://www.nytimes.com/2014/08/31/world/middleeast/isis-displaying-a-deft-command-of-varied-media.html?_r=0

Shi, P., Dillon, L., Neo, L. S., Tan, J., Wang, Y., Gold, L., & Khader, M. et al. (2014). *Syria's foreign fighters: Motivations to fight (Brief Report Series 12/2014).* Singapore: Home Team Behavioural Sciences Centre.

Siddiqui, M. (2014, August 24). ISIS: A contrived ideology justifying barbarism and sexual control. *The Guardian.* Retrieved from http://www.theguardian.com/commentisfree/2014/aug/24/isis-ideology-islamic-militants-british-appeal-iraq-syria

Siegel, P. (2014). Foreign fighters – Syria: Why we should be worried. *TRAC.* Retrieved from http://www.trackingterrorism.org/article/foreign-fighters-syria-why-we-should-be-worried

Singal, J. (2014, August 18). Why ISIS is so terrifyingly effective at seducing new recruits? *NYMag.* Retrieved from http://nymag.com/scienceofus/2014/08/how-isis-seduces-new-recruits.html

Skidmore, J. (2014). *Foreign fighter involvement in Syria.* Herzliya, Israel: International Institute for Counter-Terrorism.

Skinner, P. (2015, September 2). The power of ISIS' message. *The Cipher Brief.* Retrieved from https://www.thecipherbrief.com/article/power-isis-message-0

Sorko-Ram, S. (2012, March). Why Syria's Assad can't stop killing his own people. *MaozIsrael.* Retrieved from http://www.maozisrael.org/site/News2?id=9174#1

Stern, J., & Berger, J. M. (2015, March 8). ISIS and the foreign-fighter phenomenon. *The Atlantic.* Retrieved from http://www.theatlantic.com/international/archive/2015/03/isis-and-the-foreign-fighter-problem/387166/

Stillman, T., & Baumeister, R. (2009). Uncertainty, belongingness, and four needs for meaning. *Psychological Inquiry, 20*(4), 249–251. doi:10.1080/10478400903333544

The Islamic movement of Uzbekistan: An evolving threat. (2014, May 31). *Radio Free Europe Radio Liberty (RFERL)*. Retrieved from http://www.rferl.org/content/islamic-movement-uzbekistan-roundtable/25405614.html

The Islamic State of Iraq and Syria. (2015). *The Islamic State (2015)*. Author.

van Ginkel, B. (2015). Responding to cyber jihad: Towards an effective counter narrative. The Netherlands: International Centre for Counter-Terrorism – The Hague.

Venhaus, J. M. (2010). *Why youths join al-Qaeda. Special Report 236*. Washington, DC: United States Institute of Peace.

Wagner, M. (2014, August 23). Apparent ISIS terrorists take photos with Nutella to seem softer, friendlier to West. *New York Daily News*. Retrieved from http://www.nydailynews.com/news/world/isis-fighters-photos-nutella-friendly-article-1.1914450

Walton, G. M., Cohen, G. L., Cwir, D., & Spencer, S. J. (2012). Mere belonging: The power of social connections. *Journal of Personality and Social Psychology, 102*(3), 513–532. doi:10.1037/a0025731 PMID:22023711

Watts, C. (2014). Jihadi competition after Al-Qaeda hegemony – The 'old guard', Team ISIS and the battle for jihad hearts and minds. *Foreign Policy Research Institute*. Retrieved from http://www.fpri.org/geopoliticus/2014/02/jihadi-competition-after-al-qaeda-hegemony-old-guard-team-isis-battle-jihadi-hearts-minds

What is 'Islamic State'? (2015, October 8). *BBC News*. Retrieved from http://www.bbc.com/news/world-middle-east-29052144

Williams, D., & Marsden, S. (2014, August 11). The Cardiff jihadist who wants to die a 'martyr': Student fighting for Islamic state warns of 'fireworks' when US returns sparking fears of suicide missions. *Dailymail*. Retrieved from http://www.dailymail.co.uk/news/article-2722384/Reyaad-Khan-The-Cardiff-jihadist-wants-die-martyr.html

Wood, G. (2015, March). What ISIS Really Wants. *The Atlantic*. Retrieved from http://www.theatlantic.com/magazine/archive/2015/03/what-isis-really-wants/384980/

Young, A. (2014, October 4). Pakistan Taliban pledge support to ISIS militants. *International Business Times*. Retrieved from http://www.ibtimes.com/pakistan-taliban-pledges-support-isis-militants-1699490

Zelin, A. Y. (2013a, April 2). *ICSR Insight: European foreign fighters in Syria*. The International Centre for the Study of Radicalisation. Retrieved from http://icsr.info/2013/04/icsr-insight-european-foreign-fighters-in-syria-2/

Zelin, A. Y. (2013b, December 5). Who are the foreign fighters in Syria? *The Washington Institute*. Retrieved from http://www.washingtoninstitute.org/policy-analysis/view/who-are-the-foreign-fighters-in-syria

Zelin, A. Y. (2013c, August 7). International jihad and the Syrian conflict. *The Washington Institute for Near East Policy*. Retrieved from http://www.washingtoninstitute.org/policy-analysis/view/international-jihad-and-the-syrian-conflict

Zelin, A. Y. (2014, June). The war between ISIS and al-Qaeda for supremacy of the Global Jihadist Movement. *The Washington Institute for Near East Policy*. Retrieved from http://www.washingtoninstitute.org/uploads/Documents/pubs/ResearchNote_20_Zelin.pdf

Zuckerman, M. (1994). *Behavioural expressions and biosocial bases of sensation-seeking*. New York, NY: Cambridge Press.

Chapter 9
Psychological Effects of the Threat of ISIS:
A Preliminary Inquiry of Singapore Case Studies

Weiying Hu
Ministry of Home Affairs, Singapore

ABSTRACT

The threat of violent extremism has been considerably influenced by the self-proclaimed Islamic State in Iraq and Syria (ISIS), its inhumane brutal killings in Iraq and Syria, and exploitation of social media to recruit large numbers of foreign fighters in a scale never seen before. This development has serious implications for Singapore's security landscape. This aggressive promotion of fighting in Syria has resonated with a handful of Singaporeans, who were radicalised by radical online propaganda. In this psychological study of the Singapore cases, there are five psychological drivers that have contributed to the radicalisation process of these cases. They are: (1) justifying violence, (2) romanticising the notion of a utopian state, (3) desire to be a 'good' Muslim, (4) escaping the 'unbearable present' world, and (5) existential anxiety in relation to End Times prophecies. The preliminary findings further indicate that most of these radicalised individuals have engaged in negative activism.

INTRODUCTION

Extremist ideological narratives that are pervasive on the Internet have proven capable of gaining a foothold in the psyche of individuals who seek some form of justifications for their frustrations and anger over the plight of Muslims suffering in conflict zones. Some Singaporeans have not been immune to such narratives, nor resist the lure of the violent ideology perpetuated by the Islamic State in Iraq and Syria (ISIS). Two Singapore citizens are known to have gone to Syria with their families to partake in the conflict there (Saad, 2014). At the time of writing, a few other Singaporeans had intended to fight in Syria (among other foreign conflict zones) but were stopped in time from doing so. Thus far, a handful had been detained under the Internal Security Act (ISA) to prevent them from fighting in Syria (Lim, 2015).

DOI: 10.4018/978-1-5225-0156-5.ch009

Apart from these cases, several other Singaporeans were detected to have been radicalised by radical online propaganda. They did not have any formal religious education and relied primarily on the Internet for religious knowledge. These individuals were at different stages of radicalisation. Some had considered travelling to Syria or Iraq for jihad. Others were supportive of the armed jihad and showed their support through pro-jihadi online postings, or purchased jihadi-themed paraphernalia like ISIS flags, or apparel and stickers with captions and graphics that carried connotations of militant jihad.

A commonly asked question is whether there is a particular profile to these home-grown radicalised individuals that can help identify a person who is likely to gravitate towards violent extremism. A team of psychologists has worked with these radicalised individuals (i.e., those who have been dealt with under the ISA as well as those who were in the various stages of radicalisation) as part of Singapore's holistic approach towards the rehabilitation of these individuals. From the psychological research, no fixed profile could be distilled. The psychologists however did identify several common psychological factors that have underpinned those individuals' sympathy for the ISIS cause.

THE PSYCHOLOGY OF HOME-GROWN RADICALISED INDIVIDUALS

Ability to Justify the Use of Violence

The key feature in the radicalisation of these individuals appears to be their ability to rationalise and justify the use of violence. There are three ways in which such justifications have been made (Sabuced, Blaco, & De la Corte, 2003): (1) through attributing responsibility to the opponent, (2) by delegitimising the opponent, and (3) through the asymmetrical evaluation of suffering.

Displacing Responsibility to the Enemy

The majority of the radicalised individuals studied were found to have developed a binary worldview that enabled them to separate the 'good guys' from those they believed to be responsible for the Syrian crisis. When faced with a violent situation, they had a tendency to engage in external attribution of responsibilities (Hewstone, Jaspars, & Lallje, 1982; Taylor, & Jaggi, 1974), blaming the opponents for initiating violence (Sabuced et al., 2003). This is similar to the rhetoric used by supporters of ISIS, where the responsibility for ISIS violent and extreme actions is displaced onto its enemies. The argument used is that the 'morally reprehensible' actions of the Bashar Assad regime justified and legitimised ISIS violent retaliation, and that the violence employed was mainly in defence of the vulnerable and helpless individuals who were oppressed by the regime.

Many radicalised individuals view the West as the enemy, for being the source of evils that have corrupted and tyrannised Muslims. Given the asymmetrical nature of the balance of power between the armed forces of the West and that of ISIS, the latter's use of violent means is therefore perceived as legitimate, as it is wielded with the purpose of redressing the alleged injustices done to Muslims.

This perspective was articulated by a Singaporean subject who said that ISIS was the "good guys" protecting Iraq from the American invaders, and ISIS actions were "right" because they were protecting the land of the Muslims. He also regarded the ISIS fighters as freedom fighters.

Delegitimising the Opponent

Another psychological process used to justify the use of violence is to derogate the opponent through the attribution of 'inhuman' characteristics, like cruelty or lack of compassion (Sabuced et al., 2003). The arguments in support of ISIS rely on portraying Syrian President Bashar Assad as someone who is 'less than a human', capable of acts of atrocities that a 'normal human being' would not perform.

Another method of delegitimising the opponent is to draw connections between the enemy and other groups associated with negative values (Sabuced et al., 2003), such as cult groups. As it would be unthinkable to commit acts of violence against a member of the in-group, it is necessary to classify the opponent as members of the out-group which carries negative connotations. For instance, some extremists have disqualified Bashar Assad as a Muslim due to his alleged cruel acts against vulnerable innocents, while others have rejected his Shi'ite-Alawite religious sect as illegitimate followers of the Islamic faith. Violence against the out-group (i.e., President Bashar Assad) is justifiable because its nature and actions pose a threat to the security, existence and progress of the in-group (i.e., Sunni Muslims who adopted ISIS ideology).

Asymmetrical Evaluation of Suffering

To justify the use of violence as a form of retaliation and defence, the supporters of ISIS have adopted the asymmetrical evaluation of suffering. Asymmetrical evaluation of suffering refers to the conviction that the suffering that ISIS is inflicting is insignificant when compared to the suffering that President Bashar Assad has allegedly inflicted on the Syrian Sunni Muslims. While it cannot be denied that ISIS has committed severe acts of violence on its part in the Syrian conflict, the focus is instead placed on President Bashar Assad's alleged acts of atrocity against Muslims and the innocents in Syria. The materials published by ISIS (Alhayat Media Centre, 2014) have also highlighted the good deeds that it has done in the conflict zones, to mitigate the sufferings that ISIS violent actions have caused.

Romanticising the Notion of an Islamic Caliphate

The second driver in the radicalisation process of the Singaporeans we have studied is their tendency to romanticise the notion of an Islamic Caliphate. Many extremists have portrayed Muslim states as being ruled by corrupt governments that are under the influence of Western powers (Johnson, 2004). Consequently, there is a strong desire for peace to reign in the Middle East, and to restore the Islamic caliphate to its former glory and influence of the time of the Ottoman Empire. The romantic vision of a utopian caliphate is embodied today by the Islamic caliphate that ISIS has claimed to have established in Syria and Iraq, and which it is seeking to expand. The supporters of ISIS believe that the ISIS Islamic caliphate will bring about the ideal Muslim community, where Islamic values, governance and economic systems are in place.

Desire to be 'Good' Muslims

The third factor underpinning the radicalisation of the Singapore cases is their desire to be a 'good' Muslim. It is not unusual that in the search for meaning in life, one is confronted with existential anxiety revolving around the idea of death/afterlife and hence one's level of religious piety (i.e., whether he is considered a good Muslim and will be rewarded in the afterlife). In the face of that anxiety arising from one's perceived lack of religiosity, an individual might adopt a past-negative and present-fatalistic time perspective – i.e., to have a negative view of his past while feeling helpless about the present (Zimbardo & Boyd, 2009). For example, when faced with the idea of death, the individual might examine his past, identify the large number of sins he has committed, and feel the need to become a better person.

To assuage this existential anxiety, ISIS has attempted to replace these time perspectives with the transcendental-future and present-hedonistic time perspectives – i.e., focusing on the goals, rewards and punishments awaiting in the afterlife, and enjoying the present (Zimbardo & Boyd, 2009).

Redemption and Rewards in Afterlife (Transcendental-Future Time Perspective)

In order to assuage one's existential anxiety (in psychology, referred to as 'transcendental-future time perspective'), one focuses on the events occurring in the afterlife, including judgement, rewards, and punishments. The rhetoric by radical groups such as ISIS seeks to provide its followers with untestable but attractive notions about what happens after death. Their rhetoric provides hope, opportunity and fulfilment en route to paradise (i.e., transcendental-future time perspective). By engaging in armed jihad, these individuals are persuaded by the notion that they will not only redeem themselves by sacrificing themselves for God and rendering help to the vulnerable, they (and their families) will also be equally rewarded in paradise.

Desire for Excitement (Present-Hedonistic Time Perspective)

In achieving a present state of enjoyment (in psychology, referred to as the 'present-hedonistic time perspective'), these individuals seek activities that are "pleasurable, arousing, stimulating, exciting and novel" (Zimbardo & Boyd, 2009, p. 106). Novelty-seeking theory suggests that some individuals are drawn to violent extremism because they desire to seek adventure and participate in novel activities, particularly courses of action that carry some element of danger or risk (Victoroff, 2005). Research has shown that these individuals crave excitement and are enthralled with the arousals obtained from performing violent acts (Cottee & Hayward, 2011). This perspective is supported by Bartlett's research where he suggests that "there is something appealing about the 'violent' bit of violent extremism" (Bartlett, 2008, p. 2). Flirting with danger and being part of the action are some of the psychological mechanisms that might explain the attraction to violent extremism (Cottee & Hayward, 2011). Moreover, research has shown that engagement in war helps people accord meaning in their lives by enabling them to transcend their individuality and risk their lives for a noble cause (Mael & Ashforth, 2001).

Indeed, findings from the psychological interviews revealed that some of the radicalised Singaporeans did not subscribe to extremist ideologies or participate in the cause because of altruistic intentions (McCauley & Moskalenko, 2011). Rather they had romanticised the idea of being part of the real action or dangerous adventure (Silke, 2008). For this specific group of individuals, adrenaline-pumping adventures like taking up arms in Syria represent the elevated experience of their lives (Cottee & Hayward, 2011).

End Times Prophecies

The fourth driver is the existential anxiety generated by 'End Times' prophecies in individuals with a transcendental time perspective. The apparent relevance of End Times prophecies with the fighting in

Syria and Iraq is seen as a sign that the end is indeed near. It creates the sense that the time has come for the bodily life to end, and to transit into the next phase in the afterlife. The vision of the afterlife includes divine judgement, with the due rewards and punishments meted out, and the end of pain and suffering. ISIS has cleverly capitalised on these End Times prophecies to heighten existential anxiety and motivate people to increase their level of religious piety by engaging in a 'worthy cause'. The fear of missing the opportunity to partake in the cause is what drives this urgent need for activism (including partaking in the war).

ACTION: ENGAGING IN NEGATIVE ACTIVISM

In view of the psychological drivers mentioned above, the findings also demonstrated that the radicalised individuals are often motivated to engage in what is termed as 'misplaced activism'. For most of the individuals interviewed, they were not ready to travel to Syria to partake in the armed struggle. Thus, their need for action drove them to engage in negative activism, like buying jihadi paraphernalia or engaging in 'clicktivism' (Alexandrova, 2011). The latter refers to the act of activism achieved by clicking on an Internet-connected device, such as 'liking' or 'retweeting' a link to promote the jihadi cause.

ISIS has successfully capitalised on both online and offline social and political action. Clicking 'like' on the Facebook profile of a foreign fighter or sharing his status update suggests support for the foreign fighter. An indication of support for the foreign fighter in turn signifies the endorsement of the unlawful violence carried out in Syria. It has a similar impact to 'sharing' that picture or status on one's own page. With a click on 'like' or 'share' on social media, one could easily enable ISIS messages to be communicated to a wider audience. Thus, clicktivism has become an effective form of activism, particularly in demonstrating support explicitly and in creating awareness for the cause.

CONCLUSION

The ISIS cause continues to resonate with some owing to the psychological drivers that the psychologists have identified through interviews with the radicalised Singaporeans, who were drawn to the group and its ideology. In order to wean these individuals off the ISIS ideology, it is necessary to put forth a credible counter-argument to the ideology and legitimacy of the ISIS cause. In this regard, psychological and religious counselling can help to bring about a cognitive reframing in these individuals.

REFERENCES

Alexandrova, E. (2011). Metamorphoses of civil society and politics: From Ganko's Café to Facebook. In G. Lozanov & O. Spassov (Eds.), *Media and politics* (pp. 102–117). Konrad Adenauer Stiftung.

Alhayat Media Centre. (2014, July). The flood. *Dabiq*, *2*, 35–38.

Bartlett, J. (2008). *'Wicked' jihad and the appeal of violent extremism*. London: DEMOS.

Cottee, S., & Hayward, K. (2011). Terrorist (E)motives: The existential attractions of terrorism. *Studies in Conflict and Terrorism, 34*(12), 963–986. doi:10.1080/1057610X.2011.621116

Hewstone, M., Jaspars, J., & Lalljee, M. (1982). Social representations, social attribution and social identity: The intergroup images of 'public' and 'comprehensive' schoolboys. *European Journal of Social Psychology, 12*(3), 241–269. doi:10.1002/ejsp.2420120302

Johnson, C. (2004). *The sorrows of empire: Militarism, secrecy, and the end of republic.* New York, NY: Metropolitan Books.

Lim, Y. L. (2015, September 30). Two Singaporeans detained for making plans to travel to Syria to join ISIS. *The Straits Times.* Retrieved from http://www.straitstimes.com/singapore/courts-crime/two-singaporeans-detained-for-making-plans-to-travel-to-syria-to-join-isis

Mael, F. A., & Ashforth, B. E. (2001). Identification in work, war, sports, and religion: Contrasting the benefits and risks. *Journal for the Theory of Social Behaviour, 31*(2), 197–222. doi:10.1111/1468-5914.00154

McCauley, C., & Moskalenko, S. (2011). *Friction: How radicalization happens to them and us.* New York, NY: Oxford University Press.

Saad, I. (2014, July 9). 'Handful' of Singaporeans went to Syria to join conflict: DPM Teo. *Channel News Asia.* Retrieved from http://www.channelnewsasia.com/news/specialreports/parliament/news/handful-of-singaporeans/1248994.html

Sabuced, J. M., Blaco, A., & De la Corte, L. (2003). Beliefs which legitimize political violence against the innocents. *Psicothema, 15*(4), 550–555.

Silke, A. (2008). Holy warriors exploring the psychological processes of Jihadi radicalization. *European Journal of Criminology, 5*(1), 99–123. doi:10.1177/1477370807084226

Taylor, D. M., & Jaggi, V. (1974). Ethocentrism and casual attribution in a South Indian context. *Journal of Cross-Cultural Psychology, 5*(2), 192–171. doi:10.1177/002202217400500202

Victoroff, J. (2005). The mind of the terrorist: A review of critique of psychological approaches. *The Journal of Conflict Resolution, 49*(1), 3–42. doi:10.1177/0022002704272040

Zimbardo, P., & Boyd, J. (2009). *The Time Paradox: The New Psychology of Time that will Change Your Life.* New York, NY: Free Press.

Chapter 10

Western Female Migrants to ISIS:
Propaganda, Radicalisation, and Recruitment

Erin Marie Saltman
Institute for Strategic Dialogue, UK

ABSTRACT

Women have long been a blind spot for security, academic and think tank sectors in relation to the growing threat of global extremism. The recent spike in female recruitment to the terrorist organisation, Islamic State in Iraq and Syria (ISIS), is a strong indicator of this dangerous trend. While often assumed to be passive agents, women continue to play strong roles in online and offline recruitment to violent extremist organisations. However, women can also act as strong counter-extremism agents in the fight against radicalisation and terrorism. Looking at the issue of gender, there is a new ability through online research to retrieve valuable insight into terrorist strategies around recruitment of women from online propaganda. This chapter aims to address questions of gender within current radicalisation trends through an analysis of online data, and through tracking Western females who are migrating to territories under the control of ISIS.

INTRODUCTION

Women have long been a blind spot for security, academic and think tank sectors in relation to the growing threat of global extremism. The recent spike in female recruitment to the terrorist organisation, Islamic State in Iraq and Syria (ISIS), is a strong indicator of this dangerous trend. While often assumed to be passive agents, women continue to play strong roles in online and offline recruitment to violent extremist organisations. However, women can also act as strong counter-extremism agents in the fight against radicalisation and terrorism. It is fundamental to better understand the role women play within violent extremist organisations. It is also important to analyse whether processes of radicalisation differ between men and women, and if so, how counter-extremism efforts can be tailored to specific target audiences.

DOI: 10.4018/978-1-5225-0156-5.ch010

This chapter aims to address questions of gender within current radicalisation trends through an analysis of data being collected online, and tracking Western females who are choosing to migrate to territories under the control of ISIS. In an increasingly digital era we are given access to an abundance of data through open source information retrieval on platforms such as Facebook, Twitter and YouTube, as well as other platforms such ask.fm, BlogSpot, Instagram and Tumblr. Looking at the issue of gender, there is a new ability through online research to retrieve valuable insight into terrorist strategies around recruitment of women from online propaganda (Saltman & Smith, 2015), digital manifestos aimed at women (Winter, 2015), and testimonials from women that have tried, and been detained, from traveling to Syria.

The utilisation of online tools by violent extremist and terrorist organisations, like ISIS, has had real world consequences. The number of Western foreign terrorist fighters (FTF) and female migrants joining ISIS in Iraq and Syria was last estimated at upwards of 4,000, with over 550 women within this figure (Barrett, 2014; Hoyle, Bradford, & Frenett, 2015). While these estimates were originally given in October 2014, it is assumed the number has increased significantly since then. These are unprecedented numbers, particularly with reference to the seemingly new phenomenon of Western women migrating en masse to join ISIS. This has shocked many and forced security services to re-evaluate the risk these women pose both domestically and internationally (Hoyle et al., 2015). While the Internet cannot be considered a sole cause of these figures, there is no doubt that online pathways have facilitated violent extremist recruitment and have been catalysts for processes of radicalisation (Hussain & Saltman, 2014).

Previously, public perceptions of jihadists and members of terrorist organisations have maintained an air of mystery; viewed roughly as fear-inducing fanatics and barbaric terrorists. Messaging within Al-Qaeda and other groups has traditionally been highly centralised and secretive (Saltman & Winter, 2014). The life of a jihadist was perceived as rugged, violent and detached from civil society. However, we are now witnessing a fundamental shift. If the Vietnam War can be considered the first televised war, and the Gulf War the first 24-hour news war, we have come to a point where the current crisis in Iraq and Syria has been deemed the first social media war (Jones, 2014; O'Neil, 2013). While this digital frontline has caused a new level of fear from security services and the greater public towards online extremist propaganda and terrorist networking, it has also provided researchers and analysts with an incredible lens into the lives of FTF, their organisational support networks, and their female counterparts.

The Institute for Strategic Dialogue (ISD) has been analysing violent extremist discourse and online extremism for the last six plus years as part of its counter-extremism research and program streams. In partnership with the International Centre for the Study of Radicalisation (ICSR), ISD has cultivated a large-scale database of Western females migrating to ISIS territory as part of its Women and Extremism (WaE) program. The Western female migrant database has been expanding in breadth and depth since May 2014. At the time of writing, it is considered to be the largest database of its kind, running in parallel to the ICSR database on male FTF. This database tracks and archives social media material of over 120 female profiles across a range of online platforms. Archived data is of great importance to online research of this kind since violent extremist and terrorist-related accounts are quickly suspended or taken down from larger platforms as their more controversial content is flagged through user-based systems. From this data, the process of radicalisation is tracked from the perspective of female recruits. Likewise the role women play within modern jihadist movements like ISIS can be seen in a much more personal and direct manner than ever before.

Recognising this new and growing phenomenon, the research of this chapter is based largely on the first two publications within the WaE series: *Becoming Mulan?: Female Western Migrants to ISIS* (Hoyle et al., 2015) and *Till Martyrdom do us Part: Gender and the ISIS Phenomenon* (Saltman & Smith, 2015). While Hoyle et al. (2015) explored the emotional journey of migration for females joining ISIS and the roles they play within ISIS territory, Saltman and Smith (2015) mapped out the push and pull factors within processes of radicalisation for women and girls as well as giving an analysis on current countering violent extremism (CVE) prevention and de-radicalisation programs across Europe with a focus on gender. Adding to these research-based reports, this chapter is divided into four sections in order to best explore the topic of female radicalisation within a digital era.

Firstly, it is important to give a historical context to the subject of women within violent extremist organisations so that the current shift in trends is better understood. This gives perspective with regards to why the current ISIS phenomenon should be considered a game-changer. The second section of this chapter analyses the role that the Internet plays in contemporary processes of radicalisation and online recruitment, including how these processes differ for men and women. Progressing from this is an overview of how women are migrating to ISIS territory and the role the Internet plays in facilitating this journey, both logistically and ideologically. The chapter concludes with an examination of life for women within ISIS territory through an analysis of social media and through an evaluation of the role women play as non-combatant actors supporting a highly violent organisation.

This chapter argues that the advantages the Internet provides leaves great scope for security services, private sectors and civil society to better utilise online resources in CVE online. Surveillance, monitoring and more proactive counter-narrative developments are under-utilised pathways for CVE work. There is also a much stronger role for women to play within the CVE sector both as credible messengers within the prevention space and as practitioners on local and national levels.

HISTORICAL CONTEXT

The recruitment of women into terrorist organisations and violent extremist groups is not a new phenomenon. Since the beginning of what we consider modern terrorism, from the late 1960s, women have been documented as taking small, yet expanding, roles within terrorist groups and their revolutionary aftermath movements (Cragin & Daly, 2009). While men continue to occupy primary leadership roles, women have been documented embracing a range of important roles in carrying out logistics, recruitment of new members, protection of members, and in some cases more combatant roles; including suicide missions (Bloom, 2011; Sjoberg & Gentry, 2011). Many groups have used women to evade security forces to carry out missions. This has been seen increasingly in more modern terrorist incarnations, including Boko Haram and al-Shabaab. There are also more recent reports of ISIS, despite prohibiting women from carrying out combat, using women for more secret operations and intelligence sourcing[1].

Building upon a table developed by Cragin and Daly (2009), the following table charts the roles women have played within 26 international terrorist organisations. These roles include women as logisticians, recruiters of new members, martyrdom/suicide missions, guerrilla warfare, operational leadership positions, and political vanguard.

In many cases the roles that women play within a terrorist organisation evolve over time and can be highly affected by the availability of male forces or fluctuating responses from governments towards a specific group. One such example is the role women have played within the Chechen Separatist movement. Chechen militants, made up of those from Chechen Muslim minorities, have fought against the presence of Russian forces since the 1940s. However, violence re-emerged in the mid-1990s. At this

Table 1. Roles of women in international terrorist organisations

Group	Logistics	Recruiting	Martyr/ Combat	Guerrilla	Ops. Leader	Pol. Vanguard
Al-Aqsa Martyrs' Brigades	X	X	X			
Al-Qaeda Central	X	X				
Al-Qaeda in Iraq	X		X			
Al-Shabaab	X		X		X	
Baader-Meinhof Gang/ Red Army Faction	X				X	X
Boko Haram	X		X			
Chechen Separatists	X	X	X			
Euskadi Ta Askatasuna	X				X	X
Groupe Islamique Arme	X					
Harakat al-Muqawama al-Islamiyya/ Hamas	X		X			X
Hizballah	X					X
Islamic State in Iraq and al-Sham/ ISIS Aka Daesh/ISIL	X	X				X
Jabhat al-Nusra	X		X			
Jemaah Islamiyyah	X					
Japanese Red Army					X	X
Liberation Tigers of Tamil Eelam	X	X	X	X		
PartiyaKarkeren Kurdistan/ Kurdish Workers' Party	X		X	X		X
Palestinian Islamic Jihad	X		X			
Popular Front for the Liberation of Palestine	X		X		X	
Primea Linea/ Front Line	X				X	X
Provisional Irish Republic Army	X	X			X	X
Red Brigades	X				X	X
Revolutionary Armed Forces of Columbia	X	X		X		
Sandinista National Liberation Front	X				X	X
Sendero Luminoso/ Shining Path	X	X		X	X	X
Zapatista Revolutionary Army	X			X		X

Note: Additions to the original Cragin and Daly's (2009) table include al-Shabaab, Boko Haram, ISIS and Jabhat al-Nusra.

point a new trend of female Chechen operatives, known as 'Black Widows', emerged, and were used as suicide bombers. While some have postulated that this new wave of female Chechen terrorists were inspired by one highly effective and illusive female recruiter, known as 'Black Fatima', others have suggested that females became more necessary to continue the resistance movement as male counterparts became depleted (Murphy, 2004). A combination of socioeconomic factors and the loss of relatives are seen as a catalyst for the increased usage and willingness of women to join the Chechen movement (Cunningham, 2007). Research and interviews with families of Black Widow suicide bombers have shown that the complexity of factors leading women to join terrorist movements, are often similar to those of their male counterparts (Speckhard & Ahkmedova, 2006).

Terrorist organisations have often utilised women specifically to avoid suspicion. It was with this assessment that the Provisional Irish Republic Army (PIRA), counterpart of the political front Sinn Fein, used women to run bombs between operation cells. Cumann na mBhan was formed as a women's auxiliary branch to the Irish Republic Army in 1913; acting as nurses, couriers and intelligence agents for fighters. Starting in the late 1960s, women adapted to take on a more active role in the smuggling of weapons and bombs. Again, the active role of women became more prevalent as the conflict worsened and male forces were depleted. Many women faced charges and imprisonment for their affiliation with PIRA (Fairweather, McDonough, & McFadyean, 1984). It is important to note that most women within violent extremist organisations are not coerced into joining. Conversely, female forces often show ruthless commitment to their cause; offering their lives in devotion to the groups' larger goals.

Within more modern terrorist organisations, women have been used to send distinct international messages and are used as figureheads for propaganda. Female terrorist 'celebrities' are used both directly in strategy as well as indirectly as propaganda agents, relating the terrorist cause to a wider range of new female recruits. Sajida al-Reshawi and Hayat Boumedienne are both examples of how ISIS has utilised women as international icons and as agents for asymmetrical threat building on an international level. ISIS has given strong strategic international messages, dictating their dedication to their female constituents through their actions. The most telling example of this has been during the Jordanian hostage crisis in January 2015. In exchange for a Jordanian pilot that ISIS claimed to have hostage, Moaz al-Kasasbeh, ISIS demanded the release of an Iraqi prisoner held in Jordan, Sajida al-Rishawi. Sajida had been an Al-Qaeda suicide bomber and while her husband's bomb successfully detonated, hers did not. She was subsequently condemned to death for her participation in the deadly attack in Amman in 2005. By broadcasting through the ISIS-run Al-Bayan radio station, transmitting to ISIS controlled territory, the group called for the release of 'our sister', Sajida al-Reshawi ("Why was Sajida al-Rishawi", 2015). While there are a number of other key jihadist officials that ISIS could have requested in exchange for al-Kasasbeh, the request of a female jihadist sent a very specific message to global audiences. ISIS conveyed that they support and defend their female forces.

In a similar fashion, ISIS was quick to vocalise support for Hayat Boumedienne in the aftermath of the Charlie Hebdo attacks in Paris, January 2015. Boumedienne was the former wife of Amédy Coulibaly; who killed four men in a Jewish supermarket in coordination with the Charlie Hebdo attacks. Coulibaly is assumed to have developed ties with the Charlie Hebdo attackers, Saïd and Chérif Kouachi, while in prison together, a common vulnerable environment for radicalisation. However, security services are thought to have taken high-risk surveillance off of Coulibaly due to the perception that his relation with Boumedienne was a sign of 'softening' his ways. In fact, Boumedienne is now thought to have been integral in the logistics and communication stream that took place in the lead up to the Charlie Hebdo attacks, pledging allegiance to ISIS via video before the terrorist attack was made. In the ISIS online propaganda magazine, *Dâr Al-Islâm* (a French version of the English ISIS publication, *Dabiq*), there was a section within the magazine, in the aftermath of the Paris terrorist attacks, dedicated to an interview with Boumedienne. While the significance of this interview is discussed later, it is clear that there is an increasing focus within ISIS propaganda to convey the message that women are valued, not as sexual objects, but as mothers to the next generation and guardians of the ISIS ideology.

However, ISIS is not the only modern jihadist organisation to use women strategically to spread their messages to wider audiences. In fact, while ISIS has put guidelines and restrictions on the women within its territory against combative roles, groups like Boko Haram and al-Shabaab have used women strategically as well as employing them within suicide bombing missions. Boko Haram, or Jamā'a Ahl al-sunnah li-da'wa wa al-jihād (Sunni Group for Preaching and Jihad) in its formal Arabic title, gained international recognition for its capture and hostage holding of 276 school girls in Chibok in April 2014. The group has subsequently accumulated an estimated 500 plus women and girls, and held them in military camps. While the women held hostage have been victims of gender based violence (Zenn & Pearson, 2014), Boko Haram has also employed women and girls as young as twelve; deploying them on suicide bombing missions ("Girl Aged 12 in", 2015).

Additionally, al-Shabaab has been exposed for its usage of international networks of women for funnelling funds from abroad to the terrorist organisation. In July 2014 the Federal Bureau of Investigation cited that they had arrested three women on charges of conspiracy to funnel money to the terrorist organisation. The women were based in Washington State, Northern Virginia and the Netherlands (FBI Press Release, 2014). Women in Somalia have also carried out suicide bombing attacks in support of al-Shabaab, among other trends of an increasing number of women joining al-Shabaab's jihadist network (Bilali, 2012).

As documented, women have played a variety of roles within terrorist organisations for a long time, spanning across violent extremist ideologies and regions. The deployment of women within jihadist terrorist organisations seems to arrive as an adaptive response of groups in times of unique pressure on the male jihadist capacities (Cunningham, 2003; Ortbals & Poloni-Staudinger, 2013). Women tend to have increased capacity and roles as and when security forces have clamped down on a group, recognising that women are better positioned to avoid monitoring and surveillance, as seen during the international clamp-down on Al-Qaeda in the mid-2000s (Bloom, 2011; Sjoberg & Gentry 2011). Terrorist organisations evolve, dependent on their constraints and in parallel with the time they live. As such, with the increasing presence of the Internet in our daily lives, processes of radicalisation and the use of the Internet by terrorist and violent extremist groups has also evolved. Equally the role of women within these organisations has evolved in parallel. The next section looks deeper at the role of the Internet in modern radicalisation with reference to crucial gender dynamics being developed through an online lens.

THE ROLE OF THE INTERNET IN RADICALISATION AND GENDER DYNAMICS

We live in an age in which large parts of our daily lives are increasingly reliant upon online engagements; communications, information seeking, travel and even finding relationships are all increasingly facilitated by online tools. Activism in a range of forms has also moved into the online space. Protests, campaigns, petitions and rallies have all utilised the online space to assist, if not lead, social movements (Gerbaudo 2012). Since the Internet is a powerful tool for reaching the masses, allowing users to be highly vocal while remaining anonymous, it has always attracted those wishing to promote marginalised or socially unacceptable views. As such, violent extremist networks, from Islamist extremists to far-right fascist networks, have exploited the potential of the Internet in recent years (Hussain & Saltman 2014;

Marchive, 2013). Recruitment and extremist materials have proliferated exponentially, particularly in light of the international propaganda machine developed by ISIS – largely through online networks.

However, it is crucial to understand the measurable role the Internet plays within processes of radicalisation. In analysing the influence of propaganda on an individual it is clear that an organisation's propaganda alone is not singularly responsible for radicalisation, let along acting as the primary impetus for joining a violent extremist group or carrying out an attack. Previous research has shown that the Internet is almost never the initial 'spark' for the radicalisation process, despite many reductionist claims by media and the broader public (Hussain & Saltman 2014; Rogers & Neumann, 2007; Winters 2015). Other introductory agents or environments that are vulnerable as potential gateways for introducing violent extremist content initiating processes of radicalisation include; the way media constructs images of 'Muslims' and 'terrorists' (Moore, Mason, & Lewis, 2008; Norris, Kern, & Just, 2013; Poole, 2002), school and university campuses (Glees & Pope, 2005; Precht, 2007), religious community areas such as mosques (House of Commons Home Affairs Committee, 2012; Rogers & Neumann, 2007), and prisons (Brandon, 2009; Khosrokhavar 2004; Neumann, 2010). Despite the sensationalised notions put forth by media and certain public discourse, the Internet does not create auto-radicalisation in isolation of other socialising factors. In fact, in research conducted about online pathways towards violent extremist materials, it was highly difficult, if not impossible, to 'accidently' come across extremist propaganda by utilising terms linked to violent extremist movements. Looking at Islamist extremist related terms, it was actually more likely to haphazardly come across anti-Muslim and Islamophobic content in comparison to Islamist extremist content (Hussain & Saltman, 2014).

While the Internet is rarely, if ever, the initial introduction to violent extremist ideologies, it still plays a crucial role in contemporary processes of violent radicalisation, particularly with reference to current Islamist extremist trends and the ISIS phenomenon. However, the precise nature of the Internet's role needs to be better contextualised and understood. With regards to radicalisation by violent extremist organisation, the Internet is used in three primary ways (see Hussain & Saltman, 2014). The first is to indoctrinate individuals through deconstructing previous beliefs in order to proselytise and re-educate individuals towards a particular extremist worldview. Secondly, the Internet serves as a tool for teaching about extremist ideologies, providing fast and easily accessible learning tools, lectures and educational resources. Lastly, the Internet is used by recruiters to socialise recruits, solidifying the radical violent ideology by providing a sense of community, a like-minded social environment and alternative media that all conform to the radicalised narratives (Saltman & Winter, 2014). The Internet's role within the process of radicalisation, subsequently, takes on a variety of forms as a secondary socialiser; both reacting to the offline world while also creating its own idealised world online. Once an individual's interest around an extremist ideology has been primed, the Internet has the potential to facilitate the continuation of radicalisation, acting as a catalyst to this process by indoctrinating, teaching and socialising extremist ideologies. Once exposed to the extremist ideology, the online space can facilitate self-created vacuums of information retrieval; including extremist propaganda (Hussain & Saltman 2014).

Usage of the Internet as a tool for female recruitment into jihadist organisations is also a phenomenon that predates ISIS. Jihadist groups have used online media, platforms and forums to disseminate Islamist extremist messaging targeting women directly for a long time. In the case of insurgents in Iraq, for example, garnering support for political Islam manifested itself online. On the online forum Abu al-Boukhair Islamic Network, an author in 2011 called on women specifically to defend their religion from the 'Crusaders' as an Al-Qaeda affiliate call for women was disseminated[2]. Forums provide an outlet for women to learn about their role within jihad and to answer questions they might have about their participation. While some Muslim male leaders have issued fatwas encouraging women to participate in military jihad in a number of ways, others have argued there is no combative role for women within Islam (Qazi, 2011).

However, the usage of the Internet by ISIS since 2014 marks a clear departure from previous jihadist organisations. ISIS has proved to embrace innovation online with regards to: (1) cultivating a centralised propaganda machine, (2) managing global dissemination of threats in a variety of languages, (3) developing new coding and apps, and (4) allowing for decentralised messaging (Saltman & Winter, 2014). ISIS has a number of official media outlets producing propaganda materials which can then be distributed both through central channels as well as through FTF's personal accounts, supporters abroad and female migrants to ISIS territory. This decentralised support network has given a new depth to intimacy and personalisation of extremist messaging which has been highly important in ISIS' ability to attract new cohorts for recruitment that do not fit the traditional 'jihadist' profile.

Looking at the propaganda machinery at work, ISIS has developed a modus of operating propaganda online through both centralised and decentralised content production. Central ISIS media operations produce an average of three videos and four image-based reports circulating daily (Winter, 2015). This content tends to be produced by provincial propaganda units, and adds to radio and news bulletins also being produced on a daily basis. These propaganda outputs are times for regularity and are also produced in a stream of languages including Arabic, Turkish, English, French, Kurdish and Russian. On top of this, ISIS central produces feature-length film highlighting its most barbaric acts on a monthly basis. Within this constantly evolving and developing space, there are at least six different central ISIS media outlets serving different propaganda purposes as well as at least thirty-five provincial media offices located in different localities within Algeria, Tunisia, Libya, Egypt, Iraq, Syria, Caucasus, Yemen, Saudi Arabia, and Khorasan (Winter, 2015).

ISIS propaganda takes on two primary forms. The first, as exemplified through the centralised production, taking place via 'Al-Hayat Media', is focused on recruitment, and centres on the utopian ideals of the *Caliphate* in a range of languages, tailored to foreign audiences. In order to disseminate these messages, ISIS has also developed a range of media initiatives that are exceptionally easy to access and highly attractive to their target audiences. This target audience is primarily aimed at interested young Islamists between the ages of 16 and 25 who feel emotionally sympathetic towards the crisis in Syria and Iraq. The second category of propaganda, as exemplified by 'Mu'assissat al-Furqan', serves as a means for intimidation and dissemination of threats. Unlike Al-Hayat Media, productions coming from al-Furqan primarily target those perceived as hostile to ISIS. It is important to note that this distinction is not entirely clear sometimes, nor is ISIS propaganda limited to these two outlets, as mentioned above. Other media outlets working to produce ISIS material that show off-the-battlefield interviews with jihadists, coverage of ISIS events, religious gatherings, and elements of daily life.

The notably tech-savvy nature of ISIS as a terrorist organisation has made headlines globally. Examples of the group's technological endeavours are constantly evolving to reach new recruits, such as females, as well as to avoid authorities online. One of the most prominent developments in ISIS coding was the creation of a Twitter application in June 2014 called the 'Dawn of Glad Tidings', which was temporarily made available through the Google Play store. In essence, subscribers could download this app onto their smartphone devices, which would give centralised control of the subscriber's Twitter account to a server. The individual could still tweet their own messages, but centralised output could also be timed and controlled so that the same message would be dispersed en masse by users, disseminated in waves so that spam filters could not detect irregular output (Berger 2014). Of course, as soon as Google was notified the app was removed; however, it is a new digital era and jihadist organisations are embracing online innovation and capacities.

Although the majority of content has a predominantly male focus, within this tech savvy and prolific approach to propaganda dissemination and recruitment, there has been an increasing proliferation of gender specific propaganda being disseminated online (Hoyle et al., 2014; Saltman & Smith, 2015; Winter, 2015). The point at which ISIS leader, Abu Bakr al-Baghdadi, declared terrorist run territory spanning across parts of Iraq and Syria as being the ordained 'Caliphate', women became a more relevant part of jihadist strategy and recruitment. Declaring a Caliphate meant that new focus and resources had to be given to state-building efforts. A key aspect to solidifying statehood has subsequently been to ensure that ISIS territory, and its jihadist constituency, becomes sustainable and continues into the next generation. In other words, including women within recruitment strategy has been necessary in order to provide wives to jihadist fighters, to have mothers producing the next generation (Saltman & Smith, 2015; Saltman & Winter, 2014).

The recruitment and propaganda strategies by ISIS aimed at women have been considered highly successful given the unprecedented number of women, especially the large number of Western women, migrating to ISIS-controlled territory. This female-focused recruitment has been largely through online tools and platforms, and women have become a prevalent voice within ISIS propaganda dissemination. While ISD-based research has largely focused on Western female propaganda, there has also been an increasing amount of online propaganda aimed at Middle Eastern women. ISIS has used the online space to normalise its jihadist ideology, including the cultivation of an online environment where gender oppressive views and regulations towards females are presented as a norm (Hoyle et al., 2015). The online spaces that violent extremist groups monopolise can become a self-selected vacuum of information retrieval and interaction once an individual is introduced to these networks. In this capacity, the online world can become a catalyst for processes of radicalisation while also socialising gender-specific roles for men and women. Dictating extremist norms are conducted both in a top-down manner through centralised media and content online, but also through permitted decentralised communication. The male FTFs, female migrants and supporters living abroad are all using their abilities online to post and share ISIS content while building an online community of sympathisers (Saltman & Smith, 2015).

Through the ISD-ICSR database, monitoring the online profiles of over 120 Western female migrants to ISIS, a range of push and pull factors leading women to join ISIS have been analysed (Saltman & Smith, 2015). Tapping into the wealth of information available on open source platforms, factors have been identified based on how these women have expressed their own reasons for leaving and their online social interactions aimed at recruiting further female migrants. While for some of the women in this dataset, socio-economic status and experiences living in the West are not available to us, others are known individuals where lifestyle and life before migration to ISIS can be reviewed more in-depth. Similarly to male foreign fighter recruits, major push factors priming women to be vulnerable to extremist propaganda include: (1) feeling socially and/or culturally isolated based on ethnic or religious associations leading to feelings of uncertainty of belonging within one's own culture, (2) a sentiment that the international Muslim community as a whole is being violently persecuted (Hegghammer, 2011, 2013), and (3) anger, sadness and/or frustration over a perceived lack of international action in response to this persecution against Muslims. These push factors are usually introduced and developed initially offline, but can be solidified and reduced into increasingly extremist terms through interactions with extremist content and sympathisers online.

Push factors prime an individual through negative reinforcement of binary worldviews, reducing complicated foreign policy and geopolitical histories into a tale of good versus evil, 'us versus them'. Within the gender context, many of the Western women who have migrated to join ISIS use their various social media accounts to expose the evil and violence they believe is being conducted by the 'enemy'. Some world events have been more widely interpreted as human rights abuses, such as the treatment of certain minorities by the Assad Government; however, advancing extremist narratives begin targeting a wide interpretation of agents. As processes of radicalisation become more extreme, the enemy tends to become broader, eventually including targets such as: the Assad Regime, international coalition forces countering ISIS, the West more broadly, anyone that is not a true believer (i.e., not Muslim), anyone that is not practicing the right kind of Islamic faith or lifestyle as deemed appropriate by ISIS' interpretation of strict Shariah Law. The 'in-group' becomes more defined and elite, while the 'out-group' becomes an expansive and all-encompassing enemy (Tajfel, 1979).

While push factors lay the groundwork for extremist grievances, pull factors play a more substantial role in driving women to make the decision to leave their home countries and join ISIS-controlled territory. The primary pull factors expressed by Western women through their online profiles embrace positive incentives and motivations for migration which include: (1) idealistic goals of their own religious duty and the goal of building a utopian Caliphate, (2) finding a sense of belonging and a community embracing 'sisterhood', and (3) the romanticisation of the adventurous journey and experience in joining ISIS. Pull factors for women are similar to the reasons behind many male FTF joining ISIS. However, the narratives and propaganda defining these pull factors tend to differ greatly due to the drastic differences in roles men and women play once inside ISIS-controlled territory. While the majority of men have been recruited for military, logistics, and combatant purposes, women joining ISIS are openly told that their primary function is to embrace their duty as wives and mothers. There are also some limited cases of women taking on roles as nurses or teachers, as ISIS has recognised the need for females within this space.

The majority of women will maintain almost no official roles; however, the advancements in technology and increasing digital literacy of younger recruits have created an important unofficial role for many women joining ISIS. Similar to their male counterparts, ISIS leverages psychological vulnerabilities while promising a range of seemingly life-fulfilling opportunities on both physical and spiritual levels (Leong 2015). New female recruits to ISIS are assisted in their migration process through an elaborate stream of offline and online actors, often facilitated by females that have previously made the journey.

HOW THE INTERNET FACILITATES MIGRATION TO ISIS TERRITORY

The number of FTF and female migrants, leaving from Western countries, and many other regions, to join ISIS is unprecedented in our modern history. Modern conflicts in Afghanistan, Bosnia and Ukraine have all drawn in foreign fighters as well as women from abroad, however, both the quantity and diversity of recruits from the international community is unmatched in comparison when looking at the current crisis in Syria and Iraq. The complexities of deciding to migrate to join a conflict and planning the logistics of this act, which is inherently illegal in the case of ISIS, is one that is currently facilitated by online communications and Internet tools. The ISD-ICSR database on FTF and female migrants looks at hundreds of social media accounts tracking individuals who have chosen to leave Western countries and are now living within ISIS-controlled territory. From archiving hundreds of pages of social media account data from the women in this database alone, details about this migration process, decision-making and facilitation all become clearer.

The process of planning and carrying out the journey for Western women migrating to ISIS territory is facilitated by communications and interactions online. Many of these women are in their mid-to-late teens and early twenties – a generation which is much more digitally literate and comfortable communicating and making arrangements online. As mentioned previously, it is rare that the entire process of radicalisation will take place online, and the first introduction to violent extremism almost always comes from an offline connection or interpersonal experience (Hussain & Saltman, 2014). However, the Internet as a catalyst and socialiser can be very powerful. This online facilitation takes place both passively, through the propaganda and images that encourage women en masse to join, as well as more actively, through actual conversations with recruiters online. Once introduced to certain extremist networks online, the abundance of materials and social circles available can quickly create a self-selective vacuum of information.

The most effective types of propaganda and discourse within extremist networks play on ideas or narratives that the individual is already familiar (Ellul, 1965). In the case of the Syrian crisis, initial narratives can include geopolitical events, such as relaying the atrocities being carried out by the Assad Government on the Syrian people or criticisms of international relations with Israel and Palestine. Initial narratives can also include more personal, localised themes of isolation, the lack of belonging and feelings of hopelessness. These initial cognitive openings relating the individual are then manifested into broader narratives that become increasingly binary. The Syrian crisis becomes another global example of how the Muslim community as a whole is persecuted, and a criticism that the international community does nothing to help. Feeling socially or culturally alienated manifests into a narrative that pits this sentiment down to being Muslim and transposes the solution onto migrating, because only in the Caliphate can you truly be safe and represented as a Muslim people. This type of binary language and narration has existed in all violent extremist and fascistic movements, eventually justifying violence against the 'out group' in order to preserve the 'in group' (Tajfel, 1974; Tajfel & Turner, 1979). ISIS has utilised the Internet as a hyper-charged tool for disseminating this narrative through a range of different voices in order to recruit a range of different supporters for the terrorist organisation's cause.

In essence, ISIS has been particularly effective by allowing for decentralised voices and propaganda production so that the extremist narrative can feel localised; both with regards to language as well as content. This decentralisation has also been a catalyst for the increased recruitment of women. French propaganda for women, for example, will talk about the outlawing of the headscarf in France, feeding anger and frustration over this legislation into a wider narrative discussing international persecution of Muslims. Thus, a woman feels an emotional tie to the foreign extremist group based first on local grievances she might be feeling, which are then grown to eventually convey a much larger 'enemy' that expands beyond state actors. Ultimately, as the individual travels farther down this process of radicalisation, her helplessness within her current environment feels overwhelming and the 'solution', travelling to the Utopian idealised Caliphate, seems like a solution to *all* problems, not just locally but globally.

Internet-dissemination of female-focused ISIS propaganda and online-recruitment has been increasing since ISIS declared a Caliphate. Women represent a crucial element of the organisation's attempts at state building and great attention has been given to increase female content. This content comes in the form of centralised publications as well as decentralised content. Centralised female content is still currently much less than male-focused content. There is not a centrally existing female media wing that is currently known. This is partly due to the limitations placed on women within ISIS territory; it might be considered 'haram', or forbidden to depict women in videos. Some centrally related ISIS propaganda for females has been known to come from the *al-Khansaa Brigade*. This all-female morality-policing unit operates on the ground to ensure women are dressing and acting according to the strict Shariah Law. However, they have also published a guiding text for women entitled, *Women in the Islamic State: Manifesto and Case Study*, detailing – in Arabic – rules and regulations pertaining to women within ISIS territory. Texts like this, as well as the range of static texts, memes and images of propaganda, assist in conveying the extremist message and in finding familiarity within its recruitment base. However, more active communication and personal relational links are almost always necessary to drive a person to commit to leaving their homes to join this new cause.

Recruitment to terrorist organisations has shifted in light of the new technologies easily available online. Not only in creating great ease in planning flights and travel routes, but also in communicating across boarders easily, quickly and inexpensively. Recent research on ISIS online networks has shown that there is no one type of 'recruiter' in a traditional sense. The majority of recruitment efforts are made by active supporters, foreigners that have already made the journey and sympathisers, primarily without central command. Recruitment also involves a range of actors. First an individual must be recruited to the ideology and only then is an individual enlisted and facilitated in traveling. It should be noted as well that the online actor recruiting an individual into the ideological framework is almost always separate to the individual enlisting people to the organisation (Winter 2015).

Recruitment of women remains largely constructed through seemingly informal ties. Despite the advice and details given on open platforms online, women that are already in ISIS territory are careful not to give away details that could negatively affect the efforts of future migrants. As such, if a woman is communicating with another potential recruit, and poses questions about the practicalities of leaving, it is common that the recruiting female will urge those who want to migrate to contact them using a more secure channel, such as Surespot or Kik, rather than using larger more regulated platforms like Facebook or Twitter. They will not openly divulge the exact border crossing-points or names of pick-up point that handlers use in border countries. Women that are preparing to make their journey are diverted to conversations on private platforms and are often told to erase and get rid of their computers and/or mobile phones as they depart, to hide any evidence of their conversations.

Despite the fine details of names and places being reserved for private conversations there remains a wealth of information and practical advice given on open platforms. Blogs held by Western women living in ISIS territory are open about giving tips and advice to new females planning their own journeys. One female gives a numbered list of top tips for travel on a 'just paste it' blog link called 'Advice from a Muhajaraah' (Muhajaraah is a female migrant). This link starts with the following:

Alright... I'm gonna share my quick advice for hijrah [migration] etc please follow n RT [retweet] if you're interested... may allah guide us all aameen.[3]

While some of the #hijrahtip giving includes more spiritual and philosophical aspects about making the journey (e.g., reminding women not to do this just for marriage, popularity or revenge), other tips are much more practical so that the recruit planning her journey is not prematurely caught. The following are a sample of the tips given to exemplify this point:

3. #hijrahtip the primary sunnah act of hijrah is SECRECY. Keep your mouth shut about your plans n intentions before you know it you may have made hijrah to prison in Dar ul Kufr bc of your blabbing to everyone... stay off social media!

6. #hijrahtip study some geography. Get to know where you're headed, you're route, alternative routes if stopped and back up plan B, C, D...

9. #hijrahtip wear your best sneakers/trainers/kicks for journey. Invest in a good waterproof watch brothers g-shock if you can afford one

15. #hijrahtip practice your answers to questions you may be asked by immigration etc. Control your breathing make eye contact always smile @Umm_Adnaan #hijrahtip easily add to conversation to change the topic. It's a skill like any other to be mastered practice makes perfect! @Umm_Adnaan even my backup stories had stories! Outwit n outsmart those kuffar dogs deceive thm n humiliate them by the permission of Allah

16. #hijrahtip be very well informed wth news along the way to places you'll be traveling to and back at home to see of there are tabs on you

19. #hijrahtip there's a tweet of an ebook on how to make hijrah on my page can someone copy the link to this thread plz...READ THAT BOOK EVERY1 @Umm_Adnaan specifics on what to pack etc... I'll not be discussing routes etc due to obvious safety reasons for u still in Dar ul Kufr...

23. #hijrahtipavoid traveling by Air if there is bus/car or any ground transport it may be safer for you

24. #hijrahtip wherever possible look and dress very modern and coconutty [brown on the outside and white on the inside in reference to being a Westernised Muslim] but remember noting haraam sisters do not abandon hijab and allah knows best. If you wear niqaab i suggest not wearing any for travel

A range of information streams like this are facilitated through blogs and online social media platforms. While this list was a posting, other platforms allow for questions and answers in real time to address individual needs about preparations, packing and how to avoid security. These information streams not only provide practical information, but the informal and localised tone of these platforms creates a sense of familiarity and trust for recruits, feeling that the recruiters and/or information providers are of the same background to them. This sense of belonging and continued dialogue lowers the threshold of fears or hesitations in making the decision to 'make hijrah' (to migrate).

Once a woman has made the decision to leave her country of origin and travel to Syria there is a network of offline actors that facilitates this process. While this is similar to male FTF, women often leave in pairs or small groups. The fine details of journeys vary and are constantly evolving due to the shifting landscape on the ground. However, it is clear that while the recruitment and planning is largely taking place online, the offline networks ISIS has in place facilitating women's arrivals are expansive. Despite decentralised recruiters and propaganda accounts being careful not to give exact details, the abundance of information found on open source accounts still gives an important lens into the journeys women are taking.

One woman, *Umm Khattab,* shared her migration journey on her social media account[4]. It had been arranged that she would meet up with two other women in 'T', presumed to be Turkey, who both had young children under the age of five. The small group of women and children are stopped and detained by Turkish military. They are asked to lift their veils for identity checks, as they are in full niqab veils, and it is realised that they are not Syrian. They are asked about their links to 'Daesha' (ISIS) and the group is told they will be booked tickets back to their home countries. Despite this predicament, Umm Khattab writes that ISIS found out about their situation and was able to negotiate their release and continued journey:

So Dawlah [ISIS] found out about our predicament and sent us a lawyer who worked some magic and after a looooong tiring week in prison they let us go Alhamdulillah [thanks be to God]. So we were allowed to go T but we went crossing the boarder the normal way and me and Umm Musab and Umm Laden were all so happy cause we crossed the boarder[5]

The group's difficulties do not stop there however. Once they have crossed the Syrian border they are detained by a group identified in the blog as the 'Free Syrian Army'. Again there are negotiations, this time between an official and the husband of a travelling female; this showed the open communications between seemingly fighting factions on the ground. After negotiations they are again released and a car is waiting to drive them safely to ISIS-controlled territory. Stories such as this highlight the perseverance of dedicated women who want to join ISIS. These stories also give a glimpse into the dangerous nature of migration as well as the fluid networks ISIS has on the ground to facilitate foreigners arriving to join their cause. While recruitment and propaganda have long existed for jihadist groups, the modern digital world facilitates the expansion of these efforts, including planning travel, joining up with fellow recruits, and documenting these processes for a wider audience of new recruits so that the next waves of arrivals can prepare and avoid roadblocks experienced by previous men and women who have already made the journey.

THE ROLE OF WOMEN WITHIN ISIS TERRITORY: WIVES, PROPAGANDA DISSEMINATORS AND ASYMMETRICAL THREAT

Despite the violent ideologies women are radicalised into, their position within ISIS territory is one of social passivity and non-violence. Their roles, as dictated by a strict form of Shariah Law, focus primarily on glorifying the role of wife and mother. Their purpose for joining ISIS is not to become a 'foreign fighter', but to help produce the next generation of jihadists and pass on the jihadist ideology to their offspring. This role for women is seminal in the overarching aim of ISIS to create a sustainable statehood. Even within question forums, women already within ISIS territory warn other females that they should not come if they are expecting to remain unwed[6]. From these various platforms, it is revealed that unmarried women are placed within a sort of female-only hostel so that they are kept in accordance with their interpretation of Shariah Law. Some women arrived having previously been arranged to marry a particular individual prior to their departure. Others have unions arranged upon arrival. There is a tendency to marry foreign female women to foreign fighters of the same cultural or linguistic background so that communication between husband and wife is possible. Given that majority of FTF and female migrants from Western countries do not depart for Iraq and Syria with the ability to speak Arabic or local dialects of the region, marriages between language-compatible individuals are practical.

In the limited and constricted existence they have once in ISIS territory, one of the primary outlets for women to express themselves is online. While these platforms are openly aimed at promoting ISIS in a positive light, the realities and daily events exposed online also allow outsiders to get a closer look into the daily life of these women. Women have become increasingly active online while online-activities of many of the men fighting for ISIS have become less frequent with regards to updated posting. This is thought to be, at least in part, due to the nature of gender roles. While women spend the majority of their existence in the territory inside the home and are only allowed to leave with permission from a male guardian and with a male chaperone, men are primarily on military duty on the frontlines, with much less time to focus on disseminating online propaganda and tweeting. Many of the Western women residing in ISIS territory share everything from images of the food they cook to re-tweeting gruesome beheading images. Women are equally radicalised to praise martyrdom and glorify the deaths of their husbands on social media. These women are not naïve to the brutality of jihadist endeavours, interacting with the battlefield in the only capacity they are permitted, online.

While negativity towards life in the Caliphate is not socially permitted directly on social media platforms, it is possible to read between the lines of various online postings to get a better sense of certain realities for these women. Suggestions for new recruits on online platforms allow greater knowledge into difficulties faced. Telling potential recruits to pack warm clothes and solar powered batteries hints at the realities of severe weather, the lack of electricity, and infrequent hot and cold water. Besides the tedium of living in a severe territory, lacking many of the readily available comforts of Western societies that many of these women originate from, women are also relocating to what is essentially/in reality a terrorist-run war zone. Tweets about airstrikes overhead, images of destruction and the consistent death of 'martyred husbands' reported on these accounts, expose the violent and insecure nature of the terrain that these women have entered. Over a quarter of the women in the ISD database are widows, most within a six-month period between December 2014 and May 2015. Some widows are left pregnant or with a child. Under the regulations of the territory, women are also expected to remarry within a three to four month period. Injuries and deaths of friends and loved ones are inevitable in such an environment.

In such a harsh environment questioning one's choices and position is inevitable. Yet, even if a Western female migrant to ISIS territory questions or regrets the decision she has made, it is considerably more difficult for women to return to their countries of origin than their male counterparts. While many countries have seen a large number of male returnees, many disillusioned and often times traumatised by their experience, we have seen an extremely limited number of Western female returnees – only around ten as of the writing of this chapter. The decision to attempt to leave ISIS territory is made exponentially more difficult for women for three primary reasons: (1) ISIS is known to confiscate and/or destroy passports upon arrival into their territory as part of initiation, denouncing any previous nationality or affiliation; (2) as mentioned, movement outside of the house is highly restricted for women, so a lone female venturing towards the border would put her immediately at risk; and (3) many foreigners are still uncertain of the legislations or punishments they might face in their home countries. Even for male returnees the psychological decision of returning home, possibly facing a lifetime in prison, is weighed next to the decision to stay in a terrorist-run territory and justify one's original decision. Especially for females, once a woman has crossed into ISIS territory there is very little outsiders can do, without putting the female at great physical risk.

While outsiders may view the role of women within ISIS territory as limiting and subservient, the degree of radicalisation these women have undergone should not be discounted. To deny these women agency would be wrong. While the first process of radicalisation is highly facilitated from a distance through the digital world, a second wave of radicalisation often takes place on the ground after arrival, immersing new arrivals in an overwhelming new terrain with intensified indoctrination, reaffirming the extremist narratives from online interactions with the new norms and real-world manifestation of these narratives on the ground.

Despite the limitations in movement, speech and personal expression placed upon women living in ISIS territory, they have been given an open outlet for active service through their online activism. Each female profile gives a personal voice to the Caliphate and its cause. These decentralised messengers, creating their own memes and hashtags to support the cause, give a personal touch to online propaganda but also serve as facilitators for the recruitment of further women. As discussed above, many women make themselves available online to communicate with potential new female recruits and give consistent encouragement and advice. We are witnessing an active network of females in ISIS territory using online platforms to share propaganda, encourage others to join, and even incite violence to be carried out abroad in those who cannot make the journey. In essence, women have become a key component in ISIS' decentralised propaganda strategy online.

Despite large efforts made by leading social media platforms to take down terrorist-related accounts, both FTF and female migrants have remained active online within ISIS territory, and have developed simple online tactics for avoiding negative effects of censorship. ISIS has developed 'swarmcast' techniques whereby accounts are created for the purpose of assisting in regaining followers for previously blocked accounts (Fisher, 2015; Fisher & Prucha, 2014). Through 'just paste it' links and other proxy accounts, old accounts are listed next to the new twitter or social media handles that the person has recreated so that ISIS sympathisers and followers can simply click through these links and re-follow the new list of fellow ISIS members. New accounts therefore rapidly regain supporters. This phenomenon is just as common among females as males living within ISIS territory. New accounts have also been known to boast about the number of times their accounts have been reformed on platforms such as Twitter, with some accounts reappearing for the tenth or more time. While larger platforms such as Twitter, Facebook and YouTube are better regulated with a greater capacity to react to extremist developments online, smaller platforms with lower capacities – such as BlogSpot, Tumblr and question forums – often lack the capacities to effectively regulate content.

Moreover, the presence of Western and other international women in ISIS territory is changing the nature of asymmetrical threat assessment. By taking active roles in distributing female-targeted propaganda and helping in the recruitment of women from abroad in a range of languages, the female-factor has taken on a new level. While the jihadist ideology is nothing new, the recruitment strategy of ISIS, broadening its appeal beyond a straightforward religious narrative, has allowed for an entirely new range of actors and supporters. Jihadist propaganda and recruitment has been revolutionised by ISIS members and supporters through the creation of localised communication streams, which allows for personalised communications. In essence, ISIS has developed its own pop subculture. Memes, slang, music, catchy imagery and humour are all used to create familiar and alluring narratives. Violent extremist messaging is packaged within catchy, youthful plays on popular culture, which mainstreams this dangerous ideology.

Within this subculture, women have their own set of symbols and slogans. One popular meme that trended among ISIS fan girls and migrants was a take-off of the popular marketing campaign of the make-up line *Cover Girl*. Instead a fully veiled woman is depicted with the girlie cursive writing above it stating: 'Covered Girl ... Because I'm worth it'. What these memes and images shared online connote is something far broader than a play on words. One meme trending is actually giving great depth to the female argument for joining ISIS. In essence, what is really being said by a meme like 'Covered Girl' is something more: 'Look at the West. They sexualise women. Look at Victoria's Secret and make-up campaigns objectifying and sexualising women. We refuse to be sexual objects by taking on the full veil. We refuse to be objectified and are choosing ISIS because they respect women'. Local grievances are projected into a global movement, in a 'glocal' like way. While this term originally was developed as a way of explaining the process of international integration arising from the interchange of worldviews, ideas and other cultural aspects, it is equally relevant in current extremist movements and recruitment propaganda (Al-Rodhan & Stoudmann, 2006; Albrow & King, 1990). This 'glocalisation' discounts the nation-state and mezzo-level actors by focusing on the intimacy of the local level and the idealism conveyed on the idea of a globalist movement.

The increasing number of Western women joining the so-called Caliphate is also a powerful symbol for ISIS; legitimising their state-building efforts and mainstreaming a particular counter-culture against the West. As mentioned earlier in reference to the Paris attacks on Charlie Hebdo in January 2015, the ISIS high-gloss online publication, *Dâr Al-Islâm*, that came after the attacks dedicated two of its fourteen pages to 'sisters' of ISIS. One of these pages gives an interview supposedly with Hayat Boumedienne, the partner of attacker Coulibaly. In the online magazine, she is referred to as 'the wife of our brother Aboû Basîr 'Abdoullâh al-Ifrigî (may Allah accept him)[7]. In this brief interview, Boumedienne is quoted stating that she easily reached ISIS territory and expresses her joy in residing in ISIS territory. She is also quoted calling for all Muslims, from around the world, to join her there as their divine right and religious duty. The interview ends by citing a number of powerful female figures from the Quran, encouraging women to join, and reiterating the strong role women play. It should be noted that as of writing, Boumedienne's presence in ISIS territory is not fully confirmed. However, the personalised message for women, written and directed specifically for a French speaking audience, shows the depth at which ISIS is calculating and personalising its propaganda and targeted messaging.

The imagery being propagated around women living within ISIS territory has also changed the nature of threat assessment. Women posing with guns, hand grenades and knives have been shared among the fan girl networks. Images depicting light military training for women have also been disseminated. Despite the fact that women are currently not used for combat, the potential is there. Women have openly expressed the desire to participate more actively in the violence through posts on their online profiles. From a security perspective, it is important that women are not simply viewed as 'jihadi brides' or simply 'naïve young women'. The violent nature to their radicalisation is apparent and, as mentioned previously, the potential for women to take more active roles in the future is a possibility when looking at historical examples. The Chechen black widows only emerged after sustained conflict resulting in the depletion of male forces. If continued airstrikes and insurgent attacks deplete ISIS' male forces, their female counterparts could have the potential to be called into more combative roles. For now, onlookers are left watching through a primarily social media-driven lens, attempting to decipher the shifting landscape within which this terrorist organisation thrives.

CONCLUSION AND RECOMMENDATIONS

As discussed, women joining violent extremist and terrorist organisations are not in itself a new phenomenon. The usage of women within jihadist endeavours has its own distinct history, which far predates ISIS. However, the number of foreign females migrating to join ISIS in Syria and Iraq is unprecedented. This phenomenon has been particularly unique looking at the increasing trend of Western females joining ISIS, thought to make up between ten and twenty percent of all foreign recruits from the West. The significance of gender dynamics and female recruitment to ISIS, largely facilitated through online networks, should not be underestimated in its importance to ISIS' ultimate goal of solidifying and maintaining a global Caliphate state. As such, ISIS has created a recruitment paradigm with two crucial game-changers. Firstly, it has declared an expansive territory known as the 'Islamic State'. Notions of an existing utopia and an idealised space are seen as a tangible reality for recruits. Secondly, by allowing for decentralised messengers, including female recruits, to create and distribute propaganda in their own words. By doing this, propaganda is reaching a wider audience and appealing to a range of desires and goals. In this way, ISIS has utilised the Internet to develop a 'glocal' phenomenon, appealing to recruits on a localised level and relating their cause to a global cause.

As part of this, women are a key component to ISIS' state-building efforts, but they also serve to broaden the appeal of the terrorist organisation to a more diverse and international audience. Women give a seemingly 'soft-side' to the group's recruitment efforts, offering a personal lens into the household of jihadists, mainstreaming the appeal of the group by humanising daily life in the so-called Caliphate.

The roles women are allowed once they reach ISIS territory are physically limited, with highly gendered restrictions on activities and mobility. However, women are given an important outlet and role online. Allowing for decentralised voices, such as female migrants and fan girls, to disseminate propaganda and communicate online has changed the nature of jihadist recruitment and diversified the profile of potential recruits. Women residing within ISIS territory are providing an intimate information channel for recruiting new women, ranging in age, background and nationality. The notions and imagery around a 'jihadist' have moved away from a figure of fear and mystery. The humanisation and personalisation of the experience, both of making the journey to join ISIS and sharing a distorted account of what it is like to reside in ISIS territory, have been exposed and glorified through the online networks. This greatly diminishes the threshold of fear and hesitation of joining for potential recruits. Of course, the realities of life residing under the control of a terrorist organisation differ from the self-aware lens of ISIS supporters online. The traumas of extreme brutality, the insecurities of living within a warzone, and the realities of being unable to escape are glazed over in a veil of glorification online.

Despite the recognition by security services and governments that we are witnessing an unprecedented and dangerous trend towards violent extremism, very little has been done to constructively counter the online frontline. Governments have largely remained reliant on a range of negative measures, such as filtering and censorship methods, in their attempts to rid the Internet of 'extremist content'. This has proven largely ineffective and even counterproductive given the nature of the Internet as a tool, where content and banned accounts easily reappear and are able to re-accumulate followers quickly. Due to the diversity in extremist propaganda tactics online, an equally diverse range and scope of counter-narratives are needed to challenge the roots of the jihadist ideology. The growing trend of violent extremist propaganda targeting women, and the subsequent increasing number of Western women joining ISIS, highlights the need for better mechanisms and infrastructure for female-specific prevention and de-radicalisation programs.

The female voice within efforts to prevent and counter violent extremism and radicalisation is critical. Monitoring and analysing the online profiles of women within ISIS territory has highlighted not only the push and pull factors driving Western women to join groups like ISIS, but has also mapped significant cognitive openings for prevention and de-radicalisation. In particular for young women, leaving one's mother, abandoning one's duty as a daughter and causing emotional distress to the mother, is discussed within many blogs and social media accounts (Hoyle et al., 2015). Women have recounted the difficulty in leaving mothers and families behind. The voice of the mother as a counter-narrative is therefore an important one if adequately informed. Better communication and information networks to families, and mothers in particular, should be facilitated within countries concerned with this phenomenon, to build awareness and enable dialogue. In recent years, networks of this nature have begun to emerge, such as Women Without Borders (SAVE) and the Women and Extremism Network (WaE). SAVE, originally known as Sisters Against Violent Extremism, was developed to provide a female counter-terrorism platform to create a female security paradigm (Women Without Borders, n.d.). The WaE Network was created to bring together activists, practitioners and research experts that focus on female radicalisation as well as work to develop prevention and counter-extremism programs that are directly inclusive of women. The WaE Network includes a core group of primarily women coming from Europe, North Africa, the Middle East, and Southeast Asia in the hopes of creating an international knowledge-exchange and communication around this topic, while also promoting awareness and prevention against violent extremism (WaE network, 2015).

While networks of these kinds are crucial in countering extremist propaganda, these types of programs often lack sustainable support to have significant and lasting regional and international impact. Programs aimed at increasing credible voices against violent extremism (including female-focused efforts) need to function in a similar manner to violent extremist propaganda, by appealing to target audiences on both a local interpersonal level, as well as having international significance. CVE efforts should be creative and flexible, but also need infrastructure, sustainability and evaluation mechanisms. Governments, private sectors and civil society all have a role to play within this process (Institute for Strategic Dialogue, 2014). Governments are critical for providing necessary funding to CVE work while also creating policies and initiatives that enable this type of work to take place.

Tech companies in particular also should facilitate online CVE initiatives through their digital platforms. Beyond the need for support and information channels for families and networks that are inclusive of women in CVE efforts, there is a need to challenge online extremism directly. The Internet is a key component in the radicalisation process of aspiring female migrants and needs to be better utilised in pushing back against this phenomenon. Counter-narratives need to be targeted for a female-specific audience, just as ISIS currently tailors its own messaging. The material for this type of counter-narrative is not difficult to create or utilise, however, it demands a certain level of innovation and creativity. Successful counter-narratives rely on (1) the message, (2) the messenger, and (3) the platform being used to distribute the message (Saltman & Smith, 2015). If the credibility, authenticity or distribution of counter-narratives is not on message then the counter-narrative risks being less effective in inspiring critical thinking or presenting a credible counter message to extremism. Utilising 'credible messengers' that target emotional responses is also crucial (Briggs & Frenett, 2014). For this reason, government bodies are often not the best messengers for effective counter-narratives, while local engagement by families, religious leaders and community groups might be more effective (Leong, 2015).

Some powerful iteration of counter-narratives can be drawn directly from the few women who have returned from ISIS, exposing the harsh realities of life within ISIS territory. Successful CVE education has already been developed in places like Canada, through using the personal stories and voices of former extremists as well as victims of extremism in a program called Extreme Dialogue (Extreme Dialogue, 2015). Projects like this bring personal stories to the classroom and teach teachers how to engage with students on the topic of violent extremism, to teach critical consumption skills and develop natural resilience's towards extremist messaging. Meanwhile, other counter-narratives should not simply 'counter' terrorist propaganda directly, but offer insight and alternatives to the extremist messages. Engagement with young individuals that are already showing an appeal towards extremist groups is also needed. Pilot programs such as One2One in the United Kingdom has also used former extremists to engage directly with young people online, to provide an outlet for alternative information and discussion from someone that understands the ideological and emotional draws of extremist groups (Institute for Strategic Dialogue, 2015).

Despite some of the more ambitious and innovative programs in development, there remains a severe lack of directed counter-narrative material in circulation online on a significant scale. Ambitious initiatives need assistance in scaling up outreach and targeted messaging. This is particularly the case when looking at the important gender dynamics at play within recruitment and processes of radicalisation leading women to join violent extremist groups like ISIS. Although we see programs to counter violent extremism developing, very few campaigns or initiatives address female radicalisation narratives specifically, nor use the female voice directly. In order to effectively counter extremism it will be crucial that practitioners not only recognise the innovation and tools available through the Internet, but also diversify CVE efforts to include an adequate gender perspective.

REFERENCES

Al-Rodhan, & Stroudmann, G. (2006), *Definitions of the globalization: A comprehensive overview and a proposed definition*. Geneva: Geneva Centre for Security Policy.

Albrow, M., & King, E. (Eds.). (1990). *Globalization, knowledge and society*. London: Sage.

Barrett, R. (2014). *Foreign fighters in Syria*. New York, NY: The Soufan Group.

Berger, J. M. (2014, June 16). How IS games twitter. *The Atlantic*. Retrieved from http://www.theatlantic.com/international/archive/2014/06/isis-iraq-twitterr-social-media-strategy/372856

Bilali, A. (2012, August 13). Women and al-Shabaab: Between false empowerment and terror. *Diplomatic Courier*. Retrieved from http://www.diplomaticourier.com/women-and-al-shabab-between-false-empowerment-and-terror/

Bloom, M. (2011). *Bombshell: The many faces of women terrorists*. Philadelphia, PA: University of Pennsylvania Press. doi:10.9783/9780812208108

Brandon, J. (2009). *Unlocking Al-Qaeda: Islamist extremism in British prisons*. London: Quilliam Foundation.

Briggs, R., & Frenett, R. (2014). *Policy briefing: Foreign fighters, the challenge of counter-narratives*. London: Institute for Strategic Dialogue.

Cragin, R. K., & Daly, S. A. (2009). *Women as terrorists: Mothers, recruiters, and martyrs*. Santa Barbara, CA: ABC-CLIO.

Cunningham, K. J. (2003). Cross-regional trends in female terrorism. *Studies in Conflict and Terrorism, 26*(3), 171–195. doi:10.1080/10576100390211419

Cunningham, K. J. (2007). Countering female terrorism. *Studies in Conflict and Terrorism, 30*(2), 113–129. doi:10.1080/10576100601101067

Ellul, J. (1965). *Propaganda: The formation of men's attitudes*. New York, NY: Random House Vintage Books.

Extreme Dialogue. (2015). Retrieved from http://extremedialogue.org

Fairweather, E., McDonough, R., & McFadyean, M. (1984). *Only the rivers run free: Northern Ireland: The women's war*. London: Pluto Press.

Federal Bureau of Investigation Press Release. (2014, July 23). *Three defendants arrested on charges of providing material support to a foreign terrorist organization*. Retrieved from https://www.fbi.gov/washingtondc/press-releases/2014/three-defendants-arrested-on-charges-of-providing-material-support-to-a-foreign-terrorist-organization

Fisher, A. (2015). Swarmcast: How jihadist networks maintain a persistent online presence. *Perspectives on Terrorism, 9*(3), 3–20.

Fisher, A., & Prucha, N. (2013). Tweeting for the caliphate: Twitter as the new frontier for jihadist propaganda. *CTC Sentinel, 6*(6), 19–22.

Gerbaudo, P. (2012). *Tweets on the streets: Social media and contemporary activism*. London: Pluto Press.

Girl aged 12 in Nigeria marketplace bombing. (2015, June 24). *Al Jazeera*. Retrieved from http://www.aljazeera.com/news/2015/06/girl-aged-12-nigeria-market-suicide-bombing-150624044055589.html

Glees, A., & Pope, C. (2005). *When students turn to terror: Terrorist and extremist activity on British campuses*. London: Social Affairs Unit.

Hegghammer, T. (2011). The rise of the Muslim foreign fighters: Islam and the globalization of Jihad. *International Security, 35*(3), 53–94.

Hegghammer, T. (2013). Should I stay or should I go? Explaining variation in Western jihadists' choice between domestic and foreign fighting. *The American Political Science Review, 107*(1), 1–15. doi:10.1017/S0003055412000615

House of Commons Home Affairs Committee. (2012). *Roots of Violent Radicalization* (19th Report Session 2010-12, Vol. 1). London: The Stationery Office Limited.

Hoyle, C., Bradford, A., & Frenett, R. (2015). *Becoming Mulan? Female western migrants to ISIS*. London: Institute for Strategic Dialogue.

Hussain, G., & Saltman, E. (2014). *Jihad trending: Online extremism and how to counter it*. London: Quilliam Foundation.

Institute for Strategic Dialogue. (2014). *Government engagement and communication strategies with communities*. London: Author.

Institute for Strategic Dialogue. (2015). Retrieved from http://www.strategicdialogue.org/ISD_Brochure.pdf

Jones, S. (2014, March 28). Jihad by social media. *Financial Times Magazine*. Retrieved from http://www.ft.com/cms/s/2/907fd41c-b53c-11e3-af92-00144bdc0.html

Khosrokhavar, F. (2004). *L'Islam dans les Prisons: Voix et Regards*. Paris: Balland.

Leong, D. (2015). *Why ISIS appeals to Muslim women in Western countries: Need for counter message. RSIS Commentaries (136/2015)*. Singapore: S. Rajaratnam School of International Studies.

Marchive, V. (2013, June 4). France considers stepping up Internet monitoring to fight terrorism. *Vive la Tech*. Retrieved from http://www.zdnet.com/article/france-considers-stepping-up-internet-monitoring-to-fight-terrorism/

Moore, K., Mason, P., & Lewis, J. (2008). *Images of Islam in the UK: The representation of British Muslims in the National Print News Media 2000-2008*. Cardiff: Cardiff University.

Murphy, K. (2004, February 7). Black widows caught in web of Chechen war. *LA Times*. Retrieved from http://culteducation.com/group/1128-russian-sects/18049-black-widows-caught-up-in-web-of-chechen-war-.html

Neumann, P. (2010). *Prison and terrorism*. London: International Centre for the Study of Radicalisation.

Norris, P., Kern, M., & Just, M. (2013). *Framing terrorism: The news media, the government and the public*. London: Taylor & Francis.

O'Neill, P. H. (2013, September 18). Why the Syrian uprising is the first social media war. *The Daily Dot*. Retrieved from http://www.dailydot.com/politics/syria-civiil-social-media-war-youtube

Ortbals, C. D., & Poloni-Staudinger, L. (2013). *Terrorism and violent conflict: Women's agency, leadership and responses*. New York, NY: Springer.

Poole, E. (2002). *Reporting Islam: Media representation and British Muslims*. London: IB Tauris & Co.

Precht, T. (2007). *Home grown terrorism and Islamist radicalization in Europe: From conversion to terrorism*. Denmark: Danish Ministry of Justice.

Qazi, F. (2011). The mujahidaat – tracing the early female warriors of Islam. In L. Sjoberg & C. Gentry (Eds.), *Women, gender, and extremism* (pp. 29–56). Athens, GA: University of Georgia Press.

Rogers, B., & Neumann, P. (2007). *Recruitment and mobilisation for the Islamist militant movement in Europe*. London: Kings College London.

Saltman, E., & Smith, M. (2015). *Till martyrdom do us part: Gender and the ISIS phenomenon*. London: Institute for Strategic Dialogue.

Saltman, E., & Winter, C. (2014). *Islamic State: The changing face of modern jihadism*. London: Quilliam Foundation.

Sjoberg, L., & Gentry, C. E. (Eds.). (2011). *Women, gender and terrorism*. Athens, GA: University of Georgia Press.

Speckhard, A., & Ahkmedova, K. (2006). The making of a martyr: Chechen suicide terrorism. *Studies in Conflict and Terrorism*, *29*(5), 429–492. doi:10.1080/10576100600698550

Tajfel, H. (1974). Social identity and intergroup behaviour. *Social Sciences Information. Information Sur les Sciences Sociales*, *13*(2), 65–93. doi:10.1177/053901847401300204

Tajfel, H., & Turner, J. C. (1979). An integrative theory of intergroup conflict. In W. G. Austinm & S. Worchel (Eds.), *The social psychology of intergroup relations* (pp. 33–47). Monterey, CA: Brooks-Cole.

WaE network. (2015). Retrieved from http://www.waenetwork.org

Why was Sajida al-Rishawi important to ISIS? (2015, January 26). *Al Arabiya News*. Retrieved from http://english.alarabiya.net/en/perspective/profiles/2015/01/26/Why-is-Sajida-al-Rishawi-important-to-ISIS-.html

Winter, C. (2015). *The virtual 'caliphate': Understanding Islamic State's propaganda strategy*. London: Quilliam Foundation.

Women Without Borders. (n.d.). Retrieved from www.women-without-borders.org

Zenn, J., & Pearson, E. (2014). Women, gender and the evolving tactics of Boko Haram. *Journal of Terrorism Research*, *5*(1), 46–57. doi:10.15664/jtr.828

ENDNOTES

[1.] A number of the accounts followed in the ISD-ICSR database, as well as various media accounts, have highlighted images of Western women in ISIS territory using weaponry in light training sessions.

[2.] While this online information is username and password protected, the contents (with reference to: www.islaam.net/main/display.php?id=1126&category=13) were explored in the insightful article by Qazi (2011).

[3.] Advice from a Muhajaraah [Web log comment]. Retrieved from justpaste.it/justadvicefromamuhajaraah

[4.] As discussed in Hoyle et al. (2015). See Umm Khattab [Web log]. Retrieved from http://ummkhattab.tumblr.com (last accessed 2014, November 28).

[5.] For further analysis see Hoyle et al. (2015).

[6.] Umm Layth (2014, April 9) [Web log]. Retrieved from http://fa-tubalilghuraba.tumblr.com (last accessed 2014, November 28]. For further analysis see Hoyle et al. (2015).

[7.] Translated from French: *De l'Épouse de notre frère Aboû Basîr 'Abdoullâh al-Ifrigî (qu'Allâh l'accepte)*.

Chapter 11
An Internet–Mediated Pathway for Online Radicalisation:
RECRO

Loo Seng Neo
Home Team Behavioural Sciences Centre, Ministry of Home Affairs, Singapore

ABSTRACT

This chapter proposes an Internet-mediated radicalisation model, RECRO. It consists of five phases: (1) the Reflection phase details the triggers, needs, and vulnerabilities that an individual may have which increase one's receptiveness towards alternative belief systems; (2) the Exploration phase details the period where the individual begins making sense of the information put forth by violent extremists; (3) the Connection phase details the influence of like-minded individuals and the online community on the individual's new worldview; (4) the Resolution phase details the period during which the individual gains the momentum to translate one's radical beliefs into action; and finally (5) the Operational phase details the period during which the individual is ready to commit violence to further one's radical objectives. This model provides a basis for understanding and informing judgements about an individual's level of involvement, and paves the way for future empirical work.

INTRODUCTION

The use of the Internet by violent extremists has become the focus of an increasing amount of academic research, particularly as it pertains to the potential functions of this technological innovation in the radicalisation process. Violent extremists of all affiliations have exploited a plethora of online services to spread their ideas, connect and radicalise potential followers and sympathisers. As Shahar (2007) explains,

Without the Internet, the radical groups making up the global jihad's cadre of militants would remain as a widely dispersed and isolated group of cells that happened to claim the same historical roots ... it is the Internet which has globalised the jihad movement. The network of global jihad is a product of the communications revolution. (p. 140)

DOI: 10.4018/978-1-5225-0156-5.ch011

Hence, there is a real concern over the proliferation of radical ideas and the threat of individuals becoming radicalised in the online domain. This chapter seeks to propose a phase based model 'RECRO' to account for the phenomenon of Internet-mediated radicalisation. The first section describes the threat of violent extremism on the Internet. The next few sections then detail each of the five phases of the Internet-mediated radicalisation model (RECRO: Reflection, Exploration, Connection, Resolution, Operational). For the purposes of this chapter, a working definition of online radicalisation would be "the process by which an individual is introduced to an ideological message and belief system that encourages movement from mainstream beliefs toward extreme views, primarily through the use of online media such as Facebook, Twitter, and YouTube" (Community Oriented Policing Services [COPG], 2014, p. 1).

THE EXPLOITATION OF THE INTERNET BY VIOLENT EXTREMISTS

The advent of the Internet has altered the relationship between violent extremism and the media. The Internet and the opportunity it offers, allow violent extremists to expand the functionalities of their propaganda efforts beyond the boundaries of the traditional, mainstream media (Conway, 2012; Europol, 2014; Weimann & von Knop, 2008). Violent extremists are therefore no longer dependent on traditional media outlets to disseminate their propaganda materials.

In fact, violent extremists have become so adept at exploiting the Internet that they have developed a wide variety of digital medium (e.g., websites, forums, social media platforms) to fulfil their radical agenda. As their use of the social media proliferates, it has increased the outreach and types of information that can be shared by violent extremists. In many ways, this grants violent extremists the platform to take control of the content of their messages, undercut the legitimacy of mainstream media organisations, and sustain their movements over time (Conway & McInerney, 2008; General Intelligence and Security Service [AIVD], 2012; Seib & Janbek, 2011). Similarly, the sharp increase in online publications with violent extremist ownerships indicates that it is an increasingly important means for violent extremists to achieve their cause (Lemieux, Brachman, Levitt, & Wood, 2014; Rieger, Frischich, & Bente, 2013; Rogan, 2007).

More importantly, the Internet has afforded violent extremists the channel to influence those sympathetic to their narratives (Edwards & Gribbon, 2013; Neo, Khader, Shi, Dillon, & Ong, 2015; Torok, 2013). For example, the enormous outreach of the Internet makes it the perfect instrument to establish an online community of shared knowledge, norms and interest without temporal or geographical restrictions (Powers & Armstrong, 2014). It also offers the opportunity for violent extremists such as Abu Musab al-Zarqawi (former leader of Al-Qaeda in Iraq) to exploit the Internet to shape their audience's worldviews. Before al-Zarqawi began his online propaganda campaign, it is essential to note that he would have to kill large numbers of people in order to grab the attention of supporters and media (Conway, 2007). However, through these online videos, al-Zarqawi was able to achieve greater impact and media publicity albeit using fewer resources.

Another line of evidence comes from the use of the Internet by the Islamic State in Iraq and Syria (ISIS) to reach out and encourage others to adopt its worldview (Nuraniyah, 2014). Through social media platforms, ISIS has managed to portray a consistent public image as an organisation that delivers results (i.e., both online and offline) and establish its presence internationally (Bernard, 2014; Saifudeen, 2015). Rather than alienating potential recruits, these propaganda materials have instead succeeded in attracting more foreign fighters to join ISIS (Carter, Maher, & Neumann, 2014), and inspired established jihadist groups to pledge alliance or show support (Neo, Shi et al., 2014). Even in the face of counter-narratives directed at ISIS by law enforcement agencies, ISIS has managed to circumvent these criticisms of the group by creating its own jihadi counter-arguments. There is therefore the pressing need to be familiar with these online developments, particularly the influence of these propaganda materials on potential recruits.

The Threat of Radicalisation in the Digital Era

This marks a significant development given the fact that the increased online presence of violent extremists has raised the possibility of more individuals being influenced and radicalised by radical ideology online (Bermingham, Conway, McInerney, O'Hare, & Smeaton, 2009; Gupta, 2011; Kruglanski, Crenshaw, Post, & Victoroff, 2008). For instance, in a newspaper article by Oumar (2011), it was reported that in Mauritania, most of the violent extremists learned and assimilated the radical ideology of Al-Qaeda through its websites and online forums. Similarly, in his research on the role of the Internet on the radicalisation of youths, Samuel (2015) underline the growing hazard of radical ideas propagated online and how it has become a key medium for violent extremist groups to reach out to young people.

Across western countries, authorities are also concerned about the growing threat of online violent extremism. Roshonara Choudhry, a university student who in 2010 stabbed British MP Stephen Timms using a kitchen knife, was presented as having been radicalised by Anwar al-Awlaki's online lectures (Dillon, Neo, Ong, & Khader, 2014). Another example is the Tsarnaev brothers who shared no ties to Al-Qaeda, but are thought to have used information published on an Al-Qaeda website to plan and carry out the Boston Marathon attack (Bowman-Grieve, 2015). Furthermore, recent incidents involving other lone actors (e.g., Man Haron Monis of the Sydney Siege, Micheal Zehf-Bibeau of the Canadian Parliament attack, Michael Adebolajo and Michael Adebowale of the Lee Rigby street attack, Nidal Hasan of the Fort Hood shooting) exemplified the potential threat associated with violent extremism in the digital era. These individuals performed acts of violence against targets consistent with ideas and ideologies they had previously consumed on the Internet. These observations demonstrate the role that the Internet may play in the radicalisation process (Conway, 2012; Lennings, Amon, Brummert, & Lennings, 2010).

Perhaps nothing encapsulates the threat better than the pronounced rise in the number of Internet-mediated radicalised cases, and the emergence of lone-wolf attacks. In an analysis of the recent trends, Sageman (2010) note that: "78% of all global neo-jihadi terrorist plots in the West in the past five years came from autonomous home-grown groups without any connection, direction or control from Al-Qaeda Core or its allies" (p. 11). Broadly concurring, Weimann (2012) observe that almost all lone wolf attacks in recent years have involved the use of electronic social media.

While these high-profile cases hit the headlines, the bulk of the threat posed by online violent extremism ironically is felt through acts of non-violent mundane use of the Internet – e.g., dissemination of extremist propaganda, information provision. Those carrying out these activities are the sympathisers and supporters of violent extremist groups. Though the sympathisers and supporters differ from violent extremists in the adoption of violence, the action they take helped to sustain and propagate the ideologies of violent extremist groups.

Hence, what is more concerning is that the Internet has abetted the outreach of violent extremism right down to the individual level. The proliferation of violent extremist material online and the ease with which anyone can access online communities advocating violence and find radical materials, has inadvertently increased the capacity for violence and violent extremism. Serving as an effective conduit for communication, Cohen, Johansson, Kaati, and Mork (2014) reason that

[T]he capability threshold for individuals to carry out advanced attacks is becoming lower with time due to the power of the Internet to bring critical information, such as tutorials on bomb-making or geographical information, 'to your fingertips'. There is also a concern that the Internet is making it easier than ever to engage in the study and dissemination of extremist views. (p. 246)

Given that online events are increasingly impacting real world events, identifying individuals who are using the Internet for malevolent purposes (i.e., violent extremism) is therefore a critical concern. From a countering violent extremism perspective, understanding how the Internet has contributed to the radicalisation process is therefore important. While research on the phenomenon of radicalisation in the digital era has grown substantially in the last few years, there remain many unanswered challenges and unchartered territories of knowledge in the field. Specifically, the impact and importance of the online community, as well as the transition from online violent extremism to offline violence, remains poorly understood. Thus, there is a pressing need to study how Internet-mediated radicalisation takes place so as to find ways to educate prevention and intervention efforts.

UNDERSTANDING THE BEHAVIOUR OF ACTORS IN INTERNET-MEDIATED RADICALISATION

In the current security climate there is an ever greater need to adopt approaches that can reveal critical insights about violent extremists and how they are exploiting the features of the Internet. Edward and Gribbon (2013), in their analysis of the pathways to violent extremism, emphasise the need to take into account the influence of the Internet and the online community in order to obtain a clearer picture of the level of risk posed by such violent extremists. In like manner, Bowman-Grieve (2009) underscores the importance of examining how the virtual communities provide support for their members in order to better understand the threat of violent extremism online.

While recent cases have emphasised the relationship between violent extremist online content and its potential effects on the individual, it is important to acknowledge that these online materials are unlikely to have radicalised those arrested on their own (e.g., Dauber & Winkler, 2014; Edwards & Gribbon, 2013; Neumann 2012; Rieger et al., 2013). In this online milieu where violent extremists operate, individuals in general do not change their minds or adopt the use of violence by reading newspapers, online articles or books. Thus, to focus narrowly on violent extremist online content risks implying a degree of causality between what is found online and its influence on the individual reading it. It is integral to recognise that the physical real world interaction and networks is, and still remains a vital ingredient to buttress an already sympathetic individual's resolve to embrace radical worldviews (Conway, 2012; Yasin, 2011). As Hussain and Saltman (2014, p. 7) pointed out: "the vast majority of radicalised individuals come into contact with extremist ideology through offline socialisation prior to being further indoctrinated online". There is a need to analyse how individuals experience violent extremist online content and the possible impact of the online mediums (see Chapter 1 for more information).

However, the transition from online to offline violence remains poorly understood. While there are thousands of members of the violent extremist online communities, very few become violent extremists in the real world. The 'loudest' online members (i.e., those engaged in the most vigorous and aggressive forms of online interactions) may not, in fact, be the ones most likely to engage in violence. In this regard, Conway (2012) suggests these individuals may have utilised the Internet to dissipate their desire for violent action by only supporting and encouraging violent extremism, but not posing any real world threat. Likewise, the most passive ones are not automatically the most peaceful either. It is not possible, in other words, to draw a straight line between online chatter and offline action.

Recognising the Interaction between the Internet and the Individual

Following this line of reasoning, there is a need to acknowledge the relationships between the medium of transaction (i.e., the Internet), the constellation of like-minded individuals within the transactional structure (i.e., there may not be a physical group as the group is the virtual community), and the individual. This is in line with research which suggests individuals would actively draw on the Internet to establish new kinds of relationships (Slevin, 2000). However, while the use of the Internet as a tool for violent extremists has been well documented, the paucity of empirical research analysing the effects of Internet-mediated communications impedes law enforcement agencies actual understanding of the mechanisms at work. This problem is succinctly summarised by Saifudeen (2014),

[M]ore often than not, when incorporated into a study of the phenomenon of radicalisation in totality, the Internet is often relegated to the role of being a mere facilitator of the entire process. This unfortunately results in overlooking the significant role played by the unique attributes and online community dynamics of the Internet realm that contribute to the radicalisation process. It is these attributes and dynamics that warrant a deeper explanation that goes beyond simply talking about the 'echo chamber' effects. A pathway model specific to the online realm is thus needed to effectively understand these unique attributes of the Internet, contributing to radicalisation. (p. 1)

The question, therefore, seems obvious: how can the internal characteristics of the individual actor (i.e., from a personality and person-specific perspective) teach us about someone's propensity to become involved in violent extremism via the Internet? Are there phases of radicalisation that distinguish peaceful activists from those planning to break the law or engage in violence? If such differences exist, how can they be used to make targeting by law enforcement and intelligence agencies more efficient?

Insights from Extant Radicalisation Frameworks

Several efforts have been made to make sense of what motivates and enables violent extremist offending, and identify a pathway that explains the process of radicalisation. It has long been argued that the identification of a 'violent extremist personality' would allow law enforcement agencies to track the radicalisation process which shaped violent extremists to become what they are today. However, research suggests that there is no single pathway to violent extremism – the pathways and explanations for the propensity to behave violently are varied and are very different (Borum, 2011a; McCauley & Moskalenko, 2011); and people who hold and embrace radical ideas does not necessarily mean they will actually engage in any terrorist activity (Aly, Weimann-Saks, & Weimann, 2014; Dean, 2014).

Thus, instead of searching for a violent extremist personality, it is perhaps more constructive to emphasise a more process-oriented view, that reflects the individual being a combination of different dimensions (which includes traits and behaviours but also other dimensions of personality) that continually interact and transact with the environment. The context and experiences that the individual undergoes will shape and influence him/her to be involved in violent extremism – i.e., how do individuals come to adopt violent extremist ideology, and choose to internalise these beliefs to justify the use of violence (see Horgan, 2008). As such, these phase based frameworks represent a general sequence of stages that might shed insights on how an individual would gradually gravitate towards the use of violence.

There are many models depicting the process of radicalisation (refer to chapter 3 for a more detailed review). An influential model has been the one of Fathali Moghaddam who, in 2005, introduces the 'Staircase to Terrorism' model. This model comprises of six stages that a radicalised individual would undertake. Specifically, it uses the metaphor of a narrowing staircase that leads from the ground floor upwards to the point where one would engage in violent extremism. Moghaddam (2005) argues that feelings of perceived deprivation form the foundation and motivation for getting involved in violent extremism. The staircase leads to higher and higher floors, and whether someone remains on a particular floor depends on the 'doors' and 'spaces' that person imagines to be open to him/her on that floor. This model conceptualises how as individuals climb up the staircase, they see fewer and fewer choices, until the only possible outcome is the destruction of others, or oneself, or both.

Thus, radicalisation reflects an increasing involvement and commitment in violent extremism as well as an increasing receptiveness towards radical ideology and internalising the new beliefs as part of one's social identity. For instance, this seems to be equally true based on insights garnered from violent extremist case histories. Wilner and Dubouloz (2011) in their analysis of Islamist radicalisation also note that "cognitive shifts occur in radicalising individuals, whereby previously held conceptions, beliefs and identities along with their associated behaviours – are reconstructed and replaced" (p. 419). In the report on 'Radicalisation in the West: The homegrown threat', Silber and Bhatt (2007) demarcate the intensification of one's beliefs and commitment to the radical ideology and cause in the third stage of their radicalisation framework. The authors argue that citizen of Western home-country who ultimately adopts a jihadi-salafi ideology do so through a linear four-stage process which details the individual's acceptance of his/her duty to act on behalf of the community.

Like Silber and Bhatt's work, there have been similar efforts aimed at outlining the process of violent extremism. Based on an in-depth psychological analysis of 30 Jemaah Islamiyah members who were arrested in 2002 in Singapore, a team of psychologists managed to interview and derive a psychological profile of these offenders. Subsequently, a process model of their road to radicalisation was mapped out (see Tan, 2006). As Tan (2006, p.53) explains:

The model portrays the process of terrorism for the Jemaah Islamiyah recruit, represented by a road which transits from a predisposition phase to a socialisation phase. Personal factors which render the individual susceptible to engaging in terrorism are reflected under the predisposition phase, while situational factors which lead the individual to become radicalised and indoctrinated are reflected under the socialisation phase. Road signages situated along the route, such as individual factors, recruitment and training, represent vulnerable markers that the terrorist-to-be undergoes. (p. 53)

As in most popular models, this model posits radicalisation is a process which involves many inter-related factors and causes, and there is a need to account for the interactions between the individual and the external factors.

Internet-Mediated Radicalisation

Though the models discussed are generally consistent with each other and have become popular among law enforcement agencies, they seem more apt to explain the radicalisation process in the real world context; rather than incorporating the online element. To better understand the radicalisation process in the digital space, it is necessary to take into account the interplay and interactions over time between the person and the online environment (von Behr, Reding, Edwards, & Gribbon, 2013). For this reason, there is a need to understand how the Internet mediates the radicalisation process and shapes the user's behaviours and attitudes – i.e., understanding the individual's experience online and how he/she use the Internet in the process of radicalisation. Furthermore, understanding the transitions between the online and offline worlds is essential if law enforcement agencies are to understand how the next generation of potential violent extremists will be radicalised.

In light of these observations, some researchers (e.g., Saifudeen 2014; Torok, 2013) have attempted to hypothesise a radicalisation process in the online realm. In embarking on this effort, Saifudeen (2014), for instance, develop the 'Cyber Extremism Orbital Pathways Model'. He underscores the importance of understanding and accounting for the unique attributes of the Internet. Saifudeen (2014) proposes that it is perhaps more fruitful to focus on the wide variety and accessibility of counterculture communities that the Internet provides. In other words, rather than relegating the role of the Internet to that of a facilitator, there is the need to explain how the online communications between different entities actually contribute to the radicalisation process. Specifically,

[F]or every stage of radicalisation, there are competing forces that maintain that stage and are in equilibrium. There are tipping points that upset this equilibrium at each stage of radicalisation that ultimately plummet the individual towards manifesting radical thoughts at the cognitive level in actual violent behaviour. (Saifudeen, 2014, p. 7)

Saifudeen (2014) further emphasised that this competition of ideas may lead one to be more inclined towards violent extremist behaviours. In that sense, an individual might reach a stage where the current worldview is found to be ineffective in meeting one's expectations, or an alternative radical narrative is found to be more attractive. If that would to happen, the individual makes the conscious choice to explore further and become more entrenched with the online communities. From an operational perspective, this model provides a framework for determining possible modes or points of intervention for countering violent extremism by taking into account the context which aid in shaping new worldviews and sense of belonging.

Another much-cited contribution is that of Weimann and von Knop (2008), who have introduced a five-phase framework to understand how an individual engages with violent extremist narratives online. The framework consists of the searching phase (i.e., the individual exhibit an interest and motivation to search for radical websites); the seduction phase (i.e., the individual is exposed to the radical ideology after visiting specific websites); the captivation phase (i.e., the individual becomes attracted by the radical ideology and begins to visit more radical websites); the persuasion phase (i.e., the individual becomes an active member of the online community); and the operation phase (i.e., the individual becomes involved in the operative activities of the online community and/or violent extremist group).

This framework provides a useful starting point for conceptualising and aggregating factors that may cause an individual to support and become involved in violent extremism online. This in turn allows for the identification of phases where the individual is still 'open to' counter-narratives that challenge the ideas and messages embedded in the violent extremist narratives (Aly et al., 2014). However, the framework remains largely descriptive and underdeveloped. For instance, the framework says little about the motivations that may cause some individuals to become interested in radical ideology. Further, how do the online community of like-minded individuals and person-specific factors interact to influence the likelihood of moving from one phase to another, especially from the persuasion to operation phase? Finally, it is difficult to determine the psychological processes involved (e.g., cognitive opening, moral disengagement), and the potential barriers that prevent the individual from continuing down the path towards violent extremism. Nevertheless, it offers a useful way to organise concepts, mechanisms and processes that might be involved in Internet-mediated radicalisation, and understand the behaviour of actors in the virtual environments (i.e., how the individual interact with others online).

TOWARDS A MODEL FOR INTERNET-MEDIATED RADICALISATION: RECRO

While research on radicalisation within cyberspace has grown substantially in the recent years, there remain many unanswered challenges and unchartered territories of knowledge in the field. Against this backdrop, this chapter seeks to propose a five-phase model[1], 'RECRO', to explain the phenomenon of Internet-mediated radicalisation. Adapted from Weimann and von Knop's (2008) work, this framework can be seen as a phase model designed to demonstrate the phases in which a potential violent extremist offender chooses to desist from or continue on the path to radicalisation.

Similar to Saifudeen's (2014) work, the RECRO model seeks to account for the person-system interactions that occur in a complex, multifaceted online environment; this can only be better understood by taking into account insights from the social and psychological literature (see Mohaddam, 2005). Its' value is that it provides a working hypothesis to account for how the person and features of the online platforms recursively influence one another throughout the radicalisation and engagement process. It also points out the importance of integrating rather than viewing person-centric and system-centric factors as separate determinants of the Internet-mediated radicalisation process. The five phases of the RECRO model (see Figure 1) are summarised as follow:

1. The *Reflection* phase details the triggers, needs, and vulnerabilities that an individual may have which increase one's receptiveness towards alternative belief systems;
2. The *Exploration* phase details the period where the individual begins making sense of the online information put forth by violent extremists;
3. The *Connection* phase details the influence of like-minded individuals and the online community on the individual's new worldview;
4. The *Resolution* phase details the period during which the individual gains the momentum to translate one's radical beliefs into action; and

Figure 1. The RECRO model of Internet-mediated radicalisation

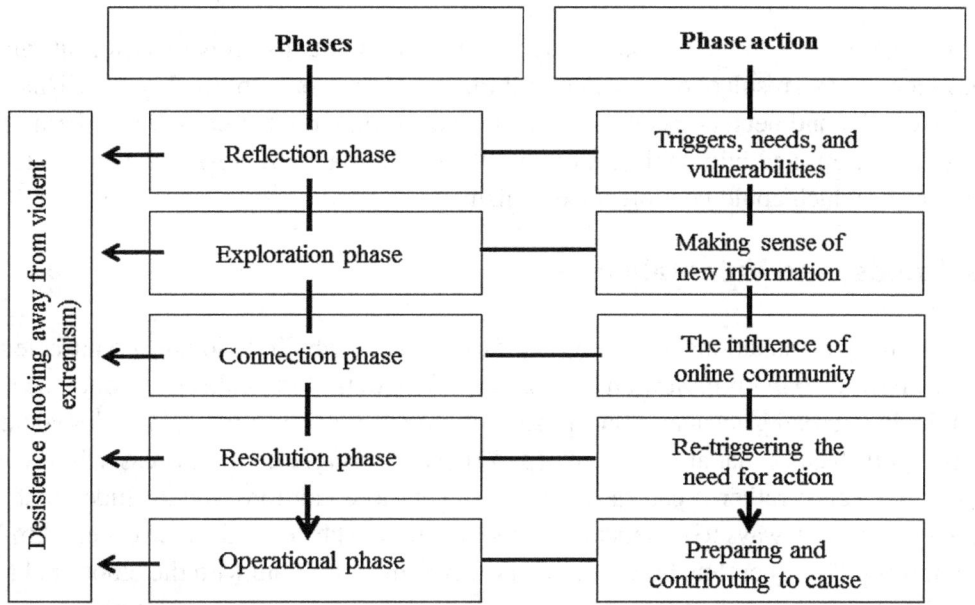

5.   The *Operational* phase details the period during which the individual is ready to commit violence to further one's radical objectives both online and/or offline.

It is important to recognise that the radicalisation process differs from person to person (i.e., individuals may move back and forth between stages or remain static), and the phases are not always as distinct from each other as they appear. Furthermore, while this chapter focuses on the online aspect of the radicalisation process, it is essential to note that radicalised attitudes and behaviours can occur in both online and offline realm (i.e., the individual is also interacting with the real world environment). When conceptualised in this manner, it is clear that the extent of Internet-mediated radicalisation can be viewed as a continuum going from no interest about the radical rhetoric presented to complete belief and trust in the narratives, and such activities often took place against a background of ongoing interaction between the individuals and their environment.

By examining the social online phenomenon of Internet-mediated radicalisation using the RECRO model, this model aims to:

- Provide a basis for understanding and informing judgements about an individual's level of involvement;
- Highlight how the Internet influences the ways the individual can relate and bond with other like-minded individuals;
- Identify the personal, cognitive, and emotional transformations that may happen as the individuals internalise new values and beliefs; and
- Pave the way for future empirical work.

THE REFLECTION PHASE: TRIGGERS, NEEDS, AND VULNERABILITIES

The reflection phase refers to the period during which an individual's propensity for alternative belief systems may increase as a result of one's vulnerabilities, needs and/or inept worldviews. This is the phase where the personality and person-specific factors and social milieu interact to create the motivation for individuals to 'open-up' and initiate the search online for alternative rhetoric or channels to fulfil their needs – i.e., one of which could be violent extremism.

Triggers, Needs, and Vulnerabilities

Over the years, many explanations have been put forward as to why individuals are attracted to radical ideology. Borum (2011b) in his review on the conceptual models of radicalisation conclude that "causal factors often include broad grievances that 'push' individuals towards a radical ideology and narrower, more specific 'pull' factors that attract them" (p. 57). These factors do not necessarily revolve around deep religious doctrines; rather it can range from triggers to conditions and attitudes that predispose the individual to find new ways to understand one's life circumstances and experiences. Similarly, Weimann and von Knop (2008) outline how radical narratives may resonate with the emotional needs faced by socially alienated and disenfranchised individuals within the diaspora communities; some of these individuals may experience certain personal circumstances that increase their readiness to subscribe to radical ideology.

Other types of motivations have also been identified. In the analysis of the 2004 Madrid bombings in Spain, Jordan, Manas, and Horsburgh (2008) highlight that the common denominator across the perpetrators is the "sense of a lack of belonging to society, hostility toward society, and the construction of an identity according to the boundaries of a virtual community that is part of the global jihad movement" (p. 23). There was no sense of affiliation to their country of residence. Instead, the perpetrators were motivated by the sense of belonging to the global jihadi movement.

In his commentary on the phenomenon of self-radicalisation, Ramakrishna (2007) suggests that a severe loss of status, such as a change in occupation, can cause an individual to be unhappy with one's status quo. As a result, he argued that there may be an increased tendency for the individual to become more susceptible to the counter-culture appeal of the violent extremist ideology.

Research also suggests that some individuals became involved in violent extremism because of the prospects for excitement, adventure, and glory (McCauley & Moskalenko, 2011; Venhaus, 2010), and that such thrill-seeking opportunities suffice as a key motivation for them to stay engage regardless of the radical ideology or cause itself. Therefore, depending on the circumstances of the individual, the main motivation for a person to become involved in violent extremism may not be due to ideology, but rather the individual is drawn towards violent extremist groups for other reasons – see chapter 3, 8, 9 and 10 for more information.

Cognitive Opening

Of particular interest here, however, is the act of re-evaluating one's life choices and belief system as a result of these factors. These personality and person-specific factors (e.g., triggers, needs, vulnerabilities) may act as disorienting dilemmas and propel individuals to re-examine and question accepted norms and beliefs (Saifudeen, 2014; Wilner & Dubouloz, 2011). There may be a loss of credibility or doubt in the ideas or solutions proposed by the current worldview one ascribes to, and the routine way of life is unable to fulfil one's needs and account for what has happened in his/her lives. Rather than simply compel an individual to participate in violence, these developments instead increase the individual's receptiveness to new experiences, perspectives and beliefs (Schmid 2013). Specifically, it emphasises the significance of exploring new ways to cope and resolve the individual's current concerns – e.g., finding the specific religious interpretation that resonate with one's own views. This follows what is termed as a 'cognitive opening' where an individual's existence can be better explained and understood by the individual if he/she would change his/her current worldview (Schmid, 2013).

For example, Wiktorowicz observed that people who join Al-Muhajiroun, a violent extremist group based in the United Kingdom,

[F]irst revealed an openness to new worldviews [cognitive opening], then came to view religion as a path to find meaning [religious seeking], eventually found the group's narrative and ethos to 'make sense' (frame alignment), and ultimately, through a process of socialisation, became fully indoctrinated into the movement. (as cited in Borum, 2011a, pp. 18-19)

In other words, the process may start by being susceptible to radical ideas as a result of personality and person-specific factors exhibited by the individual.

This reflects a crucial concern, the basis of which represents a logical argument that many have turned to the Internet for solutions to problems they have faced in their lives (Bargh & McKenna, 2004; Lennings et al., 2010; Salamon, 2007). The Internet presents many opportunities for cognitive openings to occur, given the multitude of ideas one can encounter that can offer a credible challenge to one's present worldview. Moreover, the sense of anonymity associated with online communications creates an environment where the individual is able to experiment with a whole array of alternate ideas with little regard for repercussions on oneself or consequences affecting others (Benson, 2014; Demetriou & Silke, 2003; Joinson, 2007).

To that end, the premise that individuals are susceptible to seek out alternative belief systems stem from their reaction to triggers (e.g., curiosity; unexpected life changes), needs and vulnerabilities (e.g., search for identity; need for affiliation; perceived injustice; need for excitement and adventure). Eventually, the individual 'tips' towards a decision (cognitive opening) to realise that the old reality simply no longer exists and a new one must be established. This realisation is central in creating a susceptible consciousness that increases the motivation to search for new roles, worldviews, and lifestyle routine. This resultant frame of mind may influence the individual to:

- Shape and restructure one's degree of susceptibility to new religious attitudes and beliefs;
- Be attracted by ideas championed by an alternative religious and/or spiritual guidance which helps one to comprehend one's circumstance; and
- Develop some form of expectations that the alternative novel religious and/or spiritual guidance is a good alternative to delve into.

Understanding the impact of these factors among potential violent extremists is therefore critical to map the radicalisation process. In essence, the reflection phase can be viewed as a function of triggers, needs and vulnerabilities that predispose an individual to initiate the online search for alternative religious guidance and/or channels to fulfil their needs and/or address their concerns.

THE EXPLORATION PHASE: MAKING SENSE OF NEW INFORMATION

The exploration phase refers to the period during which an individual is starting to search online for alternative belief systems – i.e., which could be radical narratives. It is essential to note that the conceptualisation of an individual's likelihood of becoming receptive to radical narratives largely hinges on how these online narratives relate to his/her life experiences and sense of self.

As mentioned earlier, the receptivity one develops towards alternative belief systems depends on the triggers, needs, and vulnerabilities of the reflection phase. Both the reflection and exploration phases are rather intertwined with each other; this affects the way the individual connects with radical ideology. In recognition of this muddled reality, these two phases occur in a parallel, rather than sequential fashion, and in reality cannot be distinctly separated. When the individual becomes receptive towards new ideas, it provides a contact point that increases the potential for him/her to establish 'connections' with the radical narratives in a manner that has well-defined consequences. Thus, this is the phase where radical ideology begins to influence the attitudes of the individual as one seeks to make sense of the new information found online.

To begin with, it is important to recognise that the visual medium, and speed, depth, volume of information heralded by the advent of the Internet has inadvertently increased the outreach of these radical narratives. Unlike traditional hardcopy version of violent extremist materials, these online propaganda materials are relatively easy to locate and access via numerous online media (Bergin, Osman, Ungerer, & Yasin, 2009; Neo et al., 2015). For example, van Ginkel (2015) observes that ISIS has been disseminating Hollywood-style high-quality videos of its actions via its fighters' social media platforms to reach out to its supporters from different parts of the world. In a way, these materials serve as channels to expose, connect and educate individuals to the propaganda created by violent extremist groups.

Coming into Contact with Radical Narratives

Arguably, in the event that the individual manages to come into contact with violent extremist narratives online (i.e., which is easily accessible as highlighted above), the individual had to make a choice either to ignore the material, or to continue the search for more relevant materials. This initial confrontation with online radical rhetoric will lead to two possible outcomes.

The 'Ignore' Response

In the first scenario, there is the possibility that the individual may abandon usage due to the nefarious nature of the radical narratives, or the inability in which the radical rhetoric correspond with the individual's existing expectation. Thus, the individual may ignore and roam uncommitted from website to website; in so doing, they are engaged with the narratives, but not connected. For example, Bartlett and Miller (2012) suggest that engaging radical narratives is not necessarily indicative of one's propensity to become a violent extremist. They argued that many individuals who have come into contact with radical narratives did not accept them. In addition, these individuals may participate in brief exchanges of information which end at a click of their mouse; the joys of the endeavour wear off quickly and the narratives cease to allure. Nonetheless, this does not mean that the individual would not be enticed in the future (Fighel, 2007).

The 'Continue' Response

Alternatively, the radical narratives may resonate with the individual's expectations and encourage one to search for more information. Mbakwe and Cunliffe (2007) in their research on the hypermedia seduction for violent extremist recruiting suggest that for some individuals, "instantaneous allure or attraction may occur simply through the existence of an extremist website, even before consideration of its content takes place" (p. 222). The act of finding the radical information may have induced feeling of gratifications and reinforced the re-occurrence of these online behaviours.

Gaining Commitment from the Individual

In this sense, online exposure to violent extremist narratives can help frame and prime the individual to a new alternative worldview. This is envisaged to create the connections through which the individual links and networks with like-minded others via the Internet. As Hussain and Saltman (2014) observe, "once the fuse has been lit, curious individuals seeking to develop their knowledge begin to search for other means through which they can learn more about their newfound ideas" (p. 74).

The radical narratives are usually framed in a way that will resonate with the interests, attitudes, and beliefs of the target audience. Upal (2015) suggests that jihadist narratives are successful primarily because they are predicated on easy-to-understand religious and emotional appeal. The prominence of jihadi materials may stem from the "rebranding many of their harsh ideas to make them sound benign and selecting emotive issues in order to elicit public sympathy" (Hussain & Saltman, 2014, p. 109). In this context, the information online may provide 'clear' answers, structures and rules for individuals who are seeking answers to concerns that they might have. Moreover, some radical narratives do demonstrate a degree of sophistication, employ logical reasoning and are further reinforced using a variety of effective media persuasion tactics.

Aly (2009) highlighted that violent extremist groups have been known to exploit and reconceptualise any newsworthy events into an immediate concern that would resonate with their following. For instance, Seib and Janbek (2011) observe that the episodes of mistreatment of prisoners at the Abu Ghraib prison have been exploited with galvanising effect by violent extremist groups who have cited retribution as their cause in their recruitment efforts. They further mentioned that "referring to someone as a terrorist or murderer rather than using resistance fighter or martyr can, over time, make a significant difference in how the public perceives particular persons and actions" (p. 9). It seems incontrovertible that through these notions of vilifying the enemy, violent extremist groups would have spread disinformation in an effort to influence the individual to adopt their point of view, and provides the vehicle to shape the individual's beliefs and behaviours.

Furthermore, a positive connection may arise as a result of the cognitive opening experienced by the individual from the reflection phase. At the individual level, the Internet removes many of the psychological inhibitions associated with face-to-face communications, and may lower the individual's resistance towards radical narratives and compel him/her to act on such information from a distinctly biased position. To that end, it may increase the likelihood of the individual to re-negotiate his/her identity within the violent extremist movement and become more supportive towards the movement (Bowman-Grieve, 2009). For example, individuals who are motivated by the need for belonging may develop the illusion that many share similar beliefs online – given that they are provided with space to explore the various online platforms to look for others who exhibit similar preference towards radical narratives. In fact, Givner-Forbes and Osman (2009) observe that online social interaction plays an important role in increasing commitment and motivation, and this in turn lowers the barriers of entry to violent extremism.

With that in mind, the individual is more likely to continue the search for more radical materials if the content on these online platforms echoes shared beliefs and champions the ideology that resonates with him/her, and/or meet the needs of him/her. The danger here therefore is that these individuals are visiting these radical narratives at various online platforms with a high degree of disciplined regularity for extended periods of time. Thus, there is an essential need to focus on the process by which the individual comes into contact with radical materials online and interpret the information.

Even in the event that such exposure fails to induce the desired outcome, the mere exposure to these radical beliefs may have also unconsciously 'familiarised' the individual with the new perspective (Fang, Singh, & Ahluwalia, 2007). In accordance to the 'mere exposure effect', these individuals may in the future become more receptive towards such radical beliefs. Thus, it would seem prudent to pay close attention to the level of resonance form between the individual and the radical narratives, and the individual's cognitions that might reflect any ongoing changes in receptiveness towards radical narratives.

THE CONNECTION PHASE: THE INFLUENCE OF THE ONLINE COMMUNITIES

The connection phase refers to the period during which an individual is ready to interact with like-minded individuals to further one's radical perspective. Following the exploration phase, the individual would have begun to connect with one another and create online communities based on similar interests and ideas, and in this case, radical narratives. These communities enable the individual to find support and reinforce his/her worldview with other like-minded individuals, which in turn facilitate the formation of a relational bond between the individual and the wider radical movement.

The Echo Chamber Effect

In many respects, the online community forms an 'echo chamber' which reinforces the commonly held shared ideology of like-minded individuals. The interactive feature of the online community allows for the exchange of ideas and validation of beliefs between its members (Bowman-Grieve, 2013; Thomas, Mcgarty, & Louis, 2014). More importantly, online social interaction is considered to be potentially more compelling and persuasive than passively receiving information (Duarte, 2007). Thus, the key perceivable danger is not that the community serves as repositories for radical rhetoric, but that it also allows the individual to gain access to a community of like-minded individuals to reinforce one's new worldview.

Moreover, given that the Internet is difficult to regulate and censor, the creators of radical online medium are therefore able to portray an image which will inculcate a more extreme perspective of the enemy by generating more arguments favouring their biased position and isolate the community members from any alternative moral interpretation. This innate feature of the online communities to present a one-sided visibility of narratives would render the individual to become increasingly impervious to contrary sources of information (Hussain & Saltman, 2014; Radlauer, 2007).

Socialisation to the Online Community

The assimilation of radical beliefs can also be attributed to the way through which the experiences of the individual's virtual encounters were normalised as part of a common online identity (Tzanetti, 2007). The resulting relaxation of constraints arising from the internalisation of the norms of the online community would fuel cognitive, emotional and behavioural changes in the individual. The nature of that implies that the individual would regress from a myriad of mainstream influences to a narrow frame of radical reference in which deviant behaviour and violence are the norm. In other words, these online platforms have been utilised to facilitate the assimilation of novel rules of social conduct, routines, and behaviours which may lead to the normalisation of violent extremist views.

For example, in his analysis of violent extremist virtual communities, Radlauer (2007) suggests that the increase in extremity and renegotiation of an individual's position in the larger context of the violent extremist movement is believed to be driven by this online mode of socialisation. The inferred common understanding has been the presence of a supportive and responsive online community to encourage and cheer the individual further down the path of radical violence. When this happens, it may increase the probability of the individual to assimilate the radical ideology into their worldviews and recognise the legitimacy of the violent extremist cause (AIVD, 2012).

As a result, the online community provides a whole new leverage for violent extremist groups to instil a strong sense of social identity by cognitively reframing an environment. Thus, this phase involves the subconscious reduction of one's inhibitions against the use of violence – especially after one has expressed solidarity with the radical narratives. In particular, the individual may go through a process of 'moral disengagement' of self-sanction in which one might change his/her opinions on the moral value of killing (Bandura, 1990). Bandura argues that

[O]nce dehumanised, the potential victims are no longer viewed as persons with feelings, hopes and concerns but as a subhuman objects. They are portrayed as mindless savages ... sub-humans are regarded as insensitive to maltreatment and capable of being influenced only by harsh methods. (Bandura, 1990, pp. 180-181)

This process of dehumanising their enemies (e.g., enemies are seen as dogs or tumours and/or are evil) would effectively remove any inherent moral inhibitions that the individual may have; increasing the likelihood for the individual to physically harm the enemies.

Development of Online Trust

The social spaces of the online communities do not transpire in a vacuum; rather they feed off the online interactions and have an indirect effect on the development of online trust. While most of the members of the online community may have not actually met in-person, there have been indications that they have developed 'mutual trust' with one another (e.g., Hegghammer, 2014; Neumann, 2012).

Thus, it can be seen that online trust is the result of an understandable and often discernible outcome of the online interactions. In a study by Fiore, LeeTeirnan, and Smith (2002), the relationship between the online users' perceptions of trust and the longevity of their participation was examined. It was found that users who contributed more and for a longer time were evaluated as more trustworthy and credible. Thus, it suggests that more active users elicit more participation from other users. In the context of violent extremism, online trust between members of the online radical community usually develops over a considerable period of time, and this in turn provides them with a renewed sense of purpose and identity.

With reference to the case of Roshonara Choundry, her trust in the teachings of Anwar al-Awlaki and Sheikh Abdullah Azzam had propelled her to embrace the use of violence, even though Choundry did not engage in any form of direct communication with them before (Dodd, 2010). Thus, the Internet influenced the way Choundry related and indirectly bonded with the online radical community. Even in cases of lone-wolf attacks, the Dutch General Intelligence and Security Service (AVID) note in 2012 that these perpetrators rarely become radicalised in complete isolation; they usually would have engaged in some form of interaction with like-minded individuals in the online communities. Likewise, Hussain and Saltman (2014) believe that the violent extremist online communities can replace the social environments that these perpetrators lack in the real world. Thus, the online communities play a role in facilitating a climate of receptivity for the violent extremist propaganda messages.

In this regards, Carter and Carter (2012) argue that individuals with no links to any violent extremist group, will enter the online community as a 'non-violent individual' and exit as a 'violent true believer'; these individuals may be radicalised but they are not yet violent extremists. In this sense, these individuals can be seen as sympathisers of violent extremist groups.

Acceptance of the Radical Narratives

Even though the potential recruits would proactively search for radical materials, violent extremist groups have been known to contact individuals who expressed a desire to be involved in the movement (COPS, 2014). Weimann (2007) noted that violent extremist recruiters have exploited the interactive online technology to roam chat-rooms and forums for receptive members. He added that these recruiters would identify people who are the most vocal and active in these online forums. Subsequently, individuals who are interested in the group's cause or radical narratives would be approached by the recruiters directly and invited to join password protected chat rooms and forums (Tokar, 2007).

Once individuals begin to be 'trapped' in such radical online communities, they may isolate themselves and withdraw from their friends and family in the real world. Their extreme views and behaviours may also be perceived by others as anti-social, which further exacerbates their sense of alienation from the real world.

In many respects, the interactive element of the Internet creates a shared online community that takes precedence over the individual's immediate physical environment. These individuals may no longer be defined by their personal identity and status. Instead, they would identify and perceive themselves to be part of the online communities. Hence, the connection phase details the process that involves the incremental changes to an individual's belief system, and the endeavour of internalising the set of radical ideas as a result of the interaction with like-minded individuals in the online community.

THE RESOLUTION PHASE: RE-TRIGGERING THE NEED FOR ACTION

The resolution phase refers to the period during which an individual gain the momentum to translate one's radical beliefs into action. It is essential to note that the act of internalising radical narratives into one's belief systems does not necessarily precipitate an act of violence (Horgan, 2005; Schuurman &

Eijkman, 2015); most people with radical ideas would never act on them. Rather, there is a need for the individual to be 'retrigger' and coerce into actions.

In some cases, the individual may encounter new issues and/or circumstances (i.e., triggers) that supplied the resolution to act in adherence to one's newly internalised radical worldview. Depending on the nature and context of these triggers, it can tip the individual towards real world action and/or seek out active engagement (see chapter 7 for more information on tipping points). It is important to note that the new issues and/or circumstances would be processed from a solidified biased perspective as compared to previous times (i.e., the exploration and connection phase) when the individual was still exploring and making the connection with radical narratives.

Mobilising Individuals to Embrace the Need for Action

To begin with, the literature suggests that the acknowledgement that one's community is under attack typically would have a powerful effect on mobilising dispersed individuals into a collective interest group for action (Huton, Long, & Page, 2009; Shayo, Olfman, Iriberri, & Igbaria, 2007; Zanini, 2004). In the context of jihadi violent extremism, this can be referred to new foreign policies introduced by governments (e.g., United States) towards the 'War on Terror', or the invasion of ISIS and Afghanistan, and other forms of actions perceived to be a 'direct attack on Islam' (Chandler, 2007). This may validate the arguments put forth in the radical narratives that are used by violent extremist groups to condemn and target their enemies. In response to these notions of perceived threats, the individuals may be incited to subvert their moral barrier and embrace the actual use of violence in an attempt to alleviate the situation (Borum, 2011b). For instance, direct contacts with Anwar al-Awlaki were noted to have provided the religious justifications for Nidal Hassan to actively pursue his jihad which eventually culminated into the 2009 Fort Hood attack (Schmitt & Lipton, 2009). Thus, these issues may act as powerful accelerants of commitment to one's violent extremist cause.

Furthermore, the need to prove oneself for the greater cause (e.g., become a 'good' Muslim) may provide the impetus to move from words to action. Silber and Bhatt (2007, p. 29) in their research on home-grown radicalisation, note that "converts ... tend to be the most zealous members of groups. Their need to prove their religious convictions to their companions often makes them the most aggressive". This intensification of religiosity has been associated with what Wilner and Dubouloz (2011) describe as the 'moment of realisation' whereby one would embrace behaviours that resonate with their new beliefs system – which has been ascribed with the use of violence. Indeed, Steinal et al. (2010) posit that there is a certain pride associated with being a part of the grander scheme of things, and such perception may reinforce the individuals' motivation to prove their worth – which in the context of violent extremism meant engaging in more extreme behaviours. Thus, the individual may feel reinvigorated and it directly impinges upon the need to act.

From a psychological perspective, it is essential to recognise that these individuals may strive to become closer to the prototype of an ideal member consistent with the ideas and ideologies they have previously 'consumed' on the Internet. In the research on identity fusion, Swann, Jetten, Gómez, Whitehouse, and Bastian (2012) suggest that the relationship an individual develops in relation to the larger group entity (i.e., online community and/or violent extremist group) will encourage him/her to channel his/her personal agency into pro-group behaviour. This in turn may encourage the individual to help and defend his/her fellow group members and enhance the propensity to engage in behaviour from the new radical worldview. For instance, the opportunity to perform martyrdom and die for a higher cause is considered by many violent extremists to be a sign of devotion towards Islam (de Bie, de Poot, & van der Leun, 2015).

In this context, the underlying principle is the mere requirement to revalidate the need to participate, in favour of the radical cause; being sympathetic or having beliefs alone was not enough; beliefs needed to be demonstrated. Thus, issues and circumstances that are considered meaningful to the individual's new outlook and worldview may have provided the trigger and resolution to embrace the actual use of violence. In other words, radical ideology that initially changed the individual's attitudes may start to change one's behaviours as well.

THE OPERATIONAL PHASE: PREPARING AND CONTRIBUTING TO THE CAUSE BOTH ONLINE AND OFFLINE

The operational phase refers to the period during which an individual is mentally and/or operationally prepared to commit violence to further one's radical objectives. Following from the resolution phase, the reconceptualised need to act may drive the individual to devote more time and resources to contribute to one's adopted cause. In the words of Wilner and Dubouloz (2011), they reason that "violent behaviour is a product of the individuals newly acquired value system, where revenge and retribution are not only justified, but expected" (p. 423). Thus, there is a need to recognise the changes in behaviours (i.e., precede the acts of violence) that the individuals may manifest on the basis of their radical worldviews.

Gaining Access to Resources

However, to be effective in an operational sense, the individual would have to obtain the right kind of 'access' to entities that can support, facilitate and prepare one to pursue the violent extremist group's cause. Irrespective of one's motivation or cause, any individuals intending to carry out an attack must plan and prepare (Clutterbuck & Warnes, 2011; Neo, Khader, Ang, Ong, & Tan, 2014). For instance, the individual may develop the intention to seek out members and/or leaders of violent extremist groups.

While some of these behavioural conducts may continue to occur in the online domain (e.g., inciting new members in the online community), there is the possibility that some individuals may bring these online relationships into the real world. This in turn increases the probability that the behaviours would eventually culminate into an attack. However, this hinges on the need to gain the right type of access to connect the 'actionated' nature of the individual with entities, which would enable the individual to realise and pursue one's cause. In this sense, access to the right entities will determine the threat that the individual pose, but also explain the potential range of modus operandi one may adopt.

Negative Access

The literature reports on findings that relate to one's inability to obtain the access which would connect the individual with any violent extremist groups (i.e., negative access). As Silke (2008) has argued, while the recent burgeoning interest in radicalisation can be attributed to its link to acts of violent extremism, not all individuals who become radicalised will eventually engage in violent extremist acts.

In his analysis of radical websites, Weimann (2007) noted that many radical online platforms "stop short of enlisting recruits for violent actions, but they do encourage supporters to show their commitment to the cause in other tangible ways" (p. 54). For example, the individual may become more active in propagating materials in support of one's radical objectives. To that extent, the individual would become a 'heightened sympathiser' with access to radical propaganda online, and has minimal or some form of interactions with violent extremist groups. In the context of ISIS, de Bie et al. (2015) note that many of the prospective foreign fighters were not successful in gaining the right access to online recruiters that can facilitate their journey to Syria and Iraq.

Thus, the individual may continue to:

- Influence others with their radical beliefs,
- Actively look for openings to communicate with violent extremist groups, and/or
- Reorganise themselves (within the online community) into smaller groups to perpetrate attacks based on the online training manuals released by violent extremist groups (see chapter 5 for more information).

To that end, the likelihood of these heightened sympathisers to conduct successful attacks is lower due to a number of reasons such as lack of opportunity, insufficient expertise, contacts or resources, or even surveillance concerns from law enforcement, which may deter them from conducting attacks. Examples of this category may include individuals such as Man Haron Monis, Micheal Zehf-Bibeau, Roshonara Choundry, etc. In sum, a radicalised individual will not necessarily become a violent extremists – a right access is required.

Positive Access

On the other hand, the literature also reports that obtaining 'positive' access to violent extremist groups would have a profound impact on one's likelihood to conduct acts of violence. Clutterbuck and Warnes (2011) in their analysis of six significant violent extremist conspiracies in the United Kingdom, found that

[T]hey must acquire or make explosives and a detonator, and devise and construct a means of initiating the explosion. If they cannot purchase or steal explosives, they must make their own from legitimately available materials. To carry out these tasks, they need to find premises in which they are safe and where their activities will not arouse suspicion. Once they have met these needs, they will require information in order to select a target and to plan the attack. They may need forged or fraudulent documents to gain access where it is denied to them and weapons to support the attack or prevent capture. They will also require somewhere to live (ideally away from the premises where they are constructing the IED), and the means to communicate with each other and to travel around. To finance all of these things, they need money. (p. iii)

In such cases, the individual would receive the right kind of information and resources to carry out an attack. The completion of these activities by these individuals can be assumed to increase their chance of launching a successful attack. The individual may operate as small autonomous cell with access to radical propaganda online, spiritual and religious guidance from recognised radical clerics, and receive operational knowledge and training from violent extremist groups. Examples of this category may include individuals such as the perpetrators from the London 7/7 attacks, Paris 2015 attacks, etc.

The individual may also continue to:

- **Engage in Preparatory Activities:** In the case of Younes Tsouli, he allegedly stole from credit card accounts to buy web hosting services, as well as various supplies off eBay such as GPS devices, pre-paid phones, and air tickets (Corera, 2008).

- **Learn New Skills from Violent Extremist Groups:** For instance, Ressa (2011) noted that Abu Musab al-Dahik, an Al-Qaeda linked leader, had posted a 23-page guide on how to effectively exploit social networking site, Facebook.

- **Influence Others with One's Radical Beliefs:** The case of Anwar al-Awlaki presents an apt example of how certain online propagator of radical narratives can incite followers to pursue acts of violence (Schmitt & Lipton, 2009).

- **Travel Overseas to Join Violent Extremist Groups:** Notably, ISIS has attracted much attention not only due to the huge influx of foreign fighters, but more importantly, through its sophisticated use of social media to convey messages about the jihad that the group is fighting for. As of 2015, approximately 20,000 individuals from 90 countries have travelled to join the fight in Iraq and Syria (van Ginkel, 2015).

Thus, there is a need to recognise the embedding environment which can provide the positive access to connect the actionated nature of the individual with violent extremist-related entities.

CONCLUSION

The radicalisation of individuals through the Internet is an emerging trend. To protect people from being radicalised online, authorities must continue to proactively study, innovate and adopt counter measures. This chapter is an attempt to account for the Internet-mediated radicalisation process. A RECRO model was proposed which focuses on the interplay and changing interactions over time between the person and the online environment. The model has introduced five phases that an individual may undergo on his/her pathway towards violent extremism.

However, this model has certain limitations as well. Some of the phases overlap and the individual may move back and forth from one phase to another. It should also be stressed that online activities need to be understood in conjunction with offline events; the Internet on the whole has complement offline activities rather than replaced it entirely. Notwithstanding the associated limitations, the model seeks to highlight key assumptions and insights into the processes of radicalisation that may occur in the digital era.

From an operational perspective, this model has the potential to provide a thorough understanding of the phenomenon law enforcement agencies want to prevent. For example, it can help to ascertain whether subjects are in nascent stages of radicalisation, which in turn can provide valuable insights to inform intervention decision.

FUTURE DIRECTIONS

For all potential recruits, the experience of the Internet-mediated radicalisation would be a gradual one. In many of the cases, these individuals tend to engage in seemingly harmless tasks, such as surfing websites in the initial reflection and exploration phases. Even though, this initial experience does not equate to radical rhetoric addiction per se, it is possible that it may inadvertently create the slippery slope to violence (Ramakrishna, 2011). The individual may gradually escalate his/her participation towards more ostracised activities such as helping to solicit funds, making videos in support of the cause, and translating radical narratives.

However, beyond merely grappling with when and how Internet-mediated radicalisation would manifest, there is also value in exploring deterrent factors that dissuade individuals from getting involved in violent extremism. Underpinning this approach is the assumption that most of the people, who were exposed to the same enabling environments as those who became violent extremists, were not radicalised (Cragin, 2014). Another line of evidence comes from the fact that while some individuals became attracted to online radical content, it is also essential to note that the majority of the Internet users are not susceptible and have not fallen prey to these materials. Even for those who have been influenced online by violent extremist ideology, only a small minority would eventually become radicalised. In fact, most of them would reject the use of violence (Rieger et al., 2013).

Furthermore, new developments (e.g., Ashour, 2009; Horgan, 2009; Rabasa, Pettyjohn, Ghez, & Boucek, 2010; Reinares, 2012) in the area of deradicalisation have revealed evidence of violent extremists disengaging from violent extremism due to a myriad of factors such as fear, disillusionment with violent extremist group, unmet expectations, changes of one's lifestyle, and perceived ineffectiveness of the cause. Thus, the presence of such factors would act as a 'protective buffer' against any form of connection that might arise from the prevailing violent extremist online ecosystem. Thus, there is value in identifying the pathways where the individual can drop out of the radicalisation process.

In conclusion, this chapter main goal is to devise a conceptual model that could provide insights into the radicalisation process. Future studies should investigate the validity of the RECRO model of Internet-mediated radicalisation by (1) mapping the model to sample of case studies (see Dillon et al., 2014; Shi, Neo, Ong, & Khader, 2014); and (2) identifying the relevant protective factors that can be used to dissuade prospective violent extremists from continuing down the path towards violent extremism.

ACKNOWLEDGMENT

The views expressed in this chapter are the author's only and do not represent the official position or view of the Ministry of Home Affairs, Singapore.

REFERENCES

Aly, A. (2009). The terrorists' audience: A model of internet radicalisation. *Journal of Australian Professional Intelligence Officers*, *17*, 3–19.

Aly, A., Weimann-Saks, D., & Weimann, G. (2014). Making 'noise' online: An analysis of the say no to terror online campaign. *Perspective on Terrorism*, *8*(5), 33–47.

Ashour, O. (2009). *The de-radicalisation of jihadists: Transforming armed Islamist movements*. New York, NY: Routledge.

Bandura, A. (1990). Mechanisms of moral disengagement. In W. Reich (Ed.), *Origins of terrorism: Psychologies, ideologies, theologies, states of mind* (pp. 161–191). Cambridge, UK: Cambridge University Press.

Bargh, J. A., & McKenna, K. Y. A. (2004). The internet and social life. *Annual Review of Psychology*, *55*(1), 573–590. doi:10.1146/annurev.psych.55.090902.141922 PMID:14744227

Bartlett, J., & Miller, C. (2012). The edge of violence: Towards telling the difference between violent and non-violent radicalisation. *Terrorism and Political Violence*, *24*(1), 1–21. doi:10.1080/09546553.2011.594923

Benson, D. C. (2014). Why the Internet is not increasing terrorism. *Security Journal*, *23*, 293–328.

Bergin, A., Osman, S. B., Ungerer, C., & Yasin, N. A. M. (2009). *Countering internet radicalisation in Southeast Asia (Special Report)*. Australian Strategic Policy Institute.

Bermingham, A., Conway, M., McInerney, L., O'Hare, N., & Smeaton, A. F. (2009). *Combining social network analysis and sentiment analysis to explore the potential for online radicalisation*. Paper presented at Advances in Social Networks Analysis and Mining, Athens, Greece. doi:10.1109/ASONAM.2009.31

Bernard, D. (2014). ISIL wages skilled social media war. *Voice of America*. Retrieved from http://www.voanews.com/content/isil-wages-skilled-social-media-war/1939505.html

Borum, R. (2011a). Radicalisation into violent extremism I: A review of social science theories. *Journal of Strategic Security*, *4*(4), 7–36. doi:10.5038/1944-0472.4.4.1

Borum, R. (2011b). Radicalisation into violent extremism II: A review of conceptual models and empirical research. *Journal of Strategic Security*, *4*(4), 37–62. doi:10.5038/1944-0472.4.4.2

Bowman-Grieve, L. (2009). Exploring "Stormfront": A virtual community of radical right. *Studies in Conflict and Terrorism*, *32*(11), 989–1007. doi:10.1080/10576100903259951

Bowman-Grieve, L. (2013). A psychological perspective on virtual communities supporting terrorist & extremist ideologies as a tool for recruitment. *Security Informatics*, *2*(9), 1–5.

Bowman-Grieve, L. (2015). Cyberterrorism and moral panics: A reflection on the discourse of cyberterrorism. In L. Jarvis, S. Macdonald, & T. M. Chen (Eds.), *Terrorism online: Politics, law and technology* (pp. 86–106). New York, NY: Routledge.

Carter, J. A., Maher, S., & Neumann, P. R. (2014, April 15). ICSR Insight: Who inspires the Syrian foreign fighters? *The International Centre for the Study of Radicalisation*. Retrieved from http://icsr.info/category/icsr-news/insights/

Carter, J. G., & Carter, D. L. (2012). Law enforcement intelligence: Implications for self-radicalized terrorism. *Police Practice and Research*, *13*(2), 138–154. doi:10.1080/15614263.2011.596685

Chandler, M. E. G. (2007). Turning the tables: Harnessing media means to counter radicalisation. In B. Ganor, K. von Knop, & C. Duarte (Eds.), *Hypermedia seduction for terrorist recruiting* (pp. 281–287). Washington, DC: IOS Press.

Clutterbuck, L., & Warnes, R. (2011). *Exploring patterns of behaviour in violent jihadist terrorists.* Santa Monica, CA: RAND Corporation.

Cohen, K., Johansson, F., Kaati, L., & Mork, J. C. (2014). Detecting linguistic markers for radical violence in social media. *Terrorism and Political Violence, 26*(1), 246–256. doi:10.1080/09546553.2014.849948

Community Oriented Policing Services (COPS). (2014). *Online radicalisation to violent extremism: Awareness brief.* Washington, DC: Office of Community Oriented Policing Services.

Conway, M. (2007). Terrorist use of the internet and the challenges of governing cyberspace. In D. Myriam, V. Mauer, & F. Krishna-Hensel (Eds.), *Power and security in the information age: Investigating the role of the state in cyberspace* (pp. 95–127). London: Ashgate.

Conway, M. (2012). Introduction: terrorism and contemporary mediascapes – reanimating research on media and terrorism. *Critical Studies on Terrorism, 5*(3), 445-453.

Conway, M., & McInerney, L. (2008). Jihadi video & auto-radicalisation: Evidence from an exploratory YouTube study. *Intelligence and Security Informatics, 5376,* 108–118.

Corera, G. (2008, January 16). The world's most wanted cyber-jihadist. *BBC News.* Retrieved from http://news.bbc.co.uk/2/hi/americas/7191248.stm

Cragin, R. K. (2014). Resisting violent extremism: A conceptual model for non-radicalisation. *Terrorism and Political Violence, 26*(2), 337–353. doi:10.1080/09546553.2012.714820

Dauber, C. E., & Winkler, C. K. (2014). Radical visual propaganda in the online environment: An introduction. In C. K. Winkler & C. E. Dauber (Eds.), *Visual propaganda and extremism in the online environment* (pp. 1–30). Carlisle, PA: Strategic Studies Institute and U.S. Army War College Press.

de Bie, J. L., de Poot, C. J., & van der Leun, J. P. (2015). Shifting modus operandi of Jjihadist foreign fighters from the Netherlands between 2000 and 2013: A crime script analysis. *Terrorism and Political Violence, 27*(3), 416–440. doi:10.1080/09546553.2015.1021038

Dean, G. (2014). *Neurocognitive risk assessment for the early detection of violent extremists.* New York, NY: Springer. doi:10.1007/978-3-319-06719-3

Demetriou, C., & Silke, A. (2003). A criminological Internet 'sting'. Experimental evidence of illegal and deviant visits to a website trap. *The British Journal of Criminology, 43*(1), 213–222. doi:10.1093/bjc/43.1.213

Dillon, L., Neo, L. S., Ong, G., & Khader, M. (2014). *Online radicalisation: A case study on Roshonara Choundry (Research report No. 14/2014).* Singapore: Home Team Behavioural Sciences Centre.

Dodd, V. (2010, November 2). Profile: Roshonara Choudary. *The Guardian.* Retrieved from http://www.guardian.co.uk/uk/2010/nov/02/profile-roshonara-choudhry-stephen-timms

Duarte, C. (2007). The seductive web: Technology as a tool for persuasion. In B. Ganor, K. von Knop, & C. Duarte (Eds.), *Hypermedia seduction for terrorist recruiting* (pp. 169–187). Washington, DC: IOS Press.

Edwards, C., & Gribbon, L. (2013). Pathways to violent extremism in the digital era. *The RUSI Journal,* *158*(5), 40–47. doi:10.1080/03071847.2013.847714

Europol. (2014). *TE-SAT 2014. European Union terrorism situation and trend report 2014.* European Law Enforcement Agency.

Fang, X., Singh, S., & Ahluwalia, R. (2007). An examination of different explanations for the mere exposure effect. *The Journal of Consumer Research,* *34*(1), 97–103. doi:10.1086/513050

Fighel, J. (2007). Radical Islamic internet propaganda: Concepts, idioms and visual motifs. In B. Ganor, K. von Knop, & C. Duarte (Eds.), *Hypermedia seduction for terrorist recruiting* (pp. 34–38). Washington, DC: IOS Press.

Fiore, A., LeeTeirnan, S., & Smith, M. (2002). Observed behavior and perceived value of authors in Usenet newsgroups: bridging the gap. *Proceedings of the 20th Annual SIGCHI Conference on Human Factors in Computing Systems.* doi:10.1145/503376.503434

General Intelligence and Security Service (AIVD). (2012). *Jihadism on the web: A breeding ground for jihad in the modern age.* The Hague: Algemene Inlichtingen en Veiligheidsdienst.

Givner-Forbes, R., & Osman, S. (2009). *How jihadist websites surmount psychological hurdles to radicalisation (policy brief).* Singapore: S. Rajaratnam School of International Studies.

Gupta, D. K. (2011). Waves of international terrorism: An exploration of the process by which ideas flood the world. In J. E. Rosenfeld (Ed.), *Terrorism, identity and legitimacy: The four waves theory and political violence* (pp. 30–43). New York, NY: Routledge.

Hegghammer, T. (2014). Interpersonal trust on jihadi internet forums. In D. Gambetta (Ed.), Fight, flight, mimic: Identity signalling in armed conflicts. Academic Press.

Horgan, J. (2005). *The psychology of terrorism.* New York, NY: Routledge. doi:10.4324/9780203496961

Horgan, J. (2008). From profiles to pathways and roots to routes: Perspectives from psychology on radicalization into terrorism. *The Annals of the American Academy of Political and Social Science,* *618*(1), 80–94. doi:10.1177/0002716208317539

Horgan, J. (2009). *Walking away from terrorism: Accounts of disengagement from radical and extremist movements.* London: Routledge.

Hussain, G., & Saltman, E. M. (2014). *Jihad trending: a comprehensive analysis of online extremism and how to counter it.* Quilliam Foundation.

Hutson, R., Long, T., & Page, M. (2009). Pathways to violent radicalisation in the Middle East: A model for future studies of transnational jihad. *The RUSI Journal,* *154*(2), 18–26. doi:10.1080/03071840902965570

Joinson, A. N. (2007). Disinhibition and the internet. In J. Gackenbach (Ed.), *Psychology and the internet: Intrapersonal, interpersonal, and transpersonal implications* (pp. 76–92). New York, NY: Academic Press. doi:10.1016/B978-012369425-6/50023-0

Jordan, J., Manas, F. M., & Horsburgh, N. (2008). Strengths and weakness of grassroot jihadist network: The Madrid bombings. *Studies in Conflict and Terrorism,* *31*(1), 17–39. doi:10.1080/10576100701767148

Kruglanski, A. W., Crenshaw, M., Post, J. M., & Victoroff, J. (2008). What should this fight be called? Metaphors of counterterrorism and their implications. *Psychological Science in the Public Interest, 8*(3), 97–133. doi:10.1111/j.1539-6053.2008.00035.x PMID:26161891

Lemieux, A. F., Brachman, J. M., Levitt, J., & Wood, J. (2014). Inspire Magazine: A Critical Analysis of its Significance and Potential Impact Through the Lens of the Information, Motivation, and Behavioral Skills Model. *Terrorism and Political Violence, 26*(2), 354–371. doi:10.1080/09546553.2013.828604

Lennings, C. J., Amon, K. L., Brummert, H., & Lennings, N. J. (2010). Grooming for terror: The internet and young people. *Psychiatry, Psychology and Law, 17*(3), 424–437. doi:10.1080/13218710903566979

Mbakwe, C., & Cunliffe, D. (2007). Hypermedia seduction: Further exploration of the process of 'seductive' online user interactions. In B. Ganor, K. von Knop, & C. Duarte (Eds.), *Hypermedia seduction for terrorist recruiting* (pp. 207–230). Washington, DC: IOS Press.

McCauley, C., & Moskalenko, S. (2011). *Friction: How radicalization happens to them and us.* Oxford University Press.

Moghaddam, F. M. (2005). The staircase to terrorism: A psychological exploration. *The American Psychologist, 60*(2), 161–169. doi:10.1037/0003-066X.60.2.161 PMID:15740448

Neo, L. S., Khader, M., Ang, J., Ong, G., & Tan, E. (2014). Developing an early screening guide for jihadi terrorism: A behavioural analysis of 30 terror attacks. *Security Journal.* doi:10.1057/sj.2014.44

Neo, L. S., Khader, M., Shi, P., Dillon, L., & Ong, G. (2015). *Extremist cyber footprints: A guide to understanding and countering online extremism.* Singapore: Home Team Behavioural Sciences Centre.

Neo, L. S., Shi, P., Dillon, L., Ong, G., Tan, E., & Khader, M. (2014). *Why is ISIS so psychologically attractive? A behavioural sciences perspective (Research report No. 18/2014).* Singapore: Home Team Behavioural Sciences Centre.

Neumann, P. R. (2012). *Countering online radicalisation in America.* Bipartisan Policy Center.

Nuraniyah, N. (2014). *Syrian conflict fallout: Time to contain hate speech in Indonesia. RSIS Commentaries (038/2014).* Singapore: S. Rajaratnam School of International Studies.

Oumar, J. (2011, July 29). Jihadist websites tempt Mauritanian boys. *Magharebia.* Retrieved from http://magharebia.com/cocoon/awi/xhtml1/en_GB/features/awi/reportage/2011/07/29/reportage-01

Powers, S., & Armstrong, M. (2014). Conceptualising radicalisation in a market for loyalties. In C. K. Winkler & C. E. Dauber (Eds.), *Visual propaganda and extremism in the online environment* (pp. 165–192). Carlisle, PA: Strategic Studies Institute and U.S. Army War College Press.

Rabasa, A., Pettyjohn, S. L., Ghez, J. J., & Boucek, C. (2010). *Deradicalising Islamist extremists.* Santa Monica, CA: RAND Corporation.

Ramakrishna, K. (2007). *Self-radicalisation: The case of Abdul Basheer Abdul Kader. RSIS Commentaries (61/2007).* Singapore: S. Rajaratnam School of International Studies.

Ramakrishna, K. (2011, October). *Identity politics and violent religious fundamentalism*. Presentation at the CENS-GFF Workshop on The impact of identity politics on violent extremism: Regional perspectives, Singapore.

Reinares, F. (2012). Exit from terrorism: A qualitative empirical study on disengagement and deradicalisation among members of ETA. *Terrorism and Political Violence, 23*(5), 780–803. doi:10.1080/09 546553.2011.613307

Ressa, M. (2011, August). *From Facebook to bin laden*. Paper presented at the Ministry of Home Affairs, Singapore. doi:10.1142/p895

Rieger, D., Frischich, L., & Bente, G. (2013). *Propaganda 2.0 Psychological effects of right-wing and Islamic extremist internet videos*. German Federal Criminal Police Office.

Rogan, H. (2007). Al-Qaeda's online media strategies: From Abu Reuter to Irhabi 007. Norway: Norwegian Defence Research Establishment (FFI).

Sageman, M. (2010). Confronting Al-Qaeda: Understanding the threat in Afghanistan. *Perspectives on Terrorism, 3*(4), 4–25.

Saifudeen, O. A. (2014). *The cyber extremism orbital pathways model*. Singapore: S. Rajaratnam School of International Studies.

Saifudeen, O. A. (2015). *Islamic state and its online recruitment formula. RSIS Commentaries (090/2015)*. Singapore: S. Rajaratnam School of International Studies.

Salamon, K. L. G. (2007). Design and identity – Visual culture and identity politics. In B. Ganor, K. von Knop, & C. Duarte (Eds.), *Hypermedia seduction for terrorist recruiting* (pp. 267–280). Washington, DC: IOS Press.

Samuel, T. K. (2015). *M.A.D. (making a difference) Amidst Mad People: Addressing Foreign Fighter Involvement in Terrorist Campaigns*. Paper presented at CENS Workshop on Countering Extremism: Islamic State and Beyond, Singapore.

Schmid, A. P. (2013). *Radicalisation, de-radicalisation, counter-radicalisation: A conceptual discussion and literature review* (ICCT Research Paper). The Netherlands: International Centre for Counter-Terrorism – The Hague.

Schmitt, E., & Lipton, E. (2009, December 31). Focus on Internet imams as Al-Qaeda recruiters. *The New York Times*. Retrieved from http://www.nytimes.com/2010/01/01/us/01imam.html

Schuurman, B., & Eijkman, Q. (2015). Indicators of terrorist intent and capability: Tools for threat assessment. *Dynamics of Asymmetric Conflict: Pathways toward terrorism and genocide*. doi: 10.1080/17467586.2015.1040426

Seib, P., & Janbek, D. M. (2011). *Global terrorism and new media: The post-Al Qaeda generation*. New York, NY: Routledge.

Shahar, Y. (2007). The internet as a tool for intelligence and counter-terrorism. In B. Ganor, K. von Knop, & C. Duarte (Eds.), *Hypermedia seduction for terrorist recruiting* (pp. 140–153). Washington, DC: IOS Press.

Shayo, C., Olfman, L., Iriberri, A., & Igbaria, M. (2007). The virtual society: Its driving forces, arrangements, practices, and implications. In J. Gackenbach (Ed.), *Psychology and the internet: Intrapersonal, interpersonal, and transpersonal implications* (pp. 187–219). New York, NY: Academic Press. doi:10.1016/B978-012369425-6/50027-8

Shi, P., Neo, L. S., Ong, G., & Khader, M. (2014). *Critical thinking, technology and terrorism: A case study analysis of Omar Shafik Hammami (Research report No. 03/2014)*. Singapore: Home Team Behavioural Sciences Centre.

Silber, M. D., & Bhatt, A. (2007). *Radicalization in the West: The Home Grown Threat*. New York, NY: New York Police Department.

Silke, A. (2008). Holy warriors: Exploring the psychological processes of jihadi radicalisation. *European Journal of Criminology, 5*(1), 99–123. doi:10.1177/1477370807084226

Slevin, J. (2000). *The internet and society*. Malden, MA: Polity Press.

Steinal, W., van Kleef, G. A., van Knippenberg, D., Hogg, M. A., Homan, A. C., & Moffitt, G. (2010). How intragroup dynamics affect behaviour in intergroup conflict: The role of group norms, prototypicality, and need to belong. *Group Processes & Intergroup Relations, 13*(6), 779–794. doi:10.1177/1368430210375702

Swann, W. B. Jr, Jetten, J., Gómez, Á., Whitehouse, H., & Bastian, B. (2012). When group membership gets personal: A theory of identity fusion. *Psychological Review, 119*(3), 441–456. doi:10.1037/a0028589 PMID:22642548

Tan, E. (2006). *Road to radicalisation: A psychological analysis of the Jemaah Islamiyah group and its members (Research report No. 01/2006)*. Singapore: Behavioural Sciences Unit.

Thomas, E. F., Mcgarty, C., & Louis, W. (2014). Social interaction and psychological pathways to political engagement and extremism. *European Journal of Social Psychology, 44*(1), 15–22. doi:10.1002/ejsp.1988

Tokar, L. (2007). Hypermedia communication as a modern means for the creation of terrorist and counterterrorist consciousness. In B. Ganor, K. von Knop, & C. Duarte (Eds.), *Hypermedia seduction for terrorist recruiting* (pp. 105–115). Washington, DC: IOS Press.

Torok, R. (2013). Developing an explanatory model for the process of online radicalisation and terrorism. *Security Informatics, 2*(1), 1–10. doi:10.1186/2190-8532-2-6

Tzanetti, T. (2007). Use of media and challenges in countering terrorist rhetoric. In B. Ganor, K. von Knop, & C. Duarte (Eds.), *Hypermedia seduction for terrorist recruiting* (pp. 231–241). Washington, DC: IOS Press.

Upal, M. (2015). Confronting Islamic jihadist movements. *Journal of Terrorism Research*. Retrieved from http://ojs.st-andrews.ac.uk/index.php/jtr/article/view/1155/900

van Ginkel, B. (2015). Responding to cyber jihad: Towards an effective counter narrative. The Netherlands: International Centre for Counter-Terrorism – The Hague.

Venhaus, J. (2010, May). *Why youth join Al-Qaeda*. United States Institute of Peace. Retrieved from http://www.usip.org/publications/why-youth-join-al-qaeda

von Behr, I., Reding, A., Edwards, C., & Gribbon, L. (2013). *Radicalisation in the digital age: The use of the internet in 15 cases of terrorism and extremism*. Santa Monica, CA: RAND Corporation.

Weimann, G. (2007). Using the internet for terrorist recruitment and mobilisation. In B. Ganor, K. von Knop, & C. Duarte (Eds.), *Hypermedia seduction for terrorist recruiting* (pp. 47–58). Washington, DC: IOS Press.

Weimann, G. (2012). Lone wolves in cyberspace. *Journal of Terrorism Research, 3*(2), 75–90. doi:10.15664/jtr.405

Weimann, G., & von Knop, K. (2008). Applying the notion of noise to countering online terrorism. *Studies in Conflict and Terrorism, 31*(10), 883–902. doi:10.1080/10576100802342601

Wilner, A. S., & Dubouloz, C. (2011). Transformative radicalisation: Applying learning theory to Islamist radicalisation. *Studies in Conflict and Terrorism, 34*(5), 418–438. doi:10.1080/1057610X.2011.561472

Yasin, N. A. (2011). *Online Indonesian Islamist extremism: A gold mine of information. RSIS Commentaries (144/2011)*. Singapore: S. Rajaratnam School of International Studies.

Zanini, M. (2004). The networking of terror in the information age. In D. M. Jones (Ed.), *Globalisation and the new terror: The Asia pacific dimension* (pp. 159–184). Cheltenham, UK: Edward Elgar Pub.

ENDNOTE

[1.] This model is developed based on insights from (i) extant literature review of radicalisation models, (ii) in-depth analysis of case studies of individuals known to be radicalised via the Internet, and (iii) discussions with subject-matter experts and practitioners who are working in the field on countering violent extremism.

Section 3
Countering Violent Extremism and Radicalisation

Chapter 12
Framing the Challenges of Online Violent Extremism:
"Policing–Public–Policies–Politics" Framework

Geoff Dean
Griffith University, Australia

ABSTRACT

This chapter argues that 'framing' the challenges posed by radicalised individuals 'online' where the path to violent extremism is just a click away, is as much about getting the framing right as it is about getting the operational plans right. A general framework based on 4 P's (Policing-Public-Policies-Politics) is proposed as the conceptual 'frame' for combating violent extremism. The metaphor of a compass is used to examine this 4P's framework from the perspective of knowledge management. The key notions of 'violent extremism', 'radicalisation' and 'digital era' are deconstructed before presenting a neurocognitive-based model of 'self-indoctrination' by those who 'inspire' a violently extreme narrative through social media technologies using the 'dark net' of cyberspace. Law enforcement's use of communication interception technologies and data retention laws is critically examined. The chapter concludes with operational implications for Policing the Public with Policy tools in the context of Political realities.

INTRODUCTION

The ability of a police organisation to effectively combat violent extremism and radicalisation in the 'online' digial era of contemporary society poses signiticant challenges. Like all challenges or problems how they are framed, in terms of the conceptual lens through which they are viewed, very much determines the parameters and hence the efficacy of any proposed solutions. Einstein's famous remark that "it is the theory that determines what can be observed" is central to this envdeavor to deal effectively with policing online violent extremism and radicalisation.

This chapter argues that the 'framing' of the challenges faced by police organisations with the rapid rise of potentially radicalised individuals online, acting alone or in tandem with tight or loose networks

DOI: 10.4018/978-1-5225-0156-5.ch012

of like-minded believers, where the path to violent extremism is just a click away is as much about getting the framing right as it is about getting the operational plans right. Therefore, the chapter proposes the starting point for 'framing the challenges' should be a general-level conceptual framework consisting of 4 big P's to do with Policing, Public, Policies and Politics.

In the first section of the chapter, the metaphor of a compass is used to explain and examine this 4P's framework for police organisations. While this framework provides the conceptual scaffolding, the actual perspective adopted for framing the challenges of online violent extremism is that of Knowledge Management (KM).

Dean and Gottschalk (2007) have written extensively about KM as it relates to a policing and law enforcement context. Dean (2012) coined the term 'Knowledge-Managed Policing' (KMP) for what he sees as consituting KM from a policing perspective. KMP is a practitioner-friendly framework combining a suite of applications for capturing and managing, systematically, the growth of tacit and explicit forms of knowledge to enhance efficient and effective policing through increasing the stock of policing knowledge and its 'knowledge value' for the betterment of society.

Furthermore, KM offers a 'systems' perspective that acts as macro analytical schematic framework that offers a helicopter view of how an organisation can best use KM to its fullest potential. Thus, a Knowledge Management System (KMS) can be understood at a broad level:

.... as a diverse array of socio-cultural, organisational and technological components (Alavi & Leidner, 2001) that come together to form a system to manage knowledge for use at the individual, group and organisational level. Hence, the main objective of a knowledge management system is to support the creation, transfer and application of knowledge in an organisation. (Dean & Gottschalk, 2007, p. 80)

Initially the chapter uses this KM perspective to explore the key notions of violent extremism, radicalisation and the digitial era. Each of these concepts in their own way are neither straightforward nor uncontested. Thus, definitions of each of these notions are critically examined to tease out their contentious elements so that a clear and coherent understanding of what each contested notion entails can be deduced. In this manner, some commonality of the core knowledge value of these problematic notions can be achieved in order to understand how best to 'combat' violent extremism and radicalisation in the current context of the digital age in which we live. This section also includes a neurocognitive-based model of the critical and central role that the process of self-indoctrination plays for individuals engaged on the road to violent extremism by those who 'inspire' them through online technologies.

The main section of the chapter, again adopts a KMS persective to inform the framing of challenges posed by online radicalisation and violent extremism. Moreover, this section focuses on three key areas. They are:

- The massive impact of social media technologies and the challenges this presents to policing in the digital age; and
- The underbelly of cyberspace and its 'dark net' which allows violently extreme groups to network in largely undetectable ways; as well as
- The use of communication interception technologies (CIT) and data retention laws to combat violent extremism.

All of these areas present different and difficult challenges to governments which have the capacity to overwhelm them. In seeking to deal with the complexity of the challenges they face, governments need a clear and concise perspective and analytical framework to forge a way forward in combating violent extremism and radicalisation in this digital era.

The chapter concludes with the key operational implications for the challenges ahead in dealing with online radicalisation and the path to violent extremism in the light of the 4 big P's of a civilised society, which is the job of **P**olicing the **P**ublic with **P**olicy tools in the context of internal and external **P**olitical realities.

4 P'S FRAMEWORK: POLICE COMPASS

The four big P's of policing are like the points on a compass. They guide police management and practitioners to know where 'True North' is to be found and how to find their way home when lost in the forest of societial expectations.

True North in a democratic society is Policing 'with the consent' of the civil society that police swear an oath to service. The 'South Pole' is the Public. They are the customers, clients, and consumers of policing. They have a direct reciprocal relationship to each other on a vertical axis like a fixed needle of a compass. The North-South connections are the defining 'poles' of a police organisation's contemporary societal/community position relative to each other.

The other two points on the policing compass lie on the 'East-West' horizontal axis. They are best understood as policing 'reference points' that either help or hinder the directional focus of the North-South needle.

The 'East Pointer' is policing Policies. Policing is kept on course by policies that are aligned with the 'public consent'. Or conversely, policing is thrown off course by having to police policies that are poorly aligned with community consent and expectations, or worse still with policies that are counter to or even destroy the fabric of public consent that allows policing to function, rightly and properly, in the first place in a democratic society.

The 'West Pointer' is policing Politics. Politics are a reality in every walk of life, probably none more so than in policing. Political manoeuvering is part and parcel of the daily rountine of policing from the street to the station to the headquarters. Playing politics in policing is driven by both internal and external political agendas.

Internal policing politics are spawned by the tight closed-shop of the police culture. Or more precisely by police cultures as there is more than one police culture. 'Street police' have a culture that is subtly different in several aspects that the 'administrative' or 'managerial culture' of police executives. One of the few times these different policing cultures present a united front as the one 'Thin Blue' line is when the police organisation is attacked and under public scrunity by the media.

External policing politics are driven by two powerful influences. The first key influence is the government-of-the-day and its poltical agenda. Governments of all political persuasions have realised the huge vote catching appeal of 'Law and Order' campaigns during election cycles. The getting 'Tough on Crime' and 'Zero Tolerance' approaches adopted by political parties across the political spectrum from the Right to the Left of politics is testament to this external reality on the police organistion. Policing is the ideal political football that gets kicked back and forth between political parties.

The second key influence that exerts powerful political pressure on the police organisation is the media. Investigative journalism often ends up with 'breaking news' media stories of incidents of police brutality, racism, corruption, or just plain incompetence that have significant potential effect on the 'reputational brand' of a police force/service, and to make or break police commissioners. Calls for Public Inquiries and Royal Commissions abound when police organisations do not engage in the politics of managing the media when under the spotlight of alleged police misconduct.

Hence, policing Politics, both internal and external, like the East pointer of Policies either helps or hinders the police compass to stay on track to True North or to be de-magnetised and thrown into confusion and chaos by machiavellian maneuvers and playing popularist politics. The diagram below (Figure 1) is a graphical representation on the 'Police Compass' discussed above.

As can be seen, the Police Compass has its 4 P's points arranged along the vertical axis of the North-South needle of Policing-Public, and the horizontal axis of the East-West 'reference pointers' of Policies-Politics.

DEFINING 'VIOLENT EXTREMISM': PROBLEMATIC CHALLENGES

The problematic nature of defining violent extremism and its closely-related offsprings, especially terrorism, presents significant challenges for countries where 'one man's terrorist can be another man's freedom fighter'.

What is abundantly clear is that defining terrorism is inordinately problematic (Resnyansky, 2007). The fact is there is no consensus in the literature regarding a universally accepted definition of terrorism (Drummond, 2002; Morgan, 2004; Schmid & Jongman, 1988; Sinai, 2007) in spite of decades of research.

Victoroff (2005, p. 4) in a review and critique of psychological approaches to terrorism noted "Schmid (1983) compiled 109 academic definitions of terrorism, suggesting that there are roughly as many available definitions as there are published experts in the field".

In 2004, Schmid quoted the conclusion Walter Laqueur from the Center for Strategic and International Studies reached when he noted "After thirty years of hard labor there is still no generally agreed definition of terrorism" (p. 395). In 2005, Schmid and Jongman found the definitional difficulties surrounding the

Figure 1. The 4 P's framework for police organisations

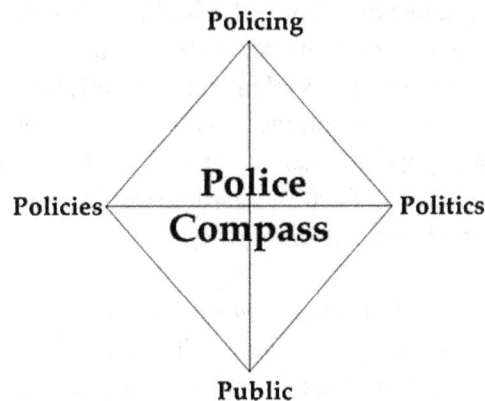

notion of terrorism have not faded. For instance, in a European Commission project (2008) on 'Defining Terrorism' it found 165 'academic' definitions and 88 'governmental' definitions of terrorism. In a 2011 publication, Schmid provides a further list of 260 definitions of terrorism.

In what is perhaps the most baffling and bizarre example of how murky the waters have gotten is provided again by Schmid in a 2013 paper when he states, "... the U.S. Government alone maintains some twenty different but simultaneously operative definitions (of terrorism) in its many agencies and departments" (p. 15).

In the final analysis, most definitions are "drowned in complexity" (Elzain, 2008, p. 10) with no clear way through the impasse of 'one side's terrorist is another side's freedom fighter' (Hoffman, 2006). Moreover, there is the political game of assigning the pejorative nature of the label 'terrorist' to one's enemies and opponents, or to those whose views one simply disagrees with or finds abhorrent (Newman, 2006). As a result of this definitional gridlock, the international community is forced to fall back on a piecemeal approach by criminalising acts which various state and national governments define as inherently terrorist in nature, and use their domestic laws to prevent and punish such acts (Maogoto, 2003).

Therefore, it comes as no surprise that the term violent extremism has emerged as the preferred notion in the political/terrorism literature to subsume the more problematic label of terrorism (Fox, 2005; United States Institute of Peace, 2012). Terms like political violence, political terrorism and terrorism are still used interchangeably in the international literature to refer to the same phenomenon that falls under the new umbrella concept of violent extremism.

Schmid (2013) notes that:

[T]he origin of the concept 'Countering Violent Extremism' (CVE) goes back to the year 2005, when some U.S. policymakers in the second Bush administration sought to replace the bellicose 'Global War on Terror' (GWOT) with some lower-key concept like 'Struggle Against Violent Extremism' (SAVE). (p. 10)

However, violent extremism like its twin, terrorism, is also problematic to define. Some researchers use the term 'militant extremism' which they define as "zealous adherence to a set of beliefs and values, with a combination of two key features: advocacy of measures beyond the norm (i.e., extremism) and intention and willingness to resort to violence (i.e., militancy)" and add the prefix 'violent' to militant extremism to refer to "not just intended but actual violence" (Saucier, Akers, Shen-Miller, Knezevic, & Stankov, 2009, p. 256).

Also, researchers have sought to draw conceptual distinctions between violent extremism and terrorism in an effort to tame the definitional beast. For instance, Mroz (2009, p. 23) sees violent extremism as "violence in the absence of reason, or rather, the belief that committing an act of violence will produce benefits that outweigh the cost of human life. Violent extremism is homicide, genocide, fratricide, and, yes, it can also be terrorism". Whereas, in contrast, terrorism has a rational purpose to coerce and intimidate a government or a civilian population, or some segment of it, through violence to further some political or social objective. Saucer et al. (2009) regard terrorism as an important subset of the larger class of militant extremists, but distinguish it as follows,

Terrorism itself, however, differs from militant extremism in being not a broad behavior pattern but rather a method or tactic: the induction of terror (i.e., intentionally creating or exploiting fear through violence, threatened or real, on unarmed civilian persons so as to achieve political objectives, in ways that subvert or ignore the requirements of law; cf Goldstick, 2002, p. 20; Hoffman, 1998, p. 43; O'Sullivan, 1986, p. 5). Although there is some overlap between militant extremism and terrorism, there are instances in which only one of these terms applies (p. 257)

Given the messy and murky waters surrounding terrorism, both 'old' political and 'new' Islamist terrorism, the move in the literature to conceptually absorb terrorism under the umbrella term of violent extremism with its wider encompassing terminology to fit in both right-wing militants, white supremacists and the like, and left-wing ideologists, does not solve all of the nagging problems associated with it. The new label of violent extremist whilst 'softer' sounding and less derogatory than terrorist, is still problematic in nature, design, and pejorative terminology if only less so.

The preferred definition of violent extremism used here is the one presented in the Australian National Counter-Terrorism Committee Framework (Nasser-Eddine, Garnham, Agostino, & Caluya, 2011) where violent extremism is defined as "A willingness to use or support the use of violence to further particular beliefs, including those of a political, social or ideological nature. This may include acts of terrorism" (p. 9).

As this definition implies, violent extremism is a broad church which encompasses different types of individuals and groups ranging from terrorists (politically-motivated), right/left-wing militants (ideologically-motivated), to active shooters (socially-motivated). Naturally, these motivational boundaries are often more fluid, blurred, multi-factorial and random in reality, and crossover in terrorists, militants, and shooters as well as other forms of mass killings like in deadly riots, fatal stabbings and so forth. All such violently extreme incidents are to a degree influenced by political-ideological-social- and cultural factors, antecedents, and drivers than any categorical definition can capture.

However, each of these groups of violent extremists has quite distinctive features at the level of specific characteristics like age, motivation, personality type, psychological characteristics, mental state, intelligence, socio-cultural background, political affiliation, and so forth. Figure 2 below is indicative of the wide variance 'in' and 'between' the three primary groups of violent extremists – terrorists, militants, and shooters.

As can be seen, the motivations, issues, and tactics are vastly different for each group and become more uniquely particular to individuals as the level of abstraction moves further down the line from general to specific characteristics and features. For example, the Department of Homeland Security [DHS] (2012) has developed a number of case studies on violent extremism groups like violent anarchists, racist skinheads, and sovereign citizen extremists.

The essential 'take-home' message of this categorical continuum is that at the highest level of generality, what unites these three disparate groups is their willingness to use and engage in violent and extreme actions to achieve their very different objectives. The common denominator between terrorists, militants, and shooters is their willingness towards violent extremism. Willingness is about beliefs which reside in the minds of individuals. Beliefs are firmly held convictions that one accepts something as true or real, generally without definitive proof of their existence.

However, what is abundantly clear is that in the contemporary world, 'extremism' however one chooses to define it, is on the rise. The Institute for Strategic Dialogue (ISD) notes with some foreboding that,

The growth of extremism – violent and non-violent – is one of the key social and political challenges facing Western societies today. Far right political parties are making headway in elections across Eu-

Figure 2. Continuum of violent extremism categories

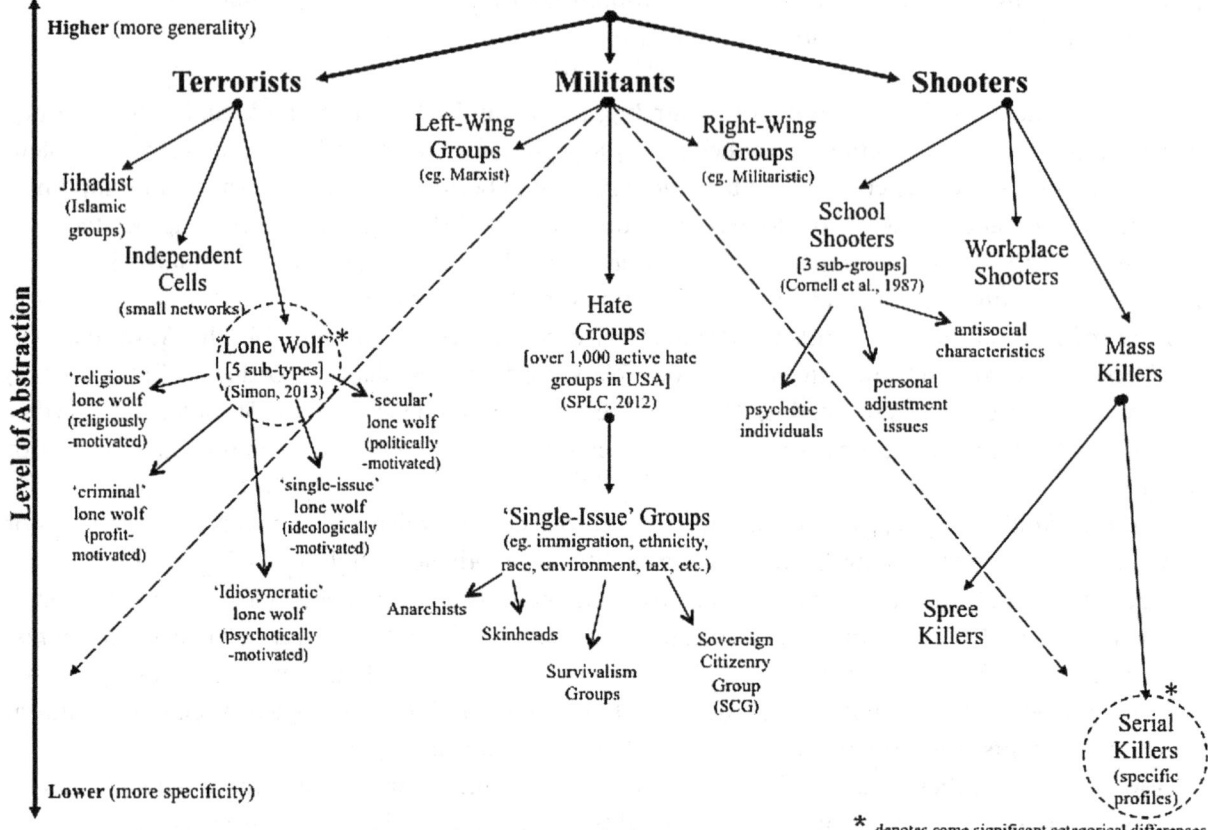

rope, populist sentiments are circulating, extremist groups and networks are growing in confidence, and terrorists groups and lone wolf individuals of different kinds continue to aim to commit violent acts and strike terror into communities. (ISD, 2012, p.10)

DEFINING 'RADICALISATION': COMPLEX CHALLENGES

Being a 'radical' had political currency, and even respectability, about it in the 1960's. Fast forward to the new millennium, and being a radical is most likely a death sentence. Consequently the notion of 'radicalisation' is much contested in the literature.

Since 9/11 the very concept of radicalisation is problematic. For instance, an expert group established by the European Commission to study the problem of violent radicalisation, described the very notion of radicalisation as "ill-defined, complex and controversial" (Coolsalet, 2011, p. 140). Moreover, an Australian research group concluded that "About the only thing that radicalisation experts agree on is that radicalisation is a process" (Nasser-Eddine et al., 2011, p. 13).

Like the term terrorism, the notion of radicalisation has been politicised by academics and governments alike which mostly only serve to confuse and confound. As Sedgwick (2010) points out "the ubiquity use of the term, 'radicalisation' suggests a consensus about its meaning, … (however) through a review of a variety of definitions … no such consensus exits" (p. 479).

Moreover, radicalisation like terrorism is a term prone to political misuse by governments, especially right-wing ones, who are often quick to label and blame minority groups who oppose their views as being 'radicalised'. The lack of consensus amongst academics about what precisely radicalisation is has spawned multiple definitions to such a degree that the term has as some academics argued is both unhelpful and indeed almost useless as a meaningful concept in the social sciences.

As a case in point, John Horgan, one of the leading researchers on radicalisation was reported as saying at a START Conference (National Consortium for the Study of Terrorism and Responses to Terrorism) held at the University of Maryland on September 1, 2011, "We should not have allowed to have radicalisation center stage. [...] We are stuck with radicalisation.' He also suggested that the focus on radicalisation may be unnecessary and that the relationship between radicalisation and terrorism is poorly understood" (as cited in Schmid, 2013, p. 19).

Moreover, too often radicalisation is muddled up with violent extremism, and defined as an absolute notion as in the U.S. Department of Homeland Security definition which is, "The process of adopting an extremist belief system, including the willingness to use, support, or facilitate violence, as a method to effect social change" (Allen, 2007, p. 4).

Whereas in the Canadian government definition, radicalisation is seen more as a relative concept in relation to mainstream politics, hence it is defined as "a process by which individuals are introduced to an overtly ideological message and belief system that encourages movement from moderate, mainstream beliefs towards extreme views" (Royal Canadian Mounted Police [RCMP], 2009, p. 1). This definition at least has the advantage of locating radicalisation as lying on a continuum of beliefs. Moghaddam (2006) further underscores the importance of disentangling radicalisation in attitudes from radicalisation of behaviour when he states: "Almost eight decades of psychological research on attitudes [...] suggest that radicalisation of attitudes need not result in radicalisation of behaviour" (p. 280).

The conflating of radicalisation with terrorism and with violent extremism in many definitions by scholars and governments has not just muddied the waters conceptually, it also has operational implications. How something is defined shapes how it is put into practice.

The centrally important message here is that it is evident there is no clear, straightforward relationship between radicalisation, terrorism and violent extremism. The relationship is one of complexity. Yet many of the models developed to deal with terrorism and violent extremism assume there is a direct relationship between being a 'radical' or holding 'radical views' or being 'perceived' as on a 'pathway to radicalisation' and automatically becoming a terrorist or violent extremist by extension.

However, there is a substantive body of research that makes it very clear that not every radical becomes a terrorist or violent extremist (Bjørgo, 2011; Borum, 2011a; Chowdhury-Fink & Heame, 2008; Freilich, Chermak, & Caspi, 2009; Hassan, 2012; Horgan, 2008a, 2008b, 2009a, 2009b, 2012; Horgan & Altier, 2012; Horgan & Braddock, 2010, 2011; Horgan & Taylor, 2010; Qatar International Academy for Security Studies [QIASS], 2010; Sedgwick, 2010).

The key point is there is no direct causal relationship between radicalisation, terrorism or violent extremism for that matter. This is not to say there is no relationship. Clearly in many cases there is a link with radical ideas. However, not every terrorist or violent extremist will necessarily hold radical views, although many may well do. As Bjørgo's (2009) work underscores, some terrorists 'drift' into terrorism for a host of reasons that have nothing to do with ideology or radical views. Some simply find it fun, or an adventure, or to escape boredom, or a way to get employment.

DEFINING THE 'DIGITAL ERA': CHANGING CHALLENGES

The digital era we are concerned about, did it begin with the Internet in 1982 or with the appearance of Web 2.0 technologies (Woolley, Limperos, & Beth, 2010) in 2004? This section's focus is on Web 2.0 applications – websites based solely on interactive user-generated content, or social media, as opposed to more traditional static websites where users can only view content (Earl & Kimport, 2011; Papic & Noonan, 2011). Over the last 10 years, Web 2.0 technologies have created a revolution in cyberspace beyond the wildest dreams of violent extremists (DHS, 2010).

The nature of the digital social media technologies like Facebook, Twitter, Instagram, blogging, and texting is different from communicating with others face-to-face, nonethless the same psychological processes are involved in seeking to radicalise an individual. Human beings are still human beings whether they are sitting in front on you or behind a computer screen or plugged into a mobile.

However, the key advantage for a radicalised individual of the online medium of communication is the anonomity it can afford the user to hide behind (Schneier, 2008). In other words, digital technologies can provide a user with a very sophisticated means for deception that is not so readily available with face-to-face communication.

Anyone who has done an introductory 101 course in psychology will find out that verbal communication only conveys about 20 percent of the meaning of a message, with about 80 percent of the meaning being read properly by 'observable' non-verbal behavours. Hence, people's ability to evaulate the 'truth' or congruence of a message is heavily dependent on being able to 'see' the other person's non-verbal behaviours.

Whilst digital technologies have come a long way in being able to enhance online communication with video software like YouTube and Skype, it is easy to 'fake' one's non-verbal communiction using such video-enhanced software programs by changing camera angles, lighting effects, mood-enhancing filters and so forth (Vergani & Zuev, 2011).

When it comes to written communication (tweets, blogs, texting) using social media technologies, then the ability to read the 'true meaning' of the message is even further reduced to about 10 percent of the communication value.

Hence, the key challenge with the digital era is the ability to easily engage in deception through projecting a 'persona' much like an avatar where the truth about who you really are is almost impossible to discern from text alone, and even harder to detect deception via online enhanced videos.

Online Radicalisation: Social Media on Steriods

The advent of social media (e.g., Facebook, Twitter, YouTube) has created new opportunities for terrorist organisations and brought with it growing challenges for law enforcement and intelligence agencies. Whilst the use of online resources by terrorist organisations is not a new occurrence, what is new is the shift to a broader focus by national intelligence agencies towards the increasing threat of home-grown terrorism ("ASIO sets up cyber", 2011; "ASIO warns of home", 2005; Johnson, 2010; Silber & Bhatt 2007; Wright 2006). A review of extant literature shows a dearth of research into the connection between theoretical and practical applications of social media by terrorist groups, and the strategies available to counteract such use.

Three of the most popular social media applications – Facebook, Twitter, and YouTube – offer examples of how online terrorism has become a new dot.com with the potential to harness the power of social media for recruiting, communicating, training, and funding home-grown terrorists.

Social Networking: Online Recruiting Sites

Facebook falls into the 'social networking' category of social media; its primary function is to build and maintain relationships between people (Alexa, 2011a; Woolley et al., 2010). Users of Facebook create an online profile using their personal details, add connections to friends or family (or strangers, if desired), and can then post 'status updates' on their pages or write messages to other users. Members can also create and join groups based on similar interests such as support for a particular political group or cause (Woolley et al., 2010).

The most important and useful Facebook feature for terrorist organisations is the groups function (Torok, 2010). The apparent strategy used by terrorist organisations is to create a Facebook group based on a seemingly innocent ideal, such as supporting Palestinians or Islam in general (DHS, 2010; Torok, 2010). As member numbers for the groups increase, jihadist material can be slowly introduced by members of the organisation to the Facebook group in a way which does not directly condone or encourage jihadist actions, and thus does not constitute a violation of Facebook policy (DHS, 2010; Torok, 2010). From this position, the group can even be directed straight to the website and forums of the terrorist organisation behind the Facebook group.

The threat posed by online recruitment is significant (al-Shishani, 2010; Stein, 2011; Weimann, 2006). There are no borders to be crossed, and no effective methods for intervention (DHS, 2010; Torok, 2010). Facebook allows terrorist organisations to recruit people from all around the world, without posing any significant threat to the security of the organisation (DHS, 2010; Torok, 2010). Importantly, once people become members of the group, the organisation can then seamlessly transit into the next phase: training.

The Blogging: Online Communication Sites

Twitter falls into the 'blogging' category of social media; however it is more aptly described as a micro-blogging service (van der Zee, 2009). Registered users of the site post publicly visible messages on their profile called 'tweets': text-based messages of up to 140 characters (van der Zee, 2009). Users can subscribe to other users to automatically receive their posts, and can follow specific topics by using 'hashtags' (#), which are used to flag posts as belonging to a certain group or topic (van der Zee, 2009), for example #terrorism to follow tweets related to the topic of terrorism.

The ability to instantaneously send small bits of information to a virtually unlimited number of people free of charge makes Twitter an extremely valuable tool for political purposes (Papic & Noonan, 2011; van der Zee, 2009). Twitter hashtag groups can function in a similar way to Facebook groups, except without a designated leader, with users often retweeting (re-posting) to ensure the message is spread (van der Zee, 2009).

This is in part where the real value of Twitter lies: in the constantly changing virtual communities that are created almost naturally during major events (Papic & Noonan, 2011; van der Zee, 2009). Political movements and protests in particular see these online communities thrive, where large amounts of people both directly and indirectly involved in an incident begin flocking to follow the relative hashtag for the event (Papic & Noonan, 2011; van der Zee, 2009).

The threat posed by Twitter arises from both its ability to send out instant messages to large numbers of people, and from the ability for people to follow particular topics as well as groups (O'Rourke, 2010). Terrorist organisations can utilise Twitter at an operation level, using the service to keep up-to-date on any new information that emerges in the public sphere (O'Rourke, 2010; U.S. 304th Military Intelligence battalion, 2008). The 2008 terrorist attack in Mumbai presents an apt example of how terrorist organisations can utilise social media sites such as Twitter.

The 2008 Mumbai terrorist attacks occurred on November 26, with more than 10 sites throughout Mumbai targeted by an Islamic terrorist organisation from Pakistan: Lashkar-e-Taiba (O'Rourke, 2010). The attacks killed 164 people and injured over 300. One of the most important issues that arose from the attacks was the technological sophistication of the attackers. All of the attackers were equipped with BlackBerry smart-phones, and not only utilised Voice over Internet Protocol (VOIP), but also carried multiple SIM cards to switch into the phones if authorities were able to block them (O'Rourke, 2010; U.S. 304th Military Intelligence battalion, 2008).

Post-attack interviews with the sole surviving attacker, combined with information from intercepted phone calls from the attackers during the events indicated that the terrorists were in constant contact with controllers based in Pakistan (O'Rourke, 2010; Rabasa et al., 2009). The controllers were able to keep track of the constant up-to-date flow of information streaming from public Twitter posts and communicate it directly to the attackers (Leggio, 2008; O'Rourke, 2010; Rabasa et al., 2009). This included critical information such as the movements and positioning of the Indian counter-terrorism units planning the assault on the hotel (Lee, 2008; Leggio, 2008; O'Rourke, 2010).

Examples such as Mumbai serve to demonstrate the increasingly advanced technological sophistication of terrorist organisations. In order to effectively combat these groups, robust counter-strategies for social media must be developed and implemented by government agencies as soon as possible.

Video Sharing: Online Training Sites

YouTube falls into the 'video sharing' category of social media; the primary function of the website is to host videos uploaded by users, which are then publicly viewed and shared around the world (Vergani & Zuev, 2011). Registered users of YouTube are able to upload videos in a wide range of formats up to 15 minutes in length, and in most cases viewers do not need to register (Vergani & Zuev, 2011). Registered members can subscribe to another user's YouTube 'channel', receiving alerts whenever a new video is posted on that channel (Vergani & Zuev, 2011). While there are a range of restrictions over what cannot be uploaded, the 'post-hoc' review system used for YouTube videos means that only those videos which have been 'reported' by viewers will be reviewed and potentially removed by YouTube staff, thus making abuse of the system possible by terrorist groups.

YouTube is free, easy to use, difficult for state authorities to control, and can be used to communicate with a tightly-knit group to the entire world (Vergani & Zuev, 2011). Furthermore, YouTube can provide a more effective means of communication than text-based social media sites such as Facebook and Twitter, simply due to the ability to use sound and video (Vergani & Zuev, 2011).

Like Facebook, YouTube has multiple uses for terrorist organisations (Bergin, Osman, Ungerer, & Yasin, 2009). Video can be a much more effective means of communicating an issue than plain text, so for this reason alone YouTube would be an invaluable tool for terrorist organisations (Torok, 2010). For example, Anwar al-Awlaki is a prominent and 'highly dangerous' planner and trainer for Al-Qaeda and all of its franchises, well-known for his utilisation of social media sites such as Facebook and YouTube to spread his extremist messages (Madhani, 2010; Shephard, 2009; Smith, 2009). As of 2010, al-Awlaki was known to have posted over 5,000 videos on YouTube (Torok, 2010). However, more important than simply relaying a message or calling for people to take action is showing them physically how to do it; this is where YouTube's value for terrorist organisations is truly shown (DHS, 2010).

Videos explaining and visually demonstrating practices such as tactical shooting or the field stripping of an AK-47 have been identified as examples of training that is effectively communicated over YouTube (DHS, 2010). Additionally, these types of training videos do not actively incite violence, and thus do not contravene YouTube's policy, and will therefore not be deleted (DHS, 2010). Terrorist organisations can also take advantage of YouTube's 'post-hoc' review system by uploading bomb making instructions and other such videos that violate YouTube policy, but which can potentially be viewed hundreds of times before the videos are reported and deleted.

New Cyber Frontier of Violent Extremism

According to Awan (2010), the Internet has surpassed all other media forms in becoming the principle arena for terrorist media activity, and the primary platform for the dissemination of jihadism. Furthermore, it is not only political activists who see the competitive advantage of using social media, as the three most popular social media sites (Facebook, Twitter, YouTube) have value-added to terrorist groups' ability to communicate, organise, recruit, and train would-be terrorists (Alexa, 2011b; Weimann, 2006; Wright, 2006). Furthermore, terrorist groups are using social media for fundraising purposes (Caldwell, 2008; Conway, 2006; Gray & Head, 2009; Strohm, 2011).

This cluster of issues is of particular relevance to countries like Pakistan with large Muslim populations where the potential target audience for social media to radicalism free of charge is greater. Moreover, countries such as Australia face their own concerns about social media, where the traditional transnational terrorism threat is being replaced by a much more pervasive and difficult to detect home-grown or grass-roots terrorism threat embedded in virtual realities ("ASIO sets up cyber", 2011; "ASIO warns of home", 2005; Johnson, 2010; Silber & Bhatt, 2007; Wright, 2006).

Moreover, there was a rapid expansion and widespread growth of jihadist websites during the period when Web 2.0 technologies began widely available around 2004 onwards. For instance, research by Weimann (2006) into the use of the Internet by terrorist groups showed that between 1997 and 2006, the number of websites dedicated to terrorist groups rose from only about 12 to over 7,000. Similarly, Stein (2011, p. 3) cites a U.S. State Department report in 1998, that "... there were only 15 Web Sites run by groups defined by U.S. as 'terrorist' groups. In 2005, this number increased to more than 4,000".

While the terrorist organisations that are advanced enough to have a presence online would traditionally stick to the use of jihadist websites and forums, where most of the users were people already supporting the cause (DHS, 2010), the transition into the more 'open' realm of social media has given them the opportunity to reach significantly larger audiences than was previously possible. For instance, Cohen (2009) found that terrorist groups actively target the large number of social media users among vulnerable populations in impoverished regions in the Middle East, Africa and Asia, and poorly integrated immigrant communities in Western Europe.

Therefore, the conceptual picture which emerges from this review is that Web 2.0 social media technologies have allowed terrorism to become a massive dot.com presence on the Internet. Figure 3 below illustrates the virtual pathways utilised by terrorists to carry out their core functions online.

Figure 3. Conceptual radicalisation pathways utilised by terrorists

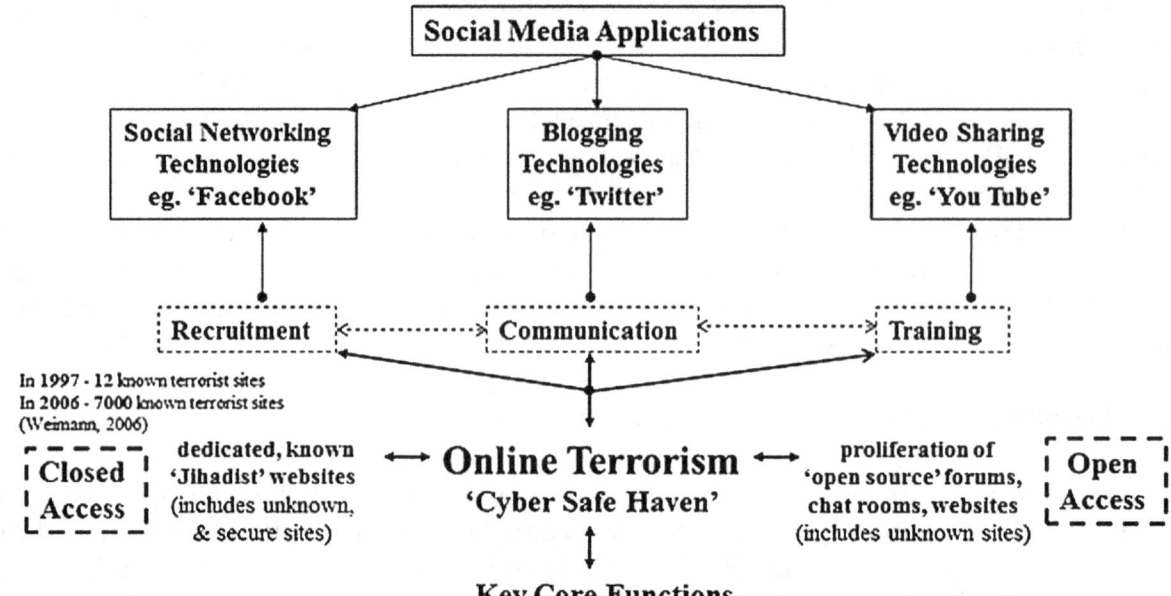

As can be seen, the conceptual mapping above depicts the phenomenal rise of jihadist expansion on the web through both closed and open access portals, as well as the various configurations of online terrorism. As such, it provides a useful starting point for an at-a-glance operational overview.

Modelling Violently Extreme Thinking

The advantage of a general level model of the key psychological processes involved in the journey to a radicalised mind-set is that it can subsume many of the specific multiple influences that come together in the 'mind' of a would-be radicalised violent extremist which have been noted and discussed in previous sections. Such a general model of the radicalisation process is contained in the diagram in Figure 4.

As noted previously, at this general psychological level, what 'unites' the disparate groups of violent extremists – terrorists, militants, shooters – is their 'cognitive willingness' to use and engage in violent and extreme actions to achieve their very different objectives. Moreover, also noted, willingness is about 'beliefs' which reside in the minds of individuals. Beliefs are also firmly held convictions that one accepts something as true or real, generally without definitive proof of their existence. A conceptual distinction needs to be made here about the very term 'beliefs' as it is often associated with the notion of ideology, especially in the political science literature where ideology is seen as a system of political beliefs.

Whilst, the notion of a 'political' set of beliefs may well hold true for militants and terrorists, it may be less applicable to active shooters, where revenge, rage, uncontrollable anger and exacting retribu-

Figure 4. NeuroCognitive radicalisation process

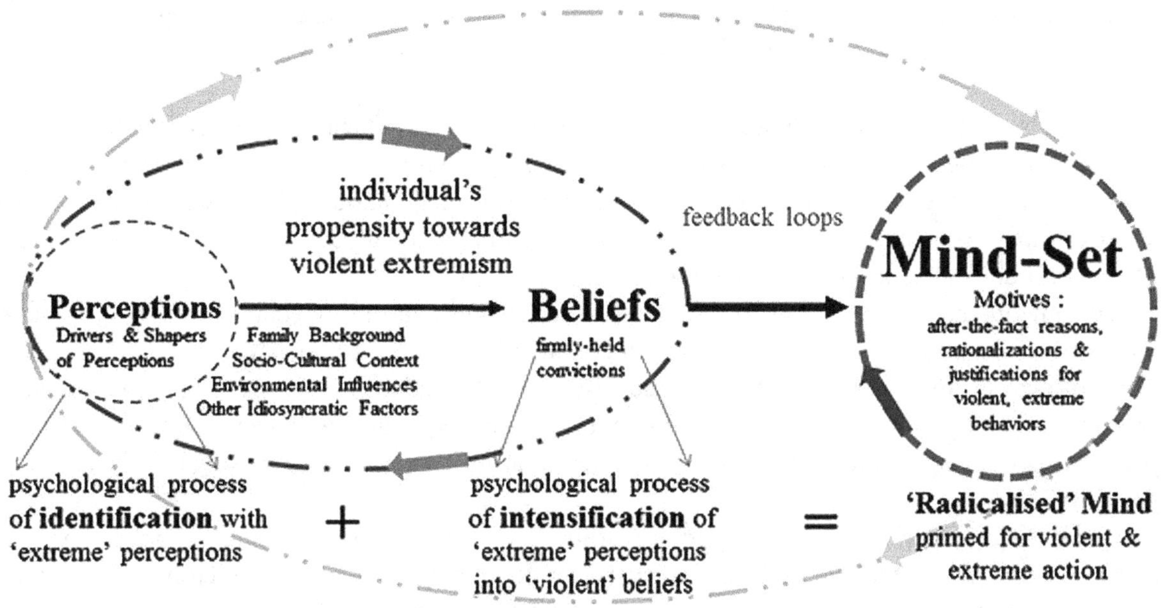

tion for 'perceived' wrongs provide the motivational fuel for violently extreme acts rather than a set of thought out and strongly held political beliefs.

Hence, for a violent extremist the cognitive willingness to use lethal violence is more about a personal set of beliefs that may or may not be mixed with political or ideological dogma. Thus, at a higher conceptually abstract level, what unites – terrorists, militants and shooters – is the set of personal, cognitive beliefs they hold that justify the use of extreme violence, even where there is considerable variance between them at the more specific motivational level of political or ideological beliefs.

A further distinction is necessary here in relation to individuals regarded a violent extremists and terrorists by virtue of being found to be associated with a terrorist/militant/extremist group, cell or network, but who for a multiplicity of reasons do not actually subscribe to a personal, cognitive set of violently extreme beliefs. Such individuals are often just plain 'caught up' in a terrorist/militant/extremist gang/group/cell/or network.

In other words, associating with a terrorist/militant/extremist gang/group/cell/or network does not automatically make one a 'true believer'. Individuals join terrorist/extremist cells for often mundane reasons like a sense of adventure, to get employment, to have an identity, or to give their life some meaning. Therefore, in theory, such individuals should be more 'cognitively open' to disengagement as they do not need to be 'deradicalised' as much as a 'true believer' would. If having to potentially kill someone is the price to be paid for adventure, fun, excitement or employment, then so be it. Of course, the risk is still there, whether they are a true believer or not makes little difference to a target.

Furthermore, at this general level of psychological abstraction, the mind of a violent extremist in most cases, with the exception of a few clearly clinically disturbed individuals, engages in normal thinking that has been taken to the 'extreme' end of 'normality' in terms of a rigid intolerance for anyone that does not agree with his/her view of the world.

Extremist thinking results from 'neuroplasticity-in-action' (Goleman, 2013; Greenfield, 2014) as repeated attentionally-focused brain-based neural patterns become over time expressed in mind-based cognitive pathways that can lead to a rigid 'mind-set' of violent extremism if left unchecked and unchallenged.

Individuals' journey along the road to a violently extreme mind-set starts with a perception of injustice or unfair treatment, real or imagined, against themselves, their race or their country. A perception is our way of interpreting reality from the multiple influences we take in through our sensory experiences made up of thoughts, feelings, emotions, cultural understandings, social, ethnic and family backgrounds. We 'see' with our eyes but 'perceive' with our brain.

Once someone has a sense of perceived injustice against oneself or on behalf of others, if this interpretation of reality is dwelt upon long enough, it has the potential to become an extreme perception. A prolonged sense of 'extreme injustice' over time will generally lead to two cognitive outcomes, anger or depression, both of which further fuel the perception of extreme injustice. Research into school shootings confirms that anger and depression are key precipitating factors in mass killings (Kiviat, Park, & Sayre, 2007).

Anger is the breeding ground for reform or revolution. It depends of where anger, born out of injustice, is directed to that determines whether it is used for good or evil. Anger directed towards the road of reform in campaigns of civil disobedience has its champions in Mahatma Gandhi, Martin Luther King, and Nelson Mandela among others. Anger directed towards the road of revolution has seen the ideals of socialism, communism, and patriotism lead to totalitarian campaigns of racial hatred, ethnic cleansing, and now jihadism. The infamous champions of revolution are many from Joseph Stalin, Adolf Hitler, Mao Zedong, and Osama bin Laden.

Depression, born out of a perceived sense of extreme injustice against oneself or on behalf of others, is often a masked form of anger turned inwards (Nelson, 2010). A person caught in a paralysing state of perceived injustice-based depression is a powder keg of raging internalised anger primed to explode. They are mentally living on the 'edge of chaos'. This does not imply or mean they are mentally ill or have an unstable personality. Just that their mind is conflicted. All that is needed is a 'trigger event' or 'tipping point'. The list is many and varied. Being fired from a job, losing a girlfriend, a marriage breakup, death of a loved one, school bulling, cyber bullying, a Facebook rejection, a demeaning YouTube video, and so forth.

Whatever the cognitive outcome – anger or depression – for a particular individual, borne out of dwelling repeated over time on a prolonged sense of extreme injustice, there are a few other ingredients needed. Add to the mix of anger/depression and the road to a violently extreme mind-set will increasingly become set like cement. These cognitive ingredients consist of a limited set of other perceptions (i.e., interpretations of reality) and beliefs (i.e., firmly-held convictions about 'our' interpreted reality) that are related or connected in some way, either through logical inference or more idiosyncratically to this foundational sense of perceived injustice. For instance, such perceptions relate to how one interprets reality about oneself or one's peers, or race, or religion, or country being victimised, being scapegoated, being humiliated, being rejected, being ostracised, being tainted or corrupted in some way and so forth.

With regard to beliefs, these primarily relate to how one should response to this foundational sense of perceived injustice and its associated perceptions. Because beliefs are firmly-held convictions about interpreted reality as perceived by that individual, they exert far more power in a person's mind than the perceptions in which they are rooted. Beliefs motivate people. Beliefs ignite people into action. For instance, if you perceive yourself as being unfairly treated at your workplace, and constantly discriminated against because of your race, and if this interpretation of reality is shared by others so that it becomes 'real' to you then over time with such daily repeated humiliations you come to the firm conviction (belief) that 'your workplace is racist' and that you must do something about it. The actions you can take range from resigning, making a formal complain to the company manager, going to a lawyer, or threating your 'racist' supervisor. If the perceptions and beliefs are extreme enough, they can escalate into you turning up at work one day with a gun supplied by an organised crime entrepreneur and shooting your supervisor. Watch what you perceive and believe as the quality of your life and others depends on it.

The following visualisation (figure 5) conceptualised by Dean (2014) depicts in extensive detail the neurocognitive theory as a general level pathway model of the inner workings of a violent extremist's mind.

This visualisation maps out the likely trajectory of an individual, identified through various means (e.g., security checks, behavioural indicators, informants, surveillance, intelligence tip-offs and so forth) as a Person-of-Concern (PoC), in relation to his/her current neurocognitive risk profile and his/her progression towards violently extreme thinking.

This NeuroCognitive Pathways Model is built around a number of critical 'pivotal points'. An individual at each pivotal point is driven by distinct motivations and combinations of push/pull factors. The net result being that individuals can 'spiral out' in different trajectories depending on the current path they choose. As can be seen, trajectories are composed of four cognitive phases – Attraction (identification), Obsession (intensification), Fixation (rigidification), and Loosing (disillusionment) – spread across three time periods (Entry, Engagement, and Disengagement) which are shaped by an individual's experiences over time.

This NeuroCognitive Pathways Model, whilst laid out in a linear structure is, in reality, a spiraling cyclical process that oscillates back and forth around pivot points in each of three time periods (Entry-

Figure 5. NeuroCognitive pathway of self-indoctrinating mind

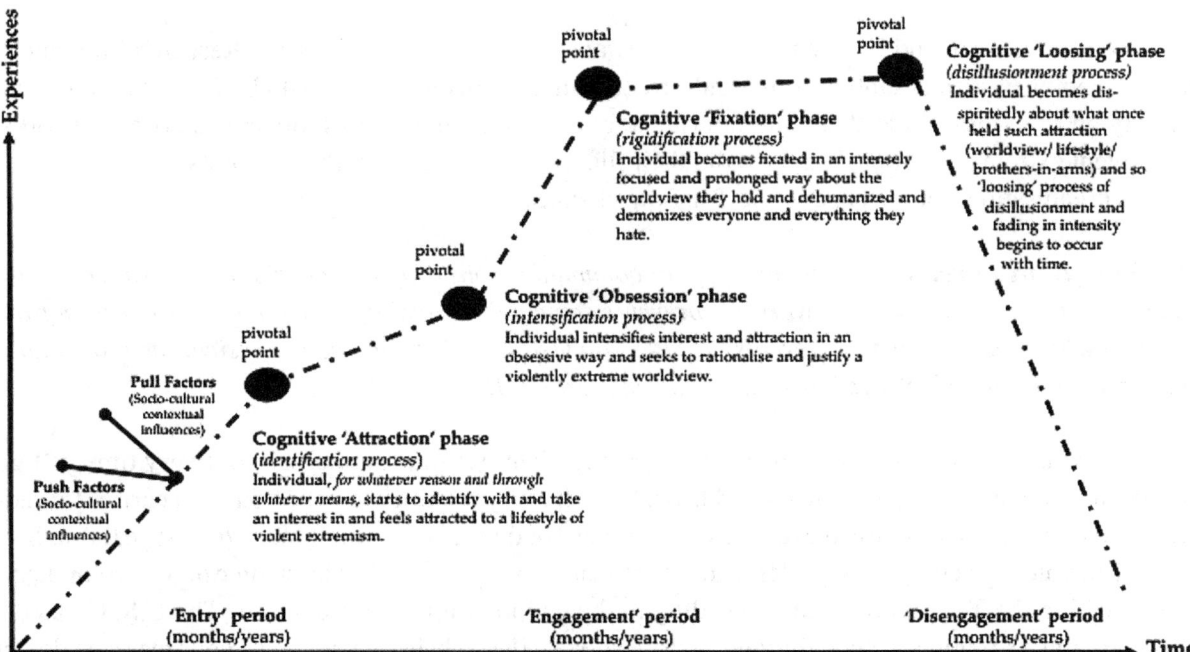

241

Engagement-Disengagement). This 'oscillating' cycle is influenced by a multiplicity of push/pull factors and 'inhibiting/constraining' factors experienced by an individual at these various pivot points.

What this framework highlights is that various combinations of these factors at some point in time 'tip' the balance towards a decision (cognitive opening) to enter or not and/or continue or not along a pathway towards extremism through psychologically identifying (identification phase) with specific perceptions and beliefs of an extreme and violent nature. Hence, the oscillating nature of a pivot point. In other words, inhibiting/constraining factors (e.g., family values, trusted peers, critical thinking, lack of determination, lack of adventure/excitement, alternative narratives) play a role in any situation which may cancel or nullify the influence of various push/pull factors to the point where a particular individual may decide not to go any further down the path of terrorism, at least at the cognitive level of committing to a firmly held belief system of violent extremism.

In summary, the utility of this visualisation model is the ability to track an individual's cognitive trajectory along neurocognitively-wired mental pathways linked to a timeline of sequential periods of Entry, Engagement and possible Disengagement (for some but not all) from a lifestyle of violent extremism.

DARK NET: THE UNDERBELLY OF CYBERSPACE

For a would-be violent extremist, the key advantage of the digital era is the anonomity it can afford the user to hide behind. In other words, digital technologies can provide a user with a very sophisticated means for deception by using browers that can access deeper, hidden layers of the Web. The most widely known example of such an anonymising software browser needed to access this hidden layer of cyberspace is called Tor. The acronym stands for 'The Onion Router'.

Anonymising Software: Tor and 'Dark Social' Technologies

The advent of the Tor and its release as free software in 2004 by the U.S. Naval Research Laboratory has been enthusiastically embraced not only by legitimate citizens concerned about their privacy and security on the World Wide Web, but unfortunately also by criminal rings, organised crime networks, and violent extremists that push and peddle their jihadist war and hate with anonymity.

The organisation's home page of the Tor Project states:

The Tor software protects you by bouncing your communications around a distributed network of relays run by volunteers all around the world: it prevents somebody watching your Internet connection from learning what sites you visit, it prevents the sites you visit from learning your physical location, and it lets you access sites which are blocked. (Torproject.org, 2015, p. 1)

Operationally, Tor provides security by separating identity from routing online. Every time you go online, the computer assigns its own IP address. Hence, every request/message you send carries this address and information is returned to that address. What Tor does is send your request/message through its network of volunteer computers (nodes) and moves your message through at least three nodes (computers) before exiting the Tor network and proceeding to the endpoint for your message ("The U.S. Created", 2014). By this re-routing method through multiple nodes, the website that receives your message do not know what your IP address is, nor does any node in the Tor network except for the final relay or endpoint.

There is considerable debate in the intelligence community about how Tor assists organised crime and online radicalisation (Schneier, 2013) and calls for it to be shut down. For instance, the NSA (National Security Agency) in America is in a constant battle with Tor to crack its encryption and break into its network. Whilst some of Tor's vulnerabilities have been exploited by the NSA and other government agencies, they had not managed to significantly infiltrate Tor nor are they even likely to be given the re-routing circuity methodology. Where some Tor weaknesses have been exposed, they are quickly patched much to the frustration of the NSA (Gellman, Timberg, & Rich, 2013; "The U.S. Created", 2014).

However, civil liberties groups are hotly opposed to taking Tor offline. They argue that "Tor's biggest problem is press. No one hears about that time someone wasn't staked by their abuser. They hear how somebody got away with downloading child porn" ("The U.S. Created", 2014, para. 5). Advocates for Tor also point out that Tor is only one, and probably the best known one, of anonymising software that criminals and violent extremists can use.

Hence, taking it offline would not stop cybercriminals. They have plenty of commerically available alternative softwares to choose from to hide their illicit activities. For instance, OTR, Cspace, ZRTP, REDPone, Tails, TrueCrypt, and other privacy tools (Electronic Privacy Information Center, 2015). This is evident in the IT literature with the notion of 'dark social'. It refers to software operating beneath the surface in the underbelly of cyberspace. Dark social is a term used by marketers and search engine optimisation specialists to describe websites' referrals that are difficult to track ("What is Metadata", 2015).

POLICING DIGITAL ERA: COMMUNICATION INTERCEPTION TECHNOLOGIES

The rapid growth of communication technology in the new millennium coupled with the rise of terrorism and the globalisation of organised crime (Gibson, 2004; Shelley, 2002; Stohl, 2006) has also witnessed a corresponding need for increasing the use of interception technologies in policing. Such 'popularity' for communication interception technologies (CIT) has spawned several concerns. Among the most prominent are definitional issues, the securitisation of a surveillance society (Norris 2006; Wood, 2006), and privacy rights (Bronitt & Stellios, 2005).

There is debate in the literature regarding the most appropriate definition for CIT (Branch, 2003; Starey, 2005). The term CIT resulted from the preconceived notions attached to the definition of telecommunications – largely associated with traditional telecommunication methods, such as telephone calls. Conversely, CIT implies a broader scope for all forms and methods of communication and is subsequently used to reference the interception methods and related technology. In Australia, the legislation concerning CIT, divides communications into two distinct categories: live communications and stored communications (Telecommunications [Interception] Amendment Act, 2006). Whilst legislation in other parts of the world is drafted differently, this distinction is generally adhered to in most countries (Starey, 2005).

Live communications addresses the category of communication that passes over a telecommunication system, such as voice telephony. The 'live' aspect concerns the fact that during a telephone call, the recipient instantly receives the message being communicated in real time (Ahmed, 2007; Starey, 2005). Starey (2005) argues the key aspect personifying live communication is that without interception (listening or recording) there is no record of the conversation once communication ceases.

Conversely, stored communication or communication stored in transit covers communication that during the course of its transmission is stored on one or more pieces of equipment of a carrier or service provider before being retrieved and accessed by the recipient. Starey (2005) and Ahmed (2007) both state that the concept of stored communication applies to most forms of electronic communication. During the transmission of electronic communication – such as email, SMS text messaging, voice mail, Internet chat or instant messaging software and VoIP telephony – the data packets transmitting this information are stored, at least momentarily, on various service provider servers and computer equipment. This information can therefore be intercepted prior to the intended recipient actually receiving the message (Ahmed, 2007; Starey, 2005).

This breakdown is especially important with regards to legislative definitions and subsequent abilities to intercept communications, where interception is defined as the act of listening to, recording or reading through any means of communication without the knowledge of the person making the communication (Ahmed, 2007; Starey, 2005; Telecommunications [Interception] Amendment Act, 2006). The following diagram in Figure 6 sketches out the dimensions of the 'balancing act' debate over security versus privacy with regard to CIT as well as defining the legislative framework.

Also, it will be noted on Figure 6 that CIT from a knowledge management perspective is an investigative tool where two distinct methodologies (overt and convert) can be employed, usually together or in parallel. Furthermore, in practice these methodologies overlap each other and are used for two quite different directions or purposes (gathering evidence and/or intelligence).

Dean, Bell, and Congram (2010) have written extensively about the significance of a Knowledge-Managed Policing (KMP) framework for CIT, and the use of CIT as an investigative tool. In essence, KMP functions as an organising framework for CIT by locating it within a wider conceptual perspective than simply a surveillance methodology. Also, KMP can act as a police governance mechanism

Figure 6. CIT as knowledge-managed investigative tool

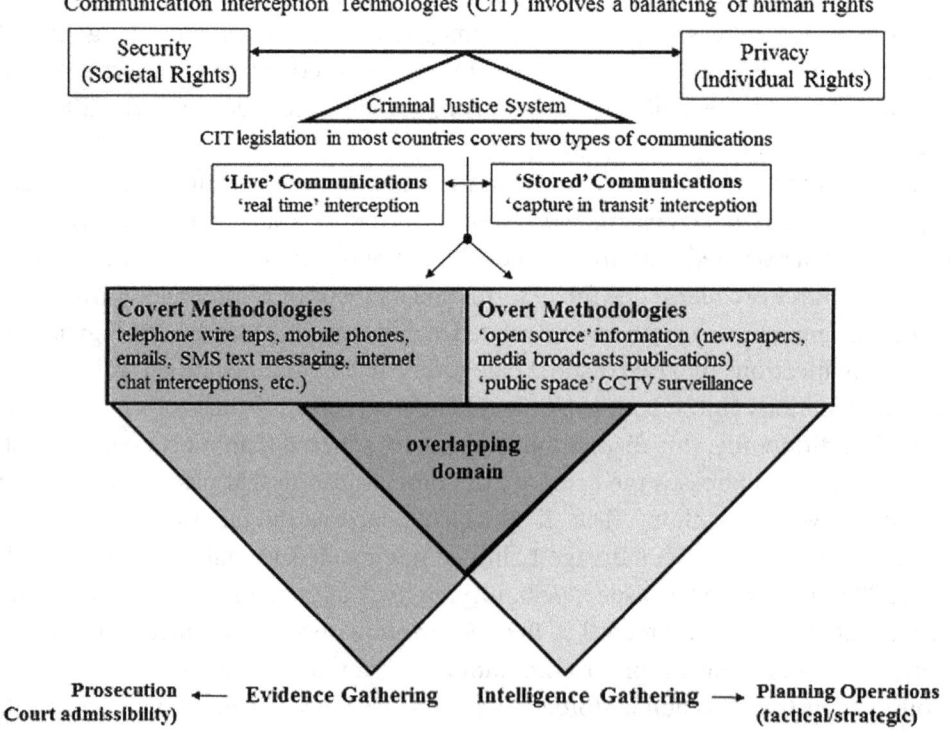

and 'regulatory' framework to ensure transparency, accountability and integrity in the use of CIT as an investigative tool by appropriate legislative bodies in the criminal justice system.

Metadata Retention Debate

Metadata retention laws are a hot topic around the world in the wake of the emergence of terrorist groups like the Islamic State in Iraq and Syria (ISIS). The central concern is the same as noted in the CIT section – how to balance individual privacy with national security.

Privacy advocates fear that metadata retention will create a totalising surveillance society much like in the Orwellian's 1984 novel where 'big brother' is watching everything. Governments, especially conservative ones, warn that metadata is essential to fight terrorism, online radicalisation, violent extremism as well as major transnational organised crime groups and networks (Braue, 2015b). The concern over metadata relates to its precision to track and identify an individual's online communications. How it does this, is explained in the following definition:

Metadata is data that describes other data. Meta is a prefix that in most information technology usages means 'an underlying definition or description'. Metadata summarises basic information about data, which can make finding and working with particular instances of data easier. For example, author, date created, and date modified and file size are examples of very basic document metadata. Having the ability to filter through that metadata makes it much easier to someone to locate a specific document. In addition to document files, metadata is used for images, videos, spreadsheet and web pages. Metadata on web pages can be very important. Metadata for web pages contain descriptions of the page's contents, as well as keyword linked to the content. These are usually expressed in the form of metatags. ("What is Metadata", 2015, para. 2)

After months of heated debate over the necessity and scope of state surveillance, the controversial data retention legislation came into effect in May 2015. The Australian Senate passed by a clear margin of 43 to 16 votes in favour of the Telecommunications (Interception and Access) Amendment (Data Retention) Bill 2014.

The metadata retention debate in Australia is mirrored in other countries. Braue (2015a) notes:

Data retention has a chequered history in other countries: Swedish authorities recently threatened an ISP in that country with a significant fine if it didn't step into line on the issue, while the European Union struck down data-retention laws as unconstitutional last year. Dutch authorities recently did away with data retention in that country, with amended laws judged to be unconsitutional and the country's telcomunications providers this week ordered to detlete data collected under data-retention laws. (p. 2)

The metadata issue is not just restricted to computers but extends to smartphones as well as with secure messaging apps like Wickr and WhatsApp. As Braue (2005b) further notes:

FBI director James Comey is among those pushing for backdoors into smartphones – but he faces resistance from within the government he serves: concers over government back doors remain so great that in December a U.S. senator introduced a bill that would prevent the government from forcing vendors to design back doors into their products to help their surveillance efforts. (p. 2)

OPERATIONALISING 4P'S FRAMEWORK: PRACTICAL IMPLICATIONS

The police compass presented initially in this chapter will now be discussed in relation to the previous sections in order to identify and operationalise practical implications for police and security services.

Reproduced below in figure 7 is the 'Police Compass' with the 4P's Framework comprised of the verrtical axis of the North-South 'Policing-Public directional needle' and the horizontal axis of the East-West 'Policies-Politics reference pointers'.

Directional Needle: 'Policing-Public' Axis

The directional needle of the police compass needs to be re-set around the central concept of radicalisation be it online or a physical time and place. As this chapter has made clear the very notion of radicalisation like terrorism is a concept in search of a meaningful definition, and is prone to political misuse by governments. What follows is a summary account of the key points from the complex, confusing, and problematic radicalisation literature in relation to those aspects of the radicalisation process which have operational utility for police and security services.

Radicalisation in the Digital Era

The extant literature makes it very clear that radicalisation like terrorism is driven by a multi-factorial mix of push-pull factors including many political, ideological, social, and cultural elements and contextual

Figure 7. Poilce compass for operational policing

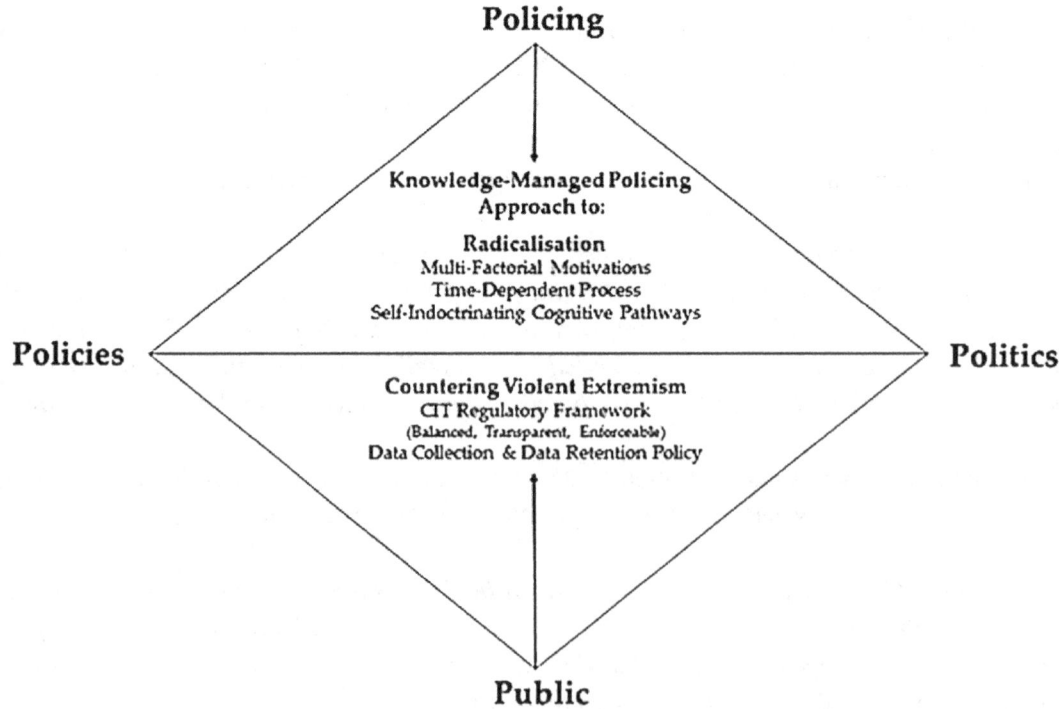

antecedents that are largely idiosyncratic and distinct to each individual. Furthermore, it is a process that is time-dependent for each individual. A summary of the key points drawn from the radicalisation literature in relation to its multi-factorial motivations, time-dependence, and self-indoctrinating nature is presented below.

Multi-Factorial Motives

Radicalisation is driven by a combination of general 'push' and specific 'pull' factors (Borum, 2011a; Borum, 2014; McCauley & Moskalenko, 2011; Schmid, 2013). They are:

- General factors that 'push' individuals towards a cognitive opening to entertain a violently extreme worldview consists of broad grievances (perceived injustices), real or imaginary.
- Specific factors that 'pull' individuals to find a violently extreme worldview cognitively attractive are more specific and local to their socio-cultural context than broad grievances, and can consist of one or more pressure, friction or tipping points, as well as other factors particular to an individual:
  - Search for social connectedness (e.g., finding acceptance in a group)
  - Search for personal meaning (e.g., a higher narrative than oneself to believe in)
  - Seeking redemption for past wrongs (e.g., doing something for justice)
  - Love of country (e.g., 'good patriot' means to an individual killing those who do not belong in one's country like migrants, illegal immigrants, asylum seekers)
  - Love of another who is already radicalised
  - Desire for martyrdom – 'fame' phenomena (e.g., being remembered in history)
  - Attraction to risk-taking, thrill-seeking, exciting adventure of jihadist lifestyle
  - Gaining employment – simply having a job even if it means pretending to be ideologically committed to a group's political agenda or philosophy
  - Access to criminal/terrorist networks to enhance personal status and/or personal advantage like more money, power, prestige
  - Getting back at others through aggression for variety of reasons:
    - Ideological hatred for those seen as responsible for injustices
    - Political cause for a 'true' believer
    - Personal outlet for aggression where taking up a jihadist cause is a cover for one's own violent tendencies

Any combination of these general and specific factors can create the necessary cognitive conditions for an individual to become involved with others either in person (individual/group meetings) and/or in combination with the virtual world of online radicalisation.

Time-Dependent Process

Radicalisation is a time-dependent process. This means that for most would-be violent extremists, the cognitive commitment necessary to a set of extreme perceptions and violent beliefs embodied in a cause/mission/purpose will subsequently strengthen their mental willingness to engage in violently extreme actions through the brain's process of neuroplasticity. For others not so cognitively committed to the ideological doctrine of the group when they first got involved for reasons more personal and particular to themselves, the very act of engaging in violent and extreme actions will strengthen their personal conviction to be more cognitively committed to the group's cause.

Moreover, as noted previously the online radicalisation path can be done through a number of forums like visiting radical websites via the open web or 'dark net' of cyberspace using Tor type browsers; searching social media sites – Facebook, blogs, Twitter, Youtube, etc. Also, online radicalisation can be done with others through digital dialogues (group context) or purely as a lone actor (wolf) to research 'how to' material for engaging in violently extreme acts.

Self-Indoctrinating Cognitive Pathways

Whether radicalisation takes place physically in a local group context or virtually online as a lone actor or in group communication/forum, the cognitive process of becoming involved will always be one of personal agency. In other words, even when substantial and influential pressure and/or brainwashing tactics are used by groups, in the final analysis the individual has the sole responsibility of giving his/her cognitive acceptance to becoming and continuing to be involved on a pathway of extremist thinking which may result in violent actions.

Hence, from a cognitive perspective, the radicalisation of an individual is always a case of self-radicalisation regardless of group influence. Groups can only apply cognitive pressure (brainwashing tactics) and persuasive arguments (rationales/justifications) to get a person's commitment. In the end, it is up to the individuals to decide what they will or will not accept for themselves.

In this sense, the problematic notion of radicalisation, like the conceptually flawed and pragmatically confused notion of legally defining terrorism, does not have to be invoked in this neurocognitive understanding on how an individual becomes involved in extreme thinking that can lead to aggressively harmful and potentially deadly actions being inflicted on others.

In fact, conceptually speaking, from a NeuroCognitive perspective the very notion of self-radicalisation can be replaced by the more accurate and precise term of 'self-indoctrination' without any lost in understanding, and a lot more operational clarity. Self-indoctrination can happen at any point in time in the process of extremist thinking. Moreover, the self-indoctrinating process can stop at any point in time as circumstances change in people's lives. Hence, self-indoctrination to a set of extreme perceptions does not necessarily equate with being a violent extremist.

Much like Borum's (2011b, p. 23) contention that "radicalisation does not equate with terrorism" per se. Hence, if someone self-indoctrinates up to the point of extreme perceptions only then they have been radicalised to a level of extremist thinking that is one step short of being a 'violent' extremist. Often this is the reality for the vast majority of a marginalised community who have a long list of grievances and injustices, but the self-indoctrination of extreme perceptions stop there as they are not willing or desire to commit to take violent actions against those they perceive as their oppressors. Thus for a theoretical point of view, such individuals may be radicalised but they are not yet terrorists or violent extremists. It is only if they go on to add to their extreme perceptions with a set of violent beliefs that, conceptually speaking, the link or connection between radicalisation and terrorism or in this case violent extremism can be assumed to be made.

Furthermore, as noted previously some individuals join extremist groups for reasons of social connectedness, personal meaning, to get employment, to mask their lust for violence, for adventure, or to get access to terrorist/criminal networks to make money without having any self-indoctrinating need for cognitive commitment to the group's belief system. Hence, this pathway model of NeuroCognitive risk of violent extremism is applicable to individuals who show some cognitive attraction to extreme perceptions with the additional possibility that such an attentional focus may lead them over time into a deep cognitive commitment to violent beliefs and a mind-set to carry out acts of violent extremism.

Case Study: Online Radicalisation or Self-Indoctrination?

The source of this case study is very recent. It was reported on May 17, 2015 by a team of investigative journalists (Passmore, Chamberlin, & Brennan, 2015) under the heading 'Trapped in Web of Terror' in The Sunday Mail, a weekend Newspaper published in Queensland, Australia. The facts as reported are below (pp. 7-8):

- Oliver Bridgeman, 18 years old, from the regional city of Toowoomba in Queensland, Australia, set up a Facebook page using the alias, Yusuf Oli, to follow the online recorded preachings of the late Sheik Ahmed Deedat, a controversial South African Muslim scholar committed to dawah, or conversion to Islam.
- Sheik Deedat's YouTube videos were also a favourite of Mohammad Ail Baryalei, a former Sydney brothel bounder who became Australia's most senior Islamic State figure who recruited dozens of Australians to fight in Syria and Iraq.
- Bridgeman also shared links to the Street Dawah group. Its Parramatta branch in Sydney was previously led by Baryalei. It is alleged that Baryalei gave the order for followers to behead random members of the public on the streets of Sydney. Baryalei was reported to have been killed fighting in Syria in October 2014.
- Bridgeman's parents reported him missing when he did not return from a trip to Indonesia, where he was understood to have been working with a humanitarian group. Intelligence services discovered that he had travelled to Turkey – a common route into Syria – and had aligned himself with the Al-Nusra Front, a terror group connected to Al-Qaeda.
- Bridgeman was seen on a few occasions at the local Garden City Mosque in Toowoomba, but he is not a regular visitor or member.
- Bridgeman's social media pages also included postings condemning extremism but they had links to online broadcasts by Egyptian cleric Mostafa Al-Adwy.
- In January 2015, Bridgeman on the Project Hope website, an organisation set up to provide aid for Syrian refugees, posted "how can we join the project?".
- Bridgeman regularly defended Islam, arguing with people who were against the religion and its customs.

What this case study reveals is that this youth has self-radicalised or to use my preferred term indoctrinated himself to the point in his thinking where he is willing to travel covertly to Syria to join in a civil war fight against an oppressive Syrian Government, defined as such by the West, and in so doing has aligned himself with an Islamic terrorist group also defined as such and blacklisted by the West.

What this implies from a NeuroCognitive pathways point of view, is that this youth has for whatever reasons been cognitively attracted (phase 1) to Islam as a religious way of life through online viewing, by his own volition, what Western authorities regard as radical Islamic teachings. This cognitive attraction would consist of a set of perceptions to do with broad grievances about Islam being misunderstood by the West and judged as evil. For example, he has defended Islam by arguing with those who disagree with his interpreted reality of Islam. Hence, this youth is embarking mentally on a cognitive journey to an extremist worldview.

At some point in time from this initial cognitive attraction to Islam phase, Bridgeman appears to have identified strongly with the plight of the Syrian population under the oppressive government. His online post of January 2015 on the Project Hope website enquiring about how to join the project set up to provide aid to Syrian refugees from the civil war, is a form of 'behavioural leaking' of intentions. This is a well-documented process in violent extremism (Bondu, Cornell, & Scheithauer, 2011).

It is surmised that Bridgeman has found at this stage a 'cause' he can in his own mind legitimately channel his energy into that 'fits' with his Islamic identification. So much so that he becomes cognitively obsessed (phase 2) as evidenced by his preparedness to travel covertly to Syria without informing his parents or any of his friends of his intentions. Here the story has yet to unfold further. But what is clear is that this self-indoctrinated youth is at least at the phase of cognitive obsession in his extremist thinking, and it remains to be seen if he will move on to the point of cognitive fixation where the extremely perceptions he already has get translated in violent beliefs that lead him to engage in violent extreme actions like killing others in the name of Allah.

This case study typifies what is happening to so many young people in search of something more than what the West has or can offer them.

Reference Pointers: 'Policies-Politics' Axis

The direction of the Policing-Public 'needle' of the police compass is influenced by the magnetising forces of the types of policies followed by the politics of the government of the day in any particular country/state context. These two 'poles' – policies and politics – are the key reference points that guide the movement of the police compass needle until a clear direction is set in policy and legitimised by governments. For example, the 'zero tolerance' policy that sweep New York city in the wake of the upsurge of petty street crime that was championed by the Major of New York City is a case in point of the operation of the 'Policies-Politics' axis on the 'Policing-Public' needle of the police compass.

Countering Violent Extremism in the Digital Era

It is evident from the previous sections of the chapter that the concept and practice of Knowledge-Managed Policing (KMP) is a highly relevant, timely and necessary perspective for policing/law enforcement/ security agencies. Adopting a salient knowledge management approach can tip the competitive advantage towards policing the multitude of harms and threats that online radicalisation presents through the medium of the dark net of social media.

CIT Regulatory Framework: Balanced, Transparent, Enforceable

The utility of KMP for managing the challenges associated with social media must, of necessity, involved a range of CIT by police and other law enforcement agencies. Such a CIT policy must be based on a balanced, transparent, and enforceable approach where national security and privacy concerns are at the forefront of its mandate.

How such a CIT policy should be formulated was the subject of a special report on 'Countering Internet radicalisation in Southeast Asia' in 2009 by Bergin, Osman, Ungerer, and Yasin. They identified three broad policy approaches and/or a combination of them which governments tend to adopt towards dealing with online terrorism. There are as stated in the report (p. 12):

- A hard strategy of 'zero tolerance' (blocking sites, prosecuting site administrators, using Internet filters);
- A softer strategy of encouraging Internet end users to directly challenge the extremist narrative (including creating websites to promote tolerance); and
- An intelligence-led strategy of monitoring leading to targeting, investigation, disruption and arrest.

Data Collection and Data Retention Policy: Operational Implications

Governments and law enforcement agencies see their two-pronged approach strategy to online radicalisation and terrorism as part of their solution by:

- Tightening control over the retention of metadata owned by private ISP companies like Google, Microsoft, Facebook, Twitter, etc.
- Forcing software manufacturers to design 'back doors' into their encryption technologies and products.

The fly in the ointment with this government solution is that there is already available 'encryption key-management' solutions that make data inaccessible even to software vendors and 'Cloud' storage providers (Braue, 2015c). For example, "SpiderOak's encryption architecture, based on an open-sourced framework, called Cryton, prevents it from ever being able to access customer's cloud data" (Braue, 2015c, p. 3). Hence, the owner of the data manages the encryption key themselves without the ISP or any third party like government agencies being able to get it as the decryption key is never transmitted. So even if law enforcement agencies are able to get both metadata and have a 'back door' into the software, it will not help them to decrypt anything without the key.

The operational ramifications of this technological solution – encryption key-management – are far reaching. It renders obsolete metadata retention. It becomes a waste of time and huge money; recent estimates for Australia's data retention scheme is around 400 million per year (Braue, 2015a) for those individuals and groups who invest in encryption key management.

Furthermore, terrorist groups like their criminal counterparts already know the surveillance capabilities of governments, and many now simply do not rely on electronic communications in any form (e.g., Facebook, twitter, smartphone) for their operational plans. They have reverted back to good old spy craft like dead letter drops, meeting in parks at odd hours, crowded shopping malls and so forth (personal communication by police researcher at Netherlands Police Academy, 2013). The cost of maintaining around-the-clock surveillance on hundreds if not thousands of suspected high-risk targets will break the budget on any government over time.

In the final analysis, the policies adopted by a police organisation will be shaped by the politics, both internal and external, that exist in any given current climate. These internal and external political forces will determine the policy agenda towards violent extremism.

CONCLUSION

The chapter has argued that the challenges facing law enforcement and security agencies in the digital era are many, varied and complex. These challenges include the definitional issues surrounding violent extremism where the belief that committing an act of violence will produce benefits that outweighs the cost of human life. Violent extremism can also be linked to terrorism where violence is used to intimidate a government or a civilian population in order to advance some political, social, or ideological objective.

Into this definitional soup is added the highly contested notion of radicalisation. The concept of radicalisation is not by definition the same as violent extremism or terrorism, yet it is often equated with these labels. As Schmid (2013, p. 8) rightly points out "… in the last two hundred years, people labelled 'radicals' have been both non-violent and violent and their radicalism has been both illegal and legal (e.g., during the Chinese Cultural Revolution)".

Radicals like everyone else have choices to make. For some its through reform, for others its through revolution. Some radicals will advocate for systemic changes that are non-violent and democratic through persuasion and reform like Mahatma Gandhi, Martin Luther King, and Nelson Mandela. While other radicals see the only way forward from an oppressive regime is through violent, non-democratic coercion and revolution like Velupillai Prabhakaran who is the founder of the Tamil Tigers, Andreas Baader from the German terrorist group the Red Army Faction, commonly known by the names of its two leaders the Baader-Meinhof gang.

Schmid (2013) succinctly sums up the situation on radicalisation when he states,

Radicals then are not per se violent and while they might share certain characteristics (e.g., alienation from the state, anger over a country's foreign policy, feelings of discrimination) with (violent) extremists, there are also important differences (such as regarding the willingness to engage in critical thinking). It does not follow that a radical attitude must result in violent behaviour – a finding well established by decades of research." (p. 8)

In an attempt to overcome the definitional quicksand of using the term radicalisation with all its associated baggage of terrorism and violent extremism, the preferred framing by the current author of the challenges posed by online radicalisation is to replace it with the notion of self-indoctrination. That is, someone with radical views, encapsulated in extreme perceptions, have self-indoctrinated themselves; if they continue to think like this, they can end up with a set of violent beliefs which lead to a cognitive pathway of engaging in acts of violent extremism.

Alongside these definitional challenges and how best to frame them so that they have operational relevance for police and security services, is the digital world we now live in, which further complicates the challenges. The advent of social media (e.g., Facebook, Twitter, YouTube) has created new opportunities for terrorist organisations and brought with it growing challenges for law enforcement and intelligence agencies. The underbelly of cyberspace is a dark net where very sophisticated means for propoganda and deception by violent extremists is the technological reality through using browers and encryption software that can access deeper, hidden layers of the Web where government authorities can do little to dismantle or disrupt them.

The current policy of law enforcement agencies relying on access to social media communications and metadata to combat and catch violent extremists will no longer be sufficient in the digital era. The argument this chapter makes is that technological advances, like we are currently seeing in the IT marketplace (e.g., anonymising software, encryption key-management), will make the security benefits for data collection and data retention by government authorities largely ineffective for smart violent extremists in the near future.

This chapter paints a picture where the future may look bleak for law enforcement efforts in combating violent extremism and radicalisation. However, it also offers a way of framing these challenges where the perspective can change to one of innovation and experimentation with new emerging digital technologies. It is a question of choice how one looks for problems or solutions.

REFERENCES

Ahmed, S. (2007). B-party intercepts and the Telecommunications (Interception) Amendment Act 2006 (Cth). *Internet Law Bulletin, 10*(1).

Al-Shishani, M. B. (2010). Taking al-Qaeda's jihad to Facebook. *Terrorism Monitor, 8*(5), 3–4.

Alexa. (2011a). *Facebook.com Site Info*. Retrieved from http://www.alexa.com/siteinfo/facebook.com

Alexa. (2011b). *Top 500 sites on the web*. Retrieved from http://www.alexa.com/topsites

Allen, C. (2007). *Threat of Islamic radicalization to the Homeland (Written testimony to the U.S. Senate Committee on Homeland Security and Governmental Affairs)*. Washington, DC: Department of Homeland Security.

ASIO sets up cyber-spook unit. (2011, March 11). *ABC News*. Retrieved from http://www.abc.net.au/news/stories/2011/03/11/3161101.htm

ASIO warns of home-grown terror threat. (2005, November 2). *ABC News*. Retrieved from http://www.abc.net.au/news/stories/2005/11/02/1495641.htm

Awan, A. N. (2010). The virtual jihad: An increasingly legitimate form of warfare. *CTC Sentinel, 3*(5), 10–13.

Bergin, A., Osman, S., Ungerer, C., & Yasin, N. A. M. (2009). *Countering internet radicalisation in Southeast Asia*. Canberra: Australian Strategic Policy Institute.

Bjørgo, T. (2009). Processes of disengagement from violent groups of the extreme right. In T. Bjørgo & J. Horgan (Eds.), *Leaving terrorism behind: Individual and collective disengagement* (pp. 30–48). Abingdon: Routledge.

Bjørgo, T. (2011). Dreams and disillusionment: Engagement in and disengagement from militant extremist groups. *Crime, Law, and Social Change, 55*(4), 277–285. doi:10.1007/s10611-011-9282-9

Bondu, R., Cornell, D. G., & Scheithauer, H. (2011). Student homicidal violence in schools: An international problem. New Directions for Youth Development: Theory, Practice, Research, 129, 13-30.

Borum, R. (2011a). Rethinking radicalization. *Journal of Strategic Security, 4*(4), 1–6.

Borum, R. (2011b). Radicalization into violent extremism: A review of social science theories. *Journal of Strategic Security, 4*(4), 7–36. doi:10.5038/1944-0472.4.4.1

Borum, R. (2014). Psychological vulnerabilities and propensities for involvement in violent extremism. *Behavioral Sciences & the Law, 32*(3), 286–305. doi:10.1002/bsl.2110 PMID:24652686

Branch, P. A. (2003). Lawful interception of the Internet. *Australian Journal of Emerging Technologies and Society, 1*(1), 1–7.

Braue, D. (2015a, March 30). *Opponents restate security, scope concerns metadata retention becomes Australian law*. Queensland: CSO Australia.

Braue, D. (2015b, April 1). *Police investigations threatened metadata retention feeds telephony* diaspora. Queensland: CSO Australia.

Braue, D. (2015c, April 3). *Avoid government, hacker snooping by owning encryption key management: lawyer*. Queensland: CSO Australia.

Bronitt, S., & Stellios, J. (2005). Telecommunications interception in Australia: Recent trends and regulatory prospects. *Telecommunications Policy, 29*(11), 875–888. doi:10.1016/j.telpol.2005.06.010

Caldwell, I. (2008). Terror on YouTube. *Forensic Examiner, 17*(3), 80–83.

Chowdhury-Fink, N., & Heame, E. B. (2008). *Beyond terrorism: Deradicalisation and disengagement from violent extremism*. New York, NY: International Peace Institute.

Cohen, J. (2009). Diverting the radicalization track. *Policy Review, 154*, 51–63.

Conway, M. (2006). Terrorism and the Internet: New media - new threat? *Parliamentary Affairs, 59*(2), 283–298. doi:10.1093/pa/gsl009

Coolsaet, R. (Ed.). (2011). *Jihadi terrorism and the radicalisation challenge: European and American experience* (2nd ed.). Farnham, MD: Ashgate.

Dean, G. (2012). *Complexity model for knowledge-managed policing of violent extremism*. Paper presented at The American Society of Criminology, Annual Meeting, Chicago, IL.

Dean, G. (2014). *Neurocogntive risk assessment for the early detection of violent extremists*. New York, NY: Springer.

Dean, G., Bell, P., & Congram, M. (2010). Knowledge-managed policing framework for communication interception technologies (CIT) in criminal justice system. *Pakistan Journal of Criminology, 2*(4), 25–41.

Dean, G., & Gottschalk, P. (2007). *Knowledge management in policing and law enforcement: Foundations, structures, applications*. Oxford, UK: Oxford University Press.

Department of Homeland Security (DHS). (2010). *Terrorist use of social networking sites: Facebook case study*. Washington, DC: Author.

Department of Homeland Security (DHS). (2012). *Case studies on violent extremism*. Washington, DC: Author.

Drummond, J. T. (2002). From northwest imperative to global jihad: Social psychological aspect of the construction of the enemy, political violence, and terror. In C. E. Stout (Ed.), *The psychology of terrorism: A public understanding - Psychological dimension to war and peace* (Vol. 1, pp. 49–96). Westport, CT: Praeger.

Earl, J., & Kimport, K. (2011). *Digitally enabled social change: Activism in the Internet age*. Cambridge, MA: Massachusetts Institute of Technology Publishing. doi:10.7551/mitpress/9780262015103.001.0001

Electronic Privacy Information Center (EPIC). (2015). *EPIC online guide to practical privacy tools*. Retrieved from https://www.epic.org/privacy/tools.html

Elzain, C. (2008). Modern Islamic terrorism and jihad. *Occasional Series in Criminal Justice and International Studies*, 1-27.

European Commission project. (2008). *Transnational terrorism, security and the rule of law*. Retrieved from http://www.transnationalterrorism.eu/tekst/publications/WP2%20Del%203.pdf

Fox, R. (2005, August 8). Gwot is history. Now for save: After the global war on terror comes the struggle against violent extremism. *New Statesman*. Retrieved from http://www.newstatesman.com/node/195357

Freilich, J. D., Chermak, S. M., & Caspi, D. (2009). Critical events in the life trajectories of domestic extremist white supremacist groups. *Criminology & Public Policy*, 8(3), 497–530. doi:10.1111/j.1745-9133.2009.00572.x

Gellman, B., Timberg, C., & Rich, S. (2013, October 4). Secret NSA documents show campaign against Tor encrypted network. *Washington Post*. Retrieved from https://www.washingtonpost.com/world/national-security/secret-nsa-documents-show-campaign-against-tor-encrypted-network/2013/10/04/610f08b6-2d05-11e3-8ade-a1f23cda135e_story.html

Gibson, S. (2004). Open source intelligence: An intelligence lifeline. *Royal United Services Institute Journal*, 149(1), 16–22.

Goleman, D. (2013). *Focus: The hidden driver of excellence*. London: Bloomsbury.

Gray, D. H., & Head, A. (2009). The importance of the Internet to the post-modern terrorist and its role as a form of safe haven. *European Journal of Scientific Research*, 25(3), 396–404.

Greenfield, S. (2014). *Mind change: How digital technologies are leaving their mark on our brains*. UK: Rider.

Hassan, M. (2012). Understanding drivers of violent extremism: The case of al-Shabab and Somali youth. *CTC Sentinel*, 5(8), 18–20.

Hoffman, B. (2006). Inside terrorism (Revised and Expanded Ed.). New York, NY: Columbia University Press.

Horgan, J. (2008a). Deradicalization or disengagement? A process in need of clarity and a counterterrorism initiative in evaluation. *Perspectives on Terrorism*, 2(4), 3–8.

Horgan, J. (2008b, May 11). From profiles to pathways: The road to recruitment. *Peace and Security*. Retrieved from http://www.america.gov/st/peacesecenglish/2008/April/20080522173120Sren oD0.3425867.html

Horgan, J. (2009a). *Walking away from terrorism: Accounts of disengagement from radical and extremist movements*. New York, NY: Routledge.

Horgan, J. (2009b). Individual disengagement: A psychological analysis. In T. Bjørgo & J. Horgan (Eds.), *Leaving terrorism behind: Individual and collective disengagement* (pp. 17–30). Abingdon: Routledge.

Horgan, J. (2012). Discussion point: The end of radicalization? *National Consortium for the Study of Terrorism and Responses to Terrorism (START)*. Retrieved from http://www.start.umd.edu/start/announcements/announcement.asp?id=416

Horgan, J., & Altier, M. B. (2012). The future of terrorist de-radicalisation programs. *Georgetown Journal of International Affairs, 13*(2), 83–90.

Horgan, J., & Braddock, K. (2010). Rehabilitating the terrorists? Challenges in assessing the effectiveness of de-radicalization programs. *Terrorism and Political Violence, 22*(2), 267–291. doi:10.1080/09546551003594748

Horgan, J., & Braddock, K. (2011). Evaluating the effectiveness of de-radicalisation programs: Towards a scientific approach to terrorism risk reduction. In S. Canna (Ed.), *Countering violent extremism: Scientific methods & strategies* (pp. 158–164). Washington, DC: NSI.

Horgan, J., & Taylor, M. (2010). Disengagement, de-radicalisation and the arc of terrorism: Future directions for research. In R. Coolsaet (Ed.), *Jihadi terrorism and the radicalisation challenge: European and American experiences* (pp. 173–187). Farnham: Ashgate.

Institute for Strategic Dialogue (ISD). (2012). *Tackling extremism: De-radicalisation and disengagement*. Retrieved from http://www.strategicdialogue.org/programmes/counter-extremism/

Johnson, T. (2010). Threat of homegrown Islamist terrorism. *Council of Foreign Affairs*. Retrieved from http://www.cfr.org/terrorism/threat-homegrown-islamist-terrorism/p11509

Kiviat, B., Park, A., & Sayre, C. (2007). Inside a mass murderer's mind. *Time*. Retrieved from http://www.time.com/time/magazine/article/0,9171.1612694,oo.html

Lee, M. (2008). Blogs feed information frenzy on Mumbai blasts. *Globe and Mail*. Retrieved from http://www.theglobeandmail.com/news/technology/article725225.ece

Leggio, J. (2008). Mumbai attack coverage demonstrates (good and bad) maturation point of social media. *ZDNet*. Retrieved from http://www.zdnet.com/blog/feeds/mumbai-attack-coverage-demonstrates-good-and-bad-maturation-point-of-social-media/339

Madhani, A. (2010). Cleric al-Awlaki dubbed 'bin Laden of the Internet'. *USA Today*. Retrieved from http://www.usatoday.com/news/nation/2010-08-25-A_Awlaki25_CV_N.htm

Maogoto, J. N. (2003). War on the enemy: Self-defence and state sponsored terrorism. *Melbourne Journal of International Law, 4*, 406–438.

McCauley, C., & Moskalenko, S. (2011). Individual and group mechanisms of radicalisation. In S. Canna (Ed.), *Protecting the homeland from international and domestic terrorism threats: Current multidisciplinary perspectives on root causes, the role of ideology, and programs for counter-radicalisation and disengagement*. College Park: START.

Morgan, M. J. (2004). The origins of the new terrorism. *Parameters*, (Spring): 29–43.

Mroz, J. (2009). *Lone wolf attacks and the difference between violent extremism and terrorism*. Retrieved from http://www.ewi.info/lone-wolf-attacks-anddifference-between-violent-extremism-and-terrorism

Nasser-Eddine, M., Garnham, B., Agostino, K., & Caluya, G. (2011). Countering violent extremism (CVE) literature review. Edinburgh, Australia: Australian Government, Department of Defence, Command and Control Division, Defence Science and Technology Organisation (DSTO).

Nelson, A. (2010). Nice girls don't do conflict. *Psychology Today*. Retrieved from https://www.psychologytoday.com/blog/he-speaks-she-speaks/201011/nice-girls-don-t-do-conflict

Newman, E. (2006). Exploring the "root causes" of terrorism. *Studies in Conflict and Terrorism*, 29(8), 749–772. doi:10.1080/10576100600704069

Norris, C. (2006). *A report on the surveillance society: For the information commissioner. Expert Report: Criminal Justice. Surveillance Studies Network*. London: Information Commissioner.

O'Rourke, S. (2010). *The emergent challenges for policing terrorism: Lessons from Mumbai*. Retrieved from http://ro.ecu.edu.au/cgi/viewcontent.cgi?article=1004&context=act

Papic, M., & Noonan, S. (2011, February 3). Social media as tool for protest. *Stratfor*. Retrieved from http://www.stratfor.com/weekly/20110202-social-media-tool-protest?utm_source=SWeekly&utm_medium=email&utm_campaign=110203&utm_content=readmore&elq=77ffb64cf0554757abe76e998eb0395b

Passmore, D., Chamberlin, T., & Brennan, R. (2015, May 17). Trapped in web of terror. *The Sunday Mail*, p. 7.

Qatar International Academy for Security Studies (QIASS). (2010). *Risk Reduction for Countering Violent Extremism: Explorative Review by the International Resource Center for Countering Violent Extremism*. Qatar: Author.

Rabasa, A., Blackwill, R., Chalk, P., Cragin, K., Fair, C., Jackson, B., & Tellis, A. et al. (2009). *The lessons of Mumbai*. Santa Monica, CA: RAND Corporation.

Resnyansky, L. (2007). *Integration of social sciences in terrorism modelling: Issues, problems and recommendations. Australia: Australian Government, Department of Defence, Command and Control Division, Defence Science and Technology Organisation*. Edinburgh, Australia: DSTO.

Royal Canadian Mounted Police (RCMP). (2009). *Radicalization: A guide for the perplexed*. Ottawa: RCMP National Security Criminal Investigations.

Saucier, G., Akers, L. G., Shen-Miller, S., Knezevic, G., & Stankov, L. (2009). Patterns of thinking in militant extremism. *Perspectives on Psychological Science, 4*(3), 256–271. doi:10.1111/j.1745-6924.2009.01123.x PMID:26158962

Schmid, A. P. (2004). Terrorism: The definitional problem. *Case Western Reserve Journal of International Law, 36*(375).

Schmid, A. P. (Ed.). (2011). *The Routledge handbook of terrorism research*. London: Routledge.

Schmid, A. P. (2013). *Radicalisation, de-radicalisation and counter-radicalisation: A conceptual discussion and literature review*. The Hague: ICCT.

Schmid, A. P., & Jongman, A. J. (1988). *Political Terrorism* (2nd ed.). Oxford, UK: North-Holland.

Schmid, A. P., & Jongman, A. J. (2005). *Political terrorism. A new guide to actors, authors, concepts, data bases, theories, & Literature*. New Brunswick: Transaction Books.

Schneier, B. (2008, April). *Internet censorship*. Retrieved from http://www.schneier.com/blog/archives/2008/04/Internet_censor.html

Schneier, B. (2013). Attacking Tor: How the NSA targets users' online anonymity. *The Guardian*. Retrieved from http://theguardian.com/world/2013/oct/04/tor-attacks-nsa-users-online-anonymity

Sedgwick, M. (2010). The concept of radicalisation as a source of confusion. *Terrorism and Political Violence, 22*(4), 479–494. doi:10.1080/09546553.2010.491009

Shelley, L. I. (2002). The nexus of organised international criminals and terrorism. *International Annals of Criminology*, 1-6.

Shephard, M. (2009). The powerful online voice of jihad. *The Star*. Retrieved from http://www.thestar.com/news/world/article/711964--the-powerful-online-voice-of-jihad

Silber, M., & Bhatt, A. (2007). *Radicalization in the West: The homegrown threat*. New York, NY: New York Police Department.

Sinai, J. (2012). Radicalisation into extremism and terrorism. *Intelligencer: Journal of U.S. Intelligence Studies, 19*(2).

Smith, H. (2009, December 30). Al-Awlaki may be Al-Qaeda recruiter. *CBS News*. Retrieved from http://www.cbsnews.com/8301-503543_162-6039811-503543.html

Starey, T. (2005). Getting the message - A comparative analysis of laws regulating law enforcement agencies' access to stored communications in Australia and the US. *Media and Arts Law Review, 10*(1), 23–55.

Stein, Y. (2011). *Social networks – Terrorism's new marketplace*. Jerusalem, Israel: Genocide Prevention Now.

Stohl, M. (2006). Cyber terrorism: A clear and present danger, the sum of all fears, breaking point or patriot games? *Crime, Law, and Social Change, 46*(4-5), 223–238. doi:10.1007/s10611-007-9061-9

Strohm, C. (2011). Facebook, YouTube aid in Al-Qaida's spread, study says. *National Journal*. Retrieved from http://search.proquest.com.ezp01.library.qut.edu.au/docview/850518421#

Telecommunications (Interception) Amendment Act Cth. (2006). Canberra: Government of Australia.

The, U. S. Created PRISM – it also created the anitdote. (2014, January 23). *Bloomberg Businessweek*. Retrieved from http://www.bloomberg.com/bw/articles/2014-01-23/tor-anonymity-software-vs-dot-the-national-security-agency

Torok, R. (2010). *Make a bomb In your mum's kitchen: Cyber recruiting and socialisation of 'white moors' and home grown jihadists*. Retrieved from http://ro.ecu.edu.au/cgi/viewcontent.cgi?article=1005&context=act

Torproject.org. (2015). *What is the Tor Brower?* Retrieved from https://www.torproject.org/projects/torbrowser.html.en

United States Institute of Peace (USIP). (2012, May 7). *Countering Violent Extremism in Pakistan*. Washington, DC: Author.

US 304th Military Intelligence Battalion. (2008). *Sample overview: alQaida-like mobile discussions & potential creative uses*. Retrieved from http://www.fas.org/irp/eprint/mobile.pdf

van der Zee, B. (2009). Twitter triumphs. *Index on Censorship*, *38*(4), 97–102. doi:10.1080/03064220903392570

Vergani, M., & Zuev, D. (2011). Analysis of YouTube videos used by activists in the Uyghur Nationalist Movement: Combining quantitative and qualitative methods. *Journal of Contemporary China*, *20*(69), 205–229. doi:10.1080/10670564.2011.541628

Victoroff, J. (2005). The mind of the terrorist: A review and critique of psychological approaches. *The Journal of Conflict Resolution*, *49*(1), 3–42. doi:10.1177/0022002704272040

Weimann, G. (2006). *Terror on the Internet: The new arena, the new challenges*. Washington, DC: United States Institute of Peace Press.

What is Metadata? (2015). *Whatis.com*. Retrieved from http://whatis.techtarget.com/defintion/metadata

Wood, D. M. (2006). *A report on the Surveillance Society: For the Information Commissioner. Surveillance Studies Network*. London: Information Commissioner.

Woolley, J. K., Limperos, A. M., & Beth, M. (2010). The 2008 presidential election, 2.0: A content analysis of user-generated political Facebook groups. *Mass Communication & Society*, *13*(5), 631–652. doi:10.1080/15205436.2010.516864

Wright, L. (2006, September 24). *ASIO scans Muslim web surfers*. Retrieved from http://www.news.com.au/national/asio-scans-muslim-web-surfers/story-e6frfkx0-1111112257310

Chapter 13

Towards a Comprehensive Approach to Combating Violent Extremist Ideology in the Digital Space:
The Counter-Ideological Response (CIR) Model

Kumar Ramakrishna
Nanyang Technological University, Singapore

ABSTRACT

Based on the assumption that ideology is the centre of gravity of a violent Islamist terrorist network, this chapter proposes a Counter-Ideological Response (CIR) Model for countering violent extremism (CVE) in Southeast Asia. The Model seeks to gradually diminish the appeal of violent extremist ideology. It comprises of five conceptual Spaces of Sender, Message, Mechanism, Recipient and Context, within which ideology-relevant policy interventions may be attempted, so as to impact the overall reach and appeal of the violent extremist narrative vis-a-vis any countervailing narrative put out against it. The model is applied to the Indonesian CVE milieu in this chapter.

INTRODUCTION

At the end of 2014, an Indonesian militant fighting with the notorious Islamic State in Iraq and Syria (ISIS) in Syria, Abu Jandal al-Yemeni al-Indonesi, posted a video on YouTube. In it, he warned that "the group will slaughter Indonesians soldiers, police or Nahdlatul Ulama (NU) members who oppose the establishment of Sharia law in Indonesia". Abu Jandal directly addressing the chief of the Indonesian armed forces, General Moeldoko, as well as the Indonesian police, the crack police counter-terrorism unit Densus (or Detachment) 88, and Banser, the security wing of the traditionalist and moderate Muslim organisation NU, declared in the four-minute video that:

DOI: 10.4018/978-1-5225-0156-5.ch013

We are awaiting your arrival here (in Syria) … If you're not coming, we will come to you. We will return to Indonesia to enforce Sharia Islam. For those who are against us, we will slaughter each of you one by one. ("Indonesian ISIS Fighter", 2015, para. 4)

Abu Jandal's warning exemplifies the current state of play in the continuing struggle of Southeast Asian states against globalised violent extremism fuelled by the virulent ideology of what has been variously referred to as Al-Qaedaism, Bin Ladenism, Jihadi Islamism or Salafi jihadism – of which ISIS is arguably the latest 'mutation' of the constantly evolving Al-Qaeda 'super-organism' (Ramakrishna, 2015). Central to this struggle has been the Internet, a great force multiplier for social media-savvy militants such as Abu Jandal and his ilk.

While 'hard' measures such as more effective law enforcement and military operations, tighter border and immigration controls, measures to cut terror financing and logistics flows, as well as enhanced intelligence sharing across and within borders remain crucial elements of a systematic grand strategy to deal with an ever-evolving violent extremist threat, a suite of 'softer' tools to complement these hard measures also appear apt. Whilst the elements of a 'soft' approach would include good governance that provides the basic public goods of security, socio-economic welfare and justice, it has been clear for a while now that countering the violent extremist ideology that legitimises the violence of the likes of Abu Jandal and his fellow travellers is also an essential part of the mix. Put another way, quite apart from the oft-discussed measures seeking to 'drain the swamp' of extremism that sustains Islamist terrorism and militancy such as the promotion of good democratic governance, socio-economic stability and growth (Australia's Regional Summit to Counter Violent Extremism, 2015), systematic counter-ideological strategy is needed. While some observers have argued in recent years that ideology is the root of terrorism, others suggest that it is more of an enabler (Ramakrishna, 2015). In any case, dealing with the ideology would have to be a central plank of any grand strategy for neutralising the terrorist threat of the type posed by Abu Jandal.

MAIN FOCUS OF THE CHAPTER

In this respect, this chapter proposes a Counter-Ideological Response (CIR) Model for consideration for possible application and requisite adaptation to the different contexts of countering violent extremism (CVE) in Europe, Southeast Asia, the Iraq/Syria region, and elsewhere[1]. The overall objective of the CIR Model would be to gradually diminish the appeal of online violent extremist ideology. The CIR Model comprises of five conceptual *Spaces* of Sender, Message, Mechanism, Recipient and Context, within which ideology-relevant policy interventions may be attempted. By the latter we mean policy interventions within each Space that impact the overall reach and appeal of the violent extremist narrative vis-a-vis any countervailing narrative put out against it. The chapter will unpack the argument in the following way. First, the role of ideology as an enabler of terrorism will be explored. This will logically lead to the next section which would lay out the need for a structured approach such as the CIR Model to counter violent extremism that animates the likes of Al-Qaeda and its latest, dangerous offshoot, ISIS. The chapter will then proceed to examine each of the five CIR Spaces in three steps. First, the conceptual structure of the Space in question will be elucidated. Second, the policy issue or question driving the relevant intervention in that Space will be examined. Third, examples from the Indonesian milieu will be brought to bear, to illustrate and flesh out the operationalisation of the CIR Model in the Space being discussed.

Issues, Controversies, Problems: Ideology as the Centre of Gravity of Violent Extremist Terrorist Networks

The nineteenth-century Prussian war philosopher Carl von Clausewitz explained that while war is animated at root by the "blind natural force" of "primordial violence, hatred, and enmity", such natural popular passions in practice are channelled in context-specific ways that differ from enemy to enemy into a centre of gravity – "the hub of all power and movement on which everything depends" (von Clausewitz, 1832/1976, pp. 595-596). Hence contingent on the specific situation and enemy, the centre of gravity could range from the enemy government; its armed forces; the armed forces of its most powerful ally; its alliance arrangements, to even enemy leaders and public opinion (von Clausewitz, 1832/1976). Later strategic theorists, taking a leaf from Clausewitz, have offered further refinements about the centre of gravity representing a critical vulnerability (Leonhard, 1991), critical strength (Andersson, 2009), or source of strength or power (Elkus, 2010) within the enemy system. Antulio Echevarria (2002), for his part, persuasively formulates the centre of gravity as a focal point in an enemy system similar to what Clausewitz had in mind:

Everything depends upon keeping the dominant characteristics of both [adversaries] in mind. From these emerge a certain centre of gravity, a focal point (Zentrum) of force and movement, upon which the larger whole depends; and it is against the enemy's centre of gravity that the collective blow of all power must be directed (emphasis mine). (p. 11)

Echevarria (2002) argues that to "find the CoG [centre of gravity] in any particular situation we must look for the thing that is providing a certain centripetal, or centre-seeking, force (as opposed to centrifugal, which is outward-seeking) for the enemy" (p. 11). In other words, the centre of gravity is "the one element within a combatant's entire structure or system that has the necessary centripetal force to hold that structure together"; implying that "a blow directed against a centre of gravity will have the greatest effect" (Lovelace, as cited in Echevarria, 2002, p. iii).

When one discusses violent extremist terrorist networks of global reach, such as Al-Qaeda and increasingly ISIS today, we note that these are not entirely hierarchically centralised entities with well-defined lines of command and control. Hence rather than top-down, rigid strategic control per se, what holds these often disparate, geographically dispersed globalised networks of affiliate regional networks, nationally-based groups – and even individual lone wolves or 'wolf packs' inspired but not necessarily directly instructed by the central Al-Qaeda or ISIS leaderships – is rather the more nebulous but still effectual commodity of strategic influence, via "common and accepted 'stories' and 'narratives'" (Jackson, 2006, p. 244). Such a 'strategic narrative' (Freedman, 2006) is in fact akin to an ideology that offers "interpretive schemata that provide a cognitive structure for comprehending the surrounding environment", and more specifically, explains "causation, evaluating situations", and "prescriptive remedies" (Wiktorowicz, 2005, pp. 15-16).

The action agenda implicit within the ideology is important. While there are several definitions, terrorism scholar Alex Schmid is on the mark in identifying ideology as "patterns of beliefs and expressions that people use to interpret and evaluate the world in a way designed to shape, mobilise, direct, organise and justify certain modes and courses of action" (Schmid, 2011, pp. 643-644). Hence without a guiding and legitimating ideology, violent extremist terrorist networks would lose not merely their systemic coherence but quite possibly their resilience in the face of incessant security force pressure. It is the ideology that thus represents the centre of gravity of the likes of Al-Qaeda, ISIS and their bedfellows in Southeast Asia and elsewhere against which – following Clausewitz – 'the collective blow of all power must be directed' (Clausewitz, 1832/1976).

SOLUTIONS AND RECOMMENDATIONS: THE COUNTER-IDEOLOGICAL RESPONSE (CIR) MODEL

The origins of the CIR Model developed in this chapter go back to an April 2011 interview in Jakarta with General Tito Karnavian, a highly respected former head of the crack Indonesian Detachment 88 counter-terrorism police unit, who later became an influential figure in the National Counter-Terrorism Agency (known as BNPT in its Indonesian acronym). Tito outlined five elements – drawn from his own extensive ground-level experience in countering violent Islamist extremism in Indonesia, coupled with his doctoral research into communications theory and counter-terrorism – that in his judgment were critical in any strategy to 'contain extremism nationally'. As he put it, these elements were the "sender or ideologue"; the "receiver or potential recruit"; the "message or ideology"; the "channel or medium of the message and methodology of spread"; and the "context that affects ease of transmission" (T. Karnavian, personal communication, April 11, 2011). As mentioned, Tito in a sense was building upon research in communications studies (e.g., Littlejohn & Foss, 2008).

In any case, adapting and considerably building upon Tito's perceptive and empirically derived inductive insights, it is proposed here that all actions under what we shall call the CIR Model must occur simultaneously within the five conceptual 'Spaces' of Sender, Message, Mechanism, Recipient and Context. More precisely, as briefly highlighted earlier, it is argued that in order to diminish the appeal of violent extremist ideologies of the type driving Al-Qaeda, ISIS and its affiliated networks and cells in Southeast Asia and beyond, ideology-relevant policy interventions that are customised to each specific geographical domain must be attempted within each of the five CIR Spaces. To elaborate further, within each national or for that matter regional or local milieu as the case may be, policy interventions by the relevant stakeholders must be attempted within the CIR Spaces of Sender, Message, Mechanism, Recipient and Context. These policy interventions across the five Spaces would be unified by one overarching aim: to diminish the overall reach and appeal of the violent extremist narrative vis-a-vis any counter-narrative put out against it. We shall now illustrate how these suggestions can be operationalised with empirical examples drawn from the Indonesian milieu.

Sender

By Sender, we mean the promulgator of the extremist message. The policy question in this Space is: how do we undercut the credibility of the Sender? It is often suggested that the best way to counter violent extremist messages emanating from a Sender like the notorious Al-Qaeda linked Jemaah Islamiyah (JI) spiritual leader and ideologue Abu Bakar Ba'asyir, who recently pledged allegiance to ISIS, is not to censor but rather censure him (Grossman, 1996). In other words, simply allow the free and open marketplace of ideational contestation to demolish and discredit both the Sender and his views. It should be noted that the concept of the marketplace of ideas has a long and distinguished history in liberal political philosophy.

The American political scientist and scholar Cass Sunstein (2009, pp. 149-152) has argued that mature democratic societies need to permit the development of numerous "deliberating enclaves, consisting of groups of like-minded people" to foster "learning, creativity and innovation". He argues that extensive enclave debates involving science, anthropology, literature, gay rights, religion or a wide range of other issues serve two crucial purposes in mature societies. First, such deliberative echo chambers promote fresh ideas and positions that can enrich the intellectual diversity of a society and in particular its 'argument pool', increasing the chances of generating 'sensible solutions' to future societal problems. Without unfettered enclave deliberation, therefore, society as a whole may well be deprived of information it needs to have. Hence, Sunstein (2010) warns against the so-called "chilling effect" on "freely expressed ideas" created by "the prospect of civil or criminal penalties for any speech" (pp. 71-72).

Second, while Sunstein (2009) admits that group polarisation towards extreme positions is well possible within such enclaves, this is generally how people 'become active, politically or otherwise'. Hence, group polarisation promotes active engagement, and "a political process might depend on a situation in which many groups of like-minded types spur their members to seek change" (Sunstein, 2009, p. 151). In his view, if individuals as a result of group polarisation 'become more outraged after talking', the wider society can only benefit. Sunstein (2009) holds that a healthy polity should refrain from too hastily condemning "new points of view without knowing whether the new points of view are better or worse" (p. 154). Importantly, though, Sunstein (2009) notes that a caveat is in order: to prevent widespread enclave deliberation and ensuing group polarisation towards political action from mutating into violence against society, it is necessary that they are not insulated; that is "not walled off from competing views – and that at many points, there is an exchange of views between enclave members and those who disagree with them" (p. 154). Sunstein (2009) is utterly persuaded that it is "total or near-total self-insulation" that often leads to "the highly unfortunate (and sometimes literally deadly) combination of extremism with marginality" (pp. 153-154). Agreeing, Susan Benesch (2013) argues that one important factor contributing to outbreaks of mass out-group violence is 'no alternative sources of information' for a particular audience who is being exposed to a certain ideological narrative.

Sunstein's views on the role of 'enclave deliberation' are pertinent to Indonesia. Tito Karnavian conceded that "extremism is a test of democracy of Indonesia", and represents the "price we have to pay, to allow extremism to grow as part of our freedom". He ventured that "if democracy is really a viable ideology, then why should we care about radical ideologies?" Nevertheless, he was fully alive to the reality that Indonesia's slow and painful transition to a "mature democracy" would entail "lots of problems" being encountered – which has in fact been the case since his comments in April 2011 (T. Karnavian, personal communication, April 11, 2011).

As of May 2015, Indonesia, like other countries throughout the world, has been deeply affected by the ISIS threat. Abu Jandal al-Yemeni al-Indonesi, the Indonesian ISIS fighter that was mentioned at the start of this chapter, is in fact only the tip of the iceberg. ISIS, whose stunning rise to prominence amidst the violent, destabilised chaos of Iraq and Syria in mid-2014, with the declaration by its leader Abu Bakar al-Baghdadi of the Caliphate has had a huge psychological impact not merely in the Middle East but in Southeast Asia as well.

The emergence of ISIS has given a worrying fillip to Southeast Asian, Indonesian-epicentered violent Islamist networks like JI and its offshoots, principally Jemaah Ansharut Tauhid (JAT) and in recent times, the violent Mujahidin Indonesia Timur (MIT) – the East Indonesian Mujahidin movement. For instance, in December 2014 BNPT reported that 514 Indonesians had joined the fighting in Iraq and Syria. It is not just an Indonesian problem either. Reports in early 2015 put the number of Malaysians joining ISIS at approximately 40, with the Philippines is said to have about 200 recruits joining the organisation, although this figure is disputed. Furthermore, in February 2015, it was reported that 110 Australians had travelled to join ISIS of whom 20 have been killed (Brennan, 2015). The concern is that just as with a previous generation of Southeast Asian fighters that returned from the Afghan conflict in the 1980s to form JI, the new generation of ISIS-trained Southeast Asians would set up a similarly dangerous alumni network, ideologically driven and trained to violently subvert their home countries, with the support of self-radicalised ISIS supporters ("Jakarta Slow to Tackle", 2015).

Tito Karnavian's long-held solution to this challenge is that "the only way is to contain and slow down the growth of extremism" (personal communication, April 11, 2011). The question is, how? Certainly, one powerful way the marketplace of ideas can help in this regard is to demolish the credibility of the Sender, by showing up variances between the former's pious rhetoric and his actual deeds. In this regard, the discovery by the U.S. Navy Seal unit of a stash of 'fairly extensive pornographic material' during the assault on Osama bin Laden's Abbotabad, Pakistan hide-out in May 2011 (Hosenball & Zakaria, 2011); as well as a documentary film producer's revelation that the JI Bali bombers Imam Samudra, Mukhlas, and Amrozi – whom he had interviewed before their executions in late 2008 – were all motivated to become martyrs by the prospect of '72 beautiful virgins ready at all times to serve them and give them sexual pleasure', represent nuggets of information that may help tilt the scales in open marketplace contestation (Cassrels, 2011b; Ramakrishna, 2009).

It should be noted however that unfettered marketplace ideational contestation to discredit the violent extremist Sender and his views might not always work. As Sunstein himself suggests, a lot depends on the nature of the deliberative enclave. A group of like-minded individuals' pre-existing attitudes, prejudices and beliefs, coupled with news – especially in the fast-paced Twitter age – that may not necessarily be truthful but certainly engages people's emotional states, is likely to generate social cascade effects and group polarisation toward the 'biased assimilation' of ideas and viewpoints that are threatening to social stability (Sunstein, 2009, 2010). He (2010, pp. 67-70) very importantly admits that there "is simply not enough evidence to justify the conclusion that false rumours on the Internet are adequately countered by the truth"; hence even "when competition among ideas is robust, bad ideas and falsehoods can become widely accepted". In the final analysis, therefore, Sunstein (2010) is compelled to concede that despite the fact that the "marketplace of ideas" has long played a "central role" in "democratic politics and constitutional law", he feels that limits on free speech – especially in the digital age – are justified (pp. 67-70). He contends that the chilling effect 'serves to reduce damaging and destructive falsehoods' that the marketplace often fails to effectively discredit and demolish. Thus what societies really need is "not the absence of 'chill,' but an optimal level" (Sunstein, 2010, p. 72).

Sunstein's remarks on the need for an optimal level of chill have certainly been pertinent in Indonesia's milieu for a number of years. In March 2011, the Setara Institute for Peace and Democracy, an Indonesian non-governmental organisation (NGO) promoting religious tolerance, called for 'radical preachers' to be banned from leading Friday prayers in some outlying districts (Nazeer, 2011a). In January 2012, the International Crisis Group also called for Jakarta to "develop a strategy, consistent with democratic values, for countering clerics who use no violence themselves but preach that it is permissible to shed the blood" of government officials and police (International Crisis Group [ICG], 2012, p. 1). At the time of writing, commentators continue to urge Jakarta to "bring hate speech within the purview of anti-terror legislation" (Pereira, 2015, para. 14).

Certainly, one useful ideology-relevant policy intervention in the Sender space would be to better drill down and identify the points, at which the Sender's pronouncements tip over into speech that clearly have the potential to incite inter-group violence and foster radicalisation into violent extremism. In this connection, Arizona State University's Centre for Strategic Communication (CSC) has suggested a four-point scale to evaluate a Sender and his pronouncements: (1) dialogue on religious differences; (2) unilateral condemnation of others' belief systems; (3) dehumanisation and demonization of certain groups with an implicit message of violence; and (4) explicit, provocative messages of violence. The CSC argues that points (1) and (2) should be considered valid criticisms of other belief systems consistent with free speech, while points (3) and (4) should really be considered as hate speech, as they clearly encourage violence against certain groups. Indonesian observers have recently suggested that such a four-point scale may have utility in the Indonesian milieu (Javadi, 2015).

Applying the CSC four-point scale to actual incidents illustrates its potential utility as an ideology-relevant policy intervention in the Sender space. That is, it may help policymakers evaluate when to 'throw the book' at a Sender, thereby diminishing the overall credibility and reach of that Sender as well as his message. For instance, on October 22, 2007, Abu Bakar Ba'asyir addressed a crowd of young people in a meeting in East Java, organised by the Persatuan Pemuda Islam Pantura or Java North Coast Islamic Youth Group. While Ba'asyir urged Muslims in Indonesia to "reject the laws of the nation's parliament" because "following state laws that contradicted Islamic Shariah law was an act of blasphemy", he directly called upon young Javanese youth to 'just beat up' foreigners who dared to venture into East Java and 'not tolerate them' (Robinson, 2008, para. 22). Moreover Ba'asyir dehumanised non-Muslim tourists in Bali, dismissing them as "worms, snakes, maggots" – that is, "animals that crawl" (Robinson, 2008, para. 13). If the CSC four-point scale were applied in this particular case as a litmus test of the intent of Ba'asyir as the Sender, it does seem that he would be prosecuted – in the process diminishing the reach of his virulent ideological narrative. It should be reiterated that linguistic dehumanisation – deliberately describing the victims-to-be as other than human, e.g., as vermin, pests, insects or animals – is increasingly acknowledged as a rhetorical hallmark of incitement to genocide, and to violence, since it dehumanises the victim or victims-to-be (Benesch, 2013).

Message

In the Message space of the CIR Model, the key policy question is: What makes a counter-narrative message 'sticky' or memorable? In a sense, there are two requirements in this Space. The first, most immediate objective is to simply and directly refute the violent extremist Sender and his own message. In the Indonesian case, it is well known for instance amongst JI activists that the notion of jihad was an individual obligation – betraying the ideological influence of Al-Qaeda. This notion has however been directly debunked by counter-messaging. For instance, the Indonesian Acehnese activist Al-Chaidar, a spokesperson for the old Darul Islam separatist movement that has been in a sense the 'tree trunk' from which the later 'branches' of JI and JAT emerged, insisted that jihad in Indonesia can only be declared by a duly constituted authority, such as the Darul Islam Imam (personal communication, January 8, 2006).

Similarly, the JI operative Imam Samudra's book-length ideological justification for the Bali bombing of October 2002 was subsequently refuted in a book by the Singaporean Muslim scholar Muhammad Haniff Hassan (Hassan, 2006). In addition, the son of the iconic Darul Islam leader S.M. Kartosoewirjo has spoken out, arguing that Darul Islam historically was relatively legitimate as his father was protecting the people; "but today they are killing civilians and Muslims in the name of jihad, and this is wrong" (T. Karnavian, personal communication, April 11, 2011).

In order for such counter-narrative messaging to have audience impact, though, they need to fulfil a second requirement in the Message space: they have to be what Malcolm Gladwell (2004, p. 25) has called "sticky", where the "presentation and structuring of information" can "make a big difference in how much of an impact" they make. The stickiness of a counter-narrative in relation to extremist ideological appeals – particularly those of ISIS, that have proven to be very well packaged and professionally done – is a crucial ideology-relevant policy intervention in the Message space that can reduce the appeal and reach of the violent Islamist[2] meme[3]. But what makes a counter-narrative sticky?

Researchers Chip and Dan Heath (2008, pp. 14-18) identify six factors that help in this regard. First, *simplicity* – the content of the message must be both simple and profound, so that it can be easily recalled, like a good meme. Second, *unexpectedness* – that message must contain counter-intuitive elements that snare attention. Third, *concreteness* – "naturally sticky ideas", the Heaths argue, "are full of concrete images – ice-filled bathtubs, apples with razors – because our brains are wired to remember concrete data". Fourth, *credibility* – "sticky ideas", the Heaths posit, "have to carry their own credentials" and need to be believable to the target audience. Fifth, *emotion* – the message must appeal viscerally to the audience. Sixth and finally, *stories* – research indicates that audiences are better able to recall messages expressed in memorable stories. Certainly, there are many moderate Muslim clerics in Indonesia who are capable of spinning sticky messages that in some ways serve as the most basic form of religious ballast against the pull of violent Islamism. In rural and urban village communities in West Java, for example, some preachers – known locally as *da'i, muballigh or pendakwah* – enjoy significant regional followings. This is because of the stickiness of their messages, which emphasise 'allegories and narrative accounts created out of daily experience' instead of abstract and 'broader social questions'. One observer recounts in this regard the impact of one such da'i, Kiai Al-Jauhari:

I have often seen audiences transfixed by Al-Jauhari's allegories and narrative accounts. He transforms Islamic messages into narrations made up of highly recognisable material, with no shortage of humour added to the mix. People are engrossed as he unfolds his creations. I have frequently asked village and mosque officials why they engage Al-Jauhari ... The most common answer is that he is able to hold people's attention for long periods of time. (Millie, 2008, pp. 82, 91-92)

Mechanism

Susan Benesch (2013) has argued that the 'means of transmission' of a narrative could well 'reinforce its capacity to persuade'. The policy question in this space therefore is: What mechanism – comprising some combination or otherwise of interlocutors, processes and technological tools – is best able to diminish the reach and appeal of the violent Islamist ideological meme, whilst at the same time expediting the dissemination of more salutary and 'sticky' counter-narratives to key target audiences? In the Indonesian case, the moderate religious scholars and teachers – the *ulama* – play a central role. Properly qualified traditionalist and modernist ulama are well positioned to lay out the theological baseline against which the highly selective interpretation of texts by Islamist ideologues can be discerned and exposed (El-Fadl, 2005).

There are limitations though. The vocal Indonesian activist and former Darul Islam member Noor Huda Ismail held that while renowned progressive Indonesian Muslim scholars are "good for youth" as well as large moderate mass civil society organisations such as the Muslim traditionalist Nahdlatul Ulama (NU) and the modernist Muhammadiyah, they tend to have little impact on "those who come from Darul Islam" (personal communication, April 6, 2011). Al-Chaidar (personal communication, January 8, 2006) for his part went even further, arguing that moderate ulama are "not effective at all". Al-Chaidar averred that the large moderate Muslim civil society organisations in Indonesia – Muhammadiyah and NU – were even "worse than the Christians" as they were regarded in radical Islamist circles as *munafiqun*, or hypocrites, who have deviated from "true Islam". To Noor Huda Ismail, for "DI, former DI members are better, who left and did different work" (personal communication, April 6, 2011).

Choice of audience-specific interlocutor aside, it appears that in the Indonesian milieu, moderated intra-faith debates, rather than open-ended dialogue per se, are useful elements of a comprehensive ideology-relevant policy intervention in the Mechanism space. In this regard, Tito Karnavian (personal communication, April 11, 2011) argued that "for the detainees", there should be much moderated dialogue and ideological contestation "between nominals, moderates, traditionalists, Salafis, let them discuss and debate". The progressive Muslim scholar Jamhari Makruf (personal communication, April 5, 2011) agreed, asserting that it is vital "to get somebody who disagrees with you, so there is quarrel or debate". Jamhari revealed he had actually tried this concept out at his university – the Universitas Islam Negeri (UIN) Syarif Hidayatullah – a couple of times previously, fostering a 'huge debate' between the Jaringan Islam Liberal (JIL or Liberal Islam Network) and Front Pembela Islam (FPI or Islamic Defenders front). When Jamhari had invited the Islamists to argue why the idea of an Islamic State in Indonesia was desirable, he at the same time ensured that Catholic speakers were present to oppose the Islamists' motion. This had the effect of compelling the Islamists to 'think about how to solve' the problem so as to win broader-based support for their platform. As Tito Karnavian (personal communication, April 11, 2011) noted, "it is important to challenge the concepts of these people".

A third and vitally important element of a comprehensive ideology-relevant policy intervention in the Mechanism space is of course the Internet – comprising websites, chatrooms, and the by-now ubiquitous social media platforms of Twitter, Facebook and YouTube. It is known for instance that ISIS has 500 to 2,000 followers "who tweet extremist messages and update their Facebook pages around the clock" (Temple-Raston, 2015, para. 3). Reports indicate that the "average ISIS-supporting account has about a thousand followers, which gives the group substantial reach" (Temple-Raston, 2015, para. 3). Little wonder therefore that the ISIS social media onslaught has found fallow soil in Indonesia. Twitter, for example, has long been exploited by 'Net-savvy radicals' to 'lobby for their causes' (Nazeer, 2011a). The radical Islamist organisation JAT itself uses several Internet and social networking sites to engage with the public and its material has also been uploaded on YouTube (ICG, 2011). It is worth remembering as well that more than a quarter of the Indonesia's 240 million people are on Facebook, "thanks in large part to cheap and fast Internet-capable phones", hence young people have long been susceptible to indoctrination and recruitment via social media by violent Islamists (Karmini, 2013, para. 6). Recent surveys suggest that in the Asia Pacific region, as of March 2015, other social media platforms such as Whatsapp, Instagram, Skype, Line and Snapchat have also gained traction with regional audiences and are hence possible platforms for exploitation by violent Islamist ideologues (Using Social Media to Communicate against Violent Extremism, 2015).

Tito Karnavian (personal communication, April 11, 2011) however opined that one must not overplay the impact of the new social media and that face-to-face contact is a more important factor for radicalising young people in the Indonesian milieu; the "final touch is the personal touch". Sidney Jones (as cited in Karmini, 2013) broadly agrees, pointing out that "although terrorists groups' Internet use is growing, they still do most of their recruiting face-to-face at traditional places such as prayer meetings" (para. 27). Noor Huda Ismail (personal communication, April 6, 2011) provided additional perspective, asserting that "Facebook, Internet, Twitter, and Blackberry" were more useful for information dissemination rather than indoctrination per se. As he put it: "You can post 'a Christian group is coming to this area, please be on the alert'". Like Tito and Jones, Huda was of the opinion that in the final analysis, "follow-up via personal face-to-face contact is crucial".

Last but not least, additional creative elements of a comprehensive ideology-relevant policy intervention in the Mechanism space include mass-market, easy-to-read and glossy publications, such as the 137-page comic *I Found the Meaning of Jihad*, chronicling the well-known life story of the former JI leader Nasir Abbas (McDowell, 2011), and award-winning locally-produced documentaries such as *Prison and Paradise*, which chronicles the children of the JI perpetrators of the October 2002 Bali bombings – as well as their victims (Nurhayati 2011). To reiterate, the key in the Mechanism space is to ask: what combination or otherwise of interlocutors, processes and technological tools – is best able to diminish the reach and appeal of the violent Islamist ideological meme, whilst at the same time expediting the dissemination of more salutary and 'sticky' counter-narratives to key target audiences?

Recipient

In the Recipient space, one needs to make a distinction between two audiences: the individual militant and the wider community from which the former emerge. The policy question in this space is: how can the appeal and reach of the violent Islamist meme be neutered for each audience?

The Individual Militant

The pertinent issue when one discusses individual militants is whether the appropriate policy is disengagement or de-radicalisation. By disengagement, following terrorism scholar John Horgan (2008), we mean that a militant individual may disengage physically from terrorist activity – without necessarily evincing a "concomitant change or reduction in ideological support" or displaying full autonomy from the "social and ideological control that the particular ideology exerts on the individual" (para. 16). On the other hand, Omar Ashour (2009, pp. 5-6) argues that "comprehensive de-radicalisation" occurs when an individual "de-legitimises the use of violent methods to achieve political goals, while also moving towards an acceptance of gradual social, political and economic changes within a pluralist context". Noor Huda Ismail (personal communication, April 6, 2011) – who has had extensive engagement with JI militant detainees past and present – observed that comprehensive de-radicalisation is "unrealistic" and the "best way is to disengage".

In other words, the aim should not be to 'stop thinking radically' but rather 'stop violence but remain in the group'. He recalled that after the October 2002 Bali bombings, most members had been opposed to the violence but had not wanted to leave JI as that would have meant losing everything that the in-group has provided for its human constituents from time immemorial – their community, security, meaning, identity. After all, as Noor Huda Ismail explained, the "group provides you with a job, a wife, so if you leave the group", you would be have "to deal with the secular system and a very difficult real world" (personal communication, April 6, 2011). The implication is that even if an individual militant, past or present detainee may well disagree with the violence, he would remain in the group.

Broadly concurring, Tito Karnavian (personal communication, April 11, 2011) for his part recalled that the New Order regime (1966-1998) of former President Soeharto had tried to tolerate the Darul Islam separatist movement and had found it "quite hard to change the mindset", but had "hoped that they will disengage the tactics of violence". Such an approach had worked to an extent, but was unable to address "the entire problem, so it was just a matter of time and opportunity to trigger and resurface". While Tito accepted that comprehensive de-radicalisation was attractive, he conceded that it was "very difficult to do in Indonesia", and hence Tito's analysis was that "disengagement is the best option here". Tito added that incarcerated JI leaders had been involved in "frank exchange" with the authorities on many occasions and had bluntly declared that it was "impossible to change the mindset", and that "Islamic shariah – whether or not it is utopian – we sacrifice for that". The curt Indonesian police response had been fine, but "please do not use violence or else government will hit you, which would be a setback for your network".

In sum, Noor Huda Ismail (personal communication, April 6, 2011) making an intriguing reference to the 2010 animated movie *How to Train Your Dragon*, likened many present and past individual JI militant detainees as "dragons" within which a violent potential will always exist. One could "use them for certain purposes", and they "won't cheat you in terms of money, as they are religious". While "outside the movement", Huda averred "people will cheat you, but not these guys, as they are trustworthy". However, there was one crucial caveat: if interlocutors discoursed about jihad, a 'shortcut' will happen and that will "get them going down the wrong route". Huda has tried to disengage his 'dragons' by immersing them in legitimate business activities.

One good example has been former JI militant Yusuf alias Mahmudi Haryono, who was jailed for five years for his involvement in the August 2003 Marriott hotel bombing by a JI splinter cell. Yusuf, who had received weapons and explosives training in Mindanao, southern Philippines, conceded in May 2011 that "jihad is still my obligation", especially in conflict areas "in Indonesia or anywhere else in the world between Muslims and non-Muslims" (N. H. Ismail, personal communication, April 6, 2011). Nevertheless, with Huda's assistance, Yusuf now runs a literary café in Semarang, Central Java, and this task has afforded him an alternate notion of "meaning in his life" (Cassrels, 2011a, para. 3). Apart from the Huda's approach of keeping individual 'dragons' busy with business activities, another practical strategy for ameliorating the appeal of the violent Islamist ideological meme is training them to better manage their emotional impulses. In this connection, the United States based 'Search for Common Ground' has worked with local NGOs to run conflict resolution role-playing exercises in Indonesian prisons, aimed at "teaching participants to respect differences and make positive choices" (Schonhardt, 2010, para. 4).

The Wider Community

Tito Karnavian (personal communication, April 11, 2011) emphasised that individual militants aside, "protecting and immunising" the wider community against the virulent ideological "virus" of violent Islamism is also very important. Ideology-relevant policy interventions in this portion of the Recipient space must involve public education programs promoting the inculcation of critical thinking skills and in particular, given the increasing salience of the Internet, digital literacy. The British think tank Demos argues that "rather than telling people what to think, it is better to teach them how to think", by encouraging "young people to critically assess propaganda, lies and half-truths themselves" (Bartlett & Miller, 2010, p. 38). The Demos study, noting how the Internet "has become the primary source of information for the majority of young people in the UK today", calls for enhanced "digital literacy" so as to enable young people to "recognise the difference between, for example, trustworthy sources of information and user generated content" (pp. 38-9).

Certainly, the University of Indonesia researcher Yon Machmudi (as cited in Afrida, 2011) complained that university students do not try to critically evaluate the content of what is online. More basically, students do not compare and contrast information sources, accepting only one point of view. As seen, given that ISIS makes extensive use of the Internet to disseminate its extremist propaganda, the relative lack of digital literacy of Indonesian young people should be a concern. Noor Huda Ismail (as cited in Sagita, 2011) thus insists that "we need to teach people to have critical thinking, teach them to ask questions" (para. 10). Huda adds elsewhere that the "poorly developed critical thinking skills" of the young men of the Tim Ightiyalat terrorist cell associated with JI had made it "easy for a charismatic figure to brainwash them" (as cited in Arnaz & Sianipar, 2011, para. 7). Tito Karnavian (personal communication, April 11, 2011) likewise informed the author that he favours "educational methods to counter or neutralise extremist initiatives", targeting "students of universities prone to infiltration of their campus groups". Tito opined that Indonesian students could be exposed to *inter alia*, the concepts of "pluralism" and "moderate Islam", the "history of Islam in Indonesia" and the well-known historical state ideology of *Pancasila* – with the ultimate objective of "encouraging a pluralistic mindset". Tito reckoned that once "the people have this, you are protecting them from the spread of the extremist ideology".

From a longer-term perspective, though, ideology-relevant policy interventions in the Recipient space involving the wider community, must involve structural, formal educational reforms. One element of this could be the wider introduction of secular humanities education which appears to have had some impact in 'immunising' young people against the appeals of violent extremist ideology. Khaled Abou El-Fadl (2005) has argued that Islamist 'puritans' seek 'modernism' rather than the cultural accoutrements of 'modernity', derided as Western and corrupt. He opined that "the majority" of the "puritan leadership comprised of people who studied the physical sciences, such as medicine, engineering, and computer science", and hence "anchor themselves in the objectivity and certitude that comes from empiricism" (p. 99). Such training rather unhelpfully predisposes them toward what Malise Ruthven (2002, p. 103) calls "mono-dimensional or literalist readings of scripture", in contrast with their "counterparts in the arts and humanities whose training requires them to approach texts multi-dimensionally, exploring contradictions and ambiguities". Interestingly, El-Fadl (2005) asserts that "self-proclaimed experts" in the shape of 'engineers, medical doctors, and physical scientists', including the 'leaders' of the "Muslim Brotherhood and al-Qa'ida", have sought to make authoritative interpretations on Islamic Law – despite the fact that they are generally "unfamiliar with the precedents and accomplishments of past generations" of Islamic scholars in developing Islamic jurisprudence (pp. 38-39).

In the Indonesian milieu, progressive Muslim scholar Jamhari Makruf (personal communication, April 5, 2011) had similarly observed that "those who study science have a greater tendency to be radical", influenced by the "one-track mind of science". He asserts – perhaps counter-intuitively – that while students on Islamic campuses have a relatively stronger tradition of debate, exposure to various perspectives such as discourse analysis and critical theory, and study the four schools of Islamic *fiqh* or jurisprudence, "it is very easy" on the other hand "to manipulate science students". Jamhari assessed that "those who study science, engineers, and architects", tend to "think 2×2 is 4, no debate at all". This mental habit, Jamhari suggests, is generally why when these young people "receive doctrine or teaching from teachers or friends" – rather than question it – "they accept it". Noor Huda Ismail (personal communication, April 6, 2011) likewise pointed out that "most of the jihadis" hailed from secular and science/technical backgrounds, and that their training had reinforced a tendency "to think in black and white" and to be "exact and precise". While the social science people had "no fixed answer" on how to get to Heaven, the "science guys", Huda mused, always tended to argue that they "must use one route'. Huda recalled in this respect that the JI militants convicted for the October 2002 Bali bombing, Imam Samudra and Mukhlas, were "very good in maths".

Having said that, it should be cautioned that even a stronger formal exposure to Islamic theology and humanities subjects on well recognised Islamic university campuses in Indonesia is increasingly – and worryingly – less effective in erecting mental barriers against violent extremist ideologies like those animating ISIS. Jamhari's own university, a genuinely prestigious Islamic institution of higher learning which emphasises a theologically sophisticated and liberal study of Islam, has seen at least six of its current and former students arrested on terrorism charges since 2010 (personal communication, April 5, 2011). These developments prompted the UIN Rector, the progressive Muslim scholar Komarudin Hidayat, to concede that his theologically sophisticated university was not entirely immune to extremist ideology after all. Tellingly, one UIN student suggested in April 2011 that extremism was growing because of a decline in academic standards of debate and critical discussion. He noted that his seniors told him that "there used to be much more discussions on the campus in the early 2000s" but nowadays "the students are more study-oriented" and "they only come to study and then go home" ("Islamic Radicalism Thriving", 2011, para. 11).

Moreover, deeper structural issues appear to have thickened the plot. Islamic tertiary institutions like UIN have found that the funding they receive annually from the Ministry of Religious Affairs is insufficient to keep operating, compelling them to approach the Education Ministry for top-up grants. While such grants have been forthcoming, there are strings attached in the form of the compulsory addition of more non-Islamic subjects into the curriculum. Certainly, on the surface this may actually be regarded as progressive attempts at modernising the curriculum. The unintended real-world consequence has been a neglect of and thus decline in the standards of the core Islamic studies teaching agenda.

In this respect, Dina Afrianty (2012) of the Center for the Study of Islam and Society at UIN has observed that increasingly undergraduates of UIN or similar institutions lack religious boarding school (*pesantren*) backgrounds, which means that coupled with the gradual decline in Islamic studies standards at university level, the net effect is that they possess increasingly weaker theological grounding. They are – ironically – thus gradually converging with their counterparts at secular institutions like University of Indonesia and the Bandung Institute of Technology in terms of lack of the systematic religious knowledge needed to reduce susceptibility to the sophisticated discourses of extremist ideologues. In sum, a better balance between technical and humanities education as well as the preservation of the traditionally high standards of Islamic education on relevant Indonesian university campuses, appear to be part of the mix of ideology-relevant policy interventions aimed at reducing the cognitive vulnerability of the wider community to the violent Islamist meme.

Context

The final space of the CIR Model is Context. This refers to environmental factors that enhance the credibility of the counter-narrative to the target audience whilst simultaneously diminishing that of the violent Islamist meme to the same audience. Susan Benesch in her recent important work on dangerous speech concurs that the context of such inflammatory rhetoric matters, arguing that factors such as "weak democratic structures and rule of law, and structural inequalities and discrimination against a group or groups", all constitute "risk factors for mass violence" (Benesch, 2013, p. 5). In this connection, the ideology-relevant policy question in this space is: what can be done to promote an environmental envelope that will enhance the believability and stickiness of the counter-narrative online message while at the same time diminishing that of the extremist online narrative? Three policy postures appear pertinent: diminishing the opportunity for terrorist groups to engage in violence; good socio-economic governance; and the calibrated use of force against terrorist networks.

Diminishing the Opportunity to be Violent

First and foremost, diminishing the opportunity for terrorists to engage in violence in the first place helps foster an environmental envelope that promotes widespread acceptance of a norm for moderation and against violent extremism. Steps in this regard have certainly been taken in the Indonesian milieu: in July 2010 under Presidential Regulation Number 46 of 2010, the National Counter-Terrorism Agency or BNPT was set up, with the aim of formulating

[P]olicy, strategy and national programs in the area of counter-terrorism; co-ordinate relevant government agencies in implementation and implementing policies in counter-terrorism; and establish Task Forces comprising elements from relevant government agencies in accordance with their respective responsibility, function and authority. (Mbai, 2010)

While BNPT absorbed the National Police (POLRI) Special Detachment 88 unit, it took care to wisely preserve the latter's lead role in investigating and arresting terrorists. Moreover, BNPT is empowered to function as a "terrorist crisis centre" in the event of a terror attack, and would assist the President in "formulating policy and taking the necessary operational steps" to deal with the incident and its aftermath (Mbai, 2010). BNPT can, through the President, request for Indonesian armed forces (Tentera Negara Indonesia or TNI) assistance in dealing with terrorism threats, should it be assessed that the "situation is beyond police capacity" (Mbai, 2010).

BNPT seeks to foster a genuine "'whole-of-government' approach to crack down on the spread of radical ideology and brewing relationships between different cells" (Lee, 2011). In this respect Tito Karnavian asserted in August 2011 that while Detachment 88 "was more than capable of arresting those who were plotting attacks", he emphasised that "neutralising radical ideology, countering its spread through Internet and printed publications" required the legally mandated contributions of "other agencies" (as cited in Lee, 2011). A central administrative challenge in this connection facing BNPT remains the prison system. Tito acknowledged that there "are many weaknesses in our prison system in terms of dealing with terrorism", and that "prisons remain ineffective in countering terrorist indoctrination" (as cited in Lee, 2011). A central challenge has been the significant number of terrorist recidivists. For example, of 100 suspected terrorists arrested in 2010 alone, "more than a dozen were repeat offenders" (Arnaz, 2011, para. 8). One joint Australian-Singaporean study noted that Indonesian "prisons provide opportunities for terrorist convicts to establish new networks" (Ungerer, 2011, p. 14). For example, detainees such as Ramli alias Iqbal Husaini ran a small business with other inmates, renting and selling mobile phones, top-up vouchers and cigarettes, whilst Solahudin made numerous friends because he was a much sought-after *tukang bekam* (traditional massage cupping therapist). According to the study, relationships formed during the period of prison incarceration tend to foster amongst detainees "a greater sense of solidarity, or even responsibility, towards one another" (Ungerer, 2011, p. 14).

A strong contributing factor to this situation is overcrowding. For instance, Porong prison, near Surabaya, in June 2011 had 27 terrorist detainees on its books. While the prison is designed to hold 1,000 inmates, it had 1,327 in June 2011, and its Block F that was supposedly designated only for terrorist detainees, also had to accommodate 50 other regular detainees because of lack of space. The resulting mixing of regular detainees with terrorist inmates, through such seemingly innocuous activities as sports or even Islam lessons, appears to have had the pernicious effect of fostering 'radicalism' amongst ordinary detainees. The latter were suitably awestruck by the "terrorists' piety and dangerous reputations", and were soon seen to have "changed their appearance, lengthening their hair and beards in imitation of the militants" (Karmini, 2011, para. 32). A related issue is the unimpressive career prospects of prison officers. Researcher Taufik Andrie observed that a massive 70 percent of prison guards would like to move on to better jobs (personal communication, October 25, 2011). It is thus no surprise that such under-motivated prison personnel have been prone to corruption and manipulation by incarcerated militants. For instance convicted JI Bali bomber Imam Samudra had managed to secure the use of a mobile phone for communication with his followers outside his prison (Forbes, 2006).

Of no less importance has been the lack of a systematic program of post-release aftercare. Brigadier-General Suryadarma Salim (as cited in Arnaz, 2011), a former Detachment 88 commander, admitted that "what we must do is open a line of communication with the former convicts, to build a solid foundation of mutual trust" (para. 12). Without a durable system of communication between "former inmates and law enforcement officers", it was not a surprise therefore that "convicted terrorists would relapse into their old ways after being released" (Arnaz, 2011, para. 9). For his part, Noor Huda Ismail (as cited in Sagita, 2011) concurred, pointing out that a former detainee whom he was engaged with had to report to the police regularly, but instead of "guidance" or "discussions" to help him "return to mainstream beliefs," all he did was "sign a document" (para. 2-3). In the final assessment therefore, a genuinely effective whole-of-government approach in which the police better coordinates 'rehabilitation efforts with the prison service' is needed. Observers have assessed in general "this has been the weakest leg of the Indonesian counter-terrorism system" (Ungerer, 2011, p. 19).

Reducing the opportunity to become violent – as part of an ideology-relevant policy intervention seeking to create an environmental envelope that diminishes the appeal of violent Islamism whilst promoting moderation – also requires a stronger line against terrorist miscreants. Former BNPT chief Ansyaad Mbai in this regard complained to the Indonesian House of Representatives in April 2011 that the 'country's poor legal system' had helped make Indonesia a 'haven for terrorists'. Mbai opined that law enforcers and intelligence personnel needed to be empowered to 'detain groups under suspicion of planning terrorist acts', though he was careful to emphasise he did not have in mind new legislation in the vein of the Soeharto New Order regime's draconian anti-subversion laws. In any case, Mbai insisted on "tougher sentences for terrorists to keep them in prison longer", as "when they are in prison, they can't attack" (as cited in Sihaloho, 2011). Certainly, radical groups have become emboldened by their apparent ability to 'get away with little or no punishment' for actions like 'raiding stalls selling alcoholic beverages and killing Ahmadiyah sect members'. This has prompted moderate leaders such as Syafi'i Anwar of the International Center for Islam and Pluralism to lament "the authorities' weak response" to such "extreme acts that draw media coverage" (Nazeer, 2011b, para. 23).

While there is much scope for improvement, one area in which the Indonesian authorities do seem to have made progress in diminishing the opportunity for terrorist groups to engage in violence – and thereby fostering an environmental envelope that mediates against the appeal of extremist ideology – is in the transnational crime-terrorism nexus. In this regard Sidney Jones (as cited in de Borchgrave, Sanderson,

& Gordon, 2009, pp. 46-47) has pointed out that "when jihadis move back and forth between Indonesia, Malaysia and the Philippines, they make occasional use of the same boatmen used by undocumented migrants", and that "some of the weapons obtained" for use in the Poso troubles had been secured from "a criminal gun mafia based in Mindanao". In light of this, it was particularly significant that in November 2011 Kuala Lumpur announced that it had detained under its previous Internal Security Act more than ten men associated with the Indonesian Kalimantan-based Abu Umar network. The arrested militants – both Indonesian and Filipinos – were arrested in Sabah State on the island of Borneo for smuggling arms from Mindanao as well as sourcing local Malaysians for training in unnamed 'neighbouring countries' ("Malaysia Detains More", 2011). Abu Umar alias Zulfikar is apparently a Darul Islam member who had trained in Mindanao in 1998, and had been implicated in violence in Jakarta, Ambon and Poso. Significantly, Abu Umar had also been fingered for 'facilitating the crossing' of JI members 'from Indonesia to Malaysia and Mindanao', and was picked up together with other cell members by the Indonesian police in July 2011. Apparently, he was also plotting an attack on the Singaporean embassy in Jakarta, because of the former's close ties with the State of Israel (Soeriaatmadja & Lee, 2011).

Good Governance, Societies and Homes

While diminishing the opportunity for terrorist groups to engage in violence can be considered as a 'negative' means of fostering an environmental envelope that promotes moderation at the expense of the violent Islamist meme, this can be balanced by more 'positive' and proactive, ideology-relevant policy measures. Foundationally, it is increasingly recognised that good governance and stable economies lay the foundation for strong families – with strong parent-child dyads at their core – and this in turn helps foster healthy and normal ego and intellectual development in youth (Jones, 2008).

The psychoanalyst Donald Winnicott (2006, pp. 148-149) has argued in this regard for the importance of "ordinary good homes" in fostering the development of emotionally well-adjusted citizens. Such citizens would *inter alia*, be expected to navigate the adolescent journey from emotional dependence on parents and seniors to mature adult independence in the context of a democratic society – with its attendant requirements for peaceful compromise across a range of issue areas between different interest groups. In like vein, Erik Erikson (1994) has pointed out that the emotionally integrated young person should display wholeness, in which "a sound, organic, progressive mutuality" exists "between diversified functions and parts within an entirety, the boundaries of which are open and fluid"; in contrast to the affectively dysregulated religious extremist who achieves only a totalism "in which an absolute boundary is emphasised" (pp. 80-81).

In Indonesia, it is well apparent that the acute shortage of Winnicott's ordinary good homes plays an important role in the 'religious radicalisation of many individuals'. A 2011 study of 32 Indonesian militants observed that "close to one-third" had "familial or marriage ties to other known extremists and militants" (Ungerer, 2011, p. 9). For instance, JI militant Solahuddin and his brothers represented their family's third generation of militants. Their grandfather had fought the Dutch whilst their father had been a Darul Islam member implicated in a 1957 plot to assassinate then-President Soekarno. Solahuddin's father, Ahmad Kandai, had taken personal charge of "their religious education", enrolling them in "schools largely run by his fellow Darul Islam members" and ultimately raising "them to observe an Islam that wasn't only deeply political but anti-establishment as well" (Ungerer, 2011, p. 9). As Solahuddin and his brothers were "constantly exposed to the militant Islamist ideology of their father and his peers" growing up, they "naturally accepted that using force was necessary to uphold the religion"

(p. 9). In a similar vein, Ervin Staub (2005, p. 76) insisted that there is such a thing as good societies in which, apart from programs to address the poverty that "creates stress and negatively affects parenting", good governance also actively shapes "cultural and societal institutions" – the aforementioned ordinary good homes for example – "in a manner that helps adults and children fulfil their needs in constructive ways and uses the resulting potential and inclinations to further develop the values and orientations that promote goodness"; rather than out-group "devaluation" and "discrimination".

Likewise, Ozerdem and Podder (2011, p. 71) argue that the "preventive capacity of communities is central to discouraging recruitment into violent extremism". Wills and Resko (2005, pp. 419-436) meanwhile emphasise that stable and positive family environments help "build commitment to mainstream values in the larger social system", and stress the importance of "social policies that are 'friendly' toward children and families" with a view to render it easier for "parents to act supportively". This is needed to generate salutary 'long-range effects in terms of prosocial behaviour' in their children – who will after all be society's future adults. Thus governance and economics do matter a great deal.

Based on a poverty measure of USD$ 2 a day, more than 100 million Indonesians would be considered poor, while the richest 40 Indonesians own as much as the poorest 60 million (de Vries, 2011). In light of this, it should be kept in mind that many Indonesian militants remain essentially 'part-time jihadis' who while occasionally participating in violent activities, still need to make a living for themselves and their families. Thus keeping such individuals "engaged in productive economic activities through employment programs and skills retraining" is an important aspect of their effective disengagement from violence (Ungerer, 2011, p. 18). Noor Huda Ismail in this respect has set former detainees up in enterprises such as 'prawn farming and restaurants' to keep them busy and in particular, isolated from their old terror networks (as cited in Cassrels, 2011a).

Calibrated Use of Force

A final but utterly important ideology-relevant policy intervention that sustains an environmental envelope hostile to violent extremist appeals is the calibrated use of force by law enforcement and counterterrorist agencies. Sulastri Osman (2013) in this connection has observed that what draws together both non-violent activists and even violent extremists at funerals of slain terrorists is a more or less generally shared perception that Muslims in Indonesia remain under physical threat from what is in recent times perceived to be an overly trigger-happy police. She asserts that distrust of the police remains high and "conspiracy theories are never in short supply" (p. 2). Osman's musings are quite on the mark. There have in fact been calls for the Indonesian police to recognise that excessive use of force actually strengthens the hand of the terrorist ideologues in Indonesia. For instance in February 2013, a 14-minute video emerged purporting to show four young suspected militants in restive Poso in Sulawesi being subjected to heavy-handed interrogation by the crack police counter-terrorist unit Detachment 88 and elements of the police mobile brigade (Brimob), which caused a major outcry from parliamentarians and moderate Muslim leaders. Some even called for the unit to be disbanded, and warned that such excessive force would likely prompt 'underground movements' in Poso and Maluku to 'do some unwanted things' ("Scrutiny Grows on Densus", 2013).

In January 2014, moreover, Detachment 88 gunned down six 'suspected militants' following a nine-hour gunfight in South Tangerang, generating a wave of criticism, not just from the likes of Ba'asyir's JAT, which deplored what it called an 'extrajudicial killing', but worryingly, even the National Commission on Human Rights (Komnas HAM), moderate civil society organisations like the Maarif Institute, and even Noor Huda Ismail, who "deplored the excessive level of force demonstrated by the elite squad in the operation" (as cited in Perdani, 2014, para. 3). To be fair, the police have suffered casualties themselves at the hands of the networks such as the notorious Poso-based MIT in recent years. Thus some angry police officers, perhaps unsurprisingly, insist that 'the best kind of de-radicalisation is through killing (such) people'. Such an attitude however is counter-productive. It is no surprise therefore that human rights observers have complained that heavy-handed Detachment 88 tactics are 'driving militancy'. More ominously, other networks like JAT have actively exploited perceived police brutality to fuel the extremist narrative, with a JAT spokesperson rallying his followers to 'Beware of this war on Islam'. Hence the importance of steadfast police professionalism – and crucially, acknowledgement of the psychological utility of minimum but surgically effective force – in the face of terrorist provocation, cannot be overstated (Ramakrishna, 2013).

FUTURE RESEARCH DIRECTIONS

In the event that the CIR Model be applied in the Indonesian milieu as a holistic, integrated medium-term analytical approach to policy interventions in the five spaces just described, at the end of a set period of time, polling and other methods of assessing the appeal and reach of violent Islamism of the type animating the steadily worsening ISIS threat should be conducted. The aim of this impact evaluation would be two-fold: to assess the degree to which public opinion in vulnerable constituencies have eschewed the violent Islamist meme; and the degree to which such a result was in part due to deliberate application of the CIR Model in a whole-of-society campaign orchestrated by the BNPT, in co-operation with other relevant stakeholders.

Since neutering violent extremism in the online space requires not just direct counter-ideological messaging in the online space but as discussed also ideology-relevant policy interventions offline, it is suggested that the Model be applied in other local contexts in Southeast Asia – southern Thailand comes to mind – and even beyond, where violent extremist ideologies have proliferated on and off-line. The cumulative knowledge generated may then be systematically collated to further refine the Model, taking into account localised, contextual nuances, while clearly teasing out general overarching themes that appear to hold true universally, such as for instance, the need for calibrated use of security force pressure, so as to not to inadvertently fuel the violent Islamist narrative.

CONCLUSION

In this chapter, we have examined a potential model – the Counter-Ideological Response (CIR) Model – to better conceptualise the policy steps needed to gradually diminish the appeal of online violent extremist ideology. As discussed, the CIR Model comprises the five conceptual spaces of Sender, Message, Mechanism, Recipient and Context, within which ideology-relevant policy interventions – that is, policy interventions within each space that impact the overall reach and appeal of the violent extremist narrative vis-a-vis any countervailing narrative put out against it – could be attempted. We illustrated the CIR Model with examples from the struggle against violent extremist ideology – including particularly that of ISIS – in the Indonesian milieu.

To conclude, it should be reiterated that while hard law enforcement and military measures are clearly needed in dealing with the rapidly evolving violent Islamist threat worldwide, diminishing the appeal and reach of the extremist ideology of the likes of ISIS remains a 'softer' but very much central, plank of any comprehensive grand strategy to neutralise the global challenge posed by the constantly mutating Al-Qaeda 'superorganism' (Ramakrishna, 2015). To cite the sagacious ancient Chinese strategist Sun Tzu, one must fight with wisdom and not merely with force alone.

REFERENCES

Afrianty, D. (2012). Islamic education and youth extremism in Indonesia. *Journal of Policing. Intelligence and Counter-Terrorism, 7*(2), 134–146. doi:10.1080/18335330.2012.719095

Afrida, N. (2011, May 18). Terror fight shifting from pesantren to campus. *The Jakarta Post*. Retrieved from http://www.thejakartapost.com/news/2011/05/18/terror-fight-shifting-'pesantren'-campus.html

Andersson, J. (2009). *Center of gravity analysis: An actual or perceived problem?* Stockholm: Swedish National Defence College.

Arnaz, F. (2011, June 27). Police say antiterror program is faulty. *The Jakarta Globe*. Retrieved from http://www.thejakartaglobe.com/archive/police-say-antiterror-program-is-faulty/

Arnaz, F., & Sianipar, O. (2011, January 27). Suspecting students with terror links, police probe Klaten technical school. *The Jakarta Globe*. Retrieved from http://www.thejakartaglobe.com/archive/suspecting-students-with-terror-links-police-probe-klaten-technical-school/

Ashour, O. (2009). *The de-radicalization of jihadists: Transforming armed Islamist movements*. New York, NY: Routledge.

Australia's Regional Summit to Counter Violent Extremism. (2015, June 12). Canberra: Attorney-General's Department, Australian Government.

Bartlett, J., & Miller, C. (2010). *The power of unreason: Conspiracy theories, extremism and counter-terrorism*. London: Demos.

Benesch, S. (2013, February 23). *The dangerous speech project: Dangerous speech – a proposal to prevent group violence*. Retrieved from http://www.dangerousspeech.org/guidelines/

Brennan, E. (2015, March 5). How Southeast Asia is responding to ISIS. *The Interpreter*. Retrieved from http://www.lowyinterpreter.org/post/2015/03/05/How-should-we-respond-to-ISIS-in-Southeast-Asia.aspx?COLLCC=651738223&COLLCC=732768703&

Cassrels, D. (2011a, May 23). How kebabs and coffee help turn inmates from the path of terror. *The Australian*. Retrieved from http://www.theaustralian.com.au/news/world/how-kebabs-and-coffee-help-turn-inmates-from-the-path-of-terror/story-e6frg6so-1226060651749

Cassrels, D. (2011b, June 25). Paving a new path for children of terror. *The Australian*. Retrieved from http://www.theaustralian.com.au/news/features/paving-a-new-path-for-children-of-terror/story-e6frg6z6-1226080886496 de Borchgrave, A., Sanderson, T., & Gordon, D. (2009). *The power of outreach: Leveraging on expertise on threats in Southeast Asia*. Washington, DC: Center for Strategic and International Studies.

de Vries, I. (2011, November 11). Amid growing inequality, it's about time our policy makers mind the wealth gap. *Jakarta Globe*. Retrieved from http://www.thejakartaglobe.com/archive/amid-growing-inequality-its-about-time-our-policy-makers-mind-the-wealth-gap/

Echevarria, A. J. II. (2002). *Clausewitz's center of gravity: Changing our warfighting doctrine-again!* Carlisle, PA: Strategic Studies Institute.

El-Fadl, K. A. (2005). *The great theft: Wrestling Islam from the extremists*. New York, NY: Harper San Francisco.

Elkus, A. (2010). Cognitive dissonance. *Red Team Journal*. Retrieved from http://redteamjournal.com/2010/09/cognitive-dissonance

Erikson, E. H. (1994). *Identity: Youth and crisis*. New York, NY: W.W. Norton.

Forbes, M. (2006, October 11). Terrorism network commanded from jail. *Sydney Morning Herald*. Retrieved from http://www.smh.com.au/news/world/terrorism-network-commanded-from-jail/2006/10/10/1160246130065.html

Freedman, L. (2006). *The transformation of strategic affairs (Adelphi Paper 379)*. London: Routledge.

Gladwell, M. (2004). *The tipping point: How little things can make a big difference*. London: Abacus.

Grossman, D. (1996). *On killing: The psychological cost of learning to kill in war and society*. New York, NY: Back Bay Books.

Hassan, M. H. (2006). *Unlicensed to kill: Countering Imam Samudra's justification for the Bali bombing*. Singapore: Peace Matters.

Heath, C., & Heath, D. (2008). *Made to stick: Why some ideas take hold And others come unstuck*. London: Arrow.

Horgan, J. (2008). Deradicalization or disengagement? A process in need of clarity and a counterterrorism initiative in need of evaluation. *Perspectives on Terrorism, 2*(4). Retrieved from http://www.terrorismanalysts.com/pt/index.php/pot/article/view/32/html

Hosenball, M., & Zakaria, T. (2011, May 13). Exclusive: Pornography found in bin Laden hideout: Officials. *Reuters*. Retrieved from http://www.reuters.com/article/2011/05/13/us-binladen-porn-idUS-TRE74C4RK20110513

Indonesian ISIS fighter sends threat message back home. (2015, January 6). *Blazingcatfur*. Retrieved from http://www.blazingcatfur.ca/2015/01/06/indonesian-isis-fighter-sends-threat-message-back-home/

International Crisis Group. (2011). *Indonesia jihadism: Small groups, big plans (Asia report 204)*. Jakarta, Brussels: International Crisis Group.

International Crisis Group. (2012). *Indonesia: From vigilantism to terrorism in Cirebon (Asia briefing 132)*. Jakarta, Brussels: International Crisis Group.

Islamic Radicalism Thriving in Indonesia's Campuses. (2011, April 26). *Yahoo News.* Retrieved from http://sg.news.yahoo.com/islamic-radicalism-thriving-indonesias-campuses-104002000.html

Jackson, B. A. (2006). Groups, networks, or movements: A command-and-control-driven approach to classifying terrorist organizations and its application to Al Qaeda. *Studies in Conflict and Terrorism, 29*(3), 241–262. doi:10.1080/10576100600564042

Jakarta slow to tackle rise of ISIS. (2015, May 29). *The Straits Times*, p. A10.

Javadi, T. (2015, May 27). Is criminalising hate speech the way to go in Indonesia? *The Malaysian Insider.* Retrieved from http://www.themalaysianinsider.com/sideviews/article/is-criminalising-hate-speech-the-way-to-go-in-indonesia-tiola-javadi

Jones, J. W. (2008). *Blood that cries out from the earth: The psychology of religious terrorism.* Oxford, UK: Oxford University Press. doi:10.1093/acprof:oso/9780195335972.001.0001

Karmini, N. (2011, June 30). Teaching jihad in Indonesian prisons. *The Jakarta Globe.* Retrieved from http://www.thejakartaglobe.com/archive/teaching-jihad-in-indonesian-prisons/

Karmini, N. (2013, June 21) Facebook broke Indonesia terror case. *Associated Press.* Retrieved from http://bigstory.ap.org/article/ap-exclusive-facebook-broke-indonesia-terror-case

Lee, L. (2011, August 18). 'Strong Case' against Umar Patek. *The Straits Times.*

Leonhard, R. R. (1991). *The art of maneuver: Maneuver-warfare theory and airland battle.* Novato, CA: Presidio Press.

Littlejohn, S. W., & Foss, K. A. (2008). *Theories of human communication* (9th ed.). Belmont, CA: Thomson Wadworth.

Malaysia detains more than 10 terror suspects linked to Abu Umar Group. (2011, November 17). *The Straits Times.*

Mbai, A. (2010, October 19). *Police-military co-operation in countering terrorism: An Indonesian perspective.* The International Seminar on Countering Terrorism, Nusa Dua, Bali, Indonesia.

McDowell, R. (2011, September 9). Captain jihad: Ex-terrorist is now comic book hero. *The Jakarta Post.* Retrieved from http://www.thejakartapost.com/news/2011/09/09/captain-jihad-ex-terrorist-now-comic-book-hero.html

Millie, J. (2008). 'Spiritual meal' or ongoing project? The dilemma of Dakwah Oratory. In G. Fealy & S. White (Eds.), *Expressing Islam: Religious life and politics in Indonesia* (pp. 80–94). Singapore: Institute of Southeast Asian Studies.

Nazeer, Z. (2011a, March 5). Indonesia faces rising intolerance. *The Straits Times.*

Nazeer, Z. (2011b, August 6). Pluralism, tolerance under growing threat. *The Straits Times.*

Nurhayati, D. (2011, October 12). 'Prison and paradise' gives a voice to terrorism survivors. *The Jakarta Post.* Retrieved from http://www.thejakartapost.com/news/2011/10/12/prison-and-paradise-gives-a-voice-terrorism-survivors.html

Osman, S. (2013). *Funerals of suspected terrorists in Indonesia: A rallying point? RSIS Commentaries (150/2013)*. Singapore: S. Rajaratnam School of International Studies.

Ozerdem, A., & Podder, S. (2011). Disarming youth combatants: Mitigating youth radicalization and violent extremism. *Journal of Strategic Security, 4*(4), 63–80. doi:10.5038/1944-0472.4.4.3

Perdani, Y. (2014, January 3). Amid criticism, police try to justify killings. *The Jakarta Post*. Retrieved from http://www.thejakartapost.com/news/2014/01/03/amid-criticism-police-try-justify-killings.html

Pereira, D. (2015, February 18). Jakarta holds key to keeping Southeast Asia safe in war on terror. *Business Times*. Retrieved from http://www.pereiraintl.com/jakarta-holds-key-to-keeping-s-e-asia-safe-in-war-on-terror/

Ramakrishna, K. (2009). *Radical pathways: Understanding Muslim radicalization in Indonesia*. Westport, CT: Praeger Security International.

Ramakrishna, K. (2013). *The east Indonesia mujahidin commandos: New faces, same ideology. RSIS Commentaries (8/2013)*. Singapore: S. Rajaratnam School of International Studies.

Ramakrishna, K. (2015). *Islamist terrorism and militancy in Indonesia: The power of the manichean mindset*. Singapore: Springer. doi:10.1007/978-981-287-194-7

Robinson, N. (2008, March 24). Bashir urges attacks on 'infidel' Australians. *The Australian*. Retrieved from http://www.theaustralian.com.au/archive/news/bashir-urges-attacks-on-infidel-australians/story-e6frg6t6-1111115870183

Ruthven, M. (2002). *A fury for God: The Islamist attack on America*. New York, NY: Granta.

Sagita, D. (2011, May 25). Government losing war against radicalism, analysts say. *The Jakarta Globe*. Retrieved from http://www.thejakartaglobe.com/archive/govt-losing-war-against-radicalism-analysts-say/

Schmid, A. (Ed.). (2011). *The Routledge handbook of terrorism research*. New York, NY: Routledge.

Schonhardt, S. (2010, July 5). Indonesia: Unlearning jihad. *Global Post*. Retrieved from http://www.globalpost.com/dispatch/indonesia/100702/indonesia-unlearning-jihad

Scrutiny grows on Densus 88 torture video. (2013, March 7). *Jakarta Globe*. Retrieved from http://thejakartaglobe.beritasatu.com/news/scrutiny-grows-on-densus-88-torture-video/

Sihaloho, M. J. (2011, April 5). Indonesia still a 'haven for terrorists': Ansyaad. *The Jakarta Globe*. Retrieved from http://jakartainformer.com/18312/indonesia-is-still-a-haven-for-terrorists-ansyaad-jakarta-globe/

Soeriaatmadja, W., & Lee, L. (2011, July 21). Singapore embassy 'targeted by terrorists'. *The Jakarta Globe*. Retrieved from http://www.thejakartaglobe.com/archive/singapore-embassy-targeted-by-terrorists/

Staub, E. (2005). Basic human needs, altruism, and aggression. In A. G. Miller (Ed.), *The social psychology of good and evil* (pp. 51–84). New York: The Guildford Press.

Sunstein, C. R. (2009). *Going to extremes: How like minds unite and divide*. New York: Oxford University Press.

Sunstein, C. R. (2010). *On rumours: How falsehoods spread, why we believe them, what can be done.* London: Penguin.

Temple-Raston, D. (2015, May 7). How to take the Internet back from ISIS. *The New Yorker.* Retrieved from http://www.newyorker.com/tech/elements/how-to-take-the-internet-back-from-isis

Ungerer, C. (2011). *Jihadists in jail: Radicalisation and the Indonesian prison experience.* Canberra: Australian Strategic Policy Institute/S. Rajaratanam School of International Studies.

Using Social Media to Communicate Against Violent Extremism. (2015). Canberra: Attorney-General's Department, Australian Government.

Von Clausewitz, C. (1976). *On war* (M. Howard & P. Paret, Trans. & Eds.). Princeton: Princeton University Press. (Original work published 1832)

Wiktorowicz, Q. (2005). *Radical Islam rising: Muslim extremism in the West.* Lanham: Rowman and Littlefield.

Wills, T. A., & Resko, J. A. (2005). Social support and behavior toward others. In A. G. Miller (Ed.), *The social psychology of good and evil* (pp. 416–443). New York: The Guildford Press.

Winnicott, D. W. (2006). *The family and individual development.* London: Routledge.

ENDNOTES

[1.] The CIR Model that is further elaborated and fleshed out in this chapter was first introduced in seminal form as part of a wider argument at the end of the author's *Islamist Terrorism and Militancy in Indonesia: The Power of the Manichean Mindset* (Singapore: Springer, 2015) as well as builds upon elements of the author's earlier short think piece entitled "The Role of Civil Society in Countering Violent Extremism in Indonesia", *Middle East Institute*, 21 July 2014, (http://www.mei.edu/content/map/role-civil-society-countering-violent-extremism-efforts-indonesia)

[2.] While there are many definitions of Islamism in the scholarly literature, that by Noorani seems particularly instructive. He describes Islamism as the "'ideologicalization' of Islam at the political level, the construction of a political ideology using symbols culled from the historical repertoire of Islam, to the exclusion of others'. He adds that while the lines between the faith and political ideology are at times blurred, "Islamism is not Islam". See Noorani, A. G. (2002). *Islam and Jihad: Prejudice versus Reality.* London and New York: Zed Books .

[3.] First introduced by evolutionary biologist Richard Dawkins in 1976, a meme is regarded as a successful unit of cultural information, an idea or a practice, passed on not genetically – like a gene – but rather via social and cultural imitation. The famous Nike advertisement 'Just Do it' is an example of a 'sticky' and enduring meme. See Ridley, M. (2004). *The Agile Gene: How Nature Turns on Nurture.* New York, NY: Perennial.

Chapter 14
Countering Online Violent Extremism:
State Action as Strategic Communication

Damien D. Cheong
Nanyang Technological University, Singapore

ABSTRACT

State action is an important form of strategic communication and therefore, significant to Countering Violent Extremism (CVE) initiatives on and offline. While non-state actors often use state action (and sometimes inaction) to incite and legitimise violence against the state as well as its citizens, generating this sort of negative sentiment does not require instigation. This is especially the case when the action(s) of a state are deemed so unacceptable and repulsive that a public backlash automatically ensues. As many violent extremists (including lone wolves) have been radicalised as a result of such controversies, it is necessary for positive state action to be carried out as well as widely publicised at the macro and micro levels. This is envisaged to counter negative narratives as well as address real world issues that push individuals towards violent extremism.

INTRODUCTION

Strategic communication or "communication through words and deeds in pursuit of national strategic objectives" has in recent times become more prominent across the globe (Cornish, Lindley-French, & York, 2011, p. ix). Many countries have not only invested or are investing in greater 'soft power' initiatives to reach out to countries around and beyond their borders, but also seem to be establishing departments/ ministries to handle various public communication functions such as the Government Communication Service in the United Kingdom. Some like the United States have even gone so far as to establish dedicated units to focus on niche/special areas such as counterterrorism communications (e.g., the Center for Strategic Counterterrorism Communications).

A key element in effective strategic communication, as underscored by Cornish, Lindley-French, and Yorke (2011), is the "potency of action" (p. 21). As "all action has a communicative value and conveys

DOI: 10.4018/978-1-5225-0156-5.ch014

a message ... words and actions are inseparable", therefore "efforts should be made to minimise ... disparities that might undermine the ... narrative" (p. 21). The same rationale holds true for state ('state', in this chapter, is defined as 'the civil government of a country') action especially since "governments will be judged as much on what they can deliver as on the promises they make and the vision they provide" (Cornish et al., 2011, p. 21).

Discussions about state action have traditionally been associated with international relations and diplomacy. However, its relevance and applicability to situations involving non-state actors are just as significant too. This is especially so when non-state actors exploit state action (or inaction) to incite and legitimise violence against the state as well as its nationals. In February 2015 for example, the Islamic State in Iraq and Syria (ISIS) justified its brutal execution of a Jordanian Air Force pilot as "retribution for his crimes against Islam and the Muslims, including his active involvement in crusader airstrikes against Muslim lands" (Dabiq, 2015, p. 5).

Incitement by religious and non-religious supporters of jihadist groups to perpetrate violence is often cited as a key driver of terrorist attacks, and has therefore been criminalised in many countries. As Bibi van Ginkel writes:

These international initiatives spurred from the belief that public provocation to commit a terrorist act creates the danger that such an offence may be committed. Furthermore, it was believed that the public expression of praise, support or justification for terrorism might create an environment and psychological climate conducive to criminal activity. (van Ginkel, 2011, p. 1)

While authorities can and have moved against radical preachers and firebrands in their jurisdictions, it is extremely challenging, if not impossible, to deal with incitement that originates from a foreign source, and is disseminated through social media and other Internet channels (e.g., Anwar al-Awlaki's video/audio messages).

Nevertheless, generating negative sentiment about a state or its nationals does not necessarily require instigation, especially when the action(s) of a state is deemed so unacceptable/repulsive that it provokes public outcry. The 2011 Arab Spring uprising in Egypt, for example, was sparked off by the death of Khaled Said, who was allegedly beaten to death in police custody ("Egypt jails police", 2011).

Many violent extremists (including lone wolves) have been radicalised through learning about controversial state action though traditional and social media. For instance, the North Carolina teenager who was arrested for terrorist-related activities in June 2015 claimed that "he was angry about U.S. airstrikes and planned revenge that would force them to stop" (Field, 2015, para. 2). In fact, the emergence of Syrian rebel groups, ironically including ISIS, has been attributed to the Assad regime's brutality towards opponents and civilians (Shoichet, 2013).

These and other similar examples suggest that, theoretically, it is incumbent upon a state to act in an unprovocative manner to avoid potential backlash and hostility. In reality, however, this can never be truly accomplished. State action, even with the best of intentions, and carried out with all necessary precautions, will antagonise, and in worse case scenarios, severely disadvantage a particular group or groups. Counter-terrorism operations and/or restoration of public order operations are cases in point. The use of force against suspects and/or protestors while lawful, can nevertheless antagonise such individuals and their supporters, for a variety of reasons (the most common being the excessive use of force). Furthermore, when operations are legally ambiguous (as in the case of drone strikes), the backlash can be expectedly severe.

How then should states deal with this conundrum where necessary armed operations might incur human casualties/fatalities, but at the same time, minimise backlash in the form of radicalising individuals, who might be motivated to carry out retributive attacks on its territory as well as against its citizens at home and abroad in the future? The problem is further complicated as incidents of this nature are often negatively framed and disseminated quickly through social and other new media channels leaving little time for the state to respond.

While communication is often always conducted in the aftermath of the incident, it may not be that effective if mistrust of the state is already pre-existing and high. Therefore, it may be better to employ a pre-crisis communication strategy of sustained positive state action at the macro and micro levels. This is envisaged to improve the state's overall image as well as its nationals, and in so doing, negate some of the backlash by increasing the likelihood that the public would give it the benefit of the doubt. This could also help increase the credibility of countering violent extremism (CVE) initiatives (private, public or non-governmental organisation [NGO]) emanating from the state or at the very least, prevent an outright rejection/dismissal of such initiatives.

HUMAN CASUALTIES FROM CRISES FEED RADICALISATION

News about human casualties from man-made and/or naturally-occurring crises has always been emotionally provocative especially in contemporary times. This, as Emma Heywood a researcher at Coventry University, argues, is because of the interesting dynamics at play between the originator of the news story and the reader/viewer (Heywood, 2015).

With regard to the reader/viewer, he/she is often predisposed to feel compassion for the victim(s). Compassion is defined here as the "painful emotion occasioned by the awareness of another person's undeserved misfortune" (Nussbaum, 2001, p. 31). This is due in part to the recognition that the strangers they learn about in these stories are also part of the human race "regardless of where, or who, they are" (Heywood, 2015, p. 41). In addition, "an element of morality" is imposed on the viewer/reader "to engage with [the] ethics of care, or to imagine putting ourselves in the position of the victim" (Silverstone, 2007, cited in Heywood, 2015, p. 41), such that some viewers/readers would ultimately be motivated to render assistance – financial or otherwise (Borum, 2003).

For the originator of news stories, particularly the mass media, there is an apparent trend towards "journalism of attachment" (Bell, 1998, cited in Heywood, 2015, p. 40). This is a form of journalism which is socially conscious and aware of the humanitarian costs of crises, and therefore actively reports on such crises/incidents to generate awareness and indirectly prompt action. This has meant that stories that elicit compassion are extremely newsworthy.

Yet, over-publishing such stories does result in 'compassion fatigue' (Campbell, 2012; Moeller, 1999; Sontag, 2003; Tester, 2001). This in turn, has compelled news generators "to manage their portrayals of victims to highlight events that are dramatic and which occur over short periods of time to heighten the newsworthiness" (Carruthers, 2000, p. 231). Some of these examples include: (a) adventure news – reports in which the distant other is presented as no cause for concern or action; (b) emergency news – news which produces pity and a demand or option for action for sufferers; and (c) ecstatic news – in which the victim is considered to be 'one of us' and the viewer can identify with the victim (Chouliaraki, 2006).

Heywood (2015, p. 41) concludes that "because cultural and geographical proximity, or relevance, is central in determining levels of compassion (we sympathise more with those we care for or relate to), the media plays a key role here as they have the ability to determine not only what is shown to viewers but how it is portrayed and the extent of the graphic nature of the suffering".

Gaza War 2014

The 2014 Gaza War is a good case in point. Briefly,

A humanitarian emergency was declared in the Gaza Strip on 7 July 2014 following a severe escalation in hostilities, involving intense Israeli aerial and navy bombardment and Palestinian rocket fire. Hostilities de-escalated following an open-ended ceasefire which entered into force on 26 August. The scale of destruction, devastation and displacement during the 50 days of conflict is unprecedented in Gaza, since at least the start of the Israeli occupation in 1967. The humanitarian impact of these hostilities comes against a backdrop of heightened vulnerability and instability in Gaza. (UN Office for the Coordination of Humanitarian Affairs [OCHA], 2014).

Images/footage of the conflict and resulting casualties were broadcasted over traditional and social media around the world.

Massive protests and demonstrations occurred in several countries as a consequence (Holland, 2014). In London for example, thousands marched to generate awareness for the plight of the Palestinians in Gaza and lament the inaction of the international community to stop the violence. When asked what had motivated her to join the demonstration, a teenager replied: "people shouldn't stand by and watch an injustice. I have little brothers and sisters and if I was in that situation I would want people globally to fight for me" (Culzac, 2014, para. 14). Such sentiments were echoed in many of the other protests as well.

In Singapore, where such demonstrations rarely occur, it was reported that over three hundred people turned up at the Speakers' Corner in Hong Lim Park to show their support for the Palestinians in Gaza. The event was organised by a civil society group called From Singapore to Palestine (FS2P), which was established in 2012 to "create awareness about the situation in Palestine" (Salleh, 2014, para. 3). An open letter imploring the Singapore government to take action to help the people of Gaza was also published on alternative media (Mastura, 2014).

While the true motivations of people to join the demonstrations may be hard to determine, the crisis and its humanitarian impact, have nevertheless reinforced a particular narrative, provoked emotive responses and could well mobilise individuals to take further action.

Air and Drone Strikes

Airstrikes are a popular tactic in counter-terrorism operations against ISIS as well as other terrorist organisations. However, the unintended civilian casualties/deaths from such attacks have the potential to radicalise individuals directly and indirectly affected by these strikes. It is the human casualties and suffering that generate the emotive response, and like the Gaza War, images/footage of this crisis is readily available on almost every news channel and outlet, in addition to social media.

Some of the incidents where airstrikes have killed civilians include: (a) a drone strike killed approximately 82 people (including children) in October 2006, when a *madrassa* in Bajaur near the Afghan border was hit (Amnesty International, 2006); (b) the July 2008 attack on a wedding party where

47 Afghanis, mostly women and children, were killed ("Afghan survivors tell", 2008). The group was reportedly escorting the bride to the wedding ceremony in the groom's village in Dih Bala district of Nangarhar province, Afghanistan; (c) the August 2008 airstrike on a Taliban commander in the village of Azizabad, killed over 90 civilians, many of them children ("Afghan bombing drives", 2008); (d) in March 2011, a series of drone strikes killed about 40 people in Datta Khel, North Waziristan, during a tribal council meeting (Amnesty International 2013); and (e) the 2013 airstrike in Yemen that killed 15 wedding guests who were mistaken for Al-Qaeda operatives ("Air strike in Yemen", 2013).

Expectedly, such errors do nothing to improve the standing of countries involved in these operations, even if they were carried out as part of wider counter-terrorism efforts. "Rapid response airstrikes have meant higher civilian casualties, while every bomb dropped in populated areas amplifies the chance of a mistake", said Brad Adams, Asia director at Human Rights Watch. "Mistakes by the US and NATO have dramatically decreased public support for the Afghan government and the presence of international forces providing security to Afghans" (Human Rights Watch, 2008, para. 4).

The use of drone strikes by the United States against terrorist targets is highly controversial. The United States has argued that this technology allows for greater precision and minimises human casualties, but the fact that civilians have been erroneously killed, and that the attacks may contravene international law, leave many uneasy. Nevertheless, it is the impact on radicalisation that is of interest here ("Drone strikes by US", 2013).

Several commentators, analysts and even military commanders have suggested that the deaths of civilians can have a radicalising effect on those directly and indirectly affected by the strikes. A 2013 Pew Research Center survey reported that anti-United States sentiment is high in communities directly affected by drone strikes (Pew Research Center, 2013). And Neda Najibi, an author associated with the Huffington Post, cautions that:

The use of drones is often justified by the fact that they (occasionally) take out some very bad people, but they actually do more harm as innocent people die and the ones they leave behind resort to terrorism as revenge for their loved ones. (Najibi, 2013, para. 8)

The Gaza as well as air and drone strikes examples underscore the fact that while individuals can be mobilised to action via an agitator, his/her involvement is not necessary if a crisis causes significant humanitarian casualties and is widely publicised. Alberto Fernandez, former Coordinator for Strategic Counterterrorism Communications, observes

[T]hat Syrian Muslims have been slaughtered in large numbers by the Assad regime. From 2012 – 2014 that was the single major factor that mobilised thousands worldwide to the war zone. But you didn't need to watch ISIS videos to see this carnage. (McCants, 2015, para. 7)

Hence, there is always a possibility that individuals who become aware of these incidents, take action (including violent action) against what they perceive as unacceptable injustices; states as well as their nationals, can easily become targets.

While the direct actions of a state may create the necessary conditions for anti-state sentiment and radicalisation, it must also be acknowledged that tacit incidents can also do the same. What they share in common with direct state action is the ability to create powerful negative sentiments.

SCANDALS AND MISINFORMATION ADVERSELY AFFECT STATE CREDIBILITY AS WELL

Scandals and misinformation involving officials, regimes or leaders can certainly generate negative sentiments against a state and its citizens, especially when cases of torture, abuse and other alleged human rights violations are documented.

Scandal: Abu Ghraib

The 2004 Abu Ghraib scandal in Iraq that involved the mistreatment and torture of captives by U.S. service personnel is a case in point. The documented abuses and subsequent findings caused severe damage to the United States' image particularly with local Iraqis and to a certain extent some circles within the Muslim world. As Martin Chulov, a reporter for The Guardian newspaper, reports: "The revelation of abuses at Abu Ghraib had a radicalising effect on many Iraqis, who saw the purported civility of American occupation as little improvement on the tyranny of Saddam" (Chulov, 2014, para. 27).

Although some observers, citing the seeming absence of anti-United States protests in the Middle East following the tenth anniversary of the scandal, have suggested that the predicted anti-United States sentiment was overplayed, the scandal did serve to radicalise individuals at the micro level. As investigations on one of the brothers behind the Charlie Hebdo massacre, Cherif Kouachi, revealed:

I was ready to go and die in battle [and] I got this idea when I saw the injustices shown by television on what was going on over there. I am speaking about the torture that the Americans have inflicted on the Iraqis. ("Terror suspect Cherif", 2015, para. 4)

Scandal: Guantanamo Bay

Publicised reports of torture and abuse by the CIA on inmates held in Guantanamo Bay during the United States' War on Terror have similarly provoked much controversy and embarrassment for the U.S. government. As a key advocate of human rights and democracy, the exposé on Guantanamo was seen as yet another example of hypocrisy (Marcus, 2006). A 2014 news report by the Sydney Morning Herald on Guantanamo Bay, cites Senator John McCain as saying that:

Torture had stained America's national honour [and that] whatever occurred here, Guantanamo has become symbolic of that torture. Obama himself has described Gitmo as a terrorist recruitment tool. It can't be an accident that Islamic State militants have taken to dressing their victims in the Gitmo's orange jumpsuits before it beheads them. ("Terror, torture and", 2014)

Both scandals have created and/or enhanced ill-feelings toward the United States and its allies.

Misinformation: The Rohingya Issue

The ease at which information and misinformation (including conspiracy theories) can be generated and disseminated today has been well-documented. Social media's appeal lies in its ability to enable 'horizontal communications', and in so doing, empower the individual. Individuals are firstly no longer dependent upon traditional sources for information (e.g., press releases, news, government/company publications) as they can easily obtain information from alternative sources on the Internet. Secondly, they can become authoritative sources of information as they can generate and disseminate findings easily. Finally, they can distribute such information expeditiously and without fear of censorship. In this context, the user is no longer just a passive consumer of news/information but a 'pro-sumer', and gives rise to more communication activity and dialogue (Scott & Jacka, 2011). This can negatively impact the reputation of a state and its citizens especially when the state cannot respond quickly enough to public reaction.

Pro-Rohingya activists have employed graphic photos and videos of victims of the conflict with Myanmar to create impact. Among the aims for doing so include: (a) generating awareness of the plight and grievances of the Rohingya; (b) mobilising support for the cause; and (c) mobilising individuals to take action. They have even resorted to using incorrectly captioned images to further these objectives. For instance, a photo by the Royal Thai Navy depicting apprehended Rohingya refugees lying on a beach and guarded by Thai authorities, which appeared originally in a 2009 Human Rights Watch report titled 'Perilous Plight: Burma's Rohingya Take to the Seas', was re-captioned as 'Hundreds of dead Muslims, killed by Buddhist terrorists in Burma – Burma government buried them in the sea' and posted on online forums such as *Jamat e-Islami Pakistan*. A photo depicting a similar scenario has also been circulated on Facebook – e.g., S-axis's Facebook page dated July 13, 2012 (Ahmed, 2012).

Another photo posted on the Facebook page of *A Heart without the Quran is like a Ship without a Compass* on July 13, 2012 shows two Muslims allegedly killed in the clashes with Myanmar troops with the caption reading 'More than 20,000 Muslims has been killed in Burma … But Electronic Media is Criminally Silent – Please Share'. This photo is believed to be a depiction of the two victims killed in the 2011 bomb blast in the Myawaddy Township along the Thai-Myanmar border (Ahmed, 2012).

The generators of these mis-captioned photos attempt to frame the Myanmar upheaval as a religious one between Buddhists and Muslims, and in so doing, mobilise the global Muslim community to take action. Expectedly, many social media users have accepted this interpretation of the conflict, and some have even called for revenge against Buddhists. Donnie Elfansyah, for instance, writes: "Islam is like sleeping tiger, never attack 1st when never being attacked, this is war! Now support our brothers n sisters in Burma! For kicking back the Kafirun!!! This is war! ALLAHU AKBAR!!! LABBAIKA YA HU-SAIN!!!" (Ahmed, 2012). Ironically, even when some users tried to reveal the truth by publishing links to the real photos, their attempts were simply ignored and dismissed (Ahmed, 2012).

Given that several Islamist groups in Indonesia have also bought into this interpretation of the upheaval is particularly significant (Zenn, 2012). They have already demonstrated in front of the Myanmar embassy in Jakarta to demand an end to the bloodshed, and some have even called for Indonesians to "go to Myanmar and carry out jihad for [their] Muslim brothers" (Zenn, 2012, para. 16). As suggested by Kyaw San Wai, an analyst at S. Rajaratnam School of International Studies, other violent extremist groups in the region could potentially hijack and leverage the Rohingya issue to revive their ailing fortunes (Kyaw, 2012).

COUNTERING VIOLENT EXTREMISM AND COUNTER-MESSAGING EFFORTS UNDERMINED

The real and perceived human suffering brought about by state actions and/or misinformation about a state can lend credence to anti-state pontification. Some of these include: (a) the state is portrayed as an acknowledged adversary (or sworn enemy), and therefore a legitimate target of attacks; (b) the state is hypocritical and should not be trusted; and (c) the state is 'immoral', and as such, at odds with one's religious beliefs. If internalised, the sense of attachment and even loyalty of some citizens could be adversely affected and state-sponsored/aligned CVE initiatives could be dismissed as propaganda (Field, 2015). The United States and Indonesian CVE efforts are cases in point.

The United States

The United States has spent considerable time and resources on CVE initiatives in recognition that these encompass "the preventative aspects of counterterrorism as well as interventions to undermine the attraction of extremist movements and ideologies that seek to promote violence" (White House, 2015, para. 2).

Internally, community engagement forms the core of such programmes, and consists of (White House, 2015):

1. **Building Awareness:** This includes identifying the drivers and indicators of radicalisation and recruitment to violence.
2. **Countering Extremist Narratives:** This is done by directly addressing and countering violent extremist recruitment narratives and encouraging civil society-led counter narratives online.
3. **Emphasising Community-Led Intervention:** Communities are empowered through various efforts designed to disrupt the radicalisation process before an individual engages in such activity.

The 'Empowering Local Partners to Prevent Violent Extremism in the United States' is an example of how such community engagement programmes are operationalised. This initiative was started in 2011 and premised on two key factors: "(a) communities provide the solution to violent extremism; and (b) CVE efforts are best pursued at the local level, tailored to local dynamics, where local officials continue to build relationships within their communities through established community policing and community outreach mechanisms" (White House, 2015, para. 4).

In addition, a whole-of-nation approach to CVE was adopted. Some of the highlights include (White House, 2015):

1. The appointment of a senior level, full-time CVE Coordinator at the Department of Homeland Security (DHS).
2. Establishing the Los Angeles-based Office for Strategic Engagement which deploys dedicated staff to: (i) facilitate information-sharing; (ii) seek engagement with local partners; (iii) strengthen community and law enforcement partnerships; and (iv) establish prevention and intervention frameworks at the local level. Plans to extend this programme to other municipalities across the country are already in place.
3. Leading a workshop with the creative arts community and community leaders to develop innovative, scalable and implementable programs and tools to counter violent extremism. These new programs and tools will include film training for disadvantaged youth and a 'CVE Hub' that will be operated by an NGO to connect, network, organise, and drive community groups, funders, academics, and the tech sector towards long-term, sustainable, creative, and nimble solutions for domestic CVE.

4. Sponsorship of a joint DHS and Department of Justice (DOJ) symposium for local partners to collaborate and share best practices on intervention and prevention framework development and implementation.

Another area of focus is counter-messaging in the social media space. This entails "working to weaken the legitimacy and resonance of violent extremist messaging and narratives" by identifying "concrete ways to build upon ongoing initiatives aimed at countering extremists' perverse message and new and innovative solutions to the challenges posed by violent extremists, especially online" (White House, 2015, para. 13). Some of the initiatives include: (a) establishing a digital communications hub that will counter ISIS's propaganda and recruitment efforts, both directly and through engagement with civil society, community, and religious leaders; (b) developing a peer-to-peer challenge to empower university students in the United States, Canada, North Africa, Middle East, Europe, Australia, and Asia to develop digital content that counters violent extremist messaging; (c) organising multiple 'technology camps' in which social media companies will work with governments, civil society, and religious leaders to develop digital content that discredits violent extremist narratives and amplifies positive alternatives (White House, 2015).

With regard to strategic communication and engagement, the United States has appointed a Special Envoy for Strategic Counterterrorism Communications at the Department of State to "drive Government efforts aimed at discrediting terrorists' propaganda and degrading their ability to disseminate messages and recruit fighters, with a particular focus on ISIL [ISIS]" (White House, 2015, para. 14).

"Fostering supportive and permissive environments in support of a vibrant civil society and identifying innovative ways to inject technical, financial, and logistical support into the civil society space" is also part of the overall initiatives (White House, 2015, para. 16). Opportunities for civil society to be an even more active partner in efforts to build local partnerships against violent extremism have been planned.

Externally, CVE efforts involve collaborating with international partners to "develop actions to counter the most immediate threats, including ISIL [ISIS], and stop the spread of violent extremism" (para. 8). Such partners include other governments, international NGOs and private sector companies (White House, 2015). For example, collaboration with Canada and the United Kingdom aims to bring together researchers from research programs to deliver practical, timely and plainspoken results to practitioners. This international compilation will ensure the best results are validated and shared with relevant stakeholders (White House, 2015).

The United States plans to also work

[W]ith religious leaders and faith communities around the world to address both religious and non-religious causes of violence and extremism, including by working with religious leaders on projects emphasising peace, tolerance, and coexistence at the community level and training religious leaders on outreach to at-risk youth. (White House, 2015, para. 15)

There are also plans to actively engage with youth around the world. The United States will support

[Y]oung leaders in the Middle East and North Africa, Sub-Saharan Africa and Southeast Asia, through projects that provide youth a sense of belonging, as well as technical skills and vocational training,

scholarships, opportunities for civic engagement, and leadership training. As part of these efforts, the United States trains, mentors, and provides seed funding to young leaders, for example, who are working to counter extremists' narratives, reintegrate former violent extremists, and promote tolerance and non-violent dispute resolution. (White House, 2015, para. 17)

These are undoubtedly very holistic and ambitious plans for CVE, and involve multiple stakeholders directly and indirectly. However, many observers have cautioned that such CVE efforts may be seriously undermined by the actions of the United States in the past as well as the present. For example, Mark Juergensmeyer, Director of the Orfalea Center for Global and International Studies, opined in a newspaper article that the United States had made a serious error by declaring a global 'War on Terror', and invading Afghanistan and Iraq in the wake of the September 11 attacks (Nirmala, 2014). He argued that the War on Terror only served to validate Osama bin Laden's view of the United States as an enemy of Islam in light of the human casualties and atrocities that were committed as part of this campaign (see Baxter & Akbarzadeh, 2008).

In a letter to Americans, bin Laden explained: "Why are we fighting and opposing you? The answer is very simple: Because you attacked us and continue to attack us ..." ("Full text: bin", 2002, para. 7). Similarly, in Anwar al-Awlaki's message inciting violence against the United States, he said:

With the American invasion of Iraq and continued US aggression against Muslims, I could not reconcile between living in the US and being a Muslim, and I eventually came to the conclusion that jihad against America is binding upon myself just as it is binding on every other Muslim. ("Purported al-awlaki", 2010, para. 2)

Furthermore, the critical missteps in United States foreign policy over the years, such as its approach to the Israeli-Palestinian conflict, have led to high levels of negative sentiment in the Middle East region (Haaretz, 2010).

The prevailing negative perception of the United States is highly detrimental to its existing and indeed future strategic communication efforts including its diplomatic and soft power initiatives. For instance, in an evaluation of why counter-messaging emanating from the DHS had not been entirely successful against ISIS narrative, Alberto Fernandez, former Coordinator for the Center for Strategic Counterterrorism Communications, argued:

It is important to remember that ISIS propaganda does not happen in a vacuum. Western governments, including the current administration, would be well served by starting from a position of humility and recognise that the problem of ISIS messaging is fundamentally a political problem reflected in social media and not the other way around. All too often the press, policymakers, and legislators have focused on the 'slickness' of the message and not on the power of the content. ISIS propaganda succeeds – when it does and it doesn't always – because a good part of it is based in real events. The best propaganda is the truth. (McCants, 2015, para. 6)

Fernandez also remarked in another interview that "saying ISIS is bad is not good enough. There has to be change on the ground. Messaging can shape and shade, but it can't turn black into white" (Cottee, 2015, para. 14).

Indonesia

In the Indonesian context, the

'[H]ard' approach is defined as measures that are employed by the state that focus on the function and role of the security apparatus (primarily the National Police and Military) and their use of force, which includes, among other things, tactical raids, arrests, infiltration and killings. The 'soft' approach, on the other hand, is seen as the function, role and activities of the non-security state apparatus (such as the Ministry of Education, as well as non-state actors (such as Islamic mass organisations), which do not resort to force. (Hasan, Hendriks, Janssen, & Meijer, 2012, p. 15)

The government has used both hard and soft measures over the last decade to deal with terrorism and violent extremism with some measure of success. Jamhari Makruf and Mutiara Pertiwi from the State Islamic University (UIN) in Jakarta, Indonesia, observe that

[B]y 2010, Indonesian Police claimed to have arrested 452 jihadi terrorists and killed some key leaders of JI, such as Dr. Azahari, Noordin M. Top, Saefudin Djaelani and Dulmatin. Additionally, the police were successful in paralysing a new al-Qaida funded-jihadi training camp in Aceh [that year]. (Makruf & Pertiwi, 2010, pp. 142-143)

However, as the hard measures have often resulted in high rates of collateral damage (e.g., death of suspects), some analysts have cautioned that counterterrorism efforts could in fact be negatively affected if the high casualty rates persist ("Indonesian anti-terror", 2013).

Manifestations of discontentment have been observed, with several groups: (a) protesting against law enforcement agencies and demanding their disbandment; (b) attacking police stations; and (c) generating and spreading rumours/conspiracy theories, which have besmirched the reputation of law enforcement agencies (Yang, 2012). Should such occurrences continue, the government risks increasing public mistrust for law enforcement agencies as well as its overall counterterrorism efforts (Taufiqurrohman, 2013).

The funerals of terrorist suspects have become rallying points for Islamist groups (violent and non-violent) in Indonesia. The men were suspected to be part of the Mujahidin Indonesia Timur terror network operating in Poso, Central Sulawesi. Sulastri Osman, an expert on Indonesian radicals, argues that this was because

[A] common identity ... [links] ... together those at the funerals. They all see themselves as 'aktivis Islam' – Islamic activists who seek to carve out a bigger public space for Islam, never mind that they often disagree over means ... [moreover, the seemingly unrestrained use of force by the police against suspects has provoked a] ... real fear ... that anyone among them can be the next victim. (Osman, 2013, p. 2)

The dead suspects are often portrayed as victims of the callous brutality of the security apparatus. This portrayal has motivated some individuals to take retaliatory action against the police (Taufiqurrohman, 2013).

The case examples mentioned above underscore that how a state carries out its counter-terrorism responses, especially when there are likely to be significant fatalities and casualties, is critical for building trust and credibility. If the state's actions are perceived to be unjust, excessive and hypocritical, its existing and future strategic communication efforts are likely to be undermined.

POSITIVE STATE ACTION AT THE MACRO LEVEL

Positive action at the macro and micro levels are important to overall CVE efforts as they help build overall trust in states. However, positive action, even if carried out perfectly, does not guarantee a full restoration of trust. This is especially so if mistrust/distrust of the state is already high. Furthermore, if the state continued with its counter-terrorism operations, and casualties occurred, its overall trust-building efforts would invariably be adversely affected. Nevertheless, it is useful for the state to carry out and publicise its positive action as it would help challenge/counter negative narratives about the state and its nationals in both the on and offline realms. It could also help address real world factors that push individuals toward violent extremism.

At the macro level, states should be mindful of three core, albeit obvious areas where communication and indeed careful management of incidents are paramount.

Minimising Collateral Damage: Israel

Many states that carry out counter-terrorism operations explicitly state that minimising civilian casualties is standard operating procedure. But how can this message be made more credible?

Israel and Hamas have been embroiled in conflict for a long time. The situation has become more complex ever since the Palestinian group won control of the Gaza Strip in 2006, and is responsible for controlling other militant groups in the Strip (e.g., Palestinian Islamic Jihad). Manifestations of conflict escalation often involve militant groups firing rockets into Israel, and the Israel Defense Forces (IDF) conducting air and ground offensives in Gaza in retaliation.

One of such offensives was *Operation Pillar of Defense* in 2012. To deal with the anticipated backlash, the IDF detailed how they attempted to minimise civilian casualties and collateral damage. Some of the methods used were: (a) phone calls to warn Gazans of airstrikes; (b) dropping leaflets to "warn civilians to avoid being present in the vicinity of Hamas operatives"; (c) diverting missiles in mid-flight when civilians are in close proximity of the target; (d) roof knocking – "a building is targeted with a loud but non-lethal bomb that warns civilians that they are in the vicinity of a weapons cache or other target. This method is used to allow all residents to leave the area before the site is hit with live ammunition"; and (e) pinpoint targeting – "where strikes will endanger few or no bystanders" (Israel Defence Forces, 2012, para. 3-7). The IDF further admitted that

[D]espite all precautions, IDF forces may have mistakenly targeted sites and hurt Palestinian civilians. The IDF is fully committed to ensuring that every allegation of wrongdoing be fully and fairly investigated, though this will happen after the conclusion of the operation. (Israel Defense Forces, 2012, para. 9)

A climate of mistrust and graphic images/videos of the casualties may do little to increase believability of such pronouncements. Yet, there are three learning points of the IDF's approach that are noteworthy:

1. Details of how civilian casualties are minimised.
2. Acknowledgement that civilian casualties will occur.
3. Identification of avenues of recourse for victims to make complaints and investigations into wrongdoings.

In addition, a programme for compensation and rebuilding should be added to the mix to help negate backlash. Also, if complaints are made, and investigations reveal wrongdoings, disciplinary or punitive action must be taken against the perpetrators to demonstrate that available recourses do, in fact, work.

Engagement with the Enemy: Thailand

States that are embroiled in armed conflict with non-state actors should, if feasible, reach out to such groups to determine ways to prevent escalation.

Since 2004, the secessionist conflict in Thailand has taken a more violent turn. Militant groups were established to fight for the independence of approximately 1.8 million ethnic Malay-Muslims in Southern Thailand. To date, approximately 5,500 people have been killed and about 10,000 injured.

In February 2013, 16 militants were killed in an attack on an army base in Narathiwat province, Thailand. Of significance is the seeming support of some members of the Malay- Muslim community for the Thai authorities. It is alleged that this group had tipped off the Thai authorities about the attack. As to why such support was forthcoming, a Thai security official opined: "We are seeing a change in attitude and sympathies among some in the Muslim community. They have had enough of the violence and the killing of innocents" (Horn, 2013, para. 4). The killing of innocents refers to the militants' penchant for attacking teachers, school officials, and schools in their armed struggle against the state ("The martyrs of the", 2012).

Violence against the Thai state has been justified on both the ideological weaving of ethno-religious sentiments as well as in retaliation against state violence. As Joseph Chinyong Liow and Don Pathan observe:

A major, if understated, motivation for violence has been the principle of reciprocity, where attacks have taken place in response to perceived injustices and crackdowns by security forces. Given that the Thai Government continues to take a heavy-handed approach in their operations in the south, it should be no surprise to find ready pools of aggrieved recruits among youths who have either loss family members or were themselves subject to abusive interrogation procedures. Not a few locals have their own vendetta against the state, and have been drawn into the insurgency, not by grandiose visions of the liberation of Patani, but by profound enmity and a quest for personal revenge. (Liow & Pathan, 2010, p. 46)

Although draconian measures were initially employed by the state to address the problem, the use of diplomacy in recent times seems to be producing some positive results. That is not to say, however, that the government has totally abandoned the use of force when dealing with the militants. What is important to note is that the Thai government has shown its willingness to address some of the key issues/grievances such as 'handing over limited powers' to the three provinces of Yala, Narathiwat, and Pattani ("Thailand mulls ceding", 2013). Such tangible and positive actions could potentially build trust, and make it easier for the government to win hearts and minds.

Increase Economic, Development and Humanitarian aid and other Soft Power Programmes: Canada

The Canadian government (under Stephen Harper) introduced several soft power initiatives as part of a broad strategy to combat violent extremism particularly in relation to ISIS. The government was also explicit in detailing how the assistance was distributed, what form it was in, and who received aid.

Humanitarian Assistance

Canada pledged over $100 million in humanitarian assistance for Iraqis affected by the violence. This included: (a) food to 1.7 million people; (b) shelter and relief supplies (such as hygiene kits, cooking materials, blankets) to 1.26 million people; and (c) improved access to education opportunities for up to 500,000 children including providing education and protection assistance for up to 150,000 conflict-affected children (Government of Canada, 2015a).

It also supported humanitarian efforts in Syria and its neighbouring countries. For instance, those in Syria were provided with funds, relief items, food, clean water, and school materials (Government of Canada, 2015a). In Jordan, "52,000 conflict-affected children and youth were able to attend child and adolescent friendly spaces, and 36,980 conflict-affected women and men were provided awareness sessions on preventing and responding to violence, protection, referral, and sexual and gender-based violence" (Government of Canada, 2015a). In Lebanon, Canada supported non-formal education for 9,170 conflict-affected school-aged children and life-skills education, as well as literacy and numeracy to 7,140 at-risk adolescents (Government of Canada, 2015a).

Refugee Resettlement

Canada expanded its commitment to help Syrian refugees by planning to resettle an additional 10,000 Syrians by the end of 2017. It is also working with humanitarian partners and private sponsors to resettle these Syrian refugees in Canadian communities (Government of Canada, 2015b). In response to the ongoing violence in Iraq, Canada also expanded its commitment to help Iraqi refugees by resettling an additional 3,000 by the end of 2015 (Government of Canada, 2015b).

Developmental Programmes

In terms of development assistance in Iraq and the region, Canada's contributions to this effort include: (a) $10 million to strengthen accountability for sexual and gender-based violence (SGBV) crimes and to support victims of SGBV in ISIS-affected areas; (b) programs to protect the rights of religious minorities in Iraq and the region; and (c) programs to build resilience and social cohesion in communities affected by conflict, and to address longer term needs, including inclusive governance (Government of Canada, 2015c).

Non-lethal security assistance is also being provided to Iraqi forces in the form of: "personal protective gear, vehicles, global positioning systems, and robots to detect and disable improvised explosive devices" (Government of Canada, 2015c, para. 5).

For countries that host significant numbers of Syrian refugees, such as Jordan, Egypt and Lebanon, Canada committed more than $230 million in aid. "This assistance is focused on building resilience in refugee-hosting communities, providing basic services such as education, municipal services, water and sanitation, and fostering social cohesion" (Government of Canada, 2015c, para. 7). In Jordan for example, "approximately 1 million Jordanians and Syrian refugee students are benefiting from improved access to quality education, water, sanitation, and hygiene initiatives" (Government of Canada, 2015c, para. 8). Also, "support for the provision of municipal services to approximately 1.1 million Jordanians and Syrian refugees" is also being offered (Government of Canada, 2015c, para. 8).

These programmes are highly commendable, and more states should incorporate such initiatives with their CVE programmes. However, attention must be paid to the realities on the ground to ensure that: (a) recipients receive the due aid; (b) abuses/scandals do not occur; and (c) lives are tangibly improved. Careful monitoring and oversight of NGOs and third parties are critical in this regard.

Minimise Inconsistencies between Rhetoric and Action

This is by far the most difficult for states to accomplish because of the ever-changing dynamics in the political and diplomatic realms, which ultimately affect its interests and priorities. Yet, reducing (as opposed to eliminating) such inconsistencies is vital in rebuilding and/or building trust. As Kirsten Mogensen, an associate professor at Roskilde University, writes: "Just as is the case in corporate branding and public relations, public diplomacy is only perceived as convincing and can only create soft power if the country behaves in accordance with what it says it does" (Mogensen, 2015, p. 320).

POSITIVE STATE ACTION AT THE MICRO LEVEL

At the micro level, state action may affect individuals at the personal level, which some would argued, is highly intrusive. Nevertheless, there are three areas that are worth focusing on: (a) creating a sense of belonging to the nation; (b) civilian management training for law enforcement; and (c) working with groups to manage religious converts.

Fostering a Sense of National Identity

Existing psychological studies have shown that a sense of "belonging is primal [and] fundamental to [an individual's] ... sense of happiness and well-being" (Enayati, 2012, para. 6). This is because "our interests, motivation, health and happiness are inextricably tied to the feeling that we belong to a greater community that may share common interests and aspirations" (para. 7). Conversely, "isolation, loneliness and low social status can harm a person's subjective sense of well-being, as well as his or her intellectual achievement, immune function and health" (para. 8).

Additional research also demonstrates "that even a single instance of exclusion can undermine well-being, IQ test performance and self-control" (Enayati, 2012, para. 8). Simply put, "if you don't feel like you belong, you are both less motivated and less likely to hang in there in the face of obstacles" (para. 9). This has implications for individuals and in particular youth who are increasingly drawn to ISIS, and are determine to join the group in Syria and Iraq.

In studies done in the United States on the factors that motivate young people to join gangs, it was revealed that 'group identity' was the major push factor. For example, Rosales (2015) notes that:

From the inner city streets of Los Angeles or Baltimore, to the rough barrios of Tegucigalpa or Guate-mala City, to the violent post-revolutionary urban districts in Tunis, youth are getting involved in gangs or extremist groups in the pursuit of one simple thing: belonging ... A young Arab who once considered joining ISIL [ISIS] told USAID staff in Tunisia, 'I just wanted to be part of something'. (para. 4-5)

Existing studies by the Soufan group and others suggest that many foreign fighters have cited similar reasons for joining ISIS. Richard Barrett of The Soufan Group (as cited in Yan, 2014) explains:

The general picture provided by foreign fighters of their lives in Syria suggests camaraderie, good mo-rale and purposeful activity, all mixed in with a sense of understated heroism, designed to attract their friends as well as to boost their own self-esteem. (para. 10)

In light of these insights, it is useful for the state to attempt to foster or improve the sense of belong-ing citizens and new migrants have for the nation. This is a complicated and challenging task because individuals must experience or witness tangible benefits for the approach to be successful. As Mona Siddiqui, professor of Islamic and Interreligious Studies at the University of Edinburgh, writes:

[L]iberal democracies thrive on people of different backgrounds and beliefs being able to live together at some level. But such democracies will only flourish when people feel that for all their material as well as cultural differences, they have a stake in the moral life and well-being of the country they call home. (Siddiqui, 2015, para. 16)

Policies as well as rhetoric must be aligned and indeed designed for this purpose, and recalibration of policies carried out if necessary.

While it is beyond the scope of this chapter to discuss specific policies that would help build na-tional identity and foster a greater sense of belonging, a few domains are worth mentioning. These are: (a) economic policies that among other things provide opportunities for individuals to make a living; (b) fund social welfare and other programmes; (c) assimilation policies; (d) migration policies; and (e) national security/law and order policies.

It must be stressed that while the state can fine-tune its policies and overall approach to help create a sense of belonging to the nation, individuals too, are responsible for the success or failure of such policies. Resistance, unwillingness, and inability to integrate will undoubtedly present challenges (Malik, 2015).

Civilian Management Training for Law Enforcement

As law enforcement and counter-terror units from the military, police and paramilitary are effectively the visible faces of the state when dealing with the public in crisis or conflict situations, it is imperative that they undergo specialised training to help them deal with crowds, especially when policing/dealing with civilians and communities.

As the military, police and paramilitary have different roles, the treatment of civilians in different crisis/conflict scenarios is expectedly different. A tongue in cheek conceptualisation of the issue was summed up as "police officers ... [are] ... better prepared to work with a population to help it achieve internal security; soldiers ... [are] ... trained, as the saying goes, to break things and kill people" (Mar-ten, 2007, p. 242).

The police in many jurisdictions are mandated to engender 'public trust' and relationship-building, as such, many officers undergo training for these purposes. For instance, in the United States, the Bureau of Justice Assistance (BJA) and the Office of Community Oriented Policing Services (COPS) "have developed guides, publications, webinars, checklists and tools for law enforcement agencies on community policing, building community trust, diversity training, privacy protections, and safeguarding first amendment rights" (Department of Justice, 2014, para. 4). The United States further acknowledges that trust-building has to be done before a crisis occurs and takes considerable time, hence regular activities are organised to keep the police engaged with communities. As a Department of Justice News Release states: "Building strong police-community relations requires a sustained effort over time, yet maintaining these relationships is exceedingly difficult during and in the aftermath of a high-profile incident or civil unrest" (Department of Justice, 2014, para. 4).

While the effectiveness of such activities can be contested, the attempts to foster better relationships between the police and the civilian population are extremely helpful.

The changing functions of the military in some countries suggest that training officers to properly manage civilian populations, especially on overseas missions, is necessary. The U.S. Army for instance includes *Civilian Casualty Mitigation* in its 'Army Tactics, Techniques, and Procedures (ATTP) 3-37.31' doctrine. This prescribes how officers and other ranks should treat civilians and combatants in foreign conflict zones, and suggests techniques/approaches. For instance, with regard to changing mind-sets: "during training and exercises, effective commanders avoid focusing exclusively on fighting against a hostile enemy, as this could reinforce a 'shoot first' mentality". And "negative attitudes, such as perceiving host-nation civilians as inferior, must be avoided because they lead to thinking that civilian casualties (CIVCAS) are not too regrettable" (Department of the Army, 2012, p. 2-3). Training programs are however only effective if the 'code of conduct' they are meant to instil is internalised, supported by senior ranks, enforceable to a certain extent, and dependent on self-discipline. Nevertheless, civilian management is increasingly becoming a necessary skill for law enforcement.

Working with Religious Groups to Help Converts[1]

Muslim converts in the West who have professed extremist beliefs, have come under the spotlight for terrorism-related activities in and outside their home countries. For instance, a Briton and a French national were identified in an ISIS video showing the mass beheadings of Syrian soldiers. The beheading of two Americans – a journalist and an aid worker – in Iraq was carried out by a Muslim convert with a British accent (i.e., Jihadi John).

In 2014, there were several attacks linked with such converts including: (a) the attack on the Canadian Parliament perpetrated by Michael Zehaf-Bibeau, a recent Muslim convert; (b) the attack on New York Police Department officers by Zale Thompson; and (c) the brutal slaying of Lee Rigby, an off-duty soldier in south-east London, by Michael Adebolajo and Michael Adebowale.

The motivations behind these acts were arguably personal and differed from individual to individual. However, what was common was the embrace of a worldview that legitimised acts of extreme violence to achieve objectives, which were premised on religious grounds. Was this the result of the convert's misinterpretation or misunderstanding of religious texts? Or was the convert influenced by radical individuals close to him or her, so-called radical influencers? Or did violent extremist groups simply appeal to the psyche of the convert?

According to psychologists, religious conversions usually happen when an individual is forced to develop a 'new meaning system' to replace the existing one as the latter has failed to adequately explain or validate the 'discrepancies' of life – e.g., the sudden death of a loved one (Paloutzian & Park, 2005). As conversion involves significant changes to a person's meaning system, it will naturally result in observable changes to his/her "self-perception, identity, life purpose, attitudes, values, goals, sensitivities, ultimate concerns and behaviour" (Paloutzian & Park, 2005, p. 334). The behavioural and attitudinal changes are stressful enough, and personal circumstances (e.g., conversion to facilitate marriage), environmental and situational factors (e.g., reaction of family and friends), as well as societal dynamics (e.g., discrimination against Muslims) may potentially add to the complexity of the conversion process.

Islam, like many other religions, is not monolithic; "its form and expression vary from one Muslim to another and from group to group" (Kusuma, 2010, para. 5). For example, Indonesian Islam, while sharing similar tenets with say Pakistani Islam, is still different in many fundamental ways. This plurality can cause confusion in the convert, and in some cases, alienation, if the convert, while Muslim, is still excluded because he/she belongs to a different ethnic group.

In fact, a 2013 Oxford Analytica report identified feelings of personal emptiness and social isolation as a major causal factor of radicalisation among Muslim converts. The study also argued that the resentment of 'modernity, globalisation and secular society'; the absence of formal education and training in Islamic doctrine and theology; and the interpretation of 'Islamic ideology as a form of protest' were key push factors towards radicalisation (Oxford Analytica, 2013).

The study found that:

[R]adicalisation is usually the result of social interaction; it is less common for converts to self-radicalise in isolation. The process, which involves the convert developing a more extreme interpretation of his/her faith to legitimise or justify violence, generally takes months or years. (Oxford Analytica, 2013)

It is for these reasons that increased psychological and community support for converts is necessary, as it can enable them to become more knowledgeable about their new faith, more confident about their place in the world, and most importantly, more discerning about alternative interpretations of religious doctrine.

The findings suggest that positive community intervention in terms of increased guidance and support is essential to help converts deal with the challenges they encounter on the religious, social, personal and sometimes financial fronts. As such, the creation of support groups for converts may be useful. For instance, in view of how "as a community, they [new Muslims] face unique challenges and have a distinct set of needs as compared to Muslims who are born into the faith", the United Arab Emirates organised a New Muslim Summit in January 2014 (Shaaban, 2014, para. 3). The summit aimed to develop effective strategies and systems to cater to the needs of new Muslims by raising awareness, educating, and providing direction to new converts (Shaaban, 2014).

Similarly in New Zealand, the New Muslim Project was founded in 2012 by a group of volunteers. It was initiated as "people in a non-Muslim country like New Zealand can be exposed to a wide range of information about Islam, (But) not all is right or authentic" (New Muslim Project NZ, 2015, para. 2). The project attempts to "provide support for people reverting to Islam, as well as those who have already reverted. We are also available to assist anyone who is interested in learning more about Islam" (New Muslim Project NZ, 2015, para. 1). It also organises social events, conducts religious courses, and provides useful information and literature about Islam.

In Singapore, the Muslim Converts' Association of Singapore (aka *Darul Arqam*), established in 1979, aims to

[P]rovide religious guidance and to render assistance (including financial assistance) to members as may be necessary; to organise religious, literary, and/or recreational activities, and to publish Islamic articles and/or literature; to participate and provide welfare services for the community where necessary; and to represent the interests of all Muslim converts residing in Singapore. (The Muslim Converts' Association of Singapore, 2015, para. 2)

In addition to community support and guidance, supportive counselling for converts is another avenue that communities can introduce to help converts during their conversion process. Supportive counselling entails a one-on-one session whereby the counsellor uses techniques to reduce the anxiety (e.g., stress arising from the conversion process) faced by the client. Such an approach may enable the counsellors to better reach out to the converts' needs and establish rapport. More importantly, it may divert the converts from turning to radical ideology to address their needs. Counselling can therefore help alleviate some of the personal, situational challenges, and stress associated with conversion.

However, supportive counselling would be useful only if converts are motivated to participate in the counselling process. Collaboration with religious authorities and/or specialists can certainly help in this regard. For instance, a possible approach, if it has not been done already, would be to explore the use of techniques that incorporate Islamic concepts into the counselling process. The common appreciation for Islam may create a facilitative platform for converts to address their needs and concerns.

The programmes and examples highlighted above would benefit tremendously from state support directly and/or indirectly.

CONCLUSION

While many of the approaches discussed in this chapter pertain to offline strategies, they nevertheless, have a significant impact on CVE initiatives online. This is because extremist narratives are often framed and premised on real world discontentment and events, which suggest that countering them, would also have to be based on tangible real world solutions.

Positive state action is vital in this regard as lives of individuals and communities can be changed for the better through various interventions. Moreover, it would be easier to counter negative messaging, perceptions and stereotypes in both the online and offline realms. Finally, it would also help overall efforts to improve public trust in states, which is a major stumbling block to effective public communications and state-initiated CVE initiatives. It should be emphasised that strategic communication on and offline is only effective if there are sound policies to back them up.

REFERENCES

Afghan bombing drives allies apart. (2008, August 27). *BBC News*. Retrieved from http://news.bbc.co.uk/2/hi/south_asia/7584464.stm

Afghan survivors tell of wedding bombing. (2008, July 13). *BBC News*. Retrieved from http://news.bbc.co.uk/2/hi/south_asia/7504574.stm

Ahmed, F. (2012, July 19). Social media is lying to you about Burma's Muslim 'cleansing'. *The Express Tribune Blog*. Retrieved from http://blogs.tribune.com.pk/story/12867/social-media-is-lying-to-you-about-burmas-muslim-cleansing/comment-page-4/

Air strike in Yemen kills 15 wedding guests mistaken for al-Qaida – officials. (2013, December 12). *The Guardian*. Retrieved from http://www.theguardian.com/world/2013/dec/12/air-strike-yemen-15-wedding-guest-killed-mistaken-al-qaida

Amnesty International. (2006). *Pakistan: Over 80 people victims of possible extrajudicial execution in Bajaur* (Amnesty International Report Index: ASA 33/046/2006). Retrieved from http://www.amnesty.org/en/library/info/ASA33/046/2006

Amnesty International. (2013). *Will I be next? US drone strikes in Pakistan*. Retrieved from http://www.amnestyusa.org/sites/default/files/asa330132013en.pdf

Baxter, K., & Akbarzadeh, S. (2008). *US foreign policy in the Middle East: The roots of anti-Americanism*. London: Routledge.

Borum, R. (2003). Understanding the terrorist mind-set. *FBI Law Enforcement Bulletin*, 72.

Campbell, D. (2012). *Myth of compassion fatigue*. Retrieved from https://www.david-campbell.org/wp-content/documents/DC_Myth_of_Compassion_Fatigue_Feb_2012.pdf

Carruthers, S. L. (2000). *The media at war: Communication and conflict in the twentieth century*. Basingstoke, UK: Palgrave Macmillan.

Cheong, D. D. (2014, December 12). Tackling extremism among western Muslim converts. *The Straits Times*. Retrieved from http://www.straitstimes.com/opinion/tackling-extremism-among-western-muslim-converts

Chouliaraki, L. (2006). *The spectatorship of suffering*. London: Sage.

Chulov, M. (2014, December 11). Isis: the inside story. *The Guardian*. Retrieved from http://www.theguardian.com/world/2014/dec/11/-sp-isis-the-inside-story

Cornish, P., Lindley-French, J., & Yorke, C. (2011). *Strategic communications and national strategy (A Chatham House Report)*. London: The Royal Institute of International Affairs.

Cottee, S. (2015, March 2). Why it's so hard to stop isis propaganda. *The Atlantic*. Retrieved from http://www.theatlantic.com/international/archive/2015/03/why-its-so-hard-to-stop-isis-propaganda/386216/

Culzac, N. (2014, August 10). Israel-Gaza conflict: 150,000 protest in London for end to 'massacre and arms trade'. *The Independent*. Retrieved from http://www.independent.co.uk/news/uk/home-news/israelgaza-conflict-thousands-protest-in-london-for-end-to-massacre-and-arms-trade-9659180.html

Dabiq. (2015). *Burning of Jordanian pilot – Retribution (Issue 7)*. Retrieved from http://media.clarionproject.org/files/islamic-state/islamic-state-dabiq-magazine-issue-7-from-hypocrisy-to-apostasy.pdf

Department of Justice. (2014, November 21). *Department of justice releases resource guide to help law enforcement strengthen relationships with communities.* Retrieved from http://www.justice.gov/opa/pr/ department-justice-releases-resource-guide-help-law-enforcement-strengthen-relationships

Department of the Army. (2012, July 31). *Civilian casualty mitigation. Army tactics, techniques, and procedures* (No. 3-37). Retrieved from https://fas.org/irp/doddir/army/attp3-37-31.pdf

Drone strikes by US may violate international law, says UN. (2013, October 18). *The Guardian.* Retrieved from http://www.theguardian.com/world/2013/oct/18/drone-strikes-us-violate-law-un

Egypt jails police over activist khaled said's death. (2011, October 26). *BBC News.* Retrieved from http:// www.bbc.com/news/15467022

Enayati, A. (2012, June 1). The importance of belonging. *CNN.* Retrieved from http://edition.cnn. com/2012/06/01/health/enayati-importance-of-belonging/

Field, C. (2015, June 22). NC teen planned to attack local bar, concert, then kill 1,000, FBI says. *WYFF4. com News.* Retrieved from http://www.wyff4.com/news/nc-teen-planned-to-attack-local-bar-concert-then-kill-1000-fbi-says/33712110

Full text: bin Laden's 'letter to America'. (2002, November 24). *The Guardian.* Retrieved from http:// www.theguardian.com/world/2002/nov/24/theobserver

Government of Canada. (2015a). *Providing humanitarian assistance.* Retrieved from http://international. gc.ca/world-monde/security-securite/isis-eiis/humanitarian_assistance-aide_humanitaire.aspx?lang=eng

Government of Canada. (2015b). *How Canada is helping Syrian and Iraqi refugees.* Retrieved from http://www.cic.gc.ca/english/refugees/crisis/canada-response.asp

Government of Canada. (2015c). *Supporting stabilization and development.* Retrieved from http:// international.gc.ca/world-monde/security-securite/isis-eiis/stabilization_development-stabilisation_developpement.aspx?lang=eng

Hasan, N., Hendriks, B., Janssen, F., & Meijer, R. (2012). *Counter terrorism strategies in Indonesia, Algeria and Saudi Arabia.* The Hague, Netherlands: Netherlands Institute of International Relations.

Heywood, E. (2015). Comparing Russian, French and UK television news. *Russian Journal of Communication, 7*(1), 40–52. doi:10.1080/19409419.2015.1008940

Holland, K. (2014, July 12). Thousands march in cities across Ireland in support of Gaza. *Irish Times.* Retrieved from http://www.irishtimes.com/news/politics/thousands-march-in-cities-across-ireland-in-support-of-gaza-1.1864826

Horn, R. (2013, February 17). In southern Thailand, 16 dead and no peace in sight. *Time Online.* Retrieved from http://world.time.com/2013/02/17/in-southern-thailand-16-dead-and-no-peace-in-sight/

Human Rights Watch. (2008, September 8). *Afghanistan: Civilian deaths from airstrikes.* Retrieved from https://www.hrw.org/news/2008/09/08/afghanistan-civilian-deaths-airstrikes

Indonesian anti-terror squad killings prompt revenge attacks. (2013, February 8). *ABC News.* Retrieved from http://www.abc.net.au/news/2013-02-08/indonesian-anti-terror-squad-killings-prompt/4507926

Israel Defense Forces. (2012, November 15). How does the IDF minimize harm to Palestinian civilians? *IDF Blog*. Retrieved from https://www.idfblog.com/blog/2012/11/15/how-does-the-idf-minimize-harm-to-palestinian-civilians/

Kusuma, M. T. (2010, October 12). Islam is a mosaic, not monolith. *The Jakarta Post*. Retrieved from http://www.thejakartapost.com/news/2010/10/12/islam-a-mosaic-not-monolith.html

Kyaw, S. W. (2012, July 18). *Western Myanmar unrest: Partisan portrayals risk extremist implications*. RSIS Commentaries (131/2012). Singapore: S. Rajaratnam School of International Studies.

Liow, C. J., & Pathan, D. (2010). *Confronting ghosts: Thailand's shapeless southern insurgency (Lowy Institute Paper 30)*. New South Wales, Australia: Lowy Institute for International Policy.

Makruf, J., & Pertiwi, M. (2010). Indonesia. In C. Ziemke-Dickens, & J. Droogan (Eds.), Asian transnational security challenges: Emerging trends, regional visions (pp. 137–149). Sydney, Australia: The Council for Asian Transnational Threat Research (CATR) & Centre for Policing, Intelligence and Counter Terrorism (PICT), Macquarie University.

Malik, K. (2015). The failure of multiculturalism: Community versus society in Europe. *Foreign Affairs*, *94*(2), 21–32.

Marcus, J. (2006, February 28). US faces sceptical world over Iraq. *BBC News*. Retrieved from http://news.bbc.co.uk/2/hi/middle_east/4755770.stm

Marten, K. (2007). Statebuilding and force: The proper role of foreign militaries. *Journal of Intervention and Statebuilding*, *1*(2), 231–247. doi:10.1080/17502970701302862

Mastura, N. (2014, July 19). Open letter to Singapore ministers – Why are we silent on Gaza? *The Online Citizen*. Retrieved from http://www.theonlinecitizen.com/2014/07/open-letter-to-singapore-ministers-why-are-we-silent-on-gaza/

McCants, W. (2015, June 19). Interview with Alberto Fernandez – Experts weigh in (part 2): Can the United States counter ISIS propaganda? *Brookings Institute's Markaz (Middle East Politics and Policy) Blog*. Retrieved from http://www.brookings.edu/blogs/markaz/posts/2015/06/19-us-counter-messaging-isis-fernandez

Moeller, S. D. (1999). *Compassion fatigue: How the media sell disease, famine, war and death*. New York, NY: Routledge.

Mogensen, K. (2015). International trust and public diplomacy. *International Communication Gazette*, *77*(4), 315–336. doi:10.1177/1748048514568764

Najibi, N. (2013, November 21). International law ignored: Pakistan at risk. *The World Post*. Retrieved from http://www.huffingtonpost.com/neda-najibi/international-law-ignored_b_4306306.html

New Muslim Project NZ. (2014). *About us*. Retrieved from http://newmuslimproject.co.nz/?page_id=2803

Nirmala, M. (2014, February 2). Don't fall for a terrorist's bait. *The Straits Times*. Retrieved from http://news.asiaone.com/news/world/dont-fall-terrorists-bait

Nussbaum, M. C. (2001). *Upheavals of thought: The intelligence of emotion.* Cambridge: Cambridge University Press. doi:10.1017/CBO9780511840715

Osman, S. (2013, August 13). *Funerals of suspected terrorists in Indonesia: a rallying point?* RSIS Commentaries (150/2013). Singapore: S. Rajaratnam School of International Studies.

Oxford Analytica. (2013, July 10). *Converts give clues to radicalisation.* Retrieved from https://www.oxan.com/display.aspx?ItemID=DB184468

Paloutzian, R. F., & Park, C. L. (2005). Religious conversion and spiritual transformation: A meaning-system analysis. In R. F. Paloutzian & C. L. Park (Eds.), *Handbook of the psychology of religion and spirituality* (pp. 331–347). New York, NY: Guilford.

Pew Research Center. (2013). *Attitudes toward the United States* (PEW Global Survey 2013). Retrieved from http://www.pewglobal.org/2013/07/18/chapter-1-attitudes-toward-the-united-states/

Purported al-awlaki message calls for jihad against US. (2010, March 18). *CNN.* Retrieved from http://edition.cnn.com/2010/WORLD/europe/03/17/al.awlaki.message/

Rosales, C. A. (2015, June 2). Fostering a sense of belonging key in preventing youth violence. *US State Department Official Blog.* Retrieved from https://blogs.state.gov/stories/2015/06/02/fostering-sense-belonging-key-preventing-youth-violence#sthash.Akq93lHV.dpuf

Salleh, N. A. M. (2014, July 26). Hundreds gather at Hong Lim Park in solidarity with people of Gaza. *The Straits Times.* Retrieved from http://www.straitstimes.com/singapore/hundreds-gather-at-hong-lim-park-in-solidarity-with-people-of-gaza

Scott, P. R., & Jacka, J. M. (2011). *Auditing social media: A governance and risk guide.* Hoboken, NJ: John Wiley & Sons, Inc.

Shaaban, A. (2014, January 20). Helping Muslim converts learn the ropes. *Khaleej Times.* Retrieved from http://www.khaleejtimes.com/article/20140119/ARTICLE/301199883/1002

Shoichet, C. (2013, September 6). Syria's rebels: 20 things you need to know. *CNN.* Retrieved from http://edition.cnn.com/2013/09/06/world/meast/syria-rebels/

Siddiqui, M. (2015, March 1). Nations flourish when people enjoy a sense of belonging. *The Guardian.* Retrieved from http://www.theguardian.com/commentisfree/2015/mar/01/muslims-in-britain-must-act-to-ensure-peace

Sontag, S. (2003). *Regarding the pain of others.* New York, NY: Farrar, Straus and Giroux.

Taufiqurrohman, M. (2013). Counterterrorism in Indonesia: Quo vadis? *Counter Terrorist Trends and Analysis, 5*(6), 7–10.

Terror suspect Cherif Kouachi: 'I was ready to go and die in battle'. (2015, January 9). *CNN.* Retrieved from http://edition.cnn.com/2015/01/09/europe/cherif-kouachi-court-documents/

Terror, torture and torpor: Inside Guantanamo bay with the 'forever prisoners'. (2014, December 13). *Sydney Morning Herald.* Retrieved from http://www.smh.com.au/world/terror-torture-and-torpor-inside-guantanamo-bay-with-the-forever-prisoners-20141212-125m1z.html

Tester, K. (2001). *Compassion, morality and the media*. Buckingham: Open University Press.

Thailand mulls ceding power to end deadly southern insurgency. (2013, June 12). *Asia One*. Retrieved from http://news.asiaone.com/print/News/AsiaOne%2BNews/Asia/Story/A1Story20130612-429225.html

The martyrs of the south. (2012, December 5). *Bangkok Post*. Retrieved from http://www.bangkokpost.com/archive/the-martyrs-of-the-south/324580

The Muslim Converts' Association of Singapore. (2014). *About us*. Retrieved from http://www.darul-arqam.org.sg/corporate/

The White House. (2015, February 18). *Fact sheet: The White House summit on countering violent extremism*. Retrieved from https://www.whitehouse.gov/the-press-office/2015/02/18/fact-sheet-white-house-summit-countering-violent-extremism

UN Office for the Coordination of Humanitarian Affairs (OCHA). (2014, October 15). *Gaza Crisis: Situation Overview*. Retrieved from http://www.ochaopt.org/content.aspx?id=1010361

U.S. general: Israel-Palestinian conflict foments anti-U.S. sentiment. (2010, March 17). *Haaretz*. Retrieved from http://www.haaretz.com/news/u-s-general-israel-palestinian-conflict-foments-anti-u-s-sentiment-1.264910

van Ginkel, B. (2011). *Incitement to terrorism: A matter of prevention or repression?* (ICCT Research Paper). Retrieved from http://www.icct.nl/download/file/ICCT-Van-Ginkel-Incitement-To-Terrorism-August-2011.pdf

Yan, H. (2014, July 10). Why is ISIS so successful at luring westerners? *CNN*. Retrieved from http://edition.cnn.com/2014/10/07/world/isis-western-draw/

Yang, J. (2012, November 7). *Attacks on Indonesian Police: Not Just Terrorism?* RSIS Commentaries (208/2012). Singapore: S. Rajaratnam School of International Studies.

Zenn, J. (2012, July 27). Islamic militants take aim at Myanmar. *Asia Times Online*. Retrieved from http://www.atimes.com/atimes/Southeast_Asia/NG27Ae04.html

ENDNOTE

[1.]   This section originates from an earlier article by Cheong (2014).

Chapter 15
Building National Resilience in the Digital Era of Violent Extremism:
Systems and People

Jethro Tan
Home Team Behavioural Sciences Centre, Ministry of Home Affairs, Singapore

Yingmin Wang
Home Team Behavioural Sciences Centre, Ministry of Home Affairs, Singapore

Danielle Gomes
Home Team Behavioural Sciences Centre, Ministry of Home Affairs, Singapore

ABSTRACT

The threat of violent extremism in the Internet age has undoubtedly become one important focus of research, policy, and government bodies all over the world. Understandably, many resources have been invested into counter violent extremism efforts, such as the identification of possible radicalised individuals, and understanding the psychology behind violent extremism. These methods adopt a resistance stance and attempt to prevent violent extremism. However, this chapter argues that resilience is equally, if not more important given the unpredictable nature of violent extremism. The first part examines 'systems' within a nation such as critical infrastructure and how concepts such as 'resilient-by-design' can be incorporated to ensure continuity in times of attacks. The second part will explore 'person' factors of crisis communication, cohesion, and social capital, and how these factors can afford a cohesive society that can overcome the cracks in social order and harmony often caused by violent extremism.

INTRODUCTION

Countering violent extremism has become a cornerstone concern of national security, especially after the notorious attack on the World Trade Centre in the United States on September 11, 2001. Subsequently, the 'war on terror' has hardly paused, with no signs of abating in the near future. Such strategies had involved security measures (e.g., surveillance) and military interventions on violent extremist groups

DOI: 10.4018/978-1-5225-0156-5.ch015

(Global Policy Forum, n.d). Evidently, relying on the strategy of resisting against violent extremists is simply inadequate. Successful attacks in cities such as the London underground bombings of 2005, the Charlie Hebdo shooting in Paris, and hostage situation in Sydney, among many other attacks all over the world, illustrate the complexity behind countering violent extremism. Indeed, nations are often reminded of the threat posed by violent extremism despite increased efforts to keep violent extremists at bay.

More recently, the presence of the Islamic State in Iraq and Syria (ISIS) on social media, the concerns of the influx of foreign fighters to Iraq and Syria, and the dissemination of videos of brutal murders of innocent people are some manifestation of online violent extremism. The strategic use of technology and the Internet has brought forth an unprecedented age of violent extremism and radicalisation through the digital space. As such, the threat of violent extremism in the Internet age has undoubtedly become one important focus for researchers, policymakers, and government bodies across the world. This goes to show that the threat of violent extremism is an evolving one, often pitting law enforcement and policymakers against the violent extremists who are constantly stepping up their game.

VIOLENT EXTREMISM IN THE DIGITAL ERA

The threat of violent extremism has become more potent in the digital era. While the advent of the Internet and subsequent info-communication technologies has brought along innovative solutions to life, it also brings about critical security concerns (Hussain & Saltman, 2014; Weimann, 2004). This implies that radical ideologies are capable of spreading at a speed previously unseen before. Cases of lone-wolf radicalisation (e.g., Roshonara Choudhry) illustrate the effectiveness of the Internet as a medium to propagate radical ideologies. Calls for attacks by radical propagators have also been found to cause critical disturbance to the functioning of the nation and compromise the safety of citizens (e.g., Sydney Siege). More importantly, these case examples raised indicate that violent extremism initiated and propagated online have the potential to cause significant harm in the offline space.

Understandably, many resources have been invested into countering violent extremism, such as the identification of possible radicalised individuals, understanding the psychology of violent extremists, or even technological warfare (e.g., drone attacks). These methods attempt to circumvent the consequences of violent extremism, which evidently will cause chaos in the highly connected world we live in. These counter violent extremism efforts adopt a 'resistance' stance (Longstaff, Armstrong, Perrin, Parker, & Hidek, 2010; Ng, 2011), and are essential to provide safety to the people and ensure growth of the economy.

However, preventive measures against violent extremism, while shown to be practical (Qatar International Academy for Security Studies, 2010), should not be the only measure taken against violent extremism. It is equally imperative to entertain the thought of how to respond to a violent extremist attack that comes into fruition. In doing so, researchers, policymakers, and government bodies can then implement strategies to enhance the ability of the nation to bounce back from the attack, and ensure continued functioning in light of the attack. In short, it is argued that resilience has to be built into individuals, communities, organisations, and nations.

RESILIENCE AS A STRATEGY FOR COUNTER VIOLENT EXTREMISM

The notion of resilience stems from psychological research which posits that there are traits, processes, and outcomes that allow individuals to bounce back from an adverse event. Since then, research on resilience has advanced to explore other levels of analysis: community resilience, organisational resilience, and national resilience.

Under the purview of national security, national resilience is of particular importance in enabling the nation to better mitigate the impact of crisis (Ellis, 2011). As seen in extensive media coverage, the impact of violent extremist attacks stretches far beyond the loss of lives. Psychological, economic, and infrastructural harm often ensue, and may take many years for the nation to recover. Besides the individual itself, such attacks affect the entire society at a national level. Thus, the authors argued that national resilience may provide valuable insights about how a nation can bounce back from a crisis (e.g., a violent extremist attack), learn from it, and ensure that the nation does not fall victim to the threat again. For the purpose of this chapter, national resilience can be defined as the ability of a nation to adapt and respond to crisis, with the goal of survival and continuity in her core structures and people, allowing the nation to thrive post-crisis (Gomes et al., 2015a).

To begin with, understanding resilience at the national level requires drawing from research across multiple disciplines (Gomes et al, 2015a). This is because such complex systems (i.e., nation) consist of both systemic and psychological components. The systemic component usually relates to the non-human aspects of the nation, which involves ensuring continued core functioning of critical systems. For example, the nation needs to ensure that systems such as water supply remain available in the event of an attack, so as to meet the needs of the citizens. Failure of such key systems to function in the event of an attack will prevent the nation from recovering quickly.

When considering the systems, one must also be cognisant that it is the people that run the systems. Thus, much thought has to be given to policymaking that targets the psychology of the nation's people. For example, in the aftermath of the Boston Bombings in 2013, research showed that effective crisis communications to the people allowed for the nation to recover from the crisis at a faster pace (Davis, Alves, & Sklansky, 2014). This illustrates the need for policies that target the psychological component of a nation. Other psychological factors that may be important at a national level will include building trust, social capital, and learning.

Applying a resilience lens to the systems and the people components of a nation allows researchers, policymakers, and government bodies to anticipate potential threats, and put into place recovery efforts that may allow nations to adapt and recovery quickly from an attack. This chapter will then explore ways for nations to build resilience against violent extremism in the digital era from the system and person perspective.

ASSUMPTIONS TO CONSIDER IN THE EVENT OF A VIOLENT EXTREMIST ATTACK

In order to build a resilient nation that recovers quickly and efficiently from a violent extremist attack, there are several key principles that need to be addressed. When considering the post-crisis efforts of a nation, it is important to discuss the potential consequences of an attack. Violent extremist attacks can present in several forms, and the modus operandi may differ. Thus, it would be unreasonable to predict and make anticipatory plans to account for all scenarios.

However, certain common characteristics of violent extremist attacks have been identified by researchers. According to Schmid (2004, p. 199), a violent extremist attack attempts to unlawfully and intentionally cause:

1. Death or serious bodily injury to any person;
2. Serious damage to public or private property, including a place of public use, a state or government facility, a public transportation system, an infrastructure facility or the environment;
3. Damage to property, places, facilities, or systems, resulting or likely to result in major economic loss, when the purpose of the conduct, by its nature or context, is to intimidate a population, or to compel a government or an international organisation to do or abstain from doing any act.

Aside from physical harm to people and infrastructure, the authors of the current chapter further argued that there is a need to consider the psychological impact of an attack. Thus, it should be appended that violent extremist attacks also aim to:

4. Cause psychological harm – through inciting fear, panic, and disorder in the public (Borum, 2004; Neo, Khader, Shi, Dillon, & Ong, 2015);
5. Raise awareness about the groups' cause and ideologies (Hoffman, 2006; Neo, et. al., 2015).

In short, a violent extremist attack would cause damage to the systemic or psychological component of the nation. Furthermore, the after effects of an attack may result in chain reactions within the society, observable both in the online and offline space. One example that illustrates the confluence of the online and offline interaction is the Arab Springs, where social media was seen to play a key role in triggering an offline protest (Eaton, 2013). Applying a resilience perspective would then denote that nations must be mindful of these potential consequences, and make preparations to deal with an attack. The following sections will discuss key principles that policymakers, researchers, and government bodies have to consider, in order to facilitate recovery from an attack.

STRATEGIES TO BUILD NATIONAL RESILIENCE IN THE DIGITAL ERA OF VIOLENT EXTREMISM

Building national resilience is a complex issue which may transcend multiple disciplines. This translates to policymaking that involves a whole-of-society approach. The authors posit that this can be achieved through strategies that focus on the 'systems' and the 'people' of the nation.

THE SYSTEMS OF A NATION: CRITICAL INFRASTRUCTURE RESILIENCE IN A DIGITAL AGE

Just as nations have capitalised on the use of digital technology, violent extremists have not overlooked the fact that they too must operate in the digital age (Conway, 2012; Neumann, 2013; U.S. Army Training and Doctrine Command [ATDC], 2006; Weimann, 2015). Violent extremists understand the benefits that can be reaped from using technology – small players can level the playing field with their larger opponents in the cyber arena equipped with a personal computer and an Internet connection (Kuehl, 2009; Singer, 2012). They can use cyber capabilities to assist in planning and conducting operations, and to infiltrate national critical infrastructures to disrupt the lives of the masses. Importantly, digital technology also affords them the anonymity to act bolder and with less inhibition (Ariely, 2008; Chen, Lee, & Macdonald, 2014).

There are systems in place within many modern cities and nations today that make use of technology to provide better quality of life to the masses. For example, one can flip a switch and have power, pick up the phone and make a call, turn a water tap to get drinking water, call the police and receive aid. However, these systems which support everyday life are often fragile and susceptible to disruptions (Aducci et al., 2008; Perrow, 1999; Rodin, 2014). Some of these infrastructures at the national level are so critical that their incapacity would have a debilitating impact on the security, safety, health or economic well-being of citizens, and on the effective functioning of the government (Gomes et al., 2015a; Labaka, Hernantes, Rich, & Sarriegi, 2013).

In the current digital era, attacks on systems through the cyber domain have also increased. Hackers affiliated with violent extremist groups have shifted to the cyber sphere to carry out their operations. International news agencies have reportedly been hacked by the group 'Syrian Electronic Army' and Malaysian Airlines claimed having been hacked by alleged ISIS sympathiser group 'Cyber Caliphate' (Ellyatt, 2015). The U.S. Central Command's social media accounts on Facebook and Twitter also reported having been hacked by the group 'Cyber Caliphate' which posted the message: "You'll see no mercy infidels. We are already here, we are in your PCs [computers], in each house, in each office" (Javers, 2015, p. 1). These examples illustrate the rising vulnerability of cyber space, particularly with regards to classified information and service continuance of systems.

With the current trend of increasing digital attacks, the obvious concern centred upon potential attacks targeted at national critical infrastructure that could cripple the nation's ability to function (Ellyatt, 2015; Cordesman & Cordesman, 2001). The threat of national critical infrastructure being targeted in digital attacks is not so far away:

[T]here are hundreds of reported online attacks taking place against the U.K. and U.S. nuclear industry and financial system every day. There is this non-stop badgering of the system by hackers who are hoping that one day the system will crack. (Ellyatt, 2015, p. 3)

Additionally, an analysis of Federal energy revealed that parts of the United States power grid have been attacked online or in person every few days (Poole-Robb, 2015). Governments need to deliberate what measures are needed to secure the nation's system from disruptions.

Eugene Kaspersky, co-founder and Chief Executive of global IT security firm Kaspersky Labs, expressed the need for a 'very serious audit' of the critical infrastructure (as cited in Ellyatt, 2015). In other words, to prepare for a digital attack on critical infrastructure, we need to test the resiliency of systems to make sure that they are able to sufficiently withstand and recover from an attack such that the system can still function.

There is a need to first understand how critical infrastructures are connected to and dependent on digital means (e.g., the Internet, online databases, computer software and hardware). This involves assessing the degree of coupling – i.e., interdependency between units of a system. This would provide an understanding on how a digital attack might infiltrate the system and what are the likely consequences. Following this, actions can be taken to allow for flexibility in the system so that core functioning can continue. The following section will elaborate on three strategies to build resilience in critical infrastructures.

Strategy 1: Know Which Critical Infrastructures Need to Continue in Times of Crisis

While it is ideal to bolster the resilience in all infrastructures to continue functioning in times of crisis, it is often not practical for governments to do so (Gomes et al., 2015b). As mentioned by Kaspersky (as cited in Ellyatt, 2015), certain infrastructures are more essential than others to sustain a nation through a crisis. Hence there is a need to identify the national critical infrastructures which would cripple a nation if they are incapacitated.

A possible way to identify what services need to continue in a crisis is to consider Maslow's hierarchy of needs (Maslow, 1943). It suggests that human needs can be represented in a hierarchy of needs, with the most basic forms of need being physiological (i.e., food, water, warmth, rest) and safety (i.e., security, safety) needs. Critical infrastructures that may be considered to meet physiological needs include healthcare, food, and water; while infrastructures which may be considered to meet safety needs include power, telecommunications, transport, and emergency services.

In the United States, the U.S. Federal Government has identified 16 national critical infrastructure sectors which provide the goods and services that contribute to the nation's defence and robust economy (ATDC, 2006; U.S. Department of Homeland Security, 2014). They include:

1. Chemical,
2. Commercial facilities,
3. Communications,
4. Critical manufacturing,
5. Dams,
6. Defence industrial base,
7. Emergency services,
8. Energy,
9. Financial services,
10. Food and agriculture,
11. Government facilities,
12. Healthcare and public health,
13. Information technology,
14. Nuclear reactors, materials, and waste,
15. Transportation, and
16. Water and wastewater systems.

In the United Kingdom, nine main sectors of national critical infrastructure have been identified by the government (U.K. Cabinet Office, 2015). They include:

1. Communications,
2. Emergency services,
3. Energy,
4. Financial services,
5. Food,
6. Government,

7. Health,
8. Transport, and
9. Water.

Hence critical infrastructures that meet and secure these basic human needs should be prioritised to ensure continued functioning after an attack.

Strategy 2: Map Interdependencies of Critical Infrastructures

Apart from identifying the critical infrastructures which need to continue functioning in times of crisis, it is equally critical to understand which parts of the system are highly interconnected, highly interdependent, and tightly coupled (Gomes et al., 2015b). Failures of tightly coupled critical infrastructures are seen to be more devastating, given that the impact of the failure is more likely to cascade down through the connected and interdependent parts of the system.

For instance, given the modern world's dependence on technology, many critical infrastructures heavily depend on power to operate their technologies – transport systems (e.g., electric trains), telecommunications systems (e.g., satellites, communication towers), water supply (e.g., water purification plants), and healthcare systems (e.g., cardiac devices) all depend on power. Hence the failure of a power grid or power plant due to a digital attack would cascade beyond the 'power' critical infrastructure to many other national critical infrastructures.

From a policymaking standpoint, it is also useful to consider both the direct and indirect effects of a critical infrastructure failure. Direct effects of a critical infrastructure attack are the disruption or failure of the functions of the critical infrastructure (ATDC, 2006). The 9/11 World Trade Centre attack is an example of a direct attack on the financial sector as critical assets such as financial data were lost. The shutdown of aviation routes and other forms of transport as a result of the 9/11 attacks were the manifestations of an indirect effect.

Additionally, there is a need to be cognisant that perpetrators can exploit a primary critical infrastructure in an attempt to damage or sabotage a secondary critical infrastructure. For example, former leader of Al-Qaeda, Osama Bin Laden, had reportedly threatened to launch a cyberattack through the Internet (telecommunications infrastructure) on the investment sector and stock market (financial infrastructure) (ATDC, 2006). These considerations allow for an understanding of how interconnections and interdependencies of critical infrastructures could be points of vulnerability for an attack.

One way of understanding these interconnections and interdependencies is through network analysis (Gomes et al., 2015b). Network analysis is a commonly used approach involving mathematical language for modelling patterns of relationships among components (Beekun & Glick, 2001; Tsai & Goshal, 1998; Vespignani, 2010). It allows for the mapping of the extent and nature of system interactions when one of the critical infrastructures fails. A clear example of network analysis is the London Anytown Project. Started in 2013 by the London Resilience Team, the Anytown Project is an infrastructure failure simulation which maps out the range and path of cascading effects of a critical infrastructure failure (Hogan, 2014).

A second way of understanding the interconnections and interdependencies of critical infrastructures is to stress-test the systems through actual deliberate attacks. An example of this is the United States and United Kingdom 'cyber war games' in 2015 ("Cyber attack war", 2015). These war games involve cyber attacks on each other's critical infrastructures (e.g., financial, energy, transport sectors) to test the resilience of the system to online attackers. The war games would also allow the nations to practise their responses to a range of cyber attacks, thereby fostering improvements to the critical infrastructures' resilience (Goel & Hong, 2015). Another way governments and companies can stress-test the cyber security of critical infrastructure systems is the recruitment of white hat hackers. These are cyber security experts hired for the purpose of identifying current and potential weaknesses of the computer and network systems (Jahankhani et al., 2015; Parker, Sachs, Shaw, Stroz, & Devost, 2004).

Strategy 3: Applying Strategies of Functional Diversity and Spare Capacity to Critical Infrastructure

Given the difficulty in identifying cyber threats today, focusing on vulnerability reduction serves a better strategy to strengthen the resilience of critical infrastructures (Parker et al., 2004). The previous strategy advocates the need to map out the interconnections and interdependencies of the critical infrastructures and identify points of vulnerability. In order for systems to persist even after an attack, buffers should also be built into the systems to strengthen their robustness and resilience (Aducci et al., 2008; Glassman, 1973; Labaka et al., 2013). Resilient-by-design, a term coined by Stephen Flynn, Founding Director of the Centre for Resilience Studies at Northeastern University, involves the intentional design of features, processes, and protocols to mitigate risk of disruptions into the initial building stage of the critical infrastructure (Flynn, 2014). According to Flynn, there is a need to distinguish between essential functioning and full functioning. He elaborated that often not all functions of critical infrastructures are required to keep the system afloat and running. Hence in the immediate aftermath of an attack, the priority should be to keep the essential functions working by allocating resources to meet the minimum threshold required to continue operating these critical infrastructures.

One strategy to ensure that there are sufficient resources to maintain essential functioning is through the process of functional diversity (Gomes et al., 2015b). Functional diversity involves the availability of different resources that serve the same function (Longstaff et al., 2010; World Economic Forum, 2013). For example, for the power critical infrastructure, sources of power can be diversified (e.g., solar panels, wind farm) to reduce the strain on the current power source (e.g., coal-burning power plant). Should the central coal-burning power plant be brought down by a physical or digital attack, the power generated from the solar panels and wind farm would still able to keep the power grid functioning at the minimum level.

A second approach to maintain essential functioning in a critical infrastructure attack is simply to stockpile spare capacities, or backups (Gomes et al., 2015b). Spare capacity serves as an operational buffer against failure, a migitation of the impact of failure, and a resilience strategy (Longstaff et al., 2010).

It is important to note that in addition to these strategies, there is the need to have disconnecting mechanisms in place to contain a disruption. This is especially relevent with many power plants and grids around the world moving towards automation and remote control (McElfresh, 2015). The 'Aurora Generator Test' carried out in 2007 by U.S. company Idaho National Laboratory showcased how a cyber attack could infiltrate the controls of the power grid to cause physical damage by instructing the generator to self-destruct (Meserve, 2007). In that experiment, researchers hacked into a replica of the power plant's control system to introduce a computer programme which caused the generator's circuit breakers to open and close rapidly. This causes the generator to shut down within three minutes.

It is worthy to note that there is evidence that a single power plant disruption can cause cascading failure of the power grid and nationwide outages (e.g., 2003 Northeast American Blackout[1]). Hence, a single digital attack by violent extremists on a single power plant control system has the potential to plunge the nation into darkness in a mere matter of minutes.

In sum, the real vulnerability of critical infrastructures to attacks and cascading failures is alarming. Nations need to remain one step ahead of violent extremist groups which are increasingly using computers and the Internet as a weapon. There is the need to build in resilience into the physical and cyber security of critical infrastructures.

THE PEOPLE OF A NATION: PEOPLE'S RESILIENCE IN A DIGITAL AGE

While due attention has to be paid to ensure that the systems of nations remain functioning, equal, if not more, weightage should be given when considering the people of nations. In this context, understanding the people component of national resilience involves looking at the social-psychological factors of a nation. This includes both the individual psychology of people, and the collective within the communities and nation.

In the aftermath of an attack, recovery efforts can be seen to be top-down (i.e., government initiated) and bottom-up (i.e., ground initiated). National leaders have to exude qualities of competence in order to successfully lead the nation through an attack. Similarly, studies have emphasised the importance of citizens of the nation banding together to tide through an attack. A highly cohesive nation will display a united citizenry, one where ground-up initiatives can complement, or even work better than government initiated policies.

The importance of national leaders and the nation's citizens illustrate that people are crucial to the recovery efforts. National leaders and the citizenry must come together to provide a whole-of-nation effort to recover from an attack. The following are selected strategies pertaining to the people of the nation that can allow a nation to tide through an attack more effectively.

Strategy 1: Utilise Social Media for Crisis Communications

In the immediate aftermath of a violent extremist attack, there is a need for leaders of the nation to communicate key information to the public. Violent extremist attacks may attempt to damage physical property and incite psychological harm (e.g., elicit fear and confusion) to the public. In this regard, crisis communications aim to provide information to the affected stakeholders. In the event of a violent extremist attack, immediate stakeholders can be the victims, the next-of-kin of victims, the public, and in some instances, even other nations. As leaders aim to push out information to avert danger and save lives, crisis communications become an integral tool.

In the aftermath of the 2013 Boston Marathon Bombing, crisis communications played a critical role in the management of the crisis. A total of about 300 people were injured, with three fatalities reported. On the social media space, photos and videos of the bombings began to propagate as members of the public started sharing information across various online platforms. Social media further served as an alternative communications tool as traditional phone communication infrastructure was overwhelmed by the surge in number of calls (Commonwealth of Massachusetts, 2014).

Furthermore, on the online space, netizens proceed to Reddit, a forum-like website for users to submit content. A subreddit (i.e., sub-communities within the Reddit website) titled '/r/FindBostonBomber' was created by netizens to identify the bomber. As Reddit users submitted pre- and post-bombing photos of the marathon, netizens banded together to analyse the images and identify the perpetrators. Eventually, Sunil Tripathi was alleged to be the bomber by the netizens[2], which turned out to be wrong (Madrigal, 2013).

As news of the Boston Marathon Bombing began to unfold, information was provided to news agencies via varying sources. This raises possibilities of inaccurate or incorrect information being reported. Furthermore, social media expedites the process through which news is being disseminated online. Misinformation and disinformation spreads faster when users of social media share news with their respective friends and followers. Additionally, one has to anticipate that netizens vigilantism becomes a source of misinformation as seen in the Reddit incident. The accessibility of online platforms (i.e., Facebook, Twitter, Reddit) allows the public to share opinions to a large audience quickly and conveniently. Likewise, as access to the Internet increases, the public becomes more exposed to the potential for encountering misinformation. This, in turn, poses a challenge in the crisis management of an attack.

There are two recommendations with regards to the crisis communications. Firstly, governments need to train leaders of the nation to address the public. In the context of a violent extremist attack, the involvement of national leaders (e.g., elected leaders, leaders of law enforcement leaders) is expected by the public. National leaders addressing the citizens can serve to provide a narrative for the nation to unite. It is imperative for compelling narratives to be delivered to the citizens during the pre-crisis and post-crisis stage. Narratives of imminent crisis (e.g., 'it is a question of when it will happen, not whether it will happen') and reinforcement of social cohesion (e.g., 'attacks are not the act of Muslims, but violent extremists') would be most beneficial before an attack as it serves as a form of psychological preparation for citizens. Narratives that provide a sense of safety, calmness, self- and community efficacy, and hope would be most beneficial after an attack hits (Hobfoll et al., 2007). Ample consideration should also be placed upon the cultural nuances within nations.

Secondly, leaders must recognise the need to refute incorrect claims by the media, where applicable. This is illustrated in the Boston Marathon Bombing, where the media was shown to present inaccurate information to the public. A fast and efficient way to do so is for the public service agencies (i.e., police and government agencies) to use an official social media account to disseminate information. The Boston Police Department (BPD) was able to execute strategic crisis communication through the use of its official twitter handle, '@BostonPolice'. The Twitter account was quick to provide accurate source of information pertaining to the bombing. Within hours of the attack, BPD released information about the details of the attacks, such as the known death and injury count. While the media speculated about the details of the attack, the BPD used Twitter to debunk misinformation from mainstream media.

The BPD social media effort on the Boston Marathon Bombing was highly lauded for exemplary crisis communications (Bindley, 2013; Davis et al., 2014; Keller, 2013). This was all made possible because the BPD had a clear mission to increase communication with the public through social media, and by extension, increase social media presence of the BPD (Bindley, 2013).

Further learning from the BPD also indicated that the success of the social media campaign was due to the ability of multiple authorised members of the police department to tweet through the BPD twitter handle. This allowed for fast and efficient message dissemination, without the usual organisational red tapes to go through (Davis et al., 2014). The implication of this is that the skill of crisis communication should not only be left to communications or public relation personnel. Thus, training of police officers on crisis communications should be a key pre-crisis agenda, so that officers are able to take on a crisis communications role in the event of an attack.

Lastly, the success of the BPD crisis communications campaign was an effort that started way before the crisis occurred. A constant effort to garner followers and engage them even during peacetime proved to be integral for the BPD to engage in a successful social media campaign after the bombing.

Strategy 2: Rebuild Trust in Government as Part of Crisis Management

Following attacks of violent extremism, there are concerns that fear and anger may fester in the population. This is especially so if the incident is regarded as a mistake or lapse in judgment of the government, which may then translate to feelings of mistrust towards the government. Interestingly, existing literature suggests that following attacks, there appears to be an observed increase in trust in government for the immediate period (Perrin & Smolek, 2009). This increase in the sense of trust is termed as a variant of a 'rally effect' in which traumatising events such as large-scale attacks results in a collective sense of loss of security (Dinesen & Jaeger, 2013; Perrin & Smolek, 2009). However, this level of trust tends to fall rapidly after some time, returning to pre-attack level (Woods, 2011).

The same effect is also observed in terms of trust in law enforcement institutions, though the rally effect is found to be not as long-lasting as compared to the effect on political institutions (Dinesen & Jaeger, 2013). Nonetheless, governments have to anticipate that there may be anger within the populace targeted towards the authorities. This is particularly so if the attack is deemed to be the result of a lapse in law enforcement capabilities.

As such, the issue of trust has profound consequences on issues pertaining to political participation and rule compliance (Levi & Stoker, 2000). A collapse in public trust is likely to lead to a decline in participation of the people regarding matters of polity. Cynicism regarding the political system will grow and upset the existing social order of the nation (Diamond, 2007). The lack of trust also brings about alienation and withdrawal from political processes where people simply do not take part in political decisions of the nation (i.e., giving up their voting rights). In addition, they are less likely to adhere to rules and policies that are implemented by the government. This then results in a shallow and fragile state, one that is unable to mobilise national resources or shape collective vision for national development (Diamond, 2007).

Public trust is a cultural phenomenon that takes a long time to emerge and is something which can be very fragile (Bicchieri, 2008). In fact, a society with strong social capital and a lot of personal trust among individuals may not necessarily translate into trust within the public sphere (Bicchieri, 2008). In order to restore trust, research suggests government has to incorporate transparency in its processes and demonstrate responsibility and accountability in its engagement with the public (Diamond, 2007). For example, acknowledgement from the government regarding existing gaps in the system, and instances where Committee of Inquiry (COI) is being set up to investigate the attacks may help in the building trust in government. In particular, following an attack, citizens should be informed of the threat in an honest, straightforward manner. Obtaining the trust of the people can enable the populace to better understand and appreciate the strategies adopted by the government, and enhance cooperation and adherence.

Strategy 3: Rebuild a Cohesive Community

After a violent extremist attack, the resulting fear and anger faced by the populace may lead to hatred being directly at specific groups and communities. For example, in the case of 9/11 attacks, the Muslim Americans and Arab Americans were targeted after the perpetrators were identified to be of Arab

Muslim descent. This is supported by figures which revealed that more hate crimes were being targeted at Muslim Americans and Arab Americans after the attack (Human Rights Watch, 2002). Thus, it is integral to ensure that the nation or community remains cohesive and persevere through the recovery of the attack. This strategy proposes two ways to build a cohesive community: dealing with post-crisis segregation; and encouraging ground-up initiatives that serve to return the community to normalcy.

Deal with Post-Crisis Segregation

Studies conducted in the United States have shown that following an attack associated with violent extremism, a heightened sense of national identity is observed (Hoyle, 2014). This heightened sense of national identity may manifest negatively, especially in a religiously motivated attack. The outcome is an 'us-versus-them' mentality (Borum, 2004). This in-group versus out-group identity may then bring about hate crimes[3] towards an otherwise innocent group.

Research suggests that hate crimes are often carried out as a form of vicarious retribution (Deloughery, King, Asal, & Rethemeyer, 2013). In fact, one study reported that after religiously motivated attacks, incidents of hate violence reported spikes at 28 percent and remains elevated for the span of a month compared to the 4.6 percent increase after other forms of attacks (Deloughery et al., 2013). Other researchers have also found similar results in terms of increased rates of hate crimes and observed that while the rate of attacks tends to reduce over time, the rates remains comparatively higher than pre-attack levels a year after (Hanes & Machin, 2014).

Promoting a common identity may prevent the occurrence of hate crime that targets any specific community or group (Levine, Prosser, Evans, & Reicher, 2005). Identity is a social construct that is highly malleable. A person's identity can be seen through different lens and one can have multiple identities. The same person can be a father, a son, doctor or a person of whatever nationality he/she may belong to. Research shows, therefore, that when an individual take up more identities, it makes it easier for them to relate to others (Levine et al., 2005). The effect of this is two-fold. It prevents certain groups from becoming the target of hate crimes, and also enables help to be rendered to these groups (Levine et al., 2005). For instance, the local Muslim community that may be victims of Islamophobic attacks should be considered as part of the nation that is negatively affected by the act (Hoyle, 2014). That is to say, these groups should not be perceived as an 'isolated Muslim community', but instead be considered as part of the nation.

An instance in which the shaping of identity has protected the community can be seen in the aftermath of the 2014 Sydney Siege. A ground-initiated social media campaign '#illridewithyou' has encouraged Australians to stand in solidarity with the local Muslims by riding home with them and protecting them from possible anti-Muslim retaliation. The campaign emphasised the identity of 'One Australia', recognising and regarding Muslim Australians as 'fellow mates' who suffered the same national tragedy at the hands of Man Haron Monis. This example illustrates the importance of perpetuating and reinforcing the idea of an inclusive national identity regardless of race, language or religion. It is therefore important that local Muslim communities (i.e., especially if they are a minority group) are regarded as having the same stake in the country as the rest of the nation (Hoyle, 2014). This notion should be reinforced in the immediate aftermath of the attack when there is still uncertainty and confusion.

Encourage Ground-Up Initiatives

Resilient communities are able to mitigate the impact of violent extremism through ground-up initiatives that encourages rapid recovery and continuity of life. One example of such an initiative can be seen in the July 7, 2011 London riot clean up brigade. The riot started off in Tottenham and gradually spread to other areas of London and United Kingdom cities such as Nottingham, Manchester, Liverpool, Birmingham, and Bristol. While the riot was attributed to an array of factors, analyses suggest that the tipping point was the result of racial tension arising over the death of Mark Duggan in a police shooting (Cooper & Nicholls, 2011). It was also said that the rioters simply participated in 'opportunistic theft' ("Nick Clegg: Riots", 2011). However, what happened as a response to the riots was the self-initiated clean-up efforts that took root from the community level.

Even as reports of riots were spreading throughout the United Kingdom, people made use of the online realm to gather resources and like-minded individuals to organise clean-up efforts the day after. The initiative gained traction and the Twitter hashtag '#londoncleanup' became a social movement. While the initiative started online, crowds showed up on the streets, armed with brooms and other cleaning tools, the day after the riots at the designated meeting points. This is an example of ground up efforts to recovery, and in this case, an attempt to regain and return the city back to normalcy. These efforts not only rally the people, they also serve to strengthen the community's identity and spirit.

Another movement '#NotInMyName' was also initiated in the online realm. The movement was started by the Active Change Foundation, which is a community based organisation. The aim of this movement was originally for British Muslims to take a stand against ISIS and its actions. This movement was picked up in Australia where it has morphed into a campaign that encourages all Australians to unite against racism and hated.

Hence, these ground-up initiatives should be supported by the government, as they empower the community to deal with the negativity following an attack. As the social media campaigns translate into offline action, governments should facilitate where possible, for these ground-up initiatives to occur. From this, an important implication can also be drawn: while the digital realm may provide an avenue for violent extremists to radicalise individuals, it is also a tool where bottom-up initiatives can propagate. The above case examples illustrate how social media can rally and unite community to fight back against the causes that brings about hatred and segregation.

Strategy 4: Galvanise Social Capital and Managing Spontaneous Volunteers

Social capital is one of the main drivers of resilience (Clifford, 2012). As part of the efforts to increase community's resilience after an attack, especially those of a large magnitude, is it important to galvanise social capital for recovery efforts. Given that response capacity by professional responders may not be optimal during the initial few hours post-crisis, volunteers play an essential role as they may come ready with a pool of unique knowledge and skills (Helsloot & Ruitenberg, 2004). As such, volunteers can augment emergency staff with basic skills, and support recovery efforts (Fernandez, Barbera, & van Dorp, 2006). Additionally, research suggests that if volunteers are disaster victims themselves, allowing them to participate in recovery efforts have psychological benefits. It empowers them and provides an avenue and outlet for them to reduce stress and channel their negative emotions (e.g., anger, fear) into something useful (Fernandez et al., 2006).

How then can such resources be galvanised in times of crisis? More often than not, there is a need to empower the people and inform them that help is required should they wish to help. In fact, studies have shown that, particularly in times of large scale disasters and crises, members of the public are more than willing to step forward and provide assistance in whatever way possible (Scanlon, Helsloot, & Groenendaal, 2014). Even if there is no official call for assistance, it is likely that communities and groups will self-initiate and self-organise themselves to assist in recovery efforts (Fernandez et al., 2006; National Research Council, 2011).

A case study depicting such an occurrence of ordinary people responding to an emergency is the 9/11 boatlift evacuations. When the planes crashed into the World Trade Centre in New York City, many people were stranded at the pier in Lower Manhattan after they were evacuated from their office buildings. Upon a call for help by the U.S. Coast Guard, boats of all shapes and sizes approached and participated in the evacuation process without incidents or injuries (Scanlon et al., 2014). It was estimated that close to half a million people were rescued from the piers and seawalls of Lower Manhattan by these boats.

Despite the rosy picture of a successful involvement of spontaneous volunteers in the boatlift case study and having numerous studies highlighting the positive effect of utilising volunteers post crisis, research also suggests that emergency services are still ill equipped in managing volunteers during crises (Fernandez et al., 2006). The lack of coordination between emergencies services and ordinary citizens may hinder and pose as an obstacle to the rescue work. An instance where such a scenario happened was in 1987, in Edmonton, Canada, where the city faced a tornado that caused widespread damage and destruction for one hour and five minutes. Many civilians rendered assistance to those who need help and delivered them to hospitals and clinics within the vicinity (Scanlon & Hiscott, 1994). Hence, by the time the professional responders arrived on scene 21 minutes later, they found that the victims and important eyewitnesses had largely been sent off to the hospitals. Rescue efforts had to start from scratch without any ground knowledge of who had survived, who had been rescued, and who might still be trapped (Scanlon et al., 2014). This lack of collaboration between spontaneous volunteers and professional responders resulted in additional work and can be better enhanced to aid recovery efforts.

Therefore, there needs to be a system for effective management and deployment of volunteers on scene. Fernandez and colleagues (2006) proposed a framework for managing volunteers. The framework has been adopted by Arlington County's volunteer management system for its public health emergencies (Fernandez et al., 2006). The model outlines processes to manage the influx of volunteers and collect relevant credentials for specific assignments that require special skills and qualifications (e.g., first aid responders). This model would then allow for a better job-fit for volunteers and also ensure sustainability of the volunteers on the ground.

Governments should also have developed ready plans to set up volunteer management centres before the crisis strikes. One way to facilitate this strategy is to collect the credentials of existing volunteers who are ready to be deployed such that appropriate help can be tapped on at critical moments. Examples of such information can include a list of organ and blood donors, people with specialised skill sets (e.g., cardiopulmonary resuscitation, first aid trained), people who are able to provide logistics support (e.g., food, water, transportation). Availability of such information in advance can facilitate the management of volunteers in the aftermath of an attack.

Strategy 5: Learn from Past Crises

The role of learning is an important one to strengthen the resilience of the nation. However, the context of learning in a crisis always begs the question of 'who or what learns'. The literature on crisis learning suggests that there exists two main forms of learning – direct and vicarious learning (Stern, 1997). Direct learning, also termed as experience-based learning, includes conscious attempts at filling gaps stemming from the system (Stern, 1997).

Learning should take a central role and the mechanisms to encourage learning should be put in place before an attack occurs. This ensures that the leaders and people are all equipped with relevant knowledge to respond to the attack. Hence, it is important to draw learning lessons by looking at the experiences of other countries. This notion has been expressed by Singapore Deputy Prime Minister Teo Chee Hean: "Whenever an incident occurs to someone else, we should ask ourselves what it means for us, what can we learn from it and how we can be better prepared for something similar" (as cited in Mokhtar, 2015, p. 1). This form of learning is cost-effective as nations are able to learn from the success and failures of others (Stern, 1997). Apart from learning from others, lessons can also be drawn from several other sources, including the nation's own history.

Analysis should be drawn from different viewpoints. Specific areas of the recovery efforts (i.e., crisis communication, role of leadership) can be looked at and explored in greater detail to yield a richer learning. For instance, lessons on the effective use of social media can be drawn through an analysis of the 2013 Boston Marathon Bombings and how the BPD utilised social media for outreach and engagement. Additionally, building up violent extremism related case studies that explores how these threats are handled can provide useful insights for future counter violent extremism initiatives. These learning lessons can be presented and passed on to the people through the use of various platforms.

CONCLUSION

Building a resilient nation has to take into account both the system and the people. This chapter seeks to provide insights to some systemic and people factors that may contribute to national resilience. Understanding critical infrastructure dependency of a nation, and ensuring its functioning in times of an attack through building spare capacity and diversity are key steps to ensure that the nation's core functions are not disrupted. Crisis communications, building trust, social capital, and learning equips the leaders and people of the nation to be resilient against threats such as a violent extremist attack.

The factors raised in this chapter, are specifically aimed at exploring how the nation can cope with potential threats in the aftermath of an attack. Even in the current digital era, the consequences of violent extremism can still be felt in the physical world. The central argument is that nations need to account and anticipate for the moment when terror strikes, and know what to do when it happens to ensure resiliency. Additionally, the cyber space is increasingly seen as an integral infrastructure of a nation, as several core functions within the nation are tied to computers. Thus, putting a resilience perspective on the threat of violent extremism in this digital age allows policymakers and leaders to contemplate how nations can continue to function in the event of an attack.

To further explore a nation's resiliency, it is also important to explore pre-crisis factors. Matrices such as the citizen's crisis preparedness, leadership capabilities, and cultural nuances are several other considerations not mentioned within this chapter that have been shown to be useful (Gomes et al., 2015a). In the current digital era of violent extremism, bearing in mind the pre- and post-crisis factors towards building resilience will be a critical tool which allows nations to mitigate the evolving threat of violent extremism.

ACKNOWLEDGMENT

The views expressed in this chapter are the authors' only and do not represent the official position or view of the Ministry of Home Affairs, Singapore.

REFERENCES

Aducci, R., Bilderbeek, P., Brown, H., Dowling, S., Freedman, N., Gantz, J., & Verma, S. et al. (2008). *The hyperconnected: Here they come! A global look at the exploding 'culture of connectivity' and its impact on the enterprise.* Framingham, MA: IDC.

Ariely, G. (2008). Knowledge management, terrorism, and cyber terrorism. In L. Janczewski & A. Colarik (Eds.), *Cyber warafe and cyber terrorism* (pp. 7–16). Hershey, PA: IGI Global.

Beekun, R., & Glick, W. (2001). Organization structure from a loose coupling perspective: A multidimensional approach. *Decision Sciences, 32*(2), 227–250. doi:10.1111/j.1540-5915.2001.tb00959.x

Bicchieri, C. (2008). Losing the trust. *Pennsylvania Arts & Sciences.* Retrieved from http://www.sas.upenn.edu/sasalum/newsltr/winter08/trust_game.pdf

Bindley, K. (2013). Boston Police Twitter: How cop team tweets from terror to joy. *Huffington Post.* Retrieved from http://www.huffingtonpost.com/2013/04/26/boston-police-twitter-marathon_n_3157472.html

Borum, R. (2004). *Psychology of terrorism.* Tampa: University of South Florida.

Chen, T., Lee, J., & Macdonald, S. (Eds.). (2014). *Cyberterrorism: Understanding, assessment, and response.* New York, NY: Springer. doi:10.1007/978-1-4939-0962-9

Clifford, M. (2012). *The keystone to community resilience: Social capital. Continuity e-Guide: A Wednesday Update by Disaster Resource Guide.* Retrieved from: http://www.disaster-resource.com/newsletter/2012/subpages/v418/meettheexperts.htm

Commonwealth of Massachusetts. (2014). *After action report for the response to the 2013 Boston Marathon Bombings.* Retrieved from http://www.mass.gov/eopss/docs/mema/after-action-report-for-the-response-to-the-2013-boston-marathon-bombings.pdf

Conway, M. (2012). From al-Zarqawi to al-Awlaki: The emergence and development of an online radical milieu. *Combating Terrorism Exchange, 2*(4), 12–22.

Cooper, C., & Nicholls, A. (2011). What caused England's riots? *The Guardian.* Retrieved from http://www.theguardian.com/society/joepublic/2011/oct/12/what-caused-england-riots

Cordesman, A., & Cordesman, J. (2001). *Cyber-threats, information warfare, and critical infrastructure protection: Defending the U.S. Homeland.* New York, NY: Praeger.

Cyber attack war games to be staged by UK and US. (2015). *BBC News.* Retrieved from www.bbc.com/news/uk-politics-30842669

Davis, E. F., Alves, A. A., & Sklansky, D. A. (2014). *Social Media and Police Leadership: Lessons from Boston. New Perspectives in Policing Bulletin.* Washington, DC: U.S. Department of Justice, National Institute of Justice.

Deloughery, K., King, R., Asal, V., & Rethemeyer, R. K. (2013). *Assessing the likelihood of hate crime in wake of Boston attacks.* National Consortium for the Study of Terrorism and Responses to Terrorism. Retrieved from http://www.start.umd.edu/sites/default/files/files/publications/research_briefs/START_HateCrimeTerrorism_QA.pdf

Diamond, L. (2007). *Building trust in government by improving governance.* Paper presented at the 7th Global Forum on Reinventing Government: Building Trust in Government, Vienna, Italy.

Dinesen, P. T., & Jaeger, M. M. (2013). The effect of terror on institutional trust: New evidence from the 3/11 Madrid terrorist attack. *Political Psychology, 34*(6), 917–926. doi:10.1111/pops.12025

Eaton, T. (2013). Internet activism and the Egyptian uprisings: Transforming online dissent into the offline world. *Westminster Papers, 9*(2). Retrieved from https://www.westminster.ac.uk/__data/assets/pdf_file/0004/220675/WPCC-vol9-issue2.pdf

Ellis, L. (2011). *Using a strengths-based approach to foster resilience.* Alberta, Canada: Mount Royal University.

Ellyatt, H. (2015, January 27). Cyberterrorists to target critical infrastructure. *CNBC.* Retrieved from http://www.cnbc.com/id/102367777

Fernandez, L., Barbera, J., & van Dorp, J. (2006). Strategies for managing volunteers during incident response: A systems approach. *Homeland Security Affairs, 2*(9). Retrieved from https://www.hsaj.org/articles/684

Flynn, S. (2014, July 30). *Understanding and embracing the resilience imperative.* Paper presented at the NIST Workshop on 'Developing a Community-Centered Approach to Disaster Resilience'. Retrieved from www.nist.gov/el/building_materials/resilience/upload/7-Flynn-NIST-Stevens-Event-7-30-14.pdf

Glassman, R. (1973). Persistence and loose coupling in living systems. *Behavioral Science, 18*(2), 83–98. doi:10.1002/bs.3830180202

Global Policy Forum. (n.d.). *War on terrorism.* Retrieved from https://www.globalpolicy.org/war-on-terrorism.html

Goel, S., & Hong, Y. (2015). Cyber war games: Strategic jostling among traditional adversaries. In S. Jajodia, P. Shakarian, V. Subrahmanian, V. Swarup, & C. Wang (Eds.), *Cyber Warfare* (pp. 1–13). Switzerland: Springer International Publishing. doi:10.1007/978-3-319-14039-1_1

Gomes, D., Tan, J., Wang, Y., Neo, L. S., Ong, G., & Khader, M. (2015a). *National resilience: HTBSC Singapore's national resilience proposed framework* (Research Report no. 3/2015). Singapore: Home Team Behavioural Sciences Centre.

Gomes, D., Tan, J., Wang, Y., Neo, L. S., Ong, G., & Khader, M. (2015b). *System de-coupling: A strategy to build national resilience* (Research Report no. 11/2015). Singapore: Home Team Behavioural Sciences Centre.

Hanes, E., & Machin, S. (2014). Hate crime research: Design and measurement strategies for improving causal inference. *Journal of Contemporary Criminal Justice, 30*(3), 228–246. doi:10.1177/1043986214536662

Helsloot, I., & Ruitenberg, A. (2004). Citizen response to disasters: A survey of literature and some practical implications. *Journal of Contingencies and Crisis Management, 12*(3), 98–111. doi:10.1111/j.0966-0879.2004.00440.x

Hobfoll, S., Watson, P., Bell, C., Bryant, R., Brymer, M., Friedman, M., & Ursano, R. J. et al. (2007). Five essential elements of immediate and mid-term mass trauma intervention: Empirical evidence. *Psychiatry, 70*(4), 283–315. doi:10.1521/psyc.2007.70.4.283 PMID:18181708

Hoffman, B. (2006). *Inside terrorism* (rev.ed). New York, NY: Columbia University Press.

Hogan, M. (2014, June 11). *Anytown: A DEFRA funded project.* Retrieved from www.london.gov.uk/sites/default/files/Blog%2042%20AnytownPoster.pdf

Hoyle, A. (2014). Breaking the Backlash – A take on the social psychology of discrimination. *ZME Science.* Retrieved from http://www.zmescience.com/other/feature-post/breaking-the-backlash/

Human Rights Watch. (2002). *"WE ARE NOT THE ENEMY". Hate crimes against Arabs, Muslims, and those perceived to be Arab or Muslim after September 111.* Retrieved from https://www.hrw.org/reports/2002/usahate/index.htm#TopOfPage

Hussain, G., & Saltman, E. M. (2014). *Jihad trending: a comprehensive analysis of online extremism and how to counter it.* London: Quilliam Foundation.

H. Jahankhani, A. Carlile, B. Akhgar, A. Taal, A. Hessami, & A. Hosseinian-Far (Eds.). (2015). Global security, safety and sustainability: Tomorrow's challenges of cyber security. In *Proceedings of the 10th International Conference on Global Security, Safety and Sustainability (ICGS3 2015).* London: Springer. doi:10.1007/978-3-319-23276-8

Javers, E. (2015). These cyberhackers may not be backed by ISIS. *CNBC News.* Retrieved from www.cnbc.com/2015/07/14/these-cyberhackers-not-backed-by-isis.html

Keller, J. (2013). How Boston Police won the Twitter wars during the Marathon Bomber hunt. *Bloomberg Business.* Retrieved from http://www.bloomberg.com/bw/articles/2013-04-26/how-boston-police-won-the-twitter-wars-during-bomber-hunt

Kuehl, D. (2009). From cyberspace to cyberpower: Defining the problem. In F. Kramer, S. Starr, & L. Wentz (Eds.), *Cyberpower and National Security* (pp. 24–42). Washington, DC: National Defense University Press.

Labaka, L., Hernantes, J., Rich, E., & Sarriegi, J. (2013). Resilience building policies and their influence in crisis prevention, absorption and recovery. *Homeland Security and Emergency Management, 10*(1), 280–317.

Lark, J., Nelson, R., & Chappelle, L. (2003). *Michigan Public Service Commission report on August 14th blackout.* Michigan, MI: Michigan Public Service Commission.

Levi, M., & Stoker, L. (2000). Political trust and trustworthiness. *Annual Review of Political Science, 3*(1), 475–507. doi:10.1146/annurev.polisci.3.1.475

Levine, M., Prosser, A., Evans, D., & Reicher, S. (2005). Identity and emergency intervention: How social group membership and inclusiveness of group boundaries shape helping behavior. *Personality and Social Psychology Bulletin, 31*(4), 443–453. doi:10.1177/0146167204271651 PMID:15743980

Longstaff, P., Armstrong, N., Perrin, K., Parker, W., & Hidek, M. (2010). *Building resilient communities: A preliminary framework for assessment.* Monterey, CA: Naval Postgraduate School, Center for Homeland Defense and Security.

Madrigal, A. C. (2013, April 19) #BostonBombing: The anatomy of a misinformation disaster. *The Atlantic.* Retrieved from http://www.theatlantic.com/technology/archive/2013/04/-bostonbombing-theanatomy-of-a-misinformation-disaster/275155/

Maslow, A. (1943). A theory of motivation. *Psychological Review, 50*(4), 370–396. doi:10.1037/h0054346

McElfresh, M. (2015, June 8). Power grid cyber attacks keep the pentagon up at night. *Scientific American.* Retrieved from www.scientificamerican.com/article/power-grid-cyber-attacks-keep-the-pentagon-up-at-night/

Meserve, J. (2007, September 27). Mouse click could plunge city into darkness, experts say. *CNN.* Retrieved from www.edition.cnn.com/2007/US/09/27/power.at.risk/index.html

Mokhtar, F. (2015). Learn from how other countries have dealt with terror threats, incidents: DPM Teo. *Channel News Asia.* Retrieved from http://www.channelnewsasia.com/news/singapore/learn-from-how-other/1824490.html

National Research Council. (2011). *Assessing national resilience to hazards and disasters: The perspective from the Gulf coast of Louisiana and Mississippi: Summary of a workshop.* Washington, DC: The National Academies Press.

Neo, L. S., Khader, M., Shi, P., Dillon, L., & Ong, G. (2015). *Extremist cyber footprints: A guide to understanding and countering online extremism.* Singapore: Home Team Behavioural Sciences Centre.

Neumann, P. (2013). Options and strategies for countering online radicalization in the United States. *Studies in Conflict and Terrorism, 36*(6), 431–459. doi:10.1080/1057610X.2013.784568

Ng, C. (2011). National resilience: Building a whole-of-society response. *Ethos (Berkeley, Calif.), 10,* 21–29.

Nick Cleggs. Riots 'completely unacceptable. (2011). *BBC News.* Retrieved from http://www.bbc.com/news/uk-politics-14443082

Parker, T., Sachs, M., Shaw, E., Stroz, E., & Devost, M. (2004). *Cyber adversary characterization: Auditing the hacker mind.* New York, NY: Syngress.

Perrin, A. J., & Smolek, S. (2009). Who trusts? Race, gender and the September 11 rally effect among young adults. *Social Science Research, 38*(1), 134–145. doi:10.1016/j.ssresearch.2008.09.001 PMID:19569296

Perrow, C. (1999). *Normal accidents: Living with high-risk technologies*. Princeton, NJ: Princeton University Press.

Poole-Robb, S. (2015, April 7). National power grids hit by cyber terrorist onslaught. *KCS Group*. Retrieved from www.kcsgroup.com/national-power-grids-hit-by-cyber-terrorist-onslaught/

Qatar International Academy for Security Studies [QIASS] (2010). *Risk reduction for countering violent extremism*. New York, NY: The Soufan Group.

Rodin, J. (2014). *The resilience dividend: Being strong in a world where things go wrong*. New York, NY: PublicAffairs.

Scanlon, J., Helsloot, I., & Groenendaal, J. (2014). Putting it all together: Integrating ordinary people into emergency response. *International Journal of Mass Emergencies and Disasters, 32*(1), 43–63.

Scanlon, J., & Hiscott, R. (1994). Despite appearances: There could be a system: Mass casualties and the Edmonton Tornado. *International Journal of Mass Emergencies and Disasters, 12*(2), 15–239.

Schmid, P. A. (2004). Frameworks for conceptualising terrorism. *Terrorism and Political Violence, 16*(2), 197–221. doi:10.1080/09546550490483134

Singer, P. (2012). The cyber terror bogeyman. *Armed Forces Journal*. Retrieved from http://www.brookings.edu/research/articles/2012/11/cyber-terror-singer

Stern, E. (1997). Crisis and learning: A conceptual balance sheet. *Journal of Contingencies and Crisis Management, 5*(2), 69–86. doi:10.1111/1468-5973.00039

Tsai, W., & Goshal, S. (1998). Social capital and value creation: The role of intrafirm networks. *Academy of Management Journal, 41*(4), 464–476. doi:10.2307/257085

U.K. Cabinet Office. (2015). *The national infrastructure*. London: Centre for the Protection of National Infrastructure.

U.S. Army Training and Doctrine Command (ATDC). (2006). *Critical infrastructure: Threats and terrorism (Handbook No. 1.02)*. Fort Leavenworth, KS: U.S. Army Training and Doctrine Command.

U.S.-Canada Power System Outage Task Force. (2014). *U.S. final report on the August 14, 2003 blackout in the United States and Canada: Causes and recommendations*. U.S. and Canada: United States Department of Energy.

U.S. Department of Homeland Security. (2014). *Critical infrastructure sectors*. Washington, DC: U.S. Department of Homeland Security.

Vespignani, A. (2010). Complex networks: The fragility of interdependency. *Nature, 464*(7291), 984–985. doi:10.1038/464984a PMID:20393545

Weimann, G. (2004). *How modern terrorism uses the Internet. Special Report No.116*. Washington, DC: United States Institute of Peace; www.terror.net

Weimann, G. (2015). *Terrorism in cyberspace*. Washington, DC: Woodrow Wilson Centre Press.

Woods, J. (2011). The 9/11 effect: Toward a social science of the terrorist threat. *The Social Science Journal, 48*(1), 213–233. doi:10.1016/j.soscij.2010.06.001

World Economic Forum. (2013). Special report: Building national resilience to global risk. *Global Risks*, 36-44.

ENDNOTES

[1.] On August 14, 2003, a massive blackout caused by cascading failure affected over 50 million people in Northeast America and some parts of Canada (U.S.-Canada Power System Outage Task Force, 2014). Investigations revealed that the blackout initiated in Ohio and quickly spread to the rest of the connected electrical grid, demonstrating that tightly interconnected critical infrastructures are highly vulnerable to cascading failure (Lark, Nelson, & Chappelle, 2003).

[2.] The actual perpetrators were identified to be brothers Dzhokhar and Tamerlan Tsarnaev. On 19 April 2013, Dzhokhar, was arrested for the bombing. His brother, Tamerlan, was killed in a shootout with the Boston Police a day earlier.

[3.] Hate crime has been defined by the U.S. Congress as "criminal offense(s) against a person or property motivated in whole or in part by an offender's bias against a race, religion, disability, ethnic origin or sexual orientation".

Chapter 16
Social Media Analytics for Intelligence and Countering Violent Extremism

Jennifer Yang Hui
Nanyang Technological University, Singapore

ABSTRACT

Social media analytics are increasingly incorporated into security practices due to the rise in online criminal and extremist activities. Social media research, however, has not become established in either intelligence practice or academic-based approach. This chapter aims to fill the gap by discussing collection methods and analytical tools for the study of social media data for intelligence and countering violent extremism: social network analysis, sentiment analysis, multilingual analysis, geo-coding, automated entity extraction, semantic search, and multimedia analysis. While technological capabilities of social media analytics are improving rapidly, it needs to be complemented with nuanced perspectives from the social sciences. Understanding of the epistemology of social media and dynamics between the online-offline interaction as well as data access will put practitioners in a better position to reap the benefits of the social media. Attention should be given to train practitioners in relevant technological skills while also incorporating social science knowledge.

INTRODUCTION

Traditional approaches to tackle violent extremism face limitations. One key area in which more effective countering violent extremism initiatives is needed is in the cyberspace. Online activities are increasingly impacting real world events as movements are organised, and communications conducted via the cyberspace. The cyberspace therefore makes up a crucial aspect of national security investigation. By 1999 most jihadist organisations had established an online presence, although the impact of radical websites and social media on radicalising individuals are debatable (Bartlett & Miller, 2013). Recent events had shown that terrorist movements around the world are increasingly aided by social media. For instance, the Islamic State in Iraq and Syria (ISIS) has proved to be extremely adept at utilising social media to

DOI: 10.4018/978-1-5225-0156-5.ch016

attract sympathisers and recruit members globally. The Europol has estimated that more than 50,000 Twitter accounts belong to ISIS supporters, and are used to send nearly 100,000 tweets every day. In Norway, the perpetrator of the 2011 attacks, Anders Breivik, distributed a manifesto via social media before committing the actual shootings. Given the role that the Internet plays in the processes of radicalisation and aiding violent movements, greater effort must be made to make sense of the vast amount of online data in order to be made into information that is actionable for security purposes.

This chapter examines various methodologies and analytical tools for online intelligence gathering and countering violent extremism on the social media. A part of the Web 2.0, social media is a series of online tools which facilitates social interactions among users as opposed to the monologue (one-to-many) approach of content delivery of the traditional media such as radio and television (Antonius & Rich, 2013). The practice of gathering data on social media in order to study patterns, sentiment of users and network is referred to as 'social media analytics'.

Social media analytics has long been utilised by private companies for gauging consumer preferences and behaviour. Its potential for analysing sentiment and conducting horizon scanning in the national security realm is similarly vast. Intelligence gathering increasingly incorporates online data in addition to traditional human resources. Social media intelligence or SOCMINT is used to refer to the gathering, processing, analysis and presentation of social media data for the purpose of law enforcement and security-related intelligence (Antonius & Rich, 2013). It comprised of a mix of open and classified sources. While sources from social media cannot replace those from traditional human sources or even from open source intelligence, they can complement the latter. Security practitioners recognised that proper harvesting of online information may yield data on events that may not have been paid attention to, which can later be confirmed through traditional collecting disciplines and news outlets (Gupta & Brooks, 2013). Security organisations such as the U.K. Ministry of Defence and the Federal Bureau of Investigation (FBI) have expressed interest in tools to monitor and analyse social media data for the purpose of enhancing situational awareness. Organisations such as the U.S. Defense Advanced Research Projects Agency (DARPA) are involved in research on advancing state-of-the-art technology in studying online data.

Using online information for intelligence and countering violent extremism, however, is not only about technological improvements, but also about the study of human interactions. The Internet and social media is a rich repository of data for the understanding of user behaviour and diffusion of information. For instance, Hal Varian, Google's chief economist famously noted the ability of Google search terms to reveal real world behaviours (Varian, 2011). Another study on the dynamics of Facebook 'likes' observed that even the most rudimentary digital records on social networking platforms can yield insights into user information and behaviours (Kosinski, Stillwell, & Graepel, 2013). There is a need for more subtle and human centric approach to studying the Internet, and the social sciences can contribute towards that end. In other words, effective mining of social media data for national security meant that there is a need to combine the data analytical capabilities of computer scientists with the ability to study human behaviour that social scientists are familiar with. Network scholar Robert Ackland (2012) noted that:

The challenge stems from the fact that social media sites such as Twitter are generating terrabytes of highly dynamic and semi-structured data each day. While computer scientists are comfortable with working at 'data scale', the behaviour that is being studied is innately social, therefore requiring behavioural models from outside of computer science. On the other hand, although social scientists have been studying social influences for decades in fields such as economics, political science, sociology and marketing science, the conceptual frameworks do not necessarily translate to social media, and the techniques in the social scientist's toolkit are not designed for research at 'data scale'.

There is therefore avenue for employing a social and behavioural lens to critically analyse online interactions that would lead to significant real world developments as well as to identify cyber footprints of individuals who possess intent detrimental to the society.

Among the works surveyed for this chapter, two agencies have published works that incorporated behavioural analysis with social media analytical tools for countering violent extremism. While their application to real life events is currently unclear, these studies have combined behavioural-based analysis with technical methods in detecting the often 'weak signals' associated with issues of interest to national security such as potential terrorists and 'complex contagion' events. For instance, researchers from Sandia National Laboratories had demonstrated that incorporating sociological models in learning algorithms significantly improve predictive abilities of social media on real life events (Colbaugh, Glass, & Bauer, 2012). In addition, while most predictive analytics calculate volume of data on medium such as social media, their systems combined volumetric analyses with well-established social scientific theory of contagion effect to track emerging events such as terrorist attacks (Colbaugh & Glass, 2012). In particular, scholars affiliated with the Swedish Defence Research Agency (FOI) have combined natural language processing techniques, text mining techniques, social network analysis, and multimedia analysis to identify the presence of lone wolf terrorists through detection of key behavioural indicators such as active participation on radical websites, radical expression in postings, leakage of indication online, identification with radical groups, and fixation with the radical cause (Brynielsson et al., 2013; Cohen, Johansson, Kaati, & Mork, 2014). It is clear, therefore, that behavioural-based analyses aid social media analytics for intelligence and countering violent extremism, and should continue to be an area for future research.

However current social media analytics for countering violent extremism have not always effectively bridged the gap between the 'hard' computer science approaches with the 'soft' humanities perspective. Effective analysis of social media for intelligence and counter violent extremism thus requires not only improvement in technology, but also a more sophisticated form of social science-derived understanding of the relationship between online and offline behaviour. In devoting a section to outlining some of these methodologies and discussing their strengths and weaknesses, this chapter hopes to highlight the existing humanities-computer science gap, and call for future work into closing the divide.

This chapter begins by reviewing the literature for the application of social media analytics to detecting extremism online. Many of these approaches focus on finding static radical content rather than detecting early indicators of extremism on fast-moving social networking platforms. It will then proceed to discuss solutions to this challenge by outlining collection methods and analytics that are not unique to, but have been found appropriate in analysing social media data. Collection methods for the retrieval of social media data include: application programming interface (API), web crawlers, and information retrieval. Social media analytical tools to be discussed include: social network analysis, natural language processing (including sentiment analysis, multilingual analysis, and geo-coding), entity extraction, semantic search, and multimedia analysis.

Social media analytics and their application to countering violent extremism will be critically evaluated in this chapter. Despite the potential benefits of social media to national security purposes, some challenges remain. Firstly, there remains technological hurdle to clear for the social media analytical tools. The challenge in mining and studying the social media is also made challenging due to the nature of social media. Finally, the lack of input from the social science perspective represents a gap that must be plugged in the analysis of online extremism. In critically evaluating social media analytical tools for intelligence and countering violent extremism, the chapter hopes to provide a framework for understanding the tools as well as the online environment they operate in.

SOCIAL MEDIA DATA COLLECTION

Data may be collected from social media using API, web crawlers or using information retrieval (Bartlett & Miller, 2013).

Application Programming Interface (API)

Automatic collection of social media data can be conducted through connection to a particular platform's API. The API is a portal that keeps the data of the social media platform and coordinates the rules for access to these data by external computer software. The data available on the API depends on the platform; some produce long-range historical data while others can only make recent data available, some provide random selection of data from the platform while others can deliver search-specific data. Some APIs, for example Facebook's and Twitter's, provide meta-data such as user information. The Twitter search API is currently capable of extracting tweets that are approximately a week old based on hashtags or text strings (Ackland, 2013).

Web Crawlers

Web crawlers are automated scripts that search the World Wide Web and catalogue information. They are able to create a copy of all the pages that have been visited. Bespoke web crawlers can be built by amateur programmers employing free online programs and tutorials. Also, data on community interaction – information users are looking for and the sources of information users utilise – may be found by web crawlers.

Information Retrieval

Data for analysis may also be found via general information retrieval methods, which searches for relevant texts or documents within a huge amount of data. Rules-based algorithms are employed to look for patterns and relevant 'objects', which are then ranked based on relevance to the search.

SOCIAL MEDIA ANALYTICAL TOOLS

Social Network Analysis (SNA)

SNA is a multidisciplinary approach to study communities and relationships that has been utilised by law enforcement agencies and national security officials, long prior to its application in social media. It assumes that the structure and composition of an individual's social network influences his or her behaviour to a greater extent than his or her individual attributes (Ackland, 2013). Therefore, mapping and measuring the social network help analysts explain the relationship between individuals and organisations, and possibly predict behaviour resulting from these ties. In terms of security, SNA has been used to track social movements, predict threats to national security, and also forecast political events. Law enforcement agencies, for example, had employed SNA concept to intervene in terrorist financing networks, map networks of terror organisations, and discover the role of their members as well as their capabilities (Barabási, 2012).

Social media has expanded the usage of SNA; studying networks has become easier with the tracking and capturing of data by mobile devices and social media applications, accompanied by the lowering of costs in creating network data sets (Hansen, Shneiderman, & Smith, 2011). SNA of social media study networks generated by the users of various online platforms: followers, communities, and the interaction among users. The activities of users on user-generated platforms such as blogs, microblogs as well as social networking platforms can yield network data such as friendships and joint memberships of groups (Ackland, 2013). These networks may be explicit or implicit. Explicit communities openly indicate membership in online communities such as Facebook communities, while implicit communities are indicated through other forms of interaction such as likes, comments, and links (Bartlett & Miller, 2013).

SNA's usefulness for intelligence and countering violent extremism purposes is based on its approximation of strength of relationships within a given network on social media. This will be used as a basis for further understanding how the strength of the network influence the course of action a particular individual might take (Bartlett & Miller, 2013). Several measures are commonly used in SNA. The first, *degree centrality*, is the number of edges a node (representing an individual) is connected to (Ackland, 2013; Skillicorn, 2009). The concept of *betweenness centrality* measures the extent to which each node lies between other individuals in the network. In this respect, someone who is the only connection between two different communities has high betweenness, whereas another person who connects people who have many other ways of reaching each other has low betweenness (Skillicorn, 2009). Another measure in SNA is *closeness*, a measure of how close each individual is to the other individuals. For instance, Mohamed Atta, an Egyptian hijacker that was responsible for driving the plane into New York's World Trade Center in the 9/11 attacks, was found to have a high score on all three of the network centrality metrics. The network metric, degree centrality, revealed Atta's active role in the network. Closeness showed his high ability to access others in the network and monitor what was taking place within the network. His role as a broker in the network revealed a high score of betweenness (Krebs, 2002).

The national security community had shown interest in utilising their knowledge of SNA in analysing online networks. In June 2006, a Canadian terror cell that was initially discovered online through its anti-Western rhetoric and calls for attack in North America was tracked down using SNA, coupled with other traditional surveillance methods (Krebs, 2002). In 2010, Michael Oates, former head of the Pentagon's bomb-fighting task force, revealed that SNA programs had been employed to track down improvised explosive device cells (ExecutiveGov, 2010). Several examples of SNA tools had been highlighted in the *Project Quantum Leap* report (Naval Special Warfare Group ONE [NSWG-1], 2012). The project was a nine-day experiment involving approximately fifty government employees and private contractors to test the feasibility of mining online data, especially social media outlet Twitter, for the purpose of gathering intelligence for a money-laundering scenario. Geospatial software 'Raptor X', and its accompanying software plug-in, 'Social Bubble', was heavily utilised during the experiment to identify human networks, businesses and locations involved in money laundering (NSWG-1, 2012). Another company, Intrusion, Inc. had developed software to index the Internet, and plot networks and Internet topography over time. Semantic Research Inc.'s *Semantica* visual analytics tool was also capable of studying structured and semi-structured data, and later transforming them into a 'triplet' format that can then be turned to identify networks.

Applying SNA to the social media, however, presents several challenges. For one, analysts need to make informed decision in determining which links, seed accounts or websites are to be targeted for analysis, for this is where the nature of the network in question is hinged (Bartlett & Miller, 2013). Defining the boundary of the network is therefore crucial in analysis. Here, behavioural-based analysis afforded by social sciences is particularly helpful in crafting the initial research, and providing models and explanatory theories.

Secondly, real-time analysis of network must be carefully considered to yield valuable strategic and tactical insights (Bartlett & Miller, 2013). SNA has been used to identify individuals, groups, and other information in a quickly unfolding situation of security interest such as riots and demonstrations. However, more work should be done about the context, individuals as well as long-term implications of the event in question. Here, again multidisciplinary perspectives from social sciences will better refine analysis.

Natural Language Processing (NLP)

NLP is a sub-field of artificial intelligence research that includes the study of the meaning of natural language and the meaning conveyed by the language user, as well as the discovery of latent insight such as geographical location within a particular text (Bartlett & Miller, 2013). Sentiment analysis and multilingual analysis are integral, generally interlinked processes in NLP. Other processes in NLP include geo-coding (i.e., the process of pinpointing geographical location). NLP has been taken further by fields such as distributional semantics, which is currently perfecting 'deep-learning' techniques that simulated the human brain and combined with multi-modal techniques, are capable of interpreting meaning across different formats in the multimedia and documents.

Sentiment Analysis

Sentiment analysis is the analysis of social media for the purpose of identifying emotional states of online users. Online conversations on social media sites reflect the feelings and opinions of its real life users, many of which are potentially security-relevant and are therefore important source of intelligence data. Effective mining of the sentiments of social media users, while still in its infancy, is therefore becoming a priority for national security officials seeking to understand public attitudes towards national security policies. Monitoring online sentiments is a part of horizon-scanning to prevent negative sentiments from snowballing into undesirable consequences such as protests, riots or even revolutions.

Research-wise, recent breakthroughs in the field of sentiment analysis include semi-supervised and unsupervised approaches that do away with the need for labelled training documents, resolving issues in:

[N]ational security-related sentiment analysis applications (that) are often characterised by the existence of only modest levels of prior knowledge, reflected in the availability of a few labelled documents and small lexicon of sentiment-laden words, and by the need to rapidly learn and adapt to new domains. (Colbaugh & Glass, 2011, p. 135; Glass & Colbaugh, 2012, p. 3)

More research is also being conducted into how to perform sentiment analysis on the multimedia, which arguably contains more expression and sentiment than words could convey. Sentiment analysis may be conducted via studying user annotations and comments in the form of tagging, ratings, and other content. In addition, some researchers are developing methodologies for analysing emotion symbols such as emoticons to bridge the language gap (Cui, Zhang, Liu, & Ma, 2011). This was particularly helpful in analysing social media exchanges such as Twitter emoticons, which are independent of languages and are thus helpful for multilingual analysis.

National security communities worldwide have been looking into utilising sentiment analysis for their operations. The U.S. Office of Naval Research was one such organisation that had expressed interest in tools that will enable them to study documents that will shed light on the ideologies and social network of criminal and terrorist groups as well as the level of 'emotional support' that users may express towards a given issue or individual ("Can you predict the future", 2013). Two projects on sentiment analysis for national security have been undertaken by students at the U.S. Naval Postgraduate School. They attempted to examine the use of social media by Syrian opposition forces, whose reliance on social media was due to the need to advertise their activities because of lack of funding (Davis, 2012). The first, called the Dynamic Twitter Network Analysis (DTNA), was a software that extracts Twitter data and sorts the information in real time by phrases, keywords or hashtags. It was capable of continuous update, and incorporates maps and geo-location features. DTNA had already been used by three of the U.S. Defense Department units overseas to gauge sentiment about issues of interest to national security. The second project incorporated the DTNA software to extract data from other social networking platforms such as Facebook and YouTube in order to secure potential sites for weapons-of-mass-destruction (Davis, 2012). The projects were interested in finding out which parts of Syria are at the most risk for losing nuclear, biological or chemical weapons in the event of the fall of the Syrian government. The researchers particularly concentrated on the city of Homs as a key point for the control of the rest of the country. The project was the first known use of sentiment analysis by the military.

Despite the potential benefits, sentiment analysis is currently in the primitive stage. Given the informal nature of online communication and the huge volume of data from which to extract relevant text for analysis, there have been few proven methodologies for extracting and analysing content tailored for social media. Demos, a think-tank based in the United Kingdom, noted the problematic methodological issue pertaining to sentiment analysis research, observing that none of the sentiment analysis literature demonstrated the "methodological standards of attitudinal research in the social sciences, or the evidentiary standards of public policy decision makers" (Bartlett & Miller, 2013, p. 24). For instance, some of the problems in sentiment analysis are related to usage of words and sentence structure such as problems in identification of entities and context, the presence of implicit sentiment such as sarcasm and other forms of 'noise' (e.g., spelling and grammatical errors), all of which are commonly found in user-generated content (Feldman, 2013; Mukherjee, 2012). Furthermore, studying social media usually means capturing only snapshots of sentiments, but effective analysis needs to capture dynamics of opinion, usually over a longer course of time. In all these areas, better understanding of human interactions and usage of speech will contribute towards improving sentiment analysis.

Multilingual Analysis

As a worldwide phenomenon with users coming from many different countries, the opinions of social media users are expressed in a variety of languages (Tromp & Pechenizky, 2011). Twitter, a microblogging site, for example, is estimated to use more than 100 languages on the site (Bartlett & Miller, 2013), and continues to add to the array of languages offered. Shifts in the world's political development have some implications on the language usage and demography of its users. For instance, the selection of the Arabic language has increased dramatically since 2011, with a sharp spike in 2014 (Berger & Morgan, 2015; Seshagiri, 2014). This was attributed to the tumultuous events in the Middle East regions and the rise of ISIS supporters worldwide.

Multilingual analysis will thus provide many benefits to national security analysts. Firstly, the researchers could have access to information from various areas of the world, deriving some form of local knowledge from the geographic areas that the language covers (Hedeland, Schmidt, & Wörner, 2011). Secondly, greater coverage of information of entities such as person and organisation may be taken from the multilingual content of social media. While the combined multilingual information sourced from various social media sites contribute towards a more comprehensive picture of the situation at hand, it also presents challenges for national security analysts seeking to understand the content and sentiments of online users.

The national security community has long been interested in finding ways to condense the multitude of information across geographical locations, which is available in different languages. The U.S. Office of Naval Research, for example, is looking for more seamless tool for machine translation and processing that is able to translate physical characters or sounds into one machine-readable language ("Can you predict the future", 2013). The aforementioned DTNA project by the U.S. Naval Postgraduate School has also taken a step further than the typical sentiment analysis software by being able to extract both English and Arabic language information (Davis, 2012). In Project Quantum Leap, private company Basis Technology was able to produce text analytics and digital forensic tools that could study text sources in a foreign language (NSWG-1, 2012). It was mentioned in the report that the company's text analytics and digital forensic tools may be applied to analyse the media or other foreign language text sources. Another company, Sherpa Analytics, demonstrated its capability to provide near real time and automated multilingual analysis of media data especially the social media.

Multilingual analysis tools are typically developed by reusing the resources from one language and adapting them to other languages (Steinberger, 2010). Within the field of multilingual analysis, machine learning and machine translation are becoming increasingly popular methods to extract texts and documents across different languages. Machine learning is a self-learning software approach to multilingual analysis that learns language rules and vocabulary automatically (Hedeland et al., 2011). It is conducted through a mark-up process (Bartlett & Miller, 2013). In this process, an analyst looks through messages, which are presented on an interface. The analyst then makes a decision on the meaning of the message and assigns it to particular categories of meaning. The algorithm will appraise the linguistic attributes that correlate with each category, and recall the category for new pieces of social media data. Machine learning is particularly suitable for multilingual sentiment analysis of the large volume of user-generated data – expressed in imprecise language – of the social media.

Despite the great interest in bridging the language gap among the national security community, multilingual analysis continues to present challenges. Researchers for the DTNA project acknowledged that foreign language analysis continued to be a major bridge to cross for social media analytics tools (Davis, 2012). Three issues present barriers to effective multilingual analysis of the social media:

1. Challenges in developing effective translation software. While most information extraction and other text mining software can theoretically be customised to incorporate many languages, most of them have only been applied to small sets of languages. This is due to the labour and cost-intensive

efforts needed to develop the software per language (Steinberger, 2010). It is also challenging for the programmers to develop machine translation that is able to produce publishable quality translations.

2. Issues inherent in translation. Translating language nuances implicit in one language to another has always been challenging in traditional translation work. Not only does this requires deep knowledge in the grammar, syntax and semantics of both languages, effective translation also demands understanding of the culture of the people under study (Birbili, 2000), as well as the context under which the communication took place.

3. Mixed usage of languages in social media postings. In an informal network such as social media, depending on their language proficiency, users may not restrict themselves to just one language. A 2015 Brookings Institution study for example, observed that ISIS supporters used more than one language in their tweets in order to increase their audience base (Berger & Morgan, 2015). In addition, tweets incorporate a variety of languages, for instance an Arabic language post may feature an English hashtag. The mixture of languages poses challenges to effective multilingual analysis.

In the future, however, multilingual analysis may be conducted in a more seamless fashion due to increasing incorporation of translation services by social media outlet. For example, Twitter has embarked on the translation of tweets of some Egyptians leaders such as the ousted President Mohammed Morsi ("Twitter translates tweets", 2013). The social media platform started the experimental translation service using Microsoft Bing translator in July 2013 on European languages and later, Arabic. Facebook is also offering a translation service for its non-English language posts. Translation feature for most social networking platforms will almost certainly be refined in the near future.

Geo-Coding

Geo-coding is the capacity to convert names and places on user-generated sites into geographic locations. Social media has demonstrated the rise of what communications technology researcher Kalev Leetaru (2012) termed 'born geographic' systems – i.e., location-aware systems with precise coordinates indicating its origins. Twitter's tweets, for example, can be geo-located very accurately as 2-3 percent of them include latitudinal and longitudinal meta-data. It was found that 15 percent of tweets can be geo-located to a specific city, based on the cross-referencing of the location of the account and time zone. Research has also shown that tying location names to longitude/ latitude coordinates raised the ability to geo-locate social media documents by a factor of 2.5 (Bartlett & Miller, 2013).

Locating places of potential security concern has long been a priority for the law enforcement. The U.S. police, for example, are already using a combination of Google maps, crime statistics, and social media to decide appropriate places to patrol (Halpern, 2013). Majority of the software demonstrated for the purpose of the Project Quantum Leap incorporated geo-locative abilities. Raptor X, for example, is a geospatial information system (GIS) that uses 'plug-ins' to extract and display heterogeneous data (NSWG-1, 2012). It has been operationally used by the U.S. Special Operations Command components. Its 'Social Bubble' is also able to extract data through the Twitter API for the platform's users' geographic locations.

While the national security and law enforcement communities have shown great interest in leveraging upon current capacity for geo-coding in the social media sphere, the capacity is limited due to the nature of social media usage during crisis situations. For instance, Bartlett and Miller (2013) observed that in the days preceding the London riots in 2011, "most tweets were negative; and very few were geo-located to the event venue" (p. 30). Therefore it appears that the reliability of geo-coding may be highly dependent on the event of interest. Using geo-coding techniques to pinpoint location for threats to security is only helpful when the data collected from social media users are large enough to form accurate and helpful information during events such as an emergency (Bartlett & Miler, 2013).

Current software is also limited in terms of the accuracy of location mapping on social media. For instance, Leetaru (2012) noted that texts generally assume that the users understand locations in a similar fashion, causing searches for country names or administrative divisions to miss some cases. Most existing geo-coding systems also cannot be modified over time, and may thus have implications on data collection on the fast-changing landscape of social media. Better integration of multidisciplinary perspectives will solve these issues in geo-coding and aid investigations.

Improved Search Capabilities for the Social Media

Social media content is unstructured. Searching for relevant content on social media will therefore require different methods from keyword-based approaches that have worked well on static web pages (Africa, 2014; Correa & Sureka, 2011). New data crawling and indexing technology, however, searches not only keywords, but also places them within the context of time and place (Africa, 2014). Two of these approaches are discussed in this chapter: automated entity extraction, and semantic search. At the time of writing, Memex Technology, a vendor for DARPA, has unveiled a search system that is able to search the 'dark web' for criminal digital traces through deep-learning techniques that simulated human search abilities (Fox-Brewster, 2015). The program aims to refine current search technology by fine-tuning entity extraction and semantic search capabilities. The advancement will integrate behavioural approach to current search capabilities.

Entity Extraction

Entity extraction is the process of identifying people, organisations and concepts such as locations, time and numbers, as well as the relationship between them in a given document. Previous methods of entity extraction used heuristics, but new developments in the field allows the usage of statistical models relying on supervised or semi-supervised learning algorithms (Johansson & Svenson, 2013). Entity extraction is performed by taking the content and sending it to an entity extractor API, which will then return the entities (Gupta & Brooks, 2013).

Entity extraction offers manifold benefits. Firstly, while traditional keyword search tends to return exact keyword matches, it often leaves out potentially relevant documents while including irrelevant ones during the course of the search. An entity extractor can be trained to recognise documents where the keyword is misspelled because it finds entities based on their context. Secondly, the process reveals patterns and upcoming trends when the same entity is flagged in multiple sources. It does not require pre-knowledge about the search, being able to spot previously unknown entities at the time of its first appearance (Gupta & Brooks, 2013). Thirdly, data extracted by entity extractor may be used for drawing relationships for analysis. Generally, entities which have a relationship will appear in the same document. Entity extractors automatically scan through files and flag those of interest. Analysts could then focus analysis on documents that contain entities of interest and give them priority. From examining the smaller set of documents, an analyst may find relationships and conclusions to feed into applications for linking, data visualisation, and alerting. Finally, employing entity extraction will tighten the intelligence feedback loop by automatically finding relevant information in huge amounts of data. While existing threat identification tools use triage rules that raise alerts upon discovering significant words or patterns, entity extraction saves time by doing away with the need to analyse false information at each stage of the analysis cycle.

The intelligence community has long been interested in funding the development of entity extraction technologies (Gupta & Brooks, 2013). They are particularly useful for helping large-scale data analysis and extraction for intelligence work. The Office of the Director of National Intelligence (ODNI) has developed a computer system called Catalyst, which is able to conduct thorough extraction of entities and their relationships as well as projecting them within powerful semantic systems, which then provides integrated database for all intelligence organisations to access ("Meet Catalyst: IARPA", 2012).

Semantic Search

The term 'semantic' refers to the study of meaning of words, phrases, and sentences in a document. A semantic search engine identifies word connections from various sources and following analysis, helps the development of actionable products. It improves on traditional search engine that retrieves results based merely on keywords, by being able to comprehend concepts and logical relationships behind search terms, understanding the intention of the searcher. Semantic search engines examine words surrounding the search terms and attempt to examine the context in which the search terms appear, as well as the different meanings in which the terms may take on. Current semantic technologies aim to learn search patterns over time and be able to better predict what the human searcher is trying to find (Hale, 2010). For example, a study by Wang, Gerber, and Brown (2012) combines semantic analysis with natural language analysis of Twitter posts to predict possible hit-and-run crime.

The intelligence community is in the process of developing systems that allow the integration of public and classified data into a semantic network that will allow new information, some from the social media, to be searched according to context. The U.S. National Security Agency (NSA) runs a program called APSTARS that integrates data from different sources, including social media, semantically for the purpose of intelligence ("Meet Catalyst: IARPA", 2012). The CIA's Quantum Leap is a semantic system as well. Several similar programs were initiated by ODNI, including 'Blackbook' and the 'Large Scale Internet Exploitation Project' (LSIE) ("Meet Catalyst: IARPA", 2012). By integrating data across government agencies, semantic analysis technologies allows the national security community to retrieve potential sources of intelligence, text analysis, and find early warning signs from social networks.

Multimedia Analysis

Social media is dominated by multimedia, hosting images, videos, audios, maps and other user-generated content that are annotated and shared among users' social networks. For instance, image-sharing website, Flickr, contains more than six billion images in 2012 (Maybury, 2012). It is estimated that more than six billion photos and approximately 12 million videos are uploaded every month on Facebook by its users in the same year. By March 2012, 48 hours of video were being uploaded every minute to the video-sharing site, YouTube, and more than three billion views per day. Network traffic involving YouTube accounts for 20 percent of web traffic, and 10 percent of all Internet traffic. In relation to extremism, some studies have confirmed jihadists' preference for YouTube to promote their causes, especially those in Western Europe (Klausen, 2014).

Given the ubiquity of multimedia on social media, analysis is crucial to national security and law enforcement operations. A study conducted by GE Global Research for the U.S. Department of Justice in 2011, for instance, examined various automated ways to detect criminal and disorderly activities within prison facilities (Krahnstoever, 2011). The intelligent video facilities employed in the study reported 70 percent success rate for the detection of violent events in prisons, with 20 percent success rate for the detection prior to the occurrence of the event. DARPA is also searching for proposals for the 'Persistent Stare Exploitation and Analysis System' that aims to automatically find and analyse images and videos for threats in urban, suburban, and rural areas.

However, in comparison to the solution for other forms of criminal challenges, multimedia analysis for countering violent extremism has proven complicated (Higham & Nakashima, 2015). For example, multimedia recognition software such as Microsoft PhotoDNA is licensed specially for the purpose of identifying child pornography, which can be matched against the database maintained by the National Center for Missing and Exploited Children. It is difficult to apply the software to detect radical content on social media because it can only find images that exist in a database. Given the agility of multimedia usage by jihadists, similar software needs to be developed with behavioural insights in mind specifically to counter extremism.

Furthermore, there is little evidence of usage of videos and images in social media platforms that can act as actionable intelligence for the prior detection of activities of national security interest. Videos and photos found on social media during the London riots of 2011, for example, tend to be for identification purposes in the aftermath of the event, rather than prior detection of potentially destabilising events in the midst of the riots. More research should therefore be conducted into finding ways to improve multimedia analysis for actionable intelligence.

FUTURE OF SOCIAL MEDIA ANALYTICS: OPERATIONAL AND PRACTICAL IMPLICATIONS

This chapter has discussed existing tools and methods for social media analytics. Strengths and challenges for each analytic tool and its relevance to national security were also explored. The positive news for the national security community is that social media analytics is undergoing continued enhancement in the technological side that should see the tools and methods becoming more helpful for intelligence and countering violent extremism purposes. On the other hand, however, it is clear that while technological advances to social media analytics have been rapid, behavioural-based approaches need to be better integrated into the tools.

The concluding section of this chapter will discuss several operational and practical implications concerning the technology of social media analytics, data availability, epistemology of social media data, dynamics of online-offline interactions, future of intelligence skills, and some ethical considerations for social media analysis for intelligence and countering violent extremism.

Technological Challenges

Despite the enthusiasm of the national security community to leverage upon social media analytics tools long used by consumer-facing companies to understand public attitudes and forecast security threats, more research needs to be put into the application of social media research for horizon scanning. There have been few multidisciplinary research programs that effectively integrate the informatics studies with perspectives from social sciences (Zeng, Chen, Lusch, & Li, 2010). Demos had also noted the gap between current social media analytics capabilities and the published capabilities implied by the research community (Bartlett & Miller, 2013).

In general, social media analytics are stronger in retrospective instead of predictive identification of threats to national security (Jonas & Harper, 2006). Current technologies used by government organisations were programmed for collection and analysis of data in structured formats that are characteristic of databases and mainframes (Antonius & Rich, 2013). To illustrate, the review of police response to the London riots of 2011 noted that the British law enforcement were "insufficiently equipped to collect and analyse the unstructured and fast-moving social media information" (Antonius & Rich, 2013, p. 42). This means that they face challenges in meeting national security needs for predictive, future-oriented research that intelligence and countering violent extremism often require.

Algorithmic limitations also limit the efficacy of social media analytics for intelligence and countering violent extremism purposes. Algorithms need patterns of behaviours to base its calculation on, an aspect which can be difficult to find on social media:

If predictive data mining is used as the basis for investigating specific people, it must meet this test: there must be a pattern that fits terrorism planning – a pattern that is exceedingly unlikely ever to exist – and the actions of investigate persons must fit that pattern while not fitting any common pattern of lawful behaviour ... Unless investigators can winnow their investigations down to data sets already known to reflect a high incidence of actual terrorist information, the high number of false positives will render any result essentially useless. (Jonas & Harper, 2006, p. 9)

Algorithms are also constrained in their ability to find contextual knowledge that humans are able to detect instinctively – e.g., facial recognition, particular objects in photos, zooming in on conversations of interest in a noisy environment, and detecting human relationships (Skillicorn, 2009). However, practitioners should leverage on the strengths that algorithms do afford: predictive patterns in languages; large, complex models found in big datasets; and datasets that are primarily symbolic. They should also keep in mind that data yielded by social media analytics tools are simply raw information which needs context in order to evaluate its usefulness (Jonas & Harper, 2006). It is obvious therefore that human behavioural analysis must be better integrated into existing social media analytics.

The gap between current technological capabilities in utilising social media analytics for national security, however, may be fast closing. As the Project Quantum Leap report concluded, there is currently a 'window' of opportunity for the exploitation of social media sources before the landscape changes (NSWG-1, 2012). Technological refinement is therefore a certainty in the future.

Data Access/ Availability

Challenges to using the Internet as a tool for intelligence and countering violent extremism do not only encompass the technological aspect, but is also the bigger question of finding relevant data. While traditional social scientific research aims to create new sets of data through solicited responses such as surveys and interviews, the objective of social media analytics is to find useful data in a sea of publicly available information. Although technological know-how is improving, collecting data via social networking platforms remains problematic due to the fact that only social media companies possess complete data that may be of interest to analysts, especially transactional data. Access to relevant data is therefore dependent on the security organisations' relationships with the social media companies, which may or may not be willing to share the information.

For instance, Twitter has been known to be very protective of its users' rights, although in April 2015 the microblogging site revealed that it had done its part in countering radicalism online by suspending 10,000 ISIS-linked accounts for disseminating violent messages (Gladstone, 2015). The urgency of cooperation was highlighted on January 15, 2015 when U.K. Prime Minister David Cameron called for pressure on social networking firms to cooperate more with British intelligence agencies so as to prevent events such as the December 2014 shootings in Paris (Townsend, 2015). Many of the big social networking companies, however, have expressed disappointment with the security organisations and responded by adding new layers of encryption to their systems to prevent spying (Bartlett & Krasodomski-Jones, 2015). The cooperation from social media companies must therefore be secured for effective intelligence gathering.

Online data may also be unavailable through conscious or unconscious choices of users and creators of platforms. Firstly, social networking platforms have inbuilt restrictions that limit access to older data. For instance, the archiving and search functions of Facebook and Twitter leave much to be desired (Boyd & Crawford 2012), which may make them difficult mediums to map out past criminal records. Secondly, there is evidence that extremists and criminals are resorting to various methods in making their online activities secret to avoid detection (Bartlett & Krasodomski-Jones, 2015). While technology such as the Memex Technology's Sourcepin is being developed to search the dark web for criminal activities, this means that catching up with online anonymity is an ongoing problem. Finally, the huge and ever-increasing volume of online data ironically compounds the challenge of finding the right data. Boyd and Crawford (2012) pointed out that the vast amount of online data "… enables the practice of apophenia: seeing patterns where none actually exist, simply because enormous quantities of data can offer connections that radiate in all directions" (p. 668). It is therefore difficult to zero in on relevant posting or content in the ocean of data. There are also few rigorous studies that examine the varieties of security challenges and the types of social media data that are most appropriate to forecast criminal and extremist activities (Gupta & Brooks, 2013). Gupta and Brooks (2013) suggested that certain types of events are more suitable than others for analysis using the social media; those that were actually discussed or organised via the social media.

Whilst collecting data across different social media platforms to form a complete picture of the threat on hand is crucial to security operations, it has proven challenging. Users use different social networking platforms for different purposes, and thus analysts need to integrate snippets of information on different platforms to better understand the issue at hand. Twitter has been the most studied social media site because it is easiest to collect data on the platform. There is evidence that other social media platforms that are trickier to access may be understudied. For example, Facebook has banned automated collection of data without its permission.

Epistemology of Social Media Data

A social science-derived lens for keeping social media data in perspective ultimately involves the understanding of online epistemology. User-generated content changes existing ways of acquiring, understanding and validating knowledge (Boyd & Crawford 2012), a development that affects not only social science researchers studying social media, but also analysts looking for intelligence online. For one, due to the multiplicity of sources, determining the credibility of online posts can be difficult. Reliability of sources is crucial in both social science disciplines as well as intelligence work. Social media data, however, contains a lot of 'noise' or irrelevant information. Also, in times of crisis, reliable first-hand accounts and helpful information may be rare. Rumours or even misleading information from users seeking to take advantage of situations may be found online. Therefore, there is a need for careful sifting of reliable from unreliable information in the evaluation of social media data for national security purposes.

Online-Offline Dynamics

Intelligence gathering and countering violent extremism efforts are interested in two online-offline implications of social media: (1) whether some aspects of the online phenomenon reflect offline realities, for example social networks; (2) whether the web impacts real life. For the first point, it should be understood that social media is a highly curated medium that may exaggerate or underrepresent reality. The existence of an account does not represent the existence of a user as well. For instance Carter, Maher, and Neumann (2014) noted that there are motivations for creating false foreign fighter accounts: desire for status or influence, or their usage for information access by news writers and intelligence organisations. In addition, sometimes fake accounts are created to provide the appearance of support for a particular cause or organisation. Conducting social network analysis and sentiment analysis in the presence of such curated content is therefore problematic.

In the case of the second point, scholars have shown that social media has been generally used as tools for propaganda dissemination and communication rather than supplanting any face-to-face interaction (Klausen, 2014; von Behr, Reding, Edwards, & Gribbon, 2013). Mining and analysis of accounts for security purposes must therefore be aware that online support and influencers need not indicate similar dynamics in the real world.

New Frontiers for Intelligence Skills

Like social science research, future directions for social media analytics for intelligence and countering violent extremism should encompass an established set of research skills. Currently, however, social media research is merely a practice and is not considered "a coherent academic discipline or distinctive intelligence tradecraft" (Bartlett & Miller, 2013, p. 3). This has implications on how security officers use social media as tool for intelligence and countering violent extremism. Additionally, researchers are still exploring the set of skills necessary for proper research on social media. For the older generation of security officers, this would mean learning new skills such as accessing APIs, data mining and analysing huge amounts of data, which represent steep learning curve for those without computational background. SNA tools, for example, require some form of training to use them (Hansen et al., 2011). A practical recommendation at this point will be for security officers to continue exploration in this area for future best practices that integrates both the perspectives and approaches of computational science and social sciences.

Ethical Considerations

The final section considers the ethical implications of social media analytics for intelligence and countering violent extremism. While it is acknowledged that social media analytics contribute to national security and law enforcement, ethical decisions must be considered to prevent possibility of misuse. For one, SOCMINT includes both open and closed forms of online data, the distinction which are at times unclear (Bartlett & Miller, 2013). Legal challenges regarding the collection of some forms of data is thus an issue that law enforcement officers face during investigation. Demos observed that most of these legal frameworks are based on the principle of 'reasonable expectation' of online privacy (Bartlett & Miller, 2013).

Online privacy has become an issue of growing public concern. On the one hand, citizens are concerned for public safety and security, and expect security services and law enforcement agencies to fulfil their obligations in keeping the country safe. They are therefore generally supportive of law enforcement access to social media data for security purposes (Bartlett & Miller, 2013; Harris, 2014; Pew Research Center, 2013, 2015; Wroe, 2015). Most Australians and New Zealanders, for example, are comfortable with their social media accounts being monitored as preventive measures against possible terrorist activities ("Kiwis okay with social media", 2015; Wroe, 2015). Americans also believed that there should be swift identification of those engaged in illegal activities such as terrorism (Pew Research Center, 2015). A Risk Assessment and Horizon Scanning (RAHS) study had found that majority of Singaporeans believed that surveillance is a necessary mechanism for the prevention of terrorism and 'self-radicalisation' (Harris, 2014).

This supportive attitude, however, is countervailed by concerns over the abuse of data sovereignty and privacy. In traditional law enforcement, the authorities need clear justification for resorting to 'invasive methods' such as wire-tapping and subsequent intervention (Cohen et al., 2014). The identity of the suspect under investigation also tends to be clear. Automated search for signs of radicalisation online, however, automatically includes unknown and potentially innocent individuals in its monitoring. Bartlett and Miller (2013, p. 53) noted that: "Often, targeting certain individuals result in the obtainment of information on other, non-targeted individual, information which these non-targeted individuals may reasonably consider to be private". Pew Research Center (2013) also found that while most Americans are supportive of the NSA's telephone and email tracking program for counterterrorism, they are less accepting of Internet monitoring programs. In a more recent study, it was found that those who have learnt more about the government's counterterrorism data collection efforts believed that social media platforms should not save user activity information (Pew Research Center, 2015).

Such concept of privacy are context-dependent, influenced by culture and behaviour of those around them (Acquisti, Brandimarte, & Loewenstein, 2015). There are also indications that attitudes towards privacy are dynamic, changing with time. Americans, for one, associate privacy closely with security, and approval for government collection of telephone and Internet data for anti-terrorism measures have fallen since Edward Snowden's disclosure of NSA surveillance program (Pew Research Center, 2014). In contrast, the aforementioned RAHS study argued that Singaporeans' tolerance for surveillance is generally higher, with most citizens believing that certain societal guarantees such as security, education, and housing are more important than civil liberties (Harris, 2014). However, the study also acknowledged the impermanence of such acceptance, which may not be embraced by the next generation of citizens. Local context should therefore be clearly understood in making ethical decisions for investigation on social media.

Another ethical consideration is the question of whether it is legally permissible for law enforcement organisations and security services to set up fictitious identities in social media, in order to obtain information posted by other users (U.S. Department of Justice and Police Executive Research Forum,

2013). Going forward, SOCMINT for intelligence gathering and countering violent extremism should therefore find ways to balance public expectation for security and privacy.

CONCLUSION

This chapter discussed various methods and tools for the collection and analysis of social media data for intelligence and countering violent extremism. These tools examine social media in the areas of user networks, sentiment, languages, and geo-location. They also provide deeper understanding through analysing relationships between entities and semantics as well as the multimedia. As the chapter argues, these capabilities are rapidly improving. Technological advancement, however, is insufficient in the long run. Through the discussion of the analytical tools' capabilities and weaknesses, it is apparent that a social science-derived lens is crucial to better our understanding of online behaviour. A possible way to close this gap is to incorporate ethnographic research on the behavioural aspects of usage of social media and radical extremism with future technological research for social media analytics.

It concludes with several observations and practical recommendations for policymakers seeking to leverage on the advantages of social media data. Social media offers analysts an exciting, yet potentially challenging prospect of finding relevant data. Availability of data, however, is dependent on the actions and choices of the users, social networking firms, as well as archiving capability of the platforms. Therefore, the traditionally mooted recommendation for more data-sharing between the authorities and social networking companies is capable of yielding relevant data only to a certain extent. The reliability of online sources, and its relation to offline dynamics should also be seriously studied by policymakers. The incorporation of social media data for intelligence and countering violent extremism also means that the future generation of officers will need new set of analytical skills that should incorporate a combination of both technological as well as social scientific knowledge. Finally, ethical considerations must be taken into account in meeting the competing public demands for security and privacy.

REFERENCES

Ackland, R. (2012). *Social media and national security: A computational social scientist's perspective.* Australia: Australian Strategic Policy Institute.

Ackland, R. (2013). *Web social science: Concepts, data and tools for social scientists in the digital age.* London: Sage Publications.

Acquisti, A., Brandimarte, L., & Loewenstein, G. (2015). Privacy and human behaviour in the age of information. *Science, 347*(6221), 509–514. doi:10.1126/science.aaa1465 PMID:25635091

Africa, C. (2014, January 29). Move beyond keyword search, expert advises. *FutureGov.* Retrieved from http://www.futuregov.asia/articles/2014/jan/29/move-beyyond-keyword-search-expert-advises/

Antonius, N., & Rich, L. (2013). Discovering collection and analysis techniques for social media to improve public safety. *The International Technology Management Review, 3*(1), 42–53. doi:10.2991/itmr.2013.3.1.4

Barabási, A. (2012). *Network science.* Boston, MA: Barabási Lab.

Bartlett, J., & Krasodomski-Jones, A. (2015). *Online anonymity: Islamic State and surveillance.* London: DEMOS.

Bartlett, J., & Miller, C. (2013). *The state of the art: A literature review of social media intelligence capabilities for counter-terrorism.* London: DEMOS.

Berger, J. M., & Morgan, J. (2015). *The ISIS twitter census: Defining and describing the population of ISIS supporters on twitter (Brooking project on U.S. Relations with the Islamic World, Analysis Paper, 20).* Washington, DC: Brookings Institution.

Birbili, M. (2000, Winter). Translating from one language to another. *Social Research Update, 31.* Retrieved from http://sru.soc.surrey.ac.uk/SRU31.html

Boyd, D., & Crawford, K. (2012). Critical questions for big data. *Information Communication and Society, 15*(5), 662–679. doi:10.1080/1369118X.2012.678878

Brynielsson, J., Horndahl, A., Johansson, F., Kaati, L., Mårtenson, C., & Svenson, P. (2013). Harvesting and analysis of weak signals for detecting lone wolf terrorists. *Security Informatics, 2*(11). doi:10.1186/2190-8532-2-11

Can you predict the future by reading Twitter? (2013, January 14). *Nexgov Newsletter.* Retrieved from http://www.nextgov.com/defense/2013/01/can-you-predict-future-reading-twitter-pentagon-thinks-maybe/60634

Carter, J., Maher, S., & Neumann, P. R. (2014). *Greenbirds: Measuring importance and influence in Syrian foreign fighters networks.* London: The International Centre for the Study of Radicalisation and Political Violence.

Cohen, K., Johansson, F., Kaati, L., & Mork, J. C. (2014). Detecting linguistic markers for radical violence in social media. *Terrorism and Political Violence, 26*(1), 246–256. doi:10.1080/09546553.2014.849948

Colbaugh, R., & Glass, K. (2010). *Estimating sentiment orientation in social media for intelligence monitoring and analysis.* Paper presented at IEEE Conference on Intelligence and Security Informatics (ISI), Vancouver, BC. doi:10.1109/ISI.2010.5484760

Colbaugh, R., & Glass, K. (2011). *Agile sentiment analysis of social media content for security informatics applications.* Paper presented at European Intelligence and Security Informatics Conference, Athens. doi:10.1109/EISIC.2011.65

Colbaugh, R., & Glass, K. (2012). *Proactive defense for evolving cyber threats (SAND2012-10177).* Livermore, CA: Sandia National Laboratories. doi:10.2172/1059470

Colbaugh, R., Glass, K., & Bauer, T. (2012). *Leveraging sociological models for predictive analytics.* Cornell University Library. Retrieved from http://arxiv.org/abs/1212.6806

Correa, D., & Sureka, A. (2013, January). Solutions to detect and analyze online radicalizations: A survey. *HITD PhD Comprehensive Report, V*(N), 1-30.

Cui, A., Zhang, M., Liu, Y., & Ma, S. (2011). Emotion tokens: Bridging the gap among multilingual Twitter sentiment analysis. *Information Retrieval Technology*, *7097*, 238–249. doi:10.1007/978-3-642-25631-8_22

Davis, K. (2012, Nov 8). Can the US military fight a war with Twitter? *Computerworld*. Retrieved from http://www.computerworld.com/article/2493445/social-media/can-the-us-military-fight-a-war-with-twitter-.html

ExecutiveGov. (2010, March 12). *Lt. Gen. Michael L. Oates of JIEDDO: Leading the fight against IEDs*. Retrieved from http://www.executivegov.com/2010/03/lt-gen-michael-l-oates-of-jieddo-leading-the-fight-against-ieds/#sthash.yjfWj0NH.dpuf

Feldman, R. (2013, April). Techniques and applications for sentiment analysis. *Communications of the ACM*, *56*(4), 82–89. doi:10.1145/2436256.2436274

Fox-Brewster, T. (2015, April 10). Memex in action: Watch DARPA Artificial Intelligence search for crime on the 'Dark Web'. *Forbes*. Retrieved from http://www.forbes.com/sites/thomasbrewster/2015/04/10/darpa-memex-search-going-open-source-check-it-out/

Gladstone, R. (2015, April 9). Twitter says it suspended 10,000 ISIS-linked accounts in one day. *The New York Times*. Retrieved from http://www.nytimes.com/2015/04/10/world/middleeast/twitter-says-it-suspended-10000-isis-linked-accounts-iin-one-day.html?_r=0

Glass, K., & Colbaugh, R. (2012). Estimating the sentiment of social media content for security informatics applications. *Security Informatics*, *1*(3). doi:10.1186/2190-8532-1-3

Gupta, R., & Brooks, H. (2013). *Using social media for global security*. Indianapolis, IN: John Wiley & Sons, Inc.

Hale, A. (2010, September 16). Sourcecon's Semantic Search Series. *Sourcecon*. Retrieved from http://www.eremedia.com/sourcecon/sourcecons-semantic-search-series/

Halpern, S. (2013, November 7). Are we puppets in a wired world? *The New York Review of Books*. Retrieved from http://www.nybooks.com/articles/archives/2013/nov/07/are-we-puppets-wired-world/

Hansen, D. L., Shneiderman, B., & Smith, M. A. (2011). *Analysing social media networks with NodeXL: Insights from a connected world*. Massachusetts, MA: Elsevier.

Harris, S. (2014, July/August). The social laboratory. *Foreign Policy*, 64–71.

Hedeland, H., Schmidt, T., & Wörner, K. (Eds.). (2011). Multilingual resources and multilingual applications. In *Proceedings of the Conference of the German Society for Computational Linguistics and Language Technology (GSCL)*. Hamburg: Universität Hamburg.

Higham, S., & Nakashima, E. (2015, July 16). Why the Islamic State leaves tech companies torn between free speech and security. *The Washington Post*. Retrieved from https://www.washingtonpost.com/world/national-security/islamic-states-embrace-of-social-media-puts-tech-companies-in-a-bind/2015/07/15/0e5624c4-169c-11e5-89f3-61410da94eb1_story.html?kmap=1

Johansson, F., & Svenson, P. (2013). Constructing and analyzing uncertain social networks from unstructured textual data. In T. Özyer, Z. Erdem, J. Rokne, & S. Khoury (Eds.), *Mining social networks and security informatics* (pp. 41–61). Dordrecht: Springer Science. doi:10.1007/978-94-007-6359-3_3

Jonas, J., & Harper, J. (2006, December 11). *Effective counterterrorism and the limited role of predictive data mining* (Policy Analysis No. 584). Washington, DC: CATO Institute.

Kiwis okay with social media monitoring for counter-terrorism, but not business. (2015, July 2). *Fairfax NZ News* Retrieved from http://www.stuff.co.nz/technology/social-networking/69883819/kiwis-okay-with-social-media-monitoring-for-counterterrorism-but-not-business

Klausen, J. (2015). Tweeting the jihad: Social media networks of western foreign fighters in Syria and Iraq. *Studies in Conflict and Terrorism, 38*(1), 1–22. doi:10.1080/1057610X.2014.974948

Kosinski, M., Stillwell, D., & Graepel, T. (2013). Private traits and attributes are predictable from digital records of human behaviour. *Proceedings of the National Academy of Sciences of the United States of America, 110*(15), 5802–5805. doi:10.1073/pnas.1218772110 PMID:23479631

Krahnstoever, N. (2011, August 15). *Automated detection and prevention of disorderly and criminal activities*. Niskayuna, NY: GE Global Research.

Krebs, V. E. (2002, April 1). Uncloaking terrorist networks. *First Monday, 7*(4). doi:10.5210/fm.v7i4.941

Leetaru, K. H. (2012). Fulltext geocoding versus spatial metadata for large text archives: Towards a geographically enriched wikipedia. *D-Lib Magazine, 18*(9/10). doi:10.1045/september2012-leetaru

Maybury, M. T. (Ed.). (2012). *Multimedia information extraction: Advances in video, audio, and imagery analysis for search, data mining, surveillance, and authoring*. IEEE Computer Society. doi:10.1002/9781118219546

Meet Catalyst. IARPA's entity and relationship extraction program. (2012, April 4). *Public Intelligence*. Retrieved from http://publicintelligence.net/meet-catalyst

Mukherjee, S. (2012, June 29). *Sentiment analysis: A literature analysis*. Mumbai: Indian Institute of Technology.

Naval Special Warfare Group ONE (NSWG-1). (2012, September 12). *Project Quantum Leap After Action Report*. Washington, DC: Author. Retrieved from http://fas.org/irp/eprint/quantum.pdf

Pew Research Center. (2013, June 10). *Public says investigate terrorism, even if it intrudes on privacy: Majority views NSA phone tracking as acceptable anti-terror tactic*. Washington, DC: Author. Retrieved from http://www.people-press.org/2013/06/10/majority-views-nsa-phone-tracking-as-acceptable-anti-terror-tactic/

Pew Research Center. (2014, January 20). *Obama's NSA Speech has little impact on sceptical public: Most say U.S. should pursue criminal case against Snowden*. Washington, DC: Author. Retrieved from http://www.people-press.org/2014/01/20/obamas-nsa-speech-has-little-impact-on-skeptical-public/

Pew Research Center. (2015, May 20). *Americans' attitudes about privacy, security and surveillance.* Washington, DC: Author. Retrieved from http://www.pewinternet.org/files/2015/05/Privacy-and-Security-Attitudes-5.19.15_FINAL.pdf

Seshagiri, A. (2014, March 9). The language of Twitter users. *The New York Times.* Retrieved from http://bits.blogs.nytimes.com/2014/03/09/the-languages-of-twitter-users/

Skillicorn, D. (2009). *Knowledge discovery for counterterrorism and law enforcement.* New York, NY: CRC Press.

Steinberger, R. (2010). Challenges and methods for multilingual text mining. In *Proceedings of the 7th International Conference on Language Resources and Evaluation (LREC).* Valletta, Malta: ELRA.

Townsend, M. (2015, January 15). How a team of social media experts is able to keep track of the UK jihadis. *The Guardian.* Retrieved from http://www.theguardian.com/world/2015/jan/17/social-media-british-jihadists-islamic-state-facebook-twitter

Tromp, E., & Pechenizky, M. (2011). *SentiCorr: Multilingual sentiment analysis of personal correspondence.* Retrieved from http://www.win.tue.nl/stressatwork/pdfs/senticorr_camera.pdf

Twitter translates tweets from leading Egyptians. (2013, July 4). *BBC News.* Retrieved from http://www.bbc.com/news/technology-23179269

U.S. Department of Justice and Police Executive Research Forum (2013, May). Social media and Tactical Considerations for Law Enforcement. Retrieved from http://www.policeforum.org/assets/docs/Free_Online_Documents/Technology/social%20media%20and%20tactical%20considerations%20for%20law%20enforcement%202013.pdf

Varian, H. (2011, September). Predicting the present. *Think with Google.* Retrieved from https://www.thinkwithgoogle.com/articles/predicting-the-present.html

von Behr, I., Reding, A., Edwards, C., & Gribbon, L. (2013). *Radicalisation in the digital era: The use of the Internet in 15 cases of terrorism and extremism.* Santa Monica, CA: RAND Corporation.

Wang, X., Gerber, M. S., & Brown, D. (2012). Automatic crime prediction using events extracted from Twitter. In S. J. Yang, A. M. Greenberg, & M. Endsley (Eds.), *Social computing, behavioral-Cultural modeling and prediction 2012, lecture notes in computer science* (pp. 231–238). Heidelberg: Springer. doi:10.1007/978-3-642-29047-3_28

Wroe, D. (2015, July 2). Most Australians happy with government watching social media to stop terror: Poll. *The Sydney Morning Herald.* Retrieved from http://www.smh.com.au/federal-politics/political-news/most-australians-happy-with-government-watching-social-media-to-stop-terror-poll-20150701-gi2uf9.html

Zeng, D., Chen, H., Lusch, R., & Li, S. (2010). Social media analytics and intelligence. *IEEE Computer Society, 25*(6), 13–16.

Chapter 17

"On the Internet, Nobody Knows You're a Dog":
The Online Risk Assessment of Violent Extremists

Neil D. Shortland
University of Massachusetts – Lowell, USA

ABSTRACT

Online behaviour can provide a unique window from which we can glean intent. From an intelligence standpoint it provides an important source of open-source information. However, making inference of intent from online activity is inherently difficult. Yet elsewhere progress is being made in incorporating information online into decisions regarding risk and offender prioritisation. This chapter synthesises lessons learnt from studies of risk assessment of violent extremists, risk assessment online, and the form and function of extremist materials online in order to begin to approach the issue of online risk assessment of violent extremism. In doing so it highlights issues associated with the diversity of online extremist behaviour, the diversity of offline extremist behaviour and the general lack of understanding related to the interaction of online and offline experiences, and how this contributes to the wider psychological process of 'radicalisation'. Implications for practitioners are discussed.

INTRODUCTION

Computers have enabled people to make more mistakes faster than almost any invention in history, with the possible exception of tequila and hand guns. (Mitch Ratcliffe)

This chapter focuses on the potential utility that online-gleaned information (i.e., information pertaining to an individual's online activities) offers for issues regarding the prioritisation and investigation of individuals who are or may in the future undertake extremist activities. Specifically this chapter presents the results of a systematic review that integrates a diverse range of literature covering extremism online, risk assessment online, and the risk assessment of extremists.

DOI: 10.4018/978-1-5225-0156-5.ch017

The earliest discussions of extremist materials on the Internet focused on how extremist organisations might use this new technology as a weapon or as a target (see Collin, 1996). Terms such as 'computer terrorism', 'cyberterror' and 'cyberjihad' have all been used to refer to activities that involve the destruction or sabotage of corporate assets achieved through hacking into computer systems (Bowman-Grieve, 2015). While cyberterrorism remains a top-tier security threat, 'cyberattacks' by extremist organisations have, as of yet, not materialised (Weimann, 2004). The more pressing concern however is the use of information technology as a facilitator for offline extremist activities rather than as a weapon or target in and unto itself. Extremist organisations currently use information technology, specifically the Internet, as a platform to recruit, deliver threats, release instructional materials to facilitate the actions of others, and plan and coordinate violent extremist attacks (Weimann, 2006). Currently the Internet is playing a central role in facilitating the process through which western individuals join foreign insurgencies (such as the Islamic State in Iraq and Syria [ISIS]) by facilitating contact and planning between would-be-recruits and recruiters. Extremist materials on the Internet have also facilitated attempts to launch domestic attacks (see Lemieux, Brachman, Levitt, & Wood, 2014). When discussing the impact of online extremist media, such as the well-known *Inspire* magazine (a media outlet of Al-Qaeda in the Arabian Peninsula [AQAP] which advocates and provides instructional materials to facilitate 'lone actor' attacks), the United Kingdom's domestic security service (MI5) states that:

... we can now say that Inspire has been read by those involved in at least seven out of the ten attacks planned within the UK since its first issue [in 2010]. We judge that it significantly enhanced the capability of individuals in four of these ten attack plots... this is pernicious. It radicalises, it exhorts violent action and it gives recipes or instructions on how to do so.

It is clear then that the Internet facilitates extremist activity. However it is also a double-edged sword. For example, in 2012 when Ted Poe, chairman of the United States Subcommittee hearing on the evolution of terrorist propaganda on Internet, requested that the Federal Bureau of Investigation (FBI) do more to counter extremists' use of the Internet, the FBI refused, stating that "they gained intelligence about groups and individuals from their social media activity, even though it is apparent that this social media activity recruits terrorists who want to kill"[1]. Discussing whether such materials should be on the Internet (and the legal/technological efforts to remove it) is outside the scope of this chapter but is covered elsewhere (e.g., McNeal, 2008); instead this chapter focuses on how, if at all, this type of materials can be used by law enforcement agencies to facilitate efforts to protect the public from the threat of terrorism.

THE ISSUES OF BEING 'ONLINE'

Issue 1: Anonymity

In 1993 Peter Steiner published a cartoon for the New Yorker titled 'On the Internet, nobody knows you're a dog'. This cartoon highlighted the core principle of the Internet that users can act with relative anonymity. While anonymity has clear counter-security benefits (see Weimann, 2004, 2006), it also has a profound psychological effect on our behaviour. Zimbardo (1969) argues that anonymity (amongst other factors) leads to de-individuation and disinhibition resulting in hostile behaviour. Prentice-Dunn and Rogers (1982, 1989) state that a reduction of 'accountability cues' and self-awareness leads to a decreased use of internal standards. At the same time, and perhaps more importantly when considering engagement in extremist materials, the Internet also removes social cues, providing an even playing field not restricted by offline realities. This effect is known as the 'equalisation hypothesis' (see Dubrovsky, Kiesler, & Sethna, 1991). Thus, the nature of the Internet has two important manifestations. It removes the psychological barriers for engaging with terroristic materials online; and it provides a platform through which individuals can project an image of themselves that they wish to portray. What this means is that the 'vulnerable border between fantasy and reality' (see Gelder, 2006) is even more vulnerable online, and decisions regarding an individual's intent (real or fanciful) will therefore be harder to discern online. What this means for counter terrorism is that when Michael Adebolajo (discussed further below) communicates with a known member of AQAP and references a desire to become a "martyr", these comments are viewed as "not unusual" and a "fairly standard example of rhetoric" (Intelligence and Security Committee Report, 2014, p. 120).

Issue 2: Increasing Proliferation of Extremist Content

A further confounding issue is that extremist material proliferates on the Internet and is increasing. The past decade has seen an exponential increase in websites, blogs and message boards advocating violent extremism, specifically jihadist materials (Brachman, 2006). Furthermore the number of individuals engaged in such materials far outweighs the number of eventual (or even possible) 'violent extremists'. The video depicting the beheading of Nick Berg by Islamic extremists in Iraq was downloaded over 15 million times, with sites hosting the video receiving over 60,000 hits per hour (Talbot, 2005). Between September and December 2014, 46,000 Twitter accounts were linked to ISIS supporters (Berger & Morgan, 2015). Linked to this, technologically savvy extremist groups also use technological tricks to increase the perceived number of supporters in their networks. Of the 36,000 accounts above, over 6,000 of these accounts were 'bots' posting terroristic material automatically and without a human user (Berger & Morgan, 2015). So, not only is the number of individuals involved in terroristic materials online vast, it is also falsely expanded by automatic software (see Berger & Stern, 2015).

On top of navigating the presence of artificial online accounts, we must acknowledge the presence of 'sock puppets'. Sock puppets – a reference to generating a puppet by putting a hand in a sock – are accounts run by a human user, that speaks to or about themselves while pretending to be another person (see Bu, Xia & Wang 2013). Sock puppets project a deceptive image and are prevalent across most areas of online activity, but are famously used as a tactic by those attempting to counter extremism. For example, Rossmiller (2007) highlights his experiences of generating cover identities to communicate with potential extremists in online forums. On the other hand, Huey and Kaylal (2015) discuss following a sock puppet account that they believed was a western female at risk of absconding to Syria to join ISIS.

Issue 3: Uncertainty and Incomplete Data

Finally, even when a potential (real) individual of interest has been identified, we must acknowledge that we are unlikely to have a complete picture of their online activity. This was demonstrated in the review of the risk assessment process for Michael Adebowale and Michael Adebolajo. Michael Adebowale and Michael Adebolajo were convicted in December 2013 for the murder of Fusilier Lee Rigby. Both offenders were known to the security services and had each been separately assessed as low priority – Adebolajo was in fact featured in five separate investigations since 2008 (see Intelligence and Security

Committee Report, 2014). After the attack, MI5 launched an investigation aimed at discerning whether the agencies acted appropriately in dealing with these individuals, given what was known at the time as well as materials that came to light in the ensuing investigation. In considering these materials, one piece of evidence was viewed as potentially decisive; an exchange between Adebowale and an individual overseas called 'FOXTROT' that was not seen until after the attack. The exchange was:

[A] substantial online exchange between Adebowale and FOXTROT in December 2012, in which Adebowale expressed his desire to murder a soldier – in the most graphic and emotive manner – because of UK military action in Iraq and Afghanistan. Adebowale had not, at that point (five months before the attack), developed a definite plan as to how he might carry out such an attack. FOXTROT encouraged him and suggested several potential attack methodologies, ranging from a martyrdom operation to use of a knife. Adebowale believed that security arrangements that guarded soldiers' places of work might make it difficult to carry out an attack, and that alternative, less secure locations should be considered. (Intelligence and Security Committee Report, 2014, p. 127)

Five months later, Adebowale killed a Royal Fusilier outside the Royal Artillery Barracks. While it is difficult to speculate on outcomes counterfactually, the Intelligence and Security Committee stated that if MI5 had access to this exchange, "Adebowale would have become a top priority … [and] there is a significant possibility that MI5 would then have been able to prevent the attack" (Intelligence and Security Committee Report, 2014, p. 7). However it also acknowledges "there may have been only a very slim chance that MI5 would have had sight of the FOXTROT exchange" (p. 7).

When investigating Adebowale's wider extremist activity online, the investigation also highlighted that he was previously subjected to seven social media account closures for (to varying degrees) engaging with extremist materials. Again while the accounts were closed prior to the attack, their closure was the result of an automatic procedure that occurs when online activity matches a series of descriptors (Intelligence and Security Committee Report, 2014) and the reasons for their closure were not examined until this review. This highlights additional issues online such as the role of third parties who own the platforms (and therefore the contents) within which these extremist online activities are hosted. At the same time, it is also important to acknowledge that those who are most visible may merely represent 'low hanging fruit' and those individuals who pose the greatest 'risk' are in fact those whose discussions are on platforms that are the hardest to obtain information from such as the 'dark web' – an online domain where users cannot be traced or identified (Bartlett, 2014) and within which we know terrorist materials proliferate (see Moon, 2007).

Extremist behaviour, in comparison to other crimes, has an incredibly low base rate (see Roberts & Horgan, 2008). Yet the Internet creates an environment in which the number of 'potential' extremists is greatly exaggerated. So while this chapter considers how information obtained online can be used to inform the risk assessment of an individual, it is important to recognise the effect that the Internet imparts on human behaviour writ large because it is viable that while, in hindsight, the Internet activities of extremists (identified post event) present clear indicators of intent, when analysed in real-time these indicators may be clouded by a large portion of individuals who present the same behavioural indicators yet possess no intent nor capability.

RISK ASSESSMENT, EXTREMISM AND THE INTERNET: A FRAMEWORK FOR ANALYSIS

With these issues in mind, the goal of this chapter is to present a theoretical framework within which we can approach online risk assessment of violent extremists. However, both conceptually and pragmatically this is a contested issue. Firstly, we are yet to satisfactorily actualise, or even conceptualise, the risk assessment of individuals who could potentially become involved in extremist activity (see Monahan, 2011). To further confound issues, while several recent developments have furthered our understanding of the process through which people become involved in terrorism (McCauley & Moskalenko, 2008, 2011), and the behaviours that they undertake when involved in terrorism (Gill, Horgan, & Deckert, 2014; Horgan, Shortland, Walsh, & Abbasciano, in press) beyond acknowledging that the Internet does play a role, we are ill-equipped to understand the process through which the Internet affects how individuals move into extremism and eventual extremist behaviour (see Horgan & Taylor, 2007). Attempting to incorporate online behaviour into an assessment as to whether an individual poses a risk of engaging in violent extremist behaviour would therefore seem problematic.

However, we are not approaching this area without precedent. Elsewhere practitioners are required to make intelligence-based decisions about the risk that child pornography offenders pose of committing a child abuse offense offline (see Long, Alison, & McManus, 2013; McManus, Long, & Alison, 2013), and mental health practitioners often make a series of assessments based on online reporting (see Buchanan, 2012). In fact, one type of these E-health initiatives is specifically aimed at responding to social media behaviour. Here "the nature of their social media use … tweets, status updates, comments or posts indicative of suicide ideation are used to classify those at risk" (Christensen, Batterham, & O'Dea, 2014, p. 8194).

Effectively synthesising influences across diverse fields requires a systematic review methodology that is flexible to both qualitative and quantitative data that can handle a large body of data (Barnett-Page & Thomas, 2009). Dixon-Woods and colleagues (2006) proposed the 'Critical Interpretive Synthesis' (CIS) as a systematic review methodology better suited to literature that covers multiple domains, methodologies and report sources (i.e., both academic and 'grey' literature). The utility here is that CIS is focused on critiquing rather than appraising each study against a series of standards – as is the case in other interpretative methodologies (Dixon-Woods et al., 2006). In doing so, the method also incorporates elements of grounded theory in that the research question(s) and search criteria can be continually adapted. Seeking, selecting and evaluating literature is therefore an iterative, rather than proscriptive stage-based approach (Barrett-Page & Thomas, 2009). Here, conceptualising the online risk assessment of violent extremists will draw influence from psychology, criminology, political science, computer science, security studies, healthcare, risk management, and communication. At the same time the data analysed will include case studies, network analyses, experimental studies, ethnographic research, and data driven behavioural analyses. CIS therefore provides a framework that is suitably adaptive for synthesis.

CIS does not use a series of pre-specified procedural steps to conduct a review (Dixon-Woods et al., 2006). However the first step of any systematic review is to assemble all (potentially) relevant literature. In identifying literature relevant to the scope of this chapter, we are between a rock and a hard place. Specifically, we cannot solely focus on literature relevant to the online risk assessment of violent extremists. A 'body' of literature in this domain does not exist. At the same time, we cannot expand the search to cover all constituent parts (i.e., the Internet, violent extremism, risk assessment) because of the sheer volume of academic work covering these three domains – a *ScienceDirect* search totals over

500,000 articles for terms 'Internet', 'Risk assessment' and 'terroris*'. To be pragmatic, the three core elements of online risk assessment of violent extremists were combined into three sets of two (see Figure 1). Variations for search terms within each element were also used to ensure all available materials were identified. Thus, searches pertaining to the Internet included terms such as 'online', searches related to violent extremism also involved the terms 'extremis*' and 'terroris*', and searches relating to risk assessment also included 'threat assessment'.

Thus, for this review, literature that addressed the risk assessment of violent extremists, the process of conducting risk assessment online, and extremism online was identified. This allowed the search strategy to be diverse enough to collect new materials that could inform the online risk assessment of violent extremists, without being so broad as to overload the initial stages of the CIS. At the same time, combining two terms inevitably means that potentially relevant materials will be excluded from this search (e.g., risk assessment of wider criminality or offline crimes were not necessarily identified in this search); that said the goal of this chapter was not to provide an exhaustive review of the literature associated with risk assessment, extremism or online writ large.

An initial search using these terms resulted in the identification of 7,262 potentially relevant papers (violent extremism online – 963 papers; risk assessment online – 4,269; risk assessment and violent extremism – 2,020). Each paper was then appraised to determine if it warranted full review (Dixon-woods et al., 2006). Based on the results of this appraisal, 84 papers were selected for full review. Below we provide a synthesis of the literature from each field, drawing implications for the online risk assessment of violent extremists.

Figure 1. A conceptual approach to the online risk assessment of violent extremists

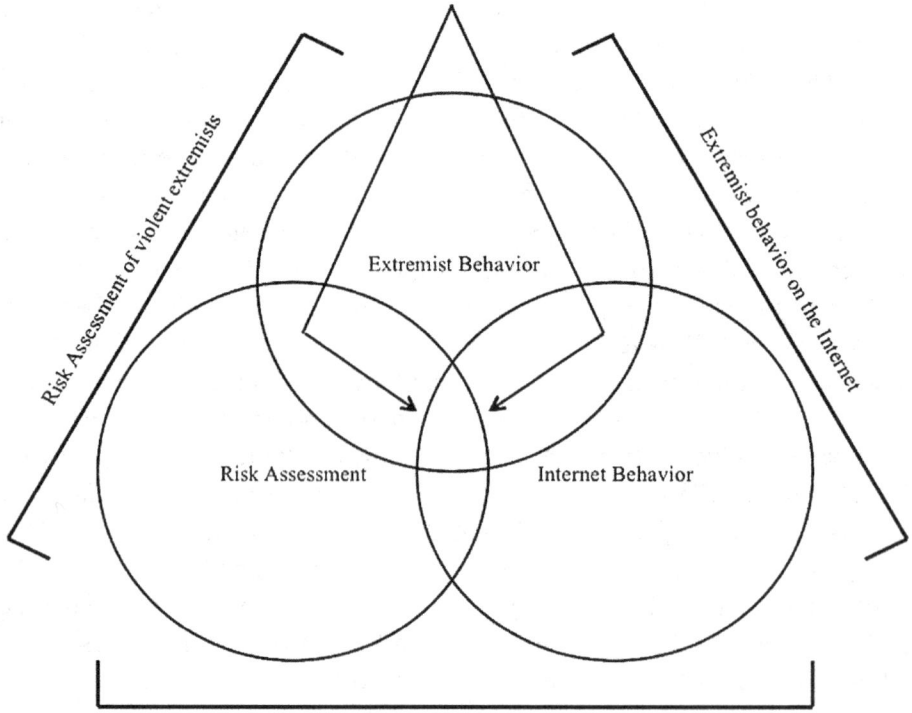

RISK ASSESSMENT AND VIOLENT EXTREMISM

There is a need to develop a capability to effectively assess the risk that an individual poses of under-taking violent extremist behaviour (Roberts & Horgan, 2008). Yet to date the majority of risk assessment literature is focused on the likelihood of a violent extremist attack (e.g., Barros, Proenca, Faria, & Gil-Alana, 2006). Whether an individual is likely to be currently (or in the future) engaged in violent extremist behaviour has received less attention (see Silke, 2014). The issue then is that in all of the most recent homegrown terrorist attacks in the United Kingdom, Australia, France, Denmark, and the United States some (if not all) of the perpetrators were, at varying points prior to their attacks, risk assessed.

Man Haron Monis, who held customers and staff hostage in a Lindt café, was subjected to many security investigations throughout his time in Australia. His latest assessment, just one week prior to the attack, was in response to 18 calls to the National Security Hotline (Commonwealth of Australia, 2015). This review however determined that "he fell well outside the threshold to be included in the 400 highest priority counter-terrorism investigations. He was only one of several thousand people of potential security concern." (Commonwealth of Australia, 2015, p. 5). Omar Abdel Hamid El-Hussein, who attempted to kill Lars Vilks (a Swedish artist) at a free speech event in Denmark, was also known to the Danish Security service ("Copenhagen gunman just out", 2015). As we saw above, Michaels Adebowale and Adebolajo were both risk assessed repeatedly. The handling of intelligence regarding the threat posed by Tamerlan Tsarnaev (one of two brothers who placed two improvised explosive devices (IEDs) at the Boston Marathon) has also been questioned (Zalkind, 2014). Most recently, Elton Smith, one of the two gunmen who attacked the controversial Prophet Mohammed cartoon contest, had been convicted of making false statements involving international and domestic terrorism (Bergen & Sterman, 2015).

While it is oft commented on that eventual perpetrators of extremist attacks are usually known, in some capacity, to those involved with counter terrorism, it is also important to emphasise their identities often emerge as part of a much larger operation. For example, Operation Crevice – a 2004 operation that intercepted a terrorist plot to bomb shopping centres in England – resulted in 45,000 hours of monitored communication, 34,000 hours of surveillance, and 4,020 telephone calls (Intelligence and Security Committee Report, 2009). Within this investigation, two individuals – Mohammed Siddique Khan and Shazad Tanweer – were associated with the terrorist cell but were not further investigated. These two individuals later detonated IEDs on the London Underground in a series of simultaneous attacks that killed 52 people and injured over 700. Furthermore it is important to mention that a known individual engaging in extremist behaviour may not necessarily be the result of 'bad' risk assessment (though in some cases that may play a role); especially if risk assessment tools are identifying those who have the greatest operational aspirations. For example, in the United States, 60 plots have been intercepted and prevented since 9/11 attacks (Zuckerman, Bucci, & Carafano, 2013). In fact when reviewing the risk assessment of Man Haron Monis, Australian Prime Minister Abbott stated "the decisions that were made were reasonable enough at the time, but plainly, in their totality, the system has let us down" ("Sydney siege report", 2015, para. 6).

The earliest efforts to develop risk assessment tools for violent extremists attempted to discern the degree to which existing tools for risk assessment of general violence can be applied such as the Psychopathy Checklist Revised (Hare, 1991, 2003; see Dernevik, Beck, Grann, Hogue, & McGuire, 2009; Pressman, 2009; Roberts & Horgan, 2008). However it is widely viewed that extremist offenders cannot be viewed as merely another type of criminals (Maghan & Kelly, 1989). Instead, ensuing research has sought out factors unique to involvement in violent extremism that can serve as risk factors to inform offender prioritisation and intelligence gathering.

To date several papers have identified groups of factors that could be used (as part of an actuarial risk assessment model) to differentiate between potentially low and high risk violent extremists. Kebbell and Porter (2011) identify 22 factors related to the desire to engage in violent extremism. These risk factors are split into four sub-categories. The first is 'standard risk factors'. These are factors that are associated with risk, but so frequent that they are unlikely to predict involvement. Standard risk factors include a super-ordinate non-Western identity, a negative view of Western foreign policy, and isolation from positive members of the out-group. The second sub-category of factors is 'moderate risk factors'. These factors are indicative of a substantially higher risk in that they are more demonstrative of support for violence. Factors include involvement in religiously motivated charity work and religious beliefs that support the use of violence. The third sub-category is 'higher risk factors' which are associated with engagement with an extremist ideology and actions that would enhance their operational capability. Risk factors include membership to a radical political group, and isolation from non-radical individuals. Finally, 'extreme risk factors' are those that represent an individual's decision to engage in violent extremist activity. These involve credible expressions of an individual's desire to kill or evidence of target selection. In a similar fashion, the Identifying Vulnerable People (IVP) tool, developed as part of the United Kingdom's PREVENT strand of the CONTEST agenda, identifies a series of factors that can be used to assess the risk that an individual may be vulnerable to become involved in extremism (see Cole, Alison, Cole, & Alison, 2010).

The Violent Extremist Risk Assessment (VERA) protocol assists the assessment of recidivism in violent extremist samples within high-security prisons. VERA-2 (the original VERA was updated in 2009; see Pressman & Flockton, 2010) consists of 31 indicator items that cover: beliefs and attitudes; content and intent; history and capability; commitment and motivation. There are also protective items (see Pressman & Flockton, 2014). VERA-2 is used as part of a multi-modal risk assessment that includes general violence risk, and provides "offense-specific supportive information on the risk of future violence of convicted and incarcerated violent extremist offenders" (Pressman & Flockton, 2014, p. 138). However more recently it has been applied to case studies of terrorist offenders to assess its utility as an intelligence tool, concluding that "the majority of factors in the VERA seem to be relevant and important to risk assessment and could be easily applied across the variety of terrorists in the sample" (Beardsley & Beech, 2013). Meloy, Hoffman, Guldmann, and James (2012), acknowledging that not all risk factors are equally indicative of violent extremist behaviour, also offer a 'typology' of warning behaviours ranging from pathway behaviours, through fixation, identification, novel aggression, energy burst, leakage, last resort, and directly communicated threat warning.

The majority of risk assessment efforts for violent extremists adopt an actuarial approach, identifying socio-demographic, behavioural or psychological markers that can be used to assess risk. The issue then is that actuarial risk assessment requires data; yet with violent extremism there are several scientific challenges that preclude the development of such data (Wetter, 2014). From a practical standpoint, validating these indicators requires data, yet there is limited accessibility to terrorist samples, and even when access is granted the available sample size is small. These samples are also non-representative of other groups, or even within that group. Open-source efforts are increasingly addressing this data-void but the inherent time delay between identifying, coding and analysing such data often means that research is analysing extremist groups that have been and gone, rather than operatives of the groups currently being risk assessed. Thus ongoing research often has to deal with an enduring question of applicability when looking at the modern subjects of risk assessment.

An addition issue is that the outcome variable (violent extremist behaviour) is diverse (see Horgan, 2014). Monahan (2011) agrees, noting that for effective risk assessment we need 'clarity from the outset' about the outcome we are aiming to assess the risk of. Here he highlights that the term 'the risk of terrorism' is an aggregated term. For example, risk assessment may differ depending on if we are assessing the likelihood that an individual will become involved, remain involved, or become re-involved (e.g., post release), as well as the 'role' that an individual may hold (see Horgan, 2014). This issue is further confounded by a lack of research into what individuals actually do when operating as part of a violent extremist organisation. Research has predominantly focused on looking at who becomes involved in violent extremism; concluding that violent extremists are not different to non-violent extremist samples (e.g., Bakker, 2006; Reinares, 2004; Sageman, 2004; Simcox & Dyer, 2013; Simcox, Stuart, Ahmed, & Murray, 2011). Yet this focus on potential socio-demographic aspects of violent extremist offenders has come at the cost of developing a behavioural understanding, directly impacting efforts to develop a scientific method for assessing risk. Recent research by Horgan and colleagues (in press) highlights this issue of behavioural diversity by showing the range of behaviours that individuals undertook when operating as part of the 'global jihadist movement' – i.e., they operated as part of Al-Qaeda, one of its affiliates, or were inspired by it (see Braniff & Moghadam, 2011).

It follows then that some of the most significant strides in addressing risk emerge from research focused on the behavioural aspects of violent extremism. For example, Gill and colleagues (2014) examined the behaviours of 113 lone actor terrorists in the United States and Europe, finding behavioural differences between those who operated under an extreme right-wing ideology, and those who were inspired by religious groups (also see Gruenewald, Chermak, & Freilich, 2013a, 2013b). At the same time, Gill et al. (2014) also identified behavioural differences between those who were, and were not successful.

Other research has looked at offender type; finding that individuals with mental illnesses (though traditionally not viewed as more likely to engage in violent extremism; Weatherston & Moran, 2003) were more likely to be a lone actor, than to operate as part of a terrorist group or cell (Corner & Gill, 2015). Research on members of the Provisional Irish Republican Army also identified role-based profiles, highlighting the need for researchers to move beyond looking at who joins a terrorist organisation, but "who becomes a bomb-maker as opposed to a gunman and so on" (Gill & Horgan, 2013, p. 454). This research highlights that attempting to assess the risk of violent extremism will continue to falter because of both the socio-demographic and behavioural diversity that exists within samples of violent extremists. At the same time, efforts to risk assess violent extremists are further confounded by the diverse nature of the threat of terrorism, in that, at any one time, the outcome variable – violent extremist behaviour – could involve a spectrum of behaviours including supporting a foreign insurgency (e.g., via financial behaviour or recruiting), attempting to join a foreign insurgency, or attempting to launch a terrorist attack in their home country on behalf of (or inspired by) a foreign insurgent group. At the same time, a key issue now is the risk assessment of 'foreign fighters', which is the risk that individuals who have been a member of a foreign insurgency will then attempt to launch a terrorist attack when they return home (see Hegghammer, 2013). So, and in accordance with Roberts and Horgan (2008), "a narrow focus of what constitutes 'terrorism' may in itself be one of the most obvious obstacles to risk management" (p. 4).

The key then is that we need to be more refined in our approach to what we are assessing; moving beyond a binary term of involvement in terrorism and towards frames of reference that accommodate the immense behavioural diversity of involvement in violent extremism (Horgan et al., in press). Risk assessing individuals involved in violent extremism is therefore in a 'catch-22' in that, theoretically, we need to be more refined as to the outcome we are trying to assess the risk of (i.e., involvement in a terrorist attack versus support functions for a terrorist attack versus joining a foreign insurgency). That said, the pragmatic constraints of violent extremism mean that in reality, any further segregation of an already-limited size of 'true-hits' would exponentially increase the number of false positives a risk system has to deal with. Finally, at the same time we are also seeing an evolution in terrorist tactics towards lower-scale attacks conducted by individuals with less tangible real-world links to a terrorist organisation (see Nesser, 2012), and who are harder to detect due to their 'weaker signal' (Brynielsson et al., 2013). Models of risk assessment may therefore have to be continually updated and re-validated to ensure that they are applicable to a continually adapting threat.

EXTREMISM ONLINE

A wide array of literature outlines what violent extremist groups and individuals do on the Internet (e.g., Bowman-Grieve, 2009; Bowman-Grieve & Conway 2012; Conway, 2006; Ekman, 2014; Holbrook & Taylor, 2013; von Behr, Reding, Edwards, & Bribbon, 2013; Weimann, 2011). Research has also begun to look at the form and function of extremist networks on the Internet (Caiani & Wagemann, 2009) as well as how such networks handle 'stress' imposed by external forces such as law enforcement (Cebrian, Torres, Huerta, & Fowler, 2012). Given the focus on the content of extremist materials online and the form of the networks that engage with it, what is less understood is the role that the Internet plays in an individual's transition towards involvement and engagement in extremist behaviour (for a full outline of the terms and process of involvement and engagement, see Horgan & Taylor, 2011).

We hold that radicalisation is the process through which an individual increasingly supports or engages in violent (and non-violent) extremist activities (Kruglanski et al., 2014), and past research efforts have aimed to identify pathways that lead an individual to violence (see McCauley & Moskalenco, 2011; McGilloway, Ghosh, & Bhui, 2015; Moghaddam, 2005). Many of these studies (and others) highlight that the Internet can play a large role in the radicalisation process. Halverson and Way (2012) for example show the role that the Internet played in the radicalisation of Colleen LaRose (Jihad Jane), a Pennsylvanian woman who travelled to Ireland to kill artist Lars Vilks. Lennings, Amon, Brummert, and Lennings (2010) also highlight the role of the Internet in radicalising, or 'grooming' youths towards terrorism. Yet beyond highlighting that the Internet increases connectivity and accessibility to extremist materials and like-minded individuals, we have little idea as to how this interacts with the process of radicalisation. For example, few people who engage in online extremist materials (or with other extremists online) will move from online engagement to offline behaviour (Holbrook & Taylor, 2013). Analysing the material itself, while important, therefore has little utility in facilitating our understanding for the role of online materials.

It is clear then that to move beyond a tacit recognition of the presence and threat of extremist materials online and towards an understanding of the role that this plays in an individual's wider movement towards extremist behaviour, our analysis is going to have to incorporate the dyadic interaction between offline and online aspects of involvement in violent extremism. Edwards and Gribbon (2013) agree, stating that researchers and policy makers need to "focus their efforts on understanding not merely the content that is available online, but the ways in which this content is used in the process of radicalisation" (p. 40).

Very few studies have investigated the online/offline interaction. Jackson and Loidolt (2013) looked at the real-world manifestations of Al-Qaeda's doctrine, questioning the degree to which the doctrine is put into practice in the real world. In the same vein, Jones (2006) discusses how the Internet facilitates the learning of 'innovative improvisers'. Lemieux and colleagues (2014) specifically looked at Inspire Magazine's influence in the real world. Applying the Information-Motivation-Behavioural Skills (IMB) framework (see Fisher & Fisher, 1992), the authors show how Inspire magazine has become so influential in real world cases of extremist violence in that it presents individuals with the information and motivation to influence actual behaviours, while at the same time ensuring individuals have the required level of behavioural skills – through the 'open source jihad' section (Lemieux et al., 2014). von Behr and colleagues (2013) have also investigated the interaction of online and offline experiences. Specifically, they analysed 15 individuals for whom the Internet played a significant role in their process of radicalisation. This allowed the authors to test a series of hypotheses from the literature against real-life cases of radicalisation (see Table 1). von Behr et al (2013)'s research supports the more general hypotheses that the Internet creates more opportunities, and acts as an echo chamber for extremists (i.e., it creates an environment within which individuals can seek only that information that conforms to their extremist viewpoints). Furthermore, while the Internet did not accelerate the process of radicalisation, it was noted that offline factors could sometimes be more influential than online factors. In most cases, radicalisation was an iterative dyadic interaction in which "events and developments in the physical world feed into online behaviour and vice versa" (von Behr et al., 2013, p. 29).

Offline experiences are therefore critical in mitigating or amplifying the effect of interacting with extremist materials online. So while online groups may act as an 'echo chamber' the offline world does not, and those who immerse themselves with ideologically-homogenous groups online, are rarely afforded the opportunity to do so offline (this is especially pertinent for 'lone actors' who may have little contact with ideologically similar individual offline). When we discuss transitioning – the process of moving from engaging with a type of material to undertaking associated behaviours offline (also called 'crossing over', see Calder, 2004) – a key issue to consider will therefore be the presence (or absence) of non-radical ties offline which may alter the influence of radical ties online.

Few studies have investigated the interaction of moderate ties offline and extremist ties online on perceptions and behaviour. By surveying members of neo-Nazi forums, Wojcieszak (2009) analysed

Table 1. Literature hypotheses and von Behr et al (2013, p. 24)'s findings regarding the role that the Internet plays in the process of radicalisation

Literature Hypotheses	Does the Primary Data Support the Hypotheses?
The Internet creates more opportunities to become radicalised	Yes in all of these cases
The Internet acts as an 'echo chamber'	Yes in the majority of these cases
The Internet accelerates the process of radicalisation	While there is no agreed length of time or template for radicalisation, it is not clear that the Internet would have accelerated this process in the majority of the cases – in these cases the Internet appears to enable rather than necessarily accelerate radicalisation
The Internet allows radicalisation to occur without physical contact	Not in the majority of these cases: most cases involve offline activity that could have played a role in the individuals' radicalisation
The Internet increases opportunities for self-radicalisation	Not in the majority of these cases: most cases of so-called 'online self-radicalisation' involve virtual communication and interaction with others

whether the similarity of offline and online groups exacerbated or attenuated radical opinions. Two opposing theories were tested. The first theory, deliberate theory, suggests that politically moderate offline ties would decrease the effect of radical social groups online. This theory holds that encountering dissimilar opinions would encourage people to take account of others' views, encouraging moderation (Arendt, 1968). Accordingly, discussing politics with family and co-workers who hold dissimilar views is shown to increase tolerance (Price, Cappella, & Nir, 2002). At the same time, exposure to opposing views can also increase uncertainty within an individual's own viewpoint, resulting in a more moderate opinion (Lavine, 2001).

On the other hand, a biased processing model suggests that exposure to dissimilar opinions offline would exacerbate an extremist mindset. Specifically, this model holds that a currently held position biases our perception, interpretation and evaluation, discounting dissimilar views in favour of those that are similar, resulting in attitude polarisation (Kunda, 1990). Wojcieszak (2009)'s surveys of neo-Nazi forums in fact found support for both hypotheses. Specifically, being embedded in a like-minded social network offline increased extremist viewpoints, supporting that those who lack exposure to dissimilar views were less able to form balanced opinions (i.e., a deliberative model). At the same time, those who have family and friends that voiced dissimilar views also showed increased extremism. These findings were also confirmed in a follow-up study looking at political similar/dissimilarities, online and offline ties, engagement in extremist materials online, and extremist behaviour offline – e.g., petitioning and attending rallies offline (see Wojcieszak, 2010).

This work has several implications; principally that offline and online interactions are highly complex and that the effect of exposure to dissimilar views is not always beneficial (Wojcieszak, 2009). For example, the negating effect of dissimilar offline ties did little to alter the views of those with strong predilections (or 'hard cores'). This is in accordance with the 'Spiral of Silence' theory which holds that individuals fear isolation, and as such, keep opposing opinions silent (Noelle-Neumann, 1993). It may therefore be that those with strong extremist views are immune to the mitigating effect of encountering dissimilar ideologies. This point has significant implications when considering the potential utility of efforts to counter violent extremism, such as the U.S. Department of Defense online campaign 'Think Now Turn Away', in that they may have little (or even a negative) effect on those with the strongest extremist viewpoints.

Thus, while the literature highlighted above shows a tacit recognition of the role that the Internet plays in the process of radicalisation, few studies (and no empirical research) have sought to investigate how the online world interacts with this process. Thus many critical questions remain unanswered. In addition, research has shown that within an individual's radicalisation, both online and offline experiences will interact and form a dynamic dyadic series of influences on an individual's transition from 'unengaged' in terrorism to 'engaged' in terrorism, as well as from online engagement to offline engagement.

RISK ASSESSMENT ONLINE

As we have seen above, there is a pressing need to use information about an individual's online behaviour when attempting to ascertain the risk that they pose. However this process is confounded by several factors inherent with being 'online' such as anonymity. In many domains the anonymity afforded by the Internet is a benefit in that it encourages disclosures, and provides a safe platform for individuals to connect and discuss sensitive or stigmatised issues, risk free. For example, those who go online for suicide related purposes report feeling less alienated, more supported, and less suicidal after discussing their issues online (Harris, McLean, & Sheffield, 2009). Yet in many other cases, as with extremist materials, the anonymity afforded by the Internet encourages individuals to engage in illegal and amoral materials. For example, 'death-porn' sites and child pornography are all widely accessible (and accessed) on the Internet (Tait, 2008). Overall, deviant online materials fall into three categories: sexual deviance; social support in promotion of negative behaviours; and hate groups/extremism (McDonald, Horstmann, Strom, & Pope, 2009). It is clear that in all three areas identifying those at risk of crossing over to offline behaviours is of critical importance, and while we have seen that efforts in this domain for extremism are in their infancy, progress has been made in the other areas.

The Internet provides a criminogenic environment that facilitates the pursuit of abhorrent sexual interests allowing individuals to network, and distribute images with others who share their prurient interest in minors (Beech, Elliott, Bridgen, & Findlater, 2008; Taylor & Quayle, 2003). Indecent images of children (IIOC) are increasingly available (Saldrini & DeRobertis, 2003), yet the Police cannot, for obvious budgetary reasons, arrest and convict everyone who is engaged in such materials. The prevalence of offline child sexual offenders within an IIOC sample is contested, and while there is considerable heterogeneity within these findings (e.g., Bourke & Hernandez, 2009 vs. Endrass et al., 2009), a recent meta-analysis concluded that 12 percent of IIOC samples would also be convicted of contact sexual offense (Seto, Hanson, & Babchishin, 2011). That said, the prevalence of contact offenders rose to 55 percent when self-report methods were used. This research has two key implications. Firstly, paedophilic interest alone is an insufficient marker for contact sexual abuse against a child (Seto, 2009; Seto, Cantor, & Blanchard, 2006). Secondly, in order for the police to focus the available resources in a way which best protect the public from serious harm, they must identify those offenders within an IIOC sample who pose the greatest risk and prioritise the arrest of these individuals. The key question facing officers investigating IIOC offenders is therefore whether an online offender is committing, or likely to commit, sexual abuse against a child offline (Eke, Seto, & Williams, 2010).

In order to assist this prioritisation, previous research has examined the association between 'contact' (offenders whose IIOC involvement co-occurs with child sexual abuse) and 'non-contact' (those whose paedophiliac offending is confined to the Internet) offenders within IIOC samples. By examining whether an offender's contact offending behaviour manifests in quantifiable differences in their IIOC collections (Elliott, Beech, Mandeville-Norden, & Hayes, 2009; Long et al., 2013, McCarthy, 2010), research aims to improve investigating officer's knowledge, capabilities and decision-making when predicting those IIOC offenders who pose the greatest risk of contact offending against a child (McManus et al., 2011).

Whilst it could be viewed that increased image severity may indicate increased risk, research has questioned the reliability of this inference. Elliott and Beech (2009) found that the majority of IIOC offenders were reported to possess images at levels 4 and 5. To further confound this association, contact offenders spent significantly larger proportions of time viewing child-modelling websites – i.e., a much lower level of image severity (Elliott et al., 2009). This means that those with lower severity images could pose a greater threat offline. With a linear correlation of IIOC severity and risk not applicable, research has focused on assessing IIOC quantity as well as their wider Internet behaviour. McCarthy (2010) found that contact offenders possessed larger amounts of IIOC. They were also more likely to engage in 'cyber-sexploitation', namely grooming behaviours and sending IIOC to children.

Long et al., (2013) found both quantitative and qualitative differences when comparing the IIOC collections of contact and non-contact offenders. They compared 30 contact and 30 non-contact IIOC offenders using data from U.K. Police Force's case files. Whilst contrary to McCarthy (2010), contact offenders had significantly lower possession of IIOC, and their IIOC possessions were also qualitatively different. Specifically, contact offenders possessed higher proportions of IIOC images at level 3, whilst non-contact offenders possessed significantly higher proportions at level 1. Thus, whilst possessing significantly lower quantities of IIOC material overall, contact offenders gravitated towards a higher severity of the images that they possessed (Long et al., 2013). Contact offenders also showed greater level of anti-forensic behaviour, in that they were less likely to pay for access and groom online. This demonstrates the quantifiable differences in IIOC behaviour between contact and non-contact indecent image offenders, which can serve as the basis for intelligence-led decisions regarding the risk that an online offender poses of offline sexual abuse (McManus et al., 2011).

This research domain contains several lessons that we can apply to the issue of online risk assessment of violent extremism, namely that 'severity' of online behaviour is not always indicative of greater risk. We saw above that discussing a willingness to become a martyr is a poor indicator of likelihood that someone will undertake a terrorist attack. At the same time, however differences between contact and non-contact offenders do exist in their Internet behaviour. This support that offline behaviours do, in some way, manifest in quantifiably different online behavioural profiles, supporting the view that online behaviour could be used to support decisions regarding risk. That said, identifying these online-behavioural differences between contact and non-contact offenders was the result of extensive behaviourally-driven data-collection activities that generates a sample of offline offenders in an online sample, and compared this to a sample of online only offenders.

To date, no research has systematically compared the online behaviours of those who also engage in extremist behaviour offline. At the same time, research that does investigate the online behaviours of individuals engaged in extremist materials online (outlined above) does not identify, nor factor in, the (albeit) small subsample of those individuals who are currently, or will in the future, move their online behaviour to offline acts of extremist violence. Thus, while the case of risk assessing IIOC offenders provides hope for the future, it also highlights the significant investment in research and data that is required if we are to be able to establish empirically valid online indicators of risk for violent extremism.

INTEGRATING THE THREE SPHERES: THE ONLINE RISK ASSESSMENT OF VIOLENT EXTREMISTS

Analysing the three spheres of influence in this area has identified several issues. The first is the homogeneity of individuals engaging in extremist materials on the Internet. Elsewhere we saw that not all individuals engaged in online depictions of child abuse had a sexual interest in children, and the majority would not engage in an act of child sexual abuse, not due to lack of opportunity, but because their prurient interests are solely confined to the online sphere. At the same time, it is viable that there will be individuals both passively (through watching and downloading extremist materials) and actively (in engaging with other extremists on social media of forums) associated with extremist materials who will have no interest of engaging in violent extremist behaviour. When it comes to risk assessment, this faction of individuals will inherently add 'noise' into a system that already has to deal with a weak and rare signal.

At the same time, those individuals who are using the Internet are using it in a plethora of different ways to support their extremist aspirations. Zachary Chesser, who was arrested for attempting to provide material support to al-Shabaab, hosted his own extremist website (themujahidblog.com) before issuing violent threats to the creators of South Park, and attempting to join al-Shabaab (Senate Committee on Homeland Security and Governmental Affairs, 2012). Other extremists have refined their online activities to obtaining instructional materials and learning operational tactics (Stenerson, 2008). The role that the Internet can play therefore varies at the individual level, from being the domain through which they act, to one that supports their activities, to merely a platform to air their grievances or allegiances. In the same vain, even though extremist materials proliferate on the Internet, this does not mean that extremists exploit such materials (it may, after all, be viewed as an operational security risk). Nesser (2008) highlights that despite the presence of online training materials, traditional military-style training is still highly desired. In fact, recent research looking at the behaviour of Al-Qaeda's operatives in the United States showed that only a small portion of these offenders used the Internet in support of their activities (Horgan et al., in press). Although this finding is confounded by the fact that the sample ranged from 1993 (when Internet use was likely to be minimal), and the degree of extremist-related Internet behaviour is not always known or reported (Horgan et al., in press).

At the same time, it is clear that we also need to understand the interaction between individuals' online experiences and their offline experiences. von Behr and colleagues (2013) argue that past and present research efforts regarding extremist materials on the Internet have focused too heavily on the 'supply' side at the cost of analysing the 'demand' – i.e., the individuals consuming and interacting with such materials. Research has yet to examine the dyadic interplay between individuals' engagement with extremist content online and their experiences offline (personal, social, and political), specifically the role that online engagement plays as part of the larger psychological process of radicalisation.

At the same time, we will also need to consider the temporal aspect of Internet engagement. For example, a survey of 6,020 16-24 year olds found that 49.5 percent had seen extremist materials on new social media, and 25.7 percent were exposed to extremist materials at least once a month. In looking at individuals association with such materials, and its effect on their political standpoints, Pauwels and Schils (2014) highlight that "political violence can only partially be explained by social learning and suggests that the impact of extremist material on new social media is mediated by real-world associations and that the offline world has to be taken into account".

Finally, the greatest progress in developing scientifically valid methods to measure risk online stem from data-driven studies of online behaviour. These are sorely lacking in research studying violent extremism, both at large and on the Internet. Yet we are replete with studies that examine the material itself (Lee & Leets, 2002). Such research is important in that it is facilitating the development of grading scales (see Holbrook & Taylor, 2013), and metrics to quantify the nature of the extremist materials that an individuals is engaging with. However, in order to be able to differentiate between the severity of risk that an individual poses, research paradigms will be required to differentiate and compare between high and low risk populations of offender behaviour. This is critical, because while several risk factors have been developed for use offline, we have very little evidence as to how these factors shift (if at all) to the online spheres. For example, Kebbell and Porter (2011, p. 223) highlight that "if the individual makes explicit expressions of their desire to achieve martyrdom, this is likely to increase their risk of being involved in violent extremism"; yet online expressions of desire to commit martyrdom (as we showed earlier) are a "fairly standard example of rhetoric" (Intelligence and Security Committee Report, 2014, p. 120).

IMPLICATIONS FOR PRACTITIONERS

Online behaviour potentially provides a unique window from which we can glean intent. From an intelligence standpoint, it provides an important source of open-source information. However, as we have showed above, assessing such materials and making the inference of intent from online activity alone, is inherently difficult in that we have to deal with questionable veracity and sincerity of an individual's online persona (amplified by the experience of being online). It is also confounded by the more general deficits in our understanding of the process through which individuals become involved in violent extremist activity. Yet elsewhere progress is being made in incorporating information online into decisions regarding risk and offender prioritisation. Based on the analysis of risk assessment of violent extremists, risk assessment online, and the nature of extremist materials online, several implications for practitioners can be identified.

Adopt a Full Spectrum Approach

An individual's online activity alone may provide little indication of risk. However, adopting a full spectrum approach will facilitate this judgment in that their online activities can be triangulated with their offline experiences (and more importantly capability). As we showed above, there is a pressing need to integrate discussions of extremist materials online, with those that focus on extremist behaviour (an offline phenomenon). In a similar vein, efforts to develop risk assessment models need to embed data points regarding online behaviour within those drawn from their offline experiences.

Understand the Diversity of the Outcome Variable

Violent extremist behaviour has many behavioural manifestations. As mentioned above, Horgan and colleagues' (in press) analysis of Al-Qaeda operatives in the United States included offenders who were directly involved in attempts to launch a terrorist attack, those who directly supported a terrorist attack, those who supported a terrorist group writ large, and those who had almost no direct connection to a terrorist attack. When considering risk assessment then, online or offline, it is important to be aware of this diversity because the risk factors for each type of behaviour (a domestic attack vs. travelling abroad to join an insurgency) may differ. Furthermore the online behaviour that these individuals engage in may also be different. The online correlates of involvement in terrorist activity and how this changes between actor types, as well as over time, is a critical question for academics and practitioners alike.

Understand how the Internet Affects Behaviour

The Internet creates an environment that can encourage extreme behaviour, further deviating expressions of intent from reality. This has several implications for the practical domain. Firstly, it decreases the moral barriers for engaging in such materials, and secondly it allows individuals to purport an alternate image of themselves that may be highly different from their offline image. When looking at individuals who are engaged in terroristic materials, and purporting a desire or intent to engage in offline acts of terrorism, it is important to note that a portion of this behaviour may be more fanciful then actual.

A second issue is to acknowledge that we do not yet understand how the Internet is affecting the process of how people become engaged in offline acts of terrorism. For example, it is not uncommon for research to purport sequential models of the process of becoming involved in terrorism (e.g., McCauley

& Moskalenko, 2008, 2011); what role does the Internet play in each stage of these processes? One advantage of assessing online-gleaned material is that it is (often but not always) accessible, meaning that progression can be monitored. For example, does an individual's narrative escalate or de-escalate, or do they become more or less active over time? It will be important that we begin to understand how an individual's progression into, or out of extremism is reflected in his/her online persona. Understanding and analysing online progression may offer a good starting point to differentiate 'true hits' from 'false positives' in online extremist samples.

Minimise Data Uncertainty through Engaging Third-Parties

Information available online may only be a partial representation of an individual's portfolio of behaviour (both online and offline), and critical aspects of their online behaviour may remain concealed. As we saw in the case of Michael Adebowale, potential intelligence was available that could have facilitated a risk assessment of his intent, and could have, arguably, resulted in a different risk assessment outcome. Dealing with uncertainty is a pervasive factor within counter terrorism operations (offline and online); however the case of Adebowale highlights that in the online sphere, data uncertainty could be minimised through effective engagement with third parties. For example, information about the need to close a social media profile because an individual was engaging with extremist materials could be an important red-flag that spurs on a larger investigation of the risk that the individual poses. While such links are important, especially given the widespread utilisation of social media platforms by extremist groups and individuals, it is important that efforts to access such information will carry with them significant concerns for security and privacy of the data. An important step will be to establish (and then share) what 'risky' online behaviour looks like so that officers are better quipped internally to identify those individuals who may pose a risk and share this information with counter terrorism practitioners.

When asked what interested him on the Internet, Zachary Chesser responded that "for [his] generation this is tantamount to asking the question, 'what interested you in the phone?'". The Internet, and now social media, is an intrinsic part of a more globalised and connected society, as such the 'use' of the Internet by extremist offenders is not a separate domain of activity but a natural extension of those activities and behaviours that they would not have undertaken in an unconnected world. Instead of viewing extremist materials on the Internet as a discrete phenomenon, or domain of extremism and extremist behaviour, it is important to maintain that it is an extension of behaviours and activities that have been occurring long before the Internet was invented. As such, and as echoed in this chapter, the most significant progress in using information gleaned from the Internet to assist efforts to prevent terrorism will result from integrating our understanding of the psychological effects of being on the Internet, with current models of how people become involved in extremism and extremist behaviour.

REFERENCES

Arendt, H. (1968). *Between past and future*. New York, NY: Viking Press.

Bakker, E. (2006). *Jihadi terrorists in Europe, their characteristics and the circumstances in which they joined the jihad (Clingendael Security Paper)*. The Netherlands: Netherlands Institute of International Relations.

Barrett-Page, E., & Thomas, J. (2009). Methods for the synthesis of qualitative research: A critical review. *BMC Medical Research Methodology, 9*(59), 1–11. PMID:19123933

Barros, C. P., Proenca, I., Faria, J. R., & Gil-Alana, L. A. (2006). Are USA citizens at risk of terrorism in Europe. *Defence and Peace Economics, 18*(6), 495–597. doi:10.1080/10242690701197605

Bartlett, J. (2014). *The dark net: Inside the digital underworld.* William Heinemann Ltd.

Beardsley, N., & Beech, A. (2013). Applying the violent extremist risk assessment (VERA) to a sample of terrorist case studies. *The Journal of Aggression. Conflict and Peace Studies, 5*, 4–15.

Beech, A. R., Elliott, I. A., Birgden, A., & Findlater, D. (2008). The internet and child sexual offending: A criminological review. *Aggression and Violent Behavior, 13*(3), 216–228. doi:10.1016/j.avb.2008.03.007

Bergen, P., & Sterman, D. (2015, May 6). Who are ISIS' American recruits? *CNN.* Retrieved from http://www.cnn.com/2015/05/06/opinions/bergen-isis-american-recruits/

Berger, J. M., & Morgan, J. (2015). *The ISIS twitter census: Defining and describing the population of ISIS supporters on twitter (Brooking project on U.S. Relations with the Islamic World, Analysis Paper, 20).* Washington, DC: Brookings Institution.

Berger, J. M., & Stern, J. (2015). *ISIS: The state of terror.* Broadway, NY: Harper Collins.

Bourke, M. L., & Hernandez, A. E. (2009). The 'Butner Study' redux: A report of the incidence of hands-on child victimization by child pornography offenders. *Journal of Family Violence, 24*(3), 183–191. doi:10.1007/s10896-008-9219-y

Bowman-Grieve, L. (2009). Exploring "Stormfront": A Virtual Community of the Radical Right. *Studies in Conflict and Terrorism, 32*(11), 989–1007. doi:10.1080/10576100903259951

Bowman-Grieve, L. (2015). Cyberterrorism and moral panics: A reflection on the discourse of cyber-terrorism. In L. Jarvis, S. M. Macdonald, & T. M. Chen (Eds.), *Terrorism online: Politics, law and technology* (pp. 86–106). New York, NY: Routledge.

Bowman-Grieve, L., & Conway, M. (2012). Exploring the form and function of dissident Irish Republican online discourses. *Media. War and Conflict, 5*(1), 71–85. doi:10.1177/1750635211434371

Brachman, J. M. (2006). High-tech terror: Al-Qaeda's use of new technology. *The Fletcher Forum of World Affairs, 30*, 149–164.

Braniff, B., & Moghadam, A. (2011). Towards global jihadism: Al-Qaeda's strategic, ideological and structural adaptations since 9/11. *Perspectives on Terrorism, 5*(2).

Brynielsson, J., Horndahl, A., Johansson, F., Kaati, L., Mårtenson, C., & Svenson, P. (2013). Harvesting and analysis of weak signals for detecting lone wolf terrorists. *Security Informatics, 2*(11). doi:10.1186/2190-8532-2-11

Bu, Z., Xia, Z., & Wang, J. (2013). A sock puppet detection algorithm on virtual spaces. *Knowledge-Based Systems, 37*, 366–377. doi:10.1016/j.knosys.2012.08.016

Buchanan, T. (2002). Online assessment: Desirable or dangerous? *Professional Psychology, Research and Practice, 33*(2), 148–154. doi:10.1037/0735-7028.33.2.148

Caiani, M., & Wagemann, C. (2009). Online networks of the Italian and German extreme right. *Information Communication and Society, 12*(1), 66–109. doi:10.1080/13691180802158482

Calder, M. (2004). *Child sexual abuse and the Internet: Tackling the new frontier.* Dorset: Russell House.

Cebrian, M., Torres, M., Huerta, R., & Fowler, J. H. (2012). Violent extremist group ecologies under stress. *Nature: Scientific Reports, 3.* doi:10.1038/srep01544 PMID:23536118

Christensen, H., Batterham, P. J., & O'Dea, B. (2014). E-health interventions for suicide prevention. *International Journal of Environmental Research and Public Health, 11*(8), 8193–8212. doi:10.3390/ijerph110808193 PMID:25119698

Cole, J., Alison, E., Cole, B., & Alison, L. J. (2012). *Guidance for identifying people vulnerable to recruitment into violent extremism.* Retrieved from https://www.counterextremism.org/resources/details/id/224/guidance-for-identifying-people-vulnerable-to-recruitment-into-violent-extremism

Collin, B. C. (1996). The future of cyberterrorism. *Crime and Justice International, 13*, 15–18.

Commonwealth of Australia. (2015). *Martin Place Siege: Joint Commonwealth - New South Wales Review.* Canberra: Department of the Prime Minister and Cabinet.

Conway, M. (2006). Terrorism and the Internet: New media—New threat? *Parliamentary Affairs, 59*(2), 283–298. doi:10.1093/pa/gsl009

Copenhagen gunman just out of prison, AP sources say. (2015, February 16). *CBS.* Retrieved from http://www.cbsnews.com/news/copenhagen-gunman-omar-abdel-hamid-el-hussein-just-out-of-prison-ap-sources/

Corner, E., & Gill, P. (2015). A false dichotomy? Mental illness and lone-actor terrorism. *Law and Human Behavior, 39*(1), 23–34. doi:10.1037/lhb0000102 PMID:25133916

Dernevik, M., Beck, A., Grann, M., Houe, T., & McGuire, J. (2009). The use of psychiatric and psychological evidence in the assessment of terrorist offenders. *Journal of Forensic Psychiatry & Psychology, 20*(4), 508–515. doi:10.1080/13501760902771217

Dixon-Woods, M., Bonas, S., Booth, A., Jones, D. R., Miller, T., Shaw, R. L., & Young, B. et al. (2006). How can systematic reviews incorporate qualitative research? A critical perspective. *Qualitative Research, 6*(1), 27–44. doi:10.1177/1468794106058867

Dubrovsky, V. J., Kiesler, S., & Sethna, B. N. (1991). The equalization phenomenon: Status effects in computer- mediated and face-to-face decision-making groups. *Human-Computer Interaction, 6*(2), 119–146. doi:10.1207/s15327051hci0602_2

Edwards, C., & Gribbon, L. (2013). Pathways to violent extremism in the digital era. *RUSI Journal, 158*(5), 40–47. doi:10.1080/03071847.2013.847714

Eke, A. W., Seto, M. C., & Williams, J. (2010). Examining the criminal history and future offending of child pornography offenders: An extended prospective follow-up study. *Law and Human Behavior*, 1–13. PMID:21088873

Ekman, M. (2014). The dark side of online activism: Swedish right-wing extremist video activism on YouTube. *Journal of Media and Communications Research*, *30*(56), 79–99.

Elliott, I. A., & Beech, A. (2009). Understanding online child pornography use: Applying sexual offense theory to Internet offenders. *Aggression and Violent Behavior*, *14*(3), 180–193. doi:10.1016/j.avb.2009.03.002

Elliott, I. A., Beech, A. R., Mandeville-Norden, R., & Hayes, E. (2009). Psychological profiles of Internet sexual offenders: Comparisons with contact sexual offenders. *Sexual Abuse*, *21*, 76–92. PMID:19218479

Endrass, J., Urbaniok, F., Hammermeister, L. C., Benz, C., Elbert, T., Laubacher, A., & Rossegger, A. (2009). The consumption of internet child pornography and violent and sex offending. *BMC Psychiatry*, *9*(43). doi:10.1186/1471-244X-9-43 PMID:19602221

Fisher, J. D., & Fisher, W. A. (1992). Changing AIDS risk behavior. *Psychological Bulletin*, *111*(3), 455–474. doi:10.1037/0033-2909.111.3.455 PMID:1594721

Gelder, K. (2006). Epic fantasy and global terrorism. In E. Mathijs & M. Pomerance (Eds.), *From hobbits to Hollywood: essays on Peter Jackson's Lord of the Rings* (pp. 101–118). The Netherlands: Rodopi.

Gill, P., & Horgan, J. (2013). Who were the volunteers? The shifting sociological and operational profile of 1240 Provisional Irish Republican Army members. *Terrorism and Political Violence*, *25*(4), 435–456. doi:10.1080/09546553.2012.664587

Gill, P., Horgan, J., & Deckert, P. (2014). Bombing alone: Tracing the motivations and antecedent behaviors of lone-actor terrorists. *Journal of Forensic Sciences*, *59*(2), 425–435. doi:10.1111/1556-4029.12312 PMID:24313297

Gruenewald, J., Chermak, S., & Freilich, J. D. (2013). Far-right lone wolf homicides in the United States. *Studies in Conflict and Terrorism*, *36*(12), 1005–1024. doi:10.1080/1057610X.2013.842123

Gruenewald, J., Chermak, S., & Freilich, J. D. (2013a). Distinguishing 'loner' attacks from other domestic extremist violence: A comparison of far-right homicide incident and offender characteristics. *Criminology & Public Policy*, *12*(1), 63–64. doi:10.1111/1745-9133.12009

Halverson, J. R., & Way, A. K. (2012). The curious case of Colleen LaRose: Social margins, new media, and online radicalization. *Media. War and Conflict*, *5*(2), 139–153. doi:10.1177/1750635212440917

Hare, R. D. (1991). *Manual for the Hare Psychopathy Check List-Revised*. Toronto, ON: Multi-Health Systems.

Hare, R. D. (2003). *Manual for the Hare Psychopathy Check-List-Revised* (2nd ed.). Toronto, ON: Multi-Health Systems.

Harris, K. M., McLean, J. P., & Sheffield, J. (2009). Examining suicide-risk individuals who go online for suicide-related purposes. *Archives of Suicide Research: The Official Journal of the Academy for Suicide Research*, *13*(3), 264–276. doi:10.1080/13811110903044419 PMID:19591000

Hegghammer, T. (2013). Should I stay or should I go? Explaining variation in western jihadists' choices between domestic and foreign fighting. *The American Political Science Review, 107*(01), 1–15. doi:10.1017/S0003055412000615

Holbrook, R. G., & Taylor, M. (2013). "Terroristic content": Towards a grading scale. *Terrorism and Political Violence, 25*(2), 202–223. doi:10.1080/09546553.2011.653893

Horgan, J. (2014). *The psychology of terrorism* (2nd ed.). New York, NY: Routledge.

Horgan, J., Shortland, N., Abbascianno, S., & Walsh, S. (in press). *Actions speak louder than words: A behavioral analysis of 183 individual convicted of Terrorist Offenses in the United States from 1989 – 2012.* Submitted to Journal of Forensic Sciences.

Horgan, J., & Taylor, M. (2007). A conceptual framework for addressing psychological process in the development of the terrorist. *Terrorism and Political Violence, 18*(4), 585–601.

Horgan, J., & Taylor, M. (2011). Disengagement, de-radicalisation and the arc of terrorism: Future directions for research. In R. Coolsaet (Ed.), *Jihadi terrorism and the radicalisation challenge: European and American experiences* (2nd ed., pp. 173–186). London: Ashgate.

Huey, L., & Kalyal, H. (2015). Questions about Dawlah. DM me, plz. The sock puppet problem in online terrorism research. Sociology Publications.

Intelligence and Security Committee Report. (2009). *Could 7/7 have been prevented? Review of the intelligence on the London terrorist attacks on 7 July 2005.* London: Controller of Her Majesty's Stationery Office.

Intelligence and Security Committee Report. (2014). *Report on the intelligence relating to the murder of Fusilier Lee Rigby.* London: Controller of Her Majesty's Stationery Office.

Jackson, B. A., & Loidolt, B. (2013). Considering al-Qa'ida's innovation doctrine: From strategic texts to 'innovation in practice'. *Terrorism and Political Violence, 25*(2), 284–310. doi:10.1080/09546553.2012.662557

Jones, C. (2006). Al-Qaeda's innovative improvisers: Learning in a diffuse transnational network. *Cambridge Review of International Affairs, 19*(4), 555–569. doi:10.1080/09557570601003205

Kebbell, M. R., & Porter, L. (2011). An intelligence assessment framework for identifying individuals at risk of committing acts of violent extremism against the West. *Security Journal, 25*(3), 212–228. doi:10.1057/sj.2011.19

Kruglanski, A. W., Gelfand, M. J., Bélanger, J. J., Sheveland, A., Hetiarachchi, M., & Gunaratna, R. (2014). The psychology of radicalization and deradicalization: How significance quest impacts violent extremism. *Political Psychology, 35*, 69–93. doi:10.1111/pops.12163

Kunda, Z. (1990). The case for motivated reasoning. *Psychological Bulletin, 108*(3), 480–498. doi:10.1037/0033-2909.108.3.480 PMID:2270237

Lavine, H. (2001). The electoral consequences of ambivalence toward presidential candidates. *American Journal of Political Science, 45*(4), 915–929. doi:10.2307/2669332

Lee, E., & Leets, L. (2002). Persuasion storytelling by hate groups online: Examining its effects on adolescents. *The American Behavioral Scientist, 45*(6), 927–957. doi:10.1177/0002764202045006003

Lemieux, A. F., Brachman, J., Levitt, J., & Wood, J. (2014). Inspire magazine: A critical analysis of its significance and potential impact through the lens of the information, motivation, and behavioral skills model. *Terrorism and Political Violence, 26*(2), 1–18. doi:10.1080/09546553.2013.828604

Lennings, C. J., Amon, K. L., Brummert, H., & Lennings, N. (2010). Grooming for terror: The Internet and young people. *Psychiatry, Psychology and Law, 17*(3), 424–437. doi:10.1080/13218710903566979

Long, M., Alison, A. J., & McManus, M. (2013). Child pornography and the likelihood of contact abuse: A comparison between contact child sexual offenders and non-contact offenders and the homologous victim selection of contact child sexual offenders. *Sexual Abuse, 25*, 370–395. doi:10.1177/1079063212464398 PMID:23160257

Maghan, J., & Kelly, R. J. (1989). Terrorism and corrections: The incarcerated radical. In J. R. Buckwalter (Ed.), *International terrorism: The decade ahead* (pp. 29–53). Chicago, IL: University of Illinois Press, Office of Criminal Justice.

McCarthy, J. (2010). Internet sexual activity: A comparison between contact and non-contact child pornography offenders. *Journal of Sexual Aggression, 16*(2), 181–195. doi:10.1080/13552601003760006

McCauley, C., & Moskalenko, S. (2008). Mechanisms of political radicalization: Pathways toward terrorism. *Terrorism and Political Violence, 20*(3), 415–433. doi:10.1080/09546550802073367

McCauley, C., & Moskalenko, S. (2011). *Friction: How radicalization happens to them and us.* Oxford, UK: Oxford University Press.

McDonald, H. S., Horstmann, N., Strom, K. J., & Pope, M. W. (2009). *The impact of the Internet on deviant behavior and deviant communities.* Durham, NC: The Institute for Homeland Security Solution.

McGilloway, A., Ghosh, P., & Bhui, K. (2015). A systematic review of pathways to and processes associated with radicalization and extremism amongst Muslims in Western societies. *International Review of Psychiatry (Abingdon, England), 27*(1), 39–50. doi:10.3109/09540261.2014.992008 PMID:25738400

McManus, M., Long, M., & Alison, L. (2011). Child pornography offenders: Towards an evidenced-based approach to prioritizing the investigation of indecent image offenses. In A. J. Alison & R. Rainbow (Eds.), *Professionalizing offender profiling: Forensic and investigative psychology in practise* (pp. 178–188). Oxon: Routledge.

McNeal, G. S. (2008). Cyber embargo: Countering the Internet jihad. *Case Western Reserve Journal of International Law, 789*, 810–812.

Meloy, R., Hoffman, J., Guldmann, A., & James, D. (2012). The role of warning behaviors in threat assessment: An exploration and suggested typology. *Behavioral Sciences & the Law, 30*(3), 256–279. doi:10.1002/bsl.999 PMID:22556034

Moghaddam, A. (2005). The staircase to terrorism: A psychological exploration. *The American Psychologist, 60*(2), 161–169. doi:10.1037/0003-066X.60.2.161 PMID:15740448

Monahan, J. (2011). The individual risk assessment of terrorism. *Psychology, Public Policy, and Law, 18*(2), 167–205. doi:10.1037/a0025792

Moon, D. B. (2007). Cyber-herding: Exploiting Islamic extremists' use of the Internet (Unpublished dissertation). Monterey, CA: Naval Postgraduate School. Retrieved from http://stinet.dtic.mil/cgi-bin/GetTRDoc?AD=ADA475919&location= U2&doc=GetTRDDoc.pdf

Nesser, P. (2008). How did Europe's global jihadis obtain training for their militant causes? *Terrorism and Political Violence, 20*(2), 234–256. doi:10.1080/09546550801920758

Nesser, P. (2012). Single actor terrorism: Scope, characteristics and explanations. *Perspectives on Terrorism, 6*, 61–73.

Noelle-Neumann, E. (1993). *The spiral of silence: Public opinion – Our social skin.* Chicago, IL: University of Chicago Press.

Pauwels, L., & Schils, N. (2014). Differential online exposure to extremist content and political violence: Testing the relative strength of social learning and competing perspectives. *Terrorism and Political Violence.* doi:10.1080/09546553.2013.876414

Prentice-Dunn, S., & Rogers, R. W. (1982). Effects of public and private self-awareness on deindividuation and aggression. *Journal of Personality and Social Psychology, 43*(3), 503–513. doi:10.1037/0022-3514.43.3.503

Prentice-Dunn, S., & Rogers, R. W. (1989). Deindividuation and the self-regulation of behavior. In P. B. Paulus (Ed.), *The psychology of group influence* (2nd ed.; pp. 86–109). Hillsdale, NJ: Lawrence Erlbaum.

Pressman, D. E. (2009). *Risk assessment decisions for violent political extremism.* Retrieved from http://www.publicsafety.gc.ca/cnt/rsrcs/pblctns/2009-02-rdv/2009-02-rdv-eng.pdf

Pressman, D. E., & Flockton, J. (2010). *VERA-2. Violent extremism risk assessment, Version 2 Manual.* Unpublished Manuscript.

Pressman, D. E., & Flockton, J. (2014). Violent extremist risk assessment: Issues and application of the VERA-2 in a high–security correctional setting. In A. Silke (Ed.), *Prisons, terrorism and extremism: Critical issues in management, radicalisation and reform* (pp. 122–143). New York, NY: Routledge.

Price, V., Cappella, J. N., & Nir, L. (2002). Does disagreement contribute to more deliberative opinion? *Political Communication, 19*(1), 97–114. doi:10.1080/105846002317246506

Reinares, F. (2004). Who are the terrorists? Analyzing changes in sociological profile among members of ETA. *Studies in Conflict and Terrorism, 27*(6), 465–488. doi:10.1080/10576100490519741

Roberts, K., & Horgan, J. (2008). Risk assessment and the terrorist. *Perspectives on Terrorism, 2*(6), 1–4.

Rossmiller, S. (2007). My cyber counter-jihad. *Middle East Quarterly, 14*(3).

Sageman, M. (2004). *Understanding terror networks.* Philadelphia, PA: University of Philadelphia Press. doi:10.9783/9780812206791

Saldarini, R. A., & DeRobertis, E. M. (2003). The impact of a technologically induced feeling of anonymity on communications and ethics: New challenges for IT pedagogy. *Journal of Information Technology Impact, 3*, 3–10.

Senate Committee on Homeland Security and Governmental Affairs. (2012). *Zachary Chesser: A case study in online Islamist radicalization and its meaning for the threat of homegrown terrorism.* Washington, DC: United States Senate.

Seto, M. C. (2009). *Assessing the risk posed by child pornography offenders.* Paper presented at the G8 Global Symposium, Chapel Hill, NC.

Seto, M. C., Cantor, J. M., & Blanchard, R. (2006). Child pornography offenses are a valid diagnostic indicator of paedophilia. *Journal of Abnormal Psychology, 115*(3), 610–615. doi:10.1037/0021-843X.115.3.610 PMID:16866601

Seto, M. C., Hanson, K. R., & Babchishin, K. M. (2011). Contact sexual offending by men with online sexual offenses. *Sexual Abuse, 23*, 124–145. PMID:21173158

Silke, A. (Ed.). (2014). *Prisons, terrorism and extremism: Critical issues in management, radicalization and reform.* Oxon, UK: Routledge.

Simcox, R., & Dyer, E. (2013). *Al Qaeda in the United States: A complete analysis of terrorism offenses.* London: The Henry Jackson Society.

Simcox, R., Stuart, H., Ahmed, H., & Murray, D. (2011). *Islamist terrorism: The British Connections* (2nd ed.). London: The Henry Jackson Society and The Center for Social Cohesion.

Stenerson, A. (2008). The Internet: A virtual training camp? *Terrorism and Political Violence, 20*(8), 215–233. doi:10.1080/09546550801920790

Sydney siege report: Tony Abbott says legal system let community down. (2015, February 22). *The Guardian.* Retrieved from http://www.theguardian.com/australia-news/2015/feb/22/sydney-siege-report-tony-abbott-more-immigration-checks-needed

Tait, S. (2008). Pornographies of violence? Internet spectatorship on body horror. *Critical Studies in Media Communication, 25*(1), 91–111. doi:10.1080/15295030701851148

Talbot, D. (2005). Terror's server. *Technology Review.* Retrieved from http://www.technologyreview.com/infotech/14150/

Taylor, M., & Quayle, E. (2003). *Child pornography: An Internet crime.* Hove, U.K.: Brunner Routledge.

von Behr, I., Reding, A., Edwards, C., & Gribbon, L. (2013). *Radicalisation in the digital era: The use of the Internet in 15 cases of terrorism and extremism.* Santa Monica, CA: RAND Corporation.

Weatherston, D., & Moran, J. (2003). Terrorism and mental illness: Is there a relationship? *International Journal of Offender Therapy and Comparative Criminology, 47*(6), 698–713. doi:10.1177/0306624X03257244 PMID:14661388

Weimann, G. (2004). *How modern terrorism uses the Internet. Special Report No.116.* Washington, DC: United States Institute of Peace; www.terror.net

Weimann, G. (2006). *Terror on the Internet: The new arena, the new challenges.* Washington, DC: United States Institute of Peace.

Weimann, G. (2011). Cyber-fatwas and terrorism. *Studies in Conflict and Terrorism, 34*(10), 765–781. doi:10.1080/1057610X.2011.604831

Wetter, O. E. (2014). Terrorism research: Should we focus on the opponent or on our own people? *Defense and Security Analysis, 30*(2), 92–105. doi:10.1080/14751798.2014.894298

Wojcieszak, M. (2009). "Carrying online participation offline"—Mobilization by radical online groups and politically dissimilar offline ties. *Journal of Communication, 59*(3), 564–586. doi:10.1111/j.1460-2466.2009.01436.x

Wojcieszak, M. (2010). 'Don't talk to me': Effects of ideologically homogeneous online groups and politically dissimilar offline ties on extremism. *New Media & Society, 12*(4), 637–655. doi:10.1177/1461444809342775

Zalkind, S. (2014, April 11). FBI admits missed opportunities to stop Tamerlan Tsarnaev. *Boston Magazine.* Retrieved from http://www.bostonmagazine.com/news/blog/2014/04/11/fbi-admits-missed-opportunities-stop-tamerlan-tsarnaev/

Zimbardo, P. G. (1969). The human choice: Individuation, reason, and order versus deindividuation, impulse, and chaos. *Nebraska Symposium on Motivation, 17*, 237–307.

Zuckerman, J., Bucci, S. P., & Carafano, J. J. (2013). *60 terrorist plots since 9/11: Continued lessons in domestic counterterrorism.* Retrieved from http://www.heritage.org/research/reports/2013/07/60-terrorist-plots-since-911-continued-lessons-in-domestic-counterterrorism

ENDNOTE

[1] For more information about the discussion on 'the evolution of terrorist propaganda: the Paris attack and social media', please refer to http://www.gpo.gov/fdsys/pkg/CHRG-114hhrg92852/html/CHRG-114hhrg92852.htm

Chapter 18
Detecting Linguistic Markers of Violent Extremism in Online Environments

Fredrik Johansson
Swedish Defence Research Agency (FOI), Sweden

Lisa Kaati
Uppsala University, Sweden

Magnus Sahlgren
Gavagai, Sweden

ABSTRACT

The ability to disseminate information instantaneously over vast geographical regions makes the Internet a key facilitator in the radicalisation process and preparations for terrorist attacks. This can be both an asset and a challenge for security agencies. One of the main challenges for security agencies is the sheer amount of information available on the Internet. It is impossible for human analysts to read through everything that is written online. In this chapter we will discuss the possibility of detecting violent extremism by identifying signs of warning behaviours in written text – what we call linguistic markers – using computers, or more specifically, natural language processing.

INTRODUCTION

In recent years, there have been many examples of various types of terrorist attacks taking place all over the world. There have also been several severe school shootings that resulted in many victims. When studying the reason behind why these attacks took place, Internet often has an important role to play. For example, the use of the Internet for terrorist recruitment and operations has increased significantly in recent years (Torok, 2013), not least due to an emergence of social media services such as Facebook, Twitter, Instagram, and YouTube.

DOI: 10.4018/978-1-5225-0156-5.ch018

There are several examples of terrorists and terrorist organisations that use or have used the Internet and social media in different ways. One example of a terrorist who used the Internet extensively is Jose Pimentel, who was arrested for planning attacks with home-made pipe bombs against police vehicles and postal facilities in the United States. Pimentel was very active on the Internet, where he maintained a website on Blogger and a YouTube channel containing radical works which connected him with like-minded individuals (Weimann, 2012). Another example of a terrorist that used the Internet is the Norwegian terrorist Anders Behring Breivik. He used the Internet to obtain the necessary knowledge on how to construct a large fertiliser bomb, and to express and discuss his critical view on Islam and socialism (Ravndal, 2013). The suicide bomber Taimour Abdulwahab al-Abdably that killed himself in the middle of Stockholm in 2010 is another example of a person that used the Internet for various reasons. Abdably was active on various forms of social media such as YouTube and Facebook and he also searched for a second wife on Islamic web pages.

Due to the nature of the Internet and social media, it is possible to communicate and express radical views and intentions as well as to connect to other persons with similar interests. This is also noted in Europol's annual terrorism situation and trend report of 2012, which states the following: "Online social media sites attract high numbers of users. Internet forums are an effective means to address targeted audiences, including supporters who have no off-line links to terrorist organisations" (Europol, 2012, p. 10).

The ability to disseminate information instantaneously over vast geographical regions makes the Internet a key facilitator in the radicalisation process and preparations for terror attacks. This can be both an asset and a challenge for intelligence and security agencies. While it is troublesome that radical and violent extremism content can be spread globally with very low costs, this fact also provides an opportunity for intelligence analysts and police to act preventively. By collecting, fusing and analysing 'weak signals' or 'digital traces' that are present on the Internet, there is a possibility to detect attackers before they strike.

One of the main challenges in doing such analysis is the sheer amount of information available on the Internet. For this reason, analysts need support from computerised tools to be able to perform analysis on a large scale. Although web data have become an important source of information for law enforcement agencies working to prevent terrorist attacks, it is impossible for human analysts to read everything that is written on the Internet.

As an example, a human analyst capable of speed-reading may be able to read up to 1,000 (or even more) words per minute (cf. the average adult reading speed is around 300 words per minute). If the analyst is able to read at the same speed consecutively for eight hours (which is perhaps not very likely), he/she will have read about 480,000 words, which given an average word length of six characters, equals 2.8 megabyte of data (cf. the average human would have read less than one megabyte of data in the same time period). It has been estimated that the Internet carries around 1.8 exabyte of data per day. Furthermore, approximately 80 percent of all available data is in unstructured form, and a large portion of this unstructured data is textual data. This means that it would require several hundred million incredibly focused speed-reading human analysts (and consequently more than a billion humans with normal reading capacity) to be able to read all the text data generated on the Internet in only one day. This example illustrates the need for computer support to be able to detect and analyse content that is of interest for law enforcement agencies if we do not know where to find the information of interest.

BACKGROUND

Tools for monitoring the Internet are not a new phenomenon. Large-scale surveillance systems and surveillance programs such as Echelon (Schmid, 2001), XKeyscore (Greenwald, 2013), and PRISM (Greenwald, 2013) have been heavily debated and criticised, mostly due to the threat towards personal integrity that monitoring of various types of communication pose. Another problem with such systems is that they often lack clear guidelines describing who and during what circumstances monitoring was allowed. Monitoring specific keywords or terms is the most common approach to obtain situational awareness using such systems. However, such approaches may generate a lot of irrelevant material due to the nature of our language – i.e., words can be used in many different contexts and have several different meanings.

Another problem with monitoring what people write (or what information they access) is the fact that even if some individuals show a great interest in radical content and participate in discussions, many of them will never become terrorists or even break the law, which makes it difficult for law enforcement agencies to identify actual terrorists (Bjelopera, 2013). For this reason, it is fundamentally important to realise that the output from such systems always have to be checked and verified by human analysts, and most often only can serve as a filtering mechanism to bring forward information that may be potentially interesting to the analysts.

MAIN FOCUS OF THE CHAPTER

In this chapter we discuss the possibility of automatically detecting signs of certain warning behaviours defined by Meloy, Hoffmann, Guldimann and James (2012). The warning behaviours might indicate that a person or a group has the intention to commit a violent attack. In the long run, our hope is that such warning behaviours can be used by systems to generate less false hits (i.e., false positives) than traditional surveillance systems.

This chapter is organised as follows. First we describe the typology of warning behaviours and then some related work and ideas for identifying a subset of such warning behaviours automatically in text using natural language processing techniques. Next, we describe the implementation of a prototype system for detecting warning behaviours in user-generated content posted on the Internet that is based on the triangulation of several linguistic markers. We also describe some preliminary results obtained when collecting data using the prototype system. It should be stressed that these are just preliminary results, but based on these we describe some operational and practical implications. There are many ethical considerations associated with these kinds of systems since there are many privacy-related issues to take into account when deciding on whether these kinds of systems should be used at all, and if so, how the intrusion of citizens' privacy can be minimised. These aspects are briefly discussed at the end of this chapter with some directions for future work.

WARNING BEHAVIOURS

It has been argued by various psychologists that violent attacks on public figures, mass murders, and acts of lone wolf terrorism, are often signalled by a set of more or less detectable warning behaviours.

Meloy and O'Toole (2011, p. 514) define warning behaviours as any behaviour that "precedes an act of targeted violence, is related to it, and may, in certain cases, predict it". Warning behaviours can in this context be viewed as indicators of increasing or accelerating risk of committing a violent attack.

Furthermore, in Meloy (2011), Meloy and O'Toole (2011), Meloy et al. (2012), and Meloy, Hoffmann, Roshdi, and Guldimann (2014), eight different warning behaviours are defined for targeted or intended violence. These warning behaviours are: (i) pathway warning behaviour, (ii) fixation warning behaviour, (iii) identification warning behaviour, (iv) novel aggression warning behaviour, (v) energy burst warning behaviour, (vi) leakage warning behaviour, (vii) last resort warning behaviour, and (viii) directly communicated threat warning behaviour. Recently, some validation research regarding the typology of warning behaviours have been done by Meloy et al. (2014). In their study, they show that some of the warning behaviours were also present in a sample of German school shooters.

In this work, we focus on a limited subset of those warning behaviours, namely the ones that have the highest potential to be discovered in textual content in social media. These warning behaviours are 'leakage', 'fixation' and 'identification', as suggested by Cohen, Johansson, Kaati, and Mork (2014). The interested reader is encouraged to read the works by Meloy et al. (2012) in order to get a full understanding of all eight warning behaviours from a psychological point of view, but for the purpose of this chapter, we will give a simplified description of leakage, fixation, and identification warning behaviours.

Leakage can basically be defined as the communication of intent to do harm to a third party. Leakage usually signals research, planning and/or implementation of an attack. It is also common that a preoccupation with the target is present. Leakage has been shown to occur in many different cases of targeted violence – everything from school shootings to attacks on public figures.

Fixation can loosely be defined as any behaviour which indicates an increasing pathological preoccupation with a person or a cause. According to Meloy, Mohandie, Knoll, and Hoffmann (2015), fixation can be measured by:

- Increasing perseveration on the person or cause;
- Increasingly strident opinion;
- Increasingly negative characterisation of the object of fixation;
- Impact on the family or other associates of the object of fixation, if present and aware; and
- Angry emotional undertone. Furthermore, fixation is typically accompanied by social or occupational deterioration.

Fixation is a behaviour that can be noted in many subjects' daily life. It could be fixation of hobbies, sports, and admiration of public figures, or in an early stage of a love affair. Fixation is considered to be pathological when it disturbs the social functions (Meloy et al., 2015). While fixation is a pathological preoccupation on an external person or cause, the identification warning behaviour is a cause or action that is within the person.

Identification can be defined as a behaviour which indicates a desire to be a 'pseudo-commando' – i.e., have a warrior mentality, closely associate with weapons or other military or law enforcement paraphernalia, identify with previous attackers or assassins, or identify oneself as an agent to advance a particular cause (Meloy et al., 2015). There are many examples of terrorist and mass murderers that showed signs of the identification warning behaviours. Meloy and colleagues (2015) use Timothy McVeigh who bombed the Alfred P. Murrah Federal Building in Oklahoma City on April 19, 1995 as an example. Due to some circumstances, McVeigh became a soldier without an army. He had developed a rigid and disciplined 'warrior mentality' and collected military paraphernalia, including weapons. Some other signs that supported McVeigh's identification warning behaviour was the fact that during the bombing he wore a T-shirt with the text "The tree of liberty must be refreshed from time to time with the blood of patriots and tyrants", and that he communicated his desire to be the 'first hero' to his sister in writing (Meloy et al., 2012).

DETECTING WARNING BEHAVIOURS

In Cohen et al. (2014), tools and techniques for detecting some of the warning behaviours described by Meloy et al. (2012) using linguistic markers were outlined. Although the article is focused on the identification of digital traces related to potential lone wolf terrorism, it can easily be extended to also cover other kinds of violence – since warning behaviours may indicate dynamic and accelerating risk of targeted violence across a variety of domains, including school shootings, mass murder, public figure attacks and assassinations, and terrorist acts (Meloy et al., 2014).

The basic idea outlined in our previous work (Brynielsson et al., 2013; Cohen et al., 2014) is to first make use of web crawlers to extract and download relevant data from websites and social media that can be readily accessed through the Internet. Next, it is suggested that various natural language processing algorithms are applied to the data in order to detect warning behaviours from digital traces that might indicate signs of violent extremism. These kinds of techniques are argued to be of great potential use by intelligence analysts for monitoring and searching for relevant information in large amounts of available data. However, it is important to stress that automated techniques can never replace a human analyst, but merely aid or support his/her work.

In Cohen et al. (2014), it is argued that the warning behaviours that are likely to be the most easily detectable in the subject's written communication in social media (e.g., extremist discussion boards) are leakage, fixation, and identification. For each of these three warning behaviours, a set of linguistic markers is proposed. The linguistic markers are intended to be used as inputs to computer algorithms so that they may be able to recognise signs of radical violence. As already mentioned, such algorithms are not supposed to make any kinds of automated decisions, but merely are intended to help the analyst navigate through the massive amounts of data and help him/her to focus on potentially relevant information.

Starting out with linguistic markers for leakage, it is observed that the leakage of one's intention to take any kind of violent action is likely to contain auxiliary verbs signalling intent (i.e., 'I will …', '… am going to …') together with words expressing violent action, either overtly or through euphemisms. As a starting point for being able to detect such linguistic markers signalling a violent intention, it is proposed that predefined word lists of violent actions are used, and to extend such a predefined list of words using lexical databases such as WordNet. Now, by lemmatising posts and tagging them with their part of speech, it would be possible to match the harvested posts to the extended word lists, and to flag hits as potential markers of leakage. Admittedly, many of such matches would probably be the result of false positives (e.g., due to ironic statements), but it is argued that the levels of false positives hopefully can be kept at an acceptable level if attention is restricted to websites or forums that are known to contain violent extremism related content.

When it comes to identification warning behaviour, this is quite complex since the definition given above covers quite a broad and complex range of phenomena. In Cohen et al. (2014), this is therefore simplified into three subcategories of identification: (i) identification with radical action (i.e., warrior mentality), (ii) identification with role-model, and (iii) group identification. For the group identification, it is argued that identification with a group (or cause) can be expressed through a usage of positive adjectives in connection with mentioning the in-group. To detect positiveness, the use of sentiment analysis or opinion mining techniques is envisioned, while references to the in-group is hypothesised to be identifiable by counting the relative frequencies of first person plural pronouns such as 'we' and 'us', and checking whether such frequencies are higher than some predefined threshold. Identification of role-models or other radical thinkers is argued to be likely to be detectable through frequent quotations and mentions, but also possibly through similarities in language, since it is not uncommon to pick up terminology of one's role model, or even adapt to similar sentence structures. For this reason, authorship analysis algorithms or content analysis algorithms could potentially be one piece of the puzzle for a working system for the detection of identification linguistic markers. Identification with radical action (i.e., warrior mentality) can probably be spotted through a certain terminology in the same manner as the intent discussion above, while a sense of moral obligation could be captured through usage of words related to duty, honour, justice, etc.

Finally, for linguistic markers of fixation, we propose to simply count the relative frequency of key terms relating to named entities such as persons, organisations, etc., after making use of named entity recognisers to identify the named entities. When named entities of interest obtain a relative frequency which is higher than some pre-specified threshold, this can be used as an indication of a potential fixation with or to the named entity. Not setting the threshold extremely high would of course generate a large number of false positives on its own, but by combining it with other linguistic markers, this is hypothesised to be a useful marker.

The article by Cohen et al. (2014) has suggested a number of natural language processing techniques for detecting linguistic markers that can be useful for intelligence analysts when analysing the content of websites or social media in order to identify online warning behaviours. However the techniques are never implemented or evaluated, making it hard to judge the usefulness of such linguistic markers. In this chapter, we therefore take the proposed techniques one step closer to a real system by implementing some of the ideas into a prototype system. The inner working of this prototype system is described in more detail in following sections, but first we review some related work.

RELATED WORK

The idea to detect terrorism-related content on the Internet is not new, as it is believed that the detection of terrorist activities on the Internet may help prevent future terrorist attacks (Elovici, Kandel, Last, Shapira, & Zaafrany, 2004). In fact, there are currently calls for research projects by the EU research and innovation programme, Horizon 2020[1], which aim at detecting and analysing terrorism-related content on the Internet with the purpose of fighting terrorism. Previous attempts described in research literature include work carried out in the EU Seventh Framework Programme (FP7) project, INDECT[2] as well as the articles by Brynielsson et al. (2013), Elovici et al. (2004), and Last, Markov, and Kandel (2006), in which data mining and machine learning algorithms are proposed for learning to classify the textual content of websites as either terror-related or non-terror-related.

In the paper by Elovici et al. (2004), a methodology is proposed that allows for processing all Internet service providers (ISPs) traffic in real-time, allowing for large-scale monitoring. This can be contrasted with the methodology presented in Brynielsson et al. (2013), in which a much smaller subset of websites, which are linked to known extremist websites, is targeted for analysis. Moreover, it is in the latter approach suggested that only user-generated content on the websites is analysed, not the web traffic as such. This is a quite important difference since the approach used in the prototype system described in this chapter, and the approach outlined in Brynielsson et al. (2013) analyse what people write; while the approach suggested in Elovici et al. (2004) builds on what information people access.

The approach described in Elovici et al. (2004) assumes that terror-related content usually viewed by terrorists and their supporters can be used by data mining tools to learn a 'Typical-Terrorist-Behaviour', but this is in our view problematic since many people who are not terrorists may be interested in reading content concerning the same topics as terrorists. For example, security researchers, intelligence analysts and journalists will be interested in reading information on terrorism websites, and are likely to be classified as 'suspected terrorists' using an approach such as the one proposed in Elovici et al. (2004). They argue that "missing one real terrorist in a haystack of legitimate users may be more costly than suspecting several legitimate users of being active terrorists" (p. 20). This may be true, but it is in general very hard for the general public to get information on how well surveillance systems work, making it hard to judge how much of our privacy it is worth losing just for the sake of a potentially more secure society.

Most readers are likely to have heard of intelligence agencies such as the National Security Agency (NSA), and various surveillance projects such as Echelon and PRISM. Although much secret information has become public knowledge due to the leak by Edward Snowden, not very much is known about the inner workings of these systems. For this reason, it is hard to compare our implementation of the prototype system with existing real systems.

IMPLEMENTATION OF LINGUISTIC MARKERS FOR DETECTING WARNING BEHAVIOURS

As explained above, the article by Cohen et al. (2014) discusses possible ways to implement a system for detecting warning behaviours based on some of the markers described by Meloy et al. (2012). Cohen et al. (2014) suggest using natural language processing techniques like lemmatisation, part of speech tagging, named entity recognition as well as lexical resources like WordNet. This is a common approach in natural language processing applications, which generally improves the quality of the resulting analysis. However, this is only true if the individual natural language processing components are accurate enough; if on the contrary, the natural language processing components are inaccurate, the errors will propagate and severely affect the end result.

This is a potential problem, since language used in social media is highly dynamic, noisy and productive, and tends to be highly multilingual. Such environments pose severe challenges for traditional natural language processing components and available natural language processing frameworks, since they are either based on precompiled lexica and rules (this tends to be the case for lemmatisers), or based on supervised machine learning where a classifier is trained on some manually annotated training data (which is normally the case for part of speech taggers and named entity recognisers). The problem with such approaches is that the trained classifiers and precompiled resources cannot keep up-to-date automatically with the constantly evolving linguistic environment in social media. Consequently, they will have limited recall, which of course is a serious deficiency in a monitoring scenario, since this means that there will be signs of violent actions that such a system will fail to identify.

Furthermore, adequate training data and lexical resources are not in abundance for languages other than English (and even for English, they can be domain-specific and less suitable to train models for application to security analysis in social media), and are costly and time-consuming to produce and maintain. We also note that the use of natural language processing components adds computational complexity to the system, which might be a limiting factor in a Big Data scenario where efficiency and scalability are important considerations.

Due to these concerns, we are aiming for a light-weight and resource-lean approach that presumes a minimum of pre-processing in order to be as efficient, scalable, and portable as possible. The proposed approach is based on simple lists of keywords, where a keyword can consist not only of single words, but also of multi-word units (e.g., the bigram 'Al-Shabab'). This means that we opt for recall rather than precision, and efficiency rather than representational sophistication. We substantiate this choice with the fact that the current application is a monitoring scenario, in which we cannot afford to miss relevant content; we thus argue that false positives are more acceptable than false negatives. This trade-off is an important consideration when dealing with monitoring tasks in user-generated content as we on the one hand would like to find as many of the real threats as possible, while on the other hand cannot afford a too high false alarm rate since this will be a burden for the analyst who in the end may stop using the system. Moreover, too low precision (i.e., low false alarm rate) also means an increased risk for privacy violations, something which is discussed in more detail in the section regarding ethical considerations.

We follow Cohen et al. (2014)'s definition of leakage in terms of 'intent to commit violent acts', and implement this marker as the combination of expressions of violent acts and intent. That is, it is not enough to mention violent acts in order for this marker to trigger; the user also has to express some form of intent in relation to the violent act. Violent acts are defined as three separate lists of terms: one relating to general expressions of violence (i.e., featuring terms like 'kill', 'assassinate', and 'bomb'), one featuring more specific terms referring to bomb ingredients, and one containing various types of weapons. Intent is defined by terms like 'going to', 'someone should', and 'plans'. This means that expressions like 'I am going to use an M-16' or 'someone should bomb the government' will trigger the marker, whereas expressions like 'I own a sniper rifle' or 'that was a good kill' will not.

For identification and fixation, we list a number of targets that could be relevant in the context of online violent extremism, ranging from individuals and organisations to ideologies and controversial topics: abortion, Anders Behring Breivik, communism, counter-jihad, cultural Marxism, EDL (European Defence League), infidels, Islamism, Jews, Kahanism, neo-nationalism, white supremacy, Charlie Hebdo, ISIS (Islamic State in Iraq and Syria), Anwar Al-Awlaki, Heil Hitler, and a list of famous mass murderers. Note that this is by no means an exhaustive list of targets that could be relevant for real-world monitoring scenarios; this list is simply meant as an example of topics that could be of relevance for the sake of demonstration. Considerably more effort would have been required from analysts and knowledge engineers to identify the relevant targets before a system like this could be put in real-world use.

For each mention of one of these targets, we count the occurrences of appreciative and depreciative expressions (i.e., we do a rudimentary form of sentiment analysis (Pang, Lee, & Vaithyanathan, 2002) of the targets), and define identification as expressions featuring a target in an appreciative context, and fixation as expressions featuring a target in a depreciative context. That is, an expression like 'I support the views of Breivik' would trigger the identification marker, whereas an expression like 'Charlie Hebdo is awful' would trigger the fixation marker. In reality, it would make sense to ensure that the thresholds of relative frequencies have to be passed before a marker (i.e., identification or fixation) is triggered –

since mentioning a named entity such as Charlie Hebdo once cannot be counted as a fixation. However, in this first prototype system this has been neglected in order to simplify the implementation.

Note that since we do not presume that the input data will be morphologically normalised (i.e., all words will be in lemma or basic form), we include morphological variants in the keyword lists (e.g., violence list contains both 'kill' and 'killed' and the list for Charlie Hebdo contains both 'Charlie Hebdo' and 'Charlie Hebdo's'). We also do not make any distinction between different parts of speech in the keyword lists, which means that the violence list contains both verbs like 'kill' and nouns like 'assassination'. The lack of part of speech tagging means that some words with polysemic meaning will trigger more often than they would have if part of speech tagging was used (e.g., the word 'conflict' can be both a noun and a verb); but as argued above, avoiding part of speech tagging allows for faster processing.

The following is a complete list of the 39 different targets used in the prototype implementation:

- violence – intent
- weapons – intent
- bomb ingredients – intent
- abortion – positive
- abortion – negative
- Anders Behring Breivik – positive
- Anders Behring Breivik – negative
- Anwar Al-Awlaki – positive
- Anwar Al-Awlaki – negative
- Charlie Hebdo – positive
- Charlie Hebdo – negative
- Columbine – positive
- Columbine – negative
- communism – positive
- communism – negative
- counter-jihad – positive
- counter-jihad – negative
- cultural Marxism – positive
- cultural Marxism – negative
- EDL – positive
- EDL – negative
- Heil Hitler – positive
- Heil Hitler – negative
- infidels – positive
- infidels – negative
- ISIS – positive
- ISIS – negative
- Islamism – positive
- Islamism – negative
- Jews – positive
- Jews – negative
- Kahanism – positive

- Kahanism – negative
- mass murderers – positive
- mass murderers – negative
- neo-nationalism – positive
- neo-nationalism – negative
- white supremacy – positive
- white supremacy – negative

Vocabulary Variation

The arguably most difficult problem when dealing with natural language in online data, and in particular when using keyword-based approaches is vocabulary variation, which is the situation when different people use different terms to refer to the same thing. As an example, consider the expressions of appreciation; there are literally hundreds, if not thousands of ways to express appreciation in English, and it would be impossible for an analyst to list them all a priori. Furthermore, language use is productive (especially in social media), which means that new expressions are invented and modified continuously. Consequently, even if we somehow could list all possible expressions of appreciation in English at this particular moment, the list would become outdated basically as soon as it was compiled (Karlgren, 2006). Keeping à jour with the productivity of language use is one of the most difficult challenges for social media monitoring in general.

One way to approach this challenge is to use unsupervised machine learning techniques that can learn to identify semantically similar terms in the data by simply reading lots of text. Such techniques are generally known as 'distributional semantic models' (Sahlgren, 2006; Turney & Pantel, 2010), and they work by collecting statistics on how terms in the data co-occur with each other. These statistics are used to identify terms that have similar co-occurrence profiles; if two terms have co-occurred significantly with the same *other* terms it means that they often can be substituted by each other in context, which is often used as criterion for semantic relationship in linguistics (Murphy, 2003).

As an example, consider a term like 'shit', which in its derogatory sense, is often used in sentiment analysis as a negative term signalling depreciation – and is thus of use in the prototype implementation as a keyword for the fixation marker. A standard lexicon will list a number of terms that are often used as synonyms to 'shit', like 'bad', 'terrible' and perhaps 'poor'. However, no single lexical resource (or, for that matter, no single human analyst) will list all possible terms used in online/social media to signal appreciation. Looking up the term 'shit' in an online lexicon continuously trained on millions of web documents each day produces the following result:

[shit: sh1t, sh*t, $hit, shyt, sht, sh-t, shite, shyte, crap, shiz, dogshit, horseshit, s--t, dog shit, crapola, crud, dipshit ...]

'Shit' in the derogatory sense may not even be listed in traditional lexica, and even human analysts would be hard pressed to come up with all these alternative terms. This means that without the use of data mining tools like distributional semantic models, we would miss all expressions that use such productive terminology. Lexical productivity might not be such a severe problem when it comes to named entities like Anders Behring Breivik and ISIS, but it will be a significant problem when looking for expressions of, for example, violence, intent and appreciation/depreciation. This demonstrates the importance of not solely relying on manually compiled knowledge bases such as WordNet or Wikipedia; we simply cannot afford to assume that vocabulary usage will remain static and predictable if we want to monitor language use in social media.

In order to handle problems with vocabulary variation, we use a distributional semantic lexicon to ensure our lists of terms are exhaustive and up-to-date with current language use. This is done by continuously consulting the online lexicon for new relevant terms; if any such terms are found, they are included in the keyword list in question. It is important to stress that each addition to the keyword lists needs to be confirmed by a human operator, since not all distributional neighbours will be relevant for the intended meaning of the keywords.

As an example, a distributional lexicon might suggest the terms 'ISIL' and 'Iowa' as related to 'ISIS'. The term 'ISIL' would be relevant in the present scenario, since it refers to the Islamic State in Iraq and the Levant, which is a synonym to ISIS. The term 'Iowa', on the other hand, would not be relevant, since it refers to another meaning of ISIS (i.e., the Iowa Student Information System).

TRIANGULATION WARNING BEHAVIOURS

The approach described above is both efficient and scalable, and manages to handle vocabulary variation by using a distributional semantic lexicon to ensure that the term lists are constantly up-to-date. As such, the proposed prototype system is geared towards high recall, and is designed to be able to capture as much relevant material as possible. However, it will also capture a considerable amount of irrelevant material, which will affect the precision of the system.

Recall is the proportion of relevant material that is detected by the system, whereas precision is the proportion of material detected by the system that is actually relevant. It is a well-known fact in information retrieval that there is a trade-off between recall and precision; a system that is geared towards recall will typically have lower precision, while a system that is geared towards precision will typically have lower recall. In the current application scenario, it is arguably more important to aim for high recall, since it may have severe consequences if we miss relevant information. However, the precision has to be reasonable as well since a too low precision will make the system more or less useless for the analysts due to the high false alarm rate. Moreover, it can cause unnecessary privacy implications as discussed further in the section on ethical considerations.

Now, looking at each individual marker by itself will likely lead to unacceptable levels of false positives (i.e., hits that are not relevant). As an example, expressions of violent intent is, unfortunately, prevalent in social media, both in expressions where the intent to commit violence is literal but perhaps not very realistic (e.g., as used by people who are upset about something), and in metaphorical expressions like 'we are going to kill tonight' (i.e., we are going to have a good time tonight). Furthermore, some keywords, like 'ISIS' may occur frequently due to their generally topical nature.

One way to reduce the amount of false positives (i.e., improve the precision) while still keeping the markers as general as possible to ensure high recall is to 'triangulate' warning behaviours based on the suggested markers. This means that we would look for content that trigger several different markers, and perhaps also over a period of time. As an example, a website that simultaneously triggers the leakage and fixation detectors would be more interesting than a website that only triggers the leakage detector. Furthermore, if the same website (i.e., trigger both the leakage and fixation markers) also triggers the identification marker but at a different time, it should further increase our interest in that website. Since we are operating with three main types of linguistic markers, we refer to this process as 'triangulation'.

Our prototype implementation is build using existing commercial tools for text analysis and social media monitoring provided by Gavagai. As already discussed above, we use a distributional semantic model to ensure the lists of keywords are exhaustive and up-to-date. We also use a monitoring tool provided by Gavagai that reads large streams (i.e., several millions of documents per day) of social media content, primarily weblogs and discussion forums. The monitoring tool performs a keyword search in the incoming data for occurrences of the keywords included in the markers that already have been described. For each marker, the monitoring tool outputs a list of Uniform Resource Identifiers[3] (URIs) and the frequency of occurrence of the marker in the document. These lists of URIs are then input to an analysis script where it is possible to define how many or which markers that have to be triggered in order for an URI to be shown as potentially interesting to the user of the system.

SOLUTIONS AND RECOMMENDATIONS

In our prototype implementation, we have collected data from a number of data sources for a few days. The data has been compared against a number of basic linguistic markers consisting of lists of keywords as described above. Each time a keyword is triggered for a particular URI, a counter is increased. It is important to highlight that in a real-world system, the keywords that are used needs to be developed further; the current keywords are just to illustrate the concept that is used in the system. For each linguistic marker we obtain a list of URIs that has triggered the particular marker, and a count of how many times the URI has triggered the marker during the time period.

Now, it must be realised that most of the URIs that hit a single linguistic marker will be completely unrelated to both violent extremism in general and specific attacks that are about to take place. Since we currently use a list of keywords consisting of terms that may occur in many contexts, the false alarm rate for a single keyword will be high. However, the idea is that by combining several such linguistic markers, the precision of the obtained results will increase.

To just give an example, for a time period of three days, we got 130 hits for URIs that contained keywords matching both violence (intent), and at least one of bomb (intent) or weapons (intent). Adding an extra filter to these results so that they also should contain a negative sentiment against the Jews, we ended up with a list consisting of only four URIs. This demonstrates how triangulation can be used to reduce the pool of 'risky' individuals or URIs. Taking a closer look at the hits, these originated from the website of a Neoconservative Right magazine, a Christian blog, and two anti-Jewish blogs. Probably none of these sites would have caused an analyst to take any further action due to their content (unless they were added to a list of websites of interest beforehand). As a first selection, this approach is obviously much faster. We only need to check a list of four websites or URIs manually compared to reading through all data from the collected sources, corresponding to an enormous amount of work.

Ethical Considerations

There are many ethical and privacy concerns that come with this kind of technologies. Some important questions that should be raised before implementing any kind of surveillance techniques are: What are the benefits of this kind of surveillance, and what is the potential harm? Who should be entitled to use this kind of techniques, and during what circumstances? Is the potential threat of violent extremism enough to warrant the use of these kinds of techniques?

First of all, it is important to think about what effect this kind of surveillance would have on citizens' privacy. As stated in Article 8 of the European Convention on Human Rights (ECHR), or more formally, the Convention for the Protection of Human Rights and Fundamental Freedoms, everyone has a right to a private life and there shall be no interference by a public authority with the exercise of this right (except such as is in accordance with the law and is necessary in a democratic society in the interests of national security, public safety, etc.).

For this reason, law enforcement agencies, security researchers, and any other actors involved in any kind of web surveillance has to balance the need for a secure society with a respect for online privacy, and make sure that this complies with laws and directives such as the EU data protection directive (or more officially Directive 95/46/EC on the protection of individuals with regard to the processing of personal data, and on the free movement of such data). Such directives obviously should be respected, but there are also additional ethical considerations that have to be made. Ultimately, if people start to censor themselves online due to the fear of being monitored by the authority or even private companies, important values of the society that we try to protect will be lost. For this reason, ethical and privacy concerns have to be considered, keeping the potential intrusion on people's privacy to an absolute minimum.

Basically, what our implemented prototype system does is that it processes publically available user generated content, and counts the number of occurrences of various terms. This is on a technical level not very different from what ordinary web spiders do when they index web pages for search engines. Few people would argue that web spiders and search engines pose a threat to online privacy. However, what mainly differs is the purpose. Search engines are intended to allow for general web searches while the purpose of our implemented system is to detect signs of radical violence, which may contain potentially sensitive information. Moreover, few would object against law enforcement officers using search engines manually to find suspicious websites; while probably more people would object against automating this endeavour in order to allow for continuous and large-scale applications of the same method.

While we are so used to search engines and manual search queries that we do not consider web spiders to be a threat against our online privacy (rather, we are more concerned about the search engines' use of tracking cookies for profiling purposes), automatic 'crawling' of crime- or terrorism-related content is something else that we are more uncomfortable with. Arguably, it is more of an intrusion on people's privacy to scan through their e-mails in order to sell targeted ads than to process publically available user generated content for any purpose. However, an important difference is that their customers in general have provided some kind of 'informed' consent.

In order to attempt to make minimal harm to online privacy, we have run our prototype system for just a short period of time. We have minimised the number of people who have access to the results (i.e., matching URIs), and limited ourselves to just look at the top-N matching results in our evaluation after triangulating several linguistic markers. Additionally, we have for ethical reasons chosen not to show any of the collected URIs to the readers and we are only presenting the results in a way to avoid re-identification of any URIs or the creators behind the user generated content. All the collected URIs where deleted after the preparation of this chapter.

Whether or not this kind of systems should be used operationally is more of a political and legislative issue than a scientific question, but in case such systems are used operationally, it is important to use various safeguards in order to protect against potential misuse. Examples of such safeguards would be to only provide authorised users access to the system, encryption of all collected data, and protected logs that would keep track of all operations and searches that the users of the system make. It could then be controlled so that the users of the system meet regulations for how such monitoring should be undertaken.

CONCLUSION

In this chapter, we have argued that the increasing use of websites and social media to spread terrorism propaganda and communicate with like-minded individuals, is both a challenge and an asset for intelligence analysts and other involved in counter-terrorism. There is a clear risk that this allows people who otherwise have no obvious connections to terrorist groups to be radicalised, but the digital communication also leave traces that potentially can be used by analysts to detect people who are about to commit violent extremism-related actions.

Psychologists have previously discovered a number of warning behaviours which often signal violent attacks on public figures, mass murders, and acts of lone wolf terrorism before they occur. The problem is that huge amounts of online textual data are generated each day, making it unfeasible (or even impossible) to manually read all available material. For this reason, we have made an attempt to implement a number of linguistic markers that might indicate that the writer shows signs of some of the warning behaviours described by Meloy et al. (2012). Our prototype system detects signs of linguistic markers automatically.

The potential advantages of such a system is that it would help intelligence analysts to focus on a smaller amount of user generated content of topical relevance for their work and thereby increase their efficiency, which in turn hopefully can lead to a more secure society. Our prototype system is a first step towards a tool that actually could be used by analysts in order to detect warning behaviours, but it also brings about ethical and privacy issues that have to be considered before putting such a system into use.

It is important to realise that the proposed system is not a way to replace the human analyst; this could never be the case for this kind of issues. Rather, we see it as a complementary way to manual approaches such as the excellent initiative by the U.K. Government (i.e., https://www.gov.uk/report-terrorism) where people can report illegal terrorism-related material they find online. Obviously, it is far from possible that all terrorist attacks can be discovered in advance using any natural language processing tool for social media analysis, since not all attackers will show warning behaviours that can be discovered on the Internet. However, there have been many cases where such warning behaviours have been identified after an attack have taken place – including recent cases such as the 2015 Charleston church shootings. Before the deed, the suspect posted photos and a manifesto on a white supremacist website. In such cases, this kind of tools could be very useful, given that a high enough classification performance can be achieved to detect such warning behaviours.

FUTURE RESEARCH DIRECTIONS

There are several directions for future work. Reducing the number of false positives and developing guidelines for how to handle false positives is one obvious direction. To reduce the number of false positives, the techniques used to detect the three types of linguistic markers described in this work needs to be refined. Detecting warning behaviours in written text is not a trivial problem and the methods and techniques that we have used in this work are promising, but there is a need for further development if this approach should be used in practice. To detect warning behaviour such as fixation, it is important to also consider the subject's changes in behaviour over time – both when it comes to perseveration and negative characterisation. Using an approach where time is a parameter is therefore a desirable way forward when detecting fixation.

Analysing written text to obtain knowledge about the psychological meaning is not something new. Tausczik and Pennebaker (2010) describe how the text analysis tool, Linguistic Inquiry and Word Count (LIWC) counts words in psychologically meaningful categories. LIWC uses a number of different categories and calculates to what degree people are using the different categories in written text. This approach has been evaluated and tested in a number of different studies such as the one described in Cohn, Mehl, and Pennebaker (2004), and Davison, Pennebaker, and Dickerson (2000). Adding a deeper psychological meaning to the analysis could be another way forward when it comes to detecting leakage and identification warning behaviours.

REFERENCES

Bjelopera, J. P. (2013). *American jihadist terrorism: Combating a complex threat. CRS Report for Congress*. Washington, DC: Congressional Research Service.

Brynielsson, J., Horndahl, A., Johansson, F., Kaati, L., Mårtenson, C., & Svenson, P. (2013). Harvesting and analysis of weak signals for detecting lone wolf terrorists. *Security Informatics*, *2*(11). doi:10.1186/2190-8532-2-11

Cohen, K., Johansson, F., Kaati, L., & Mork, J. C. (2014). Detecting linguistic markers for radical violence in social media. *Terrorism and Political Violence*, *26*(1), 246–256. doi:10.1080/09546553.2014.849948

Cohn, M. A., Mehl, M. R., & Pennebaker, J. W. (2004). Linguistic markers of psychological change surrounding September 11, 2001. *Psychological Science*, *15*(10), 687–693. doi:10.1111/j.0956-7976.2004.00741.x PMID:15447640

Davison, K. P., Pennebaker, J. W., & Dickerson, S. S. (2000). Who talks? The social psychology of illness support groups. *The American Psychologist*, *55*(2), 205–217. doi:10.1037/0003-066X.55.2.205 PMID:10717968

Elovici, Y., Kandel, A., Last, M., Shapira, B., & Zaafrany, O. (2004). Using data mining techniques for detecting terror-related activities on the web. *Journal of Information Warfare*, *3*(1), 17–29.

Europol. (2012). *TE-SAT 2012: European Union terrorism situation and trend report*. European Law Enforcement Agency.

Greenwald, G. (2013, July 31). XKeyscore: NSA tool collects 'nearly everything a user does on the internet'. *The Guardian*. Retrieved from http://www.theguardian.com/world/2013/jul/31/nsa-top-secret-program-online-data

Karlgren, J. (2006). New text - New conversations in the media landscape. *ERCIM News*. Retrieved from http://www.ercim.eu/publication/Ercim_News/enw66/karlgren_2.html

Last, M., Markov, A., & Kandel, A. (2006). Multi-lingual detection of terrorist content on the web. *Lecture Notes in Computer Science, 3917,* 16–30. doi:10.1007/11734628_3

Meloy, J. R. (2011). Approaching and attacking public figures: A contemporary analysis of communications and behaviour. In C. Chauvin (Ed.), *Threatening communications and behaviour: Perspectives on the pursuit of public figures* (pp. 75–101). Washington, DC: The National Academies Press.

Meloy, J. R., Hoffmann, J., Guldimann, A., & James, D. (2012). The role of warning behaviors in threat assessment: An exploration and suggested typology. *Behavioral Sciences & the Law, 30*(3), 256–279. doi:10.1002/bsl.999 PMID:22556034

Meloy, J. R., Hoffmann, J., Roshdi, K., & Guldimann, A. (2014). Some warning behaviors discriminate between school shooters and other students of concern. *Journal of Threat Assessment and Management, 1*(3), 203–211. doi:10.1037/tam0000020

Meloy, J. R., Mohandie, K., Knoll, J. L., & Hoffmann, J. (2015). The concept of identification in threat assessment. *Behavioral Sciences & the Law, 33*(2-3), 213–237. doi:10.1002/bsl.2166 PMID:25728417

Meloy, J. R., & O'Toole, M. E. (2011). The concept of leakage in threat assessment. *Behavioral Sciences & the Law, 29*(4), 513–527. doi:10.1002/bsl.986 PMID:21710573

Murphy, M. L. (2003). *Semantic relations and the lexicon - antonym, synonymy and other paradigms.* Cambridge, U.K.: Cambridge University Press. doi:10.1017/CBO9780511486494

Pang, B., Lee, L., & Vaithyanathan, S. (2002). Thumbs up? Sentiment classification using machine learning techniques. In *Proceedings of the Conference on Empirical Methods in Natural Language Processing (EMNLP).* Stroudsburg, PA: Association for Computational Linguistics.

Ravndal, J. A. (2013). Anders Behring Breivik's use of the Internet and social media. *Journal EXIT-Deutschland.* Retrieved from http://journals.sfu.ca/jed/index.php/jex/article/view/28

Sahlgren, M. (2006). *The word-space model: Using distributional analysis to represent syntagmatic and paradigmatic relations between words in high-dimensional vector spaces* (Doctoral dissertation). Department of Linguistics, Stockholm University, Sweden.

Schmid, G. (2001). *Report on the existence of a global system for the interception of private and commercial communications* (ECHELON Interception System, 2001/2098[INI]). European Parliament.

Tauszik, Y. R., & Pennebaker, J. W. (2010). The psychological meaning of words: LIWC and computerized text analysis methods. *Journal of Language and Social Psychology, 29*(1), 24–54. doi:10.1177/0261927X09351676

Torok, R. (2013). Developing an explanatory model for the process of online radicalisation and terrorism. *Security Informatics, 2*(6), 1–10.

Turney, P., & Pantel, P. (2010). From frequency to meaning: Vector space models of semantics. *Journal of Artificial Intelligence Research, 37*(1), 141–188.

Weimann, G. (2012). Lone wolves in cyberspace. *Journal of Terrorism Research, 3*(2). doi:10.15664/jtr.405

ENDNOTES

[1.] Horizon 2020 is the biggest European Union research and innovation programme ever with nearly €80 billion of funding available over seven years (2014 to 2020).

[2.] The INDECT project (Intelligent information system supporting observation, searching and detection for security of citizens in urban environment) is a research project, allowing new, advanced and innovative algorithms and methods aiming at detecting and counteracting threats and criminal activities, affecting citizens' safety. Please refer to http://www.indect-project.eu/ for more information.

[3.] The URI is a string of characters used to identify a name of a resource, such as a blog post.

Chapter 19
Internet Use and Violent Extremism:
A Cyber–VERA Risk Assessment Protocol

D. Elaine Pressman
Carleton University, Canada & International Centre for Counter-Terrorism (ICCT) – The Hague, The Netherlands

Cristina Ivan
Mihai Viteazul National Intelligence Academy, Romania

ABSTRACT

This chapter introduces a new approach to the risk assessment for violent extremism that is focused on cyber-related behaviour and content. The Violent Extremist Risk Assessment (VERA-2) protocol, used internationally, is augmented by an optional cyber-focused risk indicator protocol referred to as CYBERA. The risk indicators of CYBERA are elaborated and the application of CYBERA, conjointly with the VERA-2 risk assessment protocol, is described. The combined use of the two tools provides (1) a robust and cyber-focused risk assessment intended to provide early warning indicators of violent extremist action, (2) provides consistency and reliability in risk and threat assessments, (3) determines risk trajectories of individuals, and (4) assists intelligence and law enforcement analysts in their national security investigations. The tools are also relevant for use by psychologists, psychiatrists, communication analysts and provide relevant information that supports Terrorism Prevention Programs (TPP) and countering violent extremism (CVE) initiatives.

INTRODUCTION

The use of the Internet around the world is increasing. Internet use world-wide has grown from an estimated 2.03 billion users in 2010 to over 3 billion users in 2014 (Internet World Statistics, 2014). In some countries, the percentage of those accessing the Internet on wireless handheld devices has almost doubled in a scant two year period (Statistics Canada, 2013). The Internet serves as a platform for inter-

DOI: 10.4018/978-1-5225-0156-5.ch019

action between and among users, regardless of their physical locations around the world (Leiner et al., 2009) and regardless of their interests and intentions.

Cyber-expert Richard Clarke, who served as the White House Security Chief during the Clinton and George W. Bush administrations, has observed that terrorists use the Internet just like everybody else (as cited in Conway, 2006). Terrorist websites are proliferating and the use of the Internet by violent extremists is likewise increasing. The Internet offers anonymity, easy access, a lack of censorship, fast information sharing, dissemination of ideological propaganda, an inexpensive web presence and the distribution of terrorist training materials (Ogun, 2012). Ban-Ki-moon, the Secretary-General of the United Nations observed that the Internet is a prime example of how violent extremists and terrorists behave in a truly transnational way (United Nations Office on Drugs and Crime [UNODC], 2012). The United Nations is focused primarily on responses at the state level. Responses at the individual level are also essential. The individual focus is required to assess the relative risk posed by suspected or known agents and this can be accomplished with risk assessment protocols developed for national security applications.

Knowledge of the differential risk levels of potential violent extremists, returning foreign fighters and others identified as vulnerable to violent extremist actions is critical in the current volatile security context. The increasing numbers of individuals who are under some sort of surveillance and/or who may require closer monitoring is problematic for security forces with fixed resources. In order for national security personnel to keep pace with the increasing demand for monitoring of individuals, some prioritisation of these 'persons of interest' is necessary. Such prioritisation must be defensible and the decision process must be transparent in case of challenge. The current migrant situation in the Black Sea and Mediterranean regions, some of whom may represent national security risks, also calls for risk assessments. Risk clearance may become a pre-requisite demanded by European and other countries prior to resettlement.

Reliable risk judgments undertaken in a sound manner can assist in discriminating between individuals who are the target of radicalisation and recruitment from those who are disseminating terrorism related information or inciting violent extremism. Reliable risk judgments can assist in quantifying the different levels of risk that individuals may represent for a jurisdiction. These assessments are based on evidence which is available. This evidence will, in many cases, include information obtained from the subject's Internet use.

Reliable risk assessment approaches offer a framework in which one can analyse risk and determine the specific elements and indicators most pertinent to individuals. Reliable assessments can identify changing risk trajectories of individuals using controlled and repeated measures. These assessments can be supported by data acquired from Internet content, other observed behaviours, reports and background information. The prioritisation of persons identified for national security related surveillance is achievable and facilitated by the application of well-structured risk assessment protocols specific to violent extremism. The addition of detailed cyber-behavioural indicators or evidence will make such approaches more robust and relevant for the current cyber-age.

RISK ASSESSMENT, CYBER ELEMENTS AND VIOLENT EXTREMISM

Cyber information often provides the most accessible empirical evidence on individuals under surveillance. The FBI is reported to be ramping up the monitoring of Twitter and they have cited the use of suspects' tweets in several recent terrorism cases (Reilly, 2015). In one case, Bilal Abood, age 37, was arrested in Texas in part due to his Twitter activity. He had used his Twitter account to 'pledge obedience' to Abu Bakr al-Baghdadi. Although Abood originally denied that he had made the pledge of allegiance to al-Baghdadi and the Islamic State in Iraq and Syria (ISIS), the particular post which identified this undertaking was 're-tweeted by others' (United States of America v. Bilal Abood, 2015). In a second case, a 17-year-old honours high school student from the State of Virginia, Ali Shukri Amin entered a guilty plea on June 11, 2015 for knowingly conspiring and providing material support and resources to ISIS. He had created a Twitter account with over 4,000 followers. In over 7,000 tweets, evidence was obtained to document that he was supporting ISIS and providing advice on how to use 'bitcoin' to make anonymous and untraceable contributions to ISIS (U.S. Department of Justice, 2015). Amin is now subject to up to 15 years in prison for this cyber activity when he is sentenced. This activity was undertaken from his home in a quiet comfortable suburban neighbourhood outside of Washington D.C. (United States of America v. Ali Shukri Amin, 2015).

Data on the views, beliefs, attitudes, grievances, intentions and ideology of identifiable individuals can be captured from the Internet. This evidence is important for risk judgments based on a risk analysis. Such first person views and intentions are difficult to obtain except via legally sanctioned placement of audio probes, human intelligence sources, unsolicited first-hand reports and the monitoring of cyber activity.

It is often the Internet activity that provides important opportunities for law enforcement and intelligence agencies to gather insightful and incriminating information (UNODC, 2012). This information also serves as valuable data and behavioural evidence appropriate for individual risk assessment protocols. Due to the acknowledged importance of cyber elements for determining risk in potential violent extremists, these elements should be enhanced in currently available risk assessment tools. Wherever possible, explicit new cyber-focused approaches should be developed. In recruitment and radicalisation initiatives by terrorism promoters, the Internet is a primary source.

This chapter includes a description of the indicators and methodology of a new cyber risk analysis tool for violent extremism. The cyber-indicators in this new protocol, referred to as CYBERA can be integrated into the VERA-2 (Pressman & Flockton, 2012) risk assessment protocol for violent extremists. The tool can also be used independently with cyber-content.

The VERA-2 risk assessment approach is a validated and internationally used protocol that assists national security investigations. The approach includes a set of relevant indicators that are comprehensive in terms of the risk for violent extremism. This includes attitudes, beliefs, grievances, ideology, worldviews, and motivational elements that are drivers of violent extremist action, intention, capacity, networks, personal needs and criminal background. Risk mitigating elements referred to as 'protective indicators' are also included. The protocol assists analysts to make sound professional judgments of overall risk. This is accomplished via a systematic and reliable analytical approach. A comprehensive set of indicators that relates to violent extremism is rated independently for severity. All these ratings of indicators are considered together, with a weighting of their relative importance, to arrive at an overall risk judgment. The final estimation of risk together with the ratings on each of the indicators provides valuable differential information on the individual at a defined point in time. As radicalisation to violence is dynamic, it is useful to be able to compare such results on an indicator by indicator basis as well as overall risk with assessments at successive time points.

The new cyber-analysis approach developed and reported upon in this chapter will augment the current cyber content that is included in the VERA-2 tool (Pressman & Flockton, 2012). While all the cyber evidence obtained can be documented and considered in making VERA-2 judgments, the CYBERA will provide a more analytical guide for assessors. CYBERA will define more explicitly the different elements of cyber activity related to violent extremism and thus assist the analyst in this sphere.

The term CYBERA is a short form for CYBER-VERA. The name of the tool reflects the relationship between this new cyber risk assessment approach and the parent VERA-2 risk assessment protocol. The CYBERA used in concert with the VERA-2 approach will enhance the differential analysis on cyber-elements related to the risk of violent extremism. The CYBERA approach can also be used as a stand-alone addendum to other protocols in use by national security analysts.

RISK ASSESSMENT FOR VIOLENT EXTREMISM

Individual risk assessments have traditionally been related to mental health issues (Borum, 2000; Borum, Bartel, & Forth, 2006; Hare, 2003; Webster, Douglas, Eaves, & Hart, 1997) and were developed and used, in part, as psychological-diagnostic tools. They were also related to the need to predict the risk of recidivism in violent offenders. Individual risk assessment approaches also served to provide information which assisted decisions related to the security level required for the placement of violent offenders in correctional institutions.

Risk assessments provide information helpful for program planning, for rehabilitation initiatives, and for progression decisions which relate to inmate movement to lower or higher levels of security during incarceration. Risk assessments also contribute information that is pertinent to early release decisions of violent extremist offenders and others (Pressman, 2009; Pressman & Flockton, 2012).

Violent extremism focused risk assessments, such as the VERA-2, are not mental health assessments. They are national security related risk assessments. As such, they are intended to be used by non-mental health professionals such as intelligence and law enforcement personnel and/or other professionals charged by governments with making decisions pertaining to the risk of identified individuals for violent extremism actions. They may also be used by mental health professionals such as psychologists and psychiatrists who are charged with undertaking risk assessments for this population. Although violent extremist offences are not inherently mental health related, when there are such mental health disorders present, these problems should be identified and appropriate referrals made.

The VERA-2 and the CYBERA, which will be discussed in more detail later in this chapter, use a rigorous methodology comparable to other behavioural science-based risk assessment approaches. This approach, referred to as the structured professional judgment method (SPJ) has been identified as a scientific judgment method by some behavioural scientists (Webster et al., 1997) and as the most promising of available approaches for individual risk assessment of violent extremists (Monahan, 2012). Although some researchers may argue that there is always a subjective element in human judgments (McGilloway, Ghosh, & Bhui, 2015), the SPJ controls for such subjectivity in its systematic, comprehensive and transparent set of indicators and by a standardised rigor in usage that is supported by an intensive training program. This has contributed to the acceptance of the SPJ protocol by mental health professionals as well as by law enforcement and national security analysts. Violent extremism risk assessment protocols are also useful for identifying the most salient countering violent extremism (CVE) initiatives. The results obtained from risk assessments assist in identifying individual objectives and provide information pertinent to designing intervention programs sensitive to the needs of each vulnerable individual involved. Cyber-behavioural indicators will be relevant for all these applications.

There have been significant developments in risk assessment methods and validity in the past several decades (Hart & Logan, 2011; Monahan, 1981; Monahan & Stedman, 1994; Monahan et al., 2001; Webster et al., 1997; Webster, Douglas, Eaves, & Hart, 2001). These developments were integrated into the national security related risk assessment approaches identified above including the VERA (Pressman, 2009) and the VERA-2 protocols (Pressman & Flockton, 2012; Pressman & Flockton, 2014). The necessity for an individual risk assessment protocol for violent extremism that differs from general violence risk assessment in substance and objectives, was proposed less than a decade ago (Pressman, 2009). Although somewhat controversial at the time, the need for distinctive indicators relevant to violent extremists is now well accepted (Dean, 2014).

The VERA-2, which will be discussed in this chapter together with the cyber-focused risk assessment approach, CYBERA are examples of a new generation of tools. The VERA-2 protocol is in use today by national police forces, national intelligence agencies, the criminal justice system, and/or in prisons in Europe, North America, Asia and/or the Pacific region. Such tools are continuing to be developed. Some of these tools are protected by government agencies using them for analysis and are not available for review. Others, although known to be in use, are not detailed in the open-source material. In some cases, the new developments have been published (Dean, 2014; Pressman, 2009; Pressman & Flockton, 2012; Pressman & Flockton, 2014).

The first published version of a risk assessment approach for violent extremists was the VERA consultative risk assessment tool (Pressman, 2009). The VERA was revised as the VERA-2 following empirical experience by experts in the prison and national security sectors. Empirical feedback was also received from risk assessment experts in North America, Australia, Europe and Asia and contributed to the revision of the VERA as the VERA-2. The tool has been used with positive results over the past eight years. These applications have been in national security analysis, law enforcement agencies, in the criminal justice system, the prison setting and in community engagement programs with individuals convicted of or suspected of violent extremism offences. Although there are cyber-related indicators in the VERA and the VERA-2, in the current cyber rich environment, it has been deemed to be of analytical benefit to strengthen and expand the cyber-element of this tool.

The VERA has been demonstrated to have deductive, construct and face validity as well as having been shown to be a reliable approach with content validity by independent researchers (Beardsley & Beech, 2013). The VERA was also shown to be relevant for the spectrum of violent extremist ideologies as compared to being pertinent to only one type of violent extremism (Beardsley & Beech, 2013). This is valuable as it prevents the tool from being subject to the criticism of particular ideological, political or religious bias. In the current international cyber age, new cyber focused tools to assist the risk analysis and early warning of violent extremists and terrorists are required. This is the next important stage of development and the focus of this chapter.

RISK ASSESSMENT OBJECTIVES AND CYBER-LANGUAGE ANALYSIS

Two objectives of individual risk assessments have been identified. The first objective is to determine or estimate the likelihood that an individual will engage in violent action. The second objective is to identify, by means of a differential analysis, which approaches and risk elements are likely to offer the greatest opportunities to counter the risk (Borum, Fein, Vossekuil, & Berglund, 1999).

For an accurate risk assessment, the risk indicators used in tools must be relevant to the nature and characteristics of the type of violence being analysed. If the risk indicators for one type of violence are applied to a different type of violence for which dissimilar indicators are required, the risk assessment will likely be misleading and inaccurate (Maghan & Kelly, 1989; Pressman, 2009). In fact, general violence risk assessment tools have been demonstrated to be inappropriate and invalid for the population of violent extremists (Pressman & Flockton, 2012).

It is known that most violent extremists are not driven to act by mental illness, alcohol or drug addiction, psychopathy or other behavioural disorders. This is more often the case for general violent actors rather than violent extremists. Furthermore, individuals engaged in terrorist actions do not habitually demonstrate histories that include poor upbringing, educational disadvantage, childhood abuse, and early violent criminal behaviours. These facts supported the need for specialised risk assessment tools for violent extremists (Monahan, 2012; Pressman, 2009). Such risk assessment tools should contain pertinent indicators regarding the political, social or other ideological motivations of these essentially 'normal' individuals (Maghan & Kelly, 1989; Monahan, 2012; Post, 2007). Although violent extremists often hold a different worldview and may embrace a value system that supports engagement in horrific types of violence, more often than not, they are cognitively intact and functionally normal individuals (Crenshaw, 1981; Crenshaw, 2000; Post 2007). The risk assessment tools for this population must reflect this status. Cyber activity evidence is, as noted earlier, of increasing prevalence in terrorists and violent extremists. This activity could also benefit from increased delineation in risk assessment tools.

Although all cyber-evidence that is obtained can be allocated to the relevant risk elements in the VERA-2 assessment tool, a dedicated cyber risk assessment tool would provide a more discerning and insightful analysis. Cyber-behavioural data often contains person-specific language behaviour. This information can be analysed in semantic context and by other linguistic elements to provide a more specific evidence-base for personal language and imagery use.

Language and communication is fundamental to human interaction (Vygotsky, 1962, 2012). Cyber activity is a vehicle that facilitates this human interaction over time and space. The distinctive features of language use provide evidence of intention, capacity, and potential harm intended. In addition, communication is known to facilitate and promote the process of radicalisation to violence (Silber & Bhatt, 2007). Language and concept-based imagery are used to incite, convince and coerce, and language use mirrors the thoughts of the sender (Piaget, 1926, 2002). The receiver of messages may initially differ in the original denotation of words, but such reference points can be and are shaped by linguistic and visual images received. In this way, new denotations and associations are created for words and images and this can support the process of radicalisation to violence. It is this relationship between thought and language that is fundamental to future behaviour (Piaget, 1926, 2002). Messages can be amplified when the receiver becomes the message sender. Tracking of such language and imagery via cyber-communication requires a sensitive and differential analysis but can be pivotal to the assessment of risk of violent extremism.

It is also this language behaviour, identifiable from probes, human intelligence, and via the Internet, that provides the evidence of the values, attitudes, beliefs, ideological views, political and social goals, grievances, perceived injustices, and the moral compass of the user. Language can document future goals, encourage comradeship through joint action and create associations. Capturing cyber communication content can illustrate the nature of violent action planned, the tactics contemplated, strategic goals and other plans. The motivations and networks of individuals involved can be identified. In fact, cyber-language evidence functions as a megaphone of future intention and the concomitant relationship to thought (Vygotsky, 2012).

Such cyber-language evidence can be rated in terms of transparent indicators with criterion-referenced risk ratings for each indicator. A determination of relative risk per indicator based on ratings is consistent with the methodology of other so-called SPJ risk assessment tools. Cyber captured language, imagery and other behaviours provide first person evidence to assist in the determination of the ultimate risk formulation.

DEFINING AND DIFFERENTIATING RISK AND THREAT

Risk is ubiquitous. It has been described as only partially understood and not able to be predicted with certainty (Boer, Hart, Kropp, & Webster, 1997). Even tools that have claimed to have statistical predictive validity have been questioned in terms of their ability to generate correct predictions. This is despite documented research claims.

In the case of risk assessment for suspected violent extremists, the presence of uncertainty in the task of prediction is acknowledged. The objective of risk assessments for this population is the generation of defensible 'best estimates' of the likelihood of future violent action. These estimates are based on a structured methodology that evaluates the presence and level of a comprehensive list of salient indicators. The result is an early warning (risk level judgment) based on an empirical evidence-base. This is an improvement over assumptions based on general historical indicators rather than individual characteristics, unstructured assessments, or estimates based on hypothetical scenarios for forecasting.

The structured and systematic nature of the assessment is intended to overcome analyst bias as much as possible. The consideration of all potential salient indicators provides an overview of all the information that is known, and also all the information pertinent to indicators that is unknown. The structured method illustrates the difference between assumptions, intuitive reasoning and evidence. The SPJ methodology has been identified as the best of the available options for the risk assessment of violent extremists (Monahan, 2012).

A commonly held definition of risk is the exposure to danger due to injury, damage or loss, or other adverse or unwelcome circumstance. This definition is often applied to organisations, agencies, locations, identifiable groups or individuals exposed to danger of injury or damage or adverse circumstance. This context of risk pertains to the target that is exposed to the danger (Borum et al., 1999). In this context, the 'exposure to the danger' is the 'object' of the damage. Risk in this context is the probability of an attack or injury combined with the harm or severity of the loss expected to occur. In this case, *Risk = Probability (of injury or damage) × severity of the loss (harm) or R = p × h* (United States Department of Defense, 2006; Wall, 2011).

Risk assessments for individuals estimate the likelihood of an identifiable person or actor generating the harm, rather than being the object of the harm. In this case, it is the individual rather than the target that is the focus of the assessment. Individual risk assessments are those used in the criminal justice system, in mental health facilities, in the formal prison context and in detention facilities. These assessments are appropriate for intelligence and national security applications, CVE initiatives and other applications related to identifying the specific vulnerabilities of an individual to act with violence to support extremist (ideological) goals. In this case *Risk = Probability of the individual acting to cause the injury × the severity of the harm or loss*. The individual under investigation or suspicion is the focus of risk assessment for violent extremism.

There was pessimism several decades ago as to the feasibility of this type of risk assessment. Supportable prediction of individual acts of violence is a complex task and burdened with uncertainty (Webster et al., 1997). Interest was revived following important developments in methodology in the latter part of the twentieth century (Monahan, 1981). Improved methods of predicting and estimating dangerousness were developed.

There are different types of risk assessment approaches currently available (Bonta, Law, & Hanson, 1998; Hanson, 2005; Ogloff, 2009). The method that has been identified as the most useful and relevant for assessing the risk of violent extremism is the SPJ approach (Monahan, 2012; Pressman, 2009). This is a systematic approach described as a composite of empirical knowledge and professional judgment (Hart & Logan, 2011). Although the description of SPJ as an empirical and scientific method has been challenged by some in terms of its objectivity (McGilloway et al., 2015), this approach controls for human bias with the structure and criterion definitions provided and imposed them on the users.

The SPJ approach differs from other methods such as actuarial models or unstructured approaches. Actuarial models use a limited number of variables and binary type evaluations which are inappropriate for the complexity of the risk indicators associated with violent extremism. SPJ is more accurate and reliable in comparison to less structured analytical approaches and in research studies, it has been found to demonstrate a level of accuracy that exceeds unstructured approaches (Ogloff & Davis, 2005). It is more reliable than the use of intuition or scenarios as noted earlier. This does not imply that users would not demonstrate some bias in their assessments but that the method includes controls designed to minimise any such partiality.

Despite the use of SPJ as best practice, there is no certainty claimed in the prediction of violent extremist actions of individuals. The objective of risk assessments for violent extremists with tools such as the VERA-2 is a reasoned and defensible estimate of risk, based on early warnings indicators. The early warnings permit preventive or disruptive actions by law enforcement.

Risk assessments for violent extremism should be undertaken by persons lawfully charged with making such risk judgments. This further distinguishes individual risk assessment for violent extremism from other psychological and mental health based risk assessment approaches. In national security assessments, analysts are mandated to provide such judgments not on the basis of professional qualifications but on the basis of their official designated status and job requirements. They are charged with making such decisions with or without a controlled and systematic protocol. The VERA-2 and the CYBERA serve to support such analysts in making reliable and sound judgments.

Individuals who present a risk for violent extremist action also represent a potential threat. This threat may be substantial if the intention is to cause catastrophic loss of life. The term 'threat' is often confused with 'risk'. Threat is distinct albeit often associated with risk.

Threat assessments, often undertaken by law enforcement analysts, are defined as the function of an enemy's 'capability' and 'intent'. This is contrasted with risk which is a function of 'probability of action' and 'severity of the harm/loss'. Threat is often used in the context of conducting attacks but individuals can also represent a threat. Risk and threat often co-exist in the case of individuals suspected of being violent extremists and terrorists.

As noted above, individuals demonstrate 'risk' related to their likelihood of action and the harm they intend to inflict (*risk = probability of danger × severity of the harm*). They represent a 'threat' based on the function of their capacity and intention to inflict harm (*threat = capacity × intention*). Risk assessment tools for violent extremism, such as the VERA-2, include indicators related to both threat and risk. For consistency, the VERA-2 is labelled as a risk assessment tool. The users should, however, recognise that it is able to provide information pertaining to both the risk and threat presented by an individual. Similarly, the CYBERA tool will identify elements of both risk and threat. The information obtained from Internet surveillance activity can provide information pertinent to the capacity of the actor, the intention, and the propensity of the individual to act and to generate harm. This is in addition to the evidence pertinent to risk.

Predictive analytics are being explored to assess the risk of violent extremists. Large data sets are generally more useful to identify trends and mass movements rather than for individual risk assessments. No definitive mathematical algorithms have been shown to be particularly sensitive for performing individual risk assessments. There are some new promising developments (Dean, 2014; McGilloway et al., 2015) and a Bayesian mathematical approach is currently being investigated to further enhance the VERA-2. This entails the application of a Bayesian statistically sound framework for quantitative analysis (Barbieri & Pressman, 2015). Computer assisted approaches may provide the most likely applicable future developments. At present, however, human judgment, together with weightings of the indicators in terms of their importance and significance remains the 'best practice' approach (Monahan, 2012). The inclusion of increased numbers of relevant cyber indicators to capture the cyber evidence in a more analytical manner will provide enhanced good practices.

CYBER-ACTIVITY AND THE CYBERA TOOL FOR RISK ASSESSMENT

Violent extremists use the Internet for numerous purposes. These uses include indoctrination and dissemination of propaganda, recruitment, publicity, networking, planning-coordinating attacks, psychological warfare, and fundraising (Conway, 2006; Weimann, 2004). Knowledge about the functioning, activities and even targets of terrorist organisations can be derived from websites, chat rooms and other Internet communications (UNODC, 2012). A comprehensive list of the salient cyber-behaviours that provides the evidence of risk for violent extremism is possible to catalogue. These indicators can be structured into a cyber risk assessment tool.

Such an inventory was created and integrated into a framework using sectors consistent with the SPJ method. The list of indicators appears in Table 1. The approach is based on the VERA-2 risk indicators (see Table 2). Although all cyber-evidence is able to be integrated into the VERA-2 protocol, a cyber-specific tool, such as the CYBERA, provides a delineation of Internet activity and a structure for the analysis of linguistic and imagery elements. The explicit indicators identified in Table 1 lead the analyst through the significant elements of cyber risk-related behaviour.

The CYBERA tool thus provides regulation and control for the analyst. The approach is empirically grounded, flexible and practical. The CYBERA protocol uses a framework and methodology consistent with the SPJ format. It also follows the approach of other violence risk assessment tools (Borum et al., 2006; Webster et al., 1997), while using specific and relevant indicators. At this stage of development, the CYBERA should be considered a consultative tool although the indicators are supported by operational experts with empirical experience in the area of radicalisation, violent extremism, national security and cyber analysis.

Administration of the CYBERA risk assessment tool requires an evaluation for each of the identified indicators and also an overall assessment of risk levels for the individual being analysed. Each of the indicators is rated based on the cyber evidence obtained. The ratings are provided at the low, moderate or high level. A low level rating is used when the indicator is not present. A moderate rating applies if

Table 1. CYBERA indicators for risk-threat assessment of violent extremism

	CYBER-VERA (CYBERA) Indicator Items	Low	Moderate	High
	IMAGERY			
1	Uses graphic representations, symbols/logos of terrorist groups, steganography			
2	Organises site/page, rubrics to glorify violence, promote aggression, rigid worldview			
3	Uses musical background to incite hatred, recruitment to violent action			
4	Frequently changes profile and cover photos – inconsistent identity			
	SEMANTIC CONTENT			
5	Personal, terrorist narrative to promote extremist views, aggression, grievances			
6	Uses multiple/alternative narratives related to identity			
7	Uses idealised content about own community, vilifies others, dehumanisation			
8	Uses language to display extremist views, allegiance to terrorist group, narrative			
	BELIEFS, ATTITUDES, INTENTION			
9	Commitment to ideology justifying violence			
10	Perceived victim of injustice, grievances for collective group or individual			
11	Rejection of democratic society and values			
12	Adherence to conspiracy theories about the affiliated ethnic/religious group			
13	Moral emotions: hate, anger, frustration, persecution, and/or alienation			
14	Identity conflict, rejection of national collective identity			
15	Lack of understanding, tolerance outside own group			
16	Expresses intention to act violently, incites violence			
17	Expresses willingness to die for cause, achieve martyrdom			
18	Evidence planning, preparing for violent action			
	VIRTUAL SOCIAL NETWORK CONTEXT			
19	Is affiliated with an online group/social media promoting terrorist violence			
20	Repetitively accesses posts blogs, extremist forums, terrorist information, know-how			
21	Establishes friendship bonds, networks other violent extremists online			
22	Susceptible to influence, authority, indoctrination			
	INDIVIDUAL ONLINE ACTIVITY RELATED TO CAPACITY			
23	Has paramilitary, explosives training or information on explosives-bomb making			
24	Uses multiple e-mail addresses, names to obscure identity			
	LEADERSHIP, ORGANISATIONAL SKILLS			
25	Subject has large following, network, significant role as leader online			
	ADDITIONAL DESCRIPTIVE ELEMENTS (NOT RATED)			
	Circle most frequent time use of online activity (day, evening, overnight)			
	CYBER Risk Judgment (Based on information available)	**L**	**M**	**H**

the indicator is present but is infrequent, inconsistent or not considered to be substantive. A high level rating applies when the indicator is noted to be present at a significant level.

Details on specific ratings are available to trained users. All evidence must be provided for each of the indicators. The list of indicators in Table 1 is a summary document. It does not represent the expanded

Table 2. VERA-2 indicators (Pressman & Flockton, 2012)

		VERA-2 Indicator Items	Low	Moderate	High
BA.		**BELIEFS & ATTITUDES**			
BA.1		Commitment to ideology justifying violence			
BA.2		Perceived Victim of injustice and grievances			
BA.3		Dehumanisation/demonization of identified targets of injustice			
BA.4		Rejection of democratic society and values			
BA.5		Feelings of hate, frustration, persecution, alienation			
BA.6		Hostility to national collective identity			
BA.7		Lack of empathy, understanding outside own group			
CI.		**CONTEXT & INTENT**			
CI.1		Seeker, consumer, developer of violent extremist materials			
CI.2		Identification of target (person, place, group) for attack			
CI.3		Personal contact with violent extremists			
CI.4		Anger and the Expressed intent to act violently			
CI.5		Willingness to die for cause			
CI.6		Expressed intent to plan, prepare violent action			
CI.7		Susceptible to influence, authority, indoctrination			
HC.		**HISTORY & CAPABILITY**			
HC.1		Early exposure to pro-violence militant ideology			
HC.2		Network (family, friends) involved in violent action			
HC.3		Prior criminal history of violence			
HC.4		Tactical, paramilitary, explosives training			
HC.5		Extremist ideological training			
HC.6		Access to funds, resources, organisational skills			
CM.		**COMMITMENT & MOTIVATION**			
CM.1		Glorification of violent action			
CM.2		Driven by criminal opportunism			
CM.3		Commitment to group, group ideology			
CM.4		Driven by moral imperative, moral superiority			
CM.5		Driven by excitement, adventure			
P.		**PROTECTIVE ITEMS** **Note rating differences for protective items: high rating = more mitigation and less risk**			
P.1		Re-interpretation of ideology less rigid, absolute			
P.2		Rejection of violence to obtain goals			
P.3		Change of vision of enemy			
P.4		Involvement with non-violent, de-radicalisation, offence related programs			
P.5		Community support for non-violence			
P.6		Family support for non-violence			
		Additional Indicators or comments			
SPJ		**FINAL JUDGMENT**	Low	Moderate	High

working format for assessment. If information for an indicator is not available, the item is not rated and the cell is left blank. An explanation is provided for the empty cell on the worksheet provided to users. Computerised reporting to facilitate documentation can be generated. This facilitates report writing, risk formulations, the retrieval of information, and the rapid comparison of evidence over time.

All information, including that which may be available from surveillance, reports and background information, can be structured into the VERA-2 indicators. The case below illustrates how information obtained from Internet surveillance can be captured and restructured into the CYBERA framework and the VERA-2 protocol.

CASE ILLUSTRATION

United States of America v. Emerson Winfield Begolly

On July 16, 2013, the FBI released a sentencing report and information on Emerson Winfield Begolly, 24, of New Bethlehem, Pennsylvania (FBI, 2013). Begolly was sentenced to 102 months in prison in Pittsburgh, Pennsylvania for soliciting others to engage in acts of terrorism within the United States and for using a firearm during and in relation to an assault on FBI agents. He was also sentenced to serve five years of supervised release. Begolly pleaded guilty on August 9, 2011, to charges filed in the Eastern District of Virginia and the Western District of Pennsylvania (United States of America v. Emerson Winfield Begolly, 2013).

Begolly had used the Internet to encourage like-minded radical jihadists to commit atrocities and murder according to the statement of the U.S. Attorney (United States of America v Emerson Winfield Begolly, 2013), and that a mass tragedy was prevented through the use of cyber-investigations that were court sanctioned to monitor Begolly's Internet activity. Begolly solicited others to engage in acts of terrorism and used the Internet to endanger lives. The Begolly case is an illustration that online-inspired terrorism can occur anywhere, including quiet rural Pennsylvania.

The following information obtained on Begolly is pertinent to CYBERA indicators. The indicators that apply to CYBERA (and/or the VERA-2) are identified in italics after the detailed case information.

- Begolly was an active administrator on the Ansar al Mujahideen English Forum (AMEF). AMEF is an internationally used Islamist extremist Internet forum. (network association; ideological commitment to violent action; justification for the use of violence; grievances; information relevant to ideological goals; tactics supported; ideological motivation)
- Begolly had previously been a participant in the website but later became a moderator and leader of the radical forum on the Internet. (information on change in the status of the subject supports an increased risk trajectory)
- Begolly used the pseudonym of Abu Nancy. (multiple use of names to obscure identity)
- He was also known under the alias of 'Asadullah Alshishani'. (multiple names; obscuring identity)
- He repeatedly solicited jihadists on the Internet to act violently. (intention, objectives, plans, contacts, associations with other extremists)

- Begolly promoted and encouraged and solicited others on the Internet to use firearms, explosives, and propane tanks against targets. (capacity, intention, concrete plans)
- He identified specific targets including: police stations, post offices, Jewish schools and day-care centres, military facilities, train lines, bridges, cell phone towers, and a water plant. (specificity of targets; alienation from society, rejection of pluralistic society, intolerance of other faiths)
- In the summer of 2010, Begolly urged jihadists on the AMEF to 'write their legacy in blood'. (planning, encouraging violent action)
- On the Internet, Begolly promised others a special place in the afterlife for violent action in the name of Allah. (ideological motivation, glorification of action; commitment, evidence of beliefs, values)
- Following the reported shootings in Northern Virginia at the Pentagon and the Marine Corps Museum in October 2010, Begolly posted a comment online that praised the shooting. (attitudes, values, rejection of societal values, alienation)
- Begolly attempted to share responsibility for the attack and developed anti-democratic propaganda stating that 'he hoped the shooter had followed his previous postings encouraging similar acts of violence'. (rejection of democratic values)
- On December 28, 2010, Begolly further solicited his AMEF audience to violence by posting a manual on how to manufacture a bomb. (capacity, intention, planning)
- He disseminated videos on the Internet with instructions for making explosive devices with the intention of having readers perform acts of terrorism. (intention and capacity)
- The forum provided an opportunity for Begolly to express his affinity for radical views. (ideological and world view, grievances, justification for use of violence, perceived injustices)
- Begolly, while expressing his own views, encouraged other members of his faith to engage in terrorist acts within the United States (location, rejection of the law, values of the society)
- Over a period of nine months, Begolly posted on repeated occasions lengthy messages in which he extensively discussed the need for violence. (repeated Internet use, activity level, engagement level)
- His propaganda included dissemination of videos with instructions for making explosive devices to perform acts of terrorism. (capacity, intention, planning)
- Begolly's words were used to incite violence. He posted the following: "Peaceful protests do not work. The Kuffara see war as solution to their problems, so we must see war as the solution to ours. No peace, but bullets, bombs, and martyrdom operations". (willingness to be a martyr for the cause)
- He also posted links to an online document entitled 'The Explosives Course', which was made available for download. The 101-page document authored by 'The Martyred Sheik Professor Abu Khabbab al Misri' (as referred to by Begolly) contains detailed instructions on setting up a laboratory with basic chemistry components for the manufacture of explosives. A note was added that those downloading the content should be careful to use anonymity software for their own protection. (capacity building, networking with other extremists and leadership role in promoting action, deception)
- On January 4, 2011, FBI agents were assaulted by Begolly as they attempted to prevent him from reaching a loaded 9mm semi-automatic handgun, which he had concealed on his body. (willingness to be a martyr, engage in violence)

- While violently struggling with the agents, Begolly bit the agents on their fingers in an attempt to free himself to reach his firearm. His actions are consistent with a posting in which he urged his audience not to be taken alive by law enforcement, to always carry a loaded firearm, and to aggressively resist any law enforcement encounter including biting fingers if necessary. (willingness to die for the cause and martyrdom)

Begolly was 22 years old when arrested in 2011 and was sentenced in July 2013. The Sentencing Memorandum included, as key evidence, part of the propaganda that Begolly had posted on the Internet forum (United States of America v. Emerson Begolly Sentencing Memorandum, 2013). Begolly was charged with unlawful and purposeful distribution of information over the Internet related to the manufacture and distribution of explosive materials, use of weapons of mass destruction, and solicitation to commit bombings of places for public use, government buildings and public transportation systems. On August 9, 2011, Begolly had entered a guilty plea to solicitation to commit terrorist acts.

The evidence in the case illustration above is able to be re-structured into the indicators and documented on worksheets used for CYBERA assessment. The form as seen in Table 1 is the summary indicator sheet. Specific definitions for the ratings are provided for the actual assessment. These ratings are standardised. Training is used to calibrate the ratings made by users. This calibration promotes consistency and supports reliability of the tool application on repeated measures. Such repeated measures can identify risk trajectories. For example, Begolly was initially a participant rather than a moderator of the extremist website. His rhetoric change and status change would illustrate an increase on that appropriate indicator in 'risk'.

The evidence in the case illustration provided for Begolly can similarly be re-structured in terms of the pertinent indicators on the VERA-2 (see table 2 for the VERA-2 risk indicators). Information would be available for beliefs and attitudes, ideology, justification for the use of violence, grievances, worldview, associations, networks, intention, planning, capacity, and motivational elements among others based on the cyber–activity. No protective indicators were noted in the evidence-base of the case illustration and would be documented as such.

BENEFITS AND CAVEATS OF STRUCTURED PROFESSIONAL JUDGMENT CYBER-BASED RISK ASSESSMENT (CYBERA AND VERA-2)

There are benefits to the use of the CYBERA and VERA-2 risk protocols for the assessment of Internet use that is purposeful and intended to encourage and/or provide support for violent extremism. These tools are relevant and meet the growing need for cyber-relevant risk assessment tools. The CYBERA approach, like the VERA-2 uses best practice methods for violent extremism related risk assessments. Both tools use a systematic, structured and comprehensive method. Although threat assessments are not the focus of this chapter, both the VERA-2 and the CYBERA include elements that will provide insight and information related to threat assessment as well as risk.

The CYBERA protocol is currently in limited use in an expanded format. The current format is reduced in number of indicators following empirical feedback and to provide more functionality. The VERA-2 has been in use in North America, Europe, Australia and Asia over the past half-decade. The documented benefit to analysts has resulted in additional training of new analysts in national police agencies, national intelligence services, community program staff, and other professionals.

The VERA-2 and the CYBERA as well as other available tools for this population are not infallible nor are they absolute in scientific objectivity. Some subjectivity in judgment may result from an analyst's interpretation of the evidence. This is controlled as much as possible by the required documentation by the assessor of the specific evidence pertinent to and used to justify each of the indicator ratings. The overall risk assessment is based on this objective evidence-based information. The structured and rigorous approach is intended to further limit subjectivity and bias in analysis. The criterion-based definitions further enhance the objectivity and reliability. The goal of the VERA-2 and the CYBERA protocols is to generate a defensible and robust risk decision.

The independent research undertaken on the VERA protocol has documented the reliability and validity of the VERA approach (Beardsley & Beech, 2013), as well as its broad application. This has further enhanced confidence in the methods discussed.

The transparency in the analyses can prove useful in planning interventions, and the reliable repeat measures permit monitoring of the status of individuals on each of the included risk indicators at specified time intervals. The consistency of both tools permits individual risk trajectories to be obtained and to establish the efficacy of intervention programs for CVE and other rehabilitation programs.

Important caveats exist. There is no certainty in any risk assessment. The tools discussed in this chapter, as with many other tools being developed in this field, are able to offer an estimate of the 'danger' represented by a person under investigation. A definitive statistical prediction is not feasible. Users should not claim statistical certainty in the risk assessment nor absolute prediction. Furthermore, the systematic and structured behavioural approach, the criterion-level definitions for ratings, and the evidence-based methodology are all intended to limit user bias and provide an estimation of 'risk and danger'. The protocols provide early warning indicators to watch. The formal and rigorous training program required is expected to diminish user bias. The authors recognise that despite best efforts and rigorous controls, a limited amount of residual user subjectivity may exist, and should be controlled by audit whenever possible.

In the case of the CYBERA and the VERA-2 applications, there are likely to be empty cells in actual applications. This occurs when no information is available for the risk indicator. Although evidence may not be available for a rating on a particular indicator, this is still useful information. Often, missing information is not included in the risk decision process and this should be the case. That is, the 'known-unknown' should be considered as well as the 'known' information. The awareness of pertinent missing information is knowledge. Such knowledge provides direction in terms of the information to seek from other sources. When this data is able to be obtained, it assists the strength of the analysis. However, the assessment can be undertaken on the basis of the available information. In such cases, a caveat is documented and any qualification is dependent on the amount and importance of the missing information. Uncertainty does not necessarily mean lack of knowledge. The use of the risk assessment protocols provides new knowledge relevant to risk decisions.

CONCLUSION

The CYBERA tool which analyses and assesses individual cyber-behaviour in support of violent extremism is a new risk assessment tool that uses an established and accepted behavioural science methodology. This tool is specific to the assessment of individuals using social media and other computer-based systems to encourage, promote and/or support violent extremist related activities. At this time, CYBERA is a consultative tool and should be used with caution. It should also be applied in combination with other available tools.

When information additional to cyber-evidence is available (e.g., report data, human intelligence information, probe data, other relevant observations), the VERA-2 should be used in addition to the CYBERA. The VERA-2 will assist in structuring all the information available into a comprehensive risk assessment approach. When the information available is primarily from the Internet or from cyber-sources, the CYBERA should be the primary tool as it provides the most detailed analysis of cyber indicators. The use of the VERA-2 will integrate cyber-data into a multi-faceted analysis and provide additional robustness. When multiple sources of information and evidence are available including cyber-information, both tools should be employed.

Due to the uncertainty in all risk assessments, the interpretation of the data should be made with due caution. Risk decisions for the individual indicators and overall risk should be supported and justified by documented evidence used for the decision. This provides important information and support in cases of audit, reassessments and other reviews. The VERA-2 and the CYBERA are not silver bullets of prediction. Neither of these tools is intended for screening individuals from a general population to identify violent extremists. They are to be used with individuals who are already on the radar, those who are being monitored, and/or those persons suspected of violent extremist related activity. Risk assessment tools such as CYBERA and the VERA-2 do not replace professional judgment. They are intended to support professional judgment. A structured, systematic and transparent approach that can control subjectivity and bias in analysis is a step forward.

ACKNOWLEDGMENT

The authors acknowledge the assistance of Natasha Korva, Royal Canadian Mounted Police, Canada, and Irina Erhan, Mihai Viteazul National Intelligence Academy, Romania, in the preparation of this chapter.

REFERENCES

Barbieri, D., & Pressman, D. E. (2015). *Violent extremist risk assessment: A Bayesian framework*. Paper presented at the Intelligence in the Knowledge Society conference, Bucharest, Romania.

Beardsley, N. L., & Beech, A. R. (2013). Applying the violent extremist risk assessment (VERA) to a sample of terrorist case studies. *Journal of Aggression, Conflict and Peace Research, 5*(1), 4–15. doi:10.1108/17596591311290713

Boer, D. P., Hart, S. D., Kropp, P. R., & Webster, C. D. (1997). *Manual for the sexual violence risk-20: Professional guidelines for assessing risk of sexual violence*. Vancouver, Canada: Mental Health, Law & Policy Institute, Simon Fraser University.

Bonta, J., Law, M., & Hanson, R. K. (1998). The prediction of criminal and violent recidivism among mentally disordered offenders: A meta-analysis. *Psychological Bulletin, 123*(2), 123–142. doi:10.1037/0033-2909.123.2.123 PMID:9522681

Borum, R. (2000). Assessing violence risk among youth. *Journal of Clinical Psychology*, *56*(10), 1263–1288. doi:10.1002/1097-4679(200010)56:10<1263::AID-JCLP3>3.0.CO;2-D PMID:11051059

Borum, R., Bartel, P., & Forth, A. (2006). *SAVRY: Professional manual for structured assessment of violence risk in youth*. Lutz, FL: Psychological Assessment Resources Inc.

Borum, R., Fein, R. A., Vossekuil, B., & Berglund, J. (1999). Threat assessment: Defining an approach for evaluating risk of targeted violence. *Behavioral Sciences & the Law*, *17*(3), 323–333. doi:10.1002/(SICI)1099-0798(199907/09)17:3<323::AID-BSL349>3.0.CO;2-G PMID:10481132

Conway, M. (2006). Terrorism and the Internet: New media-new threat? *Parliamentary Affairs*, *59*(2), 283–298. doi:10.1093/pa/gsl009

Crenshaw, M. (1981). The causes of terrorism. *Comparative Politics*, *13*(4), 379–399. doi:10.2307/421717

Crenshaw, M. (2000). The psychology of terrorism: An agenda for the 21st century. *Political Psychology*, *21*(2), 405–420. doi:10.1111/0162-895X.00195

Dean, G. (2014). *Neurocognitive risk assessment for the early detection of violent extremists*. New York, NY: Springer. doi:10.1007/978-3-319-06719-3

FBI. (2013). *Press Release July 16, 2013 on Emerson Winfield Begolly*. Retrieved from http://www.fbi.gov/pittsburgh/press-releases/2013/pennsylvania-man-sentenced-for-terrorism-solicitation-and-firearms-offense

Hanson, R. K. (2005). Twenty Years of Progress in violence risk assessment. *Journal of Interpersonal Violence*, *20*(2), 212–217. doi:10.1177/0886260504267740 PMID:15601794

Hare, R. D. (2003). *Manual for the Hare Psychopathy Check-List-Revised* (2nd ed.). Toronto, Canada: Multi-Health Systems.

Hart, S. D., & Logan, C. (2011). Formulation of violence risk using evidence-based assessments: The Structured Professional Judgment approach. In P. Sturmey & M. McMurran (Eds.), *Forensic case formulation* (pp. 83–106). Chichester, UK: Wiley Blackwell. doi:10.1002/9781119977018.ch4

Internet World Statistics. (2014). *World Internet population and user statistics*. Retrieved from http://www.internetworldstats.com/stats.htm

Leiner, B. M., Cerf, V. G., Clark, D. D., Kahn, R. E., Kleinrock, L., Lynch, D. C., & Wolff, S. et al. (2009). A brief history of the Internet. *Computer Communication Review*, *39*(5), 22–31. doi:10.1145/1629607.1629613

Maghan, J., & Kelly, R. J. (1989). Terrorism and corrections: The incarcerated radical. In J. R. Buckwalter (Ed.), *International terrorism: The decade ahead* (pp. 29–53). Chicago, IL: University of Illinois Press, Office of Criminal Justice.

McGilloway, A., Ghosh, P., & Bhui, K. (2015). A systematic review of pathways to and processes associated with radicalization and extremism among Muslims in Western societies. *International Review of Psychiatry (Abingdon, England)*, *27*(1), 39–50. doi:10.3109/09540261.2014.992008 PMID:25738400

Monahan, J. (1981). *Predicting violent behavior: An assessment of clinical techniques*. Newbury Park, CA: Sage.

Monahan, J. (2012). The individual risk assessment of terrorism. *Psychology, Public Policy, and Law*, *18*(2), 13–28. doi:10.1037/a0025792

Monahan, J., Steadman, H., Silver, E., Appelbaum, P., Robbins, P., Mulvey, E., & Banks, S. et al. (2001). *Rethinking risk assessment: The MacArthur study of mental disorder and violence.* New York, NY: Oxford University Press.

Monahan, J., & Steadman, H. J. (1994). Violence risk assessment: A quarter century of research. In L. E. Frost & R. J. Bonnie (Eds.), *The evolution of mental health law* (pp. 195–211). Washington, DC: American Psychological Association.

Ogloff, J. (2009). *The violent client: Advances in violent risk assessment.* Melbourne, Victoria: The Australian Psychological Society.

Ogloff, J., & Davis, M. R. (2005). Assessing risk for violence in the Australian context. In D. Chappell & P. Wilson (Eds.), *Crime and justice in the new millennium* (pp. 301–338). Sydney, Australia: Lexis Nexis.

Ogun, M. N. (2012). Terrorist use of the internet: Possible suggestions to prevent the usage for terrorist purposes. *Journal of Applied Security Research*, *7*(2), 203–217. doi:10.1080/19361610.2012.656252

Piaget, J. (2002). The language and thought of the child. New York, NY: Routledge Classic.

Post, J. M. (2007). *The mind of the terrorist: The psychology of terrorism from the IRA to Al Qaeda.* New York, NY: Palgrave Macmillan.

Pressman, D. E. (2009). *Risk assessment decisions for violent political extremism.* Retrieved from http://www.publicsafety.gc.ca/res/cor/rep/_fl/2009-02-rdv-eng.pdf

Pressman, D. E., & Flockton, J. S. (2012). Calibrating risk for violent political extremists: The VERA-2 Structural Assessment. *British Journal of Forensic Practice*, *14*(4), 237–251. doi:10.1108/14636641211283057

Pressman, D. E., & Flockton, J. S. (2014). Violent extremist risk assessment: Issues and applications of the VERA-2 in a high security correctional setting. In A. Silke (Ed.), *Prisons, Terrorism and Extremism: critical Issues in Management, Radicalisation and Reform* (pp. 122–143). New York, NY: Routledge.

Reilly, R. J. (2015, August 8). FBI: When it comes to @ISIS Terror, Retweets=Endorsements which makes Twitter one of the Bureau's best informants. *Huffington Post*. Retrieved from http://www.huffingtonpost.com/entry/twitter-terrorism-fbi_55b7e25de4b0224d8834466e

Silber, M. D., & Bhatt, A. (2007). *Radicalization in the West: The homegrown threat.* New York, NY: New York City Police Department.

Statistics Canada. (2013). *Individual Internet use and e-commerce, 2012* (Catalogue no. 11-001-X). Retrieved from http://www.statcan.gc.ca/daily-quotidien/131028/dq131028a-eng

United Nations Office on Drugs and Crime (UNODC). (2012). *The use of the internet for terrorist purposes.* Retrieved from http://www.unodc.org/documents/frontpage/Use_of_Internet_for_Terrorist_Purposes.pdf

United States Department of Defense. (2006). *Risk management guide for DoD acquisition.* Washington, DC: Department of Defense.

United States of America v. Ali Shukri Amin. (2015). *In the United States District Court for the Eastern District of Virginia, Alexandria Division: Case l:15-cr-00164-CMH Document 7- Filed June 11, 2015.* Retrieved from http://www.justice.gov/opa/file/477366/download

United States of America v. Bilal Abood. (2015). *Indictment No. 3-15CR-0256K: In the United States District Court for the Northern Division of Texas Dallas Division-Filed June 10, 2015.* Retrieved from http://www.investigativeproject.org/documents/case_docs/2747.pdf

United States of America v. Emerson Winfield Begolly. (2013). *Sentencing Memorandum of Case 2:11-cr-00172-MBC Document 67 Filed 07/09/13 filed in the United States District Court for the Western District of Pennsylvania.* Retrieved from http://www.investigativeproject.org/documents/case_docs/2200.pdf

U.S. Department of Justice. (2015). *News release on Ali Shukri Amin, 17, of Manassas, Virginia June 11, 2015.* Retrieved from http://www.justice.gov/opa/pr/virginia-teen-pleads-guilty-providing-material-support-isil

Vygotsky, L. (2012). *Thought and language (First English Translation, 1962; 2012 MIT edition is revised and enlarged).* Cambridge, MA: M.I. T Press.

Wall, K. D. (2011). *The Kaplan and Garrick definition of risk and its application to managerial decisions.* DRMI Naval Postgraduate School. Retrieved from http://www.nps.edu/Academics/Centers/DRMI/docs/DRMI%20Working%20Paper%2011-3.pdf

Webster, C. D., Douglas, K. S., Eaves, D., & Hart, S. (1997). *HCR-20 assessing risk for violence: Version 2.* Vancouver, Canada: Mental Health Law & Policy Institute, Simon Fraser University.

Webster, C. D., Douglas, K. S., Eaves, D., & Hart, S. (2001). *HCR-20 violence risk management companion guide.* Vancouver, Canada: Mental Health Law & Policy Institute, Simon Fraser University.

Weimann, G. (2004). How modern terrorism uses the Internet. Special Report No.116. Washington, DC: United States Institute of Peace. Retrieved from www.terror.net

Chapter 20
A Supplementary Intervention to Deradicalisation:
CBT–Based Online Forum

Priscilla Shi
Home Team Behavioural Sciences Centre, Ministry of Home Affairs, Singapore

ABSTRACT

With today's technological advancements, common online platforms, such as Gmail, forum, websites, Facebook, Twitter, Instagram and YouTube, are used by millions to communicate and share information in the form of text, image or both with varying synchronicity. In a similar way, violent extremists are also bringing their radical agenda online. As more individuals become radicalised by online violent extremist propaganda, the need to counter such propaganda and manage existing threats, such as incarcerated detainees who are more technology-savvy, becomes increasingly urgent. This chapter propounds the idea of online deradicalisation. First, the online milieu and its concomitant social phenomena will be discussed. Second, an overview of existing elements of deradicalisation and its target audience will be covered. Third, the chapter will delve into online psychotherapy and its potential applicability to de-radicalisation. Last, the chapter will conclude with relevant implications and future research directions.

INTRODUCTION

With today's technological advancements, common online platforms such as Gmail, forum, websites, Facebook, Twitter, Instagram and YouTube, are used by millions to communicate and share information in the form of text, image or both with varying synchronicity. The term online used in this chapter refers to the whole spectrum of computer-mediated communications, including Internet-related activities. These computer-mediated communications range from "asynchronous e-mail transmissions, browsing the World Wide Web (WWW) to synchronous chat room participation … [which may occur in] a wide assortment of text-based and graphical web-based environments" (King & Moreggi, 2007, p. 223).

In a similar way, violent extremists are also bringing their radical agenda online. As more individuals become radicalised by online violent extremist propaganda, the need to counter such propaganda and

DOI: 10.4018/978-1-5225-0156-5.ch020

manage existing threats, such as incarcerated violent extremists (i.e., detainees) who are more technology-savvy, becomes increasingly urgent. Thus, this chapter propounds the idea of online deradicalisation.

The objective is to propose a supplementary intervention to current deradicalisation efforts for violent extremist rehabilitation. The author argued for the use of an online forum where detainees can openly discuss violent extremist related areas of interest with other detainees and helpers (i.e., individuals such as religious counsellors, therapists, reformed violent extremists who are charged with undertaking rehabilitation work for this population). This approach uses an online medium as an alternative to face-to-face intervention for these helpers to engage detainees (especially those who are radicalised online) to address their radical beliefs and thinking patterns.

The first section will introduce the trends of online usage by mainstream populations and violent extremists. The second section will define the phenomenon of deradicalisation. Key principles that guide deradicalisation and rehabilitation efforts will be highlighted before proposing the aforementioned supplementary intervention. Lastly, limitations and future areas of research will be discussed.

WHEN PEOPLE GO ONLINE

People interacting online do not exist alone. They are driven by similar motivations, such as the need for affiliation, information, and social support to connect with like-minded others (McKenna & Bargh, 1998). When interacting online, people gather and form virtual communities, whose functions are characterised by the interaction between human nature and the online environment (Madara, Kalafat, & Miller, 1988). According to Shayo, Olfman, Iriberri, and Igbaria (2007), the virtual community consists of

[V]arious forms of computer-mediated communications, particularly long-term, textually mediated conversations among large groups ... of people who may or may not meet one another face-to-face, and who exchange words and ideas through the mediation of computer networks and bulletin boards. (p. 206)

Such online interactions are empowering because it gives people a sense of acceptance and normality (Madara, 1999; Walter & Boyd, 2002). Furthermore, due to the less conspicuous individual differences of people interacting in online communications, group membership is enhanced by perceived similarities (Postmes, Spears, & Lea, 2002). Thus, virtual communities allow diverse, often minority, groups to be heard and members to find solidarity, "power, authority, and control over their own lives" (Shayo et al., 2007, p. 207).

Research by King and Moreggi (2007) has found two predictive factors of active participation in online communication: a lack of real world social support, and one's coping ability prior to joining the group. People with less real world social support and those who are coping well prior to joining the group tend to participate more actively online. Hence, one might infer that people communicate online to seek support from like-minded others and/or to provide support.

Like in real world interactions, people online will also establish interpersonal ties with others (Baym, 2002; Haythornthwaite, Kazmer, Robins, & Shoemaker, 2000). Interacting online, people usually seek to exchange information with others who are experiencing similar predicaments as themselves (King & Moreggi, 2007). So, they learn from like-minded others and share resources. Furthermore, research had found that members of virtual communities tend to develop strong interpersonal connections with others in their online environment (Haythornthwaite, 2001; Haythornthwaite & Wellman, 1998; Koku,

Nazer, & Wellman, 2001). Thus, some people are drawn to online communication because the technology creates meaning to interpersonal interactions, and the content created is useful and salient to them (Warschauer, 2000).

Communicating with others while sitting behind a computer screen encourages people to be less socially inhibited (Joinson, 2003). The lack of real world social feedback and the perceived sense of operating in a safe and secure environment provide a sense of safety (Wellman, 1996). As a result, people tend to feel more at ease with others and are less socially inhibited as they reciprocate self-disclosure (King & Moreggi, 2007). Moreover, the synchronicity and virtual experience of online communication enable people to communicate with ease over time and distance (Shayo et al., 2007). Depending on the online platform used, people can response to others immediately or after a time interval, and they can communicate over great distances. As a result, people may selectively participate in discussions and carefully draft their responses before replying (Haythornthwaite & Nielsen, 2007).

Thus, the online milieu is a social world in virtual space. It consists of people who communicate about issues of interest and share their opinions, thoughts and resources. More importantly, people tend to focus on shared interest, instead of random, singular pieces of information.

WHEN VIOLENT EXTREMISTS GO ONLINE

In a similar way, violent extremists use online communication for numerous purposes. Violent extremist group such as Al-Qaeda and the Islamic State in Iraq and Syria (ISIS) use the Internet for data-mining, networking with like-minded others, recruitment and mobilisation, dissemination of instructions and online manuals, planning and coordination, as well as fundraising (Weimann, 2006).

In his research on the individual radicalisation processes and the role of the Internet, Koehler (2014) argued that the Internet acts as a facilitator in bridging the gap between the individual and the radical ideology. Besides influencing those who are born into the online culture, other characteristics of online platforms, such as the quick spread of information, easy integration and expansion of functions, and permanence of radical narratives, also affect the interaction between the individual and the radical ideology. Given its affordable, detail-intensive and widespread nature, online communication has enabled its users, violent extremists included, to communicate, collaborate, and achieve critical mass (Koehler, 2014).

Violent extremist groups are increasingly efficient in their social media campaigns. For example, ISIS online campaign consists of three major components (Berger, 2015): (1) dissemination of propaganda to gain support locally and abroad; (2) designing and spreading of propaganda to manipulate enemies' perceptions and political reactions (i.e., inflame animosity); as well as (3) recruitment by cultivating members to engage fence-sitters online in different native languages to portray a sense of intimacy that comes with constant online contact. ISIS attempts to arouse sympathy for the plight of Muslims worldwide, gain understanding and support, and to instigate division between the enemies and its in-group. Also, through the use of visual and text-based social media, violent extremist groups are able to create emotionally powerful propaganda that may greatly impact people, such as the brutal executions of journalists and military personnel by ISIS. Thus, violent extremist groups target various groups of audiences by conveying different messages to different target audiences (Weimann, 2007).

Another common online communication strategy used by violent extremist groups is to directly criticise their enemies (Weimann, 2006). Either by portraying a positive image of themselves or by justifying their violent activities as responses to socio-political oppression, violent extremists may engage in the rhetoric of moral disengagement (Ganor, 2004). According to Bandura (2004), one morally disengages by justifying one's inhumane behaviours as something righteous. For example, radical Muslim cleric Anjem Choudary attempted to justify the burning of Jordanian pilot Moaz al-Kasabeh by ISIS on a television programme. Choundary explained that the execution is justified as a worthy revenge for the sufferings of Muslims killed in the opposition's bombings: this act is supported by "what Allah said in the Koran: Fight them back the way that they fight you" (Chasmar, 2015, para. 5).

Online communications of violent extremist groups are able to impact the real world in various ways. All these online strategies enable the proliferation and expansion of violent extremist groups (Weimann, 2007). Although law enforcement agencies constantly take down radical narratives online, new ones are relentlessly being created. Furthermore, convinced individuals join the violent extremist ranks ever so often and violent extremist groups publicly pledge allegiance to each other, thus further boosting their combined strength.

This means that to deal with the living threat of violent extremism, countermeasures should focus on what violent extremists are doing online and how are they doing it. By doing so, law enforcement agencies can appropriately tailor interventions to the correct target audience (Jordan & Audi, 2015), such as posting online counter-narratives that challenge existing radical ideas (Casciani, 2015). In the same vein, one might consider the possibility of an online approach to the deradicalisation of detainees (i.e., incarcerated violent extremists).

WHAT IS DERADICALISATION?

Deradicalisation refers to a fundamental change in one's beliefs and thoughts regarding violent extremism towards moderation. This concept is related but differs from that of disengagement. The latter refers to a behavioural change in one's actions towards non-violence. The distinction between these terms is also rooted in the socio-political climates of different countries where the objective of violent extremist rehabilitation may vary (International Crisis Group [ICG], 2007; Noor & Hayat, 2009). Thus, it is important for efforts related to violent extremist rehabilitation to have contextualised objectives and adopt clear definitions of key terms (Veldhuis, 2012). This will ensure that good practices and general principles drawn from research can be applied appropriately to subsequent rehabilitation for violent extremists.

This chapter defines deradicalisation programmes as "programmes that are generally directed against individuals who have become radical with the aim of re-integrating them into society or at least dissuading them from violence" (Institute for Strategic Dialogue, 2010, p. 1). As such, deradicalisation aims to reduce the risk of re-engagement of detainees, by moderating their violent extremist attitudes, beliefs, thoughts and behaviours towards non-violence, as well as to help them return to the mainstream society as functional, contributing members of that society (Horgan & Braddock, 2010).

Common Elements of Deradicalisation

Reviews of current deradicalisation and rehabilitation programmes for detainees reveal several common intervention mechanisms used: education, vocational training, psychotherapy, religious counselling (e.g., Barrett & Bokhari, 2009; Veldhuis, 2012).

Education

Based on the detainees' education level, literacy courses and basic education on other subjects (e.g., math, history) are provided to them (Mullins, 2010; Veldhuis, 2012). Education is believed to be an empowering tool for detainees to strive for social changes in peaceful ways because, not only does education improve their intellectual capabilities, it also increases their self-esteem, perceived self-efficacy, and resilience towards radical influences (Veldhuis, 2012).

Vocational Training

Often offered together with education opportunities, vocational training teaches detainees practical skills that are specific to a particular career or trade (Mullins, 2010; Veldhuis, 2012). Such training prepares detainees for their re-integration into the mainstream society by increasing their employability in skilled jobs (Veldhuis, 2012).

Religious Counselling

Religious counselling addresses the ideological concerns for the deradicalisation programmes. It aims to moderate the detainees' radical religious beliefs and worldviews by challenging them, and revealing moderate interpretations of key religious concepts (Mullins, 2010). To increase detainees' receptiveness of such religious dialogues, credible authorities on religious teachings are engaged to discuss these religious concepts with the detainees (Abuza, 2009; Boucek, 2008; ICG, 2007). The moderate degree of religiosity emphasised in religious counselling can encourage detainees to reconsider their violent extremist beliefs and adhere to more peaceful interpretations which delegitimise violent extremism (Veldhuis, 2012).

Psychotherapy

Despite the debatable presence of a relationship between psychological disorder and violent extremism in today context (e.g., "Man Haron Monis", 2014), the premise of psychotherapy, in particular cognitive behavioural therapy (CBT), seems to offer a viable tool to violent extremist rehabilitation (Mullins, 2010; Veldhuis, 2012).

CBT rests on the fundamental assumption that one's beliefs, thoughts, actions, feelings and attitudes are learned and can thus be unlearned or changed to reduce the unfavourable thoughts and behaviours (Lipsey, Landenberger, & Wilson, 2007). This means that CBT-trained individuals such as religious counsellors, therapists, reformed violent extremists who are charged with undertaking rehabilitation work, can address detainees' thought-action-consequences linkage, and discuss plausible ways to respond in a non-violent, peaceful way (e.g., by encouraging perspective taking and critical thinking). Mostly performed offline in a face-to-face context, the use of CBT in violent extremist rehabilitation is known but poorly documented (Horgan & Braddock, 2010). Thus, more research and empirical trials are needed to evaluate and validate this approach (Mullins, 2010).

RE-THINKING DERADICALISATION

With the increasing use of online platforms for a variety of purposes by violent extremists, more radical materials are made available online at an unprecedented rate. Like-minded individuals who visit such platforms to validate their radical beliefs tend to be more technology-savvy. This chapter argued for the use of online platforms and online psychotherapy in deradicalisation programmes in an attempt to augment and enhance existing programmes.

Relevance of Online Psychotherapy to Deradicalisation

The dramatic rise in the availability of information online has provided a valuable information source for people who are interested in receiving mental health services via the Internet (Alleman, 2002; Moulding, 2007). However, it is imperative to note that the search online for counselling help is not a matter of duplicating counsellor-client transactions (i.e., by anyone who has Internet access) through a computer screen.

There is a need to make sure that the help available online is professional, credible, and adheres closely to the code of ethics in the field of psychotherapy, or that there must be some sort of developments to see how existing counselling practices need to take into consideration online practices as well. To that end, online psychotherapy can be seen as another way of providing psychological advice and support over the Internet by a therapist or counsellor to a client (Cherry, 2015).

Online platforms, such as electronic mail (e-mail), forum and Internet relay chat system, offer unique advantages and disadvantages over traditional face-to-face psychotherapy. For example, e-mail is a common tool used for online psychotherapy. While it offers users convenience, more information-processing time, opportunities to elaborate and seek advice on ideas, and therapeutic reflection, it lack immediacy, verifiability of user identity, and is less applicable for less articulate users (Kennedy, 2005). On the other hand, an Internet relay chat system is more instantaneous and interactive but it gives users lesser time to carefully elaborate and think through their responses.

Online psychotherapy has been applied to a variety of conditions. It has been shown to be effective in treating conditions, such as anxiety (Cohen & Kerr, 1998), posttraumatic stress disorder (Lange, van de Ven, Schrieken, & Emmelkamp, 2001), eating disorders (Luce, Winzelberg, Zabinski, & Osborne, 2003), panic disorder with agoraphobia (Bouchard, et al., 2000), depression (Selmi, Klein, Greist, Sorell, & Erdman, 1990), as well as those who suffered from burn pain, head trauma and require cognitive retraining (Niemann, Ruff, & Baser, 1990).

Online psychotherapy shares similar therapeutic factors as offline face-to-face intervention, such as social support, practical information, shared experiences, positive role models, helper therapy, empowerment professional support, and advocacy efforts (Madara, 1999). In the context of deradicalisation, a noteworthy aspect of online psychotherapy is the benefits afforded by the Internet. This can be attributed to the following characteristics of the online platforms.

- **Overcome Physical Boundaries:** Online psychotherapy does not require people to physically meet face-to-face but enable massive amounts of information to be transmitted among its users.

Hence, it allows information dissemination over great distances and time, offering opportunities for wider networking and interaction. In the deradicalisation context, online psychotherapy minimises the need for physical exposure of counsellor to any potentially violent detainees and plausible negative repercussion, thus ensuring the safety of the counsellor.

- **Disinhibition Effect:** Considerable evidence has shown that online interactions tend to yield higher levels of self-disclosure and more candid or otherwise socially undesirable responses than face-to-face ones (e.g., Joinson, 2003). People tend to be less socially inhibited when they interact online due to the lack of direct physical contact. This, in turn, creates the perception that there is fewer social cost involved (Wellman, 1996). Walter and Boyd (2002) reported that online mutual-aid group members felt less judged by online peers than real-life acquaintances, and they were less concerned about potential embarrassment when disclosing about themselves in text-based interactions. Similarly, Cook and Doyle (2002) found that participants of online psychotherapy share a collaborative bond with their therapists, and an overall positive experience unique to online psychotherapy. In the deradicalisation context, anonymity of the online platforms may encourage unbiased interaction for the detainees with the helpers with minimal concern for judgment.

- **Asynchronous Nature of Online Communication:** Research on online communication has highlighted that the asynchronous nature of online text-based communication allows people to selectively participate in discussion (Sparks, 1992) and think carefully about their messages before posting them (Haythornthwaite & Nielsen, 2007). Furthermore, online communication provides a record of conversations where counsellors and clients can revisit, clarify, and reframe their beliefs (Gillispie, 2007). In the deradicalisation context, such continual feedback loops will encourage detainees to be more aware of their thoughts and progress over time.

Indeed, individuals (i.e., helper) such as religious counsellors, therapists, reformed violent extremists who are charged with undertaking rehabilitation work for this population, should consider the advantages of online psychotherapy and find suitable ways to incorporate these components into existing deradicalisation programmes so as to yield maximum rehabilitation gains.

However, it is essential to note that a comprehensive evaluation of online psychotherapy effectiveness is not yet possible – it is a relatively new development within the mental health field. That said, some studies have observed an increase in client participation through the use of online psychotherapy. In the study by Day and Schneider (2002), for example, they randomly assigned eight clients to one of three conditions representing three different modes of psychotherapy (i.e., face-to-face, real-time videoconference, two-way audio) to determine the participation rates from the clients. They found that participation rates were more effortful in the real-time videoconference condition than when the clients were in the face-to-face condition. This is because the former, being text-based and asynchronous, required more effort to put their thoughts into words. Thus, this study provided some support for the use of online psychotherapy.

However, online psychotherapy is a controversial intervention due to many concerns regarding ethicality, confidentiality and the qualification of the online counsellors (Cherry, 2015; Haberstroh, Barney, Foster, & Duffey, 2014). For example, counsellors cannot assume that their existing therapeutic skills are transferrable to online communication (Glueckauf, Pickett, Ketteson, Loomis, & Rozensky, 2003).

APPLYING ONLINE COGNITIVE BEHAVIOURAL THERAPY TO DERADICALISATION

CBT is a form of psychotherapy that is designed to solve current problems and change unhelpful thinking and behaviour (Lipsey et al., 2007). Counsellors used CBT techniques to help individuals challenge their beliefs and thinking patterns, and the way they react to certain activating events (i.e., triggers). The counsellors then seek to replace these maladaptive thinking patterns with adaptive ones. This, in turn, may lead to a positive change in affect and behaviours, and avoid the consequences commonly associated with the maladaptive thinking patterns.

Online Cognitive Behavioural Therapy

Recently, the online version of CBT, otherwise known as interapy is introduced. Online CBT is a web-based counsellor-assisted intervention that consists of screening, treatment, and outcome measurement (Ruwaard, Lange, Schrieken, & Emmelkamp, 2011). Conducted virtually and asynchronously via text-messaging, online CBT resembles an e-mail dialogue. This conversation is regulated by a computerised manual, which delivers a fixed sequence of assignments to the client via the Internet. Standardised feedback that emphasises on motivation for change and relationship between the counsellor and the client are also delivered to maximise the impact of the treatment. These treatments are generally short but intensive.

The concept of assignments in online CBT is a critical part of the treatment. By doing these assignments, clients are practicing what they had learnt, such as self-monitoring one's activating event, thinking patterns about the activating event, and the associated consequences in terms of behaviours and affect (Anthony & Nagel, 2010). Thus, such assignments facilitate in challenging negative assumptions that clients might have. The completed assignments can be sent to the counsellors prior to the next session. This will give the counsellors more time to prepare as well as more room for clients and counsellors to focus on the completed assignments and come up with new strategies during the next session.

Prior studies had shown significant treatment gains from online CBT on bereavement, bulimia nervosa, depression, panic disorder, posttraumatic stress, and work-related stress in controlled trials and routine clinical practice (Ruwaard et al., 2011). Significant reductions in maladaptive thinking patterns and associated affect and behaviours were also observed, and these improvements were maintained up to one year after the treatment.

Although most online therapies that are currently available attend to clinical disorders, such online therapeutic approaches may be tailored to violent extremist rehabilitation. In the context of deradicalisation, online CBT can be utilised to address detainees' thought-action-consequences linkage, and discuss plausible ways to respond in a non-violent, peaceful way.

CBT-Based Online Forum as a Supplement to Deradicalisation

To complement the existing deradicalisation efforts, a CBT-based online forum may be used as a supplementary intervention for detainees who fulfil the following criteria: (1) express preference for online communication, (2) able to articulate one's views online, and (3) was radicalised via the Internet in the first place.

To begin with, detainees should be assessed for their risk levels prior to being administered any rehabilitation intervention. If the detainees are assessed to be high risk, the level of intervention should be of high intensity (e.g., in-depth discussions, discussions that challenge beliefs, discussions that aim to change thinking patterns). However, if the detainees are assessed to be low risk, the level of intervention can be of low intensity (e.g., sharing of information, psychoeducation). Furthermore, by grouping detainees' of the same level of risk together, reduce the risk of contaminating low-risk detainees with radical influence espoused by high-risk detainees. Thus, the detainees' levels of risk can be used to guide and plan interventions.

Participating detainees are given the liberty to speak their mind on the online forum. The identity of each detainee is replaced by a generic username randomly assigned by the helper. The identity behind each username is kept anonymous to other participating detainees and helpers. This may encourage the detainees to voice queries and/or issues that they usually have difficulties in expressing via face-to-face communication. Thus, detainees can freely post their concerns and questions for discussion with other detainees and helpers (i.e., individuals such as religious counsellors, therapists, reformed violent extremists who are charged with undertaking rehabilitation work for this population).

Guided fundamentally by CBT principles, helpers may address radical beliefs of detainees by challenging negative assumptions that support the use of violence and/or any perceived grievances that the detainees have. In addition, helpers may facilitate the identification of moderate, peaceful resolutions to the negative assumptions and perceived grievances. Other principles of CBT such as rewards for behavioural improvements, as well as behavioural practice in preparation to deal with certain triggers, can also be employed to guide deradicalisation and rehabilitation efforts (Mullins, 2010). Furthermore, detainees are encouraged to practice life skills, such as perspective-taking, critical thinking and self-control (Robinson & Porporine, 2001). Thus, the ultimate goal of this online intervention is aimed at cognitive reframing or restructuring by allowing the detainees to discuss and influence each other, so that any change in thinking that emerges is formed as a group.

Role of the Helpers

Helpers are divided into two groups: primary and secondary. Primary helpers will interact anonymously with the detainees online, while secondary helpers will monitor detainees' participation and progress. These observations are recorded and used to inform subsequent intervention for all the participants of the online forum.

Primary helpers will be required to regulate the discussion (Hsiung, 2000). It is important for those detainees with grievances to have their views heard, before they can be challenged. If the detainees are not given the right to express their negative assumptions and perceived grievances and are immediately put down by the helpers, it may inadvertently increase their resistance and makes it harder for the helpers to have further conversations with them. Thus, it is crucial that an environment of unconditional regard is provided to detainees to facilitate and encourage interaction, and to share their opinions in the online forum. Helpers need to assure participating detainees that they are free to air their radical views, if any, without potential repercussion.

From a law enforcement perspective, listening to their beliefs and issues does not necessarily equate to agreeing with their worldviews. In fact, by providing the online platform for them to share their perspectives creates an opportunity for these radical beliefs and concerns to be addressed, challenged and moderated via discussion.

CONCLUSION

This chapter had briefly proposed a potential online intervention approach: CBT-based online forum as a supplementary intervention to extant deradicalisation programme. While much fine-tuning of the approach to respective rehabilitation context and targets is required, the proposed approach is a budding attempt to utilise the benefits of the Internet for violent extremist deradicalisation and rehabilitation efforts.

Given the growing technology and social media, researchers such as Beard (2005) opined of the need to merge the new technologies with psychology as a potential alternative to help people. However, it is imperative to be cognisant of the limitations associated with such approaches.

Limitations and Future Research Direction

A fundamental assumption of online interventions is that people have access to and/or understand technology. However, this is not always the case. Due to reasons such as low socio-economic status and poor literacy, some populations may not be able to afford such technology and/or express themselves adequately (Ackerman & Banks, 1990). It is important that online interventions are extended as an alternative to tradition face-to-face communication, especially for those who are familiar operating on the online sphere.

Online communication differs from face-to-face communication because the amount of and quality of information that is transmitted between the users differ. In particular, online communication may overlook situational factors, such as possible distractors and a person's arousal level. Thus, research needs to better understand what and how situational factors can affect detainees' online interactions with each other and the helpers.

Next, it is challenging to acquire unbiased outcomes of online interventions because participants who are negatively affected tend to remove themselves from the online group, and this may result in a self-selection process that positively biases the effectiveness of the intervention (King & Moreggi, 2007). Furthermore, due to information overload, some participants may selectively attend to information that interest them instead of all the messages posted online. Therefore, the helpers have to be well trained to moderate and guide the discussion with detainees on the online forum.

Lastly, rapport and trust must be established prior to the introduction of this CBT-based online forum intervention to deradicalisation efforts. Given the volatile environment of the online communication platform, it will be difficult for participating detainees to be truly committed to sharing their views if they do not trust the helpers.

ACKNOWLEDGMENT

Views expressed in this chapter belong to the author only and do not represent the official position or views of the Ministry of Home Affairs, Singapore.

REFERENCES

Abuza, Z. (2009). Rehabilitation of Jemaah Islamiyah detainees in South East Asia: A preliminary assessment. In T. Bjørgo & J. Horgan (Eds.), *Leaving terrorism behind: Individual and collective disengagement* (pp. 193–211). New York, NY: Routledge.

Ackerman, R. J., & Banks, M. E. (1990). Computers and the ethical treatment of brain-injured patients. *Social Science Computer Review, 8*(1), 83–95. doi:10.1177/089443939000800108 PMID:11659900

Alleman, J. R. (2002). Online counselling: The Internet and mental health treatment. *Psychotherapy (Chicago, Ill.), 39*(2), 199–209. doi:10.1037/0033-3204.39.2.199

Anthony, K., & Nagel, D. M. (2010). *Therapy online: A practical guide*. London: Sage Publishing. doi:10.4135/9781849204354

Bandura, A. (2004). The role of selective moral disengagement in terrorism and counterterrorism. In F. M. Moghaddam & A. J. Marsella (Eds.), *Understanding terrorism: Psychosocial roots, causes and consequences* (pp. 121–150). Washington, DC: American Psychological Association. doi:10.1037/10621-006

Barrett, R., & Bokhari, L. (2009). Deradicalization and rehabilitation programmes targeting religious terrorists and extremists in the Muslim world: An overview. In T. Bjørgo & J. Horgan (Eds.), *Leaving terrorism behind: Individual and collective disengagement*. New York, NY: Routledge.

Baym, N. K. (2002). Interpersonal life online. In L. A. Lievrouw & S. Livingstone (Eds.), *The handbook of new media* (pp. 62–76). Thousand Oaks, CA: Sage.

Beard, K. W. (2005). Internet addiction: A review of current assessment techniques and potential assessment questions. *Cyberpsychology & Behavior, 8*(1), 7–14. doi:10.1089/cpb.2005.8.7 PMID:15738688

Berger, J. M. (2015, May 7). Social Media: An Evolving Front in Radicalization. *Intel Wire*. Retrieved from http://news.intelwire.com/2015/05/social-media-evolving-front-in.html

Boucek, C. (2008). *Saudi Arabia's 'soft' counter-terrorism strategy: Prevention, rehabilitation, and aftercare (Middle East Program Report 97)*. Washington, DC: Carnegie Endowment for International Peace.

Bouchard, S., Payeur, R., Rivard, V., Allard, M., Paquin, B., Renaud, P., & Goyer, L. (2000). Cognitive behaviour therapy for panic disorder with agoraphobia in videoconference: Preliminary results. *Cyberpsychology & Behavior, 3*(6), 999–1007. doi:10.1089/109493100452264

Casciani, D. (2015, May 12). The battle of the e-Muftis. *BBC News*. Retrieved from http://www.bbc.com/news/magazine-32697424

Chasmar, J. (2015, February 5). Anjem Choudary, radical Muslim cleric: Koran justifies Jordanian pilot burning. *The Washington Times*. Retrieved from http://www.washingtontimes.com/news/2015/feb/5/anjem-choudary-radical-muslim-cleric-quran-justifi/

Cherry, K. (2015). Online therapy: What is online therapy? *About Education*. Retrieved from http://psychology.about.com/od/psychotherapy/a/onlinepsych.htm

Cohen, G. E., & Kerr, B. A. (1998). Computer-mediated counselling: An empirical study of a new mental health treatment. *Computers in Human Sciences, 15*, 13–26.

Cook, J., & Doyle, C. (2002). Working alliance in online therapy as compared to face-to-face therapy: Preliminary results. *Cyberpsychology & Behavior, 5*(2), 95–105. doi:10.1089/109493102753770480 PMID:12025884

Day, S., & Schneider, P. (2002). Psychotherapy using distance technology: A comparison to face-to-face, video, and audio treatment. *Journal of Consulting Psychology, 49*(4), 499–503. doi:10.1037/0022-0167.49.4.499

Ganor, B. (2004). Terrorism as a strategy of psychological warfare. In Y. Danieli, D. Brom, & J. Sills (Eds.), *The trauma of terrorism* (pp. 33–43). New York, NY: Haworth. doi:10.1300/J146v09n01_03

Gillispie, J. F. (2007). Cyber shrinks: Expanding the paradigm. In J. Gackenbach (Ed.), *Psychology and the Internet: Intrapersonal, interpersonal, and transpersonal implications* (pp. 245–269). London: Elsevier. doi:10.1016/B978-012369425-6/50029-1

Glueckauf, R., Pickett, T., Ketterson, T., Loomis, J., & Rozenshy, R. (2003). Preparation for the delivery of telehealth services: A self-study framework for expansion of practice. *Professional Psychology, Research and Practice, 34*(2), 159–163. doi:10.1037/0735-7028.34.2.159

Haberstroh, S., Barney, L., Foster, N., & Duffey, T. (2014). The ethical and legal practice of online counselling and psychotherapy: A review of mental health professions. *Journal of Technology in Human Sciences, 32*(3), 149–157. doi:10.1080/15228835.2013.872074

Haythornthwaite, C. (2001). Exploring multiplexity: Social network structures in a computer-supported distance learning class. *The Information Society, 17*(3), 211–226. doi:10.1080/01972240152493065

Haythornthwaite, C., Kazmer, M. M., Robins, J., & Shoemaker, S. (2000). Community development among distance learners: Temporal and technological dimensions. *Journal of Computer-Mediated Communication, 6*(1). doi:10.1111/j.1083-6101-2000.tb00114.x

Haythornthwaite, C., & Nielsen, A. L. (2007). Revisiting computer-mediated communication for work, community, and learning. In J. Gackenbach (Ed.), *Psychology and the Internet: Intrapersonal, interpersonal, and transpersonal implications* (pp. 167–180). London: Elsevier. doi:10.1016/B978-012369425-6/50026-6

Haythornthwaite, C., & Wellman, B. (1998). Work, friendship, and media use for information exchange in a networked organisation. *Journal of the American Society for Information Science, 49*(12), 1101–1114. doi:10.1002/(SICI)1097-4571(1998)49:12<1101::AID-ASI6>3.0.CO;2-Z

Horgan, J., & Braddock, K. (2010). Rehabilitating the terrorists? Challenges in assessing the effectiveness of de-radicalization programs. *Terrorism and Political Violence, 22*(2), 267–291. doi:10.1080/09546551003594748

Hsiung, R. (2000). The best of both worlds: An online mutual-aid group hosted by a mental health professional. *CyberPsychology and Behaviour, 3*(6), 935–950. doi:10.1089/109493100452200

Institute for Strategic Dialogue. (2010). *De-radicalisation*. PPN Working Paper. London: Institute for Strategic Dialogue.

International Crisis Group (ICG). (2007). *Deradicalisation' and Indonesian prisons* (Asia Report 142). Retrieved from http://www.crisisgroup.org/home/index.cfm?id1/42959andl1/41

Joinson, A. N. (2003). *Understanding the psychology of Internet behaviour: Virtual worlds, real lives*. New York, NY: Palgrave Macmillan.

Jordan, M., & Audi, T. (2015, May 6). A test case for 'Deradicalization'. *The Wall Street Journal*. Retrieved from http://www.wsj.com/articles/a-test-case-for-deradicalization-1430944585

Kennedy, A. (2005). An uneasy alliance: Two counsellors discuss technology's evolving impact on the mental health profession. *Counseling Today*, *1*, 14–16.

King, S. A., & Moreggi, D. (2007). Internet mutual-aid and support groups: The pros and cons of text-based mutual aid. In J. Gackenbach (Ed.), *Psychology and the Internet: Intrapersonal, interpersonal, and transpersonal implications* (pp. 221–243). London: Elsevier. doi:10.1016/B978-012369425-6/50028-X

Koehler, D. (2014). The radical online: Individual radicalisation processes and the role of the Internet. *Journal of Deradicalisation*, Winter 2014/15, 116-134.

Koku, E., Nazer, N., & Wellman, B. (2001). Netting scholars: Online and offline. *The American Behavioral Scientist*, *44*(10), 1752–1774. doi:10.1177/00027640121958023

Lange, A., van de Ven, J., Schrieken, B., & Emmelkamp, P. (2001). Interapy. Treatment of posttraumatic stress through the Internet: A controlled trial. *Journal of Behavior Therapy and Experimental Psychiatry*, *32*(2), 73–90. doi:10.1016/S0005-7916(01)00023-4 PMID:11764063

Lipsey, M. W., Landenberger, N. A., & Wilson, S. J. (2007). Effects of cognitive-behavioral programs for criminal offenders. *Campbell Systematic Reviews*, *6*, 1–30.

Luce, K. H., Winzelberg, A. J., Zabinski, M. F., & Osborne, M. I. (2003). Internet-delivered psychological interventions for body image dissatisfaction and disordered eating. *Psychotherapy (Chicago, Ill.)*, *40*(1-2), 148–154. doi:10.1037/0033-3204.40.1-2.148

Madara, E. J. (1999). From church basements to world wide web sites: The growth of mutual-aid support groups online. *International Journal of Self Help & Self Care*, *1*(1), 37–48. doi:10.2190/8BL4-VD3X-KV8N-T78F

Madara, E. J., Kalafat, J., & Miller, B. N. (1988). The computerised mutual-aid clearinghouse: Using "high tech" to promote "high touch" support networks. *Computers in Human Services*, *3*(3/4), 39–53. doi:10.1300/J407v03n03_04

Man Haron Monis. 'Damaged' and 'unstable'. (2014, December 16). *BBC News*. Retrieved from http://www.bbc.com/news/world-australia-30484419

McKenna, K. Y. A., & Bargh, J. A. (1998). Coming out in the age of the Internet: Identity "de-marginalisation" from virtual group participation. *Journal of Personality and Social Psychology*, *75*(3), 681–694. doi:10.1037/0022-3514.75.3.681

Moulding, N. (2007). Online counselling: With particular focus on young people and support. *Counselling, Psychotherapy, and Health*, *3*(1), 25–32.

Mullins, S. (2010). Rehabilitation of Islamist terrorists: Lessons from criminology. *Dynamics of Asymmetric Conflict*, *3*(3), 162–193. doi:10.1080/17467586.2010.528438

Neimann, H., Ruff, R., & Baser, C. (1990). Computer assisted attention retraining in head-injured individuals: A controlled efficacy study of an outpatient program. *Journal of Consulting and Clinical Psychology*, *58*(6), 811–817. doi:10.1037/0022-006X.58.6.811 PMID:2292631

Noor, S., & Hayat, S. (2009). *Deradicalisation: Approaches and models*. Indonesia: Pak Institute for Peace Studies.

Postmes, T., Spears, R., & Lea, M. (2002). Inter-group differentiation in computer-mediated communication: Effects of depersonalisation. *Group Dynamics*, *6*(1), 3–16. doi:10.1037/1089-2699.6.1.3

Ritterband, L., Gonder-Fredrick, L., Cox, D., Clifton, A., West, R., & Borowitz, S. (2003). Internet interventions: In review, in use, and into the future. *Professional Psychology, Research and Practice*, *34*(5), 527–534. doi:10.1037/0735-7028.34.5.527

Robinson, D., & Porporino, F. (2001). Programming in cognitive skills: The reasoning and rehabilitation programme. In C. Hollin (Ed.), *Handbook of offender assessment and treatment* (pp. 179–193). Chichester: John Wiley.

Ruwaard, J., Lange, A., Schrieken, B., & Emmelkamp, P. (2011). Efficacy and effectiveness of online CBT: A decade of interapy research. *Journal of Studies in Health Technology and Informatics*, *167*, 9–14. PMID:21685634

Selmi, P. M., Kleiin, M. H., Greist, J. H., Sorrell, S. P., & Erdman, H. P. (1990). Computer-administered cognitive-behavioural therapy for depression. *The American Journal of Psychiatry*, *147*(1), 51–56. doi:10.1176/ajp.147.1.51 PMID:2403473

Shayo, C., Olfman, L., Iriberri, A., & Igbaria, M. (2007). The virtual society: Its driving forces, arrangements, practices, and implications. In J. Gackenbach (Ed.), *Psychology and the Internet: Intrapersonal, interpersonal, and transpersonal implications* (pp. 187–216). London: Elsevier. doi:10.1016/B978-012369425-6/50027-8

Sparks, S. (1992). Exploring electronic social support groups. *The American Journal of Nursing*, (Dec): 62–65. PMID:1456319

Veldhuis, T. (2012). *Designing rehabilitation and reintegration programmes for violent extremist offenders: A realist approach*. ICCT Research Paper. Netherland: International Centre for Counter-Terrorism – The Hague.

Walter, J. B., & Boyd, S. (2002). Attraction to computer-mediated social support. In C. A. Lin & D. Atkin (Eds.), *Communication technology and society: Audience adoption and uses* (pp. 153–188). Cresskill, NJ: Hampton Press.

Warschauer, M. (2000). Language, identity, and the Internet. In B. E. Kolko, L. Nakamura, & G. B. Rodman (Eds.), *Race in cyberspace* (pp. 151–170). New York, NY: Routledge.

Weimann, G. (2006). *Terror on the Internet: The new arena, the new challenge.* Washington, DC: United States of Institute of Peace.

Weimann, G. (2007). Using the Internet for terrorist recruitment and mobilisation. In B. Ganor, K. V. Knop, & C. Duarte (Eds.), *Hypermedia seduction for terrorist recruiting* (pp. 47–58). Washington, DC: IOS Press.

Wellman, B. (1996). An electronic group is a virtual social network. In S. Kiesler (Ed.), *Culture of the Internet* (pp. 179–205). Mahwah, NJ: Lawrence Erlbaum.

Section 4
Emerging Trends

Chapter 21
Cyberterrorism:
Using the Internet as a Weapon of Destruction

Leevia Dillon
Home Team Behavioural Sciences Centre, Ministry of Home Affairs, Singapore

ABSTRACT

The cyber threat landscape has continued to evolve with time and enhanced technology. With the advent of new breeds of terrorists and cybercriminals, the cyberterrorism debate has again wielded global attention. In this chapter, the author will attempt to delve deeper into the concept of cyberterrorism. Firstly, it will discuss the related issues which include the definition consensus, perception, and media abuse problems. The next section draws on parallels from research on cyber threats and terrorism based on six themes (i.e., modus operandi, domain, targets, impact, antagonists and motivations) to formulate a cyberterrorism conceptual framework. The third section will provide a hypothetical four-step cyberterrorism attack sequence and suggestions for countering cyberterrorism. This chapter will then conclude by highlighting several implications of interest.

INTRODUCTION

The rapid progression of new technological advancements and its concomitant benefits has brought about a digital era in which people are so deeply embedded in. This is even more so with the advent of social media. However with such innovations, security vulnerabilities that can be exploited by individuals (i.e., equipped with the necessary systems and human manipulation skills) are inevitably introduced into the systems (Dillon, Neo, Ong, & Khader, 2015; Furnell & Warren, 1999). In other words, manipulations of the systems and/or the human operators are the common modus operandi used to execute cyber threats. Cyber threats are potential online events that may cause detrimental outcomes (e.g., massive payouts, reputational concerns, loss of lives, severe economic damages) to individuals, organisations, and countries (World Economic Forum, 2012).

Research has highlighted two types of cyber threats: non-kinetic and kinetic (Applegate, 2013). Non-kinetic threats do not precipitate violence but undermine confidentiality, integrity and availability of

DOI: 10.4018/978-1-5225-0156-5.ch021

data. The cyber espionage campaigns conducted by 'The Mask' would be an example that falls under this category. The Mask is a digital tool (*Careto* in Spanish slang, meaning 'ugly face' or 'mask') designed by Spanish-speaking perpetrators with the sole objective of conducting international cyber espionage. This tool was involved in such operations since 2007 ("Mask malware takes", 2014). Examples of its operations include web and Wi-Fi traffic interceptions, keystroke and Skype conversations monitoring, obtaining information from Nokia devices (Warren, 2014).

The main targets of The Mask fell into several categories amongst which were government institutions, diplomatic embassies, research institutions and critical infrastructure involving energy, oil and gas. Its targets included the regions of the Middle East, Europe, Africa, and North and South America. Of note, its operations ceased shortly after the publication of 'The Mask' by Kaspersky Lab, an international cybersecurity organisation (Warren, 2014). The discovery and global reach of this tool led the U.S. President Barack Obama to declare cyber threats as the next pronounced threat to national security (Harress, 2014). This example highlighted the problems with the interconnectivity brought about by advancements in online technology as physical limitations imposed by geographical boundaries become increasingly irrelevant (Dillon et al., 2015). Fortunately, there were no reported damage or injuries but it is not hard to imagine that such a tool can be used to achieve kinetic effects (Applegate, 2013).

Kinetic cyber threats result in violence or deaths through not only the exploitation of data but also of critical infrastructure. An example of which is cyberterrorism, which will be the main focus of this chapter. Though met with scepticism (see CATO Institute, 2010; Conway, 2002; Green, 2002), cyberterrorism can be a possible future threat due to the following reasons:

- The financial capabilities of terrorist organisations like Al-Qaeda (AQ) or the Islamic State in Iraq and Syria (ISIS) may enable the respective organisations to potentially purchase equipment and expertise required to execute cyber threats (Hardy & Williams, 2014; Paganini, 2012; Sherlock, Samaan, & Samaan, 2014);
- The growing interdependencies between and within critical infrastructures of a nation (Acharya, 2004; Idaho National Laboratory, 2006; Zimmerman, 2009); and
- The documented isolated cases of critical infrastructure breaches (Applegate, 2013; Dillon et al., 2015).

The objective of this chapter will present cyberterrorism as a potential threat faced by authorities. The next section of this chapter will discuss several features of cyberterrorism by exploring similarities from research on cyber threats and terrorism to determine a conceptual framework encompassing cyberterrorism. This will be followed by an outline of a hypothetical sequence of a cyberterrorism attack and suggestions for countering cyberterrorism. The chapter will then conclude by delineating several implications about cyberterrorism.

ISSUES SURROUNDING CYBERTERRORISM

The term cyberterrorism took root in 1980s by Barry Collin who had argued the term signified the combination of the physical world and cyberspace (Collin, 1997). The usage of this term gained traction during the post-Cold War period where national security was undergoing dramatic changes. During this period, the introduction of the Internet provided a global platform for people to connect with one another (Jarvis, Nouri, & Whiting, 2014). Despite the benefits reaped, the heavy dependency on the Internet was perceived by many to be a security concern.

From a psychological perspective, the combination of the fear of random and/or targeted cyber attacks from unknown perpetrators, and the unknown possibilities of cyberspace is perceived to be more threatening than a known threat (Weimann, 2004). As a result, this gave rise to the increasing attention not only on non-kinetic cyber threats but also on kinetic ones such as cyberterrorism (Stohl, 2014). Research by Singer (2012) has shown an estimated coverage of 31,300 magazines and journal articles that discuss the phenomenon of cyberterrorism.

Statistics of cyber threats recorded by the authorities are generally considered to reflect meagre indications of the actual extent of the problem as many cases go unreported (Blakemore, 2012; Rogers & Lewis, 2007). Security resources are limited and thus may not be able to monitor and attend to all known cases. This results in difficulties in estimating the extent of the problem (Blakemore, 2012). This challenge is further exacerbated by the complex interactions between the Internet and terrorism. Examples may include either terrorists' use of the Internet to facilitate their goals or using the Internet as a weapon to execute terrorist-related attacks (Jarvis et al., 2014). As such, the wide array of possible instances highlights the difficulties in defining the concept of cyberterrorism. The following section will explore the following issues surrounding cyberterrorism in greater depth: (1) lack of definition consensus, (2) perception issues, and (3) media abuse.

Lack of Definition Consensus

Similar to the concepts of terrorism and radicalisation, many observers (e.g., Ballard, Hornik, & McKenzie, 2004; McGuire, 2014) have highlighted the difficulties in understanding the concept of cyberterrorism. In part, this can be due to the lack of consensus in the definition of cyberterrorism in the extant research literature (Ahmad, Yunos, Sahib, & Yusoff, 2012). The lack of consensus can be attributed to the versatility of the meaning of cyberterrorism to fit different contexts in order to accommodate the political discourse of each consecutive epoch (Weinberg, Pedahzur, & Hirsch-Hoefler, 2004).

Despite the many definitions of cyberterrorism found in the literature, two general definitions were identified (Awan, 2014; Conway, 2002; Talihärm, 2010). The first definition described cyberterrorism to be politically, socially or ideologically motivated cyber attacks with the intention to interfere with political, social or economic functioning of an organisation or a country, and to induce grave harm – e.g., loss of lives, severe economic damages (Denning, 2009; Dillon et al., 2015; Hua & Bapna, 2012).

The second definition described cyberterrorism as the exploitation of the Internet by terrorists to perform online-based activities such as the dissemination of propaganda, communication, data mining and mobilisation of resources (Talihärm, 2010; Weimann, 2006). Research has shown that contemporary terrorists do not necessarily have the required capabilities to conduct sophisticated cyber attacks online (Reich & Gelbstein, 2012; Wilson, 2003). Instead, majority of the terrorists exploit the Internet by using the myriad of online platforms available for the aforementioned uses. Such online activities can help terrorists to achieve their radical goals and thus, must be monitored, countered and prevented.

For the purpose of this chapter, the concept of cyberterrorism, which was adapted from Denning's definition, will be defined as a kinetic cyber threat and refers to cyber attacks conducted by antagonists against critical infrastructure (1) designed to intimidate or coerce a government or the public, (2) with intent to achieve political, social or ideological goals, and (3) cause deliberate and massive damage involving the endangerment of human lives to cause psychological fear, severe disruptions of essential services and severe economic losses.

This definition will be broken down into its relevant components and examined in more detail in the next section. As our understanding of cyberterrorism continues to progress, researchers like Denning (2009) have argued that cyberterrorism is indeed a real threat. Moreover, many countries have introduced unique legislations on cyberterrorism and their acknowledgement of this threat further substantiates the point that the cyber threat is real (Awan, 2014; Hardy & Williams, 2014).

Perception Issues

Perception issues refer to the confusion of cyber attacks being classified as cyberterrorism, and the doubt over the reality of the threat, following the lack of definition consensus. For instance, Denning (2009, p. 241) highlighted the following example where "an email bomb may be considered hacktivism by some and cyberterrorism by others". Scholars have also argued that for an attack to be termed as cyberterrorism, "violence against persons or severe economic damage" must be a consequence (Conway, 2004, p. 84), while others opined that the exploitation of the Internet by terrorists is a sufficient criterion (Desouza & Hensgen, 2003). Such examples underscore the difficulty in documenting attacks as cyberterrorism.

The problems resulting from the lack of a clear definition is aptly illustrated by the case of Stuxnet (i.e., a type of complex malware which has been given the label of cyberterrorism). The creation of this malware was claimed to be a joint project between the United States and Israel to target and sabotage Iran's critical infrastructure, and place the nuclear sector under the attackers' control (Paganini, 2012).

However, Stuxnet is not a clear case of cyberterrorism based on certain definitions of cyberterrorism (e.g., Conway, 2011; Dillon et al., 2015; Talihärm, 2010). Of note, the motivation behind this cyber threat may have been political in nature but the threat did not entail a key detrimental kinetic effect – i.e., endangerment of human lives as outlined in some definitions for cyberterrorism. Alternatively, this case can also be considered as a non-kinetic nation-state cyber threat and not cyberterrorism. As such, the lack of clarity had lead scholars to discount Stuxnet to be a case of cyberterrorism, and the situation to be 'overblown' (CATO Institute, 2011; Singer, 2012).

However based on the Stuxnet incident, there are several factors illustrating the reality of the cyberterrorism threat (Dogrul, Aslan, & Celik, 2011; Weimann, 2004). They are as follow:

- **Cost Effective:** It is a cheaper alternative than traditional terrorist modus operandi. Instead of purchasing weapons to conduct attacks, only a telephone line, a computer and an online connection are needed to conduct social engineering and cyber attacks. In this case, introduction of Stuxent was via an infected USB flash drive (Chen, 2014).
- **Anonymity:** Online platforms provide a cover of anonymity for the perpetrators to conceal behind 'handles' – online monikers that prevent them from being easily identified by the authorities. In the case of Stuxnet, the perpetrators though claimed to be from the United States and Israel, were not directly confirmed but based on circumstantial evidence, and none had claimed responsibility (Kerr, Rollins, & Theohary, 2010; Lachow, 2011).
- **No Physical Borders:** The perpetrators were not restrained by physical or geographical boundaries as the malware was targeted at Iran's nuclear sector via the cyberspace.
- **Remote Access:** Cyber attacks can be conducted with remote access and does not risk incurring financial losses, mortality or travel (Chen, 2014).

- **Target and Effect Multiplier:** The effects of such cyber attacks are not only restricted to the on-line domain. There would also be real world repercussions arising from a successful cyber attack (Rogers, 2003).

Media Abuse

Cyberterrorism has made international headlines and is recognised as one of the major cyber threats worldwide (Cendrowicz, 2014; Ellyat, 2015). The term has been used interchangeably to describe any cyber-related incidences. For instance, news articles with eye-catching titles such as "Canadian boy admits cyberterrorism of his family – A 15-year-old Canadian boy has admitted he was responsible for months of notorious high-tech pranks that terrorized his own family" (as cited in Talihärm, 2010, p. 63) or "Cyber-attacks by Al-Qaeda feared, Terrorists at Threshold of Using Internet as Tool of Bloodshed, Experts Say" (as cited in Weimann, 2006, p. 151).

There is an existing and alarming gap between the assumptions made and known elements about cyberterrorism, which may devalue the term itself (Talihärm, 2010). For instance, the content analysis of 535 news items published by 31 news outlets has displayed the lack of distinction of terminologies on cyberterrorism used by media outlets (Jarvis, Macdonald, & Whiting, 2015), which may be attributed to the sensational nature of cyberterrorism.

CYBERTERRORISM CONCEPTUAL FRAMEWORK: SIMILAR FEATURES FROM CYBER THREATS AND TERRORISM

As established in the earlier section, cyberterrorism is the convergence of features of cyberspace and of terrorism. This section will explore the similarities between cyberterrorism, cyber threats and terrorism in terms of six themes which are grouped accordingly to (1) modus operandi and domain, (2) targets and impact, and (3) antagonists and motivations. The illustration of the six critical components in Figure 1 reflects the definition of cyberterrorism taken for this chapter. According to Yunos and Ahmad (2014), all the components will aid in the decision-making process to determine whether a cyber-related incident is considered an episode of cyberterrorism.

Modus Operandi and Domain

Esen (2006) stated that the Internet has increased the possibilities for cyber intrusions to occur in many folds, given the network's open architecture and that all systems connected to it are public-facing (i.e., can be accessed by anyone with an established Internet connection). Similar to other cyber threats, the modus operandi of cyberterrorism involves both systems and human manipulation skills to conduct cyber attacks and social engineering correspondingly.

Systems manipulation involves cyber attacks to deliberately exploit computer networks as a means to execute cyber threats for malicious intents. Such attacks are typically intended to disrupt the normal functioning of online infrastructures (O'Shea, 2003). Methods can include, but are not limited to the following:

Figure 1. Cyberterrorism conceptual framework (adapted from Yunos & Ahmad, 2014)

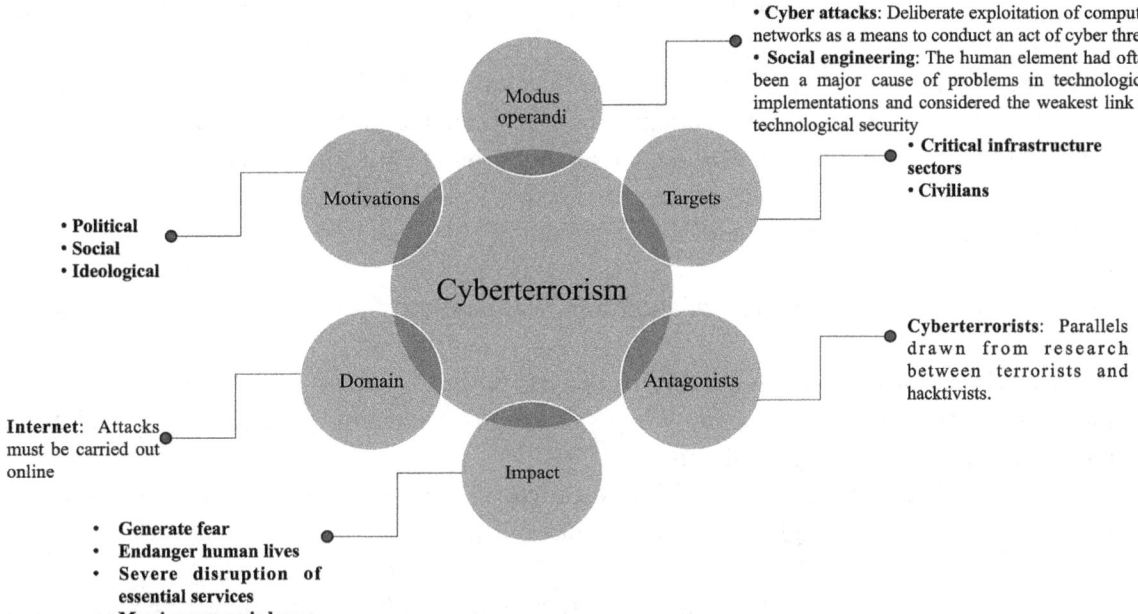

- **Malware:** Any software that contains codes that facilitate infiltration into computer systems with or without owners' consent (Pan & Fung, 2008). Examples include viruses which are small, malicious computer programs designed to spread from computer to computer by attaching themselves to existing programs to interfere with computer operations. Another example would be Trojan horses which can be disguised to look harmless or even beneficial for users.
- **Distributed Denial-of-Service Attacks (DDoS):** A form of attack that disrupts Internet users' access to the services available on the targeted system by sending large amounts of web traffic and causing server breakdown (Esen, 2002).
- **Hacking:** A general label encompassing a range of distinct attacks associated with computer intrusion, manipulation, and disruption (Yar, 2006).

Human manipulation involves attempts by perpetrators to gain information and access from the users of the online systems for malicious intents. Abraham and Chengalur-Smith (2010) averred that the human element has been a root cause of problems in technological implementations, and is considered the weakest link in technological security.

Research has shown that most cyber threats are facilitated by the lack of awareness and mistakes made by users who are victims of social engineering ("User mistakes aid", 2015). Social engineering refers to methods of deception that are utilised to deceive and manipulate their human victims into divulging confidential information (McQuade, 2006). Social engineering is considered to be easier to execute compared to efforts expended in systems manipulation (Rosoff, 2011). These tactics exploit and influence human behaviours to facilitate and enable cyber threats to be executed. According to Gragg (2002), persons that are at the highest risk of being victims of social engineering would be employees working in support-related departments of organisations (e.g., customer services, help desks, secretaries, personal assistants). This is because such professions require the employees to provide assistance to people, and it is uncommon for them to question the validity of every request due to the demanding nature of these jobs.

Establishing a sense of credibility and trust with the victim is the first step in most social engineering attacks and is considered to be the foundation for everything that follows (Mitnick & Simon, 2006). Techniques of social engineering can include, but are not limited to the following (Parker, 1998):

- **Baiting:** Usage of technical industry terminology for social engineers to appear more 'knowledgeable'.
- **Name-Dropping:** Implying close relationships with authority (i.e., familiarity) for approval to access secure information.
- **Exaggerating:** Downplaying or amplifying the criticality of a situation.
- **Asserting Authority:** Impersonating a higher authority figure/entity (can be either real or fictitious) to establish psychological dominance.
- **Intimidating, Threatening, or Shocking Scenarios:** Coerced victims into surrendering secure information or access through threats or intimidation.

One example of a cyber threat that combines both systems and human manipulation skills is spear phishing. Spear phishing is considered one of the most common threats to critical infrastructure (Wueest, 2014). It is a targeted email scam with the purpose of obtaining unauthorised access to confidential data. Furthermore, spear phishing is a targeted cyber threat which seeks out specific victims unlike phishing which does not have a specified target ("What is spear", 2015).

The following is a common scenario of spear phishing at work: An email arrives in the user's inbox from a perceived credible source (i.e., name-dropping) with a personalised subject title that may provide the user with a scenario that seems intimidating. The objective is to persuade and create panic in the user in order for him/her to let down his/her guard and click on a website link attached to the email. Once clicked, it then leads the user to a malicious website infected with malware.

Targets and Impact

As put forth by the definition, the act of cyberterrorism seeks to disrupt essential (e.g., political, social or economic) functioning of an organisation or a country. It does so by targeting critical infrastructure to induce grave harm (Applegate, 2013; Denning, 2001; Hua & Bapna, 2012). Critical infrastructure is a term used by governments to describe assets that are essential for the functioning of the society and economy (Cukier & Panjwani, 2010; Gorge, 2007). With deregulations and a focus on profits, many essential service industries are taking to the Internet to improve efficiency and reduce costs (Weimann, 2006). The online interconnectivity between critical infrastructure and 'supervisory control and data acquisition' (SCADA) systems have introduced security vulnerabilities (Verton, 2003). SCADA systems are substantially distributed networks used to control geographically dispersed critical infrastructure, and are essential to system operations (National Institute of Standards and Technology, 2006).

According to Wueest (2014), the energy sector (involving electricity, petroleum and natural gas) emerged amongst the top five major critical infrastructure sectors of targeted cyber attacks worldwide. There is a heavy reliance on the energy sector because almost all other critical infrastructure sectors are powered by electricity and fuel (Department of Homeland Security [DHS], 2014). The sheer complexity of the interconnectivity and interdependencies between and within the critical infrastructure sectors further exacerbate their security vulnerabilities which allow for malicious cyber attacks to take place (Storm, 2014).

According to a study done by security services firms, Unisys and Ponemon Institute (Kumar, 2014; Prince, 2014), alarming security gaps were found in critical infrastructure globally – 70 percent of these critical infrastructure organisations experienced at least one cyber breach in the past year. There have been many other instances that cyber attacks were launched against critical infrastructure sectors. Recognising the interconnectivity between critical infrastructure and online platforms designed to monitor and control physical processes, both security personnel and attackers know that it can be manipulated for different purposes (e.g., malicious) than what it was intended for. Below are some examples of critical infrastructure sectors where simulated or actual cyber attacks had occurred.

- **Electrical Generator:** In 2007, the U.S. Department of Homeland Security performed a hack simulation (i.e., Project Aurora) on an electrical generator, from the U.S. Department of Energy's Idaho Laboratory. The hackers managed to successfully force the motor to automatically self-destruct in 30 seconds by simply changing its operating cycle (Paganini, 2014). This exercise alarmed both the U.S. government and energy sector officials. This type of attack could potentially result in massive economic damages for regions heavily dependent on electrical power plants.
- **Sewage Processing:** From February to April 2000, Vitek Boden, a disgruntled ex-employee of Maroochy Water Services in Australia, waged a hacking campaign on approximately 46 occasions against his former company (Abrams & Weiss, 2008). He hacked into the SCADA systems that he had helped designed and installed. The attack resulted in the release of 800,000 litres of raw sewage at various locations in Queensland, which included local parks, rivers and even the vicinity surrounding a Hyatt Regency hotel. The end result of the attack led to massive environmental damage and unhealthy living conditions for the local residents (Applegate, 2013). A representative of the Australian Environmental Protection Agency, Janelle Bryant described the situation where the "marine life died, the water turned black and the stench was unbearable for the residents" (Smith, 2001, para. 2).
- **Land Traffic:** In February 2008, a fourteen-year-old Polish teenager described as a model student and an 'electronic genius' by his teachers, had rewired a television remote control to access the wireless switch junctions of the Lodz city tram system and transformed the actual system into his personal toy train set (Baker, 2008; Smith, 2008). The problem was discovered when a tram driver attempting to turn right was involuntarily taken to the left. The rear wagon derailed and collided with another passing tram. The teenager's action, which was intended as a prank, resulted in four derailed trams and minor injuries to more than a dozen passengers on board (Baker, 2008). Of note, this incident is of significance because it was the first cyber attack to directly cause injuries (Applegate, 2013).

Due to their interconnectivity, an attack on any one critical infrastructure can directly and indirectly affect other critical infrastructures, and send ripples throughout the nation (Rinaldi, Peerenboom, & Kelly, 2001). Various studies (e.g., Gorge, 2007; Loewengert, 2012; Rogers, 2003) have also outlined examples of potential risks to critical infrastructure – see Table 1.

Table 1. Examples of critical infrastructure sectors, potential vulnerabilities and consequences (adapted from Gorge, 2007; Loewengert, 2012; Rogers, 2003)

Critical Infrastructure Sector	Vulnerabilities	Potential Consequences of Cyberterrorism
Energy (electricity, petroleum and natural gas)	Disruptions in public health services	Severe economic damages
Banking and Finance	Economy	Loss of lives
Food and Drug industry	Food processing (e.g., changing food/medicine formulations) and its supply chain	Illnesses
Sewage plants	Sewage processing/disposal	Instil fear
Air/Land traffic controls	Risk of collisions, off course traffic disruption	Negative impact on credibility of industries and government
Processing of hazardous chemicals (e.g., radioactive materials)	Raw materials needed to fund weapons (e.g., bombs)	Crippled communications result in ineffective and slow recovery/response

Antagonists and Motivations

According to Heickerö (2007), antagonists are individuals or groups that have the capabilities, willingness and motivation to execute cyber threats against their chosen targets. In the field of terrorism, one of the challenges faced by authorities is the difficulty in developing a profile of a terrorist due to the lack of norms available for research (Prince, 2012). This applies to cyberterrorists as well – i.e., due to the lack of documented cyberterrorism attacks. The author argued that parallels can be drawn from the research on hacktivists and terrorists to understand the cyberterrorists, in terms of several factors. Table 2 outlines these factors.

Despite the parallels drawn in terms of motivation and online modus operandi, there is a need to distinguish between cyberterrorists and hacktivists. The objective of hacktivists is to protest and disrupt online platform functioning to draw media attention to perceived political, social and economic problems (Denning, 2009). Hacktivists do not have the intention to kill or endanger lives.

Table 2. Similar factors across the different antagonists (adapted from Heickerö, 2007)

Characteristics of Antagonists	Terrorist	Cyberterrorist	Hacktivist
Motivations	Political, social or ideological in nature (Denning, 2009)		
Online modus operandi	Use the Internet to disseminate propaganda, for communication, data mining, and mobilisation of resources (Weimann, 2006)	Use the Internet to conduct cyber attacks and social engineering to execute cyber threats (Dillon et al., 2015)	
Targets	Civilians, corporate and governments entities (Schmid, 2011)	Critical infrastructures and civilians (Denning, 2009)	Governments and corporate entities (Talihärm, 2010)
Ethics limitations	Intent to generate fear and cause deliberate and massive damage that endanger human lives and property (Prince, 2012)		Political protesting using technology and does not seek to cause harm (Weimman, 2006)

Moreover, it is important to note that the features of hacktivists and terrorists do highlight the potential threat of cyberterrorists. These are individuals who have the technical capabilities to inflict massive damage and endanger human lives (Weimann, 2006). Recent trends have highlighted several antagonists for consideration.

- **Potential Escalation of Hacktivism to Cyberterrorism:** Despite evidence of hacktivists' ethical concerns (i.e., no intention to kill or endanger lives), these individuals may still be at a higher risk of escalating their cyber threats to cyberterrorism. This can be attributed to the similarities between hacktivists and cyberterrorists as outlined in Table 2. An instance would be the 2007 Estonia politically motivated DDoS cyber attacks. The attack, which was labelled as hacktivism, targeted political parties, governments, financial networks, and Internet infrastructure amongst others (Lachow, 2009; Iasiello, 2013). The three-week long campaign was in response to the Estonian government relocating a memorial statue, which commemorates Soviet liberation of the country from the Nazis, to a less prominent spot (Herzog, 2011). Despite the political intent behind the cyber attacks, the perpetrators were able to disrupt essential services and force the Estonian government to block off international traffic and isolate the country from rest of the world. Another example would be Anonymous, a notorious international hacktivist collective with a decentralised command structure (Kelly, 2012; Stone, 2014). On April 2014, an alleged Anonymous offshoot had threatened Israel with cyberterrorism with the intention to expose their 'terrorist activities' to the world (Elis, 2014; Shamah, 2014). These examples are of significance because they illustrated the point that hacktivists themselves may have the capabilities to take their political activism to the next level.
- **Possible Collaborations between Hackers and Terrorists:** Contemporary terrorists are shifting their attention to recruit computer professionals (e.g., hackers) to their cause. These computer professionals would possess the capabilities to conduct cyber attacks for them. For instance, an AQ produced video was circulated around the Internet depicting an AQ representative calling for 'electronic jihad' by 'covert mujahideens' against the U.S. government and critical infrastructures – in particular electronic grids, water delivery systems and the finance sector (Cloherty, 2012; Mehan, 2014; Paganini, 2012; "US Senators: Al Qaeda", 2012). Another example would be that of the late Junaid Hussain, a twenty-year-old from Birmingham who had fled to Syria to join ISIS (Glum, 2015). He was dubbed the ISIS 'jihadi hacker' and went by the online moniker, Abu Hussain al-Britani (Corcoran, 2015). Hussain was believed to be the leader of ISIS CyberCaliphate and was leading efforts to recruit hackers (MacAskill, 2015). He was also the prime suspect behind the hack on the U.S. Central Command Twitter Account (Halleck, 2015). It may seem that terrorist organisations like AQ and ISIS are developing propaganda targeted at hackers in their attempt to recruit them to their cause.
- **Nation-State Threat:** Several incidents involving nation-states have illustrated the potential threat of cyberterrorism. An example would be the recent declaration of cyber war on China by the United States (Cornwell, 2014). This was in response to incidents where Chinese government-approved hackers attempted to hack into major American companies with ties to critical infrastructure sectors (e.g., nuclear energy, electrical power). Another critical example would be that of the aforementioned Stuxnet case. The complexity of this malware and its target specifications seems to suggest that the perpetrators were targeting an entire nation-state.

THE FOUR-STEP CYBERTERRORISM ATTACK SEQUENCE

This section will highlight the four-step cyberterrorism attack sequence (refer to Figure 2) based on insights gathered from experts (e.g., Gorge, 2007; Rogers, 2003).

Stage 1: Identification of Nation's Critical Infrastructure

Critical infrastructure sectors are connected to one another in complex connections, termed as cyber interdependencies. According to Rinaldi and colleagues (2001), cyber interdependencies are bidirectional relationships between two infrastructure sectors through which the state of each infrastructure depends on information transmitted through SCADA from the connected infrastructure. By targeting the critical infrastructures, their interdependencies allow for the effect of any attack to be multiplied which is also known as the 'ripple effect' phenomenon (Public Safety and Emergency Preparedness Canada, 2006).

To put things in context, the 2003 northeast blackout[1], for example, illustrated the multiplied effect a disruption of one critical infrastructure can have on other infrastructures. Even though the disruption is not a result of a cyber attack, investigations revealed that the blackout initiated in Ohio quickly spread to the rest of the connected electrical grid, demonstrating that tightly interconnected critical infrastructures are highly vulnerable to cascading failure (Lark, Nelson, & Chappelle, 2003). The power outage has significantly impacted the energy sector in terms of manufacturing and transporting products; the telecommunications sector in terms of operational difficulties; and even the food industry in terms of shipping and storage issues (Public Safety and Emergency Preparedness Canada, 2006).

Stage 2: Target Intelligence Gathering

Once critical infrastructure sectors are identified, perpetrators would start to gather intelligence about their targets. In terms of human targets, one process of gathering significant information is via social engineering. At the same time, another process to gather information on system targets would be foot-

Figure 2. Summary of the four-step cyberterrorism attack sequence (Dillon et al., 2015)

LEGEND:
** - Refers to intervention

Prevention countermeasures in place by the relevant authorities puts up a great resistance against attackers because attackers prefer a path of least resistance to reach the largest number of potential victims for the minimal amount of exploitative effort (Horacek, 2013)

** Stage 1: Identification of nation's critical infrastructure sectors

Attackers identify nation's CI sectors and its cyber interdependencies suitable to their agenda which may be influenced by the political, social or economic climate.

** Stage 2: Target intelligence gathering

Stage 3: Cyber attack launched

Cyber attacks are launched to gain complete control over the computer systems

Stage 4: Post-attack investigation

Attacks can be successful or foiled

Cyber risk management
Cyber forensic experts

printing, which is the use of cyber attack techniques to understand and identify the best way to attack these targets. Examples of techniques include but are not limited to the following:

- A digital surveillance tool known as Remote Control System (Bell, 2014). This is a furtive, spyware-based system for attacking, infecting, and monitoring computers and smart phones. Substantial amount of intelligence including encrypted communications (e.g., secure web mail) on targeted users will be provided by the software.
- The controversial anti-Google search engine, Shodan. According to Lee (2013), Shodan is a computer web search engine that allows users to search for the physical locations of electronic devices such as webcams, iPhones, routers, and even power plants.
- Conducting illegal penetration tests to simulate illegal cyber attacks (e.g., hacking) without the authorisation of relevant parties on specific websites of interest to identify security vulnerabilities or zero-day threats[2].

Stage 3: Cyber Attack Launched

Once the process of intelligence gathering is completed, cyber attacks are then launched on the identified targets. Results from a survey conducted by Trend Micro and Organisation of American States (OAS) with 575 critical infrastructure security leaders from various countries identified the most common types of attacks targeted at critical infrastructure – see Figure 3 (Walker, 2015). For example, malware can be launched to gain root (i.e., complete control) over the targeted computer systems, which may be maintained by the attackers for a period of time. Attacks on targeted critical infrastructure sectors may occur in isolation (i.e., one after another) or simultaneously. Attacks are either successful or foiled by the authorities.

Stage 4: Post-Attack Investigation

Government authorities and security agencies are involved during the post-attack investigations. Examples of actions taken by these entities include but are not limited to the following:

- Internal protocols on cyber risk management are implemented to mitigate the damages.
- Agencies made up of cyber forensic experts such as the Computer Emergency Response Teams (CERTs) can be established. These organisations are employed to implement appropriate technology and systems management practices to mitigate damages and ensure continuity of essential services of critical infrastructure sectors.

POTENTIAL INTERVENTIONS

Analysis of the hypothetical four-step cyberterrorism attack sequence may allow authorities to introduce interventions to prevent cyber attacks from occurring. In particular, the author argued that knowledge of the first and second stages of the four-step cyberterrorism attack sequence would provide valuable insights on the types of interventions that can be implemented.

Figure 3. Cyber attack trend against critical infrastructure (Walker, 2015)

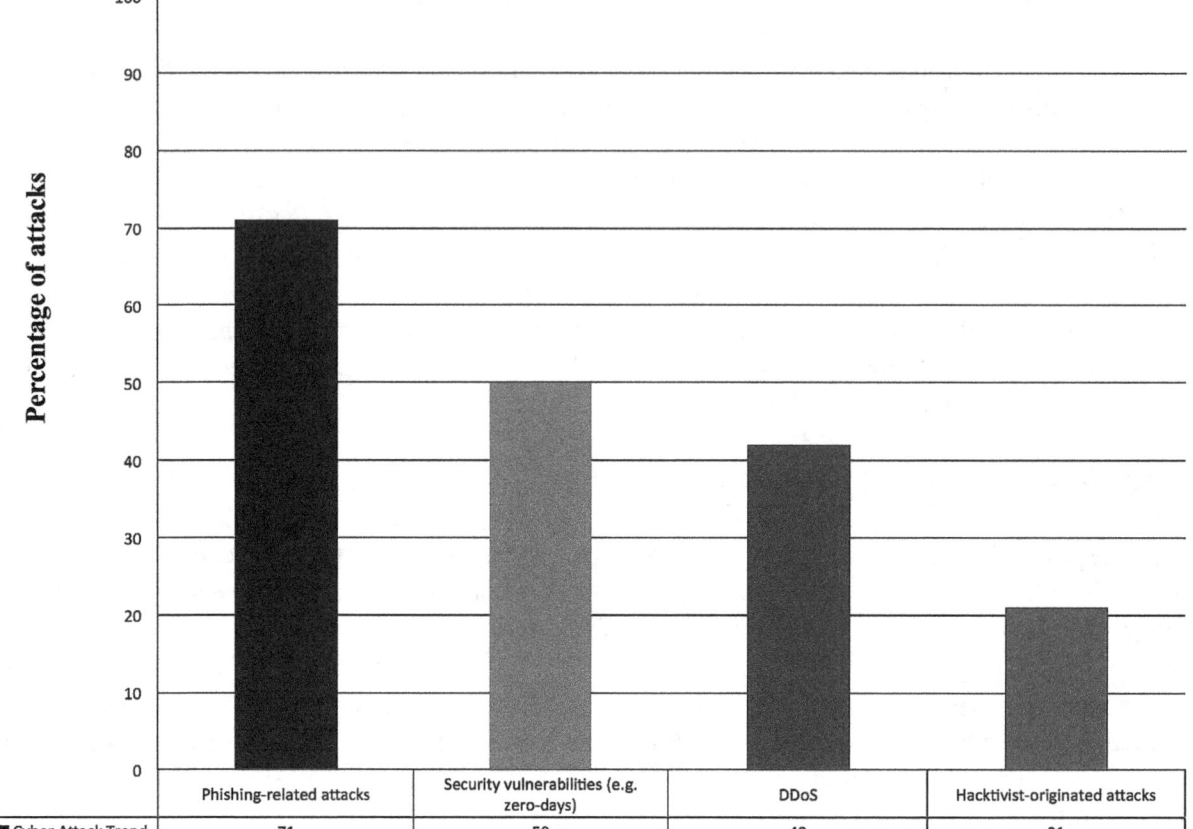

	Phishing-related attacks	Security vulnerabilities (e.g. zero-days)	DDoS	Hacktivist-originated attacks
■ Cyber Attack Trend	71	50	42	21

Interventions for Stage 1

In terms of interventions at Stage 1 (i.e., identification of nation's critical infrastructure sectors), the process of identifying the nation's critical infrastructure sectors in terms of its cyber interdependencies is essential for prioritising resources for cybersecurity protection. For instance, measures have been put in place by several countries to access and protect the cyber interdependencies of critical infrastructure sectors.

Singapore

One of Singapore's initiatives includes the setting up of the Programme on Interdependency Assessment and Studies (NIDAS) within the National Security Coordination Secretariat (NSCS) in 2012 with the objective to become the national focal point for the study of interdependencies within and across domains that impact Singapore's national security (National Security Coordination Secretariat, 2013). Another local initiative is the set-up of the National Critical Infrastructure Assurance (NCIA) in 2002 to carry out exhaustive assessments of vulnerabilities of the nation's critical infrastructure, and develop measures to mitigate these vulnerabilities. This program involves close collaborations between the private sector and the government (National Security Coordination Secretariat, 2004).

United States

One of United States's initiatives includes the National Infrastructure Protection Plan (NIPP) which was developed in 2006 by the Department of Homeland Security (DHS). It provides an overall framework for existing and potential programs, and activities to protect the nation's critical infrastructure. One key element in this initiative is the institutionalisation of public-private information sharing and partnerships in critical infrastructure protection. Another key element is its special consideration to the cyber dimension of critical infrastructure protection (Brunner & Suter, 2008; DHS, 2013a).

United Kingdom

One of United Kingdom's initiatives includes the National Information Assurance Strategy (NIAS) which was developed in 2003 by the Central Sponsor for Information Assurance (CSIA). The CSIA is a unit housed within the Cabinet Office with the objective to protect critical infrastructures from two kinds of threats – physical attacks and electronic attacks. One key element in NIAS is that the initiative recognises the interdependencies and interconnectivity of the information infrastructure, and the key role played by critical infrastructures' owners and operators (Brunner & Suter, 2008; DHS, 2013b). CSIA also collaborates with other organisations to coordinate and sponsor work programs to deliver the strategy's recommendations.

Interventions for Stage 2

At Stage 2 (i.e., target intelligence gathering), identifying defences against cyber attacks and social engineering is essential in preventing the deception of victims, and augmenting the cybersecurity of critical infrastructure. The process of gathering intelligence may work as a double-edged sword for both the attacker and the victim alike (McGreevy, 2002). Information gathering on the system and human vulnerabilities by the attacker can put the victim at a disadvantage. Similarly, victims who are aware of these vulnerabilities may have the knowledge to foil potential attacks.

According to Wueest (2014), the isolated cyber attacks that were launched against critical infrastructure sectors were not highly sophisticated and could have been prevented by adhering to best practices for cyber attack defences. Examples of best practices include but are not limited to the following:

Firewalls

Firewalls are basic devices or software programs that monitor data flow from one computer to another on a network. Accordingly, a firewall detects and deters would-be cyber attacks by providing alert messaging and management on attempted attacks to the users (Marcella & Greenfield, 2002).

Cybersecurity Professionals

These are authorised personnel employed by organisations to deliberately compromise computer systems for ethical purposes (Dillon, Neo, Ong, & Khader, 2014). These computer security professionals conduct penetration testing with the intent to test the effectiveness of the security defences of an organisation's computer systems, and identify the best ways to prevent malicious attackers from exploiting security vulnerabilities (Hoffman, 2013). For instance, cybersecurity professionals identifying zero-day threats in the computer software can provide solutions to fix the issues before malicious attackers can exploit them. These solutions can come in the forms of security patches (i.e., software updates) which serve a number of different functions (Goodrich, 2014):

- Fix security features
- Additional newer/secure features
- Remove old/unprotected features
- Increase software efficiency

Computer security professionals can also monitor attackers by using an effective method known as 'honeypots'. Honeypots are systems which function as organisational production systems that contain 'valuable data'. In other words, the data contained in these systems is not real (Government of Hong Kong Special Administrative Region, 2008). Subtle vulnerabilities have been deliberately set up within the system so that the attacker will 'take the bait'. Many organisations have used this technique to collect information on the most up-to-date malware and attack signatures so that these cyber attack techniques can be analysed to better understand the modus operandi of the attackers, and address technical vulnerabilities of their systems (Loewengart, 2012).

Centralised Security Log

This measure records suspicious online activities found within the computer systems (Marcella & Greenfield, 2002). An example would be the use of an indicator and warning checklist to detect impending cyber attacks – see table 3 (Long, 2012).

Table 3. A basic indicator and warning indicator checklist (adapted from Long, 2012)

Indicator of Activity	Yes / No
A well-known hole is found in the operating system or software that is not patched	
Port scans	
Social engineering attempts to solicit passwords, etc. Examples include employees getting email scams generated from a seemingly same person/group	
Attempted DDoS attacks	
Targeted website attacks: Defacement, SQL Injections, etc.	
Unsecured wireless access points	

For such a countermeasure to be effective, raising awareness about potential attackers throughout the organisation is required in order to alert other employees to be on their guard (Gragg, 2002). According to the Industrial Control Systems Cyber Emergency Response Team, "the ability to detect anomalous network activity and intrusions early in an incident, greatly increases the chance of successful mitigation and resolution" (Lennon, 2013, para. 22).

Profiling Potential Attackers

Profiling of attackers' modus operandi allows for security personnel to take necessary steps to protect against vulnerabilities and loopholes within computer systems. Studying past cyber threats allows cybersecurity agencies to anticipate the types of organisations (e.g., government agencies, non-profit organisations) that are being targeted by the attackers. This in turn, could help by providing forewarning of an impending cyber attack – see Table 4.

According to Mitnick and Simon (2006), social engineering techniques prey on the best qualities of human nature – i.e., our natural tendencies to be helpful, polite, and supportive, to be a team player, and the desire to get the job done. From a cognitive psychology perspective, social engineering techniques play on the heuristics that victims may have based on their unique experiences. Heuristics are used to reduce mental effort in decision-making but they may lead to systematic biases or errors in judgement especially in ambiguous situations (Tversky & Kahneman, 1974). For example, social psychologist Sagarin opined that

[W]e might comply with a request based on who the requestor claims to be, rather than the sensitivity of the information he or she has requested ... [factors like] time pressure, distractions or strong emotions can switch us to heuristic mode (as cited in Mitnick & Simon, 2006, p. 234).

According to Mitnick and Simon (2006), social engineering defences require a series of coordinated efforts which can include but are not limited to the following:

Table 4. Basic profile of a potential attacker (adapted from Long, 2012)

Attacker Profile Themes				
Targeted victims	Individual	Company	Government	Group
	• Why this victim? • Was this victim the only target?			
Attacker(s)	Individual	Group		Government
	• Any website depicting claims of responsibility • Any criminal history of the attacker(s)			
Motivations	• What is the agenda? (e.g., political, financial)			
Methods	• Presence of an attack signature • Presence of tools/techniques used			
Obstacles faced	• Presence of challenges posed to the attacker(s) by the victims (e.g., firewalls to keep out spams) • Are the attacks successful?			
Possibility of a future attack	• Based on the information gathered on the attacker(s), will the attacker(s) be likely to continue in the future?			

- **Developing a Concise Framework of Security Protocols:** These protocols must be enforced throughout the organisation by:
  - Having simple rules to define which information are considered confidential and may compromise cybersecurity in certain circumstances. For instance, developing a data classification system (e.g., sensitive, restricted, confidential) and protocols for who should be able to access such information.
  - Implementing physical staff escorts for visitors to the organisation. Staff escorts should be briefed on the security risks associated with the physical presence of an unescorted visitor. They should have the authority to address such a situation even if the visitor claims to have 'proof of identity' (e.g., access pass, badge, uniform).

    By having a framework outlining the security protocols of the organisation, this can increase employees' resistance to deception through the development of employees' perceived confidence in exerting their authority (Petty, Briñol, & Tormala, 2002). However, in order for this to be an effective countermeasure, heavy emphasis must be placed on enforcing such frameworks.

- **Performing Frequent Security Risk Assessments:** Security risk assessments may consist of 'surprise drills' to test employees' susceptibility to social engineering attacks by using professional actors to take on the role of social engineers. This can be enforced by:
  - Conducting awareness training and re-training on a frequent basis.
  - Using role-play to demonstrate personal vulnerability to social engineering attacks.
  - Examining the mechanism of such attacks, providing analysis on why they worked and then discussing how to recognise such attacks.

    Regular awareness training should be conducted for employees to keep abreast with new ways to defend against social engineering. Furthermore, this countermeasure is essential because most employees operate under the illusion of invulnerability and perceive themselves to be 'too smart' to be manipulated, and that only 'stupid' people are conned by such attacks (Mitnick & Simon, 2006).

- **Setting Personal Safety Protocols:** According to Criddle (2014), employees themselves can also adopt the following techniques as a countermeasure against these attackers:
  - Slow down. Do not let emotions overtake rational thoughts.
  - Research the facts. Keep a lookout of the URLs of the websites for misspellings.
  - Delete any requests for confidential information/passwords. Take extra caution with personal information that can compromise online assets or accounts.
  - Reject suspicious offers asking/offering help. Legitimate organisations do not initiate contact with unsolicited offers of assistance.
  - Do not let a web-link be in control of where one lands. Stay in control by finding the website using a search engine to be sure one lands as intended. Hovering over the link will show the actual URL in a pop-up box but a good fake may still steer one towards a wrong site.

CONCLUSION

This final section will highlight several concluding thoughts based on the overall content of the chapter. Firstly, with ISIS's intense propaganda war online to attract a diverse nature of audiences including computer professionals, the online terrorism threat landscape is slowly evolving (Halleck, 2015). Secondly, while the aforementioned examples provided on isolated breaches had rather mild consequences (e.g., pollution, unhealthy living conditions), they illustrated the possibility of cyberterrorism becoming a real threat that has a high possibility of occurring in the future. Thirdly, these examples illustrated that cyberterrorists have the capabilities to potentially compromise critical infrastructure sectors with ease. Lastly, attackers who have the capabilities to execute cyber attacks against critical infrastructures and can be classified as cyberterrorists are nation states (with reference to the Stuxnet case) as well as terrorist and hacker collaborators (with reference to the CyberCaliphate) (Vatis, 2001). It can be seen that the potential impact of cyberterrorism is limited only by the imagination, human and technical skills of these attackers wielding the new weapon of choice, the Internet.

REFERENCES

Abraham, S., & Chengalur-Smith, I. S. (2010). An overview of social engineering malware: Trends, tactics and implications. *Technology in Society*, *32*(3), 183–196. doi:10.1016/j.techsoc.2010.07.001

Abrams, M., & Weiss, J. (2008). Malicious control system cyber security attack case study: Maroochy water services. Australia: National Institute of Standards and Technology. Retrieved from http://csrc. nist.gov/groups/SMA/fisma/ics/documents/Maroochy-Water-Services-Case-Study_report.pdf

Acharya, A. (2004). Defending Singapore's vital infrastructure against terrorism. *IDSS Commentaries*. Retrieved from http://www.pvtr.org/pdf/commentaries/IDSS372004.pdf

Ahmad, R., Yunos, Z., Sahib, S., & Yusoff, M. (2012). Perception on cyber terrorism: A focus group discussion approach. *Journal of Information Security*, *3*(03), 231–237. doi:10.4236/jis.2012.33029

Applegate, S. D. (2013). The dawn of kinetic cyber. In K. Podins, J. Stinissen, & M. Maybaum (Eds.), *5th international conference on cyber conflict*. Estonia, Tallinn: NATO CCD COE Publication.

Awan, I. (2014). Debating the term cyber-terrorism: Issues and problems. *Internet Journal of Criminology*. Retrieved from http://www.internetjournalofcriminology.com/awan_debating_the_term_cyber-terrorism_ijc_jan_2014.pdf

Baker, G. (2008, January 11). Schoolboy hacks into city's tram system. *The Telegraph*. Retrieved from http://www.telegraph.co.uk/news/worldnews/1575293/Schoolboy-hacks-into-citys-tram-system.html

Ballard, J. D., Hornik, J. G., & McKenzie, D. (2004). Technological facilitation of terrorism. In A. O'Day (Ed.), *The international library of essays in terrorism: Cyberterrorism* (pp. 39–66). London: Ashgate Publishing Limited.

Bell, L. (2014, June 25). Hacking Team's government spy tool components uncovered by Kapersky. *The Inquirer*. Retrieved from http://www.theinquirer.net/inquirer/news/2352077/hacking-teams-government-spy-tool-components-uncovered-by-kaspersky

Blakemore, B. (2012). Cyberspace, cyber crime and cyber terrorism. In I. Awan & B. Blakemore (Eds.), *Policing cyber hate, cyber threats and cyber terrorism* (pp. 5–20). London: Ashgate Publishing Limited.

Brunner, E. M., & Suter, M. (2008). *International CIIP handbook 2008/2009: An inventory of 25 national and 7 international critical information infrastructure protection policies.* Zurich, Switzerland: Center for Security Studies.

CATO Institute. (2010). *The underwhelming threat of cyberterrorism.* Retrieved from http://www.cato.org/policy-report/januaryfebruary-2011/underwhelming-threat-cyberterrorism

Cendrowicz, L. (2014, October 30). NATO frontline in life-or-death war on cyber-terrorists. *The Guardian.* Retrieved from http://www.theguardian.com/world/2014/oct/30/nato-frontline-cyber-terrorists-war

Chen, T. M. (2014). *Cyberterrorism after Stuxnet.* Carlisle, PA: Strategic Studies Institute and U.S. Army War College Press.

Cloherty, J. (2012, May 22). Virtual terrorism: Al-Qaeda video calls for 'electronic jihad'. *ABC News.* Retrieved from http://abcnews.go.com/Politics/cyber-terrorism-al-qaeda-video-calls-electronic-jihad/story?id=16407875

Conway, M. (2002). Reality bytes: Cyberterrorism and terrorist 'use' of the internet. *First Monday, 7*(11). http://firstmonday.org/ojs/index.php/fm/article/view/1001/922 doi:10.5210/fm.v7i11.1001

Conway, M. (2004). *Cyberterrorism: Media myth or clear and present danger?* Retrieved from http://doras.dcu.ie/505/1/media_myth_2004.pdf

Conway, M. (2011). Against cyberterrorism: Why cyber-based terrorist attacks are unlikely to occur? [CACM]. *Communications of the ACM, 54*(2), 26–28. doi:10.1145/1897816.1897829

Corcoran, K. (2014, August 16). British hacker 'masterminding plan to teach jihadists how to steal from bank accounts of rich and famous to fund terror campaign'. *Daily Mail.* Retrieved from http://www.dailymail.co.uk/news/article-2726522/British-hacker-masterminding-plan-teach-jihadists-steal-bank-accounts-rich-famous-fund-terror-campaign.html

Cornwell, R. (2014, May 19). US declares cyber war on China: Chinese military hackers charged with trying to steal secrets from companies including nuclear energy firm. *The Independent.* Retrieved from http://www.independent.co.uk/life-style/gadgets-and-tech/us-charges-chinese-military-hackers-with-cyber-espionage-bid-to-gain-advantage-in-nuclear-power-metals-and-solar-product-industries-9397661.html

Criddle, L. (2014). What is social engineering? *Webroot.* Retrieved from http://www.webroot.com/us/en/home/resources/tips/online-shopping-banking/secure-what-is-social-engineering

Cukier, M., & Panjwani, S. (2010). Risk analysis methods for cyber security. In J. G. Voeller (Ed.), *Wiley handbook of science and technology for homeland security* (Vol. 1, pp. 279–289). Hoboken, NJ: John Wiley & Sons, Inc.

Denning, D. E. (2009). *Activism, hacktivism and cyberterrorism: The Internet as a tool for influencing foreign policy.* Santa Monica, CA: RAND Corporation.

Department of Homeland Security (DHS). (2013a). *NIPP 2013: Partnering for critical infrastructure security and resilience.* Retrieved from http://www.dhs.gov/sites/default/files/publications/NIPP%202013_Partnering%20for%20Critical%20Infrastructure%20Security%20and%20Resilience_508_0.pdf

Department of Homeland Security (DHS). (2013b). *National Infrastructure Protection Plan*. Retrieved from http://www.dhs.gov/sites/default/files/publications/NIPP-Fact-Sheet-508.pdf

Department of Homeland Security (DHS). (2014). *Energy sector: Sector overview*. Retrieved from http://www.dhs.gov/energy-sector

Desouza, K. C., & Hensgen, T. (2003). Semiotic emergent framework to address the reality of cyberterrorism. *Technological Forecasting and Social Change, 70*(4), 385–296. doi:10.1016/S0040-1625(03)00003-9

Dillon, L., Neo, L. S., Ong, G., & Khader, M. (2014). *Psychology behind hackers: A multiple-case study approach (Research report no. 17/2014)*. Singapore: Home Team Behavioural Sciences Centre.

Dillon, L., Neo, L. S., Ong, G., & Khader, M. (2015). *Cyberterrorism: A kinetic cyber threat (Research report no. 07/2015)*. Singapore: Home Team Behavioural Sciences Centre.

Dogrul, M., Aslan, A., & Celik, E. (2011). Developing an international cooperation on cyber defense and deterrence against cyber terrorism. In C. Czosseck, E. Tyugu, & T. Wingfield (Eds.), *3rd international conference on cyber conflict*. Estonia, Tallinn: NATO CCD COE Publications.

Elis, N. (2014, April 6). Anonymous hackers threaten Israel with cyberterrorism. *The JerusalemPost*. Retrieved from http://www.jpost.com/Defense/Anonymous-hackers-threaten-Israel-with-cyber-terrorism-347667

Ellyatt, H. (2015, January 27). Cyberterrorists to target critical infrastructure. *CNBC*. Retrieved from http://www.cnbc.com/2015/01/27/cyberterrorists-to-target-critical-infrastructure.html

Esen, R. (2002). Cybercrime: A growing problem. *Journal of Criminal Law, 66*(3), 269–283.

Furnell, S. M., & Warren, M. J. (1999). Computer hacking and cyber terrorism: The real threats in the new millennium? *Computers & Security, 18*(1), 28–34. doi:10.1016/S0167-4048(99)80006-6

Glum, J. (2015, August 28). ISIS hacker Junaid Hussain confirmed dead after US airstrike on Islamic State in Syria: Pentagon. *International Business Times*. Retrieved from http://www.ibtimes.com/isis-hacker-junaid-hussain-confirmed-dead-after-us-airstrike-islamic-state-syria-2073451

Goodrich, R. (2014). PC security and the importance of patch updates. *Top Ten Reviews*. Retrieved from http://anti-virus-software-review.toptenreviews.com/pc-security-and-the-importance-of-patch-updates.html

Gorge, M. (2007). Cyberterrorism: Hype or reality? *Computer Fraud & Security, 2*(2), 9–12. doi:10.1016/S1361-3723(07)70021-0

Government of Hong Kong Special Administrative Region. (2008). *Honeypot security*. Retrieved from http://www.infosec.gov.hk/textonly/english/technical/files/honeypots.pdf

Gragg, D. (2002). A multi-level defense against social engineering. *SANS Institute*. Retrieved from http://www.sans.org/reading-room/whitepapers/engineering/multi-level-defense-social-engineering-920

Green, J. (2002, November). The myth of cyberterrorism. *Washington Monthly*. Retrieved from http://www.washingtonmonthly.com/features/2001/0211.green.html

Halleck, T. (2015, January 13). Junaid Hussain: CyberCaliphate leader and ISIS member was behind CENTCOM hack, report says. *International Business Times*. Retrieved from http://www.ibtimes.com/junaid-hussain-cybercaliphate-leader-isis-member-was-behind-centcom-hack-report-says-1782870

Hardy, K., & Williams, G. (2012). What is 'cyberterrorism'? Computer and internet technology in legal definitions of terrorism. In T. Chen, L. Jarvis, & S. Macdonald (Eds.), *Cyberterrorism: Understanding, assessment and response* (pp. 1–23). New York, NY: Springer.

Harress, C. (2014, February 18). Obama says cyberterrorism is country's biggest threat, U.S government assembles "cyber warriors". *International Business Times*. Retrieved from http://www.ibtimes.com/obama-says-cyberterrorism-countrys-biggest-threat-us-government-assembles-cyber-warriors-1556337

Heickerö, R. (2007). Terrorism online and the change of modus operandi. *Swedish Defence Research Agency, FOI*. Retrieved from http://www.unidir.ch/files/conferences/pdfs/information-warfare-and-cyber-terrorism-en-1-69.pdf

Herzog, S. (2011). Revisiting the Estonian cyber attacks: Digital threats and multinational responses. *Journal of Strategic Security*, *4*(2), 49–60. doi:10.5038/1944-0472.4.2.3

Hoffman, C. (2013). Hacker hat colors explained: Black hats, white hats and gray hats. *How-To Geek*. Retrieved from http://www.howtogeek.com/157460/

Hua, J., & Bapna, S. (2012). How can we deter cyber terrorism? *International Security Journal: A Global Perspective, 21*, 102-114.

Iasiello, E. (2013). Cyber attack: A dull tool to shape foreign policy. In K. Podins, J. Stinissen, & M. Maybaum (Eds.), *5th international conference on cyber conflict*. Estonia, Tallinn: NATO CCD COE Publication.

Idaho National Laboratory. (2006). *Critical infrastructure interdependency modelling: A survey of U.S. and international research (INL/EXT-06-11464)*. Washington, DC: DOE Idaho Operations Office.

Jarvis, L., MacDonald, S., & Whiting, A. (2015). Constructing cyberterrorism as a security threat: A study of international news media coverage. *Perspectives on Terrorism*, *9*(1), 60–75.

Jarvis, L., Nouri, L., & Whiting, A. (2014). Understanding, locating and constructing cyberterrorism. In T. Chen, L. Jarvis, & S. Macdonald (Eds.), *Cyberterrorism: Understanding, assessment and response* (pp. 25–41). New York, NY: Springer.

Kelly, S. (2012). Cyber attacks target gas pipeline companies. *CNN*. Retrieved from http://security.blogs.cnn.com/2012/05/08/cyber-attack-targets-gas-pipeline-companies/

Kerr, P. K., Rollins, J., & Theohary, C. A. (2010). The Stuxnet computer worm: Harbinger of an emerging warfare capability (R41524). *Congressional Research Service*. Retrieved from https://www.fas.org/sgp/crs/natsec/R41524.pdf

Kumar, A. (2014, August 14). 'Alarming gaps' as 78% of Malaysian critical infrastructure providers breached, Unisys says. *Computer World*. Retrieved from http://computerworld.com.sg/print-article/64471/

Lachow, I. (2009). Cyberterrorism: Menace or myth? In F. D. Kramer, S. H. Starr, & L. K. Wentz (Eds.), *Cyberpower and national security* (pp. 123–139). Washington, DC: NDU Press.

Lachow, I. (2011). The Stuxnet enigma: Implications for the future of cybersecurity. *Georgetown Journal of International Affairs,* 118-126.

Lark, J., Nelson, R., & Chappelle, L. (2003). *Michigan Public Service Commission report on August 14th blackout.* Michigan, MI: Michigan Public Service Commission.

Lee, A. (2013, April 13). Shodan, the frightening search tool that uncovers security holes in your home, business and more. *Techno Buffalo.* Retrieved from http://www.technobuffalo.com/2013/04/13/shodan-search-sniffs-out-frightening-and-common-security-holes/

Lennon, M. (2013, July 1). Cyber attacks targeted key components of natural gas pipeline systems. *Security Week.* Retrieved from http://www.securityweek.com/cyber-attacks-targeted-key-components-natural-gas-pipeline-systems

Loewengart, V. (2012). *Proactive defense against cybercriminals: Striking back.* Retrieved from http://www.academia.edu/2215078/Proactive_Defense_against_Cyber-Criminals_Striking_Back

Long, A. (2012). Profiling hackers. *SANS Institute.* Retrieved from http://www.sans.org/reading-room/whitepapers/hackers/profiling-hackers-33864

MacAskill, E. (2015, January 14). Briton lead suspect after US Central Command's Twitter account is hacked. *The Guardian.* Retrieved from http://www.theguardian.com/us-news/2015/jan/14/briton-suspect-us-central-command-twitter-hack-junaid-hussain-tony-blair

Marcella, A. J., & Greenfield, R. S. (2002). *Cyber forensics: A field manual for collecting, examining and preserving evidence for computer crimes.* Boca Raton, FL: CRC Press LLC. doi:10.1201/9781420000115

Mask malware takes aim at governments and activists. (2014, February 11). *BBC News.* Retrieved from http://www.bbc.com/news/technology-26136412

McGreevy, J. P. (2002). Footprinting: What is it, who should do it and why? *SANS Institute.* Retrieved from http://www.sans.org/reading-room/whitepapers/auditing/footprinting-it-it-why-62

McGuire, M. R. (2014). Putting the 'cyber' into cyberterrorism: Re-reading technological risk in a hyperconnected world. In T. Chen, L. Jarvis, & S. Macdonald (Eds.), *Cyberterrorism: Understanding, assessment, and response* (pp. 63–84). New York, NY: Springer.

McQuade, S. C. (2006). *Understanding and managing cybercrime.* Boston, MA: Pearson Education, Inc.

Mehan, J. E. (Ed.). (2014). *Cyberwar, cyberterror, cybercrime and cyberactivism: An in-depth guide to the role of standards in the cybersecurity environment.* Cambridge: IT Governance Publishing.

Mitnick, K. D., & Simon, W. L. (2006). Social engineers: How they work and how to stop them. In C. Long, E. Herman, & K. Shafer (Eds.), *The art of intrusion: The real stories behind the exploits of hackers, intruders & deceivers* (pp. 221–245). Indianapolis, IN: Wiley Publishing, Inc.

National Institute of Standards and Technology. (2006). *Guide to supervisory control and data acquisition (SCADA) and industrial control systems security: Recommendations of the national institute of standards and technology (Special Publication 800-82)*. Gaithersburg, MD: Department of Commerce.

National Security Coordination Secretariat (NSCS). (2004). *The fight against terror: Singapore's national security strategy*. Retrieved from http://www.nscs.gov.sg/public/download.ashx?id=48

National Security Coordination Secretariat (NSCS). (2013). *Supporting centres*. Retrieved from http://www.nscs.gov.sg/public/content.aspx?sid=28

O'Shea, K. (2003). *Cyber attack investigative tools and technologies* [Powerpoint slides]. Hanover, NH: Darmouth College Institute for Security Technology Studies.

Paganini, P. (2012, May 26). Al Qaeda continues to frighten the U.S., cyber war has begun. *Security Affairs*. Retrieved from http://securityaffairs.co/wordpress/5745/intelligence/al-qaeda-continues-to-frighten-the-u-s-the-cyber-war-is-begun.html

Paginini, P. (2014, May 26). Critical infrastructure, hackers targeted public utility SCADA. *Security Affairs*. Retrieved from http://securityaffairs.co/wordpress/25240/hacking/critical-infrastructure-hackers-targeted-public-utility-scada.html

Pan, J. Y., & Fung, C. C. (2008). Artificial intelligence in malware: Cop or culprit? In *Proceedings of The Ninth Postgraduate Electrical Engineering and Computing Symposium*. Perth, Australia: University of Western Australia.

Parker, D. B. (1998). *Fighting computer crime: A new framework for protecting information*. New York, NY: Wiley Computer Publishing.

Petty, R. E., Briñol, P., & Tormala, Z. L. (2002). Thought confidence as a determinant of persuasion: The self-validation hypothesis. *Journal of Personality and Social Psychology, 82*(5), 722–741. doi:10.1037/0022-3514.82.5.722 PMID:12003473

Prince, B. (2014, July). Almost 70% of critical infrastructure companies breached in last 12 months: Survey. *Security Week*. Retrieved from http://www.securityweek.com/almost-70-percent-critical-infrastructure-companies-breached-last-12-months-survey

Prince, J. (2012). Psychological aspects of cyber hate and cyber terrorism. In I. Awan & B. Blakemore (Eds.), *Policing cyber hate, cyber threats and cyber terrorism* (pp. 39–55). London: Ashgate Publishing Limited.

Public Safety and Emergency Preparedness Canada. (2006). *Incident analysis: Ontario-U.S. power outage – impacts on critical infrastructure* (IA06-002). Retrieved from http://cip.management.dal.ca/publications/Ontario%20-%20US%20Power%20Outage%20-%20Impacts%20on%20Critical%20Infrastructure.pdf

Reich, P. C., & Gelbstein, E. (2012). *Law, policy and technology: Cyberterrorism, information warfare and internet immobilization*. Hershey, PA: IGI Global. doi:10.4018/978-1-61520-831-9

Rinaldi, S. M., Peerenboom, J. P., & Kelly, T. K. (2001, December). Identifying, understanding and analyzing critical infrastructure interdependencies. *IEEE Control Systems Magazines*, 11-25.

Rogers, C., & Lewis, R. (2007). *Introduction to police work*. Cullumpton, U.K.: Willan Publishing.

Rogers, M. (2003). The psychology of cyber-terrorism. In A. Silke (Ed.), *Terrorists, victims and society* (pp. 77–92). Chichester, U.K.: John Wiley & Sons, Inc. doi:10.1002/9780470713600.ch4

Rosoff, M. (2011, August 30). Former Anonymous member says hacking "all comes down to lies". *Business Insider*. Retrieved from http://www.businessinsider.com/former-anonymous-member-says-hacking-all-comes-down-to-lies-2011-8?IR=T

Schmid, A. P. (2011). The revised academic consensus definition of terrorism. *Perspectives of Terrorism*, *6*(2), 158–159.

Senators, U. S. Al Qaeda calls for 'electronic jihad'. (2012, May 12). *CNN*. Retrieved from http://edition.cnn.com/2012/05/23/politics/al-qaeda-electronic-jihad/

Shamah, D. (2014, July 9). Hackers threaten "Israhell" cyber-attack over Gaza. *The Times of Israel*. Retrieved from http://www.timesofisrael.com/hackers-threaten-israhell-cyber-attack-over-gaza/

Sherlock, R., Samaan, G., & Samaan, M. (2014). Islamic State leader Abu Bakr al-Baghdadi 'wounded in air strike'. *The Telegraph*. Retrieved from http://www.telegraph.co.uk/news/worldnews/islamic-state/11219739/Islamic-State-leader-Abu-Bakr-al-Baghdadi-wounded-in-air-strike.html

Singer, P. W. (2012). The cyber terror bogeyman. *Brookings*. Retrieved from http://www.brookings.edu/research/articles/2012/11/cyber-terror-singer

Smith, S. (2008). *Teen hacker in Poland plays trains and derails city tram system* [Web log post]. Retrieved from http://inhomelandsecurity.com/teen_hacker_in_poland_plays_tr/

Smith, T. (2001, October 31). Hacker jailed for revenge sewage attacks. *The Register*. Retrieved from http://www.theregister.co.uk/2001/10/31/hacker_jailed_for_revenge_sewage/

Stohl, M. (2014). Dr. Strangeweb: Or how they stopped worrying and learned to love cyber war. In T, Chen, L. Jarvis, & S. Macdonald (Eds.), Cyberterrorism: Understanding, assessment and response (pp. 85-102). New York, NY: Springer.

Stone, J. (2014, August 15). What is Anonymous? 'Hacktivist' involvement in Mike Brown shooting proves vigilante justice is now routine. *International Business Times*. Retrieved from http://www.ibtimes.com/what-anonymous-hacktivist-involvement-mike-brown-shooting-proves-vigilante-justice-now-1660052

Storm, D. (2014, January 15). Hackers exploit SCADA holes to take full control of critical infrastructure. *ComputerWorld*. Retrieved from http://www.computerworld.com/article/2475789/cybercrime-hacking/hackers-exploit-scada-holes-to-take-full-control-of-critical-infrastructure.html

Talihärm, A. M. (2010). Cyberterrorism: In theory or in practice? *Defence Against Terrorism Review*, *3*(2), 59–74.

Tversky, A., & Kahneman, D. (1974). *Judgement under uncertainty: Heuristics and biases, 185*(4157), 1124-1131.

U.S.-Canada Power System Outage Task Force. (2014). *U.S. final report on the August 14, 2003 blackout in the United States and Canada: Causes and recommendations*. U.S. and Canada: United States Department of Energy.

User mistakes aid most cyber attacks, Verizon and Symantec studies show. (2015, April 14). *Channel News Asia*. Retrieved from http://www.channelnewsasia.com/news/technology/user-mistakes-aid-most/1782902.html

Vatis, M. A. (2001). Cyber attacks during the war on terrorism: A predictive analysis. *Institute for Security Technology Studies*. Retrieved from http://www.ists.dartmouth.edu/docs/cyber_a1.pdf

Verton, D. (2003). *Black ice: The invisible threat of cyber-terrorism*. New York, NY: McGraw-Hill.

Walker, D. (2015, April). Critical infrastructure survey: Gov't, energy sectors targeted most by destructive attacks. *SC Magazine for IT Security Professionals*. Retrieved from http://www.scmagazine.com/critical-infrastructure-survey-govt-energy-sectors-targeted-most-by-destructive-attacks/article/407772/

Warren, Z. (2014, February 11). 'Mask' virus infected computers in government, others for seven years. *Inside Counsel*. Retrieved from http://www.insidecounsel.com/2014/02/11/mask-virus-infected-computers-in-government-others

Weimann, G. (2004). *How modern terrorism uses the Internet. Special Report No.116*. Washington, DC: United States Institute of Peace; www.terror.net

Weimman, G. (2006). *Terror on the internet: The new arena, the new challenges*. Washington, DC: United States Institute of Peace Press.

Weinberg, L., Pedahzur, A., & Hirsch-Hoefler, S. (2004). The challenges of conceptualizing terrorism. *Terrorism and Political Violence, 16*(4), 777–794. doi:10.1080/095465590899768

What is spear phishing? (2015). *Kaspersky Lab*. Retrieved from https://usa.kaspersky.com/internet-security-center/definitions/spear-phishing#.VVBupY7vPrc

Wilson, C. (2003). Computer attack and cyberterrorism: Vulnerabilities and policy issues for congress (Order Code RL32114). *CRS Report for Congress*. Retrieved from http://fas.org/irp/crs/RL32114.pdf

World Economic Forum. (2012). *Risk and responsibility in a hyper connected world pathways to global cyber resilience*. Retrieved from http:www3.weforum.org/docs/WEF_IT_PathwaysToGlobalCyberResilience_Report_2012.pdf

Wueest, C. (2014). Targeted attacks against the energy sector. *Symantec*. Retrieved from http://www.symantec.com/content/en/us/enterprise/media/security_response/whitepapers/targeted_attacks_against_the_energy_sector.pdf

Yar, M. (2006). *Cybercrime and society*. London: SAGE Publications.

Yunos, Z., & Ahmad, R. (2014). The application of qualitative method in developing a cyber terrorism framework. In *Proceedings of International Conference on Economics, Management and Development (EMD 2014)*. Interlaken, Switzerland: Europment.

Zimmerman, R. (2009). *Understanding the implications of critical infrastructure interdependencies for water* (Published Articles & Papers, Paper 7). Retrieved from http://research.create.usc.edu/cgi/view-content.cgi?article=1083&context=published_papers

ENDNOTES

[1] On August 14, 2003, a massive blackout caused by cascading failure affected over 50 million people in Northeast America and some parts of Canada (U.S.-Canada Power System Outage Task Force, 2014).

[2] Zero-day threat is a threat that exploits an unknown computer security vulnerability.

Chapter 22
Death by Hacking:
The Emerging Threat of Kinetic Cyber

Penelope Wang
Home Team Behavioural Sciences Centre, Ministry of Home Affairs, Singapore

ABSTRACT

Innovation and technological advancements have seen many devices and systems being linked up on to the Internet. Such devices and systems include personal medical devices like insulin pumps and pacemakers, cars, as well as critical infrastructure like power grids and traffic light systems. However, recent research by cyber security experts has revealed that these critical devices and systems are highly vulnerable to being hacked into and manipulated. Should such an attack be carried out successfully by bad actors, like violent extremists, this could result in physical injury or even death. Hence, this chapter aims to bring awareness on the kinetic cyber threat by highlighting various forms of kinetic cyber, and the vulnerabilities that make these devices and systems susceptible. In addition, this chapter introduces the motivations and characteristics of violent extremists who might engage in kinetic cyber, and ends off by proposing some recommended directions to counter this threat.

INTRODUCTION

The rapid technological advancements in the past few decades have brought about massive improvements and breakthroughs in many sectors of society. From the enhancement of medical devices to the creation of smart homes and smart cars as well as the implementation of technology to monitor and regulate basic systems in infrastructure, technology has indeed pervaded every aspect of the world today. Nevertheless, the benefits and convenience that technological advancements bring is not without its perils. With the rise of technology, a corresponding increase in cybercrime rates can also be observed (Mendoza, 2014).

However, the face of cybercrime is changing, and cyber attacks need not necessarily be confined to non-violent acts. The possibility for cyber attacks to cause direct or indirect physical damage, injury and even death is very real. In view of this threat, former Vice President of the United States, Dick Cheney, had had the wireless function of his pacemaker turned off for fears of an assassination attempt that can be made by remotely hacking into his pacemaker (Peterson, 2013).

DOI: 10.4018/978-1-5225-0156-5.ch022

According to Applegate (2013), the classification of these kinds of cyber attacks is known as 'Kinetic Cyber'. The threat of kinetic cyber could be more imminent than commonly believed. Europol has picked up a report by U.S. security firm, IID, which predicted that the first murder via the hacking of critical devices would happen by the end of 2014 (Peachy, 2014a). To date, while there has yet to be a murder conducted via kinetic cyber, there have been cases where kinetic cyber was used to attack and damage critical infrastructure. Given the myriad of possible attacks that could be made to cause widespread damage, it is not unthinkable then, that violent extremists could use kinetic cyber as a tool to achieve their own ends. This is especially since violent extremist groups are known to keep up to date with the latest technology and to exploit them where possible, as is the case with Al-Qaeda using encrypted and secure communications methods to conceal their tracks (The Soufan Group, 2013), as well as the Islamic State in Iraq and Syria (ISIS) using social media as an effective digital strategy to recruit members online (Bonzio, 2014).

The objective of this chapter therefore is to raise awareness of the emerging threat of kinetic cyber through highlighting the types of kinetic cyber and how such cyber attacks are carried out. In addition, this chapter seeks to outline the possible offender profiles of individuals, including violent extremists, who might engage in kinetic cyber, and provide a few recommendations on how to address this emerging threat.

TYPES OF KINETIC CYBER

In general, the primary targets for kinetic cyber are cyber-physical systems (CPS), which are computer systems that are designed to monitor and control physical processes (Applegate, 2013). The use of CPS can be found in a wide spectrum of industries, ranging from personal medical devices, automotive systems, traffic control and safety systems, to critical infrastructure control systems like electric power and water resources (Lee, 2008). The fact that these systems are connected to the cyberspace implies that they could potentially be hacked into and manipulated for purposes other than what they were originally intended for (Applegate, 2013). The idea that CPS are vulnerable to attacks is not a fantastical notion commonly found in the domain of film or television shows, but instead a very real threat that has been validated by security researchers in real life.

Hacking into Implanted Medical Devices

The primary advantage of incorporating wireless technology into implanted medical devices is to allow doctors to collect valuable patient information and modify the treatment accordingly as well as to update device software without the need to conduct surgery (Erlichman & Jack, 2012; Rubin, 2011; Wadhwa, 2012). However, when security features protecting these devices are insufficient, as is mostly the case (Higgins, 2014b), this leaves the devices vulnerable to cyber attacks. In fact, security researchers have experimented on and demonstrated how such attacks are possible.

In 2011, security analyst Jerome Radcliffe gave a presentation during the Black Hat Technical Security event on how he had hacked into his own continuous glucose monitor (CGM) and insulin pump. While he did not go so far as to manipulate the two devices he owned, he had outlined theories in which hackers could possibly manipulate the two devices. For an attack on the CGM, the goal for hackers would be to suppress legitimate sensor data from being picked up and simultaneously imitating sensor data in order to trick users into thinking that their blood sugar levels are higher or lower than it actually is (Radcliffe, 2011). This would lead users to take the corresponding action of injecting a greater dose of insulin into their bodies than required and putting their lives at risk. Similarly, for an attack on the insulin pump, hackers can alter the amount of insulin entering the body and cause the user to enter into hypoglycaemic shock, possibly leading to death (Radcliffe, 2011). However, Radcliffe outlined that distance is still one of the limitations in executing such a cyber attack, and the attacker has to be within 60 metres of the target in order to remotely hack into the medical devices.

Barnaby Jack, Director of Security Testing at computer security consultant firm, IOActive, took Radcliffe's research one step further and had not only successfully hacked into an insulin pump and instructing it to release all of its contents into a see-through mannequin, but he was also able to extend the range of an attack to about 90 metres (Erlichman & Jack, 2012; Robertson, 2012). More notably, Jack was able to exploit vulnerabilities in the device to obtain the serial number of the insulin pump to conduct a successful attack, a barrier that Radcliffe originally faced (Roberston, 2012).

CGMs and insulin pumps are not the only medical devices that have been shown to be easily exploitable. Security researchers have also demonstrated the same in implantable cardioverter defibrillator (ICD) and pacemaker, which are medical devices designed to regulate and control heart rhythm. In 2008, Halperin et al. conducted experiments where they had successfully hacked into an ICD wirelessly. In doing so, they were able to, amongst other things, obtain personal and important patient and cardiac data, turn off the ICD and prevent it from responding to potentially dangerous cardiac conditions, as well as to induce a fatal heart attack. More recently in 2012, Jack demonstrated in a Breakpoint security conference, a computer security conference covering presentations on computer security issues from international security experts, that pacemakers are highly susceptible. During the conference, Jack had successfully remotely hacked into a pacemaker to deliver a deadly 830-volt jolt, although he qualifies that the attacker has to be within a 12 metre range in order to do so (Grubb, 2012). During the same conference, Jack also highlighted how it was possible to create a computer worm that could spread to other devices of the same brand and model and repeat the same deadly effect on persons wearing the devices as it did on the original target (Grubb, 2012).

The reason often given as to why medical devices are highly vulnerable to being exploited and hacked into has to do with how security measures were hardly considered when these devices were originally designed and manufactured (Robertson, 2012; Rubin, 2011). In addition, one of the greatest limitations to include security measures into such devices is the limited amount of battery power (Wadhwa, 2012). Nevertheless, with the potential for deadly attacks and the threat of human lives at stake, security researchers are working with relevant parties to find ways to counter such threats, although implementing any such improvements are likely to take a long time (Talbot, 2013).

Hacking into Cars

Cars are known to be as vulnerable, if not more so, than implanted medical devices. With many wireless technological advancements incorporated into cars, such as the Bluetooth, keyless entry systems, cellular services, and wireless tire pressure sensors, these creates vulnerabilities for hacking into car systems remotely (Rubin, 2011). Security researchers in the United States have done so to a car that is already on the market, and have demonstrated being able to unlock the car through hacking as well as remotely inserting malicious software into the car's system, enabling the researchers to send commands to the car's electronic control unit and override various vehicle controls (Markoff, 2011). However, the group of researchers was hesitant to outline the specific controls they could override and confirm plausible scenarios where remote hacking can result in deadly car crashes. Instead, they did note the possibility that technologically savvy car thieves could hack into the car's locking system to unlock the doors and drive off with the vehicle (Markoff, 2011).

Other researchers were not as hesitant to confirm that cars can be easily hacked into, and vehicular functions taken control of. For example, Charles Miller, a computer security researcher at Twitter, and Chris Valasek, Director of Security Intelligence at IOActive, have shown that once they were able to have initial access into the wired network in cars, they could control all of the car's functions, even when a driver was present (Greenberg, 2013). Instances range from the annoying, such as blaring the car's horn, to the risky, such as manipulating the fuel meter to display a full tank when in fact the fuel level in the car is about three quarters empty, as well as to the fatal, such as controlling the steering and overriding brake control. In short, all of a car's functions can be controlled by a remote computer, with driver inputs overridden, making it fatally dangerous for the driver as well as any other road users or pedestrians in the surroundings. In their demonstration, Miller and Valasek were in the target car during the demonstration and were manipulating controls from a laptop in the backseat. However, a separate group of computer security researchers from the University of Washington and University of California, San Diego, highlighted a threat model that does not require the hackers to be physically present in the target car in order to manipulate control over the vehicle. This would involve a target car and a chase car, whereby the remote computer was in the chase car. In this model, the remote computer could still have the same amount of control of the target car as Miller and Valasek had in their experiment (Rubin, 2011).

In order to have absolute control of a car as Miller and Valasek did, it would require physical access to the car, at least for the first instance in order to access the wired systems of the targeted car. However, since others have demonstrated being able to break into cars through hacking into the car locking systems, it is entirely possible that a malicious hacker could break into the target car and access the wired systems of the car undetected, before subsequently controlling the target car remotely using a chase car. While this may only be a hypothetical scenario, the extent of vulnerabilities that cars currently possess is alarming. This is especially in light of the recent push towards developing car systems that are more integrated and interconnected (Gibbs, 2014), and the ambition of creating cars that are driverless (Greenberg, 2013). This would involve connecting many of the car systems to the Internet, leaving car systems more exposed to a remote attack (Kostadinov, 2014). In the case of driverless cars, exposing crucial driving functions to wireless technology, such as negotiating stop-and-go traffic flow, leaves the system vulnerable to a remote hack and manipulation (Greenberg, 2013). Without proper and adequate security measures, this leaves many of the cars of tomorrow vulnerable to malicious hackers that could exploit these vulnerabilities to cause injury and even death.

Hacking into Critical Infrastructures

Personal medical devices and personal vehicles are not the only systems that are vulnerable to cyber attacks. It is also the case that critical infrastructures are susceptible to an attack as well. For example, a group of cyber security researchers at the University of Michigan, led by Alex Halderman, Director of the Center for Computer Security and Society, have successfully carried out a hack into the traffic control system in an undisclosed city in Michigan. This was done under the watchful eye of local transportation officials, and they were able to change the traffic lights from a laptop in their truck (Pagliery, 2014). As traffic control systems today are interconnected to each other, it makes it easy to execute an attack on the system and cause congestions at intersections or control the lights to guarantee a particular driver a clear route to his destination.

Not only are traffic systems on the ground at risk, air traffic control systems have also been identified as vulnerable targets for kinetic cyber. Ironically, it is the new air traffic control system designed to make air traffic control more convenient and dependable that makes air traffic control systems more vulnerable to kinetic cyber (Cohn, 2013). The new air traffic control system, known as the Automated Dependent Surveillance-Broadcast (ADS-B) or the Next Generation Air Transportation System uses GPS technology to track planes instead of through the traditional radar system. This allows air control towers greater accuracy in identifying the specific location of aircraft. However, the ADS-B lacks the proper security features such as encrypted data and authentication processes that keep communications private and ensure that only genuine signals get transmitted (Greenberg, 2012). In other words, it is possible for a kinetic cyber hacker to fabricate a flight that does not exist (also known as a spoof) and have its signal appear on the air traffic detection system of an airplane or the air traffic control tower. A single spoof alone may not cause much damage as the control tower is still able to determine a genuine signal by checking back against existing radar signals or their database of flight plans, although it might lead to an airplane pilot taking sudden evasive action to avoid non-existent planes, which might injure passengers on board (Greenberg, 2012). However, the issue lies in the fact that as many as 100,000 spoofs can be created and directed at the same time to a specific air control tower (Cohn, 2013; Greenberg, 2012). This would flood the system with fake signals, which prevents the control tower from quickly distinguishing fake signals with genuine ones, likely throwing the control tower into mayhem and incapacitating it. This could result in collisions between planes in the air, or worse, the spoofs used to cover an actual aerial attack similar to the 9/11 attacks.

Apart from air traffic control systems being vulnerable, security researcher Billy Rios has also found loopholes in the Transportation Safety Administration (TSA) system at airport security checkpoints (Higgins, 2014a). His findings have highlighted that it is possible for malicious actors to hack into the TSA system and manipulate the baggage scanners such that attackers can sneak in weapons or other banned items past security checkpoints. This is indeed worrying as it reflects the possibility that violent extremists can exploit this vulnerability and conceal weapons or bombs onto planes and carry out possible hijacking plans that are similar to 9/11 attacks.

Power plants are also not invulnerable. In 2007, the Department of Homeland Security conducted an experiment, dubbed Project Aurora, and had security researchers hack into a replica of a power plant's control system to attempt a shutdown of a large generator (Applegate, 2013). The cyber attack was a success and it was noted that if such an attack were to be successfully carried out in real life, the damage would have been catastrophic. Apart from economic costs, it would have taken months before repairs could be made, and for the power plant to resume operations.

There also have been recorded successful cyber attacks by malicious hackers on critical infrastructure. For instance, the attack by a dissatisfied former employee Vitek Boden on a sewage system in Queensland, Australia, in 2000, as well as the attack on the Los Angeles traffic controls systems by two Los Angeles traffic engineers, Gabriel Murillo and Kartik Patel, during a labour union protest in 2006 (Applegate, 2013). Both these cases are considered as insider threats as all three were disgruntled employees and had used their positions to their advantage. More notable is the case of a 14-year-old Polish schoolboy who had hacked into the Lodz city tram system and built a remote control to manipulate the direction of the tram tracks, treating the entire tram system like a personal train set (Baker, 2008). The consequences of his actions resulted in the derailment of four trams and minor injuries to at least twelve passengers. The incident could have easily resulted in death but "it was lucky that nobody was killed" (Baker, 2008, para. 9).

The list of possible types of cyber attacks having physical and potentially deadly consequences is non-exhaustive and is not limited to these examples. The range of damage that could potentially be caused by kinetic cyber can range from the individual to the entire community. All it requires is for the system to be connected to a wireless network and a hacker with the necessary technical expertise. As these examples have highlighted, the threat of a cyber attack having kinetic effects is very real indeed, and there have already been real-life cases of malicious individuals who are exploiting the vulnerabilities of critical systems. The next section will look into what some of these vulnerabilities are that make such personal devices and systems so exposed to a cyber attack.

VULNERABILITIES THAT ENHANCE THE THREAT OF KINETIC CYBER

Anonymity of the Internet

The structure of the Internet is such that it provides users with visual anonymity and with a little technical know-how and effort, online anonymity as well. For hackers who seek to cover their traces, they can retain their anonymity through using anonymous servers, pseudo names, and IP spoofing, which is to change their IP address so that transmissions appear to come from another source (Armstrong & Forde, 2003). Not only does the anonymity provided by the Internet help hackers avoid getting caught, but also facilitates criminal behaviour.

There are a few theories that highlight how anonymity encourages criminal behaviour. According to Christopherson (2007), anonymity allows for the autonomy to experiment with new behaviours without the fear of being identified and negatively evaluated. This would allow an individual to freely engage in behaviours typically disapproved by others without fear of repercussions. Related to this is the concept of deindividuation, which refers to how an individual's inner restraints are lost when he or she is not being paid attention to as an individual (Demetriou & Silke, 2003). As such, these individuals are more likely to engage in deviant behaviour, and research has shown that the loss of restraints through deindividuation can lead people to behave less altruistically, more selfishly and more aggressively (Demetriou & Silke, 2003). In addition, deindividuation has been shown to be associated with stealing, cheating, violence and murder (Demetriou & Silke, 2003).

Similarly, when it comes to kinetic cyber, anonymity arising from the use of the Internet would lead to deindividuation due to how an individual can no longer be identified and regarded as an individual. This would influence an individual to be more willing to freely engage in deviant behaviour like kinetic cyber.

Low Cost of Entry

Contrary to popular belief, the equipment necessary to conduct a cyber attack on the devices and systems highlighted in the previous sections are relatively cheap and easy to obtain. With regard to personal medical devices, Radcliffe was able to get the relevant equipment from eBay for under US$100 (Radcliffe, 2011). Similarly, for hacking into a car, Miller and Valasek only required a laptop along with a particular cable (i.e., ECOM cable), which was relatively inexpensive to obtain (Valasek & Miller, 2014). A quick search online revealed the price for the cable to be about US$175.

In the case of hacking into traffic lights system, the equipment required is not as inexpensive as the rest. Chief technology officer at security research firm IOActive Labs, Cesar Cerrudo, had spent US$4,100 on the hardware required for the hacking (Panganini, 2014). Out of which, US$4,000 was used to purchase an access point from Sensys Networks, the company that installed its traffic light systems in 40 U.S. states, and has operations in nine other countries worldwide. Through this device, Cerrudo is able to intercept data from all of the sensors used by Sensys (Panganini, 2014; Zetter, 2014). However, Cerrudo mentioned that the access point was essential only because of the proprietary protocol within in. Once this protocol is learnt, the access point is in fact redundant as the device can be built by the hacker (Panganini, 2014). This means that should the threat actor be able to obtain the proprietary protocol through other means, for example through an insider, he would be able to hack into the system using equipment purchased at US$100.

As the hardware required for most hacking attempts are relatively low-priced and easy to acquire, this presents a low barrier to entry for technologically savvy individuals to engage in kinetic cyber. It therefore does not help that security measures on many personal devices and critical systems are at best, minimal, or at worst, non-existent (Cooney, 2012; Paganini, 2013).

Technical Vulnerabilities

The poor security on these critical devices and systems can be attributed to various factors. The first of which is how unencrypted data is used to communicate across wireless networks. This is especially crucial when it comes to traffic lights systems as the unencrypted data allows information on traffic signals to be monitored by an unauthorised entity easily (Zetter, 2014). Closely related to the problem of using unencrypted data is the lack of proper authentication mechanisms that are supposed to safeguard access into the system. In other words, the use of weak usernames and passwords do not help matters when it comes to enhancing the security of these traffic systems. In fact, these traffic systems often use factory-default usernames and passwords, which are found in online manuals (Bershidsky, 2014; Pagliery, 2014), making the authentication mechanism in such systems virtually non-existent. Coupled together, poor authentication mechanisms (i.e., weak usernames and passwords), alongside the use of unencrypted data, would allow the data sent over the traffic systems to be manipulated and replaced with false information (Bershidsky, 2014; Nicks, 2014; Zetter, 2014).

The problem of weak usernames and passwords do not only exist in traffic systems. The realm of personal medical devices also faces the same issues. For the medical world, there is actually a legitimate reason for having such vulnerabilities present. In emergency situations when doctors or paramedics need access to the device quickly, there is a crucial need for the authentication process to be simple and easy to remember (Grubb, 2012; Talbot, 2013). A complicated username or password that is privy to only a few individuals might in fact endanger patient lives instead. Unfortunately, this means that the username and password is often the serial and model number of the device, information that can be remotely extracted from the device and used for malicious ends (Grubb, 2012). A group of researchers from Rice University and security company RSA Laboratories is currently developing a device to address the poor security measures on these devices without compromising the need for medical professionals to have rapid access to the devices during emergencies (Talbot, 2013). However, the solution is still in its preliminary stages and it would take years for it to be implemented by the manufacturers (Talbot, 2013). Hence, personal medical devices are likely to suffer from poor security features for a fairly long time, and the threat of malicious hacks on personal medical devices to cause death is still very real at present.

The security features of cars are no better, and a security researcher has likened the vulnerabilities of modern cars to the kind found on computers when they were first being linked to the Internet in the mid-1990s (Greenberg, 2013). With such vulnerabilities that exist across all industries, it would be prudent to be mindful of them, and where possible, take steps to counter these weaknesses, such as changing usernames and passwords that control critical systems.

Social Engineering

Most of the cyber attacks described above can be carried out solely through exploiting the technical vulnerabilities in the system without the need to resort to social engineering, which refer to tactics that are used to influence people into divulging confidential information or performing a certain action. However, there are instances whereby a specific piece of critical information or protocol is required, as in the case of traffic systems. In these cases, social engineering plays a key role in obtaining such information. For example, Cesar Cerrudo's success in hacking into traffic lights systems was due to his purchase of the access point from Sensys Network, the company that had installed traffic lights systems in 40 U.S. states. Under normal circumstances, this access point is generally not sold to the public and only to city governments. However, Cerrudo had convinced the vendor that he needed a unit in order to run tests for one of his customers, and had even successfully had them ship the device to an address in Puerto Rico (Zetter, 2014). The details of how Cerrudo was successful in this piece of social engineering is not revealed, but following Dillon, Neo, Ong, and Khader's (2014) position on how establishing credibility is the crucial first step in social engineering, it could well be Cerrudo may have used certain techniques, such as name-dropping or asserting authority[1], to appear credible to the Sensys Network liaison.

The role of social engineering in kinetic cyber is at present, still relatively uncommon. However, it may slowly increase as security measures on critical systems and devices are tightened, and it becomes easier to obtain crucial information through social engineering than through technical exploits. It is therefore important that related individuals as well as employees in companies involved in relevant industries be aware of such practices in order to safeguard against potential cyber attacks.

A COMPARISON BETWEEN A TYPICAL CYBER ATTACK AND A KINETIC CYBER ATTACK

Hacking into computer systems and networks often requires gathering intelligence about the targeted system (Dillon et al., 2014). As such, hacking attacks, including those from the kinetic cyber class, are premeditated.

In terms of differences, the unique feature of kinetic cyber that stands out from typical cyber attacks is the distance between the target and the perpetrator. Typical cyber attacks are often carried out remotely, and can be executed across borders. A classic example of this is the data breach at the Office of Personnel Management in the United States, suspected to be the work of hackers based in China (Rushe, 2015). However, based on current technology, kinetic cyber is still limited by distance. In the case of personal medical devices, the perpetrator has to be within a 90-metre range for an insulin pump hack, and a 12-metre range for manipulating a pacemaker (Erlichman & Jack, 2012; Grubb, 2012). A chase car is also required in order to control systems on a target car (Rubin, 2011), and for traffic light systems, successful manipulations conducted so far are up to a range of 180 metres (Paganini, 2014).

Nevertheless, distance as a limitation of kinetic cyber may not be permanent. As technology progresses, it may be possible to circumvent the limits and expand the range of such cyber attacks. In fact, Cerrudo had explained that while his equipment only allowed him to manipulate traffic up to 180 metres, it is possible to do the same at greater distances with a powerful antenna attached to his original setup (Paganini, 2014). Given the rapid technological advances taking place in the world today, it may only be a matter of time before the limits of distance become inconsequential. It could well be the case that in the distant future, kinetic cyber can occur across borders.

POSSIBLE OFFENDER PROFILES: MOTIVATIONS AND CHARACTERISTICS OF VIOLENT EXTREMISTS WHO MIGHT ENGAGE IN KINETIC CYBER

Given that kinetic cyber is a new and emerging area, the number of reported incidents is still low. As such, there has yet to be specific research done on investigating offender profiles on individuals committing kinetic cyber. While it is fortunate that there has yet to be any known incident of kinetic cyber involving violent extremists, it would still be useful to deduce possible offender profiles for kinetic cyber in the context of violent extremism. An important first step then, is to understand why violent extremists conduct acts of violence and how does kinetic cyber fit into that context.

Revenge

A common and one of the earliest themes that emerge in the literature on reasons why individuals turn to violent extremism has to do with perceived injustice, and the associated feelings of vengeance (Borum, 2004). According to Crenshaw, "vengeance can be specific or diffuse, but it is an obsessive drive that is a powerful motive for violence toward others, especially people thought to be responsible for injustices" (as cited in Borum, 2004, p. 24). In other words, when individuals perceive themselves, or others that they identify with, to be suffering from injustice, the desire for revenge is a powerful one that can drive them towards violence.

Revenge is not a motivation that is specific solely to violent extremism. As Turgeman-Goldschmidt (2005) has highlighted, revenge is also a powerful motive for hacking offences and the act of hacking is seen as a means to address past grievances. Putting the two together, kinetic cyber may become a form of emotional expression for the violent extremist, and is fuelled by his/her anger and desire to get back at those who have hurt him/her.

Terror

A fundamental purpose for violent extremists to conduct violent acts would be to cause terror and incite fear. As Crenshaw (2000, p. 406) puts it, "the purpose of terrorism is to intimidate a watching popular audience by harming only a few"; a perspective echoed by Harari (2015), who talks about how terror acts can be seen as a 'theatrical spectacle' used by violent extremists to incite fear and push states to act irrationally, and as a result, change the political balance of power to one that is less disadvantageous for violent extremists. The most direct way to achieve this then would be to carry out an act that is unexpected and shocks the world. A classic example of this would be the 9/11 attacks, and a large part of what was shocking about the attacks was the methods employed to carry out the attacks. It is not difficult to see how kinetic cyber can be used as a tool to accomplish the purpose of inciting fear within the masses, especially considering how kinetic cyber would be a novel modus operandi.

Depending on the agenda of the violent extremists, targets of terror acts using kinetic cyber are likely to be key political figures, or public figures whose deaths might result in an adverse impact on the economy or stock market, such as CEOs of multinational corporations. In these cases, violent extremists could conduct assassinations by hacking into the personal medical devices of key political figures during public appearances. Hijacking personal vehicles and controlling them could also be a means used by violent extremists to achieve similar purposes. Alternatively, if the goal of the violent extremists is to cause widespread damage and chaos, hacking into critical infrastructures like power plants or transport systems could be another way to use kinetic cyber. As kinetic cyber has the potential for violent extremists to hack into power grids, the effect of such an attack can cripple cities and economies, and cause widespread damage and disruption. In doing so, violent extremists can then spread fear and panic amongst the targeted population. Like how the world was gripped in shock and horror during 9/11 attacks when an unorthodox method of hijacking planes to conduct mass murder was used by violent extremists, kinetic cyber could be the new unorthodox tool employed by violent extremists to cause chaos and damage on a large scale. This is especially so when a city is unprepared against kinetic cyber.

Profit

The term 'profit' as a motivation for committing kinetic cyber is used somewhat loosely in this chapter to refer to kinetic cyber that is committed in order to achieve another underlying purpose. In Turgeman-Goldschmidt's (2005) research on hackers, economic reasons for hacking refer to using hacking as a tool to conduct software piracy as this act serves as a means to oppose against the high prices charged by software companies. In addition, the desire to save or earn money can accompany such forms of hacking. For these forms of hacking, hacking is merely a tool that is used to accomplish an underlying goal.

Similarly, kinetic cyber can also be used as a tool to accomplish more instrumental purposes that are often, but not necessarily related to, money. For example, kinetic cyber may be used in blackmail attempts where the perpetrator uses the control he/she has over the victim's personal medical device or personal vehicle to coerce the victim to deposit money into a bank account. This could be a strategy violent extremists might explore in order to raise funds for their cause. On a larger scale, kinetic cyber can also be used to kill or harm CEOs of multi-national corporations and cause turmoil in the stock market. Alternatively, hacks into traffic systems can be made in order to ensure a series of green lights that guarantees perpetrators in getaway cars, a smooth and swift escape. This could potentially happen when a group of violent extremists are on the run after committing an act of terror.

While the above paragraphs dealt with how kinetic cyber can be used as a tool by violent extremists to conduct violence, it leaves the issue of why some individuals might turn to kinetic cyber instead of other means to commit acts of violent extremism. To address this, it might be useful to identify some characteristics that would differentiate violent extremists who engage in kinetic cyber and their counterparts who do not. However, as alluded to earlier, there has not been an offender profile developed for individuals committing kinetic cyber. Nevertheless, an examination into the characteristics of individuals who engage in hacking might shed some light on this issue in order to identify some characteristics of violent extremists who use kinetic cyber.

Fun, Thrill, and Excitement

Through her interviews with hackers, Turgeman-Goldschmidt (2005) found fun, thrill, and excitement to be the most prevalent theme in the interviews, and she has argued that the sense of excitement is often an underlying basis to the other motivations for hacking. This has to do with how thrill is often associated with the other motivations such that those categories of motivations often stem from feelings of fun. For example, hackers would describe how there is the 'fun of discovering', 'fun of avenging', 'fun of feeling smarter', etc. It is not difficult to see how associating excitement with other motivations might apply to kinetic cyber hackers as well.

In the context of violent extremism, research has shown that thrill is a strong factor in attracting radicals to join violent extremist groups like Al-Qaeda and ISIS (Stern & Berger, 2015; Venhaus 2010). The thrill of committing violence as part of a violent extremist group could complement the sense of excitement experienced in conducting a kinetic cyber attack.

Computer Virtuosity

Computer virtuosity refers to the pride the hacker has in his/her technical skills and his/her ability to perform hacks. It involves feelings of power and dominance over machines, and indirectly, over victims (Turgeman-Goldschmidt, 2005). Similarly, when it comes to motivations for murder, power refers to the sense of dominance and control the perpetrator has over his/her victims. In some cases where the perpetrator relishes the role of 'playing God', power also refers to the control he/she has over human lives in general (Fox & Levin, 2005). Taken together, this could mean that the feelings of power derived from the act of causing harm or death through kinetic cyber could potentially be a potent force. This is due to how the sense of power and control the perpetrator has over human lives is compounded by the pride of being able to cause harm through the use of technical skills and knowledge that are exclusive only to some. It could well be that this combination of pride and sense of dominance over other lives, that push violent extremists with the technical expertise to opt for kinetic cyber over other means of violence.

Curiosity for its Own Sake

Closely related to fun, thrill, and excitement is the motivation of curiosity for its own sake. This refers to how the hackers desire to discover and learn as much as possible, and to push the boundaries of what they can discover (Turgeman-Goldschmidt, 2005). Since kinetic cyber has the potential to result in real, sometimes fatal, consequences, curiosity may not be as strong a motivating force for malicious kinetic cyber hackers, who at the point of carrying out a kinetic cyber attack, would be more likely to be pushed by other motivations.

Instead, it would seem that security researchers are the more likely candidates who would be driven by curiosity. For these security researchers, a few of which are mentioned in the earlier paragraphs, they are likely to be driven by the curiosity of discovering how vulnerable personal devices and critical systems are. In doing so, it is their intent that their efforts raise awareness of the existing vulnerabilities, and contribute to push relevant parties to secure these devices. Nevertheless, based on a pathway illustrated in Turgeman-Goldschmidt (2005), malicious hackers may first start out as being curious about these critical devices and systems, before progressing to learn about how these systems work, and subsequently attempting a hack on these devices and systems. The implication of which is that in trying to identify and pick out violent extremists who have turned to kinetic cyber, it would be useful to look into past histories of suspected individuals who have displayed naturally curious tendencies to push the boundaries of what they can discover in cyberspace.

RECOMMENDATIONS

The threat of violent extremists using kinetic cyber as a tool to carry out their objectives is not unfounded. This is especially since the world is seeing a rise in the number of devices that are being connected to each other, a growing phenomenon known as the 'Internet of Things'. This makes devices vulnerable and open to a kinetic cyber attack if they are not sufficiently equipped with the essential security features (Kobie, 2015). However, the future is not as bleak or as terrifying as one might imagine as there can be steps taken to prepare for, and even prevent, a kinetic cyber attack.

Building Awareness

The basic step would be to build awareness on the kinetic cyber threat, especially amongst manufacturers and developers of critical devices and systems. It is imperative for these parties to understand the importance of security measures on their products, and prioritise a need for adequate security. The best practice would be to consider installing security features during the initial phase of designing the product, instead of adding these measures as an afterthought, as is the case for current products on the market (Chung, 2014; Grau, 2015). Eventually though, as more companies realise the importance of security features on such critical systems and devices, perhaps a safety culture and mindset can slowly be developed, which would result in products that are continually being updated to protect against kinetic cyber threats.

Regulating Critical Systems and Devices

From a regulatory perspective, agencies such as the Food and Drug Administration in the United States and the Therapeutic Goods Administration in Australia can take a more active role in ensuring that personal medical devices have adhered to minimum security standards that protect the user against a kinetic cyber attack before approving the launch of these products. Legislation can also make it mandatory for current critical devices and systems to undergo tests led by independent security researchers and companies in order to assess the vulnerabilities of these devices – a necessary step given the reluctance of many vendors who refuse to put their products to the test voluntarily (Kobie, 2015). This is important so that security developers can work on measures to enhance the security of current devices and systems that are in use today.

Research

Given how current trends forecast that more devices will be linked together via the Internet, it is also imperative that security research in the area of kinetic cyber be ongoing in order to address vulnerabilities in critical systems and devices. This might involve finding more sources of funding to develop research in this area as well as greater collaboration between cyber security agencies in both the public and private sector.

Protecting Key Political Figures

From the angle of protecting key political figures, in cases whereby these figures rely on personal medical devices that are vulnerable to hacking, they could consider turning off the wireless function of their devices. This is not unheard of, as mentioned in the introduction, former Vice President of the United States, Dick Cheney had indeed done so to his pacemaker for fears of an assassination attempt that can be made by remotely hacking into his pacemaker (Peterson, 2013). Certainly, should adequate security measure be put in place, the wireless features of these devices could be enabled again for the patient to enjoy the benefits of such technology.

Keeping Ahead of Trends

On the law enforcement front, it is vital that law enforcement agencies and officers are kept abreast of the latest trends in this area, and take steps to improve their infrastructure in order to be prepared for a kinetic cyber attack. For example, police forensic techniques ought to be sufficiently developed to identify and trace hacks made into critical devices and systems. In addition, efforts ought to be made to recruit enough experts whose expertise is in cyber security, which may not be easy as many of these experts draw high salaries in the private sector (Peachy, 2014b).

Monitoring Radicalised Individuals who Possess the Technological Expertise

In the area of threat assessment, it would be useful for intelligence personnel to keep a watchful eye on radicalised individuals who possess the technological expertise to conduct a kinetic cyber attack. These individuals may even display some of the characteristics of violent extremists who use kinetic cyber as outlined in the previous section. Warning behaviours from such individuals, such as an increased activity in searching for information on the target or targeted systems, could highlight the intelligence gathering phase that takes place before a perpetrator initiates an attack.

Red Teaming

Finally, the importance of red teaming in preventing a kinetic cyber attack must be emphasised. This could potentially be useful in preparing against a kinetic cyber attack from violent extremist groups. Penetration tests on critical systems could be carried out on a periodic basis in order to identify vulnerabilities and rectify them. As advocated by Cesar Cerrudo, chief technology officer at IOActive Labs, every city could create a Computer Emergency Response Team (CERT) to handle vulnerabilities and cyber attacks, and ensure that vendors actively run penetrations tests to check their own systems and fix the flaws that have been identified (Kobie, 2015).

CONCLUSION

In summary, existing vulnerabilities such as poor authentication systems as well as sending unencrypted data wirelessly put critical devices and systems at high risk of a kinetic cyber attack. This is especially true when one observes current trends and recognises that innovation and technological advances are pushing for more devices and systems to be linked to each other online.

Given how kinetic cyber can be attractive to violent extremists as it poses as a new, unorthodox method to cause terror and spread fear, it becomes a necessary priority to address the existing vulnerabilities and take steps to rectify them. Relevant industries and law enforcement agencies will have to incorporate a security mindset when developing the technologies of tomorrow in order to pre-empt and protect against such threats. Otherwise, instead of improving lives, the technologies of tomorrow might end up endangering them.

REFERENCES

Applegate, S. D. (2013). The dawn of kinetic cyber. In K. Podins, J. Stinissen, & M. Maybaum (Eds.), *Proceedings of the 5th International Conference on Cyber Conflict*. Tallinn, Estonia: NATO CCD COE Publications.

Armstrong, H. L., & Forde, P. J. (2003). Internet anonymity practices in computer crime. *Information Management & Computer Security*, *11*(5), 209–215. doi:10.1108/09685220310500117

Baker, G. (2008, January 11). Schoolboy hacks into city's tram system. *The Telegraph*. Retrieved from http://www.telegraph.co.uk/news/worldnews/1575293/Schoolboy-hacks-into-citys-tram-system.html

Bershidsky, L. (2014). Traffic hackers pull off 'Italian Job'. *Bloomberg*. Retrieved from http://www.bloombergview.com/articles/2014-08-22/traffic-hackers-pull-off-italian-job

Bonzio, A. (2014, September 15). ISIS' use of social media is not surprising; its sophisticated digital strategy is. *Huffington Post*. Retrieved from http://www.huffingtonpost.co.uk/alessandro-bonzio/isis-use-of-social-media-_b_5818720.html

Borum, R. (2004). *Psychology of Terrorism*. Tampa: University of South Florida.

Christopherson, K. M. (2007). The positive and negative implications of anonymity in Internet social interactions: "On the Internet, nobody knows you're a dog. *Computers in Human Behavior*, *23*(6), 3038–3056. doi:10.1016/j.chb.2006.09.001

Chung, E. (2014, October 27). Carmakers ignore hacking risk, security expert say. *CBC News*. Retrieved from http://www.cbc.ca/m/touch/news/story/1.2810847

Cohn, S. (2013, June 3). Hacker claims airplanes vulnerable at 30,000 feet. *CNBC*. Retrieved from http://www.cnbc.com/id/100784103# Cooney, M. (2012). Wireless medical devices face myriad security concerns. *Network World*. Retrieved from http://www.networkworld.com/article/2223222/mobile-security/wireless-medical-devices-face-myriad-security-concerns.html

Crenshaw, M. (2000). The psychology of terrorism: An agenda for the 21st century. *Political Psychology, 21*(2), 405–420. doi:10.1111/0162-895X.00195

Demetriou, C., & Silke, A. (2003). A criminological Internet 'sting'. Experimental evidence of illegal and deviant visits to a website trap. *The British Journal of Criminology, 43*(1), 213–222. doi:10.1093/bjc/43.1.213

Dillon, L., Neo, L. S., Ong, G., & Khader, M. (2014). *Psychology behind hackers: A multiple case-study approach*. Research Report No. 17/2014. Singapore: Home Team Behavioural Sciences Centre.

Erlichman, J. (Interviewer), & Jack, B. (Interviewee). (2012, February 29). *McAfee's Barnaby on Medical Device Hacking*. Bloomberg TV Website. Retrieved from http://www.bloomberg.com/video/87427352-mcafee-s-barnaby-on-medical-device-hacking.html

Fox, J. A., & Levin, J. (2005). *Extreme killing: Understanding serial and mass murder*. California: Sage Publications, Inc.

Gibbs, S. (2014, March 6). Battle for the car: Will Google, Apple or Microsoft dominate? *The Guardian*. Retrieved from http://www.theguardian.com/technology/2014/mar/06/battle-for-car-will-google-apple-microsoft-dominate

Grau, A. (2015, June 26). Securing medical devices, solving the challenge of the weakest link. *Medical Design Technology*. Retrieved from http://www.mdtmag.com/article/2015/06/securing-medical-devices-solving-challenge-weakest-link

Greenberg, A. (2012, July 25). Next-Gen air traffic control vulnerable to hackers spoofing planes out of thin air. *Forbes*. Retrieved from http://www.forbes.com/sites/andygreenberg/2012/07/25/next-gen-air-traffic-control-vulnerable-to-hackers-spoofing-planes-out-of-thin-air/

Greenberg, A. (2013, July 24). Hackers reveal nasty new car attacks – with me behind the wheel (video). *Forbes*. Retrieved from http://www.forbes.com/sites/andygreenberg/2013/07/24/hackers-reveal-nasty-new-car-attacks-with-me-behind-the-wheel-video/

Grubb, B. (2012, November 6). Fatal risk at heart of lax security. *The Sydney Morning Herald*. Retrieved from http://www.smh.com.au/digital-life/consumer-security/fatal-risk-at-heart-of-lax-security-20121105-28ore.html

Halperin, D., Heydt-Benjamin, T. S., Ransford, B., Clark, S. S., Defend, B., Morgan, W., & Maisel, W. H. et al. (2008). Pacemakers and implantable cardiac defibrillators: Software radio attacks and zero-power defenses. In *Proceedings of the 2008 IEEE Symposium on Security and Privacy*. doi:10.1109/SP.2008.31

Harari, Y. N. (2015, January 31). Yuval Noah Harai: the theatre of terror. *The Guardian*. Retrieved from http://www.theguardian.com/books/2015/jan/31/terrorism-spectacle-how-states-respond-yuval-noah-harari-sapiens

Higgins, K. J. (2014a, August 6). TSA checkpoint systems found exposed on the net. *Dark Reading*. Retrieved from http://www.darkreading.com/vulnerabilities---threats/advanced-threats/tsa-checkpoint-systems-found-exposed-on-the-net/d/d-id/1297843

Higgins, K. J. (2014b, December 11). Hiring hackers to secure the Internet of Things. *Dark Reading.* Retrieved from http://www.darkreading.com/vulnerabilities---threats/hiring-hackers-to-secure-the-internet-of-things/d/d-id/1318107

Kobie, N. (2015, May 13). Why smart cities need to get wise to security – and fast. *The Guardian.* Retrieved from http://www.theguardian.com/technology/2015/may/13/smart-cities-internet-things-security-cesar-cerrudo-ioactive-labs

Kostadinov, D. (2014, March 13). The future is now: Car hacking. *InfoSec Institute.* Retrieved from http://resources.infosecinstitute.com/future-now-car-hacking/

Lee, E. A. (2008, January 23). Cyber physical systems: Design challenges. *UC Berkeley Electrical Engineering and Computer Sciences Technical Memorandum Series, UCB/EECS-2008-8.* Retrieved from www.eecs.berkeley.edu/Pubs/TechRpts/2008/EECS-2008-8.pdf

Markoff, J. (2011, March 9). Researchers show how a car's electronics can be taken over remotely. *The New York Times.* Retrieved from http://www.nytimes.com/2011/03/10/business/10hack.html?_r=0

Mendoza, M. (2014, November 5). Cybercrime on the Rise, Survey Finds. *Huffington Post.* Retrieved from www.huffingtonpost.com/2014/05/29/cybercrime-rise-survey_n_5410280.html

Nicks, D. (2014, August 19). Hacking traffic lights is apparently really easy. *Time.* Retrieved from http://time.com/3146147/hacking-traffic-lights-is-apparently-really-easy/

Paganini, P. (2013, February 22). SCADA and security of critical infrastructures. *InfoSec Institute.* Retrieved from http://resources.infosecinstitute.com/scada-security-of-critical-infrastructures/

Paganini, P. (2014, September 2). Hacking traffic light systems. *InfoSec Institute.* Retrieved from resources.infosecinstitute.com/hacking-traffic-light-systems/

Pagliery, J. (2014, August 21). Traffic lights are dangerously easy to hack. *CNNMoney.* Retrieved from http://money.cnn.com/2014/08/21/technology/security/traffic-lights-hack/

Peachy, P. (2014a, October 5). Cyber crime: First online murder will happen by end of year, warns US firm. *The Independent.* Retrieved from www.independent.co.uk/life-style/gadgets-and-tech/news/first-online-murder-will-happen-by-end-of-year-warns-us-firm-9774955

Peachy, P. (2014b, December 7). Police 'failing to train key staff to fight growing threat of cybercrime' *The Independent.* Retrieved from http://www.independent.co.uk/news/uk/crime/police-failing-to-train-key-staff-to-fight-growing-threat-of-cyber-crime-9909334.html

Peterson, A. (2013, October 21). Yes, terrorists could have hacked Dick Cheney's heart. *The Washington Post.* Retrieved from http://www.washingtonpost.com/blogs/the-switch/wp/2013/10/21/yes-terrorists-could-have-hacked-dick-cheneys-heart/

Radcliffe, J. (2011). Hacking media devices for fun and insulin: Breaking the human SCADA system. *Black Hat Technical Security Conference.* Las Vegas: Nevada.

Robertson, J. (2012, February 29). Hacker shows off lethal attack by controlling wireless medical device. *Bloomberg.* Retrieved from http://go.bloomberg.com/tech-blog/2012-02-29-hacker-shows-off-lethal-attack-by-controlling-wireless-medical-device/

Rubin, A. (2011, October). All your devices can be hacked. *TEDxMidAtlantic.* Retrieved from http://www.ted.com/talks/avi_rubin_all_your_devices_can_be_hacked?language=en

Rushe, D. (2015, June 5). OPM hack: China blamed for massive breach of US government data. Retrieved from http://www.theguardian.com/technology/2015/jun/04/us-government-massive-data-breach-employee-records-security-clearances

Stern, J., & Berger, J. M. (2015, March 9). Thugs wanted – bring your own boots: How ISIS attracts foreign fighters to its twisted utopia. *The Guardian.* Retrieved from http://www.theguardian.com/world/2015/mar/09/how-isis-attracts-foreign-fighters-the-state-of-terror-book

Talbot, D. (2013, September 16). Encrypted heartbeats keep hackers from medical implants. *MIT Technology Review.* Retrieved from http://www.technologyreview.com/news/519266/encrypted-heartbeats-keep-hackers-from-medical-implants/

The Soufan Group. (2013, October 17). *TSG Intel Brief: The challenge of new technology adoption and violent extremist groups.* Retrieved from http://soufangroup.com/tsg-intelbrief-the-challenge-of-new-technology-adoption-and-violent-extremist-groups/

Turgeman-Goldschmidt, O. (2005). Hackers' accounts: Hacking as a social entertainment. *Social Science Computer Review, 23*(1), 8–23. doi:10.1177/0894439304271529

Valasek, C., & Miller, C. (2014). *Adventures in automotive networks and control units.* Retrieved from www.ioactive.com/pdfs/IOActive_Adventures_in_Automotive_Networks_and_Control_Units.pdf

Venhaus, J. M. (2010, May). Why youth join Al-Qaeda. *United States Institute of Peace.* Retrieved from http://www.usip.org/sites/default/files/resources/SR236Venhaus.pdf

Wadhwa, T. (2012, June 12). Yes, you can hack a pacemaker (and other medical devices too). *Forbes.* Retrieved from www.forbes.com/sites/singularity/2012/12/06/yes-you-can-hack-a-pacemaker-and-other-medical-devices-too/

Zetter, K. (2014, April 30). Hackers can mess with traffic lights to jam roads and reroute cars. *Wired.* Retrieved from www.wired.com/2014/04/traffic-lights-hacking/

ENDNOTE

[1]   The technique of name-dropping or asserting authority refers to the strategy hackers employ by assuming an identity which convinces the target to trust the hacker enough to reveal personal data or information. Examples of identities that are commonly assumed include the police as well as the corporation that hosts public email accounts (e.g., Google).

Chapter 23
Spear Phishing:
The Tip of the Spear Used by Cyber Terrorists

Arun Vishwanath
University at Buffalo, USA

ABSTRACT

The ubiquitous use of the Internet has made it possible for terrorist groups to remotely foment attacks with little risk of capture. Among the newest forms of attacks is cyber hacking, which has seen increased use by terrorist groups for acts ranging from pinpointing targets for assassination to holding organisations hostage and embarrassing governments. In almost all these attacks, spear phishing is the vector used to gain access to a computer network – making it imperative that policymakers find ways to stop it. This chapter provides an overview of the different types of spear phishing attacks and the reasons they succeed. The chapter then provides an overview of the different strategies being used to combat it and their relative effectiveness. Drawing from the latest social science research and from initiatives that have worked around the world, the chapter culminates with six policy suggestions, which could significantly reduce the effectiveness of spear phishing and protect nations from a major cyber attack.

INTRODUCTION

Terrorism is broadly defined as the unlawful use of force or violence to intimidate or coerce a civilian population or government to further political or social objectives (Federal Bureau of Investigation [FBI], n.d.). In the not so distant past, such acts required terrorists to physically enter national boundaries and conduct acts of terror. Geography, border security, and the risk of capture often limited the scope of these attacks. Our dependence on the Internet for all manner of activities, from the household monitoring of thermostats to the control of a nation's electric grid, and its democratised nature – the lack of gatekeepers (such as the editors of traditional news), the availability of standardised operating platforms, and open source software – have made it easier for today's terrorist groups to remotely foment acts of terror without the risk of capture.

DOI: 10.4018/978-1-5225-0156-5.ch023

Ongoing news reports of Al-Qaeda and the Islamic State in Iraq and Syria (ISIS) using YouTube, Twitter, and Facebook to disseminate videos of successful attacks, recruit individuals, and promote propaganda demonstrate how technically adept these groups have become (Hingham & Nakashima, 2015). But there is another troubling trend: the use of spear phishing attacks by terrorist groups.

In December 2014, ISIS launched a spear phishing attack on citizen media groups sympathetic to the Syrian government – an attack intended to place position-beacons in individual computers that could reveal the sympathisers' locations, presumably for assassination (Scott-Railton & Hardy, 2014). In another attack, ISIS used spear phishing to gain access to the U.S. Military Central Command's (Centcom) Twitter and YouTube accounts, and on the very day that U.S. President Obama made a speech on cyber security, posted images with threats against American soldiers (Zetter, 2015).

ISIS, however, is not alone. Another prolific hacker group, the Syrian Electronic Army (SEA), with links to Syria, Iran, and Hezbollah, recently hacked the Twitter account of the Associated Press (AP) and tweeted false news to AP's 2-million plus followers of two explosions in the White House that injured U.S. President Obama. Although the hack was quickly discovered and a correction sent out within three minutes of the tweet, by then the Dow Jones had dropped 143-points (Shell, 2013), and the S&P (Standard and Poor's) Index had lost USD 136 billion (Prigg, 2015). SEA has also defaced websites of news media they considered hostile to the Syrian government such as BBC News and The New York Times; defaced Facebook pages of President Obama and French President Nicholas Sarkozy; and also hacked into the recruiting websites of the U.S. Marine Corps (Acohido, 2013). Other reports of Palestinian hackers using spear phishing attacks to breach computer networks of the Israeli Defense Force (IDF) (Fisher-Ilan & Finkle, 2014); of the Iranian sponsored hacker group Tahr Andishan breaching Saudi Aramco, the state-owned national oil company of Saudi Arabia, in retaliation for Saudi Arabia government's support for sanctions against Iran (Nakashima, 2012); and of Russian hackers breaching German Chancellor Angela Merkel's computers ("Russian hackers accused", 2015), demonstrate the variety of groups utilising such modus operandi.

Almost all these major breaches have one thing in common: they all extensively utilise spear phishing. Figure 1 presents the lifecycle of a breach. As shown in the figure, spear phishing is usually the first step in a typical hacking attack that leads to a breach. It is often used early for initial information gathering, for locating individuals, and for gauging the interest of potential targets. This is usually accomplished by assessing target individuals' reactions to emails sent with varying information cues (headers, subject-line, reply-to address, etc.) or by getting access to individuals' social media accounts using fake friend requests. This data-mined information is often used to craft more targeted malware-carrying spear phishing emails, which then allow the phisher to establish a foothold, maintain presence, move laterally to other computers or vertically to other connected servers and escalate access, and finally accomplish the breach. Thus, spear phishing is the proverbial 'tip of the spear' used by cyber terrorists all over the world to launch hacking attacks with goals ranging from cyber espionage and terrorism to vandalism and acts intended to embarrass individuals, governments, and organisations – making it the focus of this chapter.

On incidence terms, the U.S Defense Department receives upwards of ten million attacks per day; many states in the United States receive twice as much; organisations, especially those in telecommunications, technology, banking and insurance industries, also receive just as many (Vishwanath, 2015a). On monetary terms, cyber breaches have shown the potential to net rich dividends. Compared to the estimated USD 120 million that Al-Qaeda netted over an eight-year period from ransoms (Callimachi, 201), a hacker group from Ukraine recently netted in excess of USD 100 million over a five-year period by spear phishing and hacking into several financial news organisations, and selling advance trade in-

Figure 1. Lifecycle of a cyber breach (Mandiant, 2013)

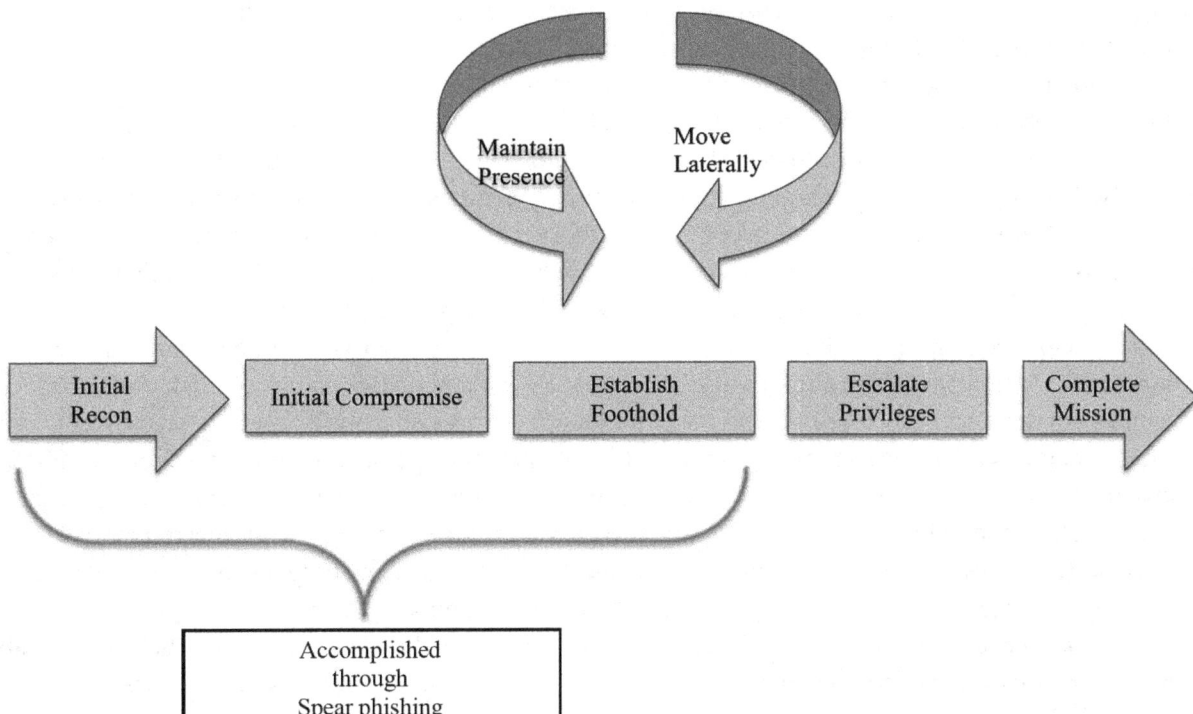

formation to 'investors' (Geiger, 2015). Thus, a successful breach, within a shorter period of time and with limited personal risk, can net enormous capital that could be used for a variety of purposes.

Stopping cyber terrorism therefore requires us to stop spear phishing. Policies for achieving this are presented in the current chapter. The chapter begins with an overview of spear phishing and how these attacks are perpetrated. It next explains the different approaches that policymakers and organisations have taken to deal with the problem and the relative success of these initiatives. It culminates with six policy suggestions that could help nations protect themselves from such attacks.

WHAT IS SPEAR PHISHING?

Spear phishing is a type of online deception where the perpetrator, a phisher, uses social engineering to gain access to individuals' personal information (Vishwanath, Herath, Chen, Wang, & Rao, 2011). Although the ruse used to gain compliance varies considerably, most spear phishing attacks fall into one of two broad types.

The first, a vector more common during the early days of spear phishing, are semantic attacks that attempt to persuade individuals to directly respond to a request. This form of phishing merely extends the 'advance fee' scams (i.e., advance a little money now with a promise of great riches in the immediate future) to the online domain. An example of this is the infamous Nigerian scam, where the phisher claims to be a Nigerian prince with vast confiscated funds, needing simply a bank account number and a small upfront fee for clearing the funds. At the core of this scam is the phisher's attempt to persuade a target to keep escalating his/her monetary and cognitive commitment, ultimately leading to his/her victimisation. Variations of this scam use Eastern European names with language that is congruent with known stereotypes of individuals in those cultures; use SMS, telephones, or cellular phone calls rather than just emails; and use threats of litigation or notification of lottery wins as bait.

Overall, these scams are thought to have a relatively low victimisation rate, with less than 1–2 percent of all emails sent netting victims (Prince, 2009). Newer forms of this type of spear phishing attempts to lure individuals by using information mined from publicly available sources, or from the target's social media feeds (Herley, 2012). As a case in point, the author received a spear phishing attack from someone claiming to be a lawyer representing a recently deceased car crash victim who shared the author's last name, and left an enormous sum of unclaimed money. Figure 2 presents this email.

The second type of spear phishing attack usually carries a malware payload hidden behind a hyperlink or attachment in the email. The aim of these attacks is to persuade the individual to click on the link or attachment in the email. Such attacks are more frequent, far more successful, and not surprisingly the dominant vector used by today's hackers. Simulated attacks net 40-60 percent success rates (Verizon, 2012; Vishwanath, Harrison, & Ng, 2015), depending on the contextual relevance of the email (e.g., sending something about the military to army cadets), its frequency (i.e., sending corrections or reminders), and its payload (i.e., certain hyperlinks garner more response rates as do certain types of file-attachments). In this type of spear phishing, clicking on the links or attachments in the email deploys the malware that opens backdoors into the individual's computer and networks. In some cases, hyperlinks open web forms or direct individual to spoofed websites that appear similar to legitimate sites that directly solicit the target's login credentials.

These attacks are less semantic driven, with some containing only a few sentences soliciting compliance, but tend to be very successful. For instance, one of the Palestinian attacks that compromised the Israeli Defense Forces had the subject line 'Breaking military news' along with an attachment; the other attack had clips claiming to showcase 'Girls of Israel Defense forces' (Waqas, 2015). Many attacks contain PDF attachments, Word documents, or Zip folders that hide malware (Mandiant, 2013). Figure 3 contains a spear phishing email with an attachment, and Figure 4 an email with a hyperlink.

Figure 2. Nigerian spear phishing email received by the author

james abufa ⚑
To: undisclosed-recipients:;   Bcc: arun.vishwanath@facebook.com
Reply-To: i.trustingod00@gmail.com
Hi,Vishwanath,

Hi,Vishwanath,

I am JAMES ABUFA, attorney to Mr J.C.Vishwanath,who passed away in a car accident in Lome Togo alongside his family members .He left behind an investment bond of about USD 18.5 Million with a bank here in my country, before his death please for more information contact me through my direct Email Address Thanks

Yours Sincerely,
JAMES ABUFA (Esq.)
Email///(i.trustingod00@gmail.com)

Figure 3. Spear phishing email with an attachment

Figure 4. Spear phishing email with a hyperlink

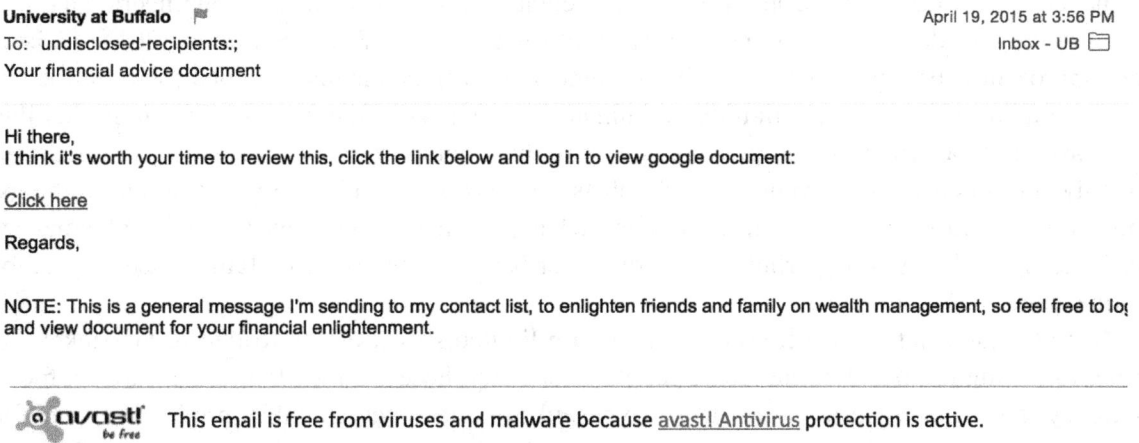

Such spear phishing is the most common attack vector used by cyber terrorist groups for three reasons. Firstly, spear phishing attacks occur via email and social media, both of which are widely diffused throughout the globe, have unified platforms, and little to no gatekeepers. Individuals also appear to be more trusting of others on platforms such as social media (Hancock, 2013) and when they use certain operating systems and devices (Vishwanath et al., 2015). These give terrorist groups a wide reach, and make it easy to achieve high victimisation rates. Secondly, spear phishing attacks require limited technical skills for deployment. Many spear phishing messages are simply constructed and require rudimentary programming skills. There is a cottage industry of off-the-shelf and open source software that can be used to deploy an attack, track responses, and open backdoors into computers. For instance, a Remote

Access Trojan (RAT) often used by hackers, Xtreme RAT, can be purchased online for 100 euros (Paganini, 2012). Likewise, one can easily find readymade code online or hire software programmers to write it inexpensively. Finally, successful spear phishing attacks are hard to detect. This is because most attacks are fomented using free email programs and there is virtually no cost to a phisher for a failed attempt. People also receive numerous emails each day, many from unknown sources, making it difficult to pinpoint which among the many emails led to the breach. Cyber breaches are become harder to detect because once a computer within a network is hacked, information requests appear to come from that computer, which antivirus software that is designed to protect networks from outside incursions find hard to detect. In fact, it takes on average over one year to detect most cyber intrusions (Mandiant, 2013).

Altogether, global reach, ease of deployment and concealment, and the difficulty of discovery make spear phishing the perfect weapon to launch cyber attacks. Not surprisingly, spear phishing is the dominant vector used by cyber terrorists. The next section presents the approaches currently used to combat spear phishing and their relative effectiveness.

CURRENT APPROACHES USED TO STOP SPEAR PHISHING

The extant approaches towards combating spear phishing can be viewed along a continuum from those that focus on technical solutions to those that attempt to intervene at the user level.

The technical focus comes from the computer sciences where the focus is on engineering a program that automates the detection and removal of spear phishing emails (Vishwanath et al., 2011). This paradigm approaches spear phishing emails in the same way as spam emails were dealt with in the recent past, with a software-based solution that eliminates user inputs in the process. Efforts in this line of work have led to a variety of anti-phishing software that attempt to block all suspicious emails, or allow only certain emails from approved 'whitelists' of servers or senders to pass through to the user's inbox. Some solutions used in conjunction with such approaches have involved blocking all emails with attachments, disabling all hyperlinks with emails, or banning the use of certain devices or platforms within a certain network.

Most of these solutions have, however, met with limited success (Wu, Miller, & Garfinkel, 2006) for the following reasons. For one, most people, especially those who work in organisations, focus on efficiency rather than security. Disallowing hyperlinks or attachments inhibits productivity and forces people to find covert workarounds to access the links, leading to even greater security risks. Two, many employees today are working in 'bring-your-own-devices (BYOD) to work' type of environment. Not only could these devices bring malware from home, but they can also be utilised to circumvent organisational access policies. Additionally, services such as Facebook's Messenger, Skype, and WhatsApp are increasingly used for business communication, and restricting their usage often increases the cost of doing business, leading to further inefficiencies and workarounds. Three, it is also easy for a phisher to use a freely available, popular email service, such as Gmail or Yahoo, whose servers are likely in the approved whitelists because of the number of people who legitimately utilise this email provider. Finally, at its core, spear phishing involves social engineering. Phishers constantly check the returns on various emails and modify their attacks, making it hard to create a set of rules that can be automatically applied to spot all spear phishing emails. In many cases, spear phishing emails that are responded to by victims (i.e., questions asked by the victims), are responded to by the phisher or followed-up with another phishing email (Mandiant, 2013). As a case in point, a recent attack involved a spear phishing email that was shortly followed by another email from the organisation's IT department asking all the employees to not click on the hyperlinks in the first email, but to use the one in the second. Both the emails were spear phishing attacks presumably from the same phisher.

Given these limitations, many organisations have instead focused on fixing the user problem by training users on how to spot a spear phishing email (Libicki, Ablon, & Webb, 2015; Vishwanath et al., 2011). There is a cottage industry of for-profit programs that promise to train an organisation's employees. There have, however, been few academic studies that directly assess the success of individual training programs primarily because the program creators do not provide their programs for testing. Hence, it is hard to evaluate each program's relative effectiveness, but evidence from academic research on general anti-phishing training suggests that these programs likely have a temporary, short-term effect (Caputo, Pfleeger, Freeman, & Johnson, 2014). In a series of studies conducted at the U.S. Military Academy from 2004 to 2007, cadets were trained in spotting spear phishing emails and subsequently phished repeatedly over a period of time. Findings revealed that training effects attenuated over time, as soon as individuals fell back into their patterns of everyday email use (Ferguson, 2005). Another line of evidence comes from the rampant increase in the number of successful breaches in the past few years, all since the advent of training, many in security sensitive organisations such as The White House, Pentagon, and Centcom, where presumably people are aware of spear phishing or trained on how to spot it.

In general, anti-phishing training appears to be ineffective because of people's established patterns of email use that are built over the long-term, and that people tend to sink into once their training is completed (Vishwanath, 2015b). Another likely reason for low education effects is the nature of email. Many legitimate emails sent by organisations appear very much like spear phishing emails. For instance, an email that was sent from the CEO of the major U.S. department store, Target, apologising to customers whose personal information was hacked appeared no different from a spear phishing email even to most security experts (Hill, 2012). The same is the case for many emails that come from government agencies and from many banks that make deception-detection difficult even for trained computer scientists. A third reason for training having a limited effect is the technical variance in email platforms. Most email platforms are built by software designers who focus on the ease of use for the user and not security. Consequently, there is considerable variance in how platforms are designed and the types of information that are presented to users. Take for instance the iOS Mail application, its design makes it impossible for a user to view the header of the email that shows the servers from which the email was sent, and that could reveal a phish. Building a training program that accommodates the different email programs and the different ways in which information is presented is, thus, an impossible task. Finally, most anti-phishing training programs are utilised by large organisations that can pay for it. This leaves out the vast majority of computer users, from students and other family members to small business owners and senior citizens, who remain vulnerable. This ultimately reduces the effectiveness of training and education because many people bring devices from home, or use devices in public places (where people who have not been trained) have already compromised their networks.

Thus, overall, both the technological and the user-focused solutions have had mixed success because of the proverbial 'people problem'. Effectively dealing with cyber attacks therefore requires a better understanding of how people utilise technology, and why they click on spear phishing emails. This is examined in the next section.

WHY DO PEOPLE GET PHISHED?

The answers to why individuals click on spear phishing emails depend on how they encounter, process, and behaviourally interact with the emails. Getting to the core of this requires an understanding of users' motivations, cognitions, and patterns of technology use. It also requires a model that can account for why certain types of spear phishing attacks are more prolific than others, why certain types of attacks work better than others, and why certain people are more susceptible to attacks. A recent model, the Suspicion, Cognition, and Automaticity Model (SCAM), developed by the author provides a comprehensive framework for such an examination (see Vishwanath et al., 2015).

SCAM accounts for the conscious and unconscious precursors of cyber actions that lead ultimately to individual victimisation. It incorporates the influence of both cognitive processing and automaticity into its explanatory model, allowing SCAM to explain why someone might fall for a payload carrying spear phishing attack more so than an attack such as the Nigerian spear phishing attack. Figure 5 presents the model.

Cognitive Processing

Forty years of research in cognitive psychology has established that people utilise one of two modes during cognitive processing (Chaiken, 1980). The first involves a systematic consideration of the content of an email message through an effortful process of deliberation, termed as systematic processing.

The second mode is heuristic processing, which involves the use of mental shortcuts or heuristics. Heuristics are generally triggered by cues in the content or context of communication. For instance, rather than read the entire text of an email, one could decide on the email's value based solely on the

Figure 5. The suspicion, cognition, automaticity model (SCAM) (Vishwanath et al., 2015)

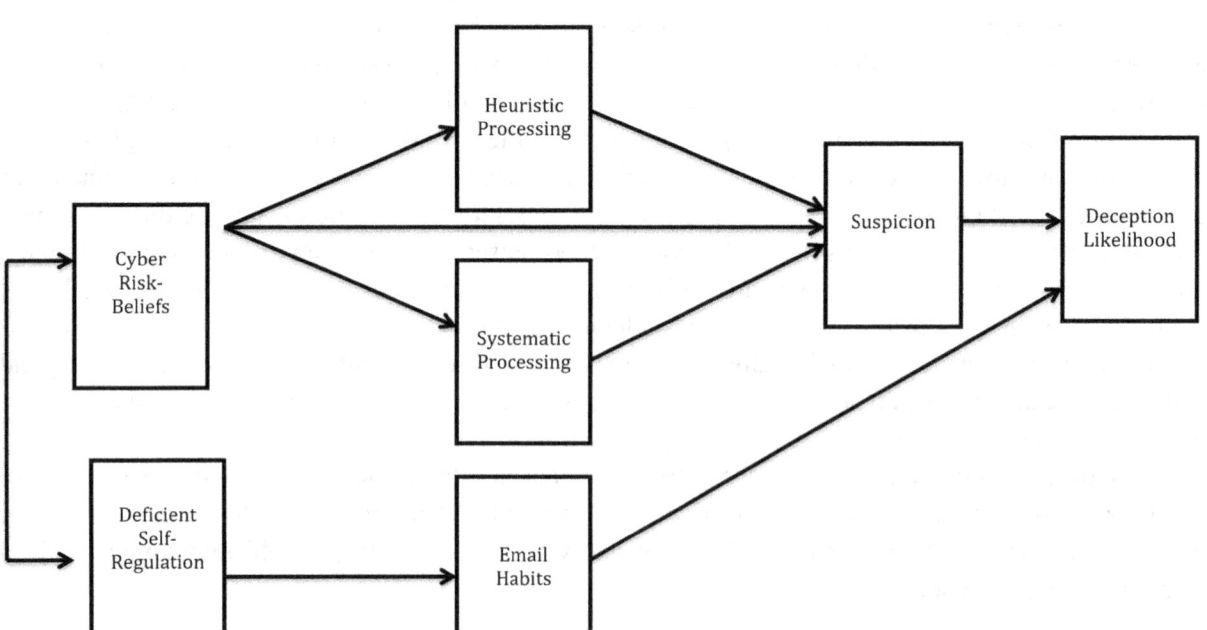

name of the sender, a graphical logo in the sender's signature, or a keyword such as 'deadline' or 'warning' highlighted in the text. Similarly, the phrase 'Sent from my iPhone' might suggest that an email was sent from a person's mobile device, and hence, unlikely to be a phish. Such heuristic processing is less effortful and is therefore the preferred and dominant mode of information evaluation. It is also an important explanation for why people fall victim to spear phishing.

Payload carrying spear phishing emails are usually crafted with specific cues that trigger heuristics. Phishers attempt to connect to individual cognitive biases by using the names of well-known organisations (e.g., the Internal Revenue Service, Apple, Facebook) and institutions relevant to the individuals (e.g., their email provider, IT help desk), the individuals' curiosity (e.g., a celebrity picture), or their sentiments (e.g., a link to support the troops or a social cause). Such cues trigger heuristics and lead to individuals clicking on the email. In contrast, the fee-forward type Nigerian emails usually contain long text and require interaction with the phisher. Their content along with the interactive process of this scam provide plenty of opportunities for users to engage in systematic processing, which is the reason why such pay-forward scams have a lower overall victimisation rate than the more simply crafted, payload-carrying spear phishing attacks.

In addition to the crafting of the email, how much cognitive energy individuals are willing to devote in a decision-making context is partly contingent on their cyber risk beliefs. In the SCAM, these risk beliefs are the people's beliefs about the inherent risk of their online actions. These beliefs stem from prior experience (e.g., having clicked on a malicious link in the past), exposure (e.g., being told not to respond to Nigerian spear phishing emails), and knowledge (e.g., knowing that .exe attachments are program files and not to be launched). Individuals' risk beliefs are, however, perceptions that are not always objectively accurate. For instance, a person may (and many people do) believe that Apple computers are safer from viruses than Microsoft's operating system. But this is an inaccurate, subjective perception that stems from the media. Objectively speaking, security against viruses does not inoculate any operating system from a RAT built to compromise that system. Likewise, people hold beliefs about the inherent security of certain file types, such as believing that Adobe PDF is somehow safer than a Word document, because they often conflate their own inability to edit the PDF with its inherent safety from viruses. In the same vein, people hold beliefs about the safety of certain devices and certain locations (e.g., public computers, open Wi-Fi networks, shared desktops), which influence how willing they are to engage cognitive resources during email use that in turn influence their likelihood of falling for a spear phishing attack.

Automaticity

Until recently, unconscious behaviours, those that are patterned, automatic responses, were given little importance by social scientists. More recent neurological work along with evidence from empirical research suggests that unconscious behaviours not only have a strong influence on online decision-making (Vishwanath, 2015b), but such actions also co-occur with conscious behaviours (Vishwanath, 2015c).

In much the same way as heuristic processing is a mental efficiency creating adaptation, the human brain also automates routine behaviours, making it easier to enact them subsequently without needing a reassessment of the rationale for the actions. Take for instance a simple, frequently enacted behaviour, such as listening to music on earphones while walking in a big city, or a relatively complex behaviour such as driving or taking the subway to work each day. For some individuals, these repeated actions are so routinized that they are performed ritualistically, often without individuals being aware of their enactment. Asking someone what they listened to, which subway stops they passed, or for how long the subway stopped along the way, and their difficulty in recalling it, usually reveals the extent of this routinization.

In general, actions such as these that are consistently performed with relatively predictable outcomes and those that provide some level of gratification at least during the early stages of forming the habit, are more likely to be routinized. For instance, listening to songs while walking, might initially improve people's mood or distract them from the effort of walking. After a certain period of repeated use, the behaviour gets routinized such that people prefer walking with music, and are often unaware of what they listened to while they walked – at which point, media scholars believe a habit has formed (Neal, Wood, & Quinn, 2006). Such habituation is stronger and more likely among individuals who are impulsive or deficient in their ability to self-regulate their behaviours (LaRose, 2010). In much the same way, media behaviours that are frequently performed and gratifying get habituated. Many media behaviours are particularly prone to habituation, because they are frequently conducted, and there are oftentimes rewards associated with it. For instance, checking email or social media feeds, actions many people frequently engage in, is easy to do and often nets gratifying information about one's friends and family. Not surprisingly, many individuals form habitual patterns of checking emails each morning, frequently checking their Facebook feeds, or visiting their favourite news webpages whenever they are online.

Email habits are, therefore, another important factor that leads to individual victimisation through spear phishing. When people encounter a spear phishing email, especially one that requires little effort to respond to, and when they have strong email habits, they are especially prone to opening the email. Experimental evidence suggests that individuals with established email habits have a significantly higher likelihood of being phished through a payload carrying hyperlink or attachment attack (Vishwanath, 2015c). Empirical evidence from experiments of social media phishing likewise shows that Facebook habits, too, have a similarly significant influence on an individual's vulnerability (Vishwanath, 2015b). Thus, at the user level, how people encounter, process and react to emails appear to influence their likelihood of victimisation. Effectively dealing with spear phishing requires policies and practices that collectively address these factors. Based on the SCAM and on initiatives that have been effective in different parts of the world, the next section presents six policy recommendations for combating spear phishing.

POLICY RECOMMENDATIONS FOR DEALING WITH SPEAR PHISHING RELATED CYBER CRIME

(1) Comprehensive Cyber Security Education

An important initiative that is urgently required is cyber security education. Much of cyber security education today, however, focuses on training people on how to spot a phish, often by repeatedly phishing them. Instead what is needed is education that focuses on improving individuals' core knowledge necessary for effectively dealing with suspicious online activity. Drawing from the SCAM, cyber security education must focus on helping users develop cyber risk beliefs that support safe online behaviours, and lead to the development of better heuristics that individuals can utilise in different online contexts. Education should focus on making people aware of the evolving threats to cyber security; guidance on ways to spot, sequester, and report suspicious online activities; and on providing users with the tools necessary for safe online browsing. Such education should be freely available and mandatory for individuals who handle personally identifiable information (PII) of customers and clients. Special efforts must also be made to educate vulnerable populations such as young children, senior citizens, and college students who are naive about information security.

In developing this initiative, nations could follow the example of the U.S. Department of Homeland Security's National Initiative for Cybersecurity Education (NICE) initiative. NICE provides virtual training and certificate programs, holds cyber competitions that allow individuals to test offensive and defensive cyber manoeuvres, and hosts research conferences, all designed to educate as well as encourage individuals into pursuing careers in cyber security.

(2) Developing Cyber Hygiene Training

During the early days of the Internet, schools and colleges all over the world focused on improving Internet literacy. In the same way, today we need to focus on teaching netizens cyber hygiene. Because many children today learn to use technology from their peers, most of who just do not have the expertise to guide them on its safe use, such training must be made a mandatory part of Kindergarten to Grade 12 curriculums. Children also increasingly post PII on social media sites, share messages on various platforms, and conduct computing and information processing tasks using mobile devices, without thinking about the inherent risk of these actions. Based on the SCAM's findings about the defining role of technology habits and rituals in predicting individual victimisation online, it is important that policy-makers and educators intervene and help children develop better cyber routines – especially during their formative years. Injecting routines such as performing security updates of one's device each morning, using separate work and personal emails, not checking email using freely available unsecured Wi-Fi networks, or using virtual private networks (VPNs) while surfing the Internet on mobile devices, must become part of everyone's online routines. While cyber security education could help teach people how to deal with specific threats, making security behaviour part of people's online rituals could inoculate people from all manner of cyber attacks for years to come.

(3) Create Dynamic IT Security Settings

Social engineering attacks target everyone in an organisation. Reports of the former director of the FBI Robert Mueller almost falling for a spear phishing attack (Krebs, 2009) speak of the reach of such attacks. Yet, the current system of according IT security privileges to employees in organisations is based on the employees' position in the organisation, and the types of information they are deemed to need. Besides, such policies are increasingly hard to implement in today's cloud-based computing, BYOD, and telecommuting work cultures. In these environments, such policies quickly become excessively restrictive leading to employees finding workarounds that increase the organisations' exposure to cyber attacks.

What is needed instead is a set of IT security policies that are not only sensitive enough to thwart incursions but also dynamic enough for implementation across varying work environments, platforms, and devices. One way to accomplish this is to use the SCAM as a guide for developing security policies. SCAM's measures could be used on a priori basis to measure individual technology habits and risk beliefs, and in conjunction with intermittent 'red team' attacks – meant to test individual and organisational cyber readiness through controlled cyber attacks – could help assess response patterns and construct an employee phishing susceptibility index (PSI). This risk profile could be amended on an ongoing basis and used to guide who receives access to different types of information in the organisation.

(4) Make Reporting Mandatory and Easy

Breaches occur because individuals click on malicious links that provide cyber terrorists a foothold into the organisation's networks. While many people fall for the deception, some become suspicious and refrain from clicking it. If more of these people would simply report their suspicion, it would help stop many attacks from spreading and infiltrating a network. There are, however, a number of different agencies in government that could potentially be reported to all using different modes (phone, email, web form) of reporting. Further complicating it is the lack of any defined feedback or reward for reporting. Many organisations which collect spear phishing reports often respond with form letters thanking individuals for the report. Together, these make reporting difficult and appear unnecessary even to individuals who have successfully identified a spear phishing attack.

What is needed instead is a simple portal that makes reporting easy. The portal could be similar to the emergency phone numbers, such as the 911 system in the United States that individuals can call in to request help. This number or email address should be easily accessible and information about its existence must be widely disseminated. When contacted, individuals should be provided with guidance on how to remediate the breach. Steps should also be taken to foster reporting such as by publicising the names of people who successfully helped stop a breach, or perhaps by naming breaches after the people whose reporting helped thwart them. Altogether, these initiatives would make reporting gratifying and help individuals form a habit of reporting suspected breaches.

Additionally, policymakers must make breach reporting mandatory for all organisations. Given the bad publicity that a breach brings, many organisations today prefer to handle the problems in-house, often without even informing the affected customers whose PII might be compromised. This creates significant problems for these individuals as well as misses an opportunity to stop further compromises that might be underway in other organisations. Hence, it is imperative that organisations mandatorily report all suspected breaches to an agency responsible for overseeing the remediation. A policy that could serve as a framework is President Obama's Cybersecurity bill, which requires all organisations in the United States to report a breach within 30 days (Steinhauer, 2015). Making reporting mandatory and easy could lead to better tracking and overtime significantly reduce the efficacy of cyber attacks.

(5) Foster Information Sharing

It is one thing to know that an attack is ongoing; it is another when other arms of the police force or the government are made aware of it. This makes it possible for the agencies to disseminate remedial measures quickly. Cyber terrorists also tend to attack multiple, related targets using the same attack vector. For instance, the SEA compromised the New York Times, The Huffington Post, and a host of other news agencies in a single attack. Thus, information of an ongoing attack also needs to be quickly shared among organisations within a sector, so they too can take steps to thwart the threat.

Such information sharing is only possible if there are specific agencies that are tasked with cumulating information, and if there is a unified mechanism of alerts that can be accessed by responsible individuals within various organisations. Cybersecurity policy must foster the creation of such an alert system as well as develop a mechanism for agencies to collect, share, and inform each other about ongoing breaches. Information sharing between different people and organisational IT, between individual IT divisions that tackle the problem and other quick reaction teams, and between policymakers should be as seamless as possible so as to effect a quick response to the attack.

(6) Develop Specialised Cyber Response Teams

Finally, it is important that there is a specialised response team that can quickly and effectively react to a cyber attack. This team should be made up of cyber security specialists as well as social-behavioural experts from academe who could not only help redress an attack but also collect incident reports, track the trajectory of incoming attacks, develop threat profiles, pinpoint the people who need to be trained, and be the gateway for cyber security related information sharing across various government agencies.

Similar response teams have been very effective in dealing with cybercrime. For instance, the City of London Police in England created a team called Action Fraud that specifically deals with cybercrime. This team is tasked with redressing all forms of computer fraud, and individuals can directly report incidents online or via telephone and get remedial help. Given the global nature of many cyber attacks, creating such a system in other nations would also allow for better information sharing and sharing of remediation strategies, which in time will greatly reduce the effectiveness of spear phishing attacks.

Many of these policy initiatives can only be effective if they are implemented together. Without individuals and organisations consistently reporting suspicious emails, the effectiveness of threat tracking is greatly reduced. Without threat tracking, the value of information sharing is significantly diminished. And without having a centralised agency responsible for the collection of data, for disseminating it, and for remediating it, there is not much value in reporting it. Again, President Obama's initiative (i.e., Cybersecurity bill) could serve as a blueprint for designing comprehensive cybersecurity policy in other nations (Daniel, 2015).

The need for an overarching cyber security policy is, however, urgent. Already, in the first six months of 2015, we have a reported 888 breaches globally leading to over 246 million PII compromises – a 10 percent increase compared to the same time frame last year ("2015 saw 888 data breaches", 2015). Not just that but these attacks are becoming more brazen because each successful breach emboldens the next. Take for instance the recent breach of the website, Ashley Madison, which is built specifically for extramarital affairs. The hacker group calling itself 'The Impact Team' held the company hostage, asking for specific changes to the website, and eventually released the user profile of over 33 million users. News of famous personalities who had signed-up on the site; of individuals worrying about persecution in nations where certain forms of sexual expression are illegal; of divorces and families being torn apart; and even reports of a few suicides (Segall, 2015), speak of the damage that such hacks create.

Osama Bin Laden had famously remarked how the reaction to the 9/11 Word Trade Center attacks would cumulatively haemorrhage the United States Economy, leading to "a death by a thousand cuts" (Ross, 2010, para. 2). Left unchecked, today's hacks will do the same. They will lead to changes in how cyber citizens behave online, on how we do business online, how we store information, in the nature of our relationships with institutions and organisations, and the cost of conducting business online. In short, the Internet will haemorrhage, leading to a death by a thousand bytes.

REFERENCES

Achiodo, B. (2012, August 30). Syria's cyber retaliation signals new era of warfare. *USA Today*. Retrieved from http://www.usatoday.com/story/cybertruth/2013/08/30/syrias-cyber-retaliation-signals--new-era-of-warfare/2740457/

Callimachi, R. (2014, July 14). Paying ransoms, Europe bankrolls qaeda terror. *The New York Times*. Retrieved from http://www.nytimes.com/2014/07/30/world/africa/ransoming-citizens-europe-becomes-al-qaedas-patron.html?_r=0

Caputo, D. D., Pfleeger, S. L., Freeman, J. D., & Johnson, M. E. (2014). Going spear phishing: Exploring embedded training and awareness. *Security & Privacy, IEEE, 12*(1), 28–38. doi:10.1109/MSP.2013.106

Chaiken, S. (1980). Heuristic versus systematic information processing and the use of source versus message cues in persuasion. *Journal of Personality and Social Psychology, 39*(5), 752–766. doi:10.1037/0022-3514.39.5.752

Daniel, M. (2015, January 14). What you need to know about President Obama's new steps on cybersecurity. *The White House*. Retrieved from https://www.whitehouse.gov/blog/2015/01/14/what-you-need-know-about-president-obama-s-new-steps-cybersecurity

Federal Bureau of Investigation (FBI). (n.d.). *Definition of terrorism*. Retrieved from https://www.fbi.gov/about-us/investigate/terrorism/terrorism-definition

Ferguson, A. J. (2005). Fostering e-mail security awareness: The West Point carronade. *EDUCASE Quarterly, 28*(1), 54–57.

Fisher-Ilan, A., & Finkle, J. (2014, January 26). Israeli defense computer hacked via tainted email: cyber firm. *Reuters*. Retrieved from http://www.reuters.com/article/2014/01/26/israel-cybersecurity-idUSL5N0L00JR20140126

Geiger, K. (2015, August 11). Hackers' $100 million insider shop sold data on demand. *Bloomberg*. Retrieved from http://www.bloomberg.com/news/articles/2015-08-11/hackers-100-million-insider-trading-shop-sold-data-on-demand

Hancock, J. B. (2013). Social media make us more honest. *TED*. Retrieved from https://www.ted.com/talks/jeff_hancock_3_types_of_digital_lies?language=en

Herley, C. (2012, June). *Why do Nigerian scammers say they are from Nigeria?* Paper presented at Workshop on the Economics of Information Security (WEIS), Berlin, Germany.

Hill, C. (2013, December 20). Email 'from Target' to customers is a phishing scam. *Market Watch*. Retrieved from http://www.marketwatch.com/story/scammers-pounce-on-target-fiasco-2013-12-20

Hingham, S., & Nakashima, E. (2015, July 16). Why the Islamic State leaves tech companies torn between free speech and security. *The Washington Post*. Retrieved from https://www.washingtonpost.com/world/national-security/islamic-states-embrace-of-social-media-puts-tech-companies-in-a-bind/2015/07/15/0e5624c4-169c-11e5-89f3-61410da94eb1_story.html

Krebs, B. (2009, October 8). Phishing scam spooked FBI director off e-banking. *The Washington Post*. Retrieved from http://voices.washingtonpost.com/securityfix/2009/10/fbi_director_on_internet_banki.html

LaRose, R. (2010). The problem of media habits. *Communication Theory, 20*(2), 194–222. doi:10.1111/j.1468-2885.2010.01360.x

Libicki, M. C., Ablon, L., & Webb, T. (2015). *The defender's dilemma: Charting a course toward cybersecurity*. Santa Monica, CA: RAND Corporation.

Mandiant. (2013). *APT1: Exposing one of China's cyber espionage units*. Alexandria, VA: Mandiant.

Nakashima, E. (2012, September 21). Iran blamed for cyberattacks on U.S. banks and companies. *The Washington Post*. Retrieved from https://www.washingtonpost.com/world/national-security/iran-blamed-for-cyberattacks/2012/09/21/afbe2be4-0412-11e2-9b24-ff730c7f6312_story.html

Neal, D. T., Wood, W., & Quinn, J. M. (2006). Habits – A repeat performance. *Current Directions in Psychological Science*, *15*(4), 198–202. doi:10.1111/j.1467-8721.2006.00435.x

Paganini, P. (2012, November 12). Cyber espionage attack against Israel is not an isolated event. *Security Affairs*. Retrieved from http://securityaffairs.co/wordpress/10243/malware/cyber-espionage-attack-against-israel-is-not-an-isolated-event.html

Prigg, M. (2015, May 20). The tweet that cost $139 billion: Researchers analyse impact of hacked 2013 message claiming President Obama had been injured by White House explosion. *The Daily Mail*. Retrieved from http://www.dailymail.co.uk/sciencetech/article-3090221/The-tweet-cost-139-BILLION-Researchers-analyse-impact-hacked-message-claiming-President-Obama-injured-White-House-explosion.html

Prince, B. (2009). Phishing attacks cost millions despite low success rate. *eWeek*. Retrieved from http://www.eweek.com/c/a/Security/Phishing-Attacks-Cost-Millions-Despite-Low-Success-Rate-879602

Ross, D. (2010, November 23). Death by a thousand cuts. *Foreign Policy*. Retrieved from http://foreignpolicy.com/2010/11/23/death-by-a-thousand-cuts-2/

Russian hackers accused of attacks on Bundestag and French TV broadcaster. (2015, June 5). *The Telegraph*. Retrieved from http://www.telegraph.co.uk/news/worldnews/europe/germany/11666815/Russian-hackers-accused-of-Bundestag-attack.html

2015 . saw 888 data breaches, 246 million records compromised worldwide. (2015, September 9). *Net-Security*. Retrieved from http://www.net-security.org/secworld.php?id=18832

Scott-Railton, J., & Hardy, S. (2014, December 18). Malware attack targeting Syrian ISIS critics. *Citizenlab*. Retrieved from https://citizenlab.org/2014/12/malware-attack-targeting-syrian-isis-critics/

Segall, L. (2015). Pastor outed on Ashley Madison commits suicide. *CNN*. Retrieved from http://money.cnn.com/2015/09/08/technology/ashley-madison-suicide/index.html

Shell, A. (2013, April 23). This stocks gyrate wildly after fake terror tweet. *USA Today*. Retrieved from http://www.usatoday.com/story/money/markets/2013/04/23/stocks-gyrate-wildly-after-fake-terror-tweet/2107089/

Steinhauer, J. (2015, April 22). House passes Cybersecurity Bill after companies fall victim to data breaches. *The New York Times*. Retrieved from http://www.nytimes.com/2015/04/23/us/politics/computer-attacks-spur-congress-to-act-on-cybersecurity-bill-years-in-making.html

Verizon. (2012). *2012 Data Breach Investigations Report*. Basking Ridge, NJ: Author. Retrieved from http://www.verizonenterprise.com/resources/reports/rp_data-breach-investigations-report-2012-ebk_en_xg.pdf

Vishwanath, A. (2015a, June 8). Why the cyberattacks keep coming. *CNN*. Retrieved from http://www.cnn.com/2015/06/08/opinions/vishwanath-stopping-hacking

Vishwanath, A. (2015b). Habitual facebook use and its impact on getting deceived on social media. *Journal of Computer-Mediated Communication, 20*(1), 83–98. doi:10.1111/jcc4.12100

Vishwanath, A. (2015c). Examining the distinct antecedents of e-mail habits and its influence on the outcomes of a phishing attack. *Journal of Computer-Mediated Communication, 20*(5), 570–584. doi:10.1111/jcc4.12126

Vishwanath, A., Harrison, B., & Ng, Y. J. (2015). *Suspicion, cognition, automaticity model (SCAM) of phishing susceptibility*. Paper presented at the Annual Conference of the International Communication Association, San Juan, Puerto Rico.

Vishwanath, A., Herath, T., Chen, R., Wang, J., & Rao, H. R. (2011). Why do people get phished? Testing individual differences in phishing vulnerability within an integrated, information processing model. *Decision Support Systems, 51*(3), 576–586. doi:10.1016/j.dss.2011.03.002

Waqas. (2015, April 18). Pics of IDF women soldiers helped hackers to breach Israeli Military Servers. *Hackread.com*. Retrieved from https://www.hackread.com/hackers-breach-israeli-military-servers/

Wu, M., Miller, R. C., & Garfinkel, S. L. (2006). Do security toolbars actually prevent phishing attacks? In *Proceedings of the SIGCHI conference on Human Factors in computing systems*. Montreal, Quebec: ACM. doi:10.1145/1124772.1124863

Zetter, K. (2015, January 12). Central command's Twitter account hacked ... As Obama speaks on cybersecurity. *Wired.com* Retrieved from http://www.wired.com/2015/01/centcoms-twitter-hack/

Section 5
Summary and Future Directions

Chapter 24
What We Know and What Else We Need to Do to Address the Problem of Violent Extremism Online:
Concluding Chapter

Majeed Khader
Home Team Behavioural Sciences Centre, Ministry of Home Affairs, Singapore

ABSTRACT

This concluding chapter is an attempt made to summarise and analyse the chapters provided by the various authors in this book. The analysis used in this chapter is based on a public health prevention model created by Quick, Quick, Nelson, and Hurrell (1997). The value of this approach is the systemic prevention angle that it undertakes to examine problems and solutions.

INTRODUCTION

This concluding chapter is an attempt made to summarise and analyse the chapters provided by the various contributors of this book. The analysis used is based on a public health prevention model created by Quick, Quick, Nelson, and Hurrell (1997). The value of this approach is the systemic prevention angle that it undertakes to examine problems and solutions. This chapter will thus be structured in a manner that discusses the various book chapters in terms of their relevance for Primary, Secondary, and Tertiary prevention efforts in countering violent extremism, and will discuss these in terms of what is working and what is lacking.

DOI: 10.4018/978-1-5225-0156-5.ch024

Public Health Prevention Model

Along the lines of Quick et al.'s (1997) framework, primary prevention serves to address risk factors and enhance an organisation's health. These initiatives refer to interventions and programs designed to reduce, modify or eliminate the risk factor in the first place. Typically, primary prevention efforts are low-cost strategies which are meant for the masses. One reason for keeping these efforts low cost or at least 'value for money' is because of the massive outreach that they are intended to have in order to have impact.

Primary prevention seeks to prevent the onset of specific diseases via risk reduction; by altering behaviours or reducing exposures that can lead to disease, or by enhancing resistance to the effects of exposure to a disease agent. Examples include smoking cessation and vaccination. Some primary approach in dental medicine has been to encourage regular tooth brushing and flossing to prevent dental cavities. Other approaches include adding fluoride to municipal drinking water to harden tooth enamel and prevent caries. Primary prevention generally targets specific causes and risk factors for specific diseases, but may also aim to promote healthy behaviours, improve host resistance, and foster safe environments that reduce the risk of diseases. In road safety, primary prevention efforts include initiatives such as the use of seatbelts and safety helmets.

Applying this to the domain of violent extremism, we should ask what are the efforts that we need to do that will be targeted at everyone in the population, no matter their risk levels. Intuitively, it could be argued that some of these efforts should be aimed at inoculating the masses against the dangers of the violent extremist propaganda with counter-narratives and anti-terrorism or anti-violent extremism campaigns.

Secondary prevention usually involves efforts aimed at those who may already be exhibiting a certain level of risk. This involves more specific, proactive efforts, which aim to influence the way in which these individuals and organisations manage the situations and risks. This is done by detecting and treating risk, disease or injury as soon as possible to halt or slow its progress, encouraging strategies to prevent re-injury or recurrence of disease, and implementing programs to return people to their original health and function to prevent long-term problems. Examples include regular examination and screening tests to detect disease in its earliest stages (e.g., mammograms to detect breast cancer); daily low-dose of aspirins and/or diet and exercise programs to prevent heart attacks or strokes; and suitably modified work so that injured or ill workers can return safely to their jobs.

Applying this to the domain of violent extremism, secondary prevention could be aimed at those who are already predisposed towards sympathising violent extremist views or already visiting violent extremist websites as well as those who have the propensity to visit such websites.

Tertiary prevention initiatives intend to be focused on aiding and healing the individual or organisational symptoms of distress and strain, and returning them to their normal state. Examples of this may include emergency medical procedures, and workplace counselling services for those who are traumatised. In the violent extremism and countering violent extremism domain, these kinds of interventions may include disengagement programs and de-radicalisation programs as well as website takedown initiatives.

Tables 1, 2, and 3 illustrate how the chapters in this book address or do not address the primary and secondary, and tertiary factors discussed earlier. These tables below are by no means comprehensive in any way, since they merely reflect the content of the chapters in this book. For example, the use of

Table 1. Ideas and solutions organised along the line of Primary Prevention: Methods to target root and fundamental causes to eliminate the risk or increase the resistance

Content Discussed in the Chapters		
Person Centred Focus	**Cyber System Centred Focus**	**Person-Cyber Combined Centred Focus**
• Understanding risk of cyber-based insider threat using reactive measures of personality (chapter 6) • Understanding the motivations Of ISIS foreign fighters (chapter 8) • Understanding Singapore's homegrown radicals (chapter 9) • Understanding the motivations of western female migrants to ISIS (chapter 10) • 4 P's: Policing, Public, Policies, and Politics (chapter 12) • Building resilience by civilian management training (chapter 14) • Building national resilience in the face of terror attacks (chapter 15)	• Understanding tipping points for online radicalisation (chapter 7) • Using the Counter-Ideological Response (CIS) model to undercut the credibility of malicious sender (chapter 13) • Understanding social media analytics for countering violent extremism (chapter 16) • Linguistic analysis Of websites to identify linguistic markers in written text (chapter 18) • Education on social engineering and its use in cyber attacks (chapter 23)	• Understanding the way ISIS uses propaganda online and offline (chapter 2) • Understanding discursive markers in social media (chapter 3) • The use of the Internet as a tool for monitoring purposes (chapter 5) • Studying cyber-based insider threats (chapter 6) • Interventions working on cyber hygiene training And cyber security education (chapter 23)
What Might Be Lacking or Insufficient/What is Needed for the Future?		
Person Centred Focus	**Cyber System Centred Focus**	**Person-Cyber Combined Centred Focus**
• Research on future trends in violent extremism. What trends will we see in 2026? 2036? • Research on culture-based understanding of violent extremism – how? • Does culture influence the motivations of violent extremists? • Learning from other violent extremist groups (e.g., animal rights, right-wing) to obtain a greater understanding of the mechanism that operate for religious violent extremism.	• Research on future trends on technological developments in terms of information technology, cyber mediums. • What cyber manifestations should be predicted in 2026? 2036? • In a world where dangerous ideas can exist, how can the state or local communities technically undercut the credibility of the malicious senders?	• What preventive messaging should we develop to prevent individuals from being radicalised? Which agencies should do this? The state, security agencies or religious Ulama (scholar)? • Exactly which messages should we be countering (e.g., Jihad, Hijrah, Bai-ah, or Ummah)? Should this done online or offline, or as a hybrid version? • How to develop a program for cyber resilience for the population at large? • How to create a globally agreed 'best practice' for countering violent extremism?

tell-tale indicators to detect and report potential violent extremist activities is certainly important for countering violent extremism efforts, but as none of the chapters had directly discussed this in detail, it is not found within the tables. However, this does not mean that it is unimportant.

For the purpose of this chapter, the content from each chapter of this book is discussed in terms of primary, secondary, and tertiary interventions. Then for each area of prevention, for example primary prevention, it is further discussed in terms of person centred, cyber system centred, and combined person-cyber centred focus. Finally, for each area of prevention, issues are discussed in terms of the content shared by the authors, and then potential areas for future research which might be lacking presently in the chapters within this book.

In analysing Tables 1, 2, and 3, several themes, issues and considerations have emerged which are further elaborated in the next section.

Table 2. Ideas and solutions organised along the line of Secondary Prevention: Methods targeted to detect and manage existing risk/persons and systems at risk

Content Discussed in the Chapters		
Person Centred Focus	**Cyber System Centred Focus**	**Person-Cyber Combined Centred Focus**
• Understanding the gender dynamics and women at risk of becoming involved with ISIS (chapter 10) • Working with converts at risk (chapter 14) • Developing risk assessment protocol – e.g., VERA-2 (chapter 19)	• Understanding the features of persuasive violent extremist online platforms (chapter 1) • Understanding what is online preaching and da'wah and how does it work? (chapter 4) • Using the Internet to plan for terror attacks (chapter 5) • Development of risk assessment protocol for online violent extremist activities – e.g., CYBERA (chapter 14) • Using social media analytics for intelligence and countering violent extremism (chapter 16)	• U.S. State Department Digital Outreach projects (chapter 2) • How the Internet facilitate the radicalisation process (chapter 11) • The use of the Internet as a reconnaissance tool for identification purposes • (chapter 5) • How the Internet facilitates migration into ISIS territory (chapter 10) • The Counter-Ideological Response (CIS) model (chapter 13) • Guidelines for developing online risk assessment of violent extremists (chapter 17)
What Might Be Lacking or Insufficient/What is Needed for the Future?		
Person Centred Focus	**Cyber System Centred Focus**	**Person-Cyber Combined Centred Focus**
• Development of checklist and screening tools for persons who may be at risk – especially risk assessment checklists for known threats.	• Automated web crawlers can be used to identify high risk online platforms – with a view to counter influence. • Working with social media companies with a view to counter social media comments, postings or videos disseminated by violent extremists.	• Continuing the counter-ideology response online by religious Ulamas to address those at risk online. • Training Ulamas to be savvy with social media, so that they may respond to those at risk. • Tackling the debate online about ISIS foreign fighters merely being about humanitarian efforts – responding to those at risk.

Table 3. Ideas and solutions organised along the line of Tertiary Prevention: Methods targeted at those affected, and introduce methods to reduce negative impact of those/systems who are affected

Content Discussed in the Chapters		
Person Centred Focus	**Cyber System Centred Focus**	**Person-Cyber Combined Centred Focus**
• Arrests • Rehabilitation • De-radicalisation programs (chapter 20) • Disengagement programs	• Take down of violent extremist online platforms	• Combination of arrests, disruption and cyber takedowns (Mentioned by several chapters) • Reporting systems in social media platforms (Mentioned by several chapters)
What Might Be Lacking or Insufficient/What is Needed for the Future?		
Person Centred Focus	**Cyber System Centred Focus**	**Person-Cyber Combined Centred Focus**

• Conduct deep level studies that examining primary data from those arrested:
   o What can ex-violent extremists tell us about the motives and appeal of joining violent extremist groups?
   o What can violent extremist veterans tell us?
 • From those arrested, what are the factors that predict re-radicalisation – when rehabilitation fails? How do we prevent re-radicalisation?
 • How do we develop a rehabilitation model based upon the Good Life for those who want to be good Muslims, living in multi-racial multi religious communities?
	• What can takedowns efforts of violent extremist online platforms tell us about the cyber and digital forensics of such online platforms?
	 • Will social network analysis and other similar social media analytics reveal anything useful?
	 • Are there cyber programs to prevent re-establishment of violent extremist online platforms?
		• How do we undertake a 'cyber-autopsy' of how an individual get radicalised online? What will this reveal that can be useful in primary prevention efforts?
		 • What prison based rehabilitation programs are designed for cyber radicals? Should cyber rehabilitation be considered?

PRIMARY PREVENTION CONSIDERATIONS

Researchers and Operational Analysts Must Better Predict the Future Trends of Violent Extremist Behaviours

The September 11 attacks occurred in 2001 and in these 15 years, the nature of violent extremism has grown in complexity and scope. Despite these many years of dealing and responding to the threat of violent extremism, we still do not predict future attacks well. For example, there have been very few successes in predicting the rise of the Islamic State in Iraq and Syria (ISIS). We did not predict the Mumbai attacks or the Paris 2015 attacks. Much of what we seem to know is very much a matter of hindsight bias, which is of course 20/20. Why is it that most researchers and operational analysts are not able to predict future attacks well? What new problems of violent extremism can we expect in 2026?

One reason could be that we do not appreciate the fundamentals well. The research enterprise is struggling to answer the question of why this problem of violent extremism comes about in the first place. What motivates violent extremists to do what they do? Another reason could be that the violent extremists are so nimble in their innovations and learning styles such that it is hard to catch up with their new developments. Whatever the reasons, we need to get better at predicting the way violent extremism is evolving if we aim to contribute to this mission of keeping our communities safe from violent extremists. More and better research needs to be done on predicting future violent extremism trends.

Build Cyber Resilience and Inoculate Our Communities and Nations

There is a need for cyber resilience. In the world of citizen journalism and increased social media presence, there is a supposed democracy of ideas. But yet some ideas are more popular than others, and some more dangerous than others (Eidelson & Eidelson, 2003). When malicious senders who appreciate how ideas may go viral on social media use these online services to propagate violent extremism, there is danger. We are not suggesting that everyone is vulnerable or naïve, because clearly some groups or some persons will be more vulnerable than others. Also, there is a natural level of resilience in most people.

Using primary prevention as a strategy, the idea should be one of cyber inoculating communities and the population to dissuade potential sympathisers and supporters. Some important questions are:

- How to design cyber resilience and cyber inoculation programs for the population at large and communities?
- Who should lead these programs (e.g., religious groups, political masters, countering violent extremism experts)?
- How should governments respond to this ocean of violent extremism propaganda? How do governments respond in way without losing their credibility? More importantly, how do governments respond in a way that does not sound alarmist?

Have a Clear International Voice Countering Violent Extremism

There is a need for a clear international mandate and voice speaking out against violence extremism. This is needed because the chapters in this book suggest that there is a wide array of diversified response strategies. Whilst each country's solution has to be customised to its own national needs, there is a need for clear international best practice guidelines in the same way that there are international guidelines for handling of victims of crime. Some early moves in this direction would be the report by the Ali Soufan Group on 'Countering Violent Extremism: The Counter Narrative Study' (The Soufan Group, 2013), which saw the compilation of counter narrative efforts undertaken by several different countries.

However, these international best practice guidelines should represent a voice which would be a harmonious set of voices from sectors including the government (to address the policy towards countering violent extremism), the religious leadership (to address the religious doctrinal issues), the Muslim community (to ensure clear buy in and customisation to different communities; cultural angles), and the counter violent extremism agencies (to ensure that the law enforcement and counter violent extremism perspective is considered). This document needs to address issues such as:

- Should Muslims make their way to ISIS to perform their *Hijrah* (emigration)? Is this the right thing to do so that they might live in an Islamic caliphate and within a Muslim community?
- How do Muslims live with other non-Muslims in a community?
- Is jihad a compulsory religious obligation for Muslims?
- Is it okay for someone to support the armed efforts even if it is from the humanitarian angle?

SECONDARY PREVENTION CONSIDERATIONS

There Is a Need to Identify Individuals, Groups and Populations 'At Risk' and To Provide Risk Management Strategies

One of the key features about secondary prevention efforts is to ask, 'who is at risk to become radicalised?' and 'what should we do for this group of individuals?' Presently, we see that at the individual level, research has found some risk factors such as those who may feel a need for cognitive closure (Webster & Kruglanski, 1994).

What about groups of individuals? Would these groups include young women who want to travel to Syria to marry jihadists? Young men who look forward to military adventure and sensation seeking? Older family-oriented men who want to live in an Islamic community under an Amir? New converts? University students? Engineering students? Scholars have suggested all of these groups previously. However, this is not a suggestion that all individuals under such groupings are vulnerable. Instead a combination of group and individual factors may contribute to a higher level of risk. Scholars and practitioners must be clear about the profile of the persons who may be at risk, and render interventions early.

A related point is that interventions must be customised for each vulnerable group. It is not a situation of 'one-size-fits-all' approach that can be recommended, but 'horses-for-courses' approach. Interventions for young men may for example involve more group-based, peer-based interactive interventions; while the interventions for those who go to Syria to seek religious fulfilment may be different from those who purport to go there for humanitarian reasons. In short, without stigmatising individuals or groups, there is a need to identify individuals and groups who may be at risk, so that they may be assisted early.

Develop 'Risk-For-Radicalisation' Assessment Tools to Assess Risk of Persons and Systems

Because secondary prevention is about mitigating the impact for those at risk, one strategy which can be used, is to develop risk assessment tools for users on how to assess the risk for radicalisation. Our own research has uncovered that when young men are arrested for radical beliefs and actions, their families always knew about their surfing habits. Most knew well that their sons and daughters were online surfing religious websites, but they just did not appreciate how bad the situation was. Therefore, there is a need to develop a risk assessment checklist that measures both individual propensities to become radicalised, and websites that facilitates the process of radicalisation.

Whilst this might sound like a common sense solution, there are not many risk assessment tools for online radicalisation. There are excellent early efforts with the development of the CYBERA (see chapter 19 by Elaine Pressman and Cristina Ivan), but more research is needed to fully understand this business of risk assessment for online violent extremism. One difficulty of doing this kind of work well is that it requires a multidisciplinary approach; it requires a blended expertise on human behaviour sciences (e.g., psychology, sociology, cultural studies, communication sciences), and also information technology and engineering sciences. Very few violent extremism research agencies appear currently to be working in this multidisciplinary way.

Study the Infrastructural Elements of Cyber Platforms that Go Viral and Contribute to Online Radicalisation

What is it about some cyber platforms that results in them going viral and becoming additive? This addictive compulsive component of some cyber platforms is not a new phenomenon, and has been seen in other areas such as cyber gaming and cyber gambling (Kuss & Griffiths, 2012). Casino designers have clearly understood the power of infrastructural design, and casinos are usually decorated to create the right ambience to allow clients to experience the sense of flow (Csikszentmihalyi, 1998) and loss of time consciousness. What is it about the mechanism of such cyber platforms that facilitates online radicalisation? Is it the interactive components of the site that allows for deep discussion? Or the fact that 'sharing' or 'liking' is so easy to do as seen in the case for many social media platforms? It is useful to study these technical aspects of such cyber platforms so that we are able to deconstruct, analyse these technical design features that may have an impact on human addiction.

TERTIARY INTERVENTIONS CONSIDERATIONS

Developing Better Interventions by Asking the Violent Extremists Themselves

From the forensic and criminal psychology field, we have learnt a lot about of criminals, gangsters, rapists, paedophiles, hackers, and white-collar criminals. Experts have specifically learnt a significant amount of information by going into prisons to interview these offenders, asking them about their motivations, values, family histories, medical and psychiatric histories, and criminal pathways. Great studies have been conducted looking at the 'life course pathways' of young offenders (see Moffitt, 1993), and much has been learnt from longitudinal studies (see Farrington, 2015). Some researchers have even lived with gangs to develop an ethnographic understanding of how it might be like to be a gangster (Levitt & Venkatesh, 2007). In our own previous projects, some of the authors of this book have spoken to young gang members in the Singapore prisons asking them about their advice on crime prevention and anti-gang crime prevention messaging. These youngsters did in fact provide useful suggestions about the things they want to see and what they did not like to see in the crime prevention publicity efforts. From all of these, much has been learnt since the 1980's on 'what works, when and how' on criminal offending. Can the same be done for violent extremism? We are not suggesting the violent extremists are similar in terms of their make up to criminals, but we are suggesting that methodologies for analysis can be transferred across these domains. Some possibilities for future research questions include:

- Is it possible to ask ex-violent extremists for their own views about what might work in terms of counter-narratives?
- What are the 'terror-genic' needs of violent extremists? What are their motivations? What are the risk and protective factors?
- Which websites and cyber platforms are frequently visited? Why are some cyber materials more addictive than others?

It must be qualified however that there are limitations of self-reports and interviews in prisons and other incarcerated settings. Apart from the fact that it requires a specialised set of skills to engage the violent extremists, deception is possible and interviewees may also provide socially desirable responses (see Turvey, Khader, Ang, Tan, & Chin, 2012). A triangulation analysis approach to understand and verify the information provided to the researchers on these abovementioned scenarios is therefore desirable.

One suggested model is to look at the totality of information obtained using a 'B-L-I-S' approach suggested by David Funder (2012) where information is obtained using behaviour, life events, inter-rater ratings and self-reports. For instance, when talking to violent extremist about the risk and protective factors that were related to radicalisation, one could interview the person involved (i.e., self-report data), interview others who could confirm the person's history, background and involvement (i.e., inter-rater data), observe significant life events the person has encountered such as divorce and marriage, number of leadership roles in violent extremist group (i.e., life events data), and observe what the person actually does, as opposed to what the person says he/she does (i.e., behaviour data). Collecting multiple data from different sources may enhance the accuracy of the information collected.

'Cyber Psychological Autopsy' and 'Cyber Technical Autopsy' Can Be Used To Study Exactly How People Get Radicalised Online

The literature on radicalisation seems abound with research on how people become radicalised. However, hardly any of this seems to be based on a detailed 'cyber psychological autopsy' or 'cyber technical autopsy'. This is probably because this methodology does not exist at this stage in the same way that it does not exist in other domains of criminal and health psychology. Psychological autopsy, for example, is a well-established methodology used in suicide research (Isometsä, 2001). This approach may be a singular case study methodology (e.g., singular suicide) or group case analysis (analysing cases as a group). In the context of violent extremism, the advantage of this approach is the detailed and granular study which can potentially reveal deep insights into motivations, preference for particular cyber platforms, nature of interactions and interconnectedness of these interactions, and the links between cyber world and real world interactions, amongst other things. Technical digital autopsies may enlighten law enforcement agencies on exactly which websites were surfed, when and how each website was linked to others, thus providing a deep insight into the processes of online radicalisation.

We Seem To Know More about De-Radicalisation than 'Re-Radicalisation'

Criminal psychologists have long confirmed the idea that a repeat offender does not have the same characteristic as most offenders. In fact, most crime is committed by repeat offenders. Using the same logic, we need to ask about what we need to know about repeat violent extremist offenders? Repeated offending groups? Failed rehabilitation programs can see ex-violent extremists being re-radicalised. Some research has suggested that re-radicalisation can be a more potent force to deal with than radicalisation, mainly because the re-radicalised person is even more fervent and stronger in his convictions and beliefs. How much do we know about re-radicalisation? How do we prevent this relapse? More research is needed in this area.

There Is a Need to Articulate the 'Right Life Model' for Muslims

Data from interviewed jihadi violent extremists seems to suggest that there is at least one group which is motivated by the need to seek the true religion or the good Muslim life. Hence, some may turn to the Internet to surf for answers and religious guidance. This may also be the reason why some are attracted to charismatic radical preachers such as Anwar al-Awlaki who spoke about what a good Muslim should do. The alternate moderate voice articulating how Muslims can live peacefully in a multi-racial and multi-religious setting is hardly discussed openly, and if it does, this material does not go viral.

In the crime literature on the other hand, a model of rehabilitation called the 'good life model (GLM)' by Ward, Goebbels, and Willis (2013) has emerged, which gives some suggestions of what it means to live the good life and a life absent of criminality. Whilst critics are sceptical of this model saying that it lacks enough clarity in its conceptualisation, the idea of the GLM is an interesting one to explore because instead of pointing why one should not live a life of criminality, it points out the kind of living that one should endeavour to have. Perhaps more work needs to be done in the area of countering violent extremism to explore the type of GLM model for Muslims who want to live a good life. This is an issue, which the Islamic religious authorities can explore and undertake more research on for the future.

CONCLUSION

In concluding this chapter and the book, it appears that there may be merits of viewing all of these issues and especially the solutions in terms of the primary, secondary, and tertiary preventive efforts; especially since prevention is always better than cure. However, using this framework also suggests to us that while much has been delivered in terms of solutions and much progress has been made, much more is still needed to address this problem of combating violent extremism and radicalisation in the digital era.

REFERENCES

Csikszentmihalyi, M. (1998). *Finding flow: The psychology of engagement with everyday life.* New York, NY: Basic Books.

Eidelson, R. J., & Eidelson, J. I. (2003). Dangerous ideas: Five beliefs that propel groups toward conflict. *The American Psychologist, 58*(3), 182–192. doi:10.1037/0003-066X.58.3.182 PMID:12772423

Farrington, D. P. (2015). Prospective longitudinal research on the development of offending. *Australian and New Zealand Journal of Criminology, 48*(3), 314–335. doi:10.1177/0004865815590461

Funder, D. C. (2012). *The personality puzzle* (6th ed.). New York, NY: Norton.

Isometsä, E. T. (2001). Psychological autopsy studies – A review. *European Psychiatry, 16*(7), 379–385. doi:10.1016/S0924-9338(01)00594-6 PMID:11728849

Kuss, D. J., & Griffiths, M. D. (2012). Online gaming addiction in adolescence: A literature review of empirical research. *Journal of Behavioral Addictions, 1*(1), 3–22. doi:10.1556/JBA.1.2012.1.1 PMID:26166826

Levitt, S. D., & Venkatesh, S. A. (2007). *An empirical analysis of street-level prostitution* (working paper). Chicago, IL: University of Chicago.

Moffitt, T. E. (1993). Adolescence-limited and life-course-persistent antisocial behaviour: A developmental taxonomy. *Psychological Review, 100*(4), 674–701. doi:10.1037/0033-295X.100.4.674 PMID:8255953

Quick, J. C., Quick, J. D., Nelson, D. L., & Hurrell, J. J. (1997). *Preventive stress management in organisations.* Washington, DC: American Psychological Association. doi:10.1037/10238-000

The Soufan Group. (2013). *Countering violent extremism: The counter narrative study.* New York, NY: The Soufan Group.

Turvey, B. E., Khader, M., Ang, J., Tan, E., & Chin, J. (2012). Introduction to terrorism: Understanding and interviewing terrorists. In B. E. Turvey (Ed.), *Criminal profiling* (4th ed., pp. 569–583). San Diego, CA: Academic Press. doi:10.1016/B978-0-12-385243-4.00023-X

Ward, T., Goebbels, S., & Willis, G. M. (2013). Offender rehabilitation: The construction of better lives and the reduction of risk. In G. Bruinsma & D. Weisburd (Eds.), *Encyclopaedia of criminology and criminal justice.* New York, NY: Springer-Verlag.

Webster, D. M., & Kruglanski, A. W. (1994). Individual differences in need for cognitive closure. *Journal of Personality and Social Psychology, 67*(6), 1049–1062. doi:10.1037/0022-3514.67.6.1049 PMID:7815301

Compilation of References

20,000 foreign fighters flock to Syria, Iraq to join terrorists. (2015, February 10). *CBS News*. Retrieved from http://www.cbsnews.com/news/ap-20000-foreign-fighters-flock-to-syria-iraq-to-join-terrorists/

2015 saw 888 data breaches, 246 million records compromised worldwide. (2015, September 9). *Net-Security*. Retrieved from http://www.net-security.org/secworld.php?id=18832

Aboul-Enein, Y. H. (2004). Osama bin-Laden interview, June 1999: Entering the mind of an adversary. *Military Review*, *84*(Sep-Oct), 109–112.

Abraham, S., & Chengalur-Smith, I. S. (2010). An overview of social engineering malware: Trends, tactics and implications. *Technology in Society*, *32*(3), 183–196. doi:10.1016/j.techsoc.2010.07.001

Abrams, M., & Weiss, J. (2008). Malicious control system cyber security attack case study: Maroochy water services. Australia: National Institute of Standards and Technology. Retrieved from http://csrc.nist.gov/groups/SMA/fisma/ics/documents/Maroochy-Water-Services-Case-Study_report.pdf

Abu Bakr al-Baghdadi urges Muslims to make hijrah to the Islamic State. (2014). *5 Pillarz*. Retrieved from http://www.5pillarz.com/2014/07/02/abu-bakr-al-baghdadi-urges-muslims-to-make-hijrah-to-the-islamic-state/

Abuza, Z. (2009). Rehabilitation of Jemaah Islamiyah detainees in South East Asia: A preliminary assessment. In T. Bjørgo & J. Horgan (Eds.), *Leaving terrorism behind: Individual and collective disengagement* (pp. 193–211). New York, NY: Routledge.

Acharya, A. (2004). Defending Singapore's vital infrastructure against terrorism. *IDSS Commentaries*. Retrieved from http://www.pvtr.org/pdf/commentaries/IDSS372004.pdf

Achiodo, B. (2012, August 30). Syria's cyber retaliation signals new era of warfare. *USA Today*. Retrieved from http://www.usatoday.com/story/cybertruth/2013/08/30/syrias-cyber-retaliation-signals--new-era-of-warfare/2740457/

Ackerman, R. J., & Banks, M. E. (1990). Computers and the ethical treatment of brain-injured patients. *Social Science Computer Review*, *8*(1), 83–95. doi:10.1177/089443939000800108 PMID:11659900

Ackland, R. (2012). *Social media and national security: A computational social scientist's perspective*. Australia: Australian Strategic Policy Institute.

Ackland, R. (2013). *Web social science: Concepts, data and tools for social scientists in the digital age*. London: Sage Publications.

Acquisti, A., Brandimarte, L., & Loewenstein, G. (2015). Privacy and human behaviour in the age of information. *Science*, *347*(6221), 509–514. doi:10.1126/science.aaa1465 PMID:25635091

Adam, F., Anuar, M., & Ali, A. H. (2014). The use of blog as a medium of Islamic da'wah in Malaysia, The use of blog as a medium of Islamic da'wah in Malaysia. *International Journal of Sustainable Human Development, 2*(2), 74–80.

Aducci, R., Bilderbeek, P., Brown, H., Dowling, S., Freedman, N., Gantz, J., & Verma, S. et al. (2008). *The hyperconnected: Here they come! A global look at the exploding 'culture of connectivity' and its impact on the enterprise.* Framingham, MA: IDC.

Afghan bombing drives allies apart. (2008, August 27). *BBC News.* Retrieved from http://news.bbc.co.uk/2/hi/south_asia/7584464.stm

Afghan survivors tell of wedding bombing. (2008, July 13). *BBC News.* Retrieved from http://news.bbc.co.uk/2/hi/south_asia/7504574.stm

Afrianty, D. (2012). Islamic education and youth extremism in Indonesia. *Journal of Policing. Intelligence and Counter-Terrorism, 7*(2), 134–146. doi:10.1080/18335330.2012.719095

Africa, C. (2014, January 29). Move beyond keyword search, expert advises. *FutureGov.* Retrieved from http://www.futuregov.asia/articles/2014/jan/29/move-beyyond-keyword-search-expert-advises/

Afrida, N. (2011, May 18). Terror fight shifting from pesantren to campus. *The Jakarta Post.* Retrieved from http://www.thejakartapost.com/news/2011/05/18/terror-fight-shifting-'pesantren'-campus.html

Ahmad, R., Yunos, Z., Sahib, S., & Yusoff, M. (2012). Perception on cyber terrorism: A focus group discussion approach. *Journal of Information Security, 3*(03), 231–237. doi:10.4236/jis.2012.33029

Ahmed, F. (2012, July 19). Social media is lying to you about Burma's Muslim 'cleansing'. *The Express Tribune Blog.* Retrieved from http://blogs.tribune.com.pk/story/12867/social-media-is-lying-to-you-about-burmas-muslim-cleansing/comment-page-4/

Ahmed, S. (2007). B-party intercepts and the Telecommunications (Interception) Amendment Act 2006 (Cth). *Internet Law Bulletin, 10*(1).

Air strike in Yemen kills 15 wedding guests mistaken for al-Qaida – officials. (2013, December 12). *The Guardian.* Retrieved from http://www.theguardian.com/world/2013/dec/12/air-strike-yemen-15-wedding-guest-killed-mistaken-al-qaida

Ajzen, I. (n.d.). *Theory of planned behavior diagram.* Retrieved from http://people.umass.edu/aizen/tpb.diag.html

Al Raffie, D. (2012). Whose hearts and minds? Narratives and counter-narratives of Salafi Jihadism. *Journal of Terrorism Research, 3*(2), 13–31. doi:10.15664/jtr.304

Albrow, M., & King, E. (Eds.). (1990). *Globalization, knowledge and society.* London: Sage.

Alexa. (2011a). *Facebook.com Site Info.* Retrieved from http://www.alexa.com/siteinfo/facebook.com

Alexa. (2011b). *Top 500 sites on the web.* Retrieved from http://www.alexa.com/topsites

Alexandrova, E. (2011). Metamorphoses of civil society and politics: From Ganko's Café to Facebook. In G. Lozanov & O. Spassov (Eds.), *Media and politics* (pp. 102–117). Konrad Adenauer Stiftung.

Alhayat Media Centre. (2014, July). The flood. *Dabiq, 2,* 35–38.

Ali, M. (2014). *'Jihad' in Syria: Fallacies of ISIS' end time prophecies. RSIS Commentaries (149/2014).* Singapore: S. Rajaratnam School of International Studies.

Alleman, J. R. (2002). Online counselling: The Internet and mental health treatment. *Psychotherapy (Chicago, Ill.), 39*(2), 199–209. doi:10.1037/0033-3204.39.2.199

Allen, C. (2007). *Threat of Islamic radicalization to the Homeland (Written testimony to the U.S. Senate Committee on Homeland Security and Governmental Affairs)*. Washington, DC: Department of Homeland Security.

Al-Majdi, M. (2014, February 8). Inna lillah, saat Jabhah Nushrah membebaskan ribuan tawanan dari penjara pusat Aleppo, ISIS menyerbu dan mengepung Jabhah Nushrah di Hasakah. *Arrahmah*. Retrieved from http://www.arrahmah.com/news/2014/02/08/inna-lillah-saat-jabhah-nushrah-membebaskan-ribuan-tawanan-dari-penjara-pusat-aleppo-isis-menyerbu-dan-mengepung-jabhah-nushrah-di-hasakah.html#sthash.RxIqckP5.dpuf

Al-Rodhan, & Stroudmann, G. (2006), *Definitions of the globalization: A comprehensive overview and a proposed definition*. Geneva: Geneva Centre for Security Policy.

Al-Shishani, M. B. (2010). Taking al-Qaeda's jihad to Facebook. *Terrorism Monitor, 8*(5), 3–4.

al-Tamimi, A. J. (2013, December 24). The Syrian rebel groups pulling in foreign fighters. *BBC News*. Retrieved from http://www.bbc.com/news/world-middle-east-25460397

Altman, A. (2014, September 22). Government veterans to take fight to extremists on online battleground. *Time*. Retrieved from http://time.com/3418918/counter-extremism-group-isis-twitter-Internet/

Aly, A. (2009). The terrorists' audience: A model of internet radicalisation. *Journal of Australian Professional Intelligence Officers, 17*, 3–19.

Aly, A. (2010). The Internet as ideological battleground. In *Proceedings of the 1st Australian Counter Terrorism Conference*. Perth, Australia: Edith Cowan University.

Aly, A., Weimann-Saks, D., & Weimann, G. (2014). Making 'noise' online: An analysis of the say no to terror online campaign. *Perspective on Terrorism, 8*(5), 33–47.

Amnesty International. (2006). *Pakistan: Over 80 people victims of possible extrajudicial execution in Bajaur* (Amnesty International Report Index: ASA 33/046/2006). Retrieved from http://www.amnesty.org/en/library/info/ASA33/046/2006

Amnesty International. (2013). *Will I be next? US drone strikes in Pakistan*. Retrieved from http://www.amnestyusa.org/sites/default/files/asa330132013en.pdf

Andersson, J. (2009). *Center of gravity analysis: An actual or perceived problem?* Stockholm: Swedish National Defence College.

Anonymous. (1895). *The protocols of the learned elders of Zion*. Author.

Anthony, K., & Nagel, D. M. (2010). *Therapy online: A practical guide*. London: Sage Publishing. doi:10.4135/9781849204354

Anti-ISIS tests show winning the Internet war is key to beating militants: Experts. (2015, February 20). *The Straits Times*. Retrieved from http://www.straitstimes.com/news/world/united-states/story/anti-isis-tests-show-winning-the-internet-war-key-beating-militants-experts/

Antoniades, D., Markatos, E. P., & Dovrolis, C. (2010). MOR: Monitoring and measurements through the onion router. In A. Krishnamurthy & B. Plattner (Eds.), *Passive and active measurement* (pp. 131–140). Berlin: Springer-Verlag. doi:10.1007/978-3-642-12334-4_14

Antonius, N., & Rich, L. (2013). Discovering collection and analysis techniques for social media to improve public safety. *The International Technology Management Review, 3*(1), 42–53. doi:10.2991/itmr.2013.3.1.4

Applegate, S. D. (2013). The dawn of kinetic cyber. In K. Podins, J. Stinissen, & M. Maybaum (Eds.), *5th international conference on cyber conflict*. Estonia, Tallinn: NATO CCD COE Publication.

Applegate, S. D. (2013). The dawn of kinetic cyber. In K. Podins, J. Stinissen, & M. Maybaum (Eds.), *Proceedings of the 5th International Conference on Cyber Conflict*. Tallinn, Estonia: NATO CCD COE Publications.

Arendt, H. (1968). *Between past and future*. New York, NY: Viking Press.

Ariely, G. (2008). Knowledge management, terrorism, and cyber terrorism. In L. Janczewski & A. Colarik (Eds.), *Cyber warafe and cyber terrorism* (pp. 7–16). Hershey, PA: IGI Global.

Ariza, L. M. (2006). Virtual Jihad. *Scientific American, 294*(1), 18–21. doi:10.1038/scientificamerican0106-18 PMID:16468423

Armstrong, H. L., & Forde, P. J. (2003). Internet anonymity practices in computer crime. *Information Management & Computer Security, 11*(5), 209–215. doi:10.1108/09685220310500117

Arnaz, F. (2011, June 27). Police say antiterror program is faulty. *The Jakarta Globe*. Retrieved from http://www.thejakartaglobe.com/archive/police-say-antiterror-program-is-faulty/

Arnaz, F., & Sianipar, O. (2011, January 27). Suspecting students with terror links, police probe Klaten technical school. *The Jakarta Globe*. Retrieved from http://www.thejakartaglobe.com/archive/suspecting-students-with-terror-links-police-probe-klaten-technical-school/

Ashour, O. (2009). *The de-radicalisation of jihadists: Transforming armed Islamist movements*. New York, NY: Routledge.

Ashour, O. (2009). *The de-radicalization of jihadists: Transforming armed Islamist movements*. New York, NY: Routledge.

ASIO sets up cyber-spook unit. (2011, March 11). *ABC News*. Retrieved from http://www.abc.net.au/news/stories/2011/03/11/3161101.htm

ASIO warns of home-grown terror threat. (2005, November 2). *ABC News*. Retrieved from http://www.abc.net.au/news/stories/2005/11/02/1495641.htm

Atran, S. (2015, April 25). Here's what the social science says about countering violent extremism. *Huffington Post*. Retrieved from http://www.huffingtonpost.com/scott-atran/violent-extremism-social-science_b_7142604.html

Australia's Regional Summit to Counter Violent Extremism. (2015, June 12). Canberra: Attorney-General's Department, Australian Government.

Awan, I. (2014). Debating the term cyber-terrorism: Issues and problems. *Internet Journal of Criminology*. Retrieved from http://www.internetjournalofcriminology.com/awan_debating_the_term_cyber-terrorism_ijc_jan_2014.pdf

Awan, A. N. (2007). Virtual jihadist media: Function, legitimacy, and radicalising efficacy. *European Journal of Cultural Studies, 10*(3), 389–408. doi:10.1177/1367549407079713

Awan, A. N. (2010). The virtual jihad: An increasingly legitimate form of warfare. *CTC Sentinel, 3*(5), 10–13.

Axelrad, E. T., Sticha, T. J., Brdiczka, O., & Shen, J. (2013). A Bayesian network model for predicting insider threats. In *IEEE Symposium on Security and Privacy Workshops*. San Francisco, CA: IEEE. doi:10.1109/SPW.2013.35

Bagby, R. M., Buis, T., & Nicholson, R. A. (1995). Relative effectiveness of the standard validity scales in detecting fake-bad and fake-good responding: Replication and extension. *Psychological Assessment, 7*(1), 84–92. doi:10.1037/1040-3590.7.1.84

Baker, G. (2008, January 11). Schoolboy hacks into city's tram system. *The Telegraph*. Retrieved from http://www.telegraph.co.uk/news/worldnews/1575293/Schoolboy-hacks-into-citys-tram-system.html

Bakker, E. (2006). *Jihadi terrorists in Europe, their characteristics and the circumstances in which they joined the jihad (Clingendael Security Paper).* The Netherlands: Netherlands Institute of International Relations.

Balkesim, S. (2014). Semantic processing of visual propaganda in the online environment. In C. K. Winkler & C. E. Dauber (Eds.), *Visual propaganda and extremism in the online environment* (pp. 193–214). Carlisle, PA: Strategic Studies Institute and U.S. Army War College Press.

Ballard, J. D., Hornik, J. G., & McKenzie, D. (2004). Technological facilitation of terrorism. In A. O'Day (Ed.), *The international library of essays in terrorism: Cyberterrorism* (pp. 39–66). London: Ashgate Publishing Limited.

Bandura, A. (1990). Mechanisms of moral disengagement. In W. Reich (Ed.), *Origins of terrorism: Psychologies, ideologies, theologies, states of mind* (pp. 161–191). Cambridge, UK: Cambridge University Press.

Bandura, A. (2004). The role of selective moral disengagement in terrorism and counterterrorism. In F. M. Moghaddam & A. J. Marsella (Eds.), *Understanding terrorism: Psychosocial roots, causes and consequences* (pp. 121–150). Washington, DC: American Psychological Association. doi:10.1037/10621-006

Barabási, A. (2012). *Network science.* Boston, MA: Barabási Lab.

Barbieri, D., & Pressman, D. E. (2015). *Violent extremist risk assessment: A Bayesian framework.* Paper presented at the Intelligence in the Knowledge Society conference, Bucharest, Romania.

Bargh, J. A., & McKenna, K. Y. A. (2004). The internet and social life. *Annual Review of Psychology, 55*(1), 573–590. doi:10.1146/annurev.psych.55.090902.141922 PMID:14744227

Barnes, B. (2012). Confronting the one-man wolf pack: Adapting law enforcement and prosecution responses to the threat of lone wolf terrorism. *Boston University Law Review. Boston University. School of Law, 92*, 1613–1662.

Barrett-Page, E., & Thomas, J. (2009). Methods for the synthesis of qualitative research: A critical review. *BMC Medical Research Methodology, 9*(59), 1–11. PMID:19123933

Barrett, R. (2014). *Foreign fighters in Syria.* New York, NY: The Soufan Group.

Barrett, R., & Bokhari, L. (2009). Deradicalization and rehabilitation programmes targeting religious terrorists and extremists in the Muslim world: An overview. In T. Bjørgo & J. Horgan (Eds.), *Leaving terrorism behind: Individual and collective disengagement.* New York, NY: Routledge.

Barros, C. P., Proenca, I., Faria, J. R., & Gil-Alana, L. A. (2006). Are USA citizens at risk of terrorism in Europe. *Defence and Peace Economics, 18*(6), 495–597. doi:10.1080/10242690701197605

Bar, S. (2006). *Jihad ideology in light of contemporary fatwas.* Washington, DC: Hudson Institute.

Bartlett, J. (2008). *'Wicked' jihad and the appeal of violent extremism.* London: DEMOS.

Bartlett, J. (2014). *The dark net: Inside the digital underworld.* William Heinemann Ltd.

Bartlett, J., & Krasodomski-Jones, A. (2015). *Online anonymity: Islamic State and surveillance.* London: DEMOS.

Bartlett, J., & Miller, C. (2010). *The power of unreason: Conspiracy theories, extremism and counter-terrorism.* London: Demos.

Bartlett, J., & Miller, C. (2012). The edge of violence: Towards telling the difference between violent and non-violent radicalisation. *Terrorism and Political Violence, 24*(1), 1–21. doi:10.1080/09546553.2011.594923

Bartlett, J., & Miller, C. (2013). *The state of the art: A literature review of social media intelligence capabilities for counter-terrorism.* London: DEMOS.

Bates, R., & Mooney, M. (2014). Distance learning and jihad: The dark side of the force. *Online Journal of Distance Learning Administration, 17*(3). Retrieved from http://www.westga.edu/~distance/ojdla/fall173/Bates_Mooney173.html

Baumeister, R., & Leary, M. R. (1995). The need to belong: Desire for interpersonal attachments as fundamental human motivation. *Psychological Bulletin, 117*(3), 497–529. doi:10.1037/0033-2909.117.3.497 PMID:7777651

Baxter, K., & Akbarzadeh, S. (2008). *US foreign policy in the Middle East: The roots of anti-Americanism.* London: Routledge.

Baym, N. K. (2002). Interpersonal life online. In L. A. Lievrouw & S. Livingstone (Eds.), *The handbook of new media* (pp. 62–76). Thousand Oaks, CA: Sage.

Beard, K. W. (2005). Internet addiction: A review of current assessment techniques and potential assessment questions. *Cyberpsychology & Behavior, 8*(1), 7–14. doi:10.1089/cpb.2005.8.7 PMID:15738688

Beardsley, N. L., & Beech, A. R. (2013). Applying the violent extremist risk assessment (VERA) to a sample of terrorist case studies. *Journal of Aggression, Conflict and Peace Research, 5*(1), 4–15. doi:10.1108/17596591311290713

Beardsley, N., & Beech, A. (2013). Applying the violent extremist risk assessment (VERA) to a sample of terrorist case studies. *The Journal of Aggression. Conflict and Peace Studies, 5*, 4–15.

Beech, A. R., Elliott, I. A., Birgden, A., & Findlater, D. (2008). The internet and child sexual offending: A criminological review. *Aggression and Violent Behavior, 13*(3), 216–228. doi:10.1016/j.avb.2008.03.007

Beekun, R., & Glick, W. (2001). Organization structure from a loose coupling perspective: A multidimensional approach. *Decision Sciences, 32*(2), 227–250. doi:10.1111/j.1540-5915.2001.tb00959.x

Behn, S. (2014, September 5). ISIS militants use 'Jihadi cool' to recruit globally. *Voices of America (VOA).* Retrieved from http://www.thecuttingedgenews.com/index.php?article=85237

Bell, L. (2014, June 25). Hacking Team's government spy tool components uncovered by Kapersky. *The Inquirer.* Retrieved from http://www.theinquirer.net/inquirer/news/2352077/hacking-teams-government-spy-tool-components-uncovered-by-kaspersky

Belsky, J. (1997). Theory testing, effect-size evaluation, and differential susceptibility to rearing influence: The case of mothering and attachment. *Child Development, 68*(4), 598–600. doi:10.2307/1132110

Benesch, S. (2013, February 23). *The dangerous speech project: Dangerous speech – a proposal to prevent group violence.* Retrieved from http://www.dangerousspeech.org/guidelines/

Benson, D. (2014). Why the Internet is not increasing terrorism. *Security Studies, 23*(2), 293–328. doi:10.1080/09636412.2014.905353

Benson, D. C. (2014). Why the Internet is not increasing terrorism. *Security Journal, 23*, 293–328.

Bergen, P., & Sterman, D. (2015, May 6). Who are ISIS' American recruits? *CNN.* Retrieved from http://www.cnn.com/2015/05/06/opinions/bergen-isis-american-recruits/

Berger, J. M. (2014). How ISIS games Twitter. *The Atlantic.* Retrieved from http://www.theatlantic.com/international/archive/2014/06/isis-iraq-twitter-social-media-strategy/372856/

Berger, J. M. (2014, June 16). How IS games twitter. *The Atlantic.* Retrieved from http://www.theatlantic.com/international/archive/2014/06/isis-iraq-twitterr-social-media-strategy/372856

Berger, J. M. (2015, May 7). Social Media: An Evolving Front in Radicalization. *Intel Wire*. Retrieved from http://news.intelwire.com/2015/05/social-media-evolving-front-in.html

Berger, J. M., & Morgan, J. (2015). *The ISIS twitter census: Defining and describing the population of ISIS supporters on twitter (Brooking project on U.S. Relations with the Islamic World, Analysis Paper, 20)*. Washington, DC: Brookings Institution.

Berger, J. M., & Stern, J. (2015). *ISIS: The state of terror*. Broadway, NY: Harper Collins.

Bergin, A., Osman, S. B., Ungerer, C., & Yasin, N. A. M. (2009). *Countering internet radicalisation in Southeast Asia (Special Report)*. Australian Strategic Policy Institute.

Bergin, A., Osman, S. B., Ungerer, C., & Yasin, N. A. M. (2009). *Countering Internet radicalisation in Southeast Asia. Special Report*. Australia: Australian Strategic Policy Institute.

Bergin, A., Osman, S., Ungerer, C., & Yasin, N. A. M. (2009). *Countering internet radicalisation in Southeast Asia*. Canberra: Australian Strategic Policy Institute.

Bermingham, A., Conway, M., McInerney, L., O'Hare, N., & Smeaton, A. F. (2009). *Combining social network analysis and sentiment analysis to explore the potential for online radicalisation*. Paper presented at Advances in Social Networks Analysis and Mining, Athens, Greece. doi:10.1109/ASONAM.2009.31

Bernard, D. (2014). ISIL wages skilled social media war. *Voice of America*. Retrieved from http://www.voanews.com/content/isil-wages-skilled-social-media-war/1939505.html

Bernays, E. (1928). *Propaganda*. New York, NY: Horace Liveright.

Bershidsky, L. (2014). Traffic hackers pull off 'Italian Job'. *Bloomberg*. Retrieved from http://www.bloombergview.com/articles/2014-08-22/traffic-hackers-pull-off-italian-job

Bhui, K., Warfa, N., & Jones, E. (2014). Is violent radicalisation associated with poverty, migration, poor self-reported health and common mental disorders? *PLoS ONE*, *9*(3), 1–10. doi:10.1371/journal.pone.0090718

Bicchieri, C. (2008). Losing the trust. *Pennsylvania Arts & Sciences*. Retrieved from http://www.sas.upenn.edu/sasalum/newsltr/winter08/trust_game.pdf

Bilali, A. (2012, August 13). Women and al-Shabaab: Between false empowerment and terror. *Diplomatic Courier*. Retrieved from http://www.diplomaticourier.com/women-and-al-shabab-between-false-empowerment-and-terror/

Bindley, K. (2013). Boston Police Twitter: How cop team tweets from terror to joy. *Huffington Post*. Retrieved from http://www.huffingtonpost.com/2013/04/26/boston-police-twitter-marathon_n_3157472.html

Birbili, M. (2000, Winter). Translating from one language to another. *Social Research Update, 31*. Retrieved from http://sru.soc.surrey.ac.uk/SRU31.html

Bjelopera, J. P. (2013). *American jihadist terrorism: Combating a complex threat. CRS Report for Congress*. Washington, DC: Congressional Research Service.

Bjørgo, T. (2009). Processes of disengagement from violent groups of the extreme right. In T. Bjørgo & J. Horgan (Eds.), *Leaving terrorism behind: Individual and collective disengagement* (pp. 30–48). Abingdon: Routledge.

Bjørgo, T. (2011). Dreams and disillusionment: Engagement in and disengagement from militant extremist groups. *Crime, Law, and Social Change*, *55*(4), 277–285. doi:10.1007/s10611-011-9282-9

Blakemore, B. (2012). Cyberspace, cyber crime and cyber terrorism. In I. Awan & B. Blakemore (Eds.), *Policing cyber hate, cyber threats and cyber terrorism* (pp. 5–20). London: Ashgate Publishing Limited.

Bloom, M. (2011). *Bombshell: The many faces of women terrorists*. Philadelphia, PA: University of Pennsylvania Press. doi:10.9783/9780812208108

Boer, D. P., Hart, S. D., Kropp, P. R., & Webster, C. D. (1997). *Manual for the sexual violence risk-20: Professional guidelines for assessing risk of sexual violence*. Vancouver, Canada: Mental Health, Law & Policy Institute, Simon Fraser University.

Boghardt, L. (2014, June 23). Saudi funding of ISIS. *The Washington Institute for Near East Policy*. Retrieved from http://www.washingtoninstitute.org/policy-analysis/view/saudi-funding-of-isis

Bondu, R., Cornell, D. G., & Scheithauer, H. (2011). Student homicidal violence in schools: An international problem. New Directions for Youth Development: Theory, Practice, Research, 129, 13-30.

Bonta, J., Law, M., & Hanson, R. K. (1998). The prediction of criminal and violent recidivism among mentally disordered offenders: A meta-analysis. *Psychological Bulletin, 123*(2), 123–142. doi:10.1037/0033-2909.123.2.123 PMID:9522681

Bonzio, A. (2014, September 15). ISIS' use of social media is not surprising; its sophisticated digital strategy is. *Huffington Post*. Retrieved from http://www.huffingtonpost.co.uk/alessandro-bonzio/isis-use-of-social-media-_b_5818720.html

Borum, R. (2003). Understanding the terrorist mind-set. *FBI Law Enforcement Bulletin, 72*.

Borum, R. (2000). Assessing violence risk among youth. *Journal of Clinical Psychology, 56*(10), 1263–1288. doi:10.1002/1097-4679(200010)56:10<1263::AID-JCLP3>3.0.CO;2-D PMID:11051059

Borum, R. (2003). Understanding the terrorist mindset. *FBI Law Enforcement Bulletin, 72*(7), 7–10.

Borum, R. (2004). *Psychology of terrorism*. Tampa: University of South Florida.

Borum, R. (2004). *Psychology of Terrorism*. Tampa: University of South Florida.

Borum, R. (2011). Radicalization into violent extremism II: A review of conceptual models and empirical research. *Journal of Strategic Security, 4*(4), 37–62. doi:10.5038/1944-0472.4.4.2

Borum, R. (2011a). Radicalisation into violent extremism I: A review of social science theories. *Journal of Strategic Security, 4*(4), 7–36. doi:10.5038/1944-0472.4.4.1

Borum, R. (2011a). Rethinking radicalization. *Journal of Strategic Security, 4*(4), 1–6.

Borum, R. (2014). Psychological vulnerabilities and propensities for involvement in violent extremism. *Behavioral Sciences & the Law, 32*(3), 286–305. doi:10.1002/bsl.2110 PMID:24652686

Borum, R., Bartel, P., & Forth, A. (2006). *SAVRY: Professional manual for structured assessment of violence risk in youth*. Lutz, FL: Psychological Assessment Resources Inc.

Borum, R., Fein, R. A., Vossekuil, B., & Berglund, J. (1999). Threat assessment: Defining an approach for evaluating risk of targeted violence. *Behavioral Sciences & the Law, 17*(3), 323–333. doi:10.1002/(SICI)1099-0798(199907/09)17:3<323::AID-BSL349>3.0.CO;2-G PMID:10481132

Boucek, C. (2008). *Saudi Arabia's 'soft' counter-terrorism strategy: Prevention, rehabilitation, and aftercare (Middle East Program Report 97)*. Washington, DC: Carnegie Endowment for International Peace.

Bouchard, S., Payeur, R., Rivard, V., Allard, M., Paquin, B., Renaud, P., & Goyer, L. (2000). Cognitive behaviour therapy for panic disorder with agoraphobia in videoconference: Preliminary results. *Cyberpsychology & Behavior*, *3*(6), 999–1007. doi:10.1089/109493100452264

Bourke, M. L., & Hernandez, A. E. (2009). The 'Butner Study' redux: A report of the incidence of hands-on child victimization by child pornography offenders. *Journal of Family Violence*, *24*(3), 183–191. doi:10.1007/s10896-008-9219-y

Bowman-Grieve, L. (2009). Exploring "Stormfront": A virtual community of radical right. *Studies in Conflict and Terrorism*, *32*(11), 989–1007. doi:10.1080/10576100903259951

Bowman-Grieve, L. (2013). A psychological perspective on virtual communities supporting terrorist & extremist ideologies as a tool for recruitment. *Security Informatics*, *2*(9), 1–5.

Bowman-Grieve, L. (2015). Cyberterrorism and moral panics: A reflection on the discourse of cyberterrorism. In L. Jarvis, S. Macdonald, & T. M. Chen (Eds.), *Terrorism online: Politics, law and technology* (pp. 86–106). New York, NY: Routledge.

Bowman-Grieve, L., & Conway, M. (2012). Exploring the form and function of dissident Irish Republican online discourses. *Media. War and Conflict*, *5*(1), 71–85. doi:10.1177/1750635211434371

Boyd, D., & Crawford, K. (2012). Critical questions for big data. *Information Communication and Society*, *15*(5), 662–679. doi:10.1080/1369118X.2012.678878

Brachman, J. (2012, February 3). The jihad hobbyists who've moved on from watching al-Qaida videos. *The Guardian*. Retrieved from http://www.guardian.co.uk/commentisfree/2012/feb/03/jihad-hobbyists-al-qaida?utm_source=twitterfeed&utm_medium=twitter

Brachman, J. (2009). A survey of Southeast Asian global jihadist websites. In S. Helfstein (Ed.), *Radical Islamic ideology in Southeast Asia* (pp. 95–114). West Point: Combating Terrorism Center.

Brachman, J. M. (2006). High-tech terror: Al-Qaeda's use of new technology. *The Fletcher Forum of World Affairs*, *30*, 149–164.

Braffman, W., & Kirsch, I. (2001). Reaction time as a predictor of imaginative suggestibility and hypnotizability. *Contemporary Hypnosis*, *18*(3), 107–119. doi:10.1002/ch.224

Branch, P. A. (2003). Lawful interception of the Internet. *Australian Journal of Emerging Technologies and Society*, *1*(1), 1–7.

Brandon, J. (2009). *Unlocking Al-Qaeda: Islamist extremism in British prisons*. London: Quilliam Foundation.

Braniff, B., & Moghadam, A. (2011). Towards global jihadism: Al-Qaeda's strategic, ideological and structural adaptations since 9/11. *Perspectives on Terrorism*, *5*(2).

Braue, D. (2015a, March 30). *Opponents restate security, scope concerns metadata retention becomes Australian law*. Queensland: CSO Australia.

Braue, D. (2015b, April 1). *Police investigations threatened metadata retention feeds telephony* diaspora. Queensland: CSO Australia.

Braue, D. (2015c, April 3). *Avoid government, hacker snooping by owning encryption key management: lawyer*. Queensland: CSO Australia.

Brennan, E. (2015, March 5). How Southeast Asia is responding to ISIS. *The Interpreter*. Retrieved from http://www.lowyinterpreter.org/post/2015/03/05/How-should-we-respond-to-ISIS-in-Southeast-Asia.aspx?COLLCC=651738223&COLLCC=732768703&

Breton, P. (2000, October 1). Wired to the counterculture. *Le Monde diplomatique*. Retrieved from http://mondediplo.com/2000/10/06internet

Briggs, R., Carlile, L., Maher, S., & Gardner, F. (2015, March 2). *Digital jihad: How online networks are changing extremists*. London: Chatham House, the Royal Institute of International Affairs.

Briggs, R., & Frenett, R. (2014). *Policy briefing: Foreign fighters, the challenge of counter-narratives*. London: Institute for Strategic Dialogue.

Brinton, L. J. (2001). Historical discourse analysis. In D. Schiffrin, D. Tannen, & H. Hamilton (Eds.), *The handbook of discourse analysis* (pp. 138–160). Massachusetts, MA: Blackwell Publishers.

Bronitt, S., & Stellios, J. (2005). Telecommunications interception in Australia: Recent trends and regulatory prospects. *Telecommunications Policy*, *29*(11), 875–888. doi:10.1016/j.telpol.2005.06.010

Brown, A., Abernethy, A., Gorsuch, R., & Dueck, A. C. (2010). Sacred violations, perceptions of injustice, and anger in Muslims. *Journal of Applied Social Psychology*, *40*(5), 1003–1027. doi:10.1111/j.1559-1816.2010.00608.x

Bruell, A., & Sebastian, M. (2015, March 2). Should Adland join the communications war on ISIS? *Ad Age*. Retrieved from http://adage.com/article/news/adland-join-communications-war-isis/297365/

Brunner, E. M., & Suter, M. (2008). *International CIIP handbook 2008/2009: An inventory of 25 national and 7 international critical information infrastructure protection policies*. Zurich, Switzerland: Center for Security Studies.

Brunst, P. W. (2010). Terrorism and the Internet: New threats posed by cyberterrorism and terrorist use of the Internet. In M. Wade & A. Maljević (Eds.), *A war on terror?: The European stance on a new threat, changing laws and human rights implications* (pp. 51–78). New York, NY: Springer. doi:10.1007/978-0-387-89291-7_3

Brynielsson, J., Horndahl, A., Johansson, F., Kaati, L., Mårtenson, C., & Svenson, P. (2013). Harvesting and analysis of weak signals for detecting lone wolf terrorists. *Security Informatics*, *2*(11). doi:10.1186/2190-8532-2-11

Buchanan, T. (2002). Online assessment: Desirable or dangerous? *Professional Psychology, Research and Practice*, *33*(2), 148–154. doi:10.1037/0735-7028.33.2.148

Bu, Z., Xia, Z., & Wang, J. (2013). A sock puppet detection algorithm on virtual spaces. *Knowledge-Based Systems*, *37*, 366–377. doi:10.1016/j.knosys.2012.08.016

Byrne, P. (2014, July 15). British ISIS militant Abdul Raqib Amin believed killed by Iraqi soldiers. *Mirror*. Retrieved from http://www.mirror.co.uk/news/uk-news/british-isis-militant-abdul-raqib-3866692

Caiani, M., & Wagemann, C. (2009). Online networks of the Italian and German extreme right. *Information Communication and Society*, *12*(1), 66–109. doi:10.1080/13691180802158482

Calais, D. C. (2014, September 7). Brussels museum shooting suspect 'beheaded baby'. *The Telegraph*. Retrieved from http://www.telegraph.co.uk/news/worldnews/middleeast/syria/11080079/Brussels-museum-shooting-suspect-beheaded-baby.html

Calder, M. (2004). *Child sexual abuse and the Internet: Tackling the new frontier*. Dorset: Russell House.

Caldwell, I. (2008). Terror on YouTube. *Forensic Examiner*, *17*(3), 80–83.

California Department of Forestry and Fire Protection (CAL FIRE). (2012). *A practical test of the 'Ember Bomb' as described in Inspire, Issue 9.* California State Threat Assessment Center.

Callimachi, R. (2014, July 14). Paying ransoms, Europe bankrolls qaeda terror. *The New York Times.* Retrieved from http://www.nytimes.com/2014/07/30/world/africa/ransoming-citizens-europe-becomes-al-qaedas-patron.html?_r=0

Campbell, D. (2012). *Myth of compassion fatigue.* Retrieved from https://www.david-campbell.org/wp-content/documents/DC_Myth_of_Compassion_Fatigue_Feb_2012.pdf

Can you predict the future by reading Twitter? (2013, January 14). *Nexgov Newsletter.* Retrieved from http://www.nextgov.com/defense/2013/01/can-you-predict-future-reading-twitter-pentagon-thinks-maybe/60634

Cappelli, D., Moore, A., & Trzeciak, R. (2012). *The CERT guide to insider threats: How to Prevent, Detect, and Respond to Information Technology Crimes.* Boston, MA: Pearson Education, Inc.

Caputo, D. D., Pfleeger, S. L., Freeman, J. D., & Johnson, M. E. (2014). Going spear phishing: Exploring embedded training and awareness. *Security & Privacy, IEEE, 12*(1), 28–38. doi:10.1109/MSP.2013.106

Card, D., Mas, A., & Rothstein, J. (2007). *Tipping and the dynamics of segregation* (Working paper 13052). Cambridge, MA: National Bureau of Economic Research.

Carré, O. (2003). *Mysticism and politics: A critical reading of Fi Zilal al-Qur'an by Sayyid Qutb (1906-1966).* Leiden: Brill.

Carruthers, S. L. (2000). *The media at war: Communication and conflict in the twentieth century.* Basingstoke, UK: Palgrave Macmillan.

Carter, J. (2013, January 23). Case study: Roshonara Choudhry. *The Risky Shift.* Retrieved from http://theriskyshift.com/2013/01/case-study-roshonara-choudhry/

Carter, J. A., Maher, S., & Neumann, P. R. (2014, April 15). *ICSR Insight: Who inspires the Syrian foreign fighters?* The International Centre for the Study of Radicalisation. Retrieved from http://icsr.info/category/icsr-news/insights/

Carter, J. A., Maher, S., & Neumann, P. R. (2014). *Greenbirds: measuring importance and influence in Syrian foreign fighter networks.* London: The International Centre for the Study of Radicalisation and Political Violence.

Carter, J. G., & Carter, D. L. (2012). Law enforcement intelligence: Implications for self-radicalized terrorism. *Police Practice and Research, 13*(2), 138–154. doi:10.1080/15614263.2011.596685

Carter, J., Maher, S., & Neumann, P. R. (2014). *Greenbirds: Measuring importance and influence in Syrian foreign fighters networks.* London: The International Centre for the Study of Radicalisation and Political Violence.

Casciani, D. (2014, October 9). How the battle against IS is being fought online. *BBC News.* Retrieved from http://www.bbc.com/news/magazine-29535343

Casciani, D. (2015, May 12). The battle of the e-Muftis. *BBC News.* Retrieved from http://www.bbc.com/news/magazine-32697424

Cassrels, D. (2011a, May 23). How kebabs and coffee help turn inmates from the path of terror. *The Australian.* Retrieved from http://www.theaustralian.com.au/news/world/how-kebabs-and-coffee-help-turn-inmates-from-the-path-of-terror/story-e6frg6so-1226060651749

Cassrels, D. (2011b, June 25). Paving a new path for children of terror. *The Australian.* Retrieved from http://www.theaustralian.com.au/news/features/paving-a-new-path-for-children-of-terror/story-e6frg6z6-1226080886496

CATO Institute. (2010). *The underwhelming threat of cyberterrorism.* Retrieved from http://www.cato.org/policy-report/januaryfebruary-2011/underwhelming-threat-cyberterrorism

Cebrian, M., Torres, M., Huerta, R., & Fowler, J. H. (2012). Violent extremist group ecologies under stress. *Nature: Scientific Reports, 3.* doi:10.1038/srep01544 PMID:23536118

Cendrowicz, L. (2014, October 30). NATO frontline in life-or-death war on cyber-terrorists. *The Guardian.* Retrieved from http://www.theguardian.com/world/2014/oct/30/nato-frontline-cyber-terrorists-war

Cervone, D., Shoda, Y., & Downey, G. (2007). Construing persons in context: On building a science of the individual. In Y. Shoda, D. Cervone, G. Downey, Y. Shoda, D. Cervone, & G. Downey (Eds.), *Persons in context: Building a science of the individual* (pp. 3–15). New York, NY: Guilford Press.

Ceyhan, A. A., & Ceyhan, E. (2008). Loneliness, depression, and computer self-efficacy as predictors of problematic Internet use. *Cyberpsychology & Behavior, 11*(6), 699–701. doi:10.1089/cpb.2007.0255 PMID:19072150

Chaiken, S. (1980). Heuristic versus systematic information processing and the use of source versus message cues in persuasion. *Journal of Personality and Social Psychology, 39*(5), 752–766. doi:10.1037/0022-3514.39.5.752

Chaiken, S. (1999). *Dual-process theories in social psychology.* New York, NY: Guilford Press.

Chakravarty, S., Portokalidis, G., Polychronakis, M., & Keromytis, A. D. (2011). Detecting traffic snooping in Tor using decoys. In *Proceedings of the 14th International Conference on Recent Advances in Intrusion Detection.* Berlin: Springer. doi:10.1007/978-3-642-23644-0_12

Chandler, M. E. G. (2007). Turning the tables: Harnessing media means to counter radicalisation. In B. Ganor, K. von Knop, & C. Duarte (Eds.), *Hypermedia seduction for terrorist recruiting* (pp. 281–287). Washington, DC: IOS Press.

Chang, I., Liu, C., & Chen, K. (2014). The push, pull and mooring effects in virtual migration for social networking sites. *Information Systems Journal, 24*(4), 323–346. doi:10.1111/isj.12030

Chang, M., & Lim, Y. (2014). Late disclosure of insider trades: Who does it and why? *Journal of Business Ethics,* 1–13.

Chasmar, J. (2015, February 5). Anjem Choudary, radical Muslim cleric: Koran justifies Jordanian pilot burning. *The Washington Times.* Retrieved from http://www.washingtontimes.com/news/2015/feb/5/anjem-choudary-radical-muslim-cleric-quran-justifi/

Chen, T. M. (2014). *Cyberterrorism after Stuxnet.* Carlisle, PA: Strategic Studies Institute and U.S. Army War College Press.

Chen, T., Lee, J., & Macdonald, S. (Eds.). (2014). *Cyberterrorism: Understanding, assessment, and response.* New York, NY: Springer. doi:10.1007/978-1-4939-0962-9

Cheong, D. D. (2014, December 12). Tackling extremism among western Muslim converts. *The Straits Times.* Retrieved from http://www.straitstimes.com/opinion/tackling-extremism-among-western-muslim-converts

Cherry, K. (2015). Online therapy: What is online therapy? *About Education.* Retrieved from http://psychology.about.com/od/psychotherapy/a/onlinepsych.htm

Cherry, K. (n.d.). How attitudes form, change and shape behavior. *about education.* Retrieved from http://psychology.about.com/od/socialpsychology/a/attitudes.htm

Chouliaraki, L. (2006). *The spectatorship of suffering.* London: Sage.

Chowdhury-Fink, N., & Heame, E. B. (2008). *Beyond terrorism: Deradicalisation and disengagement from violent extremism*. New York, NY: International Peace Institute.

Christensen, H., Batterham, P. J., & O'Dea, B. (2014). E-health interventions for suicide prevention. *International Journal of Environmental Research and Public Health, 11*(8), 8193–8212. doi:10.3390/ijerph110808193 PMID:25119698

Christmann, K. (2012). *Preventing religious radicalisation and violent extremism: A systematic review of the research evidence*. London: Youth Justice Board.

Christopherson, K. M. (2007). The positive and negative implications of anonymity in Internet social interactions: "On the Internet, nobody knows you're a dog. *Computers in Human Behavior, 23*(6), 3038–3056. doi:10.1016/j.chb.2006.09.001

Chulov, M. (2014, December 11). Isis: the inside story. *The Guardian*. Retrieved from http://www.theguardian.com/world/2014/dec/11/-sp-isis-the-inside-story

Chung, E. (2014, October 27). Carmakers ignore hacking risk, security expert say. *CBC News*. Retrieved from http://www.cbc.ca/m/touch/news/story/1.2810847

Cilluffo, F. J., Cozzens, J. B., & Ranstorp, M. (2010). *Foreign fighters: Trends, trajectories & conflict zones*. Homeland Security & Policy Institutes. Retrieved from http://www.gwumc.edu/hspi/policy/report_foreignfighters501.pdf

Clarke, R. V., & Newman, G. R. (2006). *Outsmarting the terrorists*. Westport, CA: Greenwood Publishing Group.

Clifford, M. (2012). *The keystone to community resilience: Social capital. Continuity e-Guide: A Wednesday Update by Disaster Resource Guide*. Retrieved from: http://www.disaster-resource.com/newsletter/2012/subpages/v418/meetthe-experts.htm

Cloherty, J. (2012, May 22). Virtual terrorism: Al-Qaeda video calls for 'electronic jihad'. *ABC News*. Retrieved from http://abcnews.go.com/Politics/cyber-terrorism-al-qaeda-video-calls-electronic-jihad/story?id=16407875

Clutterbuck, L., & Warnes, R. (2011). *Exploring patterns of behaviour in violent jihadist terrorists*. Santa Monica, CA: RAND Corporation.

Cohen, G. E., & Kerr, B. A. (1998). Computer-mediated counselling: An empirical study of a new mental health treatment. *Computers in Human Sciences, 15*, 13–26.

Cohen, J. (2009). Diverting the radicalization track. *Policy Review, 154*, 51–63.

Cohen, K., Fredrik, J., Lisa, K., & Jonas, C. M. (2014). Detecting linguistic markers for radical violence in social media. *Terrorism and Political Violence, 26*(1), 246–256. doi:10.1080/09546553.2014.849948

Cohn, S. (2013, June 3). Hacker claims airplanes vulnerable at 30,000 feet. *CNBC*. Retrieved from http://www.cnbc.com/id/100784103# Cooney, M. (2012). Wireless medical devices face myriad security concerns. *Network World*. Retrieved from http://www.networkworld.com/article/2223222/mobile-security/wireless-medical-devices-face-myriad-security-concerns.html

Cohn, M. A., Mehl, M. R., & Pennebaker, J. W. (2004). Linguistic markers of psychological change surrounding September 11, 2001. *Psychological Science, 15*(10), 687–693. doi:10.1111/j.0956-7976.2004.00741.x PMID:15447640

Colbaugh, R., & Glass, K. (2010). *Estimating sentiment orientation in social media for intelligence monitoring and analysis*. Paper presented at IEEE Conference on Intelligence and Security Informatics (ISI), Vancouver, BC. doi:10.1109/ISI.2010.5484760

Colbaugh, R., & Glass, K. (2011). *Agile sentiment analysis of social media content for security informatics applications*. Paper presented at European Intelligence and Security Informatics Conference, Athens. doi:10.1109/EISIC.2011.65

Colbaugh, R., Glass, K., & Bauer, T. (2012). *Leveraging sociological models for predictive analytics.* Cornell University Library. Retrieved from http://arxiv.org/abs/1212.6806

Colbaugh, R., & Glass, K. (2012). *Proactive defense for evolving cyber threats (SAND2012-10177).* Livermore, CA: Sandia National Laboratories. doi:10.2172/1059470

Cole, J., Alison, E., Cole, B., & Alison, L. J. (2012). *Guidance for identifying people vulnerable to recruitment into violent extremism.* Retrieved from https://www.counterextremism.org/resources/details/id/224/guidance-for-identifying-people-vulnerable-to-recruitment-into-violent-extremism

Collin, B. C. (1996). The future of cyberterrorism. *Crime and Justice International, 13,* 15–18.

Commonwealth of Australia. (2015). *Martin Place Siege: Joint Commonwealth - New South Wales Review.* Canberra: Department of the Prime Minister and Cabinet.

Commonwealth of Massachusetts. (2014). *After action report for the response to the 2013 Boston Marathon Bombings.* Retrieved from http://www.mass.gov/eopss/docs/mema/after-action-report-for-the-response-to-the-2013-boston-marathon-bombings.pdf

Community Oriented Policing Services (COPS). (2014). *Online radicalisation to violent extremism: Awareness brief.* Washington, DC: Office of Community Oriented Policing Services.

Community Oriented Policing Services (COPS). (2014). *YouTube and violent extremism: Awareness brief.* Washington, DC: U.S. Department of Justice.

Community Oriented Policing Services. (2014). *Online radicalisation to violent extremism: Awareness brief.* Washington, DC: Office of Community Oriented Policing Services.

Conway, M. (2004). *Cyberterrorism: Media myth or clear and present danger?* Retrieved from http://doras.dcu.ie/505/1/media_myth_2004.pdf

Conway, M. (2012). Introduction: terrorism and contemporary mediascapes – reanimating research on media and terrorism. *Critical Studies on Terrorism, 5*(3), 445-453.

Conway, M. (2002). Reality bytes: Cyberterrorism and terrorist 'use' of the internet. *First Monday, 7*(11). http://firstmonday.org/ojs/index.php/fm/article/view/1001/922 doi:10.5210/fm.v7i11.1001

Conway, M. (2005). Terrorist web sites: Their contents, functioning, and effectiveness. In P. Seib (Ed.), *Media and conflict in the twenty-first century* (pp. 185–215). New York, NY: Palgrave.

Conway, M. (2006). Terrorism and the Internet: New media – new threat. *Parliamentary Affairs, 59*(2), 283–298. doi:10.1093/pa/gsl009

Conway, M. (2007). Terrorist use of the internet and the challenges of governing cyberspace. In D. Myriam, V. Mauer, & F. Krishna-Hensel (Eds.), *Power and security in the information age: Investigating the role of the state in cyberspace* (pp. 95–127). London: Ashgate.

Conway, M. (2007). Terrorist use of the Internet and the challenges of governing cyberspace. In D. Myriam, V. Mauer, & F. Krishna-Hensel (Eds.), *Power and security in the information age: Investigating the role of the state in cyberspace* (pp. 95–127). London: Ashgate.

Conway, M. (2011). Against cyberterrorism: Why cyber-based terrorist attacks are unlikely to occur?[CACM]. *Communications of the ACM, 54*(2), 26–28. doi:10.1145/1897816.1897829

Conway, M. (2012). From al-Zarqawi to al-Awlaki: The emergence and development of an online radical milieu. *Combating Terrorism Exchange*, 2(4), 12–22.

Conway, M., & McInerney, L. (2008). Jihadi video & auto-radicalisation: Evidence from an exploratory YouTube study. *Intelligence and Security Informatics*, *5376*, 108–118.

Cook, J., & Doyle, C. (2002). Working alliance in online therapy as compared to face-to-face therapy: Preliminary results. *Cyberpsychology & Behavior*, 5(2), 95–105. doi:10.1089/109493102753770480 PMID:12025884

Coolsaet, R. (Ed.). (2011). *Jihadi terrorism and the radicalisation challenge: European and American experience* (2nd ed.). Farnham, MD: Ashgate.

Cooper, C., & Nicholls, A. (2011). What caused England's riots? *The Guardian*. Retrieved from http://www.theguardian.com/society/joepublic/2011/oct/12/what-caused-england-riots

Cooper, M. L., Barber, L. L., Zhaoyang, R., & Talley, A. E. (2011). Motivational pursuits in the context of human sexual relationships. *Journal of Personality*, 79(6), 1031–1066. doi:10.1111/j.1467-6494.2010.00713.x

Copenhagen gunman just out of prison, AP sources say. (2015, February 16). *CBS*. Retrieved from http://www.cbsnews.com/news/copenhagen-gunman-omar-abdel-hamid-el-hussein-just-out-of-prison-ap-sources/

Corcoran, K. (2014, August 16). British hacker 'masterminding plan to teach jihadists how to steal from bank accounts of rich and famous to fund terror campaign'. *Daily Mail*. Retrieved from http://www.dailymail.co.uk/news/article-2726522/British-hacker-masterminding-plan-teach-jihadists-steal-bank-accounts-rich-famous-fund-terror-campaign.html

Cordesman, A., & Cordesman, J. (2001). *Cyber-threats, information warfare, and critical infrastructure protection: Defending the U.S. Homeland*. New York, NY: Praeger.

Corera, G. (2008, January 16). The world's most wanted cyber-jihadist. *BBC News*. Retrieved from http://news.bbc.co.uk/2/hi/americas/7191248.stm

Corner, E., & Gill, P. (2015). A false dichotomy? Mental illness and lone-actor terrorism. *Law and Human Behavior*, 39(1), 23–34. doi:10.1037/lhb0000102 PMID:25133916

Cornish, P., Lindley-French, J., & Yorke, C. (2011). *Strategic communications and national strategy (A Chatham House Report)*. London: The Royal Institute of International Affairs.

Cornwell, R. (2014, May 19). US declares cyber war on China: Chinese military hackers charged with trying to steal secrets from companies including nuclear energy firm. *The Independent*. Retrieved from http://www.independent.co.uk/life-style/gadgets-and-tech/us-charges-chinese-military-hackers-with-cyber-espionage-bid-to-gain-advantage-in-nuclear-power-metals-and-solar-product-industries-9397661.html

Correa, D., & Sureka, A. (2013, January). Solutions to detect and analyze online radicalizations: A survey. *HITD PhD Comprehensive Report*, V(N), 1-30.

Costa, P. T. Jr, & McCrae, R. R. (1994). Stability and change in personality from adolescene through adulthood. In C. F. Halverson, G. A. Kohnstamm, & R. P. Martin (Eds.), *The developing structure of temperament and personality from infancy to adulthood* (pp. 139–150). Hillsdale, NJ: Erlbaum.

Cottee, S. (2015, March 2). Why it is so hard to stop ISIS propaganda. *The Atlantic*. Retrieved from http://www.theatlantic.com/international/archive/2015/03/why-its-so-hard-to-stop-isis-propaganda/386216/

Cottee, S. (2015, March 2). Why it's so hard to stop isis propaganda. *The Atlantic*. Retrieved from http://www.theatlantic.com/international/archive/2015/03/why-its-so-hard-to-stop-isis-propaganda/386216/

Cottee, S., & Hayward, K. (2011). Terrorist (E)motives: The existential attractions of terrorism. *Studies in Conflict and Terrorism, 34*(12), 963–986. doi:10.1080/1057610X.2011.621116

Cotter, C. (2001). Discourse and media. In D. Schiffrin, D. Tannen, & H. Hamilton (Eds.), *The handbook of discourse analysis* (pp. 416–436). Massachusetts, MA: Blackwell Publishers.

Cragin, R. K. (2014). Resisting violent extremism: A conceptual model for non-radicalisation. *Terrorism and Political Violence, 26*(2), 337–353. doi:10.1080/09546553.2012.714820

Cragin, R. K., & Daly, S. A. (2009). *Women as terrorists: Mothers, recruiters, and martyrs.* Santa Barbara, CA: ABC-CLIO.

Crawford, A. (2007). Crime prevention and community safety. In M. Maguire, R. Morgan, & R. Reiner (Eds.), *The oxford handbook of criminology* (4th ed.; pp. 866–909). Oxford, UK: Oxford University Press.

Crenshaw, M. (2007). *The debate over 'new' vs 'old' terrorism.* Paper presented at the annual meeting of the American Political Science Association, Chicago, IL.

Crenshaw, M. (1981). The causes of terrorism. *Comparative Politics, 13*(4), 379–399. doi:10.2307/421717

Crenshaw, M. (2000). The psychology of terrorism: An agenda for the 21st century. *Political Psychology, 21*(2), 405–420. doi:10.1111/0162-895X.00195

Criddle, L. (2014). What is social engineering? *Webroot.* Retrieved from http://www.webroot.com/us/en/home/resources/tips/online-shopping-banking/secure-what-is-social-engineering

Crossman, A. (n.d.). The tipping point: An overview of the book by Malcolm Gladwell. *about education.* Retrieved from http://sociology.about.com/od/Works/a/The-Tipping-Point.htm

Csikszentmihalyi, M. (1998). *Finding flow: The psychology of engagement with everyday life.* New York, NY: Basic Books.

Cui, A., Zhang, M., Liu, Y., & Ma, S. (2011). Emotion tokens: Bridging the gap among multilingual Twitter sentiment analysis. *Information Retrieval Technology, 7097*, 238–249. doi:10.1007/978-3-642-25631-8_22

Cukier, M., & Panjwani, S. (2010). Risk analysis methods for cyber security. In J. G. Voeller (Ed.), *Wiley handbook of science and technology for homeland security* (Vol. 1, pp. 279–289). Hoboken, NJ: John Wiley & Sons, Inc.

Culzac, N. (2014, August 10). Israel-Gaza conflict: 150,000 protest in London for end to 'massacre and arms trade'. *The Independent.* Retrieved from http://www.independent.co.uk/news/uk/home-news/israelgaza-conflict-thousands-protest-in-london-for-end-to-massacre-and-arms-trade-9659180.html

Cunningham, E. (2015, July 2). In Ramadi, the Islamic State settles in, fixing roads and restoring electricity. *The Washington Post.* Retrieved from https://www.washingtonpost.com/world/middle_east/in-ramadi-the-islamic-state-settles-in-fixing-roads-and-restoring-electricity/2015/07/01/db32ccec-19e2-11e5-bed8-1093ee58dad0_story.html

Cunningham, K. J. (2003). Cross-regional trends in female terrorism. *Studies in Conflict and Terrorism, 26*(3), 171–195. doi:10.1080/10576100390211419

Cunningham, K. J. (2007). Countering female terrorism. *Studies in Conflict and Terrorism, 30*(2), 113–129. doi:10.1080/10576100601101067

Cyber attack war games to be staged by UK and US. (2015). *BBC News.* Retrieved from www.bbc.com/news/uk-politics-30842669

Dabiq. (2015). *Burning of Jordanian pilot – Retribution (Issue 7).* Retrieved from http://media.clarionproject.org/files/islamic-state/islamic-state-dabiq-magazine-issue-7-from-hypocrisy-to-apostasy.pdf

Daniel, M. (2015, January 14). What you need to know about President Obama's new steps on cybersecurity. *The White House*. Retrieved from https://www.whitehouse.gov/blog/2015/01/14/what-you-need-know-about-president-obama-s-new-steps-cybersecurity

Dauber, C. E., & Winkler, C. K. (2014). Radical visual propaganda in the online environment: An introduction. In C. K. Winkler & C. E. Dauber (Eds.), *Visual propaganda and extremism in the online environment* (pp. 1–30). Carlisle, PA: Strategic Studies Institute and U.S. Army War College Press.

Daugherty, J. (2013). *A study of the availability of the Protocols at Manhattan newsstands*. Coral Gables, FL: University of Miami, School of Communication.

Davie, J. C. (1973). Aggression, violence, revolution and war. In J. N. Knutsen (Ed.), *Handbook of political psychology* (pp. 234–260). San Francisco, CA: Jossey-Bass.

Davis, K. (2012, Nov 8). Can the US military fight a war with Twitter? *Computerworld*. Retrieved from http://www.computerworld.com/article/2493445/social-media/can-the-us-military-fight-a-war-with-twitter-.html

Davis, E. F., Alves, A. A., & Sklansky, D. A. (2014). *Social Media and Police Leadership: Lessons from Boston. New Perspectives in Policing Bulletin*. Washington, DC: U.S. Department of Justice, National Institute of Justice.

Davison, K. P., Pennebaker, J. W., & Dickerson, S. S. (2000). Who talks? The social psychology of illness support groups. *The American Psychologist*, *55*(2), 205–217. doi:10.1037/0003-066X.55.2.205 PMID:10717968

Day, S., & Schneider, P. (2002). Psychotherapy using distance technology: A comparison to face-to-face, video, and audio treatment. *Journal of Consulting Psychology*, *49*(4), 499–503. doi:10.1037/0022-0167.49.4.499

de Bie, J. L., de Poot, C. J., & van der Leun, J. P. (2015). Shifting modus operandi of Jjihadist foreign fighters from the Netherlands between 2000 and 2013: A crime script analysis. *Terrorism and Political Violence*, *27*(3), 416–440. doi:10.1080/09546553.2015.1021038

de Borchgrave, A., Sanderson, T., & Gordon, D. (2009). *The power of outreach: Leveraging on expertise on threats in Southeast Asia*. Washington, DC: Center for Strategic and International Studies.

de Vries, I. (2011, November 11). Amid growing inequality, it's about time our policy makers mind the wealth gap. *Jakarta Globe*. Retrieved from http://www.thejakartaglobe.com/archive/amid-growing-inequality-its-about-time-our-policy-makers-mind-the-wealth-gap/

Dean, G. (2012). *Complexity model for knowledge-managed policing of violent extremism*. Paper presented at The American Society of Criminology, Annual Meeting, Chicago, IL.

Dean, G. (2014). *Neurocognitive risk assessment for the early detection of violent extremists*. New York, NY: Springer. doi:10.1007/978-3-319-06719-3

Dean, G. (2014). *Neurocogntive risk assessment for the early detection of violent extremists*. New York, NY: Springer.

Dean, G., Bell, P., & Congram, M. (2010). Knowledge-managed policing framework for communication interception technologies (CIT) in criminal justice system. *Pakistan Journal of Criminology*, *2*(4), 25–41.

Dean, G., Bell, P., & Newman, J. (2012). The dark side of social media: Review of online terrorism. *Pakistan Journal of Criminology*, *3*(3), 107–126.

Dean, G., & Gottschalk, P. (2007). *Knowledge management in policing and law enforcement: Foundations, structures, applications*. Oxford, UK: Oxford University Press.

Deci, E. L., & Ryan, R. M. (2000). The 'what' and 'why' of goal pursuits: Human needs and the self-determination of behaviour. *Psychological Inquiry, 11*(4), 227–268. doi:10.1207/S15327965PLI1104_01

Deloughery, K., King, R., Asal, V., & Rethemeyer, R. K. (2013). *Assessing the likelihood of hate crime in wake of Boston attacks.* National Consortium for the Study of Terrorism and Responses to Terrorism. Retrieved from http://www.start.umd.edu/sites/default/files/files/publications/research_briefs/START_HateCrimeTerrorism_QA.pdf

Demetriou, C., & Silke, A. (2003). A criminological Internet 'sting'. Experimental evidence of illegal and deviant visits to a website trap. *The British Journal of Criminology, 43*(1), 213–222. doi:10.1093/bjc/43.1.213

Deniz, L. (2010). Excessive Internet use and loneliness among secondary school students. *Journal of Instructional Psychology, 37*(1), 20–23.

Denning, D. E. (2009). *Activism, hacktivism and cyberterrorism: The Internet as a tool for influencing foreign policy.* Santa Monica, CA: RAND Corporation.

Department of Homeland Security (DHS). (2010). *Terrorist use of social networking sites: Facebook case study.* Washington, DC: Author.

Department of Homeland Security (DHS). (2012). *Case studies on violent extremism.* Washington, DC: Author.

Department of Homeland Security (DHS). (2013a). *NIPP 2013: Partnering for critical infrastructure security and resilience.* Retrieved from http://www.dhs.gov/sites/default/files/publications/NIPP%202013_Partnering%20for%20Critical%20Infrastructure%20Security%20and%20Resilience_508_0.pdf

Department of Homeland Security (DHS). (2013b). *National Infrastructure Protection Plan.* Retrieved from http://www.dhs.gov/sites/default/files/publications/NIPP-Fact-Sheet-508.pdf

Department of Homeland Security (DHS). (2014). *Energy sector: Sector overview.* Retrieved from http://www.dhs.gov/energy-sector

Department of Justice. (2014, November 21). *Department of justice releases resource guide to help law enforcement strengthen relationships with communities.* Retrieved from http://www.justice.gov/opa/pr/department-justice-releases-resource-guide-help-law-enforcement-strengthen-relationships

Department of the Army. (2012, July 31). *Civilian casualty mitigation. Army tactics, techniques, and procedures* (No. 3-37). Retrieved from https://fas.org/irp/doddir/army/attp3-37-31.pdf

Dernevik, M., Beck, A., Grann, M., Houe, T., & McGuire, J. (2009). The use of psychiatric and psychological evidence in the assessment of terrorist offenders. *Journal of Forensic Psychiatry & Psychology, 20*(4), 508–515. doi:10.1080/13501760902771217

Desouza, K. C., & Hensgen, T. (2003). Semiotic emergent framework to address the reality of cyberterrorism. *Technological Forecasting and Social Change, 70*(4), 385–296. doi:10.1016/S0040-1625(03)00003-9

Despite Tikrit loss, ISIS still holds large swaths of Iraq. (2015). *The New York Times.* Retrieved from http://www.nytimes.com/interactive/2014/06/12/world/middleeast/the-iraq-isis-conflict-in-maps-photos-and-video.html?_r=0

Diamond, L. (2007). *Building trust in government by improving governance.* Paper presented at the 7th Global Forum on Reinventing Government: Building Trust in Government, Vienna, Italy.

Dickinson, E. (2015, May 22). The Islamic State brings the war to Saudi Arabia. *Foreign Policy.* Retrieved from http://foreignpolicy.com/2015/05/22/isis-brings-the-war-to-saudi-arabia-qatif-mosque-bombing/

Dillon, L., Neo, L. S., Ong, G., & Khader, M. (2014). *Psychology behind hackers: A multiple case-study approach.* Research Report No. 17/2014. Singapore: Home Team Behavioural Sciences Centre.

Dillon, L., Neo, L. S., Ong, G., & Khader, M. (2014). *Online radicalisation: A case study on Roshonara Choundry (Research report No. 14/2014).* Singapore: Home Team Behavioural Sciences Centre.

Dillon, L., Neo, L. S., Ong, G., & Khader, M. (2014). *Psychology behind hackers: A multiple-case study approach (Research report no. 17/2014).* Singapore: Home Team Behavioural Sciences Centre.

Dillon, L., Neo, L. S., Ong, G., & Khader, M. (2015). *Cyberterrorism: A kinetic cyber threat (Research report no. 07/2015).* Singapore: Home Team Behavioural Sciences Centre.

Dinesen, P. T., & Jaeger, M. M. (2013). The effect of terror on institutional trust: New evidence from the 3/11 Madrid terrorist attack. *Political Psychology, 34*(6), 917–926. doi:10.1111/pops.12025

Dingledine, R., Mathewson, N., & Syverson, P. (2004). *Tor: The second-generation onion router.* Washington, DC: Naval Research Lab.

Dixon-Woods, M., Bonas, S., Booth, A., Jones, D. R., Miller, T., Shaw, R. L., & Young, B. et al. (2006). How can systematic reviews incorporate qualitative research? A critical perspective. *Qualitative Research, 6*(1), 27–44. doi:10.1177/1468794106058867

Dodd, V. (2010, November 2). Profile: Roshonara Choudary. *The Guardian.* Retrieved from http://www.guardian.co.uk/uk/2010/nov/02/profile-roshonara-choudhry-stephen-timms

Dodd, V. (2010, November 3). Roshonara Choudhry: Police interview extracts. *The Guardian.* Retrieved from http://www.theguardian.com/uk/2010/nov/03/roshonara-choudhry-police-interview

Dogrul, M., Aslan, A., & Celik, E. (2011). Developing an international cooperation on cyber defense and deterrence against cyber terrorism. In C. Czosseck, E. Tyugu, & T. Wingfield (Eds.), *3rd international conference on cyber conflict.* Estonia, Tallinn: NATO CCD COE Publications.

Doosje, B., & de Wolf, A. (2010). *Dealing with radicalism: A psychological analysis.* Amsterdam: SWP.

Doosje, B., Loseman, A., & van de Bos, K. (2013). Determinants of radicalization of Islamic youth in the Netherlands: Personal uncertainty, perceived injustice, and perceived group threat. *The Journal of Social Issues, 69*(3), 586–604. doi:10.1111/josi.12030

Double truck bombing on CIA HQ - Multiple angles. (n.d.). *Live Leak.* Retrieved from http://www.liveleak.com/view?i=0d8_1184205759

Drone strikes by US may violate international law, says UN. (2013, October 18). *The Guardian.* Retrieved from http://www.theguardian.com/world/2013/oct/18/drone-strikes-us-violate-law-un

Drummond, J. T. (2002). From northwest imperative to global jihad: Social psychological aspect of the construction of the enemy, political violence, and terror. In C. E. Stout (Ed.), *The psychology of terrorism: A public understanding - Psychological dimension to war and peace* (Vol. 1, pp. 49–96). Westport, CT: Praeger.

Duarte, C. (2007). The seductive web: Technology as a tool for persuasion. In B. Ganor, K. von Knop, & C. Duarte (Eds.), Hypermedia seduction for terrorist recruiting (pp. 169-187). Washington, DC: IOS Press.

Duarte, C. (2007). The seductive web: Technology as a tool for persuasion. In B. Ganor, K. von Knop, & C. Duarte (Eds.), *Hypermedia seduction for terrorist recruiting* (pp. 169–187). Washington, DC: IOS Press.

Dubrovsky, V. J., Kiesler, S., & Sethna, B. N. (1991). The equalization phenomenon: Status effects in computer- mediated and face-to-face decision-making groups. *Human-Computer Interaction, 6*(2), 119–146. doi:10.1207/s15327051hci0602_2

Duggan, C. (2004). Does personality change and, if so, what changes? *Criminal Behaviour and Mental Health, 14*(1), 5–16. doi:10.1002/cbm.556

Eagly, A., & Chaiken, S. (1993). *The psychology of attitudes.* Fort Worth, TX: Harcourt, Brace.

Earl, J., & Kimport, K. (2011). *Digitally enabled social change: Activism in the Internet age.* Cambridge, MA: Massachusetts Institute of Technology Publishing. doi:10.7551/mitpress/9780262015103.001.0001

Eaton, T. (2013). Internet activism and the Egyptian uprisings: Transforming online dissent into the offline world. *Westminster Papers, 9*(2). Retrieved from https://www.westminster.ac.uk/__data/assets/pdf_file/0004/220675/WPCC-vol9-issue2.pdf

Echevarria, A. J. II. (2002). *Clausewitz's center of gravity: Changing our warfighting doctrine-again!* Carlisle, PA: Strategic Studies Institute.

Edman, M., & Yener, B. (2009). On anonymity in an electronic society: A survey of anonymous communication systems. *ACM Computing Surveys, 42*(1), 1–35. doi:10.1145/1592451.1592456

Edwards, C., & Gribbon, L. (2013). Pathways to violent extremism in the digital era. *The RUSI Journal, 158*(5), 40–47. doi:10.1080/03071847.2013.847714

Edwards, D. (2005). Discursive psychology. In K. L. Fitch & R. E. Sanders (Eds.), *Handbook of language and social interaction* (pp. 257–273). Hillsdale, NJ: Erlbaum.

Edwards, D., & Potter, J. (2005). Discursive psychology, mental states and descriptions. In L. Molder & J. Potter (Eds.), *Conversation and cognition* (pp. 241–259). Cambridge: Cambridge University Press. doi:10.1017/CBO9780511489990.012

Egan, M. (2013, October 9). Does Twitter have a terrorism problem? *Fox Business.* Retrieved from http://www.foxbusiness.com/technology/2013/10/09/does-twitter-have-terrorism-problem/

Egan, V., Hughes, N., & Palmer, E. J. (2015). Moral disengagement, the dark triad, and unethical consumer attitudes. *Personality and Individual Differences, 76*, 123–128. doi:10.1016/j.paid.2014.11.054

Egypt jails police over activist khaled said's death. (2011, October 26). *BBC News.* Retrieved from http://www.bbc.com/news/15467022

Eidelson, R. J., & Eidelson, J. I. (2003). Dangerous ideas: Five beliefs that propel groups toward conflict. *The American Psychologist, 58*(3), 182–192. doi:10.1037/0003-066X.58.3.182 PMID:12772423

Eke, A. W., Seto, M. C., & Williams, J. (2010). Examining the criminal history and future offending of child pornography offenders: An extended prospective follow-up study. *Law and Human Behavior*, 1–13. PMID:21088873

Ekman, M. (2014). The dark side of online activism: Swedish right-wing extremist video activism on YouTube. *Journal of Media and Communications Research, 30*(56), 79–99.

Electronic Privacy Information Center (EPIC). (2015). *EPIC online guide to practical privacy tools.* Retrieved from https://www.epic.org/privacy/tools.html

El-Fadl, K. A. (2005). *The great theft: Wrestling Islam from the extremists.* New York, NY: Harper San Francisco.

Elis, N. (2014, April 6). Anonymous hackers threaten Israel with cyberterrorism. *The JerusalemPost.* Retrieved from http://www.jpost.com/Defense/Anonymous-hackers-threaten-Israel-with-cyber-terrorism-347667

Elkus, A. (2010). Cognitive dissonance. *Red Team Journal*. Retrieved from http://redteamjournal.com/2010/09/cognitive-dissonance

Elliott, I. A., & Beech, A. (2009). Understanding online child pornography use: Applying sexual offense theory to Internet offenders. *Aggression and Violent Behavior, 14*(3), 180–193. doi:10.1016/j.avb.2009.03.002

Elliott, I. A., Beech, A. R., Mandeville-Norden, R., & Hayes, E. (2009). Psychological profiles of Internet sexual offenders: Comparisons with contact sexual offenders. *Sexual Abuse, 21*, 76–92. PMID:19218479

Ellis, L. (2011). *Using a strengths-based approach to foster resilience*. Alberta, Canada: Mount Royal University.

Ellul, J. (1965). *Propaganda: The formation of men's attitudes*. New York, NY: Random House Vintage Books.

Ellyatt, H. (2015, January 27). Cyberterrorists to target critical infrastructure. *CNBC*. Retrieved from http://www.cnbc.com/2015/01/27/cyberterrorists-to-target-critical-infrastructure.html

Ellyatt, H. (2015, January 27). Cyberterrorists to target critical infrastructure. *CNBC*. Retrieved from http://www.cnbc.com/id/102367777

Elovici, Y., Kandel, A., Last, M., Shapira, B., & Zaafrany, O. (2004). Using data mining techniques for detecting terror-related activities on the web. *Journal of Information Warfare, 3*(1), 17–29.

Elzain, C. (2008). Modern Islamic terrorism and jihad. *Occasional Series in Criminal Justice and International Studies*, 1-27.

Enayati, A. (2012, June 1). The importance of belonging. *CNN*. Retrieved from http://edition.cnn.com/2012/06/01/health/enayati-importance-of-belonging/

Encyclopedia Britannica. (2014). *Osama bin Laden: Saudi Arabian militant*. Retrieved from http://www.britannica.com/EBchecked/topic/65507/Osama-bin-Laden

Endrass, J., Urbaniok, F., Hammermeister, L. C., Benz, C., Elbert, T., Laubacher, A., & Rossegger, A. (2009). The consumption of internet child pornography and violent and sex offending. *BMC Psychiatry, 9*(43). doi:10.1186/1471-244X-9-43 PMID:19602221

Engel, R. (2013, November 3). Analysis: Did Syria's Assad get away with chemical weapons attack? *NBC News*. Retrieved from http://www.nbcnews.com/news/other/analysis-did-syrias-assad-get-away-chemical-weapons-attack-f8C11519031

Erikson, E. H. (1994). *Identity: Youth and crisis*. New York, NY: W.W. Norton.

Erlichman, J. (Interviewer), & Jack, B. (Interviewee). (2012, February 29). *McAfee's Barnaby on Medical Device Hacking*. Bloomberg TV Website. Retrieved from http://www.bloomberg.com/video/87427352-mcafee-s-barnaby-on-medical-device-hacking.html

Esen, R. (2002). Cybercrime: A growing problem. *Journal of Criminal Law, 66*(3), 269–283.

European Commission project. (2008). *Transnational terrorism, security and the rule of law*. Retrieved from http://www.transnationalterrorism.eu/tekst/publications/WP2%20Del%203.pdf

Europol. (2012). *TE-SAT 2012: European Union terrorism situation and trend report*. European Law Enforcement Agency.

Europol. (2014). *TE-SAT 2014. European Union terrorism situation and trend report 2014*. European Law Enforcement Agency.

ExecutiveGov. (2010, March 12). *Lt. Gen. Michael L. Oates of JIEDDO: Leading the fight against IEDs.* Retrieved from http://www.executivegov.com/2010/03/lt-gen-michael-l-oates-of-jieddo-leading-the-fight-against-ieds/#sthash.yjfWj0NH.dpuf

Extreme Dialogue. (2015). Retrieved from http://extremedialogue.org

Fairclough, N. (1992). *Discourse and social change.* Cambridge: Polity Press.

Fairweather, E., McDonough, R., & McFadyean, M. (1984). *Only the rivers run free: Northern Ireland: The women's war.* London: Pluto Press.

Fang, X., Singh, S., & Ahluwalia, R. (2007). An examination of different explanations for the mere exposure effect. *The Journal of Consumer Research, 34*(1), 97–103. doi:10.1086/513050

Farrington, D. P. (2015). Prospective longitudinal research on the development of offending. *Australian and New Zealand Journal of Criminology, 48*(3), 314–335. doi:10.1177/0004865815590461

FBI. (2013). *Press Release July 16, 2013 on Emerson Winfield Begolly.* Retrieved from http://www.fbi.gov/pittsburgh/press-releases/2013/pennsylvania-man-sentenced-for-terrorism-solicitation-and-firearms-offense

Federal Bureau of Investigation (FBI). (n.d.). *Definition of terrorism.* Retrieved from https://www.fbi.gov/about-us/investigate/terrorism/terrorism-definition

Federal Bureau of Investigation Press Release. (2014, July 23). *Three defendants arrested on charges of providing material support to a foreign terrorist organization.* Retrieved from https://www.fbi.gov/washingtondc/press-releases/2014/three-defendants-arrested-on-charges-of-providing-material-support-to-a-foreign-terrorist-organization

Federal Bureau of Investigation. (n.d.). *Definitions of terrorism in the U. S. Code.* Retrieved from http://www.fbi.gov/about-us/investigate/terrorism/terrorism-definition

Feillard, G. N. (2014). Responses to the challenge of ISIS in Indonesia. In T. C. Tion (Ed.), *ISEAS Perspective* (pp. 11–18). Singapore: Institute of Southeast Asian Studies.

Feldman, R. (2013, April). Techniques and applications for sentiment analysis. *Communications of the ACM, 56*(4), 82–89. doi:10.1145/2436256.2436274

Ferencik, M., & Horvath, J. (2009). Critical discourse analysis of Obama's. In *Political Discourse, Language, Literature and Culture in a Changing Transatlantic World, International Conference Proceedings.* Presov: University of Presov.

Ferguson, A. J. (2005). Fostering e-mail security awareness: The West Point carronade. *EDUCASE Quarterly, 28*(1), 54–57.

Fernandez, L., Barbera, J., & van Dorp, J. (2006). Strategies for managing volunteers during incident response: A systems approach. *Homeland Security Affairs, 2*(9). Retrieved from https://www.hsaj.org/articles/684

Fiedler, K., Messner, C., & Bluemke, M. (2006). Unresolved problems with the "I," the "A" and the "T": Logical and psychometric critique of the Implicit Association Test (IAT). *European Review of Social Psychology, 17*(1), 74–147. doi:10.1080/10463280600681248

Field, C. (2015, June 22). NC teen planned to attack local bar, concert, then kill 1,000, FBI says. *WYFF4.com News.* Retrieved from http://www.wyff4.com/news/nc-teen-planned-to-attack-local-bar-concert-then-kill-1000-fbi-says/33712110

Fighel, J. (2007). Radical Islamic internet propaganda: Concepts, idioms and visual motifs. In B. Ganor, K. von Knop, & C. Duarte (Eds.), *Hypermedia seduction for terrorist recruiting* (pp. 34–38). Washington, DC: IOS Press.

Fighel, J. (2007). Radical Islamic Internet propaganda: Concepts, idioms and visual motifs. In B. Ganor, K. von Knop, & C. Duarte (Eds.), *Hypermedia seduction for terrorist recruiting* (pp. 34–38). Washington, DC: IOS Press.

Fiore, A., LeeTeirnan, S., & Smith, M. (2002). Observed behavior and perceived value of authors in Usenet newsgroups: bridging the gap. *Proceedings of the 20th Annual SIGCHI Conference on Human Factors in Computing Systems.* doi:10.1145/503376.503434

Fisher, A. (2015). Swarmcast: How jihadist networks maintain a persistent online presence. *Perspectives on Terrorism, 9*(3), 3–20.

Fisher, A., & Prucha, N. (2013). Tweeting for the caliphate: Twitter as the new frontier for jihadist propaganda. *CTC Sentinel, 6*(6), 19–22.

Fisher-Ilan, A., & Finkle, J. (2014, January 26). Israeli defense computer hacked via tainted email: cyber firm. *Reuters.* Retrieved from http://www.reuters.com/article/2014/01/26/israel-cybersecurity-idUSL5N0L00JR20140126

Fisher, J. D., & Fisher, W. A. (1992). Changing AIDS risk behavior. *Psychological Bulletin, 111*(3), 455–474. doi:10.1037/0033-2909.111.3.455 PMID:1594721

Flynn, S. (2014, July 30). *Understanding and embracing the resilience imperative.* Paper presented at the NIST Workshop on 'Developing a Community-Centered Approach to Disaster Resilience'. Retrieved from www.nist.gov/el/building_materials/resilience/upload/7-Flynn-NIST-Stevens-Event-7-30-14.pdf

Forbes, M. (2006, October 11). Terrorism network commanded from jail. *Sydney Morning Herald.* Retrieved from http://www.smh.com.au/news/world/terrorism-network-commanded-from-jail/2006/10/10/1160246130065.html

Foucault, M. (2006). Lectures at the College de France 1973-1974. In J. LaGrange (Ed.), *Michel Foucault: Psychiatric power* (G. Burchell, Trans.). New York, NY: Palgrave MacMillan.

Fox, R. (2005, August 8). Gwot is history. Now for save: After the global war on terror comes the struggle against violent extremism. *New Statesman.* Retrieved from http://www.newstatesman.com/node/195357

Fox-Brewster, T. (2015, April 10). Memex in action: Watch DARPA Artificial Intelligence search for crime on the 'Dark Web'. *Forbes.* Retrieved from http://www.forbes.com/sites/thomasbrewster/2015/04/10/darpa-memex-search-going-open-source-check-it-out/

Fox, J. A., & Levin, J. (2005). *Extreme killing: Understanding serial and mass murder.* California: Sage Publications, Inc.

France attack: Van driven into shoppers in Nantes. (2014, December 23). *BBC News.* Retrieved from http://www.bbc.com/news/world-europe-30583390

Frankl, V. (2000). *Recollections: An autobiography.* New York, NY: Perseus Books.

Freedman, L. (2006). *The transformation of strategic affairs (Adelphi Paper 379).* London: Routledge.

Freilich, J. D., Chermak, S. M., & Caspi, D. (2009). Critical events in the life trajectories of domestic extremist white supremacist groups. *Criminology & Public Policy, 8*(3), 497–530. doi:10.1111/j.1745-9133.2009.00572.x

Friedland, J., & Rogerson, K. (2009). *How political and social movements form on the Internet and how they change over time.* Washington, DC: Institute for Homeland Security Solutions.

Friedman, D., & Siemaszko, C. (2014, June 19). Home-grown terror: American jihadist wannabes flock to ISIS-like groups in Iraq and Syria. *Daily News.* Retrieved from http://www.nydailynews.com/news/national/jihadist-wannabes-u-s-flock-isis-like-groups-overseas-article-1.1837013

Full text: bin Laden's 'letter to America'. (2002, November 24). *The Guardian*. Retrieved from http://www.theguardian.com/world/2002/nov/24/theobserver

Funder, D. C. (2012). *The personality puzzle* (6th ed.). New York, NY: Norton.

Furnell, S. M., & Warren, M. J. (1999). Computer hacking and cyber terrorism: The real threats in the new millennium? *Computers & Security, 18*(1), 28–34. doi:10.1016/S0167-4048(99)80006-6

Gambhir, H. (2014). Backgrounder-Dabiq: The strategic messaging of the Islamic State. *Institute for the Study of War*. Retrieved from http://www.understandingwar.org/sites/default/files/Dabiq%20Backgrounder_Harleen%20Final.pdf

Ganor, B. (2004). Terrorism as a strategy of psychological warfare. In Y. Danieli, D. Brom, & J. Sills (Eds.), *The trauma of terrorism* (pp. 33–43). New York, NY: Haworth. doi:10.1300/J146v09n01_03

Gawrych, G. W. (2002). Jihad, war, and terrorism. *Small Wars Journal*. Retrieved from www.smallwarsjournal.com/documents/gawrych.pdf

Geeraerts, S. (2012). Digital radicalisation of youth. *Social Cosmos, 3*(1), 25–32.

Geiger, K. (2015, August 11). Hackers' $100 million insider shop sold data on demand. *Bloomberg*. Retrieved from http://www.bloomberg.com/news/articles/2015-08-11/hackers-100-million-insider-trading-shop-sold-data-on-demand

Gelder, K. (2006). Epic fantasy and global terrorism. In E. Mathijs & M. Pomerance (Eds.), *From hobbits to Hollywood: essays on Peter Jackson's Lord of the Rings* (pp. 101–118). The Netherlands: Rodopi.

Gellman, B., Timberg, C., & Rich, S. (2013, October 4). Secret NSA documents show campaign against Tor encrypted network. *Washington Post*. Retrieved from https://www.washingtonpost.com/world/national-security/secret-nsa-documents-show-campaign-against-tor-encrypted-network/2013/10/04/610f08b6-2d05-11e3-8ade-a1f23cda135e_story.html

General Intelligence and Security Service (AIVD). (2012). *Jihadism on the web: A breeding ground for jihad in the modern age*. The Hague: Algemene Inlichtingen en Veiligheidsdienst.

Gerbaudo, P. (2012). *Tweets on the streets: Social media and contemporary activism*. London: Pluto Press.

Gerges, F. A. (2014). ISIS and the third wave of jihadism. *Current History (New York, N.Y.), 113*(767), 339–343.

Gibbs, S. (2014, March 6). Battle for the car: Will Google, Apple or Microsoft dominate? *The Guardian*. Retrieved from http://www.theguardian.com/technology/2014/mar/06/battle-for-car-will-google-apple-microsoft-dominate

Gibson, S. (2004). Open source intelligence: An intelligence lifeline. *Royal United Services Institute Journal, 149*(1), 16–22.

Gillispie, J. F. (2007). Cyber shrinks: Expanding the paradigm. In J. Gackenbach (Ed.), *Psychology and the Internet: Intrapersonal, interpersonal, and transpersonal implications* (pp. 245–269). London: Elsevier. doi:10.1016/B978-012369425-6/50029-1

Gill, P., & Horgan, J. (2013). Who were the volunteers? The shifting sociological and operational profile of 1240 Provisional Irish Republican Army members. *Terrorism and Political Violence, 25*(4), 435–456. doi:10.1080/09546553.2012.664587

Gill, P., Horgan, J., & Deckert, P. (2014). Bombing alone: Tracing the motivations and antecedent behaviors of lone-actor terrorists. *Journal of Forensic Sciences, 59*(2), 425–435. doi:10.1111/1556-4029.12312 PMID:24313297

Girl aged 12 in Nigeria marketplace bombing. (2015, June 24). *Al Jazeera*. Retrieved from http://www.aljazeera.com/news/2015/06/girl-aged-12-nigeria-market-suicide-bombing-150624044055589.html

Givner-Forbes, R., & Osman, S. (2009). *How jihadist websites surmount psychological hurdles to radicalisation (policy brief)*. Singapore: S. Rajaratnam School of International Studies.

Gladstone, R. (2015, April 9). Twitter says it suspended 10,000 ISIS-linked accounts in one day. *The New York Times*. Retrieved from http://www.nytimes.com/2015/04/10/world/middleeast/twitter-says-it-suspended-10000-isis-linked-accounts-iin-one-day.html?_r=0

Gladwell, M. (2004). *The tipping point: How little things can make a big difference*. London: Abacus.

Glander, T. (2000). *Origins of mass communications research during the American Cold War: Educational effects and contemporary implications*. Mahwah, NJ: Lawrence Erlbaum Associates, Inc.

Glass, K., & Colbaugh, R. (2012). Estimating the sentiment of social media content for security informatics applications. *Security Informatics*, *1*(3). doi:10.1186/2190-8532-1-3

Glassman, R. (1973). Persistence and loose coupling in living systems. *Behavioral Science*, *18*(2), 83–98. doi:10.1002/bs.3830180202

Glees, A., & Pope, C. (2005). *When students turn to terror: Terrorist and extremist activity on British campuses*. London: Social Affairs Unit.

Global Policy Forum. (n.d.). *War on terrorism*. Retrieved from https://www.globalpolicy.org/war-on-terrorism.html

Glueckauf, R., Pickett, T., Ketterson, T., Loomis, J., & Rozenshy, R. (2003). Preparation for the delivery of telehealth services: A self-study framework for expansion of practice. *Professional Psychology, Research and Practice*, *34*(2), 159–163. doi:10.1037/0735-7028.34.2.159

Glum, J. (2015, August 28). ISIS hacker Junaid Hussain confirmed dead after US airstrike on Islamic State in Syria: Pentagon. *International Business Times*. Retrieved from http://www.ibtimes.com/isis-hacker-junaid-hussain-confirmed-dead-after-us-airstrike-islamic-state-syria-2073451

Goedsche, H. (1868). Biarritz. Author.

Goel, S., & Hong, Y. (2015). Cyber war games: Strategic jostling among traditional adversaries. In S. Jajodia, P. Shakarian, V. Subrahmanian, V. Swarup, & C. Wang (Eds.), *Cyber Warfare* (pp. 1–13). Switzerland: Springer International Publishing. doi:10.1007/978-3-319-14039-1_1

Goleman, D. (2013). *Focus: The hidden driver of excellence*. London: Bloomsbury.

Gomes, D., Tan, J., Wang, Y., Neo, L. S., Ong, G., & Khader, M. (2015a). *National resilience: HTBSC Singapore's national resilience proposed framework* (Research Report no. 3/2015). Singapore: Home Team Behavioural Sciences Centre.

Gomes, D., Tan, J., Wang, Y., Neo, L. S., Ong, G., & Khader, M. (2015b). *System de-coupling: A strategy to build national resilience* (Research Report no. 11/2015). Singapore: Home Team Behavioural Sciences Centre.

Goodenough, P. (2014, August 20). Al-Qaeda in Yemen announces 'solidarity' with 'our Muslims Brothers in Iraq'. *CNS News*. Retrieved from http://www.cnsnews.com/news/article/patrick-goodenough/al-qaeda-yemen-announces-solidarity-our-muslim-brothers-iraq

Goodrich, R. (2014). PC security and the importance of patch updates. *Top Ten Reviews*. Retrieved from http://anti-virus-software-review.toptenreviews.com/pc-security-and-the-importance-of-patch-updates.html

Gorge, M. (2007). Cyberterrorism: Hype or reality? *Computer Fraud & Security*, *2*(2), 9–12. doi:10.1016/S1361-3723(07)70021-0

Gorman, S., Malas, N., & Bradley, M. (2014). Brutal Efficiency: The secret to Islamic State's Success. *The Wall Street Journal*. Retrieved from http://online.wsj.com/articles/the-secret-to-the-success-of-islamic-state-1409709762

Gosling, S., Augustine, A. A., Vazire, S., Holtzman, N., & Gaddis, S. (2011). Manifestations of personality in online social networks: Self-reported Facebook-related behaviors and observable profile information. *Cyberpsychology, Behavior, and Social Networking, 14*(9), 483–488. doi:10.1089/cyber.2010.0087

Government of Canada. (2015a). *Providing humanitarian assistance*. Retrieved from http://international.gc.ca/world-monde/security-securite/isis-eiis/humanitarian_assistance-aide_humanitaire.aspx?lang=eng

Government of Canada. (2015b). *How Canada is helping Syrian and Iraqi refugees*. Retrieved from http://www.cic.gc.ca/english/refugees/crisis/canada-response.asp

Government of Canada. (2015c). *Supporting stabilization and development*. Retrieved from http://international.gc.ca/world-monde/security-securite/isis-eiis/stabilization_development-stabilisation_developpement.aspx?lang=eng

Government of Hong Kong Special Administrative Region. (2008). *Honeypot security*. Retrieved from http://www.infosec.gov.hk/textonly/english/technical/files/honeypots.pdf

Graber, E. C., Laurenceau, J., & Carver, C. S. (2011). Integrating the dynamics of personality and close relationship processes: Methodological and data analytic implications. *Journal of Personality, 79*(6), 1101–1137. doi:10.1111/j.1467-6494.2011.00725.x

Gracie, C. (2014, July 16). The knife attack that changed Kunming. *BBC News*. Retrieved from http://www.bbc.com/news/world-asia-28305109

Gragg, D. (2002). A multi-level defense against social engineering. *SANS Institute*. Retrieved from http://www.sans.org/reading-room/whitepapers/engineering/multi-level-defense-social-engineering-920

Granovetter, M. (1978). Threshold models of collective behavior. *American Journal of Sociology, 83*(6), 1420–1420. doi:10.1086/226707

Grau, A. (2015, June 26). Securing medical devices, solving the challenge of the weakest link. *Medical Design Technology*. Retrieved from http://www.mdtmag.com/article/2015/06/securing-medical-devices-solving-challenge-weakest-link

Graves, P. (1921). *The truth about the Protocols: A literary forgery*. London: The Times.

Gray, D. H., & Head, A. (2009). The importance of the Internet to the post-modern terrorist and its role as a form of safe haven. *European Journal of Scientific Research, 25*(3), 396–404.

Gray, J. R., Braver, T. S., & Raichle, M. E. (2002). Integration of emotion and cognition in the lateral prefrontal cortex. *Proceedings of the National Academy of Sciences of the United States of America, 99*(6), 4115–4120. doi:10.1073/pnas.062381899

Green, J. (2002, November). The myth of cyberterrorism. *Washington Monthly*. Retrieved from http://www.washingtonmonthly.com/features/2001/0211.green.html

Greenberg, A. (2012, July 25). Next-Gen air traffic control vulnerable to hackers spoofing planes out of thin air. *Forbes*. Retrieved from http://www.forbes.com/sites/andygreenberg/2012/07/25/next-gen-air-traffic-control-vulnerable-to-hackers-spoofing-planes-out-of-thin-air/

Greenberg, A. (2013, July 24). Hackers reveal nasty new car attacks – with me behind the wheel (video). *Forbes*. Retrieved from http://www.forbes.com/sites/andygreenberg/2013/07/24/hackers-reveal-nasty-new-car-attacks-with-me-behind-the-wheel-video/

Greenfield, S. (2014). *Mind change: How digital technologies are leaving their mark on our brains*. UK: Rider.

Greenwald, G. (2013, July 31). XKeyscore: NSA tool collects 'nearly everything a user does on the internet'. *The Guardian*. Retrieved from http://www.theguardian.com/world/2013/jul/31/nsa-top-secret-program-online-data

Grodzins, M. (2007, September 18). 50 years ago in Scientific American: Metropolitan Segregation. *Scientific American*. Retrieved from http://www.scientificamerican.com/article/50-years-ago-in-scientific-american-white-flight-1/

Grodzins, M. (1958). *The metropolitan area as a racial problem*. Pittsburgh: University of Pittsburgh Press.

Grossman, D. (1996). *On killing: The psychological cost of learning to kill in war and society*. New York, NY: Back Bay Books.

Grubb, B. (2012, November 6). Fatal risk at heart of lax security. *The Sydney Morning Herald*. Retrieved from http://www.smh.com.au/digital-life/consumer-security/fatal-risk-at-heart-of-lax-security-20121105-28ore.html

Gruenewald, J., Chermak, S., & Freilich, J. D. (2013). Far-right lone wolf homicides in the United States. *Studies in Conflict and Terrorism*, *36*(12), 1005–1024. doi:10.1080/1057610X.2013.842123

Gruenewald, J., Chermak, S., & Freilich, J. D. (2013a). Distinguishing 'loner' attacks from other domestic extremist violence: A comparison of far-right homicide incident and offender characteristics. *Criminology & Public Policy*, *12*(1), 63–64. doi:10.1111/1745-9133.12009

Gunaratna, R. (2005). *Ideology in terrorism and counter terrorism: Lessons from combating Al Qaeda and Al Jemaah Al Islamiyah in Southeast Asia*. Retrieved from http://kms1.isn.ethz.ch/serviceengine/Files/ISN/44015/ichaptersection_singledocument/0d07f910-03a4-4cc7-86ea-5b754a6e04fa/en/07.pdf

Gupta, D. K. (2011). Waves of international terrorism: An exploration of the process by which ideas flood the world. In J. E. Rosenfeld (Ed.), *Terrorism, identity and legitimacy: The four waves theory and political violence* (pp. 30–43). New York, NY: Routledge.

Gupta, R., & Brooks, H. (2013). *Using social media for global security*. Indianapolis, IN: John Wiley & Sons, Inc.

Haberstroh, S., Barney, L., Foster, N., & Duffey, T. (2014). The ethical and legal practice of online counselling and psychotherapy: A review of mental health professions. *Journal of Technology in Human Sciences*, *32*(3), 149–157. doi:10.1080/15228835.2013.872074

Hale, A. (2010, September 16). Sourcecon's Semantic Search Series. *Sourcecon*. Retrieved from http://www.eremedia.com/sourcecon/sourcecons-semantic-search-series/

Hall, J. (2014, September 19). The ISIS family tree: Sinister and organised network that begins with 'the caliph' and continues with a rigid chain of command down to foot soldiers. *Mail Online*. Retrieved from http://www.dailymail.co.uk/news/article-2761071/The-ISIS-family-tree-Sinister-organised-network-begins-caliph-continues-rigid-chain-command-level-foot-soldiers.html

Halleck, T. (2015, January 13). Junaid Hussain: CyberCaliphate leader and ISIS member was behind CENTCOM hack, report says. *International Business Times*. Retrieved from http://www.ibtimes.com/junaid-hussain-cybercaliphate-leader-isis-member-was-behind-centcom-hack-report-says-1782870

Halperin, D., Heydt-Benjamin, T. S., Ransford, B., Clark, S. S., Defend, B., Morgan, W., & Maisel, W. H. et al. (2008). Pacemakers and implantable cardiac defibrillators: Software radio attacks and zero-power defenses. In *Proceedings of the 2008 IEEE Symposium on Security and Privacy*. doi:10.1109/SP.2008.31

Halpern, S. (2013, November 7). Are we puppets in a wired world? *The New York Review of Books*. Retrieved from http://www.nybooks.com/articles/archives/2013/nov/07/are-we-puppets-wired-world/

Halverson, J. R., & Way, A. K. (2012). The curious case of Colleen LaRose: Social margins, new media, and online radicalization. *Media. War and Conflict, 5*(2), 139–153. doi:10.1177/1750635212440917

Hancock, J. B. (2013). Social media make us more honest. *TED*. Retrieved from https://www.ted.com/talks/jeff_hancock_3_types_of_digital_lies?language=en

Hanes, E., & Machin, S. (2014). Hate crime research: Design and measurement strategies for improving causal inference. *Journal of Contemporary Criminal Justice, 30*(3), 228–246. doi:10.1177/1043986214536662

Hansen, D. L., Shneiderman, B., & Smith, M. A. (2011). *Analysing social media networks with NodeXL: Insights from a connected world*. Massachusetts, MA: Elsevier.

Hanson, R. K. (2005). Twenty Years of Progress in violence risk assessment. *Journal of Interpersonal Violence, 20*(2), 212–217. doi:10.1177/0886260504267740 PMID:15601794

Harari, Y. N. (2015, January 31). Yuval Noah Harai: the theatre of terror. *The Guardian*. Retrieved from http://www.theguardian.com/books/2015/jan/31/terrorism-spectacle-how-states-respond-yuval-noah-harari-sapiens

Hardy, K., & Williams, G. (2012). What is 'cyberterrorism'? Computer and internet technology in legal definitions of terrorism. In T. Chen, L. Jarvis, & S. Macdonald (Eds.), *Cyberterrorism: Understanding, assessment and response* (pp. 1–23). New York, NY: Springer.

Hare, R. D. (1991). *Manual for the Hare Psychopathy Check List-Revised*. Toronto, ON: Multi-Health Systems.

Hare, R. D. (2003). *Manual for the Hare Psychopathy Check-List-Revised* (2nd ed.). Toronto, ON: Multi-Health Systems.

Harress, C. (2014, February 18). Obama says cyberterrorism is country's biggest threat, U.S government assembles "cyber warriors". *International Business Times*. Retrieved from http://www.ibtimes.com/obama-says-cyberterrorism-countrys-biggest-threat-us-government-assembles-cyber-warriors-1556337

Harrington, N. (2005). The frustration discomfort scale: Development and psychometric properties. *Clinical Psychology & Psychotherapy, 12*(5), 374–387. doi:10.1002/cpp.465

Harris, K. M., McLean, J. P., & Sheffield, J. (2009). Examining suicide-risk individuals who go online for suicide-related purposes. *Archives of Suicide Research: The Official Journal of the Academy for Suicide Research, 13*(3), 264–276. doi:10.1080/13811110903044419 PMID:19591000

Harris, S. (2014, July/August). The social laboratory. *Foreign Policy*, 64–71.

Hart, S. D., & Logan, C. (2011). Formulation of violence risk using evidence-based assessments: The Structured Professional Judgment approach. In P. Sturmey & M. McMurran (Eds.), *Forensic case formulation* (pp. 83–106). Chichester, UK: Wiley Blackwell. doi:10.1002/9781119977018.ch4

Hasan, N., Hendriks, B., Janssen, F., & Meijer, R. (2012). *Counter terrorism strategies in Indonesia, Algeria and Saudi Arabia*. The Hague, Netherlands: Netherlands Institute of International Relations.

Hassan, M. (2012). Understanding drivers of violent extremism: The case of al-Shabab and Somali youth. *CTC Sentinel, 5*(8), 18–20.

Hassan, M. H. (2006). *Unlicensed to kill: Countering Imam Samudra's justification for the Bali bombing*. Singapore: Peace Matters.

Haythornthwaite, C. (2001). Exploring multiplexity: Social network structures in a computer-supported distance learning class. *The Information Society, 17*(3), 211–226. doi:10.1080/01972240152493065

Haythornthwaite, C., Kazmer, M. M., Robins, J., & Shoemaker, S. (2000). Community development among distance learners: Temporal and technological dimensions. *Journal of Computer-Mediated Communication*, *6*(1). doi:10.1111/j.1083-6101-2000.tb00114.x

Haythornthwaite, C., & Nielsen, A. L. (2007). Revisiting computer-mediated communication for work, community, and learning. In J. Gackenbach (Ed.), *Psychology and the Internet: Intrapersonal, interpersonal, and transpersonal implications* (pp. 167–180). London: Elsevier. doi:10.1016/B978-012369425-6/50026-6

Haythornthwaite, C., & Wellman, B. (1998). Work, friendship, and media use for information exchange in a networked organisation. *Journal of the American Society for Information Science*, *49*(12), 1101–1114. doi:10.1002/(SICI)1097-4571(1998)49:12<1101::AID-ASI6>3.0.CO;2-Z

Heath, C., & Heath, D. (2008). *Made to stick: Why some ideas take hold and others come unstuck*. London: Arrow.

Heath, C., & Heath, D. (2008). *Made to stick: Why some ideas take hold And others come unstuck*. London: Arrow.

Heck, P. L. (2004). Jihad revisited. *The Journal of Religious Ethics*, *32*(1), 95–128. doi:10.1111/j.0384-9694.2004.00156.x

Hedeland, H., Schmidt, T., & Wörner, K. (Eds.). (2011). Multilingual resources and multilingual applications. In *Proceedings of the Conference of the German Society for Computational Linguistics and Language Technology (GSCL)*. Hamburg: Universität Hamburg.

Hegghammer, T. (2014). Interpersonal trust on jihadi internet forums. In D. Gambetta (Ed.), Fight, flight, mimic: Identity signalling in armed conflicts. Academic Press.

Hegghammer, T. (2010). *Jihad in Saudi Arabia: Violence and pan-Islamism since 1979*. Cambridge, UK: Cambridge University Press. doi:10.1017/CBO9780511809439

Hegghammer, T. (2011). The rise of the Muslim foreign fighters: Islam and the globalization of Jihad. *International Security*, *35*(3), 53–94.

Hegghammer, T. (2013). Should I stay or should I go. Explaining variation in western jihadists' choice between domestic and foreign fighting. *The American Political Science Review*, *107*(01), 1–15. doi:10.1017/S0003055412000615

Heickerö, R. (2007). Terrorism online and the change of modus operandi. *Swedish Defence Research Agency, FOI*. Retrieved from http://www.unidir.ch/files/conferences/pdfs/information-warfare-and-cyber-terrorism-en-1-69.pdf

Heider, F. (1958). *The psychology of interpersonal relations*. New York, NY: Wiley. doi:10.1037/10628-000

Helfstein, S. (2012). *Edges of radicalization: Ideas, individuals and networks in violent extremism*. Retrieved from https://www.hsdl.org/?view&did=700228

Helsloot, I., & Ruitenberg, A. (2004). Citizen response to disasters: A survey of literature and some practical implications. *Journal of Contingencies and Crisis Management*, *12*(3), 98–111. doi:10.1111/j.0966-0879.2004.00440.x

Herley, C. (2012, June). *Why do Nigerian scammers say they are from Nigeria?* Paper presented at Workshop on the Economics of Information Security (WEIS), Berlin, Germany.

Herzog, S. (2011). Revisiting the Estonian cyber attacks: Digital threats and multinational responses. *Journal of Strategic Security*, *4*(2), 49–60. doi:10.5038/1944-0472.4.2.3

Hewstone, M., Jaspars, J., & Lalljee, M. (1982). Social representations, social attribution and social identity: The intergroup images of 'public' and 'comprehensive' schoolboys. *European Journal of Social Psychology*, *12*(3), 241–269. doi:10.1002/ejsp.2420120302

Heywood, E. (2015). Comparing Russian, French and UK television news. *Russian Journal of Communication*, *7*(1), 40–52. doi:10.1080/19409419.2015.1008940

Higgins, K. J. (2014a, August 6). TSA checkpoint systems found exposed on the net. *Dark Reading*. Retrieved from http://www.darkreading.com/vulnerabilities---threats/advanced-threats/tsa-checkpoint-systems-found-exposed-on-the-net/d/d-id/1297843

Higgins, K. J. (2014b, December 11). Hiring hackers to secure the Internet of Things. *Dark Reading*. Retrieved from http://www.darkreading.com/vulnerabilities---threats/hiring-hackers-to-secure-the-internet-of-things/d/d-id/1318107

Higham, S., & Nakashima, E. (2015, July 16). Why the Islamic State leaves tech companies torn between free speech and security. *The Washington Post*. Retrieved from https://www.washingtonpost.com/world/national-security/islamic-states-embrace-of-social-media-puts-tech-companies-in-a-bind/2015/07/15/0e5624c4-169c-11e5-89f3-61410da94eb1_story.html?kmap=1

Hill, C. (2013, December 20). Email 'from Target' to customers is a phishing scam. *Market Watch*. Retrieved from http://www.marketwatch.com/story/scammers-pounce-on-target-fiasco-2013-12-20

Himmelfarb, S., & Eagly, A. H. (1974). *Readings in attitude change*. New York, NY: Wiley.

Hingham, S., & Nakashima, E. (2015, July 16). Why the Islamic State leaves tech companies torn between free speech and security. *The Washington Post*. Retrieved from https://www.washingtonpost.com/world/national-security/islamic-states-embrace-of-social-media-puts-tech-companies-in-a-bind/2015/07/15/0e5624c4-169c-11e5-89f3-61410da94eb1_story.html

Hitler, A. (1925). *Mein Kampf* (Vol. 1). Munich.

Hobfoll, S., Watson, P., Bell, C., Bryant, R., Brymer, M., Friedman, M., & Ursano, R. J. et al. (2007). Five essential elements of immediate and mid-term mass trauma intervention: Empirical evidence. *Psychiatry*, *70*(4), 283–315. doi:10.1521/psyc.2007.70.4.283 PMID:18181708

Hoffman, B. (2006). Inside terrorism (Revised and Expanded Ed.). New York, NY: Columbia University Press.

Hoffman, C. (2013). Hacker hat colors explained: Black hats, white hats and gray hats. *How-To Geek*. Retrieved from http://www.howtogeek.com/157460/

Hoffman, B. (2006). *Inside terrorism* (rev.ed). New York, NY: Columbia University Press.

Hogan, M. (2014, June 11). *Anytown: A DEFRA funded project*. Retrieved from www.london.gov.uk/sites/default/files/Blog%2042%20AnytownPoster.pdf

Holbrook, D. (2010). Using the Qur'an to justify terrorist violence: Analysing selective application of the Qur'an in English-language militant Islamist discourse. *Perspectives on Terrorism*, *4*(3), 15–28.

Holbrook, R. G., & Taylor, M. (2013). "Terroristic content": Towards a grading scale. *Terrorism and Political Violence*, *25*(2), 202–223. doi:10.1080/09546553.2011.653893

Holland, K. (2014, July 12). Thousands march in cities across Ireland in support of Gaza. *Irish Times*. Retrieved from http://www.irishtimes.com/news/politics/thousands-march-in-cities-across-ireland-in-support-of-gaza-1.1864826

Holtmann, P. (2011). *No threat at first sight: Invisible terrorist environments on Facebook and YouTube*. Retrieved from http://www.univie.ac.at/jihadism/blog/wp-content/uploads/2011/03/Philipp-Holtmann-No-threat-at-first-sight-Invisible-terrorist-environments-on-Facebook-and-Youtube.pdf

Holtz, P., Kronberger, N., & Wagner, W. (2012). Analysing Internet forums: A practical guide. *Journal of Media Psychology, 24*(2), 55–66. doi:10.1027/1864-1105/a000062

Homeland Security Institute. (2009). *The Internet as a terrorist tool for recruitment and radicalization of youth (HSI Publication Number: RP08-03.02.17-01)*. Arlington, VA: Homeland Security Institute.

Horgan, J. (2008). Deradicalization or disengagement? A process in need of clarity and a counterterrorism initiative in need of evaluation. *Perspectives on Terrorism, 2*(4). Retrieved from http://www.terrorismanalysts.com/pt/index.php/pot/article/view/32/html

Horgan, J. (2008b, May 11). From profiles to pathways: The road to recruitment. *Peace and Security*. Retrieved from http://www.america.gov/st/peacesecenglish/2008/April/20080522173120SrenoD0.3425867.html

Horgan, J. (2012). Discussion point: The end of radicalization? *National Consortium for the Study of Terrorism and Responses to Terrorism (START)*. Retrieved from http://www.start.umd.edu/start/announcements/announcement.asp?id=416

Horgan, J., Shortland, N., Abbascianno, S., & Walsh, S. (in press). *Actions speak louder than words: A behavioral analysis of 183 individual convicted of Terrorist Offenses in the United States from 1989 – 2012*. Submitted to Journal of Forensic Sciences.

Horgan, J. (2005). *The psychology of terrorism*. New York, NY: Routledge. doi:10.4324/9780203496961

Horgan, J. (2008). From profiles to pathways and roots to routes: Perspectives from psychology on radicalization into terrorism. *The Annals of the American Academy of Political and Social Science, 618*(1), 80–94. doi:10.1177/0002716208317539

Horgan, J. (2008a). Deradicalization or disengagement? A process in need of clarity and a counterterrorism initiative in evaluation. *Perspectives on Terrorism, 2*(4), 3–8.

Horgan, J. (2009). *Walking away from terrorism: Accounts of disengagement from radical and extremist movements*. London: Routledge.

Horgan, J. (2009b). Individual disengagement: A psychological analysis. In T. Bjørgo & J. Horgan (Eds.), *Leaving terrorism behind: Individual and collective disengagement* (pp. 17–30). Abingdon: Routledge.

Horgan, J., & Altier, M. B. (2012). The future of terrorist de-radicalisation programs. *Georgetown Journal of International Affairs, 13*(2), 83–90.

Horgan, J., & Braddock, K. (2010). Rehabilitating the terrorists? Challenges in assessing the effectiveness of de-radicalization programs. *Terrorism and Political Violence, 22*(2), 267–291. doi:10.1080/09546551003594748

Horgan, J., & Braddock, K. (2011). Evaluating the effectiveness of de-radicalisation programs: Towards a scientific approach to terrorism risk reduction. In S. Canna (Ed.), *Countering violent extremism: Scientific methods & strategies* (pp. 158–164). Washington, DC: NSI.

Horgan, J., & Taylor, M. (2007). A conceptual framework for addressing psychological process in the development of the terrorist. *Terrorism and Political Violence, 18*(4), 585–601.

Horgan, J., & Taylor, M. (2010). Disengagement, de-radicalisation and the arc of terrorism: Future directions for research. In R. Coolsaet (Ed.), *Jihadi terrorism and the radicalisation challenge: European and American experiences* (pp. 173–187). Farnham: Ashgate.

Horn, R. (2013, February 17). In southern Thailand, 16 dead and no peace in sight. *Time Online*. Retrieved from http://world.time.com/2013/02/17/in-southern-thailand-16-dead-and-no-peace-in-sight/

Hosenball, M., & Zakaria, T. (2011, May 13). Exclusive: Pornography found in bin Laden hideout: Officials. *Reuters.* Retrieved from http://www.reuters.com/article/2011/05/13/us-binladen-porn-idUSTRE74C4RK20110513

House of Commons Home Affairs Committee. (2012). *Roots of Violent Radicalization* (19th Report Session 2010-12, Vol. 1). London: The Stationery Office Limited.

Hovland, C., Janis, I., & Kelley, H. (1953). *Communication and persuasion.* New Haven, CT: Yale University Press.

Hoyle, A. (2014). Breaking the Backlash – A take on the social psychology of discrimination. *ZME Science.* Retrieved from http://www.zmescience.com/other/feature-post/breaking-the-backlash/

Hoyle, C., Bradford, A., & Frenett, R. (2015). *Becoming Mulan? Female western migrants to ISIS.* London: Institute for Strategic Dialogue.

Hsinchun, C., Denning, D., Roberts, N. N., Larson, C. A., Yu, X., & Huang, C. (2011). The Dark Web Forum Portal: From multi-lingual to video. In *Proceedings on the 2011 IEEE International Conference on Intelligence and Security Informatics.* Beijing: IEEE.

Hsiung, R. (2000). The best of both worlds: An online mutual-aid group hosted by a mental health professional. *Cyber-Psychology and Behaviour, 3*(6), 935–950. doi:10.1089/109493100452200

Hua, J., & Bapna, S. (2012). How can we deter cyber terrorism? *International Security Journal: A Global Perspective, 21*, 102-114.

Huey, L., & Kalyal, H. (2015). Questions about Dawlah. DM me, plz. The sock puppet problem in online terrorism research. Sociology Publications.

Hu, F., Wang, P., & Li, L. (2014). Psychometric structure of the Chinese Multiethnic Adolescent Cultural Identity Questionnaire. *Psychological Assessment, 26*(4), 1356–1368. doi:10.1037/a0037690

Hull, C. L. (1943). *Principles of behavior.* Oxford, England: Appleton-Century.

Human Rights Watch. (2002). *"WE ARE NOT THE ENEMY". Hate crimes against Arabs, Muslims, and those perceived to be Arab or Muslim after September 111.* Retrieved from https://www.hrw.org/reports/2002/usahate/index.htm#TopOfPage

Human Rights Watch. (2008, September 8). *Afghanistan: Civilian deaths from airstrikes.* Retrieved from https://www.hrw.org/news/2008/09/08/afghanistan-civilian-deaths-airstrikes

Hussain, G., & Saltman, E. (2014). *Jihad trending: Online extremism and how to counter it.* London: Quilliam Foundation.

Hussain, G., & Saltman, E. M. (2014). *Jihad trending: a comprehensive analysis of online extremism and how to counter it.* Quilliam Foundation.

Hutson, R., Long, T., & Page, M. (2009). Pathways to violent radicalisation in the Middle East: A model for future studies of transnational jihad. *The RUSI Journal, 154*(2), 18–26. doi:10.1080/03071840902965570

Iasiello, E. (2013). Cyber attack: A dull tool to shape foreign policy. In K. Podins, J. Stinissen, & M. Maybaum (Eds.), *5th international conference on cyber conflict.* Estonia, Tallinn: NATO CCD COE Publication.

Idaho National Laboratory. (2006). *Critical infrastructure interdependency modelling: A survey of U.S. and international research (INL/EXT-06-11464).* Washington, DC: DOE Idaho Operations Office.

Indonesian anti-terror squad killings prompt revenge attacks. (2013, February 8). *ABC News.* Retrieved from http://www.abc.net.au/news/2013-02-08/indonesian-anti-terror-squad-killings-prompt/4507926

Indonesian ISIS fighter sends threat message back home. (2015, January 6). *Blazingcatfur*. Retrieved from http://www.blazingcatfur.ca/2015/01/06/indonesian-isis-fighter-sends-threat-message-back-home/

Inilah Situs Online Radikal dan Pendukung ISIS. (2014, August 5). *Satu Islam*. Retrieved from http://www.satuislam.org/nasional/inilah-situs-online-radikal-dan-pendukung-isis/

Institute for Strategic Dialogue (ISD). (2012). *Tackling extremism: De-radicalisation and disengagement*. Retrieved from http://www.strategicdialogue.org/programmes/counter-extremism/

Institute for Strategic Dialogue. (2010). *De-radicalisation*. PPN Working Paper. London: Institute for Strategic Dialogue.

Institute for Strategic Dialogue. (2014). *Government engagement and communication strategies with communities*. London: Author.

Institute for Strategic Dialogue. (2015). Retrieved from http://www.strategicdialogue.org/ISD_Brochure.pdf

Intelligence and Security Committee Report. (2009). *Could 7/7 have been prevented? Review of the intelligence on the London terrorist attacks on 7 July 2005*. London: Controller of Her Majesty's Stationery Office.

Intelligence and Security Committee Report. (2014). *Report on the intelligence relating to the murder of Fusilier Lee Rigby*. London: Controller of Her Majesty's Stationery Office.

International Crisis Group (ICG). (2007). *Deradicalisation' and Indonesian prisons* (Asia Report 142). Retrieved from http://www.crisisgroup.org/home/index.cfm?id1/42959andl1/41

International Crisis Group. (2011). *Indonesia jihadism: Small groups, big plans (Asia report 204)*. Jakarta, Brussels: International Crisis Group.

International Crisis Group. (2012). *Indonesia: From vigilantism to terrorism in Cirebon (Asia briefing 132)*. Jakarta, Brussels: International Crisis Group.

Internet World Statistics. (2014). *World Internet population and user statistics*. Retrieved from http://www.internetworldstats.com/stats.htm

Internet World Stats. (2014). *Internet usage statistics: The internet big picture*. Retrieved from http://www.internetworldstats.com/stats.htm

Islamic Radicalism Thriving in Indonesia's Campuses. (2011, April 26). *Yahoo News*. Retrieved from http://sg.news.yahoo.com/islamic-radicalism-thriving-indonesias-campuses-104002000.html

Isometsä, E. T. (2001). Psychological autopsy studies – A review. *European Psychiatry*, *16*(7), 379–385. doi:10.1016/S0924-9338(01)00594-6 PMID:11728849

Israel Defense Forces. (2012, November 15). How does the IDF minimize harm to Palestinian civilians? *IDF Blog*. Retrieved from https://www.idfblog.com/blog/2012/11/15/how-does-the-idf-minimize-harm-to-palestinian-civilians/

Jackson, B. A. (2006). Groups, networks, or movements: A command-and-control-driven approach to classifying terrorist organizations and its application to Al Qaeda. *Studies in Conflict and Terrorism*, *29*(3), 241–262. doi:10.1080/10576100600564042

Jackson, B. A., & Loidolt, B. (2013). Considering al-Qa'ida's innovation doctrine: From strategic texts to 'innovation in practice'. *Terrorism and Political Violence*, *25*(2), 284–310. doi:10.1080/09546553.2012.662557

H. Jahankhani, A. Carlile, B. Akhgar, A. Taal, A. Hessami, & A. Hosseinian-Far (Eds.). (2015). Global security, safety and sustainability: Tomorrow's challenges of cyber security. In *Proceedings of the 10th International Conference on Global Security, Safety and Sustainability (ICGS3 2015)*. London: Springer. doi:10.1007/978-3-319-23276-8

Jakarta slow to tackle rise of ISIS. (2015, May 29). *The Straits Times*, p. A10.

James, W. (1890). *The principles of psychology* (Vol. I). New York, NY, US: Henry Holt and Co. doi:10.1037/11059-000

Janbek, D., & Williams, V. (2014). The role of the internet post-9/11 in terrorism and counterterrorism. *The Brown Journal of World Affairs, 20*(2), 297–308.

Jandora, J. W. (2006). Osama bin Laden's global jihad: Myth and movement. *Military Review, 86*(6), 41–50.

Jansen, R., Tschorsch, F., Johnson, A., & Scheuermann, B. (2014). *The sniper attack: Anonymously deanonymizing and disabling the Tor Network*. Arlington, VA: Office of Naval Research.

Jarvis, L., MacDonald, S., & Whiting, A. (2015). Constructing cyberterrorism as a security threat: A study of international news media coverage. *Perspectives on Terrorism, 9*(1), 60–75.

Jarvis, L., Nouri, L., & Whiting, A. (2014). Understanding, locating and constructing cyberterrorism. In T. Chen, L. Jarvis, & S. Macdonald (Eds.), *Cyberterrorism: Understanding, assessment and response* (pp. 25–41). New York, NY: Springer.

Javadi, T. (2015, May 27). Is criminalising hate speech the way to go in Indonesia? *The Malaysian Insider*. Retrieved from http://www.themalaysianinsider.com/sideviews/article/is-criminalising-hate-speech-the-way-to-go-in-indonesia-tiola-javadi

Javers, E. (2015). These cyberhackers may not be backed by ISIS. *CNBC News*. Retrieved from www.cnbc.com/2015/07/14/these-cyberhackers-not-backed-by-isis.html

Jenkins, B. M. (2015, March 20). *The allure of ISIS for young recruits*. RAND Commentary. Retrieved from http://www.rand.org/blog/2015/03/the-allure-of-isis-for-young-recruits.html

Jenkins, B. M. (2006). *Unconquerable nation: Knowing our enemy, strengthening ourselves*. Santa Monica, CA: RAND Corporation.

Jenkins, B. M. (2011). *Stray dogs and virtual armies: Radicalization and recruitment to jihadist terrorism in the United States since 9/11*. Santa Monica, CA: RAND Corporation.

Johansson, F., & Svenson, P. (2013). Constructing and analyzing uncertain social networks from unstructured textual data. In T. Özyer, Z. Erdem, J. Rokne, & S. Khoury (Eds.), *Mining social networks and security informatics* (pp. 41–61). Dordrecht: Springer Science. doi:10.1007/978-94-007-6359-3_3

John, O. P., & Srivastava, S. (1999). The Big Five trait taxonomy: History, measurement and theoretical perspectives. In L. A. Pervin & O. P. John (Eds.), *Handbook of personality: Theory and Research* (pp. 102–138). New York, NY: The Guildford Press.

Johnson, T. (2010). Threat of homegrown Islamist terrorism. *Council of Foreign Affairs*. Retrieved from http://www.cfr.org/terrorism/threat-homegrown-islamist-terrorism/p11509

Johnson, C. (2004). *The sorrows of empire: Militarism, secrecy, and the end of republic*. New York, NY: Metropolitan Books.

Joinson, A. N. (2003). *Understanding the psychology of Internet behaviour: Virtual worlds, real lives*. New York, NY: Palgrave Macmillan.

Joinson, A. N. (2007). Disinhibition and the internet. In J. Gackenbach (Ed.), *Psychology and the internet: Intrapersonal, interpersonal, and transpersonal implications* (pp. 76–92). New York, NY: Academic Press. doi:10.1016/B978-012369425-6/50023-0

Joly, M. (1864). *Dialogue in hell between Machiavelli and Montesquieu*. Brussels: A. Mertens and Son.

Jonas, J., & Harper, J. (2006, December 11). *Effective counterterrorism and the limited role of predictive data mining* (Policy Analysis No. 584). Washington, DC: CATO Institute.

Jones, S. (2014, March 28). Jihad by social media. *Financial Times Magazine*. Retrieved from http://www.ft.com/cms/s/2/907fd41c-b53c-11e3-af92-00144bdc0.html

Jones, C. (2006). Al-Qaeda's innovative improvisers: Learning in a diffuse transnational network. *Cambridge Review of International Affairs, 19*(4), 555–569. doi:10.1080/09557570601003205

Jones, J. W. (2008). *Blood that cries out from the earth: The psychology of religious terrorism*. Oxford, UK: Oxford University Press. doi:10.1093/acprof:oso/9780195335972.001.0001

Jordan, M., & Audi, T. (2015, May 6). A test case for 'Deradicalization'. *The Wall Street Journal*. Retrieved from http://www.wsj.com/articles/a-test-case-for-deradicalization-1430944585

Jordan, J., Manas, F. M., & Horsburgh, N. (2008). Strengths and weakness of grassroot jihadist network: The Madrid bombings. *Studies in Conflict and Terrorism, 31*(1), 17–39. doi:10.1080/10576100701767148

Kang, S. (2007). Disembodiment in online social interaction: Impact of online chat on social support and psychosocial well-being. *Cyberpsychology & Behavior, 10*(3), 475–477. doi:10.1089/cpb.2006.9929 PMID:17594274

Kapardis, A., & Krambia-Kapardis, M. (2004). Enhancing fraud prevention and detection by profiling fraud offenders. *Criminal Behaviour and Mental Health, 14*(3), 189–201. doi:10.1002/cbm.586

Karlgren, J. (2006). New text - New conversations in the media landscape. *ERCIM News*. Retrieved from http://www.ercim.eu/publication/Ercim_News/enw66/karlgren_2.html

Karmini, N. (2011, June 30). Teaching jihad in Indonesian prisons. *The Jakarta Globe*. Retrieved from http://www.thejakartaglobe.com/archive/teaching-jihad-in-indonesian-prisons/

Karmini, N. (2013, June 21) Facebook broke Indonesia terror case. *Associated Press*. Retrieved from http://bigstory.ap.org/article/ap-exclusive-facebook-broke-indonesia-terror-case

Katz, D. (1960). The functional approach to the study of attitudes. *Public Opinion Quarterly, 24*(2, Special Issue: Attitude Change), 163–204. doi:10.1086/266945

Kebbell, M. R., & Porter, L. (2011). An intelligence assessment framework for identifying individuals at risk of committing acts of violent extremism against the West. *Security Journal, 25*(3), 212–228. doi:10.1057/sj.2011.19

Keene, S. D. (2011). Terrorism and the Internet: A double-edged sword. *Journal of Money Laundering Control, 14*(4), 359–370. doi:10.1108/13685201111173839

Kelion, L. (2015, January 13). Facebook restricts violent video clips and photos. *BBC News*. Retrieved from http://www.bbc.com/news/technology-30793702

Keller, J. (2013). How Boston Police won the Twitter wars during the Marathon Bomber hunt. *Bloomberg Business*. Retrieved from http://www.bloomberg.com/bw/articles/2013-04-26/how-boston-police-won-the-twitter-wars-during-bomber-hunt

Keller, J., & Pfattheicher, S. (2013). The compassion-hostility paradox: The interplay of vigilant, prevention-focussed self-regulation, compassion, and hostility. *Personality and Social Psychology Bulletin, 39*(11), 1518–1529. doi:10.1177/0146167213499024

Kelly, S. (2012). Cyber attacks target gas pipeline companies. *CNN*. Retrieved from http://security.blogs.cnn.com/2012/05/08/cyber-attack-targets-gas-pipeline-companies/

Kennedy, A. (2005). An uneasy alliance: Two counsellors discuss technology's evolving impact on the mental health profession. *Counseling Today, 1*, 14–16.

Kenney, M. (2010). Beyond the Internet: Mētis, techne, and the limitations of online artifacts for Islamist terrorists. *Terrorism and Political Violence, 22*(2), 177–197. doi:10.1080/09546550903554760

Kerr, P. K., Rollins, J., & Theohary, C. A. (2010). The Stuxnet computer worm: Harbinger of an emerging warfare capability (R41524). *Congressional Research Service*. Retrieved from https://www.fas.org/sgp/crs/natsec/R41524.pdf

Khan, A. (2013, April 30). The magazine that 'inspired' the Boston bombers. *PBS: Frontline*. Retrieved from http://www.pbs.org/wgbh/pages/frontline/iraq-war-on-terror/topsecretamerica/the-magazine-that-inspired-the-boston-bombers/

Khosrokhavar, F. (2004). *L'Islam dans les Prisons: Voix et Regards*. Paris: Balland.

Kiesler, C. A., Collins, B. E., & Miller, N. (1969). *Attitude change*. New York, NY: Wiley.

Kim, J., LaRose, R., & Peng, W. (2009). Loneliness as the cause and the effect of problematic Internet use: The relationship between Internet use and psychological well-being. *Cyberpsychology & Behavior, 12*(4), 451–455. doi:10.1089/cpb.2008.0327 PMID:19514821

Kimonis, E. R., Frick, P. J., Skeem, J. L., Marsee, M. A., Cruise, K., Munoz, L. C., & Morris, A. S. et al. (2008). Assessing callous-unemotional traits in adolescent offenders: Validation of the inventory of callous-unemotional traits. *International Journal of Law and Psychiatry, 31*(3), 241–252. doi:10.1016/j.ijlp.2008.04.002

King, S. A., & Moreggi, D. (2007). Internet mutual-aid and support groups: The pros and cons of text-based mutual aid. In J. Gackenbach (Ed.), *Psychology and the Internet: Intrapersonal, interpersonal, and transpersonal implications* (pp. 221–243). London: Elsevier. doi:10.1016/B978-012369425-6/50028-X

Kiviat, B., Park, A., & Sayre, C. (2007). Inside a mass murderer's mind. *Time*. Retrieved from http://www.time.com/time/magazine/article/0,9171.1612694,oo.html

Kiwis okay with social media monitoring for counter-terrorism, but not business. (2015, July 2). *Fairfax NZ News* Retrieved from http://www.stuff.co.nz/technology/social-networking/69883819/kiwis-okay-with-social-media-monitoring-for-counterterrorism-but-not-business

Klausen, J. (2015). Tweeting the jihad: Social media networks of western foreign fighters in Syria and Iraq. *Studies in Conflict and Terrorism, 38*(1), 1–22. doi:10.1080/1057610X.2014.974948

Knapp, J. R., Smith, B. R., & Sprinkle, T. A. (2014). Clarifying the relational ties of organizational belonging: Understanding the roles of perceived insider status, psychological ownership, and organizational identification. *Journal of Leadership & Organizational Studies, 21*(3), 273–285. doi:10.1177/1548051814529826

Kobie, N. (2015, May 13). Why smart cities need to get wise to security – and fast. *The Guardian*. Retrieved from http://www.theguardian.com/technology/2015/may/13/smart-cities-internet-things-security-cesar-cerrudo-ioactive-labs

Koehler, D. (2014). The radical online: Individual radicalisation processes and the role of the Internet. *Journal of Deradicalisation*, Winter 2014/15, 116-134.

Kohlmann, E., & Alkhouri, L. (2014, September29). Profiles of Foreign Fighters in Syria and Iraq. *CTC Sentinel, 7*(9), 1–4.

Koku, E., Nazer, N., & Wellman, B. (2001). Netting scholars: Online and offline. *The American Behavioral Scientist, 44*(10), 1752–1774. doi:10.1177/00027640121958023

Kosinski, M., Stillwell, D., & Graepel, T. (2013). Private traits and attributes are predictable from digital records of human behaviour. *Proceedings of the National Academy of Sciences of the United States of America, 110*(15), 5802–5805. doi:10.1073/pnas.1218772110 PMID:23479631

Kostadinov, D. (2014, March 13). The future is now: Car hacking. *InfoSec Institute*. Retrieved from http://resources.infosecinstitute.com/future-now-car-hacking/

Krahnstoever, N. (2011, August 15). *Automated detection and prevention of disorderly and criminal activities.* Niskayuna, NY: GE Global Research.

Krebs, B. (2009, October 8). Phishing scam spooked FBI director off e-banking. *The Washington Post*. Retrieved from http://voices.washingtonpost.com/securityfix/2009/10/fbi_director_on_internet_banki.html

Krebs, V. E. (2002, April1). Uncloaking terrorist networks. *First Monday, 7*(4). doi:10.5210/fm.v7i4.941

Kruglanski, A. W. (2014, October 28). Psychology not theology: Overcoming ISIS' secret appeal. *E-International Relations*. Retrieved from http://www.e-ir.info/2014/10/28/psychology-not-theology-overcoming-isis-secret-appeal/

Kruglanski, A. W., Crenshaw, M., Post, J. M., & Victoroff, J. (2008). What should this fight be called? Metaphors of counterterrorism and their implications. *Psychological Science in the Public Interest, 8*(3), 97–133. doi:10.1111/j.1539-6053.2008.00035.x PMID:26161891

Kruglanski, A. W., Gelfand, M. J., Bélanger, J. J., Sheveland, A., Hetiarachchi, M., & Gunaratna, R. (2014). The psychology of radicalization and deradicalisation: How significance quest impacts violent extremism. *Political Psychology, 35*(S1), 69–93. doi:10.1111/pops.12163

Kruglanski, A. W., Pierro, A., Mannetti, L., & de Grada, E. (2006). Groups as epistemic providers: Need for closure and the unfolding of group-centrism. *Psychological Review, 113*(1), 84–100. doi:10.1037/0033-295X.113.1.84

Kuehl, D. (2009). From cyberspace to cyberpower: Defining the problem. In F. Kramer, S. Starr, & L. Wentz (Eds.), *Cyberpower and National Security* (pp. 24–42). Washington, DC: National Defense University Press.

Kumar, A. (2014, August 14). 'Alarming gaps' as 78% of Malaysian critical infrastructure providers breached, Unisys says. *Computer World*. Retrieved from http://computerworld.com.sg/print-article/64471/

Kunda, Z. (1990). The case for motivated reasoning. *Psychological Bulletin, 108*(3), 480–498. doi:10.1037/0033-2909.108.3.480 PMID:2270237

Kuss, D. J., & Griffiths, M. D. (2012). Online gaming addiction in adolescence: A literature review of empirical research. *Journal of Behavioral Addictions, 1*(1), 3–22. doi:10.1556/JBA.1.2012.1.1 PMID:26166826

Kusuma, M. T. (2010, October 12). Islam is a mosaic, not monolith. *The Jakarta Post*. Retrieved from http://www.thejakartapost.com/news/2010/10/12/islam-a-mosaic-not-monolith.html

Kyaw, S. W. (2012, July 18). *Western Myanmar unrest: Partisan portrayals risk extremist implications.* RSIS Commentaries (131/2012). Singapore: S. Rajaratnam School of International Studies.

Labaka, L., Hernantes, J., Rich, E., & Sarriegi, J. (2013). Resilience building policies and their influence in crisis prevention, absorption and recovery. *Homeland Security and Emergency Management, 10*(1), 280–317.

Lachow, I. (2011). The Stuxnet enigma: Implications for the future of cybersecurity. *Georgetown Journal of International Affairs,* 118-126.

Lachow, I. (2009). Cyberterrorism: Menace or myth? In F. D. Kramer, S. H. Starr, & L. K. Wentz (Eds.), *Cyberpower and national security* (pp. 123–139). Washington, DC: NDU Press.

Lachow, I., & Richardson, C. (2007). Terrorist use of the Internet: The real story. *Joint Force Quarterly, 45,* 100–103.

Landau, E. (2009, May 26). Insights on why people 'snap' and kill. *CNN.* Retrieved from http://edition.cnn.com/2009/HEALTH/05/26/snap.moments/index.html?iref=newssearch

Lange, A., van de Ven, J., Schrieken, B., & Emmelkamp, P. (2001). Interapy. Treatment of posttraumatic stress through the Internet: A controlled trial. *Journal of Behavior Therapy and Experimental Psychiatry, 32*(2), 73–90. doi:10.1016/S0005-7916(01)00023-4 PMID:11764063

Lark, J., Nelson, R., & Chappelle, L. (2003). *Michigan Public Service Commission report on August 14th blackout.* Michigan, MI: Michigan Public Service Commission.

LaRose, R. (2010). The problem of media habits. *Communication Theory, 20*(2), 194–222. doi:10.1111/j.1468-2885.2010.01360.x

Larsson, S., & Svensson, M. (2010). Compliance or obscurity? Online anonymity as a consequence of fighting unauthorised file-sharing. *Policy and Internet, 2*(4), 77–105. doi:10.2202/1944-2866.1044

Larsson, S., Svensson, M., de Kaminski, M., Rönkkö, K., & Olsson, J. A. (2012). Laws, norms, piracy and online anonymity: Practices of de-identification in the global file sharing community. *Journal of Research in Interactive Marketing, 6*(4), 260–280. doi:10.1108/17505931211282391

Last, M., Markov, A., & Kandel, A. (2006). Multi-lingual detection of terrorist content on the web. *Lecture Notes in Computer Science, 3917,* 16–30. doi:10.1007/11734628_3

Lavigne, G. L., Vallerand, R. J., & Crevier-Braud, L. (2011). The fundamental need to belong: On the distinction between growth and deficit-reduction orientations. *Personality and Social Psychology Bulletin, 37*(9), 1185–1201. doi:10.1177/0146167211405995 PMID:21540365

Lavine, H. (2001). The electoral consequences of ambivalence toward presidential candidates. *American Journal of Political Science, 45*(4), 915–929. doi:10.2307/2669332

Le Bon, G. (1896). *The crowd: A study of the popular mind.* New York, NY: Macmillan & Co.

Lee, A. (2013, April 13). Shodan, the frightening search tool that uncovers security holes in your home, business and more. *Techno Buffalo.* Retrieved from http://www.technobuffalo.com/2013/04/13/shodan-search-sniffs-out-frightening-and-common-security-holes/

Lee, E. A. (2008, January 23). Cyber physical systems: Design challenges. *UC Berkeley Electrical Engineering and Computer Sciences Technical Memorandum Series, UCB/EECS-2008-8.* Retrieved from www.eecs.berkeley.edu/Pubs/TechRpts/2008/EECS-2008-8.pdf

Lee, L. (2011, August 18). 'Strong Case' against Umar Patek. *The Straits Times.*

Lee, M. (2008). Blogs feed information frenzy on Mumbai blasts. *Globe and Mail.* Retrieved from http://www.theglobeandmail.com/news/technology/article725225.ece

Lee, E., & Leets, L. (2002). Persuasive story telling by hate groups on line. *The American Behavioral Scientist, 45,* 927–957. doi:10.1177/0002764202045006003

Leetaru, K. H. (2012). Fulltext geocoding versus spatial metadata for large text archives: Towards a geographically enriched wikipedia. *D-Lib Magazine, 18*(9/10). doi:10.1045/september2012-leetaru

Leggio, J. (2008). Mumbai attack coverage demonstrates (good and bad) maturation point of social media. *ZDNet.* Retrieved from http://www.zdnet.com/blog/feeds/mumbai-attack-coverage-demonstrates-good-and-bad-maturation-point-of-social-media/339

Legion of fighters battles for ISIS. (2015, May 20). *Al-Arabiya.* Retrieved from http://english.alarabiya.net/en/perspective/features/2015/05/20/Legion-of-foreign-fighters-battles-for-ISIS.html

Leiner, B. M., Cerf, V. G., Clark, D. D., Kahn, R. E., Kleinrock, L., Lynch, D. C., & Wolff, S. et al. (2009). A brief history of the Internet. *Computer Communication Review, 39*(5), 22–31. doi:10.1145/1629607.1629613

Lemieux, A. F., Brachman, J. M., Levitt, J., & Wood, J. (2014). Inspire Magazine: A Critical Analysis of its Significance and Potential Impact Through the Lens of the Information, Motivation, and Behavioral Skills Model. *Terrorism and Political Violence, 26*(2), 354–371. doi:10.1080/09546553.2013.828604

Lenhart, G. (1996, March 1). *Chapter 1: Introduction - Jung and the four psychological functions.* Retrieved from http://sulcus.berkeley.edu/flm/SH/MDL/GAL/GalDisChapts/galdis.chapter1.html

Lennings, C. J., Amon, K. L., Brummert, H., & Lennings, N. J. (2010). Grooming for Terror: The Internet and Young People. *Psychiatry, Psychology and Law, 17*(3), 424–437. doi:10.1080/13218710903566979

Lennon, M. (2013, July 1). Cyber attacks targeted key components of natural gas pipeline systems. *Security Week.* Retrieved from http://www.securityweek.com/cyber-attacks-targeted-key-components-natural-gas-pipeline-systems

Leong, D. (2015). *Why ISIS appeals to Muslim women in Western countries: Need for counter message. RSIS Commentaries (136/2015).* Singapore: S. Rajaratnam School of International Studies.

Leonhard, R. R. (1991). *The art of maneuver: Maneuver-warfare theory and airland battle.* Novato, CA: Presidio Press.

Levi, M., & Stoker, L. (2000). Political trust and trustworthiness. *Annual Review of Political Science, 3*(1), 475–507. doi:10.1146/annurev.polisci.3.1.475

Levine, M., Prosser, A., Evans, D., & Reicher, S. (2005). Identity and emergency intervention: How social group membership and inclusiveness of group boundaries shape helping behavior. *Personality and Social Psychology Bulletin, 31*(4), 443–453. doi:10.1177/0146167204271651 PMID:15743980

Levitt, S. D., & Venkatesh, S. A. (2007). *An empirical analysis of street-level prostitution* (working paper). Chicago, IL: University of Chicago.

Lewis, J. A. (2005). The Internet and terrorism. *Proceedings of the Annual Meeting (American Association of University Teachers of Insurance), 99*, 112–115.

Lia, B. (2008). Al-Qaida's appeal: Understanding its unique selling points. *Perspectives on Terrorism, 2*(8). Retrieved from http://www.terrorismanalysts.com/pt/index.php/pot/issue/view/14

Lia, B. (May 2008). Al-Qaida's appeal: Understanding its unique selling points. *Perspectives on Terrorism, 2*(8).

Libicki, M. C., Ablon, L., & Webb, T. (2015). *The defender's dilemma: Charting a course toward cybersecurity.* Santa Monica, CA: RAND Corporation.

Lilienfeld, S. O., Wood, J. M., & Garb, H. N. (2000). The scientific status of projective techniques. *Psychological Science in the Public Interest, 1*, 27–66.

Lim, Y. L. (2015, September 30). Two Singaporeans detained for making plans to travel to Syria to join ISIS. *The Straits Times*. Retrieved from http://www.straitstimes.com/singapore/courts-crime/two-singaporeans-detained-for-making-plans-to-travel-to-syria-to-join-isis

Liow, C. J., & Pathan, D. (2010). *Confronting ghosts: Thailand's shapeless southern insurgency (Lowy Institute Paper 30)*. New South Wales, Australia: Lowy Institute for International Policy.

Lippmann, W. (1922). *Public Opinion*. New York, NY: Harcourt, Brace and Co.

Lipsey, M. W., Landenberger, N. A., & Wilson, S. J. (2007). Effects of cognitive-behavioral programs for criminal offenders. *Campbell Systematic Reviews*, *6*, 1–30.

Littlejohn, S. W., & Foss, K. A. (2008). *Theories of human communication* (9th ed.). Belmont, CA: Thomson Wadworth.

Litvak, M. (2010). "Martyrdom is life": Jihad and martyrdom in the ideology of Hamas. *Studies in Conflict and Terrorism*, *33*(8), 716–734. doi:10.1080/1057610X.2010.494170

Loewengart, V. (2012). *Proactive defense against cybercriminals: Striking back*. Retrieved from http://www.academia.edu/2215078/Proactive_Defense_against_Cyber-Criminals_Striking_Back

Long, A. (2012). Profiling hackers. *SANS Institute*. Retrieved from http://www.sans.org/reading-room/whitepapers/hackers/profiling-hackers-33864

Long, M., Alison, A. J., & McManus, M. (2013). Child pornography and the likelihood of contact abuse: A comparison between contact child sexual offenders and non-contact offenders and the homologous victim selection of contact child sexual offenders. *Sexual Abuse*, *25*, 370–395. doi:10.1177/1079063212464398 PMID:23160257

Longstaff, P., Armstrong, N., Perrin, K., Parker, W., & Hidek, M. (2010). *Building resilient communities: A preliminary framework for assessment*. Monterey, CA: Naval Postgraduate School, Center for Homeland Defense and Security.

Lucas, R. E., & Donnellan, M. B. (2011). Personality development across the life span: Longitudinal analyses with a national sample from Germany. *Journal of Personality and Social Psychology*, *101*(4), 847–861. doi:10.1037/a0024298

Luce, K. H., Winzelberg, A. J., Zabinski, M. F., & Osborne, M. I. (2003). Internet-delivered psychological interventions for body image dissatisfaction and disordered eating. *Psychotherapy (Chicago, Ill.)*, *40*(1-2), 148–154. doi:10.1037/0033-3204.40.1-2.148

MacAskill, E. (2015, January 14). Briton lead suspect after US Central Command's Twitter account is hacked. *The Guardian*. Retrieved from http://www.theguardian.com/us-news/2015/jan/14/briton-suspect-us-central-command-twitter-hack-junaid-hussain-tony-blair

MacMillan, K., & Edwards, D. (1999). Who killed the princess? Description and blame in the British press. *Discourse Studies*, *1*(2), 151–174. doi:10.1177/1461445699001002002

Madara, E. J. (1999). From church basements to world wide web sites: The growth of mutual-aid support groups online. *International Journal of Self Help & Self Care*, *1*(1), 37–48. doi:10.2190/8BL4-VD3X-KV8N-T78F

Madara, E. J., Kalafat, J., & Miller, B. N. (1988). The computerised mutual-aid clearinghouse: Using "high tech" to promote "high touch" support networks. *Computers in Human Services*, *3*(3/4), 39–53. doi:10.1300/J407v03n03_04

Madhani, A. (2010). Cleric al-Awlaki dubbed 'bin Laden of the Internet'. *USA Today*. Retrieved from http://www.usatoday.com/news/nation/2010-08-25-A_Awlaki25_CV_N.htm

Madrigal, A. C. (2013, April 19) #BostonBombing: The anatomy of a misinformation disaster. *The Atlantic*. Retrieved from http://www.theatlantic.com/technology/archive/2013/04/-bostonbombing-theanatomy-of-a-misinformation-disaster/275155/

Mael, F. A., & Ashforth, B. E. (2001). Identification in work, war, sports, and religion: Contrasting the benefits and risks. *Journal for the Theory of Social Behaviour*, *31*(2), 197–222. doi:10.1111/1468-5914.00154

Maghan, J., & Kelly, R. J. (1989). Terrorism and corrections: The incarcerated radical. In J. R. Buckwalter (Ed.), *International terrorism: The decade ahead* (pp. 29–53). Chicago, IL: University of Illinois Press, Office of Criminal Justice.

Maher, S. (2014, November 6). From Portsmouth to Kobane: the British Jihadis fighting for ISIS. *NewStatesman*. Retrieved from http://www.newstatesman.com/2014/10/portsmouth-kobane

Maher, S. (2007). Road to jihad. *Index on Censorship*, *36*(4), 144–147. doi:10.1080/03064220701740590

Makruf, J., & Pertiwi, M. (2010). Indonesia. In C. Ziemke-Dickens, & J. Droogan (Eds.), *Asian transnational security challenges: Emerging trends, regional visions* (pp. 137–149). Sydney, Australia: The Council for Asian Transnational Threat Research (CATR) & Centre for Policing, Intelligence and Counter Terrorism (PICT), Macquarie University.

Malaysia detains more than 10 terror suspects linked to Abu Umar Group. (2011, November 17). *The Straits Times*.

Malet, D. (2009). *Foreign fighters: Transnational identity in civil conflicts* (Doctoral dissertation). Retrieved from http://davidmalet.com/uploads/Why_Foreign_Fighters_Malet.pdf

Malet, D. (2013). *Foreign fighters: Transnational identity in civil conflicts*. New York, NY: Oxford University Press. doi:10.1093/acprof:oso/9780199939459.001.0001

Malik, K. (2015). The failure of multiculturalism: Community versus society in Europe. *Foreign Affairs*, *94*(2), 21–32.

Man Haron Monis. 'Damaged' and 'unstable'. (2014, December 16). *BBC News*. Retrieved from http://www.bbc.com/news/world-australia-30484419

Mandhai, S. (2014). Muslim leaders reject Baghdadi's caliphate. *Al-Jazeera*. Retrieved from http://www.aljazeera.com/news/middleeast/2014/07/muslim-leaders-reject-baghdadi-caliphate-20147744058773906.html

Mandiant. (2013). *APT1: Exposing one of China's cyber espionage units*. Alexandria, VA: Mandiant.

Mantel, B. (2009). Terrorism and the internet: Should web sites that promote terrorism be shut down? *CQ Researcher*, *3*(1), 285–310.

Maogoto, J. N. (2003). War on the enemy: Self-defence and state sponsored terrorism. *Melbourne Journal of International Law*, *4*, 406–438.

Marcella, A. J., & Greenfield, R. S. (2002). *Cyber forensics: A field manual for collecting, examining and preserving evidence for computer crimes*. Boca Raton, FL: CRC Press LLC. doi:10.1201/9781420000115

Marchive, V. (2013, June 4). France considers stepping up Internet monitoring to fight terrorism. *Vive la Tech*. Retrieved from http://www.zdnet.com/article/france-considers-stepping-up-internet-monitoring-to-fight-terrorism/

Marcus, J. (2006, February 28). US faces sceptical world over Iraq. *BBC News*. Retrieved from http://news.bbc.co.uk/2/hi/middle_east/4755770.stm

Marcus, B., Lee, K., & Ashton, M. C. (2007). Personality dimensions explaining relationships between integrity tests and counterproductive behavior: Big five, or one in addition? *Personnel Psychology*, *60*(1), 1–34. doi:10.1111/j.1744-6570.2007.00063.x

Marcus, B., & Schuler, H. (2004). Antecedents of counterproductive behavior at work: A general perspective. *The Journal of Applied Psychology*, *89*(4), 647–660. doi:10.1037/0021-9010.89.4.647

Markoff, J. (2011, March 9). Researchers show how a car's electronics can be taken over remotely. *The New York Times*. Retrieved from http://www.nytimes.com/2011/03/10/business/10hack.html?_r=0

Marten, K. (2007). Statebuilding and force: The proper role of foreign militaries. *Journal of Intervention and Statebuilding*, *1*(2), 231–247. doi:10.1080/17502970701302862

Martinez, J. (2005). *Spatial dynamics of human populations: Some basic models*. Retrieved from http://faculty.ucr.edu/~hanneman/spatial/schelling/schelling.html

Martin, G. (2006). *Understanding terrorism: Challenges, perspectives, and issues* (2nd ed.). Thousand Oaks, CA: Sage Publications.

Masi, A. (2014, October 9). Where to find ISIS supporters: A map of militant groups aligned with the Islamic State group. *International Business Times*. Retrieved from http://www.ibtimes.com/where-find-isis-supporters-map-militant-groups-aligned-islamic-state-group-1701878

Mask malware takes aim at governments and activists. (2014, February 11). *BBC News*. Retrieved from http://www.bbc.com/news/technology-26136412

Maslow, A. (1943). A theory of motivation. *Psychological Review*, *50*(4), 370–396. doi:10.1037/h0054346

Mastors, E., & Siers, R. (2014). Omar al-Hammami: A case study in radicalization. *Behavioral Sciences & the Law*, *32*(3), 377–388. doi:10.1002/bsl.2108

Mastura, N. (2014, July 19). Open letter to Singapore ministers – Why are we silent on Gaza? *The Online Citizen*. Retrieved from http://www.theonlinecitizen.com/2014/07/open-letter-to-singapore-ministers-why-are-we-silent-on-gaza/

Mauss, I. B., Evers, C., Wilhelm, F. H., & Gross, J. J. (2006). How to bite your tongue without blowing your top: Implicit evaluation of emotion regulation predicts affective responding to anger provocation. *Personality and Social Psychology Bulletin*, *32*(5), 589–602. doi:10.1177/0146167205283841

Maybury, M. T. (Ed.). (2012). *Multimedia information extraction: Advances in video, audio, and imagery analysis for search, data mining, surveillance, and authoring*. IEEE Computer Society. doi:10.1002/9781118219546

Mbai, A. (2010, October 19). *Police-military co-operation in countering terrorism: An Indonesian perspective*. The International Seminar on Countering Terrorism, Nusa Dua, Bali, Indonesia.

Mbakwe, C., & Cunliffe, D. (2007). Hypermedia seduction: Further exploration of the process of 'seductive' online user interactions. In B. Ganor, K. von Knop, & C. Duarte (Eds.), *Hypermedia seduction for terrorist recruiting* (pp. 207–230). Washington, DC: IOS Press.

McCants, W. (2015, June 19). Interview with Alberto Fernandez – Experts weigh in (part 2): Can the United States counter ISIS propaganda? *Brookings Institute's Markaz (Middle East Politics and Policy) Blog*. Retrieved from http://www.brookings.edu/blogs/markaz/posts/2015/06/19-us-counter-messaging-isis-fernandez

McCarthy, J. (2010). Internet sexual activity: A comparison between contact and non-contact child pornography offenders. *Journal of Sexual Aggression*, *16*(2), 181–195. doi:10.1080/13552601003760006

McCauley, C., & Moskalenko, S. (2008). Mechanisms of political radicalization: Pathways toward terrorism. *Terrorism and Political Violence*, *20*(3), 415–433. doi:10.1080/09546550802073367

McCauley, C., & Moskalenko, S. (2011). *Friction: How radicalization happens to them and us*. New York, NY: Oxford University Press.

McCauley, C., & Moskalenko, S. (2011). Individual and group mechanisms of radicalisation. In S. Canna (Ed.), *Protecting the homeland from international and domestic terrorism threats: Current multi-disciplinary perspectives on root causes, the role of ideology, and programs for counter-radicalisation and disengagement*. College Park: START.

McClelland, D. C. (1987). *Human motivation*. New York, NY: Cambridge University Press.

McClelland, D. C., Koestner, R., & Weinberger, J. (1989). How do self-attributed and implicit motives differ? *Psychological Review, 96*(4), 690–702. doi:10.1037/0033-295X.96.4.690

McCrae, R. R., & Costa, P. J. Jr. (2004). A contemplated revision of the NEO Five-Factor Inventory. *Personality and Individual Differences, 36*(3), 587–596. doi:10.1016/S0191-8869(03)00118-1

McDonald, H. S., Horstmann, N., Strom, K. J., & Pope, M. W. (2009). *The impact of the Internet on deviant behavior and deviant communities*. Durham, NC: The Institute for Homeland Security Solution.

McDowell, R. (2011, September 9). Captain jihad: Ex-terrorist is now comic book hero. *The Jakarta Post*. Retrieved from http://www.thejakartapost.com/news/2011/09/09/captain-jihad-ex-terrorist-now-comic-book-hero.html

McElfresh, M. (2015, June 8). Power grid cyber attacks keep the pentagon up at night. *Scientific American*. Retrieved from www.scientificamerican.com/article/power-grid-cyber-attacks-keep-the-pentagon-up-at-night/

McFarlane, B. (2010). *Online violent radicalisation (OVeR): Challenges facing law enforcement agencies and policy stakeholders*. Peer reviewed conference paper. Global Terrorism Research Centre, Monash University.

McGilloway, A., Ghosh, P., & Bhui, K. (2015). A systematic review of pathways to and processes associated with radicalization and extremism amongst Muslims in Western societies. *International Review of Psychiatry (Abingdon, England), 27*(1), 39–50. doi:10.3109/09540261.2014.992008 PMID:25738400

McGreevy, J. P. (2002). Footprinting: What is it, who should do it and why? *SANS Institute*. Retrieved from http://www.sans.org/reading-room/whitepapers/auditing/footprinting-it-it-why-62

McGuire, M. R. (2014). Putting the 'cyber' into cyberterrorism: Re-reading technological risk in a hyperconnected world. In T. Chen, L. Jarvis, & S. Macdonald (Eds.), *Cyberterrorism: Understanding, assessment, and response* (pp. 63–84). New York, NY: Springer.

McKenna, K. Y. A., & Bargh, J. A. (1998). Coming out in the age of the Internet: Identity "de-marginalisation" from virtual group participation. *Journal of Personality and Social Psychology, 75*(3), 681–694. doi:10.1037/0022-3514.75.3.681

McLeod, S. (2009). Attitudes and behavior. *Simply Psychology*. Retrieved from http://www.simplypsychology.org/attitudes.html

McLeod, S. (2015). B. F. Skinner, operant conditioning. *Simply Psychology*. Retrieved from http://www.simplypsychology.org/operant-conditioning.html

McManus, M., Long, M., & Alison, L. (2011). Child pornography offenders: Towards an evidenced-based approach to prioritizing the investigation of indecent image offenses. In A. J. Alison & R. Rainbow (Eds.), *Professionalizing offender profiling: Forensic and investigative psychology in practise* (pp. 178–188). Oxon: Routledge.

McNeal, G. S. (2007). Cyber embargo: Countering the Internet jihad. *Case Western Reserve University School of Law, 39*(3), 789–826.

McNeal, G. S. (2008). Cyber embargo: Countering the Internet jihad. *Case Western Reserve Journal of International Law, 789*, 810–812.

McQuade, S. C. (2006). *Understanding and managing cybercrime.* Boston, MA: Pearson Education, Inc.

Meet Catalyst. IARPA's entity and relationship extraction program. (2012, April 4). *Public Intelligence.* Retrieved from http://publicintelligence.net/meet-catalyst

Mehan, J. E. (Ed.). (2014). *Cyberwar, cyberterror, cybercrime and cyberactivism: An in-depth guide to the role of standards in the cybersecurity environment.* Cambridge: IT Governance Publishing.

Meir Amit Intelligence and Terrorism Information Center (MAITIC). (2013, December). *Foreign fighters in Syria.* Retrieved from http://www.terrorism-info.org.il/en/article/20607

Melbourne shooting: Man being investigated over terrorism shot dead after stabbing police officers outside Endeavour Hills police station. (2014, September 24). *ABC News.* Retrieved from http://www.abc.net.au/news/2014-09-23/one-person-shot-dead-two-stabbed-endeavour-hills/5764408

Meleagrou-Hitchens, A. (2011, September 11). *As American as apple pie: How Anwar al-Awlaki became the face of Western jihad* (ICSR Policy Report). London: The International Centre for the Study of Radicalisation.

Meloy, J. R. (2011). Approaching and attacking public figures: A contemporary analysis of communications and behaviour. In C. Chauvin (Ed.), *Threatening communications and behaviour: Perspectives on the pursuit of public figures* (pp. 75–101). Washington, DC: The National Academies Press.

Meloy, J. R., Hoffmann, J., Guldimann, A., & James, D. (2012). The role of warning behaviors in threat assessment: An exploration and suggested typology. *Behavioral Sciences & the Law, 30*(3), 256–279. doi:10.1002/bsl.999

Meloy, J. R., Hoffmann, J., Roshdi, K., & Guldimann, A. (2014). Some warning behaviors discriminate between school shooters and other students of concern. *Journal of Threat Assessment and Management, 1*(3), 203–211. doi:10.1037/tam0000020

Meloy, J. R., Mohandie, K., Knoll, J. L., & Hoffmann, J. (2015). The concept of identification in threat assessment. *Behavioral Sciences & the Law, 33*(2-3), 213–237. doi:10.1002/bsl.2166 PMID:25728417

Meloy, J. R., & O'Toole, M. E. (2011). The concept of leakage in threat assessment. *Behavioral Sciences & the Law, 29*(4), 513–527. doi:10.1002/bsl.986 PMID:21710573

Mendoza, M. (2014, November 5). Cybercrime on the Rise, Survey Finds. *Huffington Post.* Retrieved from www.huffingtonpost.com/2014/05/29/cybercrime-rise-survey_n_5410280.html

Meserve, J. (2007, September 27). Mouse click could plunge city into darkness, experts say. *CNN.* Retrieved from www.edition.cnn.com/2007/US/09/27/power.at.risk/index.html

Michael, G. (2009). Adam Gadahn and Al-Qaeda's Internet strategy. *Middle East Policy, 16*(3), 135–152. doi:10.1111/j.1475-4967.2009.00409.x

Mielczarek, N., & Perlmutter, D. D. (2014). Big pictures and visual propaganda: The lessons of research on the "effects" of photojournalistic icons. In C. K. Winkler & C. E. Dauber (Eds.), *Visual propaganda and extremism in the online environment* (pp. 215–232). Carlisle, PA: Strategic Studies Institute and U.S. Army War College Press.

Miller, J. (2014, June 25). Can Iraqi militants be kept off social media sites? *BBC News.* Retrieved from http://www.bbc.com/news/technology-28016834

Miller, C. S., Kimonis, E. R., Otto, R. K., Kline, S. M., & Wasserman, A. L. (2012). Reliability of risk assessment measures used in sexually violent predator proceedings. *Psychological Assessment*, *24*(4), 944–953. doi:10.1037/a0028411

Millie, J. (2008). 'Spiritual meal' or ongoing project? The dilemma of Dakwah Oratory. In G. Fealy & S. White (Eds.), *Expressing Islam: Religious life and politics in Indonesia* (pp. 80–94). Singapore: Institute of Southeast Asian Studies.

Minzili, Y. (2007). *Strategic thinking of the salafi-jihadi movement*. Retrieved from http://www.herzliyaconference. org/_Uploads/2817ShmuelBarIslamistStrategic.pdf

Mischel, W., & Shoda, Y. (1995). A cognitive-affective system theory of personality: Reconceptualizing situations, dispositions, dynamics, and invariance in personality structure. *Psychological Review*, *102*(2), 246–268. doi:10.1037/0033-295X.102.2.246

Mitnick, K. D., & Simon, W. L. (2006). Social engineers: How they work and how to stop them. In C. Long, E. Herman, & K. Shafer (Eds.), *The art of intrusion: The real stories behind the exploits of hackers, intruders & deceivers* (pp. 221–245). Indianapolis, IN: Wiley Publishing, Inc.

Miyamoto, Y., & Ryff, C. D. (2011). Cultural differences in the dialectical and non-dialectical emotional styles and their implications for health. *Cognition and Emotion*, *25*(1), 22–39. doi:10.1080/02699931003612114

Moeller, S. D. (1999). *Compassion fatigue: How the media sell disease, famine, war and death*. New York, NY: Routledge.

Moffitt, T. E. (1993). Adolescence-limited and life-course-persistent antisocial behaviour: A developmental taxonomy. *Psychological Review*, *100*(4), 674–701. doi:10.1037/0033-295X.100.4.674 PMID:8255953

Mogensen, K. (2015). International trust and public diplomacy. *International Communication Gazette*, *77*(4), 315–336. doi:10.1177/1748048514568764

Moghadam, A. (2006). Suicide terrorism, occupation and the globalisation of martyrdom: A critique of dying to win. *Studies in Conflict and Terrorism*, *29*(8), 707–729. doi:10.1080/10576100600561907

Moghadam, A. (2008). *The globalization of martyrdom*. Baltimore, MD: The Johns Hopkins University Press.

Moghaddam, F. M. (2007). The staircase to terrorism: A psychological exploration. In B. Bongar, L. M. Brown, L. E., Beutler, J. N. Breckenridge, & P. G. Zimbardo (Eds.), Psychology of terrorism (pp. 69-80). New York, NY: Oxford University Press.

Moghaddam, F. M. (2005). The staircase to terrorism: A psychological exploration. *The American Psychologist*, *60*(2), 161–169. doi:10.1037/0003-066X.60.2.161 PMID:15740448

Mokhtar, F. (2015). Learn from how other countries have dealt with terror threats, incidents: DPM Teo. *Channel News Asia*. Retrieved from http://www.channelnewsasia.com/news/singapore/learn-from-how-other/1824490.html

Monahan, J. (1981). *Predicting violent behavior: An assessment of clinical techniques*. Newbury Park, CA: Sage.

Monahan, J. (2011). The individual risk assessment of terrorism. *Psychology, Public Policy, and Law*, *18*(2), 167–205. doi:10.1037/a0025792

Monahan, J., & Steadman, H. J. (1994). Violence risk assessment: A quarter century of research. In L. E. Frost & R. J. Bonnie (Eds.), *The evolution of mental health law* (pp. 195–211). Washington, DC: American Psychological Association.

Monahan, J., Steadman, H., Silver, E., Appelbaum, P., Robbins, P., Mulvey, E., & Banks, S. et al. (2001). *Rethinking risk assessment: The MacArthur study of mental disorder and violence*. New York, NY: Oxford University Press.

Moon, D. B. (2007). Cyber-herding: Exploiting Islamic extremists' use of the Internet (Unpublished dissertation). Monterey, CA: Naval Postgraduate School. Retrieved from http://stinet.dtic.mil/cgi-bin/GetTRDoc?AD=ADA475919&location= U2&doc=GetTRDDoc.pdf

Moore, A. P., Cappelli, D. M., Caron, T. C., Shaw, E. D., Spooner, D., & Trzeciak, R. F. (2011). *A preliminary model of insider theft of intellectual property (Technical report: CMU/SEI-2011-TN-013)*. Pittsburgh, PA: Software Engineering Institute.

Moore, A. P., Cappelli, D. M., & Trzeciak, R. F. (2008). *The "Big Picture" of insider IT sabotage across U.S. critical infrastructures (Technical report: CMU/SEI-2008-TR-009)*. Pittsburgh, PA: Software Engineering Institute.

Moore, C., Detert, J. R., Treviño, L. K., Baker, V. L., & Mayer, D. M. (2012). Why employees do bad things: Moral disengagement and unethical organizational behavior. *Personnel Psychology, 65*(1), 1–48. doi:10.1111/j.1744-6570.2011.01237.x

Moore, K., Mason, P., & Lewis, J. (2008). *Images of Islam in the UK: The representation of British Muslims in the National Print News Media 2000-2008*. Cardiff: Cardiff University.

Morgan, M. J. (2004). The origins of the new terrorism. *Parameters*, (Spring): 29–43.

Moulding, N. (2007). Online counselling: With particular focus on young people and support. *Counselling, Psychotherapy, and Health, 3*(1), 25–32.

Moussa, M. B. (2011). The use of the internet by Islamic social movements in collective action: The case of justice and charity. *Westminster Papers in Communication and Culture, 8*(2), 154–177.

Mroz, J. (2009). *Lone wolf attacks and the difference between violent extremism and terrorism.* Retrieved from http://www.ewi.info/lone-wolf-attacks-anddifference-between-violent-extremism-and-terrorism

Mueller, J. (2010). Assessing measures designed to protect the homeland. *Policy Studies Journal: the Journal of the Policy Studies Organization, 38*(1), 1–21. doi:10.1111/j.1541-0072.2009.00341.x

Muhammad, A. (2014, August 27). Stories of foreign fighter migration to Syria. *CTC Sentinel, 7*(8), 11–13.

Mukherjee, S. (2012, June 29). *Sentiment analysis: A literature analysis.* Mumbai: Indian Institute of Technology.

Mullins, S. (2010). Rehabilitation of Islamist terrorists: Lessons from criminology. *Dynamics of Asymmetric Conflict, 3*(3), 162–193. doi:10.1080/17467586.2010.528438

Mullins, S. (2011). Islamist terrorism in Australia: An empirical examination of the 'Home grown' threat. *Terrorism and Political Violence, 23*(2), 254–285. doi:10.1080/09546553.2010.535717

Murdoch, S. J., & Danezis, G. (2005). *Low-cost traffic analysis of TOR.* Paper presented at the 2005 IEEE Symposium on Security and Privacy, Oakland, CA. doi:10.1109/SP.2005.12

Murphy, K. (2004, February 7). Black widows caught in web of Chechen war. *LA Times.* Retrieved from http://culteducation.com/group/1128-russian-sects/18049-black-widows-caught-up-in-web-of-chechen-war-.html

Murphy, M. L. (2003). *Semantic relations and the lexicon - antonym, synonymy and other paradigms.* Cambridge, U.K.: Cambridge University Press. doi:10.1017/CBO9780511486494

Murphy, P. R., & Dacin, M. T. (2011). Psychological pathways to fraud: Understanding and preventing fraud in organization. *Journal of Business Ethics, 101*(4), 601–618. doi:10.1007/s10551-011-0741-0

Najibi, N. (2013, November 21). International law ignored: Pakistan at risk. *The World Post.* Retrieved from http://www.huffingtonpost.com/neda-najibi/international-law-ignored_b_4306306.html

Nakashima, E. (2012, September 21). Iran blamed for cyberattacks on U.S. banks and companies. *The Washington Post*. Retrieved from https://www.washingtonpost.com/world/national-security/iran-blamed-for-cyberattacks/2012/09/21/afbe2be4-0412-11e2-9b24-ff730c7f6312_story.html

Nasser-Eddine, M., Garnham, B., Agostino, K., & Caluya, G. (2011). Countering violent extremism (CVE) literature review. Edinburgh, Australia: Australian Government, Department of Defence, Command and Control Division, Defence Science and Technology Organisation (DSTO).

National Coordinator for Counterterrorism. (2010, May). *Jihadists and the Internet 2009 update*. Retrieved from http://fas.org/irp/world/netherlands/jihadists.pdf

National Institute of Standards and Technology. (2006). *Guide to supervisory control and data acquisition (SCADA) and industrial control systems security: Recommendations of the national institute of standards and technology (Special Publication 800-82)*. Gaithersburg, MD: Department of Commerce.

National Offender Management Service. (2011). *Extremism risk guidance 22*. London: Ministry of Justice Publications.

National Research Council. (2011). *Assessing national resilience to hazards and disasters: The perspective from the Gulf coast of Louisiana and Mississippi: Summary of a workshop*. Washington, DC: The National Academies Press.

National Security Coordination Secretariat (NSCS). (2004). *The fight against terror: Singapore's national security strategy*. Retrieved from http://www.nscs.gov.sg/public/download.ashx?id=48

National Security Coordination Secretariat (NSCS). (2013). *Supporting centres*. Retrieved from http://www.nscs.gov.sg/public/content.aspx?sid=28

Naval Special Warfare Group ONE (NSWG-1). (2012, September 12). *Project Quantum Leap After Action Report*. Washington, DC: Author. Retrieved from http://fas.org/irp/eprint/quantum.pdf

Nazeer, Z. (2011a, March 5). Indonesia faces rising intolerance. *The Straits Times*.

Nazeer, Z. (2011b, August 6). Pluralism, tolerance under growing threat. *The Straits Times*.

Neal, D. T., Wood, W., & Quinn, J. M. (2006). Habits – A repeat performance. *Current Directions in Psychological Science*, *15*(4), 198–202. doi:10.1111/j.1467-8721.2006.00435.x

Neimann, H., Ruff, R., & Baser, C. (1990). Computer assisted attention retraining in head-injured individuals: A controlled efficacy study of an outpatient program. *Journal of Consulting and Clinical Psychology*, *58*(6), 811–817. doi:10.1037/0022-006X.58.6.811 PMID:2292631

Nelson, A. (2010). Nice girls don't do conflict. *Psychology Today*. Retrieved from https://www.psychologytoday.com/blog/he-speaks-she-speaks/201011/nice-girls-don-t-do-conflict

Neo, L. S., Khader, M., Ang, J., Ong, G., & Tan, E. (2014). Developing an early screening guide for jihadi terrorism: A behavioural analysis of 30 terror attacks. *Security Journal*. doi:10.1057/sj.2014.44

Neo, L. S., Khader, M., Shi, P., Dillon, L., & Ong, G. (2015). *Extremist cyber footprints: A guide to understanding and countering online extremism*. Singapore: Home Team Behavioural Sciences Centre.

Neo, L. S., Shi, P., Dillon, L., Ong, G., Tan, E., & Khader, M. (2014). *Why is ISIS so psychologically attractive? A behavioural sciences perspective (Research report no. 18/2014)*. Singapore: Home Team Behavioural Sciences Centre.

Neo, L. S., Shi, P., Dillon, L., Ong, G., Tan, E., & Khader, M. (2014). *Why is ISIS so psychologically attractive? A behavioural sciences perspective (Research report No. 18/2014)*. Singapore: Home Team Behavioural Sciences Centre.

Neo, L. S., Singh, K., Khader, M., Ang, J., & Ong, G. (2013). *Understanding Internet-mediated radicalisation: A theoretical C3PO pathway framework. Research report No. 05/2013.* Singapore: Home Team Behavioural Sciences Centre.

Nesser, P. (2008). Chronology of jihadism in Western Europe 1994–2007: Planned, prepared, and executed terrorist attacks. *Studies in Conflict and Terrorism, 31*(10), 924–946. doi:10.1080/10576100802339185

Nesser, P. (2008). How did Europe's global jihadis obtain training for their militant causes? *Terrorism and Political Violence, 20*(2), 234–256. doi:10.1080/09546550801920758

Nesser, P. (2012). Single actor terrorism: Scope, characteristics and explanations. *Perspectives on Terrorism, 6,* 61–73.

Neumann, P. (2010). *Prison and terrorism.* London: International Centre for the Study of Radicalisation.

Neumann, P. R. (2012). *Countering online radicalisation in America.* Bipartisan Policy Center.

Neumann, P. R. (2013). Options and strategies for countering online radicalization in the United States. *Studies in Conflict and Terrorism, 36*(6), 431–459. doi:10.1080/1057610X.2013.784568

New Muslim Project NZ. (2014). *About us.* Retrieved from http://newmuslimproject.co.nz/?page_id=2803

Newman, E. (2006). Exploring the "root causes" of terrorism. *Studies in Conflict and Terrorism, 29*(8), 749–772. doi:10.1080/10576100600704069

Ngazis, A. N., & Haryanto, A. T. (2015, April 9). Pemerintah buka 12 Situs Islam yang. *Berita VIVA.* Retrieved from http://news.viva.co.id/news/read/611803-pemerintah-buka-12-situs-islam-yang-diblokir

Ng, C. (2011). National resilience: Building a whole-of-society response. *Ethos (Berkeley, Calif.), 10,* 21–29.

Nick Cleggs. Riots 'completely unacceptable. (2011). *BBC News.* Retrieved from http://www.bbc.com/news/uk-politics-14443082

Nicks, D. (2014, August 19). Hacking traffic lights is apparently really easy. *Time.* Retrieved from http://time.com/3146147/hacking-traffic-lights-is-apparently-really-easy/

Ningrum, B. W. (2013, March 30). Kominfo blokir 22 situs yang dianggap radikal. *Liputan6.com.* Retrieved from http://tekno.liputan6.com/read/2199730/kominfo-blokir-22-situs-yang-dianggap-radikal

Nirmala, M. (2014, February 2). Don't fall for a terrorist's bait. *The Straits Times.* Retrieved from http://news.asiaone.com/news/world/dont-fall-terrorists-bait

Nisbett, R. E., & Cohen, D. (1996). *Culture of honor: The psychology of violence in the South.* Boulder, CO: Westview Press.

Noelle-Neumann, E. (1993). *The spiral of silence: Public opinion – Our social skin.* Chicago, IL: University of Chicago Press.

Nolen-Hoeksema, S. (1998). The other end of the continuum: The costs of rumination. *Psychological Inquiry, 9*(3), 216–219. doi:10.1207/s15327965pli0903_5

Noor, S., & Hayat, S. (2009). *Deradicalisation: Approaches and models.* Indonesia: Pak Institute for Peace Studies.

Nordland, R. (2014, June 28). Iraq's Sunni militants take to social media to advance their cause and intimidate. *The New York Times.* Retrieved from http://www.nytimes.com/2014/06/29/middleeast/iraqs-sunni-militants-take-to-social-media-to-advance-their-cause-and-intimidate.html?_r=0

Norris, C. (2006). *A report on the surveillance society: For the information commissioner. Expert Report: Criminal Justice. Surveillance Studies Network.* London: Information Commissioner.

Norris, P., Kern, M., & Just, M. (2013). *Framing terrorism: The news media, the government and the public.* London: Taylor & Francis.

Nuraniyah, N. (2014, February 24). *Syrian conflict fallout: Time to contain hate speech in Indonesia.* RSIS Commentaries (038/2014). Singapore: S. Rajaratnam School of International Studies.

Nuraniyah, N. (2014). *Syrian conflict fallout: Time to contain hate speech in Indonesia. RSIS Commentaries (038/2014).* Singapore: S. Rajaratnam School of International Studies.

Nurhayati, D. (2011, October 12). 'Prison and paradise' gives a voice to terrorism survivors. *The Jakarta Post.* Retrieved from http://www.thejakartapost.com/news/2011/10/12/prison-and-paradise-gives-a-voice-terrorism-survivors.html

Nurse, J. R. C., Buckley, O., Legg, P. H., Goldsmith, M., Creese, S., Wright, G. R. T., & Whitty, M. (2014). Understanding insider threat: A framework for characterizing attacks. In *IEEE Computer Society Security and Privacy Workshops.* San Francisco, CA: IEEE. doi:10.1109/SPW.2014.38

Nussbaum, M. C. (2001). *Upheavals of thought: The intelligence of emotion.* Cambridge: Cambridge University Press. doi:10.1017/CBO9780511840715

O'Keefe, D. (1990). *Persuasion.* Newbury Park, CA: Sage.

O'Neill, P. H. (2013, September 18). Why the Syrian uprising is the first social media war. *The Daily Dot.* Retrieved from http://www.dailydot.com/politics/syria-civiil-social-media-war-youtube

O'Rourke, S. (2007). *Virtual radicalisation: Challenges for police.* Paper presented at the 8th Australian Information Warfare and Security Conference, Perth, Australia.

O'Rourke, S. (2010). *The emergent challenges for policing terrorism: Lessons from Mumbai.* Retrieved from http://ro.ecu.edu.au/cgi/viewcontent.cgi?article=1004&context=act

O'Rourke, S. (2007). Virtual radicalisation: Challenges for police. In *Proceedings of the 8th Australian Information Warfare and Security Conference.* Perth: Edith Cowan University.

O'Shea, K. (2003). *Cyber attack investigative tools and technologies* [Powerpoint slides]. Hanover, NH: Darmouth College Institute for Security Technology Studies.

Oberschall, A. (2004). Explaining terrorism: The contribution of collective action theory. *Sociological Theory, 22*(1), 26–37. doi:10.1111/j.1467-9558.2004.00202.x

Ogloff, J. (2009). *The violent client: Advances in violent risk assessment.* Melbourne, Victoria: The Australian Psychological Society.

Ogloff, J., & Davis, M. R. (2005). Assessing risk for violence in the Australian context. In D. Chappell & P. Wilson (Eds.), *Crime and justice in the new millennium* (pp. 301–338). Sydney, Australia: Lexis Nexis.

Ogun, M. N. (2012). Terrorist use of the internet: Possible suggestions to prevent the usage for terrorist purposes. *Journal of Applied Security Research, 7*(2), 203–217. doi:10.1080/19361610.2012.656252

Okon, E. (2012). The sources and schools of Islamic jurisprudence. *American Journal of Social and Management Sciences, 3*(3), 106–111. doi:10.5251/ajsms.2012.3.3.106.111

Online Radicalisation Research Community of Practice (ORRCOP). (2014, November). *ISIS and its formula for recruitment effectiveness in the online realm.* ORRCOP Commentary 1/15. Singapore: National Security Coordination Secretariat.

Ortbals, C. D., & Poloni-Staudinger, L. (2013). *Terrorism and violent conflict: Women's agency, leadership and responses.* New York, NY: Springer.

Osman, J. (2013). Al-Shabaab: Using social media to fight the jihad. *Channel 4.* Retrieved from: http://www.channel4.com/news/al-shabaab-jihadist-kenya-westgate-kenya-nairobi-twitter

Osman, S. (2013, August 13). *Funerals of suspected terrorists in Indonesia: a rallying point?* RSIS Commentaries (150/2013). Singapore: S. Rajaratnam School of International Studies.

Osman, S. (2013). *Funerals of suspected terrorists in Indonesia: A rallying point? RSIS Commentaries (150/2013).* Singapore: S. Rajaratnam School of International Studies.

Oumar, J. (2011, July 29). Jihadist websites tempt Mauritanian boys. *Magharebia.* Retrieved from http://magharebia.com/cocoon/awi/xhtml1/en_GB/features/awi/reportage/2011/07/29/reportage-01

Oxford Analytica. (2013, July 10). *Converts give clues to radicalisation.* Retrieved from https://www.oxan.com/display.aspx?ItemID=DB184468

Ozerdem, A., & Podder, S. (2011). Disarming youth combatants: Mitigating youth radicalization and violent extremism. *Journal of Strategic Security,* 4(4), 63–80. doi:10.5038/1944-0472.4.4.3

Paganini, P. (2012, May 26). Al Qaeda continues to frighten the U.S., cyber war has begun. *Security Affairs.* Retrieved from http://securityaffairs.co/wordpress/5745/intelligence/al-qaeda-continues-to-frighten-the-u-s-the-cyber-war-is-begun.html

Paganini, P. (2012, November 12). Cyber espionage attack against Israel is not an isolated event. *Security Affairs.* Retrieved from http://securityaffairs.co/wordpress/10243/malware/cyber-espionage-attack-against-israel-is-not-an-isolated-event.html

Paganini, P. (2013, February 22). SCADA and security of critical infrastructures. *InfoSec Institute.* Retrieved from http://resources.infosecinstitute.com/scada-security-of-critical-infrastructures/

Paganini, P. (2014, September 2). Hacking traffic light systems. *InfoSec Institute.* Retrieved from resources.infosecinstitute.com/hacking-traffic-light-systems/

Paginini, P. (2014, May 26). Critical infrastructure, hackers targeted public utility SCADA. *Security Affairs.* Retrieved from http://securityaffairs.co/wordpress/25240/hacking/critical-infrastructure-hackers-targeted-public-utility-scada.html

Pagliery, J. (2014, August 21). Traffic lights are dangerously easy to hack. *CNNMoney.* Retrieved from http://money.cnn.com/2014/08/21/technology/security/traffic-lights-hack/

Paloutzian, R. F., & Park, C. L. (2005). Religious conversion and spiritual transformation: A meaning-system analysis. In R. F. Paloutzian & C. L. Park (Eds.), *Handbook of the psychology of religion and spirituality* (pp. 331–347). New York, NY: Guilford.

Pang, B., Lee, L., & Vaithyanathan, S. (2002). Thumbs up? Sentiment classification using machine learning techniques. In *Proceedings of the Conference on Empirical Methods in Natural Language Processing (EMNLP).* Stroudsburg, PA: Association for Computational Linguistics.

Pan, J. Y., & Fung, C. C. (2008). Artificial intelligence in malware: Cop or culprit? In *Proceedings of The Ninth Postgraduate Electrical Engineering and Computing Symposium.* Perth, Australia: University of Western Australia.

Papic, M., & Noonan, S. (2011, February 3). Social media as tool for protest. *Stratfor*. Retrieved from http://www.stratfor.com/weekly/20110202-social-media-tool-protest?utm_source=SWeekly&utm_medium=email&utm_campaign=110203&utm_content=readmore&elq=77ffb64cf0554757abe76e998eb0395b

Parker, D. B. (1998). *Fighting computer crime: A new framework for protecting information*. New York, NY: Wiley Computer Publishing.

Parker, T., Sachs, M., Shaw, E., Stroz, E., & Devost, M. (2004). *Cyber adversary characterization: Auditing the hacker mind*. New York, NY: Syngress.

Passmore, D., Chamberlin, T., & Brennan, R. (2015, May 17). Trapped in web of terror. *The Sunday Mail*, p. 7.

Paulhus, D. L. (2014). Toward a taxonomy of dark personalities. *Current Directions in Psychological Science*, 23(6), 421–426. doi:10.1177/0963721414547737

Pauwels, L., & Schils, N. (2014). Differential online exposure to extremist content and political violence: Testing the relative strength of social learning and competing perspectives. *Terrorism and Political Violence*. doi:10.1080/09546553.2013.876414

PBNU. Ulama besar dunia tolak ISIS. (2014, August 8). *Tribunnews.com*. Retrieved from http://www.tribunnews.com/nasional/2014/08/08/pbnu-ulama-besar-dunia-tolak-isis

Peachy, P. (2014a, October 5). Cyber crime: First online murder will happen by end of year, warns US firm. *The Independent*. Retrieved from www.independent.co.uk/life-style/gadgets-and-tech/news/first-online-murder-will-happen-by-end-of-year-warns-us-firm-9774955

Peachy, P. (2014b, December 7). Police 'failing to train key staff to fight growing threat of cybercrime' *The Independent*. Retrieved from http://www.independent.co.uk/news/uk/crime/police-failing-to-train-key-staff-to-fight-growing-threat-of-cyber-crime-9909334.html

Penrose, G. (2014, July 23). Precision guided message - Radical Islam, social media and building a sleeper 'army'. *Quora*. Retrieved from http://tmgcorporateservices.quora.com/Precision-Guided-Message-Radical-Islam-Social-Media-and-Building-a-Sleeper-Army

Perdani, Y. (2014, January 3). Amid criticism, police try to justify killings. *The Jakarta Post*. Retrieved from http://www.thejakartapost.com/news/2014/01/03/amid-criticism-police-try-justify-killings.html

Pereira, D. (2015, February 18). Jakarta holds key to keeping Southeast Asia safe in war on terror. *Business Times*. Retrieved from http://www.pereiraintl.com/jakarta-holds-key-to-keeping-s-e-asia-safe-in-war-on-terror/

Perrin, A. J., & Smolek, S. (2009). Who trusts? Race, gender and the September 11 rally effect among young adults. *Social Science Research*, 38(1), 134–145. doi:10.1016/j.ssresearch.2008.09.001 PMID:19569296

Perrow, C. (1999). *Normal accidents: Living with high-risk technologies*. Princeton, NJ: Princeton University Press.

Peterson, A. (2013, October 21). Yes, terrorists could have hacked Dick Cheney's heart. *The Washington Post*. Retrieved from http://www.washingtonpost.com/blogs/the-switch/wp/2013/10/21/yes-terrorists-could-have-hacked-dick-cheneys-heart/

Petty, R. E., Briñol, P., & Tormala, Z. L. (2002). Thought confidence as a determinant of persuasion: The self-validation hypothesis. *Journal of Personality and Social Psychology*, 82(5), 722–741. doi:10.1037/0022-3514.82.5.722 PMID:12003473

Pew Forum on Religion & Public Life. (2009). *Mapping the global Muslim population*. Washington, DC: Pew Research Center.

Pew Research Center. (2013). *Attitudes toward the United States* (PEW Global Survey 2013). Retrieved from http://www.pewglobal.org/2013/07/18/chapter-1-attitudes-toward-the-united-states/

Pew Research Center. (2013, June 10). *Public says investigate terrorism, even if it intrudes on privacy: Majority views NSA phone tracking as acceptable anti-terror tactic.* Washington, DC: Author. Retrieved from http://www.people-press.org/2013/06/10/majority-views-nsa-phone-tracking-as-acceptable-anti-terror-tactic/

Pew Research Center. (2014, January 20). *Obama's NSA Speech has little impact on sceptical public: Most say U.S. should pursue criminal case against Snowden.* Washington, DC: Author. Retrieved from http://www.people-press.org/2014/01/20/obamas-nsa-speech-has-little-impact-on-skeptical-public/

Pew Research Center. (2015, May 20). *Americans' attitudes about privacy, security and surveillance.* Washington, DC: Author. Retrieved from http://www.pewinternet.org/files/2015/05/Privacy-and-Security-Attitudes-5.19.15_FINAL.pdf

Piaget, J. (2002). The language and thought of the child. New York, NY: Routledge Classic.

Poole, E. (2002). *Reporting Islam: Media representation and British Muslims.* London: IB Tauris & Co.

Poole-Robb, S. (2015, April 7). National power grids hit by cyber terrorist onslaught. *KCS Group.* Retrieved from www.kcsgroup.com/national-power-grids-hit-by-cyber-terrorist-onslaught/

Post, J. M. (2007). *The mind of the terrorist: The psychology of terrorism from the IRA to Al Qaeda.* New York, NY: Palgrave Macmillan.

Post, J. M., Ruby, K. G., & Shaw, E. C. (2002). The radical group in context: 1. An integrated framework for the analysis of group risk for terrorism. *Studies in Conflict and Terrorism, 25*(2), 73–100. doi:10.1080/105761002753502466

Postmes, T., Spears, R., & Lea, M. (2002). Inter-group differentiation in computer-mediated communication: Effects of depersonalisation. *Group Dynamics, 6*(1), 3–16. doi:10.1037/1089-2699.6.1.3

Potter, J., & Edwards, D. (2001). Discursive social psychology. In W. P. Robinson & H. Giles (Eds.), *The new handbook of language and social psychology* (pp. 103–118). London: John Wiley & Sons Ltd.

Powers, S., & Armstrong, M. (2014). Conceptualising radicalisation in a market for loyalties. In C. K. Winkler & C. E. Dauber (Eds.), *Visual propaganda and extremism in the online environment* (pp. 165–192). Carlisle, PA: Strategic Studies Institute and U.S. Army War College Press.

Precht, T. (2007). *Home grown terrorism and Islamist radicalization in Europe: From conversion to terrorism.* Denmark: Danish Ministry of Justice.

Prentice-Dunn, S., & Rogers, R. W. (1982). Effects of public and private self-awareness on deindividuation and aggression. *Journal of Personality and Social Psychology, 43*(3), 503–513. doi:10.1037/0022-3514.43.3.503

Prentice-Dunn, S., & Rogers, R. W. (1989). Deindividuation and the self-regulation of behavior. In P. B. Paulus (Ed.), *The psychology of group influence* (2nd ed.; pp. 86–109). Hillsdale, NJ: Lawrence Erlbaum.

Pressman, D. E. (2009). *Risk assessment decisions for violent political extremism.* Retrieved from http://www.publicsafety.gc.ca/cnt/rsrcs/pblctns/2009-02-rdv/2009-02-rdv-eng.pdf

Pressman, D. E. (2009). *Risk assessment decisions for violent political extremism.* Retrieved from http://www.publicsafety.gc.ca/res/cor/rep/_fl/2009-02-rdv-eng.pdf

Pressman, D. E., & Flockton, J. (2010). *VERA-2. Violent extremism risk assessment, Version 2 Manual.* Unpublished Manuscript.

Pressman, E. (2009, October 1). *Risk assessment decisions for violent political extremism 2009-02*. Retrieved from http://www.publicsafety.gc.ca/cnt/rsrcs/pblctns/2009-02-rdv/index-eng.aspx

Pressman, D. E., & Flockton, J. (2014). Violent extremist risk assessment: Issues and application of the VERA-2 in a high–security correctional setting. In A. Silke (Ed.), *Prisons, terrorism and extremism: Critical issues in management, radicalisation and reform* (pp. 122–143). New York, NY: Routledge.

Pressman, D. E., & Flockton, J. S. (2014). Violent extremist risk assessment: Issues and applications of the VERA-2 in a high security correctional setting. In A. Silke (Ed.), *Prisons, Terrorism and Extremism: critical Issues in Management, Radicalisation and Reform* (pp. 122–143). New York, NY: Routledge.

Pressman, D., & Flockton, J. (2012). Calibrating risk for violent political extremists and terrorists: The VERA 2 structured assessment. *British Journal of Forensic Practice, 14*(4), 237–251. doi:10.1108/14636641211283057

Price, V., Cappella, J. N., & Nir, L. (2002). Does disagreement contribute to more deliberative opinion? *Political Communication, 19*(1), 97–114. doi:10.1080/105846002317246506

Prigg, M. (2015, May 20). The tweet that cost $139 billion: Researchers analyse impact of hacked 2013 message claiming President Obama had been injured by White House explosion. *The Daily Mail*. Retrieved from http://www.dailymail.co.uk/sciencetech/article-3090221/The-tweet-cost-139-BILLION-Researchers-analyse-impact-hacked-message-claiming-President-Obama-injured-White-House-explosion.html

Prince, B. (2009). Phishing attacks cost millions despite low success rate. *eWeek*. Retrieved from http://www.eweek.com/c/a/Security/Phishing-Attacks-Cost-Millions-Despite-Low-Success-Rate-879602

Prince, B. (2014, July). Almost 70% of critical infrastructure companies breached in last 12 months: Survey. *Security Week*. Retrieved from http://www.securityweek.com/almost-70-percent-critical-infrastructure-companies-breached-last-12-months-survey

Prince, J. (2012). Psychological aspects of cyber hate and cyber terrorism. In I. Awan & B. Blakemore (Eds.), *Policing cyber hate, cyber threats and cyber terrorism* (pp. 39–55). London: Ashgate Publishing Limited.

Probst, C. W., Hunker, J., Bishop, M., & Gollmann, D. (Eds.). (2010). *Insider threats in cyber security*. New York, NY: Springer. doi:10.1007/978-1-4419-7133-3

Public Safety and Emergency Preparedness Canada. (2006). *Incident analysis: Ontario-U.S. power outage – impacts on critical infrastructure* (IA06-002). Retrieved from http://cip.management.dal.ca/publications/Ontario%20-%20US%20Power%20Outage%20-%20Impacts%20on%20Critical%20Infrastructure.pdf

Purported al-awlaki message calls for jihad against US. (2010, March 18). *CNN*. Retrieved from http://edition.cnn.com/2010/WORLD/europe/03/17/al.awlaki.message/

Putra, I. E., Mashuri, A., & Zaduqisti, E. (2015). Demonising the victm: Seekig the answer for how a group as the violent victim is blamed. *Psychology and Developing Societies, 27*(1), 31–57. doi:10.1177/0971333614564741

Putra, I. E., & Sukabdi, Z. A. (2013). Basic concepts and reasons behind the emergence of religious terror activities in Indonesia: An inside view. *Asian Journal of Social Psychology, 16*(2), 83–91. doi:10.1111/ajsp.12001

Pyszczynski, T., Rothschild, Z., & Abdollahi, A. (2008). Terrorism, violence, and hope for peace: A terror management perspective. *Current Directions in Psychological Science, 17*(5), 318–322. doi:10.1111/j.1467-8721.2008.00598.x

Qatar International Academy for Security Studies (QIASS). (2010). *Risk Reduction for Countering Violent Extremism: Explorative Review by the International Resource Center for Countering Violent Extremism*. Qatar: Author.

Qatar International Academy for Security Studies [QIASS] (2010). *Risk reduction for countering violent extremism.* New York, NY: The Soufan Group.

Qazi, F. (2011). The mujahidaat – tracing the early female warriors of Islam. In L. Sjoberg & C. Gentry (Eds.), *Women, gender, and extremism* (pp. 29–56). Athens, GA: University of Georgia Press.

Quick, J. C., Quick, J. D., Nelson, D. L., & Hurrell, J. J. (1997). *Preventive stress management in organisations.* Washington, DC: American Psychological Association. doi:10.1037/10238-000

Quirin, M., & Bode, R. C. (2014). An alternative to self-reports of trait and state affect: The Implicit Positive and Negative Affect Test (IPANAT). *European Journal of Psychological Assessment, 30*(3), 231–237. doi:10.1027/1015-5759/a000190

Qutb, S., & Salahi, M. (1979). *In the shade of the Qur'ān.* London: MWH.

Rabasa, A., Blackwill, R., Chalk, P., Cragin, K., Fair, C., Jackson, B., & Tellis, A. et al. (2009). *The lessons of Mumbai.* Santa Monica, CA: RAND Corporation.

Rabasa, A., Pettyjohn, S. L., Ghez, J. J., & Boucek, C. (2010). *Deradicalising Islamist extremists.* Santa Monica, CA: RAND Corporation.

Radcliffe, J. (2011). Hacking media devices for fun and insulin: Breaking the human SCADA system.*Black Hat Technical Security Conference.* Las Vegas: Nevada.

Raja, M. A. (2005). Death as a form of becoming: The Muslim imagery of death and necropolitics. *Domes, 14*(2), 1–11. doi:10.1111/j.1949-3606.2005.tb00894.x

Ramakrishna, K. (2011, October). *Identity politics and violent religious fundamentalism.* Presentation at the CENS-GFF Workshop on The impact of identity politics on violent extremism: Regional perspectives, Singapore.

Ramakrishna, K. (2007). *Self-radicalisation: The case of Abdul Basheer Abdul Kader. RSIS Commentaries (61/2007).* Singapore: S. Rajaratnam School of International Studies.

Ramakrishna, K. (2009). *Radical pathways: Understanding Muslim radicalization in Indonesia.* Westport, CT: Praeger Security International.

Ramakrishna, K. (2013). *The east Indonesia mujahidin commandos: New faces, same ideology. RSIS Commentaries (8/2013).* Singapore: S. Rajaratnam School of International Studies.

Ramakrishna, K. (2015). *Islamist Terrorism and Militancy in Indonesia: The Power of the Manichean Mindset.* Singapore: Springer. doi:10.1007/978-981-287-194-7

Ravndal, J. A. (2013). Anders Behring Breivik's use of the Internet and social media. *Journal EXIT-Deutschland.* Retrieved from http://journals.sfu.ca/jed/index.php/jex/article/view/28

Reich, P. C., & Gelbstein, E. (2012). *Law, policy and technology: Cyberterrorism, information warfare and internet immobilization.* Hershey, PA: IGI Global. doi:10.4018/978-1-61520-831-9

Reilly, R. J. (2015, August 8). FBI: When it comes to @ISIS Terror, Retweets=Endorsements which makes Twitter one of the Bureau's best informants. *Huffington Post.* Retrieved from http://www.huffingtonpost.com/entry/twitter-terrorism-fbi_55b7e25de4b0224d8834466e

Reinares, F. (2004). Who are the terrorists? Analyzing changes in sociological profile among members of ETA. *Studies in Conflict and Terrorism, 27*(6), 465–488. doi:10.1080/10576100490519741

Reinares, F. (2012). Exit from terrorism: A qualitative empirical study on disengagement and deradicalisation among members of ETA. *Terrorism and Political Violence*, *23*(5), 780–803. doi:10.1080/09546553.2011.613307

Reise, S. P., Smith, L., & Furr, R. M. (2001). Invariance on the NEO PI-R neuroticism scale. *Multivariate Behavioral Research*, *36*(1), 83–110. doi:10.1207/S15327906MBR3601_04

Rescorla, E. (2008). *Notes on P2P blocking and evasion.* IETF P@P Infrastructure Workshop (P2Pi). Retrieved from http://64.170.98.42/area/rai/trac/raw-attachment/wiki/PeerToPeerInfrastructure/27 rescorla-p2pi.pdf

Resnyansky, L. (2007). *Integration of social sciences in terrorism modelling: Issues, problems and recommendations. Australia: Australian Government, Department of Defence, Command and Control Division, Defence Science and Technology Organisation.* Edinburgh, Australia: DSTO.

Ressa, M. (2011, August). *From Facebook to bin laden.* Paper presented at the Ministry of Home Affairs, Singapore. doi:10.1142/p895

Reuter, C., Salloum, R., & Shafy, S. (2014, October 8). Inside Islamic State's Savvy PR War. *Spiegel.* Retrieved from http://www.spiegel.de/international/world/the-professional-pr-strategies-of-isis-in-syria-and-iraq-a-995611.html

Rich, E., Martinez-Moyano, I. J., Conrad, S., Cappelli, D. M., Moore, A. P., Shimeall, T. J., & Wilk, J. et al. (2005). Simulating insider cyber-threat risks: A model-based case and a case-based model. In *Proceedings of the 16th International Conference of the System Dynamics Society.* Quebec City, Canada: System Dynamics Society.

Ridings, C. M., Gefen, D., & Arinze, B. (2002). Some antecedents and effects of trust in virtual communities. *The Journal of Strategic Information Systems*, *11*(3-4), 271–295. doi:10.1016/S0963-8687(02)00021-5

Rieger, D., Frischich, L., & Bente, G. (2013). *Propaganda 2.0 Psychological effects of right-wing and Islamic extremist internet videos.* German Federal Criminal Police Office.

Rieger, D., Frischich, L., & Bente, G. (2013). *Propaganda 2.0 Psychological effects of right-wing and Islamic extremist Internet videos.* German Federal Criminal Police Office.

Rinaldi, S. M., Peerenboom, J. P., & Kelly, T. K. (2001, December). Identifying, understanding and analyzing critical infrastructure interdependencies. *IEEE Control Systems Magazines*, 11-25.

Rittel, H. W. J., & Webber, M. M. (1973). Dilemmas in a general theory of planning. *Policy Sciences*, *4*, 155–169.

Ritterband, L., Gonder-Fredrick, L., Cox, D., Clifton, A., West, R., & Borowitz, S. (2003). Internet interventions: In review, in use, and into the future. *Professional Psychology, Research and Practice*, *34*(5), 527–534. doi:10.1037/0735-7028.34.5.527

Roberts, K., & Horgan, J. (2008). Risk assessment and the terrorist. *Perspectives on Terrorism*, *2*(6), 1–4.

Robertson, J. (2012, February 29). Hacker shows off lethal attack by controlling wireless medical device. *Bloomberg.* Retrieved from http://go.bloomberg.com/tech-blog/2012-02-29-hacker-shows-off-lethal-attack-by-controlling-wireless-medical-device/

Robinson, N. (2008, March 24). Bashir urges attacks on 'infidel' Australians. *The Australian.* Retrieved from http://www.theaustralian.com.au/archive/news/bashir-urges-attacks-on-infidel-australians/story-e6frg6t6-1111115870183

Robinson, D., & Porporino, F. (2001). Programming in cognitive skills: The reasoning and rehabilitation programme. In C. Hollin (Ed.), *Handbook of offender assessment and treatment* (pp. 179–193). Chichester: John Wiley.

Rodin, J. (2014). *The resilience dividend: Being strong in a world where things go wrong.* New York, NY: PublicAffairs.

Rogan, H. (2006). Jihadism online – A study of how al-Qaeda and radical Islamist groups use the Internet for terrorist purposes. Norwegian Defence Research Establishment (FFI).

Rogan, H. (2007). Al-Qaeda's online media strategies: From Abu Reuter to Irhabi 007. Norway: Norwegian Defence Research Establishment (FFI).

Rogan, H. (2007). Al-Qaeda's online media strategies: From Abu Reuter to Irhabi 007. Norwegian Defence Research Establishment (FFI).

Rogers, B., & Neumann, P. (2007). *Recruitment and mobilisation for the Islamist militant movement in Europe*. London: Kings College London.

Rogers, C., & Lewis, R. (2007). *Introduction to police work*. Cullumpton, U.K.: Willan Publishing.

Rogers, M. (2003). The psychology of cyber-terrorism. In A. Silke (Ed.), *Terrorists, victims and society* (pp. 77–92). Chichester, U.K.: John Wiley & Sons, Inc. doi:10.1002/9780470713600.ch4

Romyn, D., & Kebbell, M. R. (2013). Terrorists' planning of attacks: A simulated 'red-team' investigation into decision-making. *Psychology, Crime & Law*, *20*(5), 480–496. doi:10.1080/1068316X.2013.793767

Romyn, D., & Kebbell, M. R. (2015). *Use of Internet to inform terrorist target selection*. Australia: Griffith University.

Rosales, C. A. (2015, June 2). Fostering a sense of belonging key in preventing youth violence. *US State Department Official Blog*. Retrieved from https://blogs.state.gov/stories/2015/06/02/fostering-sense-belonging-key-preventing-youth-violence#sthash.Akq93lHV.dpuf

Rose, S. (2014, October 7). The Isis propaganda war: a hi-tech media jihad. *The Guardian*. Retrieved from http://www.theguardian.com/world/2014/oct/07/isis-media-machine-propaganda-war

Rosoff, M. (2011, August 30). Former Anonymous member says hacking "all comes down to lies". *Business Insider*. Retrieved from http://www.businessinsider.com/former-anonymous-member-says-hacking-all-comes-down-to-lies-2011-8?IR=T

Ross, D. (2010, November 23). Death by a thousand cuts. *Foreign Policy*. Retrieved from http://foreignpolicy.com/2010/11/23/death-by-a-thousand-cuts-2/

Rossmiller, S. (2007). My cyber counter-jihad. *Middle East Quarterly*, *14*(3).

Rouse, M. (2006). Definition: Tipping points. *WhatIs.com*. Retrieved from http://whatis.techtarget.com/definition/tipping-point

Royal Canadian Mounted Police (RCMP). (2009). *Radicalization: A guide for the perplexed*. Ottawa: RCMP National Security Criminal Investigations.

Rubin, A. (2011, October). All your devices can be hacked. *TEDxMidAtlantic*. Retrieved from http://www.ted.com/talks/avi_rubin_all_your_devices_can_be_hacked?language=en

Rushe, D. (2015, June 5). OPM hack: China blamed for massive breach of US government data. Retrieved from http://www.theguardian.com/technology/2015/jun/04/us-government-massive-data-breach-employee-records-security-clearances

Rushkoff, D. (2002). Renaissance Now! Media ecology and the new global narrative. *Explorations in Media Ecology*, *1*(1), 21–32. doi:10.1386/eme.1.1.41_1

Russian hackers accused of attacks on Bundestag and French TV broadcaster. (2015, June 5). *The Telegraph*. Retrieved from http://www.telegraph.co.uk/news/worldnews/europe/germany/11666815/Russian-hackers-accused-of-Bundestag-attack.html

Ruthven, M. (2002). *A fury for God: The Islamist attack on America*. New York, NY: Granta.

Ruwaard, J., Lange, A., Schrieken, B., & Emmelkamp, P. (2011). Efficacy and effectiveness of online CBT: A decade of interapy research. *Journal of Studies in Health Technology and Informatics, 167*, 9–14. PMID:21685634

Saad, I. (2014, July 9). 'Handful' of Singaporeans went to Syria to join conflict: DPM Teo. *Channel News Asia*. Retrieved from http://www.channelnewsasia.com/news/specialreports/parliament/news/handful-of-singaporeans/1248994.html

Sabuced, J. M., Blaco, A., & De la Corte, L. (2003). Beliefs which legitimize political violence against the innocents. *Psicothema, 15*(4), 550–555.

Sackett, P. R., Berry, C. M., Wiemann, S. A., & Laczo, R. M. (2006). Citizenship and counterproductive behavior: Clarifying relations between the two domains. *Human Performance, 19*(4), 441–464. doi:10.1207/s15327043hup1904_7

Sageman, M. (2004). *Understanding terror networks*. Philadelphia, PA: University of Philadelphia Press. doi:10.9783/9780812206791

Sageman, M. (2008). *Leaderless jihad*. Philadelphia, PA: Pennsylvania University Press. doi:10.9783/9780812206784

Sageman, M. (2010). Confronting Al-Qaeda: Understanding the threat in Afghanistan. *Perspectives on Terrorism, 3*(4), 4–25.

Sagita, D. (2011, May 25). Government losing war against radicalism, analysts say. *The Jakarta Globe*. Retrieved from http://www.thejakartaglobe.com/archive/govt-losing-war-against-radicalism-analysts-say/

Sahlgren, M. (2006). *The word-space model: Using distributional analysis to represent syntagmatic and paradigmatic relations between words in high-dimensional vector spaces* (Doctoral dissertation). Department of Linguistics, Stockholm University, Sweden.

Saifudeen, O. A. (2014). *The cyber extremism orbital pathways model* (Working paper 283). Singapore: S.Rajaratnam School of International Studies.

Saifudeen, O. A. (2014). *The cyber extremism orbital pathways model*. Singapore: S. Rajaratnam School of International Studies.

Saifudeen, O. A. (2015). *Islamic state and its online recruitment formula. RSIS Commentaries (090/2015)*. Singapore: S. Rajaratnam School of International Studies.

Saj, H. E. (2012). Discourse analysis: Personal pronouns in Oprah Winfrey hosting Queen Rania of Jordan. *International Journal of Social Science and Humanity, 2*(6), 529–532.

Salamon, K. L. G. (2007). Design and identity – Visual culture and identity politics. In B. Ganor, K. von Knop, & C. Duarte (Eds.), *Hypermedia seduction for terrorist recruiting* (pp. 267–280). Washington, DC: IOS Press.

Saldarini, R. A., & DeRobertis, E. M. (2003). The impact of a technologically induced feeling of anonymity on communications and ethics: New challenges for IT pedagogy. *Journal of Information Technology Impact, 3*, 3–10.

Salgado, J. (2002). The Big Five personality dimensions and counterproductive behaviors. *International Journal of Selection and Assessment, 10*(1-2), 117–125. doi:10.1111/1468-2389.00198

Salleh, N. A. M. (2014, July 26). Hundreds gather at Hong Lim Park in solidarity with people of Gaza. *The Straits Times*. Retrieved from http://www.straitstimes.com/singapore/hundreds-gather-at-hong-lim-park-in-solidarity-with-people-of-gaza

Saltman, E., & Smith, M. (2015). *Till martyrdom do us part: Gender and the ISIS phenomenon*. London: Institute for Strategic Dialogue.

Saltman, E., & Winter, C. (2014). *Islamic State: The changing face of modern jihadism*. London: Quilliam Foundation.

Samuel, T. K. (2015). *M.A.D. (making a difference) Amidst Mad People: Addressing Foreign Fighter Involvement in Terrorist Campaigns*. Paper presented at CENS Workshop on Countering Extremism: Islamic State and Beyond, Singapore.

Sanders, C. E., Field, T. M., Diego, M., & Kaplan, M. (2000). The relationship of Internet use to depression and social isolation among adolescents. *Adolescence*, *35*(138), 237–242. PMID:11019768

Saucier, G., Akers, L. G., Shen-Miller, S., Knezevic, G., & Stankov, L. (2009). Patterns of thinking in militant extremism. *Perspectives on Psychological Science*, *4*(3), 256–271. doi:10.1111/j.1745-6924.2009.01123.x PMID:26158962

Scanlon, J., Helsloot, I., & Groenendaal, J. (2014). Putting it all together: Integrating ordinary people into emergency response. *International Journal of Mass Emergencies and Disasters*, *32*(1), 43–63.

Scanlon, J., & Hiscott, R. (1994). Despite appearances: There could be a system: Mass casualties and the Edmonton Tornado. *International Journal of Mass Emergencies and Disasters*, *12*(2), 15–239.

Schelling, T. (2006). Micromotives and macrobehaviour: With a new preface and the Nobel lecture (New ed.). New York, NY: W.W Norton & Co.

Schelling, T. (1971). Dynamic models of segregation. *The Journal of Mathematical Sociology*, *1*(2), 143–186. doi:10.1080/0022250X.1971.9989794

Scherer, K. T., Baysinger, M., Zolynsky, D., & LeBreton, J. M. (2013). Predicting counterproductive work behaviors with sub-clinical psychopathy: Beyond the Five Factor Model of personality. *Personality and Individual Differences*, *55*(3), 300–305. doi:10.1016/j.paid.2013.03.007

Schmid, A. P. (2013). *Radicalisation, de-radicalisation, counter-radicalisation: A conceptual discussion and literature review* (ICCT Research Paper). The Netherlands: International Centre for Counter-Terrorism – The Hague.

Schmid, G. (2001). *Report on the existence of a global system for the interception of private and commercial communications* (ECHELON Interception System, 2001/2098[INI]). European Parliament.

Schmid, A. (Ed.). (2011). *The Routledge Handbook of Terrorism Research*. New York, NY: Routledge.

Schmid, A. P. (2004). Terrorism: The definitional problem. *Case Western Reserve Journal of International Law*, *36*(375).

Schmid, A. P. (2011). The revised academic consensus definition of terrorism. *Perspectives of Terrorism*, *6*(2), 158–159.

Schmid, A. P. (2013). *Radicalisation, de-radicalisation and counter-radicalisation: A conceptual discussion and literature review*. The Hague: ICCT.

Schmid, A. P. (Ed.). (2011). *The Routledge handbook of terrorism research*. London: Routledge.

Schmid, A. P., & Jongman, A. J. (1988). *Political Terrorism* (2nd ed.). Oxford, UK: North-Holland.

Schmid, A. P., & Jongman, A. J. (2005). *Political terrorism. A new guide to actors, authors, concepts, data bases, theories, & Literature*. New Brunswick: Transaction Books.

Schmid, P. A. (2004). Frameworks for conceptualising terrorism. *Terrorism and Political Violence*, *16*(2), 197–221. doi:10.1080/09546550490483134

Schmitt, E. (2015, February 16). U. S. intensifies effort to blunt ISIS' message. *The New York Times*. Retrieved from http://www.nytimes.com/2015/02/17/world/middleeast/us-intensifies-effort-to-blunt-isis-message.html?_r=0

Schmitt, E., & Lipton, E. (2009, December 31). Focus on Internet imams as Al-Qaeda recruiters. *The New York Times*. Retrieved from http://www.nytimes.com/2010/01/01/us/01imam.html

Schneier, B. (2007). Did NSA put a secret backdoor in new encryption standard? *Wired*. Retrieved from http://www.wired.com/politics/security/commentary/securitymatters/2007/11/securitymatters_1115

Schneier, B. (2008, April). *Internet censorship*. Retrieved from http://www.schneier.com/blog/archives/2008/04/Internet_censor.html

Schneier, B. (2013). Attacking Tor: How the NSA targets users' online anonymity. *The Guardian*. Retrieved from http://theguardian.com/world/2013/oct/04/tor-attacks-nsa-users-online-anonymity

Schonhardt, S. (2010, July 5). Indonesia: Unlearning jihad. *Global Post*. Retrieved from http://www.globalpost.com/dispatch/indonesia/100702/indonesia-unlearning-jihad

Schultheiss, O. C., & Pang, J. S. (2007). Measuring implicit motives. In R. W. Robins, R. C. Fraley, & R. Krueger (Eds.), *Handbook of research methods in personality psychology* (pp. 322–344). New York, NY: Guilford.

Schuurman, B., & Eijkman, Q. (2015). Indicators of terrorist intent and capability: Tools for threat assessment. *Dynamics of Asymmetric Conflict: Pathways toward terrorism and genocide*. doi: 10.1080/17467586.2015.1040426

Schweitzer, Y., & Ferber, S. G. (2005). *Al-Qaeda and the internationalization of suicide terrorism*. Retrieved from http://ics-www.leeds.ac.uk/papers/pmt/exhibits/2809/memo78.pdf

Schweitzer, Y. (2006). Istishad as an ideological and practical tool in the hands of Al-Qaeda. *Journal of National Defense Studies*, *6*, 113–138.

Scott, P. R., & Jacka, J. M. (2011). *Auditing social media: A governance and risk guide*. Hoboken, NJ: John Wiley & Sons, Inc.

Scott-Railton, J., & Hardy, S. (2014, December 18). Malware attack targeting Syrian ISIS critics. *Citizenlab*. Retrieved from https://citizenlab.org/2014/12/malware-attack-targeting-syrian-isis-critics/

Scrutiny grows on Densus 88 torture video. (2013, March 7). *Jakarta Globe*. Retrieved from http://thejakartaglobe.beritasatu.com/news/scrutiny-grows-on-densus-88-torture-video/

Sedgwick, M. (2010). The concept of radicalisation as a source of confusion. *Terrorism and Political Violence*, *22*(4), 479–494. doi:10.1080/09546553.2010.491009

Segall, L. (2015). Pastor outed on Ashley Madison commits suicide. *CNN*. Retrieved from http://money.cnn.com/2015/09/08/technology/ashley-madison-suicide/index.html

Segell, G. M. (2006). Terrorism on London public transport. *Defense and Security Analysis*, *22*(1), 45–49. doi:10.1080/14751790600577132

Seib, P., & Janbek, D. M. (2011). *Global terrorism and new media: The post-Al Qaeda generation*. New York, NY: Routledge.

Selmi, P. M., Kleiin, M. H., Greist, J. H., Sorrell, S. P., & Erdman, H. P. (1990). Computer-administered cognitive-behavioural therapy for depression. *The American Journal of Psychiatry, 147*(1), 51–56. doi:10.1176/ajp.147.1.51 PMID:2403473

Senate Committee on Homeland Security and Governmental Affairs. (2012). *Zachary Chesser: A case study in online Islamist radicalization and its meaning for the threat of homegrown terrorism*. Washington, DC: United States Senate.

Senators, U. S. Al Qaeda calls for 'electronic jihad'. (2012, May 12). *CNN*. Retrieved from http://edition.cnn.com/2012/05/23/politics/al-qaeda-electronic-jihad/

Seshagiri, A. (2014, March 9). The language of Twitter users. *The New York Times*. Retrieved from http://bits.blogs.nytimes.com/2014/03/09/the-languages-of-twitter-users/

Seto, M. C. (2009). *Assessing the risk posed by child pornography offenders*. Paper presented at the G8 Global Symposium, Chapel Hill, NC.

Seto, M. C., Cantor, J. M., & Blanchard, R. (2006). Child pornography offenses are a valid diagnostic indicator of paedophilia. *Journal of Abnormal Psychology, 115*(3), 610–615. doi:10.1037/0021-843X.115.3.610 PMID:16866601

Seto, M. C., Hanson, K. R., & Babchishin, K. M. (2011). Contact sexual offending by men with online sexual offenses. *Sexual Abuse, 23*, 124–145. PMID:21173158

Shaaban, A. (2014, January 20). Helping Muslim converts learn the ropes. *Khaleej Times*. Retrieved from http://www.khaleejtimes.com/article/20140119/ARTICLE/301199883/1002

Shahar, Y. (2007). The internet as a tool for intelligence and counter-terrorism. In B. Ganor, K. von Knop, & C. Duarte (Eds.), *Hypermedia seduction for terrorist recruiting* (pp. 140–153). Washington, DC: IOS Press.

Shamah, D. (2014, July 9). Hackers threaten "Israhell" cyber-attack over Gaza. *The Times of Israel*. Retrieved from http://www.timesofisrael.com/hackers-threaten-israhell-cyber-attack-over-gaza/

Shane, S., & Hubbard, B. (2014, August 30). ISIS displaying a deft command of varied media. *The New York Times*. Retrieved from http://www.nytimes.com/2014/08/31/world/middleeast/isis-displaying-a-deft-command-of-varied-media.html?_r=0

Shayo, C., Olfman, L., Iriberri, A., & Igbaria, M. (2007). The virtual society: Its driving forces, arrangements, practices, and implications. In J. Gackenbach (Ed.), *Psychology and the internet: Intrapersonal, interpersonal, and transpersonal implications* (pp. 187–219). New York, NY: Academic Press. doi:10.1016/B978-012369425-6/50027-8

Shell, A. (2013, April 23). This stocks gyrate wildly after fake terror tweet. *USA Today*. Retrieved from http://www.usatoday.com/story/money/markets/2013/04/23/stocks-gyrate-wildly-after-fake-terror-tweet/2107089/

Shelley, L. I. (2002). The nexus of organised international criminals and terrorism. *International Annals of Criminology, 1*-6.

Shephard, M. (2009). The powerful online voice of jihad. *The Star*. Retrieved from http://www.thestar.com/news/world/article/711964--the-powerful-online-voice-of-jihad

Sherlock, R., Samaan, G., & Samaan, M. (2014). Islamic State leader Abu Bakr al-Baghdadi 'wounded in air strike'. *The Telegraph*. Retrieved from http://www.telegraph.co.uk/news/worldnews/islamic-state/11219739/Islamic-State-leader-Abu-Bakr-al-Baghdadi-wounded-in-air-strike.html

Shi, P., Dillon, L., Neo, L. S., Tan, J., Wang, Y., Gold, L., & Khader, M. et al. (2014). *Syria's foreign fighters: Motivations to fight (Brief Report Series 12/2014)*. Singapore: Home Team Behavioural Sciences Centre.

Shi, P., Neo, L. S., Ong, G., & Khader, M. (2014). *Critical thinking, technology and terrorism: A case study analysis of Omar Shafik Hammami (Research report No. 03/2014)*. Singapore: Home Team Behavioural Sciences Centre.

Shi, P., Neo, L. S., Ong, G., & Khader, M. (2014). *Understanding online protest: A system-person perspective. Research report No. 15/2014*. Singapore: Home Team Behavioural Sciences Centre.

Shoichet, C. (2013, September 6). Syria's rebels: 20 things you need to know. *CNN*. Retrieved from http://edition.cnn.com/2013/09/06/world/meast/syria-rebels/

Siddiqui, M. (2014, August 24). ISIS: A contrived ideology justifying barbarism and sexual control. *The Guardian*. Retrieved from http://www.theguardian.com/commentisfree/2014/aug/24/isis-ideology-islamic-militants-british-appeal-iraq-syria

Siddiqui, M. (2015, March 1). Nations flourish when people enjoy a sense of belonging. *The Guardian*. Retrieved from http://www.theguardian.com/commentisfree/2015/mar/01/muslims-in-britain-must-act-to-ensure-peace

Siegel, P. (2014). Foreign fighters – Syria: Why we should be worried. *TRAC*. Retrieved from http://www.trackingterrorism.org/article/foreign-fighters-syria-why-we-should-be-worried

Sihaloho, M. J. (2011, April 5). Indonesia still a 'haven for terrorists': Ansyaad. *The Jakarta Globe*. Retrieved from http://jakartainformer.com/18312/indonesia-is-still-a-haven-for-terrorists-ansyaad-jakarta-globe/

Silber, M. D., & Bhatt, A. (2007). *Radicalization in the West: The Home Grown Threat*. New York, NY: New York Police Department.

Silber, M., & Bhatt, A. (2007). *Radicalization in the West: The homegrown threat*. New York, NY: New York Police Department.

Silke, A. (2008). Holy warriors: Exploring the psychological processes of jihadi radicalisation. *European Journal of Criminology, 5*(1), 99–123. doi:10.1177/1477370807084226

Silke, A. (Ed.). (2014). *Prisons, terrorism and extremism: Critical issues in management, radicalization and reform*. Oxon, UK: Routledge.

Simcox, R., & Dyer, E. (2013). *Al Qaeda in the United States: A complete analysis of terrorism offenses*. London: The Henry Jackson Society.

Simcox, R., Stuart, H., Ahmed, H., & Murray, D. (2011). *Islamist terrorism: The British Connections* (2nd ed.). London: The Henry Jackson Society and The Center for Social Cohesion.

Sim, S., & Ismail, N. H. (2012). *Online jihad in Indonesia*. Singapore: Strategic Nexus Consultancy.

Sinai, J. (2012). Radicalisation into extremism and terrorism. *Intelligencer: Journal of U.S. Intelligence Studies, 19*(2).

Singal, J. (2014, August 18). Why ISIS is so terrifyingly effective at seducing new recruits? *NYMag*. Retrieved from http://nymag.com/scienceofus/2014/08/how-isis-seduces-new-recruits.html

Singer, P. (2012). The cyber terror bogeyman. *Armed Forces Journal*. Retrieved from http://www.brookings.edu/research/articles/2012/11/cyber-terror-singer

Singer, P. W. (2012). The cyber terror bogeyman. *Brookings*. Retrieved from http://www.brookings.edu/research/articles/2012/11/cyber-terror-singer

Sjoberg, L., & Gentry, C. E. (Eds.). (2011). *Women, gender and terrorism*. Athens, GA: University of Georgia Press.

Skidmore, J. (2014). *Foreign fighter involvement in Syria*. Herzliya, Israel: International Institute for Counter-Terrorism.

Skillicorn, D. (2009). *Knowledge discovery for counterterrorism and law enforcement*. New York, NY: CRC Press.

Skinner, P. (2015, September 2). The power of ISIS' message. *The Cipher Brief*. Retrieved from https://www.thecipher-brief.com/article/power-isis-message-0

Slevin, J. (2000). *The internet and society*. Malden, MA: Polity Press.

Smith, H. (2009, December 30). Al-Awlaki may be Al-Qaeda recruiter. *CBS News*. Retrieved from http://www.cbsnews.com/8301-503543_162-6039811-503543.html

Smith, S. (2008). *Teen hacker in Poland plays trains and derails city tram system* [Web log post]. Retrieved from http://inhomelandsecurity.com/teen_hacker_in_poland_plays_tr/

Smith, T. (2001, October 31). Hacker jailed for revenge sewage attacks. *The Register*. Retrieved from http://www.theregister.co.uk/2001/10/31/hacker_jailed_for_revenge_sewage/

Soeriaatmadja, W., & Lee, L. (2011, July 21). Singapore embassy 'targeted by terrorists'. *The Jakarta Globe*. Retrieved from http://www.thejakartaglobe.com/archive/singapore-embassy-targeted-by-terrorists/

Soghoian, C. (2010). Caught in the cloud: Privacy, encryption and government back doors in the Web 2.0 era. *Journal on Telecommunications & High Technology Law, 8*, 359–423.

Solahudin. (2013). www.teror.co.id. Depok: Center for Terrorism and Social Conflict Studies Fakultas Psikologi Universitas Indonesia.

Sontag, S. (2003). *Regarding the pain of others*. New York, NY: Farrar, Straus and Giroux.

Sorko-Ram, S. (2012, March). Why Syria's Assad can't stop killing his own people. *MaozIsrael*. Retrieved from http://www.maozisrael.org/site/News2?id=9174#1

Spaaij, R. (2010). The enigma of lone wolf terrorism: An assessment. *Studies in Conflict and Terrorism, 33*(9), 854–870. doi:10.1080/1057610X.2010.501426

Sparks, S. (1992). Exploring electronic social support groups. *The American Journal of Nursing*, (Dec): 62–65. PMID:1456319

Speckhard, A., & Ahkmedova, K. (2006). The making of a martyr: Chechen suicide terrorism. *Studies in Conflict and Terrorism, 29*(5), 429–492. doi:10.1080/10576100600698550

Starey, T. (2005). Getting the message - A comparative analysis of laws regulating law enforcement agencies' access to stored communications in Australia and the US. *Media and Arts Law Review, 10*(1), 23–55.

Statistics Canada. (2013). *Individual Internet use and e-commerce, 2012* (Catalogue no. 11-001-X). Retrieved from http://www.statcan.gc.ca/daily-quotidien/131028/dq131028a-eng

Staub, E. (2005). Basic human needs, altruism, and aggression. In A. G. Miller (Ed.), *The social psychology of good and evil* (pp. 51–84). New York: The Guildford Press.

Steinal, W., van Kleef, G. A., van Knippenberg, D., Hogg, M. A., Homan, A. C., & Moffitt, G. (2010). How intragroup dynamics affect behaviour in intergroup conflict: The role of group norms, prototypicality, and need to belong. *Group Processes & Intergroup Relations, 13*(6), 779–794. doi:10.1177/1368430210375702

Steinberger, R. (2010). Challenges and methods for multilingual text mining. In *Proceedings of the 7th International Conference on Language Resources and Evaluation (LREC)*. Valletta, Malta: ELRA.

Steinfatt, T. (2015). Measuring propaganda. In M. R. Allen (Ed.), *The Sage encyclopedia of communication research methods*. Thousand Oaks, CA: Sage Publications.

Steinhauer, J. (2015, April 22). House passes Cybersecurity Bill after companies fall victim to data breaches. *The New York Times*. Retrieved from http://www.nytimes.com/2015/04/23/us/politics/computer-attacks-spur-congress-to-act-on-cybersecurity-bill-years-in-making.html

Stein, Y. (2011). *Social networks – Terrorism's new marketplace*. Jerusalem, Israel: Genocide Prevention Now.

Stenerson, A. (2008). The Internet: A virtual training camp? *Terrorism and Political Violence, 20*(8), 215–233. doi:10.1080/09546550801920790

Stern, J., & Berger, J. M. (2015, March 8). ISIS and the foreign-fighter phenomenon. *The Atlantic*. Retrieved from http://www.theatlantic.com/international/archive/2015/03/isis-and-the-foreign-fighter-problem/387166/

Stern, J., & Berger, J. M. (2015, March 9). Thugs wanted – bring your own boots: How ISIS attracts foreign fighters to its twisted utopia. *The Guardian*. Retrieved from http://www.theguardian.com/world/2015/mar/09/how-isis-attracts-foreign-fighters-the-state-of-terror-book

Stern, E. (1997). Crisis and learning: A conceptual balance sheet. *Journal of Contingencies and Crisis Management, 5*(2), 69–86. doi:10.1111/1468-5973.00039

Stillman, T., & Baumeister, R. (2009). Uncertainty, belongingness, and four needs for meaning. *Psychological Inquiry, 20*(4), 249–251. doi:10.1080/10478400903333544

Stohl, M. (2014). Dr. Strangeweb: Or how they stopped worrying and learned to love cyber war. In T, Chen, L. Jarvis, & S. Macdonald (Eds.), Cyberterrorism: Understanding, assessment and response (pp. 85-102). New York, NY: Springer.

Stohl, M. (2006). Cyber terrorism: A clear and present danger, the sum of all fears, breaking point or patriot games? *Crime, Law, and Social Change, 46*(4-5), 223–238. doi:10.1007/s10611-007-9061-9

Stone, J. (2014, August 15). What is Anonymous? 'Hacktivist' involvement in Mike Brown shooting proves vigilante justice is now routine. *International Business Times*. Retrieved from http://www.ibtimes.com/what-anonymous-hacktivist-involvement-mike-brown-shooting-proves-vigilante-justice-now-1660052

Storm, D. (2014, January 15). Hackers exploit SCADA holes to take full control of critical infrastructure. *ComputerWorld*. Retrieved from http://www.computerworld.com/article/2475789/cybercrime-hacking/hackers-exploit-scada-holes-to-take-full-control-of-critical-infrastructure.html

Stringaris, A., Goodman, R., Ferdinando, S., Razdan, V., Muhrer, E., Leibenluft, E., & Brotman, M. A. (2012). The Affective Reactivity Index: A concise irritability scale for clinical and research settings. *Journal of Child Psychology and Psychiatry, and Allied Disciplines, 53*(11), 1109–1117. doi:10.1111/j.1469-7610.2012.02561.x

Strohm, C. (2011). Facebook, YouTube aid in Al-Qaida's spread, study says. *National Journal*. Retrieved from http://search.proquest.com.ezp01.library.qut.edu.au/docview/850518421#

Suler, J. (2004). The online disinhibition effect. *Cyberpsychology & Behavior, 7*(3), 321–326. doi:10.1089/1094931041291295

Sunstein, C. R. (2009). *Going to extremes: How like minds unite and divide*. New York: Oxford University Press.

Sunstein, C. R. (2010). *On rumours: How falsehoods spread, why we believe them, what can be done*. London: Penguin.

Swann, W. B. Jr, Jetten, J., Gómez, Á., Whitehouse, H., & Bastian, B. (2012). When group membership gets personal: A theory of identity fusion. *Psychological Review, 119*(3), 441–456. doi:10.1037/a0028589 PMID:22642548

Swink, D. (2010, March 6). The Pentagon shooting: They don't "just snap". *Psychology today*. Retrieved from http://www.psychologytoday.com/blog/threat-management/201003/the-pentagon-shooting-they-don-t-just-snap

Sydney siege report: Tony Abbott says legal system let community down. (2015, February 22). *The Guardian.* Retrieved from http://www.theguardian.com/australia-news/2015/feb/22/sydney-siege-report-tony-abbott-more-immigration-checks-needed

Tait, S. (2008). Pornographies of violence? Internet spectatorship on body horror. *Critical Studies in Media Communication, 25*(1), 91–111. doi:10.1080/15295030701851148

Tajfel, H. (1974). Social identity and intergroup behaviour. *Social Sciences Information. Information Sur les Sciences Sociales, 13*(2), 65–93. doi:10.1177/053901847401300204

Tajfel, H., & Turner, J. C. (1979). An integrative theory of intergroup conflict. In W. G. Austinm & S. Worchel (Eds.), *The social psychology of intergroup relations* (pp. 33–47). Monterey, CA: Brooks-Cole.

Talbot, D. (2005). Terror's server. *Technology Review.* Retrieved from http://www.technologyreview.com/infotech/14150/

Talbot, D. (2013, September 16). Encrypted heartbeats keep hackers from medical implants. *MIT Technology Review.* Retrieved from http://www.technologyreview.com/news/519266/encrypted-heartbeats-keep-hackers-from-medical-implants/

Talihärm, A. M. (2010). Cyberterrorism: In theory or in practice? *Defence Against Terrorism Review, 3*(2), 59–74.

Tan, E. (2006). *Road to radicalisation: A psychological analysis of the Jemaah Islamiyah group and its members (Research report No. 01/2006).* Singapore: Behavioural Sciences Unit.

Tarde, G. (1890). *Les lois de l'imitation.* Paris: Félix Alcan.

Taufiqurrohman, M. (2013). Counterterrorism in Indonesia: Quo vadis? *Counter Terrorist Trends and Analysis, 5*(6), 7–10.

Tausczik, Y. R., & Pennebaker, J. W. (2010). The psychological meaning of words: LIWC and computerized text analysis methods. *Journal of Language and Social Psychology, 29*(1), 24–54. doi:10.1177/0261927X09351676

Taylor, D. M., & Jaggi, V. (1974). Ethocentrism and casual attribution in a South Indian context. *Journal of Cross-Cultural Psychology, 5*(2), 192–171. doi:10.1177/002202217400500202

Taylor, M., & Quayle, E. (2003). *Child pornography: An Internet crime.* Hove, U.K.: Brunner Routledge.

Tekwani, S. (2007). Online networks of terrorist groups and their implications for security: a case study of Sri Lanka's Liberation Tigers of Tamil Eelam. In I. Banerjee (Ed.), *The Internet and governance in Asia: A critical reader* (pp. 173–188). Singapore: National Technological University of Singapore.

Telecommunications (Interception) Amendment Act Cth. (2006). Canberra: Government of Australia.

Temple-Raston, D. (2015, May 7). How to take the Internet back from ISIS. *The New Yorker.* Retrieved from http://www.newyorker.com/tech/elements/how-to-take-the-internet-back-from-isis

Terror suspect Cherif Kouachi: 'I was ready to go and die in battle'. (2015, January 9). *CNN.* Retrieved from http://edition.cnn.com/2015/01/09/europe/cherif-kouachi-court-documents/

Terror, torture and torpor: Inside Guantanamo bay with the 'forever prisoners'. (2014, December 13). *Sydney Morning Herald.* Retrieved from http://www.smh.com.au/world/terror-torture-and-torpor-inside-guantanamo-bay-with-the-forever-prisoners-20141212-125m1z.html

Tester, K. (2001). *Compassion, morality and the media.* Buckingham: Open University Press.

Thailand mulls ceding power to end deadly southern insurgency. (2013, June 12). *Asia One.* Retrieved from http://news.asiaone.com/print/News/AsiaOne%2BNews/Asia/Story/A1Story20130612-429225.html

The Clarion Project. (2015). Special report: The Islamic State. Clarion Project, Inc.

The Islamic movement of Uzbekistan: An evolving threat. (2014, May 31). *Radio Free Europe Radio Liberty (RFERL)*. Retrieved from http://www.rferl.org/content/islamic-movement-uzbekistan-roundtable/25405614.html

The Islamic State of Iraq and Syria. (2015). *Hijrah to the Islamic State*. Author.

The Islamic State of Iraq and Syria. (2015). *The Islamic State (2015)*. Author.

The martyrs of the south. (2012, December 5). *Bangkok Post*. Retrieved from http://www.bangkokpost.com/archive/the-martyrs-of-the-south/324580

The Meir Amit Intelligence and Terrorism Information Center. (2014). *ISIS: Portrait of a jihadi terrorist organization*. Retrieved from http://www.terrorism-info.org.il/Data/articles/Art_20733/101_14_Ef_1329270214.pdf

The Muslim Converts' Association of Singapore. (2014). *About us*. Retrieved from http://www.darul-arqam.org.sg/corporate/

The original tipping point wasn't one. (2009, July 13). *The Economist*. Retrieved from http://www.economist.com/blogs/freeexchange/2009/07/the_original_tipping_point_was

The Soufan Group. (2013). *Countering violent extremism: The counter narrative study*. New York, NY: The Soufan Group.

The Soufan Group. (2013, October 17). *TSG Intel Brief: The challenge of new technology adoption and violent extremist groups*. Retrieved from http://soufangroup.com/tsg-intelbrief-the-challenge-of-new-technology-adoption-and-violent-extremist-groups/

The White House. (2015, February 18). *Fact sheet: The White House summit on countering violent extremism*. Retrieved from https://www.whitehouse.gov/the-press-office/2015/02/18/fact-sheet-white-house-summit-countering-violent-extremism

The, U. S. Created PRISM – it also created the anitdote. (2014, January 23). *Bloomberg Businessweek*. Retrieved from http://www.bloomberg.com/bw/articles/2014-01-23/tor-anonymity-software-vs-dot-the-national-security-agency

Theories of attitude change. (2001, August 3). *The Association for Educational Communications and Technology*. Retrieved from http://www.aect.org/edtech/ed1/34/34-03.html

Thomas, E. F., Mcgarty, C., & Louis, W. (2014). Social interaction and psychological pathways to political engagement and extremism. *European Journal of Social Psychology*, *44*(1), 15–22. doi:10.1002/ejsp.1988

Thomas, T. L. (2003). Al Qaeda and the Internet: The dangers of 'cyberplanning'. *Parameters*, *33*(1), 112–123.

TODAY just published the worst article of the year. Singapore netizens tear it to shreds. (2014, November 15). *Must Share News*. Retrieved May 13, 2015, from http://mustsharenews.com/worse-story-of-year/

Toegel, G., & Conger, J. (2003). 360-degree feedback: Time for reinvention. *Academy of Management Learning & Education*, *2*(3), 297–311. doi:10.5465/AMLE.2003.10932156

Tokar, L. (2007). Hypermedia communication as a modern means for the creation of terrorist and counterterrorist consciousness. In B. Ganor, K. von Knop, & C. Duarte (Eds.), *Hypermedia seduction for terrorist recruiting* (pp. 105–115). Washington, DC: IOS Press.

Tor Project. (n.d.). Retrieved from https://www.torproject.org/index.html.en

Torok, R. (2010). *Make a bomb In your mum's kitchen: Cyber recruiting and socialisation of 'white moors' and home grown jihadists*. Retrieved from http://ro.ecu.edu.au/cgi/viewcontent.cgi?article=1005&context=act

Torok, R. (2011). *The online institution: Psychiatric power as an explanatory model for the normalisation of radicalisation and terrorism.* Paper presented at the European Intelligence and Security Informatics Conference (EISIC), Athens, Greece. doi:10.1109/EISIC.2011.43

Torok, R. (2013). Developing an explanatory model for the process of online radicalisation and terrorism. *Security Informatics, 2*(6).

Torok, R. (2013). Developing an explanatory model for the process of online radicalisation and terrorism. *Security Informatics, 2*(1), 1–10. doi:10.1186/2190-8532-2-6

Torproject.org. (2015). *What is the Tor Brower?* Retrieved from https://www.torproject.org/projects/torbrowser.html.en

Torres-Soriano, M. R. (2012). The vulnerabilities of online terrorism. *Studies in Conflict and Terrorism, 35*(4), 263–277. doi:10.1080/1057610X.2012.656345

Townsend, M. (2015, January 15). How a team of social media experts is able to keep track of the UK jihadis. *The Guardian.* Retrieved from http://www.theguardian.com/world/2015/jan/17/social-media-british-jihadists-islamic-state-facebook-twitter

Tripathy, J. (2010). What is a terrorist? *International Journal of Cultural Studies, 13*(3), 219–234. doi:10.1177/1367877909359731

Tromp, E., & Pechenizky, M. (2011). *SentiCorr: Multilingual sentiment analysis of personal correspondence.* Retrieved from http://www.win.tue.nl/stressatwork/pdfs/senticorr_camera.pdf

Tsai, W., & Goshal, S. (1998). Social capital and value creation: The role of intrafirm networks. *Academy of Management Journal, 41*(4), 464–476. doi:10.2307/257085

Tucker, D. (2010). *Jihad dramatically transformed? Sageman on Jihad and the Internet.* Washington, DC: Homeland Security Affairs.

Tuman, J. (2010). *Communicating terror: The Rhetorical dimensions of terrorism* (2nd ed.). Thousand Oaks, CA: Sage Publications.

Turgeman-Goldschmidt, O. (2005). Hackers' accounts: Hacking as a social entertainment. *Social Science Computer Review, 23*(1), 8–23. doi:10.1177/0894439304271529

Turney, P., & Pantel, P. (2010). From frequency to meaning: Vector space models of semantics. *Journal of Artificial Intelligence Research, 37*(1), 141–188.

Turvey, B. E., Khader, M., Ang, J., Tan, E., & Chin, J. (2012). Introduction to terrorism: Understanding and interviewing terrorists. In B. E. Turvey (Ed.), *Criminal profiling* (4th ed., pp. 569–583). San Diego, CA: Academic Press. doi:10.1016/B978-0-12-385243-4.00023-X

Tversky, A., & Kahneman, D. (1974). *Judgement under uncertainty: Heuristics and biases, 185*(4157), 1124-1131.

Twitter translates tweets from leading Egyptians. (2013, July 4). *BBC News.* Retrieved from http://www.bbc.com/news/technology-23179269

Tzanetti, T. (2007). Use of media and challenges in countering terrorist rhetoric. In B. Ganor, K. von Knop, & C. Duarte (Eds.), *Hypermedia seduction for terrorist recruiting* (pp. 231–241). Washington, DC: IOS Press.

U. S. Department of State. (2014). Foreign terrorist organizations. *Bureau of Counterterrorism.* Retrieved from http://www.state.gov/j/ct/rls/other/des/123085.htm

U. S. Department of State. (n.d.). *Center for Strategic Counterterrorism Communications*. Retrieved from http://www.state.gov/r/cscc/

U.K. Cabinet Office. (2015). *The national infrastructure*. London: Centre for the Protection of National Infrastructure.

U.S. Army Training and Doctrine Command (ATDC). (2006). *Critical infrastructure: Threats and terrorism (Handbook No. 1.02)*. Fort Leavenworth, KS: U.S. Army Training and Doctrine Command.

U.S. Department of Homeland Security. (2014). *Critical infrastructure sectors*. Washington, DC: U.S. Department of Homeland Security.

U.S. Department of Justice and Police Executive Research Forum (2013, May). Social media and Tactical Considerations for Law Enforcement. Retrieved from http://www.policeforum.org/assets/docs/Free_Online_Documents/Technology/social%20media%20and%20tactical%20considerations%20for%20law%20enforcement%202013.pdf

U.S. Department of Justice. (2015). *News release on Ali Shukri Amin, 17, of Manassas, Virginia June 11, 2015*. Retrieved from http://www.justice.gov/opa/pr/virginia-teen-pleads-guilty-providing-material-support-isil

U.S. general: Israel-Palestinian conflict foments anti-U.S. sentiment. (2010, March 17). *Haaretz*. Retrieved from http://www.haaretz.com/news/u-s-general-israel-palestinian-conflict-foments-anti-u-s-sentiment-1.264910

U.S.-Canada Power System Outage Task Force. (2014). *U.S. final report on the August 14, 2003 blackout in the United States and Canada: Causes and recommendations*. U.S. and Canada: United States Department of Energy.

UN Office for the Coordination of Humanitarian Affairs (OCHA). (2014, October 15). *Gaza Crisis: Situation Overview*. Retrieved from http://www.ochaopt.org/content.aspx?id=1010361

Ungerer, C. (2011). *Jihadists in jail: Radicalisation and the Indonesian prison experience*. Canberra: Australian Strategic Policy Institute/S. Rajaratanam School of International Studies.

United Nations Counterterrorism Implementation Task Force (UN CTITF). (2011). *Use of the Internet to Counter the Appeal of Extremist Violence: Conference Summary and Follow-up/ Recommendations*. Retrieved from http://www.un.org/terrorism/pdfs/CTITF%20Riyadh%20Conference%20-%20Summary%20&%20Recommendations.pdf

United Nations Office on Drugs and Crime (UNODC). (2012). *The use of the internet for terrorist purposes*. Retrieved from http://www.unodc.org/documents/frontpage/Use_of_Internet_for_Terrorist_Purposes.pdf

United Nations Office on Drugs and Crime (UNODC). (2012). *The use of the Internet for terrorist purposes*. Retrieved from http://www.unodc.org/documents/frontpage/Use_of_Internet_for_Terrorist_Purposes.pdf

United States Department of Defense. (2006). *Risk management guide for DoD acquisition*. Washington, DC: Department of Defense.

United States Institute of Peace (USIP). (2012, May 7). *Countering Violent Extremism in Pakistan*. Washington, DC: Author.

United States of America v. Ali Shukri Amin. (2015). *In the United States District Court for the Eastern District of Virginia, Alexandria Division: Case l:15-cr-00164-CMH Document 7- Filed June 11, 2015*. Retrieved from http://www.justice.gov/opa/file/477366/download

United States of America v. Bilal Abood. (2015). *Indictment No. 3-15CR-0256K: In the United States District Court for the Northern Division of Texas Dallas Division-Filed June 10, 2015*. Retrieved from http://www.investigativeproject.org/documents/case_docs/2747.pdf

United States of America v. Emerson Winfield Begolly. (2013). *Sentencing Memorandum of Case 2:11-cr-00172-MBC Document 67 Filed 07/09/13 filed in the United States District Court for the Western District of Pennsylvania.* Retrieved from http://www.investigativeproject.org/documents/case_docs/2200.pdf

Upal, M. (2015). Confronting Islamic jihadist movements. *Journal of Terrorism Research.* Retrieved from http://ojs.st-andrews.ac.uk/index.php/jtr/article/view/1155/900

Urbas, G., & Choo, K. R. (2008). *Resource materials on technology-enabled crime (Technical and Background Paper no.28).* Canberra: Australian Institute of Criminology.

US 304th Military Intelligence Battalion. (2008). *Sample overview: alQaida-like mobile discussions & potential creative uses.* Retrieved from http://www.fas.org/irp/eprint/mobile.pdf

User mistakes aid most cyber attacks, Verizon and Symantec studies show. (2015, April 14). *Channel News Asia.* Retrieved from http://www.channelnewsasia.com/news/technology/user-mistakes-aid-most/1782902.html

Using Social Media to Communicate Against Violent Extremism. (2015). Canberra: Attorney-General's Department, Australian Government.

Valasek, C., & Miller, C. (2014). *Adventures in automotive networks and control units.* Retrieved from www.ioactive.com/pdfs/IOActive_Adventures_in_Automotive_Networks_and_Control_Units.pdf

van der Zee, B. (2009). Twitter triumphs. *Index on Censorship, 38*(4), 97–102. doi:10.1080/03064220903392570

van Dijk. T. A. (1998). Ideology: A multidisciplinary approach. London: Sage Publications.

van Dijk, T. A. (1988). *News as discourse.* Lawrence Erlbaum Associates, Inc.

van Dijk, T. A. (1995). The mass media today: Discourse of domination or diversity. *Communication Beyond the Nation-State, 2*(2), 27–45.

van Ginkel, B. (2011). *Incitement to terrorism: A matter of prevention or repression?* (ICCT Research Paper). Retrieved from http://www.icct.nl/download/file/ICCT-Van-Ginkel-Incitement-To-Terrorism-August-2011.pdf

van Ginkel, B. (2015). Responding to cyber jihad: Towards an effective counter narrative. The Netherlands: International Centre for Counter-Terrorism – The Hague.

Varian, H. (2011, September). Predicting the present. *Think with Google.* Retrieved from https://www.thinkwithgoogle.com/articles/predicting-the-present.html

Vatis, M. A. (2001). Cyber attacks during the war on terrorism: A predictive analysis. *Institute for Security Technology Studies.* Retrieved from http://www.ists.dartmouth.edu/docs/cyber_a1.pdf

Veldhuis, T. (2012). *Designing rehabilitation and reintegration programmes for violent extremist offenders: A realist approach.* ICCT Research Paper. Netherland: International Centre for Counter-Terrorism – The Hague.

Veldhuis, T., & Staun, J. (2009). *Islamist radicalisation: A root cause model.* Retrieved from http://subweb.diis.dk/graphics/_IO_indsatsomraader/Religion_og_social_konflikt_og_Mellemosten/Islamist%20Radicalisation.Veldhuis%20and%20Staun.pdf

Venhaus, J. (2010, May). *Why youth join Al-Qaeda.* United States Institute of Peace. Retrieved from http://www.usip.org/publications/why-youth-join-al-qaeda

Venhaus, J. M. (2010, May). Why youth join Al-Qaeda. *United States Institute of Peace*. Retrieved from http://www.usip.org/sites/default/files/resources/SR236Venhaus.pdf

Venhaus, J. M. (2010). *Why youths join al-Qaeda. Special Report 236*. Washington, DC: United States Institute of Peace.

Venitism. (n.d.). *Distrust of mainstream media*. Retrieved from http://venitism.blogspot.sg/2011/09/distrust-of-mainstream-media.html

Venugopala, B. N. (2014). Post war disillusionment and English poetry. *International Journal of Language & Linguistics, 1*(1), 11–14.

Vergani, M., & Zuev, D. (2011). Analysis of YouTube videos used by activists in the Uyghur Nationalist Movement: Combining quantitative and qualitative methods. *Journal of Contemporary China, 20*(69), 205–229. doi:10.1080/10670564.2011.541628

Verizon. (2012). *2012 Data Breach Investigations Report*. Basking Ridge, NJ: Author. Retrieved from http://www.verizonenterprise.com/resources/reports/rp_data-breach-investigations-report-2012-ebk_en_xg.pdf

Verton, D. (2003). *Black ice: The invisible threat of cyber-terrorism*. New York, NY: McGraw-Hill.

Vespignani, A. (2010). Complex networks: The fragility of interdependency. *Nature, 464*(7291), 984–985. doi:10.1038/464984a PMID:20393545

Victoroff, J. (2005). The mind of the terrorist: A review of critique of psychological approaches. *The Journal of Conflict Resolution, 49*(1), 3–42. doi:10.1177/0022002704272040

Vishwanath, A. (2015a, June 8). Why the cyberattacks keep coming. *CNN*. Retrieved from http://www.cnn.com/2015/06/08/opinions/vishwanath-stopping-hacking

Vishwanath, A., Harrison, B., & Ng, Y. J. (2015). *Suspicion, cognition, automaticity model (SCAM) of phishing susceptibility*. Paper presented at the Annual Conference of the International Communication Association, San Juan, Puerto Rico.

Vishwanath, A. (2015b). Habitual facebook use and its impact on getting deceived on social media. *Journal of Computer-Mediated Communication, 20*(1), 83–98. doi:10.1111/jcc4.12100

Vishwanath, A. (2015c). Examining the distinct antecedents of e-mail habits and its influence on the outcomes of a phishing attack. *Journal of Computer-Mediated Communication, 20*(5), 570–584. doi:10.1111/jcc4.12126

Vishwanath, A., Herath, T., Chen, R., Wang, J., & Rao, H. R. (2011). Why do people get phished? Testing individual differences in phishing vulnerability within an integrated, information processing model. *Decision Support Systems, 51*(3), 576–586. doi:10.1016/j.dss.2011.03.002

von Behr, I., Reding, A., Edwards, C., & Gribbon, L. (2013). *Radicalisation in the digital age: The use of the internet in 15 cases of terrorism and extremism*. Santa Monica, CA: RAND Corporation.

von Behr, I., Reding, A., Edwards, C., & Gribbon, L. (2013). *Radicalisation in the digital era: The use of the Internet in 15 cases of terrorism and extremism*. Santa Monica, CA: RAND Corporation.

Von Clausewitz, C. (1976). *On war* (M. Howard & P. Paret, Trans. & Eds.). Princeton: Princeton University Press. (Original work published 1832)

von Hippel, W., & Trivers, R. (2011). The evolution and psychology of self-deception. *Behavioral and Brain Sciences, 34*(1), 1–16. doi:10.1017/S0140525X10001354

Vygotsky, L. (2012). *Thought and language (First English Translation, 1962; 2012 MIT edition is revised and enlarged)*. Cambridge, MA: M.I. T Press.

Wadhwa, T. (2012, June 12). Yes, you can hack a pacemaker (and other medical devices too). *Forbes*. Retrieved from www.forbes.com/sites/singularity/2012/12/06/yes-you-can-hack-a-pacemaker-and-other-medical-devices-too/

WaE network. (2015). Retrieved from http://www.waenetwork.org

Wagner, M. (2014, August 23). Apparent ISIS terrorists take photos with Nutella to seem softer, friendlier to West. *New York Daily News*. Retrieved from http://www.nydailynews.com/news/world/isis-fighters-photos-nutella-friendly-article-1.1914450

Walker, D. (2015, April). Critical infrastructure survey: Gov't, energy sectors targeted most by destructive attacks. *SC Magazine for IT Security Professionals*. Retrieved from http://www.scmagazine.com/critical-infrastructure-survey-govt-energy-sectors-targeted-most-by-destructive-attacks/article/407772/

Wall, K. D. (2011). *The Kaplan and Garrick definition of risk and its application to managerial decisions*. DRMI Naval Postgraduate School. Retrieved from http://www.nps.edu/Academics/Centers/DRMI/docs/DRMI%20Working%20Paper%2011-3.pdf

Walter, J. B., & Boyd, S. (2002). Attraction to computer-mediated social support. In C. A. Lin & D. Atkin (Eds.), *Communication technology and society: Audience adoption and uses* (pp. 153–188). Cresskill, NJ: Hampton Press.

Waltman, M. S. (2014). Teaching hate: The role of Internet visual imagery in the radicalisation of white ethno-terrorists in the United States. In C. K. Winkler & C. E. Dauber (Eds.), *Visual propaganda and extremism in the online environment* (pp. 83–104). Carlisle, PA: Strategic Studies Institute and U.S. Army War College Press.

Walton, G. M., Cohen, G. L., Cwir, D., & Spencer, S. J. (2012). Mere belonging: The power of social connections. *Journal of Personality and Social Psychology, 102*(3), 513–532. doi:10.1037/a0025731 PMID:22023711

Wan, C., & Chew, P. Y. (2013). Cultural knowledge, category label, and social connections: Components of cultural identity in the global, multicultural context. *Asian Journal of Social Psychology, 16*(4), 247–259. doi:10.1111/ajsp.12029

Wang, X., Gerber, M. S., & Brown, D. (2012). Automatic crime prediction using events extracted from Twitter. In S. J. Yang, A. M. Greenberg, & M. Endsley (Eds.), *Social computing, behavioral-Cultural modeling and prediction 2012, lecture notes in computer science* (pp. 231–238). Heidelberg: Springer. doi:10.1007/978-3-642-29047-3_28

Waqas. (2015, April 18). Pics of IDF women soldiers helped hackers to breach Israeli Military Servers. *Hackread.com*. Retrieved from https://www.hackread.com/hackers-breach-israeli-military-servers/

Ward, T., Goebbels, S., & Willis, G. M. (2013). Offender rehabilitation: The construction of better lives and the reduction of risk. In G. Bruinsma & D. Weisburd (Eds.), *Encyclopaedia of criminology and criminal justice*. New York, NY: Springer-Verlag.

Warren, Z. (2014, February 11). 'Mask' virus infected computers in government, others for seven years. *Inside Counsel*. Retrieved from http://www.insidecounsel.com/2014/02/11/mask-virus-infected-computers-in-government-others

Warschauer, M. (2000). Language, identity, and the Internet. In B. E. Kolko, L. Nakamura, & G. B. Rodman (Eds.), *Race in cyberspace* (pp. 151–170). New York, NY: Routledge.

Watts, C. (2014). Jihadi competition after Al-Qaeda hegemony – The 'old guard', Team ISIS and the battle for jihad hearts and minds. *Foreign Policy Research Institute*. Retrieved from http://www.fpri.org/geopoliticus/2014/02/jihadi-competition-after-al-qaeda-hegemony-old-guard-team-isis-battle-jihadi-hearts-minds

Weatherston, D., & Moran, J. (2003). Terrorism and mental illness: Is there a relationship? *International Journal of Offender Therapy and Comparative Criminology, 47*(6), 698–713. doi:10.1177/0306624X03257244 PMID:14661388

Webster, C. D., Douglas, K. S., Eaves, D., & Hart, S. (1997). *HCR-20 assessing risk for violence: Version 2.* Vancouver, Canada: Mental Health Law & Policy Institute, Simon Fraser University.

Webster, C. D., Douglas, K. S., Eaves, D., & Hart, S. (2001). *HCR-20 violence risk management companion guide.* Vancouver, Canada: Mental Health Law & Policy Institute, Simon Fraser University.

Webster, D. M., & Kruglanski, A. W. (1994). Individual differences in need for cognitive closure. *Journal of Personality and Social Psychology, 67*(6), 1049–1062. doi:10.1037/0022-3514.67.6.1049 PMID:7815301

Weimann, G. (2004). How modern terrorism uses the Internet. Special Report No.116. Washington, DC: United States Institute of Peace. Retrieved from www.terror.net

Weimann, G. (2004). *How modern terrorism uses the Internet. Special Report No.116.* Washington, DC: United States Institute of Peace; www.terror.net

Weimann, G. (2006). *Terror on the Internet: The new arena, the new challenge.* Washington, DC: United States of Institute of Peace.

Weimann, G. (2006). *Terror on the Internet: The new arena, the new challenges.* Washington, DC: United States Institute of Peace Press.

Weimann, G. (2007). Using the Internet for terrorist recruitment and mobilisation. In B. Ganor, K. V. Knop, & C. Duarte (Eds.), *Hypermedia seduction for terrorist recruiting* (pp. 47–58). Washington, DC: IOS Press.

Weimann, G. (2007). Using the internet for terrorist recruitment and mobilisation. In B. Ganor, K. von Knop, & C. Duarte (Eds.), *Hypermedia seduction for terrorist recruiting* (pp. 47–58). Washington, DC: IOS Press.

Weimann, G. (2010). Terror on Facebook, Twitter, and YouTube. *The Brown Journal of World Affairs, 16*(2), 45–54.

Weimann, G. (2011). Cyber-Fatwas and terrorism. *Studies in Conflict and Terrorism, 34*(10), 765–781. doi:10.1080/1 057610X.2011.604831

Weimann, G. (2012). Lone wolves in cyberspace. *Journal of Terrorism Research, 3*(2), 75–90. doi:10.15664/jtr.405

Weimann, G. (2015). *Terrorism in cyberspace.* Washington, DC: Woodrow Wilson Centre Press.

Weimann, G., & von Knop, K. (2008). Applying the notion of noise to countering online terrorism. *Studies in Conflict and Terrorism, 31*(10), 883–902. doi:10.1080/10576100802342601

Weimman, G. (2006). *Terror on the internet: The new arena, the new challenges.* Washington, DC: United States Institute of Peace Press.

Weinberg, L., Pedahzur, A., & Hirsch-Hoefler, S. (2004). The challenges of conceptualizing terrorism. *Terrorism and Political Violence, 16*(4), 777–794. doi:10.1080/095465590899768

Wellman, B. (1996). An electronic group is a virtual social network. In S. Kiesler (Ed.), *Culture of the Internet* (pp. 179–205). Mahwah, NJ: Lawrence Erlbaum.

West, B., & Stewart, S. (2010). Uncomfortable truths and the Times Square attack. *Stratfor.* Retrieved from https://www.stratfor.com/weekly/20100505_uncomfortable_truths_times_square_attack

Wetter, O. E. (2014). Terrorism research: Should we focus on the opponent or on our own people? *Defense and Security Analysis*, *30*(2), 92–105. doi:10.1080/14751798.2014.894298

What is 'Islamic State'? (2015, October 8). *BBC News*. Retrieved from http://www.bbc.com/news/world-middle-east-29052144

What is Metadata? (2015). *Whatis.com*. Retrieved from http://whatis.techtarget.com/defintion/metadata

What is spear phishing? (2015). *Kaspersky Lab*. Retrieved from https://usa.kaspersky.com/internet-security-center/definitions/spear-phishing#.VVBupY7vPrc

Why was Sajida al-Rishawi important to ISIS? (2015, January 26). *Al Arabiya News*. Retrieved from http://english.alarabiya.net/en/perspective/profiles/2015/01/26/Why-is-Sajida-al-Rishawi-important-to-ISIS-.html

Wiktorowicz, Q. (2005). A genealogy of radical Islam. *Studies in Conflict and Terrorism*, *28*(2), 75–97. doi:10.1080/10576100590905057

Wiktorowicz, Q. (2005). *Radical Islam rising: Muslim extremism in the West*. Lanham: Rowman and Littlefield.

Williams, D., & Marsden, S. (2014, August 11). The Cardiff jihadist who wants to die a 'martyr': Student fighting for Islamic state warns of 'fireworks' when US returns sparking fears of suicide missions. *Dailymail*. Retrieved from http://www.dailymail.co.uk/news/article-2722384/Reyaad-Khan-The-Cardiff-jihadist-wants-die-martyr.html

Wills, T. A., & Resko, J. A. (2005). Social support and behavior toward others. In A. G. Miller (Ed.), *The social psychology of good and evil* (pp. 416–443). New York: The Guildford Press.

Wilner, A. S., & Dubouloz, C. (2011). Transformative radicalisation: Applying learning theory to Islamist radicalisation. *Studies in Conflict and Terrorism*, *34*(5), 418–438. doi:10.1080/1057610X.2011.561472

Wilson, C. (2003). Computer attack and cyberterrorism: Vulnerabilities and policy issues for congress (Order Code RL32114). *CRS Report for Congress*. Retrieved from http://fas.org/irp/crs/RL32114.pdf

Winnicott, D. W. (2006). *The family and individual development*. London: Routledge.

Winter, C. (2015). *The virtual 'caliphate': Understanding Islamic State's propaganda strategy*. London: Quilliam Foundation.

Winter, D. G. (1987). Leader appeal, leader performance, and the motive profiles of leaders and followers: A study of American presidents and elections. *Journal of Personality and Social Psychology*, *52*(1), 196–202. doi:10.1037/0022-3514.52.1.196

Winter, D. G. (2004). Motivation and the escalation of conflict: Case studies of individual leaders. *Peace and Conflict*, *10*(4), 381–398. doi:10.1207/s15327949pac1004_8

Wojcieszak, M. (2009). "Carrying online participation offline"—Mobilization by radical online groups and politically dissimilar offline ties. *Journal of Communication*, *59*(3), 564–586. doi:10.1111/j.1460-2466.2009.01436.x

Wojcieszak, M. (2010). 'Don't talk to me': Effects of ideologically homogeneous online groups and politically dissimilar offline ties on extremism. *New Media & Society*, *12*(4), 637–655. doi:10.1177/1461444809342775

Women Without Borders. (n.d.). Retrieved from www.women-without-borders.org

Wood, G. (2015, March). What ISIS Really Wants. *The Atlantic*. Retrieved from http://www.theatlantic.com/magazine/archive/2015/03/what-isis-really-wants/384980/

Wood, D. M. (2006). *A report on the Surveillance Society: For the Information Commissioner. Surveillance Studies Network*. London: Information Commissioner.

Woods, J. (2011). The 9/11 effect: Toward a social science of the terrorist threat. *The Social Science Journal, 48*(1), 213–233. doi:10.1016/j.soscij.2010.06.001

Wood, W., & Neal, D. T. (2007). A new look at habits and the habit-goal interface. *Psychological Review, 114*(4), 843–863. doi:10.1037/0033-295X.114.4.843

Woolley, J. K., Limperos, A. M., & Beth, M. (2010). The 2008 presidential election, 2.0: A content analysis of user-generated political Facebook groups. *Mass Communication & Society, 13*(5), 631–652. doi:10.1080/15205436.2010.516864

Worchel, S., Lee, J., & Adewole, A. (1975). Effects of supply and demand on ratings of object value. *Journal of Personality and Social Psychology, 32*(5), 906–914. doi:10.1037/0022-3514.32.5.906

World Economic Forum. (2012). *Risk and responsibility in a hyper connected world pathways to global cyber resilience*. Retrieved from http:www3.weforum.org/docs/WEF_IT_PathwaysToGlobalCyberResilience_Report_2012.pdf

World Economic Forum. (2013). Special report: Building national resilience to global risk. *Global Risks*, 36-44.

Wright, L. (2006, September 24). *ASIO scans Muslim web surfers*. Retrieved from http://www.news.com.au/national/asio-scans-muslim-web-surfers/story-e6frfkx0-1111112257310

Wroe, D. (2015, July 2). Most Australians happy with government watching social media to stop terror: Poll. *The Sydney Morning Herald*. Retrieved from http://www.smh.com.au/federal-politics/political-news/most-australians-happy-with-government-watching-social-media-to-stop-terror-poll-20150701-gi2uf9.html

Wueest, C. (2014). Targeted attacks against the energy sector. *Symantec*. Retrieved from http://www.symantec.com/content/en/us/enterprise/media/security_response/whitepapers/targeted_attacks_against_the_energy_sector.pdf

Wu, M., Miller, R. C., & Garfinkel, S. L. (2006). Do security toolbars actually prevent phishing attacks? In *Proceedings of the SIGCHI conference on Human Factors in computing systems*. Montreal, Quebec: ACM. doi:10.1145/1124772.1124863

Yan, H. (2014, July 10). Why is ISIS so successful at luring westerners? *CNN*. Retrieved from http://edition.cnn.com/2014/10/07/world/isis-western-draw/

Yang, J. (2012, November 7). *Attacks on Indonesian Police: Not Just Terrorism?* RSIS Commentaries (208/2012). Singapore: S. Rajaratnam School of International Studies.

Yardi, S., & Boyd, D. (2010). Dynamic debates: An analysis of group polarization over time on Twitter. *Bulletin of Science, Technology & Society, 30*(5), 316–327. doi:10.1177/0270467610380011

Yar, M. (2006). *Cybercrime and society*. London: SAGE Publications.

Yasin, N. A. (2011). *Online Indonesian Islamist extremism: A gold mine of information. RSIS Commentaries (144/2011)*. Singapore: S. Rajaratnam School of International Studies.

Yasin, N. A. M. (2011). *Online Indonesian Islamist extremism: A gold mine of information. RSIS Commentaries (114/2011)*. Singapore: S. Rajaratnam School of International Studies.

Yasin, N. A. M. (2014). Understanding the contents in bahasa Indonesia extremist websites. *Counter Terrorist Trends and Analysis, 6*(3), 18–24.

Young, A. (2014, October 4). Pakistan Taliban pledge support to ISIS militants. *International Business Times*. Retrieved from http://www.ibtimes.com/pakistan-taliban-pledges-support-isis-militants-1699490

Young, H. F., Zwenk, F., & Rooze, M. (2013). *A review of the literature on radicalisation; and what it means for TERRA*. Retrieved from http://www.terra-net.eu/files/publications/20140227160036Literature%20review%20incl%20cover%20 in%20color.pdf

Young, H. F., Rooze, M., & Holsappel, J. (2015). Translating conceptualizations into practical suggestions: What the literature on radicalization can offer to practitioners. *Peace and Conflict*, *21*(2), 212–225. doi:10.1037/pac0000065

Yunos, Z., & Ahmad, R. (2014). The application of qualitative method in developing a cyber terrorism framework. In *Proceedings of International Conference on Economics, Management and Development (EMD 2014)*. Interlaken, Switzerland: Europment.

Zalkind, S. (2014, April 11). FBI admits missed opportunities to stop Tamerlan Tsarnaev. *Boston Magazine*. Retrieved from http://www.bostonmagazine.com/news/blog/2014/04/11/fbi-admits-missed-opportunities-stop-tamerlan-tsarnaev/

Zanini, M. (2004). The networking of terror in the information age. In D. M. Jones (Ed.), *Globalisation and the new terror: The Asia pacific dimension* (pp. 159–184). Cheltenham, UK: Edward Elgar Pub.

Zelin, A. Y. (2013a, April 2). *ICSR Insight: European foreign fighters in Syria*. The International Centre for the Study of Radicalisation. Retrieved from http://icsr.info/2013/04/icsr-insight-european-foreign-fighters-in-syria-2/

Zelin, A. Y. (2013b, December 5). Who are the foreign fighters in Syria? *The Washington Institute*. Retrieved from http://www.washingtoninstitute.org/policy-analysis/view/who-are-the-foreign-fighters-in-syria

Zelin, A. Y. (2013c, August 7). International jihad and the Syrian conflict. *The Washington Institute for Near East Policy*. Retrieved from http://www.washingtoninstitute.org/policy-analysis/view/international-jihad-and-the-syrian-conflict

Zelin, A. Y. (2014, June). The war between ISIS and al-Qaeda for supremacy of the Global Jihadist Movement. *The Washington Institute for Near East Policy*. Retrieved from http://www.washingtoninstitute.org/uploads/Documents/pubs/ ResearchNote_20_Zelin.pdf

Zeng, D., Chen, H., Lusch, R., & Li, S. (2010). Social media analytics and intelligence. *IEEE Computer Society*, *25*(6), 13–16.

Zenn, J. (2012, July 27). Islamic militants take aim at Myanmar. *Asia Times Online*. Retrieved from http://www.atimes. com/atimes/Southeast_Asia/NG27Ae04.html

Zenn, J., & Pearson, E. (2014). Women, gender and the evolving tactics of Boko Haram. *Journal of Terrorism Research*, *5*(1), 46–57. doi:10.15664/jtr.828

Zetter, K. (2014, April 30). Hackers can mess with traffic lights to jam roads and reroute cars. *Wired*. Retrieved from www.wired.com/2014/04/traffic-lights-hacking/

Zetter, K. (2015, January 12). Central command's Twitter account hacked … As Obama speaks on cybersecurity. *Wired. com* Retrieved from http://www.wired.com/2015/01/centcoms-twitter-hack/

Zimbardo, P. G. (1969). The human choice: Individuation, reason, and order versus deindividuation, impulse, and chaos. *Nebraska Symposium on Motivation*, *17*, 237–307.

Zimbardo, P., & Boyd, J. (2009). *The Time Paradox: The New Psychology of Time that will Change Your Life*. New York, NY: Free Press.

Zimmerman, R. (2009). *Understanding the implications of critical infrastructure interdependencies for water* (Published Articles & Papers, Paper 7). Retrieved from http://research.create.usc.edu/cgi/viewcontent.cgi?article=1083&context =published_papers

Zuckerman, J., Bucci, S. P., & Carafano, J. J. (2013). *60 terrorist plots since 9/11: Continued lessons in domestic counterterrorism*. Retrieved from http://www.heritage.org/research/reports/2013/07/60-terrorist-plots-since-911-continued-lessons-in-domestic-counterterrorism

Zuckerman, M. (1994). *Behavioural expressions and biosocial bases of sensation-seeking*. New York, NY: Cambridge Press.

About the Contributors

Majeed Khader is the Director of the Home Team Behavioural Sciences Centre under the Ministry of Home Affairs, Singapore, and Deputy Director of the Police Psychological Services Division, Police Headquarters. Dr Majeed is also the Chief Psychologist of the Singapore Police Force. A trained hostage negotiator, his previous operational duties include being the Deputy Commander of the Crisis Negotiation Unit and a trainer with the negotiation unit. He teaches criminal psychology part time as an Assistant Professor (Adjunct) at the School of Humanities and Social Sciences at Nanyang Technology University, Singapore. For the past 23 years, Dr Majeed has overseen the development of psychological services in the areas of stress, resilience, employee selection, deception psychology, leadership, crisis negotiations, crime profiling, and crisis psychology. For his work on the psychology of terrorism, he was awarded the National Day Public Administration Award (Bronze) in 2006 by the President of Singapore, and once again the Public Administration Award Silver in 2014. A forensic psychologist by training, Majeed holds a Masters degree (with Distinction) in Forensic Psychology from the University of Leicester (United Kingdom) and a PhD in Psychology (specialising in personality and crisis leadership) from the University of Aberdeen, Scotland. He also holds a degree in Economics and Sociology from the University of London. Dr Majeed has been invited as a speaker to organisations in Indonesia, Malaysia, Japan, Canada, Hong Kong, the United Kingdom and the United States to share on crime psychology, terrorism and leadership. He has also presented at the FBI, NCIS and the RCMP. He has been the Chairman of two major international conferences held in Singapore titled the 'Asian Conference of Criminal and Operations Psychology'. He has been the Asian Director and sits on the board of the United States based Society of Police and Criminal Psychology. He is a Registered Psychologist with the Singapore Psychological Society, and a member of the British, and American Psychological Societies. He has contributed several book chapters and published widely in peer-reviewed journal such as Journal of Research in Personality, Journal of Occupational Health Psychology, Psychology & Health, Cognition and Emotion, International Journal of Psychophysiology, Personality and Individual Differences, International Journal of Police Science & Management, Journal of Police and Criminal Psychology, Security Journal, etc.

Loo Seng Neo is a Senior Behavioural Sciences Research Analyst with the Home Team Behavioural Sciences Centre at the Ministry of Home Affairs, Singapore. For the past nine years, Loo Seng has been specialising on the area of violent extremism, particularly in the areas of online radicalisation, online threat assessment, pre-attack warning signs, and the psychology of violent extremism. He has presented at many international conferences, trained law enforcement officers, and published many research reports and journals on the topic of violent extremism. He is a member of the Online Radicalisation Research

Community of Practice (ORRCOP) that comprises Singaporean practitioners and subject matter experts involved in research related to online radicalisation. Academically, he teaches on the topic of psychology at a private university, and is currently pursuing his Master degree in psychology researching on the personality profiles of violent extremists at Nanyang Technology University.

Gabriel Ong is Senior Assistant Director with the Psychological and Correctional Rehabilitation Division (PCRD) of the Singapore Prison Service (SPS). Concurrently, he is Assistant Director with the Resilience, Safety and Security Psychology Branch (RSSP) of the Home Team Behavioural Sciences Centre (HTBSC). Both PCRD and HTBSC are psychology units in the Ministry of Home Affairs, Singapore. His primary roles at SPS include overseeing the evaluation of rehabilitation programmes and regimes. Prior to this, he was involved in forensic risk assessment and offender rehabilitation, specifically in the area of sexual and violent offending. His primary roles at the HTBSC include overseeing research on issues such as violent extremism and resilience. He holds a Doctor of Psychology (Clinical) from the James Cook University (Singapore). He has been with the Ministry of Home Affairs since 2001.

Eunice Tan Mingyi is a Senior Psychologist and Assistant Director of the Operations and Leadership Psychology Branch, Home Team Behavioural Sciences Centre (HTBSC), Ministry of Home Affairs, Singapore. As a pioneering member of the centre, she played an integral role in the development and setup of this research and training centre, particularly in the area of leadership assessment, selection, development and training. Her early forays into behavioural sciences research at HTBSC involved understanding the radicalisation processes of terrorists. Her presentation and work on a radicalisation model of terrorists, based on the Singapore experience with terrorism in 2002, won the Chris Hatcher Award for Best Vision during the 34th Annual Conference of the Society for Police and Criminal Psychology (SPCP) in 2007. Eunice's main research interests include understanding offending behaviour, radicalisation processes of extremists, the assessment and selection of high potentials, issues in critical incident command, crisis leadership, and command leadership in the public safety and security context. As part of her secondary duties, Eunice has been a team psychologist with the Crisis Negotiation Unit of the Singapore Police Force since 2007. In addition, she is also part of the Critical Incident Stress Intervention & Support team led by the Singapore Police Psychological Services Division. Eunice holds an MSc in Investigative and Forensic Psychology from the University of Liverpool (United Kingdom). She is also a member of the Society of Police and Criminal Psychology (SPCP), USA.

Jeffery Chin is a Senior Psychologist at the Home Team Behavioural Sciences Centre. Key areas of his work at the centre include applied research in investigative interviewing, deception and leadership during critical incidents. As a concurrent appointment, Jeffery also supports the operations of the Crisis Negotiation Unit, Singapore Police Force as a psychologist. Jeffery holds a Master degree in Investigative and Forensic Psychology from the University of Liverpool (United Kingdom). His Master's dissertation topic was on critical incident leadership.

* * *

Damien D. Cheong is Coordinator, Homeland Defence Programme and Research Fellow at the Centre of Excellence for National Security (CENS), S. Rajaratnam School of International Studies, Nanyang Technological University, Singapore. He has researched and written on a variety of issues related to homeland defence, strategic communication, security studies, political violence and Middle East politics. Damien obtained his PhD in Politics from Monash University (Australia). Prior to joining CENS, Damien was an adjunct research fellow at the Global Terrorism Research Centre (GTReC). He also lectured in strategic communications at Monash University from 2009-2010.

Geoff Dean is Professor and Director of International Programs in the School of Criminology and Criminal Justice at Griffith University in Brisbane, Australia. He publishes in a diverse range of international scholarly journals, is an international peer reviewer, and had guest editorships for Police Practice and Research: An International Journal and the Pakistan Journal of Criminology. He has been a chief investigator for the Australian Attorney-General's Departmental on the Research Panel on Countering Violent Extremism. He is the principal author of two books for Oxford University Press (OUP) in the UK on Organised Crime: Policing Illegal Business Entrepreneurialism (2012) and Knowledge Management in Policing and Law Enforcement: Foundations, Structures, Applications (2007). His latest book is on Neurocognitive Risk Assessment for the Early Detection of Violent Extremists (2014) published by Springer (NY). Prof Dean consults widely with Police Services and Universities in Asia, Europe, Scandinavia, and North America.

Leevia Dillon is a Behavioural Sciences Research Analyst with the Home Team Behavioural Sciences Centre at the Ministry of Home Affairs, Singapore and is a member of the Online Radicalisation Research Community of Practice group. For the past two years, Leevia has developed an interest in the area of violent extremism, cybercrime and how these two areas have the potential to overlap. Coming from a behavioural sciences angle, Leevia has presented at many seminars, briefed Home Team officers and have published governmental reports. Currently, Leevia is working towards publishing a paper on social engineering. Academically, Leevia is pursuing her PhD at John Jay College of Criminal Justice, City University of New York.

Fajar Erikha is a post-graduate student in Linguistic at Universitas Indonesia. He is an analyst and a researcher in the Center for Police Studies Research at Universitas Indonesia. His research interests are in discourse analysis, human empowerment, and the process of radicalisation and de-radicalisation of Terrorism in Indonesia.

Danielle Gomes is a Behavioural Sciences Research Analyst with the Resilience, Safety, and Security Psychology Branch of the Home Team Behavioural Sciences Centre, Ministry of Home Affairs in Singapore. Trained in Psychology, Danielle delves into research on national resilience, crisis response and management, and social issues like national identity, patriotism, trust, and social cohesion. Together with her research team, she was involved in the development of a framework for national resilience in Singapore. Danielle has also presented at the Social Resilience Research Roundtable chaired by Permanent Secretary Mr Benny Lim; conducted several training seminars for Home Team officers and other government personnel; and shared her research with global experts, policy-makers, and practitioners. She has also had the opportunity to dabble in terrorism work, such as understanding Jihadi counter 'counter-narratives'. Apart from research, Danielle is trained in counselling, suicide intervention, and victim care. She currently volunteers as a victim care officer with the Singapore Police Force Victim Care Cadre.

Weiying Hu is a Psychologist of a Counter-Terrorism Operations Division within the Ministry of Home Affairs, Singapore. She works with a team of psychologists in preparing psychological risk assessments, counselling services and management of the rehabilitation programme for detainees and those released under supervision, including self-radicalised individuals.

Cristina Ivan is a researcher within the National Institute for Intelligence Studies of the "Mihai Viteazul" National Intelligence Academy. Cristina Ivan holds a PhD in cultural studies from the University of Bucharest where she focused her research on identity, otherness, violence, as well as intermedia translations of violent religious extremism in discursive spaces. She has obtained a BA in philology from the Faculty of Letters, University of Bucharest and an MA with distinction in British Cultural Studies from the Faculty of Foreign Languages at the University of Bucharest. She has also graduated from a program in 'British Contemporary Studies' at the University of Edinburgh, Scotland, and a course in 'Understanding the Impact of Terrorist Ideology', jointly delivered by the George C. Marshal Centre for Security Studies and the Jordanian National Royal Academy. Over the past 6 years, she has specialised in applied research of radicalisation, terrorism, participatory democracy and active citizenship, taking part in various national and European funded projects.

Dana Janbek is Associate Professor of Public Relations at Lasell College in Newton, Massachusetts. Her research focuses on terrorist use of the Internet as a communication tool and the use of information and communication technologies in the Middle East including within refugee populations. She has published a co-authored book, a book chapter, and a number of scholarly articles on these topics. She often serves as a commentator on issues related to her research areas in Boston media outlets. Dr Janbek earned her doctoral degree in Communication from the University of Miami in FL, her Master's in Political Science from the University of Louisville in KY, and her Bachelor's in Communication from Spalding University in KY.

Fredrik Johansson received his PhD in Computer Science from Örebro University (Sweden) in 2010 and his Master of Science in Computer Science from University of Skövde (Sweden) in 2005. He has a background in the research area of information fusion but has for the last five years focused more on research in intelligence and security informatics. Dr Johansson has authored more than 30 peer-reviewed publications. He is regularly serving in the program committee of various security informatics related conferences and journals and was program chair of the 2013 European Intelligence and Security Informatics Conference in Uppsala, Sweden.

Lisa Kaati is a senior scientist at the Swedish Defense Research Agency (FOI) and the head of Arena security at Uppsala University. Dr Kaati is active in the area intelligence security informatics. Her research interests are: social network analysis, web mining, linguistics, data mining and algorithms. She is currently working on how to profile users in online environments based on their writing style, activity profiles and social network.

Mark Kebbell's research expertise is in the area of Investigative Psychology with regards the investigation and prosecution of serious crime in particular. His previous work has included writing the guidelines for police officers in England and Wales (with Wagstaff) for the assessment of eyewitness evidence and a review of factors associated with sex offending. He has worked on more than seventy criminal cases, principally involving murder or serious sexual assault, and has given expert evidence on numerous occasions including uncontested psychological evidence in an Old Bailey appeal case. He is the Editor, with Professor Graham Davies of the book 'Practical Psychology for Forensic Investigations and Prosecutions' published by Wiley.

Joyce S. Pang received her undergraduate training in psychology from Smith College, MA, USA, and her PhD in personality psychology from The University of Michigan, MI, USA. As a personality psychologist, she is interested in the assessment of individual differences and in making finer distinctions between personality dimensions in order to increase theoretical understanding of how personality affects behaviour. In all her research, Dr Pang adopts a person x situation perspective to understand how individual differences predict different reactions within different social contexts, which in turn lead to important personal and social outcomes.

D. Elaine Pressman is an international expert in the risk assessment and analysis of violent political extremism and insider threat. She is the developer of risk assessment tools for violent extremism used on four continents by national and regional police agencies, intelligence services and with detained violent extremists. The risk assessment approaches that she has developed are grounded in an evidence-base and related to the rule of law in differing legal jurisdictions. The approach uses a transparent and systematic method to assess individual risk related to radicalisation. Her work has been applied to the risk assessment of returning foreign fighters, to prospective foreign terrorist fighters, to identify early warning signs of violent extremism, for community intervention, to support integration of returnees and for the rehabilitation of convicted and/or detained extremists. Dr Pressman has a background in political science, behavioural sciences and defence-related communication sciences. She obtained her B.A. Degree from the University of Manitoba in Canada, and M.A. and Ph.D. Degrees from The Ohio State University. She completed post-doctoral training in Forensic Sciences at the Michigan State University in association with the Michigan State Police, and in Psychology in Canada and Europe. Dr Pressman has advised at the senior government level in Asia, the Pacific Region, North America and Europe. She has trained forensic specialists and law enforcement analysts around the world. Her work is being translated into German and Dutch and is available in English, French and Bahasa. She is a Senior Research Fellow in the Canadian Centre for Intelligence and Security Studies at Carleton University, Ottawa, Canada, and an Associate Fellow at the International Centre for Counter-Terrorism -The Hague. She has been a Research Fellow in the FBI Critical Incident Response Group and a regular invited lecturer at the FBI National Academy at Quantico Virginia, USA. Dr Pressman has over 25 years of clinical experience, university teaching, and research. She is the recipient of many major government grants, contracts and awards. She has published in the risk assessment field of violent extremism and has won professional peer recognition for her work. She is an Editorial Board Member of the Journal of Forensic Practice (formerly the British Journal of Forensic Practice) and the Journal of Criminological Research, Policy and Practice.

Idhamsyah Eka Putra is a lecturer and co-director of Psychology Graduate Programs at Persada Indonesia University. He holds a doctoral degree (with distinction) in Psychology from Johannes Kepler University of Linz. His research interest is in Social Psychology studying prejudice, (Islamic) terrorism, intergroup relations, social exclusions, and intergroup Conflicts.

Kumar Ramakrishna is Head of Policy Studies in the Office of the Executive Deputy Chairman, S. Rajaratnam School of International Studies (RSIS), Nanyang Technological University, Singapore. From 2006-2015, he was the Head of the Centre of Excellence for National Security at RSIS. His research interests include counter-extremism, counterinsurgency theory and practice, and the historic Communist threat to Singapore and Malaya.

David Romyn served in the Australian Army as a combat engineer for 10 years, before leaving to complete a Bachelor of Psychology with honours. He is now undertaking his Ph.D., investigating how terrorists plan and conduct terrorist attacks in Western countries, by applying a 'red-team' research design.

Magnus Sahlgren, PhD in computational linguistics from Stockholm University, has worked on computational models of meaning since 2000 at the Swedish Institute of Computer Science (SICS), and from 2010 at Gavagai. Sahlgren's dissertation "The Word-Space Model" was awarded the prize for the most prominent scholarly achievement of 2006 at the Stockholm University Faculty of Humanities. His current research focus is to develop and apply scalable and efficient distributional semantic models to various real-world text analysis problems.

Omer Ali Saifudeen is a Senior Assistant Director at the National Security Research Centre, National Security Coordination Secretariat, Prime Minister's Office, Singapore.

Erin Marie Saltman is a Senior Researcher and Networks Manager at the Institute for Strategic Dialogue. She oversees research and project development on ISD's Women and Extremism (WaE) initiative as well as the Youth Civil Activism Network (YouthCAN). Both initiatives lead action-oriented research used to strategically scale up international counter-narrative projects. WaE aims to fully analyse the recruitment and involvement of women in violent extremist networks as well as increase the role women play in countering these trends. Dr Saltman's background and expertise includes both far-right and Islamist processes of radicalisation, counter-extremism and political socialisation. Her primary research looks at online extremism, gender dynamics and counter-extremism measures. She regularly advises governments and security sectors across Europe and North America on issues related to online extremism and the role of the internet in radicalisation. Dr Saltman holds a PhD in political science from University College London. Her doctoral thesis focussed on political socialisation and processes of radicalisation in a post-Communist context, looking at youth activism and participation in alternative political and grassroots movements.

Sarlito W. Sarwono is professor in psychology, who is currently in charge of the graduate program in Police Studies, Universitas Indonesia. Since 2006 he has been conducting research in deradicalisation and counterterrorism in Indonesia until now. He has published some books concerning terrorism, such as 'Terrorism in Indonesia: A psychological review', 'Measuring ex-Terrorists' mind'.

Priscilla Shi is a Behavioural Sciences Research Analyst with the Home Team Behavioural Sciences Centre at the Ministry of Home Affairs, Singapore. She research on the areas of deradicalisation and violent extremism online. Priscilla has also written various pieces on the trend of violent extremism on online platforms and in recent conflicts in the Middle East.

Neil D. Shortland is a Senior Research Associate at the University of Massachusetts Lowell's Center for Terrorism and Security and a PhD Student at the University of Liverpool's Center for Critical and Major Incident Psychology. He conducts research on all aspects of national security including; terrorist behaviour, military operations and adaptation and high-stakes decision making. His most recent work involved collecting and analysing data on the number of civilians killed and injured by coalition and insurgent forces in Afghanistan. This work was published as part of a special feature in the journal Science.

Thomas Steinfatt is Professor of Communication and Professor of International Studies at the University of Miami, and Visiting Professor of Communication at Florida International University. His B.S. is in Mathematics and Statistics and his PhD in Communication, both from Michigan State University. A Fulbright Scholar, he specialises in Intercultural Communication, Statistical Methodology, and Propaganda, and has served as an expert witness on propaganda and corporate documents in Federal District Court and State courts. His teaching has been recognised through the University of Miami Excellence in Teaching Award. He serves on the Expert Committee on Human Trafficking for the United Nations Office of Drugs and Crime (UNODC) and on the Advisory Committee for the Walk Free Foundation of Australia in producing the yearly Global Slavery Index. His research is funded by UNESCO/UNIAP, UNDP, and the U.S. State Department through USAID. His research interests also include communication in U.S. and foreign intelligence agencies, propaganda, The JFK assassination, and interpersonal lie detection. His publications include over sixty scholarly articles, chapters, and monographs in scholarly journals including Human Communication Research, Communication Monographs, and The Journal of Personality and Social Psychology, and he has published four books. He occasionally serves as a commentator on Miami television stations and National Public Radio on political communication.

Jethro Tan is a Behavioural Sciences Research Analyst at the Home Team Behavioural Sciences Centre, Ministry of Home Affairs, Singapore. His research portfolio includes national resilience, crisis management, and crisis communications. He has shared his research findings to international and local experts, along with practitioners and policy makers. This includes training and research sharing on strategies to build a resilient nation after a violent extremist attack. He is also particularly interested in how culture plays a role in the resilience of communities and nations. He believes that technology is, and will continue to become, a key enabler in the one's quest towards resiliency.

Robyn Torok is currently completing her second PhD on social media discourses relating to radicalisation and terrorism at the Security Research Institute, Edith Cowan University, Australia. She has written extensively on the role that social media plays in radicalisation.

Arun Vishwanath, Ph.D., MBA, is Associate Professor of Communication at the University at Buffalo. His research is on the diffusion, adoption, utilisation, and mis-utilisation of information technology. His present focus is on spear phishing and spoofing attacks and on finding ways to mitigate them. This work has led to an understanding of the joint role of conscious cognitions and automatic habits in determining individual victimisation through such attacks. He is presently developing strategies for mitigating breaches and interventions that lead to better cyber hygiene.

Penelope Wang majored in Psychology at the National University of Singapore, and graduated with a Bachelor of Social Sciences (First Class Honours). She is currently working at the Home Team

Behavioural Sciences Centre (HTBSC), a research and training outfit, at the Ministry of Home Affairs. Her core area of work includes research on casino gambling in Singapore. Her previous projects include investigating the profile of local casino gamblers as well as the effect of casino environment on gambling behaviours. The findings from the first project were presented to several stakeholders such as the Casino Regulatory Authority, the National Council of Problem Gambling, as well as the Ministry of Social and Family Development. Additionally, as a member of the Crime, Investigation and Forensic Psychology Branch, Penelope has interviewed drug offenders and law enforcement officers for several key projects undertaken by the department. Penelope also forms part of the core team of trainers that conducts training for law enforcement officers on the latest evidence-based practices that could enhance their work.

Yingmin Wang is a Behavioural Sciences Research Analyst at the Home Team Behavioural Sciences Centre (HTBSC), Ministry of Home Affairs, Singapore. She has a background in Psychology and her research portfolio includes the conceptualisation and development of a National Resilience (NR) framework. Part of her research on NR also comprises people-centric factors that contribute to resilience, such as sustaining of a crisis-ready mindset. Yingmin takes a keen interest in theoretical debates especially those pertaining to resilience. Additionally, resilience of communities, how they interact and eventually give rise to self-organising behaviours, intrigues her as a researcher. At other platforms, the work she undertakes at HTBSC also provides her with exposure to violent extremism and its consequent impact on national security. She enjoys sharing her research findings with practitioners, policy makers and experts at various platforms and is enthusiastic about the dynamic and evolving research on resilience.

Jennifer Yang Hui is an Associate Research Fellow at the Centre of Excellence for National Security (CENS), a constituent unit of the S. Rajaratnam School of International Studies (RSIS), Nanyang Technological University (NTU). Jennifer graduated as a Tun Dato Sir Cheng Lock Tan Master of Arts (M.A.) scholar in Southeast Asian Studies from the National University of Singapore (NUS). She has an Honours degree in History, also from the NUS. Prior to joining RSIS, Jennifer was Research Associate at the Institute of South East Asian Studies (ISEAS). Jennifer conducts research on social media and is particularly interested in examining the role of the social media in contemporary Indonesia. Other related interests include: online epistemology, knowledge-making and their implications on digital maturity. She is currently researching on crowdsourcing and the state of public trust in the digital age.

Index

Information Resources Management Association

Become an IRMA Member

Members of the **Information Resources Management Association (IRMA)** understand the importance of community within their field of study. The Information Resources Management Association is an ideal venue through which professionals, students, and academicians can convene and share the latest industry innovations and scholarly research that is changing the field of information science and technology. Become a member today and enjoy the benefits of membership as well as the opportunity to collaborate and network with fellow experts in the field.

IRMA Membership Benefits:

- **One FREE Journal Subscription**
- **30% Off Additional Journal Subscriptions**
- **20% Off Book Purchases**
- Updates on the latest events and research on Information Resources Management through the IRMA-L listserv.
- Updates on new open access and downloadable content added to Research IRM.
- A copy of the Information Technology Management Newsletter twice a year.
- A certificate of membership.

IRMA Membership $195

Scan code to visit irma-international.org and begin by selecting your free journal subscription.

Membership is good for one full year.

9 781522 501565